INTRODUCTION TO

JAVA™

PROGRAMMING

BRIEF VERSION

Ninth Edition

Y. Daniel Liang

Armstrong Atlantic State University

PEARSON

Boston Columbus Indianapolis New York San Francisco Upper Saddle River
Amsterdam Cape Town Dubai London Madrid Milan Munich Paris Montreal Toronto
Delhi Mexico City Sao Paulo Sydney Hong Kong Seoul Singapore Taipei Tokyo

Editorial Director: Marcia Horton
Editor in Chief: Michael Hirsch
Executive Editor: Tracy Dunkelberger
Associate Editor: Carole Snyder
Director of Marketing: Patrice Jones
Marketing Manager: Yez Alayan
Marketing Coordinator: Kathryn Ferranti
Marketing Assistant: Emma Snider
Director of Production: Vince O'Brien
Managing Editor: Jeff Holcomb
Production Project Manager: Kayla Smith-Tarbox
Operations Supervisor: Alan Fischer
Manufacturing Buyer: Lisa McDowell

Art Director: Anthony Gemmellaro
Cover Designer: Anthony Gemmellaro
Manager, Visual Research: Karen Sanatar
Manager, Rights and Permissions: Mike Joyce
Text Permission Coordinator: Danielle Simon
    and Jenn Kennett
Cover Illustration: Jason Consalvo
Lead Media Project Manager: Daniel Sandin
Project Management: Gillian Hall
Composition and Art: Laserwords
Printer/Binder: Edwards Brothers
Cover Printer: Lehigh-Phoenix Color/Hagerstown
Text Font: Times 10/12

Credits and acknowledgments borrowed from other sources and reproduced, with permission, in this textbook appear on the appropriate page within text and as follows: Table 3.2 and 10.1: Data from IRS. Figures 8.1, 8.12, 12.3, 12.5, 12.7, 12.9, 12.10, 12.12–12.21, 12.26–12.30, 13.1, 13.4, 13.9, 13.11, 13.15, 13.17, 13.19, 13.21, 13.23, 13.25–13.35, 14.10, 14.14,15.9–15.11, 16.1, 16.2, 16.8, 16.11, 16.14, 16.17, 16.19–16.35, 17.1, 17.3, 17.6, 17.9, 17.12, 17.13, 17.15, 17.17–17.32, 18.6–18.8, 18.10, 18.15–18.35, 19.19, 19.20, 19.22, 20.1, 20.9, 20.12–20.14, 20.16–20.20: Screenshots © 2011 by Oracle Corporation. Reprinted with permission.

Microsoft® and Windows® are registered trademarks of the Microsoft Corporation in the U.S.A. and other countries. Screen shots and icons reprinted with permission from the Microsoft Corporation. This book is not sponsored or endorsed by or affiliated with the Microsoft Corporation.

Many of the designations by manufacturers and sellers to distinguish their products are claimed as trademarks. Where those designations appear in this book, and the publisher was aware of a trademark claim, the designations have been printed in initial caps or all caps.

Library of Congress Cataloging-in-Publication Data

Liang, Y. Daniel.
 Introduction to Java programming : brief version / Y. Daniel Liang. — 9th ed.
   p. cm.
 Includes index.
 ISBN-13: 978-0-13-292373-6
 ISBN-10: 0-13-292373-4
 1. Java (Computer program language) I. Title. II. Title: Java programming.
 QA76.73.J38L52 2013
 005.13'3—dc23
                                2012000766

Prentice Hall
is an imprint of

www.pearsonhighered.com

10 9 8 7 6 5 4 3 2 1

ISBN 13: 978-0-13-292373-6
ISBN 10: 0-13-292373-4

This book is dedicated to Professor Myers Foreman. Myers used the comprehensive version of this book in CS1, CS2, and CS3 at Lamar University and provided invaluable suggestions for improving the book. Sadly, Myers passed away after he completed the review of this edition.

To Samantha, Michael, and Michelle

PREFACE

Dear Reader,

Many of you have provided feedback on earlier editions of this book, and your comments and suggestions have greatly improved the book. This edition has been substantially enhanced in presentation, organization, examples, exercises, and supplements. We have:

what is new?

- Reorganized sections and chapters to present the subjects in a more logical order

- Included many new interesting examples and exercises to stimulate interests

- Updated to Java 7

- Created animations for algorithms and data structures to visually demonstrate the concepts

- Redesigned the support Website to make it easier to navigate

This book teaches programming in a problem-driven way that focuses on problem solving rather than syntax. We make introductory programming interesting by using thought-provoking problems in a broad context. The central thread of early chapters is on problem solving. Appropriate syntax and library are introduced to enable readers to write programs for solving the problems. To support the teaching of programming in a problem-driven way, the book provides a wide variety of problems at various levels of difficulty to motivate students. To appeal to students in all majors, the problems cover many application areas, including math, science, business, financial, gaming, animation, and multimedia.

problem-driven

The book focuses on fundamentals first by introducing basic programming concepts and techniques before designing custom classes. The fundamental concepts and techniques of loops, methods, and arrays are the foundation for programming. Building this strong foundation prepares students to learn object-oriented programming and advanced Java programming.

fundamentals-first

This book is a *brief version* of Introduction to Java Programming, *Comprehensive Version*, 9E. This version is designed for an introductory programming course, commonly known as CS1. This version contains the first twenty chapters in the comprehensive version. The brief version covers fundamentals of programming, object-oriented programming, GUI programming, exception handling, I/O, and recursion. The comprehensive version has an additional thirty chapters that cover data structures and algorithms, threads, parallel programming, networking, internationalization, advanced GUI, database, and Web programming.

brief version
comprehensive version

The best way to teach programming is *by example*, and the only way to learn programming is *by doing*. Basic concepts are explained by example, and a large number of exercises with various levels of difficulty are provided for students to practice. For our programming courses, we assign programming exercises after each lecture.

examples and exercises

Our goal is to produce a text that teaches problem solving and programming in a broad context using a wide variety of interesting examples. If you have any comments on and suggestions for improving the book, please email me.

Sincerely,

Y. Daniel Liang
y.daniel.liang@gmail.com
www.cs.armstrong.edu/liang
www.pearsonhighered.com/liang

What's New in This Edition?

This edition substantially improves *Introduction to Java Programming*, Eighth Edition. The major improvements are as follows:

complete revision

■ This edition is completely revised in every detail to enhance clarity, presentation, content, examples, and exercises.

new problems

■ New examples and exercises are provided to motivate and stimulate student interest in programming.

key point

■ Each section starts with a Key Point that highlights the important concepts covered in the section.

check point

■ Check Points provide review questions to help students track their progress and evaluate their learning after a major concept or example is covered.

test questions

■ Each chapter provides test questions online. They are grouped by sections for students to do self-test. The questions are graded online.

VideoNotes

■ New VideoNotes provide short video tutorials designed to reinforce code.

basic GUI and graphics early

■ The Java GUI API is an excellent example of how the object-oriented principle is applied. Students learn better with concrete and visual examples. So basic GUI/Graphics is moved before introducing abstract classes and interfaces. You can however still choose to cover abstract classes and interfaces before GUI or skip GUI.

numeric classes covered early

■ The numeric wrapper classes, `BigInteger`, and `BigDecimal` are now introduced in Chapter 10 to enable students to write code using these classes early.

exception handling earlier

■ Exception handling is covered before abstract classes and interfaces so that students can build robust programs early. The instructor can still choose to cover exception handling later. Text I/O is now combined with exception handling to form a new chapter.

simple generics early

■ Simple use of generics is introduced along with `ArrayList` in Chapter 11 and with `Comparable` in Chapter 15 while the complex detail on generics is introduced in the comprehensive version of the book.

Please visit www.cs.armstrong.edu/liang/intro9e/newfeatures.html for a complete list of new features as well as correlations to the previous edition.

Pedagogical Features

The book uses the following elements to help students get the most from the material:

■ The **Objectives** at the beginning of each chapter list what students should learn from the chapter. This will help them determine whether they have met the objectives after completing the chapter.

■ The **Introduction** opens the discussion with representative problems to give the reader an overview of what to expect from the chapter.

■ **Key Points** highlight the important concepts covered in each section.

■ **Check Points** provide review questions to help students track their progress as they read through the chapter and evaluate their learning.

■ **Problems and Case Studies**, carefully chosen and presented in an easy-to-follow style, teach problem solving and programming concepts. The book uses many small, simple, and stimulating examples to demonstrate important ideas.

- The **Chapter Summary** reviews the important subjects that students should understand and remember. It helps them reinforce the key concepts they have learned in the chapter.

- **Test Questions** are accessible online, grouped by sections, for students to do self-test on programming concepts and techniques.

- **Programming Exercises** are grouped by sections to provide students with opportunities to apply the new skills they have learned on their own. The level of difficulty is rated as easy (no asterisk), moderate (*), hard (**), or challenging (***). The trick of learning programming is practice, practice, and practice. To that end, the book provides a great many exercises.

- **Notes**, **Tips**, **Cautions**, and **Design Guides** are inserted throughout the text to offer valuable advice and insight on important aspects of program development.

Note
Provides additional information on the subject and reinforces important concepts.

Tip
Teaches good programming style and practice.

Caution
Helps students steer away from the pitfalls of programming errors.

Design Guide
Provides guidelines for designing programs.

Flexible Chapter Orderings

The book is designed to provide flexible chapter orderings to enable GUI, exception handling, and recursion to be covered earlier or later. The diagram shows the chapter dependencies.

Organization of the Book

The chapters in the brief version can be grouped into three parts that, taken together, form a solid introduction to Java programming. Because knowledge is cumulative, the early chapters provide the conceptual basis for understanding programming and guide students through simple examples and exercises; subsequent chapters progressively present Java programming in detail, culminating with the development of comprehensive Java applications. The appendixes contain a mixed bag of topics, including an introduction to number systems and bitwise operations.

Part I: Fundamentals of Programming (Chapters 1–7, 20)

The first part of the book is a stepping stone, preparing you to embark on the journey of learning Java. You will begin to learn about Java (Chapter 1) and fundamental programming techniques with primitive data types, variables, constants, assignments, expressions, and operators (Chapter 2), control statements (Chapters 3–4), methods (Chapter 5), and arrays (Chapters 6–7). After Chapter 6, you can jump to Chapter 20 to learn how to write recursive methods for solving inherently recursive problems.

Part II: Object-Oriented Programming (Chapters 8–11, 14–15, and 19)

This part introduces object-oriented programming. Java is an object-oriented programming language that uses abstraction, encapsulation, inheritance, and polymorphism to provide great flexibility, modularity, and reusability in developing software. You will learn programming with objects and classes (Chapters 8–10), class inheritance (Chapter 11), polymorphism (Chapter 11), exception handling and text I/O (Chapter 14), abstract classes (Chapter 15), and interfaces (Chapter 15). Processing strings is introduced in Chapter 9, and binary I/O is discussed in Chapter 19.

Part III: GUI Programming (Chapters 12–13, 16–18)

This part introduces elementary Java GUI programming in Chapters 12–13 and 16–18. Major topics include GUI basics (Chapter 12), drawing shapes (Chapter 13), event-driven programming (Chapter 16), using GUI components (Chapter 17), and writing applets (Chapter 18). You will learn the architecture of Java GUI programming and use the GUI components to develop applications and applets from these elementary GUI chapters.

Appendixes

This part of the book covers a mixed bag of topics. Appendix A lists Java keywords. Appendix B gives tables of ASCII characters and their associated codes in decimal and in hex. Appendix C shows the operator precedence. Appendix D summarizes Java modifiers and their usage. Appendix E discusses special floating-point values. Appendix F introduces number systems and conversions among binary, decimal, and hex numbers. Finally, Appendix G introduces bitwise operations.

Java Development Tools

IDE tutorials

You can use a text editor, such as the Windows Notepad or WordPad, to create Java programs and to compile and run the programs from the command window. You can also use a Java development tool, such as TextPad, NetBeans, or Eclipse. These tools support an integrated development environment (IDE) for developing Java programs quickly. Editing, compiling, building, executing, and debugging programs are integrated in one graphical user interface. Using these tools effectively can greatly increase your programming productivity. TextPad is a primitive IDE tool. NetBeans and Eclipse are more sophisticated, but they are easy to use if you follow the tutorials. Tutorials on TextPad, NetBeans, and Eclipse can be found in the supplements on the Companion Website www.cs.armstrong.edu/liang/intro9e.

Online Practice and Assessment with MyProgrammingLab

MyProgrammingLab™

MyProgrammingLab helps students fully grasp the logic, semantics, and syntax of programming. Through practice exercises and immediate, personalized feedback, MyProgrammingLab improves the programming competence of beginning students who often struggle with the basic concepts and paradigms of popular high-level programming languages.

A self-study and homework tool, a MyProgrammingLab course consists of hundreds of small practice problems organized around the structure of this textbook. For students, the system automatically detects errors in the logic and syntax of their code submissions and offers targeted hints that enable students to figure out what went wrong—and why. For instructors, a comprehensive gradebook tracks correct and incorrect answers and stores the code inputted by students for review.

MyProgrammingLab is offered to users of this book in partnership with Turing's Craft, the makers of the CodeLab interactive programming exercise system. For a full demonstration, to see feedback from instructors and students, or to get started using MyProgrammingLab in your course, visit www.myprogramminglab.com.

VideoNotes

VideoNote

We are excited about the new VideoNotes feature that is found in this new edition. These videos provide additional help by presenting examples of key topics and showing how to solve problems completely, from design through coding. VideoNotes are free to first time users and can be accessed by redeeming the access code in the front of this book at www.pearsonhighered.com/liang.

LiveLab

This book is accompanied by a complementary Web-based course assessment and management system for instructors. The system has four main components:

■ The **Automatic Grading System** can automatically grade programs.

■ The **Quiz Creation/Submission/Grading System** enables instructors to create and modify quizzes that students can take and be graded upon automatically.

■ The **Peer Evaluation System** enables peer evaluations.

■ **Tracking grades, attendance, etc.,** lets students track their grades, and enables instructors to view the grades of all students and to track students' attendance.

The main features of the Automatic Grading System include:

■ Students can run and submit exercises. (The system checks whether their program runs correctly—students can continue to run and resubmit the program before the due date.)

■ Instructors can review submissions, run programs with instructor test cases, correct them, provide feedback to students, and check plagiarism.

■ Instructors can create/modify their own exercises, create public and secret test cases, assign exercises, and set due dates for the whole class or for individuals.

■ Instructors can assign all the exercises in the text to students. Additionally, LiveLab provides extra exercises that are not printed in the text.

■ Instructors can sort and filter all exercises and check grades (by time frame, student, and/or exercise).

- Instructors can delete students from the system.

- Students and instructors can track grades on exercises.

The main features of the Quiz System are:

- Instructors can create/modify quizzes from the test bank or a text file or create completely new tests online.

- Instructors can assign the quizzes to students and set a due date and test time limit for the whole class or for individuals.

- Students and instructors can review submitted quizzes.

- Instructors can analyze quizzes and identify students' weaknesses.

- Students and instructors can track grades on quizzes.

The main features of the Peer Evaluation System include:

- Instructors can assign peer evaluation for programming exercises.

- Instructors can view peer evaluation reports.

Student Resource Website

The Student Resource Website (www.cs.armstrong.edu/liang/intro9e) contains the following resources:

- Access to VideoNotes (www.pearsonhighered.com/liang).

- Answers to check point questions

- Solutions to even-numbered programming exercises

- Source code for the examples in the book

- Interactive self-testing (organized by sections for each chapter)

- Data structures and algorithm animations

- Errata

Instructor Resource Website

The Instructor Resource Website, accessible from www.cs.armstrong.edu/liang/intro9e, contains the following resources:

- Microsoft PowerPoint slides with interactive buttons to view full-color, syntax-highlighted source code and to run programs without leaving the slides.

- Solutions to all programming exercises. Students will have access to the solutions of even-numbered programming exercises.

- Web-based quiz generator. (Instructors can choose chapters to generate quizzes from a large database of more than two thousand questions.)

- Sample exams. Most exams have four parts:

  - Multiple-choice questions or short-answer questions

  - Correct programming errors

- Trace programs
- Write programs

- Projects. In general, each project gives a description and asks students to analyze, design, and implement the project.

Some readers have requested the materials from the Instructor Resource Website. Please understand that these are for instructors only. Such requests will not be answered.

Algorithm Animations

We have provided numerous animations for algorithms. These are valuable pedagogical tools to demonstrate how algorithms work. Algorithm animations can be accessed from the Companion Website.

Acknowledgments

I would like to thank Armstrong Atlantic State University for enabling me to teach what I write and for supporting me in writing what I teach. Teaching is the source of inspiration for continuing to improve the book. I am grateful to the instructors and students who have offered comments, suggestions, bug reports, and praise.

This book has been greatly enhanced thanks to outstanding reviews for this and previous editions. The reviewers are: Elizabeth Adams (James Madison University), Syed Ahmed (North Georgia College and State University), Omar Aldawud (Illinois Institute of Technology), Yang Ang (University of Wollongong, Australia), Kevin Bierre (Rochester Institute of Technology), David Champion (DeVry Institute), James Chegwidden (Tarrant County College), Anup Dargar (University of North Dakota), Charles Dierbach (Towson University), Frank Ducrest (University of Louisiana at Lafayette), Erica Eddy (University of Wisconsin at Parkside), Deena Engel (New York University), Henry A. Etlinger (Rochester Institute of Technology), James Ten Eyck (Marist College), Myers Foreman (Lamar University), Olac Fuentes (University of Texas at El Paso), Edward F. Gehringer (North Carolina State University), Harold Grossman (Clemson University), Barbara Guillot (Louisiana State University), Stuart Hansen (University of Wisconsin, Parkside), Dan Harvey (Southern Oregon University), Ron Hofman (Red River College, Canada), Stephen Hughes (Roanoke College), Vladan Jovanovic (Georgia Southern University), Edwin Kay (Lehigh University), Larry King (University of Texas at Dallas), Nana Kofi (Langara College, Canada), George Koutsogiannakis (Illinois Institute of Technology), Roger Kraft (Purdue University at Calumet), Norman Krumpe (Miami University), Hong Lin (DeVry Institute), Dan Lipsa (Armstrong Atlantic State University), James Madison (Rensselaer Polytechnic Institute), Frank Malinowski (Darton College), Tim Margush (University of Akron), Debbie Masada (Sun Microsystems), Blayne Mayfield (Oklahoma State University), John McGrath (J.P. McGrath Consulting), Hugh McGuire (Grand Valley State), Shyamal Mitra (University of Texas at Austin), Michel Mitri (James Madison University), Kenrick Mock (University of Alaska Anchorage), Frank Murgolo (California State University, Long Beach), Jun Ni (University of Iowa), Benjamin Nystuen (University of Colorado at Colorado Springs), Maureen Opkins (CA State University, Long Beach), Gavin Osborne (University of Saskatchewan), Kevin Parker (Idaho State University), Dale Parson (Kutztown University), Mark Pendergast (Florida Gulf Coast University), Richard Povinelli (Marquette University), Roger Priebe (University of Texas at Austin), Mary Ann Pumphrey (De Anza Junior College), Pat Roth (Southern Polytechnic State University), Amr Sabry (Indiana University), Carolyn Schauble (Colorado State University), David Scuse (University of Manitoba), Ashraf Shirani (San Jose State University), Daniel Spiegel (Kutztown University), Joslyn A. Smith (Florida Atlantic University), Lixin Tao (Pace University), Ronald F. Taylor (Wright State University), Russ

Tront (Simon Fraser University), Deborah Trytten (University of Oklahoma), Kent Vidrine (George Washington University), and Bahram Zartoshty (California State University at Northridge).

It is a great pleasure, honor, and privilege to work with Pearson. I would like to thank Tracy Dunkelberger and her colleagues Marcia Horton, Michael Hirsch, Matt Goldstein, Carole Snyder, Tim Huddleston, Yez Alayan, Jeff Holcomb, Kayla Smith-Tarbox, Gillian Hall, Rebecca Greenberg, and their colleagues for organizing, producing, and promoting this project.

As always, I am indebted to my wife, Samantha, for her love, support, and encouragement.

BRIEF CONTENTS

1 Introduction to Computers, Programs, and Java   1

2 Elementary Programming   33

3 Selections   81

4 Loops   133

5 Methods   177

6 Single-Dimensional Arrays   223

7 Multidimensional Arrays   263

8 Objects and Classes   295

9 Strings   335

10 Thinking in Objects   369

11 Inheritance and Polymorphism   407

12 GUI Basics   445

13 Graphics   479

14 Exception Handling and Text I/O   517

15 Abstract Classes and Interfaces   559

16 Event-Driven Programming   599

17 GUI Components   639

18 Applets and Multimedia   671

19 Binary I/O   709

20 Recursion   737

APPENDIXES

A Java Keywords   771

B The ASCII Character Set   772

C Operator Precedence Chart   774

D Java Modifiers   776

E Special Floating-Point Values   778

F Number Systems   779

G Bitwise Operations   783

INDEX   785

CONTENTS

Chapter 1   **Introduction to Computers, Programs, and Java**   1

1.1	Introduction	2
1.2	What Is a Computer?	2
1.3	Programming Languages	9
1.4	Operating Systems	12
1.5	Java, the World Wide Web, and Beyond	13
1.6	The Java Language Specification, API, JDK, and IDE	16
1.7	A Simple Java Program	16
1.8	Creating, Compiling, and Executing a Java Program	19
1.9	Displaying Text in a Message Dialog Box	22
1.10	Programming Style and Documentation	24
1.11	Programming Errors	26

Chapter 2   **Elementary Programming**   33

2.1	Introduction	34
2.2	Writing a Simple Program	34
2.3	Reading Input from the Console	37
2.4	Identifiers	40
2.5	Variables	40
2.6	Assignment Statements and Assignment Expressions	42
2.7	Named Constants	43
2.8	Naming Conventions	44
2.9	Numeric Data Types and Operations	44
2.10	Numeric Literals	48
2.11	Evaluating Expressions and Operator Precedence	50
2.12	Case Study: Displaying the Current Time	51
2.13	Augmented Assignment Operators	53
2.14	Increment and Decrement Operators	54
2.15	Numeric Type Conversions	56
2.16	Software Development Process	58
2.17	Character Data Type and Operations	62
2.18	The String Type	68
2.19	Getting Input from Input Dialogs	70

Chapter 3   Selections   81

   3.1   Introduction   82
   3.2   boolean Data Type   82
   3.3   if Statements   84
   3.4   Case Study: Guessing Birthdays   86
   3.5   Two-Way if-else Statements   89
   3.6   Nested if and Multi-Way if-else Statements   91
   3.7   Common Errors in Selection Statements   93
   3.8   Generating Random Numbers   96
   3.9   Case Study: Computing Body Mass Index   97
   3.10   Case Study: Computing Taxes   99
   3.11   Logical Operators   101
   3.12   Case Study: Determining Leap Year   105
   3.13   Case Study: Lottery   106
   3.14   switch Statements   108
   3.15   Conditional Expressions   111
   3.16   Formatting Console Output   112
   3.17   Operator Precedence and Associativity   115
   3.18   Confirmation Dialogs   117
   3.19   Debugging   119

Chapter 4   Loops   133

   4.1   Introduction   134
   4.2   The while Loop   134
   4.3   The do-while Loop   144
   4.4   The for Loop   146
   4.5   Which Loop to Use?   150
   4.6   Nested Loops   152
   4.7   Minimizing Numeric Errors   154
   4.8   Case Studies   155
   4.9   Keywords *break* and *continue*   159
   4.10   Case Study: Displaying Prime Numbers   162
   4.11   Controlling a Loop with a Confirmation Dialog   164

Chapter 5   Methods   177

   5.1   Introduction   178
   5.2   Defining a Method   178
   5.3   Calling a Method   180
   5.4   void Method Example   183
   5.5   Passing Parameters by Values   186

5.6	Modularizing Code	189
5.7	Case Study: Converting Decimals to Hexadecimals	191
5.8	Overloading Methods	193
5.9	The Scope of Variables	196
5.10	The Math Class	197
5.11	Case Study: Generating Random Characters	201
5.12	Method Abstraction and Stepwise Refinement	203

Chapter 6   Single-Dimensional Arrays   223

6.1	Introduction	224
6.2	Array Basics	224
6.3	Case Study: Lotto Numbers	231
6.4	Case Study: Deck of Cards	234
6.5	Copying Arrays	236
6.6	Passing Arrays to Methods	237
6.7	Returning an Array from a Method	240
6.8	Case Study: Counting the Occurrences of Each Letter	241
6.9	Variable-Length Argument Lists	244
6.10	Searching Arrays	245
6.11	Sorting Arrays	248
6.12	The Arrays Class	252

Chapter 7   Multidimensional Arrays   263

7.1	Introduction	264
7.2	Two-Dimensional Array Basics	264
7.3	Processing Two-Dimensional Arrays	267
7.4	Passing Two-Dimensional Arrays to Methods	269
7.5	Case Study: Grading a Multiple-Choice Test	270
7.6	Case Study: Finding the Closest Pair	272
7.7	Case Study: Sudoku	274
7.8	Multidimensional Arrays	277

Chapter 8   Objects and Classes   295

8.1	Introduction	296
8.2	Defining Classes for Objects	296
8.3	Example: Defining Classes and Creating Objects	298
8.4	Constructing Objects Using Constructors	303
8.5	Accessing Objects via Reference Variables	304
8.6	Using Classes from the Java Library	308
8.7	Static Variables, Constants, and Methods	312
8.8	Visibility Modifiers	317

	8.9	Data Field Encapsulation	319
	8.10	Passing Objects to Methods	322
	8.11	Array of Objects	326

Chapter 9   **Strings**   335

	9.1	Introduction	336
	9.2	The String Class	336
	9.3	Case Study: Checking Palindromes	347
	9.4	Case Study: Converting Hexadecimals to Decimals	348
	9.5	The Character Class	350
	9.6	The StringBuilder and StringBuffer Classes	353
	9.7	Command-Line Arguments	358

Chapter 10   **Thinking in Objects**   369

	10.1	Introduction	370
	10.2	Immutable Objects and Classes	370
	10.3	The Scope of Variables	371
	10.4	The this Reference	373
	10.5	Class Abstraction and Encapsulation	375
	10.6	Object-Oriented Thinking	379
	10.7	Object Composition	382
	10.8	Case Study: Designing the Course Class	384
	10.9	Case Study: Designing a Class for Stacks	386
	10.10	Case Study: Designing the GuessDate Class	388
	10.11	Class Design Guidelines	391
	10.12	Processing Primitive Data Type Values as Objects	393
	10.13	Automatic Conversion between Primitive Types and Wrapper Class Types	396
	10.14	The BigInteger and BigDecimal Classes	397

Chapter 11   **Inheritance and Polymorphism**   407

	11.1	Introduction	408
	11.2	Superclasses and Subclasses	408
	11.3	Using the super Keyword	414
	11.4	Overriding Methods	418
	11.5	Overriding vs. Overloading	418
	11.6	The Object Class and Its toString() Methods	420
	11.7	Polymorphism	421
	11.8	Dynamic Binding	422
	11.9	Casting Objects and the instanceof Operator	425
	11.10	The Object's equals Method	429

11.11 The ArrayList Class 430
11.12 Case Study: A Custom Stack Class 436
11.13 The protected Data and Methods 437
11.14 Preventing Extending and Overriding 439

Chapter 12 **GUI Basics** 445

12.1 Introduction 446
12.2 Swing vs. AWT 446
12.3 The Java GUI API 446
12.4 Frames 449
12.5 Layout Managers 451
12.6 Using Panels as Subcontainers 458
12.7 The Color Class 460
12.8 The Font Class 461
12.9 Common Features of Swing GUI Components 462
12.10 Image Icons 465
12.11 JButton 467
12.12 JCheckBox 471
12.13 JRadioButton 472
12.14 Labels 473
12.15 Text Fields 474

Chapter 13 **Graphics** 479

13.1 Introduction 480
13.2 The Graphics Class 480
13.3 Drawing Strings, Lines, Rectangles, and Ovals 483
13.4 Case Study: The FigurePanel Class 485
13.5 Drawing Arcs 488
13.6 Drawing Polygons and Polylines 490
13.7 Centering a String Using the FontMetrics Class 493
13.8 Case Study: The MessagePanel Class 495
13.9 Case Study: The StillClock Class 500
13.10 Displaying Images 504
13.11 Case Study: The ImageViewer Class 506

Chapter 14 **Exception Handling and Text I/O** 517

14.1 Introduction 518
14.2 Exception-Handling Overview 518
14.3 Exception Types 523
14.4 More on Exception Handling 526
14.5 The finally Clause 534

14.6	When to Use Exceptions	535
14.7	Rethrowing Exceptions	536
14.8	Chained Exceptions	537
14.9	Defining Custom Exception Classes	538
14.10	The File Class	541
14.11	File Input and Output	544
14.12	File Dialogs	549
14.13	Reading Data from the Web	551

Chapter 15   Abstract Classes and Interfaces   559

15.1	Introduction	560
15.2	Abstract Classes	560
15.3	Case Study: the Abstract Number Class	565
15.4	Case Study: Calendar and GregorianCalendar	567
15.5	Interfaces	570
15.6	The Comparable Interface	573
15.7	The Cloneable Interface	577
15.8	Interfaces vs. Abstract Classes	581
15.9	Case Study: The Rational Class	584

Chapter 16   Event-Driven Programming   599

16.1	Introduction	600
16.2	Events and Event Sources	602
16.3	Listeners, Registrations, and Handling Events	603
16.4	Inner Classes	608
16.5	Anonymous Class Listeners	609
16.6	Alternative Ways of Defining Listener Classes	612
16.7	Case Study: Loan Calculator	615
16.8	Mouse Events	617
16.9	Listener Interface Adapters	620
16.10	Key Events	621
16.11	Animation Using the Timer Class	625

Chapter 17   GUI Components   639

17.1	Introduction	640
17.2	Events for JCheckBox, JRadioButton and JTextField	640
17.3	Text Areas	644
17.4	Combo Boxes	647
17.5	Lists	650
17.6	Scroll Bars	654

17.7	Sliders	657
17.8	Creating Multiple Windows	660

Chapter 18 Applets and Multimedia   671

18.1	Introduction	672
18.2	Developing Applets	672
18.3	The HTML File and the `<applet>`Tag	673
18.4	Applet Security Restrictions	675
18.5	Enabling Applets to Run as Applications	676
18.6	Applet Life-Cycle Methods	677
18.7	Passing Strings to Applets	679
18.8	Case Study: Bouncing Ball	683
18.9	Case Study: Developing a Tic-Tac-Toe Game	686
18.10	Locating Resources Using the URL Class	691
18.11	Playing Audio in Any Java Program	693
18.12	Case Study: National Flags and Anthems	695

Chapter 19 Binary I/O   709

19.1	Introduction	710
19.2	How Is Text I/O Handled in Java?	710
19.3	Text I/O vs. Binary I/O	711
19.4	Binary I/O Classes	712
19.5	Case Study: Copying Files	722
19.6	Object I/O	724
19.7	Random-Access Files	729

Chapter 20 Recursion   737

20.1	Introduction	738
20.2	Case Study: Computing Factorials	738
20.3	Case Study: Computing Fibonacci Numbers	741
20.4	Problem Solving Using Recursion	744
20.5	Recursive Helper Methods	746
20.6	Case Study: Finding the Directory Size	749
20.7	Case Study: Towers of Hanoi	750
20.8	Case Study: Fractals	754
20.9	Recursion vs. Iteration	757
20.10	Tail Recursion	758

APPENDIXES

Appendix A Java Keywords   771
Appendix B The ASCII Character Set   772
Appendix C Operator Precedence Chart   774
Appendix D Java Modifiers   776
Appendix E Special Floating-Point Values   778
Appendix F Number Systems   779
Appendix G Bitwise Operations   783

INDEX   785

VideoNote

VideoNotes

Locations of **VideoNotes**
http://www.pearsonhighered.com/liang

Chapter 1	Introduction to Computers, Programs, and Java	
	Your first Java program	17
	Eclipse brief tutorial	19
	NetBeans brief tutorial	19
	Compile and run a Java program	21
Chapter 2	Elementary Programming	
	Obtain input	37
	Use operators / and %	51
	Software development process	58
	Compute loan payments	59
	Compute BMI	77
Chapter 3	Selections	
	Program addition quiz	83
	Program subtraction quiz	96
	Use multi-way if-else statements	99
	Sort three integers	123
	Check point location	125
Chapter 4	Loops	
	Guess a number	137
	Multiple subtraction quiz	139
	Minimize numeric errors	154
	Display loan schedule	170
	Sum a series	170
Chapter 5	Methods	
	Define/invoke max method	180
	Use void method	183
	Modularize code	189
	Stepwise refinement	203
	Reverse an integer	212
	Estimate π	215
Chapter 6	Single-Dimensional Arrays	
	Random shuffling	228
	Lotto numbers	231
	Selection sort	249
	Coupon collector's problem	260
	Consecutive four	261
Chapter 7	Multidimensional Arrays	
	Find the row with the largest sum	268
	Grade multiple-choice test	270
	Sudoku	274
	Multiply two matrices	282
	Even number of 1s	289
Chapter 8	Objects and Classes	
	Define classes and objects	296
	Use classes	311
	Static vs. instance	312
	Data field encapsulation	319
	The Fan class	331

Chapter 9	Strings	
	Check palindrome	347
	Command-line argument	359
	Number conversion	364
	Check ISBN-10	367

Chapter 10	Thinking in Objects	
	Immutable objects and `this` keyword	370
	The `Loan` class	376
	The BMI class	380
	The `StackOfIntegers` class	386
	Process large numbers	397
	The `MyPoint` class	400

Chapter 11	Inheritance and Polymorphism	
	Geometric class hierarchy	408
	Polymorphism and dynamic binding demo	423
	The `ArrayList` class	430
	The `MyStack` class	436
	New `Account` class	443

Chapter 12	GUI Basics	
	Use `FlowLayout`	452
	Use panels as subcontainers	458
	Use Swing common properties	462
	Display a checkerboard	477
	Display a random matrix	478

Chapter 13	Graphics	
	The `FigurePanel` class	485
	The `MessagePanel` class	495
	The `StillClock` class	500
	Plot a function	511
	Plot a bar chart	512

Chapter 14	Exception Handling and Text I/O	
	Exception-handling advantages	518
	Create custom exception classes	538
	Write and read data	544
	`HexFormatException`	555

Chapter 15	Abstract Classes and Interfaces	
	Abstract `GeometricObject` class	560
	`Calendar` and `GregorianCalendar` classes	567
	The concept of interface	570
	Redesign the `Rectangle` class	593

Chapter 16	Event-Driven Programming	
	Listener and its registration	607
	Anonymous listener	610
	Move message using the mouse	618
	Animate a clock	628
	Animate a rising flag	632
	Check mouse point location	632

Chapter 17	GUI Components	
	Use text areas	668

Chapter 18	Applets and Multimedia	
	First applet	672
	Run applets standalone	676

	TicTacToe	686
	Audio and image	695
	Control a group of clocks	701
Chapter 19	**Binary I/O**	
	Copy file	722
	Object I/O	724
	Split a large file	734
Chapter 20	**Recursion**	
	Binary search	748
	Directory size	749
	Fractal (Sierpinski triangle)	754
	Search a string in a directory	764

INTRODUCTION TO COMPUTERS, PROGRAMS, AND JAVA

Objectives

- To understand computer basics, programs, and operating systems (§§1.2–1.4).

- To describe the relationship between Java and the World Wide Web (§1.5).

- To understand the meaning of Java language specification, API, JDK, and IDE (§1.6).

- To write a simple Java program (§1.7).

- To display output on the console (§1.7).

- To explain the basic syntax of a Java program (§1.7).

- To create, compile, and run Java programs (§1.8).

- To display output using the `JOptionPane` message dialog boxes (§1.9).

- To become familiar with Java programming style and documentation (§1.10).

- To explain the differences between syntax errors, runtime errors, and logic errors (§1.11).

1.1 Introduction

The central theme of this book is to learn how to solve problems by writing a program.

what is programming?
programming
program

This book is about programming. So, what is programming? The term *programming* means to create (or develop) software, which is also called a *program.* In basic terms, software contains the instructions that tell a computer—or a computerized device—what to do.

Software is all around you, even in devices that you might not think would need it. Of course, you expect to find and use software on a personal computer, but software also plays a role in running airplanes, cars, cell phones, and even toasters. On a personal computer, you use word processors to write documents, Web browsers to explore the Internet, and e-mail programs to send messages. These programs are all examples of software. Software developers create software with the help of powerful tools called *programming languages.*

This book teaches you how to create programs by using the Java programming language. There are many programming languages, some of which are decades old. Each language was invented for a specific purpose—to build on the strengths of a previous language, for example, or to give the programmer a new and unique set of tools. Knowing that there are so many programming languages available, it would be natural for you to wonder which one is best. But, in truth, there is no "best" language. Each one has its own strengths and weaknesses. Experienced programmers know that one language might work well in some situations, whereas a different language may be more appropriate in other situations. For this reason, seasoned programmers try to master as many different programming languages as they can, giving them access to a vast arsenal of software-development tools.

If you learn to program using one language, you should find it easy to pick up other languages. The key is to learn how to solve problems using a programming approach. That is the main theme of this book.

You are about to begin an exciting journey: learning how to program. At the outset, it is helpful to review computer basics, programs, and operating systems. If you are already familiar with such terms as CPU, memory, disks, operating systems, and programming languages, you may skip the review in Sections 1.2–1.4.

1.2 What Is a Computer?

A computer is an electronic device that stores and processes data.

hardware
software

A computer includes both *hardware* and *software.* In general, hardware comprises the visible, physical elements of the computer, and software provides the invisible instructions that control the hardware and make it perform specific tasks. Knowing computer hardware isn't essential to learning a programming language, but it can help you better understand the effects that a program's instructions have on the computer and its components. This section introduces computer hardware components and their functions.

A computer consists of the following major hardware components (Figure 1.1):

- A central processing unit (CPU)

- Memory (main memory)

- Storage devices (such as disks and CDs)

- Input devices (such as the mouse and keyboard)

- Output devices (such as monitors and printers)

- Communication devices (such as modems and network interface cards)

bus

A computer's components are interconnected by a subsystem called a *bus.* You can think of a bus as a sort of system of roads running among the computer's components; data and

FIGURE 1.1 A computer consists of a CPU, memory, storage devices, input devices, output devices, and communication devices.

power travel along the bus from one part of the computer to another. In personal computers, the bus is built into the computer's *motherboard,* which is a circuit case that connects all of the parts of a computer together, as shown in Figure 1.2.

motherboard

1.2.1 Central Processing Unit

The *central processing unit (CPU)* is the computer's brain. It retrieves instructions from memory and executes them. The CPU usually has two components: a *control unit* and an *arithmetic/logic unit.* The control unit controls and coordinates the actions of the other components. The arithmetic/logic unit performs numeric operations (addition, subtraction, multiplication, division) and logical operations (comparisons).

CPU

Today's CPUs are built on small silicon semiconductor chips that contain millions of tiny electric switches, called *transistors,* for processing information.

Every computer has an internal clock, which emits electronic pulses at a constant rate. These pulses are used to control and synchronize the pace of operations. A higher clock *speed* enables more instructions to be executed in a given period of time. The unit of measurement of clock speed is the *hertz (Hz),* with 1 hertz equaling 1 pulse per second. In the 1990s computers measured clocked speed in *megahertz (MHz),* but CPU speed has been improving continuously,

speed

hertz
megahertz

CPU is placed
under the fan

Memory

Motherboard

FIGURE 1.2 The motherboard connects all parts of a computer together.

gigahertz

and the clock speed of a computer is now usually stated in *gigahertz (GHz)*. Intel's newest processors run at about 3 GHz.

core

CPUs were originally developed with only one core. The *core* is the part of the processor that performs the reading and executing of instructions. In order to increase CPU processing power, chip manufacturers are now producing CPUs that contain multiple cores. A multicore CPU is a single component with two or more independent processors. Today's consumer computers typically have two, three, and even four separate cores. Soon, CPUs with dozens or even hundreds of cores will be affordable.

1.2.2 Bits and Bytes

Before we discuss memory, let's look at how information (data and programs) are stored in a computer.

A computer is really nothing more than a series of switches. Each switch exists in two states: on or off. Storing information in a computer is simply a matter of setting a sequence of switches on or off. If the switch is on, its value is 1. If the switch is off, its value is 0.

bits

These 0s and 1s are interpreted as digits in the binary number system and are called *bits* (binary digits).

byte

The minimum storage unit in a computer is a *byte*. A byte is composed of eight bits. A small number such as 3 can be stored as a single byte. To store a number that cannot fit into a single byte, the computer uses several bytes.

Data of various kinds, such as numbers and characters, are encoded as a series of bytes. As a programmer, you don't need to worry about the encoding and decoding of data, which the

encoding scheme

computer system performs automatically, based on the encoding scheme. An *encoding scheme* is a set of rules that govern how a computer translates characters, numbers, and symbols into data the computer can actually work with. Most schemes translate each character into a predetermined string of numbers. In the popular ASCII encoding scheme, for example, the character C is represented as 01000011 in one byte.

A computer's storage capacity is measured in bytes and multiples of the byte, as follows:

- A *kilobyte (KB)* is about 1,000 bytes.
- A *megabyte (MB)* is about 1 million bytes.
- A *gigabyte (GB)* is about 1 billion bytes.
- A *terabyte (TB)* is about 1 trillion bytes.

kilobyte (KB)

megabyte (MB)

gigabyte (GB)

terabyte (TB)

A typical one-page word document might take 20 KB. Therefore, 1 MB can store 50 pages of documents and 1 GB can store 50,000 pages of documents. A typical two-hour high-resolution movie might take 8 GB, so it would require 160 GB to store 20 movies.

1.2.3 Memory

A computer's *memory* consists of an ordered sequence of bytes for storing programs as well as data that the program is working with. You can think of memory as the computer's work area for executing a program. A program and its data must be moved into the computer's memory before they can be executed by the CPU.

memory

Every byte in the memory has a *unique address*, as shown in Figure 1.3. The address is used to locate the byte for storing and retrieving the data. Since the bytes in the memory can be accessed in any order, the memory is also referred to as *random-access memory (RAM)*.

unique address

RAM

FIGURE 1.3 Memory stores data and program instructions in uniquely addressed memory locations. Each memory location can store one byte of data.

Today's personal computers usually have at least 1 gigabyte of RAM, but they more commonly have 2 to 4 GB installed. Generally speaking, the more RAM a computer has, the faster it can operate, but there are limits to this simple rule of thumb.

A memory byte is never empty, but its initial content may be meaningless to your program. The current content of a memory byte is lost whenever new information is placed in it.

Like the CPU, memory is built on silicon semiconductor chips that have millions of transistors embedded on their surface. Compared to CPU chips, memory chips are less complicated, slower, and less expensive.

1.2.4 Storage Devices

A computer's memory (RAM) is a volatile form of data storage: any information that has been stored in memory (that is, saved) is lost when the system's power is turned off. Programs and data are permanently stored on *storage devices* and are moved, when the computer actually uses them, to memory, which operates at much faster speeds than permanent storage devices can.

storage devices

There are three main types of storage devices:

- Magnetic disk drives
- Optical disc drives (CD and DVD)
- USB flash drives

drive

Drives are devices for operating a medium, such as disks and CDs. A storage medium physically stores data and program instructions. The drive reads data from the medium and writes data onto the medium.

Disks

hard disk

A computer usually has at least one hard disk drive (Figure 1.4). *Hard disks* are used for permanently storing data and programs. Newer computers have hard disks that can store from 200 to 800 gigabytes of data. Hard disk drives are usually encased inside the computer, but removable hard disks are also available.

FIGURE 1.4 A hard disk is a device for permanently storing programs and data.

CDs and DVDs

CD-R

CD stands for compact disc. There are two types of CD drives: CD-R and CD-RW. A *CD-R* is for read-only permanent storage; the user cannot modify its contents once they are recorded.

CD-RW

A *CD-RW* can be used like a hard disk; that is, you can write data onto the disc, and then overwrite that data with new data. A single CD can hold up to 700 MB. Most new PCs are equipped with a CD-RW drive that can work with both CD-R and CD-RW discs.

DVD

DVD stands for digital versatile disc or digital video disc. DVDs and CDs look alike, and you can use either to store data. A DVD can hold more information than a CD; a standard DVD's storage capacity is 4.7 GB. Like CDs, there are two types of DVDs: DVD-R (read-only) and DVD-RW (rewritable).

USB Flash Drives

Universal serial bus (USB) connectors allow the user to attach many kinds of peripheral devices to the computer. You can use a USB to connect a printer, digital camera, mouse, external hard disk drive, and other devices to the computer.

A USB *flash drive* is a device for storing and transporting data. A flash drive is small—about the size of a pack of gum, as shown in Figure 1.5. It acts like a portable hard drive that can be plugged into your computer's USB port. USB flash drives are currently available with up to 256 GB storage capacity.

FIGURE 1.5 USB flash drives are very portable and can store a lot of data.

1.2.5 Input and Output Devices

Input and output devices let the user communicate with the computer. The most common input devices are *keyboards* and *mice*. The most common output devices are *monitors* and *printers*.

The Keyboard

A keyboard is a device for entering input. Figure 1.6 shows a typical keyboard. Compact keyboards are available without a numeric keypad.

FIGURE 1.6 A computer keyboard consists of the keys for sending input to a computer.

Function keys are located across the top of the keyboard and are prefaced with the letter *F.* Their functions depend on the software currently being used.   function key

modifier key

A *modifier key* is a special key (such as the *Shift*, *Alt*, and *Ctrl* keys) that modifies the normal action of another key when the two are pressed simultaneously.

numeric keypad

The *numeric keypad*, located on the right side of most keyboards, is a separate set of keys styled like a calculator to use for entering numbers quickly.

arrow keys

Arrow keys, located between the main keypad and the numeric keypad, are used to move the mouse pointer up, down, left, and right on the screen in many kinds of programs.

Insert key
Delete key
Page Up key
Page Down key

The *Insert*, *Delete*, *Page Up*, and *Page Down keys* are used in word processing and other programs for inserting text and objects, deleting text and objects, and moving up or down through a document one screen at a time.

The Mouse

A *mouse* is a pointing device. It is used to move a graphical pointer (usually in the shape of an arrow) called a *cursor* around the screen or to click on-screen objects (such as a button) to trigger them to perform an action.

The Monitor

The *monitor* displays information (text and graphics). The screen resolution and dot pitch determine the quality of the display.

screen resolution
pixels

The *screen resolution* specifies the number of pixels in horizontal and vertical dimensions of the display device. *Pixels* (short for "picture elements") are tiny dots that form an image on the screen. A common resolution for a 17-inch screen, for example, is 1,024 pixels wide and 768 pixels high. The resolution can be set manually. The higher the resolution, the sharper and clearer the image is.

dot pitch

The *dot pitch* is the amount of space between pixels, measured in millimeters. The smaller the dot pitch, the sharper the display.

1.2.6 Communication Devices

modem

Computers can be networked through communication devices, such as a dial-up *modem* (*mo*dulator/*dem*odulator), a DSL or cable modem, a wired network interface card, or a wireless adapter.

- A dial-up modem uses a phone line and can transfer data at a speed up to 56,000 bps (bits per second).

digital subscriber line (DSL)

- A *digital subscriber line (DSL)* connection also uses a standard phone line, but it can transfer data 20 times faster than a standard dial-up modem.

cable modem

- A *cable modem* uses the cable TV line maintained by the cable company and is generally faster than DSL.

network interface card (NIC)
local area network (LAN)

- A *network interface card (NIC)* is a device that connects a computer to a *local area network (LAN)*, as shown in Figure 1.7. LANs are commonly used in universities, businesses, and government agencies. A high-speed NIC called *1000BaseT* can transfer data at 1,000 million bits per second (mbps).

million bits per second (mbps)

- Wireless networking is now extremely popular in homes, businesses, and schools. Every laptop computer sold today is equipped with a wireless adapter that enables the computer to connect to a local area network and the Internet.

Note

Answers to checkpoint questions are on the Companion Website.

Check Point

1.1 What are hardware and software?

1.2 List five major hardware components of a computer.

MyProgrammingLab™

1.3 What does the acronym "CPU" stand for?

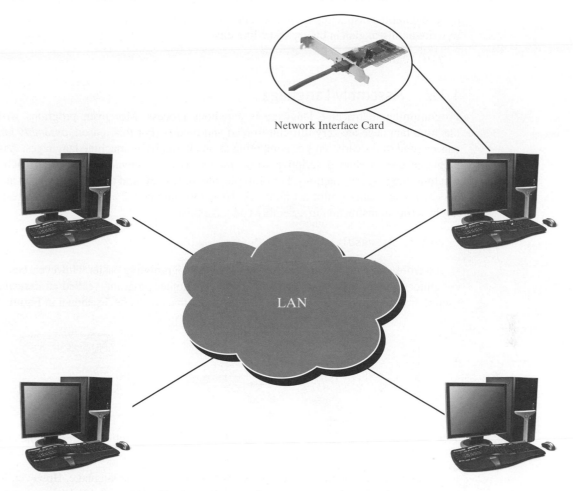

FIGURE 1.7 A local area network connects computers in close proximity to each other.

1.4 What unit is used to measure CPU speed?

1.5 What is a bit? What is a byte?

1.6 What is memory for? What does RAM stand for? Why is memory called RAM?

1.7 What unit is used to measure memory size?

1.8 What unit is used to measure disk size?

1.9 What is the primary difference between memory and a storage device?

1.3 Programming Languages

Computer programs, known as software, are instructions that tell a computer what to do.

Key Point

Computers do not understand human languages, so programs must be written in a language a computer can use. There are hundreds of programming languages, and they were developed to make the programming process easier for people. However, all programs must be converted into a language the computer can understand.

1.3.1 Machine Language

A computer's native language, which differs among different types of computers, is its *machine language*—a set of built-in primitive instructions. These instructions are in the form of binary code, so if you want to give a computer an instruction in its native language, you

machine language

have to enter the instruction as binary code. For example, to add two numbers, you might have to write an instruction in binary code, like this:

```
1101101010011010
```

1.3.2 Assembly Language

assembly language

Programming in machine language is a tedious process. Moreover, programs written in machine language are very difficult to read and modify. For this reason, *assembly language* was created in the early days of computing as an alternative to machine languages. Assembly language uses a short descriptive word, known as a *mnemonic*, to represent each of the machine-language instructions. For example, the mnemonic **add** typically means to add numbers and **sub** means to subtract numbers. To add the numbers **2** and **3** and get the result, you might write an instruction in assembly code like this:

```
add 2, 3, result
```

assembler

Assembly languages were developed to make programming easier. However, because the computer cannot understand assembly language, another program—called an *assembler*—is used to translate assembly-language programs into machine code, as shown in Figure 1.8.

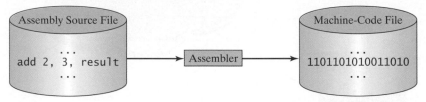

FIGURE 1.8 An assembler translates assembly-language instructions into machine code.

low-level language

Writing code in assembly language is easier than in machine language. However, it is still tedious to write code in assembly language. An instruction in assembly language essentially corresponds to an instruction in machine code. Writing in assembly requires that you know how the CPU works. Assembly language is referred to as a *low-level language*, because assembly language is close in nature to machine language and is machine dependent.

1.3.3 High-Level Language

high-level language

In the 1950s, a new generation of programming languages known as *high-level languages* emerged. They are platform-independent, which means that you can write a program in a high-level language and run it in different types of machines. High-level languages are English-like and easy to learn and use. The instructions in a high-level programming language are called *statements*. Here, for example, is a high-level language statement that computes the area of a circle with a radius of **5**:

statement

```
area = 5 * 5 * 3.1415
```

There are many high-level programming languages, and each was designed for a specific purpose. Table 1.1 lists some popular ones.

source program

source code

A program written in a high-level language is called a *source program* or *source code*. Because a computer cannot understand a source program, a source program must be translated into machine code for execution. The translation can be done using another programming tool called an *interpreter* or a *compiler*.

interpreter

compiler

■ An interpreter reads one statement from the source code, translates it to the machine code or virtual machine code, and then executes it right away, as shown in Figure 1.9a.

TABLE 1.1 Popular High-Level Programming Languages

Language	Description
Ada	Named for Ada Lovelace, who worked on mechanical general-purpose computers. The Ada language was developed for the Department of Defense and is used mainly in defense projects.
BASIC	Beginner's All-purpose Symbolic Instruction Code. It was designed to be learned and used easily by beginners.
C	Developed at Bell Laboratories. C combines the power of an assembly language with the ease of use and portability of a high-level language.
C++	C++ is an object-oriented language, based on C.
C#	Pronounced "C Sharp." It is a hybrid of Java and C++ and was developed by Microsoft.
COBOL	COmmon Business Oriented Language. Used for business applications.
FORTRAN	FORmula TRANslation. Popular for scientific and mathematical applications.
Java	Developed by Sun Microsystems, now part of Oracle. It is widely used for developing platform-independent Internet applications.
Pascal	Named for Blaise Pascal, who pioneered calculating machines in the seventeenth century. It is a simple, structured, general-purpose language primarily for teaching programming.
Python	A simple general-purpose scripting language good for writing short programs.
Visual Basic	Visual Basic was developed by Microsoft and it enables the programmers to rapidly develop graphical user interfaces.

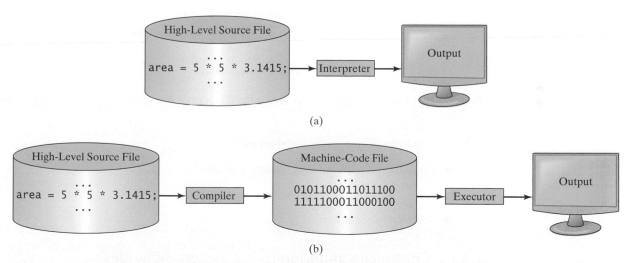

FIGURE 1.9 (a) An interpreter translates and executes a program one statement at a time. (b) A compiler translates the entire source program into a machine-language file for execution.

Note that a statement from the source code may be translated into several machine instructions.

- A compiler translates the entire source code into a machine-code file, and the machine-code file is then executed, as shown in Figure 1.9b.

1.10 What language does the CPU understand?

1.11 What is an assembly language?

Check Point

MyProgrammingLab™

1.12   What is an assembler?

1.13   What is a high-level programming language?

1.14   What is a source program?

1.15   What is an interpreter?

1.16   What is a compiler?

1.17   What is the difference between an interpreted language and a compiled language?

1.4 Operating Systems

🔑 **Key Point**

The operating system (OS) *is the most important program that runs on a computer. The OS manages and controls a computer's activities.*

operating system (OS)

The popular *operating systems* for general-purpose computers are Microsoft Windows, Mac OS, and Linux. Application programs, such as a Web browser or a word processor, cannot run unless an operating system is installed and running on the computer. Figure 1.10 shows the interrelationship of hardware, operating system, application software, and the user.

FIGURE 1.10   Users and applications access the computer's hardware via the operating system.

The major tasks of an operating system are:

- Controlling and monitoring system activities

- Allocating and assigning system resources

- Scheduling operations

1.4.1   Controlling and Monitoring System Activities

Operating systems perform basic tasks, such as recognizing input from the keyboard, sending output to the monitor, keeping track of files and folders on storage devices, and controlling peripheral devices, such as disk drives and printers. An operating system must also ensure that different programs and users working at the same time do not interfere with each other. In addition, the OS is responsible for security, ensuring that unauthorized users and programs do not access the system.

1.4.2   Allocating and Assigning System Resources

The operating system is responsible for determining what computer resources a program needs (such as CPU time, memory space, disks, input and output devices) and for allocating and assigning them to run the program.

1.4.3   Scheduling Operations

The OS is responsible for scheduling programs' activities to make efficient use of system resources. Many of today's operating systems support such techniques as *multiprogramming*, *multithreading*, and *multiprocessing* to increase system performance.

Multiprogramming allows multiple programs to run simultaneously by sharing the same CPU. The CPU is much faster than the computer's other components. As a result, it is idle most of the time—for example, while waiting for data to be transferred from a disk or waiting for other system resources to respond. A multiprogramming OS takes advantage of this situation by allowing multiple programs to use the CPU when it would otherwise be idle. For example, multiprogramming enables you to use a word processor to edit a file at the same time as your Web browser is downloading a file.

multiprogramming

Multithreading allows a single program to execute multiple tasks at the same time. For instance, a word-processing program allows users to simultaneously edit text and save it to a disk. In this example, editing and saving are two tasks within the same application. These two tasks may run concurrently.

multithreading

Multiprocessing, or *parallel processing*, uses two or more processors together to perform subtasks concurrently and then combine solutions of the subtasks to obtain a solution for the entire task. It is like a surgical operation where several doctors work together on one patient.

multiprocessing

1.18   What is an operating system? List some popular operating systems.

1.19   What are the major responsibilities of an operating system?

1.20   What are multiprogramming, multithreading, and multiprocessing?

MyProgrammingLab™

1.5   Java, the World Wide Web, and Beyond

Java is a powerful and versatile programming language for developing software running on mobile devices, desktop computers, and servers.

This book introduces Java programming. Java was developed by a team led by James Gosling at Sun Microsystems. Sun Microsystems was purchased by Oracle in 2010. Originally called *Oak,* Java was designed in 1991 for use in embedded chips in consumer electronic appliances. In 1995, renamed *Java,* it was redesigned for developing Web applications. For the history of Java, see www.java.com/en/javahistory/index.jsp.

Java has become enormously popular. Its rapid rise and wide acceptance can be traced to its design characteristics, particularly its promise that you can write a program once and run it anywhere. As stated by its designer, Java is *simple, object oriented, distributed, interpreted, robust, secure, architecture neutral, portable, high performance, multithreaded,* and *dynamic*. For the anatomy of Java characteristics, see www.cs.armstrong.edu/liang/JavaCharacteristics.pdf.

Java is a full-featured, general-purpose programming language that can be used to develop robust mission-critical applications. Today, it is employed not only for Web programming, but also for developing standalone applications across platforms on servers, desktop computers, and mobile devices. It was used to develop the code to communicate with and control the robotic rover on Mars. Many companies that once considered Java to be more hype than substance are now using it to create distributed applications accessed by customers and partners across the Internet. For every new project being developed today, companies are asking how they can use Java to make their work easier.

The World Wide Web is an electronic information repository that can be accessed on the Internet from anywhere in the world. The Internet, the Web's infrastructure, has been around for more than forty years. The colorful World Wide Web and sophisticated Web browsers are the major reason for the Internet's popularity.

applet

HTML

Java initially became attractive because Java programs can be run from a Web browser. Such programs are called *applets*. Applets employ a modern graphical interface with buttons, text fields, text areas, radio buttons, and so on, to interact with users on the Web and process their requests. Applets make the Web responsive, interactive, and fun to use. Applets are embedded in an HTML file. *HTML (Hypertext Markup Language)* is a simple scripting language for laying out documents, linking documents on the Internet, and bringing images, sound, and video alive on the Web. Figure 1.11 shows an applet running from a Web browser for playing a tic-tac-toe game.

Enter this URL from a Web browser

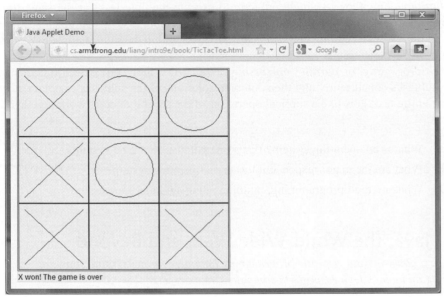

FIGURE 1.11 A Java applet for playing tic-tac-toe runs from a Web browser.

 Tip
For a demonstration of Java applets, visit java.sun.com/applets. This site provides a rich Java resource as well as links to other cool applet demo sites.

Java is now very popular for developing applications on Web servers. These applications process data, perform computations, and generate dynamic Web pages. The LiveLab automatic grading system, shown in Figure 1.12 and which you can use with this book, was developed using Java.

Java is a versatile programming language: You can use it to develop applications for desktop computers, servers, and small hand-held devices. The software for Android cell phones is developed using Java. Figure 1.13 shows an emulator for developing Android phone applications.

 ✓ Check Point

1.21 Who invented Java? Which company owns Java now?

1.22 What is a Java applet?

MyProgrammingLab™ **1.23** What programming language does Android use?

FIGURE 1.12   Java was used to develop LiveLab, the automatic grading system that accompanies this book.

FIGURE 1.13   Java is used in Android phones.

1.6 The Java Language Specification, API, JDK, and IDE

Java syntax is defined in the Java language specification, and the Java library is defined in the Java API. The JDK is the software for developing and running Java programs. An IDE is an integrated development environment for rapidly developing programs.

Computer languages have strict rules of usage. If you do not follow the rules when writing a program, the computer will not be able to understand it. The Java language specification and the Java API define the Java standards.

Java language specification

The *Java language specification* is a technical definition of the Java programming language's syntax and semantics. You can find the complete Java language specification at java.sun.com/docs/books/jls.

API
library

The *application program interface (API)*, also known as *library*, contains predefined classes and interfaces for developing Java programs. The API is still expanding. You can view and download the latest version of the Java API at www.oracle.com/technetwork/java/index.html.

Java is a full-fledged and powerful language that can be used in many ways. It comes in three editions:

Java SE, EE, and ME

- Java *Standard Edition (Java SE)* to develop client-side standalone applications or applets.

- *Java Enterprise Edition (Java EE)* to develop server-side applications, such as Java servlets, JavaServer Pages (JSP), and JavaServer Faces (JSF).

- *Java Micro Edition (Java ME)* to develop applications for mobile devices, such as cell phones.

This book uses Java SE to introduce Java programming. Java SE is the foundation upon which all other Java technology is based. There are many versions of Java SE. The latest, Java SE 7, is used in this book. Oracle releases each version with a *Java Development Toolkit (JDK)*. For Java SE 7, the Java Development Toolkit is called *JDK 1.7* (also known as *Java 7* or *JDK 7*).

Java Development Toolkit (JDK)
JDK 1.7 = JDK 7

The JDK consists of a set of separate programs, each invoked from a command line, for developing and testing Java programs. Instead of using the JDK, you can use a Java development tool (e.g., NetBeans, Eclipse, and TextPad)—software that provides an *integrated development environment (IDE)* for developing Java programs quickly. Editing, compiling, building, debugging, and online help are integrated in one graphical user interface. You simply enter source code in one window or open an existing file in a window, and then click a button or menu item or press a function key to compile and run the program.

Integrated development environment

Check Point
MyProgrammingLab™

1.24 What is the Java language specification?

1.25 What does JDK stand for?

1.26 What does IDE stand for?

1.27 Are tools like NetBeans and Eclipse different languages from Java, or are they dialects or extensions of Java?

1.7 A Simple Java Program

A Java program is executed from the `main` *method in the class.*

Let's begin with a simple Java program that displays the message `Welcome to Java!` on the console. (The word *console* is an old computer term that refers to the text entry and display device of a computer. *Console input* means to receive input from the keyboard, and *console output* means to display output on the monitor.) The program is shown in Listing 1.1.

what is a console?
console input
console output

LISTING 1.1 Welcome.java

```
1  public class Welcome {
2    public static void main(String[] args) {
3      // Display message Welcome to Java! on the console
4      System.out.println("Welcome to Java!");
5    }
6  }
```

class
main method
display message

VideoNote
Your first Java program

```
Welcome to Java!
```

Note that the line numbers are for reference purposes only; they are not part of the program. So, don't type line numbers in your program.

Line 1 defines a class. Every Java program must have at least one class. Each class has a name. By convention, class names start with an uppercase letter. In this example, the class name is `Welcome`.

Line 2 defines the `main` method. The program is executed from the `main` method. A class may contain several methods. The `main` method is the entry point where the program begins execution.

A method is a construct that contains statements. The `main` method in this program contains the `System.out.println` statement. This statement displays the string `Welcome to Java!` on the console (line 4). *String* is a programming term meaning a sequence of characters. A string must be enclosed in double quotation marks. Every statement in Java ends with a semicolon (`;`), known as the *statement terminator*.

Reserved words, or *keywords*, have a specific meaning to the compiler and cannot be used for other purposes in the program. For example, when the compiler sees the word `class`, it understands that the word after `class` is the name for the class. Other reserved words in this program are `public`, `static`, and `void`.

Line 3 is a *comment* that documents what the program is and how it is constructed. Comments help programmers to communicate and understand the program. They are not programming statements and thus are ignored by the compiler. In Java, comments are preceded by two slashes (`//`) on a line, called a *line comment,* or enclosed between `/*` and `*/` on one or several lines, called a *block comment* or *paragraph comment*. When the compiler sees `//`, it ignores all text after `//` on the same line. When it sees `/*`, it scans for the next `*/` and ignores any text between `/*` and `*/`. Here are examples of comments:

line numbers

class name

main method

string

statement terminator
reserved word
keyword

comment

line comment
block comment

```
// This application program displays Welcome to Java!
/* This application program displays Welcome to Java! */
/* This application program
   displays Welcome to Java! */
```

A pair of curly braces in a program forms a *block* that groups the program's components. In Java, each block begins with an opening brace (`{`) and ends with a closing brace (`}`). Every class has a *class block* that groups the data and methods of the class. Similarly, every method has a *method block* that groups the statements in the method. Blocks can be *nested*, meaning that one block can be placed within another, as shown in the following code.

block

Tip
An opening brace must be matched by a closing brace. Whenever you type an opening brace, immediately type a closing brace to prevent the missing-brace error. Most Java IDEs automatically insert the closing brace for each opening brace.

match braces

```
public class Welcome {                          Class block
   public static void main(String[] args) {
      System.out.println("Welcome to Java!");   Method block
   }
}
```

Caution

case sensitive

Java source programs are case sensitive. It would be wrong, for example, to replace `main` in the program with `Main`.

special characters

You have seen several special characters (e.g., { }, //, ;) in the program. They are used in almost every program. Table 1.2 summarizes their uses.

TABLE 1.2 Special Characters

Character	Name	Description
{}	Opening and closing braces	Denote a block to enclose statements.
()	Opening and closing parentheses	Used with methods.
[]	Opening and closing brackets	Denote an array.
//	Double slashes	Precede a comment line.
" "	Opening and closing quotation marks	Enclose a string (i.e., sequence of characters).
;	Semicolon	Mark the end of a statement.

common errors

syntax rules

The most common errors you will make as you learn to program will be syntax errors. Like any programming language, Java has its own syntax, and you need to write code that conforms to the *syntax rules.* If your program violates a rule—for example, if the semicolon is missing, a brace is missing, a quotation mark is missing, or a word is misspelled—the Java compiler will report syntax errors. Try to compile the program with these errors and see what the compiler reports.

Note

You are probably wondering why the `main` method is defined this way and why `System.out.println(...)` is used to display a message on the console. For the time being, simply accept that this is how things are done. Your questions will be fully answered in subsequent chapters.

The program in Listing 1.1 displays one message. Once you understand the program, it is easy to extend it to display more messages. For example, you can rewrite the program to display three messages, as shown in Listing 1.2.

LISTING 1.2 WelcomeWithThreeMessages.java

class
main method
display message

```
1  public class WelcomeWithThreeMessages {
2    public static void main(String[] args) {
3      System.out.println("Programming is fun!");
4      System.out.println("Fundamentals First");
5      System.out.println("Problem Driven");
6    }
7  }
```

```
Programming is fun!
Fundamentals First
Problem Driven
```

Further, you can perform mathematical computations and display the result on the console. Listing 1.3 gives an example of evaluating $\dfrac{10.5 + 2 \times 3}{45 - 3.5}$.

LISTING 1.3 ComputeExpression.java

```
1  public class ComputeExpression {
2    public static void main(String[] args) {
3      System.out.println((10.5 + 2 * 3) / (45 - 3.5));
4    }
5  }
```

class
main method
compute expression

```
0.39759036144578314
```

The multiplication operator in Java is *. As you can see, it is a straightforward process to translate an arithmetic expression to a Java expression. We will discuss Java expressions further in Chapter 2.

1.28   What is a keyword? List some Java keywords.

1.29   Is Java case sensitive? What is the case for Java keywords?

1.30   What is a comment? Is the comment ignored by the compiler? How do you denote a comment line and a comment paragraph?

1.31   What is the statement to display a string on the console?

1.32   Show the output of the following code:

```
public class Test {
  public static void main(String[] args) {
    System.out.println("3.5 * 4 / 2 - 2.5 is ");
    System.out.println(3.5 * 4 / 2 - 2.5);
  }
}
```

Check
Point

MyProgrammingLab™

1.8 Creating, Compiling, and Executing a Java Program

You save a Java program in a .java file and compile it into a .class file. The .class file is executed by the Java Virtual Machine.

You have to create your program and compile it before it can be executed. This process is repetitive, as shown in Figure 1.14. If your program has compile errors, you have to modify the program to fix them, then recompile it. If your program has runtime errors or does not produce the correct result, you have to modify the program, recompile it, and execute it again.

You can use any text editor or IDE to create and edit a Java source-code file. This section demonstrates how to create, compile, and run Java programs from a command window. If you wish to use an *IDE* such as Eclipse, NetBeans, or TextPad, refer to Supplement II for tutorials. From the command window, you can use a text editor such as Notepad to create the Java source-code file, as shown in Figure 1.15.

Key
Point

VideoNote
Eclipse brief tutorial

command window
IDE Supplements

VideoNote
NetBeans brief tutorial

file name

Note
The source file must end with the extension `.java` and must have the same exact name as the public class name. For example, the file for the source code in Listing 1.1 should be named **Welcome.java**, since the public class name is `Welcome`.

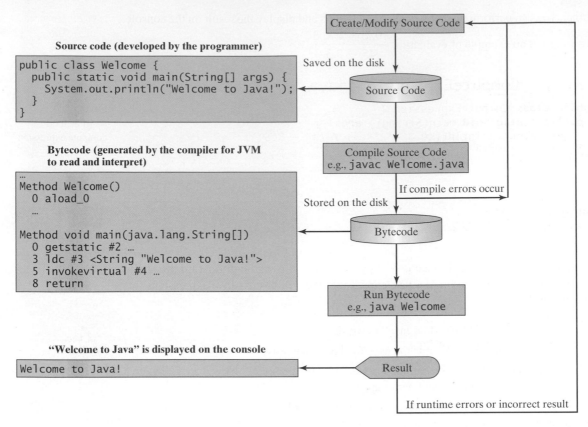

FIGURE 1.14 The Java program-development process consists of repeatedly creating/modifying source code, compiling, and executing programs.

FIGURE 1.15 You can create a Java source file using Windows Notepad.

A Java compiler translates a Java source file into a Java bytecode file. The following command compiles **Welcome.java**:

compile

```
javac Welcome.java
```

Note

You must first install and configure the JDK before you can compile and run programs. See Supplement I.B, Installing and Configuring JDK 7, for how to install the JDK and set up the environment to compile and run Java programs. If you have trouble compiling and running programs, see Supplement I.C, Compiling and Running Java from the Command Window. This supplement also explains how to use basic DOS commands and how to use Windows Notepad and WordPad to create and edit files. All the supplements are accessible from the Companion Website.

Supplement I.B

Supplement I.C

.class bytecode file

If there aren't any syntax errors, the *compiler* generates a bytecode file with a **.class** extension. Thus, the preceding command generates a file named **Welcome.class**, as shown in

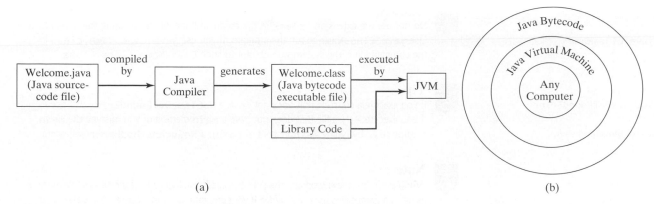

FIGURE 1.16 (a) Java source code is translated into bytecode. (b) Java bytecode can be executed on any computer with a Java Virtual Machine.

Figure 1.16a. The Java language is a high-level language, but Java bytecode is a low-level language. The *bytecode* is similar to machine instructions but is architecture neutral and can run on any platform that has a *Java Virtual Machine (JVM)*, as shown in Figure 1.16b. Rather than a physical machine, the virtual machine is a program that interprets Java bytecode. This is one of Java's primary advantages: *Java bytecode can run on a variety of hardware platforms and operating systems.* Java source code is compiled into Java bytecode and Java bytecode is interpreted by the JVM. Your Java code may use the code in the Java library. The JVM executes your code along with the code in the library.

bytecode
Java Virtual Machine (JVM)

To execute a Java program is to run the program's bytecode. You can execute the bytecode on any platform with a JVM, which is an interpreter. It translates the individual instructions in the bytecode into the target machine language code one at a time rather than the whole program as a single unit. Each step is executed immediately after it is translated.

interpret bytecode

The following command runs the bytecode for Listing 1.1:

run

```
java Welcome
```

Figure 1.17 shows the `javac` command for compiling **Welcome.java**. The compiler generates the **Welcome.class** file, and this file is executed using the `java` command.

javac command
java command

 Note
For simplicity and consistency, all source-code and class files used in this book are placed under **c:\book** unless specified otherwise.

c:\book

Compile ⟶
Show files ⟶
Run ⟶

VideoNote
Compile and run a Java program

FIGURE 1.17 The output of Listing 1.1 displays the message "Welcome to Java!"

java ClassName

Caution

Do not use the extension **.class** in the command line when executing the program. Use **java ClassName** to run the program. If you use **java ClassName.class** in the command line, the system will attempt to fetch **ClassName.class.class**.

NoClassDefFoundError

NoSuchMethodError

Tip

If you execute a class file that does not exist, a **NoClassDefFoundError** will occur. If you execute a class file that does not have a **main** method or you mistype the **main** method (e.g., by typing **Main** instead of **main**), a **NoSuchMethodError** will occur.

class loader

bytecode verifier

Note

When executing a Java program, the JVM first loads the bytecode of the class to memory using a program called the *class loader*. If your program uses other classes, the class loader dynamically loads them just before they are needed. After a class is loaded, the JVM uses a program called the *bytecode verifier* to check the validity of the bytecode and to ensure that the bytecode does not violate Java's security restrictions. Java enforces strict security to make sure that Java class files are not tampered and do not harm your computer.

use package

Pedagogical Note

Your instructor may require you to use packages for organizing programs. For example, you may place all programs in this chapter in a package named *chapter1*. For instructions on how to use packages, see Supplement I.F, Using Packages to Organize the Classes in the Text.

Check Point

MyProgrammingLab™

1.33 What is the Java source filename extension, and what is the Java bytecode filename extension?

1.34 What are the input and output of a Java compiler?

1.35 What is the command to compile a Java program?

1.36 What is the command to run a Java program?

1.37 What is the JVM?

1.38 Can Java run on any machine? What is needed to run Java on a computer?

1.39 If a **NoClassDefFoundError** occurs when you run a program, what is the cause of the error?

1.40 If a **NoSuchMethodError** occurs when you run a program, what is the cause of the error?

1.9 Displaying Text in a Message Dialog Box

Key Point

You can display text in a graphical dialog box.

The program in Listing 1.1 displays the text on the console, as shown in Figure 1.17. You can rewrite the program to display the text in a message dialog box. To do so, you need to use the **showMessageDialog** method in the **JOptionPane** class. **JOptionPane** is one of the many predefined classes in the Java library that you can reuse rather than "reinvent the wheel." You can use the **showMessageDialog** method to display any text in a message dialog box, as shown in Figure 1.18. The new program is given in Listing 1.4.

JOptionPane

showMessageDialog

LISTING 1.4 WelcomeInMessageDialogBox.java

block comment

```
1  /* This application program displays Welcome to Java!
2   * in a message dialog box.
3   */
```

FIGURE 1.18 "Welcome to Java!" is displayed in a message box.

```
4  import javax.swing.JOptionPane;                                    import
5
6  public class WelcomeInMessageDialogBox {
7    public static void main(String[] args) {                        main method
8      // Display Welcome to Java! in a message dialog box
9      JOptionPane.showMessageDialog(null,"Welcome to Java!");        display message
10   }
11 }
```

The first three lines are block comments. The first line begins with /* and the last line ends with */. By convention, all other lines begin with an asterisk (*).

This program uses the Java class **JOptionPane** (line 9). Java's predefined classes are grouped into packages. **JOptionPane** is in the **javax.swing** package. **JOptionPane** is   package
imported into the program using the **import** statement in line 4 so that the compiler can locate the class without the full name **javax.swing.JOptionPane**.

 Note
If you replace **JOptionPane** in line 9 with **javax.swing.JOptionPane**, you don't need to import it in line 4. **javax.swing.JOptionPane** is the full name for the **JOptionPane** class.

The **showMessageDialog** method is a *static* method. Such a method should be invoked by using the class name followed by a dot operator (**.**) and the method name with arguments. Details of methods will be discussed in Chapter 5. The **showMessageDialog** method can be invoked with two arguments, as shown below.

The first argument can always be **null**. **null** is a Java keyword that will be fully discussed in Chapter 8. The second argument is a string for text to be displayed.

There are several ways to use the **showMessageDialog** method. For the time being, you   two versions of
need to know only two ways. One is to use a statement, as shown in the example: showMessageDialog

```
JOptionPane.showMessageDialog(null, x);
```

where x is a string for the text to be displayed.

The other is to use a statement like this one:

```
JOptionPane.showMessageDialog(null, x,
  y, JOptionPane.INFORMATION_MESSAGE);
```

where **x** is a string for the text to be displayed, and **y** is a string for the title of the message box. The fourth argument can be `JOptionPane.INFORMATION_MESSAGE`, which causes the information icon ( ) to be displayed in the message box, as shown in the following example.

```
JOptionPane.showMessageDialog(null,
    "Welcome to Java!",
    "Display Message",
    JOptionPane.INFORMATION_MESSAGE);
```

Note

There are two types of **import** statements: *specific import* and *wildcard import*. The *specific import* specifies a single class in the import statement. For example, the following statement imports `JOptionPane` from the package `javax.swing`.

specific import

```
import javax.swing.JOptionPane;
```

wildcard import

The *wildcard import* imports all the classes in a package by using the asterisk as the wildcard. For example, the following statement imports all the classes from the package `javax.swing`.

```
import javax.swing.*;
```

no performance difference

The information for the classes in an imported package is not read in at compile time or runtime unless the class is used in the program. The import statement simply tells the compiler where to locate the classes. There is no performance difference between a specific import and a wildcard import declaration.

Note

Recall that you have used the `System` class in the statement `System.out.println
("Welcome to Java");` in Listing 1.1. The `System` class is not imported because it is in the `java.lang` package. All the classes in the `java.lang` package are *implicitly* imported in every Java program.

`java.lang` package
implicitly imported

**Check
Point**

MyProgrammingLab™

1.41 What is the statement to display the message "Hello world" in a message dialog box?

1.42 Why does the `System` class not need to be imported?

1.43 Are there any performance differences between the following two `import` statements?

```
import javax.swing.JOptionPane;
import javax.swing.*;
```

1.10 Programming Style and Documentation

**Key
Point**

Good programming style and proper documentation make a program easy to read and help programmers prevent errors.

programming style

documentation

Programming style deals with what programs look like. A program can compile and run properly even if written on only one line, but writing it all on one line would be bad programming style because it would be hard to read. *Documentation* is the body of explanatory remarks and comments pertaining to a program. Programming style and documentation are as important as coding. Good programming style and appropriate documentation reduce the chance of errors and make programs easy to read. This section gives several guidelines. For more detailed guidelines, see Supplement I.D, Java Coding Style Guidelines, on the Companion Website.

1.10.1 Appropriate Comments and Comment Styles

Include a summary at the beginning of the program that explains what the program does, its key features, and any unique techniques it uses. In a long program, you should also include comments that introduce each major step and explain anything that is difficult to read. It is important to make comments concise so that they do not crowd the program or make it difficult to read.

In addition to line comments (beginning with //) and block comments (beginning with /*), Java supports comments of a special type, referred to as *javadoc comments*. javadoc comments begin with /** and end with */. They can be extracted into an HTML file using the JDK's **javadoc** command. For more information, see java.sun.com/j2se/javadoc.

javadoc comment

Use javadoc comments (/** ... */) for commenting on an entire class or an entire method. These comments must precede the class or the method header in order to be extracted into a javadoc HTML file. For commenting on steps inside a method, use line comments (//). To see an example of a javadoc HTML file, check out www.cs.armstrong.edu/liang/javadoc/Exercise1.html. Its corresponding Java code is shown in www.cs.armstrong.edu/liang/javadoc/Exercise1.java.

1.10.2 Proper Indentation and Spacing

A consistent indentation style makes programs clear and easy to read, debug, and maintain. *Indentation* is used to illustrate the structural relationships between a program's components or statements. Java can read the program even if all of the statements are on the same long line, but humans find it easier to read and maintain code that is aligned properly. Indent each subcomponent or statement at least *two* spaces more than the construct within which it is nested.

indent code

A single space should be added on both sides of a binary operator, as shown in the following statement:

```
System.out.println(3+4*4);
```
◄──── Bad style

```
System.out.println(3 + 4 * 4);
```
◄──── Good style

1.10.3 Block Styles

A *block* is a group of statements surrounded by braces. There are two popular styles, *next-line* style and *end-of-line* style, as shown below.

```
public class Test
{
  public static void main(String[] args)
  {
    System.out.println("Block Styles");
  }
}
```
Next-line style

```
public class Test {
  public static void main(String[] args) {
    System.out.println("Block Styles");
  }
}
```
End-of-line style

The next-line style aligns braces vertically and makes programs easy to read, whereas the end-of-line style saves space and may help avoid some subtle programming errors. Both are acceptable block styles. The choice depends on personal or organizational preference. You should use a block style consistently—mixing styles is not recommended. This book uses the *end-of-line* style to be consistent with the Java API source code.

MyProgrammingLab™

1.44 Reformat the following program according to the programming style and documentation guidelines. Use the end-of-line brace style.

```java
public class Test
{
  // Main method
  public static void main(String[] args) {
  /** Display output */
  System.out.println("Welcome to Java");
  }
}
```

1.11 Programming Errors

Programming errors can be categorized into three types: syntax errors, runtime errors, *and* logic errors.

1.11.1 Syntax Errors

syntax errors
compile errors

Errors that are detected by the compiler are called *syntax errors* or *compile errors*. Syntax errors result from errors in code construction, such as mistyping a keyword, omitting some necessary punctuation, or using an opening brace without a corresponding closing brace. These errors are usually easy to detect, because the compiler tells you where they are and what caused them. For example, the program in Listing 1.5 has a syntax error, as shown in Figure 1.19.

LISTING 1.5 ShowSyntaxErrors.java

```java
1  public class ShowSyntaxErrors {
2    public static main(String[] args) {
3      System.out.println("Welcome to Java);
4    }
5  }
```

Four errors are reported, but the program actually has two errors:

- The keyword **void** is missing before **main** in line 2.

- The string **Welcome to Java** should be closed with a closing quotation mark in line 3.

Since a single error will often display many lines of compile errors, it is a good practice to fix errors from the top line and work downward. Fixing errors that occur earlier in the program may also fix additional errors that occur later.

Compile ───▶

```
Administrator: Command Prompt                                          _ □ X
c:\book>javac ShowSyntaxErrors.java
ShowSyntaxErrors.java:2: error: invalid method declaration; return type required

   public static main(String[] args) {
                 ^
ShowSyntaxErrors.java:3: error: unclosed string literal
     System.out.println("Welcome to Java);
                        ^
ShowSyntaxErrors.java:3: error: ';' expected
     System.out.println("Welcome to Java);
                                          ^
ShowSyntaxErrors.java:5: error: reached end of file while parsing
}
 ^
4 errors

c:\book>_
```

FIGURE 1.19 The compiler reports syntax errors.

Tip
If you don't know how to correct it, compare your program closely, character by character, with similar examples in the text. In the first few weeks of this course, you will probably spend a lot of time fixing syntax errors. Soon you will be familiar with Java syntax and can quickly fix syntax errors.

fix syntax errors

1.11.2 Runtime Errors

Runtime errors are errors that cause a program to terminate abnormally. They occur while a program is running if the environment detects an operation that is impossible to carry out. Input mistakes typically cause runtime errors. An *input error* occurs when the program is waiting for the user to enter a value, but the user enters a value that the program cannot handle. For instance, if the program expects to read in a number, but instead the user enters a string, this causes data-type errors to occur in the program.

runtime errors

Another example of runtime errors is division by zero. This happens when the divisor is zero for integer divisions. For instance, the program in Listing 1.6 would cause a runtime error, as shown in Figure 1.20.

LISTING 1.6 ShowRuntimeErrors.java

```
1  public class ShowRuntimeErrors {
2    public static void main(String[] args) {
3      System.out.println(1 / 0);
4    }
5  }
```

runtime error

Run

FIGURE 1.20 The runtime error causes the program to terminate abnormally.

1.11.3 Logic Errors

Logic errors occur when a program does not perform the way it was intended to. Errors of this kind occur for many different reasons. For example, suppose you wrote the program in Listing 1.7 to convert Celsius 35 degrees to a Fahrenheit degree:

logic errors

LISTING 1.7 ShowLogicErrors.java

```
1  public class ShowLogicErrors {
2    public static void main(String[] args) {
3      System.out.println("Celsius 35 is Fahrenheit degree ");
4      System.out.println((9 / 5) * 35 + 32);
5    }
6  }
```

```
Celsius 35 is Fahrenheit degree
67
```

You will get Fahrenheit **67** degrees, which is wrong. It should be **95.0**. In Java, the division for integers is an integer—the fractional part is truncated—so in Java **9 / 5** is **1**. To get the correct result, you need to use **9.0 / 5**, which results in **1.8**.

In general, syntax errors are easy to find and easy to correct, because the compiler gives indications as to where the errors came from and why they are wrong. Runtime errors are not difficult to find, either, since the reasons and locations for the errors are displayed on the console when the program aborts. Finding logic errors, on the other hand, can be very challenging. In the upcoming chapters, you will learn the techniques of tracing programs and finding logic errors.

MyProgrammingLab™

1.45 What are syntax errors (compile errors), runtime errors, and logic errors?

1.46 Give examples of syntax errors, runtime errors, and logic errors.

1.47 If you forget to put a closing quotation mark on a string, what kind error will be raised?

1.48 If your program needs to read integers, but the user entered strings, an error would occur when running this program. What kind of error is this?

1.49 Suppose you write a program for computing the perimeter of a rectangle and you mistakenly write your program so that it computes the area of a rectangle. What kind of error is this?

1.50 Identify and fix the errors in the following code:

```
1  public class Welcome {
2    public void Main(String[] args) {
3      System.out.println('Welcome to Java!);
4    }
5  }
```

1.51 The following program is wrong. Reorder the lines so that the program displays **morning** followed by **afternoon**.

```
1      public static void main(String[] args) {
2      }
3  public class Welcome {
4      System.out.println("afternoon");
5      System.out.println("morning");
6  }
```

KEY TERMS

Application Program Interface (API) 16	dot pitch 8
assembler 10	DSL (digital subscriber line) 8
assembly language 10	encoding scheme 4
bit 4	hardware 2
block 17	high-level language 10
block comment 17	integrated development environment
bus 2	(IDE) 16
byte 4	interpreter 10
bytecode 21	java command 21
bytecode verifier 22	Java Development Toolkit (JDK) 16
cable modem 8	Java language specification 16
central processing unit (CPU) 3	Java Virtual Machine (JVM) 21
class loader 22	javac command 21
comment 17	keyword (or reserved word) 17
compiler 10	library 16
console 16	line comment 17

logic error   27
low-level language   10
machine language   9
`main` method   17
memory   5
modem   8
motherboard   3
network interface card (NIC)   8
operating system (OS)   12
pixel   8
program   2

programming   2
runtime error   27
screen resolution   8
software   2
source code   10
source program   10
specific import   24
statement   10
storage devices   5
syntax error   26
wildcard import   24

Note
The above terms are defined in this chapter. Supplement I.A, Glossary, lists all the key terms and descriptions in the book, organized by chapters.

Supplement I.A

CHAPTER SUMMARY

1. A computer is an electronic device that stores and processes data.

2. A computer includes both *hardware* and *software*.

3. Hardware is the physical aspect of the computer that can be touched.

4. Computer *programs*, known as *software*, are the invisible instructions that control the hardware and make it perform tasks.

5. Computer *programming* is the writing of instructions (i.e., code) for computers to perform.

6. The *central processing unit (CPU)* is a computer's brain. It retrieves instructions from *memory* and executes them.

7. Computers use zeros and ones because digital devices have two stable states, referred to by convention as zero and one.

8. A *bit* is a binary digit 0 or 1.

9. A *byte* is a sequence of 8 bits.

10. A kilobyte is about 1,000 bytes, a megabyte about 1 million bytes, a gigabyte about 1 billion bytes, and a terabyte about 1,000 gigabytes.

11. Memory stores data and program instructions for the CPU to execute.

12. A memory unit is an ordered sequence of bytes.

13. Memory is volatile, because information is lost when the power is turned off.

14. Programs and data are permanently stored on *storage devices* and are moved to memory when the computer actually uses them.

15. The *machine language* is a set of primitive instructions built into every computer.

16. *Assembly language* is a *low-level programming language* in which a mnemonic is used to represent each machine-language instruction.

17. *High-level languages* are English-like and easy to learn and program.

18. A program written in a high-level language is called a *source program.*

19. A *compiler* is a software program that translates the source program into a *machine-language program.*

20. The *operating system (OS)* is a program that manages and controls a computer's activities.

21. Java is platform independent, meaning that you can write a program once and run it on any computer.

22. Java programs can be embedded in HTML pages and downloaded by Web browsers to bring live animation and interaction to Web clients.

23. The Java source file name must match the public class name in the program. Java source code files must end with the `.java` extension.

24. Every class is compiled into a separate bytecode file that has the same name as the class and ends with the `.class` extension.

25. To compile a Java source-code file from the command line, use the *javac command.*

26. To run a Java class from the command line, use the *java command.*

27. Every Java program is a set of class definitions. The keyword `class` introduces a class definition. The contents of the class are included in a *block.*

28. A block begins with an opening brace ({) and ends with a closing brace (}).

29. Methods are contained in a class. To run a Java program, the program must have a `main` method. The `main` method is the entry point where the program starts when it is executed.

30. Every *statement* in Java ends with a semicolon (;), known as the *statement terminator.*

31. *Reserved words,* or *keywords,* have a specific meaning to the compiler and cannot be used for other purposes in the program.

32. In Java, comments are preceded by two slashes (//) on a line, called a *line comment,* or enclosed between /* and */ on one or several lines, called a *block comment* or *paragraph comment.* Comments are ignored by the compiler.

33. Java source programs are case sensitive.

34. There are two types of `import` statements: *specific import* and *wildcard import*. The specific import specifies a single class in the import statement; the wildcard import imports all the classes in a package.

35. Programming errors can be categorized into three types: *syntax errors*, *runtime errors*, and *logic errors*. Errors that occur during compilation are called syntax errors or *compile errors*. Runtime errors are errors that cause a program to terminate abnormally. Logic errors occur when a program does not perform the way it was intended to.

TEST QUESTIONS

Do the test questions for this chapter online at www.cs.armstrong.edu/liang/intro9e/test.html.

PROGRAMMING EXERCISES

MyProgrammingLab™

Note
Solutions to even-numbered exercises are on the Companion Website. Solutions to all exercises are on the Instructor Resource Website. The level of difficulty is rated easy (no star), moderate (*), hard (**), or challenging (***).

level of difficulty

1.1 (*Display three messages*) Write a program that displays `Welcome to Java`, `Welcome to Computer Science`, and `Programming is fun`.

1.2 (*Display five messages*) Write a program that displays `Welcome to Java` five times.

*__1.3__ (*Display a pattern*) Write a program that displays the following pattern:

```
J     A     V     V     A
 J    A A    V   V   A A
J  J  AAAAA   V V    AAAAA
 J J  A   A    V    A     A
```

1.4 (*Print a table*) Write a program that displays the following table:

```
a     a^2    a^3
1     1      1
2     4      8
3     9      27
4     16     64
```

1.5 (*Compute expressions*) Write a program that displays the result of
$$\frac{9.5 \times 4.5 - 2.5 \times 3}{45.5 - 3.5}.$$

1.6 (*Summation of a series*) Write a program that displays the result of
$$1 + 2 + 3 + 4 + 5 + 6 + 7 + 8 + 9.$$

1.7 (*Approximate* π) π can be computed using the following formula:
$$\pi = 4 \times \left(1 - \frac{1}{3} + \frac{1}{5} - \frac{1}{7} + \frac{1}{9} - \frac{1}{11} + \cdots \right)$$

Write a program that displays the result of $4 \times \left(1 - \frac{1}{3} + \frac{1}{5} - \frac{1}{7} + \frac{1}{9} - \frac{1}{11} \right)$

and $4 \times \left(1 - \frac{1}{3} + \frac{1}{5} - \frac{1}{7} + \frac{1}{9} - \frac{1}{11} + \frac{1}{13} \right)$. Use `1.0` instead of `1` in your program.

1.8 (*Area and perimeter of a circle*) Write a program that displays the area and perimeter of a circle that has a radius of 5.5 using the following formula:

$$perimeter = 2 \times radius \times \pi$$
$$area = radius \times radius \times \pi$$

1.9 (*Area and perimeter of a rectangle*) Write a program that displays the area and perimeter of a rectangle with the width of 4.5 and height of 7.9 using the following formula:

$$area = width \times height$$

1.10 (*Average speed in miles*) Assume a runner runs 14 kilometers in 45 minutes and 30 seconds. Write a program that displays the average speed in miles per hour. (Note that 1 mile is 1.6 kilometers.)

*1.11 (*Population projection*) The U.S. Census Bureau projects population based on the following assumptions:

- One birth every 7 seconds
- One death every 13 seconds
- One new immigrant every 45 seconds

Write a program to display the population for each of the next five years. Assume the current population is 312,032,486 and one year has 365 days. *Hint*: In Java, if two integers perform division, the result is an integer. The fraction part is truncated. For example, 5 / 4 is 1 (not 1.25) and 10 / 4 is 2 (not 2.5).

1.12 (*Average speed in kilometers*) Assume a runner runs 24 miles in 1 hour, 40 minutes, and 35 seconds. Write a program that displays the average speed in kilometers per hour. (Note that 1 mile is 1.6 kilometers.)

ELEMENTARY PROGRAMMING

Objectives

- To write Java programs to perform simple computations (§2.2).
- To obtain input from the console using the `Scanner` class (§2.3).
- To use identifiers to name variables, constants, methods, and classes (§2.4).
- To use variables to store data (§§2.5–2.6).
- To program with assignment statements and assignment expressions (§2.6).
- To use constants to store permanent data (§2.7).
- To name classes, methods, variables, and constants by following their naming conventions (§2.8).
- To explore Java numeric primitive data types: `byte`, `short`, `int`, `long`, `float`, and `double` (§2.9.1).
- To perform operations using operators +, -, *, /, and % (§2.9.2).
- To perform exponent operations using `Math.pow(a, b)` (§2.9.3).
- To write integer literals, floating-point literals, and literals in scientific notation (§2.10).
- To write and evaluate numeric expressions (§2.11).
- To obtain the current system time using `System.currentTimeMillis()` (§2.12).
- To use augmented assignment operators (§2.13).
- To distinguish between postincrement and preincrement and between postdecrement and predecrement (§2.14).
- To cast the value of one type to another type (§2.15).
- To describe the software development process and apply it to develop the loan payment program (§2.16).
- To represent characters using the `char` type (§2.17).
- To represent a string using the `String` type (§2.18).
- To obtain input using the `JOptionPane` input dialog boxes (§2.19).

2.1 Introduction

Key
Point

The focus of this chapter is on learning elementary programming techniques to solve problems.

In Chapter 1 you learned how to create, compile, and run very basic Java programs. Now you will learn how to solve problems by writing programs. Through these problems, you will learn elementary programming using primitive data types, variables, constants, operators, expressions, and input and output.

Suppose, for example, that you need to take out a student loan. Given the loan amount, loan term, and annual interest rate, can you write a program to compute the monthly payment and total payment? This chapter shows you how to write programs like this. Along the way, you learn the basic steps that go into analyzing a problem, designing a solution, and implementing the solution by creating a program.

2.2 Writing a Simple Program

Key
Point

Writing a program involves designing a strategy for solving the problem and then using a programming language to implement that strategy.

problem

algorithm

pseudocode

Let's first consider the simple problem of computing the area of a circle. How do we write a program for solving this problem?

Writing a program involves designing algorithms and translating algorithms into programming instructions, or code. An *algorithm* describes how a problem is solved by listing the actions that need to be taken and the order of their execution. Algorithms can help the programmer plan a program before writing it in a programming language. Algorithms can be described in natural languages or in *pseudocode* (natural language mixed with some programming code). The algorithm for calculating the area of a circle can be described as follows:

1. Read in the circle's radius.

2. Compute the area using the following formula:

$$area = radius \times radius \times \pi$$

3. Display the result.

Tip
It's always good practice to outline your program (or its underlying problem) in the form of an algorithm before you begin coding.

When you *code*—that is, when you write a program—you translate an algorithm into a program. You already know that every Java program begins with a class definition in which the keyword **class** is followed by the class name. Assume that you have chosen **ComputeArea** as the class name. The outline of the program would look like this:

```
public class ComputeArea {
  // Details to be given later
}
```

As you know, every Java program must have a **main** method where program execution begins. The program is then expanded as follows:

```
public class ComputeArea {
  public static void main(String[] args) {
    // Step 1: Read in radius

    // Step 2: Compute area
```

```
    // Step 3: Display the area
  }
}
```

The program needs to read the radius entered by the user from the keyboard. This raises two important issues:

- Reading the radius.
- Storing the radius in the program.

Let's address the second issue first. In order to store the radius, the program needs to declare a symbol called a *variable*. A variable represents a value stored in the computer's memory.

Rather than using x and y as variable names, choose descriptive names: in this case, radius for radius, and area for area. To let the compiler know what radius and area are, specify their data types. That is the kind of the data stored in a variable, whether integer, *floating-point number*, or something else. This is known as *declaring variables.* Java provides simple data types for representing integers, floating-point numbers (i.e., numbers with a decimal point), characters, and Boolean types. These types are known as *primitive data types* or *fundamental types.*

Declare radius and area as double-precision floating-point numbers. The program can be expanded as follows:

```
public class ComputeArea {
  public static void main(String[] args) {
    double radius;
    double area;

    // Step 1: Read in radius

    // Step 2: Compute area

    // Step 3: Display the area
  }
}
```

The program declares radius and area as variables. The reserved word double indicates that radius and area are double-precision floating-point values stored in the computer.

The first step is to prompt the user to designate the circle's radius. You will learn how to prompt the user for information shortly. For now, to learn how variables work, you can assign a fixed value to radius in the program as you write the code; later, you'll modify the program to prompt the user for this value.

The second step is to compute area by assigning the result of the expression radius * radius * 3.14159 to area.

In the final step, the program will display the value of area on the console by using the System.out.println method.

Listing 2.1 shows the complete program, and a sample run of the program is shown in Figure 2.1.

LISTING 2.1 ComputeArea.java

```
1  public class ComputeArea {
2    public static void main(String[] args) {
3      double radius; // Declare radius
4      double area; // Declare area
5
6      // Assign a radius
7      radius = 20; // radius is now 20
```

Margin notes: variable; descriptive names; data type; declare variables; floating-point number; primitive data types

```
 8
 9      // Compute area
10      area = radius * radius * 3.14159;
11
12      // Display results
13      System.out.println("The area for the circle of radius " +
14        radius + " is " + area);
15    }
16  }
```

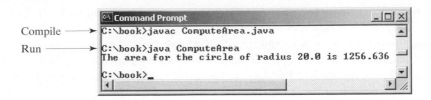

Compile
Run

FIGURE 2.1   The program displays the area of a circle.

declare variable
assign value

Variables such as **radius** and **area** correspond to memory locations. Every variable has a name, a type, a size, and a value. Line 3 declares that **radius** can store a **double** value. The value is not defined until you assign a value. Line 7 assigns **20** into variable **radius**. Similarly, line 4 declares variable **area**, and line 10 assigns a value into **area**. The following table shows the value in the memory for **area** and **radius** as the program is executed. Each row in the table shows the values of variables after the statement in the corresponding line in the program is executed. This method of reviewing how a program works is called *tracing a program*. Tracing programs are helpful for understanding how programs work, and they are useful tools for finding errors in programs.

tracing program

line#	radius	area
3	no value	
4		no value
7	20	
10		1256.636

concatenate strings

concatenate strings with
numbers

The plus sign (+) has two meanings: one for addition and the other for concatenating (combining) strings. The plus sign (+) in lines 13–14 is called a *string concatenation operator*. It combines two strings into one. If a string is combined with a number, the number is converted into a string and concatenated with the other string. Therefore, the plus signs (+) in lines 13–14 concatenate strings into a longer string, which is then displayed in the output. Strings and string concatenation will be discussed further in Section 2.18.

Caution
A string cannot cross lines in the source code. Thus, the following statement would result in a compile error:

```
System.out.println("Introduction to Java Programming,
   by Y. Daniel Liang");
```

To fix the error, break the string into separate substrings, and use the concatenation operator (+) to combine them:

break a long string

```
System.out.println("Introduction to Java Programming, " +
    "by Y. Daniel Liang");
```

Tip
This example consists of three steps. It is a good approach to develop and test these steps incrementally by adding them one at a time.

incremental development and testing

2.1 Identify and fix the errors in the following code:

```
 1  public class Test {
 2    public void main(string[] args) {
 3      int i;
 4      int k = 100.0;
 5      int j = i + 1;
 6
 7      System.out.println("j is " + j + " and
 8        k is " + k);
 9    }
10  }
```

MyProgrammingLab™

2.3 Reading Input from the Console

Reading input from the console enables the program to accept input from the user.

In Listing 2.1, the radius is fixed in the source code. To use a different radius, you have to modify the source code and recompile it. Obviously, this is not convenient, so instead you can use the **Scanner** class for console input.

VideoNote
Obtain input

Java uses **System.out** to refer to the standard output device and **System.in** to the standard input device. By default, the output device is the display monitor and the input device is the keyboard. To perform console output, you simply use the **println** method to display a primitive value or a string to the console. Console input is not directly supported in Java, but you can use the **Scanner** class to create an object to read input from **System.in**, as follows:

```
Scanner input = new Scanner(System.in);
```

The syntax **new Scanner(System.in)** creates an object of the **Scanner** type. The syntax **Scanner input** declares that **input** is a variable whose type is **Scanner**. The whole line **Scanner input = new Scanner(System.in)** creates a **Scanner** object and assigns its reference to the variable **input**. An object may invoke its methods. To invoke a method on an object is to ask the object to perform a task. You can invoke the methods listed in Table 2.1 to read various types of input.

For now, we will see how to read a number that includes a decimal point by invoking the **nextDouble()** method. Other methods will be covered when they are used. Listing 2.2 rewrites Listing 2.1 to prompt the user to enter a radius.

LISTING 2.2 ComputeAreaWithConsoleInput.java

```
1  import java.util.Scanner; // Scanner is in the java.util package
2
3  public class ComputeAreaWithConsoleInput {
4    public static void main(String[] args) {
5      // Create a Scanner object
6      Scanner input = new Scanner(System.in);
7
```

import class

create a Scanner

TABLE 2.1 Methods for Scanner Objects

Method	Description
nextByte()	reads an integer of the **byte** type.
nextShort()	reads an integer of the **short** type.
nextInt()	reads an integer of the **int** type.
nextLong()	reads an integer of the **long** type.
nextFloat()	reads a number of the **float** type.
nextDouble()	reads a number of the **double** type.
next()	reads a string that ends before a whitespace character.
nextLine()	reads a line of text (i.e., a string ending with the *Enter* key pressed).

read a double

```
 8      // Prompt the user to enter a radius
 9      System.out.print("Enter a number for radius: ");
10      double radius = input.nextDouble();
11
12      // Compute area
13      double area = radius * radius * 3.14159;
14
15      // Display results
16      System.out.println("The area for the circle of radius " +
17        radius + " is " + area);
18    }
19  }
```

```
Enter a number for radius: 2.5 ⏎Enter
The area for the circle of radius 2.5 is 19.6349375
```

```
Enter a number for radius: 23 ⏎Enter
The area for the circle of radius 23.0 is 1661.90111
```

The **Scanner** class is in the **java.util** package. It is imported in line 1. Line 6 creates a **Scanner** object.

The statement in line 9 displays a message to prompt the user for input.

```
System.out.print("Enter a number for radius: ");
```

print vs. println

The **print** method is identical to the **println** method except that **println** moves to the beginning of the next line after displaying the string, but **print** does not advance to the next line when completed.

The statement in line 10 reads input from the keyboard.

```
double radius = input.nextDouble();
```

After the user enters a number and presses the *Enter* key, the program reads the number and assigns it to **radius**.

More details on objects will be introduced in Chapter 8. For the time being, simply accept that this is how to obtain input from the console.

Listing 2.3 gives an example of reading multiple input from the keyboard. The program reads three numbers and displays their average.

LISTING 2.3 ComputeAverage.java

```java
 1  import java.util.Scanner; // Scanner is in the java.util package
 2
 3  public class ComputeAverage {
 4    public static void main(String[] args) {
 5      // Create a Scanner object
 6      Scanner input = new Scanner(System.in);
 7
 8      // Prompt the user to enter three numbers
 9      System.out.print("Enter three numbers: ");
10      double number1 = input.nextDouble();
11      double number2 = input.nextDouble();
12      double number3 = input.nextDouble();
13
14      // Compute average
15      double average = (number1 + number2 + number3) / 3;
16
17      // Display results
18      System.out.println("The average of " + number1 + " " + number2
19        + " " + number3 + " is " + average);
20    }
21  }
```

import class

create a Scanner

read a double

```
Enter three numbers: 1 2 3 ⏎Enter
The average of 1.0 2.0 3.0 is 2.0
```

enter input in one line

```
Enter three numbers: 10.5 ⏎Enter
11 ⏎Enter
11.5 ⏎Enter
The average of 10.5 11.0 11.5 is 11.0
```

enter input in multiple lines

The code for importing the **Scanner** class (line 1) and creating a **Scanner** object (line 6) are the same as in the preceding example as well as in all new programs you will write for reading input from the keyboard.

Line 9 prompts the user to enter three numbers. The numbers are read in lines 10–12. You may enter three numbers separated by spaces, then press the *Enter* key, or enter each number followed by a press of the *Enter* key, as shown in the sample runs of this program.

If you entered an input other than a numeric value, a runtime error would occur. In Chapter 14, you will learn how to handle the exception so that the program can continue to run.

runtime error

Note

Most of the programs in the early chapters of this book perform three steps: input, process, and output, called *IPO*. Input is receiving input from the user; process is producing results using the input; and output is displaying the results.

IPO

MyProgrammingLab™

2.2   How do you write a statement to let the user enter an integer or a double value from the keyboard?

2.3   What happens if you entered `5a` when executing the following code?

```
double radius = input.nextDouble();
```

2.4 Identifiers

Identifiers are the names that identify the elements such as classes, methods, and variables in a program.

identifiers
identifier naming rules

As you see in Listing 2.3, `ComputeAverage`, `main`, `input`, `number1`, `number2`, `number3`, and so on are the names of things that appear in the program. In programming terminology, such names are called *identifiers*. All identifiers must obey the following rules:

- An identifier is a sequence of characters that consists of letters, digits, underscores (_), and dollar signs ($).

- An identifier must start with a letter, an underscore (_), or a dollar sign ($). It cannot start with a digit.

- An identifier cannot be a reserved word. (See Appendix A for a list of reserved words.)

- An identifier cannot be `true`, `false`, or `null`.

- An identifier can be of any length.

For example, `$2`, `ComputeArea`, `area`, `radius`, and `showMessageDialog` are legal identifiers, whereas `2A` and `d+4` are not because they do not follow the rules. The Java compiler detects illegal identifiers and reports syntax errors.

case sensitive

Note

Since Java is case sensitive, `area`, `Area`, and `AREA` are all different identifiers.

Tip

Identifiers are for naming variables, constants, methods, classes, and packages. Descriptive identifiers make programs easy to read. Avoid using abbreviations for identifiers. Using complete words is more descriptive. For example, `numberOfStudents` is better than `numStuds`, `numOfStuds`, or `numOfStudents`. We use descriptive names for complete programs in the text. However, we will occasionally use variables names such as `i`, `j`, `k`, `x`, and `y` in the code snippets for brevity. These names also provide a generic tone to the code snippets.

descriptive names

the $ character

Tip

Do not name identifiers with the $ character. By convention, the $ character should be used only in mechanically generated source code.

MyProgrammingLab™

2.4   Which of the following identifiers are valid? Which are Java keywords?

```
miles, Test, a++, --a, 4#R, $4, #44, apps
class, public, int, x, y, radius
```

2.5 Variables

Variables are used to represent values that may be changed in the program.

why called variables?

As you see from the programs in the preceding sections, variables are used to store values to be used later in a program. They are called variables because their values can be changed. In the program in Listing 2.2, `radius` and `area` are variables of the double-precision, floating-point type. You can assign any numerical value to `radius` and `area`, and the values of `radius` and `area` can be reassigned. For example, in the following code, `radius` is initially `1.0` (line 2) and then changed to `2.0` (line 7), and area is set to `3.14159` (line 3) and then reset to `12.56636` (line 8).

```
1  // Compute the first area
2  radius = 1.0;                                        radius: | 1.0     |
3  area = radius * radius * 3.14159;                       area: | 3.14159 |
4  System.out.println("The area is "+ area +" for radius "+ radius);
5
6  // Compute the second area
7  radius = 2.0;                                        radius: | 2.0      |
8  area = radius * radius * 3.14159;                       area: | 12.56636 |
9  System.out.println("The area is "+ area +" for radius "+ radius);
```

Variables are for representing data of a certain type. To use a variable, you declare it by telling the compiler its name as well as what type of data it can store. The *variable declaration* tells the compiler to allocate appropriate memory space for the variable based on its data type. The syntax for declaring a variable is

```
datatype variableName;
```

Here are some examples of variable declarations:

declare variable

```
int count;          // Declare count to be an integer variable
double radius;      // Declare radius to be a double variable
double interestRate; // Declare interestRate to be a double variable
```

These examples use the data types `int` and `double`. Later you will be introduced to additional data types, such as `byte`, `short`, `long`, `float`, `char`, and `boolean`.

If variables are of the same type, they can be declared together, as follows:

```
datatype variable1, variable2, ..., variablen;
```

The variables are separated by commas. For example,

```
int i, j, k; // Declare i, j, and k as int variables
```

Variables often have initial values. You can declare a variable and initialize it in one step. Consider, for instance, the following code:

initialize variables

```
int count = 1;
```

This is equivalent to the next two statements:

```
int count;
count = 1;
```

You can also use a shorthand form to declare and initialize variables of the same type together. For example,

```
int i = 1, j = 2;
```

Tip

A variable must be declared before it can be assigned a value. A variable declared in a method must be assigned a value before it can be used.

Whenever possible, declare a variable and assign its initial value in one step. This will make the program easy to read and avoid programming errors.

scope of a variable

Every variable has a scope. The *scope of a variable* is the part of the program where the variable can be referenced. The rules that define the scope of a variable will be introduced gradually later in the book. For now, all you need to know is that a variable must be declared and initialized before it can be used. Consider the following code:

```
int interestRate = 0.05
int interest = interestrate * 45
```

This code is wrong, because `interestRate` is assigned a value `0.05`, but `interestrate` has not been declared and initialized. Java is case sensitive, so it considers `interestRate` and `interestrate` to be two different variables.

2.6 Assignment Statements and Assignment Expressions

 Key Point

An assignment statement designates a value for a variable. An assignment statement can be used as an expression in Java.

assignment statement
assignment operator

After a variable is declared, you can assign a value to it by using an *assignment statement*. In Java, the equal sign (=) is used as the *assignment operator*. The syntax for assignment statements is as follows:

```
variable = expression;
```

expression

An *expression* represents a computation involving values, variables, and operators that, taking them together, evaluates to a value. For example, consider the following code:

```
int y = 1;              // Assign 1 to variable y
double radius = 1.0;    // Assign 1.0 to variable radius
int x = 5 * (3 / 2);    // Assign the value of the expression to x
x = y + 1;              // Assign the addition of y and 1 to x
area = radius * radius * 3.14159; // Compute area
```

You can use a variable in an expression. A variable can also be used in both sides of the = operator. For example,

```
x = x + 1;
```

In this assignment statement, the result of `x + 1` is assigned to `x`. If `x` is `1` before the statement is executed, then it becomes `2` after the statement is executed.

To assign a value to a variable, you must place the variable name to the left of the assignment operator. Thus, the following statement is wrong:

```
1 = x; // Wrong
```

 Note

In mathematics, `x = 2 * x + 1` denotes an equation. However, in Java, `x = 2 * x + 1` is an assignment statement that evaluates the expression `2 * x + 1` and assigns the result to `x`.

assignment expression

In Java, an assignment statement is essentially an expression that evaluates to the value to be assigned to the variable on the left side of the assignment operator. For this reason, an assignment statement is also known as an *assignment expression*. For example, the following statement is correct:

```
System.out.println(x = 1);
```

which is equivalent to

```
x = 1;
System.out.println(x);
```

If a value is assigned to multiple variables, you can use this syntax:

```
i = j = k = 1;
```

which is equivalent to

```
k = 1;
j = k;
i = j;
```

 Note

In an assignment statement, the data type of the variable on the left must be compatible with the data type of the value on the right. For example, `int x = 1.0` would be illegal, because the data type of `x` is `int`. You cannot assign a `double` value (`1.0`) to an `int` variable without using type casting. Type casting is introduced in Section 2.15.

2.7 Named Constants

A named constant is an identifier that represents a permanent value.

 Key Point

The value of a variable may change during the execution of a program, but a *named constant,* or simply *constant,* represents permanent data that never changes. In our `ComputeArea` program, π is a constant. If you use it frequently, you don't want to keep typing `3.14159`; instead, you can declare a constant for π. Here is the syntax for declaring a constant:

constant

```
final datatype CONSTANTNAME = value;
```

A constant must be declared and initialized in the same statement. The word `final` is a Java keyword for declaring a constant. For example, you can declare π as a constant and rewrite Listing 2.1 as follows:

final keyword

```java
// ComputeArea.java: Compute the area of a circle
public class ComputeArea {
  public static void main(String[] args) {
    final double PI = 3.14159; // Declare a constant

    // Assign a radius
    double radius = 20;

    // Compute area
    double area = radius * radius * PI;

    // Display results
    System.out.println("The area for the circle of radius " +
      radius + " is " + area);
  }
}
```

There are three benefits of using constants: (1) You don't have to repeatedly type the same value if it is used multiple times; (2) if you have to change the constant value (e.g., from `3.14` to `3.14159` for `PI`), you need to change it only in a single location in the source code; and (3) a descriptive name for a constant makes the program easy to read.

benefits of constants

2.8 Naming Conventions

Sticking with the Java naming conventions makes your programs easy to read and avoids errors.

Make sure that you choose descriptive names with straightforward meanings for the variables, constants, classes, and methods in your program. As mentioned earlier, names are case sensitive. Listed below are the conventions for naming variables, methods, and classes.

name variables and methods

■ Use lowercase for variables and methods. If a name consists of several words, concatenate them into one, making the first word lowercase and capitalizing the first letter of each subsequent word—for example, the variables `radius` and `area` and the method `showMessageDialog`.

name classes

■ Capitalize the first letter of each word in a class name—for example, the class names `ComputeArea`, `System`, and `JOptionPane`.

name constants

■ Capitalize every letter in a constant, and use underscores between words—for example, the constants `PI` and `MAX_VALUE`.

It is important to follow the naming conventions to make your programs easy to read.

name classes

 Caution

Do not choose class names that are already used in the Java library. For example, since the `System` class is defined in Java, you should not name your class `System`.

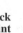 **Check Point**

MyProgrammingLab

2.5 What are the benefits of using constants? Declare an `int` constant `SIZE` with value `20`.

2.6 What are the naming conventions for class names, method names, constants, and variables? Which of the following items can be a constant, a method, a variable, or a class according to the Java naming conventions?

```
MAX_VALUE, Test, read, readInt
```

2.7 Translate the following algorithm into Java code:

Step 1: Declare a `double` variable named `miles` with initial value `100`.

Step 2: Declare a `double` constant named `KILOMETERS_PER_MILE` with value `1.609`.

Step 3: Declare a `double` variable named `kilometers`, multiply `miles` and `KILOMETERS_PER_MILE`, and assign the result to `kilometers`.

Step 4: Display `kilometers` to the console.

What is kilometers after Step 4?

2.9 Numeric Data Types and Operations

*Java has six numeric types for integers and floating-point numbers with operators +, -, *, /, and %.*

2.9.1 Numeric Types

Every data type has a range of values. The compiler allocates memory space for each variable or constant according to its data type. Java provides eight primitive data types for numeric values, characters, and Boolean values. This section introduces numeric data types and operators.

Table 2.2 lists the six numeric data types, their ranges, and their storage sizes.

TABLE 2.2 Numeric Data Types

Name	Range	Storage Size	
byte	-2^7 to 2^7-1 $(-128$ to $127)$	8-bit signed	byte type
short	-2^{15} to $2^{15}-1$ $(-32768$ to $32767)$	16-bit signed	short type
int	-2^{31} to $2^{31}-1$ $(-2147483648$ to $2147483647)$	32-bit signed	int type
long	-2^{63} to $2^{63}-1$ (i.e., -9223372036854775808 to 9223372036854775807)	64-bit signed	long type
float	Negative range: $-3.4028235E+38$ to $-1.4E-45$ Positive range: $1.4E-45$ to $3.4028235E+38$	32-bit IEEE 754	float type
double	Negative range: $-1.7976931348623157E+308$ to $-4.9E-324$ Positive range: $4.9E-324$ to $1.7976931348623157E+308$	64-bit IEEE 754	double type

Note

IEEE 754 is a standard approved by the Institute of Electrical and Electronics Engineers for representing floating-point numbers on computers. The standard has been widely adopted. Java uses the 32-bit **IEEE 754** for the `float` type and the 64-bit **IEEE 754** for the `double` type. The **IEEE 754** standard also defines special floating-point values, which are listed in Appendix E.

Java uses four types for integers: `byte`, `short`, `int`, and `long`. Choose the type that is most appropriate for your variable. For example, if you know an integer stored in a variable is within a range of a byte, declare the variable as a `byte`. For simplicity and consistency, we will use `int` for integers most of the time in this book.

Java uses two types for floating-point numbers: `float` and `double`. The `double` type is twice as big as `float`, so the `double` is known as *double precision* and `float` as *single precision*. Normally you should use the `double` type, because it is more accurate than the `float` type.

integer types

floating-point types

Caution

When a variable is assigned a value that is too large (*in size*) to be stored, it causes *overflow*. For example, executing the following statement causes overflow, because the largest value that can be stored in a variable of the `int` type is `2147483647`. `2147483648` will be too large for an `int` value.

what is overflow?

```
int value = 2147483647 + 1;
// value will actually be -2147483648
```

Likewise, executing the following statement causes overflow, because the smallest value that can be stored in a variable of the `int` type is `-2147483648`. `-2147483649` will be too large in size to be stored in an `int` variable.

```
int value = -2147483648 - 1;
// value will actually be 2147483647
```

Java does not report warnings or errors on overflow, so be careful when working with numbers close to the maximum or minimum range of a given type.

what is underflow?

When a floating-point number is too small (i.e., too close to zero) to be stored, it causes *underflow*. Java approximates it to zero, so normally you don't need to be concerned about underflow.

2.9.2 Numeric Operators

operators +, -, *, /, %

operands

The operators for numeric data types include the standard arithmetic operators: addition (+), subtraction (–), multiplication (*), division (/), and remainder (%), as shown in Table 2.3. The *operands* are the values operated by an operator.

TABLE 2.3 Numeric Operators

Name	Meaning	Example	Result
+	Addition	34 + 1	35
–	Subtraction	34.0 – 0.1	33.9
*	Multiplication	300 * 30	9000
/	Division	1.0 / 2.0	0.5
%	Remainder	20 % 3	2

integer division

When both operands of a division are integers, the result of the division is an integer and the fractional part is truncated. For example, **5 / 2** yields **2**, not **2.5**, and **–5 / 2** yields **–2**, not **–2.5**. To perform regular mathematical division, one of the operands must be a floating-point number. For example, **5.0 / 2** yields **2.5**.

The **%** operator, known as *remainder* or *modulo* operator, yields the remainder after division. The operand on the left is the dividend and the operand on the right is the divisor. Therefore, **7 % 3** yields **1**, **3 % 7** yields **3**, **12 % 4** yields **0**, **26 % 8** yields **2**, and **20 % 13** yields **7**.

$$
\begin{array}{ccccc}
2 & 0 & 3 & 3 & 1 \leftarrow \text{Quotient}\\
3\overline{)7} & 7\overline{)3} & 4\overline{)12} & 8\overline{)26} & \text{Divisor} \longrightarrow 13\overline{)20} \leftarrow \text{Dividend}\\
\underline{6} & \underline{0} & \underline{12} & \underline{24} & \underline{13}\\
1 & 3 & 0 & 2 & 7 \leftarrow \text{Remainder}
\end{array}
$$

The **%** operator is often used for positive integers, but it can also be used with negative integers and floating-point values. The remainder is negative only if the dividend is negative. For example, **–7 % 3** yields **–1**, **–12 % 4** yields **0**, **–26 % –8** yields **–2**, and **20 % –13** yields **7**.

Remainder is very useful in programming. For example, an even number **% 2** is always **0** and an odd number **% 2** is always **1**. Thus, you can use this property to determine whether a number is even or odd. If today is Saturday, it will be Saturday again in 7 days. Suppose you and your friends are going to meet in 10 days. What day is in 10 days? You can find that the day is Tuesday using the following expression:

The program in Listing 2.4 obtains minutes and remaining seconds from an amount of time in seconds. For example, **500** seconds contains **8** minutes and **20** seconds.

LISTING **2.4** DisplayTime.java

```
 1  import java.util.Scanner;
 2
 3  public class DisplayTime {
 4    public static void main(String[] args) {
 5      Scanner input = new Scanner(System.in);
 6      // Prompt the user for input
 7      System.out.print("Enter an integer for seconds: ");
 8      int seconds = input.nextInt();
 9
10      int minutes = seconds / 60; // Find minutes in seconds
11      int remainingSeconds = seconds % 60; // Seconds remaining
12      System.out.println(seconds + " seconds is " + minutes +
13        " minutes and " + remainingSeconds + " seconds");
14    }
15  }
```

import Scanner

create a Scanner

read an integer

divide
remainder

```
Enter an integer for seconds: 500  ↵Enter
500 seconds is 8 minutes and 20 seconds
```

line#	seconds	minutes	remainingSeconds
8	500		
10		8	
11			20

The `nextInt()` method (line 8) reads an integer for **seconds**. Line 10 obtains the minutes using **seconds / 60**. Line 11 (**seconds % 60**) obtains the remaining seconds after taking away the minutes.

The + and – operators can be both unary and binary. A *unary* operator has only one operand; a *binary* operator has two. For example, the – operator in **-5** is a unary operator to negate number **5**, whereas the – operator in **4 - 5** is a binary operator for subtracting **5** from **4**.

unary operator
binary operator

Note

Calculations involving floating-point numbers are approximated because these numbers are not stored with complete accuracy. For example,

floating-point approximation

```
System.out.println(1.0 - 0.1 - 0.1 - 0.1 - 0.1 - 0.1);
```

displays **0.5000000000000001**, not **0.5**, and

```
System.out.println(1.0 - 0.9);
```

displays **0.09999999999999998**, not **0.1**. Integers are stored precisely. Therefore, calculations with integers yield a precise integer result.

2.9.3 Exponent Operations

Math.pow(a, b) method

The `Math.pow(a, b)` method can be used to compute a^b. The `pow` method is defined in the `Math` class in the Java API. You invoke the method using the syntax `Math.pow(a, b)` (i.e., `Math.pow(2, 3)`), which returns the result of a^b (2^3). Here `a` and `b` are parameters for the `pow` method and the numbers `2` and `3` are actual values used to invoke the method. For example,

```
System.out.println(Math.pow(2, 3)); // Displays 8.0
System.out.println(Math.pow(4, 0.5)); // Displays 2.0
System.out.println(Math.pow(2.5, 2)); // Displays 6.25
System.out.println(Math.pow(2.5, -2)); // Displays 0.16
```

Chapter 5 introduces more details on methods. For now, all you need to know is how to invoke the `pow` method to perform the exponent operation.

Check
Point

MyProgrammingLab™

2.8 Find the largest and smallest `byte`, `short`, `int`, `long`, `float`, and `double`. Which of these data types requires the least amount of memory?

2.9 Show the result of the following remainders.

```
56 % 6
78 % -4
-34 % 5
-34 % -5
5 % 1
1 % 5
```

2.10 If today is Tuesday, what will be the day in 100 days?

2.11 What is the result of `25 / 4`? How would you rewrite the expression if you wished the result to be a floating-point number?

2.12 Are the following statements correct? If so, show the output.

```
System.out.println("25 / 4 is " + 25 / 4);
System.out.println("25 / 4.0 is " + 25 / 4.0);
System.out.println("3 * 2 / 4 is " + 3 * 2 / 4);
System.out.println("3.0 * 2 / 4 is " + 3.0 * 2 / 4);
```

2.13 Write a statement to display the result of $2^{3.5}$.

2.14 Suppose `m` and `r` are integers. Write a Java expression for mr^2 to obtain a floating-point result.

2.10 Numeric Literals

Key
Point

literal

A literal is a constant value that appears directly in a program.

For example, `34` and `0.305` are literals in the following statements:

```
int numberOfYears = 34;
double weight = 0.305;
```

2.10.1 Integer Literals

An integer literal can be assigned to an integer variable as long as it can fit into the variable. A compile error will occur if the literal is too large for the variable to hold. The statement `byte b = 128`, for example, will cause a compile error, because `128` cannot be stored in a variable of the `byte` type. (Note that the range for a byte value is from `-128` to `127`.)

An integer literal is assumed to be of the `int` type, whose value is between -2^{31} (-2147483648) and $2^{31} - 1$ (2147483647). To denote an integer literal of the `long` type, append the letter `L` or `l` to it. For example, to write integer `2147483648` in a Java program, you have to write it as `2147483648L` or `2147483648l`, because `2147483648` exceeds the range for the `int` value. `L` is preferred because `l` (lowercase `L`) can easily be confused with 1 (the digit one).

long type

Note

By default, an integer literal is a decimal integer number. To denote an octal integer literal, use a leading *0* (zero), and to denote a hexadecimal integer literal, use a leading *0x* or *0X* (zero x). For example, the following code displays the decimal value `65535` for hexadecimal number `FFFF`.

octal and hex literals

```
System.out.println(0xFFFF);
```

Hexadecimal numbers, binary numbers, and octal numbers are introduced in Appendix F.

2.10.2 Floating-Point Literals

Floating-point literals are written with a decimal point. By default, a floating-point literal is treated as a `double` type value. For example, `5.0` is considered a `double` value, not a `float` value. You can make a number a `float` by appending the letter `f` or `F`, and you can make a number a `double` by appending the letter `d` or `D`. For example, you can use `100.2f` or `100.2F` for a `float` number, and `100.2d` or `100.2D` for a `double` number.

suffix f or F
suffix d or D

Note

The `double` type values are more accurate than the `float` type values. For example,

double vs. float

```
System.out.println("1.0 / 3.0 is " + 1.0 / 3.0);
```

displays `1.0 / 3.0 is 0.3333333333333333`.

```
System.out.println("1.0F / 3.0F is " + 1.0F / 3.0F);
```

displays `1.0F / 3.0F is 0.33333334`.

2.10.3 Scientific Notation

Floating-point literals can be written in scientific notation in the form of a $\times 10^b$. For example, the scientific notation for 123.456 is 1.23456×10^2 and for 0.0123456 is 1.23456×10^{-2}. A special syntax is used to write scientific notation numbers. For example, 1.23456×10^2 is written as `1.23456E2` or `1.23456E+2` and 1.23456×10^{-2} as `1.23456E-2`. `E` (or `e`) represents an exponent and can be in either lowercase or uppercase.

Note

The `float` and `double` types are used to represent numbers with a decimal point. Why are they called *floating-point numbers*? These numbers are stored in scientific notation internally. When a number such as `50.534` is converted into scientific notation, such as `5.0534E+1`, its decimal point is moved (i.e., floated) to a new position.

why called floating-point?

2.15 Which of the following are correct literals for floating-point numbers?

`12.3`, `12.3e+2`, `23.4e-2`, `-334.4`, `20.5`, `39F`, `40D`

2.16 Which of the following are the same as `52.534`?

`5.2534e+1`, `0.52534e+2`, `525.34e-1`, `5.2534e+0`

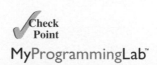

2.11 Evaluating Expressions and Operator Precedence

Key
Point

Java expressions are evaluated in the same way as arithmetic expressions.

Writing a numeric expression in Java involves a straightforward translation of an arithmetic expression using Java operators. For example, the arithmetic expression

$$\frac{3 + 4x}{5} - \frac{10(y - 5)(a + b + c)}{x} + 9\left(\frac{4}{x} + \frac{9 + x}{y}\right)$$

can be translated into a Java expression as:

```
(3 + 4 * x) / 5 - 10 * (y - 5) * (a + b + c) / x +
9 * (4 / x + (9 + x) / y)
```

evaluating an expression

Though Java has its own way to evaluate an expression behind the scene, the result of a Java expression and its corresponding arithmetic expression are the same. Therefore, you can safely apply the arithmetic rule for evaluating a Java expression. Operators contained within pairs of parentheses are evaluated first. Parentheses can be nested, in which case the expression in the inner parentheses is evaluated first. When more than one operator is used in an expression, the following operator precedence rule is used to determine the order of evaluation.

operator precedence rule

- Multiplication, division, and remainder operators are applied first. If an expression contains several multiplication, division, and remainder operators, they are applied from left to right.

- Addition and subtraction operators are applied last. If an expression contains several addition and subtraction operators, they are applied from left to right.

Here is an example of how an expression is evaluated:

```
3 + 4 * 4 + 5 * (4 + 3) - 1
                                    (1) inside parentheses first
3 + 4 * 4 + 5 * 7 - 1
                                    (2) multiplication
3 + 16 + 5 * 7 - 1
                                    (3) multiplication
3 + 16 + 35 - 1
                                    (4) addition
19 + 35 - 1
                                    (5) addition
54 - 1
                                    (6) subtraction
53
```

Listing 2.5 gives a program that converts a Fahrenheit degree to Celsius using the formula $celsius = (\frac{5}{9})(fahrenheit - 32)$.

LISTING 2.5 FahrenheitToCelsius.java

```
1  import java.util.Scanner;
2
3  public class FahrenheitToCelsius {
4    public static void main(String[] args) {
5      Scanner input = new Scanner(System.in);
6
7      System.out.print("Enter a degree in Fahrenheit: ");
```

```
 8        double fahrenheit = input.nextDouble();
 9
10        // Convert Fahrenheit to Celsius
11        double celsius = (5.0 / 9) * (fahrenheit - 32);
12        System.out.println("Fahrenheit " + fahrenheit + " is " +
13          celsius + " in Celsius");
14    }
15 }
```

divide

```
Enter a degree in Fahrenheit: 100 ↵Enter
Fahrenheit 100.0 is 37.77777777777778 in Celsius
```

line#	fahrenheit	celsius
8	100	
11		37.77777777777778

Be careful when applying division. Division of two integers yields an integer in Java. $\frac{5}{9}$ is translated to **5.0 / 9** instead of **5 / 9** in line 11, because **5 / 9** yields **0** in Java.

integer vs. decimal division

2.17 How would you write the following arithmetic expression in Java?

$$\frac{4}{3(r + 34)} - 9(a + bc) + \frac{3 + d(2 + a)}{a + bd}$$

Check Point

MyProgrammingLab

2.12 Case Study: Displaying the Current Time

You can invoke `System.currentTimeMillis()` *to return the current time.*

Key Point

The problem is to develop a program that displays the current time in GMT (Greenwich Mean Time) in the format hour:minute:second, such as 13:19:8.

The `currentTimeMillis` method in the `System` class returns the current time in milliseconds elapsed since the time **00:00:00** on January 1, 1970 GMT, as shown in Figure 2.2. This time is known as the *UNIX epoch*. The epoch is the point when time starts, and **1970** was the year when the UNIX operating system was formally introduced.

VideoNote

Use operators / and %

`currentTimeMillis`
UNIX epoch

FIGURE 2.2 The `System.currentTimeMillis()` returns the number of milliseconds since the UNIX epoch.

You can use this method to obtain the current time, and then compute the current second, minute, and hour as follows.

1. Obtain the total milliseconds since midnight, January 1, 1970, in **totalMilliseconds** by invoking `System.currentTimeMillis()` (e.g., **1203183068328** milliseconds).

2. Obtain the total seconds **totalSeconds** by dividing **totalMilliseconds** by **1000** (e.g., **1203183068328** milliseconds / **1000** = **1203183068** seconds).

3. Compute the current second from **totalSeconds % 60** (e.g., **1203183068** seconds % **60** = **8**, which is the current second).

4. Obtain the total minutes **totalMinutes** by dividing **totalSeconds** by **60** (e.g., **1203183068** seconds / **60** = **20053051** minutes).

5. Compute the current minute from **totalMinutes % 60** (e.g., **20053051** minutes % **60** = **31**, which is the current minute).

6. Obtain the total hours **totalHours** by dividing **totalMinutes** by **60** (e.g., **20053051** minutes / **60** = **334217** hours).

7. Compute the current hour from **totalHours % 24** (e.g., **334217** hours % 24 = **17**, which is the current hour).

Listing 2.6 gives the complete program.

LISTING 2.6 ShowCurrentTime.java

totalMilliseconds

totalSeconds

currentSecond

totalMinutes

currentMinute

totalHours

currentHour

preparing output

```
1   public class ShowCurrentTime {
2     public static void main(String[] args) {
3       // Obtain the total milliseconds since midnight, Jan 1, 1970
4       long totalMilliseconds = System.currentTimeMillis();
5
6       // Obtain the total seconds since midnight, Jan 1, 1970
7       long totalSeconds = totalMilliseconds / 1000;
8
9       // Compute the current second in the minute in the hour
10      long currentSecond = totalSeconds % 60;
11
12      // Obtain the total minutes
13      long totalMinutes = totalSeconds / 60;
14
15      // Compute the current minute in the hour
16      long currentMinute = totalMinutes % 60;
17
18      // Obtain the total hours
19      long totalHours = totalMinutes / 60;
20
21      // Compute the current hour
22      long currentHour = totalHours % 24;
23
24      // Display results
25      System.out.println("Current time is " + currentHour + ":"
26        + currentMinute + ":" + currentSecond + " GMT");
27    }
28  }
```

```
Current time is 17:31:8 GMT
```

Line 4 invokes **System.currentTimeMillis()** to obtain the current time in milliseconds as a long value. Thus, all the variables are declared as the long type in this program. The seconds, minutes, and hours are extracted from the current time using the **/** and **%** operators (lines 6–22).

variables \ line#	4	7	10	13	16	19	22
totalMilliseconds	1203183068328						
totalSeconds		1203183068					
currentSecond			8				
totalMinutes				20053051			
currentMinute					31		
totalHours						334217	
currentHour							17

In the sample run, a single digit 8 is displayed for the second. The desirable output would be 08. This can be fixed by using a function that formats a single digit with a prefix 0 (see Exercise 5.37).

2.13 Augmented Assignment Operators

The operators +, -, *, /, and % can be combined with the assignment operator to form augmented operators.

Key Point

Very often the current value of a variable is used, modified, and then reassigned back to the same variable. For example, the following statement increases the variable count by 1:

```
count = count + 1;
```

Java allows you to combine assignment and addition operators using an augmented (or compound) assignment operator. For example, the preceding statement can be written as:

```
count += 1;
```

The += is called the *addition assignment operator*. Table 2.4 shows other augmented assignment operators.

addition assignment operator

TABLE 2.4 Augmented Assignment Operators

Operator	Name	Example	Equivalent
+=	Addition assignment	i += 8	i = i + 8
-=	Subtraction assignment	i -= 8	i = i - 8
*=	Multiplication assignment	i *= 8	i = i * 8
/=	Division assignment	i /= 8	i = i / 8
%=	Remainder assignment	i %= 8	i = i % 8

Caution

There are no spaces in the augmented assignment operators. For example, + = should be +=.

Note

Like the assignment operator (=), the operators (+=, -=, *=, /=, %=) can be used to form an assignment statement as well as an expression. For example, in the following code, x += 2 is a statement in the first line and an expression in the second line.

```
x += 2; // Statement
System.out.println(x += 2); // Expression
```

2.14 Increment and Decrement Operators

Key Point

The increment (++) and decrement (−−) operators are for incrementing and decrementing a variable by 1.

increment operator (++)
decrement operator (−−)

The ++ and −− are two shorthand operators for incrementing and decrementing a variable by 1. These are handy, because that's often how much the value needs to be changed in many programming tasks. For example, the following code increments i by 1 and decrements j by 1.

```
int i = 3, j = 3;
i++; // i becomes 4
j--; // j becomes 2
```

postincrement
postdecrement

i++ is pronounced as i plus plus and i−− as i minus minus. These operators are known as *postfix increment* (or postincrement) and *postfix decrement* (or postdecrement), because the operators ++ and −− are placed after the variable. These operators can also be placed before the variable. For example,

```
int i = 3, j = 3;
++i; // i becomes 4
--j; // j becomes 2
```

preincrement
predecrement

++i increments i by 1 and −−j decrements j by 1. These operators are known as *prefix increment* (or preincrement) and *prefix decrement* (or predecrement).

As you see, the effect of i++ and ++i or i−− and −−i are the same in the preceding examples. However, their effects are different when they are used in statements that do more than just increment and decrement. Table 2.5 describes their differences and gives examples.

TABLE 2.5 Increment and Decrement Operators

Operator	Name	Description	Example (assume i = 1)
++var	preincrement	Increment var by 1, and use the new var value in the statement	int j = ++i; // j is 2, i is 2
var++	postincrement	Increment var by 1, but use the original var value in the statement	int j = i++; // j is 1, i is 2
--var	predecrement	Decrement var by 1, and use the new var value in the statement	int j = --i; // j is 0, i is 0
var--	postdecrement	Decrement var by 1, and use the original var value in the statement	int j = i--; // j is 1, i is 0

Here are additional examples to illustrate the differences between the prefix form of ++ (or −−) and the postfix form of ++ (or −−). Consider the following code:

```
int i = 10;
int newNum = 10 * i++;
```
Same effect as →
```
int newNum = 10 * i;
i = i + 1;
```

```
System.out.print("i is " + i
    + ", newNum is " + newNum);
```

```
i is 11, newNum is 100
```

In this case, i is incremented by 1, then the *old* value of i is used in the multiplication. So newNum becomes 100. If i++ is replaced by ++i as follows,

```
int i = 10;
int newNum = 10 * (++i);
```
Same effect as →
```
i = i + 1;
int newNum = 10 * i;
```

```
System.out.print("i is " + i
    + ", newNum is " + newNum);
```

```
i is 11, newNum is 110
```

i is incremented by 1, and the new value of i is used in the multiplication. Thus newNum becomes 110.

Here is another example:

```
double x = 1.0;
double y = 5.0;
double z = x-- + (++y);
```

After all three lines are executed, y becomes 6.0, z becomes 7.0, and x becomes 0.0.

Tip

Using increment and decrement operators makes expressions short, but it also makes them complex and difficult to read. Avoid using these operators in expressions that modify multiple variables or the same variable multiple times, such as this one: int k = ++i + i.

2.18 Which of these statements are true?

a. Any expression can be used as a statement.

b. The expression x++ can be used as a statement.

c. The statement x = x + 5 is also an expression.

d. The statement x = y = x = 0 is illegal.

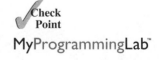

2.19 Assume that int a = 1 and double d = 1.0, and that each expression is independent. What are the results of the following expressions?

```
a = 46 / 9;
a = 46 % 9 + 4 * 4 - 2;
a = 45 + 43 % 5 * (23 * 3 % 2);
a %= 3 / a + 3;
d = 4 + d * d + 4;
d += 1.5 * 3 + (++a);
d -= 1.5 * 3 + a++;
```

2.20 How do you obtain the current minute using the `System.currentTimeMillis()` method?

2.15 Numeric Type Conversions

Key Point

Floating-point numbers can be converted into integers using explicit casting.

Can you perform binary operations with two operands of different types? Yes. If an integer and a floating-point number are involved in a binary operation, Java automatically converts the integer to a floating-point value. So, `3 * 4.5` is same as `3.0 * 4.5`.

You can always assign a value to a numeric variable whose type supports a larger range of values; thus, for instance, you can assign a `long` value to a `float` variable. You cannot, however, assign a value to a variable of a type with a smaller range unless you use *type casting*. *Casting* is an operation that converts a value of one data type into a value of another data type. Casting a type with a small range to a type with a larger range is known as *widening a type*. Casting a type with a large range to a type with a smaller range is known as *narrowing a type*. Java will automatically widen a type, but you must narrow a type explicitly.

casting
widening a type
narrowing a type

The syntax for casting a type is to specify the target type in parentheses, followed by the variable's name or the value to be cast. For example, the following statement

```
System.out.println((int)1.7);
```

displays `1`. When a `double` value is cast into an `int` value, the fractional part is truncated. The following statement

```
System.out.println((double)1 / 2);
```

displays `0.5`, because `1` is cast to `1.0` first, then `1.0` is divided by `2`. However, the statement

```
System.out.println(1 / 2);
```

displays `0`, because `1` and `2` are both integers and the resulting value should also be an integer.

possible loss of precision

Caution
Casting is necessary if you are assigning a value to a variable of a smaller type range, such as assigning a `double` value to an `int` variable. A compile error will occur if casting is not used in situations of this kind. However, be careful when using casting, as loss of information might lead to inaccurate results.

Note
Casting does not change the variable being cast. For example, `d` is not changed after casting in the following code:

```
double d = 4.5;
int i = (int)d;  // i becomes 4, but d is still 4.5
```

casting in an augmented
 expression

Note
In Java, an augmented expression of the form `x1 op= x2` is implemented as `x1 = (T)(x1 op x2)`, where `T` is the type for `x1`. Therefore, the following code is correct.

```
int sum = 0;
sum += 4.5; // sum becomes 4 after this statement
```

`sum += 4.5` is equivalent to `sum = (int)(sum + 4.5)`.

Note

To assign a variable of the **int** type to a variable of the **short** or **byte** type, explicit casting must be used. For example, the following statements have a compile error:

```
int i = 1;
byte b = i; // Error because explicit casting is required
```

However, so long as the integer literal is within the permissible range of the target variable, explicit casting is not needed to assign an integer literal to a variable of the **short** or **byte** type (see Section 2.10, Numeric Literals).

The program in Listing 2.7 displays the sales tax with two digits after the decimal point.

LISTING 2.7 SalesTax.java

```
1  import java.util.Scanner;
2
3  public class SalesTax {
4    public static void main(String[] args) {
5      Scanner input = new Scanner(System.in);
6
7      System.out.print("Enter purchase amount: ");
8      double purchaseAmount = input.nextDouble();
9
10     double tax = purchaseAmount * 0.06;                              casting
11     System.out.println("Sales tax is $" + (int)(tax * 100) / 100.0);
12   }
13 }
```

```
Enter purchase amount: 197.55  ↵Enter
Sales tax is $11.85
```

line#	purchaseAmount	tax	output
8	197.55		
10		11.853	
11			11.85

The variable **purchaseAmount** is **197.55** (line 8). The sales tax is **6%** of the purchase, so the **tax** is evaluated as **11.853** (line 10). Note that   formatting numbers

```
tax * 100 is 1185.3
(int)(tax * 100) is 1185
(int)(tax * 100) / 100.0 is 11.85
```

So, the statement in line 11 displays the tax **11.85** with two digits after the decimal point.

2.21 Can different types of numeric values be used together in a computation?

2.22 What does an explicit casting from a **double** to an **int** do with the fractional part of the **double** value? Does casting change the variable being cast?

2.23 Show the following output:

```
float f = 12.5F;
int i = (int)f;
```

✓**Check Point**

MyProgrammingLab™

```
System.out.println("f is " + f);
System.out.println("i is " + i);
```

2.24 If you change `(int)(tax * 100) / 100.0` to `(int)(tax * 100) / 100` in line 11 in Listing 2.7, what will be the output for the input purchase amount of **197.556**?

2.16 Software Development Process

Key Point

VideoNote
Software development process

The software development life cycle is a multi-stage process that includes requirements specification, analysis, design, implementation, testing, deployment, and maintenance.

Developing a software product is an engineering process. Software products, no matter how large or how small, have the same life cycle: requirements specification, analysis, design, implementation, testing, deployment, and maintenance, as shown in Figure 2.3.

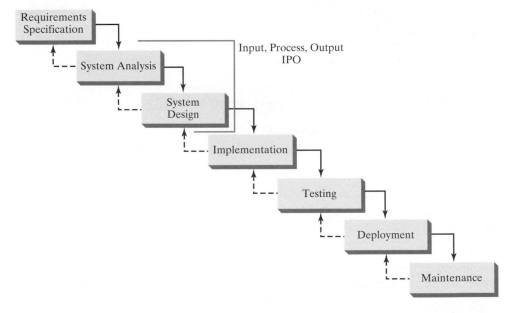

FIGURE 2.3 At any stage of the software development life cycle, it may be necessary to go back to a previous stage to correct errors or deal with other issues that might prevent the software from functioning as expected.

requirements specification

    Requirements specification is a formal process that seeks to understand the problem that the software will address and to document in detail what the software system needs to do. This phase involves close interaction between users and developers. Most of the examples in this book are simple, and their requirements are clearly stated. In the real world, however, problems are not always well defined. Developers need to work closely with their customers (the individuals or organizations that will use the software) and study the problem carefully to identify what the software needs to do.

system analysis

    System analysis seeks to analyze the data flow and to identify the system's input and output. When you do analysis, it helps to identify what the output is first, and then figure out what input data you need in order to produce the output.

system design

    System design is to design a process for obtaining the output from the input. This phase involves the use of many levels of abstraction to break down the problem into manageable components and design strategies for implementing each component. You can view each component as a subsystem that performs a specific function of the system. The essence of system analysis and design is input, process, and output (IPO).

IPO

Implementation involves translating the system design into programs. Separate programs are written for each component and then integrated to work together. This phase requires the use of a programming language such as Java. The implementation involves coding, self-testing, and debugging (that is, finding errors, called *bugs,* in the code).

Testing ensures that the code meets the requirements specification and weeds out bugs. An independent team of software engineers not involved in the design and implementation of the product usually conducts such testing.

Deployment makes the software available for use. Depending on the type of the software, it may be installed on each user's machine or installed on a server accessible on the Internet.

Maintenance is concerned with updating and improving the product. A software product must continue to perform and improve in an ever-evolving environment. This requires periodic upgrades of the product to fix newly discovered bugs and incorporate changes.

To see the software development process in action, we will now create a program that computes loan payments. The loan can be a car loan, a student loan, or a home mortgage loan. For an introductory programming course, we focus on requirements specification, analysis, design, implementation, and testing.

implementation

testing

deployment

maintenance

VideoNote
Compute loan payments

Stage 1: Requirements Specification

The program must satisfy the following requirements:

- It must let the user enter the interest rate, the loan amount, and the number of years for which payments will be made.

- It must compute and display the monthly payment and total payment amounts.

Stage 2: System Analysis

The output is the monthly payment and total payment, which can be obtained using the following formulas:

$$monthlyPayment = \frac{loanAmount \times monthlyInterestRate}{1 - \dfrac{1}{(1 + monthlyInterestRate)^{numberOfYears \times 12}}}$$

$$totalPayment = monthlyPayment \times numberOfYears \times 12$$

So, the input needed for the program is the monthly interest rate, the length of the loan in years, and the loan amount.

Note
The requirements specification says that the user must enter the annual interest rate, the loan amount, and the number of years for which payments will be made. During analysis, however, it is possible that you may discover that input is not sufficient or that some values are unnecessary for the output. If this happens, you can go back and modify the requirements specification.

Note
In the real world, you will work with customers from all walks of life. You may develop software for chemists, physicists, engineers, economists, and psychologists, and of course you will not have (or need) complete knowledge of all these fields. Therefore, you don't have to know how formulas are derived, but given the monthly interest rate, the number of years, and the loan amount, you can compute the monthly payment in this program. You will, however, need to communicate with customers and understand how a mathematical model works for the system.

Stage 3: System Design

During system design, you identify the steps in the program.

Step 1. Prompt the user to enter the annual interest rate, the number of years, and the loan amount.

Step 2. The input for the annual interest rate is a number in percent format, such as 4.5%. The program needs to convert it into a decimal by dividing it by **100**. To obtain the monthly interest rate from the annual interest rate, divide it by **12**, since a year has 12 months. So, to obtain the monthly interest rate in decimal format, you need to divide the annual interest rate in percentage by **1200**. For example, if the annual interest rate is 4.5%, then the monthly interest rate is 4.5/1200 = 0.00375.

Step 3. Compute the monthly payment using the preceding formula.

Step 4. Compute the total payment, which is the monthly payment multiplied by **12** and multiplied by the number of years.

Step 5. Display the monthly payment and total payment.

Stage 4: Implementation

Implementation is also known as *coding* (writing the code). In the formula, you have to compute $(1 + monthlyInterestRate)^{numberOfYears \times 12}$, which can be obtained using `Math.pow(1 + monthlyInterestRate, numberOfYears * 12)`.

Math.pow(a, b) method

Listing 2.8 gives the complete program.

LISTING 2.8 ComputeLoan.java

import class

```java
1  import java.util.Scanner;
2
3  public class ComputeLoan {
4    public static void main(String[] args) {
5      // Create a Scanner
6      Scanner input = new Scanner(System.in);
7
8      // Enter annual interest rate in percentage, e.g., 7.25%
9      System.out.print("Enter annual interest rate, e.g., 7.25%: ");
10     double annualInterestRate = input.nextDouble();
11
12     // Obtain monthly interest rate
13     double monthlyInterestRate = annualInterestRate / 1200;
14
15     // Enter number of years
16     System.out.print(
17       "Enter number of years as an integer, e.g., 5: ");
18     int numberOfYears = input.nextInt();
19
20     // Enter loan amount
21     System.out.print("Enter loan amount, e.g., 120000.95: ");
22     double loanAmount = input.nextDouble();
23
24     // Calculate payment
25     double monthlyPayment = loanAmount * monthlyInterestRate / (1
26       - 1 / Math.pow(1 + monthlyInterestRate, numberOfYears * 12));
27     double totalPayment = monthlyPayment * numberOfYears * 12;
28
29     // Display results
```

create a Scanner

enter interest rate

enter years

enter loan amount

monthlyPayment

totalPayment

```
30        System.out.println("The monthly payment is $" +
31            (int)(monthlyPayment * 100) / 100.0);                casting
32        System.out.println("The total payment is $" +
33            (int)(totalPayment * 100) / 100.0);                  casting
34    }
35  }
```

```
Enter annual interest rate, e.g., 5.75%: 5.75  ↵Enter
Enter number of years as an integer, e.g., 5: 15  ↵Enter
Enter loan amount, e.g., 120000.95: 250000  ↵Enter
The monthly payment is $2076.02
The total payment is $373684.53
```

variables \ line#	10	13	18	22	25	27
annualInterestRate	5.75					
monthlyInterestRate		0.0047916666666				
numberOfYears			15			
loanAmount				250000		
monthlyPayment					2076.0252175	
totalPayment						373684.539

Line 10 reads the annual interest rate, which is converted into the monthly interest rate in line 13.

Choose the most appropriate data type for the variable. For example, `numberOfYears` is best declared as an `int` (line 18), although it could be declared as a `long`, `float`, or `double`. Note that `byte` might be the most appropriate for `numberOfYears`. For simplicity, however, the examples in this book will use `int` for integer and `double` for floating-point values.

The formula for computing the monthly payment is translated into Java code in lines 25–27.

Casting is used in lines 31 and 33 to obtain a new `monthlyPayment` and `totalPayment` with two digits after the decimal points.

The program uses the `Scanner` class, imported in line 1. The program also uses the `Math` class, and you might be wondering why that class isn't imported into the program. The `Math` class is in the `java.lang` package, and all classes in the `java.lang` package are implicitly imported. Therefore, you don't need to explicitly import the `Math` class.

java.lang package

Stage 5: Testing

After the program is implemented, test it with some sample input data and verify whether the output is correct. Some of the problems may involve many cases, as you will see in later chapters. For these types of problems, you need to design test data that cover all cases.

Tip

The system design phase in this example identified several steps. It is a good approach to developing and testing these steps incrementally by adding them one at a time. This approach makes it much easier to pinpoint problems and debug the program.

incremental development and testing

Check
Point

MyProgrammingLab™

2.25 How would you write the following arithmetic expression?

$$\frac{-b + \sqrt{b^2 - 4ac}}{2a}$$

2.17 Character Data Type and Operations

Key
Point

A character data type represents a single character.

char type

In addition to processing numeric values, you can process characters in Java. The character data type, **char**, is used to represent a single character. A character literal is enclosed in single quotation marks. Consider the following code:

```
char letter = 'A';
char numChar = '4';
```

The first statement assigns character **A** to the **char** variable **letter**. The second statement assigns digit character **4** to the **char** variable **numChar**.

char literal

> **Caution**
>
> A string literal must be enclosed in quotation marks (**" "**). A character literal is a single character enclosed in single quotation marks (**' '**). Therefore, **"A"** is a string, but **'A'** is a character.

2.17.1 Unicode and ASCII code

Computers use binary numbers internally. A character is stored in a computer as a sequence of 0s and 1s. Mapping a character to its binary representation is called *encoding*. There are different ways to encode a character. How characters are encoded is defined by an *encoding scheme*.

encoding

Unicode

original Unicode

Java supports *Unicode,* an encoding scheme established by the Unicode Consortium to support the interchange, processing, and display of written texts in the world's diverse languages. Unicode was originally designed as a 16-bit character encoding. The primitive data type **char** was intended to take advantage of this design by providing a simple data type that could hold any character. However, it turned out that the 65,536 characters possible in a 16-bit encoding are not sufficient to represent all the characters in the world. The Unicode standard therefore has been extended to allow up to 1,112,064 characters. Those characters that go beyond the original 16-bit limit are called *supplementary characters*. Java supports the supplementary characters. The processing and representing of supplementary characters are beyond the scope of this book. For simplicity, this book considers only the original 16-bit Unicode characters. These characters can be stored in a **char** type variable.

supplementary Unicode

A 16-bit Unicode takes two bytes, preceded by **\u**, expressed in four hexadecimal digits that run from **\u0000** to **\uFFFF**. Hexadecimal numbers are introduced in Appendix F, Number Systems. For example, the English word **welcome** is translated into Chinese using two characters, 欢迎. The Unicodes of these two characters are **\u6B22\u8FCE**.

Listing 2.9 gives a program that displays two Chinese characters and three Greek letters.

LISTING 2.9 DisplayUnicode.java

```
1 import javax.swing.JOptionPane;
2
3 public class DisplayUnicode {
4   public static void main(String[] args) {
5     JOptionPane.showMessageDialog(null,
6       "\u6B22\u8FCE \u03b1 \u03b2 \u03b3",
7       "\u6B22\u8FCE Welcome",
```

```
 8          JOptionPane.INFORMATION_MESSAGE);
 9    }
10 }
```

If no Chinese font is installed on your system, you will not be able to see the Chinese characters. The Unicodes for the Greek letters α β γ are **\u03b1** **\u03b2** **\u03b3**.

Most computers use *ASCII (American Standard Code for Information Interchange)*, a 7-bit encoding scheme for representing all uppercase and lowercase letters, digits, punctuation marks, and control characters. Unicode includes ASCII code, with **\u0000** to **\u007F** corresponding to the 128 ASCII characters. (See Appendix B for a list of ASCII characters and their decimal and hexadecimal codes.) You can use ASCII characters such as **'X'**, **'1'**, and **'$'** in a Java program as well as Unicodes. Thus, for example, the following statements are equivalent:

ASCII

```
char letter = 'A';
char letter = '\u0041'; // Character A's Unicode is 0041
```

Both statements assign character **A** to the **char** variable **letter**.

> **Note**
> The increment and decrement operators can also be used on **char** variables to get the next or preceding Unicode character. For example, the following statements display character **b**.
>
> ```
> char ch = 'a';
> System.out.println(++ch);
> ```

char increment and decrement

2.17.2   Escape Characters

Suppose you want to print a message with quotation marks in the output. Can you write a statement like this?

```
System.out.println("He said "Java is fun"");
```

No, this statement has a compile error. The compiler thinks the second quotation character is the end of the string and does not know what to do with the rest of the characters.

To overcome this problem, Java uses a special notation to represent special characters, as shown in Table 2.6. This special notation, called an *escape character*, consists of a backslash (\) followed by a character or a character sequence. For example, **\t** is an escape character for the Tab character and an escape character such as **\u03b1** is used to represent a Unicode. The symbols in an escape character are interpreted as a whole rather than individually.

escape character

So, now you can print the quoted message using the following statement:

```
System.out.println("He said \"Java is fun\"");
```

The output is

```
He said "Java is fun"
```

Note that the symbols \ and " together represent one character.

2.17.3   Casting between **char** and Numeric Types

A **char** can be cast into any numeric type, and vice versa. When an integer is cast into a **char**, only its lower 16 bits of data are used; the other part is ignored. For example:

```
char ch = (char)0XAB0041;  // The lower 16 bits hex code 0041 is
                           // assigned to ch
System.out.println(ch);    // ch is character A
```

TABLE 2.6 Escape Characters

Escape Character	Name	Unicode Code	Decimal Value
\b	Backspace	\u0008	8
\t	Tab	\u0009	9
\n	Linefeed	\u000A	10
\f	Formfeed	\u000C	12
\r	Carriage Return	\u000D	13
\\	Backslash	\u005C	92
\"	Double Quote	\u0022	34

When a floating-point value is cast into a **char**, the floating-point value is first cast into an **int**, which is then cast into a **char**.

```
char ch = (char)65.25;    // Decimal 65 is assigned to ch
System.out.println(ch);   // ch is character A
```

When a **char** is cast into a numeric type, the character's Unicode is cast into the specified numeric type.

```
int i = (int)'A'; // The Unicode of character A is assigned to i
System.out.println(i);  // i is 65
```

Implicit casting can be used if the result of a casting fits into the target variable. Otherwise, explicit casting must be used. For example, since the Unicode of **'a'** is **97**, which is within the range of a byte, these implicit castings are fine:

```
byte b = 'a';
int i = 'a';
```

But the following casting is incorrect, because the Unicode \uFFF4 cannot fit into a byte:

```
byte b = '\uFFF4';
```

To force this assignment, use explicit casting, as follows:

```
byte b = (byte)'\uFFF4';
```

Any positive integer between **0** and **FFFF** in hexadecimal can be cast into a character implicitly. Any number not in this range must be cast into a **char** explicitly.

numeric operators on
characters

 Note

All numeric operators can be applied to **char** operands. A **char** operand is automatically cast into a number if the other operand is a number or a character. If the other operand is a string, the character is concatenated with the string. For example, the following statements

```
int i = '2' + '3'; // (int)'2' is 50 and (int)'3' is 51
System.out.println("i is " + i); // i is 101
```

```
int j = 2 + 'a'; // (int)'a' is 97
System.out.println("j is " + j); // j is 99
System.out.println(j + " is the Unicode for character "
    + (char)j); // j is the Unicode for character c
System.out.println("Chapter " + '2');
```

display

```
i is 101
j is 99
99 is the Unicode for character c
Chapter 2
```

> **Note**
> The Unicodes for lowercase letters are consecutive integers starting from the Unicode for
> `'a'`, then for `'b'`, `'c'`, . . . , and `'z'`. The same is true for the uppercase letters. Fur-
> thermore, the Unicode for `'a'` is greater than the Unicode for `'A'`, so `'a'` − `'A'` is
> the same as `'b'` − `'B'`. For a lowercase letter *ch*, its corresponding uppercase letter is
> `(char)('A' + (ch - 'a'))`.

2.17.4   Case Study: Counting Monetary Units

Suppose you want to develop a program that changes a given amount of money into smaller
monetary units. The program lets the user enter an amount as a **double** value representing a
total in dollars and cents, and outputs a report listing the monetary equivalent in the maximum
number of dollars, quarters, dimes, nickels, and pennies, in this order, to result in the
minimum number of coins, as shown in the sample run.

Here are the steps in developing the program:

1. Prompt the user to enter the amount as a decimal number, such as `11.56`.

2. Convert the amount (e.g., `11.56`) into cents (`1156`).

3. Divide the cents by `100` to find the number of dollars. Obtain the remaining cents using
   the cents remainder `100`.

4. Divide the remaining cents by `25` to find the number of quarters. Obtain the remaining
   cents using the remaining cents remainder `25`.

5. Divide the remaining cents by `10` to find the number of dimes. Obtain the remaining
   cents using the remaining cents remainder `10`.

6. Divide the remaining cents by `5` to find the number of nickels. Obtain the remaining
   cents using the remaining cents remainder `5`.

7. The remaining cents are the pennies.

8. Display the result.

The complete program is given in Listing 2.10.

LISTING 2.10   ComputeChange.java

```
1  import java.util.Scanner;                                        import class
2
3  public class ComputeChange {
4    public static void main(String[] args) {
5      // Create a Scanner
6      Scanner input = new Scanner(System.in);
7
8      // Receive the amount
9      System.out.print(
```

enter input

dollars

quarters

dimes

nickels

pennies

output

```
10          "Enter an amount, for example, 11.56: ");
11      double amount = input.nextDouble();
12
13      int remainingAmount = (int)(amount * 100);
14
15      // Find the number of one dollars
16      int numberOfOneDollars = remainingAmount / 100;
17      remainingAmount = remainingAmount % 100;
18
19      // Find the number of quarters in the remaining amount
20      int numberOfQuarters = remainingAmount / 25;
21      remainingAmount = remainingAmount % 25;
22
23      // Find the number of dimes in the remaining amount
24      int numberOfDimes = remainingAmount / 10;
25      remainingAmount = remainingAmount % 10;
26
27      // Find the number of nickels in the remaining amount
28      int numberOfNickels = remainingAmount / 5;
29      remainingAmount = remainingAmount % 5;
30
31      // Find the number of pennies in the remaining amount
32      int numberOfPennies = remainingAmount;
33
34      // Display results
35      System.out.println("Your amount " + amount + " consists of \n" +
36          "\t" + numberOfOneDollars + " dollars\n" +
37          "\t" + numberOfQuarters + " quarters\n" +
38          "\t" + numberOfDimes + " dimes\n" +
39          "\t" + numberOfNickels + " nickels\n" +
40          "\t" + numberOfPennies + " pennies");
41    }
42  }
```

```
Enter an amount, for example, 11.56: 11.56  ↵Enter
Your amount 11.56 consists of
        11 dollars
        2 quarters
        0 dimes
        1 nickels
        1 pennies
```

variables \ line#	11	13	16	17	20	21	24	25	28	29	32
amount	11.56										
remainingAmount		1156		56		6		6		1	
numberOfOneDollars			11								
numberOfQuarters					2						
numberOfDimes							0				
numberOfNickels									1		
numberOfPennies											1

The variable `amount` stores the amount entered from the console (line 11). This variable is not changed, because the amount has to be used at the end of the program to display the results. The program introduces the variable `remainingAmount` (line 13) to store the changing remaining amount.

The variable `amount` is a `double` decimal representing dollars and cents. It is converted to an `int` variable `remainingAmount`, which represents all the cents. For instance, if `amount` is `11.56`, then the initial `remainingAmount` is `1156`. The division operator yields the integer part of the division, so `1156 / 100` is `11`. The remainder operator obtains the remainder of the division, so `1156 % 100` is `56`.

The program extracts the maximum number of singles from the remaining amount and obtains a new remaining amount in the variable `remainingAmount` (lines 16–17). It then extracts the maximum number of quarters from `remainingAmount` and obtains a new `remainingAmount` (lines 20–21). Continuing the same process, the program finds the maximum number of dimes, nickels, and pennies in the remaining amount.

One serious problem with this example is the possible loss of precision when casting a `double` amount to an `int remainingAmount`. This could lead to an inaccurate result. If you try to enter the amount `10.03`, `10.03 * 100` becomes `1002.9999999999`. You will find that the program displays `10` dollars and `2` pennies. To fix the problem, enter the amount as an integer value representing cents (see Exercise 2.24).

loss of precision

As shown in the sample run, `0` dimes, `1` nickels, and `1` pennies are displayed in the result. It would be better not to display `0` dimes, and to display `1` nickel and `1` penny using the singular forms of the words. You will learn how to use selection statements to modify this program in the next chapter (see Exercise 3.7).

2.26 Use print statements to find out the ASCII code for `'1'`, `'A'`, `'B'`, `'a'`, and `'b'`. Use print statements to find out the character for the decimal codes 40, 59, 79, 85, and 90. Use print statements to find out the character for the hexadecimal code 40, 5A, 71, 72, and 7A.

✓ Check Point

MyProgrammingLab™

2.27 Which of the following are correct literals for characters?
`'1'`, `'\u345dE'`, `'\u3fFa'`, `'\b'`, `'\t'`

2.28 How do you display the characters \ and "?

2.29 Evaluate the following:

```
int i = '1';
int j = '1' + '2' * ('4' - '3') + 'b' / 'a';
int k = 'a';
char c = 90;
```

2.30 Can the following conversions involving casting be allowed? If so, find the converted result.

```
char c = 'A';
int i = (int)c;

float f = 1000.34f;
int i = (int)f;

double d = 1000.34;
int i = (int)d;

int i = 97;
char c = (char)i;
```

2.31 Show the output of the following program:

```java
public class Test {
  public static void main(String[] args) {
    char x = 'a';
    char y = 'c';

    System.out.println(++x);
    System.out.println(y++);
    System.out.println(x - y);
  }
}
```

2.18 The **String** Type

Key
Point

A string is a sequence of characters.

The **char** type represents only one character. To represent a string of characters, use the data type called **String**. For example, the following code declares the message to be a string with the value **"Welcome to Java"**.

```java
String message = "Welcome to Java";
```

String is a predefined class in the Java library, just like the classes **System**, **JOptionPane**, and **Scanner**. The **String** type is not a primitive type. It is known as a *reference type*. Any Java class can be used as a reference type for a variable. Reference data types will be thoroughly discussed in Chapter 8, Objects and Classes. For the time being, you need to know only how to declare a **String** variable, how to assign a string to the variable, and how to concatenate strings.

concatenate strings and numbers

As first shown in Listing 2.1, two strings can be concatenated. The plus sign (+) is the concatenation operator if one of the operands is a string. If one of the operands is a nonstring (e.g., a number), the nonstring value is converted into a string and concatenated with the other string. Here are some examples:

```java
// Three strings are concatenated
String message = "Welcome " + "to " + "Java";

// String Chapter is concatenated with number 2
String s = "Chapter" + 2; // s becomes Chapter2

// String Supplement is concatenated with character B
String s1 = "Supplement" + 'B'; // s1 becomes SupplementB
```

If neither of the operands is a string, the plus sign (+) is the addition operator that adds two numbers.

The augmented += operator can also be used for string concatenation. For example, the following code appends the string **"and Java is fun"** with the string **"Welcome to Java"** in **message**.

```java
message += " and Java is fun";
```

So the new **message** is **"Welcome to Java and Java is fun"**.
If **i = 1** and **j = 2**, what is the output of the following statement?

```java
System.out.println("i + j is " + i + j);
```

The output is **"i + j is 12"** because **"i + j is "** is concatenated with the value of **i** first. To force **i + j** to be executed first, enclose **i + j** in the parentheses, as follows:

```java
System.out.println("i + j is " + (i + j));
```

To read a string from the console, invoke the **next()** method on a **Scanner** object. For example, the following code reads three strings from the keyboard:

read strings

```
Scanner input = new Scanner(System.in);
System.out.println("Enter three words separated by spaces: ");
String s1 = input.next();
String s2 = input.next();
String s3 = input.next();
System.out.println("s1 is " + s1);
System.out.println("s2 is " + s2);
System.out.println("s3 is " + s3);
```

```
Enter three words separated by spaces: Welcome to Java  ↵ Enter
s1 is Welcome
s2 is to
s3 is Java
```

The **next()** method reads a string that ends with a whitespace character. The characters ' ', \t, \f, \r, or \n are known as *whitespace characters*.

whitespace character

You can use the **nextLine()** method to read an entire line of text. The **nextLine()** method reads a string that ends with the *Enter* key pressed. For example, the following statements read a line of text.

```
Scanner input = new Scanner(System.in);
System.out.println("Enter a line: ");
String s = input.nextLine();
System.out.println("The line entered is " + s);
```

```
Enter a line: Welcome to Java  ↵ Enter
The line entered is Welcome to Java
```

 Important Caution

To *avoid input errors,* do not use **nextLine()** after **nextByte()**, **nextShort()**, **nextInt()**, **nextLong()**, **nextFloat()**, **nextDouble()**, or **next()**. The reasons will be explained in Section 14.1!.3, "How Does **Scanner** Work?"

avoid input errors

2.32   Show the output of the following statements (write a program to verify your results):

```
System.out.println("1" + 1);
System.out.println('1' + 1);
System.out.println("1" + 1 + 1);
System.out.println("1" + (1 + 1));
System.out.println('1' + 1 + 1);
```

2.33   Evaluate the following expressions (write a program to verify your results):

```
1 + "Welcome " + 1 + 1
1 + "Welcome " + (1 + 1)
1 + "Welcome " + ('\u0001' + 1)
1 + "Welcome " + 'a' + 1
```

Check
Point

MyProgrammingLab™

2.19 Getting Input from Input Dialogs

Key Point

An input dialog box prompts the user to enter an input graphically.

JOptionPane class

You can obtain input from the console. Alternatively, you can obtain input from an input dialog box by invoking the `JOptionPane.showInputDialog` method, as shown in Figure 2.4.

FIGURE 2.4 The input dialog box enables the user to enter a string.

When this method is executed, a dialog is displayed to enable you to enter an input value. After entering a string, click *OK* to accept the input and close the dialog box. The input is returned from the method as a string.

showInputDialog method

There are several ways to use the `showInputDialog` method. For the time being, you need to know only two ways to invoke it.

One is to use a statement like this one:

```
JOptionPane.showInputDialog(x);
```

where `x` is a string for the prompting message.

The other is to use a statement such as the following:

```
String string = JOptionPane.showInputDialog(null, x,
    y, JOptionPane.QUESTION_MESSAGE);
```

where `x` is a string for the prompting message and `y` is a string for the title of the input dialog box, as shown in the example below.

2.19.1 Converting Strings to Numbers

The input returned from the input dialog box is a string. If you enter a numeric value such as **123**, it returns **"123"**. You have to convert a string into a number to obtain the input as a number.

Integer.parseInt method

To convert a string into an **int** value, use the **Integer.parseInt** method, as follows:

```
int intValue = Integer.parseInt(intString);
```

where **intString** is a numeric string such as **123**.

Double.parseDouble method

To convert a string into a **double** value, use the **Double.parseDouble** method, as follows:

```
double doubleValue = Double.parseDouble(doubleString);
```

where **doubleString** is a numeric string such as **123.45**.

The **Integer** and **Double** classes are both included in the **java.lang** package, and thus they are automatically imported.

2.19.2   Using Input Dialog Boxes

Having learned how to read input from an input dialog box, you can rewrite the program in Listing 2.8, ComputeLoan.java, to read from input dialog boxes rather than from the console. Listing 2.11 gives the complete program. Figure 2.5 shows a sample run of the program.

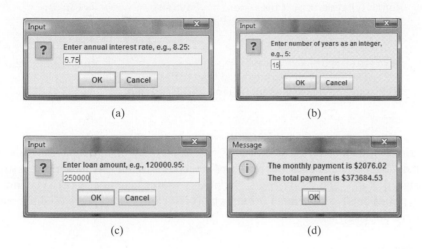

(a)   (b)

(c)   (d)

FIGURE 2.5   The program accepts the annual interest rate (a), number of years (b), and loan amount (c), then displays the monthly payment and total payment (d).

LISTING 2.11   ComputeLoanUsingInputDialog.java

```
 1  import javax.swing.JOptionPane;
 2
 3  public class ComputeLoanUsingInputDialog {
 4    public static void main(String[] args) {
 5      // Enter annual interest rate
 6      String annualInterestRateString = JOptionPane.showInputDialog(
 7        "Enter annual interest rate, for example, 8.25:");
 8
 9      // Convert string to double
10      double annualInterestRate =
11        Double.parseDouble(annualInterestRateString);
12
13      // Obtain monthly interest rate
14      double monthlyInterestRate = annualInterestRate / 1200;
15
16      // Enter number of years
17      String numberOfYearsString = JOptionPane.showInputDialog(
18        "Enter number of years as an integer, for example, 5:");
19
20      // Convert string to int
21      int numberOfYears = Integer.parseInt(numberOfYearsString);
22
23      // Enter loan amount
24      String loanString = JOptionPane.showInputDialog(
25        "Enter loan amount, for example, 120000.95:");
26
27      // Convert string to double
28      double loanAmount = Double.parseDouble(loanString);
29
```

enter interest rate

convert string to double

monthlyPayment

totalPayment

preparing output

```
30        // Calculate payment
31        double monthlyPayment = loanAmount * monthlyInterestRate / (1
32          - 1 / Math.pow(1 + monthlyInterestRate, numberOfYears * 12));
33        double totalPayment = monthlyPayment * numberOfYears * 12;
34
35        // Format to keep two digits after the decimal point
36        monthlyPayment = (int)(monthlyPayment * 100) / 100.0;
37        totalPayment = (int)(totalPayment * 100) / 100.0;
38
39        // Display results
40        String output = "The monthly payment is $" + monthlyPayment +
41          "\nThe total payment is $" + totalPayment;
42        JOptionPane.showMessageDialog(null, output);
43    }
44 }
```

The **showInputDialog** method in lines 6–7 displays an input dialog. Enter the interest rate as a double value and click *OK* to accept the input. The value is returned as a string that is assigned to the **String** variable **annualInterestRateString**. The **Double.parseDouble (annualInterestRateString)** (line 11) is used to convert the string into a **double** value.

JOptionPane or Scanner?

Pedagogical Note

For obtaining input you can use either **JOptionPane** or **Scanner**—whichever is more convenient. For consistency and simplicity, the examples in this book use **Scanner** for getting input. You can easily revise the examples using **JOptionPane** for getting input.

MyProgrammingLab™

2.34 Why do you have to import **JOptionPane** but not the **Math** class?

2.35 How do you prompt the user to enter an input using a dialog box?

2.36 How do you convert a string to an integer? How do you convert a string to a double?

KEY TERMS

algorithm   34
assignment operator (=)   42
assignment statement   42
byte type   45
casting   56
char type   62
constant   43
data type   35
declare variables   35
decrement operator (−−)   54
double type   45
encoding   62
escape character   63
expression   42
final keyword   43
float type   45
floating-point number   35
identifier   40

increment operator (++)   54
incremental development
  and testing   37
int type   45
IPO   39
literal   48
long type   45
narrowing (of types)   56
operands   46
operator   46
overflow   45
postdecrement   54
postincrement   54
predecrement   54
preincrement   54
primitive data type   35
pseudocode   34
requirements specification   58

scope of a variable   42
short type   45
supplementary Unicode   62
system analysis   58
system design   58
underflow   46

Unicode   62
UNIX epoch   51
variable   35
whitespace character   69
widening (of types)   56

CHAPTER SUMMARY

1. *Identifiers* are names for naming elements such as variables, constants, methods, classes, packages in a program.

2. An identifier is a sequence of characters that consists of letters, digits, underscores (_), and dollar signs ($). An identifier must start with a letter or an underscore. It cannot start with a digit. An identifier cannot be a reserved word. An identifier can be of any length.

3. *Variables* are used to store data in a program.

4. To declare a variable is to tell the compiler what type of data a variable can hold.

5. In Java, the equal sign (=) is used as the *assignment operator.*

6. A variable declared in a method must be assigned a value before it can be used.

7. A *named constant* (or simply a *constant*) represents permanent data that never changes.

8. A named constant is declared by using the keyword `final`.

9. Java provides four integer types (`byte`, `short`, `int`, and `long`) that represent integers of four different sizes.

10. Java provides two *floating-point types* (`float` and `double`) that represent floating-point numbers of two different precisions.

11. Java provides *operators* that perform numeric operations: + (addition), – (subtraction), * (multiplication), / (division), and % (remainder).

12. Integer arithmetic (/) yields an integer result.

13. The numeric operators in a Java expression are applied the same way as in an arithmetic expression.

14. Java provides the augmented assignment operators += (addition assignment), –= (subtraction assignment), *= (multiplication assignment), /= (division assignment), and %= (remainder assignment).

15. The *increment operator* (++) and the *decrement operator* (−−) increment or decrement a variable by 1.

16. When evaluating an expression with values of mixed types, Java automatically converts the operands to appropriate types.

17. You can explicitly convert a value from one type to another using the `(type)value` notation.

18. *Casting* a variable of a type with a small range to a variable of a type with a larger range is known as *widening a type.*

19. Casting a variable of a type with a large range to a variable of a type with a smaller range is known as *narrowing a type.*

20. Widening a type can be performed automatically without explicit casting. Narrowing a type must be performed explicitly.

21. The character type **char** represents a single character.

22. An *escape character* is a notation for representing a special character. An escape character consists of a backslash (\\) followed by a character or a character sequence.

23. The characters ' ', \\t, \\f, \\r, and \\n are known as the whitespace characters.

24. In computer science, midnight of January 1, 1970, is known as the *UNIX epoch.*

TEST QUESTIONS

Do the test questions for this chapter online at www.cs.armstrong.edu/liang/intro9e/test.html.

PROGRAMMING EXERCISES

sample runs

Note
You can run all exercises by downloading **exercise9e.zip** from www.cs.armstrong.edu/liang/intro9e/exercise9e.zip and use the command `java -cp exercise9e.zip Exercisei_j` to run Exercise*i_j*. For example, to run Exercise 2.1, use

```
java -cp exercise9e.zip Exercise02_01
```

This will give you an idea how the program runs.

Debugging TIP
The compiler usually gives a reason for a syntax error. If you don't know how to correct it, compare your program closely, character by character, with similar examples in the text.

learn from examples

document analysis and design

Pedagogical Note
Instructors may ask you to document your analysis and design for selected exercises. Use your own words to analyze the problem, including the input, output, and what needs to be computed, and describe how to solve the problem in pseudocode.

Sections 2.2–2.12

2.1 (*Convert Celsius to Fahrenheit*) Write a program that reads a Celsius degree in a **double** value from the console, then converts it to Fahrenheit and displays the result. The formula for the conversion is as follows:

$$\text{fahrenheit} = (9 / 5) * \text{celsius} + 32$$

Hint: In Java, **9 / 5** is **1**, but **9.0 / 5** is **1.8**.

Here is a sample run:

```
Enter a degree in Celsius: 43 ↵Enter
43 Celsius is 109.4 Fahrenheit
```

2.2 (*Compute the volume of a cylinder*) Write a program that reads in the radius and length of a cylinder and computes the area and volume using the following formulas:

```
area = radius * radius * π
volume = area * length
```

Here is a sample run:

```
Enter the radius and length of a cylinder: 5.5 12 ↵Enter
The area is 95.0331
The volume is 1140.4
```

2.3 (*Convert feet into meters*) Write a program that reads a number in feet, converts it to meters, and displays the result. One foot is `0.305` meter. Here is a sample run:

```
Enter a value for feet: 16.5 ↵Enter
16.5 feet is 5.0325 meters
```

2.4 (*Convert pounds into kilograms*) Write a program that converts pounds into kilograms. The program prompts the user to enter a number in pounds, converts it to kilograms, and displays the result. One pound is `0.454` kilograms. Here is a sample run:

```
Enter a number in pounds: 55.5 ↵Enter
55.5 pounds is 25.197 kilograms
```

*2.5 (*Financial application: calculate tips*) Write a program that reads the subtotal and the gratuity rate, then computes the gratuity and total. For example, if the user enters **10** for subtotal and **15%** for gratuity rate, the program displays **$1.5** as gratuity and **$11.5** as total. Here is a sample run:

```
Enter the subtotal and a gratuity rate: 10 15 ↵Enter
The gratuity is $1.5 and total is $11.5
```

2.6 (*Sum the digits in an integer*) Write a program that reads an integer between **0 and **1000** and adds all the digits in the integer. For example, if an integer is **932**, the sum of all its digits is **14**.

Hint: Use the **%** operator to extract digits, and use the **/** operator to remove the extracted digit. For instance, **932 % 10 = 2** and **932 / 10 = 93**.

Here is a sample run:

```
Enter a number between 0 and 1000: 999 ↵Enter
The sum of the digits is 27
```

*2.7 (*Find the number of years*) Write a program that prompts the user to enter the minutes (e.g., 1 billion), and displays the number of years and days for the minutes. For simplicity, assume a year has **365** days. Here is a sample run:

```
Enter the number of minutes: 1000000000  ↵Enter
1000000000 minutes is approximately 1902 years and 214 days
```

*2.8 (*Current time*) Listing 2.6, ShowCurrentTime.java, gives a program that displays the current time in GMT. Revise the program so that it prompts the user to enter the time zone offset to GMT and displays the time in the specified time zone. Here is a sample run:

```
Enter the time zone offset to GMT: -5  ↵Enter
The current time is 4:50:34
```

2.9 (*Physics: acceleration*) Average acceleration is defined as the change of velocity divided by the time taken to make the change, as shown in the following formula:

$$a = \frac{v_1 - v_0}{t}$$

Write a program that prompts the user to enter the starting velocity v_0 in meters/second, the ending velocity v_1 in meters/second, and the time span t in seconds, and displays the average acceleration. Here is a sample run:

```
Enter v0, v1, and t: 5.5 50.9 4.5  ↵Enter
The average acceleration is 10.0889
```

2.10 (*Science: calculating energy*) Write a program that calculates the energy needed to heat water from an initial temperature to a final temperature. Your program should prompt the user to enter the amount of water in kilograms and the initial and final temperatures of the water. The formula to compute the energy is

```
Q = M * (finalTemperature - initialTemperature) * 4184
```

where **M** is the weight of water in kilograms, temperatures are in degrees Celsius, and energy **Q** is measured in joules. Here is a sample run:

```
Enter the amount of water in kilograms: 55.5  ↵Enter
Enter the initial temperature: 3.5  ↵Enter
Enter the final temperature: 10.5  ↵Enter
The energy needed is 1625484.0
```

2.11 (*Population projection*) Rewrite Exercise 1.11 to prompt the user to enter the number of years and displays the population after the number of years. Here is a sample run of the program:

```
Enter the number of years: 5  ↵Enter
The population in 5 years is 325932970
```

2.12 (*Physics: finding runway length*) Given an airplane's acceleration *a* and take-off speed *v,* you can compute the minimum runway length needed for an airplane to take off using the following formula:

$$length = \frac{v^2}{2a}$$

Write a program that prompts the user to enter *v* in meters/second (m/s) and the acceleration *a* in meters/second squared (m/s²), and displays the minimum runway length. Here is a sample run:

```
Enter speed and acceleration: 60 3.5  ↵Enter
The minimum runway length for this airplane is 514.286
```

**2.13 (*Financial application: compound value*) Suppose you save $100 *each* month into a savings account with the annual interest rate 5%. Thus, the monthly interest rate is 0.05/12 = 0.00417. After the first month, the value in the account becomes

```
100 * (1 + 0.00417) = 100.417
```

After the second month, the value in the account becomes

```
(100 + 100.417) * (1 + 0.00417) = 201.252
```

After the third month, the value in the account becomes

```
(100 + 201.252) * (1 + 0.00417) = 302.507
```

and so on.

Write a program that prompts the user to enter a monthly saving amount and displays the account value after the sixth month. (In Exercise 4.30, you will use a loop to simplify the code and display the account value for any month.)

```
Enter the monthly saving amount: 100  ↵Enter
After the sixth month, the account value is $608.81
```

*2.14 (*Health application: computing BMI*) Body Mass Index (BMI) is a measure of health on weight. It can be calculated by taking your weight in kilograms and dividing by the square of your height in meters. Write a program that prompts the user to enter a weight in pounds and height in inches and displays the BMI. Note that one pound is 0.45359237 kilograms and one inch is 0.0254 meters. Here is a sample run:

VideoNote

Compute BMI

```
Enter weight in pounds: 95.5  ⏎Enter
Enter height in inches: 50  ⏎Enter
BMI is 26.8573
```

*2.15 (*Geometry: area of a triangle*) Write a program that prompts the user to enter three points (x1, y1), (x2, y2), (x3, y3) of a triangle and displays its area. The formula for computing the area of a triangle is

$$s = (side1 + side2 + side3)/2;$$

$$area = \sqrt{s(s - side1)(s - side2)(s - side3)}$$

Here is a sample run:

```
Enter three points for a triangle: 1.5 -3.4 4.6 5 9.5 -3.4  ⏎Enter
The area of the triangle is 33.6
```

2.16 (*Geometry: area of a hexagon*) Write a program that prompts the user to enter the side of a hexagon and displays its area. The formula for computing the area of a hexagon is

$$Area = \frac{3\sqrt{3}}{2}s^2,$$

where *s* is the length of a side. Here is a sample run:

```
Enter the side: 5.5  ⏎Enter
The area of the hexagon is 78.5895
```

*2.17 (*Science: wind-chill temperature*) How cold is it outside? The temperature alone is not enough to provide the answer. Other factors including wind speed, relative humidity, and sunshine play important roles in determining coldness outside. In 2001, the National Weather Service (NWS) implemented the new wind-chill temperature to measure the coldness using temperature and wind speed. The formula is:

$$t_{wc} = 35.74 + 0.6215t_a - 35.75v^{0.16} + 0.4275t_a v^{0.16}$$

where t_a is the outside temperature measured in degrees Fahrenheit and *v* is the speed measured in miles per hour. t_{wc} is the wind-chill temperature. The formula cannot be used for wind speeds below 2 mph or temperatures below $-58°F$ or above $41°F$.

Write a program that prompts the user to enter a temperature between $-58°F$ and $41°F$ and a wind speed greater than or equal to 2 and displays the wind-chill temperature. Use **Math.pow(a, b)** to compute $v^{0.16}$. Here is a sample run:

```
Enter the temperature in Fahrenheit: 5.3  ⏎Enter
Enter the wind speed in miles per hour: 6  ⏎Enter
The wind chill index is -5.56707
```

2.18 (*Print a table*) Write a program that displays the following table:

```
a       b       pow(a, b)
1       2       1
2       3       8
3       4       81
4       5       1024
5       6       15625
```

2.19 (*Geometry: distance of two points*) Write a program that prompts the user to enter two points (x1, y1) and (x2, y2) and displays their distance between them. The formula for computing the distance is $\sqrt{(x_2 - x_1)^2 + (y_2 - y_1)^2}$. Note that you can use Math.pow(a, 0.5) to compute $\sqrt{a}$. Here is a sample run:

```
Enter x1 and y1: 1.5 -3.4  ↵Enter
Enter x2 and y2: 4 5   ↵Enter
The distance between the two points is 8.764131445842194
```

Sections 2.13–2.16

*2.20 (*Financial application: calculate interest*) If you know the balance and the annual percentage interest rate, you can compute the interest on the next monthly payment using the following formula:

$$interest = balance \times (annualInterestRate / 1200)$$

Write a program that reads the balance and the annual percentage interest rate and displays the interest for the next month. Here is a sample run:

```
Enter balance and interest rate (e.g., 3 for 3%): 1000 3.5  ↵Enter
The interest is 2.91667
```

*2.21 (*Financial application: calculate future investment value*) Write a program that reads in investment amount, annual interest rate, and number of years, and displays the future investment value using the following formula:

```
futureInvestmentValue =
  investmentAmount x (1 + monthlyInterestRate)numberOfYears*12
```

For example, if you enter amount **1000**, annual interest rate **3.25%**, and number of years **1**, the future investment value is **1032.98**.

Here is a sample run:

```
Enter investment amount: 1000  ↵Enter
Enter annual interest rate in percentage: 4.25  ↵Enter
Enter number of years: 1  ↵Enter
Accumulated value is $1043.34
```

Sections 2.17–2.18

2.22 (*Random character*) Write a program that displays a random uppercase letter using the `System.CurrentTimeMillis()` method.

2.23 (*Find the character of an ASCII code*) Write a program that receives an ASCII code (an integer between 0 and 127) and displays its character. For example, if the user enters **97**, the program displays character **a**. Here is a sample run:

```
Enter an ASCII code: 69  ↵Enter
The character is E
```

*2.24 (*Financial application: monetary units*) Rewrite Listing 2.10, ComputeChange.java, to fix the possible loss of accuracy when converting a `double` value to an `int` value. Enter the input as an integer whose last two digits represent the cents. For example, the input **1156** represents **11** dollars and **56** cents.

*2.25 (*Financial application: payroll*) Write a program that reads the following information and prints a payroll statement:

Employee's name (e.g., Smith)
Number of hours worked in a week (e.g., 10)
Hourly pay rate (e.g., 6.75)
Federal tax withholding rate (e.g., 20%)
State tax withholding rate (e.g., 9%)

```
Enter employee's name: Smith  ↵Enter
Enter number of hours worked in a week: 10  ↵Enter
Enter hourly pay rate: 6.75  ↵Enter
Enter federal tax withholding rate: 0.20  ↵Enter
Enter state tax withholding rate: 0.09  ↵Enter

Employee Name: Smith
Hours Worked:  10.0
Pay Rate:  $6.75
Gross Pay:  $67.5
Deductions:
   Federal Withholding (20.0%):  $13.5
   State Withholding (9.0%):  $6.07
   Total Deduction:  $19.57
Net Pay:  $47.92
```

Section 2.19

*2.26 (*Use input dialog*) Rewrite Listing 2.10, ComputeChange.java, using input and output dialog boxes.

*2.27 (*Financial application: payroll*) Rewrite Exercise 2.25 using GUI input and output dialog boxes.

SELECTIONS

Objectives

- To declare `boolean` variables and write Boolean expressions using comparison operators (§3.2).

- To implement selection control using one-way `if` statements (§3.3).

- To program using one-way `if` statements (`GuessBirthday`) (§3.4).

- To implement selection control using two-way `if-else` statements (§3.5).

- To implement selection control using nested `if` and multi-way `if` statements (§3.6).

- To avoid common errors in `if` statements (§3.7).

- To generate random numbers using the `Math.random()` method (§3.8).

- To program using selection statements for a variety of examples (`SubtractionQuiz`, `BMI`, `ComputeTax`) (§§3.8–3.10).

- To combine conditions using logical operators (`&&`, `||`, and `!`) (§3.11).

- To program using selection statements with combined conditions (`LeapYear`, `Lottery`) (§§3.12–3.13).

- To implement selection control using `switch` statements (§3.14).

- To write expressions using the conditional operator (§3.15).

- To format output using the `System.out.printf` method (§3.16).

- To examine the rules governing operator precedence and associativity (§3.17).

- To get user confirmation using confirmation dialogs (§3.18).

- To apply common techniques to debug errors (§3.19).

3.1 Introduction

The program can decide which statements to execute based on a condition.

problem

If you enter a negative value for `radius` in Listing 2.2, ComputeAreaWithConsoleInput.java, the program displays an invalid result. If the radius is negative, you don't want the program to compute the area. How can you deal with this situation?

selection statements

Like all high-level programming languages, Java provides *selection statements*: statements that let you choose actions with two or more alternative courses. You can use the following selection statement to replace lines 12–17 in Listing 2.2:

```java
if (radius < 0) {
  System.out.println("Incorrect input");
}
else {
  area = radius * radius * 3.14159;
  System.out.println("Area is " + area);
}
```

Boolean expression
Boolean value

Selection statements use conditions that are Boolean expressions. A *Boolean expression* is an expression that evaluates to a *Boolean value*: `true` or `false`. We now introduce Boolean types and comparison operators.

3.2 `boolean` Data Type

A `boolean` data type declares a variable with the value either `true` or `false`.

boolean data type
comparison operators

How do you compare two values, such as whether a radius is greater than **0**, equal to **0**, or less than **0**? Java provides six *comparison operators* (also known as *relational operators*), shown in Table 3.1, which can be used to compare two values (assume radius is **5** in the table).

TABLE 3.1 Comparison Operators

Java Operator	Mathematics Symbol	Name	Example (radius is 5)	Result
<	<	less than	`radius < 0`	`false`
<=	≤	less than or equal to	`radius <= 0`	`false`
>	>	greater than	`radius > 0`	`true`
>=	≥	greater than or equal to	`radius >= 0`	`true`
==	=	equal to	`radius == 0`	`false`
!=	≠	not equal to	`radius != 0`	`true`

compare characters

Note

You can also compare characters. Comparing characters is the same as comparing their Unicodes. For example, `a` is larger than `A` because the Unicode of `a` is larger than the Unicode of `A`. See Appendix B, The ASCII Character Set, to find the order of characters.

== vs. =

Caution

The equality comparison operator is two equal signs (`==`), not a single equal sign (`=`). The latter symbol is for assignment.

The result of the comparison is a Boolean value: `true` or `false`. For example, the following statement displays `true`:

```java
double radius = 1;
System.out.println(radius > 0);
```

A variable that holds a Boolean value is known as a *Boolean variable*. The **boolean** data type is used to declare Boolean variables. A **boolean** variable can hold one of the two values: **true** or **false**. For example, the following statement assigns **true** to the variable **lightsOn**:

Boolean variable

```java
boolean lightsOn = true;
```

true and **false** are literals, just like a number such as **10**. They are reserved words and cannot be used as identifiers in your program.

Boolean literals

Suppose you want to develop a program to let a first-grader practice addition. The program randomly generates two single-digit integers, **number1** and **number2**, and displays to the student a question such as "What is 1 + 7?", as shown in the sample run in Listing 3.1. After the student types the answer, the program displays a message to indicate whether it is true or false.

VideoNote

Program addition quiz

There are several ways to generate random numbers. For now, generate the first integer using **System.currentTimeMillis() % 10** and the second using **System.currentTimeMillis() / 7 % 10**. Listing 3.1 gives the program. Lines 5–6 generate two numbers, **number1** and **number2**. Line 14 obtains an answer from the user. The answer is graded in line 18 using a Boolean expression **number1 + number2 == answer**.

LISTING 3.1   AdditionQuiz.java

```java
1   import java.util.Scanner;
2
3   public class AdditionQuiz {
4     public static void main(String[] args) {
5       int number1 = (int)(System.currentTimeMillis() % 10);
6       int number2 = (int)(System.currentTimeMillis() / 7 % 10);
7
8       // Create a Scanner
9       Scanner input = new Scanner(System.in);
10
11      System.out.print(
12        "What is " + number1 + " + " + number2 + "? ");
13
14      int answer = input.nextInt();
15
16      System.out.println(
17        number1 + " + " + number2 + " = " + answer + " is " +
18        (number1 + number2 == answer));
19    }
20  }
```

generate number1
generate number2

show question

display result

```
What is 1 + 7? 8 ⏎Enter
1 + 7 = 8 is true
```

```
What is 4 + 8? 9 ⏎Enter
4 + 8 = 9 is false
```

line#	number1	number2	answer	output
5	4			
6		8		
14			9	
16				4 + 8 = 9 is false

3.1 List six comparison operators.

3.2 Show the printout of the following statements:

```
System.out.println('a' < 'b');
System.out.println('a' <= 'A');
System.out.println('a' > 'b');
System.out.println('a' >= 'A');
System.out.println('a' == 'a');
System.out.println('a' != 'b');
```

3.3 Can the following conversions involving casting be allowed? If so, find the converted result.

```
boolean b = true;
i = (int)b;

int i = 1;
boolean b = (boolean)i;
```

3.3 `if` Statements

Key
Point

An `if` statement executes the statements if the condition is true.

The preceding program displays a message such as "6 + 2 = 7 is false." If you wish the message to be "6 + 2 = 7 is incorrect," you have to use a selection statement to make this

why `if` statement?   minor change.

Java has several types of selection statements: one-way `if` statements, two-way `if-else` statements, nested `if` statements, `switch` statements, and conditional expressions.

A one-way `if` statement executes an action if and only if the condition is `true`. The syntax for a one-way `if` statement is:

`if` statement
```
if (boolean-expression) {
    statement(s);
}
```

The flowchart in Figure 3.1 illustrates how Java executes the syntax of an `if` statement.

flowchart   A *flowchart* is a diagram that describes an algorithm or process, showing the steps as boxes of various kinds, and their order by connecting these with arrows. Process operations are represented in these boxes, and arrows connecting them represent the flow of control. A diamond box is used to denote a Boolean condition and a rectangle box is for representing statements.

If the `boolean-expression` evaluates to `true`, the statements in the block are executed. As an example, see the following code:

```
if (radius >= 0) {
    area = radius * radius * PI;
    System.out.println("The area for the circle of radius " +
        radius + " is " + area);
}
```

The flowchart of the preceding statement is shown in Figure 3.1b. If the value of **radius** is greater than or equal to **0**, then the **area** is computed and the result is displayed; otherwise, the two statements in the block will not be executed.

The **boolean-expression** is enclosed in parentheses. For example, the code in (a) below is wrong. It should be corrected, as shown in (b).

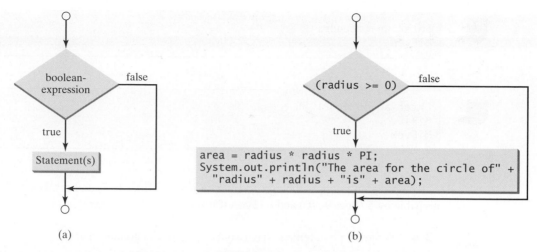

FIGURE 3.1 An **if** statement executes statements if the **boolean-expression** evaluates to **true**.

```
if i > 0 {
   System.out.println("i is positive");
}
```
(a) Wrong

```
if (i > 0) {
   System.out.println("i is positive");
}
```
(b) Correct

The block braces can be omitted if they enclose a single statement. For example, the following statements are equivalent.

```
if (i > 0) {
   System.out.println("i is positive");
}
```
(a)

Equivalent

```
if (i > 0)
   System.out.println("i is positive");
```
(b)

 Note

Omitting braces makes the code shorter, but it is prone to errors. It is a common mistake to forget the braces when you go back to modify the code that omits the braces.

Omitting braces or not

Listing 3.2 gives a program that prompts the user to enter an integer. If the number is a multiple of **5**, the program displays **HiFive**. If the number is divisible by **2**, it displays **HiEven**.

LISTING 3.2 SimpleIfDemo.java

```
 1  import java.util.Scanner;
 2
 3  public class SimpleIfDemo {
 4    public static void main(String[] args) {
 5      Scanner input = new Scanner(System.in);
 6      System.out.println("Enter an integer: ");
 7      int number = input.nextInt();                    enter input
 8
 9      if (number % 5 == 0)                              check 5
10        System.out.println("HiFive");
11
12      if (number % 2 == 0)                             check even
13        System.out.println("HiEven");
14    }
15  }
```

```
Enter an integer: 4 [↵Enter]
HiEven
```

```
Enter an integer: 30 [↵Enter]
HiFive
HiEven
```

The program prompts the user to enter an integer (lines 6–7) and displays `HiFive` if it is divisible by **5** (lines 9–10) and `HiEven` if it is divisible by **2** (lines 12–13).

3.4 Write an `if` statement that assigns **1** to **x** if **y** is greater than **0**.

3.5 Write an `if` statement that increases pay by 3% if **score** is greater than **90**.

MyProgrammingLab™

3.4 Case Study: Guessing Birthdays

Key Point

Guessing birthdays is an interesting problem with a simple programming solution.

You can find out the date of the month when your friend was born by asking five questions. Each question asks whether the day is in one of the five sets of numbers.

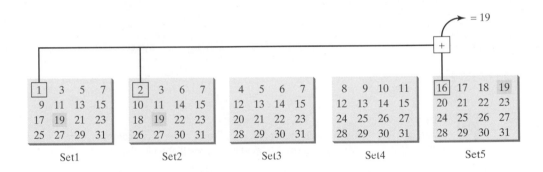

The birthday is the sum of the first numbers in the sets where the day appears. For example, if the birthday is **19**, it appears in Set1, Set2, and Set5. The first numbers in these three sets are **1**, **2**, and **16**. Their sum is **19**.

Listing 3.3 gives a program that prompts the user to answer whether the day is in Set1 (lines 41–44), in Set2 (lines 50–53), in Set3 (lines 59–62), in Set4 (lines 68–71), and in Set5 (lines 77–80). If the number is in the set, the program adds the first number in the set to **day** (lines 47, 56, 65, 74, 83).

LISTING **3.3** GuessBirthday.java

```
1  import java.util.Scanner;
2
3  public class GuessBirthday {
4    public static void main(String[] args) {
5      String set1 =
6        " 1  3  5  7\n" +
```

```
 7          "  9 11 13 15\n" +
 8          " 17 19 21 23\n" +
 9          " 25 27 29 31";
10
11      String set2 =
12          "  2  3  6  7\n" +
13          " 10 11 14 15\n" +
14          " 18 19 22 23\n" +
15          " 26 27 30 31";
16
17      String set3 =
18          "  4  5  6  7\n" +
19          " 12 13 14 15\n" +
20          " 20 21 22 23\n" +
21          " 28 29 30 31";
22
23      String set4 =
24          "  8  9 10 11\n" +
25          " 12 13 14 15\n" +
26          " 24 25 26 27\n" +
27          " 28 29 30 31";
28
29      String set5 =
30          " 16 17 18 19\n" +
31          " 20 21 22 23\n" +
32          " 24 25 26 27\n" +
33          " 28 29 30 31";
34
35      int day = 0;                                             day to be determined
36
37      // Create a Scanner
38      Scanner input = new Scanner(System.in);
39
40      // Prompt the user to answer questions
41      System.out.print("Is your birthday in Set1?\n");
42      System.out.print(set1);
43      System.out.print("\nEnter 0 for No and 1 for Yes: ");
44      int answer = input.nextInt();
45
46      if (answer == 1)                                         in Set1?
47          day += 1;
48
49      // Prompt the user to answer questions
50      System.out.print("\nIs your birthday in Set2?\n");
51      System.out.print(set2);
52      System.out.print("\nEnter 0 for No and 1 for Yes: ");
53      answer = input.nextInt();
54
55      if (answer == 1)                                         in Set2?
56          day += 2;
57
58      // Prompt the user to answer questions
59      System.out.print("Is your birthday in Set3?\n");
60      System.out.print(set3);
61      System.out.print("\nEnter 0 for No and 1 for Yes: ");
62      answer = input.nextInt();
63
64      if (answer == 1)                                         in Set3?
65          day += 4;
66
```

```
67         // Prompt the user to answer questions
68         System.out.print("\nIs your birthday in Set4?\n");
69         System.out.print(set4);
70         System.out.print("\nEnter 0 for No and 1 for Yes: ");
71         answer = input.nextInt();
72
73         if (answer == 1)
74            day += 8;
75
76         // Prompt the user to answer questions
77         System.out.print("\nIs your birthday in Set5?\n");
78         System.out.print(set5);
79         System.out.print("\nEnter 0 for No and 1 for Yes: ");
80         answer = input.nextInt();
81
82         if (answer == 1)
83            day += 16;
84
85         System.out.println("\nYour birthday is " + day + "!");
86      }
87   }
```

in Set4?

in Set5?

```
Is your birthday in Set1?
 1  3  5  7
 9 11 13 15
17 19 21 23
25 27 29 31
Enter 0 for No and 1 for Yes: 1  ↵Enter

Is your birthday in Set2?
 2  3  6  7
10 11 14 15
18 19 22 23
26 27 30 31
Enter 0 for No and 1 for Yes: 1  ↵Enter

Is your birthday in Set3?
 4  5  6  7
12 13 14 15
20 21 22 23
28 29 30 31
Enter 0 for No and 1 for Yes: 0  ↵Enter

Is your birthday in Set4?
 8  9 10 11
12 13 14 15
24 25 26 27
28 29 30 31
Enter 0 for No and 1 for Yes: 0  ↵Enter

Is your birthday in Set5?
16 17 18 19
20 21 22 23
24 25 26 27
28 29 30 31
Enter 0 for No and 1 for Yes: 1  ↵Enter
Your birthday is 19!
```

line#	day	answer	output
35	0		
44		1	
47	1		
53		1	
56	3		
62		0	
71		0	
80		1	
83	19		
85			Your birthday is 19!

This game is easy to program. You may wonder how the game was created. The mathematics behind the game is actually quite simple. The numbers are not grouped together by accident—the way they are placed in the five sets is deliberate. The starting numbers in the five sets are **1**, **2**, **4**, **8**, and **16**, which correspond to **1**, **10**, **100**, **1000**, and **10000** in binary (binary numbers are introduced in Appendix F, Number Systems). A binary number for decimal integers between **1** and **31** has at most five digits, as shown in Figure 3.2a. Let it be $b_5b_4b_3b_2b_1$. Thus, $b_5b_4b_3b_2b_1 = b_50000 + b_4000 + b_300 + b_20 + b_1$, as shown in Figure 3.2b. If a day's binary number has a digit **1** in b_k, the number should appear in Set$k$. For example, number **19** is binary **10011**, so it appears in Set1, Set2, and Set5. It is binary **1** + **10** + **10000** = **10011** or decimal **1** + **2** + **16** = **19**. Number **31** is binary **11111**, so it appears in Set1, Set2, Set3, Set4, and Set5. It is binary **1** + **10** + **100** + **1000** + **10000** = **11111** or decimal **1** + **2** + **4** + **8** + **16** = **31**.

mathematics behind the game

Decimal	Binary
1	00001
2	00010
3	00011
...	
19	10011
...	
31	11111

(a)

$$
\begin{array}{rrr}
b_5\ 0\ 0\ 0\ 0 & & 10000 \\
b_4\ 0\ 0\ 0 & & 1000 \\
b_3\ 0\ 0 & 10000 & 100 \\
b_2\ 0 & 10 & 10 \\
+\ \underline{\quad b_1} & +\ \underline{\quad 1} & +\ \underline{\quad 1} \\
b_5\ b_4\ b_3\ b_2\ b_1 & 10011 & 11111 \\
& 19 & 31
\end{array}
$$

(b)

FIGURE 3.2 (a) A number between **1** and **31** can be represented using a 5-digit binary number. (b) A 5-digit binary number can be obtained by adding binary numbers **1**, **10**, **100**, **1000**, or **10000**.

3.5 Two-Way `if-else` Statements

An `if-else` statement decides which statements to execute based on whether the condition is true or false.

🔑 **Key Point**

A one-way `if` statement takes an action if the specified condition is `true`. If the condition is `false`, nothing is done. But what if you want to take alternative actions when the condition is `false`? You can use a two-way `if-else` statement. The actions that a two-way `if-else` statement specifies differ based on whether the condition is `true` or `false`.

Here is the syntax for a two-way **if-else** statement:

```
if (boolean-expression) {
  statement(s)-for-the-true-case;
}
else {
  statement(s)-for-the-false-case;
}
```

The flowchart of the statement is shown in Figure 3.3.

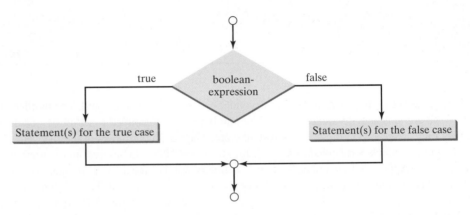

FIGURE 3.3 An **if-else** statement executes statements for the true case if the **Boolean-expression** evaluates to **true**; otherwise, statements for the false case are executed.

If the **boolean-expression** evaluates to **true**, the statement(s) for the true case are executed; otherwise, the statement(s) for the false case are executed. For example, consider the following code:

two-way if-else statement

```
if (radius >= 0) {
  area = radius * radius * PI;
  System.out.println("The area for the circle of radius " +
    radius + " is " + area);
}
else {
  System.out.println("Negative input");
}
```

If **radius >= 0** is **true**, **area** is computed and displayed; if it is **false**, the message **"Negative input"** is displayed.

As usual, the braces can be omitted if there is only one statement within them. The braces enclosing the **System.out.println("Negative input")** statement can therefore be omitted in the preceding example.

Here is another example of using the **if-else** statement. The example checks whether a number is even or odd, as follows:

```
if (number % 2 == 0)
  System.out.println(number + " is even.");
else
  System.out.println(number + " is odd.");
```

3.6   Write an **if** statement that increases **pay** by 3% if **score** is greater than **90**, otherwise increases **pay** by 1%.

3.7   What is the printout of the code in (a) and (b) if **number** is 30? What if **number** is **35**?

```
if (number % 2 == 0)
  System.out.println(number + " is even.");

System.out.println(number + " is odd.");
```

(a)

```
if (number % 2 == 0)
  System.out.println(number + " is even.");
else
  System.out.println(number + " is odd.");
```

(b)

3.6 Nested **if** and Multi-Way **if-else** Statements

*An **if** statement can be inside another **if** statement to form a nested **if** statement.*

The statement in an **if** or **if-else** statement can be any legal Java statement, including another **if** or **if-else** statement. The inner **if** statement is said to be *nested* inside the outer **if** statement. The inner **if** statement can contain another **if** statement; in fact, there is no limit to the depth of the nesting. For example, the following is a nested **if** statement:

nested **if** statement

```
if (i > k) {
  if (j > k)
    System.out.println("i and j are greater than k");
}
else
  System.out.println("i is less than or equal to k");
```

The **if (j > k)** statement is nested inside the **if (i > k)** statement.

The nested **if** statement can be used to implement multiple alternatives. The statement given in Figure 3.4a, for instance, assigns a letter grade to the variable **grade** according to the score, with multiple alternatives.

```
if (score >= 90.0)
  grade = 'A';
else
  if (score >= 80.0)
    grade = 'B';
  else
    if (score >= 70.0)
      grade = 'C';
    else
      if (score >= 60.0)
        grade = 'D';
      else
        grade = 'F';
```

(a)

Equivalent

This is better

```
if (score >= 90.0)
  grade = 'A';
else if (score >= 80.0)
  grade = 'B';
else if (score >= 70.0)
  grade = 'C';
else if (score >= 60.0)
  grade = 'D';
else
  grade = 'F';
```

(b)

FIGURE 3.4   A preferred format for multiple alternatives is shown in (b) using a multi-way **if-else** statement.

The execution of this **if** statement proceeds as shown in Figure 3.5. The first condition (**score >= 90.0**) is tested. If it is **true**, the grade becomes **A**. If it is **false**, the second condition (**score >= 80.0**) is tested. If the second condition is **true**, the grade becomes **B**. If that condition is **false**, the third condition and the rest of the conditions (if necessary) are tested until a condition is met or all of the conditions prove to be **false**. If all of the conditions are **false**, the grade becomes **F**. Note that a condition is tested only when all of the conditions that come before it are **false**.

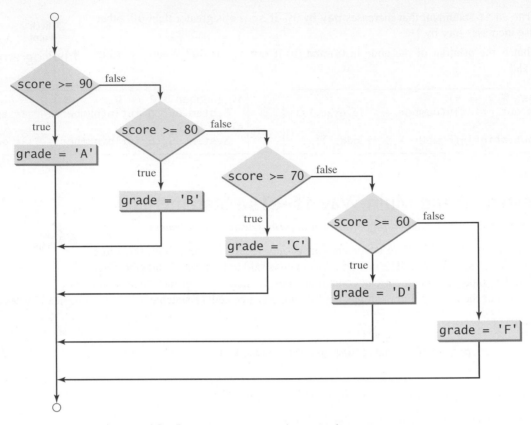

FIGURE 3.5 You can use a multi-way `if-else` statement to assign a grade.

multi-way `if` statement

The `if` statement in Figure 3.4a is equivalent to the `if` statement in Figure 3.4b. In fact, Figure 3.4b is the preferred coding style for multiple alternative `if` statements. This style, called *multi-way `if-else` statements*, avoids deep indentation and makes the program easy to read.

MyProgrammingLab™

3.8 Suppose x = 3 and y = 2; show the output, if any, of the following code. What is the output if x = 3 and y = 4? What is the output if x = 2 and y = 2? Draw a flowchart of the code.

```
if (x > 2) {
  if (y > 2) {
    z = x + y;
    System.out.println("z is " + z);
  }
}
else
  System.out.println("x is " + x);
```

3.9 Suppose x = 2 and y = 3. Show the output, if any, of the following code. What is the output if x = 3 and y = 2? What is the output if x = 3 and y = 3? (*Hint:* Indent the statement correctly first.)

```
if (x > 2)
  if (y > 2) {
    int z = x + y;
    System.out.println("z is " + z);
  }
else
  System.out.println("x is " + x);
```

3.10 What is wrong in the following code?

```
if (score >= 60.0)
   grade = 'D';
else if (score >= 70.0)
   grade = 'C';
else if (score >= 80.0)
   grade = 'B';
else if (score >= 90.0)
   grade = 'A';
else
   grade = 'F';
```

3.7 Common Errors in Selection Statements

*Forgetting necessary braces, ending an `if` statement in the wrong place, mistaking `==`
for `=`, and dangling `else` clauses are common errors in selection statements.*

 **Key
Point**

The following errors are common among new programmers.

Common Error 1: Forgetting Necessary Braces

The braces can be omitted if the block contains a single statement. However, forgetting the
braces when they are needed for grouping multiple statements is a common programming
error. If you modify the code by adding new statements in an `if` statement without braces,
you will have to insert the braces. For example, the following code in (a) is wrong. It should
be written with braces to group multiple statements, as shown in (b).

```
if (radius >= 0)
   area = radius * radius * PI;
   System.out.println("The area "
      + " is " + area);
```
(a) Wrong

```
if (radius >= 0) {
   area = radius * radius * PI;
   System.out.println("The area "
      + " is " + area);
}
```
(b) Correct

Common Error 2: Wrong Semicolon at the `if` Line

Adding a semicolon at the end of an `if` line, as shown in (a) below, is a common mistake.

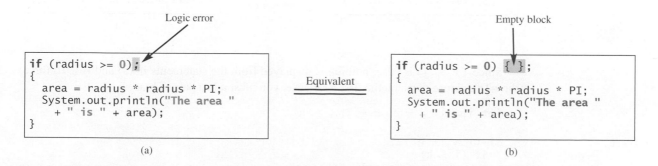

Logic error

```
if (radius >= 0);
{
   area = radius * radius * PI;
   System.out.println("The area "
      + " is " + area);
}
```
(a)

Equivalent

Empty block

```
if (radius >= 0) { };
{
   area = radius * radius * PI;
   System.out.println("The area "
      + " is " + area);
}
```
(b)

This mistake is hard to find, because it is neither a compile error nor a runtime error; it is a
logic error. The code in (a) is equivalent to that in (b) with an empty block.

This error often occurs when you use the next-line block style. Using the end-of-line block
style can help prevent this error.

Common Error 3: Redundant Testing of Boolean Values

To test whether a **boolean** variable is **true** or **false** in a test condition, it is redundant to use the equality comparison operator like the code in (a):

```
if (even == true)
    System.out.println(
        "It is even.");
```
(a)

Equivalent

This is better

```
if (even)
    System.out.println(
        "It is even.");
```
(b)

Instead, it is better to test the **boolean** variable directly, as shown in (b). Another good reason for doing this is to avoid errors that are difficult to detect. Using the = operator instead of the == operator to compare the equality of two items in a test condition is a common error. It could lead to the following erroneous statement:

```
if (even = true)
    System.out.println("It is even.");
```

This statement does not have compile errors. It assigns **true** to **even**, so that **even** is always **true**.

Common Error 4: Dangling `else` Ambiguity

The code in (a) below has two **if** clauses and one **else** clause. Which **if** clause is matched by the **else** clause? The indentation indicates that the **else** clause matches the first **if** clause. However, the **else** clause actually matches the second **if** clause. This situation is known as the *dangling else ambiguity*. The **else** clause always matches the most recent unmatched **if** clause in the same block. So, the statement in (a) is equivalent to the code in (b).

dangling else ambiguity

```
int i = 1, j = 2, k = 3;

if (i > j)
  if (i > k)
    System.out.println("A");
else
    System.out.println("B");
```
(a)

Equivalent

This is better
with correct
indentation

```
int i = 1, j = 2, k = 3;

if (i > j)
  if (i > k)
    System.out.println("A");
else
    System.out.println("B");
```
(b)

Since `(i > j)` is false, nothing is displayed from the statements in (a) and (b). To force the **else** clause to match the first **if** clause, you must add a pair of braces:

```
int i = 1, j = 2, k = 3;

if (i > j) {
  if (i > k)
    System.out.println("A");
}
else
  System.out.println("B");
```

This statement displays **B**.

Tip

Often new programmers write the code that assigns a test condition to a **boolean**   assign **boolean** variable
variable like the code in (a):

```
if (number % 2 == 0)
  even = true;
else
  even = false;
```

Equivalent   ═══════

This is shorter

```
boolean even
  = number % 2 == 0;
```

(a)   (b)

The code can be simplified by assigning the test value directly to the variable, as shown
in (b).

3.11   Which of the following statements are equivalent? Which ones are correctly indented?

```
if (i > 0) if
(j > 0)
x = 0; else
if (k > 0) y = 0;
else z = 0;
```

```
if (i > 0) {
  if (j > 0)
    x = 0;
  else if (k > 0)
    y = 0;
}
else
  z = 0;
```

```
if (i > 0)
  if (j > 0)
    x = 0;
  else if (k > 0)
    y = 0;
  else
    z = 0;
```

```
if (i > 0)
  if (j > 0)
    x = 0;
  else if (k > 0)
    y = 0;
else
  z = 0;
```

(a)   (b)   (c)   (d)

3.12   Rewrite the following statement using a Boolean expression:

```
if (count % 10 == 0)
  newLine = true;
else
  newLine = false;
```

3.13   Are the following statements correct? Which one is better?

```
if (age < 16)
  System.out.println
    ("Cannot get a driver's license");
if (age >= 16)
  System.out.println
    ("Can get a driver's license");
```

```
if (age < 16)
  System.out.println
    ("Cannot get a driver's license");
else
  System.out.println
    ("Can get a driver's license");
```

(a)   (b)

3.14   What is the output of the following code if **number** is 14, 15, and 30?

```
if (number % 2 == 0)
  System.out.println
    (number + " is even");
if (number % 5 == 0)
  System.out.println
    (number + " is multiple of 5");
```

```
if (number % 2 == 0)
  System.out.println
    (number + " is even");
else if (number % 5 == 0)
  System.out.println
    (number + " is multiple of 5");
```

(a)   (b)

3.8 Generating Random Numbers

You can use `Math.random()` *to obtain a random double value between* `0.0` *and* `1.0`, *excluding* `1.0`.

VideoNote

Program subtraction quiz

Suppose you want to develop a program for a first-grader to practice subtraction. The program randomly generates two single-digit integers, **number1** and **number2**, with **number1 >= number2**, and it displays to the student a question such as "What is 9 − 2?" After the student enters the answer, the program displays a message indicating whether it is correct.

The previous programs generate random numbers using `System.currentTimeMillis()`. A better approach is to use the **random()** method in the **Math** class. Invoking this method

random() method

returns a random double value **d** such that $0.0 \le d < 1.0$. Thus, **(int)(Math.random() * 10)** returns a random single-digit integer (i.e., a number between **0** and **9**).

The program can work as follows:

1. Generate two single-digit integers into **number1** and **number2**.

2. If **number1 < number2**, swap **number1** with **number2**.

3. Prompt the student to answer, **"What is number1 - number2?"**

4. Check the student's answer and display whether the answer is correct.

The complete program is shown in Listing 3.4.

LISTING 3.4 SubtractionQuiz.java

```java
1  import java.util.Scanner;
2
3  public class SubtractionQuiz {
4    public static void main(String[] args) {
5      // 1. Generate two random single-digit integers
6      int number1 = (int)(Math.random() * 10);
7      int number2 = (int)(Math.random() * 10);
8
9      // 2. If number1 < number2, swap number1 with number2
10     if (number1 < number2) {
11       int temp = number1;
12       number1 = number2;
13       number2 = temp;
14     }
15
16     // 3. Prompt the student to answer "What is number1 – number2?"
17     System.out.print
18       ("What is " + number1 + " - " + number2 + "? ");
19     Scanner input = new Scanner(System.in);
20     int answer = input.nextInt();
21
22     // 4. Grade the answer and display the result
23     if (number1 - number2 == answer)
24       System.out.println("You are correct!");
25     else
26       System.out.println("Your answer is wrong\n" + number1 + " - "
27         + number2 + " is " + (number1 - number2));
28   }
29 }
```

random number

get answer

check the answer

```
What is 6 - 6? 0  ↵Enter
You are correct!
```

```
What is 9 - 2? 5  ↵Enter
Your answer is wrong
9 - 2 is 7
```

line#	number1	number2	temp	answer	output
6	2				
7		9			
11			2		
12	9				
13		2			
20				5	
26					Your answer is wrong 9 - 2 should be 7

To swap two variables **number1** and **number2**, a temporary variable **temp** (line 11) is used to first hold the value in **number1**. The value in **number2** is assigned to **number1** (line 12), and the value in **temp** is assigned to **number2** (line 13).

3.15 Which of the following is a possible output from invoking **Math.random()**?

323.4, 0.5, 34, 1.0, 0.0, 0.234

3.16 a. How do you generate a random integer **i** such that $0 \le i < 20$?

b. How do you generate a random integer **i** such that $10 \le i < 20$?

c. How do you generate a random integer **i** such that $10 \le i \le 50$?

3.9 Case Study: Computing Body Mass Index

*You can use nested **if** statements to write a program that interprets body mass index.*

Body Mass Index (BMI) is a measure of health based on height and weight. It can be calculated by taking your weight in kilograms and dividing it by the square of your height in meters. The interpretation of BMI for people 20 years or older is as follows:

BMI	Interpretation
Below 18.5	Underweight
18.5–24.9	Normal
25.0–29.9	Overweight
Above 30.0	Obese

Write a program that prompts the user to enter a weight in pounds and height in inches and displays the BMI. Note that one pound is **0.45359237** kilograms and one inch is **0.0254** meters. Listing 3.5 gives the program.

LISTING 3.5 ComputeAndInterpretBMI.java

```java
 1  import java.util.Scanner;
 2
 3  public class ComputeAndInterpretBMI {
 4    public static void main(String[] args) {
 5      Scanner input = new Scanner(System.in);
 6
 7      // Prompt the user to enter weight in pounds
 8      System.out.print("Enter weight in pounds: ");
 9      double weight = input.nextDouble();
10
11      // Prompt the user to enter height in inches
12      System.out.print("Enter height in inches: ");
13      double height = input.nextDouble();
14
15      final double KILOGRAMS_PER_POUND = 0.45359237; // Constant
16      final double METERS_PER_INCH = 0.0254; // Constant
17
18      // Compute BMI
19      double weightInKilograms = weight * KILOGRAMS_PER_POUND;
20      double heightInMeters = height * METERS_PER_INCH;
21      double bmi = weightInKilograms /
22        (heightInMeters * heightInMeters);
23
24      // Display result
25      System.out.println("BMI is " + bmi);
26      if (bmi < 18.5)
27        System.out.println("Underweight");
28      else if (bmi < 25)
29        System.out.println("Normal");
30      else if (bmi < 30)
31        System.out.println("Overweight");
32      else
33        System.out.println("Obese");
34    }
35  }
```

input weight

input height

compute bmi

display output

```
Enter weight in pounds: 146  ↵Enter
Enter height in inches: 70  ↵Enter
BMI is 20.948603801493316
Normal
```

line#	weight	height	weightInKilograms	heightInMeters	bmi	output
9	146					
13		70				
19			66.22448602			
20				1.778		
21					20.9486	
25						BMI is 20.95
31						Normal

The constants KILOGRAMS_PER_POUND and METERS_PER_INCH are defined in lines 15–16. Using constants here makes programs easy to read.

3.10 Case Study: Computing Taxes

You can use nested if *statements to write a program for computing taxes.*

Key Point

VideoNote

Use multi-way if-else statements

The United States federal personal income tax is calculated based on filing status and taxable income. There are four filing statuses: single filers, married filing jointly or qualified widow(er), married filing separately, and head of household. The tax rates vary every year. Table 3.2 shows the rates for 2009. If you are, say, single with a taxable income of $10,000, the first $8,350 is taxed at 10% and the other $1,650 is taxed at 15%, so, your total tax is $1,082.50.

TABLE 3.2 2009 U.S. Federal Personal Tax Rates

Marginal Tax Rate	Single	Married Filing Jointly or Qualifying Widow(er)	Married Filing Separately	Head of Household
10%	$0 – $8,350	$0 – $16,700	$0 – $8,350	$0 – $11,950
15%	$8,351– $33,950	$16,701 – $67,900	$8,351 – $33,950	$11,951 – $45,500
25%	$33,951 – $82,250	$67,901 – $137,050	$33,951 – $68,525	$45,501 – $117,450
28%	$82,251 – $171,550	$137,051 – $208,850	$68,526 – $104,425	$117,451 – $190,200
33%	$171,551 – $372,950	$208,851 – $372,950	$104,426 – $186,475	$190,201 – $372,950
35%	$372,951 +	$372,951 +	$186,476 +	$372,951 +

You are to write a program to compute personal income tax. Your program should prompt the user to enter the filing status and taxable income and compute the tax. Enter 0 for single filers, 1 for married filing jointly or qualified widow(er), 2 for married filing separately, and 3 for head of household.

Your program computes the tax for the taxable income based on the filing status. The filing status can be determined using if statements outlined as follows:

```
if (status == 0) {
  // Compute tax for single filers
}
else if (status == 1) {
  // Compute tax for married filing jointly or qualifying widow(er)
}
else if (status == 2) {
  // Compute tax for married filing separately
}
else if (status == 3) {
  // Compute tax for head of household
}
else {
  // Display wrong status
}
```

For each filing status there are six tax rates. Each rate is applied to a certain amount of taxable income. For example, of a taxable income of $400,000 for single filers, $8,350 is taxed at 10%, (33,950 – 8,350) at 15%, (82,250 – 33,950) at 25%, (171,550 – 82,250) at 28%, (372,950 – 171,550) at 33%, and (400,000 – 372,950) at 35%.

Listing 3.6 gives the solution for computing taxes for single filers. The complete solution is left as an exercise.

LISTING 3.6 ComputeTax.java

```java
1  import java.util.Scanner;
2
3  public class ComputeTax {
4    public static void main(String[] args) {
5      // Create a Scanner
6      Scanner input = new Scanner(System.in);
7
8      // Prompt the user to enter filing status
9      System.out.print(
10       "(0-single filer, 1-married jointly or qualifying widow(er),
11       + "\n2-married separately, 3-head of household)\n" +
12       "Enter the filing status: ");
13     int status = input.nextInt();
14
15     // Prompt the user to enter taxable income
16     System.out.print("Enter the taxable income: ");
17     double income = input.nextDouble();
18
19     // Compute tax
20     double tax = 0;
21
22     if (status == 0) { // Compute tax for single filers
23       if (income <= 8350)
24         tax = income * 0.10;
25       else if (income <= 33950)
26         tax = 8350 * 0.10 + (income - 8350) * 0.15;
27       else if (income <= 82250)
28         tax = 8350 * 0.10 + (33950 - 8350) * 0.15 +
29           (income - 33950) * 0.25;
30       else if (income <= 171550)
31         tax = 8350 * 0.10 + (33950 - 8350) * 0.15 +
32           (82250 - 33950) * 0.25 + (income - 82250) * 0.28;
33       else if (income <= 372950)
34         tax = 8350 * 0.10 + (33950 - 8350) * 0.15 +
35           (82250 - 33950) * 0.25 + (171550 - 82250) * 0.28 +
36           (income - 171550) * 0.33;
37       else
38         tax = 8350 * 0.10 + (33950 - 8350) * 0.15 +
39           (82250 - 33950) * 0.25 + (171550 - 82250) * 0.28 +
40           (372950 - 171550) * 0.33 + (income - 372950) * 0.35;
41     }
42     else if (status == 1) { // Left as exercise
43       // Compute tax for married file jointly or qualifying widow(er)
44     }
45     else if (status == 2) { // Compute tax for married separately
46       // Left as exercise
47     }
48     else if (status == 3) { // Compute tax for head of household
49       // Left as exercise
50     }
51     else {
52       System.out.println("Error: invalid status");
53       System.exit(1);
54     }
55
56     // Display the result
57     System.out.println("Tax is " + (int)(tax * 100) / 100.0);
58   }
59 }
```

Margin notes:
- input status (line 13)
- input income (line 17)
- compute tax (line 22)
- exit program (line 53)
- display output (line 57)

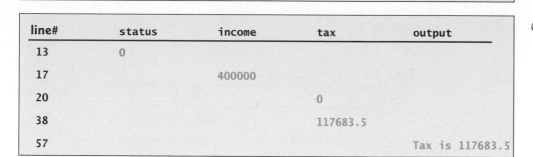

```
(0-single filer, 1-married jointly or qualifying widow(er),
2-married separately, 3-head of household)
Enter the filing status: 0 ↵Enter
Enter the taxable income: 400000 ↵Enter
Tax is 117683.5
```

line#	status	income	tax	output
13	0			
17		400000		
20			0	
38			117683.5	
57				Tax is 117683.5

The program receives the filing status and taxable income. The multi-way `if-else` statements (lines 22, 42, 45, 48, 51) check the filing status and compute the tax based on the filing status.

`System.exit(status)` (line 53) is defined in the `System` class. Invoking this method terminates the program. The status `0` indicates that the program is terminated normally. A nonzero status code indicates abnormal termination.

System.exit(status)

An initial value of `0` is assigned to `tax` (line 20). A compile error would occur if it had no initial value, because all of the other statements that assign values to `tax` are within the `if` statement. The compiler thinks that these statements may not be executed and therefore reports a compile error.

To test a program, you should provide the input that covers all cases. For this program, your input should cover all statuses (`0`, `1`, `2`, `3`). For each status, test the tax for each of the six brackets. So, there are a total of 24 cases.

test all cases

 Tip
For all programs, you should write a small amount of code and test it before moving on to add more code. This is called *incremental development and testing*. This approach makes testing easier, because the errors are likely in the new code you just added.

incremental development and testing

3.17 Are the following two statements equivalent?

✓**Check Point**

MyProgrammingLab™

```
if (income <= 10000)
  tax = income * 0.1;
else if (income <= 20000)
  tax = 1000 +
    (income - 10000) * 0.15;
```

```
if (income <= 10000)
  tax = income * 0.1;
else if (income > 10000 &&
        income <= 20000)
  tax = 1000 +
    (income - 10000) * 0.15;
```

3.11 Logical Operators

The logical operators !, &&, ||, *and* ∧ *can be used to create a compound Boolean expression.*

 Key Point

Sometimes, whether a statement is executed is determined by a combination of several conditions. You can use logical operators to combine these conditions to form a compound Boolean expression. *Logical operators*, also known as *Boolean operators*, operate on Boolean values to create a new Boolean value. Table 3.3 lists the Boolean operators. Table 3.4 defines the not (!) operator, which negates `true` to `false` and `false` to `true`. Table 3.5 defines the and (&&) operator. The and (&&) of two Boolean operands is `true` if and only if both operands are `true`. Table 3.6 defines the or (||) operator. The or (||) of two Boolean operands is `true` if at least one of the operands is `true`. Table 3.7 defines the exclusive or (∧) operator. The exclusive or (∧) of two Boolean operands is `true` if and only if the two operands have differ-ent Boolean values. Note that `p1 ∧ p2` is the same as `p1 != p2`.

TABLE 3.3 Boolean Operators

Operator	Name	Description
!	not	logical negation
&&	and	logical conjunction
||	or	logical disjunction
∧	exclusive or	logical exclusion

TABLE 3.4 Truth Table for Operator !

p	!p	Example (assume **age = 24, gender = 'F'**)
true	false	`!(age > 18)` is `false`, because `(age > 18)` is `true`.
false	true	`!(gender == 'M')` is `true`, because `(gender == 'M')` is `false`.

TABLE 3.5 Truth Table for Operator &&

p_1	p_2	p_1 && p_2	Example (assume **age = 24, gender = 'F'**)
false	false	false	`(age > 18) && (gender == 'F')` is `true`, because `(age > 18)` and `(gender == 'F')` are both `true`.
false	true	false	
true	false	false	`(age > 18) && (gender != 'F')` is `false`, because `(gender != 'F')` is `false`.
true	true	true	

TABLE 3.6 Truth Table for Operator ||

p_1	p_2	p_1 || p_2	Example (assume **age = 24, gender = 'F'**)
false	false	false	`(age > 34) || (gender == 'F')` is `true`, because `(gender == 'F')` is `true`.
false	true	true	
true	false	true	`(age > 34) || (gender == 'M')` is `false`, because `(age > 34)` and `(gender == 'M')` are both `false`.
true	true	true	

TABLE 3.7 Truth Table for Operator ∧

p₁	p₂	p₁ ∧ p₂	Example (assume **age = 24, gender = 'F'**)
false	false	false	**(age > 34) ∧ (gender == 'F')** is **true**, because **(age > 34)** is **false** but **(gender == 'F')** is **true**.
false	true	true	
true	false	true	**(age > 34) ∧ (gender == 'M')** is **false**, because **(age > 34)** and **(gender == 'M')** are both **false**.
true	true	false	

Listing 3.7 gives a program that checks whether a number is divisible by **2** and **3**, by **2** or **3**, and by **2** or **3** but not both:

LISTING 3.7 TestBooleanOperators.java

```
1  import java.util.Scanner;                                      import class
2
3  public class TestBooleanOperators {
4    public static void main(String[] args) {
5      // Create a Scanner
6      Scanner input = new Scanner(System.in);
7
8      // Receive an input
9      System.out.print("Enter an integer: ");
10     int number = input.nextInt();                              input
11
12     if (number % 2 == 0 && number % 3 == 0)                    and
13       System.out.println(number + " is divisible by 2 and 3.");
14
15     if (number % 2 == 0 || number % 3 == 0)                    or
16       System.out.println(number + " is divisible by 2 or 3.");
17
18     if (number % 2 == 0 ^ number % 3 == 0)                     exclusive or
19       System.out.println(number +
20         " is divisible by 2 or 3, but not both.");
21   }
22 }
```

```
Enter an integer: 4  ↵Enter
4 is divisible by 2 or 3.
4 is divisible by 2 or 3, but not both.
```

```
Enter an integer: 18  ↵Enter
18 is divisible by 2 and 3.
18 is divisible by 2 or 3.
```

(number % 2 == 0 && number % 3 == 0) (line 12) checks whether the number is divisible by both **2** and **3**. **(number % 2 == 0 || number % 3 == 0)** (line 15) checks whether the number is divisible by **2** and/or by **3**. **(number % 2 == 0 ^ number % 3 == 0)** (line 18) checks whether the number is divisible by **2** or **3**, but not both.

Caution

In mathematics, the expression

```
1 <= numberOfDaysInAMonth <= 31
```

incompatible operands

is correct. However, it is incorrect in Java, because `1 <= numberOfDaysInAMonth` is evaluated to a `boolean` value, which cannot be compared with `31`. Here, two operands (a `boolean` value and a numeric value) are *incompatible*. The correct expression in Java is

```
(1 <= numberOfDaysInAMonth) && (numberOfDaysInAMonth <= 31)
```

Note

cannot cast `boolean`

As shown in the preceding chapter, a `char` value can be cast into an `int` value, and vice versa. A `boolean` value, however, cannot be cast into a value of another type, nor can a value of another type be cast into a `boolean` value.

Note

De Morgan's law

De Morgan's law, named after Indian-born British mathematician and logician Augustus De Morgan (1806–1871), can be used to simplify Boolean expressions. The law states:

```
!(condition1 && condition2) is the same as
    !condition1 || !condition2
!(condition1 || condition2) is the same as
    !condition1 && !condition2
```

For example,

```
! (number % 2 == 0 && number % 3 == 0)
```

can be simplified using an equivalent expression:

```
(number % 2 != 0 || number % 3 != 0)
```

As another example,

```
!(number == 2 || number == 3)
```

is better written as

```
number != 2 && number != 3
```

conditional operator
short-circuit operator

If one of the operands of an `&&` operator is `false`, the expression is `false`; if one of the operands of an `||` operator is `true`, the expression is `true`. Java uses these properties to improve the performance of these operators. When evaluating `p1 && p2`, Java first evaluates `p1` and then, if `p1` is `true`, evaluates `p2`; if `p1` is `false`, it does not evaluate `p2`. When evaluating `p1 || p2`, Java first evaluates `p1` and then, if `p1` is `false`, evaluates `p2`; if `p1` is `true`, it does not evaluate `p2`. Therefore, `&&` is referred to as the *conditional* or *short-circuit AND* operator, and `||` is referred to as the *conditional* or *short-circuit OR* operator. Java also provides the conditional AND (`&`) and OR (`|`) operators, which are covered in Supplement III.C and III.D for advanced readers.

3.18 Assuming that `x` is `1`, show the result of the following Boolean expressions.

```
(true) && (3 > 4)
!(x > 0) && (x > 0)
(x > 0) || (x < 0)

(x != 0) || (x == 0)
(x >= 0) || (x < 0)
(x != 1) == !(x == 1)
```

3.19 Write a Boolean expression that evaluates to `true` if a number stored in variable `num` is between `1` and `100`.

3.20 Write a Boolean expression that evaluates to `true` if a number stored in variable `num` is between `1` and `100` or the number is negative.

3.21 Assume that x and y are **int** type. Which of the following are legal Java expressions?

```
x > y > 0
x = y && y
x /= y
x or y
x and y
(x != 0) || (x = 0)
```

3.22 Suppose that x is 1. What is x after the evaluation of the following expression?

```
a. (x >= 1) && (x++ > 1)
b. (x > 1) && (x++ > 1)
```

3.23 What is the value of the expression ch >= 'A' && ch <= 'Z' if ch is 'A', 'p', 'E', or '5'?

3.24 Suppose, when you run the program, you enter input 2 3 6 from the console. What is the output?

```java
public class Test {
  public static void main(String[] args) {
    java.util.Scanner input = new java.util.Scanner(System.in);
    double x = input.nextDouble();
    double y = input.nextDouble();
    double z = input.nextDouble();

    System.out.println("(x < y && y < z) is " + (x < y && y < z));
    System.out.println("(x < y || y < z) is " + (x < y || y < z));
    System.out.println("!(x < y) is " + !(x < y));
    System.out.println("(x + y < z) is " + (x + y < z));
    System.out.println("(x + y < z) is " + (x + y < z));
  }
}
```

3.25 Write a Boolean expression that evaluates **true** if **age** is greater than **13** and less than **18**.

3.26 Write a Boolean expression that evaluates **true** if **weight** is greater than **50** pounds or height is greater than **60** inches.

3.27 Write a Boolean expression that evaluates **true** if **weight** is greater than **50** pounds and height is greater than **60** inches.

3.28 Write a Boolean expression that evaluates **true** if either **weight** is greater than **50** pounds or height is greater than **60** inches, but not both.

3.12 Case Study: Determining Leap Year

A year is a leap year *if it is divisible by 4 but not by 100, or if it is divisible by 400.*

Key
Point

You can use the following Boolean expressions to check whether a year is a leap year:

```java
// A leap year is divisible by 4
boolean isLeapYear = (year % 4 == 0);

// A leap year is divisible by 4 but not by 100
isLeapYear = isLeapYear && (year % 100 != 0);

// A leap year is divisible by 4 but not by 100 or divisible by 400
isLeapYear = isLeapYear || (year % 400 == 0);
```

Or you can combine all these expressions into one like this:

```java
isLeapYear = (year % 4 == 0 && year % 100 != 0) || (year % 400 == 0);
```

Listing 3.8 gives the program that lets the user enter a year and checks whether it is a leap year.

LISTING 3.8 LeapYear.java

```java
 1  import java.util.Scanner;
 2
 3  public class LeapYear {
 4    public static void main(String[] args) {
 5      // Create a Scanner
 6      Scanner input = new Scanner(System.in);
 7      System.out.print("Enter a year: ");
 8      int year = input.nextInt();
 9
10      // Check if the year is a leap year
11      boolean isLeapYear =
12        (year % 4 == 0 && year % 100 != 0) || (year % 400 == 0);
13
14      // Display the result
15      System.out.println(year + " is a leap year? " + isLeapYear);
16    }
17  }
```

input

leap year?

display result

```
Enter a year: 2012  ↵Enter
2008 is a leap year? true
```

```
Enter a year: 1900  ↵Enter
1900 is a leap year? false
```

```
Enter a year: 2002  ↵Enter
2002 is a leap year? false
```

3.13 Case Study: Lottery

Key Point

The lottery program involves generating random numbers, comparing digits, and using Boolean operators.

Suppose you want to develop a program to play lottery. The program randomly generates a lottery of a two-digit number, prompts the user to enter a two-digit number, and determines whether the user wins according to the following rules:

1. If the user input matches the lottery number in the exact order, the award is $10,000.

2. If all the digits in the user input match all the digits in the lottery number, the award is $3,000.

3. If one digit in the user input matches a digit in the lottery number, the award is $1,000.

The complete program is shown in Listing 3.9.

LISTING 3.9 Lottery.java

```java
 1  import java.util.Scanner;
 2
 3  public class Lottery {
 4    public static void main(String[] args) {
 5      // Generate a lottery number
```

```
 6        int lottery = (int)(Math.random() * 100);                          generate a lottery number
 7
 8        // Prompt the user to enter a guess
 9        Scanner input = new Scanner(System.in);
10        System.out.print("Enter your lottery pick (two digits): ");
11        int guess = input.nextInt();                                        enter a guess
12
13        // Get digits from lottery
14        int lotteryDigit1 = lottery / 10;
15        int lotteryDigit2 = lottery % 10;
16
17        // Get digits from guess
18        int guessDigit1 = guess / 10;
19        int guessDigit2 = guess % 10;
20
21        System.out.println("The lottery number is " + lottery);
22
23        // Check the guess
24        if (guess == lottery)                                               exact match?
25          System.out.println("Exact match: you win $10,000");
26        else if (guessDigit2 == lotteryDigit1                               match all digits?
27               && guessDigit1 == lotteryDigit2)
28          System.out.println("Match all digits: you win $3,000");
29        else if (guessDigit1 == lotteryDigit1                               match one digit?
30               || guessDigit1 == lotteryDigit2
31               || guessDigit2 == lotteryDigit1
32               || guessDigit2 == lotteryDigit2)
33          System.out.println("Match one digit: you win $1,000");
34        else
35          System.out.println("Sorry, no match");
36      }
37  }
```

```
Enter your lottery pick (two digits): 45  [↵Enter]
The lottery number is 12
Sorry, no match
```

```
Enter your lottery pick: 23  [↵Enter]
The lottery number is 34
Match one digit: you win $1,000
```

line# variable	6	11	14	15	18	19	33
lottery	34						
guess		23					
lotteryDigit1			3				
lotteryDigit2				4			
guessDigit1					2		
guessDigit2						3	
Output							Match one digit: you win $1,000

The program generates a lottery using the `random()` method (line 6) and prompts the user to enter a guess (line 11). Note that `guess % 10` obtains the last digit from `guess` and `guess / 10` obtains the first digit from `guess`, since `guess` is a two-digit number (lines 18–19). The program checks the guess against the lottery number in this order:

1. First, check whether the guess matches the lottery exactly (line 24).

2. If not, check whether the reversal of the guess matches the lottery (lines 26–27).

3. If not, check whether one digit is in the lottery (lines 29–32).

4. If not, nothing matches and display `"Sorry, no match"` (lines 34–35).

3.14 `switch` Statements

Key Point

A `switch` statement executes statements based on the value of a variable or an expression.

The `if` statement in Listing 3.6, ComputeTax.java, makes selections based on a single `true` or `false` condition. There are four cases for computing taxes, which depend on the value of `status`. To fully account for all the cases, nested `if` statements were used. Overuse of nested `if` statements makes a program difficult to read. Java provides a `switch` statement to simplify coding for multiple conditions. You can write the following `switch` statement to replace the nested `if` statement in Listing 3.6:

```
switch (status) {
  case 0:  compute tax for single filers;
           break;
  case 1:  compute tax for married jointly or qualifying widow(er);
           break;
  case 2:  compute tax for married filing separately;
           break;
  case 3:  compute tax for head of household;
           break;
  default: System.out.println("Error: invalid status");
           System.exit(1);
}
```

The flowchart of the preceding `switch` statement is shown in Figure 3.6.

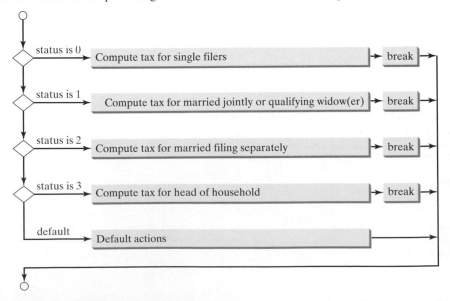

FIGURE 3.6   The `switch` statement checks all cases and executes the statements in the matched case.

This statement checks to see whether the status matches the value 0, 1, 2, or 3, in that order. If matched, the corresponding tax is computed; if not matched, a message is displayed. Here is the full syntax for the **switch** statement:

```
switch (switch-expression) {
  case value1: statement(s)1;
               break;
  case value2: statement(s)2;
               break;
  ...
  case valueN: statement(s)N;
               break;
  default:     statement(s)-for-default;
}
```

switch statement

The **switch** statement observes the following rules:

- The **switch-expression** must yield a value of **char**, **byte**, **short**, **int**, or **String** type and must always be enclosed in parentheses. (Using **String** type in the **switch** expression is new in JDK 7.)

- The **value1**, . . ., and **valueN** must have the same data type as the value of the **switch-expression**. Note that **value1**, . . ., and **valueN** are constant expressions, meaning that they cannot contain variables, such as 1 + x.

- When the value in a **case** statement matches the value of the **switch-expression**, the statements *starting from this case* are executed until either a **break** statement or the end of the **switch** statement is reached.

- The **default** case, which is optional, can be used to perform actions when none of the specified cases matches the **switch-expression**.

- The keyword **break** is optional. The **break** statement immediately ends the **switch** statement.

 Caution

Do not forget to use a **break** statement when one is needed. Once a case is matched, the statements starting from the matched case are executed until a **break** statement or the end of the **switch** statement is reached. This is referred to as *fall-through* behavior. For example, the following code displays the character **a** three times if **ch** is **a**:

without break

fall-through behavior

```
switch (ch) {
  case 'a': System.out.println(ch);
  case 'b': System.out.println(ch);
  case 'c': System.out.println(ch);
}
```

 Tip

To avoid programming errors and improve code maintainability, it is a good idea to put a comment in a case clause if **break** is purposely omitted.

Now let us write a program to find out the Chinese Zodiac sign for a given year. The Chinese Zodiac is based on a twelve-year cycle, with each year represented by an animal—monkey, rooster, dog, pig, rat, ox, tiger, rabbit, dragon, snake, horse, or sheep—in this cycle, as shown in Figure 3.7.

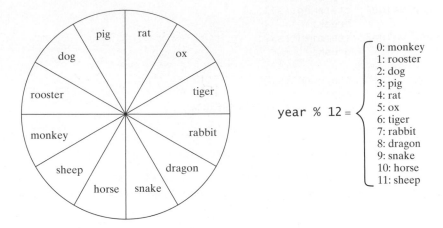

FIGURE 3.7 The Chinese Zodiac is based on a twelve-year cycle.

Note that **year % 12** determines the Zodiac sign. 1900 is the year of the rat because **1900 % 12** is **4**. Listing 3.10 gives a program that prompts the user to enter a year and displays the animal for the year.

LISTING 3.10 ChineseZodiac.java

```
 1  import java.util.Scanner;
 2
 3  public class ChineseZodiac {
 4    public static void main(String[] args) {
 5      Scanner input = new Scanner(System.in);
 6
 7      System.out.print("Enter a year: ");
 8      int year = input.nextInt();
 9
10      switch (year % 12) {
11        case 0: System.out.println("monkey"); break;
12        case 1: System.out.println("rooster"); break;
13        case 2: System.out.println("dog"); break;
14        case 3: System.out.println("pig"); break;
15        case 4: System.out.println("rat"); break;
16        case 5: System.out.println("ox"); break;
17        case 6: System.out.println("tiger"); break;
18        case 7: System.out.println("rabbit"); break;
19        case 8: System.out.println("dragon"); break;
20        case 9: System.out.println("snake"); break;
21        case 10: System.out.println("horse"); break;
22        case 11: System.out.println("sheep");
23      }
24    }
25  }
```

enter year

determine Zodiac sign

```
Enter a year: 1963  ⏎ Enter
rabbit
```

```
Enter a year: 1877  ⏎ Enter
ox
```

3.29 What data types are required for a `switch` variable? If the keyword `break` is not used after a case is processed, what is the next statement to be executed? Can you convert a `switch` statement to an equivalent `if` statement, or vice versa? What are the advantages of using a `switch` statement?

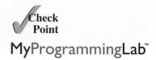
Check Point

MyProgrammingLab™

3.30 What is `y` after the following `switch` statement is executed? Rewrite the code using the `if-else` statement.

```
x = 3; y = 3;
switch (x + 3) {
  case 6:  y = 1;
  default: y += 1;
}
```

3.31 What is `x` after the following `if-else` statement is executed? Use a `switch` statement to rewrite it and draw the flowchart for the new `switch` statement.

```
int x = 1, a = 3;
if (a == 1)
  x += 5;
else if (a == 2)
  x += 10;
else if (a == 3)
  x += 16;
else if (a == 4)
  x += 34;
```

3.32 Write a `switch` statement that assigns a `String` variable `dayName` with Sunday, Monday, Tuesday, Wednesday, Thursday, Friday, Saturday, if `day` is 0, 1, 2, 3, 4, 5, 6, accordingly.

3.15 Conditional Expressions

A conditional expression evaluates an expression based on a condition.

Key Point

You might want to assign a value to a variable that is restricted by certain conditions. For example, the following statement assigns 1 to `y` if `x` is greater than 0, and -1 to `y` if `x` is less than or equal to 0.

```
if (x > 0)
  y = 1;
else
  y = -1;
```

Alternatively, as in the following example, you can use a conditional expression to achieve the same result.

```
y = (x > 0) ? 1 : -1;
```

Conditional expressions are in a completely different style, with no explicit `if` in the statement. The syntax is:

conditional expression

```
boolean-expression ? expression1 : expression2;
```

The result of this conditional expression is **expression1** if **boolean-expression** is true; otherwise the result is **expression2**.

Suppose you want to assign the larger number of variable **num1** and **num2** to **max**. You can simply write a statement using the conditional expression:

```
max = (num1 > num2) ? num1 : num2;
```

For another example, the following statement displays the message "num is even" if **num** is even, and otherwise displays "num is odd."

```
System.out.println((num % 2 == 0) ? "num is even" : "num is odd");
```

As you can see from these examples, conditional expressions enable you to write short and concise code.

> **Note**
> The symbols **?** and **:** appear together in a conditional expression. They form a conditional operator called a *ternary operator* because it uses three operands. It is the only ternary operator in Java.

MyProgrammingLab™

3.33   Suppose that, when you run the following program, you enter input **2 3 6** from the console. What is the output?

```java
public class Test {
  public static void main(String[] args) {
    java.util.Scanner input = new java.util.Scanner(System.in);
    double x = input.nextDouble();
    double y = input.nextDouble();
    double z = input.nextDouble();

    System.out.println((x < y && y < z) ? "sorted" : "not sorted");
  }
}
```

3.34   Rewrite the following **if** statements using the conditional operator.

```
if (ages >= 16)
  ticketPrice = 20;
else
  ticketPrice = 10;
```

```
if (count % 10 == 0)
  System.out.print(count + "\n");
else
  System.out.print(count);
```

3.35   Rewrite the following conditional expressions using **if-else** statements.

a. score = (x > 10) ? 3 * scale : 4 * scale;
b. tax = (income > 10000) ? income * 0.2 : income * 0.17 + 1000;
c. System.out.println((number % 3 == 0) ? i : j);

3.16 Formatting Console Output

Key Point

You can use the **System.out.printf** *method to display formatted output on the console.*

Often it is desirable to display numbers in a certain format. For example, the following code computes interest, given the amount and the annual interest rate.

```
double amount = 12618.98;
double interestRate = 0.0013;
```

```java
double interest = amount * interestRate;
System.out.println("Interest is " + interest);
```

```
Interest is 16.404674
```

Because the interest amount is currency, it is desirable to display only two digits after the decimal point. To do this, you can write the code as follows:

```java
double amount = 12618.98;
double interestRate = 0.0013;
double interest = amount * interestRate;
System.out.println("Interest is "
  + (int)(interest * 100) / 100.0);
```

```
Interest is 16.4
```

However, the format is still not correct. There should be two digits after the decimal point: **16.40** rather than **16.4**. You can fix it by using the `printf` method, like this:

printf

```java
double amount = 12618.98;
double interestRate = 0.0013;
double interest = amount * interestRate;
System.out.printf("Interest is %4.2f", interest);
```

%[4].[2][f] ← format specifier

field width   conversion code

precision

```
Interest is 16.40
```

The syntax to invoke this method is

```java
System.out.printf(format, item1, item2, ..., itemk)
```

where `format` is a string that may consist of substrings and format specifiers.

A *format specifier* specifies how an item should be displayed. An item may be a numeric value, a character, a Boolean value, or a string. A simple format specifier consists of a percent sign (%) followed by a conversion code. Table 3.8 lists some frequently used simple format specifiers.

format specifier

TABLE 3.8 Frequently Used Format Specifiers

Format Specifier	Output	Example
%b	a Boolean value	true or false
%c	a character	'a'
%d	a decimal integer	200
%f	a floating-point number	45.460000
%e	a number in standard scientific notation	4.556000e+01
%s	a string	"Java is cool"

Here is an example:

```
int count = 5;
double amount = 45.56;
System.out.printf("count is %d and amount is %f", count, amount);
```

display   count is 5 and amount is 45.560000

Items must match the format specifiers in order, in number, and in exact type. For example, the format specifier for **count** is **%d** and for **amount** is **%f**. By default, a floating-point value is displayed with six digits after the decimal point. You can specify the width and precision in a format specifier, as shown in the examples in Table 3.9.

TABLE 3.9   Examples of Specifying Width and Precision

Example	Output
%5c	Output the character and add four spaces before the character item, because the width is 5.
%6b	Output the Boolean value and add one space before the false value and two spaces before the true value.
%5d	Output the integer item with width at least 5. If the number of digits in the item is <5, add spaces before the number. If the number of digits in the item is >5, the width is automatically increased.
%10.2f	Output the floating-point item with width at least 10 including a decimal point and two digits after the point. Thus there are 7 digits allocated before the decimal point. If the number of digits before the decimal point in the item is <7, add spaces before the number. If the number of digits before the decimal point in the item is >7, the width is automatically increased.
%10.2e	Output the floating-point item with width at least 10 including a decimal point, two digits after the point and the exponent part. If the displayed number in scientific notation has width less than 10, add spaces before the number.
%12s	Output the string with width at least 12 characters. If the string item has fewer than 12 characters, add spaces before the string. If the string item has more than 12 characters, the width is automatically increased.

If an item requires more spaces than the specified width, the width is automatically increased. For example, the following code

```
System.out.printf("%3d#%2s#%3.2f\n", 1234, "Java", 51.6653);
```

displays

```
1234#Java#51.67
```

The specified width for **int** item **1234** is **3**, which is smaller than its actual size **4**. The width is automatically increased to **4**. The specified width for string item **Java** is **2**, which is smaller than its actual size **4**. The width is automatically increased to **4**. The specified width for **double** item **51.6653** is **3**, but it needs width 5 to display 51.67, so the width is automatically increased to **5**.

right justify
left justify

By default, the output is right justified. You can put the minus sign (-) in the format specifier to specify that the item is left justified in the output within the specified field. For example, the following statements

```
System.out.printf("%8d%8s%8.1f\n", 1234, "Java", 5.63);
System.out.printf("%-8d%-8s%-8.1f \n", 1234, "Java", 5.63);
```

display

```
    |←— 8 —→|←— 8 —→|←— 8 —→|
    ☐☐☐☐ 1234 ☐☐☐☐ Java ☐☐☐☐☐ 5.6
    1234 ☐☐☐☐ Java ☐☐☐☐ 5.6 ☐☐☐☐☐
```

where the square box (☐) denotes a blank space.

Caution

The items must match the format specifiers in exact type. The item for the format specifier **%f** or **%e** must be a floating-point type value such as **40.0**, not **40**. Thus, an **int** variable cannot match **%f** or **%e**.

Tip

The **%** sign denotes a format specifier. To output a literal **%** in the format string, use **%%**.

3.36 What are the format specifiers for outputting a Boolean value, a character, a decimal integer, a floating-point number, and a string?

3.37 What is wrong in the following statements?

    a. `System.out.printf("%5d %d", 1, 2, 3);`

    b. `System.out.printf("%5d %f", 1);`

    c. `System.out.printf("%5d %f", 1, 2);`

3.38 Show the output of the following statements.

    a. `System.out.printf("amount is %f %e\n", 32.32, 32.32);`

    b. `System.out.printf("amount is %5.4f %5.4e\n", 32.32, 32.32);`

    c. `System.out.printf("%6b\n", (1 > 2));`

    d. `System.out.printf("%6s\n", "Java");`

    e. `System.out.printf("%-6b%s\n", (1 > 2), "Java");`

    f. `System.out.printf("%6b%-8s\n", (1 > 2), "Java");`

3.17 Operator Precedence and Associativity

Operator precedence and associativity determine the order in which operators are evaluated.

Section 2.11 introduced operator precedence involving arithmetic operators. This section discusses operator precedence in more details. Suppose that you have this expression:

```
3 + 4 * 4 > 5 * (4 + 3) - 1 && (4 - 3 > 5)
```

What is its value? What is the execution order of the operators?

The expression in the parentheses is evaluated first. (Parentheses can be nested, in which case the expression in the inner parentheses is executed first.) When evaluating an expression without parentheses, the operators are applied according to the precedence rule and the associativity rule.

The precedence rule defines precedence for operators, as shown in Table 3.10, which contains the operators you have learned so far. Operators are listed in decreasing order of precedence from top to bottom. The logical operators have lower precedence than the relational operators and the relational operators have lower precedence than the arithmetic operators. Operators with the same precedence appear in the same group. (See Appendix C, *Operator Precedence Chart*, for a complete list of Java operators and their precedence.)

operator precedence

TABLE 3.10   Operator Precedence Chart

Precedence	Operator
	`var++` and `var--` (Postfix)
	`+`, `-` (Unary plus and minus), `++var` and `--var` (Prefix)
	(type) (Casting)
	`!`(Not)
	`*`, `/`, `%` (Multiplication, division, and remainder)
	`+`, `-` (Binary addition and subtraction)
	`<`, `<=`, `>`, `>=` (Comparison)
	`==`, `!=` (Equality)
	`^` (Exclusive OR)
	`&&` (AND)
	`||` (OR)
	`=`, `+=`, `-=`, `*=`, `/=`, `%=` (Assignment operator)

operator associativity

If operators with the same precedence are next to each other, their *associativity* determines the order of evaluation. All binary operators except assignment operators are *left associative*. For example, since + and – are of the same precedence and are left associative, the expression

$$a - b + c - d \quad \overset{\text{is equivalent to}}{=\!=\!=\!=\!=\!=\!=\!=} \quad ((a - b) + c) - d$$

Assignment operators are *right associative*. Therefore, the expression

$$a = b \mathrel{+}= c = 5 \quad \overset{\text{is equivalent to}}{=\!=\!=\!=\!=\!=\!=\!=} \quad a = (b \mathrel{+}= (c = 5))$$

Suppose a, b, and c are 1 before the assignment; after the whole expression is evaluated, a becomes 6, b becomes 6, and c becomes 5. Note that left associativity for the assignment operator would not make sense.

Note

Java has its own way to evaluate an expression internally. The result of a Java evaluation is the same as that of its corresponding arithmetic evaluation. Advanced readers may refer to Supplement III.B for more discussions on how an expression is evaluated in Java *behind the scenes.*

behind the scenes

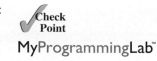

3.39 List the precedence order of the Boolean operators. Evaluate the following expressions:

```
true || true && false
true && true || false
```

3.40 True or false? All the binary operators except = are left associative.

3.41 Evaluate the following expressions:

```
2 * 2 - 3 > 2 && 4 - 2 > 5
2 * 2 - 3 > 2 || 4 - 2 > 5
```

3.42 Is $(x > 0 \&\& x < 10)$ the same as $((x > 0) \&\& (x < 10))$? Is $(x > 0 || x < 10)$ the same as $((x > 0) || (x < 10))$? Is $(x > 0 || x < 10 \&\& y < 0)$ the same as $(x > 0 || (x < 10 \&\& y < 0))$?

3.18 Confirmation Dialogs

You can use a confirmation dialog to obtain a confirmation from the user.

Key
Point

You have used `showMessageDialog` to display a message dialog box and `showInputDialog` to display an input dialog box. Occasionally it is useful to answer a question with a confirmation dialog box. A confirmation dialog can be created using the following statement:

```
int option =
    JOptionPane.showConfirmDialog
        (null, "Continue");
```

When a button is clicked, the method returns an option value. The value is `JOptionPane.YES_OPTION` (0) for the *Yes* button, `JOptionPane.NO_OPTION` (1) for the *No* button, and `JOptionPane.CANCEL_OPTION` (2) for the *Cancel* button.

You may rewrite the guess-birthday program in Listing 3.3 using confirmation dialog boxes, as shown in Listing 3.11. Figure 3.8 shows a sample run of the program for the day 19.

LISTING 3.11 GuessBirthdayUsingConfirmationDialog.java

```
1  import javax.swing.JOptionPane;
2
3  public class GuessBirthdayUsingConfirmationDialog {
4    public static void main(String[] args) {
5      String set1 =
6        "  1   3   5   7\n" +
7        "  9 11 13 15\n" +
8        "17 19 21 23\n" +
9        "25 27 29 31";
10
11     String set2 =
12       "  2   3   6   7\n" +
13       "10 11 14 15\n" +
14       "18 19 22 23\n" +
15       "26 27 30 31";
16
```

import class

set1

set2

118 Chapter 3 Selections

```
set3              17        String set3 =
                  18          " 4  5  6  7\n" +
                  19          "12 13 14 15\n" +
                  20          "20 21 22 23\n" +
                  21          "28 29 30 31";
                  22
set4              23        String set4 =
                  24          " 8  9 10 11\n" +
                  25          "12 13 14 15\n" +
                  26          "24 25 26 27\n" +
                  27          "28 29 30 31";
                  28
set5              29        String set5 =
                  30          "16 17 18 19\n" +
                  31          "20 21 22 23\n" +
                  32          "24 25 26 27\n" +
                  33          "28 29 30 31";
                  34
                  35        int day = 0;
                  36
                  37        // Prompt the user to answer questions
confirmation      38        int answer = JOptionPane.showConfirmDialog(null,
dialog            39          "Is your birthday in these numbers?\n" + set1);
                  40
in set1?          41        if (answer == JOptionPane.YES_OPTION)
                  42          day += 1;
                  43
                  44        answer = JOptionPane.showConfirmDialog(null,
                  45          "Is your birthday in these numbers?\n" + set2);
                  46
in set2?          47        if (answer == JOptionPane.YES_OPTION)
                  48          day += 2;
                  49
                  50        answer = JOptionPane.showConfirmDialog(null,
                  51          "Is your birthday in these numbers?\n" + set3);
                  52
in set3?          53        if (answer == JOptionPane.YES_OPTION)
                  54          day += 4;
                  55
                  56        answer = JOptionPane.showConfirmDialog(null,
                  57          "Is your birthday in these numbers?\n" + set4);
                  58
in set4?          59        if (answer == JOptionPane.YES_OPTION)
                  60          day += 8;
                  61
                  62        answer = JOptionPane.showConfirmDialog(null,
                  63          "Is your birthday in these numbers?\n" + set5);
                  64
in set5?          65        if (answer == JOptionPane.YES_OPTION)
                  66          day += 16;
                  67
                  68        JOptionPane.showMessageDialog(null, "Your birthday is " +
                  69          day + "!");
                  70      }
                  71    }
```

The program displays confirmation dialog boxes to prompt the user to answer whether a number is in Set1 (line 38), Set2 (line 44), Set3 (line 50), Set4 (line 56), and Set5 (line 62). If the answer is Yes, the first number in the set is added to **day** (lines 42, 48, 54, 60, and 66).

FIGURE 3.8 Click Yes in (a), Yes in (b), No in (c), No in (d), and Yes in (e).

3.43 How do you display a confirmation dialog? What value is returned when invoking `JOptionPane.showConfirmDialog`?

MyProgrammingLab™

3.19 Debugging

Debugging is the process of finding and fixing errors in a program.

Key
Point

As mentioned in Section 1.11,1, syntax errors are easy to find and easy to correct because the compiler gives indications as to where the errors came from and why they are there. Runtime errors are not difficult to find either, because the Java interpreter displays them on the console when the program aborts. Finding logic errors, on the other hand, can be very challenging.

Logic errors are called *bugs*. The process of finding and correcting errors is called *debugging*. A common approach to debugging is to use a combination of methods to help pinpoint the part of the program where the bug is located. You can *hand-trace* the program (i.e., catch errors by reading the program), or you can insert print statements in order to show the values of the variables or the execution flow of the program. These approaches might work for debugging a short, simple program, but for a large, complex program, the most effective approach is to use a debugger utility.

bugs
debugging
hand-traces

JDK includes a command-line debugger, jdb, which is invoked with a class name. jdb is itself a Java program, running its own copy of Java interpreter. All the Java IDE tools, such as Eclipse and NetBeans, include integrated debuggers. The debugger utilities let you follow the execution of a program. They vary from one system to another, but they all support most of the following helpful features.

- **Executing a single statement at a time:** The debugger allows you to execute one statement at a time so that you can see the effect of each statement.

- **Tracing into or stepping over a method:** If a method is being executed, you can ask the debugger to enter the method and execute one statement at a time in the method, or you can ask it to step over the entire method. You should step over the entire method if you know that the method works. For example, always step over system-supplied methods, such as `System.out.println`.

- **Setting breakpoints:** You can also set a breakpoint at a specific statement. Your program pauses when it reaches a breakpoint. You can set as many breakpoints as you want. Breakpoints are particularly useful when you know where your programming error starts. You can set a breakpoint at that statement and have the program execute until it reaches the breakpoint.

- **Displaying variables:** The debugger lets you select several variables and display their values. As you trace through a program, the content of a variable is continuously updated.

- **Displaying call stacks:** The debugger lets you trace all of the method calls. This feature is helpful when you need to see a large picture of the program-execution flow.

- **Modifying variables:** Some debuggers enable you to modify the value of a variable when debugging. This is convenient when you want to test a program with different samples but do not want to leave the debugger.

debugging in IDE

 Tip

If you use an IDE such as Eclipse or NetBeans, please refer to *Learning Java Effectively with Eclipse/NetBeans* in Supplements II.C and II.E on the Companion Website. The supplement shows you how to use a debugger to trace programs and how debugging can help in learning Java effectively.

KEY TERMS

Boolean expression 82	flowchart 84
`boolean` data type 82	format specifier 113
Boolean value 82	operator associativity 116
conditional operator 104	operator precedence 116
dangling else ambiguity 94	selection statement 82
debugging 119	short-circuit operator 104
fall-through behavior 109	

CHAPTER SUMMARY

1. A `boolean` type variable can store a `true` or `false` value.

2. The relational operators (`<`, `<=`, `==`, `!=`, `>`, `>=`) work with numbers and characters, and yield a Boolean value.

3. The Boolean operators `&&`, `||`, `!`, and `^` operate with Boolean values and variables.

4. When evaluating `p1 && p2`, Java first evaluates `p1` and then evaluates `p2` if `p1` is `true`; if `p1` is `false`, it does not evaluate `p2`. When evaluating `p1 || p2`, Java first evaluates `p1` and then evaluates `p2` if `p1` is `false`; if `p1` is `true`, it does not evaluate `p2`. Therefore, `&&` is referred to as the *conditional* or *short-circuit AND operator*, and `||` is referred to as the *conditional* or *short-circuit OR operator*.

5. *Selection statements* are used for programming with alternative courses of actions. There are several types of selection statements: `if` statements, two-way `if-else` statements, nested `if` statements, multi-way `if-else` statements, `switch` statements, and conditional expressions.

6. The various `if` statements all make control decisions based on a *Boolean expression*. Based on the `true` or `false` evaluation of the expression, these statements take one of two possible courses.

7. The `switch` statement makes control decisions based on a switch expression of type `char`, `byte`, `short`, `int`, or `String`.

8. The keyword `break` is optional in a `switch` statement, but it is normally used at the end of each case in order to skip the remainder of the `switch` statement. If the `break` statement is not present, the next `case` statement will be executed.

9. The operators in expressions are evaluated in the order determined by the rules of parentheses, *operator precedence*, and *operator associativity*.

10. Parentheses can be used to force the order of evaluation to occur in any sequence.

11. Operators with higher precedence are evaluated earlier. For operators of the same precedence, their associativity determines the order of evaluation.

12. All binary operators except assignment operators are left-associative; assignment operators are right-associative.

TEST QUESTIONS

Do the test questions for this chapter online at www.cs.armstrong.edu/liang/intro9e/test.html.

PROGRAMMING EXERCISES   MyProgrammingLab™

 Pedagogical Note
For each exercise, carefully analyze the problem requirements and design strategies for solving the problem before coding.

think before coding

 Debugging Tip
Before you ask for help, read and explain the program to yourself, and trace it using several representative inputs by hand or using an IDE debugger. You learn how to program by debugging your own mistakes.

learn from mistakes

Section 3.2

*3.1 (*Algebra: solve quadratic equations*) The two roots of a quadratic equation $ax^2 + bx + c = 0$ can be obtained using the following formula:

$$r_1 = \frac{-b + \sqrt{b^2 - 4ac}}{2a} \quad \text{and} \quad r_2 = \frac{-b - \sqrt{b^2 - 4ac}}{2a}$$

$b^2 - 4ac$ is called the discriminant of the quadratic equation. If it is positive, the equation has two real roots. If it is zero, the equation has one root. If it is negative, the equation has no real roots.

Write a program that prompts the user to enter values for a, b, and c and displays the result based on the discriminant. If the discriminant is positive, display two roots. If the discriminant is 0, display one root. Otherwise, display "The equation has no real roots".

Note that you can use `Math.pow(x, 0.5)` to compute $\sqrt{x}$. Here are some sample runs.

```
Enter a, b, c: 1.0 3 1  ⏎Enter
The roots are -0.381966 and -2.61803
```

```
Enter a, b, c: 1 2.0 1  ⏎Enter
The root is -1
```

```
Enter a, b, c: 1 2 3  ⏎Enter
The equation has no real roots
```

3.2 (*Game: add three numbers*) The program in Listing 3.1 generates two integers and prompts the user to enter the sum of these two integers. Revise the program to generate three single-digit integers and prompt the user to enter the sum of these three integers.

Sections 3.3–3.8

*3.3 (*Algebra: solve 2 × 2 linear equations*) You can use Cramer's rule to solve the following 2 × 2 system of linear equation:

$$ax + by = e \qquad x = \frac{ed - bf}{ad - bc} \qquad y = \frac{af - ec}{ad - bc}$$
$$cx + dy = f$$

Write a program that prompts the user to enter a, b, c, d, e, and f and displays the result. If $ad - bc$ is **0**, report that "The equation has no solution".

```
Enter a, b, c, d, e, f: 9.0 4.0 3.0 -5.0 -6.0 -21.0  ⏎Enter
x is -2.0 and y is 3.0
```

```
Enter a, b, c, d, e, f: 1.0 2.0 2.0 4.0 4.0 5.0  ⏎Enter
The equation has no solution
```

**3.4 (*Game: learn addition*) Write a program that generates two integers under 100 and prompts the user to enter the sum of these two integers. The program then reports true if the answer is correct, false otherwise. The program is similar to Listing 3.1.

*3.5 (*Find future dates*) Write a program that prompts the user to enter an integer for today's day of the week (Sunday is 0, Monday is 1, . . ., and Saturday is 6). Also prompt the user to enter the number of days after today for a future day and display the future day of the week. Here is a sample run:

```
Enter today's day: 1  ⏎Enter
Enter the number of days elapsed since today: 3  ⏎Enter
Today is Monday and the future day is Thursday
```

```
Enter today's day: 0  ↵Enter
Enter the number of days elapsed since today: 31  ↵Enter
Today is Sunday and the future day is Wednesday
```

*3.6 (*Health application: BMI*) Revise Listing 3.5, ComputeAndInterpretBMI.java, to let the user enter weight, feet, and inches. For example, if a person is 5 feet and 10 inches, you will enter **5** for feet and **10** for inches. Here is a sample run:

```
Enter weight in pounds: 140  ↵Enter
Enter feet: 5  ↵Enter
Enter inches: 10  ↵Enter
BMI is 20.087702275404553
Normal
```

3.7 (*Financial application: monetary units*) Modify Listing 2.10, ComputeChange.java, to display the nonzero denominations only, using singular words for single units such as 1 dollar and 1 penny, and plural words for more than one unit such as 2 dollars and 3 pennies.

VideoNote
Sort three integers

*3.8 (*Sort three integers*) Write a program that sorts three integers. The integers are entered from the input dialogs and stored in variables **num1**, **num2**, and **num3**, respectively. The program sorts the numbers so that $num1 \leq num2 \leq num3$.

3.9 (*Business: check ISBN-10*) An **ISBN-10 (International Standard Book Number) consists of 10 digits: $d_1d_2d_3d_4d_5d_6d_7d_8d_9d_{10}$. The last digit, d_{10}, is a checksum, which is calculated from the other nine digits using the following formula:

$$(d_1 \times 1 + d_2 \times 2 + d_3 \times 3 + d_4 \times 4 + d_5 \times 5 +$$
$$d_6 \times 6 + d_7 \times 7 + d_8 \times 8 + d_9 \times 9) \% 11$$

If the checksum is **10**, the last digit is denoted as X according to the ISBN-10 convention. Write a program that prompts the user to enter the first 9 digits and displays the 10-digit ISBN (including leading zeros). Your program should read the input as an integer. Here are sample runs:

```
Enter the first 9 digits of an ISBN as integer: 013601267  ↵Enter
The ISBN-10 number is 0136012671
```

```
Enter the first 9 digits of an ISBN as integer: 013031997  ↵Enter
The ISBN-10 number is 013031997X
```

3.10 (*Game: addition quiz*) Listing 3.4, SubtractionQuiz.java, randomly generates a subtraction question. Revise the program to randomly generate an addition question with two integers less than 100.

Sections 3.9–3.19

*3.11 (*Find the number of days in a month*) Write a program that prompts the user to enter the month and year and displays the number of days in the month. For example, if the user entered month 2 and year 2012, the program should display that February 2012 had 29 days. If the user entered month 3 and year 2015, the program should display that March 2015 had 31 days.

3.12 (*Check a number*) Write a program that prompts the user to enter an integer and checks whether the number is divisible by both 5 and 6, or neither of them, or just one of them. Here are some sample runs for inputs 10, 30, and 23.

```
10 is divisible by 5 or 6, but not both
30 is divisible by both 5 and 6
23 is not divisible by either 5 or 6
```

*3.13 (*Financial application: compute taxes*) Listing 3.6, ComputeTax.java, gives the source code to compute taxes for single filers. Complete Listing 3.6 to give the complete source code.

3.14 (*Game: heads or tails*) Write a program that lets the user guess whether the flip of a coin results in heads or tails. The program randomly generates an integer 0 or 1, which represents head or tail. The program prompts the user to enter a guess and reports whether the guess is correct or incorrect.

**3.15 (*Game: lottery*) Revise Listing 3.9, Lottery.java, to generate a lottery of a three-digit number. The program prompts the user to enter a three-digit number and determines whether the user wins according to the following rules:

1. If the user input matches the lottery number in the exact order, the award is $10,000.
2. If all the digits in the user input match all the digits in the lottery number, the award is $3,000.
3. If one digit in the user input matches a digit in the lottery number, the award is $1,000.

3.16 (*Random character*) Write a program that displays a random uppercase letter using the `Math.random()` method.

*3.17 (*Game: scissor, rock, paper*) Write a program that plays the popular scissor-rock-paper game. (A scissor can cut a paper, a rock can knock a scissor, and a paper can wrap a rock.) The program randomly generates a number 0, 1, or 2 representing scissor, rock, and paper. The program prompts the user to enter a number 0, 1, or 2 and displays a message indicating whether the user or the computer wins, loses, or draws. Here are sample runs:

```
scissor (0), rock (1), paper (2): 1  ↵Enter
The computer is scissor. You are rock. You won
```

```
scissor (0), rock (1), paper (2): 2  ↵Enter
The computer is paper. You are paper too. It is a draw
```

*3.18 (*Use the input dialog box*) Rewrite Listing 3.8, LeapYear.java, using the input dialog box.

**3.19 (*Compute the perimeter of a triangle*) Write a program that reads three edges for a triangle and computes the perimeter if the input is valid. Otherwise, display that the input is invalid. The input is valid if the sum of every pair of two edges is greater than the remaining edge.

*3.20 (*Science: wind-chill temperature*) Programming Exercise 2.17 gives a formula to compute the wind-chill temperature. The formula is valid for temperatures in the range between −58°F and 41°F and wind speed greater than or equal to 2. Write a program that prompts the user to enter a temperature and a wind speed. The program displays the wind-chill temperature if the input is valid; otherwise, it displays a message indicating whether the temperature and/or wind speed is invalid.

Comprehensive

**3.21 (*Science: day of the week*) Zeller's congruence is an algorithm developed by Christian Zeller to calculate the day of the week. The formula is

$$h = \left(q + \frac{26(m+1)}{10} + k + \frac{k}{4} + \frac{j}{4} + 5j \right) \% 7$$

where

- h is the day of the week (0: Saturday, 1: Sunday, 2: Monday, 3: Tuesday, 4: Wednesday, 5: Thursday, 6: Friday).
- q is the day of the month.
- m is the month (3: March, 4: April, . . ., 12: December). January and February are counted as months 13 and 14 of the previous year.
- j is the century (i.e., $\frac{year}{100}$).
- k is the year of the century (i.e., *year* % 100).

Note that the division in the formula performs an integer division. Write a program that prompts the user to enter a year, month, and day of the month, and displays the name of the day of the week. Here are some sample runs:

```
Enter year: (e.g., 2012): 2015  ↵Enter
Enter month: 1-12: 1  ↵Enter
Enter the day of the month: 1-31: 25  ↵Enter
Day of the week is Sunday
```

```
Enter year: (e.g., 2012): 2012  ↵Enter
Enter month: 1-12: 5  ↵Enter
Enter the day of the month: 1-31: 12  ↵Enter
Day of the week is Saturday
```

(*Hint*: January and February are counted as 13 and 14 in the formula, so you need to convert the user input 1 to 13 and 2 to 14 for the month and change the year to the previous year.)

VideoNote

Check point location

**3.22 (*Geometry: point in a circle?*) Write a program that prompts the user to enter a point (x, y) and checks whether the point is within the circle centered at (0, 0) with radius 10. For example, (4, 5) is inside the circle and (9, 9) is outside the circle, as shown in Figure 3.9a.

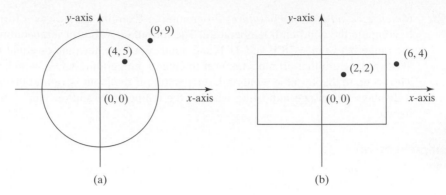

(a)　　　　　　　　　　　(b)

FIGURE 3.9 (a) Points inside and outside of the circle. (b) Points inside and outside of the rectangle.

(*Hint*: A point is in the circle if its distance to (**0**, **0**) is less than or equal to **10**. The formula for computing the distance is $\sqrt{(x_2 - x_1)^2 + (y_2 - y_1)^2}$. Test your program to cover all cases.) Two sample runs are shown below.

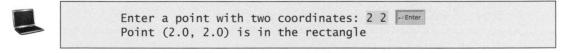

```
Enter a point with two coordinates: 4 5  ↵Enter
Point (4.0, 5.0) is in the circle
```

```
Enter a point with two coordinates: 9 9  ↵Enter
Point (9.0, 9.0) is not in the circle
```

3.23 (*Geometry: point in a rectangle?*) Write a program that prompts the user to enter a point (x**, **y**) and checks whether the point is within the rectangle centered at (**0**, **0**) with width **10** and height **5**. For example, (**2**, **2**) is inside the rectangle and (**6**, **4**) is outside the rectangle, as shown in Figure 3.9b. (*Hint*: A point is in the rectangle if its horizontal distance to (**0**, **0**) is less than or equal to **10** / **2** and its vertical distance to (**0**, **0**) is less than or equal to **5.0** / **2**. Test your program to cover all cases.) Here are two sample runs.

```
Enter a point with two coordinates: 2 2  ↵Enter
Point (2.0, 2.0) is in the rectangle
```

```
Enter a point with two coordinates: 6 4  ↵Enter
Point (6.0, 4.0) is not in the rectangle
```

3.24 (*Game: pick a card*) Write a program that simulates picking a card from a deck of **52 cards. Your program should display the rank (**Ace**, **2**, **3**, **4**, **5**, **6**, **7**, **8**, **9**, **10**, **Jack**, **Queen**, **King**) and suit (**Clubs**, **Diamonds**, **Hearts**, **Spades**) of the card Here is a sample run of the program:

```
The card you picked is Jack of Hearts
```

*3.25 (*Geometry: intersecting point*) Two points on line 1 are given as (**x1, y1**) and (**x2, y2**) and on line 2 as (**x3, y3**) and (**x4, y4**), as shown in Figure 3.10a–b.

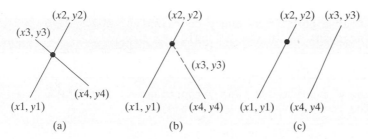

FIGURE 3.10   Two lines intersect in (a and b) and two lines are parallel in (c).

The intersecting point of the two lines can be found by solving the following linear equation:

$$(y_1 - y_2)x - (x_1 - x_2)y = (y_1 - y_2)x_1 - (x_1 - x_2)y_1$$

$$(y_3 - y_4)x - (x_3 - x_4)y = (y_3 - y_4)x_3 - (x_3 - x_4)y_3$$

This linear equation can be solved using Cramer's rule (see Exercise 3.3). If the equation has no solutions, the two lines are parallel (Figure 3.10c). Write a program that prompts the user to enter four points and displays the intersecting point. Here are sample runs:

```
Enter x1, y1, x2, y2, x3, y3, x4, y4: 2 2 5 -1.0 4.0 2.0 -1.0 -2.0 ⏎Enter
The intersecting point is at (2.88889, 1.1111)
```

```
Enter x1, y1, x2, y2, x3, y3, x4, y4: 2 2 7 6.0 4.0 2.0 -1.0 -2.0 ⏎Enter
The two lines are parallel
```

3.26   (*Use the &&, || and ∧ operators*) Write a program that prompts the user to enter an integer and determines whether it is divisible by 5 and 6, whether it is divisible by 5 or 6, and whether it is divisible by 5 or 6, but not both. Here is a sample run of this program:

```
Enter an integer: 10 ⏎Enter
Is 10 divisible by 5 and 6? false
Is 10 divisible by 5 or 6? true
Is 10 divisible by 5 or 6, but not both? true
```

**3.27   (*Geometry: points in triangle?*) Suppose a right triangle is placed in a plane as shown below. The right-angle point is placed at (0, 0), and the other two points are placed at (200, 0), and (0, 100). Write a program that prompts the user to enter a point with x- and y-coordinates and determines whether the point is inside the triangle. Here are the sample runs:

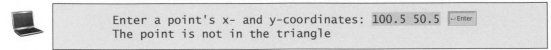

**3.28 (*Geometry: two rectangles*) Write a program that prompts the user to enter the center x-, y-coordinates, width, and height of two rectangles and determines whether the second rectangle is inside the first or overlaps with the first, as shown in Figure 3.11. Test your program to cover all cases.

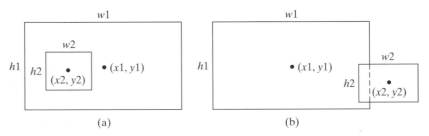

(a)   (b)

FIGURE 3.11   (a) A rectangle is inside another one. (b) A rectangle overlaps another one.

Here are the sample runs:

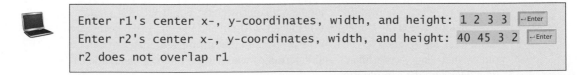

3.29 (*Geometry: two circles*) Write a program that prompts the user to enter the center coordinates and radii of two circles and determines whether the second circle is inside the first or overlaps with the first, as shown in Figure 3.12. (*Hint*: circle2 is inside circle1 if the distance between the two centers <= |r1** - **r2**| and circle2 overlaps circle1 if the distance between the two centers <= **r1** + **r2**. Test your program to cover all cases.)

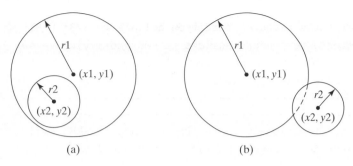

FIGURE 3.12 (a) A circle is inside another circle. (b) A circle overlaps another circle.

Here are the sample runs:

```
Enter circle1's center x-, y-coordinates, and radius: 0.5 5.1 13  ↵Enter
Enter circle2's center x-, y-coordinates, and radius: 1 1.7 4.5  ↵Enter
circle2 is inside circle1
```

```
Enter circle1's center x-, y-coordinates, and radius: 3.4 5.7 5.5  ↵Enter
Enter circle2's center x-, y-coordinates, and radius: 6.7 3.5 3  ↵Enter
circle2 overlaps circle1
```

```
Enter circle1's center x-, y-coordinates, and radius: 3.4 5.5 1  ↵Enter
Enter circle2's center x-, y-coordinates, and radius: 5.5 7.2 1  ↵Enter
circle2 does not overlap circle1
```

*3.30 (*Current time*) Revise Programming Exercise 2.8 to display the hour using a 12-hour clock. Here is a sample run:

```
Enter the time zone offset to GMT: -5  ↵Enter
The current time is 4:50:34 AM
```

*3.31 (*Financials: currency exchange*) Write a program that prompts the user to enter the exchange rate from currency in U.S. dollars to Chinese RMB. Prompt the user to enter 0 to convert from U.S. dollars to Chinese RMB and 1 to convert from Chinese RMB and U.S. dollars. Prompt the user to enter the amount in U.S. dollars or Chinese RMB to convert it to Chinese RMB or U.S. dollars, respectively. Here are the sample runs:

```
Enter the exchange rate from dollars to RMB: 6.81  ↵Enter
Enter 0 to convert dollars to RMB and 1 vice versa: 0  ↵Enter
Enter the dollar amount: 100  ↵Enter
$100.0 is 681.0 yuan
```

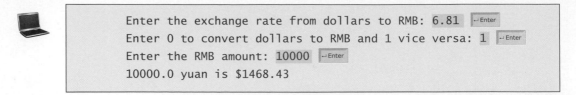

```
Enter the exchange rate from dollars to RMB: 6.81  ↵Enter
Enter 0 to convert dollars to RMB and 1 vice versa: 1  ↵Enter
Enter the RMB amount: 10000  ↵Enter
10000.0 yuan is $1468.43
```

```
Enter the exchange rate from dollars to RMB: 6.81  ↵Enter
Enter 0 to convert dollars to RMB and 1 vice versa: 5  ↵Enter
Incorrect input
```

*3.32 (*Geometry: point position*) Given a directed line from point p0(x0, y0) to p1(x1, y1), you can use the following condition to decide whether a point p2(x2, y2) is on the left of the line, on the right, or on the same line (see Figure 3.13):

$$(x1 - x0)*(y2 - y0) - (x2 - x0)*(y1 - y0) \begin{cases} >0 & \text{p2 is on the left side of the line} \\ =0 & \text{p2 is on the same line} \\ <0 & \text{p2 is on the right side of the line} \end{cases}$$

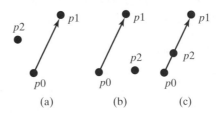

FIGURE 3.13 (a) p2 is on the left of the line. (b) p2 is on the right of the line. (c) p2 is on the same line.

Write a program that prompts the user to enter the three points for p0, p1, and p2 and displays whether p2 is on the left of the line from p0 to p1, to the right, or on the same line. Here are some sample runs:

```
Enter three points for p0, p1, and p2: 4.4 2 6.5 9.5 -5 4  ↵Enter
p2 is on the left side of the line
```

```
Enter three points for p0, p1, and p2: 1 1 5 5 2 2  ↵Enter
p2 is on the same line
```

```
Enter three points for p0, p1, and p2: 3.4 2 6.5 9.5 5 2.5  ↵Enter
p2 is on the right side of the line
```

*3.33 (*Financial: compare costs*) Suppose you shop for rice in two different packages. You would like to write a program to compare the cost. The program prompts the user to enter the weight and price of the each package and displays the one with the better price. Here is a sample run:

```
Enter weight and price for package 1: 50 24.59 ↵Enter
Enter weight and price for package 2: 25 11.99 ↵Enter
Package 1 has a better price.
```

*3.34 (*Geometry: point on line segment*) Exercise 3.32 shows how to test whether a point is on an unbounded line. Revise Exercise 3.32 to test whether a point is on a line segment. Write a program that prompts the user to enter the three points for p0, p1, and p2 and displays whether p2 is on the line segment from p0 to p1. Here are some sample runs:

```
Enter three points for p0, p1, and p2: 1 1 2.5 2.5 1.5 1.5 ↵Enter
(1.5, 1.5) is on the line segment from (1.0, 1.0) to (2.5, 2.5)
```

```
Enter three points for p0, p1, and p2: 1 1 2 2 3.5 3.5 ↵Enter
(3.5, 3.5) is not on the line segment from (1.0, 1.0) to (2.0, 2.0)
```

*3.35 (*Decimal to hex*) Write a program that prompts the user to enter an integer between 0 and 15 and displays its corresponding hex number. Here are some sample runs:

```
Enter a decimal value (0 to 15): 11 ↵Enter
The hex value is B
```

```
Enter a decimal value (0 to 15): 5 ↵Enter
The hex value is 5
```

```
Enter a decimal value (0 to 15): 31 ↵Enter
Invalid input
```

LOOPS

Objectives

- To write programs for executing statements repeatedly using a `while` loop (§4.2).
- To follow the loop design strategy to develop loops (§§4.2.1–4.2.3).
- To control a loop with a sentinel value (§4.2.4).
- To obtain large input from a file using input redirection rather than typing from the keyboard (§4.2.5).
- To write loops using `do-while` statements (§4.3).
- To write loops using `for` statements (§4.4).
- To discover the similarities and differences of three types of loop statements (§4.5).
- To write nested loops (§4.6).
- To learn the techniques for minimizing numerical errors (§4.7).
- To learn loops from a variety of examples (`GCD`, `FutureTuition`, `MonteCarloSimulation`) (§4.8).
- To implement program control with `break` and `continue` (§4.9).
- To write a program that displays prime numbers (§4.10).
- To control a loop with a confirmation dialog (§4.11).

4.1 Introduction

problem

A loop can be used to tell a program to execute statements repeatedly.

Suppose that you need to display a string (e.g., `Welcome to Java!`) a hundred times. It would be tedious to have to write the following statement a hundred times:

$$100 \text{ times} \begin{cases} \texttt{System.out.println("Welcome to Java!");} \\ \texttt{System.out.println("Welcome to Java!");} \\ \texttt{...} \\ \texttt{System.out.println("Welcome to Java!");} \end{cases}$$

So, how do you solve this problem?

loop

Java provides a powerful construct called a *loop* that controls how many times an operation or a sequence of operations is performed in succession. Using a loop statement, you simply tell the computer to display a string a hundred times without having to code the print statement a hundred times, as follows:

```java
int count = 0;
while (count < 100) {
  System.out.println("Welcome to Java!");
  count++;
}
```

The variable `count` is initially `0`. The loop checks whether `count < 100` is `true`. If so, it executes the loop body to display the message `Welcome to Java!` and increments `count` by `1`. It repeatedly executes the loop body until `count < 100` becomes `false`. When `count < 100` is `false` (i.e., when `count` reaches `100`), the loop terminates and the next statement after the loop statement is executed.

Loops are constructs that control repeated executions of a block of statements. The concept of looping is fundamental to programming. Java provides three types of loop statements: `while` loops, `do-while` loops, and `for` loops.

4.2 The `while` Loop

A `while` loop executes statements repeatedly while the condition is true.

The syntax for the `while` loop is:

while loop

```java
while (loop-continuation-condition) {
  // Loop body
  Statement(s);
}
```

Figure 4.1a shows the `while`-loop flowchart. The part of the loop that contains the statements to be repeated is called the *loop body*. A one-time execution of a loop body is referred to as an *iteration (or repetition) of the loop*. Each loop contains a *loop-continuation-condition*, a Boolean expression that controls the execution of the body. It is evaluated each time to determine if the loop body is executed. If its evaluation is `true`, the loop body is executed; if its evaluation is `false`, the entire loop terminates and the program control turns to the statement that follows the `while` loop.

loop body
iteration
`loop-continuation-condition`

The loop for displaying `Welcome to Java!` a hundred times introduced in the preceding section is an example of a `while` loop. Its flowchart is shown in Figure 4.1b. The

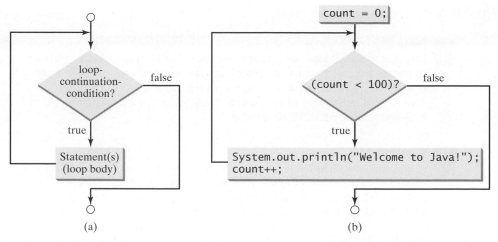

FIGURE 4.1 The `while` loop repeatedly executes the statements in the loop body when the `loop-continuation-condition` evaluates to `true`.

`loop-continuation-condition` is `count < 100` and the loop body contains the following two statements:

```
                           loop-continuation-condition
int count = 0;
while (count < 100) {
  System.out.println("Welcome to Java!");  } loop body
  count++;
}
```

In this example, you know exactly how many times the loop body needs to be executed because the control variable `count` is used to count the number of executions. This type of loop is known as a *counter-controlled loop*.

counter-controlled loop

 Note

The `loop-continuation-condition` must always appear inside the parentheses. The braces enclosing the loop body can be omitted only if the loop body contains one or no statement.

Here is another example to help understand how a loop works.

```
int sum = 0, i = 1;
while (i < 10) {
  sum = sum + i;
  i++;
}
System.out.println("sum is " + sum); // sum is 45
```

If `i < 10` is `true`, the program adds `i` to `sum`. Variable `i` is initially set to `1`, then is incremented to `2`, `3`, and up to `10`. When `i` is `10`, `i < 10` is `false`, so the loop exits. Therefore, the sum is `1 + 2 + 3 + ... + 9 = 45`.

What happens if the loop is mistakenly written as follows?

```
int sum = 0, i = 1;
while (i < 10) {
  sum = sum + i;
}
```

This loop is infinite, because i is always 1 and i < 10 will always be true.

infinite loop

Note

Make sure that the `loop-continuation-condition` eventually becomes `false` so that the loop will terminate. A common programming error involves *infinite loops* (i. e., the loop runs forever). If your program takes an unusually long time to run and does not stop, it may have an infinite loop. If you are running the program from the command window, press *CTRL+C* to stop it.

off-by-one error

Caution

Programmers often make the mistake of executing a loop one more or less time. This is commonly known as the *off-by-one error*. For example, the following loop displays `Welcome to Java` 101 times rather than 100 times. The error lies in the condition, which should be `count < 100` rather than `count <= 100`.

```java
int count = 0;
while (count <= 100) {
  System.out.println("Welcome to Java!");
  count++;
}
```

Recall that Listing 3.1, AdditionQuiz.java, gives a program that prompts the user to enter an answer for a question on addition of two single digits. Using a loop, you can now rewrite the program to let the user repeatedly enter a new answer until it is correct, as shown in Listing 4.1.

LISTING 4.1 RepeatAdditionQuiz.java

generate number1
generate number2

show question

get first answer

check answer

read an answer

```java
1  import java.util.Scanner;
2
3  public class RepeatAdditionQuiz {
4    public static void main(String[] args) {
5      int number1 = (int)(Math.random() % 10);
6      int number2 = (int)(Math.random() % 10);
7
8      // Create a Scanner
9      Scanner input = new Scanner(System.in);
10
11     System.out.print(
12       "What is " + number1 + " + " + number2 + "? ");
13     int answer = input.nextInt();
14
15     while (number1 + number2 != answer) {
16       System.out.print("Wrong answer. Try again. What is "
17         + number1 + " + " + number2 + "? ");
18       answer = input.nextInt();
19     }
20
21     System.out.println("You got it!");
22   }
23 }
```

```
What is 5 + 9? 12  ↵Enter
Wrong answer. Try again. What is 5 + 9? 34  ↵Enter
Wrong answer. Try again. What is 5 + 9? 14  ↵Enter
You got it!
```

The loop in lines 15–19 repeatedly prompts the user to enter an `answer` when `number1 + number2 != answer` is `true`. Once `number1 + number2 != answer` is `false`, the loop exits.

4.2.1 Case Study: Guessing Numbers

VideoNote
Guess a number

The problem is to guess what number a computer has in mind. You will write a program that randomly generates an integer between **0** and **100**, inclusive. The program prompts the user to enter a number continuously until the number matches the randomly generated number. For each user input, the program tells the user whether the input is too low or too high, so the user can make the next guess intelligently. Here is a sample run:

```
Guess a magic number between 0 and 100
Enter your guess: 50  ↵Enter
Your guess is too high
Enter your guess: 25  ↵Enter
Your guess is too low
Enter your guess: 42  ↵Enter
Your guess is too high
Enter your guess: 39  ↵Enter
Yes, the number is 39
```

The magic number is between **0** and **100**. To minimize the number of guesses, enter **50** first. If your guess is too high, the magic number is between **0** and **49**. If your guess is too low, the magic number is between **51** and **100**. So, you can eliminate half of the numbers from further consideration after one guess.

intelligent guess

How do you write this program? Do you immediately begin coding? No. It is important to *think before coding.* Think how you would solve the problem without writing a program. You need first to generate a random number between **0** and **100**, inclusive, then to prompt the user to enter a guess, and then to compare the guess with the random number.

think before coding

It is a good practice to *code incrementally* one step at a time. For programs involving loops, if you don't know how to write a loop right away, you may first write the code for executing the loop one time, and then figure out how to repeatedly execute the code in a loop. For this program, you may create an initial draft, as shown in Listing 4.2.

code incrementally

LISTING 4.2 GuessNumberOneTime.java

```java
1  import java.util.Scanner;
2
3  public class GuessNumberOneTime {
4    public static void main(String[] args) {
5      // Generate a random number to be guessed
6      int number = (int)(Math.random() * 101);
7
8      Scanner input = new Scanner(System.in);
9      System.out.println("Guess a magic number between 0 and 100");
10
11      // Prompt the user to guess the number
12      System.out.print("\nEnter your guess: ");
13      int guess = input.nextInt();
14
15      if (guess == number)
16        System.out.println("Yes, the number is " + number);
17      else if (guess > number)
18        System.out.println("Your guess is too high");
19      else
```

generate a number

enter a guess

correct guess?

too high?

too low?

```
20        System.out.println("Your guess is too low");
21      }
22  }
```

When you run this program, it prompts the user to enter a guess only once. To let the user enter a guess repeatedly, you may put the code in lines 11–20 in a loop as follows:

```
while (true) {
  // Prompt the user to guess the number
  System.out.print("\nEnter your guess: ");
  guess = input.nextInt();

  if (guess == number)
    System.out.println("Yes, the number is " + number);
  else if (guess > number)
    System.out.println("Your guess is too high");
  else
    System.out.println("Your guess is too low");
} // End of loop
```

This loop repeatedly prompts the user to enter a guess. However, this loop is not correct, because it never terminates. When **guess** matches **number**, the loop should end. So, the loop can be revised as follows:

```
while (guess != number) {
  // Prompt the user to guess the number
  System.out.print("\nEnter your guess: ");
  guess = input.nextInt();

  if (guess == number)
    System.out.println("Yes, the number is " + number);
  else if (guess > number)
    System.out.println("Your guess is too high");
  else
    System.out.println("Your guess is too low");
} // End of loop
```

The complete code is given in Listing 4.3.

LISTING 4.3 GuessNumber.java

```
1  import java.util.Scanner;
2
3  public class GuessNumber {
4    public static void main(String[] args) {
5      // Generate a random number to be guessed
6      int number = (int)(Math.random() * 101);
7
8      Scanner input = new Scanner(System.in);
9      System.out.println("Guess a magic number between 0 and 100");
10
11     int guess = -1;
12     while (guess != number) {
13       // Prompt the user to guess the number
14       System.out.print("\nEnter your guess: ");
15       guess = input.nextInt();
16
17       if (guess == number)
18         System.out.println("Yes, the number is " + number);
19       else if (guess > number)
```

generate a number

enter a guess

```
20         System.out.println("Your guess is too high");          too high?
21      else
22         System.out.println("Your guess is too low");           too low?
23    } // End of loop
24   }
25 }
```

	line#	number	guess	output
	6	39		
	11		-1	
iteration 1	15		50	
	20			Your guess is too high
iteration 2	15		25	
	22			Your guess is too low
iteration 3	15		42	
	20			Your guess is too high
iteration 4	15		39	
	18			Yes, the number is 39

The program generates the magic number in line 6 and prompts the user to enter a guess continuously in a loop (lines 12–23). For each guess, the program checks whether the guess is correct, too high, or too low (lines 17–22). When the guess is correct, the program exits the loop (line 12). Note that **guess** is initialized to **-1**. Initializing it to a value between **0** and **100** would be wrong, because that could be the number to be guessed.

4.2.2 Loop Design Strategies

Writing a correct loop is not an easy task for novice programmers. Consider three steps when writing a loop.

Step 1: Identify the statements that need to be repeated.

Step 2: Wrap these statements in a loop like this:

```
while (true) {
  Statements;
}
```

Step 3: Code the **loop-continuation-condition** and add appropriate statements for controlling the loop.

```
while (loop-continuation-condition) {
  Statements;
  Additional statements for controlling the loop;
}
```

4.2.3 Case Study: Multiple Subtraction Quiz

The Math subtraction learning tool program in Listing 3.4, SubtractionQuiz.java, generates just one question for each run. You can use a loop to generate questions repeatedly. How do you write the code to generate five questions? Follow the loop design strategy. First identify the statements that need to be repeated. These are the statements for obtaining two random numbers, prompting

VideoNote

Multiple subtraction quiz

the user with a subtraction question, and grading the question. Second, wrap the statements in a loop. Third, add a loop control variable and the **loop-continuation-condition** to execute the loop five times.

Listing 4.4 gives a program that generates five questions and, after a student answers all five, reports the number of correct answers. The program also displays the time spent on the test and lists all the questions.

LISTING 4.4 SubtractionQuizLoop.java

```java
 1  import java.util.Scanner;
 2
 3  public class SubtractionQuizLoop {
 4    public static void main(String[] args) {
 5      final int NUMBER_OF_QUESTIONS = 5; // Number of questions
 6      int correctCount = 0; // Count the number of correct answers
 7      int count = 0; // Count the number of questions
 8      long startTime = System.currentTimeMillis();
 9      String output = " "; // output string is initially empty
10      Scanner input = new Scanner(System.in);
11
12      while (count < NUMBER_OF_QUESTIONS) {
13        // 1. Generate two random single-digit integers
14        int number1 = (int)(Math.random() * 10);
15        int number2 = (int)(Math.random() * 10);
16
17        // 2. If number1 < number2, swap number1 with number2
18        if (number1 < number2) {
19          int temp = number1;
20          number1 = number2;
21          number2 = temp;
22        }
23
24        // 3. Prompt the student to answer "What is number1 - number2?"
25        System.out.print(
26          "What is " + number1 + " - " + number2 + "? ");
27        int answer = input.nextInt();
28
29        // 4. Grade the answer and display the result
30        if (number1 - number2 == answer) {
31          System.out.println("You are correct!");
32          correctCount++; // Increase the correct answer count
33        }
34        else
35          System.out.println("Your answer is wrong.\n" + number1
36            + " - " + number2 + " should be " + (number1 - number2));
37
38        // Increase the question count
39        count++;
40
41        output += "\n" + number1 + "-" + number2 + "=" + answer +
42          ((number1 - number2 == answer) ? " correct" : " wrong");
43      }
44
45      long endTime = System.currentTimeMillis();
46      long testTime = endTime - startTime;
47
48      System.out.println("Correct count is " + correctCount +
49        "\nTest time is " + testTime / 1000 + " seconds\n" + output);
50    }
51  }
```

Margin notes:
- get start time (line 8)
- loop (line 12)
- display a question (line 25)
- grade an answer (line 30)
- increase correct count (line 32)
- increase control variable (line 39)
- prepare output (line 41)
- end loop (line 43)
- get end time (line 45)
- test time (line 46)
- display result (line 48)

```
What is 9 - 2? 7  [↵ Enter]
You are correct!

What is 3 - 0? 3  [↵ Enter]
You are correct!

What is 3 - 2? 1  [↵ Enter]
You are correct!

What is 7 - 4? 4  [↵ Enter]
Your answer is wrong.

7 - 4 should be 3
What is 7 - 5? 4  [↵ Enter]

Your answer is wrong.
7 - 5 should be 2

Correct count is 3
Test time is 1021 seconds

9-2=7 correct
3-0=3 correct
3-2=1 correct
7-4=4 wrong
7-5=4 wrong
```

The program uses the control variable **count** to control the execution of the loop. **count** is initially **0** (line 7) and is increased by **1** in each iteration (line 39). A subtraction question is displayed and processed in each iteration. The program obtains the time before the test starts in line 8 and the time after the test ends in line 45, and computes the test time in line 46. The test time is in milliseconds and is converted to seconds in line 49.

4.2.4 Controlling a Loop with a Sentinel Value

Another common technique for controlling a loop is to designate a special value when reading and processing a set of values. This special input value, known as a *sentinel value*, signifies the end of the input. A loop that uses a sentinel value to control its execution is called a *sentinel-controlled loop*.

Listing 4.5 writes a program that reads and calculates the sum of an unspecified number of integers. The input **0** signifies the end of the input. Do you need to declare a new variable for each input value? No. Just use one variable named **data** (line 12) to store the input value and use a variable named **sum** (line 15) to store the total. Whenever a value is read, assign it to **data** and, if it is not zero, add it to **sum** (line 17).

sentinel value

sentinel-controlled loop

LISTING 4.5   SentinelValue.java

```java
1  import java.util.Scanner;
2
3  public class SentinelValue {
4    /** Main method */
5    public static void main(String[] args) {
6      // Create a Scanner
7      Scanner input = new Scanner(System.in);
8
9      // Read an initial data
10     System.out.print(
11       "Enter an integer (the input ends if it is 0): ");
12     int data = input.nextInt();
```

input

```
13
14      // Keep reading data until the input is 0
15      int sum = 0;
16      while (data != 0) {
17        sum += data;
18
19        // Read the next data
20        System.out.print(
21          "Enter an integer (the input ends if it is 0): ");
22        data = input.nextInt();
23      }
24
25      System.out.println("The sum is " + sum);
26    }
27  }
```

loop (next to line 16)

end of loop (next to line 23)

display result (next to line 25)

```
Enter an integer (the input ends if it is 0): 2  ↵Enter
Enter an integer (the input ends if it is 0): 3  ↵Enter
Enter an integer (the input ends if it is 0): 4  ↵Enter
Enter an integer (the input ends if it is 0): 0  ↵Enter
The sum is 9
```

	line#	data	sum	output
	12	2		
	15		0	
iteration 1	17		2	
	22	3		
iteration 2	17		5	
	22	4		
iteration 3	17		9	
	22	0		
	25			The sum is 9

If **data** is not **0**, it is added to **sum** (line 17) and the next item of input data is read (lines 20–22). If **data** is **0**, the loop body is no longer executed and the **while** loop terminates. The input value **0** is the sentinel value for this loop. Note that if the first input read is **0**, the loop body never executes, and the resulting sum is **0**.

 Caution

Don't use floating-point values for equality checking in a loop control. Because floating-point values are approximations for some values, using them could result in imprecise counter values and inaccurate results.

Consider the following code for computing $1 + 0.9 + 0.8 + ... + 0.1$:

```
double item = 1; double sum = 0;
while (item != 0) { // No guarantee item will be 0
  sum += item;
  item -= 0.1;
}
System.out.println(sum);
```

Variable **item** starts with **1** and is reduced by **0.1** every time the loop body is executed. The loop should terminate when **item** becomes **0**. However, there is no guarantee that item will be exactly **0**, because the floating-point arithmetic is approximated. This loop seems okay on the surface, but it is actually an infinite loop.

numeric error

4.2.5 Input and Output Redirections

In the preceding example, if you have a large number of data to enter, it would be cumbersome to type from the keyboard. You can store the data separated by whitespaces in a text file, say **input.txt**, and run the program using the following command:

```
java SentinelValue < input.txt
```

This command is called *input redirection*. The program takes the input from the file **input.txt** rather than having the user type the data from the keyboard at runtime. Suppose the contents of the file are

input redirection

```
2 3 4 5 6 7 8 9 12 23 32
23 45 67 89 92 12 34 35 3 1 2 4 0
```

The program should get **sum** to be **518**.

Similarly, there is *output redirection*, which sends the output to a file rather than displaying it on the console. The command for output redirection is:

output redirection

```
java ClassName > output.txt
```

Input and output redirection can be used in the same command. For example, the following command gets input from **input.txt** and sends output to **output.txt**:

```
java SentinelValue < input.txt > output.txt
```

Try running the program to see what contents are in **output.txt**.

4.1 Analyze the following code. Is **count < 100** always **true**, always **false**, or sometimes **true** or sometimes **false** at Point A, Point B, and Point C?

✓ Check Point

MyProgrammingLab™

```java
int count = 0;
while (count < 100) {
  // Point A
  System.out.println("Welcome to Java!\n");
  count++;
  // Point B
}
// Point C
```

4.2 What is wrong if **guess** is initialized to **0** in line 11 in Listing 4.3?

4.3 How many times are the following loop bodies repeated? What is the printout of each loop?

```java
int i = 1;
while (i < 10)
  if (i % 2 == 0)
    System.out.println(i);
```
(a)

```java
int i = 1;
while (i < 10)
  if (i % 2 == 0)
    System.out.println(i++);
```
(b)

```java
int i = 1;
while (i < 10)
  if ((i++) % 2 == 0)
    System.out.println(i);
```
(c)

4.4   Suppose the input is 2 3 4 5 0. What is the output of the following code?

```java
import java.util.Scanner;

public class Test {
  public static void main(String[] args) {

    Scanner input = new Scanner(System.in);

    int number, max;
    number = input.nextInt();
    max = number;

    while (number != 0) {
      number = input.nextInt();
      if (number > max)
        max = number;
    }

    System.out.println("max is " + max);
    System.out.println("number " + number);
  }
}
```

4.5   What is the output of the following code? Explain the reason.

```java
int x = 80000000;

while (x > 0)
  x++;

System.out.println("x is " + x);
```

4.3 The **do-while** Loop

 Key Point

A do-while *loop is the same as a* while *loop except that it executes the loop body first and then checks the loop continuation condition.*

The do-while loop is a variation of the while loop. Its syntax is:

do-while loop

```java
do {
  // Loop body;
  Statement(s);
} while (loop-continuation-condition);
```

Its execution flowchart is shown in Figure 4.2.

The loop body is executed first, and then the loop-continuation-condition is evaluated. If the evaluation is true, the loop body is executed again; if it is false, the do-while loop terminates. The difference between a while loop and a do-while loop is the order in which the loop-continuation-condition is evaluated and the loop body executed. You can write a loop using either the while loop or the do-while loop. Sometimes one is a more convenient choice than the other. For example, you can rewrite the while loop in Listing 4.5 using a do-while loop, as shown in Listing 4.6.

LISTING 4.6   TestDoWhile.java

```java
1  import java.util.Scanner;
2
3  public class TestDoWhile {
```

FIGURE 4.2 The do-while loop executes the loop body first, then checks the loop-continuation-condition to determine whether to continue or terminate the loop.

```
4    /** Main method */
5    public static void main(String[] args) {
6      int data;
7      int sum = 0;
8
9      // Create a Scanner
10     Scanner input = new Scanner(System.in);
11
12     // Keep reading data until the input is 0
13     do {                                                    loop
14       // Read the next data
15       System.out.print(
16         "Enter an integer (the input ends if it is 0): ");
17       data = input.nextInt();
18
19       sum += data;
20     } while (data != 0);                                    end loop
21
22     System.out.println("The sum is " + sum);
23   }
24 }
```

```
Enter an integer (the input ends if it is 0): 3 ↵Enter
Enter an integer (the input ends if it is 0): 5 ↵Enter
Enter an integer (the input ends if it is 0): 6 ↵Enter
Enter an integer (the input ends if it is 0): 0 ↵Enter
The sum is 14
```

Tip
Use the do-while loop if you have statements inside the loop that must be executed *at least once*, as in the case of the do-while loop in the preceding TestDoWhile program. These statements must appear before the loop as well as inside it if you use a while loop.

4.6 Suppose the input is 2 3 4 5 0. What is the output of the following code?

```java
import java.util.Scanner;

public class Test {
  public static void main(String[] args) {
    Scanner input = new Scanner(System.in);

    int number, max;
    number = input.nextInt();
    max = number;

    do {
      number = input.nextInt();
      if (number > max)
        max = number;
    } while (number != 0);

    System.out.println("max is " + max);
    System.out.println("number " + number);
  }
}
```

4.7 What are the differences between a `while` loop and a `do-while` loop? Convert the following `while` loop into a `do-while` loop.

```java
Scanner input = new Scanner(System.in);
int sum = 0;
System.out.println("Enter an integer " +
  "(the input ends if it is 0)");
int number = input.nextInt();
while (number != 0) {
  sum += number;
  System.out.println("Enter an integer " +
    "(the input ends if it is 0)");
  number = input.nextInt();
}
```

4.4 The **for** Loop

A **for** *loop has a concise syntax for writing loops.*

Often you write a loop in the following common form:

```java
i = initialValue;  // Initialize loop control variable
while (i < endValue) {
  // Loop body
  ...
  i++; // Adjust loop control variable
}
```

A **for** loop can be used to simplify the preceding loop as:

```java
for (i = initialValue; i < endValue; i++) {
  // Loop body
  ...
}
```

In general, the syntax of a **for** loop is:

```
for (initial-action; loop-continuation-condition;
        action-after-each-iteration) {
  // Loop body;
  Statement(s);
}
```

for loop

The flowchart of the **for** loop is shown in Figure 4.3a.

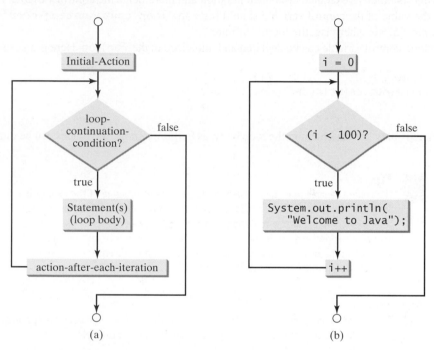

(a)   (b)

FIGURE 4.3   A **for** loop performs an initial action once, then repeatedly executes the statements in the loop body, and performs an action after an iteration when the **loop-continuation-condition** evaluates to **true**.

The **for** loop statement starts with the keyword **for**, followed by a pair of parentheses enclosing the control structure of the loop. This structure consists of **initial-action**, **loop-continuation-condition**, and **action-after-each-iteration**. The control structure is followed by the loop body enclosed inside braces. The **initial-action**, **loop-continuation-condition**, and **action-after-each-iteration** are separated by semicolons.

A **for** loop generally uses a variable to control how many times the loop body is executed and when the loop terminates. This variable is referred to as a *control variable*. The **initial-action** often initializes a control variable, the **action-after-each-iteration** usually increments or decrements the control variable, and the **loop-continuation-condition** tests whether the control variable has reached a termination value. For example, the following **for** loop prints **Welcome to Java!** a hundred times:

control variable

```
int i;
for (i = 0; i < 100; i++) {
  System.out.println("Welcome to Java!");
}
```

The flowchart of the statement is shown in Figure 4.3b. The `for` loop initializes `i` to `0`, then repeatedly executes the `println` statement and evaluates `i++` while `i` is less than `100`.

initial-action

The `initial-action`, `i = 0`, initializes the control variable, `i`. The `loop-continuation-condition`, `i < 100`, is a Boolean expression. The expression is evaluated right after the initialization and at the beginning of each iteration. If this condition is `true`, the loop body is executed. If it is `false`, the loop terminates and the program control turns to the line following the loop.

action-after-each-iteration

The `action-after-each-iteration`, `i++`, is a statement that adjusts the control variable. This statement is executed after each iteration and increments the control variable. Eventually, the value of the control variable should force the `loop-continuation-condition` to become `false`; otherwise, the loop is infinite.

The loop control variable can be declared and initialized in the `for` loop. Here is an example:

```
for (int i = 0; i < 100; i++) {
  System.out.println("Welcome to Java!");
}
```

omitting braces

If there is only one statement in the loop body, as in this example, the braces can be omitted.

declare control variable

Tip
The control variable must be declared inside the control structure of the loop or before the loop. If the loop control variable is used only in the loop, and not elsewhere, it is good programming practice to declare it in the `initial-action` of the `for` loop. If the variable is declared inside the loop control structure, it cannot be referenced outside the loop. In the preceding code, for example, you cannot reference `i` outside the `for` loop, because it is declared inside the `for` loop.

for loop variations

Note
The `initial-action` in a `for` loop can be a list of zero or more comma-separated variable declaration statements or assignment expressions. For example:

```
for (int i = 0, j = 0; (i + j < 10); i++, j++) {
  // Do something
}
```

The `action-after-each-iteration` in a `for` loop can be a list of zero or more comma-separated statements. For example:

```
for (int i = 1; i < 100; System.out.println(i), i++);
```

This example is correct, but it is a bad example, because it makes the code difficult to read. Normally, you declare and initialize a control variable as an initial action and increment or decrement the control variable as an action after each iteration.

Note
If the `loop-continuation-condition` in a `for` loop is omitted, it is implicitly `true`. Thus the statement given below in (a), which is an infinite loop, is the same as in (b). To avoid confusion, though, it is better to use the equivalent loop in (c).

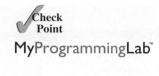

4.8 Do the following two loops result in the same value in **sum**?

```
for (int i = 0; i < 10; ++i) {
  sum += i;
}
```
(a)

```
for (int i = 0; i < 10; i++) {
  sum += i;
}
```
(b)

4.9 What are the three parts of a **for** loop control? Write a **for** loop that prints the numbers from **1** to **100**.

4.10 Suppose the input is **2 3 4 5 0**. What is the output of the following code?

```
import java.util.Scanner;

public class Test {
  public static void main(String[] args) {
    Scanner input = new Scanner(System.in);

    int number, sum = 0, count;

    for (count = 0; count < 5; count++) {
      number = input.nextInt();
      sum += number;
    }

    System.out.println("sum is " + sum);
    System.out.println("count is " + count);
  }
}
```

4.11 What does the following statement do?

```
for ( ; ; ) {
  // Do something
}
```

4.12 If a variable is declared in the **for** loop control, can it be used after the loop exits?

4.13 Convert the following **for** loop statement to a **while** loop and to a **do-while** loop:

```
long sum = 0;
for (int i = 0; i <= 1000; i++)
  sum = sum + i;
```

4.14 Count the number of iterations in the following loops.

```
int count = 0;
while (count < n) {
  count++;
}
```
(a)

```
for (int count = 0;
     count <= n; count++) {
}
```
(b)

```
int count = 5;
while (count < n) {
  count++;
}
```
(c)

```
int count = 5;
while (count < n) {
  count = count + 3;
}
```
(d)

4.5 Which Loop to Use?

pretest loop
posttest loop

You can use a `for` *loop, a* `while` *loop, or a* `do-while` *loop, whichever is convenient.*

The `while` loop and `for` loop are called *pretest loops* because the continuation condition is checked before the loop body is executed. The `do-while` loop is called a *posttest loop* because the condition is checked after the loop body is executed. The three forms of loop statements—`while`, `do-while`, and `for`—are expressively equivalent; that is, you can write a loop in any of these three forms. For example, a `while` loop in (a) in the following figure can always be converted into the `for` loop in (b).

```
while (loop-continuation-condition) {
   // Loop body
}
```
Equivalent
```
for ( ; loop-continuation-condition; ) {
   // Loop body
}
```

(a)   (b)

A `for` loop in (a) in the next figure can generally be converted into the `while` loop in (b) except in certain special cases (see Checkpoint Question 4.23 for such a case).

```
for (initial-action;
     loop-continuation-condition;
     action-after-each-iteration) {
   // Loop body;
}
```
Equivalent
```
initial-action;
while (loop-continuation-condition) {
   // Loop body;
   action-after-each-iteration;
}
```

(a)   (b)

Use the loop statement that is most intuitive and comfortable for you. In general, a `for` loop may be used if the number of repetitions is known in advance, as, for example, when you need to display a message a hundred times. A `while` loop may be used if the number of repetitions is not fixed, as in the case of reading the numbers until the input is **0**. A `do-while` loop can be used to replace a `while` loop if the loop body has to be executed before the continuation condition is tested.

Caution

Adding a semicolon at the end of the `for` clause before the loop body is a common mistake, as shown below in (a). In (a), the semicolon signifies the end of the loop prematurely. The loop body is actually empty, as shown in (b). (a) and (b) are equivalent. Both are incorrect.

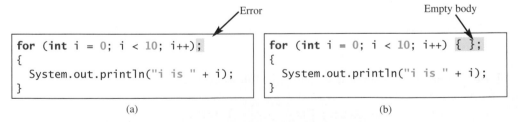

Error   Empty body

```
for (int i = 0; i < 10; i++);
{
   System.out.println("i is " + i);
}
```
```
for (int i = 0; i < 10; i++) { };
{
   System.out.println("i is " + i);
}
```

(a)   (b)

Similarly, the loop in (c) is also wrong. (c) is equivalent to (d). Both are incorrect.

Error   Empty body

```
int i = 0;
while (i < 10);
{
   System.out.println("i is " + i);
   i++;
}
```
```
int i = 0;
while (i < 10) { };
{
   System.out.println("i is " + i);
   i++;
}
```

(c)   (d)

These errors often occur when you use the next-line block style. Using the end-of-line block style can avoid errors of this type.

In the case of the **do-while** loop, the semicolon is needed to end the loop.

```
int i = 0;
do {
  System.out.println("i is " + i);
  i++;
} while (i < 10);
```

Correct

4.15 Can you convert a **for** loop to a **while** loop? List the advantages of using **for** loops.

4.16 Can you always convert a **while** loop into a **for** loop? Convert the following **while** loop into a **for** loop.

```
int i = 1;
int sum = 0;
while (sum < 10000) {
  sum = sum + i;
  i++;
}
```

4.17 Identify and fix the errors in the following code:

```
1   public class Test {
2     public void main(String[] args) {
3       for (int i = 0; i < 10; i++);
4         sum += i;
5
6       if (i < j);
7         System.out.println(i)
8       else
9         System.out.println(j);
10
11      while (j < 10);
12      {
13        j++;
14      }
15
16      do {
17        j++;
18      } while (j < 10)
19    }
20  }
```

4.18 What is wrong with the following programs?

```
1 public class ShowErrors {
2   public static void main(String[] args) {
3     int i;
4     int j = 5;
5
6     if (j > 3)
7       System.out.println(i + 4);
8   }
9 }
```

(a)

```
1 public class ShowErrors {
2   public static void main(String[] args) {
3     for (int i = 0; i < 10; i++);
4       System.out.println(i + 4);
5   }
6 }
```

(b)

4.6 Nicht Loops

Key
Point

A loop can be nested inside another loop.

nested loop

Nested loops consist of an outer loop and one or more inner loops. Each time the outer loop is repeated, the inner loops are reentered, and started anew.

Listing 4.7 presents a program that uses nested **for** loops to display a multiplication table.

LISTING 4.7 `MultiplicationTable.java`

table title

outer loop

inner loop

```java
1  public class MultiplicationTable {
2    /** Main method */
3    public static void main(String[] args) {
4      // Display the table heading
5      System.out.println("            Multiplication Table");
6
7      // Display the number title
8      System.out.print("    ");
9      for (int j = 1; j <= 9; j++)
10       System.out.print("   " + j);
11
12     System.out.println("\n---------------------------------------");
13
14     // Display table body
15     for (int i = 1; i <= 9; i++) {
16       System.out.print(i + " | ");
17       for (int j = 1; j <= 9; j++) {
18         // Display the product and align properly
19         System.out.printf("%4d", i * j);
20       }
21       System.out.println();
22     }
23   }
24 }
```

```
        Multiplication Table
     1   2   3   4   5   6   7   8   9
   ---------------------------------------
1 |  1   2   3   4   5   6   7   8   9
2 |  2   4   6   8  10  12  14  16  18
3 |  3   6   9  12  15  18  21  24  27
4 |  4   8  12  16  20  24  28  32  36
5 |  5  10  15  20  25  30  35  40  45
6 |  6  12  18  24  30  36  42  48  54
7 |  7  14  21  28  35  42  49  56  63
8 |  8  16  24  32  40  48  56  64  72
9 |  9  18  27  36  45  54  63  72  81
```

The program displays a title (line 5) on the first line in the output. The first **for** loop (lines 9–10) displays the numbers 1 through 9 on the second line. A dashed (–) line is displayed on the third line (line 12).

The next loop (lines 15–22) is a nested **for** loop with the control variable i in the outer loop and j in the inner loop. For each i, the product i * j is displayed on a line in the inner loop, with j being 1, 2, 3, ..., 9.

> **Note**
> Be aware that a nested loop may take a long time to run. Consider the following loop nested in three levels:
>
> ```
> for (int i = 0; i < 10000; i++)
>   for (int j = 0; j < 10000; j++)
>     for (int k = 0; k < 10000; k++)
>       Perform an action
> ```
>
> The action is performed one trillion times. If it takes 1 microsecond to perform the action, the total time to run the loop would be more than 277 hours. Note that 1 microsecond is one millionth (10^{-6}) of a second.

4.19 How many times is the `println` statement executed?

```
for (int i = 0; i < 10; i++)
  for (int j = 0; j < i; j++)
    System.out.println(i * j)
```

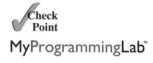

4.20 Show the output of the following programs. (*Hint*: Draw a table and list the variables in the columns to trace these programs.)

```java
public class Test {
  /** Main method */
  public static void main(String[] args) {
    for (int i = 1; i < 5; i++) {
      int j = 0;
      while (j < i) {
        System.out.print(j + " ");
        j++;
      }
    }
  }
}
```
(a)

```java
public class Test {
  /** Main method */
  public static void main(String[] args) {
    int i = 0;
    while (i < 5) {
      for (int j = i; j > 1; j--)
        System.out.print(j + " ");
      System.out.println("****");
      i++;
    }
  }
}
```
(b)

```java
public class Test {
  public static void main(String[] args) {
    int i = 5;
    while (i >= 1) {
      int num = 1;
      for (int j = 1; j <= i; j++) {
        System.out.print(num + "xxx");
        num *= 2;
      }

      System.out.println();
      i--;
    }
  }
}
```
(c)

```java
public class Test {
  public static void main(String[] args) {
    int i = 1;
    do {
      int num = 1;
      for (int j = 1; j <= i; j++) {
        System.out.print(num + "G");
        num += 2;
      }

      System.out.println();
      i++;
    } while (i <= 5);
  }
}
```
(d)

4.7 Minimizing Numeric Errors

Using floating-point numbers in the loop continuation condition may cause numeric errors.

Numeric errors involving floating-point numbers are inevitable. This section discusses how to minimize such errors through an example.

Listing 4.8 presents an example summing a series that starts with `0.01` and ends with `1.0`. The numbers in the series will increment by `0.01`, as follows: `0.01 + 0.02 + 0.03`, and so on.

VideoNote

Minimize numeric errors

LISTING 4.8 TestSum.java

```
1  public class TestSum {
2    public static void main(String[] args) {
3      // Initialize sum
4      float sum = 0;
5
6      // Add 0.01, 0.02, ..., 0.99, 1 to sum
7      for (float i = 0.01f; i <= 1.0f; i = i + 0.01f)
8        sum += i;
9
10     // Display result
11     System.out.println("The sum is " + sum);
12   }
13 }
```

loop

```
The sum is 50.499985
```

The `for` loop (lines 7–8) repeatedly adds the control variable `i` to `sum`. This variable, which begins with `0.01`, is incremented by `0.01` after each iteration. The loop terminates when `i` exceeds `1.0`.

The `for` loop initial action can be any statement, but it is often used to initialize a control variable. From this example, you can see that a control variable can be a `float` type. In fact, it can be any data type.

double precision

The exact `sum` should be `50.50`, but the answer is `50.499985`. The result is imprecise because computers use a fixed number of bits to represent floating-point numbers, and thus they cannot represent some floating-point numbers exactly. If you change `float` in the program to `double`, as follows, you should see a slight improvement in precision, because a `double` variable holds 64 bits, whereas a `float` variable holds 32 bits.

```
// Initialize sum
double sum = 0;

// Add 0.01, 0.02, ..., 0.99, 1 to sum
for (double i = 0.01; i <= 1.0; i = i + 0.01)
  sum += i;
```

numeric error

However, you will be stunned to see that the result is actually `49.50000000000003`. What went wrong? If you display `i` for each iteration in the loop, you will see that the last `i` is slightly larger than `1` (not exactly `1`). This causes the last `i` not to be added into `sum`. The fundamental problem is that the floating-point numbers are represented by approximation. To fix the problem, use an integer count to ensure that all the numbers are added to `sum`. Here is the new loop:

```
double currentValue = 0.01;

for (int count = 0; count < 100; count++) {
```

```
      sum += currentValue;
      currentValue += 0.01;
  }
```

After this loop, **sum** is **50.50000000000003**. This loop adds the numbers from smallest to biggest. What happens if you add numbers from biggest to smallest (i.e., **1.0**, **0.99**, **0.98**, . . . , **0.02**, **0.01** in this order) as follows:

```
  double currentValue = 1.0;

  for (int count = 0; count < 100; count++) {
    sum += currentValue;
    currentValue -= 0.01;
  }
```

After this loop, **sum** is **50.49999999999995**. Adding from biggest to smallest is less accurate than adding from smallest to biggest. This phenomenon is an artifact of the finite-precision arithmetic. Adding a very small number to a very big number can have no effect if the result requires more precision than the variable can store. For example, the inaccurate result of **100000000.0 + 0.000000001** is **100000000.0**. To obtain more accurate results, carefully select the order of computation. Adding smaller numbers before bigger numbers is one way to minimize errors.

avoiding numeric error

4.8 Case Studies

Loops are fundamental in programming. The ability to write loops is essential in learning Java programming.

Key
Point

If you can write programs using loops, you know how to program! For this reason, this section presents three additional examples of solving problems using loops.

4.8.1   Case Study: Finding the Greatest Common Divisor

The greatest common divisor (gcd) of the two integers **4** and **2** is **2**. The greatest common divisor of the two integers **16** and **24** is **8**. How do you find the greatest common divisor? Let the two input integers be **n1** and **n2**. You know that number **1** is a common divisor, but it may not be the greatest common divisor. So, you can check whether **k** (for **k** = **2**, **3**, **4**, and so on) is a common divisor for **n1** and **n2**, until **k** is greater than **n1** or **n2**. Store the common divisor in a variable named **gcd**. Initially, **gcd** is **1**. Whenever a new common divisor is found, it becomes the new gcd. When you have checked all the possible common divisors from **2** up to **n1** or **n2**, the value in variable **gcd** is the greatest common divisor. The idea can be translated into the following loop:

gcd

```
  int gcd = 1; // Initial gcd is 1
  int k = 2; // Possible gcd

  while (k <= n1 && k <= n2) {
    if (n1 % k == 0 && n2 % k == 0)
      gcd = k; // Update gcd
    k++; // Next possible gcd
  }

  // After the loop, gcd is the greatest common divisor for n1 and n2
```

Listing 4.9 presents the program that prompts the user to enter two positive integers and finds their greatest common divisor.

LISTING 4.9 GreatestCommonDivisor.java

```java
 1  import java.util.Scanner;
 2
 3  public class GreatestCommonDivisor {
 4    /** Main method */
 5    public static void main(String[] args) {
 6      // Create a Scanner
 7      Scanner input = new Scanner(System.in);
 8
 9      // Prompt the user to enter two integers
10      System.out.print("Enter first integer: ");
11      int n1 = input.nextInt();
12      System.out.print("Enter second integer: ");
13      int n2 = input.nextInt();
14
15      int gcd = 1; // Initial gcd is 1
16      int k = 2; // Possible gcd
17      while (k <= n1 && k <= n2) {
18        if (n1 % k == 0 && n2 % k == 0)
19          gcd = k; // Update gcd
20        k++;
21      }
22
23      System.out.println("The greatest common divisor for " + n1 +
24        " and " + n2 + " is " + gcd);
25    }
26  }
```

input (line 11)
input (line 13)
gcd (line 15)
check divisor (line 18)
output (line 23)

```
Enter first integer: 125 ↵Enter
Enter second integer: 2525 ↵Enter
The greatest common divisor for 125 and 2525 is 25
```

think before you type

How would you write this program? Would you immediately begin to write the code? No. It is important to *think before you type*. Thinking enables you to generate a logical solution for the problem without concern about how to write the code. Once you have a logical solution, type the code to translate the solution into a Java program. The translation is not unique. For example, you could use a `for` loop to rewrite the code as follows:

```java
for (int k = 2; k <= n1 && k <= n2; k++) {
  if (n1 % k == 0 && n2 % k == 0)
    gcd = k;
}
```

multiple solutions

A problem often has multiple solutions, and the gcd problem can be solved in many ways. Programming Exercise 4.14 suggests another solution. A more efficient solution is to use the classic Euclidean algorithm (see www.cut-the-knot.org/blue/Euclid.shtml for more information).

erroneous solutions

You might think that a divisor for a number `n1` cannot be greater than `n1 / 2` and would attempt to improve the program using the following loop:

```java
for (int k = 2; k <= n1 / 2 && k <= n2 / 2; k++) {
  if (n1 % k == 0 && n2 % k == 0)
    gcd = k;
}
```

This revision is wrong. Can you find the reason? See Checkpoint Question 4.21 for the answer.

4.8.2 Case Study: Predicting the Future Tuition

Suppose that the tuition for a university is **$10,000** this year and tuition increases **7%** every year. In how many years will the tuition be doubled?

Before you can write a program to solve this problem, first consider how to solve it by hand. The tuition for the second year is the tuition for the first year * **1.07**. The tuition for a future year is the tuition of its preceding year * **1.07**. Thus, the tuition for each year can be computed as follows:

```
double tuition = 10000;   int year = 0;   // Year 0
tuition = tuition * 1.07; year++;         // Year 1
tuition = tuition * 1.07; year++;         // Year 2
tuition = tuition * 1.07; year++;         // Year 3
...
```

Keep computing the tuition for a new year until it is at least **20000**. By then you will know how many years it will take for the tuition to be doubled. You can now translate the logic into the following loop:

```
double tuition = 10000;   // Year 0
int year = 0;
while (tuition < 20000) {
  tuition = tuition * 1.07;
  year++;
}
```

The complete program is shown in Listing 4.10.

LISTING 4.10 FutureTuition.java

```
1  public class FutureTuition {
2    public static void main(String[] args) {
3      double tuition = 10000;   // Year 0
4      int year = 0;
5      while (tuition < 20000) {                        loop
6        tuition = tuition * 1.07;                      next year's tuition
7        year++;
8      }
9
10     System.out.println("Tuition will be doubled in "
11       + year + " years");
12     System.out.printf("Tuition will be $%.2f in %1d years",
13       tuition, year);
14   }
15 }
```

```
Tuition will be doubled in 11 years
Tuition will be $21048.52 in 11 years
```

The `while` loop (lines 5–8) is used to repeatedly compute the tuition for a new year. The loop terminates when the tuition is greater than or equal to **20000**.

4.8.3 Case Study: Monte Carlo Simulation

Monte Carlo simulation uses random numbers and probability to solve problems. This method has a wide range of applications in computational mathematics, physics, chemistry, and finance. This section gives an example of using Monte Carlo simulation for estimating π.

To estimate π using the Monte Carlo method, draw a circle with its bounding square as shown below.

Assume the radius of the circle is 1. Therefore, the circle area is π and the square area is 4. Randomly generate a point in the square. The probability for the point to fall in the circle is `circleArea / squareArea` = $\pi / 4$.

Write a program that randomly generates 1,000,000 points in the square and let `numberOfHits` denote the number of points that fall in the circle. Thus, `numberOfHits` is approximately `1000000` * ($\pi / 4$). π can be approximated as `4 * numberOfHits / 1000000`. The complete program is shown in Listing 4.11.

LISTING 4.11 `MonteCarloSimulation.java`

```
 1  public class MonteCarloSimulation {
 2    public static void main(String[] args) {
 3      final int NUMBER_OF_TRIALS = 10000000;
 4      int numberOfHits = 0;
 5
 6      for (int i = 0; i < NUMBER_OF_TRIALS; i++) {
 7        double x = Math.random() * 2.0 - 1;
 8        double y = Math.random() * 2.0 - 1;
 9        if (x * x + y * y <= 1)
10          numberOfHits++;
11      }
12
13      double pi = 4.0 * numberOfHits / NUMBER_OF_TRIALS;
14      System.out.println("PI is " + pi);
15    }
16  }
```

generate random points
check inside circle
estimate pi

```
PI is 3.14124
```

The program repeatedly generates a random point (x, y) in the square in lines 7–8:

```
double x = Math.random() * 2.0 - 1;
double y = Math.random() * 2.0 - 1;
```

If $x^2 + y^2 \le 1$, the point is inside the circle and `numberOfHits` is incremented by 1. π is approximately `4 * numberOfHits / NUMBER_OF_TRIALS` (line 13).

4.21 Will the program work if **n1** and **n2** are replaced by **n1 / 2** and **n2 / 2** in line 17 in Listing 4.9?

4.9 Keywords *break* and *continue*

The break *and* continue *keywords provide additional controls in a loop.*

 Pedagogical Note

Two keywords, break and continue, can be used in loop statements to provide additional controls. Using break and continue can simplify programming in some cases. Overusing or improperly using them, however, can make programs difficult to read and debug. (*Note to instructors*: You may skip this section without affecting students' understanding of the rest of the book.)

You have used the keyword **break** in a **switch** statement. You can also use **break** in a loop to immediately terminate the loop. Listing 4.12 presents a program to demonstrate the effect of using **break** in a loop.

break statement

LISTING 4.12 TestBreak.java

```java
1  public class TestBreak {
2    public static void main(String[] args) {
3      int sum = 0;
4      int number = 0;
5
6      while (number < 20) {
7        number++;
8        sum += number;
9        if (sum >= 100)
10         break;
11     }
12
13     System.out.println("The number is " + number);
14     System.out.println("The sum is " + sum);
15   }
16 }
```

break

```
The number is 14
The sum is 105
```

The program in Listing 4.12 adds integers from **1** to **20** in this order to **sum** until **sum** is greater than or equal to **100**. Without the **if** statement (line 9), the program calculates the sum of the numbers from **1** to **20**. But with the **if** statement, the loop terminates when **sum** becomes greater than or equal to **100**. Without the **if** statement, the output would be:

```
The number is 20
The sum is 210
```

You can also use the **continue** keyword in a loop. When it is encountered, it ends the current iteration and program control goes to the end of the loop body. In other words, **continue** breaks out of an iteration while the **break** keyword breaks out of a loop. Listing 4.13 presents a program to demonstrate the effect of using **continue** in a loop.

continue statement

LISTING 4.13   TestContinue.java

```
1  public class TestContinue {
2    public static void main(String[] args) {
3      int sum = 0;
4      int number = 0;
5
6      while (number < 20) {
7        number++;
8        if (number == 10 || number == 11)
9          continue;
10       sum += number;
11     }
12
13     System.out.println("The sum is " + sum);
14   }
15 }
```

continue

```
The sum is 189
```

The program in Listing 4.13 adds integers from 1 to 20 except 10 and 11 to sum. With the if statement in the program (line 8), the continue statement is executed when number becomes 10 or 11. The continue statement ends the current iteration so that the rest of the statement in the loop body is not executed; therefore, number is not added to sum when it is 10 or 11. Without the if statement in the program, the output would be as follows:

```
The sum is 210
```

In this case, all of the numbers are added to sum, even when number is 10 or 11. Therefore, the result is 210, which is 21 more than it was with the if statement.

Note

The continue statement is always inside a loop. In the while and do-while loops, the loop-continuation-condition is evaluated immediately after the continue statement. In the for loop, the action-after-each-iteration is performed, then the loop-continuation-condition is evaluated, immediately after the continue statement.

You can always write a program without using break or continue in a loop (see Checkpoint Question 4.24). In general, though, using break and continue is appropriate if it simplifies coding and makes programs easier to read.

Suppose you need to write a program to find the smallest factor other than 1 for an integer n (assume n >= 2). You can write a simple and intuitive code using the break statement as follows:

```
int factor = 2;
while (factor <= n) {
  if (n % factor == 0)
    break;
  factor++;
}
```

```
System.out.println("The smallest factor other than 1 for "
  + n + " is " + factor);
```

You may rewrite the code without using break as follows:

```
boolean found = false;
int factor = 2;
while (factor <= n && !found ) {
  if (n % factor == 0)
    found = true;
  else
    factor++;
}
System.out.println("The smallest factor other than 1 for "
  + n + " is " + factor);
```

Obviously, the break statement makes this program simpler and easier to read in this case. However, you should use break and continue with caution. Too many break and continue statements will produce a loop with many exit points and make the program difficult to read.

Note

Some programming languages have a goto statement. The goto statement indiscriminately transfers control to any statement in the program and executes it. This makes your program vulnerable to errors. The break and continue statements in Java are different from goto statements. They operate only in a loop or a switch statement. The break statement breaks out of the loop, and the continue statement breaks out of the current iteration in the loop.

goto

4.22 What is the keyword break for? What is the keyword continue for? Will the following programs terminate? If so, give the output.

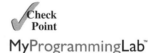

```
int balance = 10;
while (true) {
  if (balance < 9)
    break;
  balance = balance - 9;
}

System.out.println("Balance is "
  + balance);
```
(a)

```
int balance = 10;
while (true) {
  if (balance < 9)
    continue;
  balance = balance - 9;
}

System.out.println("Balance is "
  + balance);
```
(b)

4.23 The for loop on the left is converted into the while loop on the right. What is wrong? Correct it.

```
for (int i = 0; i < 4; i++) {
  if (i % 3 == 0) continue;
  sum += i;
}
```
Converted
→
Wrong conversion
```
int i = 0;
while (i < 4) {
  if (i % 3 == 0) continue;
  sum += i;
  i++;
}
```

4.24 Rewrite the programs `TestBreak` and `TestContinue` in Listings 4.12 and 4.13 without using `break` and `continue`.

4.25 After the `break` statement in (a) is executed in the following loop, which statement is executed? Show the output. After the `continue` statement in (b) is executed in the following loop, which statement is executed? Show the output.

```
for (int i = 1; i < 4; i++) {
  for (int j = 1; j < 4; j++) {
    if (i * j > 2)
      break;

    System.out.println(i * j);
  }

  System.out.println(i);
}
```
(a)

```
for (int i = 1; i < 4; i++) {
  for (int j = 1; j < 4; j++) {
    if (i * j > 2)
      continue;

    System.out.println(i * j);
  }

  System.out.println(i);
}
```
(b)

4.10 Case Study: Displaying Prime Numbers

Key Point

This section presents a program that displays the first fifty prime numbers in five lines, each containing ten numbers.

An integer greater than 1 is *prime* if its only positive divisor is 1 or itself. For example, 2, 3, 5, and 7 are prime numbers, but 4, 6, 8, and 9 are not.

The problem is to display the first 50 prime numbers in five lines, each of which contains ten numbers. The problem can be broken into the following tasks:

- Determine whether a given number is prime.
- For number = 2, 3, 4, 5, 6, ..., test whether it is prime.
- Count the prime numbers.
- Display each prime number, and display ten numbers per line.

Obviously, you need to write a loop and repeatedly test whether a new number is prime. If the number is prime, increase the count by 1. The count is 0 initially. When it reaches 50, the loop terminates.

Here is the algorithm for the problem:

```
Set the number of prime numbers to be printed as
  a constant NUMBER_OF_PRIMES;
Use count to track the number of prime numbers and
  set an initial count to 0;
Set an initial number to 2;

while (count < NUMBER_OF_PRIMES) {
  Test whether number is prime;

  if number is prime {
    Display the prime number and increase the count;
  }

  Increment number by 1;
}
```

To test whether a number is prime, check whether it is divisible by 2, 3, 4, and so on up to number/2. If a divisor is found, the number is not a prime. The algorithm can be described as follows:

```
Use a boolean variable isPrime to denote whether
  the number is prime; Set isPrime to true initially;

for (int divisor = 2; divisor <= number / 2; divisor++) {
  if (number % divisor == 0) {
    Set isPrime to false
    Exit the loop;
  }
}
```

The complete program is given in Listing 4.14.

LISTING 4.14 PrimeNumber.java

```
1  public class PrimeNumber {
2    public static void main(String[] args) {
3      final int NUMBER_OF_PRIMES = 50; // Number of primes to display
4      final int NUMBER_OF_PRIMES_PER_LINE = 10; // Display 10 per line
5      int count = 0; // Count the number of prime numbers
6      int number = 2; // A number to be tested for primeness
7
8      System.out.println("The first 50 prime numbers are \n");
9
10     // Repeatedly find prime numbers
11     while (count < NUMBER_OF_PRIMES) {                              count prime numbers
12       // Assume the number is prime
13       boolean isPrime = true; // Is the current number prime?
14
15       // Test whether number is prime
16       for (int divisor = 2; divisor <= number / 2; divisor++) {    check primeness
17         if (number % divisor == 0) { // If true, number is not prime
18           isPrime = false; // Set isPrime to false
19           break; // Exit the for loop                              exit loop
20         }
21       }
22
23       // Display the prime number and increase the count
24       if (isPrime) {                                               display if prime
25         count++; // Increase the count
26
27         if (count % NUMBER_OF_PRIMES_PER_LINE == 0) {
28           // Display the number and advance to the new line
29           System.out.println(number);
30         }
31         else
32           System.out.print(number + " ");
33       }
34
35       // Check if the next number is prime
36       number++;
37     }
38   }
39 }
```

```
The first 50 prime numbers are
2  3  5  7  11 13 17 19 23 29
31 37 41 43 47 53 59 61 67 71
73 79 83 89 97 101 103 107 109 113
127 131 137 139 149 151 157 163 167 173
179 181 191 193 197 199 211 223 227 229
```

subproblem

This is a complex program for novice programmers. The key to developing a programmatic solution for this problem, and for many other problems, is to break it into subproblems and develop solutions for each of them in turn. Do not attempt to develop a complete solution in the first trial. Instead, begin by writing the code to determine whether a given number is prime, then expand the program to test whether other numbers are prime in a loop.

To determine whether a number is prime, check whether it is divisible by a number between 2 and number/2 inclusive (lines 16–21). If so, it is not a prime number (line 18); otherwise, it is a prime number. For a prime number, display it. If the count is divisible by 10 (lines 27–30), advance to a new line. The program ends when the count reaches 50.

The program uses the **break** statement in line 19 to exit the **for** loop as soon as the number is found to be a nonprime. You can rewrite the loop (lines 16–21) without using the **break** statement, as follows:

```java
for (int divisor = 2; divisor <= number / 2 && isPrime;
    divisor++) {
  // If true, the number is not prime
  if (number % divisor == 0) {
    // Set isPrime to false, if the number is not prime
    isPrime = false;
  }
}
```

However, using the **break** statement makes the program simpler and easier to read in this case.

4.11 Controlling a Loop with a Confirmation Dialog

Key Point

You can use a confirmation dialog to prompt the user to confirm whether to continue or exit a loop.

confirmation dialog

A sentinel-controlled loop can be implemented using a confirmation dialog. The answers *Yes* or *No* continue or terminate the loop. The template of the loop may look as follows:

```java
int option = JOptionPane.YES_OPTION;
while (option == JOptionPane.YES_OPTION) {
  System.out.println("continue loop");
  option = JOptionPane.showConfirmDialog(null, "Continue?");
}
```

Listing 4.15 rewrites Listing 4.5, SentinelValue.java, using a confirmation dialog box. A sample run is shown in Figure 4.4.

LISTING 4.15 SentinelValueUsingConfirmationDialog.java

```java
1  import javax.swing.JOptionPane;
2
3  public class SentinelValueUsingConfirmationDialog {
4    public static void main(String[] args) {
5      int sum = 0;
```

```
6
7        // Keep reading data until the user answers No
8        int option = JOptionPane.YES_OPTION;                              confirmation option
9        while (option == JOptionPane.YES_OPTION) {                        check option
10         // Read the next data
11         String dataString = JOptionPane.showInputDialog(                input dialog
12           "Enter an integer: ");
13         int data = Integer.parseInt(dataString);
14
15         sum += data;
16
17         option = JOptionPane.showConfirmDialog(null, "Continue?");       confirmation dialog
18       }
19
20       JOptionPane.showMessageDialog(null, "The sum is " + sum);         message dialog
21     }
22 }
```

|(a)|(b)|

|(c)|(d)|(e)|

FIGURE 4.4 The user enters 3 in (a), clicks Yes in (b), enters 5 in (c), clicks No in (d), and the result is shown in (e).

The program displays an input dialog to prompt the user to enter an integer (line 11) and adds it to sum (line 15). Line 17 displays a confirmation dialog to let the user decide whether to continue the input. If the user clicks *Yes,* the loop continues; otherwise, the loop exits. Finally, the program displays the result in a message dialog box (line 20).

The showConfirmDialog method (line 17) returns an integer JOptionPane.YES_OPTION, JOptionPane.NO_OPTION, or JOptionPane.CANCEL_OPTION, if the user clicks *Yes, No,* or *Cancel.* The return value is assigned to the variable option (line 17). If this value is JOptionPane.YES_OPTION, the loop continues (line 9).

KEY TERMS

break statement   159
continue statement   159
do-while loop   144
for loop   147
infinite loop   136
input redirection   143
iteration   134
loop   134
loop body   134
nested loop   152
off-by-one error   136
output redirection   143
posttest loop   150
pretest loop   150
sentinel value   141
while loop   134

CHAPTER SUMMARY

1. There are three types of repetition statements: the `while` loop, the `do-while` loop, and the `for` loop.

2. The part of the loop that contains the statements to be repeated is called the *loop body*.

3. A one-time execution of a loop body is referred to as an *iteration of the loop*.

4. An *infinite loop* is a loop statement that executes infinitely.

5. In designing loops, you need to consider both the *loop control structure* and the loop body.

6. The `while` loop checks the `loop-continuation-condition` first. If the condition is `true`, the loop body is executed; if it is `false`, the loop terminates.

7. The `do-while` loop is similar to the `while` loop, except that the `do-while` loop executes the loop body first and then checks the `loop-continuation-condition` to decide whether to continue or to terminate.

8. The `while` loop and the `do-while` loop often are used when the number of repetitions is not predetermined.

9. A *sentinel value* is a special value that signifies the end of the loop.

10. The `for` loop generally is used to execute a loop body a predictable number of times; this number is not determined by the loop body.

11. The `for` loop control has three parts. The first part is an initial action that often initializes a control variable. The second part, the `loop-continuation-condition`, determines whether the loop body is to be executed. The third part is executed after each iteration and is often used to adjust the control variable. Usually, the loop control variables are initialized and changed in the control structure.

12. The `while` loop and `for` loop are called *pretest loops* because the continuation condition is checked before the loop body is executed.

13. The `do-while` loop is called a *posttest loop* because the condition is checked after the loop body is executed.

14. Two keywords, `break` and `continue`, can be used in a loop.

15. The `break` keyword immediately ends the innermost loop, which contains the break.

16. The `continue` keyword only ends the current iteration.

TEST QUESTIONS

Do the test questions for this chapter online at www.cs.armstrong.edu/liang/intro9e/test.html.

MyProgrammingLab™

PROGRAMMING EXERCISES

read and think before coding

Pedagogical Note
Read each problem several times until you understand it. Think how to solve the problem before starting to write code. Translate your logic into a program.

A problem often can be solved in many different ways. Students are encouraged to explore various solutions.

explore solutions

Sections 4.2–4.7

*4.1 (*Count positive and negative numbers and compute the average of numbers*) Write a program that reads an unspecified number of integers, determines how many positive and negative values have been read, and computes the total and average of the input values (not counting zeros). Your program ends with the input **0**. Display the average as a floating-point number. Here is a sample run:

```
Enter an integer, the input ends if it is 0: 1 2 -1 3 0  ↵Enter
The number of positives is 3
The number of negatives is 1
The total is 5
The average is 1.25
```

```
Enter an integer, the input ends if it is 0: 0  ↵Enter
No numbers are entered except 0
```

4.2 (*Repeat additions*) Listing 4.4, SubtractionQuizLoop.java, generates five random subtraction questions. Revise the program to generate ten random addition questions for two integers between **1** and **15**. Display the correct count and test time.

4.3 (*Conversion from kilograms to pounds*) Write a program that displays the following table (note that **1** kilogram is **2.2** pounds):

```
Kilograms       Pounds
1                2.2
3                6.6
...
197             433.4
199             437.8
```

4.4 (*Conversion from miles to kilometers*) Write a program that displays the following table (note that 1 mile is 1.609 kilometers):

```
Miles       Kilometers
1            1.609
2            3.218
...
9           14.481
10          16.090
```

4.5 (*Conversion from kilograms to pounds and pounds to kilograms*) Write a program that displays the following two tables side by side (note that 1 kilogram is 2.2 pounds and that 1 pound is .453 kilograms):

```
Kilograms   Pounds  |   Pounds    Kilograms
1            2.2     |   20         9.09
3            6.6     |   25        11.36
...
197        433.4     |   510      231.82
199        437.8     |   515      234.09
```

4.6 *(Conversion from miles to kilometers)* Write a program that displays the following two tables side by side (note that 1 mile is 1.609 kilometers and that 1 kilometer is .621 miles):

```
Miles        Kilometers  |  Kilometers      Miles
1            1.609       |  20              12.430
2            3.218       |  25              15.538
...
9            14.481      |  60              37.290
10           16.090      |  65              40.398
```

**4.7 *(Financial application: compute future tuition)* Suppose that the tuition for a university is $10,000 this year and increases 5% every year. Write a program that computes the tuition in ten years and the total cost of four years' worth of tuition starting ten years from now.

4.8 *(Find the highest score)* Write a program that prompts the user to enter the number of students and each student's name and score, and finally displays the name of the student with the highest score.

*4.9 *(Find the two highest scores)* Write a program that prompts the user to enter the number of students and each student's name and score, and finally displays the student with the highest score and the student with the second-highest score.

4.10 *(Find numbers divisible by 5 and 6)* Write a program that displays all the numbers from 100 to 1,000, ten per line, that are divisible by 5 and 6. Numbers are separated by exactly one space.

4.11 *(Find numbers divisible by 5 or 6, but not both)* Write a program that displays all the numbers from 100 to 200, ten per line, that are divisible by 5 or 6, but not both. Numbers are separated by exactly one space.

4.12 *(Find the smallest n such that $n^2 > 12,000$)* Use a `while` loop to find the smallest integer n such that n^2 is greater than 12,000.

4.13 *(Find the largest n such that $n^3 < 12,000$)* Use a `while` loop to find the largest integer n such that n^3 is less than 12,000.

Sections 4.8–4.10

*4.14 *(Compute the greatest common divisor)* Another solution for Listing 4.9 to find the greatest common divisor of two integers n1 and n2 is as follows: First find d to be the minimum of n1 and n2, then check whether d, d–1, d–2, ..., 2, or 1 is a divisor for both n1 and n2 in this order. The first such common divisor is the greatest common divisor for n1 and n2. Write a program that prompts the user to enter two positive integers and displays the gcd.

*4.15 *(Display the ASCII character table)* Write a program that prints the characters in the ASCII character table from ! to ~. Display ten characters per line. The ASCII table is shown in Appendix B. Characters are separated by exactly one space.

*4.16 *(Find the factors of an integer)* Write a program that reads an integer and displays all its smallest factors in increasing order. For example, if the input integer is 120, the output should be as follows: 2, 2, 2, 3, 5.

**4.17 *(Display pyramid)* Write a program that prompts the user to enter an integer from 1 to 15 and displays a pyramid, as shown in the following sample run:

```
Enter the number of lines: 7  ↵Enter
                                  1
                              2   1   2
                          3   2   1   2   3
                      4   3   2   1   2   3   4
                  5   4   3   2   1   2   3   4   5
              6   5   4   3   2   1   2   3   4   5   6
          7   6   5   4   3   2   1   2   3   4   5   6   7
```

*4.18 (*Display four patterns using loops*) Use nested loops that display the following patterns in four separate programs:

```
Pattern A           Pattern B           Pattern C           Pattern D
1                   1 2 3 4 5 6                       1     1 2 3 4 5 6
1 2                 1 2 3 4 5                        2 1      1 2 3 4 5
1 2 3               1 2 3 4                         3 2 1       1 2 3 4
1 2 3 4             1 2 3                          4 3 2 1        1 2 3
1 2 3 4 5           1 2                           5 4 3 2 1         1 2
1 2 3 4 5 6         1                           6 5 4 3 2 1           1
```

4.19 (*Display numbers in a pyramid pattern*) Write a nested **for loop that prints the following output:

```
                              1
                          1   2   1
                      1   2   4   2   1
                  1   2   4   8   4   2   1
              1   2   4   8  16   8   4   2   1
          1   2   4   8  16  32  16   8   4   2   1
      1   2   4   8  16  32  64  32  16   8   4   2   1
  1   2   4   8  16  32  64 128  64  32  16   8   4   2   1
```

*4.20 (*Display prime numbers between 2 and 1,000*) Modify Listing 4.14 to display all the prime numbers between 2 and 1,000, inclusive. Display eight prime numbers per line. Numbers are separated by exactly one space.

Comprehensive

**4.21 (*Financial application: compare loans with various interest rates*) Write a program that lets the user enter the loan amount and loan period in number of years and displays the monthly and total payments for each interest rate starting from 5% to 8%, with an increment of 1/8. Here is a sample run:

```
Loan Amount: 10000  ↵Enter
Number of Years: 5  ↵Enter
Interest Rate    Monthly Payment    Total Payment

5.000%           188.71             11322.74
5.125%           189.28             11357.13
5.250%           189.85             11391.59
...
7.875%           202.17             12129.97
8.000%           202.76             12165.83
```

For the formula to compute monthly payment, see Listing 2.8, ComputeLoan.java.

VideoNote
Display loan schedule

**4.22 (*Financial application: loan amortization schedule*) The monthly payment for a given loan pays the principal and the interest. The monthly interest is computed by multiplying the monthly interest rate and the balance (the remaining principal). The principal paid for the month is therefore the monthly payment minus the monthly interest. Write a program that lets the user enter the loan amount, number of years, and interest rate and displays the amortization schedule for the loan. Here is a sample run:

```
Loan Amount: 10000  ↵Enter
Number of Years: 1  ↵Enter
Annual Interest Rate: 7  ↵Enter

Monthly Payment: 865.26
Total Payment: 10383.21

Payment#      Interest      Principal      Balance
1             58.33         806.93         9193.07
2             53.62         811.64         8381.43
...
11            10.0          855.26          860.27
12             5.01         860.25            0.01
```

> **Note**
> The balance after the last payment may not be zero. If so, the last payment should be the normal monthly payment plus the final balance.

Hint: Write a loop to display the table. Since the monthly payment is the same for each month, it should be computed before the loop. The balance is initially the loan amount. For each iteration in the loop, compute the interest and principal, and update the balance. The loop may look like this:

```
for (i = 1; i <= numberOfYears * 12; i++) {
  interest = monthlyInterestRate * balance;
  principal = monthlyPayment - interest;
  balance = balance - principal;
  System.out.println(i + "\t\t" + interest
    + "\t\t" + principal + "\t\t" + balance);
}
```

*4.23 (*Obtain more accurate results*) In computing the following series, you will obtain more accurate results by computing from right to left rather than from left to right:

$$1 + \frac{1}{2} + \frac{1}{3} + \ldots + \frac{1}{n}$$

Write a program that computes the results of the summation of the preceding series from left to right and from right to left with **n = 50000**.

*4.24 (*Sum a series*) Write a program to sum the following series:

$$\frac{1}{3} + \frac{3}{5} + \frac{5}{7} + \frac{7}{9} + \frac{9}{11} + \frac{11}{13} + \ldots + \frac{95}{97} + \frac{97}{99}$$

VideoNote
Sum a series

**4.25 (*Compute π*) You can approximate π by using the following series:

$$\pi = 4\left(1 - \frac{1}{3} + \frac{1}{5} - \frac{1}{7} + \frac{1}{9} - \frac{1}{11} + \cdots + \frac{(-1)^{i+1}}{2i - 1}\right)$$

Write a program that displays the π value for i = 10000, 20000, ..., and 100000.

**4.26 (*Compute e*) You can approximate e using the following series:

$$e = 1 + \frac{1}{1!} + \frac{1}{2!} + \frac{1}{3!} + \frac{1}{4!} + \cdots + \frac{1}{i!}$$

Write a program that displays the e value for i = 10000, 20000, ..., and 100000. (*Hint*: Because $i! = i \times (i - 1) \times \cdots \times 2 \times 1$, then

$$\frac{1}{i!} \text{ is } \frac{1}{i(i - 1)!}$$

Initialize e and item to be 1 and keep adding a new item to e. The new item is the previous item divided by i for i = 2, 3, 4, ...)

**4.27 (*Display leap years*) Write a program that displays all the leap years, ten per line, in the twenty-first century (from 2001 to 2100), separated by exactly one space.

**4.28 (*Display the first days of each month*) Write a program that prompts the user to enter the year and first day of the year, and displays the first day of each month in the year on the console. For example, if the user entered the year 2013, and 2 for Tuesday, January 1, 2013, your program should display the following output:

```
January 1, 2013 is Tuesday
...
December 1, 2013 is Sunday
```

**4.29 (*Display calendars*) Write a program that prompts the user to enter the year and first day of the year and displays the calendar table for the year on the console. For example, if the user entered the year 2013, and 2 for Tuesday, January 1, 2013, your program should display the calendar for each month in the year, as follows:

January 2013						
Sun	Mon	Tue	Wed	Thu	Fri	Sat
		1	2	3	4	5
6	7	8	9	10	11	12
13	14	15	16	17	18	19
20	21	22	23	24	25	26
27	28	29	30	31		

.
.
.

December 2013						
Sun	Mon	Tue	Wed	Thu	Fri	Sat
1	2	3	4	5	6	7
8	9	10	11	12	13	14
15	16	17	18	19	20	21
22	23	24	25	26	27	28
29	30	31				

*4.30 (*Financial application: compound value*) Suppose you save $100 *each* month into a savings account with the annual interest rate 5%. So, the monthly interest rate is `0.05 / 12 = 0.00417`. After the first month, the value in the account becomes

$$100 * (1 + 0.00417) = 100.417$$

After the second month, the value in the account becomes

$$(100 + 100.417) * (1 + 0.00417) = 201.252$$

After the third month, the value in the account becomes

$$(100 + 201.252) * (1 + 0.00417) = 302.507$$

and so on.

Write a program that prompts the user to enter an amount (e.g., **100**), the annual interest rate (e.g., **5**), and the number of months (e.g., **6**) and displays the amount in the savings account after the given month.

*4.31 (*Financial application: compute CD value*) Suppose you put $10,000 into a CD with an annual percentage yield of 5.75%. After one month, the CD is worth

$$10000 + 10000 * 5.75 / 1200 = 10047.91$$

After two months, the CD is worth

$$10047.91 + 10047.91 * 5.75 / 1200 = 10096.06$$

After three months, the CD is worth

$$10096.06 + 10096.06 * 5.75 / 1200 = 10144.43$$

and so on.

Write a program that prompts the user to enter an amount (e.g., **10000**), the annual percentage yield (e.g., **5.75**), and the number of months (e.g., **18**) and displays a table as shown in the sample run.

```
Enter the initial deposit amount: 10000  ↵Enter
Enter annual percentage yield: 5.75  ↵Enter
Enter maturity period (number of months): 18  ↵Enter

Month  CD Value
1      10047.91
2      10096.06
...
17     10846.56
18     10898.54
```

**4.32 (*Game: lottery*) Revise Listing 3.9, Lottery.java, to generate a lottery of a two-digit number. The two digits in the number are distinct. (*Hint*: Generate the first digit. Use a loop to continuously generate the second digit until it is different from the first digit.)

**4.33 (*Perfect number*) A positive integer is called a *perfect number* if it is equal to the sum of all of its positive divisors, excluding itself. For example, 6 is the first perfect number because 6 = 3 + 2 + 1. The next is 28 = 14 + 7 + 4 + 2 + 1. There are four perfect numbers less than 10,000. Write a program to find all these four numbers.

***4.34 (*Game: scissor, rock, paper*) Exercise 3.17 gives a program that plays the scissor-rock-paper game. Revise the program to let the user continuously play until either the user or the computer wins more than two times.

*4.35 (*Summation*) Write a program to compute the following summation.

$$\frac{1}{1 + \sqrt{2}} + \frac{1}{\sqrt{2} + \sqrt{3}} + \frac{1}{\sqrt{3} + \sqrt{4}} + \dots + \frac{1}{\sqrt{624} + \sqrt{625}}$$

**4.36 (*Business application: checking ISBN*) Use loops to simplify Exercise 3.9.

**4.37 (*Decimal to binary*) Write a program that prompts the user to enter a decimal integer and displays its corresponding binary value. Don't use Java's `Integer.toBinaryString(int)` in this program.

**4.38 (*Decimal to hex*) Write a program that prompts the user to enter a decimal integer and displays its corresponding hexadecimal value. Don't use Java's `Integer.toHexString(int)` in this program.

*4.39 (*Financial application: find the sales amount*) You have just started a sales job in a department store. Your pay consists of a base salary and a commission. The base salary is \$5,000. The scheme shown below is used to determine the commission rate.

Sales Amount	Commission Rate
\$0.01–\$5,000	8 percent
\$5,000.01–\$10,000	10 percent
\$10,000.01 and above	12 percent

Your goal is to earn \$30,000 a year. Write a program that finds out the minimum number of sales you have to generate in order to make \$30,000.

4.40 (*Simulation: heads or tails*) Write a program that simulates flipping a coin one million times and displays the number of heads and tails.

**4.41 (*Occurrence of max numbers*) Write a program that reads integers, finds the largest of them, and counts its occurrences. Assume that the input ends with number 0. Suppose that you entered 3 5 2 5 5 5 0; the program finds that the largest is 5 and the occurrence count for 5 is 4.

(*Hint*: Maintain two variables, `max` and `count`. `max` stores the current max number, and `count` stores its occurrences. Initially, assign the first number to `max` and 1 to `count`. Compare each subsequent number with `max`. If the number is greater than `max`, assign it to `max` and reset `count` to 1. If the number is equal to `max`, increment `count` by 1.)

```
Enter numbers: 3 5 2 5 5 5 0  ↵Enter
The largest number is 5
The occurrence count of the largest number is 4
```

*4.42   (*Financial application: find the sales amount*) Rewrite Exercise 4.39 as follows:
- Use a `for` loop instead of a `do-while` loop.
- Let the user enter `COMMISSION_SOUGHT` instead of fixing it as a constant.

*4.43   (*Simulation: clock countdown*) Write a program that prompts the user to enter the number of seconds, displays a message at every second, and terminates when the time expires. Here is a sample run:

```
Enter the number of seconds: 3 ⏎Enter
2 seconds remaining
1 second remaining
Stopped
```

**4.44   (*Monte Carlo simulation*) A square is divided into four smaller regions as shown below in (a). If you throw a dart into the square 1,000,000 times, what is the probability for a dart to fall into an odd-numbered region? Write a program to simulate the process and display the result.

(*Hint*: Place the center of the square in the center of a coordinate system, as shown in (b). Randomly generate a point in the square and count the number of times for a point to fall into an odd-numbered region.)

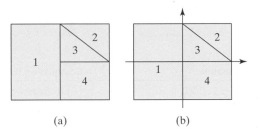

(a)   (b)

*4.45   (*Math: combinations*) Write a program that displays all possible combinations for picking two numbers from integers 1 to 7. Also display the total number of all combinations.

```
1 2
1 3
...
...

The total number of all combinations is 21
```

*4.46   (*Computer architecture: bit-level operations*) A `short` value is stored in 16 bits. Write a program that prompts the user to enter a short integer and displays the 16 bits for the integer. Here are sample runs:

```
Enter an integer: 5 ⏎Enter
The bits are 0000000000000101
```

```
Enter an integer: -5  ↵Enter
The bits are 1111111111111011
```

(*Hint*: You need to use the bitwise right shift operator (>>) and the bitwise AND operator (&), which are covered in Appendix G, Bitwise Operations.)

**4.47 (*Statistics: compute mean and standard deviation*) In business applications, you are often asked to compute the mean and standard deviation of data. The mean is simply the average of the numbers. The standard deviation is a statistic that tells you how tightly all the various data are clustered around the mean in a set of data. For example, what is the average age of the students in a class? How close are the ages? If all the students are the same age, the deviation is 0.

Write a program that prompts the user to enter ten numbers, and displays the mean and standard deviations of these numbers using the following formula:

$$mean = \frac{\sum_{i=1}^{n} x_i}{n} = \frac{x_1 + x_2 + \ldots + x_n}{n} \qquad deviation = \sqrt{\frac{\sum_{i=1}^{n} x_i^2 - \frac{\left(\sum_{i=1}^{n} x_i\right)^2}{n}}{n - 1}}$$

Here is a sample run:

```
Enter ten numbers: 1 2 3 4.5 5.6 6 7 8 9 10  ↵Enter
The mean is 5.61
The standard deviation is 2.99794
```

METHODS

Objectives

- To define methods with formal parameters (§5.2).

- To invoke methods with actual parameters (i.e., arguments) (§5.2).

- To define methods with a return value (§5.3).

- To define methods without a return value (§5.4).

- To pass arguments by value (§5.5).

- To develop reusable code that is modular, easy to read, easy to debug, and easy to maintain (§5.6).

- To write a method that converts decimals to hexadecimals (§5.7).

- To use method overloading and understand ambiguous overloading (§5.8).

- To determine the scope of variables (§5.9).

- To solve mathematics problems using the methods in the `Math` class (§§5.10–5.11).

- To apply the concept of method abstraction in software development (§5.12).

- To design and implement methods using stepwise refinement (§5.12).

5.1 Introduction

Methods can be used to define reusable code and organize and simplify code.

problem

Suppose that you need to find the sum of integers from 1 to 10, from 20 to 37, and from 35 to 49, respectively. You may write the code as follows:

```
int sum = 0;
for (int i = 1; i <= 10; i++)
  sum += i;
System.out.println("Sum from 1 to 10 is " + sum);

sum = 0;
for (int i = 20; i <= 37; i++)
  sum += i;
System.out.println("Sum from 20 to 37 is " + sum);

sum = 0;
for (int i = 35; i <= 49; i++)
  sum += i;
System.out.println("Sum from 35 to 49 is " + sum);
```

why methods?

You may have observed that computing these sums from 1 to 10, from 20 to 37, and from 35 to 49 are very similar except that the starting and ending integers are different. Wouldn't it be nice if we could write the common code once and reuse it? We can do so by defining a method and invoking it.

The preceding code can be simplified as follows:

define sum method

```
1  public static int sum(int i1, int i2) {
2    int result = 0;
3    for (int i = i1; i <= i2; i++)
4      result += i;
5
6    return result;
7  }
8
9  public static void main(String[] args) {
10   System.out.println("Sum from 1 to 10 is " + sum(1, 10));
11   System.out.println("Sum from 20 to 37 is " + sum(20, 37));
12   System.out.println("Sum from 35 to 49 is " + sum(35, 49));
13 }
```

main method
invoke sum

Lines 1–7 define the method named `sum` with two parameters `i1` and `i2`. The statements in the `main` method invoke `sum(1, 10)` to compute the sum from 1 to 10, `sum(20, 37)` to compute the sum from 20 to 37, and `sum(35, 49)` to compute the sum from 35 to 49.

method

A *method* is a collection of statements grouped together to perform an operation. In earlier chapters you have used predefined methods such as `System.out.println`, `JOptionPane.showMessageDialog`, `System.exit`, `Math.pow`, and `Math.random`. These methods are defined in the Java library. In this chapter, you will learn how to define your own methods and apply method abstraction to solve complex problems.

5.2 Defining a Method

A method definition consists of its method name, parameters, return value type, and body.

The syntax for defining a method is:

```
modifier returnValueType methodName(list of parameters) {
  // Method body;
}
```

Let's look at a method defined to find the larger between two integers. This method, named `max`, has two `int` parameters, `num1` and `num2`, the larger of which is returned by the method. Figure 5.1 illustrates the components of this method.

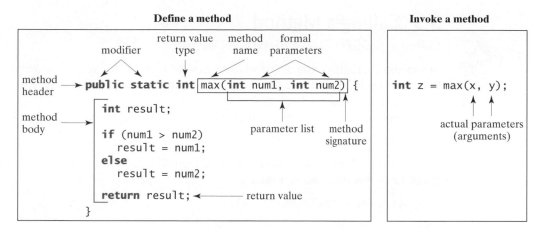

FIGURE 5.1 A method definition consists of a method header and a method body.

The *method header* specifies the *modifiers*, *return value type*, *method name*, and *parameters* of the method. The `static` modifier is used for all the methods in this chapter. The reason for using it will be discussed in Chapter 8, Objects and Classes.

method header
modifier

A method may return a value. The `returnValueType` is the data type of the value the method returns. Some methods perform desired operations without returning a value. In this case, the `returnValueType` is the keyword `void`. For example, the `returnValueType` is `void` in the `main` method, as well as in `System.exit`, `System.out.println`, and `JOptionPane.showMessageDialog`. If a method returns a value, it is called a *value-returning method*, otherwise it is called a *void method*.

value-returning method
void method

The variables defined in the method header are known as *formal parameters* or simply *parameters*. A parameter is like a placeholder: When a method is invoked, you pass a value to the parameter. This value is referred to as an *actual parameter or argument*. The *parameter list* refers to the method's type, order, and number of the parameters. The method name and the parameter list together constitute the *method signature*. Parameters are optional; that is, a method doesn't have to contain any parameters. For example, the `Math.random()` method has no parameters.

formal parameter
parameter
actual parameter
argument
parameter list
method signature

The method body contains a collection of statements that implement the method. The method body of the `max` method uses an `if` statement to determine which number is larger and return the value of that number. In order for a value-returning method to return a result, a return statement using the keyword `return` is *required*. The method terminates when a return statement is executed.

Note

Some programming languages refer to methods as *procedures* and *functions*. In those languages, a value-returning method is called a *function* and a void method is called a *procedure*.

Caution

In the method header, you need to declare each parameter separately. For instance, `max(int num1, int num2)` is correct, but `max(int num1, num2)` is wrong.

define vs. declare

Note

We say "*define* a method" and "*declare* a variable." We are making a subtle distinction here. A definition defines what the defined item is, but a declaration usually involves allocating memory to store data for the declared item.

5.3 Calling a Method

Key
Point

Calling a method executes the code in the method.

In a method definition, you define what the method is to do. To execute the method, you have to *call* or *invoke* it. There are two ways to call a method, depending on whether the method returns a value or not.

If a method returns a value, a call to the method is usually treated as a value. For example,

```java
int larger = max(3, 4);
```

calls `max(3, 4)` and assigns the result of the method to the variable `larger`. Another example of a call that is treated as a value is

```java
System.out.println(max(3, 4));
```

which prints the return value of the method call `max(3, 4)`.

If a method returns `void`, a call to the method must be a statement. For example, the method `println` returns `void`. The following call is a statement:

```java
System.out.println("Welcome to Java!");
```

Note

A value-returning method can also be invoked as a statement in Java. In this case, the caller simply ignores the return value. This is not often done, but it is permissible if the caller is not interested in the return value.

When a program calls a method, program control is transferred to the called method. A called method returns control to the caller when its return statement is executed or when its method-ending closing brace is reached.

Listing 5.1 shows a complete program that is used to test the `max` method.

LISTING 5.1   TestMax.java

VideoNote

Define/invoke `max` method

main method

invoke max

define method

```java
 1  public class TestMax {
 2    /** Main method */
 3    public static void main(String[] args) {
 4      int i = 5;
 5      int j = 2;
 6      int k = max(i, j);
 7      System.out.println("The maximum of " + i +
 8        " and " + j + " is " + k);
 9    }
10
11    /** Return the max of two numbers */
12    public static int max(int num1, int num2) {
13      int result;
14
15      if (num1 > num2)
16        result = num1;
17      else
18        result = num2;
19
20      return result;
21    }
22  }
```

```
The maximum of 5 and 2 is 5
```

	line#	i	j	k	num1	num2	result
	4	5					
	5		2				
Invoking max	12				5	2	
	13						undefined
	16						5
	6			5			

This program contains the `main` method and the `max` method. The `main` method is just like any other method except that it is invoked by the JVM to start the program.   **main method**

The `main` method's header is always the same. Like the one in this example, it includes the modifiers `public` and `static`, return value type `void`, method name `main`, and a parameter of the `String[]` type. `String[]` indicates that the parameter is an array of `String`, a subject addressed in Chapter 6.

The statements in `main` may invoke other methods that are defined in the class that contains the `main` method or in other classes. In this example, the `main` method invokes `max(i, j)`, which is defined in the same class with the `main` method.

When the `max` method is invoked (line 6), variable `i`'s value `5` is passed to `num1`, and variable `j`'s value `2` is passed to `num2` in the `max` method. The flow of control transfers to the `max` method, and the `max` method is executed. When the `return` statement in the `max` method is executed, the `max` method returns the control to its caller (in this case the caller is the `main` method). This process is illustrated in Figure 5.2.   **max method**

pass the value `i`

pass the value `j`

```
public static void main(String[] args) {
   int i = 5;
   int j = 2;
   int k = max(i, j);

   System.out.println(
      "The maximum of " + i +
      " and " + j + " is " + k);
}
```

```
public static int max(int num1, int num2) {
   int result;

   if (num1 > num2)
      result = num1;
   else
      result = num2;

   return result;
}
```

FIGURE 5.2 When the `max` method is invoked, the flow of control transfers to it. Once the `max` method is finished, it returns control back to the caller.

Caution

A `return` statement is required for a value-returning method. The method shown below in (a) is logically correct, but it has a compile error because the Java compiler thinks that this method might not return a value.

```
public static int sign(int n) {
  if (n > 0)
    return 1;
  else if (n == 0)
    return 0;
  else if (n < 0)
    return -1;
}
```

Should be →

```
public static int sign(int n) {
  if (n > 0)
    return 1;
  else if (n == 0)
    return 0;
  else
    return -1;
}
```

(a)   (b)

To fix this problem, delete `if (n < 0)` in (a), so the compiler will see a `return` statement to be reached regardless of how the `if` statement is evaluated.

reusing method

Note
Methods enable code sharing and reuse. The `max` method can be invoked from any class, not just `TestMax`. If you create a new class, you can invoke the `max` method using `ClassName.methodName` (i.e., `TestMax.max`).

activation record

call stack

Each time a method is invoked, the system creates an *activation record* (also called an *activation frame*) that stores parameters and variables for the method and places the activation record in an area of memory known as a *call stack*. A call stack is also known as an *execution stack*, *runtime stack*, or *machine stack*, and it is often shortened to just "the stack." When a method calls another method, the caller's activation record is kept intact, and a new activation record is created for the new method called. When a method finishes its work and returns to its caller, its activation record is removed from the call stack.

A call stack stores the activation records in a last-in, first-out fashion: The activation record for the method that is invoked last is removed first from the stack. For example, suppose method `m1` calls method `m2`, and then `m3`. The runtime system pushes `m1`'s activation record into the stack, then `m2`'s, and then `m3`'s. After `m3` is finished, its activation record is removed from the stack. After `m2` is finished, its activation record is removed from the stack. After `m1` is finished, its activation record is removed from the stack.

Understanding call stacks helps you to comprehend how methods are invoked. The variables defined in the `main` method in Listing 5.1 are `i`, `j`, and `k`. The variables defined in the `max` method are `num1`, `num2`, and `result`. The variables `num1` and `num2` are defined in the method signature and are parameters of the `max` method. Their values are passed through method invocation. Figure 5.3 illustrates the activation records for method calls in the stack.

(a) The `main` method is invoked.

(b) The `max` method is invoked.

(c) The `max` method is being executed.

(d) The `max` method is finished and the return value is sent to k.

(e) The `main` method is finished.

FIGURE 5.3 When the `max` method is invoked, the flow of control transfers to the `max` method. Once the `max` method is finished, it returns control back to the caller.

5.4 **void** Method Example

A void *method does not return a value.*

The preceding section gives an example of a value-returning method. This section shows how to define and invoke a void method. Listing 5.2 gives a program that defines a method named printGrade and invokes it to print the grade for a given score.

LISTING 5.2   TestVoidMethod.java

```java
1  public class TestVoidMethod {
2    public static void main(String[] args) {
3      System.out.print("The grade is ");
4      printGrade(78.5);
5
6      System.out.print("The grade is ");
7      printGrade(59.5);
8    }
9
10   public static void printGrade(double score) {
11     if (score >= 90.0) {
12       System.out.println('A');
13     }
14     else if (score >= 80.0) {
15       System.out.println('B');
16     }
17     else if (score >= 70.0) {
18       System.out.println('C');
19     }
20     else if (score >= 60.0) {
21       System.out.println('D');
22     }
23     else {
24       System.out.println('F');
25     }
26   }
27 }
```

main method

invoke printGrade

printGrade method

```
The grade is C
The grade is F
```

The printGrade method is a void method because it does not return any value. A call to a void method must be a statement. Therefore, it is invoked as a statement in line 4 in the main method. Like any Java statement, it is terminated with a semicolon.

invoke void method

To see the differences between a void and value-returning method, let's redesign the printGrade method to return a value. The new method, which we call getGrade, returns the grade as shown in Listing 5.3.

void vs. value-returned

LISTING 5.3   TestReturnGradeMethod.java

```java
1  public class TestReturnGradeMethod {
2    public static void main(String[] args) {
3      System.out.print("The grade is " + getGrade(78.5));
4      System.out.print("\nThe grade is " + getGrade(59.5));
5    }
6
```

main method

invoke getGrade

getGrade method

```
7    public static char getGrade(double score) {
8      if (score >= 90.0)
9        return 'A';
10     else if (score >= 80.0)
11       return 'B';
12     else if (score >= 70.0)
13       return 'C';
14     else if (score >= 60.0)
15       return 'D';
16     else
17       return 'F';
18   }
19 }
```

```
The grade is C
The grade is F
```

The **getGrade** method defined in lines 7–18 returns a character grade based on the numeric score value. The caller invokes this method in lines 3–4.

The **getGrade** method can be invoked by a caller wherever a character may appear. The **printGrade** method does not return any value, so it must be invoked as a statement.

Note

return in void method

A **return** statement is not needed for a **void** method, but it can be used for terminating the method and returning to the method's caller. The syntax is simply

```
return;
```

This is not often done, but sometimes it is useful for circumventing the normal flow of control in a **void** method. For example, the following code has a return statement to terminate the method when the score is invalid.

```
public static void printGrade(double score) {
  if (score < 0 || score > 100) {
    System.out.println("Invalid score");
    return;
  }

  if (score >= 90.0) {
    System.out.println('A');
  }
  else if (score >= 80.0) {
    System.out.println('B');
  }
  else if (score >= 70.0) {
    System.out.println('C');
  }
  else if (score >= 60.0) {
    System.out.println('D');
  }
  else {
    System.out.println('F');
  }
}
```

5.1 What are the benefits of using a method?

5.2 How do you define a method? How do you invoke a method?

5.3 How do you simplify the `max` method in Listing 5.1 using the conditional operator?

5.4 True or false? A call to a method with a `void` return type is always a statement itself, but a call to a value-returning method cannot be a statement by itself.

5.5 What is the `return` type of a `main` method?

5.6 What would be wrong with not writing a `return` statement in a value-returning method? Can you have a `return` statement in a `void` method? Does the `return` statement in the following method cause syntax errors?

```
public static void xMethod(double x, double y) {
  System.out.println(x + y);
  return x + y;
}
```

5.7 Define the terms parameter, argument, and method signature.

5.8 Write method headers (not the bodies) for the following methods:

a. Compute a sales commission, given the sales amount and the commission rate.

b. Display the calendar for a month, given the month and year.

c. Compute a square root of a number.

d. Test whether a number is even, and returning `true` if it is.

e. Display a message a specified number of times.

f. Compute the monthly payment, given the loan amount, number of years, and annual interest rate.

g. Find the corresponding uppercase letter, given a lowercase letter.

5.9 Identify and correct the errors in the following program:

```
1  public class Test {
2    public static method1(int n, m) {
3      n += m;
4      method2(3.4);
5    }
6
7    public static int method2(int n) {
8      if (n > 0) return 1;
9      else if (n == 0) return 0;
10     else if (n < 0) return -1;
11    }
12 }
```

5.10 Reformat the following program according to the programming style and documentation guidelines proposed in Section 1.10, Programming Style and Documentation. Use the next-line brace style.

```
public class Test {
  public static double method1(double i, double j)
  {
  while (i < j) {
    j--;
  }

  return j;
  }
}
```

5.5 Passing Parameters by Values

Key Point

The arguments are passed by value to parameters when invoking a method.

The power of a method is its ability to work with parameters. You can use `println` to print any string and `max` to find the maximum of any two `int` values. When calling a method, you need to provide arguments, which must be given in the same order as their respective parameters in the method signature. This is known as *parameter order association*. For example, the following method prints a message `n` times:

parameter order association

```
public static void nPrintln(String message, int n) {
  for (int i = 0; i < n; i++)
    System.out.println(message);
}
```

You can use `nPrintln("Hello", 3)` to print `Hello` three times. The `nPrintln("Hello", 3)` statement passes the actual string parameter `Hello` to the parameter `message`, passes `3` to `n`, and prints `Hello` three times. However, the statement `nPrintln(3, "Hello")` would be wrong. The data type of `3` does not match the data type for the first parameter, `message`, nor does the second argument, `Hello`, match the second parameter, `n`.

Caution

The arguments must match the parameters in *order, number,* and *compatible type,* as defined in the method signature. Compatible type means that you can pass an argument to a parameter without explicit casting, such as passing an `int` value argument to a `double` value parameter.

When you invoke a method with an argument, the value of the argument is passed to the parameter. This is referred to as *pass-by-value*. If the argument is a variable rather than a literal value, the value of the variable is passed to the parameter. The variable is not affected, regardless of the changes made to the parameter inside the method. As shown in Listing 5.4, the value of `x` (`1`) is passed to the parameter `n` to invoke the `increment` method (line 5). The parameter `n` is incremented by `1` in the method (line 10), but `x` is not changed no matter what the method does.

pass-by-value

LISTING 5.4 Increment.java

```
1  public class Increment {
2    public static void main(String[] args) {
3      int x = 1;
4      System.out.println("Before the call, x is " + x);
5      increment(x);
6      System.out.println("After the call, x is " + x);
7    }
8
9    public static void increment(int n) {
10     n++;
11     System.out.println("n inside the method is " + n);
12   }
13 }
```

invoke increment

increment n

```
Before the call, x is 1
n inside the method is 2?
After the call, x is 1
```

Listing 5.5 gives another program that demonstrates the effect of passing by value. The program creates a method for swapping two variables. The **swap** method is invoked by passing two arguments. Interestingly, the values of the arguments are not changed after the method is invoked.

LISTING 5.5 TestPassByValue.java

```
1  public class TestPassByValue {
2    /** Main method */
3    public static void main(String[] args) {
4      // Declare and initialize variables
5      int num1 = 1;
6      int num2 = 2;
7
8      System.out.println("Before invoking the swap method, num1 is " +
9        num1 + " and num2 is " + num2);
10
11      // Invoke the swap method to attempt to swap two variables
12      swap(num1, num2);                                              false swap
13
14      System.out.println("After invoking the swap method, num1 is " +
15        num1 + " and num2 is " + num2);
16    }
17
18    /** Swap two variables */
19    public static void swap(int n1, int n2) {
20      System.out.println("\tInside the swap method");
21      System.out.println("\t\tBefore swapping, n1 is " + n1
22        + " and n2 is " + n2);
23
24      // Swap n1 with n2
25      int temp = n1;
26      n1 = n2;
27      n2 = temp;
28
29      System.out.println("\t\tAfter swapping, n1 is " + n1
30        + " and n2 is " + n2);
31    }
32  }
```

```
Before invoking the swap method, num1 is 1 and num2 is 2
  Inside the swap method
    Before swapping, n1 is 1 and n2 is 2
    After swapping, n1 is 2 and n2 is 1
After invoking the swap method, num1 is 1 and num2 is 2
```

Before the **swap** method is invoked (line 12), **num1** is 1 and **num2** is 2. After the **swap** method is invoked, **num1** is still 1 and **num2** is still 2. Their values have not been swapped. As shown in Figure 5.4, the values of the arguments **num1** and **num2** are passed to **n1** and **n2**, but **n1** and **n2** have their own memory locations independent of **num1** and **num2**. Therefore, changes in **n1** and **n2** do not affect the contents of **num1** and **num2**.

Another twist is to change the parameter name **n1** in **swap** to **num1**. What effect does this have? No change occurs, because it makes no difference whether the parameter and the argument have the same name. The parameter is a variable in the method with its own memory space. The variable is allocated when the method is invoked, and it disappears when the method is returned to its caller.

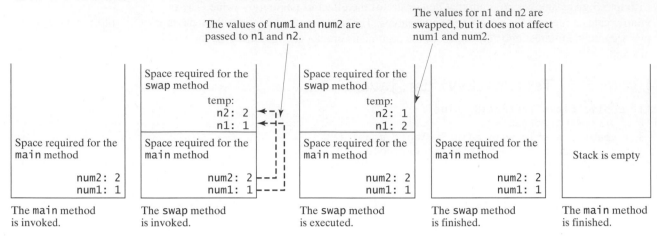

FIGURE 5.4 The values of the variables are passed to the method's parameters.

Note

For simplicity, Java programmers often say *passing x to y*, which actually means *passing the value of argument x to parameter y*.

5.11 How is an argument passed to a method? Can the argument have the same name as its parameter?

5.12 Identify and correct the errors in the following program:

```
1   public class Test {
2     public static void main(String[] args) {
3       nPrintln(5, "Welcome to Java!");
4     }
5
6     public static void nPrintln(String message, int n) {
7       int n = 1;
8       for (int i = 0; i < n; i++)
9         System.out.println(message);
10    }
11  }
```

5.13 What is pass-by-value? Show the result of the following programs.

```
public class Test {
  public static void main(String[] args) {
    int max = 0;
    max(1, 2, max);
    System.out.println(max);
  }

  public static void max(
      int value1, int value2, int max) {
    if (value1 > value2)
      max = value1;
    else
      max = value2;
  }
}
```

(a)

```
public class Test {
  public static void main(String[] args) {
    int i = 1;
    while (i <= 6) {
      method1(i, 2);
      i++;
    }
  }

  public static void method1(
      int i, int num) {
    for (int j = 1; j <= i; j++) {
      System.out.print(num + " ");
      num *= 2;
    }

    System.out.println();
  }
}
```

(b)

```
public class Test {
  public static void main(String[] args) {
    // Initialize times
    int times = 3;
    System.out.println("Before the call,"
      + " variable times is " + times);

    // Invoke nPrintln and display times
    nPrintln("Welcome to Java!", times);
    System.out.println("After the call,"
      + " variable times is " + times);
  }

  // Print the message n times
  public static void nPrintln(
      String message, int n) {
    while (n > 0) {
      System.out.println("n = " + n);
      System.out.println(message);
      n--;
    }
  }
}
```

(c)

```
public class Test {
  public static void main(String[] args) {
    int i = 0;
    while (i <= 4) {
      method1(i);
      i++;
    }

    System.out.println("i is " + i);
  }

  public static void method1(int i) {
    do {
      if (i % 3 != 0)
        System.out.print(i + " ");
      i--;
    }
    while (i >= 1);

    System.out.println();
  }
}
```

(d)

5.14 For (a) in the preceding question, show the contents of the activation records in the call stack just before the method `max` is invoked, just as `max` is entered, just before `max` is returned, and right after `max` is returned.

5.6 Modularizing Code

Modularizing makes the code easy to maintain and debug and enables the code to be reused.

Key Point

Methods can be used to reduce redundant code and enable code reuse. Methods can also be used to modularize code and improve the quality of the program.

Listing 4.9 gives a program that prompts the user to enter two integers and displays their greatest common divisor. You can rewrite the program using a method, as shown in Listing 5.6.

VideoNote

Modularize code

LISTING 5.6 GreatestCommonDivisorMethod.java

```
1  import java.util.Scanner;
2
3  public class GreatestCommonDivisorMethod {
4    /** Main method */
5    public static void main(String[] args) {
6      // Create a Scanner
7      Scanner input = new Scanner(System.in);
8
9      // Prompt the user to enter two integers
10     System.out.print("Enter first integer: ");
11     int n1 = input.nextInt();
12     System.out.print("Enter second integer: ");
13     int n2 = input.nextInt();
14
```

invoke gcd

```
15      System.out.println("The greatest common divisor for " + n1 +
16        " and " + n2 + " is " + gcd(n1, n2));
17    }
18
```

compute gcd

```
19    /** Return the gcd of two integers */
20    public static int gcd(int n1, int n2) {
21      int gcd = 1; // Initial gcd is 1
22      int k = 2;   // Possible gcd
23
24      while (k <= n1 && k <= n2) {
25        if (n1 % k == 0 && n2 % k == 0)
26          gcd = k; // Update gcd
27        k++;
28      }
29
```

return gcd

```
30      return gcd; // Return gcd
31    }
32  }
```

```
Enter first integer: 45 ↵Enter
Enter second integer: 75 ↵Enter
The greatest common divisor for 45 and 75 is 15
```

By encapsulating the code for obtaining the gcd in a method, this program has several advantages:

1. It isolates the problem for computing the gcd from the rest of the code in the main method. Thus, the logic becomes clear and the program is easier to read.

2. The errors on computing the gcd are confined in the **gcd** method, which narrows the scope of debugging.

3. The **gcd** method now can be reused by other programs.

Listing 5.7 applies the concept of code modularization to improve Listing 4.14, PrimeNumber.java.

LISTING 5.7 PrimeNumberMethod.java

```
1  public class PrimeNumberMethod {
2    public static void main(String[] args) {
3      System.out.println("The first 50 prime numbers are \n");
```
invoke printPrimeNumbers
```
4      printPrimeNumbers(50);
5    }
6
```
printPrimeNumbers
method
```
7    public static void printPrimeNumbers(int numberOfPrimes) {
8      final int NUMBER_OF_PRIMES_PER_LINE = 10; // Display 10 per line
9      int count = 0; // Count the number of prime numbers
10     int number = 2; // A number to be tested for primeness
11
12     // Repeatedly find prime numbers
13     while (count < numberOfPrimes) {
14       // Print the prime number and increase the count
```
invoke isPrime
```
15       if (isPrime(number)) {
16         count++; // Increase the count
17
```

```
18            if (count % NUMBER_OF_PRIMES_PER_LINE == 0) {
19                // Print the number and advance to the new line
20                System.out.printf("%-5s\n", number);
21            }
22            else
23                System.out.printf("%-5s", number);
24        }
25
26        // Check whether the next number is prime
27        number++;
28      }
29    }
30
31    /** Check whether number is prime */
32    public static boolean isPrime(int number) {
33      for (int divisor = 2; divisor <= number / 2; divisor++) {
34        if (number % divisor == 0) { // If true, number is not prime
35          return false; // Number is not a prime
36        }
37      }
38
39      return true; // Number is prime
40    }
41  }
```

isPrime method

```
The first 50 prime numbers are

2    3    5    7    11   13   17   19   23   29
31   37   41   43   47   53   59   61   67   71
73   79   83   89   97   101  103  107  109  113
127  131  137  139  149  151  157  163  167  173
179  181  191  193  197  199  211  223  227  229
```

We divided a large problem into two subproblems: determining whether a number is a prime and printing the prime numbers. As a result, the new program is easier to read and easier to debug. Moreover, the methods `printPrimeNumbers` and `isPrime` can be reused by other programs.

5.7 Case Study: Converting Decimals to Hexadecimals

This section presents a program that converts a decimal number to a hexadecimal number.

Key Point

Hexadecimals are often used in computer systems programming (see Appendix F for an introduction to number systems). To convert a decimal number d to a hexadecimal number is to find the hexadecimal digits $h_n, h_{n-1}, h_{n-2}, \ldots, h_2, h_1,$ and h_0 such that

$$d = h_n \times 16^n + h_{n-1} \times 16^{n-1} + h_{n-2} \times 16^{n-2} + \ldots$$
$$+ h_2 \times 16^2 + h_1 \times 16^1 + h_0 \times 16^0$$

These hexadecimal digits can be found by successively dividing d by 16 until the quotient is 0. The remainders are $h_0, h_1, h_2, \ldots, h_{n-2}, h_{n-1},$ and h_n. The hexadecimal digits include the decimal digits 0, 1, 2, 3, 4, 5, 6, 7, 8, and 9, plus A, which is the decimal value 10; B, which is the decimal value 11; C, which is 12; D, which is 13; E, which is 14; and F, which is 15.

For example, the decimal number **123** is **7B** in hexadecimal. The conversion is done as follows. Divide **123** by **16**. The remainder is **11** (**B** in hexadecimal) and the quotient is **7**. Continue to divide **7** by **16**. The remainder is **7** and the quotient is **0**. Therefore **7B** is the hexadecimal number for **123**.

Listing 5.8 gives a program that prompts the user to enter a decimal number and converts it into a hex number as a string.

LISTING 5.8 Decimal2HexConversion.java

```java
 1  import java.util.Scanner;
 2
 3  public class Decimal2HexConversion {
 4    /** Main method */
 5    public static void main(String[] args) {
 6      // Create a Scanner
 7      Scanner input = new Scanner(System.in);
 8
 9      // Prompt the user to enter a decimal integer
10      System.out.print("Enter a decimal number: ");
11      int decimal = input.nextInt();
12
13      System.out.println("The hex number for decimal " +
14        decimal + " is " + decimalToHex(decimal));
15    }
16
17    /** Convert a decimal to a hex as a string */
18    public static String decimalToHex(int decimal) {
19      String hex = "";
20
21      while (decimal != 0) {
22        int hexValue = decimal % 16;
23        hex = toHexChar(hexValue) + hex;
24        decimal = decimal / 16;
25      }
26
27      return hex;
28    }
29
30    /** Convert an integer to a single hex digit in a character */
31    public static char toHexChar(int hexValue) {
32      if (hexValue <= 9 && hexValue >= 0)
33        return (char)(hexValue + '0');
34      else  // hexValue <= 15 && hexValue >= 10
35        return (char)(hexValue - 10 + 'A');
36    }
37  }
```

input decimal

decimal to hex

get a hex char

get a letter

```
Enter a decimal number: 1234  ↵ Enter
The hex number for decimal 1234 is 4D2
```

	line#	decimal	hex	hexValue	toHexChar(hexValue)
	19	1234	""		
iteration 1	22			2	
	23		"2"		2
	24	77			
iteration 2	22			13	
	23		"D2"		D
	24	4			
iteration 3	22			4	
	23		"4D2"		4
	24	0			

The program uses the `decimalToHex` method (lines 18–28) to convert a decimal integer to a hex number as a string. The method gets the remainder of the division of the decimal integer by `16` (line 22). The remainder is converted into a character by invoking the `toHexChar` method (line 23). The character is then appended to the hex string (line 23). The hex string is initially empty (line 19). Divide the decimal number by `16` to remove a hex digit from the number (line 24). The `decimalToHex` method repeatedly performs these operations in a loop until quotient becomes `0` (lines 21–25).

The `toHexChar` method (lines 31–36) converts a `hexValue` between 0 and 15 into a hex character. If `hexValue` is between `0` and `9`, it is converted to `(char)(hexValue + '0')` (line 33). Recall that when adding a character with an integer, the character's Unicode is used in the evaluation. For example, if `hexValue` is 5, `(char)(hexValue + '0')` returns 5. Similarly, if `hexValue` is between `10` and `15`, it is converted to `(char)(hexValue - 10 + 'A')` (line 35). For instance, if `hexValue` is 11, `(char)(hexValue - 10 + 'A')` returns B.

5.15 What is the return value from invoking `toHexChar(5)`? What is the return value from invoking `toHexChar(15)`?

5.16 What is the return value from invoking `decimalToHex(245)`? What is the return value from invoking `decimalToHex(3245)`?

5.8 Overloading Methods

Overloading methods enables you to define the methods with the same name as long as their signatures are different.

The `max` method that was used earlier works only with the `int` data type. But what if you need to determine which of two floating-point numbers has the maximum value? The solution is to create another method with the same name but different parameters, as shown in the following code:

```java
public static double max(double num1, double num2) {
  if (num1 > num2)
    return num1;
  else
    return num2;
}
```

method overloading

If you call `max` with `int` parameters, the `max` method that expects `int` parameters will be invoked; if you call `max` with `double` parameters, the `max` method that expects `double` parameters will be invoked. This is referred to as *method overloading*; that is, two methods have the same name but different parameter lists within one class. The Java compiler determines which method to use based on the method signature.

Listing 5.9 is a program that creates three methods. The first finds the maximum integer, the second finds the maximum double, and the third finds the maximum among three double values. All three methods are named `max`.

LISTING 5.9 TestMethodOverloading.java

```
1  public class TestMethodOverloading {
2    /** Main method */
3    public static void main(String[] args) {
4      // Invoke the max method with int parameters
5      System.out.println("The maximum of 3 and 4 is "
6        + max(3, 4));
7
8      // Invoke the max method with the double parameters
9      System.out.println("The maximum of 3.0 and 5.4 is "
10       + max(3.0, 5.4));
11
12     // Invoke the max method with three double parameters
13     System.out.println("The maximum of 3.0, 5.4, and 10.14 is "
14       + max(3.0, 5.4, 10.14));
15   }
16
17   /** Return the max of two int values */
18   public static int max(int num1, int num2) {
19     if (num1 > num2)
20       return num1;
21     else
22       return num2;
23   }
24
25   /** Find the max of two double values */
26   public static double max(double num1, double num2) {
27     if (num1 > num2)
28       return num1;
29     else
30       return num2;
31   }
32
33   /** Return the max of three double values */
34   public static double max(double num1, double num2, double num3) {
35     return max(max(num1, num2), num3);
36   }
37 }
```

overloaded max (line 18)
overloaded max (line 26)
overloaded max (line 34)

```
The maximum of 3 and 4 is 4
The maximum of 3.0 and 5.4 is 5.4
The maximum of 3.0, 5.4, and 10.14 is 10.14
```

When calling `max(3, 4)` (line 6), the `max` method for finding the maximum of two integers is invoked. When calling `max(3.0, 5.4)` (line 10), the `max` method for finding the maximum of two doubles is invoked. When calling `max(3.0, 5.4, 10.14)` (line 14), the `max` method for finding the maximum of three double values is invoked.

Can you invoke the `max` method with an `int` value and a `double` value, such as `max(2, 2.5)`? If so, which of the `max` methods is invoked? The answer to the first question is yes. The answer to the second question is that the `max` method for finding the maximum of two `double` values is invoked. The argument value 2 is automatically converted into a `double` value and passed to this method.

You may be wondering why the method `max(double, double)` is not invoked for the call `max(3, 4)`. Both `max(double, double)` and `max(int, int)` are possible matches for `max(3, 4)`. The Java compiler finds the most specific method for a method invocation. Since the method `max(int, int)` is more specific than `max(double, double)`, `max(int, int)` is used to invoke `max(3, 4)`.

Tip

Overloading methods can make programs clearer and more readable. Methods that perform the same function with different types of parameters should be given the same name.

Note

Overloaded methods must have different parameter lists. You cannot overload methods based on different modifiers or return types.

Note

Sometimes there are two or more possible matches for an invocation of a method, but the compiler cannot determine the most specific match. This is referred to as *ambiguous invocation*. Ambiguous invocation causes a compile error. Consider the following code:

ambiguous invocation

```java
public class AmbiguousOverloading {
  public static void main(String[] args) {
    System.out.println(max(1, 2));
  }

  public static double max(int num1, double num2) {
    if (num1 > num2)
      return num1;
    else
      return num2;
  }

  public static double max(double num1, int num2) {
    if (num1 > num2)
      return num1;
    else
      return num2;
  }
}
```

Both `max(int, double)` and `max(double, int)` are possible candidates to match `max(1, 2)`. Because neither is more specific than the other, the invocation is ambiguous, resulting in a compile error.

5.17 What is method overloading? Is it permissible to define two methods that have the same name but different parameter types? Is it permissible to define two methods in a class that have identical method names and parameter lists but different return value types or different modifiers?

5.18 What is wrong in the following program?

```java
public class Test {
  public static void method(int x) {
  }
```

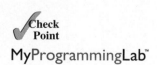

```
        public static int method(int y) {
          return y;
        }
      }
```

5.19 Given two method definitions,

public static double m(double x, **double** y)

public static double m(int x, **double** y)

tell which of the two methods is invoked for:

a. **double** z = m(4, 5);

b. **double** z = m(4, 5.4);

c. **double** z = m(4.5, 5.4);

5.9 The Scope of Variables

Key Point

The scope of a variable *is the part of the program where the variable can be referenced.*

scope of a variable
local variable

Section 2.5 introduced the scope of a variable. This section discusses the scope of variables in more details. A variable defined inside a method is referred to as a *local variable*. The scope of a local variable starts from its declaration and continues to the end of the block that contains the variable. A local variable must be declared and assigned a value before it can be used.

A parameter is actually a local variable. The scope of a method parameter covers the entire method. A variable declared in the initial-action part of a **for**-loop header has its scope in the entire loop. However, a variable declared inside a **for**-loop body has its scope limited in the loop body from its declaration to the end of the block that contains the variable, as shown in Figure 5.5.

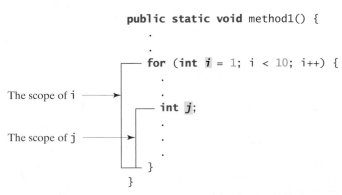

FIGURE 5.5 A variable declared in the initial action part of a **for**-loop header has its scope in the entire loop.

You can declare a local variable with the same name in different blocks in a method, but you cannot declare a local variable twice in the same block or in nested blocks, as shown in Figure 5.6.

It is fine to declare i in two
nonnested blocks.

```
public static void method1() {
  int x = 1;
  int y = 1;

  for (int i = 1; i < 10; i++) {
    x += i;
  }

  for (int i = 1; i < 10; i++) {
    y += i;
  }
}
```

It is wrong to declare i in two
nested blocks.

```
public static void method2() {

  int i = 1;
  int sum = 0;

  for (int i = 1; i < 10; i++)
    sum += i;
  }

}
```

FIGURE 5.6 A variable can be declared multiple times in nonnested blocks, but only once in nested blocks.

Caution

Do not declare a variable inside a block and then attempt to use it outside the block. Here is an example of a common mistake:

```
for (int i = 0; i < 10; i++) {
}

System.out.println(i);
```

The last statement would cause a syntax error, because variable i is not defined outside of the **for** loop.

5.20 What is a local variable?

5.21 What is the scope of a local variable?

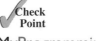

Check Point

MyProgrammingLab

5.10 The **Math** Class

Key Point

The Math class contains the methods needed to perform basic mathematical functions.

You have already used the **pow(a, b)** method to compute a^b in Section 2.9.3, Exponent Operations, and the **Math.random()** method in Section 3.8, Generating Random Numbers. This section introduces other useful methods in the **Math** class. They can be categorized as *trigonometric methods*, *exponent methods*, and *service methods*. Service methods include the rounding, min, max, absolute, and random methods. In addition to methods, the **Math** class provides two useful **double** constants, **PI** and **E** (the base of natural logarithms). You can use these constants as **Math.PI** and **Math.E** in any program.

5.10.1 Trigonometric Methods

The **Math** class contains the following trigonometric methods:

```
/** Return the trigonometric sine of an angle in radians */
public static double sin(double radians)

/** Return the trigonometric cosine of an angle in radians */
public static double cos(double radians)

/** Return the trigonometric tangent of an angle in radians */
public static double tan(double radians)
```

```
/** Convert the angle in degrees to an angle in radians */
public static double toRadians(double degree)

/** Convert the angle in radians to an angle in degrees */
public static double toDegrees(double radians)

/** Return the angle in radians for the inverse of sin */
public static double asin(double a)

/** Return the angle in radians for the inverse of cos */
public static double acos(double a)

/** Return the angle in radians for the inverse of tan */
public static double atan(double a)
```

The parameter for **sin**, **cos**, and **tan** is an angle in radians. The return value for **asin**, **acos**, and **atan** is a degree in radians in the range between $-\pi/2$ and $\pi/2$. One degree is equal to $\pi/180$ in radians, 90 degrees is equal to $\pi/2$ in radians, and 30 degrees is equal to $\pi/6$ in radians.

For example,

```
Math.toDegrees(Math.PI / 2) returns 90.0
Math.toRadians(30) returns 0.5236 (same as π/6)
Math.sin(0) returns 0.0
Math.sin(Math.toRadians(270)) returns -1.0
Math.sin(Math.PI / 6) returns 0.5
Math.sin(Math.PI / 2) returns 1.0
Math.cos(0) returns 1.0
Math.cos(Math.PI / 6) returns 0.866
Math.cos(Math.PI / 2) returns 0
Math.asin(0.5) returns 0.523598333 (same as π/6)
```

5.10.2 Exponent Methods

There are five methods related to exponents in the **Math** class:

```
/** Return e raised to the power of x (e^x) */
public static double exp(double x)

/** Return the natural logarithm of x (ln(x) = log_e(x)) */
public static double log(double x)

/** Return the base 10 logarithm of x (log_10(x)) */
public static double log10(double x)

/** Return a raised to the power of b (a^b) */
public static double pow(double a, double b)

/** Return the square root of x √x for x >= 0 */
public static double sqrt(double x)
```

For example,

```
Math.exp(1) returns 2.71828
Math.log(Math.E) returns 1.0
Math.log10(10) returns 1.0
Math.pow(2, 3) returns 8.0
Math.pow(3, 2) returns 9.0
Math.pow(3.5, 2.5) returns 22.91765
```

```
Math.sqrt(4) returns 2.0
Math.sqrt(10.5) returns 3.24
```

5.10.3   The Rounding Methods

The **Math** class contains five rounding methods:

```
/** x is rounded up to its nearest integer. This integer is
 * returned as a double value. */
public static double ceil(double x)

/** x is rounded down to its nearest integer. This integer is
 * returned as a double value. */
public static double floor(double x)

/** x is rounded to its nearest integer. If x is equally close
 * to two integers, the even one is returned as a double. */
public static double rint(double x)

/** Return (int)Math.floor(x + 0.5). */
public static int round(float x)

/** Return (long)Math.floor(x + 0.5). */
public static long round(double x)
```

For example,

```
Math.ceil(2.1) returns 3.0
Math.ceil(2.0) returns 2.0
Math.ceil(-2.0) returns -2.0
Math.ceil(-2.1) returns -2.0
Math.floor(2.1) returns 2.0
Math.floor(2.0) returns 2.0
Math.floor(-2.0) returns -2.0
Math.floor(-2.1) returns -3.0
Math.rint(2.1) returns 2.0
Math.rint(-2.0) returns -2.0
Math.rint(-2.1) returns -2.0
Math.rint(2.5) returns 2.0
Math.rint(3.5) returns 4.0
Math.rint(-2.5) returns -2.0
Math.round(2.6f) returns 3 // Returns int
Math.round(2.0) returns 2  // Returns long
Math.round(-2.0f) returns -2  // Returns int
Math.round(-2.6) returns -3  // Returns long
Math.round(-2.4) returns -2  // Returns long
```

5.10.4   The **min**, **max**, and **abs** Methods

The **min** and **max** methods are overloaded to return the minimum and maximum numbers of two numbers (**int**, **long**, **float**, or **double**). For example, **max(3.4, 5.0)** returns **5.0**, and **min(3, 2)** returns **2**.

The **abs** method is overloaded to return the absolute value of the number (**int**, **long**, **float**, or **double**). For example,

```
Math.max(2, 3) returns 3
Math.max(2.5, 3) returns 3.0
Math.min(2.5, 3.6) returns 2.5
```

```
Math.abs(-2) returns 2
Math.abs(-2.1) returns 2.1
```

5.10.5 The random Method

You have used the `random()` method to generate a random `double` value greater than or equal to `0.0` and less than `1.0` (`0 <= Math.random() < 1.0`). This method is very useful. You can use it to write a simple expression to generate random numbers in any range. For example,

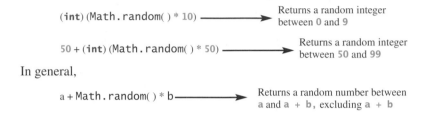

(**int**)(Math.random( ) * 10) ⟶ Returns a random integer between **0** and **9**

50 + (**int**)(Math.random( ) * 50) ⟶ Returns a random integer between **50** and **99**

In general,

a + Math.random( ) * b ⟶ Returns a random number between **a** and **a + b**, excluding **a + b**

Tip
You can view the complete documentation for the **Math** class online at download .oracle.com/javase/7/docs/api, as shown in Figure 5.7.

Note
Not all classes need a `main` method. The **Math** class and the **JOptionPane** class do not have `main` methods. These classes contain methods for other classes to use.

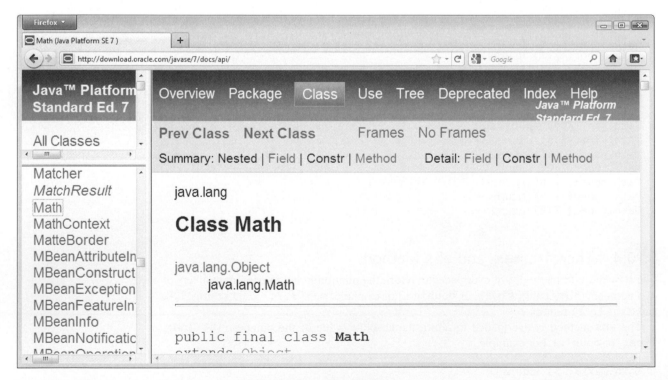

FIGURE 5.7 You can view the documentation for the Java API online.

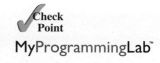

5.22 True or false? The argument for trigonometric methods is an angle in radians.

5.23 Write an expression that obtains a random integer between 34 and 55. Write an expression that obtains a random integer between 0 and 999. Write an expression that obtains a random number between 5.5 and 55.5. Write an expression that obtains a random lowercase letter.

5.24 Evaluate the following method calls:

a. `Math.sqrt(4)`

b. `Math.sin(2 * Math.PI)`

c. `Math.cos(2 * Math.PI)`

d. `Math.pow(2, 2)`

e. `Math.log(Math.E)`

f. `Math.exp(1)`

g. `Math.max(2, Math.min(3, 4))`

h. `Math.rint(-2.5)`

i. `Math.ceil(-2.5)`

j. `Math.floor(-2.5)`

k. `Math.round(-2.5f)`

l. `Math.round(-2.5)`

m. `Math.rint(2.5)`

n. `Math.ceil(2.5)`

o. `Math.floor(2.5)`

p. `Math.round(2.5f)`

q. `Math.round(2.5)`

r. `Math.round(Math.abs(-2.5))`

5.11 Case Study: Generating Random Characters

A character is coded using an integer. Generating a random character is to generate an integer.

Computer programs process numerical data and characters. You have seen many examples that involve numerical data. It is also important to understand characters and how to process them. This section presents an example of generating random characters.

As introduced in Section 2.17, every character has a unique Unicode between 0 and FFFF in hexadecimal (65535 in decimal). To generate a random character is to generate a random integer between 0 and 65535 using the following expression (note that since 0 <= `Math.random()` < 1.0, you have to add 1 to 65535):

```
(int)(Math.random() * (65535 + 1))
```

Now let's consider how to generate a random lowercase letter. The Unicodes for lowercase letters are consecutive integers starting from the Unicode for a, then that for b, c, ..., and z. The Unicode for a is

```
(int)'a'
```

Thus, a random integer between `(int)'a'` and `(int)'z'` is

```
(int)((int)'a' + Math.random() * ((int)'z' - (int)'a' + 1))
```

As discussed in Section 2.17.3, all numeric operators can be applied to the **char** operands. The **char** operand is cast into a number if the other operand is a number or a character. Therefore, the preceding expression can be simplified as follows:

```
'a' + Math.random() * ('z' - 'a' + 1)
```

and a random lowercase letter is

```
(char)('a' + Math.random() * ('z' - 'a' + 1))
```

Hence, a random character between any two characters **ch1** and **ch2** with **ch1 < ch2** can be generated as follows:

```
(char)(ch1 + Math.random() * (ch2 - ch1 + 1))
```

This is a simple but useful discovery. Listing 5.10 creates a class named **RandomCharacter** with five overloaded methods to get a certain type of character randomly. You can use these methods in your future projects.

LISTING 5.10 RandomCharacter.java

```
 1  public class RandomCharacter {
 2    /** Generate a random character between ch1 and ch2 */
 3    public static char getRandomCharacter(char ch1, char ch2) {
 4      return (char)(ch1 + Math.random() * (ch2 - ch1 + 1));
 5    }
 6
 7    /** Generate a random lowercase letter */
 8    public static char getRandomLowerCaseLetter() {
 9      return getRandomCharacter('a', 'z');
10    }
11
12    /** Generate a random uppercase letter */
13    public static char getRandomUpperCaseLetter() {
14      return getRandomCharacter('A', 'Z');
15    }
16
17    /** Generate a random digit character */
18    public static char getRandomDigitCharacter() {
19      return getRandomCharacter('0', '9');
20    }
21
22    /** Generate a random character */
23    public static char getRandomCharacter() {
24      return getRandomCharacter('\u0000', '\uFFFF');
25    }
26  }
```

getRandomCharacter

getRandomLower
  CaseLetter()

getRandomUpper
  CaseLetter()

getRandomDigit
  Character()

getRandomCharacter()

Listing 5.11 gives a test program that displays 175 random lowercase letters.

LISTING 5.11 TestRandomCharacter.java

```
 1  public class TestRandomCharacter {
 2    /** Main method */
 3    public static void main(String[] args) {
 4      final int NUMBER_OF_CHARS = 175;
 5      final int CHARS_PER_LINE = 25;
 6
 7      // Print random characters between 'a' and 'z', 25 chars per line
 8      for (int i = 0; i < NUMBER_OF_CHARS; i++) {
 9        char ch = RandomCharacter.getRandomLowerCaseLetter();
10        if ((i + 1) % CHARS_PER_LINE == 0)
11          System.out.println(ch);
12        else
13          System.out.print(ch);
14      }
15    }
16  }
```

constants

lower-case letter

```
gmjsohezfkgtazqgmswfclrao
pnrunulnwmaztlfjedmpchcif
lalqdgivxkxpbzulrmqmbhikr
lbnrjlsopfxahssqhwuuljvbe
xbhdotzhpehbqmuwsfktwsoli
cbuwkzgxpmtzihgatdslvbwbz
bfesoklwbhnooygiigzdxuqni
```

Line 9 invokes `getRandomLowerCaseLetter()` defined in the `RandomCharacter` class. Note that `getRandomLowerCaseLetter()` does not have any parameters, but you still have to use the parentheses when defining and invoking the method.

parentheses required

5.12 Method Abstraction and Stepwise Refinement

The key to developing software is to apply the concept of abstraction.

Key Point

You will learn many levels of abstraction from this book. *Method abstraction* is achieved by separating the use of a method from its implementation. The client can use a method without knowing how it is implemented. The details of the implementation are encapsulated in the method and hidden from the client who invokes the method. This is also known as *information hiding* or *encapsulation*. If you decide to change the implementation, the client program will not be affected, provided that you do not change the method signature. The implementation of the method is hidden from the client in a "black box," as shown in Figure 5.8.

VideoNote

Stepwise refinement

method abstraction

information hiding

FIGURE 5.8 The method body can be thought of as a black box that contains the detailed implementation for the method.

You have already used the `System.out.print` method to display a string and the `max` method to find the maximum number. You know how to write the code to invoke these methods in your program, but as a user of these methods, you are not required to know how they are implemented.

The concept of method abstraction can be applied to the process of developing programs. When writing a large program, you can use the *divide-and-conquer* strategy, also known as *stepwise refinement*, to decompose it into subproblems. The subproblems can be further decomposed into smaller, more manageable problems.

divide and conquer

stepwise refinement

Suppose you write a program that displays the calendar for a given month of the year. The program prompts the user to enter the year and the month, then displays the entire calendar for the month, as shown in the following sample run.

```
Enter full year (e.g., 2012): 2012 ↵Enter

Enter month as a number between 1 and 12: 3 ↵Enter

         March 2012
------------------------------
Sun Mon Tue Wed Thu Fri Sat
                  1   2   3
  4   5   6   7   8   9  10
 11  12  13  14  15  16  17
 18  19  20  21  22  23  24
 25  26  27  28  29  30  31
```

Let us use this example to demonstrate the divide-and-conquer approach.

5.12.1 Top-Down Design

How would you get started on such a program? Would you immediately start coding? Beginning programmers often start by trying to work out the solution to every detail. Although details are important in the final program, concern for detail in the early stages may block the problem-solving process. To make problem solving flow as smoothly as possible, this example begins by using method abstraction to isolate details from design and only later implements the details.

For this example, the problem is first broken into two subproblems: get input from the user, and print the calendar for the month. At this stage, you should be concerned with what the subproblems will achieve, not with how to get input and print the calendar for the month. You can draw a structure chart to help visualize the decomposition of the problem (see Figure 5.9a).

FIGURE 5.9   The structure chart shows that the `printCalendar` problem is divided into two subproblems, `readInput` and `printMonth` in (a), and that `printMonth` is divided into two smaller subproblems, `printMonthTitle` and `printMonthBody` in (b).

You can use **Scanner** to read input for the year and the month. The problem of printing the calendar for a given month can be broken into two subproblems: print the month title, and print the month body, as shown in Figure 5.9b. The month title consists of three lines: month and year, a dashed line, and the names of the seven days of the week. You need to get the month name (e.g., January) from the numeric month (e.g., 1). This is accomplished in **getMonthName** (see Figure 5.10a).

In order to print the month body, you need to know which day of the week is the first day of the month (**getStartDay**) and how many days the month has (**getNumberOfDaysInMonth**),

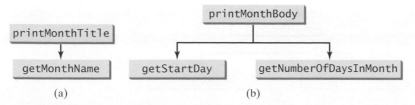

FIGURE 5.10 (a) To `printMonthTitle`, you need `getMonthName`. (b) The `printMonthBody` problem is refined into several smaller problems.

as shown in Figure 5.10b. For example, December 2013 has 31 days, and December 1, 2013, is a Sunday.

How would you get the start day for the first date in a month? There are several ways to do so. For now, we'll use an alternative approach. Assume you know that the start day for January 1, 1800, was a Wednesday (`START_DAY_FOR_JAN_1_1800 = 3`). You could compute the total number of days (`totalNumberOfDays`) between January 1, 1800, and the first date of the calendar month. The start day for the calendar month is `(totalNumberOfDays + startDay1800) % 7`, since every week has seven days. Thus, the `getStartDay` problem can be further refined as `getTotalNumberOfDays`, as shown in Figure 5.11a.

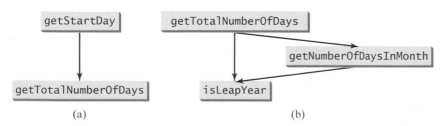

FIGURE 5.11 (a) To `getStartDay`, you need `getTotalNumberOfDays`. (b) The `getTotalNumberOfDays` problem is refined into two smaller problems.

To get the total number of days, you need to know whether the year is a leap year and the number of days in each month. Thus, `getTotalNumberOfDays` can be further refined into two subproblems: `isLeapYear` and `getNumberOfDaysInMonth`, as shown in Figure 5.11b. The complete structure chart is shown in Figure 5.12.

5.12.2 Top-Down and/or Bottom-Up Implementation

Now we turn our attention to implementation. In general, a subproblem corresponds to a method in the implementation, although some are so simple that this is unnecessary. You would need to decide which modules to implement as methods and which to combine in other methods. Decisions of this kind should be based on whether the overall program will be easier to read as a result of your choice. In this example, the subproblem `readInput` can be simply implemented in the `main` method.

You can use either a "top-down" or a "bottom-up" approach. The top-down approach implements one method in the structure chart at a time from the top to the bottom. *Stubs*—a simple but incomplete version of a method—can be used for the methods waiting to be implemented. The use of stubs enables you to quickly build the framework of the program. Implement the `main` method first, then use a stub for the `printMonth` method. For example,

top-down approach

stub

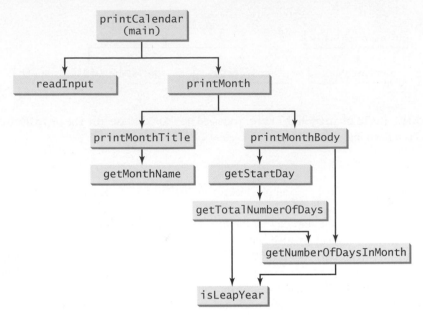

FIGURE 5.12 The structure chart shows the hierarchical relationship of the subproblems in the program.

let `printMonth` display the year and the month in the stub. Thus, your program may begin like this:

```java
public class PrintCalendar {
  /** Main method */
  public static void main(String[] args) {
    Scanner input = new Scanner(System.in);

    // Prompt the user to enter year
    System.out.print("Enter full year (e.g., 2012): ");
    int year = input.nextInt();

    // Prompt the user to enter month
    System.out.print("Enter month as a number between 1 and 12: ");
    int month = input.nextInt();

    // Print calendar for the month of the year
    printMonth(year, month);
  }

  /** A stub for printMonth may look like this */
  public static void printMonth(int year, int month) {
    System.out.print(month + " " + year);
  }

  /** A stub for printMonthTitle may look like this */
  public static void printMonthTitle(int year, int month) {
  }

  /** A stub for getMonthBody may look like this */
  public static void printMonthBody(int year, int month) {
  }
```

```
/** A stub for getMonthName may look like this */
public static String getMonthName(int month) {
  return "January"; // A dummy value
}

/** A stub for getStartDay may look like this */
public static int getStartDay(int year, int month) {
  return 1; // A dummy value
}

/** A stub for getTotalNumberOfDays may look like this */
public static int getTotalNumberOfDays(int year, int month) {
  return 10000; // A dummy value
}

/** A stub for getNumberOfDaysInMonth may look like this */
public static int getNumberOfDaysInMonth(int year, int month) {
  return 31; // A dummy value
}

/** A stub for isLeapYear may look like this */
public static Boolean isLeapYear(int year) {
  return true; // A dummy value
  }
}
```

Compile and test the program, and fix any errors. You can now implement the `printMonth` method. For methods invoked from the `printMonth` method, you can again use stubs.

The bottom-up approach implements one method in the structure chart at a time from the bottom to the top. For each method implemented, write a test program, known as the *driver*, to test it. The top-down and bottom-up approaches are equally good: Both approaches implement methods incrementally, help to isolate programming errors, and make debugging easy. They can be used together.

bottom-up approach
driver

5.12.3 Implementation Details

The `isLeapYear(int year)` method can be implemented using the following code from Section 3.12:

```
return (year % 400 == 0 || (year % 4 == 0 && year % 100 != 0));
```

Use the following facts to implement `getTotalNumberOfDaysInMonth(int year, int month)`:

- January, March, May, July, August, October, and December have 31 days.
- April, June, September, and November have 30 days.
- February has 28 days during a regular year and 29 days during a leap year. A regular year, therefore, has 365 days, a leap year 366 days.

To implement `getTotalNumberOfDays(int year, int month)`, you need to compute the total number of days (`totalNumberOfDays`) between January 1, 1800, and the first day of the calendar month. You could find the total number of days between the year 1800 and the calendar year and then figure out the total number of days prior to the calendar month in the calendar year. The sum of these two totals is `totalNumberOfDays`.

To print a body, first pad some space before the start day and then print the lines for every week.

The complete program is given in Listing 5.12.

LISTING 5.12 PrintCalendar.java

```java
 1  import java.util.Scanner;
 2
 3  public class PrintCalendar {
 4    /** Main method */
 5    public static void main(String[] args) {
 6      Scanner input = new Scanner(System.in);
 7
 8      // Prompt the user to enter year
 9      System.out.print("Enter full year (e.g., 2012): ");
10      int year = input.nextInt();
11
12      // Prompt the user to enter month
13      System.out.print("Enter month as a number between 1 and 12: ");
14      int month = input.nextInt();
15
16      // Print calendar for the month of the year
17      printMonth(year, month);
18    }
19
20    /** Print the calendar for a month in a year */
21    public static void printMonth(int year, int month) {
22      // Print the headings of the calendar
23      printMonthTitle(year, month);
24
25      // Print the body of the calendar
26      printMonthBody(year, month);
27    }
28
29    /** Print the month title, e.g., March 2012 */
30    public static void printMonthTitle(int year, int month) {
31      System.out.println("          " + getMonthName(month)
32        + " " + year);
33      System.out.println("-----------------------------");
34      System.out.println(" Sun Mon Tue Wed Thu Fri Sat");
35    }
36
37    /** Get the English name for the month */
38    public static String getMonthName(int month) {
39      String monthName = "";
40      switch (month) {
41        case 1: monthName = "January"; break;
42        case 2: monthName = "February"; break;
43        case 3: monthName = "March"; break;
44        case 4: monthName = "April"; break;
45        case 5: monthName = "May"; break;
46        case 6: monthName = "June"; break;
47        case 7: monthName = "July"; break;
48        case 8: monthName = "August"; break;
49        case 9: monthName = "September"; break;
50        case 10: monthName = "October"; break;
51        case 11: monthName = "November"; break;
52        case 12: monthName = "December";
53      }
54
55      return monthName;
56    }
57
58    /** Print month body */
```

printMonth

printMonthTitle

getMonthName

```
59   public static void printMonthBody(int year, int month) {                printMonthBody
60     // Get start day of the week for the first date in the month
61     int startDay = getStartDay(year, month);
62
63     // Get number of days in the month
64     int numberOfDaysInMonth = getNumberOfDaysInMonth(year, month);
65
66     // Pad space before the first day of the month
67     int i = 0;
68     for (i = 0; i < startDay; i++)
69       System.out.print("    ");
70
71     for (i = 1; i <= numberOfDaysInMonth; i++) {
72       System.out.printf("%4d", i);
73
74       if ((i + startDay) % 7 == 0)
75         System.out.println();
76     }
77
78     System.out.println();
79   }
80
81   /** Get the start day of month/1/year */
82   public static int getStartDay(int year, int month) {                     getStartDay
83     final int START_DAY_FOR_JAN_1_1800 = 3;
84     // Get total number of days from 1/1/1800 to month/1/year
85     int totalNumberOfDays = getTotalNumberOfDays(year, month);
86
87     // Return the start day for month/1/year
88     return (totalNumberOfDays + START_DAY_FOR_JAN_1_1800) % 7;
89   }
90
91   /** Get the total number of days since January 1, 1800 */
92   public static int getTotalNumberOfDays(int year, int month) {            getTotalNumberOfDays
93     int total = 0;
94
95     // Get the total days from 1800 to 1/1/year
96     for (int i = 1800; i < year; i++)
97       if (isLeapYear(i))
98         total = total + 366;
99       else
100        total = total + 365;
101
102    // Add days from Jan to the month prior to the calendar month
103    for (int i = 1; i < month; i++)
104      total = total + getNumberOfDaysInMonth(year, i);
105
106    return total;
107  }
108
109  /** Get the number of days in a month */
110  public static int getNumberOfDaysInMonth(int year, int month) {          getNumberOfDaysInMonth
111    if (month == 1 || month == 3 || month == 5 || month == 7 ||
112      month == 8 || month == 10 || month == 12)
113      return 31;
114
115    if (month == 4 || month == 6 || month == 9 || month == 11)
116      return 30;
117
118    if (month == 2) return isLeapYear(year) ? 29 : 28;
```

```
119
120      return 0; // If month is incorrect
121    }
122
123    /** Determine if it is a leap year */
124    public static boolean isLeapYear(int year) {
125      return year % 400 == 0 || (year % 4 == 0 && year % 100 != 0);
126    }
127  }
```

isLeapYear

The program does not validate user input. For instance, if the user enters either a month not in the range between 1 and 12 or a year before 1800, the program displays an erroneous calendar. To avoid this error, add an if statement to check the input before printing the calendar.

This program prints calendars for a month but could easily be modified to print calendars for a whole year. Although it can print months only after January 1800, it could be modified to print months before 1800.

5.12.4 Benefits of Stepwise Refinement

Stepwise refinement breaks a large problem into smaller manageable subproblems. Each subproblem can be implemented using a method. This approach makes the program easier to write, reuse, debug, test, modify, and maintain.

Simpler Program

The print calendar program is long. Rather than writing a long sequence of statements in one method, stepwise refinement breaks it into smaller methods. This simplifies the program and makes the whole program easier to read and understand.

Reusing Methods

Stepwise refinement promotes code reuse within a program. The isLeapYear method is defined once and invoked from the getTotalNumberOfDays and getNumberOfDayInMonth methods. This reduces redundant code.

Easier Developing, Debugging, and Testing

Since each subproblem is solved in a method, a method can be developed, debugged, and tested individually. This isolates the errors and makes developing, debugging, and testing easier.

When implementing a large program, use the top-down and/or bottom-up approach. Do not write the entire program at once. Using these approaches seems to take more development time (because you repeatedly compile and run the program), but it actually saves time and makes debugging easier.

incremental development and
testing

Better Facilitating Teamwork

When a large problem is divided into subprograms, subproblems can be assigned to different programmers. This makes it easier for programmers to work in teams.

KEY TERMS

actual parameter   179
ambiguous invocation   195
argument   179
divide and conquer   203
formal parameter (i.e., parameter)   179
information hiding   203
method   178
method abstraction   203

method overloading   194
method signature   179
modifier   179
parameter   179
pass-by-value   186
scope of a variable   196
stepwise refinement   203
stub   205

CHAPTER SUMMARY

1. Making programs modular and reusable is one of the central goals in software engineering. Java provides many powerful constructs that help to achieve this goal. *Methods* are one such construct.

2. The method header specifies the *modifiers*, *return value type*, *method name*, and *parameters* of the method. The `static` modifier is used for all the methods in this chapter.

3. A method may return a value. The `returnValueType` is the data type of the value the method returns. If the method does not return a value, the `returnValueType` is the keyword `void`.

4. The *parameter list* refers to the type, order, and number of a method's parameters. The method name and the parameter list together constitute the *method signature*. Parameters are optional, that is, a method doesn't need to contain any parameters.

5. A return statement can also be used in a `void` method for terminating the method and returning to the method's caller. This is useful occasionally for circumventing the normal flow of control in a method.

6. The arguments that are passed to a method should have the same number, type, and order as the parameters in the method signature.

7. When a program calls a method, program control is transferred to the called method. A called method returns control to the caller when its return statement is executed or when its method-ending closing brace is reached.

8. A value-returning method can also be invoked as a statement in Java. In this case, the caller simply ignores the return value.

9. A method can be overloaded. This means that two methods can have the same name, as long as their method parameter lists differ.

10. A variable declared in a method is called a local variable. The *scope of a local variable* starts from its declaration and continues to the end of the block that contains the variable. A local variable must be declared and initialized before it is used.

11. *Method abstraction* is achieved by separating the use of a method from its implementation. The client can use a method without knowing how it is implemented. The details of the implementation are encapsulated in the method and hidden from the client who invokes the method. This is known as *information hiding* or *encapsulation*.

12. Method abstraction modularizes programs in a neat, hierarchical manner. Programs written as collections of concise methods are easier to write, debug, maintain, and modify than would otherwise be the case. This writing style also promotes method reusability.

13. When implementing a large program, use the top-down and/or bottom-up coding approach. Do not write the entire program at once. This approach may seem to take more time for coding (because you are repeatedly compiling and running the program), but it actually saves time and makes debugging easier.

TEST QUESTIONS

Do the test questions for this chapter online at www.cs.armstrong.edu/liang/intro9e/test.html.

PROGRAMMING EXERCISES

Sections 5.2–5.9

5.1 (*Math: pentagonal numbers*) A pentagonal number is defined as $n(3n–1)/2$ for $n = 1, 2, \ldots$, and so on. Therefore, the first few numbers are 1, 5, 12, 22, ... Write a method with the following header that returns a pentagonal number:

```
public static int getPentagonalNumber(int n)
```

Write a test program that uses this method to display the first 100 pentagonal numbers with 10 numbers on each line.

*5.2 (*Sum the digits in an integer*) Write a method that computes the sum of the digits in an integer. Use the following method header:

```
public static int sumDigits(long n)
```

For example, **sumDigits(234)** returns **9** (2 + 3 + 4). (*Hint*: Use the **%** operator to extract digits, and the **/** operator to remove the extracted digit. For instance, to extract 4 from 234, use **234 % 10** (= 4). To remove 4 from 234, use **234 / 10** (= 23). Use a loop to repeatedly extract and remove the digit until all the digits are extracted. Write a test program that prompts the user to enter an integer and displays the sum of all its digits.

**5.3 (*Palindrome integer*) Write the methods with the following headers

```
// Return the reversal of an integer, i.e., reverse(456) returns 654
public static int reverse(int number)

// Return true if number is a palindrome
public static boolean isPalindrome(int number)
```

Use the **reverse** method to implement **isPalindrome**. A number is a palindrome if its reversal is the same as itself. Write a test program that prompts the user to enter an integer and reports whether the integer is a palindrome.

*5.4 (*Display an integer reversed*) Write a method with the following header to display an integer in reverse order:

```
public static void reverse(int number)
```

For example, **reverse(3456)** displays **6543**. Write a test program that prompts the user to enter an integer and displays its reversal.

*5.5 (*Sort three numbers*) Write a method with the following header to display three numbers in increasing order:

```
public static void displaySortedNumbers(
    double num1, double num2, double num3)
```

Write a test program that prompts the user to enter three numbers and invokes the method to display them in increasing order.

*5.6 (*Display patterns*) Write a method to display a pattern as follows:

```
            1
          2 1
        3 2 1
...
n n-1 ... 3 2 1
```

VideoNote

Reverse an integer

The method header is

```
public static void displayPattern(int n)
```

*5.7 (*Financial application: compute the future investment value*) Write a method that computes future investment value at a given interest rate for a specified number of years. The future investment is determined using the formula in Programming Exercise 2.21.

Use the following method header:

```
public static double futureInvestmentValue(
  double investmentAmount, double monthlyInterestRate, int years)
```

For example, `futureInvestmentValue(10000, 0.05/12, 5)` returns `12833.59`.

Write a test program that prompts the user to enter the investment amount (e.g., 1000) and the interest rate (e.g., 9%) and prints a table that displays future value for the years from 1 to 30, as shown below:

```
The amount invested: 1000 ⏎Enter
Annual interest rate: 9 ⏎Enter
Years          Future Value
1                  1093.80
2                  1196.41
...
29                13467.25
30                14730.57
```

5.8 (*Conversions between Celsius and Fahrenheit*) Write a class that contains the following two methods:

```
/** Convert from Celsius to Fahrenheit */
public static double celsiusToFahrenheit(double celsius)

/** Convert from Fahrenheit to Celsius */
public static double fahrenheitToCelsius(double fahrenheit)
```

The formula for the conversion is:

```
fahrenheit = (9.0 / 5) * celsius + 32
celsius = (5.0 / 9) * (fahrenheit - 32)
```

Write a test program that invokes these methods to display the following tables:

Celsius	Fahrenheit		Fahrenheit	Celsius
40.0	104.0		120.0	48.89
39.0	102.2		110.0	43.33
...				
32.0	89.6		40.0	4.44
31.0	87.8		30.0	-1.11

5.9 (*Conversions between feet and meters*) Write a class that contains the following two methods:

```
/** Convert from feet to meters */
public static double footToMeter(double foot)
```

```
/** Convert from meters to feet */
public static double meterToFoot(double meter)
```

The formula for the conversion is:

```
meter = 0.305 * foot
foot = 3.279 * meter
```

Write a test program that invokes these methods to display the following tables:

Feet	Meters		Meters	Feet
1.0	0.305	|	20.0	65.574
2.0	0.610	|	25.0	81.967
...				
9.0	2.745	|	60.0	196.721
10.0	3.050	|	65.0	213.115

5.10 (*Use the isPrime Method*) Listing 5.7, PrimeNumberMethod.java, provides the isPrime(int number) method for testing whether a number is prime. Use this method to find the number of prime numbers less than **10000**.

5.11 (*Financial application: compute commissions*) Write a method that computes the commission, using the scheme in Programming Exercise 4.39. The header of the method is as follows:

```
public static double computeCommission(double salesAmount)
```

Write a test program that displays the following table:

Sales Amount	Commission
10000	900.0
15000	1500.0
...	
95000	11100.0
100000	11700.0

5.12 (*Display characters*) Write a method that prints characters using the following header:

```
public static void printChars(char ch1, char ch2, int
   numberPerLine)
```

This method prints the characters between **ch1** and **ch2** with the specified numbers per line. Write a test program that prints ten characters per line from **1** to **Z**. Characters are separated by exactly one space.

*5.13 (*Sum series*) Write a method to compute the following series:

$$m(i) = \frac{1}{2} + \frac{2}{3} + \ldots + \frac{i}{i+1}$$

Write a test program that displays the following table:

i	m(i)
1	0.5000
2	1.1667
...	
19	16.4023
20	17.3546

VideoNote

Estimate π

*5.14 (*Estimate* π) π can be computed using the following series:

$$m(i) = 4\left(1 - \frac{1}{3} + \frac{1}{5} - \frac{1}{7} + \frac{1}{9} - \frac{1}{11} + \cdots + \frac{(-1)^{i+1}}{2i - 1}\right)$$

Write a method that returns m(i) for a given i and write a test program that displays the following table:

i	m(i)
1	4.0000
101	3.1515
201	3.1466
301	3.1449
401	3.1441
501	3.1436
601	3.1433
701	3.1430
801	3.1428
901	3.1427

*5.15 (*Financial application: print a tax table*) Listing 3.6 gives a program to compute tax. Write a method for computing tax using the following header:

public static double computetax(**int** status, **double** taxableIncome)

Use this method to write a program that prints a tax table for taxable income from $50,000 to $60,000 with intervals of $50 for all the following statuses:

Taxable Income	Single	Married Joint or Qualifying Widow(er)	Married Separate	Head of a House
50000	8688	6665	8688	7352
50050	8700	6673	8700	7365
...				
59950	11175	8158	11175	9840
60000	11188	8165	11188	9852

*5.16 (*Number of days in a year*) Write a method that returns the number of days in a year using the following header:

public static int numberOfDaysInAYear(**int** year)

Write a test program that displays the number of days in year from 2000 to 2020.

Sections 5.10–5.11

*5.17 (*Display matrix of 0s and 1s*) Write a method that displays an *n*-by-*n* matrix using the following header:

public static void printMatrix(**int** n)

Each element is 0 or 1, which is generated randomly. Write a test program that prompts the user to enter n and displays an *n*-by-*n* matrix. Here is a sample run:

```
Enter n: 3 ⏎Enter
0 1 0
0 0 0
1 1 1
```

5.18 (*Use the* `Math.sqrt` *method*) Write a program that prints the following table using the `sqrt` method in the `Math` class.

Number	SquareRoot
0	0.0000
2	1.4142
...	
18	4.2426
20	4.4721

*5.19 (*The* `MyTriangle` *class*) Create a class named `MyTriangle` that contains the following two methods:

```
/** Return true if the sum of any two sides is
 *  greater than the third side. */
public static boolean isValid(
   double side1, double side2, double side3)

/** Return the area of the triangle. */
public static double area(
   double side1, double side2, double side3)
```

Write a test program that reads three sides for a triangle and computes the area if the input is valid. Otherwise, it displays that the input is invalid. The formula for computing the area of a triangle is given in Programming Exercise 2.15.

5.20 (*Use trigonometric methods*) Print the following table to display the `sin` value and `cos` value of degrees from 0 to 360 with increments of 10 degrees. Round the value to keep four digits after the decimal point.

Degree	Sin	Cos
0	0.0000	1.0000
10	0.1736	0.9848
...		
350	-0.1736	0.9848
360	0.0000	1.0000

*5.21 (*Geometry: great circle distance*) The great circle distance is the distance between two points on the surface of a sphere. Let (x1, y1) and (x2, y2) be the geographical latitude and longitude of two points. The great circle distance between the two points can be computed using the following formula:

$$d = radius \times \arccos(\sin(x_1) \times \sin(x_2) + \cos(x_1) \times \cos(x_2) \times \cos(y_1 - y_2))$$

Write a program that prompts the user to enter the latitude and longitude of two points on the earth in degrees and displays its great circle distance. The average earth radius is 6,371.01 km. Note that you need to convert the degrees into radians using the `Math.toRadians` method since the Java trigonometric methods use radians. The latitude and longitude degrees in the formula are for North and West. Use negative to indicate South and East degrees. Here is a sample run:

```
Enter point 1 (latitude and longitude) in degrees:
  39.55 -116.25  ⏎Enter
Enter point 2 (latitude and longitude) in degrees:
  41.5 87.37  ⏎Enter
The distance between the two points is 10691.79183231593 km
```

**5.22 (*Math: approximate the square root*) There are several techniques for implementing the `sqrt` method in the `Math` class. One such technique is known as the *Babylonian method.* It approximates the square root of a number, `n`, by repeatedly performing a calculation using the following formula:

```
nextGuess = (lastGuess + n / lastGuess) / 2
```

When `nextGuess` and `lastGuess` are almost identical, `nextGuess` is the approximated square root. The initial guess can be any positive value (e.g., `1`). This value will be the starting value for `lastGuess`. If the difference between `nextGuess` and `lastGuess` is less than a very small number, such as `0.0001`, you can claim that `nextGuess` is the approximated square root of `n`. If not, `nextGuess` becomes `lastGuess` and the approximation process continues. Implement the following method that returns the square root of `n`.

public static double sqrt(**long** n)

*5.23 (*Geometry: display angles*) Write a program that prompts the user to enter three points of a triangle and displays the angles in degrees. Round the value to keep two digits after the decimal point. The formula to compute angles A, B, and C are as follows:

```
A = arccos((a * a - b * b - c * c) / (-2 * b * c))
B = arccos((b * b - a * a - c * c) / (-2 * a * c))
C = arccos((c * c - b * b - a * a) / (-2 * a * b))
```

Here is a sample run of the program:

```
Enter three points: 1 1 6.5 1 6.5 2.5 ⏎Enter
The three angles are 15.26 90.0 74.74
```

Sections 5.10–5.12

**5.24 (*Display current date and time*) Listing 2.6, ShowCurrentTime.java, displays the current time. Improve this example to display the current date and time. The calendar example in Listing 5.12, PrintCalendar.java, should give you some ideas on how to find the year, month, and day.

**5.25 (*Convert milliseconds to hours, minutes, and seconds*) Write a method that converts milliseconds to hours, minutes, and seconds using the following header:

public static String convertMillis(**long** millis)

The method returns a string as *hours:minutes:seconds.* For example, `convertMillis(5500)` returns a string 0:0:5, `convertMillis(100000)` returns a string 0:1:40, and `convertMillis(555550000)` returns a string 154:19:10.

Comprehensive

**5.26 (*Palindromic prime*) A *palindromic prime* is a prime number and also palindromic. For example, 131 is a prime and also a palindromic prime, as are 313 and 757. Write a program that displays the first 100 palindromic prime numbers. Display 10 numbers per line, separated by exactly one space, as follows:

```
2  3  5  7  11 101 131 151 181 191
313 353 373 383 727 757 787 797 919 929
...
```

**5.27 (*Emirp*) An *emirp* (prime spelled backward) is a nonpalindromic prime number whose reversal is also a prime. For example, 17 is a prime and 71 is a prime, so 17 and 71 are emirps. Write a program that displays the first 100 emirps. Display 10 numbers per line, separated by exactly one space, as follows:

```
13 17 31 37 71 73 79 97 107 113
149 157 167 179 199 311 337 347 359 389
...
```

**5.28 (*Mersenne prime*) A prime number is called a *Mersenne prime* if it can be written in the form $2^p - 1$ for some positive integer p. Write a program that finds all Mersenne primes with $p \leq 31$ and displays the output as follows:

```
p            2^p - 1

2               3
3               7
5              31
...
```

**5.29 (*Twin primes*) Twin primes are a pair of prime numbers that differ by 2. For example, 3 and 5 are twin primes, 5 and 7 are twin primes, and 11 and 13 are twin primes. Write a program to find all twin primes less than 1,000. Display the output as follows:

```
(3, 5)
(5, 7)
...
```

**5.30 (*Game: craps*) Craps is a popular dice game played in casinos. Write a program to play a variation of the game, as follows:

Roll two dice. Each die has six faces representing values 1, 2, . . ., and 6, respectively. Check the sum of the two dice. If the sum is 2, 3, or 12 (called *craps*), you lose; if the sum is 7 or 11 (called *natural*), you win; if the sum is another value (i.e., 4, 5, 6, 8, 9, or 10), a point is established. Continue to roll the dice until either a 7 or the same point value is rolled. If 7 is rolled, you lose. Otherwise, you win.

Your program acts as a single player. Here are some sample runs.

```
You rolled 5 + 6 = 11
You win
```

```
You rolled 1 + 2 = 3
You lose
```

```
You rolled 4 + 4 = 8
point is 8
You rolled 6 + 2 = 8
You win
```

```
You rolled 3 + 2 = 5
point is 5
You rolled 2 + 5 = 7
You lose
```

**5.31 (*Financial: credit card number validation*) Credit card numbers follow certain patterns. A credit card number must have between 13 and 16 digits. It must start with:

- 4 for Visa cards
- 5 for Master cards
- 37 for American Express cards
- 6 for Discover cards

In 1954, Hans Luhn of IBM proposed an algorithm for validating credit card numbers. The algorithm is useful to determine whether a card number is entered correctly or whether a credit card is scanned correctly by a scanner. Credit card numbers are generated following this validity check, commonly known as the *Luhn check* or the *Mod 10 check,* which can be described as follows (for illustration, consider the card number 4388576018402626):

1. Double every second digit from right to left. If doubling of a digit results in a two-digit number, add up the two digits to get a single-digit number.

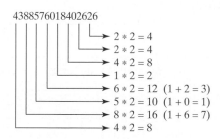

```
4388576018402626
                  ► 2 * 2 = 4
                  ► 2 * 2 = 4
                  ► 4 * 2 = 8
                  ► 1 * 2 = 2
                  ► 6 * 2 = 12  (1 + 2 = 3)
                  ► 5 * 2 = 10  (1 + 0 = 1)
                  ► 8 * 2 = 16  (1 + 6 = 7)
                  ► 4 * 2 = 8
```

2. Now add all single-digit numbers from Step 1.

$$4 + 4 + 8 + 2 + 3 + 1 + 7 + 8 = 37$$

3. Add all digits in the odd places from right to left in the card number.

$$6 + 6 + 0 + 8 + 0 + 7 + 8 + 3 = 38$$

4. Sum the results from Step 2 and Step 3.

$$37 + 38 = 75$$

5. If the result from Step 4 is divisible by 10, the card number is valid; otherwise, it is invalid. For example, the number 4388576018402626 is invalid, but the number 4388576018410707 is valid.

Write a program that prompts the user to enter a credit card number as a **long** integer. Display whether the number is valid or invalid. Design your program to use the following methods:

```
/** Return true if the card number is valid */
public static boolean isValid(long number)

/** Get the result from Step 2 */
public static int sumOfDoubleEvenPlace(long number)

/** Return this number if it is a single digit, otherwise,
 * return the sum of the two digits */
public static int getDigit(int number)

/** Return sum of odd-place digits in number */
public static int sumOfOddPlace(long number)

/** Return true if the digit d is a prefix for number */
public static boolean prefixMatched(long number, int d)

/** Return the number of digits in d */
public static int getSize(long d)

/** Return the first k number of digits from number. If the
 * number of digits in number is less than k, return number. */
public static long getPrefix(long number, int k)
```

Here are sample runs of the program:

```
Enter a credit card number as a long integer:
   4388576018410707  ↵Enter
4388576018410707 is valid
```

```
Enter a credit card number as a long integer:
   4388576018402626  ↵Enter
4388576018402626 is invalid
```

**5.32 (*Game: chance of winning at craps*) Revise Exercise 5.30 to run it 10,000 times and display the number of winning games.

5.33 (*Current date and time*) Invoking **System.currentTimeMillis() returns the elapsed time in milliseconds since midnight of January 1, 1970. Write a program that displays the date and time. Here is a sample run:

```
Current date and time is May 16, 2012 10:34:23
```

**5.34 (*Print calendar*) Programming Exercise 3.21 uses Zeller's congruence to calculate the day of the week. Simplify Listing 5.12, PrintCalendar.java, using Zeller's algorithm to get the start day of the month.

5.35 (*Geometry: area of a pentagon*) The area of a pentagon can be computed using the following formula:

$$Area = \frac{5 \times s^2}{4 \times \tan\left(\dfrac{\pi}{5}\right)}$$

Write a program that prompts the user to enter the side of a pentagon and displays the area. Here is a sample run:

```
Enter the side: 5.5  ↵Enter
The area of the pentagon is 52.04444136781625
```

*5.36 (*Geometry: area of a regular polygon*) A regular polygon is an *n*-sided polygon in which all sides are of the same length and all angles have the same degree (i.e., the polygon is both equilateral and equiangular). The formula for computing the area of a regular polygon is

$$Area = \frac{n \times s^2}{4 \times \tan\left(\dfrac{\pi}{n}\right)}$$

Write a method that returns the area of a regular polygon using the following header:

```
public static double area(int n, double side)
```

Write a main method that prompts the user to enter the number of sides and the side of a regular polygon and displays its area. Here is a sample run:

```
Enter the number of sides: 5  ↵Enter
Enter the side: 6.5  ↵Enter
The area of the polygon is 72.69017017488385
```

5.37 (*Format an integer*) Write a method with the following header to format the integer with the specified width.

```
public static String format(int number, int width)
```

The method returns a string for the number with one or more prefix 0s. The size of the string is the width. For example, `format(34,   4)` returns `0034` and `format(34,   5)` returns `00034`. If the number is longer than the width, the method returns the string representation for the number. For example, `format(34,  1)` returns `34`.

Write a test program that prompts the user to enter a number and its width and displays a string returned by invoking `format(number, width)`.

*5.38 (*Generate random characters*) Use the methods in **RandomCharacter** in Listing 5.10 to print 100 uppercase letters and then 100 single digits, printing ten per line.

5.39 (*Geometry: point position*) Programming Exercise 3.32 shows how to test whether a point is on the left side of a directed line, on the right, or on the same line. Write the methods with the following headers:

```
/** Return true if point (x2, y2) is on the left side of the
 *  directed line from (x0, y0) to (x1, y1) */
public static boolean leftOfTheLine(double x0, double y0,
  double x1, double y1, double x2, double y2)

/** Return true if point (x2, y2) is on the same
 *  line from (x0, y0) to (x1, y1) */
public static boolean onTheSameLine(double x0, double y0,
  double x1, double y1, double x2, double y2)

/** Return true if point (x2, y2) is on the
 *  line segment from (x0, y0) to (x1, y1) */
public static boolean onTheLineSegment(double x0, double y0,
  double x1, double y1, double x2, double y2)
```

Write a program that prompts the user to enter the three points for **p0**, **p1**, and **p2** and displays whether **p2** is on the left of the line from **p0** to **p1**, right, the same line, or on the line segment. Here are some sample runs:

```
Enter three points for p0, p1, and p2: 1 1 2 2 1.5 1.5  ↵Enter
(1.5, 1.5) is on the line segment from (1.0, 1.0) to (2.0, 2.0)
```

```
Enter three points for p0, p1, and p2: 1 1 2 2 3 3  ↵Enter
(3.0, 3.0) is on the same line from (1.0, 1.0) to (2.0, 2.0)
```

```
Enter three points for p0, p1, and p2: 1 1 2 2 1 1.5  ↵Enter
(1.0, 1.5) is on the left side of the line
   from (1.0, 1.0) to (2.0, 2.0)
```

```
Enter three points for p0, p1, and p2: 1 1 2 2 1 -1  ↵Enter
(1.0, -1.0) is on the right side of the line
   from (1.0, 1.0) to (2.0, 2.0)
```

SINGLE-DIMENSIONAL ARRAYS

Objectives

- To describe why arrays are necessary in programming (§6.1).

- To declare array reference variables and create arrays (§§6.2.1–6.2.2).

- To obtain array size using `arrayRefVar.length` and know default values in an array (§6.2.3).

- To access array elements using indexed variables (§6.2.4).

- To declare, create, and initialize an array using an array initializer (§6.2.5).

- To program common array operations (displaying arrays, summing all elements, finding the minimum and maximum elements, random shuffling, and shifting elements) (§6.2.6).

- To simplify programming using the for-each loops (§6.2.7).

- To apply arrays in application development (`LottoNumbers`, `DeckOfCards`) (§§6.3–6.4).

- To copy contents from one array to another (§6.5).

- To develop and invoke methods with array arguments and return values (§§6.6–6.8).

- To define a method with a variable-length argument list (§6.9).

- To search elements using the linear (§6.10.1) or binary (§6.10.2) search algorithm.

- To sort an array using the selection sort approach (§6.11.1).

- To sort an array using the insertion sort approach (§6.11.2).

- To use the methods in the `java.util.Arrays` class (§6.12).

6.1 Introduction

A single array variable can reference a large collection of data.

problem
why array?

Often you will have to store a large number of values during the execution of a program. Suppose, for instance, that you need to read 100 numbers, compute their average, and find out how many numbers are above the average. Your program first reads the numbers and computes their average, then compares each number with the average to determine whether it is above the average. In order to accomplish this task, the numbers must all be stored in variables. You have to declare 100 variables and repeatedly write almost identical code 100 times. Writing a program this way would be impractical. So, how do you solve this problem?

what is array?

An efficient, organized approach is needed. Java and most other high-level languages provide a data structure, the *array*, which stores a fixed-size sequential collection of elements of the same type. In the present case, you can store all 100 numbers into an array and access them through a single array variable. The solution may look like this:

```
 1   public class AnalyzeNumbers {
 2     public static void main(String[] args) {
 3       final int NUMBER_OF_ELEMENTS = 100;
 4       double[] numbers = new double[NUMBER_OF_ELEMENTS];
 5       double sum = 0;
 6
 7       java.util.Scanner input = new java.util.Scanner(System.in);
 8       for (int i = 0; i < NUMBER_OF_ELEMENTS; i++) {
 9         System.out.print("Enter a new number: ");
10         numbers[i] = input.nextDouble();
11         sum += numbers[i];
12       }
13
14       double average = sum / NUMBER_OF_ELEMENTS;
15
16       int count = 0; // The number of elements above average
17       for (int i = 0; i < NUMBER_OF_ELEMENTS; i++)
18         if (numbers[i] > average)
19           count++;
20
21       System.out.println("Average is " + average);
22       System.out.println("Number of elements above the average "
23         + count);
24     }
25   }
```

create array

store number in array

get average

above average?

numbers	array
numbers[0]:	
numbers[1]:	
numbers[2]:	
.	
numbers[i]	.
.	
numbers[97]:	
numbers[98]:	
numbers[99]:	

The program creates an array of **100** elements in line 4, stores numbers into the array in line 10, adds each number to **sum** in line 11, and obtains the average in line 14. It then compares each number in the array with the average to count the number of values above the average (lines 16–19).

This chapter introduces single-dimensional arrays. The next chapter will introduce two-dimensional and multidimensional arrays.

6.2 Array Basics

Once an array is created, its size is fixed. An array reference variable is used to access the elements in an array using an index.

index

An array is used to store a collection of data, but often we find it more useful to think of an array as a collection of variables of the same type. Instead of declaring individual variables, such as **number0**, **number1**, . . . , and **number99**, you declare one array variable such as **numbers** and use **numbers[0]**, **numbers[1]**, . . . , and **numbers[99]** to represent individual variables.

This section introduces how to declare array variables, create arrays, and process arrays using indexed variables.

6.2.1 Declaring Array Variables

To use an array in a program, you must declare a variable to reference the array and specify the array's *element type*. Here is the syntax for declaring an array variable:

element type

```
elementType[] arrayRefVar;
```

The `elementType` can be any data type, and all elements in the array will have the same data type. For example, the following code declares a variable `myList` that references an array of double elements.

```
double[] myList;
```

> **Note**
> You can also use `elementType arrayRefVar[]` to declare an array variable. This style comes from the C language and was adopted in Java to accommodate C programmers. The style `elementType[] arrayRefVar` is preferred.

preferred syntax

6.2.2 Creating Arrays

Unlike declarations for primitive data type variables, the declaration of an array variable does not allocate any space in memory for the array. It creates only a storage location for the reference to an array. If a variable does not contain a reference to an array, the value of the variable is `null`. You cannot assign elements to an array unless it has already been created. After an array variable is declared, you can create an array by using the `new` operator with the following syntax:

null

```
arrayRefVar = new elementType[arraySize];
```

new operator

This statement does two things: (1) it creates an array using `new elementType[array-Size]`; (2) it assigns the reference of the newly created array to the variable `arrayRefVar`.

Declaring an array variable, creating an array, and assigning the reference of the array to the variable can be combined in one statement as:

```
elementType[] arrayRefVar = new elementType[arraySize];
```

or

```
elementType arrayRefVar[] = new elementType[arraySize];
```

Here is an example of such a statement:

```
double[] myList = new double[10];
```

This statement declares an array variable, `myList`, creates an array of ten elements of `double` type, and assigns its reference to `myList`. To assign values to the elements, use the syntax:

```
arrayRefVar[index] = value;
```

For example, the following code initializes the array.

```
myList[0] = 5.6;
myList[1] = 4.5;
myList[2] = 3.3;
myList[3] = 13.2;
```

```
myList[4] = 4.0;
myList[5] = 34.33;
myList[6] = 34.0;
myList[7] = 45.45;
myList[8] = 99.993;
myList[9] = 11123;
```

This array is illustrated in Figure 6.1.

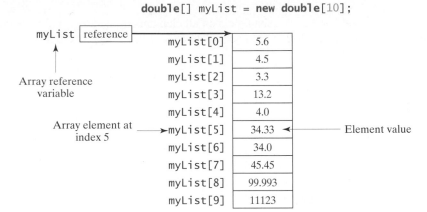

FIGURE 6.1 The array `myList` has ten elements of `double` type and `int` indices from `0` to `9`.

Note

array vs. array variable

An array variable that appears to hold an array actually contains a reference to that array. Strictly speaking, an array variable and an array are different, but most of the time the distinction can be ignored. Thus it is all right to say, for simplicity, that `myList` is an array, instead of stating, at greater length, that `myList` is a variable that contains a reference to an array of ten double elements.

6.2.3 Array Size and Default Values

array length

When space for an array is allocated, the array size must be given, specifying the number of elements that can be stored in it. The size of an array cannot be changed after the array is created. Size can be obtained using `arrayRefVar.length`. For example, `myList.length` is `10`.

default values

When an array is created, its elements are assigned the default value of `0` for the numeric primitive data types, `\u0000` for `char` types, and `false` for `boolean` types.

6.2.4 Array Indexed Variables

0 based

The array elements are accessed through the index. Array indices are `0` based; that is, they range from `0` to `arrayRefVar.length-1`. In the example in Figure 6.1, `myList` holds ten `double` values, and the indices are from `0` to `9`.

indexed variable

Each element in the array is represented using the following syntax, known as an *indexed variable*:

```
arrayRefVar[index];
```

For example, `myList[9]` represents the last element in the array `myList`.

Caution

Some programming languages use parentheses to reference an array element, as in `myList(9)`, but Java uses brackets, as in `myList[9]`.

After an array is created, an indexed variable can be used in the same way as a regular variable. For example, the following code adds the values in `myList[0]` and `myList[1]` to `myList[2]`.

```
myList[2] = myList[0] + myList[1];
```

The following loop assigns 0 to `myList[0]`, 1 to `myList[1]`, ..., and 9 to `myList[9]`:

```
for (int i = 0; i < myList.length; i++) {
  myList[i] = i;
}
```

6.2.5   Array Initializers

Java has a shorthand notation, known as the *array initializer*, which combines the declaration, creation, and initialization of an array in one statement using the following syntax:

array initializer

```
elementType[] arrayRefVar = {value0, value1, ..., valuek};
```

For example, the statement

```
double[] myList = {1.9, 2.9, 3.4, 3.5};
```

declares, creates, and initializes the array `myList` with four elements, which is equivalent to the following statements:

```
double[] myList = new double[4];
myList[0] = 1.9;
myList[1] = 2.9;
myList[2] = 3.4;
myList[3] = 3.5;
```

Caution

The **new** operator is not used in the array-initializer syntax. Using an array initializer, you have to declare, create, and initialize the array all in one statement. Splitting it would cause a syntax error. Thus, the next statement is wrong:

```
double[] myList;
myList = {1.9, 2.9, 3.4, 3.5};
```

6.2.6   Processing Arrays

When processing array elements, you will often use a `for` loop—for two reasons:

- All of the elements in an array are of the same type. They are evenly processed in the same fashion repeatedly using a loop.

- Since the size of the array is known, it is natural to use a `for` loop.

Assume the array is created as follows:

```
double[] myList = new double[10];
```

The following are some examples of processing arrays.

1. *Initializing arrays with input values:* The following loop initializes the array `myList` with user input values.

```
java.util.Scanner input = new java.util.Scanner(System.in);
System.out.print("Enter " + myList.length + " values: ");
for (int i = 0; i < myList.length; i++)
  myList[i] = input.nextDouble();
```

2. *Initializing arrays with random values:* The following loop initializes the array `myList` with random values between `0.0` and `100.0`, but less than `100.0`.

```
for (int i = 0; i < myList.length; i++) {
  myList[i] = Math.random() * 100;
}
```

3. *Displaying arrays:* To print an array, you have to print each element in the array using a loop like the following:

```
for (int i = 0; i < myList.length; i++) {
  System.out.print(myList[i] + " ");
}
```

print character array

> **Tip**
>
> For an array of the `char[]` type, it can be printed using one print statement. For example, the following code displays `Dallas`:
>
> ```
> char[] city = {'D', 'a', 'l', 'l', 'a', 's'};
> System.out.println(city);
> ```

4. *Summing all elements:* Use a variable named `total` to store the sum. Initially `total` is `0`. Add each element in the array to `total` using a loop like this:

```
double total = 0;
for (int i = 0; i < myList.length; i++) {
  total += myList[i];
}
```

5. *Finding the largest element:* Use a variable named `max` to store the largest element. Initially `max` is `myList[0]`. To find the largest element in the array `myList`, compare each element with `max`, and update `max` if the element is greater than `max`.

```
double max = myList[0];
for (int i = 1; i < myList.length; i++) {
  if (myList[i] > max) max = myList[i];
}
```

6. *Finding the smallest index of the largest element:* Often you need to locate the largest element in an array. If an array has more than one largest element, find the smallest index of such an element. Suppose the array `myList` is {1, 5, 3, 4, 5, 5}. The largest element is `5` and the smallest index for `5` is `1`. Use a variable named `max` to store the largest element and a variable named `indexOfMax` to denote the index of the largest element. Initially `max` is `myList[0]`, and `indexOfMax` is `0`. Compare each element in `myList` with `max`, and update `max` and `indexOfMax` if the element is greater than `max`.

```
double max = myList[0];
int indexOfMax = 0;
for (int i = 1; i < myList.length; i++) {
  if (myList[i] > max) {
    max = myList[i];
    indexOfMax = i;
  }
}
```

VideoNote

Random shuffling

7. *Random shuffling:* In many applications, you need to randomly reorder the elements in an array. This is called *shuffling*. To accomplish this, for each element

`myList[i]`, randomly generate an index `j` and swap `myList[i]` with `myList[j]`, as follows:

```
for (int i = 0; i < myList.length; i++) {
  // Generate an index j randomly
  int j = (int) (Math.random()
    * mylist.length);

  // Swap myList[i] with myList[j]
  double temp = myList[i];
  myList[i] = myList[j];
  myList[j] = temp;
}
```

8. *Shifting elements:* Sometimes you need to shift the elements left or right. Here is an example of shifting the elements one position to the left and filling the last element with the first element:

```
double temp = myList[0]; // Retain the first element

// Shift elements left
for (int i = 1; i < myList.length; i++) {
  myList[i - 1] = myList[i];
}
```

```
// Move the first element to fill in the last position
myList[myList.length - 1] = temp;
```

9. *Simplifying coding:* Arrays can be used to greatly simplify coding for certain tasks. For example, suppose you wish to obtain the English name of a given month by its number. If the month names are stored in an array, the month name for a given month can be accessed simply via the index. The following code prompts the user to enter a month number and displays its month name:

```
String[] months = {"January", "February", ..., "December"};
System.out.print("Enter a month number (1 to 12): ");
int monthNumber = input.nextInt();
System.out.println("The month is " + months[monthNumber - 1]);
```

If you didn't use the `months` array, you would have to determine the month name using a lengthy multi-way `if-else` statement as follows:

```
if (monthNumber == 1)
  System.out.println("The month is January");
else if (monthNumber == 2)
  System.out.println("The month is February");
...
else
  System.out.println("The month is December");
```

6.2.7 for-each Loops

Java supports a convenient **for** loop, known as a *for-each loop* or *enhanced for loop*, which enables you to traverse the array sequentially without using an index variable. For example, the following code displays all the elements in the array `myList`:

```
for (double u: myList) {
  System.out.println(u);
}
```

You can read the code as "for each element **u** in **myList**, do the following." Note that the variable, **u**, must be declared as the same type as the elements in **myList**.

In general, the syntax for a for-each loop is

```
for (elementType element: arrayRefVar) {
  // Process the element
}
```

You still have to use an index variable if you wish to traverse the array in a different order or change the elements in the array.

Caution

ArrayIndexOutOfBounds-
Exception

Accessing an array out of bounds is a common programming error that throws a runtime **ArrayIndexOutOfBoundsException**. To avoid it, make sure that you do not use an index beyond **arrayRefVar.length - 1**.

off-by-one error

Programmers often mistakenly reference the first element in an array with index **1**, but it should be **0**. This is called the *off-by-one error*. Another common error in a loop is using <= where < should be used. For example, the following loop is wrong.

```
for (int i = 0; i <= list.length; i++)
  System.out.print(list[i] + " ");
```

The <= should be replaced by <.

6.1 How do you declare an array reference variable and how do you create an array?

6.2 When is the memory allocated for an array?

6.3 What is the printout of the following code?

```
int x = 30;
int[] numbers = new int[x];
x = 60;
System.out.println("x is " + x);
System.out.println("The size of numbers is " + numbers.length);
```

6.4 Indicate **true** or **false** for the following statements:

■ Every element in an array has the same type.

■ The array size is fixed after an array reference variable is declared.

■ The array size is fixed after it is created.

■ The elements in an array must be a primitive data type.

6.5 Which of the following statements are valid?

```
int i = new int(30);
double d[] = new double[30];
char[] r = new char(1..30);
int i[] = (3, 4, 3, 2);
float f[] = {2.3, 4.5, 6.6};
char[] c = new char();
```

6.6 How do you access elements in an array? What is an array indexed variable?

6.7 What is the array index type? What is the lowest index? What is the representation of the third element in an array named **a**?

6.8 Write statements to do the following:

a. Create an array to hold **10** double values.

b. Assign the value **5.5** to the last element in the array.

c. Display the sum of the first two elements.

d. Write a loop that computes the sum of all elements in the array.

e. Write a loop that finds the minimum element in the array.

f. Randomly generate an index and display the element of this index in the array.

g. Use an array initializer to create another array with the initial values 3.5, 5.5, 4.52, and 5.6.

6.9 What happens when your program attempts to access an array element with an invalid index?

6.10 Identify and fix the errors in the following code:

```
1  public class Test {
2    public static void main(String[] args) {
3      double[100] r;
4
5      for (int i = 0; i < r.length(); i++);
6        r(i) = Math.random * 100;
7    }
8  }
```

6.11 What is the output of the following code?

```
1   public class Test {
2     public static void main(String[] args) {
3       int list[] = {1, 2, 3, 4, 5, 6};
4       for (int i = 1; i < list.length; i++)
5         list[i] = list[i - 1];
6
7       for (int i = 0; i < list.length; i++)
8         System.out.print(list[i] + " ");
9     }
10  }
```

6.3 Case Study: Lotto Numbers

The problem is to write a program that checks if all the input numbers cover 1 to 99.

Key Point

Each ticket for the Pick-10 lotto has 10 unique numbers ranging from 1 to 99. Suppose you buy a lot of tickets and like to have them cover all numbers from 1 to 99. Write a program that reads the ticket numbers from a file and checks whether all numbers are covered. Assume the last number in the file is 0. Suppose the file contains the numbers

VideoNote

Lotto numbers

```
80 3 87 62 30 90 10 21 46 27
12 40 83 9 39 88 95 59 20 37
80 40 87 67 31 90 11 24 56 77
11 48 51 42 8 74 1 41 36 53
52 82 16 72 19 70 44 56 29 33
54 64 99 14 23 22 94 79 55 2
60 86 34 4 31 63 84 89 7 78
43 93 97 45 25 38 28 26 85 49
47 65 57 67 73 69 32 71 24 66
92 98 96 77 6 75 17 61 58 13
35 81 18 15 5 68 91 50 76
0
```

Your program should display

```
The tickets cover all numbers
```

Suppose the file contains the numbers

```
11 48 51 42 8 74 1 41 36 53
52 82 16 72 19 70 44 56 29 33
0
```

Your program should display

```
The tickets don't cover all numbers
```

How do you mark a number as covered? You can create an array with **99 boolean** elements. Each element in the array can be used to mark whether a number is covered. Let the array be **isCovered**. Initially, each element is **false**, as shown in Figure 6.2a. Whenever a number is read, its corresponding element is set to **true**. Suppose the numbers entered are **1, 2, 3, 99, 0**. When number **1** is read, **isCovered[0]** is set to **true** (see Figure 6.2b). When number **2** is read, **isCovered[2 - 1]** is set to **true** (see Figure 6.2c). When number **3** is read, **isCovered[3 - 1]** is set to **true** (see Figure 6.2d). When number **99** is read, **isCovered[98]** is set to **true** (see Figure 6.2e).

isCovered	isCovered	isCovered	isCovered	isCovered
[0] false	[0] true	[0] true	[0] true	[0] true
[1] false	[1] false	[1] true	[1] true	[1] true
[2] false	[2] false	[2] false	[2] true	[2] true
[3] false	[3] false	[3] false	[3] false	[3] false
.	.	.	.	.
.	.	.	.	.
.	.	.	.	.
[97] false	[97] false	[97] false	[97] false	[97] false
[98] false	[98] false	[98] false	[98] false	[98] true
(a)	(b)	(c)	(d)	(e)

FIGURE 6.2 If number i appears in a Lotto ticket, **isCovered[i-1]** is set to **true**.

The algorithm for the program can be described as follows:

```
for each number k read from the file,
  mark number k as covered by setting isCovered[k - 1] true;
if every isCovered[i] is true
  The tickets cover all numbers
else
  The tickets don't cover all numbers
```

The complete program is given in Listing 6.1.

LISTING 6.1 LottoNumbers.java

```
 1  import java.util.Scanner;
 2
 3  public class LottoNumbers {
 4    public static void main(String[] args) {
 5      Scanner input = new Scanner(System.in);
 6      boolean[] isCovered = new boolean[99]; // Default is false
 7
 8      // Read each number and mark its corresponding element covered
 9      int number = input.nextInt();
10      while (number != 0) {
11        isCovered[number - 1] = true;
12        number = input.nextInt();
13      }
14
```

create and initialize array

read number

mark number covered
read number

```
15        // Check whether all covered
16        boolean allCovered = true; // Assume all covered initially
17        for (int i = 0; i < isCovered.length; i++)
18          if (!isCovered[i]) {
19            allCovered = false; // Find one number not covered
20            break;
21          }
22
23        // Display result
24        if (allCovered)
25          System.out.println("The tickets cover all numbers");
26        else
27          System.out.println("The tickets don't cover all numbers");
28      }
29  }
```

check allCovered?

Suppose you have created a text file named LottoNumbers.txt that contains the input data 2 5 6 5 4 3 23 43 2 0. You can run the program using the following command:

```
java LottoNumbers < LottoNumbers.txt
```

The program can be traced as follows:

Line#	\[1]	\[2]	\[3]	\[4]	\[5]	\[22]	\[42]	number	allCovered
	\[1]	\[2]	\[3]	\[4]	\[5]	\[22]	\[42]		
6	false	false	false	false	false	false	false		
9								2	
11	true								
12								5	
11				true					
12								6	
11					true				
12								5	
11				true					
12								4	
11			true						
12								3	
11		true							
12								23	
11						true			
12								43	
11							true		
12								2	
11	true								
12								0	
16									true
18(i=0)									false

where the header "Representative elements in array isCovered" spans columns [1] through [42].

The program creates an array of **99 boolean** elements and initializes each element to **false** (line 6). It reads the first number from the file (line 9). The program then repeats the following operations in a loop:

- If the number is not zero, set its corresponding value in array **isCovered** to **true** (line 11);

- Read the next number (line 12).

When the input is **0**, the input ends. The program checks whether all numbers are covered in lines 16–21 and displays the result in lines 24–27.

6.4 Case Study: Deck of Cards

Key Point

The problem is to create a program that will randomly select four cards from a deck of cards.

Say you want to write a program that will pick four cards at random from a deck of **52** cards. All the cards can be represented using an array named **deck**, filled with initial values **0** to **51**, as follows:

```
int[] deck = new int[52];

// Initialize cards
for (int i = 0; i < deck.length; i++)
  deck[i] = i;
```

Card numbers **0** to **12**, **13** to **25**, **26** to **38**, and **39** to **51** represent 13 Spades, 13 Hearts, 13 Diamonds, and 13 Clubs, respectively, as shown in Figure 6.3. **cardNumber / 13** determines the suit of the card and **cardNumber % 13** determines the rank of the card, as shown in Figure 6.4. After shuffling the array **deck**, pick the first four cards from **deck**. The program displays the cards from these four card numbers.

FIGURE 6.3 52 cards are stored in an array named **deck**.

$$\text{cardNumber} / 13 = \begin{cases} 0 \longrightarrow \text{Spades} \\ 1 \longrightarrow \text{Hearts} \\ 2 \longrightarrow \text{Diamonds} \\ 3 \longrightarrow \text{Clubs} \end{cases} \qquad \text{cardNumber} \% 13 = \begin{cases} 0 \longrightarrow \text{Ace} \\ 1 \longrightarrow 2 \\ \cdot \\ \cdot \\ 10 \longrightarrow \text{Jack} \\ 11 \longrightarrow \text{Queen} \\ 12 \longrightarrow \text{King} \end{cases}$$

FIGURE 6.4 How `cardNumber` identifies a card's suit and rank number.

Listing 6.2 gives the solution to the problem.

LISTING 6.2 `DeckOfCards.java`

```java
public class DeckOfCards {
  public static void main(String[] args) {
    int[] deck = new int[52];                                          // create array deck
    String[] suits = {"Spades", "Hearts", "Diamonds", "Clubs"};        // array of strings
    String[] ranks = {"Ace", "2", "3", "4", "5", "6", "7", "8", "9",   // array of strings
      "10", "Jack", "Queen", "King"};

    // Initialize the cards
    for (int i = 0; i < deck.length; i++)                              // initialize deck
      deck[i] = i;

    // Shuffle the cards
    for (int i = 0; i < deck.length; i++) {                            // shuffle deck
      // Generate an index randomly
      int index = (int)(Math.random() * deck.length);
      int temp = deck[i];
      deck[i] = deck[index];
      deck[index] = temp;
    }

    // Display the first four cards
    for (int i = 0; i < 4; i++) {
      String suit = suits[deck[i] / 13];                               // suit of a card
      String rank = ranks[deck[i] % 13];                               // rank of a card
      System.out.println("Card number " + deck[i] + ": "
        + rank + " of " + suit);
    }
  }
}
```

```
Card number 6: 7 of Spades
Card number 48: 10 of Clubs
Card number 11: Queen of Spades
Card number 24: Queen of Hearts
```

The program defines an array **suits** for four suits (line 4) and an array **ranks** for 13 cards in a suit (lines 5–6). Each element in these arrays is a string.

The program initializes **deck** with values **0** to **51** in lines 9–10. The **deck** value **0** represents the card Ace of Spades, **1** represents the card 2 of Spades, **13** represents the card Ace of Hearts, and **14** represents the card 2 of Hearts.

Lines 13–19 randomly shuffle the deck. After a deck is shuffled, **deck[i]** contains an arbitrary value. **deck[i] / 13** is **0, 1, 2,** or **3**, which determines the suit (line 23). **deck[i] % 13** is a value between **0** and **12**, which determines the rank (line 24). If the **suits** array is not defined, you would have to determine the suit using a lengthy multi-way **if-else** statement as follows:

```
if (deck[i] / 13 == 0)
  System.out.print("suit is Spades");
else if (deck[i] / 13 == 1)
  System.out.print("suit is Hearts");
else if(deck[i] / 13 == 2)
  System.out.print("suit is Diamonds");
else
  System.out.print("suit is Clubs");
```

With **suits = {"Spades", "Hearts", "Diamonds", "Clubs"}** created in an array, **suits[deck / 13]** gives the suit for the **deck**. Using arrays greatly simplifies the solution for this program.

6.5 Copying Arrays

Key
Point

To copy the contents of one array into another, you have to copy the array's individual elements into the other array.

Often, in a program, you need to duplicate an array or a part of an array. In such cases you could attempt to use the assignment statement (=), as follows:

```
list2 = list1;
```

copy reference

However, this statement does not copy the contents of the array referenced by **list1** to **list2**, but instead merely copies the reference value from **list1** to **list2**. After this statement, **list1** and **list2** reference the same array, as shown in Figure 6.5. The array previously referenced by **list2** is no longer referenced; it becomes garbage, which will be automatically collected by the Java Virtual Machine (this process is called *garbage collection*).

garbage collection

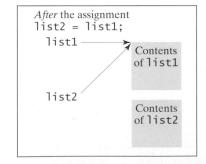

FIGURE 6.5 Before the assignment statement, **list1** and **list2** point to separate memory locations. After the assignment, the reference of the **list1** array is passed to **list2**.

In Java, you can use assignment statements to copy primitive data type variables, but not arrays. Assigning one array variable to another array variable actually copies one reference to another and makes both variables point to the same memory location.

There are three ways to copy arrays:

- Use a loop to copy individual elements one by one.
- Use the static `arraycopy` method in the `System` class.
- Use the `clone` method to copy arrays; this will be introduced in Chapter 15, Abstract Classes and Interfaces.

You can write a loop to copy every element from the source array to the corresponding element in the target array. The following code, for instance, copies `sourceArray` to `targetArray` using a `for` loop.

```java
int[] sourceArray = {2, 3, 1, 5, 10};
int[] targetArray = new int[sourceArray.length];
for (int i = 0; i < sourceArray.length; i++) {
  targetArray[i] = sourceArray[i];
}
```

Another approach is to use the `arraycopy` method in the `java.lang.System` class to copy arrays instead of using a loop. The syntax for `arraycopy` is:

arraycopy method

```java
arraycopy(sourceArray, src_pos, targetArray, tar_pos, length);
```

The parameters `src_pos` and `tar_pos` indicate the starting positions in `sourceArray` and `targetArray`, respectively. The number of elements copied from `sourceArray` to `targetArray` is indicated by `length`. For example, you can rewrite the loop using the following statement:

```java
System.arraycopy(sourceArray, 0, targetArray, 0, sourceArray.length);
```

The `arraycopy` method does not allocate memory space for the target array. The target array must have already been created with its memory space allocated. After the copying takes place, `targetArray` and `sourceArray` have the same content but independent memory locations.

Note

The `arraycopy` method violates the Java naming convention. By convention, this method should be named `arrayCopy` (i.e., with an uppercase C).

6.12 Use the `arraycopy()` method to copy the following array to a target array `t`:

```java
int[] source = {3, 4, 5};
```

6.13 Once an array is created, its size cannot be changed. Does the following code resize the array?

```java
int[] myList;
myList = new int[10];
// Sometime later you want to assign a new array to myList
myList = new int[20];
```

Check
Point

MyProgrammingLab™

6.6 Passing Arrays to Methods

When passing an array to a method, the reference of the array is passed to the method.

Key
Point

Just as you can pass primitive type values to methods, you can also pass arrays to methods. For example, the following method displays the elements in an `int` array:

```java
public static void printArray(int[] array) {
  for (int i = 0; i < array.length; i++) {
```

```
          System.out.print(array[i] + " ");
      }
  }
```

You can invoke it by passing an array. For example, the following statement invokes the **printArray** method to display **3**, **1**, **2**, **6**, **4**, and **2**.

```
printArray(new int[]{3, 1, 2, 6, 4, 2});
```

Note

The preceding statement creates an array using the following syntax:

```
new elementType[]{value0, value1, ..., valuek};
```

anonymous array

There is no explicit reference variable for the array. Such array is called an *anonymous array*.

pass-by-value

Java uses *pass-by-value* to pass arguments to a method. There are important differences between passing the values of variables of primitive data types and passing arrays.

- For an argument of a primitive type, the argument's value is passed.

pass-by-sharing

- For an argument of an array type, the value of the argument is a reference to an array; this reference value is passed to the method. Semantically, it can be best described as *pass-by-sharing*, that is, the array in the method is the same as the array being passed. Thus, if you change the array in the method, you will see the change outside the method.

Take the following code, for example:

```
public class Test {
  public static void main(String[] args) {
    int x = 1; // x represents an int value
    int[] y = new int[10]; // y represents an array of int values

    m(x, y); // Invoke m with arguments x and y

    System.out.println("x is " + x);
    System.out.println("y[0] is " + y[0]);
  }

  public static void m(int number, int[] numbers) {
    number = 1001; // Assign a new value to number
    numbers[0] = 5555; // Assign a new value to numbers[0]
  }
}
```

```
x is 1
y[0] is 5555
```

You may wonder why after **m** is invoked, **x** remains **1**, but **y[0]** become **5555**. This is because **y** and **numbers**, although they are independent variables, reference the same array, as illustrated in Figure 6.6. When **m(x, y)** is invoked, the values of **x** and **y** are passed to **number** and **numbers**. Since **y** contains the reference value to the array, **numbers** now contains the same reference value to the same array.

FIGURE 6.6 The primitive type value in x is passed to number, and the reference value in y is passed to numbers.

Note

Arrays are objects in Java (objects are introduced in Chapter 8). The JVM stores the objects in an area of memory called the *heap*, which is used for dynamic memory allocation.

heap

Listing 6.3 gives another program that shows the difference between passing a primitive data type value and an array reference variable to a method.

The program contains two methods for swapping elements in an array. The first method, named swap, fails to swap two int arguments. The second method, named swapFirstTwoInArray, successfully swaps the first two elements in the array argument.

LISTING 6.3 TestPassArray.java

```java
 1  public class TestPassArray {
 2    /** Main method */
 3    public static void main(String[] args) {
 4      int[] a = {1, 2};
 5
 6      // Swap elements using the swap method
 7      System.out.println("Before invoking swap");
 8      System.out.println("array is {" + a[0] + ", " + a[1] + "}");
 9      swap(a[0], a[1]);                                                      false swap
10      System.out.println("After invoking swap");
11      System.out.println("array is {" + a[0] + ", " + a[1] + "}");
12
13      // Swap elements using the swapFirstTwoInArray method
14      System.out.println("Before invoking swapFirstTwoInArray");
15      System.out.println("array is {" + a[0] + ", " + a[1] + "}");
16      swapFirstTwoInArray(a);                                               swap array elements
17      System.out.println("After invoking swapFirstTwoInArray");
18      System.out.println("array is {" + a[0] + ", " + a[1] + "}");
19    }
20
21    /** Swap two variables */
22    public static void swap(int n1, int n2) {
23      int temp = n1;
24      n1 = n2;
25      n2 = temp;
26    }
27
28    /** Swap the first two elements in the array */
29    public static void swapFirstTwoInArray(int[] array) {
30      int temp = array[0];
31      array[0] = array[1];
32      array[1] = temp;
33    }
34  }
```

```
Before invoking swap
array is {1, 2}
After invoking swap
array is {1, 2}
Before invoking swapFirstTwoInArray
array is {1, 2}
After invoking swapFirstTwoInArray
array is {2, 1}
```

As shown in Figure 6.7, the two elements are not swapped using the **swap** method. However, they are swapped using the **swapFirstTwoInArray** method. Since the parameters in the **swap** method are primitive type, the values of **a[0]** and **a[1]** are passed to **n1** and **n2** inside the method when invoking **swap(a[0], a[1])**. The memory locations for **n1** and **n2** are independent of the ones for **a[0]** and **a[1]**. The contents of the array are not affected by this call.

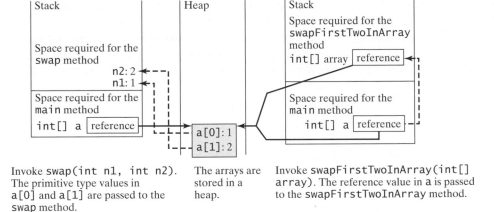

FIGURE 6.7   When passing an array to a method, the reference of the array is passed to the method.

The parameter in the **swapFirstTwoInArray** method is an array. As shown in Figure 6.7, the reference of the array is passed to the method. Thus the variables **a** (outside the method) and **array** (inside the method) both refer to the same array in the same memory location. Therefore, swapping **array[0]** with **array[1]** inside the method **swapFirstTwoInArray** is the same as swapping **a[0]** with **a[1]** outside of the method.

6.7 Returning an Array from a Method

Key Point

When a method returns an array, the reference of the array is returned.

You can pass arrays when invoking a method. A method may also return an array. For example, the following method returns an array that is the reversal of another array.

create array

return array

```
 1  public static int[] reverse(int[] list) {
 2    int[] result = new int[list.length];
 3
 4    for (int i = 0, j = result.length - 1;
 5         i < list.length; i++, j--) {
 6      result[j] = list[i];
 7    }
 8
 9    return result;
10  }
```

Line 2 creates a new array `result`. Lines 4–7 copy elements from array `list` to array `result`. Line 9 returns the array. For example, the following statement returns a new array `list2` with elements **6, 5, 4, 3, 2, 1**.

```
int[] list1 = {1, 2, 3, 4, 5, 6};
int[] list2 = reverse(list1);
```

6.8 Case Study: Counting the Occurrences of Each Letter

This section presents a program to count the occurrences of each letter in an array of characters.

Key
Point

The program given in Listing 6.4 does the following:

1. Generates **100** lowercase letters randomly and assigns them to an array of characters, as shown in Figure 6.8a. You can obtain a random letter by using the **getRandomLower-CaseLetter()** method in the **RandomCharacter** class in Listing 5.10.

2. Count the occurrences of each letter in the array. To do so, create an array, say **counts**, of **26 int** values, each of which counts the occurrences of a letter, as shown in Figure 6.8b. That is, **counts[0]** counts the number of **a**'s, **counts[1]** counts the number of **b**'s, and so on.

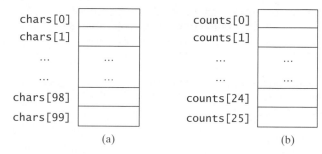

(a)   (b)

FIGURE 6.8   The **chars** array stores **100** characters, and the **counts** array stores **26** counts, each of which counts the occurrences of a letter.

LISTING 6.4 CountLettersInArray.java

```
 1  public class CountLettersInArray {
 2    /** Main method */
 3    public static void main(String[] args) {
 4      // Declare and create an array
 5      char[] chars = createArray();
 6
 7      // Display the array
 8      System.out.println("The lowercase letters are:");
 9      displayArray(chars);
10
11      // Count the occurrences of each letter
12      int[] counts = countLetters(chars);
13
14      // Display counts
15      System.out.println();
16      System.out.println("The occurrences of each letter are:");
17      displayCounts(counts);
18    }
19
20    /** Create an array of characters */
```

create array

pass array

return array

pass array

```
21    public static char[] createArray() {
22      // Declare an array of characters and create it
23      char[] chars = new char[100];
24
25      // Create lowercase letters randomly and assign
26      // them to the array
27      for (int i = 0; i < chars.length; i++)
28        chars[i] = RandomCharacter.getRandomLowerCaseLetter();
29
30      // Return the array
31      return chars;
32    }
33
34    /** Display the array of characters */
35    public static void displayArray(char[] chars) {
36      // Display the characters in the array 20 on each line
37      for (int i = 0; i < chars.length; i++) {
38        if ((i + 1) % 20 == 0)
39          System.out.println(chars[i]);
40        else
41          System.out.print(chars[i] + " ");
42      }
43    }
44
45    /** Count the occurrences of each letter */
46    public static int[] countLetters(char[] chars) {
47      // Declare and create an array of 26 int
48      int[] counts = new int[26];
49
50      // For each lowercase letter in the array, count it
51      for (int i = 0; i < chars.length; i++)
52        counts[chars[i] - 'a']++;
53
54      return counts;
55    }
56
57    /** Display counts */
58    public static void displayCounts(int[] counts) {
59      for (int i = 0; i < counts.length; i++) {
60        if ((i + 1) % 10 == 0)
61          System.out.println(counts[i] + " " + (char)(i + 'a'));
62        else
63          System.out.print(counts[i] + " " + (char)(i + 'a') + " ");
64      }
65    }
66  }
```

increase count

```
The lowercase letters are:
e y l s r i b k j v j h a b z n w b t v
s c c k r d w a m p w v u n q a m p l o
a z g d e g f i n d x m z o u l o z j v
h w i w n t g x w c d o t x h y v z y z
q e a m f w p g u q t r e n n w f c r f

The occurrences of each letter are:
5 a 3 b 4 c 4 d 4 e 4 f 4 g 3 h 3 i 3 j
2 k 3 l 4 m 6 n 4 o 3 p 3 q 4 r 2 s 4 t
3 u 5 v 8 w 3 x 3 y 6 z
```

The `createArray` method (lines 21–32) generates an array of 100 random lowercase letters. Line 5 invokes the method and assigns the array to `chars`. What would be wrong if you rewrote the code as follows?

```
char[] chars = new char[100];
chars = createArray();
```

You would be creating two arrays. The first line would create an array by using `new char[100]`. The second line would create an array by invoking `createArray()` and assign the reference of the array to `chars`. The array created in the first line would be garbage because it is no longer referenced, and as mentioned earlier Java automatically collects garbage behind the scenes. Your program would compile and run correctly, but it would create an array unnecessarily.

Invoking `getRandomLowerCaseLetter()` (line 28) returns a random lowercase letter. This method is defined in the `RandomCharacter` class in Listing 5.10.

The `countLetters` method (lines 46–55) returns an array of 26 `int` values, each of which stores the number of occurrences of a letter. The method processes each letter in the array and increases its count by one. A brute-force approach to count the occurrences of each letter might be as follows:

```
for (int i = 0; i < chars.length; i++)
  if (chars[i] == 'a')
    counts[0]++;
  else if (chars[i] == 'b')
    counts[1]++;
  ...
```

But a better solution is given in lines 51–52.

```
for (int i = 0; i < chars.length; i++)
  counts[chars[i] - 'a']++;
```

If the letter (`chars[i]`) is `a`, the corresponding count is `counts['a' - 'a']` (i.e., `counts[0]`). If the letter is `b`, the corresponding count is `counts['b' - 'a']` (i.e., `counts[1]`), since the Unicode of `b` is one more than that of `a`. If the letter is `z`, the corresponding count is `counts['z' - 'a']` (i.e., `counts[25]`), since the Unicode of `z` is 25 more than that of `a`.

Figure 6.9 shows the call stack and heap *during* and *after* executing `createArray`. See Checkpoint Question 6.16 to show the call stack and heap for other methods in the program.

(a) Executing
`createArray` in line 5

(b) After exiting
`createArray` in line 5

FIGURE 6.9 (a) An array of 100 characters is created when executing `createArray`. (b) This array is returned and assigned to the variable `chars` in the `main` method.

6.14 True or false? When an array is passed to a method, a new array is created and passed to the method.

MyProgrammingLab™ **6.15** Show the output of the following two programs:

```java
public class Test {
  public static void main(String[] args) {
    int number = 0;
    int[] numbers = new int[1];

    m(number, numbers);

    System.out.println("number is " + number
      + " and numbers[0] is " + numbers[0]);
  }

  public static void m(int x, int[] y) {
    x = 3;
    y[0] = 3;
  }
}
```

(a)

```java
public class Test {
  public static void main(String[] args) {
    int[] list = {1, 2, 3, 4, 5};
    reverse(list);
    for (int i = 0; i < list.length; i++)
      System.out.print(list[i] + " ");
  }

  public static void reverse(int[] list) {
    int[] newList = new int[list.length];

    for (int i = 0; i < list.length; i++)
      newList[i] = list[list.length - 1 - i];

    list = newList;
  }
}
```

(b)

6.16 Where are the arrays stored during execution? Show the contents of the stack and heap during and after executing `displayArray`, `countLetters`, `displayCounts` in Listing 6.4.

6.9 Variable-Length Argument Lists

A variable number of arguments of the same type can be passed to a method and treated as an array.

You can pass a variable number of arguments of the same type to a method. The parameter in the method is declared as follows:

```
typeName... parameterName
```

In the method declaration, you specify the type followed by an ellipsis (`...`). Only one variable-length parameter may be specified in a method, and this parameter must be the last parameter. Any regular parameters must precede it.

Java treats a variable-length parameter as an array. You can pass an array or a variable number of arguments to a variable-length parameter. When invoking a method with a variable number of arguments, Java creates an array and passes the arguments to it. Listing 6.5 contains a method that prints the maximum value in a list of an unspecified number of values.

LISTING 6.5 VarArgsDemo.java

```java
public class VarArgsDemo {
  public static void main(String[] args) {
    printMax(34, 3, 3, 2, 56.5);
    printMax(new double[]{1, 2, 3});
  }

  public static void printMax(double... numbers) {
    if (numbers.length == 0) {
      System.out.println("No argument passed");
```

pass variable-length arg list
pass an array arg

a variable-length arg
parameter

```
10        return;
11      }
12
13      double result = numbers[0];
14
15      for (int i = 1; i < numbers.length; i++)
16        if (numbers[i] > result)
17          result = numbers[i];
18
19      System.out.println("The max value is " + result);
20    }
21  }
```

Line 3 invokes the `printMax` method with a variable-length argument list passed to the array `numbers`. If no arguments are passed, the length of the array is `0` (line 8).

Line 4 invokes the `printMax` method with an array.

6.17 What is wrong in the following method header?

```
public static void print(String... strings, double... numbers)
public static void print(double... numbers, String name)
public static double... print(double d1, double d2)
```

6.18 Can you invoke the `printMax` method in Listing 6.5 using the following statements?

```
printMax(1, 2, 2, 1, 4);
printMax(new double[]{1, 2, 3});
printMax(new int[]{1, 2, 3});
```

6.10 Searching Arrays

If an array is sorted, binary search is more efficient than linear search for finding an element in the array.

Searching is the process of looking for a specific element in an array—for example, discovering whether a certain score is included in a list of scores. Searching is a common task in computer programming. Many algorithms and data structures are devoted to searching. This section discusses two commonly used approaches, *linear search* and *binary search*.

linear search
binary search

6.10.1 The Linear Search Approach

The linear search approach compares the key element `key` sequentially with each element in the array. It continues to do so until the key matches an element in the array or the array is exhausted without a match being found. If a match is made, the linear search returns the index of the element in the array that matches the key. If no match is found, the search returns `-1`. The `linearSearch` method in Listing 6.6 gives the solution.

linear search animation on Companion Website

LISTING 6.6 LinearSearch.java

```
1  public class LinearSearch {
2    /** The method for finding a key in the list */
3    public static int linearSearch(int[] list, int key) {
4      for (int i = 0; i < list.length; i++) {
5        if (key == list[i])
6          return i;
7      }
8      return -1;
9    }
10  }
```

[0] [1] [2] ...
list
key Compare key with `list[i]` for i = 0, 1, ...

To better understand this method, trace it with the following statements:

```
1  int[] list = {1, 4, 4, 2, 5, -3, 6, 2};
2  int i = linearSearch(list, 4);   // Returns 1
3  int j = linearSearch(list, -4);  // Returns -1
4  int k = linearSearch(list, -3);  // Returns 5
```

The linear search method compares the key with each element in the array. The elements can be in any order. On average, the algorithm will have to examine half of the elements in an array before finding the key, if it exists. Since the execution time of a linear search increases linearly as the number of array elements increases, linear search is inefficient for a large array.

6.10.2   The Binary Search Approach

Binary search is the other common search approach for a list of values. For binary search to work, the elements in the array must already be ordered. Assume that the array is in ascending order. The binary search first compares the key with the element in the middle of the array. Consider the following three cases:

- If the key is less than the middle element, you need to continue to search for the key only in the first half of the array.

- If the key is equal to the middle element, the search ends with a match.

- If the key is greater than the middle element, you need to continue to search for the key only in the second half of the array.

binary search animation on Companion Website

Clearly, the binary search method eliminates at least half of the array after each comparison. Sometimes you eliminate half of the elements, and sometimes you eliminate half plus one. Suppose that the array has n elements. For convenience, let n be a power of 2. After the first comparison, $n/2$ elements are left for further search; after the second comparison, $(n/2)/2$ elements are left. After the kth comparison, $n/2^k$ elements are left for further search. When $k = \log_2 n$, only one element is left in the array, and you need only one more comparison. Therefore, in the worst case when using the binary search approach, you need $\log_2 n + 1$ comparisons to find an element in the sorted array. In the worst case for a list of 1024 (2^{10}) elements, binary search requires only 11 comparisons, whereas a linear search requires 1023 comparisons in the worst case.

The portion of the array being searched shrinks by half after each comparison. Let `low` and `high` denote, respectively, the first index and last index of the array that is currently being searched. Initially, `low` is `0` and `high` is `list.length-1`. Let `mid` denote the index of the middle element, so `mid` is `(low + high)/2`. Figure 6.10 shows how to find key `11` in the list {2, 4, 7, 10, 11, 45, 50, 59, 60, 66, 69, 70, 79} using binary search.

You now know how the binary search works. The next task is to implement it in Java. Don't rush to give a complete implementation. Implement it incrementally, one step at a time. You may start with the first iteration of the search, as shown in Figure 6.11a. It compares the key with the middle element in the list whose `low` index is `0` and `high` index is `list.length - 1`. If `key < list[mid]`, set the `high` index to `mid - 1`; if `key == list[mid]`, a match is found and return `mid`; if `key > list[mid]`, set the `low` index to `mid + 1`.

Next consider implementing the method to perform the search repeatedly by adding a loop, as shown in Figure 6.11b. The search ends if the key is found, or if the key is not found when `low > high`.

why not −1?

When the key is not found, `low` is the insertion point where a key would be inserted to maintain the order of the list. It is more useful to return the insertion point than `-1`. The method must return a negative value to indicate that the key is not in the list. Can it simply return `-low`? No. If the key is less than `list[0]`, `low` would be `0`. `-0` is `0`. This would

FIGURE 6.10 Binary search eliminates half of the list from further consideration after each comparison.

```
public static int binarySearch(
    int[] list, int key) {
  int low = 0;
  int high = list.length - 1;

  int mid = (low + high) / 2;
  if (key < list[mid])
    high = mid - 1;
  else if (key == list[mid])
    return mid;
  else
    low = mid + 1;



}
```
(a) Version 1

```
public static int binarySearch(
    int[] list, int key) {
  int low = 0;
  int high = list.length - 1;

  while (high >= low) {
    int mid = (low + high) / 2;
    if (key < list[mid])
      high = mid - 1;
    else if (key == list[mid])
      return mid;
    else
      low = mid + 1;
  }

  return -1; // Not found
}
```
(b) Version 2

FIGURE 6.11 Binary search is implemented incrementally.

indicate that the key matches `list[0]`. A good choice is to let the method return `-low - 1` if the key is not in the list. Returning `-low - 1` indicates not only that the key is not in the list, but also where the key would be inserted.

The complete program is given in Listing 6.7.

LISTING 6.7 BinarySearch.java

```
1  public class BinarySearch {
2    /** Use binary search to find the key in the list */
3    public static int binarySearch(int[] list, int key) {
4      int low = 0;
5      int high = list.length - 1;
6
7      while (high >= low) {
8        int mid = (low + high) / 2;
9        if (key < list[mid])
10         high = mid - 1;
11       else if (key == list[mid])
```

first half

```
12              return mid;
13          else
14              low = mid + 1;
15      }
16
17      return -low - 1; // Now high < low, key not found
18  }
19 }
```

second half

The binary search returns the index of the search key if it is contained in the list (line 12). Otherwise, it returns `-low - 1` (line 17).

What would happen if we replaced `(high >= low)` in line 7 with `(high > low)`? The search would miss a possible matching element. Consider a list with just one element. The search would miss the element.

Does the method still work if there are duplicate elements in the list? Yes, as long as the elements are sorted in increasing order. The method returns the index of one of the matching elements if the element is in the list.

To better understand this method, trace it with the following statements and identify `low` and `high` when the method returns.

```
int[] list = {2, 4, 7, 10, 11, 45, 50, 59, 60, 66, 69, 70, 79};
int i = BinarySearch.binarySearch(list, 2); // Returns 0
int j = BinarySearch.binarySearch(list, 11); // Returns 4
int k = BinarySearch.binarySearch(list, 12); // Returns -6
int l = BinarySearch.binarySearch(list, 1); // Returns -1
int m = BinarySearch.binarySearch(list, 3); // Returns -2
```

Here is the table that lists the `low` and `high` values when the method exits and the value returned from invoking the method.

Method	Low	High	Value Returned
binarySearch(list, 2)	0	1	0
binarySearch(list, 11)	3	5	4
binarySearch(list, 12)	5	4	-6
binarySearch(list, 1)	0	-1	-1
binarySearch(list, 3)	1	0	-2

Note

Linear search is useful for finding an element in a small array or an unsorted array, but it is inefficient for large arrays. Binary search is more efficient, but it requires that the array be presorted.

binary search benefits

6.11 Sorting Arrays

Key Point

There are many strategies for sorting elements in an array. Selection sort and insertion sort are two common approaches.

Sorting, like searching, is a common task in computer programming. Many different algorithms have been developed for sorting. This section introduces two simple, intuitive sorting algorithms: *selection sort* and *insertion sort*.

selection sort

insertion sort

6.11.1   Selection Sort

Suppose that you want to sort a list in ascending order. Selection sort finds the smallest number in the list and swaps it with the first element. It then finds the smallest number remaining and swaps it with the second element, and so on, until only a single number remains. Figure 6.12 shows how to sort the list {2, 9, 5, 4, 8, 1, 6} using selection sort.

VideoNote

Selection sort

selection sort animation on Companion Website

Select 1 (the smallest) and swap it with 2 (the first) in the list.

The number 1 is now in the correct position and thus no longer needs to be considered.

Select 2 (the smallest) and swap it with 9 (the first) in the remaining list.

The number 2 is now in the correct position and thus no longer needs to be considered.

Select 4 (the smallest) and swap it with 5 (the first) in the remaining list.

The number 4 is now in the correct position and thus no longer needs to be considered.

5 is the smallest and in the right position. No swap is necessary.

The number 5 is now in the correct position and thus no longer needs to be considered.

Select 6 (the smallest) and swap it with 8 (the first) in the remaining list.

The number 6 is now in the correct position and thus no longer needs to be considered.

Select 8 (the smallest) and swap it with 9 (the first) in the remaining list.

The number 8 is now in the correct position and thus no longer needs to be considered.

Since there is only one element remaining in the list, the sort is completed.

FIGURE 6.12   Selection sort repeatedly selects the smallest number and swaps it with the first number in the list.

You know how the selection-sort approach works. The task now is to implement it in Java. Beginners find it difficult to develop a complete solution on the first attempt. Start by writing the code for the first iteration to find the smallest element in the list and swap it with the first element, and then observe what would be different for the second iteration, the third, and so on. The insight this gives will enable you to write a loop that generalizes all the iterations.

The solution can be described as follows:

```
for (int i = 0; i < list.length - 1; i++) {
  select the smallest element in list[i..list.length-1];
  swap the smallest with list[i], if necessary;
  // list[i] is in its correct position.
  // The next iteration apply on list[i+1..list.length-1]
}
```

Listing 6.8 implements the solution.

LISTING 6.8 `SelectionSort.java`

```java
 1  public class SelectionSort {
 2    /** The method for sorting the numbers */
 3    public static void selectionSort(double[] list) {
 4      for (int i = 0; i < list.length - 1; i++) {
 5        // Find the minimum in the list[i..list.length-1]
 6        double currentMin = list[i];
 7        int currentMinIndex = i;
 8
 9        for (int j = i + 1; j < list.length; j++) {
10          if (currentMin > list[j]) {
11            currentMin = list[j];
12            currentMinIndex = j;
13          }
14        }
15
16        // Swap list[i] with list[currentMinIndex] if necessary
17        if (currentMinIndex != i) {
18          list[currentMinIndex] = list[i];
19          list[i] = currentMin;
20        }
21      }
22    }
23  }
```

select

swap

The `selectionSort(double[] list)` method sorts any array of `double` elements. The method is implemented with a nested `for` loop. The outer loop (with the loop control variable `i`) (line 4) is iterated in order to find the smallest element in the list, which ranges from `list[i]` to `list[list.length-1]`, and exchange it with `list[i]`.

The variable `i` is initially `0`. After each iteration of the outer loop, `list[i]` is in the right place. Eventually, all the elements are put in the right place; therefore, the whole list is sorted.

To understand this method better, trace it with the following statements:

```java
double[] list = {1, 9, 4.5, 6.6, 5.7, -4.5};
SelectionSort.selectionSort(list);
```

6.11.2 Insertion Sort

insertion sort animation on Companion Website

Suppose that you want to sort a list in ascending order. The insertion-sort algorithm sorts a list of values by repeatedly inserting a new element into a sorted sublist until the whole list is sorted. Figure 6.13 shows how to sort the list {2, 9, 5, 4, 8, 1, 6} using insertion sort.

The algorithm can be described as follows:

```java
for (int i = 1; i < list.length; i++) {
  insert list[i] into a sorted sublist list[0..i-1] so that
  list[0..i] is sorted.
}
```

To insert `list[i]` into `list[0..i-1]`, save `list[i]` into a temporary variable, say `currentElement`. Move `list[i-1]` to `list[i]` if `list[i-1] > currentElement`, move `list[i-2]` to `list[i-1]` if `list[i-2] > currentElement`, and so on, until `list[i-k] <= currentElement` or `k > i` (we pass the first element of the sorted list). Assign `currentElement` to `list[i-k+1]`. For example, to insert `4` into {2, 5, 9} in Step 4 in Figure 6.14, move `list[2]` (9) to `list[3]` since `9 > 4`, and move `list[1]` (5) to `list[2]` since `5 > 4`. Finally, move `currentElement` (4) to `list[1]`.

Step 1: Initially, the sorted sublist contains the first element in the list. Insert 9 into the sublist.

2   9   5   4   8   1   6

Step 2: The sorted sublist is {2, 9}. Insert 5 into the sublist.

2   9→5   4   8   1   6

Step 3: The sorted sublist is {2, 5, 9}. Insert 4 into the sublist.

2   5→9→4   8   1   6

Step 4: The sorted sublist is {2, 4, 5, 9}. Insert 8 into the sublist.

2   4   5   9→8   1   6

Step 5: The sorted sublist is {2, 4, 5, 8, 9}. Insert 1 into the sublist.

2→4→5→8→9→1   6

Step 6: The sorted sublist is {1, 2, 4, 5, 8, 9}. Insert 6 into the sublist.

1   2   4   5   8→9→6

Step 7: The entire list is now sorted.

1   2   4   5   6   8   9

FIGURE 6.13 Insertion sort repeatedly inserts a new element into a sorted sublist.

```
        [0][1][2][3][4][5][6]
list    | 2  5  9  4           |    Step 1: Save 4 to a temporary variable currentElement

        [0][1][2][3][4][5][6]
list    | 2  5     9           |    Step 2: Move list[2] to list[3]

        [0][1][2][3][4][5][6]
list    | 2     5  9           |    Step 3: Move list[1] to list[2]

        [0][1][2][3][4][5][6]
list    | 2  4  5  9           |    Step 4: Assign currentElement to list[1]
```

FIGURE 6.14 A new element is inserted into a sorted sublist.

The algorithm can be expanded and implemented as in Listing 6.9.

LISTING 6.9 InsertionSort.java

```java
1  public class InsertionSort {
2    /** The method for sorting the numbers */
3    public static void insertionSort(double[] list) {
4      for (int i = 1; i < list.length; i++) {
5        /** Insert list[i] into a sorted sublist list[0..i-1] so that
6             list[0..i] is sorted. */
7        double currentElement = list[i];
8        int k;
9        for (k = i - 1; k >= 0 && list[k] > currentElement; k--) {     shift
10         list[k + 1] = list[k];
11       }
12
13       // Insert the current element into list[k + 1]
```

insert

```
14              list[k + 1] = currentElement;
15          }
16      }
17  }
```

The `insertionSort(double[] list)` method sorts any array of `double` elements. The method is implemented with a nested `for` loop. The outer loop (with the loop control variable `i`) (line 4) is iterated in order to obtain a sorted sublist, which ranges from `list[0]` to `list[i]`. The inner loop (with the loop control variable `k`) inserts `list[i]` into the sublist from `list[0]` to `list[i-1]`.

To better understand this method, trace it with the following statements:

```
double[] list = {1, 9, 4.5, 6.6, 5.7, -4.5};
InsertionSort.insertionSort(list);
```

Check Point

MyProgrammingLab™

6.19 Use Figure 6.10 as an example to show how to apply the binary search approach to a search for key **10** and key **12** in list {2, 4, 7, 10, 11, 45, 50, 59, 60, 66, 69, 70, 79}.

6.20 If the binary search method returns –4, is the key in the list? Where should the key be inserted if you wish to insert the key into the list?

6.21 Use Figure 6.12 as an example to show how to apply the selection-sort approach to sort {3.4, 5, 3, 3.5, 2.2, 1.9, 2}.

6.22 Use Figure 6.13 as an example to show how to apply the insertion-sort approach to sort {3.4, 5, 3, 3.5, 2.2, 1.9, 2}.

6.23 How do you modify the `selectionSort` method in Listing 6.8 to sort numbers in decreasing order?

6.24 How do you modify the `insertionSort` method in Listing 6.9 to sort numbers in decreasing order?

6.12 The **Arrays** Class

Key Point

The `java.util.Arrays` class contains useful methods for common array operations such as sorting and searching.

The `java.util.Arrays` class contains various static methods for sorting and searching arrays, comparing arrays, filling array elements, and returning a string representation of the array. These methods are overloaded for all primitive types.

sort

You can use the `sort` method to sort a whole array or a partial array. For example, the following code sorts an array of numbers and an array of characters.

```
double[] numbers = {6.0, 4.4, 1.9, 2.9, 3.4, 3.5};
java.util.Arrays.sort(numbers); // Sort the whole array

char[] chars = {'a', 'A', '4', 'F', 'D', 'P'};
java.util.Arrays.sort(chars, 1, 3); // Sort part of the array
```

Invoking `sort(numbers)` sorts the whole array `numbers`. Invoking `sort(chars, 1, 3)` sorts a partial array from `chars[1]` to `chars[3-1]`.

binarySearch

You can use the `binarySearch` method to search for a key in an array. The array must be presorted in increasing order. If the key is not in the array, the method returns `–(insertionindex + 1)`. For example, the following code searches the keys in an array of integers and an array of characters.

```
int[] list = {2, 4, 7, 10, 11, 45, 50, 59, 60, 66, 69, 70, 79};
System.out.println("(1) Index is " +
        java.util.Arrays.binarySearch(list, 11));
```

```
System.out.println("(2) Index is " +
      java.util.Arrays.binarySearch(list, 12));

char[] chars = {'a', 'c', 'g', 'x', 'y', 'z'};
System.out.println("(3) Index is " +
      java.util.Arrays.binarySearch(chars, 'a'));
System.out.println("(4) Index is " +
      java.util.Arrays.binarySearch(chars, 't'));
```

The output of the preceding code is

1. Index is 4

2. Index is –6

3. Index is 0

4. Index is –4

You can use the **equals** method to check whether two arrays are equal. Two arrays are equal   equals
if they have the same contents. In the following code, **list1** and **list2** are equal, but **list2**
and **list3** are not.

```
int[] list1 = {2, 4, 7, 10};
int[] list2 = {2, 4, 7, 10};
int[] list3 = {4, 2, 7, 10};
System.out.println(java.util.Arrays.equals(list1, list2)); // true
System.out.println(java.util.Arrays.equals(list2, list3)); // false
```

You can use the **fill** method to fill in all or part of the array. For example, the following code   fill
fills **list1** with **5** and fills **8** into elements **list2[1]** and **list2[3-1]**.

```
int[] list1 = {2, 4, 7, 10};
int[] list2 = {2, 4, 7, 10};
java.util.Arrays.fill(list1, 5); // Fill 5 to the whole array
java.util.Arrays.fill(list2, 1, 3, 8); // Fill 8 to a partial array
```

You can also use the **toString** method to return a string that represents all elements in the   toString
array. This is a quick and simple way to display all elements in the array. For example, the following code

```
int[] list = {2, 4, 7, 10};
System.out.println(Arrays.toString(list));
```

displays **[2, 4, 7, 10]**.

6.25 What types of array can be sorted using the **java.util.Arrays.sort** method?
Does this **sort** method create a new array?

6.26 To apply **java.util.Arrays.binarySearch(array, key)**, should the array be
sorted in increasing order, in decreasing order, or neither?

6.27 Show the output of the following code:

```
int[] list1 = {2, 4, 7, 10};
java.util.Arrays.fill(list1, 7);
System.out.println(java.util.Arrays.toString(list1));

int[] list2 = {2, 4, 7, 10};
System.out.println(java.util.Arrays.toString(list2));
System.out.print(java.util.Arrays.equals(list1, list2));
```

**Check
Point**

MyProgrammingLab™

KEY TERMS

anonymous array   238
array   224
array initializer   227
binary search   245
garbage collection   236
index   224

indexed variable   226
insertion sort   248
linear search   245
off-by-one error   230
selection sort   248

CHAPTER SUMMARY

1. A variable is declared as an *array* type using the syntax `elementType[] arrayRefVar` or `elementType arrayRefVar[]`. The style `elementType[] arrayRefVar` is preferred, although `elementType arrayRefVar[]` is legal.

2. Unlike declarations for primitive data type variables, the declaration of an array variable does not allocate any space in memory for the array. An array variable is not a primitive data type variable. An array variable contains a reference to an array.

3. You cannot assign elements to an array unless it has already been created. You can create an array by using the `new` operator with the following syntax: `new elementType[arraySize]`.

4. Each element in the array is represented using the syntax `arrayRefVar[index]`. An *index* must be an integer or an integer expression.

5. After an array is created, its size becomes permanent and can be obtained using `arrayRefVar.length`. Since the index of an array always begins with `0`, the last index is always `arrayRefVar.length - 1`. An out-of-bounds error will occur if you attempt to reference elements beyond the bounds of an array.

6. Programmers often mistakenly reference the first element in an array with index `1`, but it should be `0`. This is called the index *off-by-one error*.

7. When an array is created, its elements are assigned the default value of `0` for the numeric primitive data types, `\u0000` for char types, and `false` for `boolean` types.

8. Java has a shorthand notation, known as the *array initializer*, which combines declaring an array, creating an array, and initializing an array in one statement, using the syntax `elementType[] arrayRefVar = {value0, value1, ..., value`*k*`}`.

9. When you pass an array argument to a method, you are actually passing the reference of the array; that is, the called method can modify the elements in the caller's original array.

10. If an array is sorted, *binary search* is more efficient than *linear search* for finding an element in the array.

11. *Selection sort* finds the smallest number in the list and swaps it with the first element. It then finds the smallest number remaining and swaps it with the first element in the remaining list, and so on, until only a single number remains.

12. The *insertion-sort algorithm* sorts a list of values by repeatedly inserting a new element into a sorted sublist until the whole list is sorted.

TEST QUESTIONS

Do the test questions for this chapter online at www.cs.armstrong.edu/liang/intro9e/test.html.

PROGRAMMING EXERCISES

MyProgrammingLab™

Sections 6.2–6.5

*6.1 (*Assign grades*) Write a program that reads student scores, gets the best score, and then assigns grades based on the following scheme:

Grade is A if score is >= best − 10

Grade is B if score is >= best − 20;

Grade is C if score is >= best − 30;

Grade is D if score is >= best − 40;

Grade is F otherwise.

The program prompts the user to enter the total number of students, then prompts the user to enter all of the scores, and concludes by displaying the grades. Here is a sample run:

```
Enter the number of students: 4 ↵Enter
Enter 4 scores: 40 55 70 58 ↵Enter
Student 0 score is 40 and grade is C
Student 1 score is 55 and grade is B
Student 2 score is 70 and grade is A
Student 3 score is 58 and grade is B
```

6.2 (*Reverse the numbers entered*) Write a program that reads ten integers and displays them in the reverse of the order in which they were read.

**6.3 (*Count occurrence of numbers*) Write a program that reads the integers between 1 and 100 and counts the occurrences of each. Assume the input ends with 0. Here is a sample run of the program:

```
Enter the integers between 1 and 100: 2 5 6 5 4 3 23 43 2 0 ↵Enter
2 occurs 2 times
3 occurs 1 time
4 occurs 1 time
5 occurs 2 times
6 occurs 1 time
23 occurs 1 time
43 occurs 1 time
```

Note that if a number occurs more than one time, the plural word "times" is used in the output.

6.4 (*Analyze scores*) Write a program that reads an unspecified number of scores and determines how many scores are above or equal to the average and how many scores are below the average. Enter a negative number to signify the end of the input. Assume that the maximum number of scores is 100.

**6.5 (*Print distinct numbers*) Write a program that reads in ten numbers and displays distinct numbers (i.e., if a number appears multiple times, it is displayed only once). (*Hint*: Read a number and store it to an array if it is new. If the number is already in the array, ignore it.) After the input, the array contains the distinct numbers. Here is the sample run of the program:

```
Enter ten numbers: 1 2 3 2 1 6 3 4 5 2  ↵Enter
The distinct numbers are: 1 2 3 6 4 5
```

*6.6 (*Revise Listing 4.14, PrimeNumber.java*) Listing 4.14 determines whether a number n is prime by checking whether 2, 3, 4, 5, 6, ..., n/2 is a divisor. If a divisor is found, n is not prime. A more efficient approach is to check whether any of the prime numbers less than or equal to $\sqrt{n}$ can divide n evenly. If not, n is prime. Rewrite Listing 4.14 to display the first 50 prime numbers using this approach. You need to use an array to store the prime numbers and later use them to check whether they are possible divisors for n.

*6.7 (*Count single digits*) Write a program that generates 100 random integers between 0 and 9 and displays the count for each number. (*Hint*: Use `(int)(Math.random() * 10)` to generate a random integer between 0 and 9. Use an array of ten integers, say `counts`, to store the counts for the number of 0s, 1s, ..., 9s.)

Sections 6.6–6.8

6.8 (*Average an array*) Write two overloaded methods that return the average of an array with the following headers:

```java
public static int average(int[] array)
public static double average(double[] array)
```

Write a test program that prompts the user to enter ten double values, invokes this method, and displays the average value.

6.9 (*Find the smallest element*) Write a method that finds the smallest element in an array of double values using the following header:

```java
public static double min(double[] array)
```

Write a test program that prompts the user to enter ten numbers, invokes this method to return the minimum value, and displays the minimum value. Here is a sample run of the program:

```
Enter ten numbers: 1.9 2.5 3.7 2 1.5 6 3 4 5 2  ↵Enter
The minimum number is: 1.5
```

6.10 (*Find the index of the smallest element*) Write a method that returns the index of the smallest element in an array of integers. If the number of such elements is greater than 1, return the smallest index. Use the following header:

```java
public static int indexOfSmallestElement(double[] array)
```

Write a test program that prompts the user to enter ten numbers, invokes this method to return the index of the smallest element, and displays the index.

*6.11 (*Statistics: compute deviation*) Programming Exercise 5.37 computes the standard deviation of numbers. This exercise uses a different but equivalent formula to compute the standard deviation of n numbers.

$$mean = \frac{\sum_{i=1}^{n} x_i}{n} = \frac{x_1 + x_2 + \ldots + x_n}{n} \qquad deviation = \sqrt{\frac{\sum_{i=1}^{n} (x_i - mean)^2}{n - 1}}$$

To compute the standard deviation with this formula, you have to store the individual numbers using an array, so that they can be used after the mean is obtained.

Your program should contain the following methods:

```
/** Compute the deviation of double values */
public static double deviation(double[] x)

/** Compute the mean of an array of double values */
public static double mean(double[] x)
```

Write a test program that prompts the user to enter ten numbers and displays the mean and standard deviation, as shown in the following sample run:

```
Enter ten numbers: 1.9 2.5 3.7 2 1 6 3 4 5 2  ↵Enter
The mean is 3.11
The standard deviation is 1.55738
```

*6.12 (*Reverse an array*) The `reverse` method in Section 6.7 reverses an array by copying it to a new array. Rewrite the method that reverses the array passed in the argument and returns this array. Write a test program that prompts the user to enter ten numbers, invokes the method to reverse the numbers, and displays the numbers.

Section 6.9

*6.13 (*Random number chooser*) Write a method that returns a random number between 1 and 54, excluding the numbers passed in the argument. The method header is specified as follows:

```
public static int getRandom(int... numbers)
```

6.14 (*Computing gcd*) Write a method that returns the gcd of an unspecified number of integers. The method header is specified as follows:

```
public static int gcd(int... numbers)
```

Write a test program that prompts the user to enter five numbers, invokes the method to find the gcd of these numbers, and displays the gcd.

Sections 6.10–6.12

6.15 (*Eliminate duplicates*) Write a method that returns a new array by eliminating the duplicate values in the array using the following method header:

```
public static int[] eliminateDuplicates(int[] list)
```

Write a test program that reads in ten integers, invokes the method, and displays the result. Here is the sample run of the program:

```
Enter ten numbers: 1 2 3 2 1 6 3 4 5 2  ↵Enter
The distinct numbers are: 1 2 3 6 4 5
```

6.16 (*Execution time*) Write a program that randomly generates an array of 100,000 integers and a key. Estimate the execution time of invoking the `linearSearch` method in Listing 6.6. Sort the array and estimate the execution time of invoking the `binarySearch` method in Listing 6.7. You can use the following code template to obtain the execution time:

```
long startTime = System.currentTimeMillis();
perform the task;
long endTime = System.currentTimeMillis();
long executionTime = endTime - startTime;
```

**6.17 (*Sort students*) Write a program that prompts the user to enter the number of students, the students' names, and their scores, and prints student names in decreasing order of their scores.

**6.18 (*Bubble sort*) Write a sort method that uses the bubble-sort algorithm. The bubble-sort algorithm makes several passes through the array. On each pass, successive neighboring pairs are compared. If a pair is not in order, its values are swapped; otherwise, the values remain unchanged. The technique is called a *bubble sort* or *sinking sort* because the smaller values gradually "bubble" their way to the top and the larger values "sink" to the bottom. Write a test program that reads in ten double numbers, invokes the method, and displays the sorted numbers.

**6.19 (*Sorted?*) Write the following method that returns true if the list is already sorted in increasing order.

public static boolean isSorted(**int**[] list)

Write a test program that prompts the user to enter a list and displays whether the list is sorted or not. Here is a sample run. Note that the first number in the input indicates the number of the elements in the list.

```
Enter list: 8 10 1 5 16 61 9 11 1  ↵Enter
The list is not sorted
```

```
Enter list: 10 1 1 3 4 4 5 7 9 11 21  ↵Enter
The list is already sorted
```

*6.20 (*Revise selection sort*) In Section 6.11.1, you used selection sort to sort an array. The selection-sort method repeatedly finds the smallest number in the current array and swaps it with the first. Rewrite this program by finding the largest number and swapping it with the last. Write a test program that reads in ten double numbers, invokes the method, and displays the sorted numbers.

***6.21 (*Game: bean machine*) The bean machine, also known as a quincunx or the Galton box, is a device for statistics experiments named after English scientist Sir Francis Galton. It consists of an upright board with evenly spaced nails (or pegs) in a triangular form, as shown in Figure 6.15.

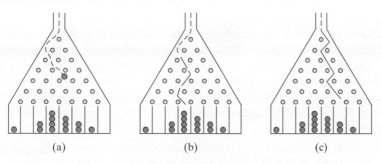

FIGURE 6.15 Each ball takes a random path and falls into a slot.

Balls are dropped from the opening of the board. Every time a ball hits a nail, it has a 50% chance of falling to the left or to the right. The piles of balls are accumulated in the slots at the bottom of the board.

Write a program that simulates the bean machine. Your program should prompt the user to enter the number of the balls and the number of the slots in the machine. Simulate the falling of each ball by printing its path. For example, the path for the ball in Figure 6.15b is LLRRLLR and the path for the ball in Figure 6.15c is RLRRLRR. Display the final buildup of the balls in the slots in a histogram. Here is a sample run of the program:

```
Enter the number of balls to drop: 5  ↵Enter
Enter the number of slots in the bean machine: 7  ↵Enter

LRLRLRR
RRLLLRR
LLRLLRR
RRLLLLL
LRLRRLR


       0
       0
     000
```

(*Hint*: Create an array named `slots`. Each element in `slots` stores the number of balls in a slot. Each ball falls into a slot via a path. The number of Rs in a path is the position of the slot where the ball falls. For example, for the path LRLRLRR, the ball falls into `slots[4]`, and for the path is RRLLLLL, the ball falls into `slots[2]`.)

***6.22 (*Game: Eight Queens*) The classic Eight Queens puzzle is to place eight queens on a chessboard such that no two queens can attack each other (i.e., no two queens are on the same row, same column, or same diagonal). There are many possible solutions. Write a program that displays one such solution. A sample output is shown below:

```
|Q| | | | | | | |
| | | | |Q| | | |
| | | | | | | |Q|
| | | | |Q| | | |
| | |Q| | | | | |
| | | | | | |Q| |
| |Q| | | | | | |
| | | |Q| | | | |
```

**6.23 *(Game: locker puzzle)* A school has 100 lockers and 100 students. All lockers are closed on the first day of school. As the students enter, the first student, denoted S1, opens every locker. Then the second student, S2, begins with the second locker, denoted L2, and closes every other locker. Student S3 begins with the third locker and changes every third locker (closes it if it was open, and opens it if it was closed). Student S4 begins with locker L4 and changes every fourth locker. Student S5 starts with L5 and changes every fifth locker, and so on, until student S100 changes L100.

After all the students have passed through the building and changed the lockers, which lockers are open? Write a program to find your answer.

(Hint: Use an array of 100 Boolean elements, each of which indicates whether a locker is open (`true`) or closed (`false`). Initially, all lockers are closed.)

VideoNote

Coupon collector's problem

**6.24 *(Simulation: coupon collector's problem)* Coupon collector is a classic statistics problem with many practical applications. The problem is to pick objects from a set of objects repeatedly and find out how many picks are needed for all the objects to be picked at least once. A variation of the problem is to pick cards from a shuffled deck of 52 cards repeatedly and find out how many picks are needed before you see one of each suit. Assume a picked card is placed back in the deck before picking another. Write a program to simulate the number of picks needed to get four cards from each suit and display the four cards picked (it is possible a card may be picked twice). Here is a sample run of the program:

```
Queen of Spades
5 of Clubs
Queen of Hearts
4 of Diamonds
Number of picks: 12
```

6.25 *(Algebra: solve quadratic equations)* Write a method for solving a quadratic equation using the following header:

```
public static int solveQuadratic(double[] eqn, double[] roots)
```

The coefficients of a quadratic equation $ax^2 + bx + c = 0$ are passed to the array eqn and the noncomplex roots are stored in roots. The method returns the number of roots. See Programming Exercise 3.1 on how to solve a quadratic equation.

Write a program that prompts the user to enter values for *a*, *b*, and *c* and displays the number of roots and all noncomplex roots.

6.26 *(Strictly identical arrays)* The arrays `list1` and `list2` are *strictly identical* if their corresponding elements are equal. Write a method that returns `true` if `list1` and `list2` are strictly identical, using the following header:

```
public static boolean equals(int[] list1, int[] list2)
```

Write a test program that prompts the user to enter two lists of integers and displays whether the two are strictly identical. Here are the sample runs. Note that the first number in the input indicates the number of the elements in the list.

```
Enter list1: 5 2 5 6 1 6  ↵Enter
Enter list2: 5 2 5 6 1 6  ↵Enter
Two lists are strictly identical
```

```
Enter list1: 5 2 5 6 6 1 ⏎Enter
Enter list2: 5 2 5 6 1 6 ⏎Enter
Two lists are not strictly identical
```

6.27 (*Identical arrays*) The arrays `list1` and `list2` are *identical* if they have the same contents. Write a method that returns `true` if `list1` and `list2` are identical, using the following header:

public static boolean equals(**int**[] list1, **int**[] list2)

Write a test program that prompts the user to enter two lists of integers and displays whether the two are identical. Here are the sample runs. Note that the first number in the input indicates the number of the elements in the list.

```
Enter list1: 5 2 5 6 6 1 ⏎Enter
Enter list2: 5 5 2 6 1 6 ⏎Enter
Two lists are identical
```

```
Enter list1: 5 5 5 6 6 1 ⏎Enter
Enter list2: 5 2 5 6 1 6 ⏎Enter
Two lists are not identical
```

*6.28 (*Math: combinations*) Write a program that prompts the user to enter 10 integers and displays all combinations of picking two numbers from the 10.

*6.29 (*Game: pick four cards*) Write a program that picks four cards from a deck of 52 cards and computes their sum. An Ace, King, Queen, and Jack represent 1, 13, 12, and 11, respectively. Your program should display the number of picks that yields the sum of 24.

*6.30 (*Pattern recognition: consecutive four equal numbers*) Write the following method that tests whether the array has four consecutive numbers with the same value.

VideoNote

Consecutive four

public static boolean isConsecutiveFour(**int**[] values)

Write a test program that prompts the user to enter a series of integers and displays true if the series contains four consecutive numbers with the same value. Otherwise, display false. Your program should first prompt the user to enter the input size—i.e., the number of values in the series.

**6.31 (*Merge two sorted lists*) Write the following method that merges two sorted lists into a new sorted list.

public static int[] merge(**int**[] list1, **int**[] list2)

Implement the method in a way that takes `list1.length + list2.length` comparisons. Write a test program that prompts the user to enter two sorted lists and displays the merged list. Here is a sample run. Note that the first number in the input indicates the number of the elements in the list.

```
Enter list1: 5 1 5 16 61 111  ↵Enter
Enter list2: 4 2 4 5 6  ↵Enter
The merged list is 1 2 4 5 5 6 16 61 111
```

**6.32 (*Partition of a list*) Write the following method that partitions the list using the first element, called a *pivot*.

public static int partition(**int**[] list)

After the partition, the elements in the list are rearranged so that all the elements before the pivot are less than or equal to the pivot and the elements after the pivot are greater than the pivot. The method returns the index where the pivot is located in the new list. For example, suppose the list is {5, 2, 9, 3, 6, 8}. After the partition, the list becomes {3, 2, 5, 9, 6, 8}. Implement the method in a way that takes list.length comparisons. Write a test program that prompts the user to enter a list and displays the list after the partition. Here is a sample run. Note that the first number in the input indicates the number of the elements in the list.

```
Enter list: 8 10 1 5 16 61 9 11 1  ↵Enter
After the partition, the list is 9 1 5 1 10 61 11 16
```

*6.33 (*Culture: Chinese Zodiac*) Simplify Listing 3.10 using an array of strings to store the animal names.

***6.34 (*Game: multiple Eight Queens solutions*) Exercise 6.22 finds one solution for the Eight Queens problem. Write a program to count all possible solutions for the Eight Queens problem and display all solutions.

MULTIDIMENSIONAL ARRAYS

Objectives

- To give examples of representing data using two-dimensional arrays (§7.1).

- To declare variables for two-dimensional arrays, create arrays, and access array elements in a two-dimensional array using row and column indexes (§7.2).

- To program common operations for two-dimensional arrays (displaying arrays, summing all elements, finding the minimum and maximum elements, and random shuffling) (§7.3).

- To pass two-dimensional arrays to methods (§7.4).

- To write a program for grading multiple-choice questions using two-dimensional arrays (§7.5).

- To solve the closest-pair problem using two-dimensional arrays (§7.6).

- To check a Sudoku solution using two-dimensional arrays (§7.7).

- To use multidimensional arrays (§7.8).

7.1 Introduction

Data in a table or a matrix can be represented using a two-dimensional array.

The preceding chapter introduced how to use one-dimensional arrays to store linear collections of elements. You can use a two-dimensional array to store a matrix or a table. For example, the following table that lists the distances between cities can be stored using a two-dimensional array named `distances`.

problem

| Distance Table (in miles) | | | | | | |
	Chicago	Boston	New York	Atlanta	Miami	Dallas	Houston
Chicago	0	983	787	714	1375	967	1087
Boston	983	0	214	1102	1763	1723	1842
New York	787	214	0	888	1549	1548	1627
Atlanta	714	1102	888	0	661	781	810
Miami	1375	1763	1549	661	0	1426	1187
Dallas	967	1723	1548	781	1426	0	239
Houston	1087	1842	1627	810	1187	239	0

```java
double[][] distances = {
    {0, 983, 787, 714, 1375, 967, 1087},
    {983, 0, 214, 1102, 1763, 1723, 1842},
    {787, 214, 0, 888, 1549, 1548, 1627},
    {714, 1102, 888, 0, 661, 781, 810},
    {1375, 1763, 1549, 661, 0, 1426, 1187},
    {967, 1723, 1548, 781, 1426, 0, 239},
    {1087, 1842, 1627, 810, 1187, 239, 0},
};
```

7.2 Two-Dimensional Array Basics

An element in a two-dimensional array is accessed through a row and column index.

How do you declare a variable for two-dimensional arrays? How do you create a two-dimensional array? How do you access elements in a two-dimensional array? This section addresses these issues.

7.2.1 Declaring Variables of Two-Dimensional Arrays and Creating Two-Dimensional Arrays

The syntax for declaring a two-dimensional array is:

```java
elementType[][] arrayRefVar;
```

or

```java
elementType arrayRefVar[][]; // Allowed, but not preferred
```

As an example, here is how you would declare a two-dimensional array variable `matrix` of `int` values:

```java
int[][] matrix;
```

or

```
int matrix[][]; // This style is allowed, but not preferred
```

You can create a two-dimensional array of 5-by-5 `int` values and assign it to `matrix` using this syntax:

```
matrix = new int[5][5];
```

Two subscripts are used in a two-dimensional array, one for the row and the other for the column. As in a one-dimensional array, the index for each subscript is of the `int` type and starts from `0`, as shown in Figure 7.1a.

```
           [0][1][2][3][4]              [0][1][2][3][4]                [0][1][2]
      [0]  0  0  0  0  0           [0]  0  0  0  0  0            [0]  1  2  3
      [1]  0  0  0  0  0           [1]  0  0  0  0  0            [1]  4  5  6
      [2]  0  0  0  0  0           [2]  0  7  0  0  0            [2]  7  8  9
      [3]  0  0  0  0  0           [3]  0  0  0  0  0            [3] 10 11 12
      [4]  0  0  0  0  0           [4]  0  0  0  0  0

                                                           int[][] array = {
                                                              {1, 2, 3},
      matrix = new int[5][5];      matrix[2][1] = 7;           {4, 5, 6},
                                                              {7, 8, 9},
                                                              {10, 11, 12}
                                                           };

           (a)                          (b)                            (c)
```

FIGURE 7.1 The index of each subscript of a two-dimensional array is an `int` value, starting from `0`.

To assign the value `7` to a specific element at row `2` and column `1`, as shown in Figure 7.1b, you can use the following syntax:

```
matrix[2][1] = 7;
```

 Caution

It is a common mistake to use `matrix[2, 1]` to access the element at row `2` and column `1`. In Java, each subscript must be enclosed in a pair of square brackets.

You can also use an array initializer to declare, create, and initialize a two-dimensional array. For example, the following code in (a) creates an array with the specified initial values, as shown in Figure 7.1c. This is equivalent to the code in (b).

```
int[][] array = {
   {1, 2, 3},
   {4, 5, 6},
   {7, 8, 9},
   {10, 11, 12}
};
```

Equivalent

```
int[][] array = new int[4][3];
array[0][0] = 1; array[0][1] = 2; array[0][2] = 3;
array[1][0] = 4; array[1][1] = 5; array[1][2] = 6;
array[2][0] = 7; array[2][1] = 8; array[2][2] = 9;
array[3][0] = 10; array[3][1] = 11; array[3][2] = 12;
```

(a)

(b)

7.2.2 Obtaining the Lengths of Two-Dimensional Arrays

A two-dimensional array is actually an array in which each element is a one-dimensional array. The length of an array `x` is the number of elements in the array, which can be obtained using `x.length`. `x[0]`, `x[1]`, . . . , and `x[x.length-1]` are arrays. Their lengths can be obtained using `x[0].length`, `x[1].length`, . . . , and `x[x.length-1].length`.

For example, suppose x = new int[3][4], x[0], x[1], and x[2] are one-dimensional arrays and each contains four elements, as shown in Figure 7.2. x.length is 3, and x[0].length, x[1].length, and x[2].length are 4.

FIGURE 7.2 A two-dimensional array is a one-dimensional array in which each element is another one-dimensional array.

7.2.3 Ragged Arrays

ragged array

Each row in a two-dimensional array is itself an array. Thus, the rows can have different lengths. An array of this kind is known as a *ragged array*. Here is an example of creating a ragged array:

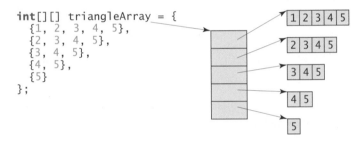

```
int[][] triangleArray = {
  {1, 2, 3, 4, 5},
  {2, 3, 4, 5},
  {3, 4, 5},
  {4, 5},
  {5}
};
```

As you can see, triangleArray[0].length is 5, triangleArray[1].length is 4, triangleArray[2].length is 3, triangleArray[3].length is 2, and triangle-Array[4].length is 1.

If you don't know the values in a ragged array in advance, but do know the sizes—say, the same as before—you can create a ragged array using the following syntax:

```
int[][] triangleArray = new int[5][];
triangleArray[0] = new int[5];
triangleArray[1] = new int[4];
triangleArray[2] = new int[3];
triangleArray[3] = new int[2];
triangleArray[4] = new int[1];
```

You can now assign values to the array. For example,

```
triangleArray[0][3] = 50;
triangleArray[4][0] = 45;
```

Note
The syntax new int[5][] for creating an array requires the first index to be specified. The syntax new int[][] would be wrong.

7.1 Declare an array reference variable for a two-dimensional array of **int** values, create a 4-by-5 **int** matrix, and assign it to the variable.

7.2   Can the rows in a two-dimensional array have different lengths?

7.3   What is the output of the following code?

```java
int[][] array = new int[5][6];
int[] x = {1, 2};
array[0] = x;
System.out.println("array[0][1] is " + array[0][1]);
```

7.4   Which of the following statements are valid?

```java
int[][] r = new int[2];
int[] x = new int[];
int[][] y = new int[3][];
int[][] z = {{1, 2}};
int[][] m = {{1, 2}, {2, 3}};
int[][] n = {{1, 2}, {2, 3}, };
```

7.3 Processing Two-Dimensional Arrays

Nested for loops are often used to process a two-dimensional array.

Key
Point

Suppose an array `matrix` is created as follows:

```java
int[][] matrix = new int[10][10];
```

The following are some examples of processing two-dimensional arrays.

1. *Initializing arrays with input values.* The following loop initializes the array with user input values:

```java
java.util.Scanner input = new Scanner(System.in);
System.out.println("Enter " + matrix.length + " rows and " +
  matrix[0].length + " columns: ");
for (int row = 0; row < matrix.length; row++) {
  for (int column = 0; column < matrix[row].length; column++) {
    matrix[row][column] = input.nextInt();
  }
}
```

2. *Initializing arrays with random values.* The following loop initializes the array with random values between 0 and 99:

```java
for (int row = 0; row < matrix.length; row++) {
  for (int column = 0; column < matrix[row].length; column++) {
    matrix[row][column] = (int)(Math.random() * 100);
  }
}
```

3. *Printing arrays.* To print a two-dimensional array, you have to print each element in the array using a loop like the following:

```java
for (int row = 0; row < matrix.length; row++) {
  for (int column = 0; column < matrix[row].length; column++) {
    System.out.print(matrix[row][column] + " ");
  }

  System.out.println();
}
```

4. *Summing all elements.* Use a variable named `total` to store the sum. Initially `total` is 0. Add each element in the array to `total` using a loop like this:

```
int total = 0;
for (int row = 0; row < matrix.length; row++) {
  for (int column = 0; column < matrix[row].length; column++) {
    total += matrix[row][column];
  }
}
```

5. *Summing elements by column.* For each column, use a variable named `total` to store its sum. Add each element in the column to `total` using a loop like this:

```
for (int column = 0; column < matrix[0].length; column++) {
  int total = 0;
  for (int row = 0; row < matrix.length; row++)
    total += matrix[row][column];
  System.out.println("Sum for column " + column + " is "
    + total);
}
```

6. *Which row has the largest sum?* Use variables `maxRow` and `indexOfMaxRow` to track the largest sum and index of the row. For each row, compute its sum and update `maxRow` and `indexOfMaxRow` if the new sum is greater.

VideoNote

Find the row with the largest sum

```
int maxRow = 0;
int indexOfMaxRow = 0;

// Get sum of the first row in maxRow
for (int column = 0; column < matrix[0].length; column++) {
  maxRow += matrix[0][column];
}

for (int row = 1; row < matrix.length; row++) {
  int totalOfThisRow = 0;
  for (int column = 0; column < matrix[row].length; column++)
    totalOfThisRow += matrix[row][column];

  if (totalOfThisRow > maxRow) {
    maxRow = totalOfThisRow;
    indexOfMaxRow = row;
  }
}

System.out.println("Row " + indexOfMaxRow
  + " has the maximum sum of " + maxRow);
```

7. *Random shuffling.* Shuffling the elements in a one-dimensional array was introduced in Section 6.2.6. How do you shuffle all the elements in a two-dimensional array? To accomplish this, for each element `matrix[i][j]`, randomly generate indices `i1` and `j1` and swap `matrix[i][j]` with `matrix[i1][j1]`, as follows:

```
for (int i = 0; i < matrix.length; i++) {
  for (int j = 0; j < matrix[i].length; j++) {
    int i1 = (int)(Math.random() * matrix.length);
    int j1 = (int)(Math.random() * matrix[i].length);

    // Swap matrix[i][j] with matrix[i1][j1]
    int temp = matrix[i][j];
    matrix[i][j] = matrix[i1][j1];
    matrix[i1][j1] = temp;
  }
}
```

7.5 Show the printout of the following code:

```
int[][] array = {{1, 2}, {3, 4}, {5, 6}};
for (int i = array.length - 1; i >= 0; i--) {
  for (int j = array[i].length - 1; j >= 0; j--)
    System.out.print(array[i][j] + " ");
  System.out.println();
}
```

Check
Point

MyProgrammingLab™

7.6 Show the printout of the following code:

```
int[][] array = {{1, 2}, {3, 4}, {5, 6}};
int sum = 0;
for (int i = 0; i < array.length; i++)
  sum += array[i][0];
System.out.println(sum);
```

7.4 Passing Two-Dimensional Arrays to Methods

When passing a two-dimensional array to a method, the reference of the array is passed to the method.

Key
Point

You can pass a two-dimensional array to a method just as you pass a one-dimensional array. You can also return an array from a method. Listing 7.1 gives an example with two methods. The first method, `getArray()`, returns a two-dimensional array, and the second method, `sum(int[][] m)`, returns the sum of all the elements in a matrix.

LISTING 7.1 PassTwoDimensionalArray.java

```
 1  import java.util.Scanner;
 2
 3  public class PassTwoDimensionalArray {
 4    public static void main(String[] args) {
 5      int[][] m = getArray(); // Get an array          get array
 6
 7      // Display sum of elements
 8      System.out.println("\nSum of all elements is " + sum(m));   pass array
 9    }
10
11    public static int[][] getArray() {                  getArray method
12      // Create a Scanner
13      Scanner input = new Scanner(System.in);
14
15      // Enter array values
16      int[][] m = new int[3][4];
17      System.out.println("Enter " + m.length + " rows and "
18        + m[0].length + " columns: ");
19      for (int i = 0; i < m.length; i++)
20        for (int j = 0; j < m[i].length; j++)
21          m[i][j] = input.nextInt();
22
23      return m;                                         return array
24    }
25
26    public static int sum(int[][] m) {                  sum method
27      int total = 0;
28      for (int row = 0; row < m.length; row++) {
29        for (int column = 0; column < m[row].length; column++) {
30          total += m[row][column];
31        }
```

```
32       }
33
34       return total;
35    }
36 }
```

```
Enter 3 rows and 4 columns:
1 2 3 4  ↵Enter
5 6 7 8  ↵Enter
9 10 11 12  ↵Enter

Sum of all elements is 78
```

The method `getArray` prompts the user to enter values for the array (lines 11–24) and returns the array (line 23).

The method `sum` (lines 26–35) has a two-dimensional array argument. You can obtain the number of rows using `m.length` (line 28) and the number of columns in a specified row using `m[row].length` (line 29).

7.7 Show the printout of the following code:

```java
public class Test {
  public static void main(String[] args) {
    int[][] array = {{1, 2, 3, 4}, {5, 6, 7, 8}};
    System.out.println(m1(array)[0]);
    System.out.println(m1(array)[1]);
  }

  public static int[] m1(int[][] m) {
    int[] result = new int[2];
    result[0] = m.length;
    result[1] = m[0].length;
    return result;
  }
}
```

7.5 Case Study: Grading a Multiple-Choice Test

The problem is to write a program that will grade multiple-choice tests.

Suppose you need to write a program that grades multiple-choice tests. Assume there are eight students and ten questions, and the answers are stored in a two-dimensional array. Each row records a student's answers to the questions, as shown in the following array.

VideoNote

Grade multiple-choice test

Students' Answers to the Questions:

	0	1	2	3	4	5	6	7	8	9
Student 0	A	B	A	C	C	D	E	E	A	D
Student 1	D	B	A	B	C	A	E	E	A	D
Student 2	E	D	D	A	C	B	E	E	A	D
Student 3	C	B	A	E	D	C	E	E	A	D
Student 4	A	B	D	C	C	D	E	E	A	D
Student 5	B	B	E	C	C	D	E	E	A	D
Student 6	B	B	A	C	C	D	E	E	A	D
Student 7	E	B	E	C	C	D	E	E	A	D

The key is stored in a one-dimensional array:

Key to the Questions:

```
           0 1 2 3 4 5 6 7 8 9
    Key   D B D C C D A E A D
```

Your program grades the test and displays the result. It compares each student's answers with the key, counts the number of correct answers, and displays it. Listing 7.2 gives the program.

LISTING 7.2 GradeExam.java

```java
 1  public class GradeExam {
 2    /** Main method */
 3    public static void main(String[] args) {
 4      // Students' answers to the questions
 5      char[][] answers = {                                          2-D array
 6        {'A', 'B', 'A', 'C', 'C', 'D', 'E', 'E', 'A', 'D'},
 7        {'D', 'B', 'A', 'B', 'C', 'A', 'E', 'E', 'A', 'D'},
 8        {'E', 'D', 'D', 'A', 'C', 'B', 'E', 'E', 'A', 'D'},
 9        {'C', 'B', 'A', 'E', 'D', 'C', 'E', 'E', 'A', 'D'},
10        {'A', 'B', 'D', 'C', 'C', 'D', 'E', 'E', 'A', 'D'},
11        {'B', 'B', 'E', 'C', 'C', 'D', 'E', 'E', 'A', 'D'},
12        {'B', 'B', 'A', 'C', 'C', 'D', 'E', 'E', 'A', 'D'},
13        {'E', 'B', 'E', 'C', 'C', 'D', 'E', 'E', 'A', 'D'}};
14
15      // Key to the questions
16      char[] keys = {'D', 'B', 'D', 'C', 'C', 'D', 'A', 'E', 'A', 'D'};   1-D array
17
18      // Grade all answers
19      for (int i = 0; i < answers.length; i++) {
20        // Grade one student
21        int correctCount = 0;
22        for (int j = 0; j < answers[i].length; j++) {
23          if (answers[i][j] == keys[j])                              compare with key
24            correctCount++;
25        }
26
27        System.out.println("Student " + i + "'s correct count is " +
28          correctCount);
29      }
30    }
31  }
```

```
Student 0's correct count is 7
Student 1's correct count is 6
Student 2's correct count is 5
Student 3's correct count is 4
Student 4's correct count is 8
Student 5's correct count is 7
Student 6's correct count is 7
Student 7's correct count is 7
```

The statement in lines 5–13 declares, creates, and initializes a two-dimensional array of characters and assigns the reference to answers of the char[][] type.

The statement in line 16 declares, creates, and initializes an array of char values and assigns the reference to keys of the char[] type.

Each row in the array **answers** stores a student's answer, which is graded by comparing it with the key in the array **keys**. The result is displayed immediately after a student's answer is graded.

7.6 Case Study: Finding the Closest Pair

 This section presents a geometric problem for finding the closest pair of points.

closest-pair animation on the Companion Website

Given a set of points, the closest-pair problem is to find the two points that are nearest to each other. In Figure 7.3, for example, points **(1, 1)** and **(2, 0.5)** are closest to each other. There are several ways to solve this problem. An intuitive approach is to compute the distances between all pairs of points and find the one with the minimum distance, as implemented in Listing 7.3.

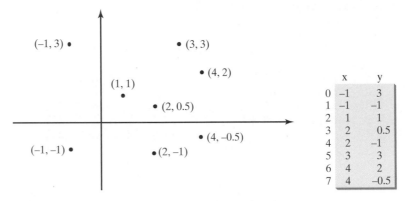

FIGURE 7.3 Points can be represented in a two-dimensional array.

LISTING 7.3 FindNearestPoints.java

```
1  import java.util.Scanner;
2
3  public class FindNearestPoints {
4    public static void main(String[] args) {
5      Scanner input = new Scanner(System.in);
6      System.out.print("Enter the number of points: ");
7      int numberOfPoints = input.nextInt();
8
9      // Create an array to store points
10     double[][] points = new double[numberOfPoints][2];
11     System.out.print("Enter " + numberOfPoints + " points: ");
12     for (int i = 0; i < points.length; i++) {
13       points[i][0] = input.nextDouble();
14       points[i][1] = input.nextDouble();
15     }
16
17     // p1 and p2 are the indices in the points' array
18     int p1 = 0, p2 = 1; // Initial two points
19     double shortestDistance = distance(points[p1][0], points[p1][1],
20       points[p2][0], points[p2][1]); // Initialize shortestDistance
21
22     // Compute distance for every two points
23     for (int i = 0; i < points.length; i++) {
```

number of points (7)

2-D array (10)

read points (12)

track two points (18)
track shortestDistance (19)

for each point i (23)

```
24            for (int j = i + 1; j < points.length; j++) {          for each point j
25                double distance = distance(points[i][0], points[i][1],   distance between i and j
26                    points[j][0], points[j][1]); // Find distance        distance between two points
27
28                if (shortestDistance > distance) {
29                    p1 = i; // Update p1
30                    p2 = j; // Update p2
31                    shortestDistance = distance; // Update shortestDistance   update shortestDistance
32                }
33            }
34        }
35
36        // Display result
37        System.out.println("The closest two points are " +
38            "(" + points[p1][0] + ", " + points[p1][1] + ") and (" +
39            points[p2][0] + ", " + points[p2][1] + ")");
40    }
41
42    /** Compute the distance between two points (x1, y1) and (x2, y2)*/
43    public static double distance(
44        double x1, double y1, double x2, double y2) {
45        return Math.sqrt((x2 - x1) * (x2 - x1) + (y2 - y1) * (y2 - y1));
46    }
47 }
```

```
Enter the number of points: 8  ↵Enter
Enter 8 points: -1 3   -1 -1   1 1   2 0.5   2 -1   3 3   4 2 4 -0.5  ↵Enter
The closest two points are (1, 1) and (2, 0.5)
```

The program prompts the user to enter the number of points (lines 6–7). The points are read from the console and stored in a two-dimensional array named **points** (lines 12–15). The program uses the variable **shortestDistance** (line 19) to store the distance between the two nearest points, and the indices of these two points in the **points** array are stored in **p1** and **p2** (line 18).

For each point at index **i**, the program computes the distance between **points[i]** and **points[j]** for all **j > i** (lines 23–34). Whenever a shorter distance is found, the variable **shortestDistance** and **p1** and **p2** are updated (lines 28–32).

The distance between two points **(x1, y1)** and **(x2, y2)** can be computed using the formula $\sqrt{(x_2 - x_1)^2 + (y_2 - y_1)^2}$ (lines 43–46).

The program assumes that the plane has at least two points. You can easily modify the program to handle the case if the plane has zero or one point.

Note that there might be more than one closest pair of points with the same minimum distance. The program finds one such pair. You may modify the program to find all closest pairs in Programming Exercise 7.8.

multiple closest pairs

Tip

It is cumbersome to enter all points from the keyboard. You may store the input in a file, say **FindNearestPoints.txt**, and compile and run the program using the following command:

input file

```
java FindNearestPoints < FindNearestPoints.txt
```

7.7 Case Study: Sudoku

The problem is to check whether a given Sudoku solution is correct.

This section presents an interesting problem of a sort that appears in the newspaper every day. It is a number-placement puzzle, commonly known as *Sudoku*. This is a very challenging problem. To make it accessible to the novice, this section presents a solution to a simplified version of the Sudoku problem, which is to verify whether a solution is correct. The complete solution for solving the Sudoku problem is presented in Supplement VI.A.

Sudoku is a 9 × 9 grid divided into smaller 3 × 3 boxes (also called *regions* or *blocks*), as shown in Figure 7.4a. Some cells, called *fixed cells*, are populated with numbers from 1 to 9. The objective is to fill the empty cells, also called *free cells*, with the numbers 1 to 9 so that every row, every column, and every 3 × 3 box contains the numbers 1 to 9, as shown in Figure 7.4b.

FIGURE 7.4 The Sudoku puzzle in (a) is solved in (b).

For convenience, we use value 0 to indicate a free cell, as shown in Figure 7.5a. The grid can be naturally represented using a two-dimensional array, as shown in Figure 7.5b.

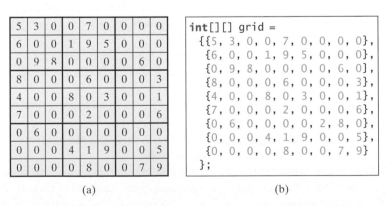

```
int[][] grid =
  {{5, 3, 0, 0, 7, 0, 0, 0, 0},
   {6, 0, 0, 1, 9, 5, 0, 0, 0},
   {0, 9, 8, 0, 0, 0, 0, 6, 0},
   {8, 0, 0, 0, 6, 0, 0, 0, 3},
   {4, 0, 0, 8, 0, 3, 0, 0, 1},
   {7, 0, 0, 0, 2, 0, 0, 0, 6},
   {0, 6, 0, 0, 0, 0, 2, 8, 0},
   {0, 0, 0, 4, 1, 9, 0, 0, 5},
   {0, 0, 0, 0, 8, 0, 0, 7, 9}
  };
```

(a)   (b)

FIGURE 7.5 A grid can be represented using a two-dimensional array.

To find a solution for the puzzle, we must replace each 0 in the grid with an appropriate number from 1 to 9. For the solution to the puzzle in Figure 7.5, the grid should be as shown in Figure 7.6.

Once a solution to a Sudoku puzzle is found, how do you verify that it is correct? Here are two approaches:

■ Check if every row has numbers from 1 to 9, every column has numbers from 1 to 9, and every small box has numbers from 1 to 9.

■ Check each cell. Each cell must be a number from 1 to 9 and the cell must be unique on every row, every column, and every small box.

```
A solution grid is
 {{5, 3, 4, 6, 7, 8, 9, 1, 2},
  {6, 7, 2, 1, 9, 5, 3, 4, 8},
  {1, 9, 8, 3, 4, 2, 5, 6, 7},
  {8, 5, 9, 7, 6, 1, 4, 2, 3},
  {4, 2, 6, 8, 5, 3, 7, 9, 1},
  {7, 1, 3, 9, 2, 4, 8, 5, 6},
  {9, 6, 1, 5, 3, 7, 2, 8, 4},
  {2, 8, 7, 4, 1, 9, 6, 3, 5},
  {3, 4, 5, 2, 8, 6, 1, 7, 9}
 };
```

FIGURE 7.6 A solution is stored in `grid`.

The program in Listing 7.4 prompts the user to enter a solution and reports whether it is valid. We use the second approach in the program to check whether the solution is correct.

LISTING 7.4 CheckSudokuSolution.java

```java
1  import java.util.Scanner;
2
3  public class CheckSudokuSolution {
4    public static void main(String[] args) {
5      // Read a Sudoku solution
6      int[][] grid = readASolution();                          read input
7
8      System.out.println(isValid(grid) ? "Valid solution" :     solution valid?
9        "Invalid solution");
10   }
11
12   /** Read a Sudoku solution from the console */
13   public static int[][] readASolution() {                     read solution
14     // Create a Scanner
15     Scanner input = new Scanner(System.in);
16
17     System.out.println("Enter a Sudoku puzzle solution:");
18     int[][] grid = new int[9][9];
19     for (int i = 0; i < 9; i++)
20       for (int j = 0; j < 9; j++)
21         grid[i][j] = input.nextInt();
22
23     return grid;
24   }
25
26   /** Check whether a solution is valid */
27   public static boolean isValid(int[][] grid) {               check solution
28     for (int i = 0; i < 9; i++)
29       for (int j = 0; j < 9; j++)
30         if (grid[i][j] < 1 || grid[i][j] > 9
31             || !isValid(i, j, grid))
32           return false;
33     return true; // The solution is valid
34   }
35
36   /** Check whether grid[i][j] is valid in the grid */
37   public static boolean isValid(int i, int j, int[][] grid) {
38     // Check whether grid[i][j] is valid in i's row
```

check rows

```
39      for (int column = 0; column < 9; column++)
40        if (column != j && grid[i][column] == grid[i][j])
41          return false;
42
43      // Check whether grid[i][j] is valid in j's column
44      for (int row = 0; row < 9; row++)
```

check columns

```
45        if (row != i && grid[row][j] == grid[i][j])
46          return false;
47
48      // Check whether grid[i][j] is valid in the 3-by-3 box
49      for (int row = (i / 3) * 3; row < (i / 3) * 3 + 3; row++)
```

check small boxes

```
50        for (int col = (j / 3) * 3; col < (j / 3) * 3 + 3; col++)
51          if (row != i && col != j && grid[row][col] == grid[i][j])
52            return false;
53
54      return true; // The current value at grid[i][j] is valid
55    }
56  }
```

```
Enter a Sudoku puzzle solution:
9 6 3 1 7 4 2 5 8  ↵Enter
1 7 8 3 2 5 6 4 9  ↵Enter
2 5 4 6 8 9 7 3 1  ↵Enter
8 2 1 4 3 7 5 9 6  ↵Enter
4 9 6 8 5 2 3 1 7  ↵Enter
7 3 5 9 6 1 8 2 4  ↵Enter
5 8 9 7 1 3 4 6 2  ↵Enter
3 1 7 2 4 6 9 8 5  ↵Enter
6 4 2 5 9 8 1 7 3  ↵Enter
Valid solution
```

The program invokes the `readASolution()` method (line 6) to read a Sudoku solution and return a two-dimensional array representing a Sudoku grid.

isValid method

The `isValid(grid)` method checks whether the values in the grid are valid by verifying that each value is between 1 and 9 and that each value is valid in the grid (lines 27–34).

overloaded isValid method

The `isValid(i, j, grid)` method checks whether the value at `grid[i][j]` is valid. It checks whether `grid[i][j]` appears more than once in row i (lines 39–41), in column j (lines 44–46), and in the 3 × 3 box (lines 49–52).

How do you locate all the cells in the same box? For any `grid[i][j]`, the starting cell of the 3 × 3 box that contains it is `grid[(i / 3) * 3][(j / 3) * 3]`, as illustrated in Figure 7.7.

grid[0][0]

grid[0][6]

For any grid[i][j] in this 3 by 3 box, its starting cell is grid[3*(i/3)][3*(j/3)] (i.e., grid[0][6]). For example, for grid[2][8], i=2 and j=8, 3*(i/3)=0 and 3*(j/3)=6.

grid[6][3]

For any grid[i][j] in this 3 by 3 box, its starting cell is grid[3*(i/3)][3*(j/3)] (i.e., grid[6][3]). For example, grid[8][5], i=8 and j=5, 3*(i/3)=6 and 3*(j/3)=3.

FIGURE 7.7 The location of the first cell in a 3 × 3 box determines the locations of other cells in the box.

With this observation, you can easily identify all the cells in the box. For instance, if `grid[r][c]` is the starting cell of a 3 × 3 box, the cells in the box can be traversed in a nested loop as follows:

```
// Get all cells in a 3-by-3 box starting at grid[r][c]
for (int row = r; row < r + 3; row++)
  for (int col = c; col < c + 3; col++)
    // grid[row][col] is in the box
```

It is cumbersome to enter 81 numbers from the console. When you test the program, you may store the input in a file, say **CheckSudokuSolution.txt** (see www.cs.armstrong.edu/liang/data/ CheckSudokuSolution.txt), and run the program using the following command:

input file

```
java CheckSudokuSolution < CheckSudokuSolution.txt
```

7.8 Multidimensional Arrays

A two-dimensional array consists of an array of one-dimensional arrays and a three-dimensional array consists of an array of two-dimensional arrays.

Key Point

In the preceding section, you used a two-dimensional array to represent a matrix or a table. Occasionally, you will need to represent *n*-dimensional data structures. In Java, you can create *n*-dimensional arrays for any integer *n*.

The way to declare two-dimensional array variables and create two-dimensional arrays can be generalized to declare *n*-dimensional array variables and create *n*-dimensional arrays for *n* >= 3. For example, you may use a three-dimensional array to store exam scores for a class of six students with five exams, and each exam has two parts (multiple-choice and essay). The following syntax declares a three-dimensional array variable `scores`, creates an array, and assigns its reference to `scores`.

```
double[][][] scores = new double[6][5][2];
```

You can also use the short-hand notation to create and initialize the array as follows:

```
double[][][] scores = {
  {{7.5, 20.5}, {9.0, 22.5}, {15, 33.5}, {13, 21.5}, {15, 2.5}},
  {{4.5, 21.5}, {9.0, 22.5}, {15, 34.5}, {12, 20.5}, {14, 9.5}},
  {{6.5, 30.5}, {9.4, 10.5}, {11, 33.5}, {11, 23.5}, {10, 2.5}},
  {{6.5, 23.5}, {9.4, 32.5}, {13, 34.5}, {11, 20.5}, {16, 7.5}},
  {{8.5, 26.5}, {9.4, 52.5}, {13, 36.5}, {13, 24.5}, {16, 2.5}},
  {{9.5, 20.5}, {9.4, 42.5}, {13, 31.5}, {12, 20.5}, {16, 6.5}}};
```

`scores[0][1][0]` refers to the multiple-choice score for the first student's second exam, which is `9.0`. `scores[0][1][1]` refers to the essay score for the first student's second exam, which is `22.5`. This is depicted in the following figure:

A multidimensional array is actually an array in which each element is another array. A three-dimensional array consists of an array of two-dimensional arrays. A two-dimensional array consists of an array of one-dimensional arrays. For example, suppose `x = new int[2][2][5]`, and `x[0]` and `x[1]` are two-dimensional arrays. `X[0][0]`, `x[0][1]`, `x[1][0]`, and `x[1][1]` are one-dimensional arrays and each contains five elements.

x.length is 2, x[0].length and x[1].length are 2, and X[0][0].length, x[0][1].length, x[1][0].length, and x[1][1].length are 5.

7.8.1 Case Study: Daily Temperature and Humidity

Suppose a meteorology station records the temperature and humidity every hour of every day and stores the data for the past ten days in a text file named **Weather.txt** (see www.cs.armstrong.edu/liang/data/Weather.txt). Each line of the file consists of four numbers that indicate the day, hour, temperature, and humidity. The contents of the file may look like the one in (a).

Day	Hour	Temperature	Humidity
1	1	76.4	0.92
1	2	77.7	0.93
. . .			
10	23	97.7	0.71
10	24	98.7	0.74

(a)

Day	Hour	Temperature	Humidity
10	24	98.7	0.74
1	2	77.7	0.93
. . .			
10	23	97.7	0.71
1	1	76.4	0.92

(b)

Note that the lines in the file are not necessarily in increasing order of day and hour. For example, the file may appear as shown in (b).

Your task is to write a program that calculates the average daily temperature and humidity for the 10 days. You can use the input redirection to read the file and store the data in a three-dimensional array named **data**. The first index of **data** ranges from 0 to 9 and represents 10 days, the second index ranges from 0 to 23 and represents 24 hours, and the third index ranges from 0 to 1 and represents temperature and humidity, as depicted in the following figure:

Which day Which hour Temperature or humidity

data [i] [j] [k]

Note that the days are numbered from 1 to 10 and the hours from 1 to 24 in the file. Because the array index starts from 0, **data[0][0][0]** stores the temperature in day 1 at hour 1 and **data[9][23][1]** stores the humidity in day 10 at hour 24.

The program is given in Listing 7.5.

LISTING 7.5 Weather.java

three-dimensional array

```
1   import java.util.Scanner;
2
3   public class Weather {
4     public static void main(String[] args) {
5       final int NUMBER_OF_DAYS = 10;
6       final int NUMBER_OF_HOURS = 24;
7       double[][][] data
8         = new double[NUMBER_OF_DAYS][NUMBER_OF_HOURS][2];
9
10      Scanner input = new Scanner(System.in);
11      // Read input using input redirection from a file
12      for (int k = 0; k < NUMBER_OF_DAYS * NUMBER_OF_HOURS; k++) {
13        int day = input.nextInt();
14        int hour = input.nextInt();
15        double temperature = input.nextDouble();
16        double humidity = input.nextDouble();
17        data[day - 1][hour - 1][0] = temperature;
```

```
18        data[day - 1][hour - 1][1] = humidity;
19      }
20
21      // Find the average daily temperature and humidity
22      for (int i = 0; i < NUMBER_OF_DAYS; i++) {
23        double dailyTemperatureTotal = 0, dailyHumidityTotal = 0;
24        for (int j = 0; j < NUMBER_OF_HOURS; j++) {
25          dailyTemperatureTotal += data[i][j][0];
26          dailyHumidityTotal += data[i][j][1];
27        }
28
29        // Display result
30        System.out.println("Day " + i + "'s average temperature is "
31          + dailyTemperatureTotal / NUMBER_OF_HOURS);
32        System.out.println("Day " + i + "'s average humidity is "
33          + dailyHumidityTotal / NUMBER_OF_HOURS);
34      }
35    }
36  }
```

```
Day 0's average temperature is 77.7708
Day 0's average humidity is 0.929583
Day 1's average temperature is 77.3125
Day 1's average humidity is 0.929583
. . .
Day 9's average temperature is 79.3542
Day 9's average humidity is 0.9125
```

You can use the following command to run the program:

```
java Weather < Weather.txt
```

A three-dimensional array for storing temperature and humidity is created in line 8. The loop in lines 12–19 reads the input to the array. You can enter the input from the keyboard, but doing so will be awkward. For convenience, we store the data in a file and use input redirection to read the data from the file. The loop in lines 24–27 adds all temperatures for each hour in a day to dailyTemperatureTotal and all humidity for each hour to dailyHumidityTotal. The average daily temperature and humidity are displayed in lines 30–33.

7.8.2 Case Study: Guessing Birthdays

Listing 3.3, GuessBirthday.java, gives a program that guesses a birthday. The program can be simplified by storing the numbers in five sets in a three-dimensional array, and it prompts the user for the answers using a loop, as shown in Listing 7.6. The sample run of the program can be the same as shown in Listing 3.3.

LISTING 7.6 GuessBirthdayUsingArray.java

```
1  import java.util.Scanner;
2
3  public class GuessBirthdayUsingArray {
4    public static void main(String[] args) {
5      int day = 0; // Day to be determined
6      int answer;
7
8      int[][][] dates = {                            three-dimensional array
9        {{ 1,  3,  5,  7},
10        { 9, 11, 13, 15},
```

```
11            {17, 19, 21, 23},
12            {25, 27, 29, 31}},
13           {{ 2,  3,  6,  7},
14            {10, 11, 14, 15},
15            {18, 19, 22, 23},
16            {26, 27, 30, 31}},
17           {{ 4,  5,  6,  7},
18            {12, 13, 14, 15},
19            {20, 21, 22, 23},
20            {28, 29, 30, 31}},
21           {{ 8,  9, 10, 11},
22            {12, 13, 14, 15},
23            {24, 25, 26, 27},
24            {28, 29, 30, 31}},
25           {{16, 17, 18, 19},
26            {20, 21, 22, 23},
27            {24, 25, 26, 27},
28            {28, 29, 30, 31}}};
29
30         // Create a Scanner
31         Scanner input = new Scanner(System.in);
32
33         for (int i = 0; i < 5; i++) {
34           System.out.println("Is your birthday in Set" + (i + 1) + "?");
35           for (int j = 0; j < 4; j++) {
36             for (int k = 0; k < 4; k++)
37               System.out.printf("%4d", dates[i][j][k]);
38             System.out.println();
39           }
40
41           System.out.print("\nEnter 0 for No and 1 for Yes: ");
42           answer = input.nextInt();
43
44           if (answer == 1)
45             day += dates[i][0][0];
46         }
47
48         System.out.println("Your birthday is " + day);
49       }
50     }
```

(margin note, line 34) Set i

(margin note, line 45) add to day

A three-dimensional array `dates` is created in Lines 8–28. This array stores five sets of numbers. Each set is a 4-by-4 two-dimensional array.

The loop starting from line 33 displays the numbers in each set and prompts the user to answer whether the birthday is in the set (lines 41–42). If the day is in the set, the first number (`dates[i][0][0]`) in the set is added to variable `day` (line 45).

Check Point

MyProgrammingLab™

7.8   Declare an array variable for a three-dimensional array, create a $4 \times 6 \times 5$ `int` array, and assign its reference to the variable.

7.9   Assume `int[][][] x = new char[12][5][2]`, how many elements are in the array? What are `x.length`, `x[2].length`, and `x[0][0].length`?

7.10   Show the printout of the following code:

```
int[][][] array = {{{1, 2}, {3, 4}}, {{5, 6},{7, 8}}};
System.out.println(array[0][0][0]);
System.out.println(array[1][1][1]);
```

CHAPTER SUMMARY

1. A two-dimensional array can be used to store a table.

2. A variable for two-dimensional arrays can be declared using the syntax: `elementType[][] arrayVar`.

3. A two-dimensional array can be created using the syntax: `new elementType [ROW_SIZE][COLUMN_SIZE]`.

4. Each element in a two-dimensional array is represented using the syntax: `arrayVar[rowIndex][columnIndex]`.

5. You can create and initialize a two-dimensional array using an array initializer with the syntax: `elementType[][] arrayVar = {{row values}, . . . , {row values}}`.

6. You can use arrays of arrays to form multidimensional arrays. For example, a variable for three-dimensional arrays can be declared as `elementType[][][] arrayVar`, and a three-dimensional array can be created using `new elementType[size1][size2] [size3]`.

TEST QUESTIONS

Do the test questions for this chapter online at www.cs.armstrong.edu/liang/intro9e/test.html.

PROGRAMMING EXERCISES

MyProgrammingLab™

*7.1 (*Sum elements column by column*) Write a method that returns the sum of all the elements in a specified column in a matrix using the following header:

public static double sumColumn(**double**[][] m, **int** columnIndex)

Write a test program that reads a 3-by-4 matrix and displays the sum of each column. Here is a sample run:

```
Enter a 3-by-4 matrix row by row:
1.5 2 3 4  ↵Enter
5.5 6 7 8  ↵Enter
9.5 1 3 1  ↵Enter
Sum of the elements at column 0 is 16.5
Sum of the elements at column 1 is 9.0
Sum of the elements at column 2 is 13.0
Sum of the elements at column 3 is 13.0
```

*7.2 (*Sum the major diagonal in a matrix*) Write a method that sums all the numbers in the major diagonal in an $n \times n$ matrix of integers using the following header:

public static double sumMajorDiagonal(**double**[][] m)

Write a test program that reads a 4-by-4 matrix and displays the sum of all its elements on the major diagonal. Here is a sample run:

```
Enter a 4-by-4 matrix row by row:
1 2 3 4.0  ↵Enter
5 6.5 7 8  ↵Enter
9 10 11 12  ↵Enter
13 14 15 16  ↵Enter
Sum of the elements in the major diagonal is 34.5
```

*7.3 (*Sort students on grades*) Rewrite Listing 7.2, GradeExam.java, to display the students in increasing order of the number of correct answers.

**7.4 (*Compute the weekly hours for each employee*) Suppose the weekly hours for all employees are stored in a two-dimensional array. Each row records an employee's seven-day work hours with seven columns. For example, the following array stores the work hours for eight employees. Write a program that displays employees and their total hours in decreasing order of the total hours.

	Su	M	T	W	Th	F	Sa
Employee 0	2	4	3	4	5	8	8
Employee 1	7	3	4	3	3	4	4
Employee 2	3	3	4	3	3	2	2
Employee 3	9	3	4	7	3	4	1
Employee 4	3	5	4	3	6	3	8
Employee 5	3	4	4	6	3	4	4
Employee 6	3	7	4	8	3	8	4
Employee 7	6	3	5	9	2	7	9

7.5 (*Algebra: add two matrices*) Write a method to add two matrices. The header of the method is as follows:

public static double[][] addMatrix(double[][] a, double[][] b)

In order to be added, the two matrices must have the same dimensions and the same or compatible types of elements. Let **c** be the resulting matrix. Each element c_{ij} is $a_{ij} + b_{ij}$. For example, for two 3×3 matrices **a** and **b**, **c** is

VideoNote

Multiply two matrices

$$\begin{pmatrix} a_{11} & a_{12} & a_{13} \\ a_{21} & a_{22} & a_{23} \\ a_{31} & a_{32} & a_{33} \end{pmatrix} + \begin{pmatrix} b_{11} & b_{12} & b_{13} \\ b_{21} & b_{22} & b_{23} \\ b_{31} & b_{32} & b_{33} \end{pmatrix} = \begin{pmatrix} a_{11} + b_{11} & a_{12} + b_{12} & a_{13} + b_{13} \\ a_{21} + b_{21} & a_{22} + b_{22} & a_{23} + b_{23} \\ a_{31} + b_{31} & a_{32} + b_{32} & a_{33} + b_{33} \end{pmatrix}$$

Write a test program that prompts the user to enter two 3×3 matrices and displays their sum. Here is a sample run:

```
Enter matrix1: 1 2 3 4 5 6 7 8 9  ↵Enter
Enter matrix2: 0 2 4 1 4.5 2.2 1.1 4.3 5.2  ↵Enter
The matrices are added as follows
1.0 2.0 3.0       0.0 2.0 4.0       1.0 4.0 7.0
4.0 5.0 6.0   +   1.0 4.5 2.2   =   5.0 9.5 8.2
7.0 8.0 9.0       1.1 4.3 5.2       8.1 12.3 14.2
```

**7.6 (*Algebra: multiply two matrices*) Write a method to multiply two matrices. The header of the method is:

```
public static double[][]
    multiplyMatrix(double[][] a, double[][] b)
```

To multiply matrix a by matrix b, the number of columns in a must be the same as the number of rows in b, and the two matrices must have elements of the same or compatible types. Let c be the result of the multiplication. Assume the column size of matrix a is n. Each element c_{ij} is $a_{i1} \times b_{1j} + a_{i2} \times b_{2j} + \ldots + a_{in} \times b_{nj}$. For example, for two 3×3 matrices a and b, c is

$$\begin{pmatrix} a_{11} & a_{12} & a_{13} \\ a_{21} & a_{22} & a_{23} \\ a_{31} & a_{32} & a_{33} \end{pmatrix} \times \begin{pmatrix} b_{11} & b_{12} & b_{13} \\ b_{21} & b_{22} & b_{23} \\ b_{31} & b_{32} & b_{33} \end{pmatrix} = \begin{pmatrix} c_{11} & c_{12} & c_{13} \\ c_{21} & c_{22} & c_{23} \\ c_{31} & c_{32} & c_{33} \end{pmatrix}$$

where $c_{ij} = a_{i1} \times b_{1j} + a_{i2} \times b_{2j} + a_{i3} \times b_{3j}$.

Write a test program that prompts the user to enter two 3×3 matrices and displays their product. Here is a sample run:

```
Enter matrix1: 1 2 3 4 5 6 7 8 9 ↵Enter
Enter matrix2: 0 2 4 1 4.5 2.2 1.1 4.3 5.2 ↵Enter
The multiplication of the matrices is
1 2 3      0 2.0 4.0        5.3 23.9 24
4 5 6   *  1 4.5 2.2   =    11.6 56.3 58.2
7 8 9      1.1 4.3 5.2      17.9 88.7 92.4
```

*7.7 (*Points nearest to each other*) Listing 7.3 gives a program that finds two points in a two-dimensional space nearest to each other. Revise the program so that it finds two points in a three-dimensional space nearest to each other. Use a two-dimensional array to represent the points. Test the program using the following points:

```
double[][] points = {{-1, 0, 3}, {-1, -1, -1}, {4, 1, 1},
    {2, 0.5, 9}, {3.5, 2, -1}, {3, 1.5, 3}, {-1.5, 4, 2},
    {5.5, 4, -0.5}};
```

The formula for computing the distance between two points (x1, y1, z1) and (x2, y2, z2) is $\sqrt{(x_2 - x_1)^2 + (y_2 - y_1)^2 + (z_2 - z_1)^2}$.

**7.8 (*All closest pairs of points*) Revise Listing 7.3, FindNearestPoints.java, to find all closest pairs of points with the same minimum distance.

***7.9 (*Game: play a tic-tac-toe game*) In a game of tic-tac-toe, two players take turns marking an available cell in a 3×3 grid with their respective tokens (either X or O). When one player has placed three tokens in a horizontal, vertical, or diagonal row on the grid, the game is over and that player has won. A draw (no winner) occurs when all the cells on the grid have been filled with tokens and neither player has achieved a win. Create a program for playing tic-tac-toe.

The program prompts two players to enter an X token and O token alternately. Whenever a token is entered, the program redisplays the board on the console and determines the status of the game (win, draw, or continue). Here is a sample run:

```
---------------
|   |   |   |
---------------
|   |   |   |
---------------
|   |   |   |
---------------
Enter a row (0, 1, or 2) for player X: 1 [↵Enter]
Enter a column (0, 1, or 2) for player X: 1 [↵Enter]

---------------
|   |   |   |
---------------
|   | X |   |
---------------
|   |   |   |
---------------
Enter a row (0, 1, or 2) for player O: 1 [↵Enter]
Enter a column (0, 1, or 2) for player O: 2 [↵Enter]

---------------
|   |   |   |
---------------
|   | X | O |
---------------
|   |   |   |
---------------
Enter a row (0, 1, or 2) for player X:

  . . .

---------------
| X |   |   |
---------------
| O | X | O |
---------------
|   |   | X |
---------------
X player won
```

*7.10 (*Largest row and column*) Write a program that randomly fills in 0s and 1s into a 4-by-4 matrix, prints the matrix, and finds the first row and column with the most 1s. Here is a sample run of the program:

```
0011
0011
1101
1010
The largest row index: 2
The largest column index: 2
```

**7.11 (*Game: nine heads and tails*) Nine coins are placed in a 3-by-3 matrix with some face up and some face down. You can represent the state of the coins using a 3-by-3 matrix with values 0 (heads) and 1 (tails). Here are some examples:

```
0 0 0     1 0 1     1 1 0     1 0 1     1 0 0
0 1 0     0 0 1     1 0 0     1 1 0     1 1 1
0 0 0     1 0 0     0 0 1     1 0 0     1 1 0
```

Each state can also be represented using a binary number. For example, the preceding matrices correspond to the numbers

000010000 101001100 110100001 101110100 100111110

There are a total of 512 possibilities, so you can use decimal numbers 0, 1, 2, 3, . . . , and 511 to represent all states of the matrix. Write a program that prompts the user to enter a number between 0 and 511 and displays the corresponding matrix with the characters H and T. Here is a sample run:

```
Enter a number between 0 and 511: 7  ↵Enter
H H H
H H H
T T T
```

The user entered 7, which corresponds to 000000111. Since 0 stands for H and 1 for T, the output is correct.

**7.12 (*Financial application: compute tax*) Rewrite Listing 3.6, ComputeTax.java, using arrays. For each filing status, there are six tax rates. Each rate is applied to a certain amount of taxable income. For example, from the taxable income of $400,000 for a single filer, $8,350 is taxed at 10%, (33,950 – 8,350) at 15%, (82,250 – 33,950) at 25%, (171,550 – 82,550) at 28%, (372,550 – 82,250) at 33%, and (400,000 – 372,950) at 36%. The six rates are the same for all filing statuses, which can be represented in the following array:

```
double[] rates = {0.10, 0.15, 0.25, 0.28, 0.33, 0.35};
```

The brackets for each rate for all the filing statuses can be represented in a two-dimensional array as follows:

```
int[][] brackets = {
  {8350, 33950, 82250, 171550, 372950},  // Single filer
  {16700, 67900, 137050, 20885, 372950}, // Married jointly
                                          // or qualifying widow(er)
  {8350, 33950, 68525, 104425, 186475},  // Married separately
  {11950, 45500, 117450, 190200, 372950} // Head of household
};
```

Suppose the taxable income is $400,000 for single filers. The tax can be computed as follows:

```
tax = brackets[0][0] * rates[0] +
  (brackets[0][1] - brackets[0][0]) * rates[1] +
  (brackets[0][2] - brackets[0][1]) * rates[2] +
  (brackets[0][3] - brackets[0][2]) * rates[3] +
  (brackets[0][4] - brackets[0][3]) * rates[4] +
  (400000 - brackets[0][4]) * rates[5]
```

*7.13 (*Locate the largest element*) Write the following method that returns the location of the largest element in a two-dimensional array.

```
public static int[] locateLargest(double[][] a)
```

The return value is a one-dimensional array that contains two elements. These two elements indicate the row and column indices of the largest element in the two-dimensional array. Write a test program that prompts the user to enter a two-dimensional array and displays the location of the largest element in the array. Here is a sample run:

```
Enter the number of rows and columns of the array: 3 4 ↵Enter
Enter the array:
23.5 35 2 10 ↵Enter
4.5 3 45 3.5 ↵Enter
35 44 5.5 9.6 ↵Enter
The location of the largest element is at (1, 2)
```

**7.14 (*Explore matrix*) Write a program that prompts the user to enter the length of a square matrix, randomly fills in 0s and 1s into the matrix, prints the matrix, and finds the rows, columns, and diagonals with all 0s or 1s. Here is a sample run of the program:

```
Enter the size for the matrix: 4 ↵Enter
0111
0000
0100
1111
All 0s on row 1
All 1s on row 3
No same numbers on a column
No same numbers on the major diagonal
No same numbers on the sub-diagonal
```

*7.15 (*Geometry: same line?*) Programming Exercise 5.39 gives a method for testing whether three points are on the same line.

Write the following method to test whether all the points in the array **points** are on the same line.

public static boolean sameLine(**double**[][] points)

Write a program that prompts the user to enter five points and displays whether they are on the same line. Here are sample runs:

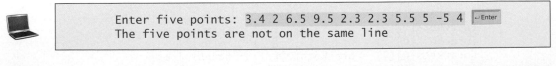

```
Enter five points: 3.4 2 6.5 9.5 2.3 2.3 5.5 5 -5 4 ↵Enter
The five points are not on the same line
```

```
Enter five points: 1 1 2 2 3 3 4 4 5 5 ↵Enter
The five points are on the same line
```

*7.16 (*Sort two-dimensional array*) Write a method to sort a two-dimensional array using the following header:

public static void sort(**int** m[][])

The method performs a primary sort on rows and a secondary sort on columns. For example, the following array

`{{4, 2},{1, 7},{4, 5},{1, 2},{1, 1},{4, 1}}`

will be sorted to

`{{1, 1},{1, 2},{1, 7},{4, 1},{4, 2},{4, 5}}`.

***7.17 (*Financial tsunami*) Banks lend money to each other. In tough economic times, if a bank goes bankrupt, it may not be able to pay back the loan. A bank's total assets are its current balance plus its loans to other banks. The diagram in Figure 7.8 shows five banks. The banks' current balances are 25, 125, 175, 75, and 181 million dollars, respectively. The directed edge from node 1 to node 2 indicates that bank 1 lends 40 million dollars to bank 2.

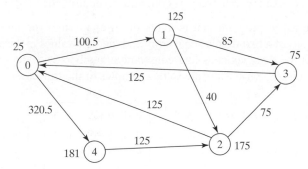

FIGURE 7.8 Banks lend money to each other.

If a bank's total assets are under a certain limit, the bank is unsafe. The money it borrowed cannot be returned to the lender, and the lender cannot count the loan in its total assets. Consequently, the lender may also be unsafe, if its total assets are under the limit. Write a program to find all the unsafe banks. Your program reads the input as follows. It first reads two integers `n` and `limit`, where `n` indicates the number of banks and `limit` is the minimum total assets for keeping a bank safe. It then reads `n` lines that describe the information for `n` banks with IDs from `0` to `n-1`.

The first number in the line is the bank's balance, the second number indicates the number of banks that borrowed money from the bank, and the rest are pairs of two numbers. Each pair describes a borrower. The first number in the pair is the borrower's ID and the second is the amount borrowed. For example, the input for the five banks in Figure 7.8 is as follows (note that the limit is 201):

```
5 201
25 2 1 100.5 4 320.5
125 2 2 40 3 85
175 2 0 125 3 75
75 1 0 125
181 1 2 125
```

The total assets of bank 3 are (75 + 125), which is under 201, so bank 3 is unsafe. After bank 3 becomes unsafe, the total assets of bank 1 fall below (125 + 40). Thus, bank 1 is also unsafe. The output of the program should be

`Unsafe banks are 3 1`

(*Hint*: Use a two-dimensional array **borrowers** to represent loans. **borrowers[i][j]** indicates the loan that bank **i** loans to bank **j**. Once bank **j** becomes unsafe, **borrowers[i][j]** should be set to **0**.)

*7.18 (*Shuffle rows*) Write a method that shuffles the rows in a two-dimensional **int** array using the following header:

public static void shuffle(**int**[][] m)

Write a test program that shuffles the following matrix:

int[][] m = {{1, 2}, {3, 4}, {5, 6}, {7, 8}, {9, 10}};

**7.19 (*Pattern recognition: four consecutive equal numbers*) Write the following method that tests whether a two-dimensional array has four consecutive numbers of the same value, either horizontally, vertically, or diagonally.

public static boolean isConsecutiveFour(**int**[][] values)

Write a test program that prompts the user to enter the number of rows and columns of a two-dimensional array and then the values in the array and displays true if the array contains four consecutive numbers with the same value. Otherwise, display false. Here are some examples of the true cases:

0 1 0 3 1 6 1	0 1 0 3 1 6 1	0 1 0 3 1 6 1	0 1 0 3 1 6 1
0 1 6 8 6 0 1	0 1 6 8 6 0 1	0 1 6 8 6 0 1	0 1 6 8 6 0 1
5 6 2 1 8 2 9	5 5 2 1 8 2 9	5 6 2 1 6 2 9	9 6 2 1 8 2 9
6 5 6 1 1 9 1	6 5 6 1 1 9 1	6 5 6 6 1 9 1	6 9 6 1 1 9 1
1 3 6 1 4 0 7	1 5 6 1 4 0 7	1 3 6 1 4 0 7	1 3 9 1 4 0 7
3 3 3 3 4 0 7	3 5 3 3 4 0 7	3 6 3 3 4 0 7	3 3 3 9 4 0 7

***7.20 (*Game: connect four*) Connect four is a two-player board game in which the players alternately drop colored disks into a seven-column, six-row vertically suspended grid, as shown below.

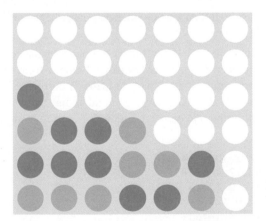

The objective of the game is to connect four same-colored disks in a row, a column, or a diagonal before your opponent can do likewise. The program prompts two players to drop a red or yellow disk alternately. In the preceding figure, the red disk is shown in a dark color and the yellow in a light color. Whenever a disk is dropped, the program redisplays the board on the console and determines the status of the game (win, draw, or continue). Here is a sample run:

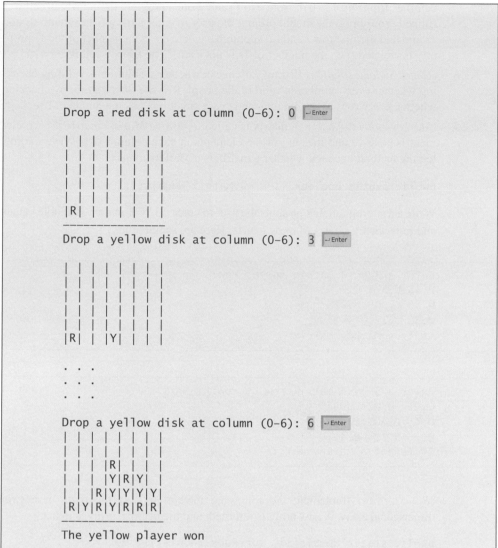

```
| | | | | | | |
| | | | | | | |
| | | | | | | |
| | | | | | | |
| | | | | | | |
| | | | | | | |
-------------------
Drop a red disk at column (0-6): 0  ↵Enter

| | | | | | | |
| | | | | | | |
| | | | | | | |
| | | | | | | |
| | | | | | | |
|R| | | | | | |
-------------------
Drop a yellow disk at column (0-6): 3  ↵Enter

| | | | | | | |
| | | | | | | |
| | | | | | | |
| | | | | | | |
| | | | | | | |
|R| | |Y| | | |
-------------------

. . .
. . .
. . .

Drop a yellow disk at column (0-6): 6  ↵Enter
| | | | | | | |
| | | | |R| | | |
| | | |R| | | |
| | | |Y|R|Y| |
| | |R|Y|Y|Y|Y|
|R|Y|R|Y|R|R|R|
-------------------
The yellow player won
```

*7.21 (*Central city*) Given a set of cities, the central point is the city that has the shortest total distance to all other cities. Write a program that prompts the user to enter the number of the cities and the locations of the cities (coordinates), and finds the central city.

```
Enter the number of cities: 5  ↵Enter
Enter the coordinates of the cities:
  2.5 5 5.1 3 1 9 5.4 54 5.5 2.1  ↵Enter
The central city is at (2.5, 5.0)
```

*7.22 (*Even number of 1s*) Write a program that generates a 6-by-6 two-dimensional matrix filled with 0s and 1s, displays the matrix, and checks if every row and every column have an even number of 1s.

*7.23 (*Game: find the flipped cell*) Suppose you are given a 6-by-6 matrix filled with 0s and 1s. All rows and all columns have an even number of 1s. Let the user flip one

VideoNote
Even number of 1s

cell (i.e., flip from 1 to 0 or from 0 to 1) and write a program to find which cell was flipped. Your program should prompt the user to enter a 6-by-6 array with 0s and 1s and find the first row r and first column c where the even number of the 1s property is violated (i.e., the number of 1s is not even). The flipped cell is at (r, c).

*7.24 (*Check Sudoku solution*) Listing 7.4 checks whether a solution is valid by checking whether every number is valid in the board. Rewrite the program by checking whether every row, every column, and every small box has the numbers 1 to 9.

*7.25 (*Markov matrix*) An $n \times n$ matrix is called a *positive Markov matrix* if each element is positive and the sum of the elements in each column is 1. Write the following method to check whether a matrix is a Markov matrix.

```
public static boolean isMarkovMatrix(double[][] m)
```

Write a test program that prompts the user to enter a 3×3 matrix of double values and tests whether it is a Markov matrix. Here are sample runs:

```
Enter a 3-by-3 matrix row by row:
0.15 0.875 0.375  ↵Enter
0.55 0.005 0.225  ↵Enter
0.30 0.12 0.4  ↵Enter
It is a Markov matrix
```

```
Enter a 3-by-3 matrix row by row:
0.95 -0.875 0.375  ↵Enter
0.65 0.005 0.225  ↵Enter
0.30 0.22 -0.4  ↵Enter
It is not a Markov matrix
```

*7.26 (*Row sorting*) Implement the following method to sort the rows in a two-dimensional array. A new array is returned and the original array is intact.

```
public static double[][] sortRows(double[][] m)
```

Write a test program that prompts the user to enter a 3×3 matrix of double values and displays a new row-sorted matrix. Here is a sample run:

```
Enter a 3-by-3 matrix row by row:
0.15 0.875 0.375  ↵Enter
0.55 0.005 0.225  ↵Enter
0.30 0.12 0.4  ↵Enter

The row-sorted array is
0.15 0.375 0.875
0.005 0.225 0.55
0.12 0.30 0.4
```

*7.27 (*Column sorting*) Implement the following method to sort the columns in a two-dimensional array. A new array is returned and the original array is intact.

```
public static double[][] sortColumns(double[][] m)
```

Write a test program that prompts the user to enter a 3 × 3 matrix of double values and displays a new column-sorted matrix. Here is a sample run:

```
Enter a 3-by-4 matrix row by row:
0.15 0.875 0.375 ⏎Enter
0.55 0.005 0.225 ⏎Enter
0.30 0.12 0.4 ⏎Enter

The column-sorted array is
0.15 0.0050 0.225
0.3  0.12   0.375
0.55 0.875  0.4
```

7.28   (*Strictly identical arrays*) The two-dimensional arrays m1 and m2 are *strictly identical* if their corresponding elements are equal. Write a method that returns true if m1 and m2 are strictly identical, using the following header:

public static boolean equals(**int**[][] m1, **int**[][] m2)

Write a test program that prompts the user to enter two 3 × 3 arrays of integers and displays whether the two are strictly identical. Here are the sample runs.

```
Enter list1: 51 22 25 6 1 4 24 54 6 ⏎Enter
Enter list2: 51 22 25 6 1 4 24 54 6 ⏎Enter
The two arrays are strictly identical
```

```
Enter list1: 51 25 22 6 1 4 24 54 6 ⏎Enter
Enter list2: 51 22 25 6 1 4 24 54 6 ⏎Enter
The two arrays are not strictly identical
```

7.29   (*Identical arrays*) The two-dimensional arrays m1 and m2 are *identical* if they have the same contents. Write a method that returns true if m1 and m2 are identical, using the following header:

public static boolean equals(**int**[][] m1, **int**[][] m2)

Write a test program that prompts the user to enter two lists of integers and displays whether the two are identical. Here are the sample runs.

```
Enter list1: 51 25 22 6 1 4 24 54 6 ⏎Enter
Enter list2: 51 22 25 6 1 4 24 54 6 ⏎Enter
The two arrays are identical
```

```
Enter list1: 51 5 22 6 1 4 24 54 6 ⏎Enter
Enter list2: 51 22 25 6 1 4 24 54 6 ⏎Enter
The two arrays are not identical
```

*7.30 (*Algebra: solve linear equations*) Write a method that solves the following 2×2 system of linear equations:

$$a_{00}x + a_{01}y = b_0 \qquad x = \frac{b_0 a_{11} - b_1 a_{01}}{a_{00}a_{11} - a_{01}a_{10}} \qquad y = \frac{b_1 a_{00} - b_0 a_{10}}{a_{00}a_{11} - a_{01}a_{10}}$$
$$a_{10}x + a_{11}y = b_1$$

The method header is

```
public static double[] linearEquation(double[][] a, double[] b)
```

The method returns `null` if $a_{00}a_{11} - a_{01}a_{10}$ is `0`. Write a test program that prompts the user to enter a_{00}, a_{01}, a_{10}, a_{11}, b_0, and b_1, and displays the result. If $a_{00}a_{11} - a_{01}a_{10}$ is `0`, report that "The equation has no solution." A sample run is similar to Programming Exercise 3.3.

*7.31 (*Geometry: intersecting point*) Write a method that returns the intersecting point of two lines. The intersecting point of the two lines can be found by using the formula shown in Programming Exercise 3.25. Assume that (`x1`, `y1`) and (`x2`, `y2`) are the two points on line 1 and (`x3`, `y3`) and (`x4`, `y4`) are on line 2. The method header is

```
public static double[] getIntersectingPoint(double[][] points)
```

The points are stored in a 4-by-2 two-dimensional array `points` with (`points[0][0]`, `points[0][1]`) for (`x1`, `y1`). The method returns the intersecting point or `null` if the two lines are parallel. Write a program that prompts the user to enter four points and displays the intersecting point. See Programming Exercise 3.25 for a sample run.

*7.32 (*Geometry: area of a triangle*) Write a method that returns the area of a triangle using the following header:

```
public static double getTriangleArea(double[][] points)
```

The points are stored in a 3-by-2 two-dimensional array `points` with `points[0][0]` and `points[0][1]` for (`x1`, `y1`). The triangle area can be computed using the formula in Programming Exercise 2.15. The method returns `0` if the three points are on the same line. Write a program that prompts the user to enter two lines and displays the intersecting point. Here is a sample run of the program:

```
Enter x1, y1, x2, y2, x3, y3: 2.5 2 5 -1.0 4.0 2.0  ↵Enter
The area of the triangle is 2.25
```

```
Enter x1, y1, x2, y2, x3, y3: 2 2 4.5 4.5 6 6  ↵Enter
The three points are on the same line
```

*7.33 (*Geometry: polygon subareas*) A convex 4-vertex polygon is divided into four triangles, as shown in Figure 7.9.

Write a program that prompts the user to enter the coordinates of four vertices and displays the areas of the four triangles in increasing order. Here is a sample run:

```
Enter x1, y1, x2, y2, x3, y3, x4, y4:
  -2.5 2 4 4 3 -2 -2 -3.5  ↵Enter
The areas are 6.17 7.96 8.08 10.42
```

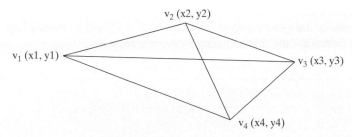

FIGURE 7.9 A 4-vertex polygon is defined by four vertices.

*7.34 (*Geometry: rightmost lowest point*) In computational geometry, often you need to find the rightmost lowest point in a set of points. Write the following method that returns the rightmost lowest point in a set of points.

```
public static double[]
        getRightmostLowestPoint(double[][] points)
```

Write a test program that prompts the user to enter the coordinates of six points and displays the rightmost lowest point. Here is a sample run:

```
Enter 6 points: 1.5 2.5 -3 4.5 5.6 -7 6.5 -7 8 1 10 2.5  ↵Enter
The rightmost lowest point is (6.5, -7.0)
```

**7.35 (*Largest block*) Given a square matrix with the elements 0 or 1, write a program to find a maximum square submatrix whose elements are all 1s. Your program should prompt the user to enter the number of rows in the matrix. The program then displays the location of the first element in the maximum square submatrix and the number of the rows in the submatrix. Here is a sample run:

```
Enter the number of rows in the matrix: 5  ↵Enter
Enter the matrix row by row:
1 0 1 0 1  ↵Enter
1 1 1 0 1  ↵Enter
1 0 1 1 1  ↵Enter
1 0 1 1 1  ↵Enter
1 0 1 1 1  ↵Enter

The maximum square submatrix is at (2, 2) with size 3
```

Your program should implement and use the following method to find the maximum square submatrix:

```
public static int[] findLargestBlock(int[][] m)
```

The return value is an array that consists of three values. The first two values are the row and column indices for the first element in the submatrix, and the third value is the number of the rows in the submatrix.

7.36 (*Latin square*) A Latin square is an n-by-n array filled with **n different Latin letters, each occurring exactly once in each row and once in each column. Write a program that prompts the user to enter the number **n** and the array of characters, as shown in the sample output, and checks if the input array is a Latin square. The characters are the first **n** characters starting from **A**.

```
Enter number n: 4 ↵Enter
Enter 4 rows of letters separated by spaces:
A B C D ↵Enter
B A D C ↵Enter
C D B A ↵Enter
D C A B ↵Enter
The input array is a Latin square
```

```
Enter number n: 3 ↵Enter
Enter 3 rows of letters separated by spaces:
A F D ↵Enter
Wrong input: the letters must be from A to C
```

OBJECTS AND CLASSES

Objectives

- To describe objects and classes, and use classes to model objects (§8.2).

- To use UML graphical notation to describe classes and objects (§8.2).

- To demonstrate how to define classes and create objects (§8.3).

- To create objects using constructors (§8.4).

- To access objects via object reference variables (§8.5).

- To define a reference variable using a reference type (§8.5.1).

- To access an object's data and methods using the object member access operator (.) (§8.5.2).

- To define data fields of reference types and assign default values for an object's data fields (§8.5.3).

- To distinguish between object reference variables and primitive data type variables (§8.5.4).

- To use the Java library classes `Date`, `Random`, and `JFrame` (§8.6).

- To distinguish between instance and static variables and methods (§8.7).

- To define private data fields with appropriate `get` and `set` methods (§8.8).

- To encapsulate data fields to make classes easy to maintain (§8.9).

- To develop methods with object arguments and differentiate between primitive-type arguments and object-type arguments (§8.10).

- To store and process objects in arrays (§8.11).

8.1 Introduction

Object-oriented programming enables you to develop large-scale software and GUIs effectively.

Having learned the material in the preceding chapters, you are able to solve many programming problems using selections, loops, methods, and arrays. However, these Java features are not sufficient for developing graphical user interfaces and large-scale software systems. Suppose you want to develop a graphical user interface (GUI, pronounced *goo-ee*) as shown in Figure 8.1. How would you program it? You will learn how in this chapter.

why OOP?

FIGURE 8.1 The GUI objects are created from classes.

This chapter introduces object-oriented programming, which you can use to develop GUI and large-scale software systems.

8.2 Defining Classes for Objects

A class defines the properties and behaviors for objects.

VideoNote

Define classes and objects

object
state of an object
properties
attributes
data fields
behavior
actions

Object-oriented programming (OOP) involves programming using objects. An *object* represents an entity in the real world that can be distinctly identified. For example, a student, a desk, a circle, a button, and even a loan can all be viewed as objects. An object has a unique identity, state, and behavior.

■ The *state* of an object (also known as its *properties* or *attributes*) is represented by *data fields* with their current values. A circle object, for example, has a data field `radius`, which is the property that characterizes a circle. A rectangle object has the data fields `width` and `height`, which are the properties that characterize a rectangle.

■ The *behavior* of an object (also known as its *actions*) is defined by methods. To invoke a method on an object is to ask the object to perform an action. For example, you may define methods named `getArea()` and `getPerimeter()` for circle objects. A circle object may invoke `getArea()` to return its area and `getPerimeter()` to return its perimeter. You may also define the `setRadius(radius)` method. A circle object can invoke this method to change its radius.

class
contract

instantiation
instance

Objects of the same type are defined using a common class. A *class* is a template, blueprint, or *contract* that defines what an object's data fields and methods will be. An object is an instance of a class. You can create many instances of a class. Creating an instance is referred to as *instantiation*. The terms *object* and *instance* are often interchangeable. The relationship between classes and objects is analogous to that between an apple-pie recipe and apple pies: You can make as many apple pies as you want from a single recipe. Figure 8.2 shows a class named `Circle` and its three objects.

data field
method
constructors

A Java class uses variables to define data fields and methods to define actions. Additionally, a class provides methods of a special type, known as *constructors*, which are invoked to create a new object. A constructor can perform any action, but constructors are designed to perform initializing actions, such as initializing the data fields of objects. Figure 8.3 shows an example of defining the class for circle objects.

FIGURE 8.2   A class is a template for creating objects.

```
class Circle {
  /** The radius of this circle */
  double radius = 1;                             ← Data field

  /** Construct a circle object */
  Circle() {
  }

  /** Construct a circle object */              ← Constructors
  Circle(double newRadius) {
    radius = newRadius;
  }

  /** Return the area of this circle */
  double getArea() {
    return radius * radius * Math.PI;
  }

  /** Return the perimeter of this circle */
  double getPerimeter() {                        ← Method
    return 2 * radius * Math.PI;
  }

  /** Set new radius for this circle */
  double setRadius(double newRadius) {
    radius = newRadius;
  }
}
```

FIGURE 8.3   A class is a construct that defines objects of the same type.

The `Circle` class is different from all of the other classes you have seen thus far. It does not have a `main` method and therefore cannot be run; it is merely a definition for circle objects. The class that contains the `main` method will be referred to in this book, for convenience, as the *main class*.

The illustration of class templates and objects in Figure 8.2 can be standardized using *Unified Modeling Language (UML)* notation. This notation, as shown in Figure 8.4, is called a *UML class diagram*, or simply a *class diagram*. In the class diagram, the data field is denoted as

main class

Unified Modeling Language
  (UML)

class diagram

```
dataFieldName: dataFieldType
```

The constructor is denoted as

```
ClassName(parameterName: parameterType)
```

UML Class Diagram

Circle	← Class name
radius: double	← Data fields
Circle() Circle(newRadius: double) getArea(): double getPerimeter(): double setRadius(newRadius: double): void	← Constructors and methods

circle1: Circle	circle2: Circle	circle3: Circle	← UML notation for objects
radius = 1	radius = 25	radius = 125	

FIGURE 8.4 Classes and objects can be represented using UML notation.

The method is denoted as

```
methodName(parameterName: parameterType): returnType
```

8.3 Example: Defining Classes and Creating Objects

Classes are definitions for objects and objects are created from classes.

This section gives two examples of defining classes and uses the classes to create objects. Listing 8.1 is a program that defines the `Circle` class and uses it to create objects. The program constructs three circle objects with radius **1**, **25**, and **125** and displays the radius and area of each of the three circles. It then changes the radius of the second object to **100** and displays its new radius and area.

Note

avoid naming conflicts

To avoid a naming conflict with several enhanced versions of the `Circle` class introduced later in the chapter, the `Circle` class in this example is named `SimpleCircle`. For simplicity, we will still refer to the class in the text as `Circle`.

LISTING 8.1 TestSimpleCircle.java

main class

main method

create object

create object

create object

create object

```java
 1  public class TestSimpleCircle {
 2    /** Main method */
 3    public static void main(String[] args) {
 4      // Create a circle with radius 1
 5      SimpleCircle circle1 = new SimpleCircle();
 6      System.out.println("The area of the circle of radius "
 7        + circle1.radius + " is " + circle1.getArea());
 8
 9      // Create a circle with radius 25
10      SimpleCircle circle2 = new SimpleCircle(25);
11      System.out.println("The area of the circle of radius "
12        + circle2.radius + " is " + circle2.getArea());
13
14      // Create a circle with radius 125
15      SimpleCircle circle3 = new SimpleCircle(125);
16      System.out.println("The area of the circle of radius "
17        + circle3.radius + " is " + circle3.getArea());
18
19      // Modify circle radius
20      circle2.radius = 100; // or circle2.setRadius(100)
21      System.out.println("The area of the circle of radius "
22        + circle2.radius + " is " + circle2.getArea());
23    }
```

```
24  }
25
26  // Define the circle class with two constructors
27  class SimpleCircle {
28    double radius;
29
30    /** Construct a circle with radius 1 */
31    SimpleCircle() {
32      radius = 1;
33    }
34
35    /** Construct a circle with a specified radius */
36    SimpleCircle(double newRadius) {
37      radius = newRadius;
38    }
39
40    /** Return the area of this circle */
41    double getArea() {
42      return radius * radius * Math.PI;
43    }
44
45    /** Return the perimeter of this circle */
46    double getPerimeter() {
47      return 2 * radius * Math.PI;
48    }
49
50    /** Set a new radius for this circle */
51    void setRadius(double newRadius) {
52      radius = newRadius;
53    }
54  }
```

class SimpleCircle
data field

no-arg constructor

second constructor

getArea

getPerimeter

setRadius

```
The area of the circle of radius 1.0 is 3.141592653589793
The area of the circle of radius 25.0 is 1963.4954084936207
The area of the circle of radius 125.0 is 49087.385212340516
The area of the circle of radius 100.0 is 31415.926535897932
```

The program contains two classes. The first of these, `TestSimpleCircle`, is the main class. Its sole purpose is to test the second class, `SimpleCircle`. Such a program that uses the class is often referred to as a *client* of the class. When you run the program, the Java runtime system invokes the `main` method in the main class.

client

You can put the two classes into one file, but only one class in the file can be a *public class*. Furthermore, the public class must have the same name as the file name. Therefore, the file name is **TestSimpleCircle.java**, since `TestSimpleCircle` is public. Each class in the source code is compiled into a **.class** file. When you compile **TestSimpleCircle.java**, two class files **TestSimpleCircle.class** and **SimpleCircle.class** are generated, as shown in Figure 8.5.

public class

FIGURE 8.5 Each class in the source code file is compiled into a **.class** file.

The main class contains the `main` method (line 3) that creates three objects. As in creating an array, the `new` operator is used to create an object from the constructor. `new SimpleCircle()` creates an object with radius 1 (line 5), `new SimpleCircle(25)` creates an object with radius 25 (line 10), and `new SimpleCircle(125)` creates an object with radius 125 (line 15).

These three objects (referenced by `circle1`, `circle2`, and `circle3`) have different data but the same methods. Therefore, you can compute their respective areas by using the `getArea()` method. The data fields can be accessed via the reference of the object using `circle1.radius`, `circle2.radius`, and `circle3.radius`, respectively. The object can invoke its method via the reference of the object using `circle1.getArea()`, `circle2.getArea()`, and `circle3.getArea()`, respectively.

These three objects are independent. The radius of `circle2` is changed to `100` in line 20. The object's new radius and area are displayed in lines 21–22.

There are many ways to write Java programs. For instance, you can combine the two classes in the example into one, as shown in Listing 8.2.

LISTING 8.2 SimpleCircle.java

```
 1  public class SimpleCircle {
 2    /** Main method */
 3    public static void main(String[] args) {
 4      // Create a circle with radius 1
 5      SimpleCircle circle1 = new SimpleCircle();
 6      System.out.println("The area of the circle of radius "
 7        + circle1.radius + " is " + circle1.getArea());
 8
 9      // Create a circle with radius 25
10      SimpleCircle circle2 = new SimpleCircle(25);
11      System.out.println("The area of the circle of radius "
12        + circle2.radius + " is " + circle2.getArea());
13
14      // Create a circle with radius 125
15      SimpleCircle circle3 = new SimpleCircle(125);
16      System.out.println("The area of the circle of radius "
17        + circle3.radius + " is " + circle3.getArea());
18
19      // Modify circle radius
20      circle2.radius = 100;
21      System.out.println("The area of the circle of radius "
22        + circle2.radius + " is " + circle2.getArea());
23    }
24
25    double radius;
26
27    /** Construct a circle with radius 1 */
28    SimpleCircle() {
29      radius = 1;
30    }
31
32    /** Construct a circle with a specified radius */
33    SimpleCircle(double newRadius) {
34      radius = newRadius;
35    }
36
37    /** Return the area of this circle */
38    double getArea() {
39      return radius * radius * Math.PI;
40    }
41
```

main method (line 3)

data field (line 25)

no-arg constructor (line 28)

second constructor (line 33)

method (line 38)

```
42     /** Return the perimeter of this circle */
43     double getPerimeter() {
44       return 2 * radius * Math.PI;
45     }
46
47     /** Set a new radius for this circle */
48     void setRadius(double newRadius) {
49       radius = newRadius;
50     }
51   }
```

Since the combined class has a **main** method, it can be executed by the Java interpreter. The **main** method is the same as in Listing 8.1. This demonstrates that you can test a class by simply adding a **main** method in the same class.

As another example, consider television sets. Each TV is an object with states (current channel, current volume level, power on or off) and behaviors (change channels, adjust volume, turn on/off). You can use a class to model TV sets. The UML diagram for the class is shown in Figure 8.6.

FIGURE 8.6   The TV class models TV sets.

Listing 8.3 gives a program that defines the **TV** class.

LISTING 8.3 TV.java

```
1   public class TV {
2     int channel = 1; // Default channel is 1                           data fields
3     int volumeLevel = 1; // Default volume level is 1
4     boolean on = false; // TV is off
5
6     public TV() {                                                       constructor
7     }
8
9     public void turnOn() {                                              turn on TV
10       on = true;
11     }
12
13     public void turnOff() {                                            turn off TV
```

```
                        14        on = false;
                        15      }
                        16
set a new channel       17      public void setChannel(int newChannel) {
                        18        if (on && newChannel >= 1 && newChannel <= 120)
                        19          channel = newChannel;
                        20      }
                        21
set a new volume        22      public void setVolume(int newVolumeLevel) {
                        23        if (on && newVolumeLevel >= 1 && newVolumeLevel <= 7)
                        24          volumeLevel = newVolumeLevel;
                        25      }
                        26
increase channel        27      public void channelUp() {
                        28        if (on && channel < 120)
                        29          channel++;
                        30      }
                        31
decrease channel        32      public void channelDown() {
                        33        if (on && channel > 1)
                        34          channel--;
                        35      }
                        36
increase volume         37      public void volumeUp() {
                        38        if (on && volumeLevel < 7)
                        39          volumeLevel++;
                        40      }
                        41
decrease volume         42      public void volumeDown() {
                        43        if (on && volumeLevel > 1)
                        44          volumeLevel--;
                        45      }
                        46    }
```

The constructor and methods in the TV class are defined public so they can be accessed from other classes. Note that the channel and volume level are not changed if the TV is not on. Before either of these is changed, its current value is checked to ensure that it is within the correct range.

Listing 8.4 gives a program that uses the TV class to create two objects.

LISTING 8.4 TestTV.java

```
                    1   public class TestTV {
main method         2     public static void main(String[] args) {
create a TV         3       TV tv1 = new TV();
turn on             4       tv1.turnOn();
set a new channel   5       tv1.setChannel(30);
set a new volume    6       tv1.setVolume(3);
                    7
create a TV         8       TV tv2 = new TV();
turn on             9       tv2.turnOn();
increase channel    10      tv2.channelUp();
                    11      tv2.channelUp();
increase volume     12      tv2.volumeUp();
                    13
display state       14      System.out.println("tv1's channel is " + tv1.channel
                    15        + " and volume level is " + tv1.volumeLevel);
                    16      System.out.println("tv2's channel is " + tv2.channel
                    17        + " and volume level is " + tv2.volumeLevel);
                    18    }
                    19  }
```

```
tv1's channel is 30 and volume level is 3
tv2's channel is 3 and volume level is 2
```

The program creates two objects in lines 3 and 8 and invokes the methods on the objects to perform actions for setting channels and volume levels and for increasing channels and volumes. The program displays the state of the objects in lines 14–17. The methods are invoked using syntax such as `tv1.turnOn()` (line 4). The data fields are accessed using syntax such as `tv1.channel` (line 14).

These examples have given you a glimpse of classes and objects. You may have many questions regarding constructors, objects, reference variables, accessing data fields, and invoking object's methods. The sections that follow discuss these issues in detail.

8.1 Describe the relationship between an object and its defining class.

8.2 How do you define a class?

8.3 How do you declare an object's reference variable?

8.4 How do you create an object?

8.4 Constructing Objects Using Constructors

A constructor is invoked to create an object using the new *operator.*

Constructors are a special kind of method. They have three peculiarities:

- A constructor must have the same name as the class itself.

- Constructors do not have a return type—not even `void`.

- Constructors are invoked using the `new` operator when an object is created. Constructors play the role of initializing objects.

The constructor has exactly the same name as its defining class. Like regular methods, constructors can be overloaded (i.e., multiple constructors can have the same name but different signatures), making it easy to construct objects with different initial data values.

It is a common mistake to put the `void` keyword in front of a constructor. For example,

```
public void Circle() {
}
```

In this case, `Circle()` is a method, not a constructor.

Constructors are used to construct objects. To construct an object from a class, invoke a constructor of the class using the `new` operator, as follows:

```
new ClassName(arguments);
```

For example, `new Circle()` creates an object of the `Circle` class using the first constructor defined in the `Circle` class, and `new Circle(25)` creates an object using the second constructor defined in the `Circle` class.

A class normally provides a constructor without arguments (e.g., `Circle()`). Such a constructor is referred to as a *no-arg* or *no-argument constructor*.

A class may be defined without constructors. In this case, a public no-arg constructor with an empty body is implicitly defined in the class. This constructor, called a *default constructor*, is provided automatically *only if no constructors are explicitly defined in the class.*

8.5 What are the differences between constructors and methods?

8.6 When will a class have a default constructor?

Key marginal notes: constructor's name / no return type / new operator / overloaded constructors / no void / constructing objects / no-arg constructor / default constructor

8.5 Accessing Objects via Reference Variables

Key Point

An object's data and methods can be accessed through the dot (.) operator via the object's reference variable.

Newly created objects are allocated in the memory. They can be accessed via reference variables.

8.5.1 Reference Variables and Reference Types

reference variable

Objects are accessed via the object's *reference variables*, which contain references to the objects. Such variables are declared using the following syntax:

```
ClassName objectRefVar;
```

reference type

A class is essentially a programmer-defined type. A class is a *reference type*, which means that a variable of the class type can reference an instance of the class. The following statement declares the variable `myCircle` to be of the `Circle` type:

```
Circle myCircle;
```

The variable `myCircle` can reference a `Circle` object. The next statement creates an object and assigns its reference to `myCircle`:

```
myCircle = new Circle();
```

You can write a single statement that combines the declaration of an object reference variable, the creation of an object, and the assigning of an object reference to the variable with the following syntax:

```
ClassName objectRefVar = new ClassName();
```

Here is an example:

```
Circle myCircle = new Circle();
```

The variable `myCircle` holds a reference to a `Circle` object.

object vs. object reference variable

Note

An object reference variable that appears to hold an object actually contains a reference to that object. Strictly speaking, an object reference variable and an object are different, but most of the time the distinction can be ignored. Therefore, it is fine, for simplicity, to say that `myCircle` is a `Circle` object rather than use the longer-winded description that `myCircle` is a variable that contains a reference to a `Circle` object.

array object

Note

Arrays are treated as objects in Java. Arrays are created using the `new` operator. An array variable is actually a variable that contains a reference to an array.

8.5.2 Accessing an Object's Data and Methods

dot operator (.)

In OOP terminology, an object's member refers to its data fields and methods. After an object is created, its data can be accessed and its methods invoked using the *dot operator (.)*, also known as the *object member access operator*:

- `objectRefVar.dataField` references a data field in the object.
- `objectRefVar.method(arguments)` invokes a method on the object.

For example, `myCircle.radius` references the radius in `myCircle`, and `myCircle.getArea()` invokes the `getArea` method on `myCircle`. Methods are invoked as operations on objects.

The data field `radius` is referred to as an *instance variable*, because it is dependent on a specific instance. For the same reason, the method `getArea` is referred to as an *instance method*, because you can invoke it only on a specific instance. The object on which an instance method is invoked is called a *calling object*.

instance variable
instance method

calling object

Caution

Recall that you use `Math.methodName(arguments)` (e.g., `Math.pow(3, 2.5)`) to invoke a method in the `Math` class. Can you invoke `getArea()` using `Circle.getArea()`? The answer is no. All the methods in the `Math` class are static methods, which are defined using the `static` keyword. However, `getArea()` is an instance method, and thus nonstatic. It must be invoked from an object using `objectRefVar.methodName(arguments)` (e.g., `myCircle.getArea()`). Further explanation is given in Section 8.7, Static Variables, Constants, and Methods.

invoking methods

Note

Usually you create an object and assign it to a variable, and then later you can use the variable to reference the object. Occasionally an object does not need to be referenced later. In this case, you can create an object without explicitly assigning it to a variable using the syntax:

```
new Circle();
```

or

```
System.out.println("Area is " + new Circle(5).getArea());
```

The former statement creates a `Circle` object. The latter creates a `Circle` object and invokes its `getArea` method to return its area. An object created in this way is known as an *anonymous object*.

anonymous object

8.5.3 Reference Data Fields and the `null` Value

The data fields can be of reference types. For example, the following `Student` class contains a data field `name` of the `String` type. `String` is a predefined Java class.

reference data fields

```
class Student {
  String name; // name has the default value null
  int age; // age has the default value 0
  boolean isScienceMajor; // isScienceMajor has default value false
  char gender; // gender has default value '\u0000'
}
```

If a data field of a reference type does not reference any object, the data field holds a special Java value, `null`. `null` is a literal just like `true` and `false`. While `true` and `false` are Boolean literals, `null` is a literal for a reference type.

null value

The default value of a data field is `null` for a reference type, `0` for a numeric type, `false` for a `boolean` type, and `\u0000` for a `char` type. However, Java assigns no default value to a local variable inside a method. The following code displays the default values of the data fields `name`, `age`, `isScienceMajor`, and `gender` for a `Student` object:

default field values

```
class Test {
  public static void main(String[] args) {
    Student student = new Student();
    System.out.println("name? " + student.name);
```

```
            System.out.println("age? " + student.age );
            System.out.println("isScienceMajor? " + student.isScienceMajor );
            System.out.println("gender? " + student.gender );
    }
}
```

The following code has a compile error, because the local variables x and y are not initialized:

```
class Test {
    public static void main(String[] args) {
        int x;  // x has no default value
        String y;  // y has no default value
        System.out.println("x is " + x );
        System.out.println("y is " + y );
    }
}
```

NullPointerException

> **Caution**
>
> **NullPointerException** is a common runtime error. It occurs when you invoke a method on a reference variable with a **null** value. Make sure you assign an object reference to the variable before invoking the method through the reference variable.

8.5.4 Differences between Variables of Primitive Types and Reference Types

Every variable represents a memory location that holds a value. When you declare a variable, you are telling the compiler what type of value the variable can hold. For a variable of a primitive type, the value is of the primitive type. For a variable of a reference type, the value is a reference to where an object is located. For example, as shown in Figure 8.7, the value of int variable i is int value 1, and the value of Circle object c holds a reference to where the contents of the Circle object are stored in memory.

When you assign one variable to another, the other variable is set to the same value. For a variable of a primitive type, the real value of one variable is assigned to the other variable. For a variable of a reference type, the reference of one variable is assigned to the other variable. As shown in Figure 8.8, the assignment statement i = j copies the contents of j into i for

Created using new Circle()

Primitive type	int i = 1 i	1
Object type	Circle c c	reference - - - → c: Circle / radius = 1

FIGURE 8.7 A variable of a primitive type holds a value of the primitive type, and a variable of a reference type holds a reference to where an object is stored in memory.

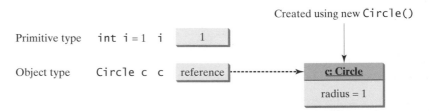

Primitive type assignment i = j

Before: After:

i   1   i   2

j   2   j   2

FIGURE 8.8 Primitive variable j is copied to variable i.

primitive variables. As shown in Figure 8.9, the assignment statement `c1 = c2` copies the reference of `c2` into `c1` for reference variables. After the assignment, variables `c1` and `c2` refer to the same object.

FIGURE 8.9 Reference variable `c2` is copied to variable `c1`.

Note
As illustrated in Figure 8.9, after the assignment statement `c1 = c2`, `c1` points to the same object referenced by `c2`. The object previously referenced by `c1` is no longer use-ful and therefore is now known as *garbage*. Garbage occupies memory space, so the Java runtime system detects garbage and automatically reclaims the space it occupies. This process is called *garbage collection*.

garbage

garbage collection

Tip
If you know that an object is no longer needed, you can explicitly assign `null` to a ref-erence variable for the object. The JVM will automatically collect the space if the object is not referenced by any reference variable.

8.7 Which operator is used to access a data field or invoke a method from an object?

8.8 What is an anonymous object?

8.9 What is `NullPointerException`?

8.10 Is an array an object or a primitive type value? Can an array contain elements of an object type as well as a primitive type? Describe the default value for the elements of an array.

8.11 What is wrong with each of the following programs?

✓Check Point

MyProgrammingLab™

```
1  public class ShowErrors {
2    public static void main(String[] args) {
3      ShowErrors t = new ShowErrors(5);
4    }
5  }
```

(a)

```
1  public class ShowErrors {
2    public static void main(String[] args) {
3      ShowErrors t = new ShowErrors();
4      t.x();
5    }
6  }
```

(b)

```
1  public class ShowErrors {
2    public void method1() {
3      Circle c;
4      System.out.println("What is radius "
5        + c.getRadius());
6      c = new Circle();
7    }
8  }
```

(c)

```
1  public class ShowErrors {
2    public static void main(String[] args) {
3      C c = new C(5.0);
4      System.out.println(c.value);
5    }
6  }
7
8  class C {
9    int value = 2;
10 }
```

(d)

8.12 What is wrong in the following code?

```
1  class Test {
2    public static void main(String[] args) {
3      A a = new A();
4      a.print();
5    }
6  }
7
8  class A {
9    String s;
10
11   A(String newS) {
12     s = newS;
13   }
14
15   public void print() {
16     System.out.print(s);
17   }
18 }
```

8.13 What is the printout of the following code?

```
public class A {
  private boolean x;

  public static void main(String[] args) {
    A a = new A();
    System.out.println(a.x);
  }
}
```

8.6 Using Classes from the Java Library

The Java API contains a rich set of classes for developing Java programs.

Listing 8.1 defined the SimpleCircle class and created objects from the class. You will frequently use the classes in the Java library to develop programs. This section gives some examples of the classes in the Java library.

8.6.1 The Date Class

In Listing 2.6, ShowCurrentTime.java, you learned how to obtain the current time using System.currentTimeMillis(). You used the division and remainder operators to extract the current second, minute, and hour. Java provides a system-independent encapsulation of date and time in the `java.util.Date` class, as shown in Figure 8.10.

java.util.Date class

java.util.Date	
+Date()	Constructs a Date object for the current time.
+Date(elapseTime: long)	Constructs a Date object for a given time in milliseconds elapsed since January 1, 1970, GMT.
+toString(): String	Returns a string representing the date and time.
+getTime(): long	Returns the number of milliseconds since January 1, 1970, GMT.
+setTime(elapseTime: long): void	Sets a new elapse time in the object.

FIGURE 8.10 A `Date` object represents a specific date and time.

You can use the no-arg constructor in the `Date` class to create an instance for the current date and time, the `getTime()` method to return the elapsed time since January 1, 1970, GMT, and the `toString()` method to return the date and time as a string. For example, the following code

```
java.util.Date date = new java.util.Date();                          create object
System.out.println("The elapsed time since Jan 1, 1970 is " +
  date.getTime() + " milliseconds");                                 get elapsed time
System.out.println(date.toString());                                 invoke toString
```

displays the output like this:

```
The elapsed time since Jan 1, 1970 is 1324903419651 milliseconds
Mon Dec 26 07:43:39 EST 2011
```

The `Date` class has another constructor, `Date(long elapseTime)`, which can be used to construct a `Date` object for a given time in milliseconds elapsed since January 1, 1970, GMT.

8.6.2 The Random Class

You have used `Math.random()` to obtain a random `double` value between `0.0` and `1.0` (excluding `1.0`). Another way to generate random numbers is to use the `java.util.Random` class, as shown in Figure 8.11, which can generate a random `int`, `long`, `double`, `float`, and `boolean` value.

java.util.Random	
+Random()	Constructs a Random object with the current time as its seed.
+Random(seed: long)	Constructs a Random object with a specified seed.
+nextInt(): int	Returns a random int value.
+nextInt(n: int): int	Returns a random int value between 0 and n (excluding n).
+nextLong(): long	Returns a random long value.
+nextDouble(): double	Returns a random double value between 0.0 and 1.0 (excluding 1.0).
+nextFloat(): float	Returns a random float value between 0.0F and 1.0F (excluding 1.0F).
+nextBoolean(): boolean	Returns a random boolean value.

FIGURE 8.11 A `Random` object can be used to generate random values.

When you create a Random object, you have to specify a seed or use the default seed. A seed is a number used to initialize a random number generator. The no-arg constructor creates a Random object using the current elapsed time as its seed. If two Random objects have the same seed, they will generate identical sequences of numbers. For example, the following code creates two Random objects with the same seed, 3.

```
Random random1 = new Random(3);
System.out.print("From random1: ");
for (int i = 0; i < 10; i++)
  System.out.print(random1.nextInt(1000) + " ");

Random random2 = new Random(3);
System.out.print("\nFrom random2: ");
for (int i = 0; i < 10; i++)
  System.out.print(random2.nextInt(1000) + " ");
```

The code generates the same sequence of random int values:

```
From random1: 734 660 210 581 128 202 549 564 459 961
From random2: 734 660 210 581 128 202 549 564 459 961
```

same sequence

Note

The ability to generate the same sequence of random values is useful in software testing and many other applications. In software testing, often you need to reproduce the test cases from a fixed sequence of random numbers.

8.6.3 Displaying GUI Components

Pedagogical Note

Graphical user interface (GUI) components are good examples for teaching OOP. Simple GUI examples are introduced here for this purpose. The full introduction to GUI programming begins with Chapter 12, GUI Basics.

When you develop programs to create graphical user interfaces, you will use Java classes such as JFrame, JButton, JRadioButton, JComboBox, and JList to create frames, buttons, radio buttons, combo boxes, lists, and so on. Listing 8.5 is an example that creates two windows using the JFrame class. The output of the program is shown in Figure 8.12.

FIGURE 8.12 The program creates two windows using the JFrame class.

LISTING 8.5 TestFrame.java

create an object
invoke a method

```
1  import javax.swing.JFrame;
2
3  public class TestFrame {
4    public static void main(String[] args) {
5      JFrame frame1 = new JFrame();
6      frame1.setTitle("Window 1");
7      frame1.setSize(200, 150);
8      frame1.setLocation(200, 100);
9      frame1.setDefaultCloseOperation(JFrame.EXIT_ON_CLOSE);
10     frame1.setVisible(true);
```

```
11
12        JFrame frame2 = new JFrame();                                create an object
13        frame2.setTitle("Window 2");                                 invoke a method
14        frame2.setSize(200, 150);
15        frame2.setLocation(410, 100);
16        frame2.setDefaultCloseOperation(JFrame.EXIT_ON_CLOSE);
17        frame2.setVisible(true);
18    }
19 }
```

This program creates two objects of the `JFrame` class (lines 5, 12) and then uses the methods
`setTitle`, `setSize`, `setLocation`, `setDefaultCloseOperation`, and `setVisible` to
set the properties of the objects. The `setTitle` method sets a title for the window (lines 6,
13). The `setSize` method sets the window's width and height (lines 7, 14). The
`setLocation` method specifies the location of the window's upper-left corner (lines 8, 15).
The `setDefaultCloseOperation` method terminates the program when the frame is
closed (lines 9, 16). The `setVisible` method displays the window.

You can add graphical user interface components, such as buttons, labels, text fields, check
boxes, and combo boxes to the window. The components are defined using classes. Listing
8.6 gives an example of creating a graphical user interface, as shown in Figure 8.1.

LISTING 8.6 GUIComponents.java

```
1  import javax.swing.*;                                                VideoNote
2                                                                       Use classes
3  public class GUIComponents {
4    public static void main(String[] args) {
5      // Create a button with text OK
6      JButton jbtOK = new JButton("OK");                               create a button
7
8      // Create a button with text Cancel
9      JButton jbtCancel = new JButton("Cancel");                       create a button
10
11     // Create a label with text "Enter your name: "
12     JLabel jlblName = new JLabel("Enter your name: ");               create a label
13
14     // Create a text field with text "Type Name Here"
15     JTextField jtfName = new JTextField("Type Name Here");           create a text field
16
17     // Create a check box with text Bold
18     JCheckBox jchkBold = new JCheckBox("Bold");                      create a check box
19
20     // Create a check box with text Italic
21     JCheckBox jchkItalic = new JCheckBox("Italic");                  create a check box
22
23     // Create a radio button with text Red
24     JRadioButton jrbRed = new JRadioButton("Red");                   create a radio button
25
26     // Create a radio button with text Yellow
27     JRadioButton jrbYellow = new JRadioButton("Yellow");             create a radio button
28
29     // Create a combo box with several choices
30     JComboBox jcboColor = new JComboBox(new String[]{"Freshman",     create a combo box
31       "Sophomore", "Junior", "Senior"});
32
33     // Create a panel to group components
34     JPanel panel = new JPanel();                                     create a panel
35     panel.add(jbtOK); // Add the OK button to the panel              add to panel
36     panel.add(jbtCancel); // Add the Cancel button to the panel
```

```
37    panel.add(jlblName); // Add the label to the panel
38    panel.add(jtfName); // Add the text field to the panel
39    panel.add(jchkBold); // Add the check box to the panel
40    panel.add(jchkItalic); // Add the check box to the panel
41    panel.add(jrbRed); // Add the radio button to the panel
42    panel.add(jrbYellow); // Add the radio button to the panel
43    panel.add(jcboColor); // Add the combo box to the panel
44
```

create a frame
add panel to frame

```
45    JFrame frame = new JFrame(); // Create a frame
46    frame.add(panel); // Add the panel to the frame
47    frame.setTitle("Show GUI Components");
48    frame.setSize(450, 100);
49    frame.setLocation(200, 100);
50    frame.setDefaultCloseOperation(JFrame.EXIT_ON_CLOSE);
```

display frame

```
51    frame.setVisible(true);
52  }
53 }
```

This program creates GUI objects using the classes **JButton**, **JLabel**, **JTextField**, **JCheckBox**, **JRadioButton**, and **JComboBox** (lines 6–31). Then, using the **JPanel** class (line 34), it then creates a panel object and adds the button, label, text field, check box, radio button, and combo box to it (lines 35–43). The program then creates a frame and adds the panel to the frame (line 45). The frame is displayed in line 51.

Check
Point

MyProgrammingLab™

8.14 How do you create a **Date** for the current time? How do you display the current time?

8.15 How do you create a **JFrame**, set a title in a frame, and display a frame?

8.16 Which packages contain the classes **Date**, **JFrame**, **JOptionPane**, **System**, and **Math**?

8.7 Static Variables, Constants, and Methods

Key
Point

A static variable is shared by all objects of the class. A static method cannot access instance members of the class.

VideoNote

Static vs. instance

instance variable

The data field **radius** in the circle class is known as an *instance variable*. An instance variable is tied to a specific instance of the class; it is not shared among objects of the same class. For example, suppose that you create the following objects:

```
Circle circle1 = new Circle();
Circle circle2 = new Circle(5);
```

The **radius** in **circle1** is independent of the **radius** in **circle2** and is stored in a different memory location. Changes made to **circle1**'s **radius** do not affect **circle2**'s **radius**, and vice versa.

static variable

If you want all the instances of a class to share data, use *static variables*, also known as *class variables*. Static variables store values for the variables in a common memory location. Because of this common location, if one object changes the value of a static variable, all objects of the same class are affected. Java supports static methods as well as static variables.

static method

Static methods can be called without creating an instance of the class.

Let's modify the **Circle** class by adding a static variable **numberOfObjects** to count the number of circle objects created. When the first object of this class is created, **numberOfObjects** is **1**. When the second object is created, **numberOfObjects** becomes **2**. The UML of the new circle class is shown in Figure 8.13. The **Circle** class defines the instance variable **radius** and the static variable **numberOfObjects**, the instance methods **getRadius**, **setRadius**, and **getArea**, and the static method **getNumberOfObjects**. (Note that static variables and methods are underlined in the UML class diagram.)

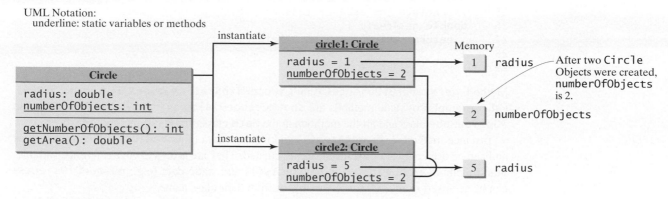

FIGURE 8.13 Instance variables belong to the instances and have memory storage independent of one another. Static variables are shared by all the instances of the same class.

To declare a static variable or define a static method, put the modifier `static` in the variable or method declaration. The static variable `numberOfObjects` and the static method `getNumberOfObjects()` can be declared as follows:

```
static int numberOfObjects;
```
declare static variable

```
static int getNumberObjects() {
  return numberOfObjects;
}
```
define static method

Constants in a class are shared by all objects of the class. Thus, constants should be declared as `final static`. For example, the constant `PI` in the `Math` class is defined as:

declare constant

```
final static double PI = 3.14159265358979323846;
```

The new circle class, named `CircleWithStaticMembers`, is defined in Listing 8.7:

LISTING 8.7 CircleWithStaticMembers.java

```
1  public class CircleWithStaticMembers {
2    /** The radius of the circle */
3    double radius;
4
5    /** The number of objects created */
6    static int numberOfObjects = 0;
7
8    /** Construct a circle with radius 1 */
9    CircleWithStaticMembers() {
10     radius = 1;
11     numberOfObjects++;
12   }
13
14   /** Construct a circle with a specified radius */
15   CircleWithStaticMembers(double newRadius) {
16     radius = newRadius;
17     numberOfObjects++;
18   }
19
20   /** Return numberOfObjects */
21   static int getNumberOfObjects() {
22     return numberOfObjects;
23   }
24
```

static variable

increase by 1

increase by 1

static method

```
25    /** Return the area of this circle */
26    double getArea() {
27      return radius * radius * Math.PI;
28    }
29  }
```

Method **getNumberOfObjects()** in **CircleWithStaticMembers** is a static method. Other examples of static methods are **showMessageDialog** and **showInputDialog** in the **JOptionPane** class and all the methods in the **Math** class. The **main** method is static, too.

Instance methods (e.g., **getArea()**) and instance data (e.g., **radius**) belong to instances and can be used only after the instances are created. They are accessed via a reference variable. Static methods (e.g., **getNumberOfObjects()**) and static data (e.g., **numberOfObjects**) can be accessed from a reference variable or from their class name.

The program in Listing 8.8 demonstrates how to use instance and static variables and methods and illustrates the effects of using them.

LISTING 8.8 TestCircleWithStaticMembers.java

```
1  public class TestCircleWithStaticMembers {
2    /** Main method */
3    public static void main(String[] args) {
4      System.out.println("Before creating objects");
5      System.out.println("The number of Circle objects is " +
6        CircleWithStaticMembers.numberOfObjects );
7
8      // Create c1
9      CircleWithStaticMembers c1 = new CircleWithStaticMembers();
10
11     // Display c1 BEFORE c2 is created
12     System.out.println("\nAfter creating c1");
13     System.out.println("c1: radius (" + c1.radius +
14       ") and number of Circle objects (" +
15       c1.numberOfObjects + ")");
16
17     // Create c2
18     CircleWithStaticMembers c2 = new CircleWithStaticMembers(5);
19
20     // Modify c1
21     c1.radius = 9;
22
23     // Display c1 and c2 AFTER c2 was created
24     System.out.println("\nAfter creating c2 and modifying c1");
25     System.out.println("c1: radius (" + c1.radius +
26       ") and number of Circle objects (" +
27       c1.numberOfObjects + ")");
28     System.out.println("c2: radius (" + c2.radius +
29       ") and number of Circle objects (" +
30       c2.numberOfObjects + ")");
31   }
32 }
```

static variable — lines 5–6
instance variable — lines 13–14
static variable — line 15
instance variable — line 21
static variable — line 27
static variable — line 30

```
Before creating objects
The number of Circle objects is 0
After creating c1
c1: radius (1.0) and number of Circle objects (1)
After creating c2 and modifying c1
c1: radius (9.0) and number of Circle objects (2)
c2: radius (5.0) and number of Circle objects (2)
```

When you compile `TestCircleWithStaticMembers.java`, the Java compiler automatically compiles `CircleWithStaticMembers.java` if it has not been compiled since the last change.

Static variables and methods can be accessed without creating objects. Line 6 displays the number of objects, which is `0`, since no objects have been created.

The `main` method creates two circles, `c1` and `c2` (lines 9, 18). The instance variable `radius` in `c1` is modified to become `9` (line 21). This change does not affect the instance variable `radius` in `c2`, since these two instance variables are independent. The static variable `numberOfObjects` becomes `1` after `c1` is created (line 9), and it becomes `2` after `c2` is created (line 18).

Note that `PI` is a constant defined in `Math`, and `Math.PI` references the constant. `c1.numberOfObjects` (line 27) and `c2.numberOfObjects` (line 30) are better replaced by `CircleWithStaticMembers.numberOfObjects`. This improves readability, because other programmers can easily recognize the static variable. You can also replace `CircleWithStaticMembers.numberOfObjects` with `CircleWithStaticMembers.getNumberOfObjects()`.

Tip

Use `ClassName.methodName(arguments)` to invoke a static method and `ClassName.staticVariable` to access a static variable. This improves readability, because other programmers can easily recognize the static method and data in the class.

use class name

An instance method can invoke an instance or static method and access an instance or static data field. A static method can invoke a static method and access a static data field. However, a static method cannot invoke an instance method or access an instance data field, since static methods and static data fields don't belong to a particular object. The relationship between static and instance members is summarized in the following diagram:

For example, the following code is wrong.

```
1  public class A {
2    int i = 5;
3    static int k = 2;
4
5    public static void main(String[] args) {
6      int j = i; // Wrong because i is an instance variable
7      m1(); // Wrong because m1() is an instance method
8    }
9
10   public void m1() {
11     // Correct since instance and static variables and methods
12     // can be used in an instance method
13     i = i + k + m2(i, k);
14   }
15
16   public static int m2(int i, int j) {
17     return (int)(Math.pow(i, j));
18   }
19 }
```

Note that if you replace the preceding code with the following new code, the program would be fine, because the instance data field `i` and method `m1` are now accessed from an object `a` (lines 7–8):

```
1  public class A {
2    int i = 5;
3    static int k = 2;
4
5    public static void main(String[] args) {
6      A a = new A();
7      int j = a.i; // OK, a.i accesses the object's instance variable
8      a.m1(); // OK. a.m1() invokes the object's instance method
9    }
10
11   public void m1() {
12     i = i + k + m2(i, k);
13   }
14
15   public static int m2(int i, int j) {
16     return (int)(Math.pow(i, j));
17   }
18 }
```

instance or static?

Design Guide

How do you decide whether a variable or method should be an instance one or a static one? A variable or method that is dependent on a specific instance of the class should be an instance variable or method. A variable or method that is not dependent on a specific instance of the class should be a static variable or method. For example, every circle has its own radius, so the radius is dependent on a specific circle. Therefore, `radius` is an instance variable of the `Circle` class. Since the `getArea` method is dependent on a specific circle, it is an instance method. None of the methods in the `Math` class, such as `random`, `pow`, `sin`, and `cos`, is dependent on a specific instance. Therefore, these methods are static methods. The `main` method is static and can be invoked directly from a class.

common design error

Caution

It is a common design error to define an instance method that should have been defined as static. For example, the method `factorial(int n)` should be defined as static, as shown next, because it is independent of any specific instance.

```
public class Test {
  public int factorial(int n) {
    int result = 1;
    for (int i = 1; i <= n; i++)
      result *= i;

    return result;
  }
}
```

(a) Wrong design

```
public class Test {
  public static int factorial(int n) {
    int result = 1;
    for (int i = 1; i <= n; i++)
      result *= i;

    return result;
  }
}
```

(b) Correct design

8.17 Suppose that the class `F` is defined in (a). Let `f` be an instance of `F`. Which of the statements in (b) are correct?

```
public class F {              System.out.println(f.i);
  int i;                      System.out.println(f.s);
  static String s;            f.imethod();
                              f.smethod();
  void imethod() {            System.out.println(F.i);
  }                           System.out.println(F.s);
                              F.imethod();
  static void smethod() {     F.smethod();
  }
}
```
            (a)   (b)

8.18   Add the `static` keyword in the place of `?` if appropriate.

```
public class Test {
  private int count;

  public ? void main(String[] args) {
    ...
  }

  public ? int getCount() {
    return count;
  }

  public ? int factorial(int n) {
    int result = 1;
    for (int i = 1; i <= n; i++)
      result *= i;

    return result;
  }
}
```

8.19   Can you invoke an instance method or reference an instance variable from a static method? Can you invoke a static method or reference a static variable from an instance method? What is wrong in the following code?

```
1  public class C {
2    public static void main(String[] args) {
3      method1();
4    }
5
6    public void method1() {
7      method2();
8    }
9
10   public static void method2() {
11     System.out.println("What is radius " + c.getRadius());
12   }
13
14   Circle c = new Circle();
15 }
```

8.8 Visibility Modifiers

Visibility modifiers can be used to specify the visibility of a class and its members.

**Key
Point**

You can use the `public` visibility modifier for classes, methods, and data fields to denote that they can be accessed from any other classes. If no visibility modifier is used, then by default the classes, methods, and data fields are accessible by any class in the same package. This is known as *package-private* or *package-access*.

package-private (or package-access)

using packages

Note

Packages can be used to organize classes. To do so, you need to add the following line as the first noncomment and nonblank statement in the program:

package packageName;

If a class is defined without the package statement, it is said to be placed in the *default package*.

Java recommends that you place classes into packages rather using a default package. For simplicity, however, this book uses default packages. For more information on packages, see Supplement III.G, Packages.

In addition to the `public` and default visibility modifiers, Java provides the `private` and `protected` modifiers for class members. This section introduces the `private` modifier. The `protected` modifier will be introduced in Section 11.13, The `protected` Data and Methods.

The `private` modifier makes methods and data fields accessible only from within its own class. Figure 8.14 illustrates how a public, default, and private data field or method in class `C1` can be accessed from a class `C2` in the same package and from a class `C3` in a different package.

```
package p1;

public class C1 {
  public int x;
  int y;
  private int z;

  public void m1() {
  }
  void m2() {
  }
  private void m3() {
  }
}
```

```
package p1;

public class C2 {
  void aMethod() {
    C1 o = new C1();
    can access o.x;
    can access o.y;
    cannot access o.z;

    can invoke o.m1();
    can invoke o.m2();
    cannot invoke o.m3();
  }
}
```

```
package p2;

public class C3 {
  void aMethod() {
    C1 o = new C1();
    can access o.x;
    cannot access o.y;
    cannot access o.z;

    can invoke o.m1();
    cannot invoke o.m2();
    cannot invoke o.m3();
  }
}
```

FIGURE 8.14 The private modifier restricts access to its defining class, the default modifier restricts access to a package, and the public modifier enables unrestricted access.

If a class is not defined as public, it can be accessed only within the same package. As shown in Figure 8.15, `C1` can be accessed from `C2` but not from `C3`.

```
package p1;

class C1 {
   ...
}
```

```
package p1;

public class C2 {
   can access C1
}
```

```
package p2;

public class C3 {
   cannot access C1;
   can access C2;
}
```

FIGURE 8.15 A nonpublic class has package-access.

inside access

A visibility modifier specifies how data fields and methods in a class can be accessed from outside the class. There is no restriction on accessing data fields and methods from inside the class. As shown in Figure 8.16b, an object `c` of class `C` cannot access its private members, because `c` is in the `Test` class. As shown in Figure 8.16a, an object `c` of class `C` can access its private members, because `c` is defined inside its own class.

```
public class C {
  private boolean x;

  public static void main(String[] args) {
    C c = new C();
    System.out.println(c.x);
    System.out.println(c.convert());
  }

  private int convert() {
    return x ? 1 : -1;
  }
}
```

```
public class Test {
  public static void main(String[] args) {
    C c = new C();
    System.out.println(c.x);
    System.out.println(c.convert());
  }
}
```

(a) This is okay because object c is used inside the class C.   (b) This is wrong because x and convert are private in class C.

FIGURE 8.16 An object can access its private members if it is defined in its own class.

Caution

The `private` modifier applies only to the members of a class. The `public` modifier can apply to a class or members of a class. Using the modifiers `public` and `private` on local variables would cause a compile error.

Note

In most cases, the constructor should be public. However, if you want to prohibit the user from creating an instance of a class, use a *private constructor*. For example, there is no reason to create an instance from the `Math` class, because all of its data fields and methods are static. To prevent the user from creating objects from the `Math` class, the constructor in `java.lang.Math` is defined as follows:

private constructor

```
private Math() {
}
```

8.9 Data Field Encapsulation

Making data fields private protects data and makes the class easy to maintain.

The data fields `radius` and `numberOfObjects` in the `CircleWithStaticMembers` class in Listing 8.7 can be modified directly (e.g., `c1.radius = 5` or `CircleWithStaticMembers.numberOfObjects = 10`). This is not a good practice—for two reasons:

Key Point

VideoNote

Data field encapsulation

- First, data may be tampered with. For example, `numberOfObjects` is to count the number of objects created, but it may be mistakenly set to an arbitrary value (e.g., `CircleWithStaticMembers.numberOfObjects = 10`).

- Second, the class becomes difficult to maintain and vulnerable to bugs. Suppose you want to modify the `CircleWithStaticMembers` class to ensure that the radius is nonnegative after other programs have already used the class. You have to change not only the `CircleWithStaticMembers` class but also the programs that use it, because the clients may have modified the radius directly (e.g., `c1.radius = -5`).

To prevent direct modifications of data fields, you should declare the data fields private, using the `private` modifier. This is known as *data field encapsulation*.

data field encapsulation

A private data field cannot be accessed by an object from outside the class that defines the private field. However, a client often needs to retrieve and modify a data field. To make a private data field accessible, provide a *get* method to return its value. To enable a private data field to be updated, provide a *set* method to set a new value.

> **Note**
>
> Colloquially, a **get** method is referred to as a *getter* (or *accessor*), and a **set** method is referred to as a *setter* (or *mutator*).

getter (or accessor)
setter (or mutator)

A **get** method has the following signature:

public returnType get*PropertyName*()

boolean accessor

If the **returnType** is **boolean**, the **get** method should be defined as follows by convention:

public boolean is*PropertyName*()

A **set** method has the following signature:

public void set*PropertyName*(*dataType propertyValue*)

Let's create a new circle class with a private data-field radius and its associated accessor and mutator methods. The class diagram is shown in Figure 8.17. The new circle class, named **CircleWithPrivateDataFields**, is defined in Listing 8.9:

The - sign indicates a private modifier →

Circle
-radius: double
-numberOfObjects: int
+Circle()
+Circle(radius: double)
+getRadius(): double
+setRadius(radius: double): void
+getNumberOfObjects(): int
+getArea(): double

The radius of this circle (default: 1.0).
The number of circle objects created.

Constructs a default circle object.
Constructs a circle object with the specified radius.
Returns the radius of this circle.
Sets a new radius for this circle.
Returns the number of circle objects created.
Returns the area of this circle.

FIGURE 8.17 The **Circle** class encapsulates circle properties and provides get/set and other methods.

LISTING 8.9 CircleWithPrivateDataFields.java

encapsulate radius

encapsulate numberOfObjects

```java
1  public class CircleWithPrivateDataFields {
2    /** The radius of the circle */
3    private double radius = 1;
4
5    /** The number of objects created */
6    private static int numberOfObjects = 0;
7
8    /** Construct a circle with radius 1 */
9    public CircleWithPrivateDataFields() {
10     numberOfObjects++;
11   }
12
13   /** Construct a circle with a specified radius */
14   public CircleWithPrivateDataFields(double newRadius) {
15     radius = newRadius;
```

```
16        numberOfObjects++;
17    }
18
19    /** Return radius */
20    public double getRadius() {                              accessor method
21      return radius;
22    }
23
24    /** Set a new radius */
25    public void setRadius(double newRadius) {                mutator method
26      radius = (newRadius >= 0) ? newRadius : 0;
27    }
28
29    /** Return numberOfObjects */
30    public static int getNumberOfObjects() {                 accessor method
31      return numberOfObjects;
32    }
33
34    /** Return the area of this circle */
35    public double getArea() {
36      return radius * radius * Math.PI;
37    }
38  }
```

The **getRadius()** method (lines 20–22) returns the radius, and the **setRadius(newRadius)** method (line 25–27) sets a new radius for the object. If the new radius is negative, **0** is set as the radius for the object. Since these methods are the only ways to read and modify the radius, you have total control over how the **radius** property is accessed. If you have to change the implementation of these methods, you don't need to change the client programs. This makes the class easy to maintain.

Listing 8.10 gives a client program that uses the **Circle** class to create a **Circle** object and modifies the radius using the **setRadius** method.

LISTING 8.10 TestCircleWithPrivateDataFields.java

```
1  public class TestCircleWithPrivateDataFields {
2    /** Main method */
3    public static void main(String[] args) {
4      // Create a circle with radius 5.0
5      CircleWithPrivateDataFields myCircle =
6        new CircleWithPrivateDataFields(5.0);
7      System.out.println("The area of the circle of radius "
8        + myCircle.getRadius() + " is " + myCircle.getArea());    invoke public method
9
10     // Increase myCircle's radius by 10%
11     myCircle.setRadius(myCircle.getRadius() * 1.1);
12     System.out.println("The area of the circle of radius "
13       + myCircle.getRadius() + " is " + myCircle.getArea());    invoke public method
14
15     System.out.println("The number of objects created is "
16       + CircleWithPrivateDataFields.getNumberOfObjects());       invoke public method
17   }
18 }
```

The data field **radius** is declared private. Private data can be accessed only within their defining class, so you cannot use **myCircle.radius** in the client program. A compile error would occur if you attempted to access private data from a client.

Since `numberOfObjects` is private, it cannot be modified. This prevents tampering. For example, the user cannot set `numberOfObjects` to 100. The only way to make it 100 is to create 100 objects of the `Circle` class.

Suppose you combined `TestCircleWithPrivateDataFields` and `Circle` into one class by moving the `main` method in `TestCircleWithPrivateDataFields` into `Circle`. Could you use `myCircle.radius` in the `main` method? See Checkpoint Question 8.22 for the answer.

 Design Guide
To prevent data from being tampered with and to make the class easy to maintain, declare data fields private.

 Check Point

MyProgrammingLab™

8.20 What is an accessor method? What is a mutator method? What are the naming conventions for accessor methods and mutator methods?

8.21 What are the benefits of data field encapsulation?

8.22 In the following code, `radius` is private in the `Circle` class, and `myCircle` is an object of the `Circle` class. Does the highlighted code cause any problems? If so, explain why.

```
public class Circle {
  private double radius = 1;

  /** Find the area of this circle */
  public double getArea() {
    return radius * radius * Math.PI;
  }

  public static void main(String[] args) {
    Circle myCircle = new Circle();
    System.out.println("Radius is " + myCircle.radius);
  }
}
```

8.10 Passing Objects to Methods

 Key Point

Passing an object to a method is to pass the reference of the object.

You can pass objects to methods. Like passing an array, passing an object is actually passing the reference of the object. The following code passes the `myCircle` object as an argument to the `printCircle` method:

pass an object

```
1  public class Test {
2    public static void main(String[] args) {
3      // CircleWithPrivateDataFields is defined in Listing 8.9
4      CircleWithPrivateDataFields myCircle = new
5        CircleWithPrivateDataFields(5.0);
6      printCircle(myCircle);
7    }
8
9    public static void printCircle(CircleWithPrivateDataFields c) {
10     System.out.println("The area of the circle of radius "
11       + c.getRadius() + " is " + c.getArea());
12   }
13 }
```

pass-by-value

Java uses exactly one mode of passing arguments: pass-by-value. In the preceding code, the value of `myCircle` is passed to the `printCircle` method. This value is a reference to a `Circle` object.

The program in Listing 8.11 demonstrates the difference between passing a primitive type value and passing a reference value.

LISTING 8.11   TestPassObject.java

```
 1  public class TestPassObject {
 2    /** Main method */
 3    public static void main(String[] args) {
 4      // Create a Circle object with radius 1
 5      CircleWithPrivateDataFields myCircle =
 6        new CircleWithPrivateDataFields(1);
 7
 8      // Print areas for radius 1, 2, 3, 4, and 5.
 9      int n = 5;
10      printAreas(myCircle, n);                                    pass object
11
12      // See myCircle.radius and times
13      System.out.println("\n" + "Radius is " + myCircle.getRadius());
14      System.out.println("n is " + n);
15    }
16
17    /** Print a table of areas for radius */
18    public static void printAreas(                               object parameter
19        CircleWithPrivateDataFields c, int times) {
20      System.out.println("Radius \t\tArea");
21      while (times >= 1) {
22        System.out.println(c.getRadius() + "\t\t" + c.getArea());
23        c.setRadius(c.getRadius() + 1);
24        times--;
25      }
26    }
27  }
```

```
Radius      Area
1.0         3.141592653589793
2.0         12.566370614359172
3.0         29.274333882308138
4.0         50.26548245743669
5.0         79.53981633974483
Radius is 6.0
n is 5
```

The `CircleWithPrivateDataFields` class is defined in Listing 8.9. The program passes a `CircleWithPrivateDataFields` object `myCircle` and an integer value from `n` to invoke `printAreas(myCircle, n)` (line 9), which prints a table of areas for radii 1, 2, 3, 4, 5, as shown in the sample output.

Figure 8.18 shows the call stack for executing the methods in the program. Note that the objects are stored in a heap (see Section 6.6).

When passing an argument of a primitive data type, the value of the argument is passed. In this case, the value of `n` (5) is passed to `times`. Inside the `printAreas` method, the content of `times` is changed; this does not affect the content of `n`.

When passing an argument of a reference type, the reference of the object is passed. In this case, `c` contains a reference for the object that is also referenced via `myCircle`. Therefore, changing the properties of the object through `c` inside the `printAreas` method has the same effect as doing so outside the method through the variable `myCircle`. Pass-by-value on references can be best described semantically as *pass-by-sharing*; that is, the object referenced in   pass-by-sharing
the method is the same as the object being passed.

FIGURE 8.18 The value of n is passed to `times`, and the reference to `myCircle` is passed to c in the `printAreas` method.

8.23 Describe the difference between passing a parameter of a primitive type and passing a parameter of a reference type. Show the output of the following programs:

MyProgrammingLab™

```java
public class Test {
  public static void main(String[] args) {
    Count myCount = new Count();
    int times = 0;

    for (int i = 0; i < 100; i++)
      increment(myCount, times);

    System.out.println("count is " + myCount.count);
    System.out.println("times is " + times);
  }

  public static void increment(Count c, int times) {
    c.count++;
    times++;
  }
}
```

```java
public class Count {
  public int count;

  public Count(int c) {
    count = c;
  }

  public Count() {
    count = 1;
  }
}
```

8.24 Show the output of the following program:

```java
public class Test {
  public static void main(String[] args) {
    Circle circle1 = new Circle(1);
    Circle circle2 = new Circle(2);

    swap1(circle1, circle2);
    System.out.println("After swap1: circle1 = " +
      circle1.radius + " circle2 = " + circle2.radius);

    swap2(circle1, circle2);
    System.out.println("After swap2: circle1 = " +
      circle1.radius + " circle2 = " + circle2.radius);
  }

  public static void swap1(Circle x, Circle y) {
    Circle temp = x;
    x = y;
    y = temp;
```

```
        }

        public static void swap2(Circle x, Circle y) {
            double temp = x.radius;
            x.radius = y.radius;
            y.radius = temp;
        }
    }

    class Circle {
        double radius;

        Circle(double newRadius) {
            radius = newRadius;
        }
    }
```

8.25   Show the printout of the following code:

```
public class Test {
  public static void main(String[] args) {
    int[] a = {1, 2};
    swap(a[0], a[1]);
    System.out.println("a[0] = " + a[0]
      + " a[1] = " + a[1]);
  }

  public static void swap(int n1, int n2) {
    int temp = n1;
    n1 = n2;
    n2 = temp;
  }
}
```
(a)

```
public class Test {
  public static void main(String[] args) {
    int[] a = {1, 2};
    swap(a);
    System.out.println("a[0] = " + a[0]
      + " a[1] = " + a[1]);
  }

  public static void swap(int[] a) {
    int temp = a[0];
    a[0] = a[1];
    a[1] = temp;
  }
}
```
(b)

```
public class Test {
  public static void main(String[] args) {
    T t = new T();
    swap(t);
    System.out.println("e1 = " + t.e1
      + " e2 = " + t.e2);
  }

  public static void swap(T t) {
    int temp = t.e1;
    t.e1 = t.e2;
    t.e2 = temp;
  }
}

class T {
  int e1 = 1;
  int e2 = 2;
}
```
(c)

```
public class Test {
  public static void main(String[] args) {
    T t1 = new T();
    T t2 = new T();
    System.out.println("t1's i = " +
      t1.i + " and j = " + t1.j);
    System.out.println("t2's i = " +
      t2.i + " and j = " + t2.j);
  }
}

class T {
  static int i = 0;
  int j = 0;

  T() {
    i++;
    j = 1;
  }
}
```
(d)

8.26 What is the output of the following programs?

```java
import java.util.Date;

public class Test {
  public static void main(String[] args) {
    Date date = null;
    m1(date);
    System.out.println(date);
  }

  public static void m1(Date date) {
    date = new Date();
  }
}
```

(a)

```java
import java.util.Date;

public class Test {
  public static void main(String[] args) {
    Date date = new Date(1234567);
    m1(date);
    System.out.println(date.getTime());
  }

  public static void m1(Date date) {
    date = new Date(7654321);
  }
}
```

(b)

```java
import java.util.Date;

public class Test {
  public static void main(String[] args) {
    Date date = new Date(1234567);
    m1(date);
    System.out.println(date.getTime());
  }

  public static void m1(Date date) {
    date.setTime(7654321);
  }
}
```

(c)

```java
import java.util.Date;

public class Test {
  public static void main(String[] args) {
    Date date = new Date(1234567);
    m1(date);
    System.out.println(date.getTime());
  }

  public static void m1(Date date) {
    date = null;
  }
}
```

(d)

8.11 Array of Objects

Key Point

An array can hold objects as well as primitive type values.

Chapter 6, Single-Dimensional Arrays, described how to create arrays of primitive type elements. You can also create arrays of objects. For example, the following statement declares and creates an array of ten `Circle` objects:

```java
Circle[] circleArray = new Circle[10];
```

To initialize `circleArray`, you can use a `for` loop like this one:

```java
for (int i = 0; i < circleArray.length; i++) {
  circleArray[i] = new Circle();
}
```

An array of objects is actually an *array of reference variables*. So, invoking `circleArray[1].getArea()` involves two levels of referencing, as shown in Figure 8.19. `circleArray` references the entire array; `circleArray[1]` references a `Circle` object.

Note
When an array of objects is created using the **new** operator, each element in the array is a reference variable with a default value of **null**.

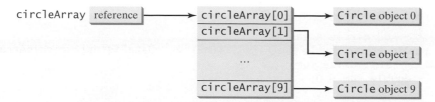

FIGURE 8.19 In an array of objects, an element of the array contains a reference to an object.

Listing 8.12 gives an example that demonstrates how to use an array of objects. The program summarizes the areas of an array of circles. The program creates `circleArray`, an array composed of five `Circle` objects; it then initializes circle radii with random values and displays the total area of the circles in the array.

LISTING 8.12 TotalArea.java

```
 1  public class TotalArea {
 2    /** Main method */
 3    public static void main(String[] args) {
 4      // Declare circleArray
 5      CircleWithPrivateDataFields[] circleArray;                    array of objects
 6
 7      // Create circleArray
 8      circleArray = createCircleArray();
 9
10      // Print circleArray and total areas of the circles
11      printCircleArray(circleArray);
12    }
13
14    /** Create an array of Circle objects */
15    public static CircleWithPrivateDataFields[] createCircleArray() {
16      CircleWithPrivateDataFields[] circleArray =
17        new CircleWithPrivateDataFields[5];
18
19      for (int i = 0; i < circleArray.length; i++) {
20        circleArray[i] =
21          new CircleWithPrivateDataFields(Math.random() * 100);
22      }
23
24      // Return Circle array
25      return circleArray;                                          return array of objects
26    }
27
28    /** Print an array of circles and their total area */
29    public static void printCircleArray(
30        CircleWithPrivateDataFields[] circleArray) {               pass array of objects
31      System.out.printf("%-30s%-15s\n", "Radius", "Area");
32      for (int i = 0; i < circleArray.length; i++) {
33        System.out.printf("%-30f%-15f\n", circleArray[i].getRadius(),
34          circleArray[i].getArea());
35      }
36
37      System.out.println("-----------------------------------------------");
38
39      // Compute and display the result
40      System.out.printf("%-30s%-15f\n", "The total area of circles is",
41        sum(circleArray) );
```

pass array of objects

```
42    }
43
44    /** Add circle areas */
45    public static double sum(CircleWithPrivateDataFields[] circleArray) {
46      // Initialize sum
47      double sum = 0;
48
49      // Add areas to sum
50      for (int i = 0; i < circleArray.length; i++)
51        sum += circleArray[i].getArea();
52
53      return sum;
54    }
55  }
```

```
Radius                          Area
70.577708                       15648.941866
44.152266                       6124.291736
24.867853                       1942.792644
 5.680718                       101.380949
36.734246                       4239.280350
-----------------------------------------------
The total area of circles is  28056.687544
```

The program invokes `createCircleArray()` (line 8) to create an array of five circle objects. Several circle classes were introduced in this chapter. This example uses the `CircleWithPrivateDataFields` class introduced in Section 8.9, Data Field Encapsulation.

The circle radii are randomly generated using the `Math.random()` method (line 21). The `createCircleArray` method returns an array of `CircleWithPrivateDataFields` objects (line 25). The array is passed to the `printCircleArray` method, which displays the radius and area of each circle and the total area of the circles.

The sum of the circle areas is computed by invoking the `sum` method (line 41), which takes the array of `CircleWithPrivateDataFields` objects as the argument and returns a `double` value for the total area.

8.27 What is wrong in the following code?

```
1  public class Test {
2    public static void main(String[] args) {
3      java.util.Date[] dates = new java.util.Date[10];
4      System.out.println(dates[0]);
5      System.out.println(dates[0].toString());
6    }
7  }
```

KEY TERMS

action   296
anonymous object   305
attribute   296
behavior   296
class   296
client   299

constructor   296
data field   296
data field encapsulation   319
default constructor   303
dot operator (.)   304
getter (or accessor)   320

instance   296
instance method   305
instance variable   305
instantiation   296
no-arg constructor   303
`null` value   305
object   296
object-oriented programming (OOP)
package-private (or package-
   access)   317
private constructor   319

property   296
public class   299
reference type   304
reference variable   304
setter (or mutator)   320
state   296
static method   312
static variable   312
Unified Modeling Language
   (UML)   297

CHAPTER SUMMARY

1. A *class* is a template for *objects*. It defines the *properties* of objects and provides *constructors* for creating objects and methods for manipulating them.

2. A class is also a data type. You can use it to declare object *reference variables*. An object reference variable that appears to hold an object actually contains a reference to that object. Strictly speaking, an object reference variable and an object are different, but most of the time the distinction can be ignored.

3. An object is an *instance* of a class. You use the `new` operator to create an object, and the *dot operator* (`.`) to access members of that object through its reference variable.

4. An *instance variable* or *method* belongs to an instance of a class. Its use is associated with individual instances. A *static variable* is a variable shared by all instances of the same class. A *static method* is a method that can be invoked without using instances.

5. Every instance of a class can access the class's static variables and methods. For clarity, however, it is better to invoke static variables and methods using `ClassName.variable` and `ClassName.method`.

6. Modifiers specify how the class, method, and data are accessed. A `public` class, method, or data is accessible to all clients. A `private` method or data is accessible only inside the class.

7. You can provide a `get` method or a `set` method to enable clients to see or modify the data. Colloquially, a `get` method is referred to as a *getter* (or *accessor*), and a `set` method as a *setter* (or *mutator*).

8. A `get` method has the signature `public returnType getPropertyName()`. If the `returnType` is `boolean`, the `get` method should be defined as `public boolean isPropertyName()`. A `set` method has the signature `public void setPropertyName(dataType propertyValue)`.

9. All parameters are passed to methods using pass-by-value. For a parameter of a primitive type, the actual value is passed; for a parameter of a *reference type*, the reference for the object is passed.

10. A Java array is an object that can contain primitive type values or object type values. When an array of objects is created, its elements are assigned the default value of `null`.

TEST QUESTIONS

Do the test questions for this chapter online at www.cs.armstrong.edu/liang/intro9e/test.html.

MyProgrammingLab™

PROGRAMMING EXERCISES

three objectives

 Pedagogical Note
The exercises in Chapters 8–11, 15 help you achieve three objectives:

- Design classes and draw UML class diagrams
- Implement classes from the UML
- Use classes to develop applications

Students can download solutions for the UML diagrams for the even-numbered exercises from the Companion Website, and instructors can download all solutions from the same site.

Sections 8.2–8.5

8.1 (*The Rectangle class*) Following the example of the `Circle` class in Section 8.2, design a class named `Rectangle` to represent a rectangle. The class contains:

- Two `double` data fields named `width` and `height` that specify the width and height of the rectangle. The default values are `1` for both `width` and `height`.
- A no-arg constructor that creates a default rectangle.
- A constructor that creates a rectangle with the specified `width` and `height`.
- A method named `getArea()` that returns the area of this rectangle.
- A method named `getPerimeter()` that returns the perimeter.

Draw the UML diagram for the class and then implement the class. Write a test program that creates two `Rectangle` objects—one with width `4` and height `40` and the other with width `3.5` and height `35.9`. Display the width, height, area, and perimeter of each rectangle in this order.

8.2 (*The Stock class*) Following the example of the `Circle` class in Section 8.2, design a class named `Stock` that contains:

- A string data field named `symbol` for the stock's symbol.
- A string data field named `name` for the stock's name.
- A `double` data field named `previousClosingPrice` that stores the stock price for the previous day.
- A `double` data field named `currentPrice` that stores the stock price for the current time.
- A constructor that creates a stock with the specified symbol and name.
- A method named `getChangePercent()` that returns the percentage changed from `previousClosingPrice` to `currentPrice`.

Draw the UML diagram for the class and then implement the class. Write a test program that creates a `Stock` object with the stock symbol `ORCL`, the name `Oracle Corporation`, and the previous closing price of `34.5`. Set a new current price to `34.35` and display the price-change percentage.

Section 8.6

*8.3 (*Use the Date class*) Write a program that creates a `Date` object, sets its elapsed time to `10000`, `100000`, `1000000`, `10000000`, `100000000`, `1000000000`, `10000000000`, and `100000000000`, and displays the date and time using the `toString()` method, respectively.

*8.4 (*Use the Random class*) Write a program that creates a `Random` object with seed `1000` and displays the first 50 random integers between `0` and `100` using the `nextInt(100)` method.

*8.5 (*Use the GregorianCalendar class*) Java API has the `GregorianCalendar` class in the `java.util` package, which you can use to obtain the year, month, and day of a date. The no-arg constructor constructs an instance for the current date, and the methods `get(GregorianCalendar.YEAR)`, `get(GregorianCalendar.MONTH)`, and `get(GregorianCalendar.DAY_OF_MONTH)` return the year, month, and day. Write a program to perform two tasks:

- Display the current year, month, and day.
- The `GregorianCalendar` class has the `setTimeInMillis(long)`, which can be used to set a specified elapsed time since January 1, 1970. Set the value to `1234567898765L` and display the year, month, and day.

Sections 8.7–8.9

**8.6 (*Display calendars*) Rewrite the `PrintCalendar` class in Listing 5.12 to display calendars in a message dialog box. Since the output is generated from several static methods in the class, you may define a static `String` variable `output` for storing the output and display it in a message dialog box.

8.7 (*The Account class*) Design a class named `Account` that contains:

- A private `int` data field named `id` for the account (default `0`).
- A private `double` data field named `balance` for the account (default `0`).
- A private `double` data field named `annualInterestRate` that stores the current interest rate (default `0`). Assume all accounts have the same interest rate.
- A private `Date` data field named `dateCreated` that stores the date when the account was created.
- A no-arg constructor that creates a default account.
- A constructor that creates an account with the specified id and initial balance.
- The accessor and mutator methods for `id`, `balance`, and `annualInterestRate`.
- The accessor method for `dateCreated`.
- A method named `getMonthlyInterestRate()` that returns the monthly interest rate.
- A method named `getMonthlyInterest()` that returns the monthly interest.
- A method named `withdraw` that withdraws a specified amount from the account.
- A method named `deposit` that deposits a specified amount to the account.

Draw the UML diagram for the class and then implement the class. (*Hint*: The method `getMonthlyInterest()` is to return monthly interest, not the interest rate. Monthly interest is `balance * monthlyInterestRate`. `monthlyInterestRate` is `annualInterestRate / 12`. Note that `annualInterestRate` is a percentage, e.g.,like 4.5%. You need to divide it by 100.)

Write a test program that creates an `Account` object with an account ID of 1122, a balance of $20,000, and an annual interest rate of 4.5%. Use the `withdraw` method to withdraw $2,500, use the `deposit` method to deposit $3,000, and print the balance, the monthly interest, and the date when this account was created.

8.8 (*The Fan class*) Design a class named `Fan` to represent a fan. The class contains:

- Three constants named `SLOW`, `MEDIUM`, and `FAST` with the values `1`, `2`, and `3` to denote the fan speed.

VideoNote

The `Fan` class

- A private `int` data field named `speed` that specifies the speed of the fan (the default is `SLOW`).
- A private `boolean` data field named `on` that specifies whether the fan is on (the default is `false`).
- A private `double` data field named `radius` that specifies the radius of the fan (the default is `5`).
- A string data field named `color` that specifies the color of the fan (the default is `blue`).
- The accessor and mutator methods for all four data fields.
- A no-arg constructor that creates a default fan.
- A method named `toString()` that returns a string description for the fan. If the fan is on, the method returns the fan speed, color, and radius in one combined string. If the fan is not on, the method returns the fan color and radius along with the string "fan is off" in one combined string.

Draw the UML diagram for the class and then implement the class. Write a test program that creates two `Fan` objects. Assign maximum speed, radius `10`, color `yellow`, and turn it on to the first object. Assign medium speed, radius `5`, color `blue`, and turn it off to the second object. Display the objects by invoking their `toString` method.

**8.9 (*Geometry: n-sided regular polygon*) In an *n*-sided regular polygon, all sides have the same length and all angles have the same degree (i.e., the polygon is both equilateral and equiangular). Design a class named `RegularPolygon` that contains:

- A private `int` data field named `n` that defines the number of sides in the polygon with default value `3`.
- A private `double` data field named `side` that stores the length of the side with default value `1`.
- A private `double` data field named `x` that defines the *x*-coordinate of the polygon's center with default value `0`.
- A private `double` data field named `y` that defines the *y*-coordinate of the polygon's center with default value `0`.
- A no-arg constructor that creates a regular polygon with default values.
- A constructor that creates a regular polygon with the specified number of sides and length of side, centered at (`0`, `0`).
- A constructor that creates a regular polygon with the specified number of sides, length of side, and *x*-and *y*-coordinates.
- The accessor and mutator methods for all data fields.
- The method `getPerimeter()` that returns the perimeter of the polygon.
- The method `getArea()` that returns the area of the polygon. The formula for computing the area of a regular polygon is $Area = \dfrac{n \times s^2}{4 \times \tan\left(\dfrac{\pi}{n}\right)}$.

Draw the UML diagram for the class and then implement the class. Write a test program that creates three `RegularPolygon` objects, created using the no-arg constructor, using `RegularPolygon(6, 4)`, and using `RegularPolygon(10, 4, 5.6, 7.8)`. For each object, display its perimeter and area.

*8.10 (*Algebra: quadratic equations*) Design a class named `QuadraticEquation` for a quadratic equation $ax^2 + bx + x = 0$. The class contains:

- Private data fields `a`, `b`, and `c` that represent three coefficients.
- A constructor for the arguments for `a`, `b`, and `c`.

- Three `get` methods for `a`, `b`, and `c`.
- A method named `getDiscriminant()` that returns the discriminant, which is $b^2 - 4ac$.
- The methods named `getRoot1()` and `getRoot2()` for returning two roots of the equation

$$r_1 = \frac{-b + \sqrt{b^2 - 4ac}}{2a} \quad \text{and} \quad r_2 = \frac{-b - \sqrt{b^2 - 4ac}}{2a}$$

These methods are useful only if the discriminant is nonnegative. Let these methods return `0` if the discriminant is negative.

Draw the UML diagram for the class and then implement the class. Write a test program that prompts the user to enter values for a, b, and c and displays the result based on the discriminant. If the discriminant is positive, display the two roots. If the discriminant is 0, display the one root. Otherwise, display "The equation has no roots." See Programming Exercise 3.1 for sample runs.

*8.11 (*Algebra: 2 × 2 linear equations*) Design a class named `LinearEquation` for a 2 × 2 system of linear equations:

$$\begin{array}{cc} ax + by = e \\ cx + dy = f \end{array} \quad x = \frac{ed - bf}{ad - bc} \quad y = \frac{af - ec}{ad - bc}$$

The class contains:

- Private data fields `a`, `b`, `c`, `d`, `e`, and `f`.
- A constructor with the arguments for `a`, `b`, `c`, `d`, `e`, and `f`.
- Six `get` methods for `a`, `b`, `c`, `d`, `e`, and `f`.
- A method named `isSolvable()` that returns true if $ad - bc$ is not 0.
- Methods `getX()` and `getY()` that return the solution for the equation.

Draw the UML diagram for the class and then implement the class. Write a test program that prompts the user to enter `a`, `b`, `c`, `d`, `e`, and `f` and displays the result. If $ad - bc$ is 0, report that "The equation has no solution." See Programming Exercise 3.3 for sample runs.

**8.12 (*Geometry: intersection*) Suppose two line segments intersect. The two endpoints for the first line segment are (`x1`, `y1`) and (`x2`, `y2`) and for the second line segment are (`x3`, `y3`) and (`x4`, `y4`). Write a program that prompts the user to enter these four endpoints and displays the intersecting point. (*Hint*: Use the `LinearEquation` class in Exercise 8.11.)

```
Enter the endpoints of the first line segment: 2.0 2.0 0 0  ↵ Enter
Enter the endpoints of the second line segment: 0 2.0 2.0 0  ↵ Enter
The intersecting point is: (1.0, 1.0)
```

**8.13 (*The Location class*) Design a class named `Location` for locating a maximal value and its location in a two-dimensional array. The class contains public data fields `row`, `column`, and `maxValue` that store the maximal value and its indices in a two-dimensional array with `row` and `column` as `int` types and `maxValue` as a `double` type.

Write the following method that returns the location of the largest element in a two-dimensional array:

```java
public static Location locateLargest(double[][] a)
```

The return value is an instance of `Location`. Write a test program that prompts the user to enter a two-dimensional array and displays the location of the largest element in the array. Here is a sample run:

```
Enter the number of rows and columns in the array: 3 4  ⏎Enter
Enter the array:
23.5 35 2 10  ⏎Enter
4.5 3 45 3.5  ⏎Enter
35 44 5.5 9.6  ⏎Enter
The location of the largest element is 45 at (1, 2)
```

*8.14   (*Stopwatch*) Design a class named `StopWatch`. The class contains:

- Private data fields `startTime` and `endTime` with get methods.
- A no-arg constructor that initializes `startTime` with the current time.
- A method named `start()` that resets the `startTime` to the current time.
- A method named `stop()` that sets the `endTime` to the current time.
- A method named `getElapsedTime()` that returns the elapsed time for the stopwatch in milliseconds.

Draw the UML diagram for the class and then implement the class. Write a test program that measures the execution time of sorting 100,000 numbers using selection sort.

STRINGS

Objectives

- To use the `String` class to process fixed strings (§9.2).

- To construct strings (§9.2.1).

- To understand that strings are immutable and to create an interned string (§9.2.2).

- To compare strings (§9.2.3).

- To get string length and characters, and combine strings (§9.2.4).

- To obtain substrings (§9.2.5).

- To convert, replace, and split strings (§9.2.6).

- To match, replace, and split strings by patterns (§9.2.7).

- To search for a character or substring in a string (§9.2.8).

- To convert between a string and an array (§9.2.9).

- To convert characters and numbers into a string (§9.2.10).

- To obtain a formatted string (§9.2.11).

- To check whether a string is a palindrome (§9.3).

- To convert hexadecimal numbers to decimal numbers (§9.4).

- To use the `Character` class to process a single character (§9.5).

- To use the `StringBuilder` and `StringBuffer` classes to process flexible strings (§9.6).

- To distinguish among the `String`, `StringBuilder`, and `StringBuffer` classes (§9.2–9.6).

- To learn how to pass arguments to the `main` method from the command line (§9.7).

9.1 Introduction

Key Point

The classes `String`, `StringBuilder`, *and* `StringBuffer` *are used for processing strings.*

A *string* is a sequence of characters. Strings are frequently used in programming. In many languages, strings are treated as an array of characters, but in Java a string is treated as an object. This chapter introduces the classes for processing strings.

9.2 The `String` Class

A `String` *object is immutable: Its content cannot be changed once the string is created.*

The `String` class has 13 constructors and more than 40 methods for manipulating strings. Not only is it very useful in programming, but it is also a good example for learning classes and objects.

9.2.1 Constructing a String

You can create a string object from a string literal or from an array of characters. To create a string from a string literal, use the syntax:

```
String newString = new String(stringLiteral);
```

The argument `stringLiteral` is a sequence of characters enclosed inside double quotes. The following statement creates a `String` object `message` for the string literal `"Welcome to Java"`:

```
String message = new String("Welcome to Java");
```

string literal object

Java treats a string literal as a `String` object. Thus, the following statement is valid:

```
String message = "Welcome to Java";
```

You can also create a string from an array of characters. For example, the following statements create the string `"Good Day"`:

```
char[] charArray = {'G', 'o', 'o', 'd', ' ', 'D', 'a', 'y'};
String message = new String(charArray);
```

Note

String variable, String object, string value

A `String` variable holds a reference to a `String` object that stores a string value. Strictly speaking, the terms *String variable*, *String object*, and *string value* are different, but most of the time the distinctions between them can be ignored. For simplicity, the term *string* will often be used to refer to `String` variable, `String` object, and string value.

9.2.2 Immutable Strings and Interned Strings

immutable

A `String` *object is immutable; its contents cannot be changed.* Does the following code change the contents of the string?

```
String s = "Java";
s = "HTML";
```

The answer is no. The first statement creates a `String` object with the content `"Java"` and assigns its reference to `s`. The second statement creates a new `String` object with the content

"HTML" and assigns its reference to **s**. The first **String** object still exists after the assignment, but it can no longer be accessed, because variable **s** now points to the new object, as shown in Figure 9.1.

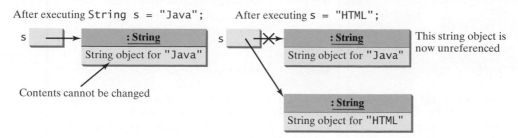

FIGURE 9.1   Strings are immutable; once created, their contents cannot be changed.

Because strings are immutable and are ubiquitous in programming, the JVM uses a unique instance for string literals with the same character sequence in order to improve efficiency and save memory. Such an instance is called an *interned string*. For example, the following statements:

interned string

```
String s1 = "Welcome to Java";

String s2 = new String("Welcome to Java");

String s3 = "Welcome to Java";

System.out.println("s1 == s2 is " + (s1 == s2));
System.out.println("s1 == s3 is " + (s1 == s3));
```

display

```
s1 == s2 is false
s1 == s3 is true
```

In the preceding statements, **s1** and **s3** refer to the same interned string—"Welcome to Java"—so **s1 == s3** is **true**. However, **s1 == s2** is **false**, because **s1** and **s2** are two different string objects, even though they have the same contents.

9.2.3   String Comparisons

The **String** class provides the methods for comparing strings, as shown in Figure 9.2.

How do you compare the contents of two strings? You might attempt to use the **==** operator, as follows:

==

```
if (string1 == string2)
  System.out.println("string1 and string2 are the same object");
else
  System.out.println("string1 and string2 are different objects");
```

However, the **==** operator checks only whether **string1** and **string2** refer to the same object; it does not tell you whether they have the same contents. Therefore, you cannot use the **==** operator to find out whether two string variables have the same contents. Instead, you should use the **equals** method. The following code, for instance, can be used to compare two strings:

string1.equals(string2)

```
if (string1.equals(string2))
  System.out.println("string1 and string2 have the same contents");
else
  System.out.println("string1 and string2 are not equal");
```

java.lang.String	
+equals(s1: Object): boolean	Returns true if this string is equal to string s1.
+equalsIgnoreCase(s1: String): boolean	Returns true if this string is equal to string s1 case insensitive.
+compareTo(s1: String): int	Returns an integer greater than 0, equal to 0, or less than 0 to indicate whether this string is greater than, equal to, or less than s1.
+compareToIgnoreCase(s1: String): int	Same as compareTo except that the comparison is case insensitive.
+regionMatches(index: int, s1: String, s1Index: int, len: int): boolean	Returns true if the specified subregion of this string exactly matches the specified subregion in string s1.
+regionMatches(ignoreCase: boolean, index: int, s1: String, s1Index: int, len: int): boolean	Same as the preceding method except that you can specify whether the match is case sensitive.
+startsWith(prefix: String): boolean	Returns true if this string starts with the specified prefix.
+endsWith(suffix: String): boolean	Returns true if this string ends with the specified suffix.

FIGURE 9.2 The String class contains the methods for comparing strings.

Note that parameter type for the equals method is Object. We will introduce the Object class in Chapter 11. For now, you can replace Object by String for using the equals method to compare two strings. For example, the following statements display true and then false.

```java
String s1 = new String("Welcome to Java");
String s2 = "Welcome to Java";
String s3 = "Welcome to C++";
System.out.println(s1.equals(s2)); // true
System.out.println(s1.equals(s3)); // false
```

The compareTo method can also be used to compare two strings. For example, consider the following code:

s1.compareTo(s2)

s1.compareTo(s2)

The method returns the value 0 if s1 is equal to s2, a value less than 0 if s1 is lexicographically (i.e., in terms of Unicode ordering) less than s2, and a value greater than 0 if s1 is lexicographically greater than s2.

The actual value returned from the compareTo method depends on the offset of the first two distinct characters in s1 and s2 from left to right. For example, suppose s1 is abc and s2 is abg, and s1.compareTo(s2) returns -4. The first two characters (a vs. a) from s1 and s2 are compared. Because they are equal, the second two characters (b vs. b) are compared. Because they are also equal, the third two characters (c vs. g) are compared. Since the character c is 4 less than g, the comparison returns -4.

Caution
Syntax errors will occur if you compare strings by using comparison operators >, >=, <, or <=. Instead, you have to use s1.compareTo(s2).

Note
The equals method returns true if two strings are equal and false if they are not. The compareTo method returns 0, a positive integer, or a negative integer, depending on whether one string is equal to, greater than, or less than the other string.

The String class also provides the equalsIgnoreCase, compareToIgnoreCase, and regionMatches methods for comparing strings. The equalsIgnoreCase and compareToIgnoreCase methods ignore the case of the letters when comparing two strings. The regionMatches method compares portions of two strings for equality. You can also use str.startsWith(prefix) to check whether string str starts with a specified prefix, and str.endsWith(suffix) to check whether string str ends with a specified suffix.

9.2.4 Getting String Length and Characters, and Combining Strings

The String class provides the methods for obtaining a string's length, retrieving individual characters, and concatenating strings, as shown in Figure 9.3.

java.lang.String	
+length(): int	Returns the number of characters in this string.
+charAt(index: int): char	Returns the character at the specified index from this string.
+concat(s1: String): String	Returns a new string that concatenates this string with string s1.

FIGURE 9.3 The String class contains the methods for getting string length, individual characters, and combining strings.

You can get the length of a string by invoking its length() method. For example, message.length() returns the length of the string message.

Caution

length is a method in the String class but is a property of an array object. Therefore, you have to use s.length() to get the number of characters in string s, and a.length to get the number of elements in array a.

length()

string length vs. array length

The s.charAt(index) method can be used to retrieve a specific character in a string s, where the index is between 0 and s.length()-1. For example, message.charAt(0) returns the character W, as shown in Figure 9.4.

charAt(index)

Note

When you use a string, you often know its literal value. For convenience, Java allows you to use the string literal to refer directly to strings without creating new variables. Thus, "Welcome to Java".charAt(0) is correct and returns W.

string literal

Indices   0   1   2   3   4   5   6   7   8   9   10   11   12   13   14

message | W | e | l | c | o | m | e | | t | o | | J | a | v | a |

message.charAt(0)   message.length() is 15   message.charAt(14)

FIGURE 9.4 The characters in a String object are stored using an array internally.

Note

The String class uses an array to store characters internally. The array is private and cannot be accessed outside of the String class. The String class provides many public methods, such as length() and charAt(index), to retrieve the string information. This is a good example of encapsulation: the data field of the class is hidden from the user through the private modifier, and thus the user cannot directly manipulate it. If the array were not private, the user would be able to change the string content by modifying the array. This would violate the tenet that the String class is immutable.

encapsulating string

string index range

Caution

Attempting to access characters in a string **s** out of bounds is a common programming error. To avoid it, make sure that you do not use an index beyond `s.length()` – 1. For example, `s.charAt(s.length())` would cause a `StringIndexOutOfBoundsException`.

You can use the `concat` method to concatenate two strings. The statement shown below, for example, concatenates strings **s1** and **s2** into **s3**:

s1.concat(s2)

```
String s3 = s1.concat(s2);
```

Because string concatenation is heavily used in programming, Java provides a convenient way to accomplish it. You can use the plus (+) operator to concatenate two strings, so the previous statement is equivalent to

s1 + s2

```
String s3 = s1 + s2;
```

The following code combines the strings **message**, " and ", and "HTML" into one string:

```
String myString = message + " and " + "HTML";
```

Recall that the + operator can also concatenate a number with a string. In this case, the number is converted into a string and then concatenated. Note that at least one of the operands must be a string in order for concatenation to take place.

9.2.5 Obtaining Substrings

You can obtain a single character from a string using the `charAt` method, as shown in Figure 9.3. You can also obtain a substring from a string using the `substring` method in the `String` class, as shown in Figure 9.5.

For example,

```
String message = "Welcome to Java".substring(0, 11) + "HTML";
```

The string `message` now becomes `Welcome to HTML`.

java.lang.String	
+substring(beginIndex: int): String	Returns this string's substring that begins with the character at the specified beginIndex and extends to the end of the string, as shown in Figure 9.6.
+substring(beginIndex: int, endIndex: int): String	Returns this string's substring that begins at the specified beginIndex and extends to the character at index endIndex – 1, as shown in Figure 9.6. Note that the character at endIndex is not part of the substring.

FIGURE 9.5 The `String` class contains the methods for obtaining substrings.

FIGURE 9.6 The `substring` method obtains a substring from a string.

> **Note**
> If **beginIndex** is **endIndex**, **substring(beginIndex, endIndex)** returns an
> empty string with length **0**. If **beginIndex > endIndex**, it would be a runtime error.

beginIndex <= endIndex

9.2.6 Converting, Replacing, and Splitting Strings

The **String** class provides the methods for converting, replacing, and splitting strings, as
shown in Figure 9.7.

java.lang.String	
+toLowerCase(): String	Returns a new string with all characters converted to lowercase.
+toUpperCase(): String	Returns a new string with all characters converted to uppercase.
+trim(): String	Returns a new string with whitespace characters trimmed on both sides.
+replace(oldChar: char, newChar: char): String	Returns a new string that replaces all matching characters in this string with the new character.
+replaceFirst(oldString: String, newString: String): String	Returns a new string that replaces the first matching substring in this string with the new substring.
+replaceAll(oldString: String, newString: String): String	Returns a new string that replaces all matching substrings in this string with the new substring.
+split(delimiter: String): String[]	Returns an array of strings consisting of the substrings split by the delimiter.

FIGURE 9.7 The **String** class contains the methods for converting, replacing, and splitting strings.

Once a string is created, its contents cannot be changed. The methods **toLowerCase**,
toUpperCase, **trim**, **replace**, **replaceFirst**, and **replaceAll** return a new string
derived from the original string (without changing the original string!). The **toLowerCase** and
toUpperCase methods return a new string by converting all the characters in the string to
lowercase or uppercase. The **trim** method returns a new string by eliminating whitespace
characters from both ends of the string. Several versions of the **replace** methods are provided
to replace a character or a substring in the string with a new character or a new substring.
For example,

"Welcome". toLowerCase() returns a new string, welcome.   toLowerCase()
"Welcome". toUpperCase() returns a new string, WELCOME.   toUpperCase()
"\t Good Night \n". trim() returns a new string, Good Night.   trim()
"Welcome". replace('e', 'A') returns a new string, WAlcomA.   replace
"Welcome". replaceFirst("e", "AB") returns a new string, WABlcome.   replaceFirst
"Welcome". replace("e", "AB") returns a new string, WABlcomAB.   replace
"Welcome". replace("el", "AB") returns a new string, WABcome.   replace

The **split** method can be used to extract tokens from a string with the specified delimiters.   split
For example, the following code

```
String[] tokens = "Java#HTML#Perl".split("#");
for (int i = 0; i < tokens.length; i++)
  System.out.print(tokens[i] + " ");
```

displays

Java HTML Perl

9.2.7 Matching, Replacing and Splitting by Patterns

Often you will need to write code that validates user input, such as to check whether the input is a number, a string with all lowercase letters, or a Social Security number. How do you write this type of code? A simple and effective way to accomplish this task is to use the regular expression.

A *regular expression* (abbreviated *regex*) is a string that describes a pattern for matching a set of strings. You can match, replace, or split a string by specifying a pattern. This is an extremely useful and powerful feature.

Let us begin with the **matches** method in the **String** class. At first glance, the **matches** method is very similar to the **equals** method. For example, the following two statements both evaluate to **true**.

```
"Java".matches("Java");
"Java".equals("Java");
```

However, the **matches** method is more powerful. It can match not only a fixed string, but also a set of strings that follow a pattern. For example, the following statements all evaluate to **true**:

```
"Java is fun".matches("Java.*")
"Java is cool".matches("Java.*")
"Java is powerful".matches("Java.*")
```

`Java.*` in the preceding statements is a regular expression. It describes a string pattern that begins with Java followed by *any* zero or more characters. Here, the substring `.*` matches any zero or more characters.

The following statement evaluates to **true**.

```
"440-02-4534".matches("\\d{3}-\\d{2}-\\d{4}")
```

Here `\\d` represents a single digit, and `\\d{3}` represents three digits.

The **replaceAll**, **replaceFirst**, and **split** methods can be used with a regular expression. For example, the following statement returns a new string that replaces $, +, or # in a+b$#c with the string NNN.

```
String s = "a+b$#c".replaceAll("[$+#]", "NNN");
System.out.println(s);
```

Here the regular expression `[$+#]` specifies a pattern that matches $, +, or #. So, the output is aNNNbNNNNNNc.

The following statement splits the string into an array of strings delimited by punctuation marks.

```
String[] tokens = "Java,C?C#,C++".split("[.,:;?]");

for (int i = 0; i < tokens.length; i++)
  System.out.println(tokens[i]);
```

In this example, the regular expression `[.,:;?]` specifies a pattern that matches ., ,, :, ;, or ?. Each of these characters is a delimiter for splitting the string. Thus, the string is split into Java, C, C#, and C++, which are stored in array **tokens**.

Regular expression patterns are complex for beginning students to understand. For this reason, simple patterns are introduced in this section. Please refer to Supplement III.H, Regular Expressions, to learn more about these patterns.

9.2.8 Finding a Character or a Substring in a String

The **String** class provides several overloaded **indexOf** and **lastIndexOf** methods to find a character or a substring in a string, as shown in Figure 9.8.

(margin notes)
why regular expression?
regular expression
regex

matches(regex)

replaceAll(regex)

split(regex)

further studies

java.lang.String	
+indexOf(ch: char): int	Returns the index of the first occurrence of ch in the string. Returns –1 if not matched.
+indexOf(ch: char, fromIndex: int): int	Returns the index of the first occurrence of ch after fromIndex in the string. Returns –1 if not matched.
+indexOf(s: String): int	Returns the index of the first occurrence of string s in this string. Returns –1 if not matched.
+indexOf(s: String, fromIndex: int): int	Returns the index of the first occurrence of string s in this string after fromIndex. Returns –1 if not matched.
+lastIndexOf(ch: int): int	Returns the index of the last occurrence of ch in the string. Returns –1 if not matched.
+lastIndexOf(ch: int, fromIndex: int): int	Returns the index of the last occurrence of ch before fromIndex in this string. Returns –1 if not matched.
+lastIndexOf(s: String): int	Returns the index of the last occurrence of string s. Returns –1 if not matched.
+lastIndexOf(s: String, fromIndex: int): int	Returns the index of the last occurrence of string s before fromIndex. Returns –1 if not matched.

FIGURE 9.8   The **String** class contains the methods for matching substrings.

For example,

```
"Welcome to Java".indexOf('W') returns 0.
"Welcome to Java".indexOf('o') returns 4.
"Welcome to Java".indexOf('o', 5) returns 9.
"Welcome to Java".indexOf("come") returns 3.
"Welcome to Java".indexOf("Java", 5) returns 11.
"Welcome to Java".indexOf("java", 5) returns -1.

"Welcome to Java".lastIndexOf('W') returns 0.
"Welcome to Java".lastIndexOf('o') returns 9.
"Welcome to Java".lastIndexOf('o', 5) returns 4.
"Welcome to Java".lastIndexOf("come") returns 3.
"Welcome to Java".lastIndexOf("Java", 5) returns -1.
"Welcome to Java".lastIndexOf("Java") returns 11.
```

indexOf

lastIndexOf

9.2.9   Conversion between Strings and Arrays

Strings are not arrays, but a string can be converted into an array, and vice versa. To convert a string into an array of characters, use the **toCharArray** method. For example, the following statement converts the string **Java** to an array.

toCharArray

```
char[] chars = "Java".toCharArray();
```

Thus, **chars[0]** is **J**, **chars[1]** is **a**, **chars[2]** is **v**, and **chars[3]** is **a**.

You can also use the **getChars(int srcBegin, int srcEnd, char[] dst, int dstBegin)** method to copy a substring of the string from index **srcBegin** to index **srcEnd-1** into a character array **dst** starting from index **dstBegin**. For example, the following code copies a substring "3720" in "CS3720" from index **2** to index **6-1** into the character array **dst** starting from index **4**.

getChars

```
char[] dst = {'J', 'A', 'V', 'A', '1', '3', '0', '1'};
"CS3720".getChars(2, 6, dst, 4);
```

Thus, **dst** becomes {'J', 'A', 'V', 'A', '3', '7', '2', '0'}.

To convert an array of characters into a string, use the `String(char[])` constructor or the `valueOf(char[])` method. For example, the following statement constructs a string from an array using the `String` constructor.

```
String str = new String(new char[]{'J', 'a', 'v', 'a'});
```

`valueOf`

The next statement constructs a string from an array using the `valueOf` method.

```
String str = String.valueOf(new char[]{'J', 'a', 'v', 'a'});
```

9.2.10 Converting Characters and Numeric Values to Strings

overloaded `valueOf`

The static `valueOf` method can be used to convert an array of characters into a string. There are several overloaded versions of the `valueOf` method that can be used to convert a character and numeric values to strings with different parameter types, `char`, `double`, `long`, `int`, and `float`, as shown in Figure 9.9.

java.lang.String	
+valueOf(c: char): String	Returns a string consisting of the character c.
+valueOf(data: char[]): String	Returns a string consisting of the characters in the array.
+valueOf(d: double): String	Returns a string representing the double value.
+valueOf(f: float): String	Returns a string representing the float value.
+valueOf(i: int): String	Returns a string representing the int value.
+valueOf(l: long): String	Returns a string representing the long value.
+valueOf(b: boolean): String	Returns a string representing the boolean value.

FIGURE 9.9 The `String` class contains the static methods for creating strings from primitive type values.

For example, to convert a `double` value `5.44` to a string, use `String.valueOf(5.44)`. The return value is a string consisting of the characters `'5'`, `'.'`, `'4'`, and `'4'`.

Note
You can use `Double.parseDouble(str)` or `Integer.parseInt(str)` to convert a string to a `double` value or an `int` value. `Double` and `Integer` are two classes in the `java.lang` package.

9.2.11 Formatting Strings

The `String` class contains the static `format` method to create a formatted string. The syntax to invoke this method is:

```
String.format(format, item1, item2, ..., itemk)
```

This method is similar to the `printf` method except that the `format` method returns a formatted string, whereas the `printf` method displays a formatted string. For example,

```
String s = String.format("%7.2f%6d%-4s", 45.556, 14, "AB");
System.out.println(s);
```

displays

```
□□45.56□□□□14AB□□
```

Note that

```
System.out.printf(format, item1, item2, ..., itemk);
```

is equivalent to

```
System.out.printf(
  String.format(format, item1, item2, ..., itemk));
```

where the square box (□) denotes a blank space.

9.1 Suppose that s1, s2, s3, and s4 are four strings, given as follows:

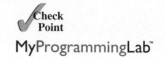

```
String s1 = "Welcome to Java";
String s2 = s1;
String s3 = new String("Welcome to Java");
String s4 = "Welcome to Java";
```

What are the results of the following expressions?

a. s1 == s2   m. s1.length()

b. s2 == s3   n. s1.substring(5)

c. s1.equals(s2)   o. s1.substring(5, 11)

d. s2.equals(s3)   p. s1.startsWith("Wel")

e. s1.compareTo(s2) q. s1.endsWith("Java")

f. s2.compareTo(s3) r. s1.toLowerCase()

g. s1 == s4   s. s1.toUpperCase()

h. s1.charAt(0)   t. "Welcome ".trim()

i. s1.indexOf('j')   u. s1.replace('o', 'T')

j. s1.indexOf("to") v. s1.replaceAll("o", "T")

k. s1.lastIndexOf('a') w. s1.replaceFirst("o", "T")

l. s1.lastIndexOf("o", 15) x. s1.toCharArray()

9.2 To create the string Welcome to Java, you may use a statement like this:

```
String s = "Welcome to Java";
```

or:

```
String s = new String("Welcome to Java");
```

Which one is better? Why?

9.3 Suppose that s1 and s2 are two strings. Which of the following statements or expressions are incorrect?

```
String s = new String("new string");
String s3 = s1 + s2;
String s3 = s1 - s2;
s1 == s2;
s1 >= s2;
s1.compareTo(s2);
int i = s1.length();
char c = s1(0);
char c = s1.charAt(s1.length());
```

9.4 What is the printout of the following code?

```
String s1 = "Welcome to Java";
String s2 = s1.replace("o", "abc");
System.out.println(s1);
System.out.println(s2);
```

9.5 Let s1 be " Welcome " and s2 be " welcome ". Write the code for the following statements:

    a. Check whether s1 is equal to s2 and assign the result to a Boolean variable isEqual.

    b. Check whether s1 is equal to s2, ignoring case, and assign the result to a Boolean variable isEqual.

    c. Compare s1 with s2 and assign the result to an int variable x.

    d. Compare s1 with s2, ignoring case, and assign the result to an int variable x.

    e. Check whether s1 has the prefix AAA and assign the result to a Boolean variable b.

    f. Check whether s1 has the suffix AAA and assign the result to a Boolean variable b.

    g. Assign the length of s1 to an int variable x.

    h. Assign the first character of s1 to a char variable x.

    i. Create a new string s3 that combines s1 with s2.

    j. Create a substring of s1 starting from index 1.

    k. Create a substring of s1 from index 1 to index 4.

    l. Create a new string s3 that converts s1 to lowercase.

    m. Create a new string s3 that converts s1 to uppercase.

    n. Create a new string s3 that trims blank spaces on both ends of s1.

    o. Replace all occurrences of the character e with E in s1 and assign the new string to s3.

    p. Split Welcome to Java and HTML into an array tokens delimited by a space.

    q. Assign the index of the first occurrence of the character e in s1 to an int variable x.

    r. Assign the index of the last occurrence of the string abc in s1 to an int variable x.

9.6 Does any method in the String class change the contents of the string?

9.7 Suppose string s is created using new String(); what is s.length()?

9.8 How do you convert a char, an array of characters, or a number to a string?

9.9 Why does the following code cause a NullPointerException?

```
1  public class Test {
2    private String text;
3
4    public Test(String s) {
5      String text = s;
6    }
7
8    public static void main(String[] args) {
9      Test test = new Test("ABC");
10     System.out.println(test.text.toLowerCase());
11   }
12 }
```

9.10 What is wrong in the following program?

```
1  public class Test {
2    String text;
3
```

```
4      public void Test(String s) {
5        text = s;
6      }
7
8      public static void main(String[] args) {
9        Test test = new Test("ABC");
10       System.out.println(test);
11     }
12   }
```

9.11   Show the output of the following code.

```
public class Test {
  public static void main(String[] args) {
    System.out.println("Hi, ABC, good".matches("ABC "));
    System.out.println("Hi, ABC, good".matches(".*ABC.*"));
    System.out.println("A,B;C".replaceAll(",;", "#"));
    System.out.println("A,B;C".replaceAll("[,;]", "#"));

    String[] tokens = "A,B;C".split("[,;]");
    for (int i = 0; i < tokens.length; i++)
      System.out.print(tokens[i] + " ");
  }
}
```

9.3 Case Study: Checking Palindromes

This section presents a program that checks whether a string is a palindrome.

Key Point

A string is a palindrome if it reads the same forward and backward. The words "mom," "dad," and "noon," for instance, are all palindromes.

The problem is to write a program that prompts the user to enter a string and reports whether the string is a palindrome. One solution is to check whether the first character in the string is the same as the last character. If so, check whether the second character is the same as the second-to-last character. This process continues until a mismatch is found or all the characters in the string are checked, except for the middle character if the string has an odd number of characters.

VideoNote
Check palindrome

To implement this idea, use two variables, say **low** and **high**, to denote the position of the two characters at the beginning and the end in a string **s**, as shown in Listing 9.1 (lines 22, 25). Initially, **low** is **0** and **high** is **s.length() - 1**. If the two characters at these positions match, increment **low** by **1** and decrement **high** by **1** (lines 31–32). This process continues until (**low >= high**) or a mismatch is found.

LISTING 9.1   CheckPalindrome.java

```
1   import java.util.Scanner;
2
3   public class CheckPalindrome {
4     /** Main method */
5     public static void main(String[] args) {
6       // Create a Scanner
7       Scanner input = new Scanner(System.in);
8
9       // Prompt the user to enter a string
10      System.out.print("Enter a string: ");
11      String s = input.nextLine();
12
13      if (isPalindrome(s))
```

input string

```
14              System.out.println(s + " is a palindrome");
15          else
16              System.out.println(s + " is not a palindrome");
17      }
18
19      /** Check if a string is a palindrome */
20      public static boolean isPalindrome(String s) {
21          // The index of the first character in the string
22          int low = 0;
23
24          // The index of the last character in the string
25          int high = s.length() - 1;
26
27          while (low < high) {
28              if (s.charAt(low) != s.charAt(high))
29                  return false; // Not a palindrome
30
31              low++;
32              high--;
33          }
34
35          return true; // The string is a palindrome
36      }
37  }
```

low index

high index

update indices

```
Enter a string: noon  ⏎ Enter
noon is a palindrome
```

```
Enter a string: moon  ⏎ Enter
moon is not a palindrome
```

The `nextLine()` method in the `Scanner` class (line 11) reads a line into `s`, and then `isPalindrome(s)` checks whether `s` is a palindrome (line 13).

9.4 Case Study: Converting Hexadecimals to Decimals

Key Point

This section presents a program that converts a hexadecimal number into a decimal number.

Section 5.7 gives a program that converts a decimal to a hexadecimal. How do you convert a hex number into a decimal?

Given a hexadecimal number $h_n h_{n-1} h_{n-2} \ldots h_2 h_1 h_0$, the equivalent decimal value is

$$h_n \times 16^n + h_{n-1} \times 16^{n-1} + h_{n-2} \times 16^{n-2} + \ldots + h_2 \times 16^2 + h_1 \times 16^1 + h_0 \times 16^0$$

For example, the hex number **AB8C** is

$$10 \times 16^3 + 11 \times 16^2 + 8 \times 16^1 + 12 \times 16^0 = 43916$$

Our program will prompt the user to enter a hex number as a string and convert it into a decimal using the following method:

```
public static int hexToDecimal(String hex)
```

A brute-force approach is to convert each hex character into a decimal number, multiply it by 16^i for a hex digit at the i's position, and then add all the items together to obtain the equivalent decimal value for the hex number.

Note that

$$h_n \times 16^n + h_{n-1} \times 16^{n-1} + h_{n-2} \times 16^{n-2} + \ldots + h_1 \times 16^1 + h_0 \times 16^0$$

$$= (\ldots ((h_n \times 16 + h_{n-1}) \times 16 + h_{n-2}) \times 16 + \ldots + h_1) \times 16 + h_0$$

This observation, known as the Horner's algorithm, leads to the following efficient code for converting a hex string to a decimal number:

```
int decimalValue = 0;
for (int i = 0; i < hex.length(); i++) {
  char hexChar = hex.charAt(i);
  decimalValue = decimalValue * 16 + hexCharToDecimal(hexChar);
}
```

Here is a trace of the algorithm for hex number **AB8C**:

	i	hexChar	hexCharToDecimal(hexChar)	decimalValue
before the loop				0
after the 1st iteration	0	A	10	10
after the 2nd iteration	1	B	11	10 * 16 + 11
after the 3rd iteration	2	8	8	(10 * 16 + 11) * 16 + 8
after the 4th iteration	3	C	12	((10 * 16 + 11) * 16 + 8) * 16 + 12

Listing 9.2 gives the complete program.

LISTING 9.2 HexToDecimalConversion.java

```
1  import java.util.Scanner;
2
3  public class HexToDecimalConversion {
4    /** Main method */
5    public static void main(String[] args) {
6      // Create a Scanner
7      Scanner input = new Scanner(System.in);
8
9      // Prompt the user to enter a string
10     System.out.print("Enter a hex number: ");
11     String hex = input.nextLine();                          input string
12
13     System.out.println("The decimal value for hex number "
14       + hex + " is " + hexToDecimal(hex.toUpperCase()));    hex to decimal
15   }
16
17   public static int hexToDecimal(String hex) {
18     int decimalValue = 0;
19     for (int i = 0; i < hex.length(); i++) {
20       char hexChar = hex.charAt(i);
21       decimalValue = decimalValue * 16 + hexCharToDecimal(hexChar);
22     }
23
24     return decimalValue;
25   }
26
```

```
27    public static int hexCharToDecimal(char ch) {
28      if (ch >= 'A' && ch <= 'F')
29        return 10 + ch - 'A';
30      else // ch is '0', '1', ..., or '9'
31        return ch - '0';
32    }
33  }
```

```
Enter a hex number: AB8C  ⏎Enter
The decimal value for hex number AB8C is 43916
```

```
Enter a hex number: af71  ⏎Enter
The decimal value for hex number af71 is 44913
```

The program reads a string from the console (line 11), and invokes the **hexToDecimal** method to convert a hex string to decimal number (line 14). The characters can be in either lowercase or uppercase. They are converted to uppercase before invoking the **hexToDecimal** method.

The **hexToDecimal** method is defined in lines 17–25 to return an integer. The length of the string is determined by invoking **hex.length()** in line 19.

The **hexCharToDecimal** method is defined in lines 27–32 to return a decimal value for a hex character. The character can be in either lowercase or uppercase. Recall that to subtract two characters is to subtract their Unicodes. For example, **'5' – '0'** is **5**.

9.5 The **Character** Class

Key Point

*You can create an object for a character using the **Character** class. A **Character** object contains a character value.*

Many methods in the Java API require an object argument. To enable the primitive data values to be treated as objects, Java provides a class for every primitive data type. These classes are **Character**, **Boolean**, **Byte**, **Short**, **Integer**, **Long**, **Float**, and **Double** for **char**, **boolean**, **byte**, **short**, **int**, **long**, **float**, and **double**, respectively. These classes are called *wrapper classes* because each wraps or encapsulates a primitive type value in an object. All these classes are in the **java.lang** package, and they contain useful methods for processing primitive values. This section introduces the **Character** class. The other wrapper classes will be introduced in Chapter 10, Thinking in Objects.

wrapper class

The **Character** class has a constructor and several methods for determining a character's category (uppercase, lowercase, digit, and so on) and for converting characters from uppercase to lowercase, and vice versa, as shown in Figure 9.10.

You can create a **Character** object from a **char** value. For example, the following statement creates a **Character** object for the character **a**.

```
Character character = new Character('a');
```

The **charValue** method returns the character value wrapped in the **Character** object. The **compareTo** method compares this character with another character and returns an integer that is the difference between the Unicode of this character and the Unicode of the other character. The **equals** method returns **true** if and only if the two characters are the same. For example, suppose **charObject** is **new Character('b')**:

```
charObject.compareTo(new Character('a')) returns 1
charObject.compareTo(new Character('b')) returns 0
charObject.compareTo(new Character('c')) returns -1
```

```
charObject.compareTo(new Character('d')) returns -2
charObject.equals(new Character('b')) returns true
charObject.equals(new Character('d')) returns false
```

java.lang.Character	
+Character(value: char)	Constructs a character object with char value.
+charValue(): char	Returns the char value from this object.
+compareTo(anotherCharacter: Character): int	Compares this character with another.
+equals(anotherCharacter: Character): boolean	Returns true if this character is equal to another.
+isDigit(ch: char): boolean	Returns true if the specified character is a digit.
+isLetter(ch: char): boolean	Returns true if the specified character is a letter.
+isLetterOrDigit(ch: char): boolean	Returns true if the character is a letter or a digit.
+isLowerCase(ch: char): boolean	Returns true if the character is a lowercase letter.
+isUpperCase(ch: char): boolean	Returns true if the character is an uppercase letter.
+toLowerCase(ch: char): char	Returns the lowercase of the specified character.
+toUpperCase(ch: char): char	Returns the uppercase of the specified character.

FIGURE 9.10 The Character class provides the methods for manipulating a character.

Most of the methods in the Character class are static methods. The isDigit(char ch) method returns true if the character is a digit, and the isLetter(char ch) method returns true if the character is a letter. The isLetterOrDigit(char ch) method returns true if the character is a letter or a digit. The isLowerCase(char ch) method returns true if the character is a lowercase letter, and the isUpperCase(char ch) method returns true if the character is an uppercase letter. The toLowerCase(char ch) method returns the lowercase letter for the character, and the toUpperCase(char ch) method returns the uppercase letter for the character.

Now let's write a program that prompts the user to enter a string and counts the number of occurrences of each letter in the string regardless of case.

Here are the steps to solve this problem:

1. Convert all the uppercase letters in the string to lowercase using the toLowerCase method in the String class.

2. Create an array, say counts of 26 int values, each of which counts the occurrences of a letter. That is, counts[0] counts the number of as, counts[1] counts the number of bs, and so on.

3. For each character in the string, check whether it is a (lowercase) letter. If so, increment the corresponding count in the array.

Listing 9.3 gives the complete program.

LISTING 9.3 CountEachLetter.java

```
1  import java.util.Scanner;
2
3  public class CountEachLetter {
4    /** Main method */
5    public static void main(String[] args) {
6      // Create a Scanner
7      Scanner input = new Scanner(System.in);
8
```

input string

count letters

```
 9        // Prompt the user to enter a string
10        System.out.print("Enter a string: ");
11        String s = input.nextLine();
12
13        // Invoke the countLetters method to count each letter
14        int[] counts = countLetters(s.toLowerCase());
15
16        // Display results
17        for (int i = 0; i < counts.length; i++) {
18          if (counts[i] != 0)
19            System.out.println((char)('a' + i) + " appears   " +
20              counts[i] + ((counts[i] == 1) ? " time" : " times"));
21        }
22      }
23
24      /** Count each letter in the string */
25      public static int[] countLetters(String s) {
26        int[] counts = new int[26];
27
28        for (int i = 0; i < s.length(); i++) {
29          if (Character.isLetter(s.charAt(i)))
30            counts[s.charAt(i) - 'a']++;
31        }
32
33        return counts;
34      }
35    }
```

count a letter

```
Enter a string: abababx  ↵Enter
a appears   3 times
b appears   3 times
x appears   1 time
```

The main method reads a line (line 11) and counts the number of occurrences of each letter in the string by invoking the **countLetters** method (line 14). Since the case of the letters is ignored, the program uses the **toLowerCase** method to convert the string into all lowercase and pass the new string to the **countLetters** method.

The **countLetters** method (lines 25–34) returns an array of **26** elements. Each element counts the number of occurrences of a letter in the string **s**. The method processes each character in the string. If the character is a letter, its corresponding count is increased by **1**. For example, if the character (**s.charAr(i)**) is **a**, the corresponding count is **counts['a' - 'a']** (i.e., **counts[0]**). If the character is **b**, the corresponding count is **counts['b' - 'a']** (i.e., **counts[1]**), since the Unicode of **b** is **1** more than that of **a**. If the character is **z**, the corresponding count is **counts['z' - 'a']** (i.e., **counts[25]**), since the Unicode of **z** is **25** more than that of **a**.

Check Point

MyProgrammingLab

9.12 How do you determine whether a character is in lowercase or uppercase?

9.13 How do you determine whether a character is alphanumeric?

9.14 Show the output of the following code.

```
public class Test {
  public static void main(String[] args) {
    String s = "Hi, Good Morning";
    System.out.println(m(s));
  }
```

```
    public static int m(String s) {
      int count = 0;
      for (int i = 0; i < s.length(); i++)
        if (Character.isUpperCase(s.charAt(i)))
          count++;

      return count;
    }
  }
```

9.6 The **StringBuilder** and **StringBuffer** Classes

The **StringBuilder** *and* **StringBuffer** *classes are similar to the* **String** *class except that the* **String** *class is immutable.*

Key Point

In general, the **StringBuilder** and **StringBuffer** classes can be used wherever a string is used. **StringBuilder** and **StringBuffer** are more flexible than **String**. You can add, insert, or append new contents into **StringBuilder** and **StringBuffer** objects, whereas the value of a **String** object is fixed once the string is created.

The **StringBuilder** class is similar to **StringBuffer** except that the methods for modify-   StringBuilder
ing the buffer in **StringBuffer** are *synchronized*, which means that only one task is allowed to execute the methods. Use **StringBuffer** if the class might be accessed by multiple tasks concurrently. Concurrent programming will be introduced in Chapter 32. Using **StringBuilder** is more efficient if it is accessed by just a single task. The constructors and methods in **StringBuffer** and **StringBuilder** are almost the same. This section covers **StringBuilder**. You can replace **StringBuilder** in all occurrences in this section by **StringBuffer**. The program can compile and run without any other changes.

The **StringBuilder** class has three constructors and more than 30 methods for manag-   StringBuilder
ing the builder and modifying strings in the builder. You can create an empty string builder or   constructors
a string builder from a string using the constructors, as shown in Figure 9.11.

java.lang.StringBuilder	
+StringBuilder()	Constructs an empty string builder with capacity 16.
+StringBuilder(capacity: int)	Constructs a string builder with the specified capacity.
+StringBuilder(s: String)	Constructs a string builder with the specified string.

FIGURE 9.11   The **StringBuilder** class contains the constructors for creating instances of **StringBuilder**.

9.6.1   Modifying Strings in the **StringBuilder**

You can append new contents at the end of a string builder, insert new contents at a specified position in a string builder, and delete or replace characters in a string builder, using the methods listed in Figure 9.12.

The **StringBuilder** class provides several overloaded methods to append **boolean**, **char**, **char[]**, **double**, **float**, **int**, **long**, and **String** into a string builder. For example, the following code appends strings and characters into **stringBuilder** to form a new string, **Welcome to Java**.

```
StringBuilder stringBuilder = new StringBuilder();
stringBuilder.append("Welcome");
stringBuilder.append(' ');
stringBuilder.append("to");
stringBuilder.append(' ');
stringBuilder.append("Java");
```
append

java.lang.StringBuilder	
+append(data: char[]): StringBuilder	Appends a char array into this string builder.
+append(data: char[], offset: int, len: int): StringBuilder	Appends a subarray in data into this string builder.
+append(v: *aPrimitiveType*): StringBuilder	Appends a primitive type value as a string to this builder.
+append(s: String): StringBuilder	Appends a string to this string builder.
+delete(startIndex: int, endIndex: int): StringBuilder	Deletes characters from startIndex to endIndex-1.
+deleteCharAt(index: int): StringBuilder	Deletes a character at the specified index.
+insert(index: int, data: char[], offset: int, len: int): StringBuilder	Inserts a subarray of the data in the array into the builder at the specified index.
+insert(offset: int, data: char[]): StringBuilder	Inserts data into this builder at the position offset.
+insert(offset: int, b: *aPrimitiveType*): StringBuilder	Inserts a value converted to a string into this builder.
+insert(offset: int, s: String): StringBuilder	Inserts a string into this builder at the position offset.
+replace(startIndex: int, endIndex: int, s: String): StringBuilder	Replaces the characters in this builder from startIndex to endIndex-1 with the specified string.
+reverse(): StringBuilder	Reverses the characters in the builder.
+setCharAt(index: int, ch: char): void	Sets a new character at the specified index in this builder.

FIGURE 9.12 The StringBuilder class contains the methods for modifying string builders.

The StringBuilder class also contains overloaded methods to insert **boolean**, **char**, **char array**, **double**, **float**, **int**, **long**, and **String** into a string builder. Consider the following code:

insert

```
stringBuilder.insert(11, "HTML and ");
```

Suppose stringBuilder contains Welcome to Java before the insert method is applied. This code inserts "HTML and " at position 11 in stringBuilder (just before the J). The new stringBuilder is Welcome to HTML and Java.

You can also delete characters from a string in the builder using the two delete methods, reverse the string using the reverse method, replace characters using the replace method, or set a new character in a string using the setCharAt method.

For example, suppose stringBuilder contains Welcome to Java before each of the following methods is applied:

delete   stringBuilder.delete(8, 11) changes the builder to Welcome Java.
deleteCharAt   stringBuilder.deleteCharAt(8) changes the builder to Welcome o Java.
reverse   stringBuilder.reverse() changes the builder to avaJ ot emocleW.
replace   stringBuilder.replace(11, 15, "HTML") changes the builder to Welcome to HTML.
setCharAt   stringBuilder.setCharAt(0, 'w') sets the builder to welcome to Java.

All these modification methods except setCharAt do two things:

■ Change the contents of the string builder

ignore return value   ■ Return the reference of the string builder

For example, the following statement

```
StringBuilder stringBuilder1 = stringBuilder.reverse();
```

reverses the string in the builder and assigns the builder's reference to `stringBuilder1`. Thus, `stringBuilder` and `stringBuilder1` both point to the same `StringBuilder` object. Recall that a value-returning method can be invoked as a statement, if you are not interested in the return value of the method. In this case, the return value is simply ignored. For example, in the following statement

```
stringBuilder.reverse();
```

the return value is ignored.

Tip
If a string does not require any change, use `String` rather than `StringBuilder`. Java can perform some optimizations for `String`, such as sharing interned strings.

String or StringBuilder?

9.6.2 The `toString`, `capacity`, `length`, `setLength`, and `charAt` Methods

The `StringBuilder` class provides the additional methods for manipulating a string builder and obtaining its properties, as shown in Figure 9.13.

java.lang.StringBuilder	
+toString(): String	Returns a string object from the string builder.
+capacity(): int	Returns the capacity of this string builder.
+charAt(index: int): char	Returns the character at the specified index.
+length(): int	Returns the number of characters in this builder.
+setLength(newLength: int): void	Sets a new length in this builder.
+substring(startIndex: int): String	Returns a substring starting at `startIndex`.
+substring(startIndex: int, endIndex: int): String	Returns a substring from `startIndex` to `endIndex-1`.
+trimToSize(): void	Reduces the storage size used for the string builder.

FIGURE 9.13 The `StringBuilder` class contains the methods for modifying string builders.

The `capacity()` method returns the current capacity of the string builder. The capacity is the number of characters the string builder is able to store without having to increase its size.

The `length()` method returns the number of characters actually stored in the string builder. The `setLength(newLength)` method sets the length of the string builder. If the `newLength` argument is less than the current length of the string builder, the string builder is truncated to contain exactly the number of characters given by the `newLength` argument. If the `newLength` argument is greater than or equal to the current length, sufficient null characters (`\u0000`) are appended to the string builder so that `length` becomes the `newLength` argument. The `newLength` argument must be greater than or equal to `0`.

The `charAt(index)` method returns the character at a specific `index` in the string builder. The index is `0` based. The first character of a string builder is at index `0`, the next at index `1`, and so on. The `index` argument must be greater than or equal to `0`, and less than the length of the string builder.

capacity()

length()
setLength(int)

charAt(int)

Note
The length of the string is always less than or equal to the capacity of the builder. The length is the actual size of the string stored in the builder, and the capacity is the current size of the builder. The builder's capacity is automatically increased if more characters are added to exceed its capacity. Internally, a string builder is an array of characters, so

length and capacity

the builder's capacity is the size of the array. If the builder's capacity is exceeded, the array is replaced by a new array. The new array size is `2 * (the previous array size + 1)`.

Tip
You can use `new StringBuilder(initialCapacity)` to create a `StringBuilder` with a specified initial capacity. By carefully choosing the initial capacity, you can make your program more efficient. If the capacity is always larger than the actual length of the builder, the JVM will never need to reallocate memory for the builder. On the other hand, if the capacity is too large, you will waste memory space. You can use the `trimToSize()` method to reduce the capacity to the actual size.

initial capacity

trimToSize()

9.6.3 Case Study: Ignoring Nonalphanumeric Characters When Checking Palindromes

Listing 9.1, CheckPalindrome.java, considered all the characters in a string to check whether it was a palindrome. Write a new program that ignores nonalphanumeric characters in checking whether a string is a palindrome.

Here are the steps to solve the problem:

1. Filter the string by removing the nonalphanumeric characters. This can be done by creating an empty string builder, adding each alphanumeric character in the string to a string builder, and returning the string from the string builder. You can use the `isLetterOrDigit(ch)` method in the `Character` class to check whether character `ch` is a letter or a digit.

2. Obtain a new string that is the reversal of the filtered string. Compare the reversed string with the filtered string using the `equals` method.

The complete program is shown in Listing 9.4.

LISTING **9.4** `PalindromeIgnoreNonAlphanumeric.java`

check palindrome

```
 1  import java.util.Scanner;
 2
 3  public class PalindromeIgnoreNonAlphanumeric {
 4    /** Main method */
 5    public static void main(String[] args) {
 6      // Create a Scanner
 7      Scanner input = new Scanner(System.in);
 8
 9      // Prompt the user to enter a string
10      System.out.print("Enter a string: ");
11      String s = input.nextLine();
12
13      // Display result
14      System.out.println("Ignoring nonalphanumeric characters, \nis "
15        + s + " a palindrome? " + isPalindrome(s));
16    }
17
18    /** Return true if a string is a palindrome */
19    public static boolean isPalindrome(String s) {
20      // Create a new string by eliminating nonalphanumeric chars
21      String s1 = filter(s);
22
23      // Create a new string that is the reversal of s1
24      String s2 = reverse(s1);
25
26      // Check if the reversal is the same as the original string
```

```
27        return s2.equals(s1);
28    }
29
30    /** Create a new string by eliminating nonalphanumeric chars */
31    public static String filter(String s) {
32        // Create a string builder
33        StringBuilder stringBuilder = new StringBuilder();
34
35        // Examine each char in the string to skip alphanumeric char
36        for (int i = 0; i < s.length(); i++) {
37            if (Character.isLetterOrDigit(s.charAt(i))) {
38                stringBuilder.append(s.charAt(i));               add letter or digit
39            }
40        }
41
42        // Return a new filtered string
43        return stringBuilder.toString();
44    }
45
46    /** Create a new string by reversing a specified string */
47    public static String reverse(String s) {
48        StringBuilder stringBuilder = new StringBuilder(s);
49        stringBuilder.reverse(); // Invoke reverse in StringBuilder
50        return stringBuilder.toString();
51    }
52 }
```

```
Enter a string: ab<c>cb?a  ↵Enter
Ignoring nonalphanumeric characters,
is ab<c>cb?a a palindrome? true
```

```
Enter a string: abcc><?cab  ↵Enter
Ignoring nonalphanumeric characters,
is abcc><?cab a palindrome? false
```

The `filter(String s)` method (lines 31–44) examines each character in string `s` and copies it to a string builder if the character is a letter or a numeric character. The `filter` method returns the string in the builder. The `reverse(String s)` method (lines 47–51) creates a new string that reverses the specified string `s`. The `filter` and `reverse` methods both return a new string. The original string is not changed.

The program in Listing 9.1 checks whether a string is a palindrome by comparing pairs of characters from both ends of the string. Listing 9.4 uses the `reverse` method in the `StringBuilder` class to reverse the string, then compares whether the two strings are equal to determine whether the original string is a palindrome.

9.15 What is the difference between `StringBuilder` and `StringBuffer`?

9.16 How do you create a string builder from a string? How do you return a string from a string builder?

9.17 Write three statements to reverse a string `s` using the `reverse` method in the `StringBuilder` class.

9.18 Write three statements to delete a substring from a string `s` of 20 characters, starting at index 4 and ending with index 10. Use the `delete` method in the `StringBuilder` class.

9.19 What is the internal storage for characters in a string and a string builder?

✓Check
 Point

MyProgrammingLab™
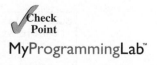

9.20 Suppose that `s1` and `s2` are given as follows:

```
StringBuilder s1 = new StringBuilder("Java");
StringBuilder s2 = new StringBuilder("HTML");
```

Show the value of `s1` after each of the following statements. Assume that the statements are independent.

a. `s1.append(" is fun");`
b. `s1.append(s2);`
c. `s1.insert(2, "is fun");`
d. `s1.insert(1, s2);`
e. `s1.charAt(2);`
f. `s1.length();`

g. `s1.deleteCharAt(3);`
h. `s1.delete(1, 3);`
i. `s1.reverse();`
j. `s1.replace(1, 3, "Computer");`
k. `s1.substring(1, 3);`
l. `s1.substring(2);`

9.21 Show the output of the following program:

```java
public class Test {
  public static void main(String[] args) {
    String s = "Java";
    StringBuilder builder = new StringBuilder(s);
    change(s, builder);

    System.out.println(s);
    System.out.println(builder);
  }

  private static void change(String s, StringBuilder builder) {
    s = s + " and HTML";
    builder.append(" and HTML");
  }
}
```

9.7 Command-Line Arguments

Key Point

The `main` method can receive string arguments from the command line.

Perhaps you have already noticed the unusual header for the `main` method, which has the parameter `args` of `String[]` type. It is clear that `args` is an array of strings. The `main` method is just like a regular method with a parameter. You can call a regular method by passing actual parameters. Can you pass arguments to `main`? Yes, of course you can. In the following examples, the `main` method in class `TestMain` is invoked by a method in `A`.

```java
public class A {
  public static void main(String[] args) {
    String[] strings = {"New York",
      "Boston", "Atlanta"};
    TestMain.main(strings);
  }
}
```

```java
public class TestMain {
  public static void main(String[] args) {
    for (int i = 0; i < args.length; i++)
      System.out.println(args[i]);
  }
}
```

A `main` method is just a regular method. Furthermore, you can pass arguments from the command line.

9.7.1 Passing Strings to the `main` Method

You can pass strings to a `main` method from the command line when you run the program. The following command line, for example, starts the program `TestMain` with three strings: `arg0`, `arg1`, and `arg2`:

```
java TestMain arg0 arg1 arg2
```

`arg0`, `arg1`, and `arg2` are strings, but they don't have to appear in double quotes on the command line. The strings are separated by a space. A string that contains a space must be enclosed in double quotes. Consider the following command line:

```
java TestMain "First num" alpha 53
```

It starts the program with three strings: `First num`, `alpha`, and `53`. Since `First num` is a string, it is enclosed in double quotes. Note that `53` is actually treated as a string. You can use `"53"` instead of `53` in the command line.

When the `main` method is invoked, the Java interpreter creates an array to hold the command-line arguments and pass the array reference to `args`. For example, if you invoke a program with `n` arguments, the Java interpreter creates an array like this one:

```
args = new String[n];
```

The Java interpreter then passes `args` to invoke the `main` method.

> **Note**
>
> If you run the program with no strings passed, the array is created with `new String[0]`. In this case, the array is empty with length `0`. `args` references to this empty array. Therefore, `args` is not `null`, but `args.length` is `0`.

9.7.2 Case Study: Calculator

Suppose you are to develop a program that performs arithmetic operations on integers. The program receives an expression in one string argument. The expression consists of an integer followed by an operator and another integer. For example, to add two integers, use this command:

VideoNote

Command-line argument

```
java Calculator "2 + 3"
```

The program will display the following output:

```
2 + 3 = 5
```

Figure 9.14 shows sample runs of the program.

The strings passed to the main program are stored in `args`, which is an array of strings. In this case, we pass the expression as one string. Therefore, the array contains only one element in `args[0]` and `args.length` is `1`.

Here are the steps in the program:

1. Use `args.length` to determine whether the expression has been provided as one argument in the command line. If not, terminate the program using `System.exit(1)`.

2. Split the expression in the string `args[0]` into three tokens in `tokens[0]`, `tokens[1]`, and `tokens[2]`.

3. Perform a binary arithmetic operation on the operands `tokens[0]` and `tokens[2]` using the operator in `tokens[1]`.

FIGURE 9.14 The program takes an expression in one argument (**operand1 operator operand2**) from the command line and displays the expression and the result of the arithmetic operation.

The program is shown in Listing 9.5.

LISTING 9.5 Calculator.java

```java
1  public class Calculator {
2    /** Main method */
3    public static void main(String[] args) {
4      // Check number of strings passed
5      if (args.length != 1) {
6        System.out.println(
7          "Usage: java Calculator \"operand1 operator operand2\"");
8        System.exit(1);
9      }
10
11     // The result of the operation
12     int result = 0;
13
14     // The result of the operation
15     String[] tokens = args[0].split(" ");
16
17     // Determine the operator
18     switch (tokens[1].charAt(0) ) {
19       case '+': result = Integer.parseInt(tokens[0]) +
20                          Integer.parseInt(tokens[2]);
21               break;
22       case '-': result = Integer.parseInt(tokens[0]) -
23                          Integer.parseInt(tokens[2]);
24               break;
25       case '*': result = Integer.parseInt(tokens[0]) *
26                          Integer.parseInt(tokens[2]);
27               break;
28       case '/': result = Integer.parseInt(tokens[0]) /
29                          Integer.parseInt(tokens[2]);
30     }
31
32     // Display result
33     System.out.println(tokens[0] + ' ' + tokens[1] + ' '
34       + tokens[2] + " = " + result);
35   }
36 }
```

check argument (line 5)

split string (line 15)

check operator (line 18)

The expression is passed as a string in one argument and it is split into three parts—`tokens[0]`, `tokens[1]`, and `tokens[2]`—using the `split` method (line 15) with a space as a delimiter.

`Integer.parseInt(tokens[0])` (line 19) converts a digital string into an integer. The string must consist of digits. If it doesn't, the program will terminate abnormally.

For this program to work, the expression must be entered in the form of "operand1 operator operand2". The operands and operator are separated by exactly one space. You can modify the program to accept the expressions in different forms (see Programming Exercise 9.28).

9.22 This book declares the `main` method as

```
public static void main(String[] args)
```

Can it be replaced by one of the following lines?

```
public static void main(String args[])
public static void main(String[] x)
public static void main(String x[])
static void main(String x[])
```

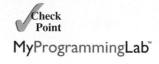

9.23 Show the output of the following program when invoked using

1. **java Test I have a dream**

2. **java Test "1 2 3"**

3. **java Test**

```
public class Test {
  public static void main(String[] args) {
    System.out.println("Number of strings is " + args.length);
    for (int i = 0; i < args.length; i++)
      System.out.println(args[i]);
  }
}
```

KEY TERMS

interned string   337

wrapper class   350

CHAPTER SUMMARY

1. Strings are objects encapsulated in the `String` class. A string can be constructed using one of the 13 constructors or simply using a string literal. Java treats a string literal as a `String` object.

2. A `String` object is immutable; its contents cannot be changed. To improve efficiency and save memory, the JVM stores two literal strings that have the same character sequence in a unique object. This unique object is called an *interned string object*.

3. You can get the length of a string by invoking its `length()` method, retrieve a character at the specified `index` in the string using the `charAt(index)` method, and use the `indexOf` and `lastIndexOf` methods to find a character or a substring in a string.

4. You can use the `concat` method to concatenate two strings, or the plus (+) operator to concatenate two or more strings.

5. You can use the `substring` method to obtain a substring from the string.

6. You can use the `equals` and `compareTo` methods to compare strings. The `equals` method returns `true` if two strings are equal, and `false` if they are not equal. The `compareTo` method returns `0`, a positive integer, or a negative integer, depending on whether one string is equal to, greater than, or less than the other string.

7. A *regular expression* (abbreviated *regex*) is a string that describes a pattern for matching a set of strings. You can match, replace, or split a string by specifying a pattern.

8. The `Character` class is a wrapper class for a single character. The `Character` class provides useful static methods to determine whether a character is a letter (`isLetter(char)`), a digit (`isDigit(char)`), uppercase (`isUpperCase(char)`), or lowercase (`isLowerCase(char)`).

9. The `StringBuilder` and `StringBuffer` classes can be used to replace the `String` class. The `String` object is immutable, but you can add, insert, or append new contents into `StringBuilder` and `StringBuffer` objects. Use `String` if the string contents do not require any change, and use `StringBuilder` or `StringBuffer` if they might change.

10. You can pass strings to the `main` method from the command line. Strings passed to the `main` program are stored in `args`, which is an array of strings. The first string is represented by `args[0]`, and `args.length` is the number of strings passed.

TEST QUESTIONS

Do the test questions for this chapter online at www.cs.armstrong.edu/liang/intro9e/test.html.

MyProgrammingLab™ ## PROGRAMMING EXERCISES

Sections 9.2–9.3

*9.1 (*Check SSN*) Write a program that prompts the user to enter a Social Security number in the format DDD-DD-DDDD, where D is a digit. The program displays `Valid SSN` for a correct Social Security number and `Invalid SSN` otherwise.

**9.2 (*Check substrings*) You can check whether a string is a substring of another string by using the `indexOf` method in the `String` class. Write your own method for this function. Write a program that prompts the user to enter two strings, and checks whether the first string is a substring of the second.

**9.3 (*Check password*) Some websites impose certain rules for passwords. Write a method that checks whether a string is a valid password. Suppose the password rules are as follows:

- A password must have at least eight characters.
- A password consists of only letters and digits.
- A password must contain at least two digits.

Write a program that prompts the user to enter a password and displays `Valid Password` if the rules are followed or `Invalid Password` otherwise.

9.4   (*Occurrences of a specified character*) Write a method that finds the number of occurrences of a specified character in a string using the following header:

```
public static int count(String str, char a)
```

For example, `count("Welcome", 'e')` returns 2. Write a test program that prompts the user to enter a string followed by a character and displays the number of occurrences of the character in the string.

**9.5   (*Occurrences of each digit in a string*) Write a method that counts the occurrences of each digit in a string using the following header:

```
public static int[] count(String s)
```

The method counts how many times a digit appears in the string. The return value is an array of ten elements, each of which holds the count for a digit. For example, after executing `int[] counts = count("12203AB3")`, `counts[0]` is 1, `counts[1]` is 1, `counts[2]` is 2, and `counts[3]` is 2.

Write a test program that prompts the user to enter a string and displays the number of occurrences of each digit in the string.

*9.6   (*Count the letters in a string*) Write a method that counts the number of letters in a string using the following header:

```
public static int countLetters(String s)
```

Write a test program that prompts the user to enter a string and displays the number of letters in the string.

*9.7   (*Phone keypads*) The international standard letter/number mapping found on the telephone is:

1	2 ABC	3 DEF
4 GHI	5 JKL	6 MNO
7 PQRS	8 TUV	9 WXYZ
	0	

Write a method that returns a number, given an uppercase letter, as follows:

```
public static int getNumber(char uppercaseLetter)
```

Write a test program that prompts the user to enter a phone number as a string. The input number may contain letters. The program translates a letter (upper- or lower-case) to a digit and leaves all other characters intact. Here is a sample run of the program:

```
Enter a string: 1-800-Flowers  ↵Enter
1-800-3569377
```

```
Enter a string: 1800flowers
18003569377
```

*9.8 (*Binary to decimal*) Write a method that parses a binary number as a string into a decimal integer. The method header is:

public static int binaryToDecimal(String binaryString)

For example, binary string 10001 is 17 ($1 \times 2^4 + 0 \times 2^3 + 0 \times 2^2 + 0 \times 2 + 1 = 17$). Therefore, **binaryToDecimal("10001")** returns **17**. Note that **Integer.parseInt("10001", 2)** parses a binary string to a decimal value. Do not use this method in this exercise.

Write a test program that prompts the user to enter a binary string and displays the corresponding decimal integer value.

Section 9.4

**9.9 (*Binary to hex*) Write a method that parses a binary number into a hex number. The method header is:

public static String binaryToHex(String binaryValue)

Write a test program that prompts the user to enter a binary number and displays the corresponding hexadecimal value.

**9.10 (*Decimal to binary*) Write a method that parses a decimal number into a binary number as a string. The method header is:

public static String decimalToBinary(**int** value)

Write a test program that prompts the user to enter a decimal integer value and displays the corresponding binary value.

**9.11 (*Sort characters in a string*) Write a method that returns a sorted string using the following header:

public static String sort(String s)

For example, **sort("acb")** returns **abc**.

Write a test program that prompts the user to enter a string and displays the sorted string.

9.12 (*Anagrams*) Write a method that checks whether two words are anagrams. Two words are anagrams if they contain the same letters in any order. For example, **silent and **listen** are anagrams. The header of the method is:

public static boolean isAnagram(String s1, String s2)

Write a test program that prompts the user to enter two strings and, if they are anagrams, displays **two strings are anagrams**, and displays **two strings are not anagrams** if they are not anagrams.

Section 9.5

*9.13 (*Pass a string to check palindromes*) Rewrite Listing 9.1 by passing the string as a command-line argument.

*9.14 (*Sum integers*) Write two programs. The first program passes an unspecified number of integers as separate strings to the **main** method and displays their total. The

VideoNote

Number conversion

second program passes an unspecified number of integers delimited by one space in a string to the `main` method and displays their total. Name the two programs `Exercise9_14a` and `Exercise9_14b`, as shown in Figure 9.15.

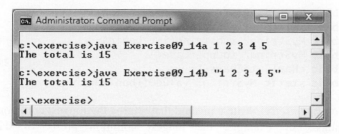

```
Administrator: Command Prompt
c:\exercise>java Exercise09_14a 1 2 3 4 5
The total is 15

c:\exercise>java Exercise09_14b "1 2 3 4 5"
The total is 15

c:\exercise>
```

FIGURE 9.15 The program adds all the numbers passed from the command line.

*9.15 (*Find the number of uppercase letters in a string*) Write a program that passes a string to the `main` method and displays the number of uppercase letters in the string.

Comprehensive

**9.16 (*Implement the String class*) The `String` class is provided in the Java library. Provide your own implementation for the following methods (name the new class `MyString1`):

```java
public MyString1(char[] chars);
public char charAt(int index);
public int length();
public MyString1 substring(int begin, int end);
public MyString1 toLowerCase();
public boolean equals(MyString1 s);
public static MyString1 valueOf(int i);
```

9.17 (*Guess the capitals*) Write a program that repeatedly prompts the user to enter a capital for a state. Upon receiving the user input, the program reports whether the answer is correct. Assume that **50 states and their capitals are stored in a two-dimensional array, as shown in Figure 9.16. The program prompts the user to answer all states' capitals and displays the total correct count. The user's answer is not case-sensitive.

```
Alabama          Montgomery
Alaska           Juneau
Arizona          Phoenix
...              ...
...              ...
```

FIGURE 9.16 A two-dimensional array stores states and their capitals.

Here is a sample run:

```
What is the capital of Alabama? Montogomery  ↵Enter
The correct answer should be Montgomery
What is the capital of Alaska? Juneau  ↵Enter
Your answer is correct
What is the capital of Arizona? ...
...
The correct count is 35
```

**9.18 (*Implement the String class*) The `String` class is provided in the Java library. Provide your own implementation for the following methods (name the new class `MyString2`):

```
public MyString2(String s);
public int compare(String s);
public MyString2 substring(int begin);
public MyString2 toUpperCase();
public char[] toChars();
public static MyString2 valueOf(boolean b);
```

*9.19 (*Common prefix*) Write a method that returns the longest common prefix of two strings. For example, the longest common prefix of `distance` and `disinfection` is `dis`. The header of the method is:

```
public static String prefix(String s1, String s2)
```

If the two strings don't have a common prefix, the method returns an empty string.

Write a `main` method that prompts the user to enter two strings and displays their longest common prefix.

9.20 (*Implement the Character class*) The `Character` class is provided in the Java library. Provide your own implementation for this class. Name the new class `MyCharacter`.

**9.21 (*New string split method*) The `split` method in the `String` class returns an array of strings consisting of the substrings split by the delimiters. However, the delimiters are not returned. Implement the following new method that returns an array of strings consisting of the substrings split by the matching delimiters, including the matching delimiters.

```
public static String[] split(String s, String regex)
```

For example, `split("ab#12#453", "#")` returns `ab, #, 12, #, 453` in an array of `String`, and `split("a?b?gf#e", "[?#]")` returns `a, b, ?, b, gf, #,` and `e` in an array of `String`.

**9.22 (*Implement the StringBuilder class*) The `StringBuilder` class is provided in the Java library. Provide your own implementation for the following methods (name the new class `MyStringBuilder1`):

```
public MyStringBuilder1(String s);
public MyStringBuilder1 append(MyStringBuilder1 s);
public MyStringBuilder1 append(int i);
public int length();
public char charAt(int index);
public MyStringBuilder1 toLowerCase();
public MyStringBuilder1 substring(int begin, int end);
public String toString();
```

**9.23 (*Financial: credit card number validation*) Rewrite Programming Exercise 5.31 using a string input for the credit card number. Redesign the program using the following methods:

```
/** Return true if the card number is valid */
public static boolean isValid(String cardNumber)

/** Get the result from Step 2 */
public static int sumOfDoubleEvenPlace(String cardNumber)
```

```
/** Return this number if it is a single digit; otherwise,
 * return the sum of the two digits */
public static int getDigit(int number)

/** Return sum of odd-place digits in number */
public static int sumOfOddPlace(String cardNumber)
```

**9.24 (*Implement the `StringBuilder` class*) The `StringBuilder` class is provided in the Java library. Provide your own implementation for the following methods (name the new class `MyStringBuilder2`):

```
public MyStringBuilder2();
public MyStringBuilder2(char[] chars);
public MyStringBuilder2(String s);
public MyStringBuilder2 insert(int offset, MyStringBuilder2 s);
public MyStringBuilder2 reverse();
public MyStringBuilder2 substring(int begin);
public MyStringBuilder2 toUpperCase();
```

***9.25 (*Game: hangman*) Write a hangman game that randomly generates a word and prompts the user to guess one letter at a time, as shown in the sample run. Each letter in the word is displayed as an asterisk. When the user makes a correct guess, the actual letter is then displayed. When the user finishes a word, display the number of misses and ask the user whether to continue to play with another word. Declare an array to store words, as follows:

```
// Add any words you wish in this array
String[] words = {"write", "that", ...};
```

```
(Guess) Enter a letter in word ******* > p  ⏎Enter
(Guess) Enter a letter in word p****** > r  ⏎Enter
(Guess) Enter a letter in word pr**r** > p  ⏎Enter
      p is already in the word
(Guess) Enter a letter in word pr**r** > o  ⏎Enter
(Guess) Enter a letter in word pro*r** > g  ⏎Enter
(Guess) Enter a letter in word progr** > n  ⏎Enter
      n is not in the word
(Guess) Enter a letter in word progr** > m  ⏎Enter
(Guess) Enter a letter in word progr*m > a  ⏎Enter
The word is program. You missed 1 time
Do you want to guess another word? Enter y or n>
```

**9.26 (*Check ISBN-10*) Use string operations to simplify Programming Exercise 3.9. Enter the first 9 digits of an ISBN number as a string.

VideoNote
Check ISBN-10

*9.27 (*Bioinformatics: find genes*) Biologists use a sequence of the letters A, C, T, and G to model a *genome*. A *gene* is a substring of a genome that starts after a triplet ATG and ends before a triplet TAG, TAA, or TGA. Furthermore, the length of a gene string is a multiple of 3, and the gene does not contain any of the triplets ATG, TAG, TAA, or TGA. Write a program that prompts the user to enter a genome and displays all genes in the genome. If no gene is found in the input sequence, display "no gene is found". Here are the sample runs:

```
Enter a genome string: TTATGTTTTAAGGATGGGGCGTTAGTT  ⏎Enter
TTT
GGGCGT
```

```
Enter a genome string: TGTGTGTATAT  ↵Enter
no gene is found
```

*9.28 (*Calculator*) Revise Listing 9.5, Calculator.java, to accept an expression in which the operands and operator are separated by zero or more spaces. For example, 3+4 and 3 + 4 are acceptable expressions.

*9.29 (*Business: check ISBN-13*) **ISBN-13** is a new standard for identifying books. It uses the 13 digits $d_1d_2d_3d_4d_5d_6d_7d_8d_9d_{10}d_{11}d_{12}d_{13}$. The last digit, d_{13}, is a checksum, which is calculated from the other digits using the following formula:

$$10 - (d_1 + 3d_2 + d_3 + 3d_4 + d_5 + 3d_6 + d_7 + 3d_8 + d_9 + 3d_{10} + d_{11} + 3d_{12}) \% 10$$

If the checksum is 10, replace it with 0. Your program should read the input as a string. Here are sample runs:

```
Enter the first 12 digits of an ISBN-13 as a string:
 978013213080  ↵Enter
The ISBN-13 number is 9780132130806
```

```
Enter the first 12 digits of an ISBN-13 as a string:
 978013213079  ↵Enter
The ISBN-13 number is 9780132130790
```

*9.30 (*Capitalize first letter of each word*) Write the following method that returns a new string in which the first letter in each word is capitalized.

public static void title(String s)

Write a test program that prompts the user to enter a string and invokes this method, and displays the return value from this method. Here is a sample run:

```
Enter a string: london   england 2015  ↵Enter
The new string is: London   England 2015
```

Note that words may be separated by multiple blank spaces.

*9.31 (*Swap case*) Write the following method that returns a new string in which the uppercase letters are changed to lowercase and lowercase letters are changed to uppercase.

public static String swapCase(String s)

Write a test program that prompts the user to enter a string and invokes this method, and displays the return value from this method. Here is a sample run:

```
Enter a string: I'm here  ↵Enter
The new string is: i'M HERE
```

THINKING IN OBJECTS

Objectives

- To create immutable objects from immutable classes to protect the contents of objects (§10.2).

- To determine the scope of variables in the context of a class (§10.3).

- To use the keyword `this` to refer to the calling object itself (§10.4).

- To apply class abstraction to develop software (§10.5).

- To explore the differences between the procedural paradigm and object-oriented paradigm (§10.6).

- To develop classes for modeling composition relationships (§10.7).

- To design programs using the object-oriented paradigm (§§10.8–10.10).

- To design classes that follow the class-design guidelines (§10.11).

- To create objects for primitive values using the wrapper classes (`Byte`, `Short`, `Integer`, `Long`, `Float`, `Double`, `Character`, and `Boolean`) (§10.12).

- To simplify programming using automatic conversion between primitive types and wrapper class types (§10.13).

- To use the `BigInteger` and `BigDecimal` classes for computing very large numbers with arbitrary precisions (§10.14).

10.1 Introduction

The focus of this chapter is on class design and explores the differences between procedural programming and object-oriented programming.

The preceding two chapters introduced objects and classes. You learned how to define classes, create objects, and use objects from several classes in the Java API (e.g., **Date**, **Random**, **String**, **StringBuilder**, and **Scanner**). This book's approach is to teach problem solving and fundamental programming techniques before object-oriented programming. This chapter shows how procedural and objcct-oriented programming differ. You will see the benefits of object-oriented programming and learn to use it effectively.

We will use several examples to illustrate the advantages of the object-oriented approach. The examples involve designing new classes and using them in applications. We first introduce some language features supporting these examples.

10.2 Immutable Objects and Classes

Key
Point

You can define immutable classes to create immutable objects. The contents of immutable objects cannot be changed.

VideoNote

Immutable objects and `this` keyword

immutable object

immutable class

Normally, you create an object and allow its contents to be changed later. However, occasionally it is desirable to create an object whose contents cannot be changed once the object has been created. We call such an object an *immutable object* and its class an *immutable class*. The **String** class, for example, is immutable. If you deleted the **set** method in the **CircleWithPrivateDataFields** class in Listing 8.9, the class would be immutable, because radius is private and cannot be changed without a **set** method.

If a class is immutable, then all its data fields must be private and it cannot contain public **set** methods for any data fields. A class with all private data fields and no mutators is not necessarily immutable. For example, the following **Student** class has all private data fields and no **set** methods, but it is not an immutable class.

Student class

```
1  public class Student {
2    private int id;
3    private String name;
4    private java.util.Date dateCreated;
5
6    public Student(int ssn, String newName) {
7      id = ssn;
8      name = newName;
9      dateCreated = new java.util.Date();
10   }
11
12   public int getId() {
13     return id;
14   }
15
16   public String getName() {
17     return name;
18   }
19
20   public java.util.Date getDateCreated() {
21     return dateCreated;
22   }
23 }
```

As shown in the following code, the data field **dateCreated** is returned using the **getDateCreated()** method. This is a reference to a **Date** object. Through this reference, the content for **dateCreated** can be changed.

```java
public class Test {
  public static void main(String[] args) {
    Student student = new Student(111223333, "John");
    java.util.Date dateCreated = student.getDateCreated();
    dateCreated.setTime(200000); // Now dateCreated field is changed!
  }
}
```

For a class to be immutable, it must meet the following requirements:

- All data fields must be private.

- There can't be any mutator methods for data fields.

- No accessor methods can return a reference to a data field that is mutable.

Interested readers may refer to Supplement III.AB for an extended discussion on immutable objects.

10.1 If a class contains only private data fields and no **set** methods, is the class immutable?

10.2 If all the data fields in a class are private and primitive types, and the class doesn't contain any **set** methods, is the class immutable?

10.3 Is the following class immutable?

```java
public class A {
  private int[] values;

  public int[] getValues() {
    return values;
  }
}
```

✓ **Check Point**

MyProgrammingLab™

10.3 The Scope of Variables

The scope of instance and static variables is the entire class, regardless of where the variables are declared.

🔑 **Key Point**

Chapter 5, Methods, discussed local variables and their scope rules. Local variables are declared and used inside a method locally. This section discusses the scope rules of all the variables in the context of a class.

Instance and static variables in a class are referred to as the *class's variables* or *data fields*. A variable defined inside a method is referred to as a *local variable*. The scope of a class's variables is the entire class, regardless of where the variables are declared. A class's variables and methods can appear in any order in the class, as shown in Figure 10.1a. The exception is when a data field is initialized based on a reference to another data field. In such cases, the

class's variables

```java
public class Circle {
  public double findArea() {
    return radius * radius * Math.PI;
  }

  private double radius = 1;
}
```

```java
public class F {
  private int i;
  private int j = i + 1;
}
```

(a) The variable `radius` and method `findArea()` can be declared in any order.

(b) `i` has to be declared before `j` because `j`'s initial value is dependent on `i`.

FIGURE 10.1 Members of a class can be declared in any order, with one exception.

other data field must be declared first, as shown in Figure 10.1b. For consistency, this book declares data fields at the beginning of the class.

You can declare a class's variable only once, but you can declare the same variable name in a method many times in different nonnesting blocks.

hidden variables

If a local variable has the same name as a class's variable, the local variable takes precedence and the class's variable with the same name is *hidden*. For example, in the following program, x is defined both as an instance variable and as a local variable in the method.

```java
public class F {
  private int x = 0; // Instance variable
  private int y = 0;

  public F() {
  }

  public void p() {
    int x = 1; // Local variable
    System.out.println("x = " + x);
    System.out.println("y = " + y);
  }
}
```

What is the printout for f.p(), where f is an instance of F? The printout for f.p() is 1 for x and 0 for y. Here is why:

- x is declared as a data field with the initial value of 0 in the class, but it is also declared in the method p() with an initial value of 1. The latter x is referenced in the System.out.println statement.

- y is declared outside the method p(), but y is accessible inside the method.

Tip
To avoid confusion and mistakes, do not use the names of instance or static variables as local variable names, except for method parameters.

10.4 What is the output of the following program?

MyProgrammingLab™

```java
public class Test {
  private static int i = 0;
  private static int j = 0;

  public static void main(String[] args) {
    int i = 2;
    int k = 3;

    {
      int j = 3;
      System.out.println("i + j is " + i + j);
    }

    k = i + j;
    System.out.println("k is " + k);
    System.out.println("j is " + j);
  }
}
```

10.4 The **this** Reference

The keyword this *refers to the object itself. It can also be used inside a constructor to invoke another constructor of the same class.*

Key Point

The this *keyword* is the name of a reference that an object can use to refer to itself. You can use the this keyword to refer to the object's instance members. For example, the following code in (a) uses this to reference the object's radius and invokes its getArea() method explicitly. The this reference is normally omitted, as shown in (b). However, the this reference is needed to reference hidden data fields or invoke an overloaded constructor.

this keyword

```
public class Circle {
  private double radius;

  ...

  public double getArea() {
    return this.radius * this.radius
      * Math.PI;
  }

  public String toString() {
    return "radius: " + this.radius
      + "area: " + this.getArea();
  }
}
```

Equivalent

```
public class Circle {
  private double radius;

  ...

  public double getArea() {
    return radius * radius * Math.PI;
  }

  public String toString() {
    return "radius: " + radius
      + "area: " + getArea();
  }
}
```

(a)

(b)

10.4.1 Using **this** to Reference Hidden Data Fields

The this keyword can be used to reference a class's *hidden data fields*. For example, a data-field name is often used as the parameter name in a set method for the data field. In this case, the data field is hidden in the set method. You need to reference the hidden data-field name in the method in order to set a new value to it. A hidden static variable can be accessed simply by using the ClassName.staticVariable reference. A hidden instance variable can be accessed by using the keyword this, as shown in Figure 10.2a.

hidden data fields

```
public class F {
  private int i = 5;
  private static double k = 0;

  public void setI(int i) {
    this.i = i;
  }

  public static void setK(double k) {
    F.k = k;
  }

  // Other methods omitted
}
```

```
Suppose that f1 and f2 are two objects of F.

Invoking f1.setI(10) is to execute
    this.i = 10, where this refers f1

Invoking f2.setI(45) is to execute
    this.i = 45, where this refers f2

Invoking F.setK(33) is to execute
    F.k = 33. setK is a static method
```

(a)

(b)

FIGURE 10.2 The keyword this refers to the calling object that invokes the method.

The this keyword gives us a way to refer to the object that invokes an instance method. To invoke f1.setI(10), this.i = i is executed, which assigns the value of parameter i to the data field i of this calling object f1. The keyword this refers to the object that invokes the instance method `setI`, as shown in Figure 10.2b. The line `F.k = k` means that the value in parameter `k` is assigned to the static data field `k` of the class, which is shared by all the objects of the class.

10.4.2 Using `this` to Invoke a Constructor

The `this` keyword can be used to invoke another constructor of the same class. For example, you can rewrite the `Circle` class as follows:

```java
public class Circle {
  private double radius;

  public Circle(double radius) {
    this.radius = radius;
  }

  public Circle() {
    this(1.0);
  }
  ...
}
```

The **this** keyword is used to reference the hidden data field radius of the object being constructed.

The **this** keyword is used to invoke another constructor.

The line `this(1.0)` in the second constructor invokes the first constructor with a `double` value argument.

Note

Java requires that the `this(arg-list)` statement appear first in the constructor before any other executable statements.

Tip

If a class has multiple constructors, it is better to implement them using `this(arg-list)` as much as possible. In general, a constructor with no or fewer arguments can invoke a constructor with more arguments using `this(arg-list)`. This syntax often simplifies coding and makes the class easier to read and to maintain.

Check
Point

MyProgrammingLab™

10.5 Describe the role of the `this` keyword.

10.6 What is wrong in the following code?

```java
1  public class C {
2    private int p;
3
4    public C() {
5      System.out.println("C's no-arg constructor invoked");
6      this(0);
7    }
8
9    public C(int p) {
10     p = p;
11   }
12
13   public void setP(int p) {
14     p = p;
15   }
16 }
```

10.7 What is wrong in the following code?

```
public class Test {
  private int id;

  public void m1() {
    this.id = 45;
  }

  public void m2() {
    Test.id = 45;
  }
}
```

10.5 Class Abstraction and Encapsulation

Class abstraction is the separation of class implementation from the use of a class. The details of implementation are encapsulated and hidden from the user. This is known as class encapsulation.

Key
Point

In Chapter 5, you learned about method abstraction and used it in stepwise refinement. Java provides many levels of abstraction, and *class abstraction* separates class implementation from how the class is used. The creator of a class describes the functions of the class and lets the user know how the class can be used. The collection of methods and fields that are accessible from outside the class, together with the description of how these members are expected to behave, serves as the *class's contract*. As shown in Figure 10.3, the user of the class does not need to know how the class is implemented. The details of implementation are encapsulated and hidden from the user. This is called *class encapsulation*. For example, you can create a `Circle` object and find the area of the circle without knowing how the area is computed. For this reason, a class is also known as an *abstract data type* (ADT).

class abstraction

class's contract

class encapsulation

abstract data type

FIGURE 10.3 Class abstraction separates class implementation from the use of the class.

Class abstraction and encapsulation are two sides of the same coin. Many real-life examples illustrate the concept of class abstraction. Consider, for instance, building a computer system. Your personal computer has many components—a CPU, memory, disk, motherboard, fan, and so on. Each component can be viewed as an object that has properties and methods. To get the components to work together, you need know only how each component is used and how it interacts with the others. You don't need to know how the components work internally. The internal implementation is encapsulated and hidden from you. You can build a computer without knowing how a component is implemented.

The computer-system analogy precisely mirrors the object-oriented approach. Each component can be viewed as an object of the class for the component. For example, you might have a class that models all kinds of fans for use in a computer, with properties such as fan size and speed and methods such as start and stop. A specific fan is an instance of this class with specific property values.

As another example, consider getting a loan. A specific loan can be viewed as an object of a `Loan` class. The interest rate, loan amount, and loan period are its data properties, and computing the monthly payment and total payment are its methods. When you buy a car, a loan object is created by instantiating the class with your loan interest rate, loan amount, and loan period. You can then use the methods to find the monthly payment and total payment of your loan. As a user of the **Loan** class, you don't need to know how these methods are implemented.

Listing 2.8, ComputeLoan.java, presented a program for computing loan payments. That program cannot be reused in other programs because the code for computing the payments is in the **main** method. One way to fix this problem is to define static methods for computing the monthly payment and total payment. However, this solution has limitations. Suppose you wish to associate a date with the loan. There is no good way to tie a date with a loan without using objects. The traditional procedural programming paradigm is action-driven, and data are separated from actions. The object-oriented programming paradigm focuses on objects, and actions are defined along with the data in objects. To tie a date with a loan, you can define a loan class with a date along with other of the loan's properties as data fields. A loan object now contains data and actions for manipulating and processing data, and the loan data and actions are integrated in one object. Figure 10.4 shows the UML class diagram for the **Loan** class.

Loan
-annualInterestRate: double
-numberOfYears: int
-loanAmount: double
-loanDate: java.util.Date
+Loan()
+Loan(annualInterestRate: double, numberOfYears: int,loanAmount: double)
+getAnnualInterestRate(): double
+getNumberOfYears(): int
+getLoanAmount(): double
+getLoanDate(): java.util.Date
+setAnnualInterestRate(annualInterestRate: double): void
+setNumberOfYears(numberOfYears: int): void
+setLoanAmount(loanAmount: double): void
+getMonthlyPayment(): double
+getTotalPayment(): double

The annual interest rate of the loan (default: 2.5).
The number of years for the loan (default: 1).
The loan amount (default: 1000).
The date this loan was created.

Constructs a default **Loan** object.
Constructs a loan with specified interest rate, years, and loan amount.

Returns the annual interest rate of this loan.
Returns the number of the years of this loan.
Returns the amount of this loan.
Returns the date of the creation of this loan.
Sets a new annual interest rate for this loan.

Sets a new number of years for this loan.

Sets a new amount for this loan.

Returns the monthly payment for this loan.
Returns the total payment for this loan.

FIGURE 10.4 The **Loan** class models the properties and behaviors of loans.

The UML diagram in Figure 10.4 serves as the contract for the **Loan** class. Throughout this book, you will play the roles of both class user and class developer. Remember that a class user can use the class without knowing how the class is implemented.

Assume that the **Loan** class is available. The program in Listing 10.1 uses that class.

LISTING 10.1 TestLoanClass.java

```
1  import java.util.Scanner;
2
3  public class TestLoanClass {
4    /** Main method */
5    public static void main(String[] args) {
```

```
6      // Create a Scanner
7      Scanner input = new Scanner(System.in);
8
9      // Enter annual interest rate
10     System.out.print(
11       "Enter annual interest rate, for example, 8.25: ");
12     double annualInterestRate = input.nextDouble();
13
14     // Enter number of years
15     System.out.print("Enter number of years as an integer: ");
16     int numberOfYears = input.nextInt();
17
18     // Enter loan amount
19     System.out.print("Enter loan amount, for example, 120000.95: ");
20     double loanAmount = input.nextDouble();
21
22     // Create a Loan object
23     Loan loan =
24       new Loan(annualInterestRate, numberOfYears, loanAmount);          create Loan object
25
26     // Display loan date, monthly payment, and total payment
27     System.out.printf("The loan was created on %s\n" +
28       "The monthly payment is %.2f\nThe total payment is %.2f\n",
29       loan.getLoanDate().toString(), loan.getMonthlyPayment(),         invoke instance method
30       loan.getTotalPayment());                                        invoke instance method
31   }
32 }
```

```
Enter annual interest rate, for example, 8.25: 2.5 ⏎Enter
Enter number of years as an integer: 5 ⏎Enter
Enter loan amount, for example, 120000.95: 1000 ⏎Enter
The loan was created on Sat Jun 16 21:12:50 EDT 2012
The monthly payment is 17.75
The total payment is 1064.84
```

The `main` method reads the interest rate, the payment period (in years), and the loan amount; creates a **Loan** object; and then obtains the monthly payment (line 29) and the total payment (line 30) using the instance methods in the **Loan** class.

The **Loan** class can be implemented as in Listing 10.2.

LISTING 10.2 Loan.java

```
1  public class Loan {
2    private double annualInterestRate;
3    private int numberOfYears;
4    private double loanAmount;
5    private java.util.Date loanDate;
6
7    /** Default constructor */
8    public Loan() {                                                    no-arg constructor
9      this(2.5, 1, 1000);
10   }
11
12   /** Construct a loan with specified annual interest rate,
13       number of years, and loan amount
14    */
```

constructor

```
15  public Loan(double annualInterestRate, int numberOfYears,
16      double loanAmount) {
17    this.annualInterestRate = annualInterestRate;
18    this.numberOfYears = numberOfYears;
19    this.loanAmount = loanAmount;
20    loanDate = new java.util.Date();
21  }
22
23  /** Return annualInterestRate */
24  public double getAnnualInterestRate() {
25    return annualInterestRate;
26  }
27
28  /** Set a new annualInterestRate */
29  public void setAnnualInterestRate(double annualInterestRate) {
30    this.annualInterestRate = annualInterestRate;
31  }
32
33  /** Return numberOfYears */
34  public int getNumberOfYears() {
35    return numberOfYears;
36  }
37
38  /** Set a new numberOfYears */
39  public void setNumberOfYears(int numberOfYears) {
40    this.numberOfYears = numberOfYears;
41  }
42
43  /** Return loanAmount */
44  public double getLoanAmount() {
45    return loanAmount;
46  }
47
48  /** Set a new loanAmount */
49  public void setLoanAmount(double loanAmount) {
50    this.loanAmount = loanAmount;
51  }
52
53  /** Find monthly payment */
54  public double getMonthlyPayment() {
55    double monthlyInterestRate = annualInterestRate / 1200;
56    double monthlyPayment = loanAmount * monthlyInterestRate / (1 -
57      (1 / Math.pow(1 + monthlyInterestRate, numberOfYears * 12)));
58    return monthlyPayment;
59  }
60
61  /** Find total payment */
62  public double getTotalPayment() {
63    double totalPayment = getMonthlyPayment() * numberOfYears * 12;
64    return totalPayment;
65  }
66
67  /** Return loan date */
68  public java.util.Date getLoanDate() {
69    return loanDate;
70  }
71 }
```

From a class developer's perspective, a class is designed for use by many different customers. In order to be useful in a wide range of applications, a class should provide a variety of ways for customization through constructors, properties, and methods.

The `Loan` class contains two constructors, four `get` methods, three `set` methods, and the methods for finding the monthly payment and the total payment. You can construct a `Loan` object by using the no-arg constructor or the constructor with three parameters: annual interest rate, number of years, and loan amount. When a loan object is created, its date is stored in the `loanDate` field. The `getLoanDate` method returns the date. The three `get` methods—`getAnnualInterest`, `getNumberOfYears`, and `getLoanAmount`—return the annual interest rate, payment years, and loan amount, respectively. All the data properties and methods in this class are tied to a specific instance of the `Loan` class. Therefore, they are instance variables and methods.

Important Pedagogical Tip

Use the UML diagram for the `Loan` class shown in Figure 10.4 to write a test program that uses the `Loan` class even though you don't know how the `Loan` class is implemented. This has three benefits:

■   It demonstrates that developing a class and using a class are two separate tasks.

■   It enables you to skip the complex implementation of certain classes without interrupting the sequence of this book.

■   It is easier to learn how to implement a class if you are familiar with it by using the class.

For all the class examples from now on, create an object from the class and try using its methods before turning your attention to its implementation.

10.8 If you redefine the `Loan` class in Listing 10.2 without `set` methods, is the class immutable?

10.6 Object-Oriented Thinking

The procedural paradigm focuses on designing methods. The object-oriented paradigm couples data and methods together into objects. Software design using the object-oriented paradigm focuses on objects and operations on objects.

Chapters 1–7 introduced fundamental programming techniques for problem solving using loops, methods, and arrays. Knowing these techniques lays a solid foundation for object-oriented programming. Classes provide more flexibility and modularity for building reusable software. This section improves the solution for a problem introduced in Chapter 3 using the object-oriented approach. From these improvements, you will gain insight into the differences between procedural and object-oriented programming and see the benefits of developing reusable code using objects and classes.

Listing 3.5, ComputeAndInterpretBMI.java, presented a program for computing body mass index. The code cannot be reused in other programs, because the code is in the `main` method. To make it reusable, define a static method to compute body mass index as follows:

```
public static double getBMI(double weight, double height)
```

This method is useful for computing body mass index for a specified weight and height. However, it has limitations. Suppose you need to associate the weight and height with a person's name and birth date. You could declare separate variables to store these values, but these values would not be tightly coupled. The ideal way to couple them is to create an object that contains them all. Since these values are tied to individual objects, they should be stored in instance data fields. You can define a class named `BMI` as shown in Figure 10.5.

The get methods for these data fields are provided in the class, but omitted in the UML diagram for brevity.

BMI
-name: String -age: int -weight: double -height: double
+BMI(name: String, age: int, weight: double, height: double) +BMI(name: String, weight: double, height: double) +getBMI(): double +getStatus(): String

The name of the person.
The age of the person.
The weight of the person in pounds.
The height of the person in inches.

Creates a BMI object with the specified name, age, weight, and height.
Creates a BMI object with the specified name, weight, height, and a default age 20.
Returns the BMI
Returns the BMI status (e.g., normal, overweight, etc.)

FIGURE 10.5 The BMI class encapsulates BMI information.

Assume that the BMI class is available. Listing 10.3 gives a test program that uses this class.

LISTING 10.3 UseBMIClass.java

```
1  public class UseBMIClass {
2    public static void main(String[] args) {
3      BMI bmi1 = new BMI("Kim Yang", 18, 145, 70);
4      System.out.println("The BMI for " + bmi1.getName() + " is "
5        + bmi1.getBMI() + " " + bmi1.getStatus());
6
7      BMI bmi2 = new BMI("Susan King", 215, 70);
8      System.out.println("The BMI for " + bmi2.getName() + " is "
9        + bmi2.getBMI() + " " + bmi2.getStatus());
10   }
11 }
```

create an object
invoke instance method

create an object
invoke instance method

```
The BMI for Kim Yang is 20.81 Normal
The BMI for Susan King is 30.85 Obese
```

Line 3 creates the object **bmi1** for **Kim Yang** and line 7 creates the object **bmi2** for **Susan King**. You can use the instance methods **getName()**, **getBMI()**, and **getStatus()** to return the BMI information in a BMI object.

The BMI class can be implemented as in Listing 10.4.

LISTING 10.4 BMI.java

```
1  public class BMI {
2    private String name;
3    private int age;
4    private double weight; // in pounds
5    private double height; // in inches
6    public static final double KILOGRAMS_PER_POUND = 0.45359237;
```

```
 7      public static final double METERS_PER_INCH = 0.0254;
 8
 9      public BMI(String name, int age, double weight, double height) {        constructor
10        this.name = name;
11        this.age = age;
12        this.weight = weight;
13        this.height = height;
14      }
15
16      public BMI(String name, double weight, double height) {                 constructor
17        this(name, 20, weight, height);
18      }
19
20      public double getBMI() {                                                getBMI
21        double bmi = weight * KILOGRAMS_PER_POUND /
22          ((height * METERS_PER_INCH) * (height * METERS_PER_INCH));
23        return Math.round(bmi * 100) / 100.0;
24      }
25
26      public String getStatus() {                                             getStatus
27        double bmi = getBMI();
28        if (bmi < 18.5)
29          return "Underweight";
30        else if (bmi < 25)
31          return "Normal";
32        else if (bmi < 30)
33          return "Overweight";
34        else
35          return "Obese";
36      }
37
38      public String getName() {
39        return name;
40      }
41
42      public int getAge() {
43        return age;
44      }
45
46      public double getWeight() {
47        return weight;
48      }
49
50      public double getHeight() {
51        return height;
52      }
53    }
```

The mathematical formula for computing the BMI using weight and height is given in Section 3.9. The instance method **getBMI()** returns the BMI. Since the weight and height are instance data fields in the object, the **getBMI()** method can use these properties to compute the BMI for the object.

The instance method **getStatus()** returns a string that interprets the BMI. The interpretation is also given in Section 3.9.

This example demonstrates the advantages of the object-oriented paradigm over the procedural paradigm. The procedural paradigm focuses on designing methods. The object-oriented paradigm couples data and methods together into objects. Software design using the object-oriented paradigm focuses on objects and operations on objects. The object-oriented approach

procedural vs. object-oriented paradigms

combines the power of the procedural paradigm with an added dimension that integrates data with operations into objects.

In procedural programming, data and operations on the data are separate, and this methodology requires sending data to methods. Object-oriented programming places data and the operations that pertain to them in an object. This approach solves many of the problems inherent in procedural programming. The object-oriented programming approach organizes programs in a way that mirrors the real world, in which all objects are associated with both attributes and activities. Using objects improves software reusability and makes programs easier to develop and easier to maintain. Programming in Java involves thinking in terms of objects; a Java program can be viewed as a collection of cooperating objects.

Check Point

MyProgrammingLab™

10.9 Is the `BMI` class defined in Listing 10.4 immutable?

Key Point

10.7 Object Composition

An object can contain another object. The relationship between the two is called composition.

In Listing 10.2, you defined the `Loan` class to contain a `Date` data field. The relationship between `Loan` and `Date` is composition. In Listing 10.4, you defined the `BMI` class to contain a `String` data field. The relationship between `BMI` and `String` is composition.

aggregation
has-a relationship

Composition is actually a special case of the aggregation relationship. Aggregation models *has-a* relationships and represents an ownership relationship between two objects. The owner object is called an *aggregating object* and its class an *aggregating class*. The subject object is called an *aggregated object* and its class an *aggregated class*.

composition

An object may be owned by several other aggregating objects. If an object is exclusively owned by an aggregating object, the relationship between them is referred to as *composition*. For example, "a student has a name" is a composition relationship between the `Student` class and the `Name` class, whereas "a student has an address" is an aggregation relationship between the `Student` class and the `Address` class, because an address may be shared by several students. In UML notation, a filled diamond is attached to an aggregating class (e.g., `Student`) to denote the composition relationship with an aggregated class (e.g., `Name`), and an empty diamond is attached to an aggregating class (e.g., `Student`) to denote the aggregation relationship with an aggregated class (e.g., `Address`), as shown in Figure 10.6.

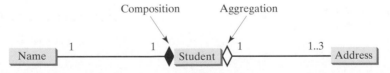

FIGURE 10.6 A student has a name and an address.

multiplicity

Each class involved in a relationship may specify a *multiplicity*. A multiplicity could be a number or an interval that specifies how many of the class's objects are involved in the relationship. The character * means an unlimited number of objects, and the interval `m..n` means that the number of objects should be between `m` and `n`, inclusive. In Figure 10.6, each student has only one address, and each address may be shared by up to **3** students. Each student has one name, and a name is unique for each student.

An aggregation relationship is usually represented as a data field in the aggregating class. For example, the relationship in Figure 10.6 can be represented as follows:

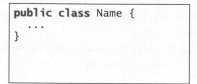

```
public class Name {
   ...
}
```
Aggregated class

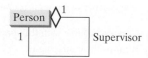

```
public class Student {
   private Name name;
   private Address address;

   ...
}
```
Aggregating class

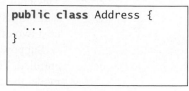

```
public class Address {
   ...
}
```
Aggregated class

Aggregation may exist between objects of the same class. For example, a person may have a supervisor. This is illustrated in Figure 10.7.

```
Person ◇ 1
   1    |
        | Supervisor
```

FIGURE 10.7   A person may have a supervisor.

In the relationship "a person has a supervisor," as shown in Figure 10.7, a supervisor can be represented as a data field in the **Person** class, as follows:

```
public class Person {
   // The type for the data is the class itself
   private Person supervisor;

   ...
}
```

If a person can have several supervisors, as shown in Figure 10.8a, you may use an array to store supervisors, as shown in Figure 10.8b.

```
Person        ◇ 1
   m            |
                | Supervisor
```
(a)

```
public class Person {
   ...
   private Person[] supervisors;
}
```
(b)

FIGURE 10.8   A person can have several supervisors.

> **Note**
> Since aggregation and composition relationships are represented using classes in the same way, many texts don't differentiate them and call both compositions. We will do the same in this book for simplicity.

aggregation or composition

10.10 What is an aggregation relationship between two objects?

10.11 What is a composition relationship between two objects?

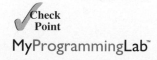

✓ Check Point

MyProgrammingLab™

10.8 Case Study: Designing the **Course** Class

Key Point

This section designs a class for modeling courses.

This book's philosophy is *teaching by example and learning by doing*. The book provides a wide variety of examples to demonstrate object-oriented programming. This section and the next two offer additional examples on designing classes.

Suppose you need to process course information. Each course has a name and has students enrolled. You should be able to add/drop a student to/from the course. You can use a class to model the courses, as shown in Figure 10.9.

Course
-courseName: String
-students: String[]
-numberOfStudents: int
+Course(courseName: String)
+getCourseName(): String
+addStudent(student: String): void
+dropStudent(student: String): void
+getStudents(): String[]
+getNumberOfStudents(): int

The name of the course.
An array to store the students for the course.
The number of students (default: 0).

Creates a course with the specified name.
Returns the course name.
Adds a new student to the course.
Drops a student from the course.
Returns the students for the course.
Returns the number of students for the course.

FIGURE 10.9 The Course class models the courses.

A **Course** object can be created using the constructor **Course(String name)** by passing a course name. You can add students to the course using the **addStudent(String student)** method, drop a student from the course using the **dropStudent(String student)** method, and return all the students in the course using the **getStudents()** method. Suppose the class is available; Listing 10.5 gives a test class that creates two courses and adds students to them.

LISTING 10.5 TestCourse.java

```java
1  public class TestCourse {
2    public static void main(String[] args) {
3      Course course1 = new Course("Data Structures");
4      Course course2 = new Course("Database Systems");
5
6      course1.addStudent("Peter Jones");
7      course1.addStudent("Kim Smith");
8      course1.addStudent("Anne Kennedy");
9
10     course2.addStudent("Peter Jones");
11     course2.addStudent("Steve Smith");
12
13     System.out.println("Number of students in course1: "
14       + course1.getNumberOfStudents());
15     String[] students = course1.getStudents();
16     for (int i = 0; i < course1.getNumberOfStudents(); i++)
17       System.out.print(students[i] + ", ");
18
19     System.out.println();
20     System.out.print("Number of students in course2: "
```

create a course

add a student

number of students
return students

```
21        + course2.getNumberOfStudents());
22    }
23 }
```

```
Number of students in course1: 3
Peter Jones, Kim Smith, Anne Kennedy,
Number of students in course2: 2
```

The **Course** class is implemented in Listing 10.6. It uses an array to store the students in the course. For simplicity, assume that the maximum course enrollment is **100**. The array is created using **new String[100]** in line 3. The **addStudent** method (line 10) adds a student to the array. Whenever a new student is added to the course, **numberOfStudents** is increased (line 12). The **getStudents** method returns the array. The **dropStudent** method (line 27) is left as an exercise.

LISTING 10.6 Course.java

```
1  public class Course {
2    private String courseName;
3    private String[] students = new String[100];          create students
4    private int numberOfStudents;
5
6    public Course(String courseName) {                     add a course
7      this.courseName = courseName;
8    }
9
10   public void addStudent(String student) {
11     students[numberOfStudents] = student;
12     numberOfStudents++;
13   }
14
15   public String[] getStudents() {                        return students
16     return students;
17   }
18
19   public int getNumberOfStudents() {                     number of students
20     return numberOfStudents;
21   }
22
23   public String getCourseName() {
24     return courseName;
25   }
26
27   public void dropStudent(String student) {
28     // Left as an exercise in Programming Exercise 10.9
29   }
30 }
```

The array size is fixed to be **100** (line 3), so you cannot have more than 100 students in the course. You can improve the class by automatically increasing the array size in Programming Exercise 10.9.

When you create a **Course** object, an array object is created. A **Course** object contains a reference to the array. For simplicity, you can say that the **Course** object contains the array.

The user can create a **Course** object and manipulate it through the public methods **addStudent**, **dropStudent**, **getNumberOfStudents**, and **getStudents**. However, the user doesn't need to know how these methods are implemented. The `Course` class encapsulates the internal implementation. This example uses an array to store students, but you could use a different data structure to store `students`. The program that uses `Course` does not need to change as long as the contract of the public methods remains unchanged.

10.9 Case Study: Designing a Class for Stacks

This section designs a class for modeling stacks.

Recall that a *stack* is a data structure that holds data in a last-in, first-out fashion, as shown in Figure 10.10.

stack

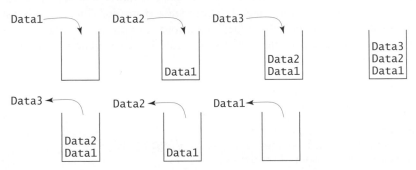

FIGURE 10.10 A stack holds data in a last-in, first-out fashion.

Stacks have many applications. For example, the compiler uses a stack to process method invocations. When a method is invoked, its parameters and local variables are pushed into a stack. When a method calls another method, the new method's parameters and local variables are pushed into the stack. When a method finishes its work and returns to its caller, its associated space is released from the stack.

You can define a class to model stacks. For simplicity, assume the stack holds the `int` values. So name the stack class `StackOfIntegers`. The UML diagram for the class is shown in Figure 10.11.

VideoNote

The `StackOfIntegers` class

StackOfIntegers	
-elements: int[] -size: int	An array to store integers in the stack. The number of integers in the stack.
+StackOfIntegers() +StackOfIntegers(capacity: int) +empty(): boolean +peek(): int +push(value: int): void +pop(): int +getSize(): int	Constructs an empty stack with a default capacity of 16. Constructs an empty stack with a specified capacity. Returns true if the stack is empty. Returns the integer at the top of the stack without removing it from the stack. Stores an integer into the top of the stack. Removes the integer at the top of the stack and returns it. Returns the number of elements in the stack.

FIGURE 10.11 The `StackOfIntegers` class encapsulates the stack storage and provides the operations for manipulating the stack.

Suppose that the class is available. The test program in Listing 10.7 uses the class to create a stack (line 3), store ten integers 0, 1, 2, . . . , and 9 (line 6), and displays them in reverse order (line 9).

Listing 10.7 TestStackOfIntegers.java

```
1  public class TestStackOfIntegers {
2    public static void main(String[] args) {
3      StackOfIntegers stack = new StackOfIntegers();
4
5      for (int i = 0; i < 10; i++)
6        stack.push(i);
7
8      while (!stack.empty())
9        System.out.print(stack.pop() + " ");
10   }
11 }
```

create a stack

push to stack

pop from stack

```
9 8 7 6 5 4 3 2 1 0
```

How do you implement the `StackOfIntegers` class? The elements in the stack are stored in an array named `elements`. When you create a stack, the array is also created. The no-arg constructor creates an array with the default capacity of `16`. The variable `size` counts the number of elements in the stack, and `size - 1` is the index of the element at the top of the stack, as shown in Figure 10.12. For an empty stack, `size` is `0`.

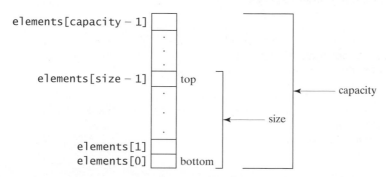

Figure 10.12 The `StackOfIntegers` class encapsulates the stack storage and provides the operations for manipulating the stack.

The `StackOfIntegers` class is implemented in Listing 10.8. The methods `empty()`, `peek()`, `pop()`, and `getSize()` are easy to implement. To implement `push(int value)`, assign `value` to `elements[size]` if `size < capacity` (line 24). If the stack is full (i.e., `size >= capacity`), create a new array of twice the current capacity (line 19), copy the contents of the current array to the new array (line 20), and assign the reference of the new array to the current array in the stack (line 21). Now you can add the new value to the array (line 24).

Listing 10.8 StackOfIntegers.java

```
1  public class StackOfIntegers {
2    private int[] elements;
3    private int size;
4    public static final int DEFAULT_CAPACITY = 16;
5
6    /** Construct a stack with the default capacity 16 */
7    public StackOfIntegers() {
8      this (DEFAULT_CAPACITY);
```

max capacity 16

```
 9    }
10
11    /** Construct a stack with the specified maximum capacity */
12    public StackOfIntegers(int capacity) {
13      elements = new int[capacity];
14    }
15
16    /** Push a new integer to the top of the stack */
17    public void push(int value) {
18      if (size >= elements.length) {
19        int[] temp = new int[elements.length * 2];
20        System.arraycopy(elements, 0, temp, 0, elements.length);
21        elements = temp;
22      }
23
24      elements[size++] = value;
25    }
26
27    /** Return and remove the top element from the stack */
28    public int pop() {
29      return elements[--size];
30    }
31
32    /** Return the top element from the stack */
33    public int peek() {
34      return elements[size - 1];
35    }
36
37    /** Test whether the stack is empty */
38    public boolean empty() {
39      return size == 0;
40    }
41
42    /** Return the number of elements in the stack */
43    public int getSize() {
44      return size;
45    }
46  }
```

double the capacity

add to stack

10.10 Case Study: Designing the **GuessDate** Class

Key Point

You can define utility classes that contain static methods and static data.

Listing 3.3, GuessBirthday.java, and Listing 7.6, GuessBirthdayUsingArray.java, presented two programs for guessing birthdays. Both programs use the same data developed with the procedural paradigm. The majority of the code in these two programs is to define the five sets of data. You cannot reuse the code in these two programs, because the code is in the **main** method. To make the code reusable, design a class to encapsulate the data, as defined in Figure 10.13.

Note that **getValue** is defined as a static method because it is not dependent on a specific object of the **GuessDate** class. The **GuessDate** class encapsulates **dates** as a private member. The user of this class doesn't need to know how **dates** is implemented or even that the **dates** field exists in the class. All that the user needs to know is how to use this method to access dates. Suppose this class is available. As shown in Section 3.4, there are five sets of dates. Invoking **getValue(setNo, row, column)** returns the date at the specified row and column in the given set. For example, **getValue(1, 0, 0)** returns **2**.

GuessDate
-dates: int[][][]
+getValue(setNo: int, row: int, column: int): int

The static array to hold dates.

Returns a date at the specified row and column in a given set.

FIGURE 10.13 The GuessDate class defines data for guessing birthdays.

Assume that the **GuessDate** class is available. Listing 10.9 is a test program that uses this class.

LISTING 10.9 UseGuessDateClass.java

```java
1  import java.util.Scanner;
2
3  public class UseGuessDateClass {
4    public static void main(String[] args) {
5      int date = 0; // Date to be determined
6      int answer;
7
8      // Create a Scanner
9      Scanner input = new Scanner(System.in);
10
11     for (int i = 0; i < 5; i++) {
12       System.out.println("Is your birthday in Set" + (i + 1) + "?");
13       for (int j = 0; j < 4; j++) {
14         for (int k = 0; k < 4; k++)
15           System.out.print(GuessDate.getValue(i, j, k) + "  ");    invoke static method
16         System.out.println();
17       }
18
19       System.out.print("\nEnter 0 for No and 1 for Yes: ");
20       answer = input.nextInt();
21
22       if (answer == 1)
23         date += GuessDate.getValue(i, 0, 0);                       invoke static method
24     }
25
26     System.out.println("Your birthday is " + date);
27   }
28 }
```

```
Is your birthday in Set1?
1    3    5    7
9    11   13   15
17   19   21   23
25   27   29   31
Enter 0 for No and 1 for Yes: 0  ↵Enter

Is your birthday in Set2?
2    3    6    7
10   11   14   15
18   19   22   23
26   27   30   31
Enter 0 for No and 1 for Yes: 1  ↵Enter
```

```
Is your birthday in Set3?
4    5    6    7
12   13   14   15
20   21   22   23
28   29   30   31
Enter 0 for No and 1 for Yes: 0  ↵Enter

Is your birthday in Set4?
8    9    10   11
12   13   14   15
24   25   26   27
28   29   30   31
Enter 0 for No and 1 for Yes: 1  ↵Enter

Is your birthday in Set5?
16   17   18   19
20   21   22   23
24   25   26   27
28   29   30   31
Enter 0 for No and 1 for Yes: 1  ↵Enter

Your birthday is 26
```

Since `getValue` is a static method, you don't need to create an object in order to invoke it. `GuessDate.getValue(i, j, k)` (line 15) returns the date at row `j` and column `k` in Set `i`. The `GuessDate` class can be implemented as in Listing 10.10.

LISTING 10.10 GuessDate.java

```java
 1 public class GuessDate {
 2   private final static int[][][] dates = {        // static field
 3     {{ 1,  3,  5,  7},
 4      { 9, 11, 13, 15},
 5      {17, 19, 21, 23},
 6      {25, 27, 29, 31}},
 7     {{ 2,  3,  6,  7},
 8      {10, 11, 14, 15},
 9      {18, 19, 22, 23},
10      {26, 27, 30, 31}},
11     {{ 4,  5,  6,  7},
12      {12, 13, 14, 15},
13      {20, 21, 22, 23},
14      {28, 29, 30, 31}},
15     {{ 8,  9, 10, 11},
16      {12, 13, 14, 15},
17      {24, 25, 26, 27},
18      {28, 29, 30, 31}},
19     {{16, 17, 18, 19},
20      {20, 21, 22, 23},
21      {24, 25, 26, 27},
22      {28, 29, 30, 31}}};
23
24   /** Prevent the user from creating objects from GuessDate */
25   private GuessDate() {        // private constructor
26   }
27
28   /** Return a date at the specified row and column in a given set */
```

```
29    public static int getValue(int setNo, int i, int j) {
30      return dates[setNo][i][j];
31    }
32  }
```

static method

This class uses a three-dimensional array to store dates (lines 2–22). You could use a different data structure (i.e., five two-dimensional arrays for representing five sets of numbers). The implementation of the `getValue` method would change, but the program that uses `GuessDate` wouldn't need to change as long as the contract of the public method `getValue` remains unchanged. This shows the benefit of data encapsulation.

benefit of data encapsulation

The class defines a private no-arg constructor (line 25) to prevent the user from creating objects for this class. Since all methods are static in this class, there is no need to create objects from this class.

private constructor

10.12 Why is the no-arg constructor in the `Math` class defined private?

 Check Point

10.11 Class Design Guidelines

MyProgrammingLab™

Key Point

Class design guidelines are helpful for designing sound classes.

You have learned how to design classes from the preceding two examples and from many other examples in the preceding chapters. This section summarizes some of the guidelines.

10.11.1 Cohesion

A class should describe a single entity, and all the class operations should logically fit together to support a coherent purpose. You can use a class for students, for example, but you should not combine students and staff in the same class, because students and staff are different entities.

coherent purpose

A single entity with many responsibilities can be broken into several classes to separate the responsibilities. The classes `String`, `StringBuilder`, and `StringBuffer` all deal with strings, for example, but have different responsibilities. The `String` class deals with immutable strings, the `StringBuilder` class is for creating mutable strings, and the `StringBuffer` class is similar to `StringBuilder` except that `StringBuffer` contains synchronized methods for updating strings.

separating responsibilities

10.11.2 Consistency

Follow standard Java programming style and naming conventions. Choose informative names for classes, data fields, and methods. A popular style is to place the data declaration before the constructor and place constructors before methods.

naming conventions

Make the names consistent. It is not a good practice to choose different names for similar operations. For example, the `length()` method returns the size of a `String`, a `StringBuilder`, and a `StringBuffer`. It would be inconsistent if different names were used for this method in these classes.

naming consistency

In general, you should consistently provide a public no-arg constructor for constructing a default instance. If a class does not support a no-arg constructor, document the reason. If no constructors are defined explicitly, a public default no-arg constructor with an empty body is assumed.

no-arg constructor

If you want to prevent users from creating an object for a class, you can declare a private constructor in the class, as is the case for the `Math` class and the `GuessDate` class.

10.11.3 Encapsulation

A class should use the `private` modifier to hide its data from direct access by clients. This makes the class easy to maintain.

encapsulating data fields

Provide a `get` method only if you want the field to be readable, and provide a `set` method only if you want the field to be updateable. For example, the `Course` class provides a `get` method for `courseName`, but no `set` method, because the user is not allowed to change the course name once it is created.

10.11.4 Clarity

Cohesion, consistency, and encapsulation are good guidelines for achieving design clarity. Additionally, a class should have a clear contract that is easy to explain and easy to understand.

easy to explain

Users can incorporate classes in many different combinations, orders, and environments. Therefore, you should design a class that imposes no restrictions on how or when the user can use it, design the properties in a way that lets the user set them in any order and with any combination of values, and design methods that function independently of their order of occur-

independent methods

rence. For example, the `Loan` class contains the properties `loanAmount`, `numberOfYears`, and `annualInterestRate`. The values of these properties can be set in any order.

intuitive meaning

Methods should be defined intuitively without causing confusion. For example, the `substring(int beginIndex, int endIndex)` method in the `String` class is some-what confusing. The method returns a substring from `beginIndex` to `endIndex - 1`, rather than to `endIndex`. It would be more intuitive to return a substring from `beginIndex` to `endIndex`.

independent properties

You should not declare a data field that can be derived from other data fields. For example, the following `Person` class has two data fields: `birthDate` and `age`. Since `age` can be derived from `birthDate`, `age` should not be declared as a data field.

```java
public class Person {
  private java.util.Date birthDate;
  private int age;

  ...
}
```

10.11.5 Completeness

Classes are designed for use by many different customers. In order to be useful in a wide range of applications, a class should provide a variety of ways for customization through properties and methods. For example, the `String` class contains more than 40 methods that are useful for a variety of applications.

10.11.6 Instance vs. Static

A variable or method that is dependent on a specific instance of the class must be an instance variable or method. A variable that is shared by all the instances of a class should be declared static. For example, the variable `numberOfObjects` in `CircleWithPrivateDataFields` in Listing 8.9 is shared by all the objects of the `CircleWithPrivateDataFields` class and therefore is declared static. A method that is not dependent on a specific instance should be defined as a static method. For instance, the `getNumberOfObjects` method in `CircleWithPrivateDataFields` is not tied to any specific instance and therefore is defined as a static method.

Always reference static variables and methods from a class name (rather than a reference variable) to improve readability and avoid errors.

Do not pass a parameter from a constructor to initialize a static data field. It is better to use a `set` method to change the static data field. Thus, the following class in (a) is better replaced by (b).

```
public class SomeThing {
  private int t1;
  private static int t2;

  public SomeThing(int t1, int t2) {
    ...
  }
}
```

(a)

```
public class SomeThing {
  private int t1;
  private static int t2;

  public SomeThing(int t1) {
    ...
  }

  public static void setT2(int t2) {
    SomeThing.t2 = t2;
  }
}
```

(b)

Instance and static are integral parts of object-oriented programming. A data field or method is either instance or static. Do not mistakenly overlook static data fields or methods. It is a common design error to define an instance method that should have been static. For example, the `factorial(int n)` method for computing the factorial of `n` should be defined static, because it is independent of any specific instance.

common design error

A constructor is always instance, because it is used to create a specific instance. A static variable or method can be invoked from an instance method, but an instance variable or method cannot be invoked from a static method.

10.13 Describe class design guidelines.

Check Point

10.12 Processing Primitive Data Type Values as Objects

MyProgrammingLab™

A primitive type value is not an object, but it can be wrapped in an object using a wrapper class in the Java API.

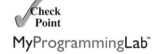
Key Point

Owing to performance considerations, primitive data type values are not objects in Java. Because of the overhead of processing objects, the language's performance would be adversely affected if primitive data type values were treated as objects. However, many Java methods require the use of objects as arguments. Java offers a convenient way to incorporate, or wrap, a primitive data type into an object (e.g., wrapping `int` into the `Integer` class, and wrapping `double` into the `Double` class). Recall that a `char` value can be wrapped into a `Character` object in Section 9.5. By using a wrapper class, you can process primitive data type values as objects. Java provides `Boolean`, `Character`, `Double`, `Float`, `Byte`, `Short`, `Integer`, and `Long` wrapper classes in the `java.lang` package for primitive data types. The `Boolean` class wraps a Boolean value `true` or `false`. This section uses `Integer` and `Double` as examples to introduce the numeric wrapper classes.

why wrapper class?

>
> **Note**
> Most wrapper class names for a primitive type are the same as the primitive data type name with the first letter capitalized. The exceptions are `Integer` and `Character`.

naming convention

Numeric wrapper classes are very similar to each other. Each contains the methods `doubleValue()`, `floatValue()`, `intValue()`, `longValue()`, `shortValue()`, and `byteValue()`. These methods "convert" objects into primitive type values. The key features of `Integer` and `Double` are shown in Figure 10.14.

You can construct a wrapper object either from a primitive data type value or from a string representing the numeric value—for example, `new Double(5.0)`, `new Double("5.0")`, `new Integer(5)`, and `new Integer("5")`.

constructors

java.lang.Integer
-value: int
+MAX_VALUE: int
+MIN_VALUE: int
+Integer(value: int)
+Integer(s: String)
+byteValue(): byte
+shortValue(): short
+intValue(): int
+longVlaue(): long
+floatValue(): float
+doubleValue(): double
+compareTo(o: Integer): int
+toString(): String
+valueOf(s: String): Integer
+valueOf(s: String, radix: int): Integer
+parseInt(s: String): int
+parseInt(s: String, radix: int): int

java.lang.Double
-value: double
+MAX_VALUE: double
+MIN_VALUE: double
+Double(value: double)
+Double(s: String)
+byteValue(): byte
+shortValue(): short
+intValue(): int
+longVlaue(): long
+floatValue(): float
+doubleValue(): double
+compareTo(o: Double): int
+toString(): String
+valueOf(s: String): Double
+valueOf(s: String, radix: int): Double
+parseDouble(s: String): double
+parseDouble(s: String, radix: int): double

FIGURE 10.14 The wrapper classes provide constructors, constants, and conversion methods for manipulating various data types.

no no-arg constructor
immutable

The wrapper classes do not have no-arg constructors. The instances of all wrapper classes are immutable; this means that, once the objects are created, their internal values cannot be changed.

constants

Each numeric wrapper class has the constants MAX_VALUE and MIN_VALUE. MAX_VALUE represents the maximum value of the corresponding primitive data type. For Byte, Short, Integer, and Long, MIN_VALUE represents the minimum byte, short, int, and long values. For Float and Double, MIN_VALUE represents the minimum *positive* float and double values. The following statements display the maximum integer (2,147,483,647), the minimum positive float (1.4E–45), and the maximum double floating-point number (1.79769313486231570c+308d).

```
System.out.println("The maximum integer is " + Integer.MAX_VALUE);
System.out.println("The minimum positive float is " +
  Float.MIN_VALUE);
System.out.println(
  "The maximum double-precision floating-point number is " +
  Double.MAX_VALUE);
```

conversion methods

Each numeric wrapper class contains the methods doubleValue(), floatValue(), intValue(), longValue(), and shortValue() for returning a double, float, int, long, or short value for the wrapper object. For example,

```
new Double("12.4").intValue() returns 12;
new Integer("12").doubleValue() returns 12.0;
```

compareTo method

Recall that the String class contains the compareTo method for comparing two strings. The numeric wrapper classes contain the compareTo method for comparing two numbers and returns 1, 0, or -1, if this number is greater than, equal to, or less than the other number. For example,

```
new Double("12.4").compareTo(new Double("12.3")) returns 1;
new Double("12.3").compareTo(new Double("12.3")) returns 0;
new Double("12.3").compareTo(new Double("12.51")) returns -1;
```

The numeric wrapper classes have a useful static method, **valueOf (String s)**. This   static valueOf methods
method creates a new object initialized to the value represented by the specified string. For
example,

```
Double doubleObject = Double.valueOf("12.4");
Integer integerObject = Integer.valueOf("12");
```

You have used the **parseInt** method in the **Integer** class to parse a numeric string into   static parsing methods
an **int** value and the **parseDouble** method in the **Double** class to parse a numeric string
into a **double** value. Each numeric wrapper class has two overloaded parsing methods to
parse a numeric string into an appropriate numeric value based on **10** (decimal) or any specified radix (e.g., **2** for binary, **8** for octal, and **16** for hexadecimal). The following examples
show how to use these methods.

```
// These two methods are in the Byte class
public static byte parseByte(String s)
public static byte parseByte(String s, int radix)

// These two methods are in the Short class
public static short parseShort(String s)
public static short parseShort(String s, int radix)

// These two methods are in the Integer class
public static int parseInt(String s)
public static int parseInt(String s, int radix)

// These two methods are in the Long class
public static long parseLong(String s)
public static long parseLong(String s, int radix)

// These two methods are in the Float class
public static float parseFloat(String s)
public static float parseFloat(String s, int radix)

// These two methods are in the Double class
public static double parseDouble(String s)
public static double parseDouble(String s, int radix)
```

For example,

```
Integer.parseInt("11", 2) returns 3;
Integer.parseInt("12", 8) returns 10;
Integer.parseInt("13", 10) returns 13;
Integer.parseInt("1A", 16) returns 26;
```

Integer.parseInt("12", 2) would raise a runtime exception because **12** is not a
binary number.

Note that you can convert a decimal number into a hex number using the **format** method.   converting decimal to hex
For example,

```
String.format("%x", 26) returns 1A;
```

10.14 Describe primitive-type wrapper classes.

10.15 Can each of the following statements be compiled?

    a. `Integer i = new Integer("23");`

    b. `Integer i = new Integer(23);`

    c. `Integer i = Integer.valueOf("23");`

    d. `Integer i = Integer.parseInt("23", 8);`

    e. `Double d = new Double();`

    f. `Double d = Double.valueOf("23.45");`

    g. `int i = (Integer.valueOf("23")).intValue();`

    h. `double d = (Double.valueOf("23.4")).doubleValue();`

    i. `int i = (Double.valueOf("23.4")).intValue();`

    j. `String s = (Double.valueOf("23.4")).toString();`

10.16 How do you convert an integer into a string? How do you convert a numeric string into an integer? How do you convert a double number into a string? How do you convert a numeric string into a double value?

10.17 Show the output of the following code.

```java
public class Test {
  public static void main(String[] args) {
    Integer x = new Integer(3);
    System.out.println(x.intValue());
    System.out.println(x.compareTo(new Integer(4)));
  }
}
```

10.18 What is the output of the following code?

```java
public class Test {
  public static void main(String[] args) {
    System.out.println(Integer.parseInt("10"));
    System.out.println(Integer.parseInt("10", 10));
    System.out.println(Integer.parseInt("10", 16));
    System.out.println(Integer.parseInt("11"));
    System.out.println(Integer.parseInt("11", 10));
    System.out.println(Integer.parseInt("11", 16));
  }
}
```

10.13 Automatic Conversion between Primitive Types and Wrapper Class Types

A primitive type value can be automatically converted to an object using a wrapper class, and vice versa, depending on the context.

boxing
unboxing

autoboxing
autounboxing

Converting a primitive value to a wrapper object is called *boxing*. The reverse conversion is called *unboxing*. Java allows primitive types and wrapper classes to be converted automatically. The compiler will automatically box a primitive value that appears in a context requiring an object, and will unbox an object that appears in a context requiring a primitive value. This is called *autoboxing* and *autounboxing*.

For instance, the following statement in (a) can be simplified as in (b) due to autoboxing.

```
Integer intObject = new Integer(2);
```
(a)

Equivalent

```
Integer intObject = 2;
```
(b)

autoboxing

Consider the following example:

```
1  Integer[] intArray = {1, 2, 3};
2  System.out.println(intArray[0] + intArray[1] + intArray[2]);
```

In line 1, the primitive values 1, 2, and 3 are automatically boxed into objects **new Integer(1)**, **new Integer(2)**, and **new Integer(3)**. In line 2, the objects **intArray[0]**, **intArray[1]**, and **intArray[2]** are automatically converted into **int** values that are added together.

10.19 What are autoboxing and autounboxing? Are the following statements correct?

a. `Integer x = 3 + new Integer(5);`

b. `Integer x = 3;`

c. `Double x = 3;`

d. `Double x = 3.0;`

e. `int x = new Integer(3);`

f. `int x = new Integer(3) + new Integer(4);`

10.20 Show the output of the following code?

```
public class Test {
  public static void main(String[] args) {
    Double x = new Double(3.5);
    System.out.println(x.intValue());
    System.out.println(x.compareTo(4.5));
  }
}
```

10.14 The **BigInteger** and **BigDecimal** Classes

The BigInteger and BigDecimal classes can be used to represent integers or decimal numbers of any size and precision.

VideoNote

Process large numbers

immutable

If you need to compute with very large integers or high-precision floating-point values, you can use the **BigInteger** and **BigDecimal** classes in the **java.math** package. Both are *immutable*. The largest integer of the **long** type is **Long.MAX_VALUE** (i.e., **9223372036854775807**). An instance of **BigInteger** can represent an integer of any size. You can use **new BigInteger(String)** and **new BigDecimal(String)** to create an instance of **BigInteger** and **BigDecimal**, use the **add**, **subtract**, **multiple**, **divide**, and **remainder** methods to perform arithmetic operations, and use the **compareTo** method to compare two big numbers. For example, the following code creates two **BigInteger** objects and multiplies them.

```
BigInteger a = new BigInteger("9223372036854775807");
BigInteger b = new BigInteger("2");
BigInteger c = a.multiply(b); // 9223372036854775807 * 2
System.out.println(c);
```

The output is **18446744073709551614**.

There is no limit to the precision of a `BigDecimal` object. The `divide` method may throw an `ArithmeticException` if the result cannot be terminated. However, you can use the overloaded `divide(BigDecimal d, int scale, int roundingMode)` method to specify a scale and a rounding mode to avoid this exception, where `scale` is the maximum number of digits after the decimal point. For example, the following code creates two `BigDecimal` objects and performs division with scale `20` and rounding mode `BigDecimal.ROUND_UP`.

```java
BigDecimal a = new BigDecimal(1.0);
BigDecimal b = new BigDecimal(3);
BigDecimal c = a.divide(b, 20, BigDecimal.ROUND_UP);
System.out.println(c);
```

The output is `0.33333333333333333334`.

Note that the factorial of an integer can be very large. Listing 10.11 gives a method that can return the factorial of any integer.

LISTING 10.11 LargeFactorial.java

```java
 1  import java.math.*;
 2
 3  public class LargeFactorial {
 4    public static void main(String[] args) {
 5      System.out.println("50! is \n" + factorial(50));
 6    }
 7
 8    public static BigInteger factorial(long n) {
 9      BigInteger result = BigInteger.ONE;
10      for (int i = 1; i <= n; i++)
11        result = result.multiply(new BigInteger(i + ""));
12
13      return result;
14    }
15  }
```

constant (line 9)

multiply (line 11)

```
50! is
30414093201713378043612608166064768844377641568960512000000000000
```

`BigInteger.ONE` (line 9) is a constant defined in the `BigInteger` class. `BigInteger.ONE` is the same as `new BigInteger("1")`.

A new result is obtained by invoking the `multiply` method (line 11).

10.21 What is the output of the following code?

```java
public class Test {
  public static void main(String[] args) {
    java.math.BigInteger x = new java.math.BigInteger("3");
    java.math.BigInteger y = new java.math.BigInteger("7");
    x.add(y);
    System.out.println(x);
  }
}
```

KEY TERMS

abstract data type (ADT)   375
aggregation   382
boxing   396
class abstraction   375
class encapsulation   375
class's contract   375
class's variable   371
composition   382

has-a relationship   382
immutable class   370
immutable object   370
multiplicity   382
stack   386
`this` keyword   373
unboxing   396

CHAPTER SUMMARY

1. Once it is created, an *immutable object* cannot be modified. To prevent users from modifying an object, you can define *immutable classes*.

2. The scope of instance and static variables is the entire class, regardless of where the variables are declared. Instance and static variables can be declared anywhere in the class. For consistency, they are declared at the beginning of the class in this book.

3. The keyword `this` can be used to refer to the calling object. It can also be used inside a constructor to invoke another constructor of the same class.

4. The procedural paradigm focuses on designing methods. The object-oriented paradigm couples data and methods together into objects. Software design using the object-oriented paradigm focuses on objects and operations on objects. The object-oriented approach combines the power of the procedural paradigm with an added dimension that integrates data with operations into objects.

5. Many Java methods require the use of objects as arguments. Java offers a convenient way to incorporate, or wrap, a primitive data type into an object (e.g., wrapping `int` into the `Integer` class, and wrapping `double` into the `Double` class).

6. Java can automatically convert a primitive type value to its corresponding wrapper object in the context and vice versa.

7. The `BigInteger` class is useful for computing and processing integers of any size. The `BigDecimal` class can be used to compute and process floating-point numbers with any arbitrary precision.

TEST QUESTIONS

Do the test questions for this chapter online at www.cs.armstrong.edu/liang/intro9e/test.html.

PROGRAMMING EXERCISES

Sections 10.2–10.6

*10.1 (*The Time class*) Design a class named `Time`. The class contains:

- The data fields `hour`, `minute`, and `second` that represent a time.
- A no-arg constructor that creates a `Time` object for the current time. (The values of the data fields will represent the current time.)

■ A constructor that constructs a `Time` object with a specified elapsed time since midnight, January 1, 1970, in milliseconds. (The values of the data fields will represent this time.)

■ A constructor that constructs a `Time` object with the specified hour, minute, and second.

■ Three `get` methods for the data fields `hour`, `minute`, and `second`, respectively.

■ A method named `setTime(long elapseTime)` that sets a new time for the object using the elapsed time. For example, if the elapsed time is `555550000` milliseconds, the hour is `10`, the minute is `19`, and the second is `10`.

Draw the UML diagram for the class and then implement the class. Write a test program that creates two `Time` objects (using `new Time()` and `new Time(555550000)`) and displays their hour, minute, and second in the format hour:minute:second.

(*Hint*: The first two constructors will extract the hour, minute, and second from the elapsed time. For the no-arg constructor, the current time can be obtained using `System.currentTimeMillis()`, as shown in Listing 2.6, ShowCurrentTime.java.)

10.2 (*The* `BMI` *class*) Add the following new constructor in the `BMI` class:

```
/** Construct a BMI with the specified name, age, weight,
 * feet, and inches
 */
public BMI(String name, int age, double weight, double feet,
    double inches)
```

10.3 (*The* `MyInteger` *class*) Design a class named `MyInteger`. The class contains:

■ An `int` data field named `value` that stores the `int` value represented by this object.

■ A constructor that creates a `MyInteger` object for the specified `int` value.

■ A `get` method that returns the `int` value.

■ The methods `isEven()`, `isOdd()`, and `isPrime()` that return `true` if the value in this object is even, odd, or prime, respectively.

■ The static methods `isEven(int)`, `isOdd(int)`, and `isPrime(int)` that return `true` if the specified value is even, odd, or prime, respectively.

■ The static methods `isEven(MyInteger)`, `isOdd(MyInteger)`, and `isPrime(MyInteger)` that return `true` if the specified value is even, odd, or prime, respectively.

■ The methods `equals(int)` and `equals(MyInteger)` that return `true` if the value in this object is equal to the specified value.

■ A static method `parseInt(char[])` that converts an array of numeric characters to an `int` value.

■ A static method `parseInt(String)` that converts a string into an `int` value.

Draw the UML diagram for the class and then implement the class. Write a client program that tests all methods in the class.

10.4 (*The* `MyPoint` *class*) Design a class named `MyPoint` to represent a point with x- and y-coordinates. The class contains:

■ The data fields `x` and `y` that represent the coordinates with `get` methods.

■ A no-arg constructor that creates a point (`0`, `0`).

■ A constructor that constructs a point with specified coordinates.

■ Two `get` methods for the data fields `x` and `y`, respectively.

VideoNote

The `MyPoint` class

■ A method named `distance` that returns the distance from this point to another point of the `MyPoint` type.

■ A method named `distance` that returns the distance from this point to another point with specified x- and y-coordinates.

Draw the UML diagram for the class and then implement the class. Write a test program that creates the two points (0, 0) and (10, 30.5) and displays the distance between them.

Sections 10.7–10.11

*10.5 (*Displaying the prime factors*) Write a program that prompts the user to enter a positive integer and displays all its smallest factors in decreasing order. For example, if the integer is 120, the smallest factors are displayed as 5, 3, 2, 2, 2. Use the `StackOfIntegers` class to store the factors (e.g., 2, 2, 2, 3, 5) and retrieve and display them in reverse order.

*10.6 (*Displaying the prime numbers*) Write a program that displays all the prime numbers less than 120 in decreasing order. Use the `StackOfIntegers` class to store the prime numbers (e.g., 2, 3, 5, . . .) and retrieve and display them in reverse order.

**10.7 (*Game: ATM machine*) Use the `Account` class created in Programming Exercise 8.7 to simulate an ATM machine. Create ten accounts in an array with id 0, 1, . . . , 9, and initial balance $100. The system prompts the user to enter an id. If the id is entered incorrectly, ask the user to enter a correct id. Once an id is accepted, the main menu is displayed as shown in the sample run. You can enter a choice 1 for viewing the current balance, 2 for withdrawing money, 3 for depositing money, and 4 for exiting the main menu. Once you exit, the system will prompt for an id again. Thus, once the system starts, it will not stop.

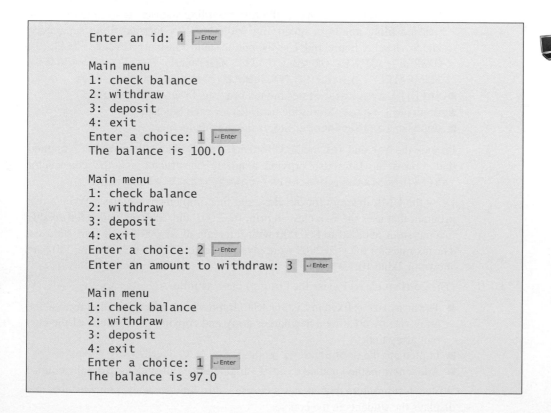

```
Enter an id: 4  ↵Enter

Main menu
1: check balance
2: withdraw
3: deposit
4: exit
Enter a choice: 1  ↵Enter
The balance is 100.0

Main menu
1: check balance
2: withdraw
3: deposit
4: exit
Enter a choice: 2  ↵Enter
Enter an amount to withdraw: 3  ↵Enter

Main menu
1: check balance
2: withdraw
3: deposit
4: exit
Enter a choice: 1  ↵Enter
The balance is 97.0
```

```
                    Main menu
                    1: check balance
                    2: withdraw
                    3: deposit
                    4: exit
                    Enter a choice: 3  ↵Enter
                    Enter an amount to deposit: 10  ↵Enter

                    Main menu
                    1: check balance
                    2: withdraw
                    3: deposit
                    4: exit
                    Enter a choice: 1  ↵Enter
                    The balance is 107.0

                    Main menu
                    1: check balance
                    2: withdraw
                    3: deposit
                    4: exit
                    Enter a choice: 4  ↵Enter

                    Enter an id:
```

***10.8 (*Financial: the* Tax *class*) Programming Exercise 7.12 writes a program for computing taxes using arrays. Design a class named Tax to contain the following instance data fields:

- int filingStatus: One of the four tax-filing statuses: 0—single filer, 1—married filing jointly or qualifying widow(er), 2—married filing separately, and 3—head of household. Use the public static constants SINGLE_FILER (0), MARRIED_JOINTLY_OR_QUALIFYING_WIDOW(ER) (1), MARRIED_SEPARATELY (2), HEAD_OF_HOUSEHOLD (3) to represent the statuses.
- int[][] brackets: Stores the tax brackets for each filing status.
- double[] rates: Stores the tax rates for each bracket.
- double taxableIncome: Stores the taxable income.

Provide the get and set methods for each data field and the getTax() method that returns the tax. Also provide a no-arg constructor and the constructor Tax(filingStatus, brackets, rates, taxableIncome).

Draw the UML diagram for the class and then implement the class. Write a test program that uses the Tax class to print the 2001 and 2009 tax tables for taxable income from $50,000 to $60,000 with intervals of $1,000 for all four statuses. The tax rates for the year 2009 were given in Table 3.2. The tax rates for 2001 are shown in Table 10.1.

**10.9 (*The* Course *class*) Revise the Course class as follows:

- The array size is fixed in Listing 10.6. Improve it to automatically increase the array size by creating a new larger array and copying the contents of the current array to it.
- Implement the dropStudent method.
- Add a new method named clear() that removes all students from the course.

Write a test program that creates a course, adds three students, removes one, and displays the students in the course.

TABLE 10.1   2001 United States Federal Personal Tax Rates

Tax rate	Single filers	Married filing jointly or qualifying widow(er)	Married filing separately	Head of household
15%	Up to $27,050	Up to $45,200	Up to $22,600	Up to $36,250
27.5%	$27,051–$65,550	$45,201–$109,250	$22,601–$54,625	$36,251–$93,650
30.5%	$65,551–$136,750	$109,251–$166,500	$54,626–$83,250	$93,651–$151,650
35.5%	$136,751–$297,350	$166,501–$297,350	$83,251–$148,675	$151,651–$297,350
39.1%	$297,351 or more	$297,351 or more	$ 148,676 or more	$297,351 or more

*10.10   (*Game: The* `GuessDate` *class*) Modify the `GuessDate` class in Listing 10.10. Instead of representing dates in a three-dimensional array, use five two-dimensional arrays to represent the five sets of numbers. Thus, you need to declare:

```
private static int[][] set1 = {{1,  3,  5,  7}, ... };
private static int[][] set2 = {{2,  3,  6,  7}, ... };
private static int[][] set3 = {{4,  5,  6,  7}, ... };
private static int[][] set4 = {{8,  9, 10, 11}, ... };
private static int[][] set5 = {{16, 17, 18, 19}, ... };
```

*10.11   (*Geometry: The* `Circle2D` *class*) Define the `Circle2D` class that contains:

- Two `double` data fields named `x` and `y` that specify the center of the circle with `get` methods.
- A data field `radius` with a `get` method.
- A no-arg constructor that creates a default circle with (0, 0) for (x, y) and 1 for `radius`.
- A constructor that creates a circle with the specified `x`, `y`, and `radius`.
- A method `getArea()` that returns the area of the circle.
- A method `getPerimeter()` that returns the perimeter of the circle.
- A method `contains(double x, double y)` that returns `true` if the specified point (x, y) is inside this circle (see Figure 10.15a).
- A method `contains(Circle2D circle)` that returns `true` if the specified circle is inside this circle (see Figure 10.15b).
- A method `overlaps(Circle2D circle)` that returns `true` if the specified circle overlaps with this circle (see Figure 10.15c).

(a)   (b)   (c)

FIGURE 10.15   (a) A point is inside the circle. (b) A circle is inside another circle. (c) A circle overlaps another circle.

Draw the UML diagram for the class and then implement the class. Write a test program that creates a `Circle2D` object `c1 (new Circle2D(2, 2, 5.5))`, displays its area and perimeter, and displays the result of `c1.contains(3, 3)`, `c1.contains(new Circle2D(4, 5, 10.5))`, and `c1.overlaps(new Circle2D(3, 5, 2.3))`.

***10.12 (*Geometry: The* `Triangle2D` *class*) Define the `Triangle2D` class that contains:

- Three points named `p1`, `p2`, and `p3` of the type `MyPoint` with `get` and `set` methods. `MyPoint` is defined in Exercise 10.4.
- A no-arg constructor that creates a default triangle with the points (0, 0), (1, 1), and (2, 5).
- A constructor that creates a triangle with the specified points.
- A method `getArea()` that returns the area of the triangle.
- A method `getPerimeter()` that returns the perimeter of the triangle.
- A method `contains(MyPoint p)` that returns `true` if the specified point `p` is inside this triangle (see Figure 10.16a).
- A method `contains(Triangle2D t)` that returns `true` if the specified triangle is inside this triangle (see Figure 10.16b).
- A method `overlaps(Triangle2D t)` that returns `true` if the specified triangle overlaps with this triangle (see Figure 10.16c).

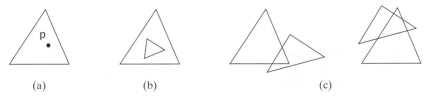

(a)   (b)   (c)

FIGURE 10.16 (a) A point is inside the triangle. (b) A triangle is inside another triangle. (c) A triangle overlaps another triangle.

Draw the UML diagram for the class and then implement the class. Write a test program that creates a `Triangle2D` objects `t1` using the constructor `new Triangle2D(new MyPoint(2.5, 2), new MyPoint(4.2, 3), new MyPoint(5, 3.5))`, displays its area and perimeter, and displays the result of `t1.contains(3, 3)`, `r1.contains(new Triangle2D(new MyPoint(2.9, 2), new MyPoint(4, 1), MyPoint(1, 3.4)))`, and `t1.overlaps(new Triangle2D(new MyPoint(2, 5.5), new MyPoint(4, -3), MyPoint(2, 6.5)))`.

(*Hint*: For the formula to compute the area of a triangle, see Programming Exercise 2.15. Use the `java.awt.geo.Line2D` class in the Java API to implement the `contains` and `overlaps` methods. The `Line2D` class contains the methods for checking whether two line segments intersect and whether a line contains a point, and so on. Please see the Java API for more information on `Line2D`. To detect whether a point is inside a triangle, draw three dashed lines, as shown in Figure 10.17. If the point is inside a triangle, each dashed line should intersect a side only once. If a dashed line intersects a side twice, then the point must be outside the triangle.)

(a)   (b)

FIGURE 10.17 (a) A point is inside the triangle. (b) A point is outside the triangle.

*10.13 (*Geometry: the* `MyRectangle2D` *class*) Define the `MyRectangle2D` class that contains:

- Two **double** data fields named x and y that specify the center of the rectangle with **get** and **set** methods. (Assume that the rectangle sides are parallel to x- or y- axes.)
- The data fields `width` and `height` with **get** and **set** methods.
- A no-arg constructor that creates a default rectangle with (0, 0) for (x, y) and 1 for both `width` and `height`.
- A constructor that creates a rectangle with the specified x, y, `width`, and `height`.
- A method `getArea()` that returns the area of the rectangle.
- A method `getPerimeter()` that returns the perimeter of the rectangle.
- A method `contains(double x, double y)` that returns **true** if the specified point (x, y) is inside this rectangle (see Figure 10.18a).
- A method `contains(MyRectangle2D r)` that returns **true** if the specified rectangle is inside this rectangle (see Figure 10.18b).
- A method `overlaps(MyRectangle2D r)` that returns **true** if the specified rectangle overlaps with this rectangle (see Figure 10.18c).

     (a)   (b)   (c)   (d)

FIGURE 10.18 A point is inside the rectangle. (b) A rectangle is inside another rectangle. (c) A rectangle overlaps another rectangle. (d) Points are enclosed inside a rectangle.

Draw the UML diagram for the class and then implement the class. Write a test program that creates a `MyRectangle2D` object r1 (**new MyRectangle2D(2, 2, 5.5, 4.9)**), displays its area and perimeter, and displays the result of `r1.contains(3, 3)`, `r1.contains(new MyRectangle2D(4, 5, 10.5, 3.2))`, and `r1.overlaps(new MyRectangle2D(3, 5, 2.3, 5.4))`.

*10.14 (*The* `MyDate` *class*) Design a class named `MyDate`. The class contains:

- The data fields `year`, `month`, and `day` that represent a date. `month` is 0-based, i.e., 0 is for January.
- A no-arg constructor that creates a `MyDate` object for the current date.
- A constructor that constructs a `MyDate` object with a specified elapsed time since midnight, January 1, 1970, in milliseconds.
- A constructor that constructs a `MyDate` object with the specified year, month, and day.
- Three **get** methods for the data fields `year`, `month`, and `day`, respectively.
- A method named `setDate(long elapsedTime)` that sets a new date for the object using the elapsed time.

Draw the UML diagram for the class and then implement the class. Write a test program that creates two `MyDate` objects (using **new MyDate()** and **new MyDate(34355555133101L)**) and displays their year, month, and day.

(*Hint*: The first two constructors will extract the year, month, and day from the elapsed time. For example, if the elapsed time is **561555550000** milliseconds, the year is

1987, the month is **9**, and the day is **18**. You may use the `GregorianCalendar` class discussed in Programming Exercise 8.5 to simplify coding.)

*10.15 (*Geometry: finding the bounding rectangle*) A bounding rectangle is the minimum rectangle that encloses a set of points in a two-dimensional plane, as shown in Figure 10.18d. Write a method that returns a bounding rectangle for a set of points in a two-dimensional plane, as follows:

public static MyRectangle2D getRectangle(**double**[][] points)

The `Rectangle2D` class is defined in Exercise 10.13. Write a test program that prompts the user to enter five points and displays the bounding rectangle's center, width, and height. Here is a sample run:

```
Enter five points: 1.0 2.5 3 4 5 6 7 8 9 10  ↵Enter
The bounding rectangle's center (5.0, 6.25), width 8.0, height 7.5
```

Sections 10.12–10.14

*10.16 (*Divisible by* **2** *or* **3**) Find the first ten numbers with **50** decimal digits that are divisible by **2** or **3**.

*10.17 (*Square numbers*) Find the first ten square numbers that are greater than `Long.MAX_VALUE`. A square number is a number in the form of n^2.

*10.18 (*Large prime numbers*) Write a program that finds five prime numbers larger than `Long.MAX_VALUE`.

*10.19 (*Mersenne prime*) A prime number is called a *Mersenne prime* if it can be written in the form $2^p - 1$ for some positive integer p. Write a program that finds all Mersenne primes with $p \leq 100$ and displays the output as shown below. (*Hint:* You have to use `BigInteger` to store the number, because it is too big to be stored in `long`. Your program may take several hours to run.)

```
p           2^p - 1

2           3
3           7
5           31
...
```

*10.20 (*Approximate e*) Programming Exercise 4.26 approximates *e* using the following series:

$$e = 1 + \frac{1}{1!} + \frac{1}{2!} + \frac{1}{3!} + \frac{1}{4!} + \ldots + \frac{1}{i!}$$

In order to get better precision, use `BigDecimal` with **25** digits of precision in the computation. Write a program that displays the **e** value for $i = $ **100, 200,** . . . , and **1000**.

10.21 (*Divisible by* **5** *or* **6**) Find the first ten numbers (greater than `Long.MAX_VALUE`) that are divisible by **5** or **6**.

INHERITANCE AND POLYMORPHISM

Objectives

- To define a subclass from a superclass through inheritance (§11.2).
- To invoke the superclass's constructors and methods using the `super` keyword (§11.3).
- To override instance methods in the subclass (§11.4).
- To distinguish differences between overriding and overloading (§11.5).
- To explore the `toString()` method in the `Object` class (§11.6).
- To discover polymorphism and dynamic binding (§§11.7–11.8).
- To describe casting and explain why explicit downcasting is necessary (§11.9).
- To explore the `equals` method in the `Object` class (§11.10).
- To store, retrieve, and manipulate objects in an `ArrayList` (§11.11).
- To implement a `Stack` class using `ArrayList` (§11.12).
- To enable data and methods in a superclass accessible from subclasses using the `protected` visibility modifier (§11.13).
- To prevent class extending and method overriding using the `final` modifier (§11.14).

11.1 Introduction

Object-oriented programming allows you to define new classes from existing classes. This is called inheritance.

inheritance

As discussed earlier in the book, the procedural paradigm focuses on designing methods and the object-oriented paradigm couples data and methods together into objects. Software design using the object-oriented paradigm focuses on objects and operations on objects. The object-oriented approach combines the power of the procedural paradigm with an added dimension that integrates data with operations into objects.

why inheritance?

Inheritance is an important and powerful feature for reusing software. Suppose you need to define classes to model circles, rectangles, and triangles. These classes have many common features. What is the best way to design these classes so as to avoid redundancy and make the system easy to comprehend and easy to maintain? The answer is to use inheritance.

11.2 Superclasses and Subclasses

Inheritance enables you to define a general class (e.g., a superclass) and later extend it to more specialized classes (e.g., subclasses).

You use a class to model objects of the same type. Different classes may have some common properties and behaviors, which can be generalized in a class that can be shared by other classes. You can define a specialized class that extends the generalized class. The specialized classes inherit the properties and methods from the general class.

VideoNote

Geometric class hierarchy

Consider geometric objects. Suppose you want to design the classes to model geometric objects such as circles and rectangles. Geometric objects have many common properties and behaviors. They can be drawn in a certain color and be filled or unfilled. Thus a general class `GeometricObject` can be used to model all geometric objects. This class contains the properties `color` and `filled` and their appropriate `get` and `set` methods. Assume that this class also contains the `dateCreated` property and the `getDateCreated()` and `toString()` methods. The `toString()` method returns a string representation of the object. Since a circle is a special type of geometric object, it shares common properties and methods with other geometric objects. Thus it makes sense to define the `Circle` class that extends the `GeometricObject` class. Likewise, `Rectangle` can also be defined as a subclass of `GeometricObject`. Figure 11.1 shows the relationship among these classes. A triangular arrow pointing to the superclass is used to denote the inheritance relationship between the two classes involved.

subclass
superclass

In Java terminology, a class `C1` extended from another class `C2` is called a *subclass*, and `C2` is called a *superclass*. A superclass is also referred to as a *parent class* or a *base class*, and a subclass as a *child class*, an *extended class*, or a *derived class*. A subclass inherits accessible data fields and methods from its superclass and may also add new data fields and methods.

The `Circle` class inherits all accessible data fields and methods from the `GeometricObject` class. In addition, it has a new data field, `radius`, and its associated `get` and `set` methods. The `Circle` class also contains the `getArea()`, `getPerimeter()`, and `getDiameter()` methods for returning the area, perimeter, and diameter of the circle.

The `Rectangle` class inherits all accessible data fields and methods from the `GeometricObject` class. In addition, it has the data fields `width` and `height` and their associated `get` and `set` methods. It also contains the `getArea()` and `getPerimeter()` methods for returning the area and perimeter of the rectangle.

The `GeometricObject`, `Circle`, and `Rectangle` classes are shown in Listings 11.1, 11.2, and 11.3.

avoid naming conflicts

Note

To avoid a naming conflict with the improved `GeometricObject`, `Circle`, and `Rectangle` classes introduced in Chapter 15, we'll name these classes

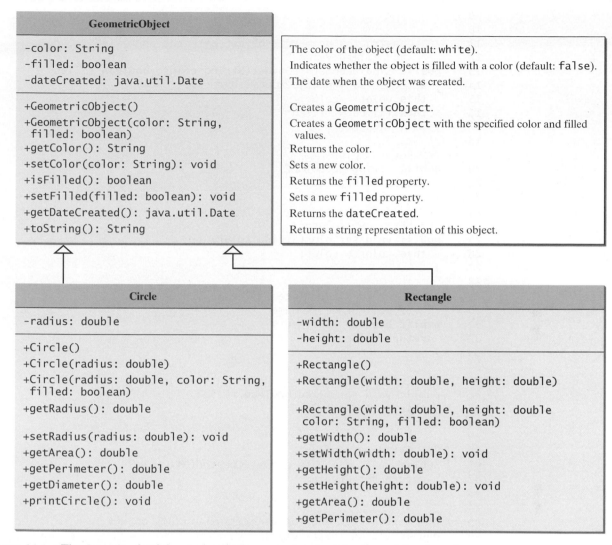

FIGURE 11.1 The **GeometricObject** class is the superclass for **Circle** and **Rectangle**.

SimpleGeometricObject, **CircleFromSimpleGeometricObject**, and **RectangleFromSimpleGeometricObject** in this chapter. For simplicity, we will still refer to them in the text as **GeometricObject**, **Circle**, and **Rectangle** classes. The best way to avoid naming conflicts is to place these classes in different packages. However, for simplicity and consistency, all classes in this book are placed in the default package.

Listing 11.1 SimpleGeometricObject.java

```
1  public class SimpleGeometricObject {
2    private String color = "white";
3    private boolean filled;
4    private java.util.Date dateCreated;
5
6    /** Construct a default geometric object */
7    public SimpleGeometricObject() {
8      dateCreated = new java.util.Date();
```

data fields

constructor
date constructed

```
 9    }
10
11    /** Construct a geometric object with the specified color
12     *   and filled value */
13    public SimpleGeometricObject(String color, boolean filled) {
14      dateCreated = new java.util.Date();
15      this.color = color;
16      this.filled = filled;
17    }
18
19    /** Return color */
20    public String getColor() {
21      return color;
22    }
23
24    /** Set a new color */
25    public void setColor(String color) {
26      this.color = color;
27    }
28
29    /** Return filled. Since filled is boolean,
30       its get method is named isFilled */
31    public boolean isFilled() {
32      return filled;
33    }
34
35    /** Set a new filled */
36    public void setFilled(boolean filled) {
37      this.filled = filled;
38    }
39
40    /** Get dateCreated */
41    public java.util.Date getDateCreated() {
42      return dateCreated;
43    }
44
45    /** Return a string representation of this object */
46    public String toString() {
47      return "created on " + dateCreated + "\ncolor: " + color +
48        " and filled: " | filled;
49    }
50  }
```

LISTING 11.2 CircleFromSimpleGeometricObject.java

extends superclass
data fields

constructor

```
 1  public class CircleFromSimpleGeometricObject
 2      extends SimpleGeometricObject  {
 3    private double radius;
 4
 5    public CircleFromSimpleGeometricObject() {
 6    }
 7
 8    public CircleFromSimpleGeometricObject(double radius) {
 9      this.radius = radius;
10    }
11
12    public CircleFromSimpleGeometricObject(double radius,
13        String color, boolean filled) {
14      this.radius = radius;
15      setColor(color);
```

```
16        setFilled(filled);
17      }
18
19      /** Return radius */
20      public double getRadius() {
21        return radius;
22      }
23
24      /** Set a new radius */
25      public void setRadius(double radius) {
26        this.radius = radius;
27      }
28
29      /** Return area */
30      public double getArea() {
31        return radius * radius * Math.PI;
32      }
33
34      /** Return diameter */
35      public double getDiameter() {
36        return 2 * radius;
37      }
38
39      /** Return perimeter */
40      public double getPerimeter() {
41        return 2 * radius * Math.PI;
42      }
43
44      /** Print the circle info */
45      public void printCircle() {
46        System.out.println("The circle is created " + getDateCreated() +
47          " and the radius is " + radius);
48      }
49    }
```

methods

The `Circle` class (Listing 11.2) extends the `GeometricObject` class (Listing 11.1) using the following syntax:

Subclass   Superclass

public class Circle **extends** GeometricObject

The keyword **extends** (lines 1–2) tells the compiler that the `Circle` class extends the `GeometricObject` class, thus inheriting the methods `getColor`, `setColor`, `isFilled`, `setFilled`, and `toString`.

The overloaded constructor `Circle(double radius, String color, boolean filled)` is implemented by invoking the `setColor` and `setFilled` methods to set the `color` and `filled` properties (lines 12–17). These two public methods are defined in the base class `GeometricObject` and are inherited in `Circle`, so they can be used in the derived class.

You might attempt to use the data fields `color` and `filled` directly in the constructor as follows:

private member in base class

```
public CircleFromSimpleGeometricObject(
    double radius, String color, boolean filled) {
```

```
      this.radius = radius;
      this.color = color; // Illegal
      this.filled = filled; // Illegal
   }
```

This is wrong, because the private data fields **color** and **filled** in the **GeometricObject** class cannot be accessed in any class other than in the **GeometricObject** class itself. The only way to read and modify **color** and **filled** is through their **get** and **set** methods.

The **Rectangle** class (Listing 11.3) extends the **GeometricObject** class (Listing 11.1) using the following syntax:

The keyword **extends** (lines 1–2) tells the compiler that the **Rectangle** class extends the **GeometricObject** class, thus inheriting the methods **getColor**, **setColor**, **isFilled**, **setFilled**, and **toString**.

LISTING 11.3 RectangleFromSimpleGeometricObject.java

```
 1  public class RectangleFromSimpleGeometricObject
 2      extends SimpleGeometricObject {
 3    private double width;
 4    private double height;
 5
 6    public RectangleFromSimpleGeometricObject() {
 7    }
 8
 9    public RectangleFromSimpleGeometricObject(
10        double width, double height) {
11      this.width = width;
12      this.height = height;
13    }
14
15    public RectangleFromSimpleGeometricObject(
16        double width, double height, String color, boolean filled) {
17      this.width = width;
18      this.height = height;
19      setColor(color);
20      setFilled(filled);
21    }
22
23    /** Return width */
24    public double getWidth() {
25      return width;
26    }
27
28    /** Set a new width */
29    public void setWidth(double width) {
30      this.width = width;
31    }
32
```

extends superclass
data fields

constructor

methods

```
33    /** Return height */
34    public double getHeight() {
35      return height;
36    }
37
38    /** Set a new height */
39    public void setHeight(double height) {
40      this.height = height;
41    }
42
43    /** Return area */
44    public double getArea() {
45      return width * height;
46    }
47
48    /** Return perimeter */
49    public double getPerimeter() {
50      return 2 * (width + height);
51    }
52 }
```

The code in Listing 11.4 creates objects of `Circle` and `Rectangle` and invokes the methods on these objects. The `toString()` method is inherited from the `GeometricObject` class and is invoked from a `Circle` object (line 5) and a `Rectangle` object (line 13).

LISTING 11.4 TestCircleRectangle.java

```
1  public class TestCircleRectangle {
2    public static void main(String[] args) {
3      CircleFromSimpleGeometricObject circle =
4        new CircleFromSimpleGeometricObject(1);              Circle object
5      System.out.println("A circle " + circle.toString());   invoke toString
6      System.out.println("The color is " + circle.getColor());  invoke getColor
7      System.out.println("The radius is " + circle.getRadius());
8      System.out.println("The area is " + circle.getArea());
9      System.out.println("The diameter is " + circle.getDiameter());
10
11     RectangleFromSimpleGeometricObject rectangle =
12       new RectangleFromSimpleGeometricObject(2, 4);         Rectangle object
13     System.out.println("\nA rectangle " + rectangle.toString());  invoke toString
14     System.out.println("The area is " + rectangle.getArea());
15     System.out.println("The perimeter is " +
16       rectangle.getPerimeter());
17   }
18 }
```

```
A circle created on Thu Feb 10 19:54:25 EST 2011
color: white and filled: false
The color is white
The radius is 1.0
The area is 3.141592653589793
The diameter is 2.0
A rectangle created on Thu Feb 10 19:54:25 EST 2011
color: white and filled: false
The area is 8.0
The perimeter is 12.0
```

Note the following points regarding inheritance:

more in subclass

- Contrary to the conventional interpretation, a subclass is not a subset of its superclass. In fact, a subclass usually contains more information and methods than its superclass.

private data fields

- Private data fields in a superclass are not accessible outside the class. Therefore, they cannot be used directly in a subclass. They can, however, be accessed/mutated through public accessors/mutators if defined in the superclass.

nonextensible is-a

- Not all is-a relationships should be modeled using inheritance. For example, a square is a rectangle, but you should not extend a `Square` class from a `Rectangle` class, because the `width` and `height` properties are not appropriate for a square. Instead, you should define a `Square` class to extend the `GeometricObject` class and define the `side` property for the side of a square.

no blind extension

- Inheritance is used to model the is-a relationship. Do not blindly extend a class just for the sake of reusing methods. For example, it makes no sense for a `Tree` class to extend a `Person` class, even though they share common properties such as height and weight. A subclass and its superclass must have the is-a relationship.

multiple inheritance

single inheritance

- Some programming languages allow you to derive a subclass from several classes. This capability is known as *multiple inheritance*. Java, however, does not allow multiple inheritance. A Java class may inherit directly from only one superclass. This restriction is known as *single inheritance*. If you use the `extends` keyword to define a subclass, it allows only one parent class. Nevertheless, multiple inheritance can be achieved through interfaces, which will be introduced in Section 15.4.

Check
Point

MyProgrammingLab™

11.1 True or false? A subclass is a subset of a superclass.

11.2 What keyword do you use to define a subclass?

11.3 What is single inheritance? What is multiple inheritance? Does Java support multiple inheritance?

11.3 Using the **super** Keyword

Key
Point

The keyword **super** *refers to the superclass and can be used to invoke the superclass's methods and constructors.*

A subclass inherits accessible data fields and methods from its superclass. Does it inherit constructors? Can the superclass's constructors be invoked from a subclass? This section addresses these questions and their ramifications.

Section 10.4, The `this` Reference, introduced the use of the keyword `this` to reference the calling object. The keyword `super` refers to the superclass of the class in which `super` appears. It can be used in two ways:

- To call a superclass constructor.
- To call a superclass method.

11.3.1 Calling Superclass Constructors

A constructor is used to construct an instance of a class. Unlike properties and methods, the constructors of a superclass are not inherited by a subclass. They can only be invoked from the constructors of the subclasses using the keyword `super`.

The syntax to call a superclass's constructor is:

super(), or **super**(parameters);

The statement **super**() invokes the no-arg constructor of its superclass, and the statement **super(arguments)** invokes the superclass constructor that matches the **arguments**. The statement **super**() or **super(arguments)** must appear in the first line of the subclass's constructor; this is the only way to explicitly invoke a superclass constructor. For example, the constructor in lines 12–17 in Listing 11.2 can be replaced by the following code:

```
public CircleFromSimpleGeometricObject(
    double radius, String color, boolean filled) {
  super(color, filled);
  this.radius = radius;
}
```

 Caution
You must use the keyword **super** to call the superclass constructor, and the call must be the first statement in the constructor. Invoking a superclass constructor's name in a subclass causes a syntax error.

11.3.2   Constructor Chaining

A constructor may invoke an overloaded constructor or its superclass constructor. If neither is invoked explicitly, the compiler automatically puts **super**() as the first statement in the constructor. For example:

```
public ClassName() {
  // some statements
}
```
Equivalent
```
public ClassName() {
  super();
  // some statements
}
```

```
public ClassName(double d) {
  // some statements
}
```
Equivalent
```
public ClassName(double d) {
  super();
  // some statements
}
```

In any case, constructing an instance of a class invokes the constructors of all the superclasses along the inheritance chain. When constructing an object of a subclass, the subclass constructor first invokes its superclass constructor before performing its own tasks. If the superclass is derived from another class, the superclass constructor invokes its parent-class constructor before performing its own tasks. This process continues until the last constructor along the inheritance hierarchy is called. This is called *constructor chaining*.

constructor chaining

Consider the following code:

```
1  public class Faculty extends Employee {
2    public static void main(String[] args) {
3      new Faculty();
4    }
5
6    public Faculty() {
```

```
 7        System.out.println("(4) Performs Faculty's tasks");
 8      }
 9    }
10
11    class Employee extends Person {
12      public Employee() {
13        this("(2) Invoke Employee's overloaded constructor");
14        System.out.println("(3) Performs Employee's tasks ");
15      }
16
17      public Employee(String s) {
18        System.out.println(s);
19      }
20    }
21
22    class Person {
23      public Person() {
24        System.out.println("(1) Performs Person's tasks");
25      }
26    }
```

invoke overloaded
constructor

```
(1) Performs Person's tasks
(2) Invoke Employee's overloaded constructor
(3) Performs Employee's tasks
(4) Performs Faculty's tasks
```

The program produces the preceding output. Why? Let us discuss the reason. In line 3, **new Faculty()** invokes **Faculty**'s no-arg constructor. Since **Faculty** is a subclass of **Employee**, **Employee**'s no-arg constructor is invoked before any statements in **Faculty**'s constructor are executed. **Employee**'s no-arg constructor invokes **Employee**'s second constructor (line 12). Since **Employee** is a subclass of **Person**, **Person**'s no-arg constructor is invoked before any statements in **Employee**'s second constructor are executed. This process is illustrated in the following figure.

Caution

no-arg constructor

If a class is designed to be extended, it is better to provide a no-arg constructor to avoid programming errors. Consider the following code:

```
1    public class Apple extends Fruit {
2    }
3
4    class Fruit {
5      public Fruit(String name) {
6        System.out.println("Fruit's constructor is invoked");
7      }
8    }
```

Since no constructor is explicitly defined in `Apple`, `Apple`'s default no-arg constructor is defined implicitly. Since `Apple` is a subclass of `Fruit`, `Apple`'s default constructor automatically invokes `Fruit`'s no-arg constructor. However, `Fruit` does not have a no-arg constructor, because `Fruit` has an explicit constructor defined. Therefore, the program cannot be compiled.

Design Guide

If possible, you should provide a no-arg constructor for every class to make the class easy to extend and to avoid errors.

no-arg constructor

11.3.3   Calling Superclass Methods

The keyword **super** can also be used to reference a method other than the constructor in the superclass. The syntax is:

```
super.method(parameters);
```

You could rewrite the `printCircle()` method in the `Circle` class as follows:

```
public void printCircle() {
  System.out.println("The circle is created " +
    super.getDateCreated() + " and the radius is " + radius);
}
```

It is not necessary to put **super** before `getDateCreated()` in this case, however, because `getDateCreated` is a method in the `GeometricObject` class and is inherited by the `Circle` class. Nevertheless, in some cases, as shown in the next section, the keyword **super** is needed.

11.4   What is the printout of running the class `C` in (a)? What problem arises in compiling the program in (b)?

```
class A {
  public A() {
    System.out.println(
      "A's no-arg constructor is invoked");
  }
}

class B extends A {
}

public class C {
  public static void main(String[] args) {
    B b = new B();
  }
}
```

(a)

```
class A {
  public A(int x) {
  }
}

class B extends A {
  public B() {
  }
}

public class C {
  public static void main(String[] args) {
    B b = new B();
  }
}
```

(b)

11.5   How does a subclass invoke its superclass's constructor?

11.6   True or false? When invoking a constructor from a subclass, its superclass's no-arg constructor is always invoked.

11.4 Overriding Methods

Key Point

To override a method, the method must be defined in the subclass using the same signature and the same return type as in its superclass.

method overriding

A subclass inherits methods from a superclass. Sometimes it is necessary for the subclass to modify the implementation of a method defined in the superclass. This is referred to as *method overriding*.

The **toString** method in the **GeometricObject** class (lines 46–49 in Listing 11.1) returns the string representation of a geometric object. This method can be overridden to return the string representation of a circle. To override it, add the following new method in the **Circle** class in Listing 11.2.

```
1  public class CircleFromSimpleGeometricObject
2      extends SimpleGeometricObject {
3    // Other methods are omitted
4
5    // Override the toString method defined in the superclass
6    public String toString() {
7      return super.toString() + "\nradius is " + radius;
8    }
9  }
```

toString in superclass

The **toString()** method is defined in the **GeometricObject** class and modified in the **Circle** class. Both methods can be used in the **Circle** class. To invoke the **toString** method defined in the **GeometricObject** class from the **Circle** class, use **super.toString()** (line 7).

no super.super.methodName()

Can a subclass of **Circle** access the **toString** method defined in the **GeometricObject** class using syntax such as **super.super.toString()**? No. This is a syntax error.

Several points are worth noting:

override accessible instance method

■ An instance method can be overridden only if it is accessible. Thus a private method cannot be overridden, because it is not accessible outside its own class. If a method defined in a subclass is private in its superclass, the two methods are completely unrelated.

cannot override static method

■ Like an instance method, a static method can be inherited. However, a static method cannot be overridden. If a static method defined in the superclass is redefined in a subclass, the method defined in the superclass is hidden. The hidden static methods can be invoked using the syntax **SuperClassName.staticMethodName**.

Check Point

11.7 True or false? You can override a private method defined in a superclass.

11.8 True or false? You can override a static method defined in a superclass.

MyProgrammingLab™

11.9 How do you explicitly invoke a superclass's constructor from a subclass?

11.10 How do you invoke an overridden superclass method from a subclass?

11.5 Overriding vs. Overloading

Key Point

Overloading means to define multiple methods with the same name but different signatures. Overriding means to provide a new implementation for a method in the subclass.

You learned about overloading methods in Section 5.8. To override a method, the method must be defined in the subclass using the same signature and the same return type.

Let us use an example to show the differences between overriding and overloading. In (a) below, the method p(double i) in class A overrides the same method defined in class B. In (b), however, the class A has two overloaded methods: p(double i) and p(int i). The method p(double i) is inherited from B.

```
public class Test {
  public static void main(String[] args) {
    A a = new A();
    a.p(10);
    a.p(10.0);
  }
}

class B {
  public void p(double i) {
    System.out.println(i * 2);
  }
}

class A extends B {
  // This method overrides the method in B
  public void p(double i) {
    System.out.println(i);
  }
}
```

(a)

```
public class Test {
  public static void main(String[] args) {
    A a = new A();
    a.p(10);
    a.p(10.0);
  }
}

class B {
  public void p(double i) {
    System.out.println(i * 2);
  }
}

class A extends B {
  // This method overloads the method in B
  public void p(int i) {
    System.out.println(i);
  }
}
```

(b)

When you run the Test class in (a), both a.p(10) and a.p(10.0) invoke the p(double i) method defined in class A to display 10.0. When you run the Test class in (b), a.p(10) invokes the p(int i) method defined in class A to display 10, and a.p(10.0) invokes the p(double i) method defined in class B to display 20.0.

Note the following:

- Overridden methods are in different classes related by inheritance; overloaded methods can be either in the same class or different classes related by inheritance.

- Overridden methods have the same signature and return type; overloaded methods have the same name but a different parameter list.

To avoid mistakes, you can use a special Java syntax, called *override annotation*, to place @Override before the method in the subclass. For example:

override annotation

```
1  public class CircleFromSimpleGeometricObject
2      extends SimpleGeometricObject {
3    // Other methods are omitted
4
5    @Override
6    public String toString() {
7      return super.toString() + "\nradius is " + radius;
8    }
9  }
```

toString in superclass

This annotation denotes that the annotated method is required to override a method in the superclass. If a method with this annotation does not override its superclass's method, the compiler will report an error. For example, if toString is mistyped as tostring, a compile error is reported. If the override annotation isn't used, the compile won't report an error. Using annotation avoids mistakes.

11.11 Identify the problems in the following code:

```
1   public class Circle {
2     private double radius;
3
4     public Circle(double radius) {
5       radius = radius;
6     }
7
8     public double getRadius() {
9       return radius;
10    }
11
12    public double getArea() {
13      return radius * radius * Math.PI;
14    }
15  }
16
17  class B extends Circle {
18    private double length;
19
20    B(double radius, double length) {
21      Circle(radius);
22      length = length;
23    }
24
25    @Override
26    public double getArea() {
27      return getArea() * length;
28    }
29  }
```

11.12 Explain the difference between method overloading and method overriding.

11.13 If a method in a subclass has the same signature as a method in its superclass with the same return type, is the method overridden or overloaded?

11.14 If a method in a subclass has the same signature as a method in its superclass with a different return type, will this be a problem?

11.15 If a method in a subclass has the same name as a method in its superclass with different parameter types, is the method overridden or overloaded?

11.16 What is the benefit of using the `@Override` annotation?

11.6 The **Object** Class and Its **toString()** Method

Key Point

Every class in Java is descended from the `java.lang.Object` class.

If no inheritance is specified when a class is defined, the superclass of the class is `Object` by default. For example, the following two class definitions are the same:

`public class ClassName {`
`  ...`
`}`
	Equivalent	`public class ClassName extends Object {`
		`  ...`
		`}`

Classes such as `String`, `StringBuilder`, `Loan`, and `GeometricObject` are implicitly subclasses of `Object` (as are all the main classes you have seen in this book so far). It is important to be familiar with the methods provided by the `Object` class so that you can use them in your classes. This section introduces the `toString` method in the `Object` class.

The signature of the `toString()` method is:

toString()

```
public String toString()
```

Invoking `toString()` on an object returns a string that describes the object. By default, it returns a string consisting of a class name of which the object is an instance, an at sign (@), and the object's memory address in hexadecimal. For example, consider the following code for the `Loan` class defined in Listing 10.2:

string representation

```
Loan loan = new Loan();
System.out.println(loan.toString());
```

The output for this code displays something like `Loan@15037e5`. This message is not very helpful or informative. Usually you should override the `toString` method so that it returns a descriptive string representation of the object. For example, the `toString` method in the `Object` class was overridden in the `GeometricObject` class in lines 46–49 in Listing 11.1 as follows:

```
public String toString() {
  return "created on " + dateCreated + "\ncolor: " + color +
    " and filled: " + filled;
}
```

Note

You can also pass an object to invoke `System.out.println(object)` or `System.out.print(object)`. This is equivalent to invoking `System.out.println(object.toString())` or `System.out.print(object.toString())`. Thus, you could replace `System.out.println(loan.toString())` with `System.out.println(loan)`.

print object

11.7 Polymorphism

Polymorphism *means that a variable of a supertype can refer to a subtype object.*

Key Point

The three pillars of object-oriented programming are encapsulation, inheritance, and polymorphism. You have already learned the first two. This section introduces polymorphism.

First, let us define two useful terms: subtype and supertype. A class defines a type. A type defined by a subclass is called a *subtype*, and a type defined by its superclass is called a *supertype*. Therefore, you can say that `Circle` is a subtype of `GeometricObject` and `GeometricObject` is a supertype for `Circle`.

subtype
supertype

The inheritance relationship enables a subclass to inherit features from its superclass with additional new features. A subclass is a specialization of its superclass; every instance of a subclass is also an instance of its superclass, but not vice versa. For example, every circle is a geometric object, but not every geometric object is a circle. Therefore, you can always pass an instance of a subclass to a parameter of its superclass type. Consider the code in Listing 11.5.

LISTING 11.5 PolymorphismDemo.java

```
1  public class PolymorphismDemo {
2    /** Main method */
3    public static void main(String[] args) {
```

polymorphic call

polymorphic call

```
 4      // Display circle and rectangle properties
 5      displayObject(new CircleFromSimpleGeometricObject
 6                            (1, "red", false));
 7      displayObject(new RectangleFromSimpleGeometricObject
 8                            (1, 1, "black", true));
 9    }
10
11    /** Display geometric object properties */
12    public static void displayObject(SimpleGeometricObject object) {
13      System.out.println("Created on " + object.getDateCreated() +
14        ". Color is " + object.getColor());
15    }
16  }
```

```
Created on Mon Mar 09 19:25:20 EDT 2011. Color is white
Created on Mon Mar 09 19:25:20 EDT 2011. Color is black
```

The method **displayObject** (line 12) takes a parameter of the **GeometricObject** type. You can invoke **displayObject** by passing any instance of **GeometricObject** (e.g., **new CircleFromSimpleGeometricObject(1, "red", false)** and **new Rectangle-FromSimpleGeometricObject(1, 1, "black", false)** in lines 5–8). An object of a subclass can be used wherever its superclass object is used. This is commonly known as *polymorphism* (from a Greek word meaning "many forms"). In simple terms, polymorphism means that a variable of a supertype can refer to a subtype object.

what is polymorphism?

11.8 Dynamic Binding

 Key Point

A method can be implemented in several classes along the inheritance chain. The JVM decides which method is invoked at runtime.

A method can be defined in a superclass and overridden in its subclass. For example, the **toString()** method is defined in the **Object** class and overridden in **GeometricObject**. Consider the following code:

```
Object o = new GeometricObject();
System.out.println(o.toString());
```

declared type

actual type

dynamic binding

Which **toString()** method is invoked by **o**? To answer this question, we first introduce two terms: declared type and actual type. A variable must be declared a type. The type that declares a variable is called the variable's *declared type*. Here **o**'s declared type is **Object**. A variable of a reference type can hold a **null** value or a reference to an instance of the declared type. The instance may be created using the constructor of the declared type or its subtype. The *actual type* of the variable is the actual class for the object referenced by the variable. Here **o**'s actual type is **GeometricObject**, because **o** references an object created using **new GeometricObject()**. Which **toString()** method is invoked by **o** is determined by **o**'s actual type. This is known as *dynamic binding*.

Dynamic binding works as follows: Suppose an object **o** is an instance of classes C_1, C_2, ..., C_{n-1}, and C_n, where C_1 is a subclass of C_2, C_2 is a subclass of C_3, ..., and C_{n-1} is a subclass of C_n, as shown in Figure 11.2. That is, C_n is the most general class, and C_1 is the most specific class. In Java, C_n is the **Object** class. If **o** invokes a method **p**, the JVM searches for the implementation of the method **p** in C_1, C_2, ..., C_{n-1}, and C_n, in this order, until it is found. Once an implementation is found, the search stops and the first-found implementation is invoked.

If o is an instance of C_1, o is also an
instance of C_2, C_3, ..., C_{n-1}, and C_n

java.lang.Object

FIGURE 11.2 The method to be invoked is dynamically bound at runtime.

Listing 11.6 gives an example to demonstrate dynamic binding.

VideoNote

Polymorphism and dynamic
binding demo

LISTING 11.6 DynamicBindingDemo.java

```
1  public class DynamicBindingDemo {
2    public static void main(String[] args) {
3      m(new GraduateStudent());
4      m(new Student());
5      m(new Person());
6      m(new Object());
7    }
8
9    public static void m(Object x) {
10     System.out.println(x.toString());
11   }
12 }
13
14 class GraduateStudent extends Student {
15 }
16
17 class Student extends Person {
18   @Override
19   public String toString() {
20     return "Student";
21   }
22 }
23
24 class Person extends Object {
25   @Override
26   public String toString() {
27     return "Person";
28   }
29 }
```

polymorphic call

dynamic binding

override toString()

override toString()

```
Student
Student
Person
java.lang.Object@130c19b
```

Method m (line 9) takes a parameter of the **Object** type. You can invoke m with any object
(e.g., new GraduateStudent(), new Student(), new Person(), and new Object())
in lines 3–6.

When the method m(Object x) is executed, the argument x's toString method is
invoked. x may be an instance of **GraduateStudent**, **Student**, **Person**, or **Object**. The
classes **GraduateStudent**, **Student**, **Person**, and **Object** have their own implementations of the **toString** method. Which implementation is used will be determined by x's
actual type at runtime. Invoking m(new GraduateStudent()) (line 3) causes the
toString method defined in the **Student** class to be invoked.

Invoking m(new Student()) (line 4) causes the **toString** method defined in the
Student class to be invoked; invoking m(new Person()) (line 5) causes the **toString**

method defined in the **Person** class to be invoked; and invoking **m(new Object())** (line 6) causes the **toString** method defined in the **Object** class to be invoked.

matching vs. binding

Matching a method signature and binding a method implementation are two separate issues. The *declared type* of the reference variable decides which method to match at compile time. The compiler finds a matching method according to the parameter type, number of parameters, and order of the parameters at compile time. A method may be implemented in several classes along the inheritance chain. The JVM dynamically binds the implementation of the method at runtime, decided by the actual type of the variable.

Check Point

MyProgrammingLab™

11.17 What is polymorphism? What is dynamic binding?

11.18 Describe the difference between method matching and method binding.

11.19 Can you assign **new int[50]**, **new Integer[50]**, **new String[50]**, or **new Object[50]**, into a variable of **Object[]** type?

11.20 What is wrong in the following code?

```
1   public class Test {
2     public static void main(String[] args) {
3       Integer[] list1 = {12, 24, 55, 1};
4       Double[] list2 = {12.4, 24.0, 55.2, 1.0};
5       int[] list3 = {1, 2, 3};
6       printArray(list1);
7       printArray(list2);
8       printArray(list3);
9     }
10
11    public static void printArray(Object[] list) {
12      for (Object o: list)
13        System.out.print(o + " ");
14      System.out.println();
15    }
16  }
```

11.21 Show the output of the following code:

```
public class Test {
  public static void main(String[] args) {
    new Person().printPerson();
    new Student().printPerson();
  }
}

class Student extends Person {
  @Override
  public String getInfo() {
    return "Student";
  }
}

class Person {
  public String getInfo() {
    return "Person";
  }

  public void printPerson() {
    System.out.println(getInfo());
  }
}
```

(a)

```
public class Test {
  public static void main(String[] args) {
    new Person().printPerson();
    new Student().printPerson();
  }
}

class Student extends Person {
  private String getInfo() {
    return "Student";
  }
}

class Person {
  private String getInfo() {
    return "Person";
  }

  public void printPerson() {
    System.out.println(getInfo());
  }
}
```

(b)

11.22 Show the output of following program:

```
1  public class Test {
2    public static void main(String[] args) {
3      A a = new A(3);
4    }
5  }
6
7  class A extends B {
8    public A(int t) {
9      System.out.println("A's constructor is invoked");
10   }
11 }
12
13 class B {
14   public B() {
15     System.out.println("B's constructor is invoked");
16   }
17 }
```

Is the no-arg constructor of **Object** invoked when **new A(3)** is invoked?

11.9 Casting Objects and the **instanceof** Operator

One object reference can be typecast into another object reference. This is called casting object.

Key Point

casting object

In the preceding section, the statement

```
m(new Student());
```

assigns the object **new Student()** to a parameter of the **Object** type. This statement is equivalent to

```
Object o = new Student(); // Implicit casting
m(o);
```

The statement **Object o = new Student()**, known as *implicit casting*, is legal because an instance of **Student** is an instance of **Object**.

implicit casting

Suppose you want to assign the object reference **o** to a variable of the **Student** type using the following statement:

```
Student b = o;
```

In this case a compile error would occur. Why does the statement **Object o = new Student()** work but **Student b = o** doesn't? The reason is that a **Student** object is always an instance of **Object**, but an **Object** is not necessarily an instance of **Student**. Even though you can see that **o** is really a **Student** object, the compiler is not clever enough to know it. To tell the compiler that **o** is a **Student** object, use *explicit casting*. The syntax is similar to the one used for casting among primitive data types. Enclose the target object type in parentheses and place it before the object to be cast, as follows:

explicit casting

```
Student b = (Student)o; // Explicit casting
```

It is always possible to cast an instance of a subclass to a variable of a superclass (known as *upcasting*), because an instance of a subclass is *always* an instance of its superclass. When casting an instance of a superclass to a variable of its subclass (known as *downcasting*), explicit casting must be used to confirm your intention to the compiler with the

upcasting
downcasting

ClassCastException

instanceof

(`SubclassName`) cast notation. For the casting to be successful, you must make sure that the object to be cast is an instance of the subclass. If the superclass object is not an instance of the subclass, a runtime *ClassCastException* occurs. For example, if an object is not an instance of `Student`, it cannot be cast into a variable of `Student`. It is a good practice, therefore, to ensure that the object is an instance of another object before attempting a casting. This can be accomplished by using the *instanceof* operator. Consider the following code:

```
Object myObject = new Circle();
... // Some lines of code
/** Perform casting if myObject is an instance of Circle */
if (myObject instanceof Circle) {
  System.out.println("The circle diameter is " +
    ((Circle)myObject) .getDiameter());
  ...
}
```

You may be wondering why casting is necessary. The variable `myObject` is declared `Object`. The *declared type* decides which method to match at compile time. Using `myObject.getDiameter()` would cause a compile error, because the `Object` class does not have the `getDiameter` method. The compiler cannot find a match for `myObject.getDiameter()`. Therefore, it is necessary to cast `myObject` into the `Circle` type to tell the compiler that `myObject` is also an instance of `Circle`.

Why not define `myObject` as a `Circle` type in the first place? To enable generic programming, it is a good practice to define a variable with a supertype, which can accept a value of any subtype.

lowercase keywords

Note
instanceof is a Java keyword. Every letter in a Java keyword is in lowercase.

casting analogy

Tip
To help understand casting, you may also consider the analogy of fruit, apple, and orange, with the `Fruit` class as the superclass for `Apple` and `Orange`. An apple is a fruit, so you can always safely assign an instance of `Apple` to a variable for `Fruit`. However, a fruit is not necessarily an apple, so you have to use explicit casting to assign an instance of `Fruit` to a variable of `Apple`.

Listing 11.7 demonstrates polymorphism and casting. The program creates two objects (lines 5–6), a circle and a rectangle, and invokes the `displayObject` method to display them (lines 9–10). The `displayObject` method displays the area and diameter if the object is a circle (line 15), and the area if the object is a rectangle (lines 21–22).

LISTING 11.7 CastingDemo.java

```
1  public class CastingDemo {
2    /** Main method */
3    public static void main(String[] args) {
4      // Create and initialize two objects
5      Object object1 = new CircleFromSimpleGeometricObject(1);
6      Object object2 = new RectangleFromSimpleGeometricObject(1, 1);
7
8      // Display circle and rectangle
9      displayObject(object1);
10     displayObject(object2);
11   }
12
```

```
13    /** A method for displaying an object */
14    public static void displayObject(Object object) {
15      if (object instanceof CircleFromSimpleGeometricObject) {
16        System.out.println("The circle area is " +
17          ((CircleFromSimpleGeometricObject)object).getArea());
18        System.out.println("The circle diameter is " +
19          ((CircleFromSimpleGeometricObject)object).getDiameter());
20      }
21      else if (object instanceof
22                    RectangleFromSimpleGeometricObject ) {
23        System.out.println("The rectangle area is " +
24          ((RectangleFromSimpleGeometricObject)object).getArea());
25      }
26    }
27  }
```

polymorphic call

polymorphic call

```
The circle area is 3.141592653589793
The circle diameter is 2.0
The rectangle area is 1.0
```

The `displayObject(Object object)` method is an example of generic programming. It can be invoked by passing any instance of `Object`.

The program uses implicit casting to assign a `Circle` object to `object1` and a `Rectangle` object to `object2` (lines 5–6), then invokes the `displayObject` method to display the information on these objects (lines 9–10).

In the `displayObject` method (lines 14–26), explicit casting is used to cast the object to `Circle` if the object is an instance of `Circle`, and the methods `getArea` and `getDiameter` are used to display the area and diameter of the circle.

Casting can be done only when the source object is an instance of the target class. The program uses the `instanceof` operator to ensure that the source object is an instance of the target class before performing a casting (line 15).

Explicit casting to `Circle` (lines 17, 19) and to `Rectangle` (line 24) is necessary because the `getArea` and `getDiameter` methods are not available in the `Object` class.

Caution

The object member access operator (`.`) precedes the casting operator. Use parentheses to ensure that casting is done before the `.` operator, as in

precedes casting

```
((Circle)object).getArea());
```

Casting a primitive type value is different from casting an object reference. Casting a primitive type value returns a new value. For example:

```
int age = 45;
byte newAge = (int)age; // A new value is assigned to newAge
```

However, casting an object reference does not create a new object. For example:

```
Object o = new Circle();
Circle c = (Circle)o; // No new object is created
```

Now reference variables `o` and `c` point to the same object.

MyProgrammingLab™

11.23 Indicate true or false for the following statements:

- You can always successfully cast an instance of a subclass to a superclass.
- You can always successfully cast an instance of a superclass to a subclass.

11.24 For the `GeometricObject` and `Circle` classes in Listings 11.1 and 11.2, answer the following questions:

a. Are the following Boolean expressions true or false?

```
Circle circle = new Circle(1);
GeometricObject object1 = new GeometricObject();
(circle instanceof GeometricObject)
(object1 instanceof GeometricObject)
(circle instanceof Circle)
(object1 instanceof Circle)
```

b. Can the following statements be compiled?

```
Circle circle = new Circle(5);
GeometricObject object = circle;
```

c. Can the following statements be compiled?

```
GeometricObject object = new GeometricObject();
Circle circle = (Circle)object;
```

11.25 Suppose that `Fruit`, `Apple`, `Orange`, `GoldenDelicious`, and `McIntosh` are defined in the following inheritance hierarchy:

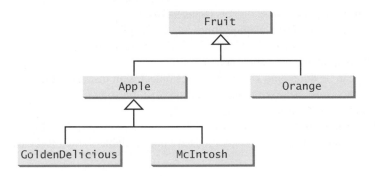

Assume that the following code is given:

```
Fruit fruit = new GoldenDelicious();
Orange orange = new Orange();
```

Answer the following questions:

a. Is **fruit instanceof Fruit**?

b. Is **fruit instanceof Orange**?

c. Is **fruit instanceof Apple**?

d. Is **fruit instanceof GoldenDelicious**?

e. Is **fruit instanceof McIntosh**?

f. Is **orange instanceof Orange**?

g. Is `orange instanceof Fruit`?

h. Is `orange instanceof Apple`?

i. Suppose the method `makeAppleCider` is defined in the `Apple` class. Can `fruit` invoke this method? Can `orange` invoke this method?

j. Suppose the method `makeOrangeJuice` is defined in the `Orange` class. Can `orange` invoke this method? Can `fruit` invoke this method?

k. Is the statement `Orange p = new Apple()` legal?

l. Is the statement `McIntosh p = new Apple()` legal?

m. Is the statement `Apple p = new McIntosh()` legal?

11.26 What is wrong in the following code?

```
1  public class Test {
2    public static void main(String[] args) {
3      Object fruit = new Fruit();
4      Object apple = (Apple)fruit;
5    }
6  }
7
8  class Apple extends Fruit {
9  }
10
11 class Fruit {
12 }
```

11.10 The **Object**'s **equals** Method

Like the `toString()` method, the `equals(Object)` method is another method defined in the `Object` class.

 Key Point

Another method defined in the `Object` class that is often used is the `equals` method. Its signature is

`equals(Object)`

```
public boolean equals(Object o)
```

This method tests whether two objects are equal. The syntax for invoking it is:

```
object1.equals(object2);
```

The default implementation of the `equals` method in the `Object` class is:

```
public boolean equals(Object obj) {
  return (this == obj);
}
```

This implementation checks whether two reference variables point to the same object using the `==` operator. You should override this method in your custom class to test whether two distinct objects have the same content.

The `equals` method is overridden in many classes in the Java API, such as `java.lang.String` and `java.util.Date`, to compare whether the contents of two objects are equal. You have already used the `equals` method to compare two strings in Section 9.2, The `String` Class. The `equals` method in the `String` class is inherited from the `Object` class and is overridden in the `String` class to test whether two strings are identical in content.

You can override the **equals** method in the **Circle** class to compare whether two circles are equal based on their radius as follows:

```
public boolean equals(Object o) {
  if (o instanceof Circle) {
    return radius == ((Circle)o).radius;
  }
  else
    return false;
}
```

== vs. equals

Note

The == comparison operator is used for comparing two primitive data type values or for determining whether two objects have the same references. The **equals** method is intended to test whether two objects have the same contents, provided that the method is overridden in the defining class of the objects. The == operator is stronger than the **equals** method, in that the == operator checks whether the two reference variables refer to the same object.

Caution

Using the signature **equals(SomeClassName obj)** (e.g., **equals(Circle c)**) to override the **equals** method in a subclass is a common mistake. You should use **equals(Object obj)**. See CheckPoint Question 11.28.

equals(Object)

11.27 Does every object have a **toString** method and an **equals** method? Where do they come from? How are they used? Is it appropriate to override these methods?

MyProgrammingLab

11.28 When overriding the **equals** method, a common mistake is mistyping its signature in the subclass. For example, the **equals** method is incorrectly written as **equals(Circle circle)**, as shown in (a) in following the code; instead, it should be **equals(Object circle)**, as shown in (b). Show the output of running class **Test** with the **Circle** class in (a) and in (b), respectively.

```
public class Test {
  public static void main(String[] args) {
    Object circle1 = new Circle();
    Object circle2 = new Circle();
    System.out.println(circle1.equals(circle2));
  }
}
```

```
class Circle {
  double radius;

  public boolean equals(Circle circle) {
    return this.radius == circle.radius;
  }
}
```

```
class Circle {
  double radius;

  public boolean equals(Object circle) {
    return this.radius ==
      ((Circle)circle).radius;
  }
}
```

            (a)   (b)

11.11 The **ArrayList** Class

VideoNote

The ArrayList class

Key Point

An ArrayList object can be used to store a list of objects.

Now we are ready to introduce a very useful class for storing objects. You can create an array to store objects. But, once the array is created, its size is fixed. Java provides the **ArrayList** class, which can be used to store an unlimited number of objects. Figure 11.3 shows some methods in `ArrayList`.

java.util.ArrayList<E>	
+ArrayList()	Creates an empty list.
+add(o: E): void	Appends a new element o at the end of this list.
+add(index: int, o: E): void	Adds a new element o at the specified index in this list.
+clear(): void	Removes all the elements from this list.
+contains(o: Object): boolean	Returns true if this list contains the element o.
+get(index: int): E	Returns the element from this list at the specified index.
+indexOf(o: Object): int	Returns the index of the first matching element in this list.
+isEmpty(): boolean	Returns true if this list contains no elements.
+lastIndexOf(o: Object): int	Returns the index of the last matching element in this list.
+remove(o: Object): boolean	Removes the element o from this list.
+size(): int	Returns the number of elements in this list.
+remove(index: int): boolean	Removes the element at the specified index.
+set(index: int, o: E): E	Sets the element at the specified index.

FIGURE 11.3 An `ArrayList` stores an unlimited number of objects.

`ArrayList` is known as a generic class with a generic type `E`. You can specify a concrete type to replace `E` when creating an `ArrayList`. For example, the following statement creates an `ArrayList` and assigns its reference to variable `cities`. This `ArrayList` object can be used to store strings.

```
ArrayList<String> cities = new ArrayList<String>();
```

The following statement creates an `ArrayList` and assigns its reference to variable `dates`. This `ArrayList` object can be used to store dates.

```
ArrayList<java.util.Date> dates = new ArrayList<java.util.Date> ();
```

Note
In JDK 7, the statement

```
ArrayList<AConcreteType> list = new ArrayList<AConcreteType> ();
```

can be simplified by

```
ArrayList<AConcreteType> list = new ArrayList<> ();
```

The concrete type is no longer required in the constructor thanks to a feature called *type inference*. The compiler is able to infer the type from the variable declaration. More discussions on generics including how to define custom generic classes and methods will be introduced in Chapter 21, Generics.

type inference

Listing 11.8 gives an example of using `ArrayList` to store objects.

LISTING 11.8 TestArrayList.java

```
1  import java.util.ArrayList;
2
```

import ArrayList

```
 3  public class TestArrayList {
 4    public static void main(String[] args) {
 5      // Create a list to store cities
 6      ArrayList<String> cityList = new ArrayList<String>();
 7
 8      // Add some cities in the list
 9      cityList.add("London");
10      // cityList now contains [London]
11      cityList.add("Denver");
12      // cityList now contains [London, Denver]
13      cityList.add("Paris");
14      // cityList now contains [London, Denver, Paris]
15      cityList.add("Miami");
16      // cityList now contains [London, Denver, Paris, Miami]
17      cityList.add("Seoul");
18      // Contains [London, Denver, Paris, Miami, Seoul]
19      cityList.add("Tokyo");
20      // Contains [London, Denver, Paris, Miami, Seoul, Tokyo]
21
22      System.out.println("List size? " + cityList.size());
23      System.out.println("Is Miami in the list? " +
24        cityList.contains("Miami"));
25      System.out.println("The location of Denver in the list? "
26        + cityList.indexOf("Denver"));
27      System.out.println("Is the list empty? " +
28        cityList.isEmpty()); // Print false
29
30      // Insert a new city at index 2
31      cityList.add(2, "Xian");
32      // Contains [London, Denver, Xian, Paris, Miami, Seoul, Tokyo]
33
34      // Remove a city from the list
35      cityList.remove("Miami");
36      // Contains [London, Denver, Xian, Paris, Seoul, Tokyo]
37
38      // Remove a city at index 1
39      cityList.remove(1);
40      // Contains [London, Xian, Paris, Seoul, Tokyo]
41
42      // Display the contents in the list
43      System.out.println(cityList.toString());
44
45      // Display the contents in the list in reverse order
46      for (int i = cityList.size() - 1; i >= 0; i--)
47        System.out.print(cityList.get(i) + " ");
48      System.out.println();
49
50      // Create a list to store two circles
51      ArrayList<CircleFromSimpleGeometricObject> list
52        = new ArrayList<CircleFromSimpleGeometricObject>();
53
54      // Add two circles
55      list.add(new CircleFromSimpleGeometricObject(2));
56      list.add(new CircleFromSimpleGeometricObject(3));
57
58      // Display the area of the first circle in the list
59      System.out.println("The area of the circle? " +
60        ((CircleFromSimpleGeometricObject)list.get(0)).getArea());
61    }
62  }
```

Margin annotations:

create ArrayList (line 6)
add element (line 9)
list size (line 22)
contains element? (line 24)
element index (line 26)
is empty? (line 28)
remove element (line 35)
remove element (line 39)
toString() (line 43)
get element (line 47)
create ArrayList (line 52)

```
List size? 6
Is Miami in the list? True
The location of Denver in the list? 1
Is the list empty? false
[London, Xian, Paris, Seoul, Tokyo]
Tokyo Seoul Paris Xian London
The area of the circle? 12.566370614359172
```

Since the `ArrayList` is in the `java.util` package, it is imported in line 1. The program creates an `ArrayList` of strings using its no-arg constructor and assigns the reference to `cityList` (line 6). The `add` method (lines 9–19) adds strings to the end of list. So, after `cityList.add("London")` (line 9), the list contains

    `[London]`

add(Object)

After `cityList.add("Denver")` (line 11), the list contains

    `[London, Denver]`

After adding `Paris`, `Miami`, `Seoul`, and `Tokyo` (lines 13–19), the list contains

    `[London, Denver, Paris, Miami, Seoul, Tokyo]`

Invoking `size()` (line 22) returns the size of the list, which is currently **6**. Invoking `contains("Miami")` (line 24) checks whether the object is in the list. In this case, it returns `true`, since `Miami` is in the list. Invoking `indexOf("Denver")` (line 26) returns the index of `Denver` in the list, which is **1**. If `Denver` were not in the list, it would return `-1`. The `isEmpty()` method (line 28) checks whether the list is empty. It returns `false`, since the list is not empty.

size()

The statement `cityList.add(2, "Xian")` (line 31) inserts an object into the list at the specified index. After this statement, the list becomes

add(index, Object)

    `[London, Denver, Xian, Paris, Miami, Seoul, Tokyo]`

The statement `cityList.remove("Miami")` (line 35) removes the object from the list. After this statement, the list becomes

remove(Object)

    `[London, Denver, Xian, Paris, Seoul, Tokyo]`

The statement `cityList.remove(1)` (line 39) removes the object at the specified index from the list. After this statement, the list becomes

remove(index)

    `[London, Xian, Paris, Seoul, Tokyo]`

The statement in line 43 is same as

    `System.out.println(cityList);`

The `toString()` method returns a string representation of the list in the form of `[e0.toString(), e1.toString(), ..., ek.toString()]`, where `e0, e1, . . . ,` and `ek` are the elements in the list.

toString()

The `get(index)` method (line 47) returns the object at the specified index.

getIndex()

`ArrayList` objects can be used like arrays, but there are many differences. Table 11.1 lists their similarities and differences.

array vs. ArrayList

Once an array is created, its size is fixed. You can access an array element using the square-bracket notation (e.g., `a[index]`). When an `ArrayList` is created, its size is **0**.

TABLE 11.1 Differences and Similarities between Arrays and `ArrayList`

Operation	Array	ArrayList
Creating an array/ArrayList	`String[] a = new String[10]`	`ArrayList<String> list = new ArrayList<>();`
Accessing an element	`a[index]`	`list.get(index);`
Updating an element	`a[index] = "London";`	`list.set(index, "London");`
Returning size	`a.length`	`list.size();`
Adding a new element		`list.add("London");`
Inserting a new element		`list.add(index, "London");`
Removing an element		`list.remove(index);`
Removing an element		`list.remove(Object);`
Removing all elements		`list.clear();`

You cannot use the `get` and `set` methods if the element is not in the list. It is easy to add, insert, and remove elements in a list, but it is rather complex to add, insert, and remove elements in an array. You have to write code to manipulate the array in order to perform these operations.

Suppose you want to create an `ArrayList` for storing integers. Can you use the following code to create a list?

```
ArrayList<int> list = new ArrayList<int>();
```

No. This will not work because the elements stored in an `ArrayList` must be of an object type. You cannot use a primitive data type such as `int` to replace a generic type. However, you can create an `ArrayList` for storing `Integer` objects as follows:

```
ArrayList<Integer> list = new ArrayList<Integer>();
```

Listing 11.9 gives a program that prompts the user to enter a sequence of numbers and displays the distinct numbers in the sequence. Assume that the input ends with 0 and 0 is not counted as a number in the sequence.

LISTING 11.9 DistinctNumbers.java

```
 1  import java.util.ArrayList;
 2  import java.util.Scanner;
 3
 4  public class DistinctNumbers {
 5    public static void main(String[] args) {
 6      ArrayList<Integer> list = new ArrayList<Integer>();
 7
 8      Scanner input = new Scanner(System.in);
 9      System.out.print("Enter integers (input ends with 0): ");
10      int value;
11
12      do {
13        value = input.nextInt(); // Read a value from the input
14
15        if (!list.contains(value) && value != 0)
16          list.add(value);  // Add the value if it is not in the list
17      } while (value != 0);
```

create an array list

contained in list?
add to list

```
18
19      // Display the distinct numbers
20      for (int i = 0; i < list.size(); i++)
21        System.out.print(list.get(i) + " ");
22    }
23 }
```

```
Enter numbers (input ends with 0): 1 2 3 2 1 6 3 4 5 4 5 1 2 3 0  ↵Enter
The distinct numbers are: 1 2 3 6 4 5
```

The program creates an **ArrayList** for **Integer** objects (line 6) and repeatedly reads a value in the loop (lines 12–17). For each value, if it is not in the list (line 15), add it to the list (line 16). You can rewrite this program using an array to store the elements rather than using an **ArrayList**. However, it is simpler to implement this program using an **ArrayList** for two reasons.

■ First, the size of an **ArrayList** is flexible so you don't have to specify its size in advance. When creating an array, its size must be specified.

■ Second, **ArrayList** contains many useful methods. For example, you can test whether an element is in the list using the **contains** method. If you use an array, you have to write additional code to implement this method.

11.29 How do you do the following?

    a. Create an **ArrayList** for storing double values?

    b. Append an object to a list?

    c. Insert an object at the beginning of a list?

    d. Find the number of objects in a list?

    e. Remove a given object from a list?

    f. Remove the last object from the list?

    g. Check whether a given object is in a list?

    h. Retrieve an object at a specified index from a list?

✓ **Check Point**

MyProgrammingLab™

11.30 Identify the errors in the following code.

```
ArrayList<String> list = new ArrayList<String> ();
list.add("Denver");
list.add("Austin");
list.add(new java.util.Date());
String city = list.get(0);
list.set(3, "Dallas");
System.out.println(list.get(3));
```

11.31 Suppose the **ArrayList list** contains duplicate elements. Does the following code correctly remove the element from the array list? If not, correct the code.

```
for (int i = 0; i < list.size(); i++)
  list.remove(element);
```

11.32 Explain why the following code displays [1, 3] rather than [2, 3].

```
ArrayList<Integer> list = new ArrayList<Integer>();
list.add(1);
```

```
        list.add(2);
        list.add(3);
        list.remove(1);
        System.out.println(list);
```

11.12 Case Study: A Custom Stack Class

VideoNote

The MyStack class

This section designs a stack class for holding objects.

Section 10.9 presented a stack class for storing **int** values. This section introduces a stack class to store objects. You can use an **ArrayList** to implement **Stack**, as shown in Listing 11.10. The UML diagram for the class is shown in Figure 11.4.

MyStack	
-list: ArrayList<Object>	A list to store elements.
+isEmpty(): boolean	Returns true if this stack is empty.
+getSize(): int	Returns the number of elements in this stack.
+peek(): Object	Returns the top element in this stack without removing it.
+pop(): Object	Returns and removes the top element in this stack.
+push(o: Object): void	Adds a new element to the top of this stack.

FIGURE 11.4 The MyStack class encapsulates the stack storage and provides the operations for manipulating the stack.

LISTING 11.10 MyStack.java

```
1  import java.util.ArrayList;
2
3  public class MyStack {
4    private ArrayList<Object> list = new ArrayList<Object>();
5
6    public boolean isEmpty() {
7      return list.isEmpty();
8    }
9
10   public int getSize() {
11     return list.size();
12   }
13
14   public Object peek() {
15     return list.get(getSize() - 1);
16   }
17
18   public Object pop() {
19     Object o = list.get(getSize() - 1);
20     list.remove(getSize() - 1);
21     return o;
22   }
23
24   public void push(Object o) {
25     list.add(o);
26   }
27
```

array list

stack empty?

get stack size

peek stack

remove

push

```
28    @Override
29    public String toString() {
30      return "stack: " + list.toString();
31    }
32  }
```

An array list is created to store the elements in the stack (line 4). The `isEmpty()` method (lines 6–8) returns `list.isEmpty()`. The `getSize()` method (lines 10–12) returns `list.size()`. The `peek()` method (lines 14–16) retrieves the element at the top of the stack without removing it. The end of the list is the top of the stack. The `pop()` method (lines 18–22) removes the top element from the stack and returns it. The `push(Object element)` method (lines 24–26) adds the specified element to the stack. The `toString()` method (lines 28–31) defined in the `Object` class is overridden to display the contents of the stack by invoking `list.toString()`. The `toString()` method implemented in `ArrayList` returns a string representation of all the elements in an array list.

Design Guide

In Listing 11.10, `MyStack` contains `ArrayList`. The relationship between `MyStack` and `ArrayList` is *composition*. While inheritance models an *is-a* relationship, composition models a *has-a* relationship. You could also implement `MyStack` as a subclass of `ArrayList` (see Programming Exercise 11.4). Using composition is better, however, because it enables you to define a completely new stack class without inheriting the unnecessary and inappropriate methods from `ArrayList`.

composition
is-a
has-a

11.13 The **protected** Data and Methods

A protected member of a class can be accessed from a subclass.

Key Point

So far you have used the `private` and `public` keywords to specify whether data fields and methods can be accessed from outside of the class. Private members can be accessed only from inside of the class, and public members can be accessed from any other classes.

Often it is desirable to allow subclasses to access data fields or methods defined in the superclass, but not to allow nonsubclasses to access these data fields and methods. To accomplish this, you can use the `protected` keyword. This way you can access protected data fields or methods in a superclass from its subclasses.

why `protected`?

The modifiers `private`, `protected`, and `public` are known as *visibility* or *accessibility modifiers* because they specify how classes and class members are accessed. The visibility of these modifiers increases in this order:

Visibility increases

private, default (no modifier), protected, public

Table 11.2 summarizes the accessibility of the members in a class. Figure 11.5 illustrates how a public, protected, default, and private datum or method in class `C1` can be accessed from a class `C2` in the same package, from a subclass `C3` in the same package, from a subclass `C4` in a different package, and from a class `C5` in a different package.

Use the `private` modifier to hide the members of the class completely so that they cannot be accessed directly from outside the class. Use no modifiers (the default) in order to allow the members of the class to be accessed directly from any class within the same package but not from other packages. Use the `protected` modifier to enable the members of the class to be accessed by the subclasses in any package or classes in the same package. Use the `public` modifier to enable the members of the class to be accessed by any class.

Your class can be used in two ways: (1) for creating instances of the class and (2) for defining subclasses by extending the class. Make the members `private` if they are not intended

TABLE 11.2 Data and Methods Visibility

Modifier on members in a class	Accessed from the same class	Accessed from the same package	Accessed from a subclass in a different package	Accessed from a different package
public	✓	✓	✓	✓
protected	✓	✓	✓	–
default (no modifier)	✓	✓	–	–
private	✓	–	–	–

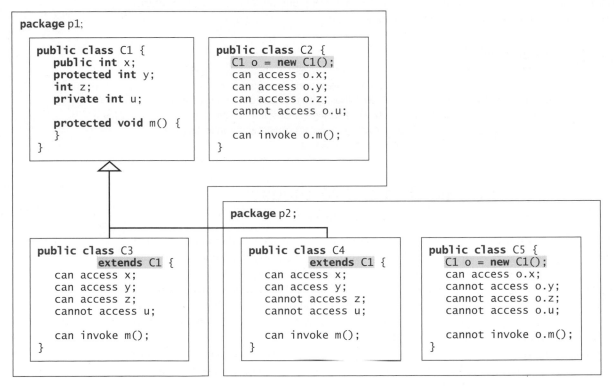

FIGURE 11.5 Visibility modifiers are used to control how data and methods are accessed.

for use from outside the class. Make the members **public** if they are intended for the users of the class. Make the fields or methods **protected** if they are intended for the extenders of the class but not for the users of the class.

The **private** and **protected** modifiers can be used only for members of the class. The **public** modifier and the default modifier (i.e., no modifier) can be used on members of the class as well as on the class. A class with no modifier (i.e., not a public class) is not accessible by classes from other packages.

change visibility

Note

A subclass may override a protected method defined in its superclass and change its visibility to public. However, a subclass cannot weaken the accessibility of a method defined in the superclass. For example, if a method is defined as public in the superclass, it must be defined as public in the subclass.

11.33 What modifier should you use on a class so that a class in the same package can access it, but a class in a different package cannot access it?

11.34 What modifier should you use so that a class in a different package cannot access the class, but its subclasses in any package can access it?

11.35 In the following code, the classes **A** and **B** are in the same package. If the question marks in (a) are replaced by blanks, can class **B** be compiled? If the question marks are replaced by **private**, can class **B** be compiled? If the question marks are replaced by **protected**, can class **B** be compiled?

```
package p1;

public class A {
    ?    int i;

    ?    void m() {
        ...
    }
}
```
(a)

```
package p1;

public class B extends A {
    public void m1(String[] args) {
        System.out.println(i);
        m();
    }
}
```
(b)

11.36 In the following code, the classes **A** and **B** are in different packages. If the question marks in (a) are replaced by blanks, can class **B** be compiled? If the question marks are replaced by **private**, can class **B** be compiled? If the question marks are replaced by **protected**, can class **B** be compiled?

```
package p1;

public class A {
    ?    int i;

    ?    void m() {
        ...
    }
}
```
(a)

```
package p2;

public class B extends A {
    public void m1(String[] args) {
        System.out.println(i);
        m();
    }
}
```
(b)

11.14 Preventing Extending and Overriding

Neither a final class nor a final method can be extended. A final data field is a constant.

You may occasionally want to prevent classes from being extended. In such cases, use the **final** modifier to indicate that a class is final and cannot be a parent class. The **Math** class is a final class. The **String**, **StringBuilder**, and **StringBuffer** classes are also final classes. For example, the following class **A** is final and cannot be extended:

```
public final class A {
    // Data fields, constructors, and methods omitted
}
```

You also can define a method to be final; a final method cannot be overridden by its subclasses.

For example, the following method `m` is final and cannot be overridden:

```
public class Test {
  // Data fields, constructors, and methods omitted

  public final void m() {
    // Do something
  }
}
```

> **Note**
> The modifiers `public`, `protected`, `private`, `static`, `abstract`, and `final` are used on classes and class members (data and methods), except that the `final` modifier can also be used on local variables in a method. A `final` local variable is a constant inside a method.

Check Point

MyProgrammingLab™

11.37 How do you prevent a class from being extended? How do you prevent a method from being overridden?

11.38 Indicate true or false for the following statements:

a. A protected datum or method can be accessed by any class in the same package.

b. A protected datum or method can be accessed by any class in different packages.

c. A protected datum or method can be accessed by its subclasses in any package.

d. A final class can have instances.

e. A final class can be extended.

f. A final method can be overridden.

KEY TERMS

actual type   422
casting objects   425
constructor chaining   415
declared type   422
dynamic binding   422
inheritance   408
`instanceof`   426
is-a relationship   437
method overriding   419
multiple inheritance   414

override   419
polymorphism   422
`protected`   437
single inheritance   414
subclass   408
subtype   421
superclass   408
supertype   421
type inference   431

CHAPTER SUMMARY

1. You can define a new class from an existing class. This is known as class *inheritance*. The new class is called a *subclass*, *child class*, or *extended class*. The existing class is called a *superclass*, *parent class*, or *base class*.

2. A constructor is used to construct an instance of a class. Unlike properties and methods, the constructors of a superclass are not inherited in the subclass. They can be invoked only from the constructors of the subclasses, using the keyword `super`.

3. A constructor may invoke an overloaded constructor or its superclass's constructor. The call must be the first statement in the constructor. If none of them is invoked explicitly, the compiler puts `super()` as the first statement in the constructor, which invokes the superclass's no-arg constructor.

4. To *override* a method, the method must be defined in the subclass using the same signature and the same return type as in its superclass.

5. An instance method can be overridden only if it is accessible. Thus, a private method cannot be overridden because it is not accessible outside its own class. If a method defined in a subclass is private in its superclass, the two methods are completely unrelated.

6. Like an instance method, a static method can be inherited. However, a static method cannot be overridden. If a static method defined in the superclass is redefined in a subclass, the method defined in the superclass is hidden.

7. Every class in Java is descended from the `java.lang.Object` class. If no superclass is specified when a class is defined, its superclass is `Object`.

8. If a method's parameter type is a superclass (e.g., `Object`), you may pass an object to this method of any of the parameter's subclasses (e.g., `Circle` or `String`). This is known as polymorphism.

9. It is always possible to cast an instance of a subclass to a variable of a superclass, because an instance of a subclass is *always* an instance of its superclass. When casting an instance of a superclass to a variable of its subclass, explicit casting must be used to confirm your intention to the compiler with the (`SubclassName`) cast notation.

10. A class defines a type. A type defined by a subclass is called a *subtype* and a type defined by its superclass is called a *supertype*.

11. When invoking an instance method from a reference variable, the *actual type of* the variable decides which implementation of the method is used *at runtime*. This is known as dynamic binding.

12. You can use `obj instanceof AClass` to test whether an object is an instance of a class.

13. You can use the `ArrayList` class to create an object to store a list of objects.

14. You can use the `protected` modifier to prevent the data and methods from being accessed by nonsubclasses from a different package.

15. You can use the `final` modifier to indicate that a class is final and cannot be extended and to indicate that a method is final and cannot be overridden.

TEST QUESTIONS

Do the test questions for this chapter online at www.cs.armstrong.edu/liang/intro9e/test.html.

MyProgrammingLab™

PROGRAMMING EXERCISES

Sections 11.2–11.4

11.1 (*The Triangle class*) Design a class named `Triangle` that extends `GeometricObject`. The class contains:

- Three `double` data fields named `side1`, `side2`, and `side3` with default values `1.0` to denote three sides of the triangle.
- A no-arg constructor that creates a default triangle.
- A constructor that creates a triangle with the specified `side1`, `side2`, and `side3`.
- The accessor methods for all three data fields.
- A method named `getArea()` that returns the area of this triangle.
- A method named `getPerimeter()` that returns the perimeter of this triangle.
- A method named `toString()` that returns a string description for the triangle.

For the formula to compute the area of a triangle, see Programming Exercise 2.15. The `toString()` method is implemented as follows:

```
return "Triangle: side1 = " + side1 + " side2 = " + side2 +
  " side3 = " + side3;
```

Draw the UML diagrams for the classes `Triangle` and `GeometricObject` and implement the classes. Write a test program that prompts the user to enter three sides of the triangle, a color, and a Boolean value to indicate whether the triangle is filled. The program should create a `Triangle` object with these sides and set the `color` and `filled` properties using the input. The program should display the area, perimeter, color, and true or false to indicate whether it is filled or not.

Sections 11.5–11.14

11.2 (*The Person, Student, Employee, Faculty, and Staff classes*) Design a class named `Person` and its two subclasses named `Student` and `Employee`. Make `Faculty` and `Staff` subclasses of `Employee`. A person has a name, address, phone number, and email address. A student has a class status (freshman, sophomore, junior, or senior). Define the status as a constant. An employee has an office, salary, and date hired. Use the `MyDate` class defined in Programming Exercise 10.14 to create an object for date hired. A faculty member has office hours and a rank. A staff member has a title. Override the `toString` method in each class to display the class name and the person's name.

Draw the UML diagram for the classes and implement them. Write a test program that creates a `Person`, `Student`, `Employee`, `Faculty`, and `Staff`, and invokes their `toString()` methods.

11.3 (*Subclasses of Account*) In Programming Exercise 8.7, the `Account` class was defined to model a bank account. An account has the properties account number, balance, annual interest rate, and date created, and methods to deposit and withdraw funds. Create two subclasses for checking and saving accounts. A checking account has an overdraft limit, but a savings account cannot be overdrawn.

Draw the UML diagram for the classes and then implement them. Write a test program that creates objects of `Account`, `SavingsAccount`, and `CheckingAccount` and invokes their `toString()` methods.

11.4 (*Maximum element in ArrayList*) Write the following method that returns the maximum value in an `ArrayList` of integers. The method returns `null` if the list is `null` or the list size is `0`.

```
public static Integer max(ArrayList<Integer> list)
```

Write a test program that prompts the user to enter a sequence of numbers ending with `0`, and invokes this method to return the largest number in the input.

11.5 (*The Course class*) Rewrite the `Course` class in Listing 10.6. Use an `ArrayList` to replace an array to store students. You should not change the original contract of the `Course` class (i.e., the definition of the constructors and methods should not be changed).

11.6 (*Use ArrayList*) Write a program that creates an `ArrayList` and adds a `Loan` object, a `Date` object, a string, a `JFrame` object, and a `Circle` object to the list, and use a loop to display all the elements in the list by invoking the object's `toString()` method.

11.7 (*Shuffle ArrayList*) Write the following method that shuffles the elements in an `ArrayList` of integers.

```
public static void shuffle(ArrayList<Integer> list)
```

**11.8 (*New Account class*) An `Account` class was specified in Programming Exercise 8.7. Design a new `Account` class as follows:

VideoNote

New `Account` class

- Add a new data field `name` of the `String` type to store the name of the customer.
- Add a new constructor that constructs an account with the specified name, id, and balance.
- Add a new data field named `transactions` whose type is `ArrayList` that stores the transaction for the accounts. Each transaction is an instance of the `Transaction` class. The `Transaction` class is defined as shown in Figure 11.6.

> The get and set methods for these data fields are provided in the class, but omitted in the UML diagram for brevity.

Transaction
-date: java.util.Date
-type: char
-amount: double
-balance: double
-description: String
+Transaction(type: char, amount: double, balance: double, description: String)

The date of this transaction.

The type of the transaction, such as 'W' for withdrawal, 'D' for deposit.

The amount of the transaction.

The new balance after this transaction.

The description of this transaction.

Construct a `Transaction` with the specified date, type, balance, and description.

FIGURE 11.6 The `Transaction` class describes a transaction for a bank account.

■ Modify the `withdraw` and `deposit` methods to add a transaction to the `transactions` array list.

■ All other properties and methods are the same as in Programming Exercise 8.7.

Write a test program that creates an `Account` with annual interest rate **1.5%**, balance **1000**, id **1122**, and name **George**. Deposit $30, $40, and $50 to the account and withdraw $5, $4, and $2 from the account. Print an account summary that shows account holder name, interest rate, balance, and all transactions.

*11.9 (*Largest rows and columns*) Write a program that randomly fills in **0**s and **1**s into an n-by-n matrix, prints the matrix, and finds the rows and columns with the most **1**s. (*Hint*: Use two `ArrayList`s to store the row and column indices with the most **1**s.) Here is a sample run of the program:

```
Enter the array size n: 4  ⏎Enter
The random array is
0011
0011
1101
1010
The largest row index: 2
The largest column index: 2, 3
```

11.10 (*Implement MyStack using inheritance*) In Listing 11.10, `MyStack` is implemented using composition. Define a new stack class that extends `ArrayList`.

Draw the UML diagram for the classes and then implement `MyStack`. Write a test program that prompts the user to enter five strings and displays them in reverse order.

11.11 (*Sort ArrayList*) Write the following method that sorts an `ArrayList` of numbers:

```
public static void sort(ArrayList<Integer> list)
```

Write a test program that prompts the user to enter 5 numbers, stores them in an array list, and displays them in increasing order.

11.12 (*Sum ArrayList*) Write the following method that returns the sum of all numbers in an `ArrayList`:

```
public static double sum(ArrayList<Double> list)
```

Write a test program that prompts the user to enter 5 numbers, stores them in an array list, and displays their sum.

GUI Basics

Objectives

- To distinguish between Swing and AWT (§12.2).

- To describe the Java GUI API hierarchy (§12.3).

- To create user interfaces using frames, panels, and simple GUI components (§12.4).

- To understand the role of layout managers and use the `FlowLayout`, `GridLayout`, and `BorderLayout` managers to lay out components in a container (§12.5).

- To use `JPanel` to group components in a subcontainer (§12.6).

- To create objects for colors using the `Color` class (§12.7).

- To create objects for fonts using the `Font` class (§12.8).

- To apply common features such as borders, tool tips, fonts, and colors on Swing components (§12.9).

- To decorate the border of GUI components (§12.9).

- To create image icons using the `ImageIcon` class (§12.10).

- To create and use buttons using the `JButton` class (§12.11).

- To create and use check boxes using the `JCheckBox` class (§12.12).

- To create and use radio buttons using the `JRadioButton` class (§12.13).

- To create and use labels using the `JLabel` class (§12.14).

- To create and use text fields using the `JTextField` class (§12.15).

12.1 Introduction

Java GUI is an excellent pedagogical tool for learning object-oriented programming.

The design of the API for Java GUI programming is an excellent example of how the object-oriented principle is applied. This chapter serves two purposes. First, it presents the basics of Java GUI programming. Second, it uses GUI to demonstrate OOP. Specifically, this chapter introduces the framework of the Java GUI API and discusses GUI components and their relationships, containers and layout managers, colors, fonts, borders, image icons, and tool tips. It also introduces some of the most frequently used GUI components.

12.2 Swing vs. AWT

AWT GUI components are replaced by more versatile and stable Swing GUI components.

We used simple GUI examples to demonstrate OOP in Section 8.6.3, Displaying GUI Components. We used the GUI components such as `JButton`, `JLabel`, `JTextField`, `JRadioButton`, and `JComboBox`. Why do the GUI component classes have the prefix *J*? Instead of `JButton`, why not name it simply `Button`? In fact, there is a class already named `Button` in the `java.awt` package.

AWT

Swing components

lightweight component
heavyweight component
why prefix J?

When Java was introduced, the GUI classes were bundled in a library known as the *Abstract Windows Toolkit (AWT)*. AWT is fine for developing simple graphical user interfaces, but not for developing comprehensive GUI projects. In addition, AWT is prone to platform-specific bugs. The AWT user-interface components were replaced by a more robust, versatile, and flexible library known as *Swing components*. Swing components are painted directly on canvases using Java code, except for components that are subclasses of `java.awt.Window` or `java.awt.Panel`, which must be drawn using native GUI on a specific platform. Swing components depend less on the target platform and use less of the native GUI resource. For this reason, Swing components that don't rely on native GUI are referred to as *lightweight components*, and AWT components are referred to as *heavyweight components*.

To distinguish new Swing component classes from their AWT counterparts, the Swing GUI component classes are named with a prefixed *J*. Although AWT components are still supported in Java, it is better to learn how to program using Swing components, because the AWT user-interface components will eventually fade away. This book uses Swing GUI components exclusively.

MyProgrammingLab™

12.1 Why are the Swing GUI classes named with the prefix *J*?

12.2 Explain the difference between AWT GUI components and Swing GUI components.

12.3 The Java GUI API

The GUI API contains classes that can be classified into three groups: component classes, container classes, *and* helper classes.

The hierarchical relationships of the Java GUI API are shown in Figure 12.1. Recall that the triangular arrow denotes the inheritance relationship, the diamond denotes the composition relationship, and the filled diamond denotes the exclusive composition relationship. The object composition relationship was introduced in Section 10.7.

component class
container class

helper class

The subclasses of `Component` are called *component classes* for creating the user interface. The classes, such as `JFrame`, `JPanel`, and `JApplet`, are called *container classes* used to contain other components. The classes, such as `Graphics`, `Color`, `Font`, `FontMetrics`, and `Dimension`, are called *helper classes* used to support GUI components.

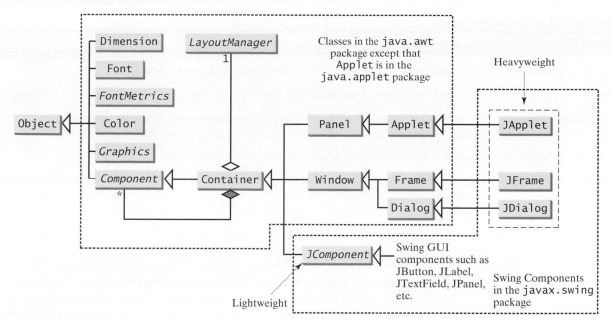

FIGURE 12.1 Java GUI programming utilizes the classes shown in this hierarchical diagram.

 Note
The JFrame, JApplet, JDialog, and JComponent classes and their subclasses are grouped in the **javax.swing** package. Applet is in the **java.applet** class. All the other classes in Figure 12.1 are grouped in the **java.awt** package.

12.3.1 Component Classes

An instance of **Component** can be displayed on the screen. **Component** is the root class of all the user-interface classes including container classes, and **JComponent** is the root class of all the lightweight Swing components. Both **Component** and **JComponent** are abstract classes (abstract classes will be introduced in Chapter 15). For now, all you need to know is that abstract classes are the same as classes except that you cannot create instances using the **new** operator. For example, you cannot use **new   JComponent()** to create an instance of **JComponent**. However, you can use the constructors of concrete subclasses of **JComponent** to create **JComponent** instances. It is important to become familiar with the class inheritance hierarchy. For example, the following statements all display true:

abstract class

```
JButton jbtOK = new JButton("OK");
System.out.println(jbtOK instanceof JButton);
System.out.println(jbtOK instanceof JComponent);
System.out.println(jbtOK instanceof Container);
System.out.println(jbtOK instanceof Component);
System.out.println(jbtOK instanceof Object);
```

12.3.2 Container Classes

An instance of **Container** can hold instances of **Component**. A container is called a *top-level container* if it can be displayed without being embedded in another container. **Window**, **Frame**, **Dialog**, **JFrame**, and **JDialog** are top-level containers. **Window**, **Panel**, **Applet**, **Frame**, and **Dialog** are the container classes for AWT components. To work with Swing components, use **Container**, **JFrame**, **JDialog**, **JApplet**, and **JPanel**, as described in Table 12.1.

top-level container

TABLE 12.1 GUI Container Classes

Container Class	Description
`java.awt.Container`	is used to hold components. Frames, panels, and applets are its subclasses.
`javax.swing.JFrame`	is a top-level container for holding other Swing user-interface components in Java GUI applications.
`javax.swing.JPanel`	is an invisible container for grouping user-interface components. Panels can be nested. You can place panels inside another panel. `JPanel` is also often used as a canvas to draw graphics.
`javax.swing.JApplet`	is a base class for creating a Java applet using Swing components.
`javax.swing.JDialog`	is a popup window generally used as a temporary window to receive additional information from the user or to provide notification to the user.

12.3.3 GUI Helper Classes

The helper classes, such as **Graphics**, **Color**, **Font**, **FontMetrics**, **Dimension**, and **LayoutManager**, are not subclasses of **Component**. They are used to describe the properties of GUI components, such as graphics context, colors, fonts, and dimension, as described in Table 12.2.

TABLE 12.2 GUI Helper Classes

Helper Class	Description
`java.awt.Graphics`	is an abstract class that provides the methods for drawing strings, lines, and simple shapes.
`java.awt.Color`	deals with the colors of GUI components. For example, you can specify background or foreground colors in components like `JFrame` and `JPanel`, or you can specify colors of lines, shapes, and strings in drawings.
`java.awt.Font`	specifies fonts for the text and drawings on GUI components. For example, you can specify the font type (e.g., SansSerif), style (e.g., bold), and size (e.g., 24 points) for the text on a button.
`java.awt.FontMetrics`	is an abstract class used to get the properties of the fonts.
`java.awt.Dimension`	encapsulates the width and height of a component (in integer precision) in a single object.
`java.awt.LayoutManager`	specifies how components are arranged in a container.

Note
The helper classes are in the `java.awt` package. The Swing components do not replace all the classes in the AWT, only the AWT GUI component classes (e.g., `Button`, `TextField`, `TextArea`). The AWT helper classes are still useful in GUI programming.

12.3 Which class is the root of the Java GUI component classes? Is a container class a subclass of **Component**? Which class is the root of the Swing GUI component classes?

12.4 Which of the following statements have syntax errors?

```
Component c1 = new Component();
JComponent c2 = new JComponent();
Component c3 = new JButton();
JComponent c4 = new JButton();
```

12.4 Frames

A frame is a window for holding other GUI components.

Key
Point

To create a user interface, you need to create either a frame or an applet to hold the user-interface components. This section introduces frames. Creating Java applets will be introduced in Chapter 18.

12.4.1 Creating a Frame

To create a frame, use the `JFrame` class, as shown in Figure 12.2.

javax.swing.JFrame	
+JFrame()	Creates a default frame with no title.
+JFrame(title: String)	Creates a frame with the specified title.
+setSize(width: int, height: int): void	Sets the size of the frame.
+setLocation(x: int, y: int): void	Sets the upper-left-corner location of the frame.
+setVisible(visible: boolean): void	Sets true to display the frame.
+setDefaultCloseOperation(mode: int): void	Specifies the operation when the frame is closed.
+setLocationRelativeTo(c: Component): void	Sets the location of the frame relative to the specified component. If the component is null, the frame is centered on the screen.
+pack(): void	Automatically sets the frame size to hold the components in the frame.

FIGURE 12.2 The *JFrame* class is used to create a window for displaying GUI components.

The program in Listing 12.1 creates a frame.

LISTING 12.1 MyFrame.java

```
1  import javax.swing.JFrame;                                              import package
2
3  public class MyFrame {
4    public static void main(String[] args) {
5      JFrame frame = new JFrame("MyFrame"); // Create a frame        create frame
6      frame.setSize(400, 300); // Set the frame size                 set size
7      frame.setLocationRelativeTo(null); // Center a frame           center frame
8      frame.setDefaultCloseOperation(JFrame.EXIT_ON_CLOSE);          close upon exit
9      frame.setVisible(true); // Display the frame                   display the frame
10   }
11 }
```

The frame is not displayed until the `frame.setVisible(true)` method is invoked. `frame.setSize(400, 300)` specifies that the frame is **400** pixels wide and **300** pixels high. If the `setSize` method is not used, the frame will be sized to display just the title bar. Since the `setSize` and `setVisible` methods are both defined in the `Component` class, they are inherited by the `JFrame` class. Later you will see that these methods are also useful in many other subclasses of `Component`.

When you run the `MyFrame` program, a window will be displayed on the screen (see Figure 12.3a).

Invoking `setLocationRelativeTo(null)` (line 7) centers the frame on the screen. Invoking `setDefaultCloseOperation(JFrame.EXIT_ON_CLOSE)` (line 8) tells the program to terminate when the frame is closed. If this statement is not used, the program does not terminate when the frame is closed. In that case, you have to stop the program by pressing *Ctrl+C* at the DOS prompt window in Windows or stop the process by using the kill command

(a)   (b)

FIGURE 12.3 (a) The program creates and displays a frame with the title MyFrame. (b) An OK button is added to the frame.

in UNIX. If you run the program from an IDE such as Eclipse or NetBeans, you need to click the red *Terminate* button in the Console pane to stop the program.

Note

pixel and resolution

Recall that a pixel is the smallest unit of space available for drawing on the screen. You can think of a pixel as a small rectangle and think of the screen as paved with pixels. The *resolution* specifies the number of pixels in horizontal and vertical dimensions of the screen. The more pixels the screen has, the higher the screen's resolution. The higher the resolution, the finer the detail you can see.

Note

setSize before centering

You should invoke the setSize(w, h) method before invoking setLocationRelativeTo(null) to center the frame.

12.4.2 Adding Components to a Frame

The frame shown in Figure 12.3a is empty. Using the **add** method, you can add components to the frame, as shown in Listing 12.2.

LISTING 12.2 MyFrameWithComponents.java

```
1  import javax.swing.*;
2
3  public class MyFrameWithComponents {
4    public static void main(String[] args) {
5      JFrame frame = new JFrame("MyFrameWithComponents");
6
7      // Add a button to the frame
8      JButton jbtOK = new JButton("OK");
9      frame.add(jbtOK);
10
11     frame.setSize(400, 300);
12     frame.setDefaultCloseOperation(JFrame.EXIT_ON_CLOSE);
13     frame.setLocationRelativeTo(null); // Center the frame
14     frame.setVisible(true);
15   }
16 }
```

create a button
add to frame

set size
exit upon closing window
center the frame
set visible

Each **JFrame** contains a *content pane*, which is an instance of **java.awt.Container**. The GUI components such as buttons are placed in the content pane in a frame. In earlier versions of Java, you had to use the **getContentPane** method in the **JFrame** class to return the content pane of the frame, then invoke the content pane's **add** method to place a component in the content pane, as follows:

```
java.awt.Container container = frame.getContentPane();
container.add(jbtOK);
```

This was cumbersome. Versions of Java since Java 5 allow you to place components in the content pane by invoking a frame's **add** method, as follows:

```
frame.add(jbtOK);
```

This feature is called *content-pane delegation*. Strictly speaking, a component is added to the content pane of a frame. For simplicity, we say that a component is added to a frame.

content-pane delegation

In Listing 12.2, an object of **JButton** was created using **new JButton("OK")**, and this object was added to the content pane of the frame (line 9).

The **add(Component comp)** method defined in the **Container** class adds an instance of **Component** to the container. Since **JButton** is a subclass of **Component**, an instance of **JButton** is also an instance of **Component**. To remove a component from a container, use the **remove** method. The following statement removes the button from the container:

```
container.remove(jbtOK);
```

When you run the program **MyFrameWithComponents**, the window will be displayed as in Figure 12.3b. The button is always centered in the frame and occupies the entire frame no matter how you resize it. This is because components are put in the frame by the content pane's layout manager, and the default layout manager for the content pane places the button in the center. In the next section, you will use several different layout managers to place components in the desired locations.

12.5 How do you create a frame? How do you set the size for a frame? How do you add components to a frame? What would happen if the statements **frame.setSize(400, 300)** and **frame.setVisible(true)** were swapped in Listing 12.2?

✔**Check Point**
MyProgrammingLab™

12.5 Layout Managers

Each container contains a layout manager, which is an object responsible for laying out the GUI components in the container.

🔑**Key Point**

In many other window systems, the user-interface components are arranged by using hard-coded pixel measurements. For example, when placing a button at location (**10, 10**) in a window using hard-coded pixel measurements, the user interface might look fine on one system but be unusable on another. Java's *layout managers* provide a level of abstraction that automatically maps your user interface on all window systems.

layout manager

The Java GUI components are placed in containers, where they are arranged by the container's layout manager. In the preceding program, you did not specify where to place the *OK* button in the frame, but Java knows where to place it, because the layout manager works behind the scenes to place components in the correct locations. A layout manager is created using a layout manager class.

Layout managers are set in containers using the **setLayout(aLayoutManager)** method. For example, you can use the following statements to create an instance of *X*Layout and set it in a container:

```
LayoutManager layoutManager = new XLayout();
container.setLayout(layoutManager);
```

This section introduces three basic layout managers: **FlowLayout**, **GridLayout**, and **BorderLayout**.

12.5.1 FlowLayout

`FlowLayout` is the simplest layout manager. The components are arranged in the container from left to right in the order in which they were added. When one row is filled, a new row is started. You can specify the way the components are aligned by using one of three constants: `FlowLayout.RIGHT`, `FlowLayout.CENTER`, or `FlowLayout.LEFT`. You can also specify the gap between components in pixels. The class diagram for `FlowLayout` is shown in Figure 12.4.

FIGURE 12.4 `FlowLayout` lays out components row by row.

Listing 12.3 gives a program that demonstrates flow layout. The program adds three labels and text fields to the frame with a `FlowLayout` manager, as shown in Figure 12.5.

LISTING 12.3 ShowFlowLayout.java

```
1  import javax.swing.JLabel;
2  import javax.swing.JTextField;
3  import javax.swing.JFrame;
4  import java.awt.FlowLayout;
5
6  public class ShowFlowLayout extends JFrame {
7    public ShowFlowLayout() {
8      // Set FlowLayout, aligned left with horizontal gap 10
9      // and vertical gap 20 between components
10     setLayout(new FlowLayout(FlowLayout.LEFT, 10, 20));
11
12     // Add labels and text fields to the frame
13     add(new JLabel("First Name"));
14     add(new JTextField(8));
15     add(new JLabel("MI"));
16     add(new JTextField(1));
17     add(new JLabel("Last Name"));
18     add(new JTextField(8));
19   }
20
21   /** Main method */
22   public static void main(String[] args) {
23     ShowFlowLayout frame = new ShowFlowLayout();
24     frame.setTitle("ShowFlowLayout");
25     frame.setSize(200, 200);
```

extends JFrame

set layout

add label
add text field

```
26      frame.setLocationRelativeTo(null); // Center the frame
27      frame.setDefaultCloseOperation(JFrame.EXIT_ON_CLOSE);
28      frame.setVisible(true);
29    }
30  }
```

create frame

set visible

(a)   (b)

FIGURE 12.5 The components are added by the `FlowLayout` manager to fill in the rows in the container one after another.

This example creates a program using a style different from the programs in the preceding section, where frames were created using the `JFrame` class. This example creates a class named `ShowFlowLayout` that extends the `JFrame` class (line 6). The `main` method in this program creates an instance of `ShowFlowLayout` (line 23). The constructor of `ShowFlowLayout` constructs and places the components in the frame. This is the preferred style of creating GUI applications—for three reasons:

■ Creating a GUI application means creating a frame, so it is natural to define a frame to extend `JFrame`.

■ The frame may be further extended to add new components or functions.

■ The class can be easily reused. For example, you can create multiple frames by creating multiple instances of the class.

Using one style consistently makes programs easy to read. From now on, most of the GUI main classes will extend the `JFrame` class. The constructor of the main class constructs the user interface. The `main` method creates an instance of the main class and then displays the frame.

Will the program work if line 23 is replaced by the following code?

```
JFrame frame = new ShowFlowLayout();
```

Yes. The program will still work because `ShowFlowLayout` is a subclass of `JFrame` and the methods `setTitle`, `setSize`, `setLocationRelativeTo`, `setDefaultCloseOperation`, and `setVisible` (lines 24–28) are all available in the `JFrame` class.

In this example, the `FlowLayout` manager is used to place components in a frame. If you resize the frame, the components are automatically rearranged to fit. In Figure 12.5a, the first row has three components, but in Figure 12.5b, the first row has four components, because the width has been increased.

If you replace the `setLayout` statement (line 10) with `setLayout(new FlowLayout(FlowLayout.RIGHT, 0, 0))`, all the rows of buttons will be right aligned with no gaps.

An anonymous `FlowLayout` object was created in the statement (line 10):

```
setLayout(new FlowLayout(FlowLayout.LEFT, 10, 20));
```

which is equivalent to:

```
FlowLayout layout = new FlowLayout(FlowLayout.LEFT, 10, 20);
setLayout(layout);
```

This code creates an explicit reference to the object `layout` of the `FlowLayout` class. The explicit reference is not necessary, because the object is not directly referenced in the `ShowFlowLayout` class.

Suppose you add the same button to the frame ten times; will ten buttons appear in the frame? No, a GUI component such as a button can be added to only one container and only once in a container. Adding a button to a container multiple times is the same as adding it once.

Note

GUI components cannot be shared by containers, because only one GUI component can appear in only one container at a time. Therefore, the relationship between a component and a container is the composition denoted by a filled diamond, as shown in Figure 12.1.

Caution

Do not forget to put the `new` operator before a layout manager class when setting a layout style—for example, `setLayout(new FlowLayout())`.

Note

The constructor `ShowFlowLayout()` does not explicitly invoke the constructor `JFrame()`, but the constructor `JFrame()` is invoked implicitly. See Section 11.3.2, Constructor Chaining.

12.5.2 GridLayout

The `GridLayout` manager arranges components in a grid (matrix) formation. The components are placed in the grid from left to right, starting with the first row, then the second, and so on, in the order in which they are added. The class diagram for `GridLayout` is shown in Figure 12.6.

> The `get` and `set` methods for these data fields are provided in the class, but omitted in the UML diagram for brevity.

java.awt.GridLayout	
-rows: int	The number of rows in the grid (default: 1).
-columns: int	The number of columns in the grid (default: 1).
-hgap: int	The horizontal gap between the components (default: 0).
-vgap: int	The vertical gap between the components (default: 0).
+GridLayout()	Creates a default `GridLayout` manager.
+GridLayout(rows: int, columns: int)	Creates a `GridLayout` with a specified number of rows and columns.
+GridLayout(rows: int, columns: int, hgap: int, vgap: int)	Creates a `GridLayout` manager with a specified number of rows and columns, horizontal gap, and vertical gap.

Figure 12.6 `GridLayout` lays out components in equal-sized cells on a grid.

You can specify the number of rows and columns in the grid. The basic rules are as follows:

■ The number of rows or the number of columns can be zero, but not for both. If one is zero and the other is nonzero, the nonzero dimension is fixed, while the zero dimension is determined dynamically by the layout manager. For example, if you specify zero rows and three columns for a grid that has ten components, `GridLayout` creates three fixed columns of four rows, with the last row containing one component. If you specify three rows and zero columns for a grid that has ten components, `GridLayout` creates three fixed rows of four columns, with the last row containing two components.

■ If both the number of rows and the number of columns are nonzero, the number of rows is the dominating parameter; that is, the number of rows is fixed, and the layout manager dynamically calculates the number of columns. For example, if you specify three rows and three columns for a grid that has ten components, `GridLayout` creates three fixed rows of four columns, with the last row containing two components.

Listing 12.4 gives a program that demonstrates grid layout. The program is similar to the one in Listing 12.3, except that it adds three labels and three text fields to the frame of `GridLayout` instead of `FlowLayout`, as shown in Figure 12.7.

FIGURE 12.7 The `GridLayout` manager divides the container into grids; then the components are added to fill in the cells row by row.

LISTING 12.4 ShowGridLayout.java

```java
 1  import javax.swing.JLabel;
 2  import javax.swing.JTextField;
 3  import javax.swing.JFrame;
 4  import java.awt.GridLayout;
 5
 6  public class ShowGridLayout extends JFrame {
 7    public ShowGridLayout() {
 8      // Set GridLayout, 3 rows, 2 columns, and gaps 5 between
 9      // components horizontally and vertically
10      setLayout(new GridLayout(3, 2, 5, 5));                    set layout
11
12      // Add labels and text fields to the frame
13      add(new JLabel("First Name"));                           add label
14      add(new JTextField(8));                                  add text field
15      add(new JLabel("MI"));
16      add(new JTextField(1));
17      add(new JLabel("Last Name"));
18      add(new JTextField(8));
19    }
20
21    /** Main method */
22    public static void main(String[] args) {
23      ShowGridLayout frame = new ShowGridLayout();
24      frame.setTitle("ShowGridLayout");
25      frame.setSize(200, 125);
26      frame.setLocationRelativeTo(null); // Center the frame    create the frame
27      frame.setDefaultCloseOperation(JFrame.EXIT_ON_CLOSE);
28      frame.setVisible(true);                                  set visible
29    }
30  }
```

If you resize the frame, the layout of the components remains unchanged (i.e., the number of rows and columns does not change, and the gaps don't change either).

All components are given equal size in the container of `GridLayout`.

Replacing the `setLayout` statement (line 10) with `setLayout(new GridLayout(3, 10))` would still yield three rows and *two* columns. The `columns` parameter is ignored because the `rows` parameter is nonzero. The actual number of columns is calculated by the layout manager.

What would happen if the `setLayout` statement (line 10) were replaced with `setLayout(new GridLayout(4, 2))` or with `setLayout(new GridLayout(2, 2))`? Please try it yourself.

Note

In `FlowLayout` and `GridLayout`, the order in which the components are added to the container is important. The order determines the location of the components in the container.

12.5.3   BorderLayout

The `BorderLayout` manager divides a container into five areas: East, South, West, North, and Center. Components are added to a `BorderLayout` by using `add(Component, index)`, where `index` is a constant `BorderLayout.EAST`, `BorderLayout.SOUTH`, `BorderLayout.WEST`, `BorderLayout.NORTH`, or `BorderLayout.CENTER`. The class diagram for `BorderLayout` is shown in Figure 12.8.

FIGURE 12.8   `BorderLayout` lays out components in five areas.

The components are laid out according to their preferred sizes and their placement in the container. The North and South components can stretch horizontally; the East and West components can stretch vertically; the Center component can stretch both horizontally and vertically to fill any empty space.

Listing 12.5 gives a program that demonstrates border layout. The program adds five buttons labeled `East`, `South`, `West`, `North`, and `Center` to the frame with a `BorderLayout` manager, as shown in Figure 12.9.

FIGURE 12.9   `BorderLayout` divides the container into five areas, each of which can hold a component.

LISTING 12.5   ShowBorderLayout.java

```
1  import javax.swing.JButton;
2  import javax.swing.JFrame;
3  import java.awt.BorderLayout;
```

```
 4
 5   public class ShowBorderLayout extends JFrame {
 6     public ShowBorderLayout() {
 7       // Set BorderLayout with horizontal gap 5 and vertical gap 10
 8       setLayout(new BorderLayout(5, 10));                                 set layout
 9
10       // Add buttons to the frame
11       add(new JButton("East"), BorderLayout.EAST);                       add buttons
12       add(new JButton("South"), BorderLayout.SOUTH);
13       add(new JButton("West"), BorderLayout.WEST);
14       add(new JButton("North"), BorderLayout.NORTH);
15       add(new JButton("Center"), BorderLayout.CENTER);
16     }
17
18     /** Main method */
19     public static void main(String[] args) {
20       ShowBorderLayout frame = new ShowBorderLayout();
21       frame.setTitle("ShowBorderLayout");
22       frame.setSize(300, 200);
23       frame.setLocationRelativeTo(null); // Center the frame     create the frame
24       frame.setDefaultCloseOperation(JFrame.EXIT_ON_CLOSE);
25       frame.setVisible(true);                                            set visible
26     }
27   }
```

The buttons are added to the frame (lines 11–15). Note that the **add** method for **BorderLayout** is different from the one for `FlowLayout` and `GridLayout`. With **BorderLayout**, you specify where to put the components.

It is unnecessary to place components to occupy all the areas. If you remove the East button from the program and rerun it, you will see that the Center button stretches rightward to occupy the East area.

Note

`BorderLayout` interprets the absence of an index specification as `BorderLayout.CENTER`. For example, `add(component)` is the same as `add(Component, BorderLayout.CENTER)`. If you add two components to a container of `BorderLayout`, as follows,

```
container.add(component1);
container.add(component2);
```

only the last component is displayed.

12.5.4   Properties of Layout Managers

Layout managers have properties that can be changed dynamically.

- `FlowLayout` has `alignment`, `hgap`, and `vgap` properties. You can use the `setAlignment`, `setHgap`, and `setVgap` methods to specify the alignment and the horizontal and vertical gaps.

- `GridLayout` has the `rows`, `columns`, `hgap`, and `vgap` properties. You can use the `setRows`, `setColumns`, `setHgap`, and `setVgap` methods to specify the number of rows, the number of columns, and the horizontal and vertical gaps.

- `BorderLayout` has the `hgap` and `vgap` properties. You can use the `setHgap` and `setVgap` methods to specify the horizontal and vertical gaps.

In the preceding sections an anonymous layout manager is used because the properties of a layout manager do not change once it is created. If you have to change the properties of a layout manager dynamically, the layout manager must be explicitly referenced by a variable. You can then change the properties of the layout manager through the variable. For example, the following code creates a layout manager and sets its properties:

```
// Create a layout manager
FlowLayout flowLayout = new FlowLayout();

// Set layout properties
flowLayout.setAlignment(FlowLayout.RIGHT);
flowLayout.setHgap(10);
flowLayout.setVgap(20);
```

MyProgrammingLab

12.6 Will the program work if **ShowFlowLayout** in line 23 in Listing 12.3 is replaced by **JFrame**?

Will the program work if **ShowGridLayout** in line 23 in Listing 12.4 is replaced by **JFrame**?

Will the program work if **ShowBorderLayout** line 20 in Listing 12.5 is replaced by **JFrame**?

12.7 Why do you need to use layout managers? What is the default layout manager for a frame? How do you add a component to a frame?

12.8 Describe **FlowLayout**. How do you create a **FlowLayout** manager? How do you add a component to a **FlowLayout** container? Is there a limit to the number of components that can be added to a **FlowLayout** container? What are the properties for setting the horizontal and vertical gaps between the components in the container? Can you specify alignment?

12.9 Describe **GridLayout**. How do you create a **GridLayout** manager? How do you add a component to a **GridLayout** container? Is there a limit to the number of components that can be added to a **GridLayout** container? What are the properties for setting the horizontal and vertical gaps between the components in the container?

12.10 Describe **BorderLayout**. How do you create a **BorderLayout** manager? How do you add a component to a **BorderLayout** container? What are the properties for setting the horizontal and vertical gaps between the components in the container?

12.11 The following program is supposed to display a button in a frame, but nothing is displayed. What is the problem?

```
1  public class Test extends javax.swing.JFrame {
2    public Test() {
3      add(new javax.swing.JButton("OK"));
4    }
5
6    public static void main(String[] args) {
7      javax.swing.JFrame frame = new javax.swing.JFrame();
8      frame.setSize(100, 200);
9      frame.setVisible(true);
10   }
11 }
```

12.6 Using Panels as Subcontainers

A container can be placed inside another container. Panels can be used as subcontainers to group GUI components to achieve the desired layout.

Suppose that you want to place ten buttons and a text field in a frame. The buttons are placed in grid formation, but the text field is placed on a separate row. It is difficult to achieve the desired look by placing all the components in a single container. With Java GUI programming, you can divide a window into panels. Panels act as subcontainers to group user-interface components. You add the buttons in one panel, then add the panel to the frame.

VideoNote

Use panels as subcontainers

The Swing version of panel is `JPanel`. You can use **new** `JPanel()` to create a panel with a default `FlowLayout` manager or **new** `JPanel(LayoutManager)` to create a panel with the specified layout manager. Use the **add(Component)** method to add a component to the panel. For example, the following code creates a panel and adds a button to it:

```
JPanel p = new JPanel();
p.add(new JButton("OK"));
```

Panels can be placed inside a frame or inside another panel. The following statement places panel **p** in frame **f**:

```
f.add(p);
```

Listing 12.6 gives an example that demonstrates using panels as subcontainers. The program creates a user interface for a microwave oven, as shown in Figure 12.10.

FIGURE 12.10   The program uses panels to organize components.

LISTING 12.6 `TestPanels.java`

```
1   import java.awt.*;
2   import javax.swing.*;
3
4   public class TestPanels extends JFrame {
5     public TestPanels() {
6       // Create panel p1 for the buttons and set GridLayout
7       JPanel p1 = new JPanel();                                        panel p1
8       p1.setLayout(new GridLayout(4, 3));
9
10      // Add buttons to the panel
11      for (int i = 1; i <= 9; i++) {
12        p1.add(new JButton("" + i));
13      }
14
15      p1.add(new JButton("" + 0));
16      p1.add(new JButton("Start"));
17      p1.add(new JButton("Stop"));
18
19      // Create panel p2 to hold a text field and p1
20      JPanel p2 = new JPanel(new BorderLayout());                      panel p2
21      p2.add(new JTextField("Time to be displayed here"),
22        BorderLayout.NORTH);
23      p2.add(p1, BorderLayout.CENTER);
24
25      // Add contents to the frame
26      add(p2, BorderLayout.EAST);                                      add p2 to frame
27      add(new JButton("Food to be placed here"),
28        BorderLayout.CENTER);
29    }
30
```

```
31     /** Main method */
32     public static void main(String[] args) {
33       TestPanels frame = new TestPanels();
34       frame.setTitle("The Front View of a Microwave Oven");
35       frame.setSize(400, 250);
36       frame.setLocationRelativeTo(null); // Center the frame
37       frame.setDefaultCloseOperation(JFrame.EXIT_ON_CLOSE);
38       frame.setVisible(true);
39     }
40   }
```

The `setLayout` method is defined in `java.awt.Container`. Since `JPanel` is a subclass of `Container`, you can use `setLayout` to set a new layout manager in the panel (line 8). Lines 7–8 can be replaced by `JPanel p1 = new JPanel(new GridLayout(4, 3))`.

To achieve the desired layout, the program uses panel `p1` of `GridLayout` to group the number buttons, the *Stop* button, and the *Start* button, and panel `p2` of `BorderLayout` to hold a text field in the north and `p1` in the center. The button representing the food is placed in the center of the frame, and `p2` is placed in the east of the frame.

The statement (lines 21–22)

```
p2.add(new JTextField("Time to be displayed here"),
   BorderLayout.NORTH);
```

creates an instance of `JTextField` and adds it to `p2`. `JTextField` is a GUI component that can be used for user input as well as to display values.

superclass `Container`

Note

It is worthwhile to note that the `Container` class is the superclass for GUI component classes, such as `JButton`. Every GUI component is a container. In theory, you could use the `setLayout` method to set the layout in a button and add components to a button, because all the public methods in the `Container` class are inherited by `JButton`, but for practical reasons you should not use buttons as containers.

Check Point

MyProgrammingLab™

12.12 How do you create a panel with a specified layout manager?

12.13 What is the default layout manager for a `JPanel`? How do you add a component to a `JPanel`?

12.14 Can you use the `setTitle` method in a panel? What is the purpose of using a panel?

12.15 Since a GUI component class such as `JButton` is a subclass of `Container`, can you add components to a button?

12.7 The **Color** Class

Key Point

Each GUI component has background and foreground colors. Colors are objects created from the `Color` class.

You can set colors for GUI components by using the `java.awt.Color` class. Colors are made of red, green, and blue components, each represented by an `int` value that describes its intensity, ranging from **0** (darkest shade) to **255** (lightest shade). This is known as the *RGB model*.

You can create a color using the following constructor:

```
public Color(int r, int g, int b);
```

in which `r`, `g`, and `b` specify a color by its red, green, and blue components. For example,

```
Color color = new Color(128, 100, 100);
```

Note

The arguments `r`, `g`, `b` are between **0** and **255**. If a value beyond this range is passed to the argument, an `IllegalArgumentException` will occur.

`IllegalArgumentException`

You can use the **setBackground(Color c)** and **setForeground(Color c)** methods defined in the **java.awt.Component** class to set a component's background and foreground colors. Here is an example of setting the background and foreground of a button:

```
JButton jbtOK = new JButton("OK");
jbtOK.setBackground(color);
jbtOK.setForeground(new Color(100, 1, 1));
```

Alternatively, you can use one of the 13 standard colors (**BLACK**, **BLUE**, **CYAN**, **DARK_GRAY**, **GRAY**, **GREEN**, **LIGHT_GRAY**, **MAGENTA**, **ORANGE**, **PINK**, **RED**, **WHITE**, and **YELLOW**) defined as constants in **java.awt.Color**. The following code, for instance, sets the foreground color of a button to red:

```
jbtOK.setForeground(Color.RED);
```

12.16 How do you create a color? What is wrong about creating a **Color** using **new Color(400, 200, 300)**? Which of two colors is darker, **new Color(10, 0, 0)** or **new Color(200, 0, 0)**?

12.17 How do you create a **Color** object with a random color?

12.18 How do you set a button object **jbtOK** with blue background?

✓ Check Point
MyProgrammingLab™

12.8 The **Font** Class

Key Point

Each GUI component has the font property. Fonts are objects created from the Font class.

You can create a font using the **java.awt.Font** class and set fonts for the components using the **setFont** method in the **Component** class.

The constructor for **Font** is:

```
public Font(String name, int style, int size);
```

You can choose a font name from **SansSerif**, **Serif**, **Monospaced**, **Dialog**, and **DialogInput**, choose a style from **Font.PLAIN** (0), **Font.BOLD** (1), **Font.ITALIC** (2), and **Font.BOLD + Font.ITALIC** (3), and specify a font size of any positive integer. For example, the following statements create two fonts and set one font to a button.

```
Font font1 = new Font("SansSerif", Font.BOLD, 16);
Font font2 = new Font("Serif", Font.BOLD + Font.ITALIC, 12);

JButton jbtOK = new JButton("OK");
jbtOK.setFont(font1);
```

> **Tip**
> If your system supports other fonts, such as "Times New Roman," you can use the font to create a **Font** object. To find the fonts available on your system, you need to obtain an instance of **java.awt.GraphicsEnvironment** using its static method **getLocalGraphicsEnvironment()**. **GraphicsEnvironment** is an abstract class that describes the graphics environment on a particular system. You can use its **getAllFonts()** method to obtain all the available fonts on the system and its **getAvailableFontFamilyNames()** method to obtain the names of all the available fonts. For example, the following statements print all the available font names in the system:
>
> ```
> GraphicsEnvironment e =
>   GraphicsEnvironment.getLocalGraphicsEnvironment();
> String[] fontnames = e.getAvailableFontFamilyNames();
>
> for (int i = 0; i < fontnames.length; i++)
>   System.out.println(fontnames[i]);
> ```

find available fonts

MyProgrammingLab™

Check Point

12.19 How do you create a `Font` object with font name `Courier`, size `20`, and style `bold`?

12.20 How do you find all available fonts on your system?

12.9 Common Features of Swing GUI Components

Key Point

GUI components have common features. They are defined in the superclasses `Component`, `Container`, *and* `JComponent`.

VideoNote

Use Swing common properties

So far in this chapter you have used several GUI components (e.g., `JFrame`, `Container`, `JPanel`, `JButton`, `JLabel`, and `JTextField`). Many more GUI components will be introduced in this book. It is important to understand the common features of Swing GUI components. The `Component` class is the root for all GUI components and containers. All Swing GUI components (except `JFrame`, `JApplet`, and `JDialog`) are subclasses of `JComponent`, as shown in Figure 12.1. Figure 12.11 lists some frequently used methods in

Component
Container
JComponent
tool tip

`Component`, `Container`, and `JComponent` for manipulating properties such as font, color, mouse cursor, size, tool tip text, and border.

A *tool tip* is text displayed on a component when you move the mouse onto the component. It is often used to describe the function of a component.

The `get` and `set` methods for these data fields are provided in the class, but omitted in the UML diagram for brevity.

java.awt.Component	
-font: java.awt.Font	The font of this component.
-background: java.awt.Color	The background color of this component.
-foreground: java.awt.Color	The foreground color of this component.
-preferredSize: java.awt.Dimension	The preferred size of this component.
-visible: boolean	Indicates whether this component is visible.
-cursor: java.awt.Cursor	The mouse cursor shape.
+getWidth(): int	Returns the width of this component.
+getHeight(): int	Returns the height of this component.
+getX(): int	`getX()` and `getY()` return the coordinate of the
+getY(): int	component's upper-left corner within its parent component.

java.awt.Container	
+add(comp: Component): Component	Adds a component to the container.
+add(comp: Component, index: int): Component	Adds a component to the container with the specified index.
+remove(comp: Component): void	Removes the component from the container.
+getLayout(): LayoutManager	Returns the layout manager for this container.
+setLayout(l: LayoutManager): void	Sets the layout manager for this container.

The `get` and `set` methods for these data fields are provided in the class, but omitted in the UML diagram for brevity.

javax.swing.JComponent	
-toolTipText: String	The tool tip text for this component. Tool tip text is displayed when the mouse points on the component without clicking.
-border: javax.swing.border.Border	The border for this component.

FIGURE 12.11 All the Swing GUI components inherit the public methods from `Component`, `Container`, and `JComponent`.

You can set a border for any object of the `JComponent` class. Swing has several types of borders. To create a titled border, use `new TitledBorder(String title)`. To create a line border, use `new LineBorder(Color color, int width)`, where `width` specifies the thickness of the line.

Listing 12.7 is an example to demonstrate Swing common features. The example creates a panel **p1** to hold three buttons (line 8) and a panel **p2** to hold two labels (line 26), as shown in Figure 12.12. The background of the button `jbtLeft` is set to white (line 12) and the foreground of the button `jbtCenter` is set to green (line 13). The tool tip of the button `jbtRight` is set in line 14. Titled borders are set on panels **p1** and **p2** (lines 18, 37) and line borders are set on the labels (lines 33–34).

FIGURE 12.12 The font, color, border, and tool tip text are set in the message panel.

The mouse cursor is set to the cross-hair shape in **p1** (line 19). The `Cursor` class contains the constants for specifying the cursor shape such as `DEFAULT_CURSOR(` ➤ `)`, `CROSSHAIR_CURSOR` (✛), `HAND_CURSOR(` ☝ `)`, `MOVE_CURSOR(` ✤ `)`, `TEXT_CURSOR(` I `)`, and so on. A `Cursor` object for the cross-hair cursor is created using `new Cursor(Cursor.CROSSHAIR_CURSOR)` (line 19) and this cursor is set for **p1**. Note that the default mouse cursor is still used in **p2**, because the program does not explicitly set a mouse cursor for **p2**.

LISTING 12.7 `TestSwingCommonFeatures.java`

```
1   import java.awt.*;
2   import javax.swing.*;
3   import javax.swing.border.*;
4
5   public class TestSwingCommonFeatures extends JFrame {
6     public TestSwingCommonFeatures() {
7       // Create a panel to group three buttons
8       JPanel p1 = new JPanel(new FlowLayout(FlowLayout.LEFT, 2, 2));
9       JButton jbtLeft = new JButton("Left");
10      JButton jbtCenter = new JButton("Center");
11      JButton jbtRight = new JButton("Right");
12      jbtLeft.setBackground(Color.WHITE);
13      jbtCenter.setForeground(Color.GREEN);
14      jbtRight.setToolTipText("This is the Right button");
15      p1.add(jbtLeft);
16      p1.add(jbtCenter);
17      p1.add(jbtRight);
18      p1.setBorder(new TitledBorder("Three Buttons"));
19      p1.setCursor(new Cursor(Cursor.CROSSHAIR_CURSOR));
20
21      // Create a font and a line border
22      Font largeFont = new Font("TimesRoman", Font.BOLD, 20);
23      Border lineBorder = new LineBorder(Color.BLACK, 2);
```

border

set background
set foreground
set tool tip text

set titled border
set mouse cursor

create a font
create a border

set foreground

set font

set line border

set titled border

```
24
25      // Create a panel to group two labels
26      JPanel p2 = new JPanel(new GridLayout(1, 2, 5, 5));
27      JLabel jlblRed = new JLabel("Red");
28      JLabel jlblOrange = new JLabel("Orange");
29      jlblRed.setForeground(Color.RED);
30      jlblOrange.setForeground(Color.ORANGE);
31      jlblRed.setFont(largeFont);
32      jlblOrange.setFont(largeFont);
33      jlblRed.setBorder(lineBorder);
34      jlblOrange.setBorder(lineBorder);
35      p2.add(jlblRed);
36      p2.add(jlblOrange);
37      p2.setBorder(new TitledBorder("Two Labels"));
38
39      // Add two panels to the frame
40      setLayout(new GridLayout(2, 1, 5, 5));
41      add(p1);
42      add(p2);
43    }
44
45    public static void main(String[] args) {
46      // Create a frame and set its properties
47      JFrame frame = new TestSwingCommonFeatures();
48      frame.setTitle("TestSwingCommonFeatures");
49      frame.setSize(300, 150);
50      frame.setLocationRelativeTo(null); // Center the frame
51      frame.setDefaultCloseOperation(JFrame.EXIT_ON_CLOSE);
52      frame.setVisible(true);
53    }
54  }
```

property default values

Note

The same property may have different default values in different components. For example, the **visible** property in **JFrame** is **false** by default, but it is **true** in every instance of **JComponent** (e.g., **JButton** and **JLabel**) by default. To display a **JFrame**, you have to invoke **setVisible(true)** to set the **visible** property **true**, but you don't have to set this property for a **JButton** or a **JLabel**, because it is already **true**. To make a **JButton** or a **JLabel** invisible, you can invoke **setVisible(false)**. Please run the program and see the effect after inserting the following two statements in line 38:

```
jbtLeft.setVisible(false);
jlblRed.setVisible(false);
```

MyProgrammingLab™

12.21 How do you set background color, foreground color, font, and tool tip text on a Swing GUI component?

12.22 Why is the tool tip text not displayed in the following code?

```
1   import javax.swing.*;
2
3   public class Test extends JFrame {
4     private JButton jbtOK = new JButton("OK");
5
6     public static void main(String[] args) {
7       // Create a frame and set its properties
8       JFrame frame = new Test();
9       frame.setTitle("Logic Error");
10      frame.setSize(200, 100);
11      frame.setDefaultCloseOperation(JFrame.EXIT_ON_CLOSE);
```

```
12        frame.setVisible(true);
13      }
14
15      public Test() {
16        jbtOK.setToolTipText("This is a button");
17        add(new JButton("OK"));
18      }
19    }
```

12.23 Show the output of the following code:

```
import javax.swing.*;

public class Test {
  public static void main(String[] args) {
    JButton jbtOK = new JButton("OK");
    System.out.println(jbtOK.isVisible());

    JFrame frame = new JFrame();
    System.out.println(frame.isVisible());
  }
}
```

12.24 What happens if you add a button to a container several times, as shown below? Does it cause syntax errors? Does it cause runtime errors?

```
JButton jbt = new JButton();
JPanel panel = new JPanel();
panel.add(jbt);
panel.add(jbt);
panel.add(jbt);
```

12.10 Image Icons

Image icons can be displayed in many GUI components. Image icons are objects created using the `ImageIcon` *class.*

Key
Point

An icon is a fixed-size picture; typically it is small and used to decorate components. Images are normally stored in image files. Java currently supports three image formats: GIF (Graphics Interchange Format), JPEG (Joint Photographic Experts Group), and PNG (Portable Network Graphics). The image file names for these types end with **.gif**, **.jpg**, and **.png**, respectively. If you have a bitmap file or image files in other formats, you can use image-processing utilities to convert them into the GIF, JPEG, or PNG format for use in Java.

To display an image icon, first create an `ImageIcon` object using `new javax.swing.ImageIcon(filename)`. For example, the following statement creates an icon from an image file **us.gif** in the **image** directory under the current class path:

image-file format

```
ImageIcon icon = new ImageIcon("image/us.gif");
```

create ImageIcon

image/us.gif is located in **c:\book\image\us.gif**. The back slash (\) is the Windows file path notation. In UNIX, the forward slash (/) should be used. In Java, the forward slash (/) is used to denote a relative file path under the Java classpath (e.g., **image/us.gif**, as in this example).

file path character

Tip
File names are not case sensitive in Windows but are case sensitive in UNIX. To enable your programs to run on all platforms, name all the image files consistently, using lowercase.

naming files consistently

An image icon can be displayed in a label or a button using **new JLabel(imageIcon)** or **new JButton(imageIcon)**. Listing 12.8 demonstrates displaying icons in labels and buttons. The example creates two labels and two buttons with icons, as shown in Figure 12.13.

FIGURE 12.13 The image icons are displayed in labels and buttons.

LISTING 12.8 TestImageIcon.java

```
1  import javax.swing.*;
2  import java.awt.*;
3
4  public class TestImageIcon extends JFrame {
5    private ImageIcon usIcon = new ImageIcon("image/us.gif");
6    private ImageIcon myIcon = new ImageIcon("image/my.jpg");
7    private ImageIcon frIcon = new ImageIcon("image/fr.gif");
8    private ImageIcon ukIcon = new ImageIcon("image/uk.gif");
9
10   public TestImageIcon() {
11     setLayout(new GridLayout(1, 4, 5, 5));
12     add(new JLabel(usIcon));
13     add(new JLabel(myIcon));
14     add(new JButton(frIcon));
15     add(new JButton(ukIcon));
16   }
17
18   /** Main method */
19   public static void main(String[] args) {
20     TestImageIcon frame = new TestImageIcon();
21     frame.setTitle("TestImageIcon");
22     frame.setSize(200, 200);
23     frame.setLocationRelativeTo(null); // Center the frame
24     frame.setDefaultCloseOperation(JFrame.EXIT_ON_CLOSE);
25     frame.setVisible(true);
26   }
27 }
```

create image icons (line 5)

a label with image (line 12)

a button with image (line 14)

Note

sharing borders and icons

Borders and icons can be shared. Thus, you can create a border or icon and use it to set the **border** or **icon** property for any GUI component. For example, the following statements set a border **b** for the panels **p1** and **p2**:

```
p1.setBorder(b);
p2.setBorder(b);
```

The following statements set an icon in the buttons **jbt1** and **jbt2**:

```
jbt1.setIcon(icon);
jbt2.setIcon(icon);
```

Tip

A *splash screen* is an image that is displayed while the application is starting up. If your program takes a long time to load, you may display a splash screen to alert the user. For example, the following command:

splash screen

```
java –splash:image/us.gif TestImageIcon
```

displays an image while the program **TestImageIcon** is being loaded.

12.25 How do you create an **ImageIcon** from the file **image/us.gif** in the class directory?

12.26 Will the following code display three buttons? Will the buttons display the same icon?

```java
1   import javax.swing.*;
2   import java.awt.*;
3
4   public class Test extends JFrame  {
5     public static void main(String[] args) {
6       // Create a frame and set its properties
7       JFrame frame = new Test();
8       frame.setTitle("ButtonIcons");
9       frame.setSize(200, 100);
10      frame.setDefaultCloseOperation(JFrame.EXIT_ON_CLOSE);
11      frame.setVisible(true);
12    }
13
14    public Test() {
15      ImageIcon usIcon = new ImageIcon("image/us.gif");
16      JButton jbt1 = new JButton(usIcon);
17      JButton jbt2 = new JButton(usIcon);
18
19      JPanel p1 = new JPanel();
20      p1.add(jbt1);
21
22      JPanel p2 = new JPanel();
23      p2.add(jbt2);
24
25      JPanel p3 = new JPanel();
26      p2.add(jbt1);
27
28      add(p1, BorderLayout.NORTH);
29      add(p2, BorderLayout.SOUTH);
30      add(p3, BorderLayout.CENTER);
31    }
32  }
```

12.27 Can a border or an icon be shared by GUI components?

12.11 **JButton**

*To create a push button, use the **JButton** class.*

We have used **JButton** in the examples to demonstrate the basics of GUI programming. This section will introduce more features of **JButton**. The following sections will introduce GUI components **JCheckBox**, **JRadioButton**, **JLabel**, **JTextField**, and **JPasswordField**. More GUI components such as **JTextArea**, **JComboBox**, **JList**, **JScrollBar**, and **JSlider** will be introduced in Chapter 17. The relationship of these classes is pictured in Figure 12.14.

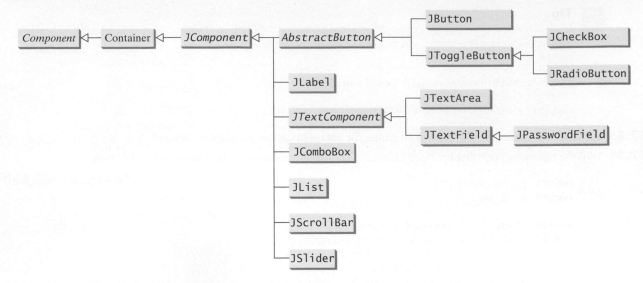

FIGURE 12.14 These Swing GUI components are frequently used to create user interfaces.

naming convention for
   components

 Note

Throughout this book, the prefixes `jbt`, `jchk`, `jrb`, `jlbl`, `jtf`, `jpf`, `jta`, `jcbo`, `jlst`, `jscb`, and `jsld` are used to name reference variables for `JButton`, `JCheckBox`, `JRadioButton`, `JLabel`, `JTextField`, `JPasswordField`, `JTextArea`, `JComboBox`, `JList`, `JScrollBar`, and `JSlider`.

AbstractButton

A *button* is a component that triggers an action when clicked. Swing provides regular buttons, toggle buttons, check box buttons, and radio buttons. The common features of these buttons are defined in `javax.swing.AbstractButton`, as shown in Figure 12.15.

FIGURE 12.15 `AbstractButton` defines common features of different types of buttons.

JButton inherits AbstractButton and provides several constructors to create buttons, as shown in Figure 12.16.

javax.swing.AbstractButton

javax.swing.JButton
+JButton()
+JButton(icon: javax.swing.Icon)
+JButton(text: String)
+JButton(text: String, icon: Icon)

Creates a default button without any text or icons.
Creates a button with an icon.
Creates a button with text.
Creates a button with text and an icon.

FIGURE 12.16 JButton defines a regular push button.

12.11.1 Icons, Pressed Icons, and Rollover Icons

A button has a default icon, a pressed icon, and a rollover icon. Normally you use the default icon, because the other icons are for special effects. A pressed icon is displayed when a button is pressed, and a rollover icon is displayed when the mouse is over the button but not pressed. For example, Listing 12.9 displays the U.S. flag as a regular icon, the Canadian flag as a pressed icon, and the British flag as a rollover icon, as shown in Figure 12.17.

LISTING 12.9 TestButtonIcons.java

```
 1 import javax.swing.*;
 2
 3 public class TestButtonIcons extends JFrame  {
 4   public static void main(String[] args) {
 5     // Create a frame and set its properties
 6     JFrame frame = new TestButtonIcons();
 7     frame.setTitle("ButtonIcons");
 8     frame.setSize(200, 100);
 9     frame.setLocationRelativeTo(null); // Center the frame
10     frame.setDefaultCloseOperation(JFrame.EXIT_ON_CLOSE);
11     frame.setVisible(true);
12   }
13
14   public TestButtonIcons() {
15     ImageIcon usIcon = new ImageIcon("image/usIcon.gif");      create icons
16     ImageIcon caIcon = new ImageIcon("image/caIcon.gif");
17     ImageIcon ukIcon = new ImageIcon("image/ukIcon.gif");
18
19     JButton jbt = new JButton("Click it", usIcon);             regular icon
20     jbt.setPressedIcon(caIcon);                                pressed icon
21     jbt.setRolloverIcon(ukIcon);                               rollover icon
22
23     add(jbt);                                                  add a button
24   }
25 }
```

(a) Default icon   (b) Pressed icon   (c) Rollover icon

FIGURE 12.17 A button can have several types of icons.

12.11.2 Alignments

horizontal alignment

Horizontal alignment specifies how the icon and text are placed horizontally on a button. You can set the horizontal alignment using `setHorizontalAlignment(int)` with one of the five constants `LEADING`, `LEFT`, `CENTER`, `RIGHT`, or `TRAILING`, as shown in Figure 12.18. At present, `LEADING` and `LEFT` are the same, and `TRAILING` and `RIGHT` are the same. Future implementation may distinguish them. The default horizontal alignment is `AbstractButton.CENTER`.

FIGURE 12.18 You can specify how the icon and text are placed on a button horizontally.

vertical alignment

Vertical alignment specifies how the icon and text are placed vertically on a button. You can set the vertical alignment using `setVerticalAlignment(int)` with one of the three constants `TOP`, `CENTER`, or `BOTTOM`, as shown in Figure 12.19. The default vertical alignment is `AbstractButton.CENTER`.

FIGURE 12.19 You can specify how the icon and text are placed on a button vertically.

12.11.3 Text Positions

horizontal text position

Horizontal text position specifies the horizontal position of the text relative to the icon. You can set the horizontal text position using `setHorizontalTextPosition(int)` with one of the five constants `LEADING`, `LEFT`, `CENTER`, `RIGHT`, or `TRAILING`, as shown in Figure 12.20. At present, `LEADING` and `LEFT` are the same, and `TRAILING` and `RIGHT` are the same. Future implementation may distinguish them. The default horizontal text position is `AbstractButton.RIGHT`.

FIGURE 12.20 You can specify the horizontal position of the text relative to the icon.

vertical text position

Vertical text position specifies the vertical position of the text relative to the icon. You can set the vertical text position using `setVerticalTextPosition(int)` with one of the three constants TOP, CENTER, or BOTTOM, as shown in Figure 12.21. The default vertical text position is AbstractButton.CENTER.

Text positioned top   Text centered   Text positioned bottom
                        vertically

FIGURE 12.21   You can specify the vertical position of the text relative to the icon.

12.28 How do you create a button with the text OK? How do you change text on a button? How do you set an icon, a pressed icon, and a rollover icon in a button?

12.29 Given a JButton object jbtOK, write statements to set the button's foreground to red, background to yellow, mnemonic to K, tool tip text to Click OK to proceed, horizontal alignment to RIGHT, vertical alignment to BOTTOM, horizontal text position to LEFT, vertical text position to TOP, and icon text gap to 5.

12.30 List at least five properties defined in the AbstractButton class.

12.12 **JCheckBox**

To create a check box button, use the JCheckBox class.

 Key Point

A *toggle button* is a two-state button like a light switch. JToggleButton *inherits* AbstractButton *and* implements a toggle button. Often JToggleButton's subclasses JCheckBox and JRadioButton are used to enable the user to toggle a choice on or off. This section introduces JCheckBox. JRadioButton will be introduced in the next section.

toggle button

   JCheckBox inherits all the properties from AbstractButton, such as text, icon, mnemonic, verticalAlignment, horizontalAlignment, horizontalTextPosition, verticalTextPosition, and selected, and provides several constructors to create check boxes, as shown in Figure 12.22.

javax.swing.JCheckBox	
+JCheckBox()	Creates a default check box without any text or icon.
+JCheckBox(text: String)	Creates a check box with text.
+JCheckBox(text: String, selected: boolean)	Creates a check box with text and specifies whether the check box is initially selected.
+JCheckBox(icon: Icon)	Creates a check box with an icon.
+JCheckBox(text: String, icon: Icon)	Creates a check box with text and an icon.
+JCheckBox(text: String, icon: Icon, selected: boolean)	Creates a check box with text and an icon, and specifies whether the check box is initially selected.

FIGURE 12.22   JCheckBox defines a check box button.

Here is an example for creating a check box with the text *Student*. Its foreground is **red**, the background is **white**, its mnemonic key is **S**, and it is initially selected.

```java
JCheckBox jchk = new JCheckBox("Student", true);
jchk.setForeground(Color.RED);
jchk.setBackground(Color.WHITE);
jchk.setMnemonic('S');
```

☑ Student

mnemonics

The button can also be accessed by using the keyboard mnemonics. Pressing *Alt+S* is equivalent to clicking the check box.

isSelected?

To see if a check box is selected, use the `isSelected()` method.

✓Check Point

12.31 How do you create a check box? How do you create a check box with the box checked initially? How do you determine whether a check box is selected?

MyProgrammingLab™

12.13 JRadioButton

🔑 Key Point

To create a radio button, use the JRadioButton class.

Radio buttons, also known as *option buttons*, enable you to choose a single item from a group of choices. In appearance radio buttons resemble check boxes, but check boxes display a square that is either checked or blank, whereas radio buttons display a circle that is either filled (if selected) or blank (if not selected).

`JRadioButton` inherits `AbstractButton` and provides several constructors to create radio buttons, as shown in Figure 12.23. These constructors are similar to the constructors for `JCheckBox`.

javax.swing.JRadioButton	
+JRadioButton()	Creates a default radio button without any text or icon.
+JRadioButton(text: String)	Creates a radio button with text.
+JRadioButton(text: String, selected: boolean)	Creates a radio button with text and specifies whether the radio button is initially selected.
+JRadioButton(icon: Icon)	Creates a radio button with an icon.
+JRadioButton(text: String, icon: Icon)	Creates a radio button with text and an icon.
+JRadioButton(text: String, icon: Icon, selected: boolean)	Creates a radio button with text and an icon, and specifies whether the radio button is initially selected.

FIGURE 12.23 `JRadioButton` defines a radio button.

Here is an example for creating a radio button with the text Student. The code specifies **red** foreground, **white** background, mnemonic key **S**, and initially selected.

```java
JRadioButton jrb = new JRadioButton("Student", true);
jrb.setForeground(Color.RED);
jrb.setBackground(Color.WHITE);
jrb.setMnemonic('S');
```

◉ Student

To group radio buttons, you need to create an instance of `java.swing.ButtonGroup` and use the **add** method to add them to it, as follows:

```
ButtonGroup group = new ButtonGroup();
group.add(jrb1);
group.add(jrb2);
```

This code creates a radio-button group for the radio buttons **jrb1** and **jrb2** so that they are selected mutually exclusively. Without grouping, **jrb1** and **jrb2** would be independent.

> **Note**
>
> **ButtonGroup** is not a subclass of `java.awt.Component`, so a **ButtonGroup** object cannot be added to a container.
>
> To see if a radio button is selected, use the `isSelected()` method.

GUI helper class

12.32 How do you create a radio button? How do you create a radio button with the button selected initially? How do you group radio buttons together? How do you determine whether a radio button is selected?

MyProgrammingLab™

12.14 Labels

To create a label, use the `JLabel` *class.*

A *label* is a display area for a short text, an image, or both. It is often used to label other components (usually text fields). Figure 12.24 lists the constructors and methods in the **JLabel** class.

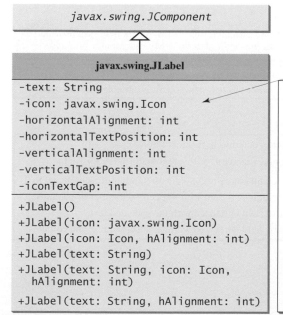

The get and set methods for these data fields are provided in the class, but omitted in the UML diagram for brevity.

javax.swing.JLabel	
-text: String	The label's text.
-icon: javax.swing.Icon	The label's image icon.
-horizontalAlignment: int	The horizontal alignment of the text and icon on the label.
-horizontalTextPosition: int	The horizontal text position relative to the icon on the label.
-verticalAlignment: int	The vertical alignment of the text and icon on the label.
-verticalTextPosition: int	The vertical text position relative to the icon on the label.
-iconTextGap: int	The gap between the text and the icon on the label.
+JLabel()	Creates a default label without any text or icons.
+JLabel(icon: javax.swing.Icon)	Creates a label with an icon.
+JLabel(icon: Icon, hAlignment: int)	Creates a label with an icon and the specified horizontal alignment.
+JLabel(text: String)	Creates a label with text.
+JLabel(text: String, icon: Icon, hAlignment: int)	Creates a label with text, an icon, and the specified horizontal alignment.
+JLabel(text: String, hAlignment: int)	Creates a label with text and the specified horizontal alignment.

FIGURE 12.24 `JLabel` displays text or an icon, or both.

JLabel inherits all the properties from **JComponent** and has many properties similar to the ones in **JButton**, such as **text**, **icon**, **horizontalAlignment**, **verticalAlignment**, **horizontalTextPosition**, **verticalTextPosition**, and **iconTextGap**. For example, the following code displays a label with text and an icon:

```
// Create an image icon from an image file
ImageIcon icon = new ImageIcon("image/grapes.gif");

// Create a label with a text, an icon,
// with centered horizontal alignment
JLabel jlbl = new JLabel("Grapes", icon, JLabel.CENTER);

//Set label's text alignment and gap between text and icon
jlbl.setHorizontalTextPosition(JLabel.CENTER);
jlbl.setVerticalTextPosition(JLabel.BOTTOM);
jlbl.setIconTextGap(5);
```

Check Point

MyProgrammingLab™

12.33 How do you create a label named **Address**? How do you change the name on a label? How do you set an icon in a label?

12.34 Given a **JLabel** object **jlblMap**, write statements to set the label's foreground to **red**, background to **yellow**, mnemonic to **M**, tool tip text to **Map image**, horizontal alignment to **RIGHT**, vertical alignment to **BOTTOM**, horizontal text position to **LEFT**, vertical text position to **TOP**, and icon text gap to **5**.

12.15 Text Fields

Key Point

To create a text field, use the JTextField class.

A *text field* can be used to enter or display a string. **JTextField** is a subclass of **JTextComponent**. Figure 12.25 lists the constructors and methods in **JTextField**.

javax.swing.text.JTextComponent	
-text: String -editable: boolean	The text contained in this text component. Indicates whether this text component is editable (default: true).

The get and set methods for these data fields are provided in the class, but omitted in the UML diagram for brevity.

javax.swing.JTextField	
-columns: int -horizontalAlignment: int	The number of columns in this text field. The horizontal alignment of this text field (default: LEFT).
+JTextField() +JTextField(column: int) +JTextField(text: String) +JTextField(text: String, columns: int)	Creates a default empty text field with number of columns set to 0. Creates an empty text field with a specified number of columns. Creates a text field initialized with the specified text. Creates a text field initialized with the specified text and columns.

FIGURE 12.25 JTextField enables you to enter or display a string.

JTextField inherits JTextComponent, which inherits JComponent. Here is an example of creating a text field with red foreground color and right horizontal alignment:

```
JTextField jtfMessage = new JTextField("T-Storm");
jtfMessage.setForeground(Color.RED);
jtfMessage.setHorizontalAlignment(JTextField.RIGHT);
```

To set new text in a text field, use the **setText(newText)** method. To get the text from a text field, use the **getText()** method.

Note

If a text field is used for entering a password, use `JPasswordField` to replace `JTextField`. `JPasswordField` extends `JTextField` and hides the input text with echo characters (e.g., ******). By default, the echo character is *. You can specify a new echo character using the `setEchoChar(char)` method.

`JPasswordField`

12.35 How do you create a text field with `10` columns and the default text `Welcome to Java`? How do you write the code to check whether a text field is empty?

12.36 How do you create text field for entering passwords?

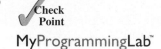

KEY TERMS

AWT   446
component class   446
container class   446
heavyweight component   446
helper class   446

layout manager   451
lightweight component   446
Swing components   446
splash screen   467
top-level container   447

CHAPTER SUMMARY

1. Every container has a *layout manager* that is used to position and place components in the container in the desired locations. Three simple and frequently used layout managers are `FlowLayout`, `GridLayout`, and `BorderLayout`.

2. You can use a `JPanel` as a subcontainer to group components to achieve a desired layout.

3. Use the `add` method to place components in a `JFrame` or a `JPanel`. By default, the frame's layout is `BorderLayout`, and the `JPanel`'s layout is `FlowLayout`.

4. Colors are made of red, green, and blue components, each represented by an unsigned byte value that describes its intensity, ranging from `0` (darkest shade) to `255` (lightest shade). This is known as the *RGB model*.

5. To create a `Color` object, use `new Color(r, g, b)`, in which r, g, and b specify a color by its red, green, and blue components. Alternatively, you can use one of the 13 standard colors (`BLACK`, `BLUE`, `CYAN`, `DARK_GRAY`, `GRAY`, `GREEN`, `LIGHT_GRAY`, `MAGENTA`, `ORANGE`, `PINK`, `RED`, `WHITE`, `YELLOW`) defined as constants in `java.awt.Color`.

6. Every *Swing* GUI component is a subclass of `javax.swing.JComponent`, and `JComponent` is a subclass of `java.awt.Component`. The properties `font`, `background`, `foreground`, `height`, `width`, and `preferredSize` in `Component` are inherited in these subclasses, as are `toolTipText` and `border` in `JComponent`.

7. You can use borders on any Swing components. You can create an image icon using the `ImageIcon` class and display it in a label and a button. Icons and borders can be shared.

8. You can display a text and icon on buttons (`JButton`, `JCheckBox`, `JRadioButton`) and labels (`JLabel`).

9. You can specify the horizontal and vertical text alignment in `JButton`, `JCheckBox`, `JRadioButton`, and `JLabel`, and the horizontal text alignment in `JTextField`.

10. You can specify the horizontal and vertical text position relative to the icon in `JButton`, `JCheckBox`, `JRadioButton`, and `JLabel`.

TEST QUESTIONS

Do the test questions for this chapter online at www.cs.armstrong.edu/liang/intro9e/test.html.

MyProgrammingLab™

PROGRAMMING EXERCISES

download image files

 Note

The image icons used in the exercises can be obtained from www.cs.armstrong.edu/liang/intro9e/book.zip under the image folder.

Sections 12.2–12.6

12.1 (*Use the `FlowLayout` manager*) Write a program that meets the following requirements (see Figure 12.26):

- Create a frame and set its layout to `FlowLayout`.
- Create two panels and add them to the frame.
- Each panel contains three buttons. The panel uses `FlowLayout`.

FIGURE 12.26 Exercise 12.1 places the first three buttons in one panel and the other three buttons in another panel.

12.2 (*Use the `BorderLayout` manager*) Rewrite the preceding program to create the same user interface, but instead of using `FlowLayout` for the frame, use `BorderLayout`. Place one panel in the south of the frame and the other in the center.

12.3 (*Use the `GridLayout` manager*) Rewrite Programming Exercise 12.1 to add six buttons into a frame. Use a `GridLayout` of two rows and three columns for the frame.

12.4 (*Use `JPanel` to group buttons*) Rewrite Programming Exercise 12.1 to create the same user interface. Instead of creating buttons and panels separately, define a class that extends the `JPanel` class. Place three buttons in your panel class, and create two panels from the user-defined panel class.

12.5 (*Display labels*) Write a program that displays four lines of text in four labels, as shown in Figure 12.27a. Add a line border around each label.

(a)   (b)   (c)

FIGURE 12.27 (a) Exercise 12.5 displays four labels. (b) Exercise 12.6 displays four icons. (c) Exercise 12.7 displays a tic-tac-toe board with image icons in labels.

Sections 12.7–12.15

12.6 (*Display icons*) Write a program that displays four icons in four labels, as shown in Figure 12.27b. Add a line border around each label.

12.7 (*Game: display a tic-tac-toe board*) Display a frame that contains nine labels. A label may display an image icon for X or an image icon for O, as shown in Figure 12.27c. What to display is randomly decided. Use the `Math.random()` method to generate an integer `0` or `1`, which corresponds to displaying an X or O image icon. These images are in the files **x.gif and **o.gif**.

*12.8 (*Swing common features*) Display a frame that contains six labels. Set the background of the labels to white. Set the foreground of the labels to black, blue, cyan, green, magenta, and orange, respectively, as shown in Figure 12.28a. Set the border of each label to a line border with the color yellow. Set the font of each label to Times Roman, bold, and 20 pixels. Set the text and tool tip text of each label to the name of its foreground color.

(a)   (b)   (c)

FIGURE 12.28 (a) Six labels are placed in the frame. (b) Three cards are randomly selected. (c) A checkerboard is displayed using buttons.

*12.9 (*Game: display three cards*) Display a frame that contains three labels. Each label displays a card, as shown in Figure 12.28b. The card image files are named **1.png**, **2.png**, . . ., **54.png** (including jokers) and stored in the **image/card** directory. All three cards are distinct and selected randomly.

*12.10 (*Game: display a checkerboard*) Write a program that displays a checkerboard in which each white and black cell is a `JButton` with a background black or white, as shown in Figure 12.28c.

*12.11 (*Game: display four cards*) Use the same cards from Exercise 12.9 to display a frame that contains four buttons. All buttons have the same icon from **backCard.png**, as shown in Figure 12.29a. The pressed icons are four cards randomly selected from the 54 cards in a deck, as shown in Figure 12.29b.

VideoNote

Display a checkerboard

(a)   (b)   (c)

FIGURE 12.29 (a) The four buttons have the same icon. (b) Each button's pressed icon is randomly picked from the deck. (c) The image icons and texts are displayed in four labels.

12.12 (*Use labels*) Write a program that displays the image icon and the text in four labels, as shown Figure 12.29c.

12.13 (*Display 54 cards*) Expand Exercise 12.9 to display all 54 cards in 54 labels, nine per row.

VideoNote

Display a random matrix

*12.14 (*Display random 0 or 1*) Write a program that displays a 10-by-10 square matrix, as shown in Figure 12.30. Each element in the matrix is **0** or **1**, randomly generated. Display each number centered in a label.

FIGURE 12.30 The program randomly generates 0s and 1s.

GRAPHICS

Objectives

- To draw graphics using the methods in the `Graphics` class (§13.2).

- To override the `paintComponent` method to draw graphics on a GUI component (§13.2).

- To use a panel as a canvas to draw graphics (§13.2).

- To draw strings, lines, rectangles, ovals, arcs, and polygons (§§13.3, 13.5–13.6).

- To obtain font properties using `FontMetrics` and to display a text centered in a panel (§13.7).

- To display an image on a GUI component (§13.10).

- To develop the reusable GUI components `FigurePanel`, `MessagePanel`, `StillClock`, and `ImageViewer` (§§13.4, 13.8, 13.9, 13.11).

13.1 Introduction

Problem

Key Point

You can draw custom shapes on a GUI component.

Suppose you want to draw shapes such as a bar chart, a clock, or a stop sign, as shown in Figure 13.1. How do you do so?

| (a) | (b) | (c) |

FIGURE 13.1 You can draw shapes using the drawing methods in the **Graphics** class.

This chapter describes how to use the methods in the **Graphics** class to draw strings, lines, rectangles, ovals, arcs, polygons, and images, and how to develop reusable GUI components.

13.2 The **Graphics** Class

Key Point

Each GUI component has a graphics context, which is an object of the **Graphics** *class. The* **Graphics** *class contains the methods for drawing various shapes.*

The **Graphics** class provides the methods for drawing strings, lines, rectangles, ovals, arcs, polygons, and polylines, as shown in Figure 13.2.

Think of a GUI component as a piece of paper and the **Graphics** object as a pencil or paintbrush. You can apply the methods in the **Graphics** class to draw graphics on a GUI component.

To paint, you need to specify where to paint. Each component has its own coordinate system with the origin (**0, 0**) at the upper-left corner. The *x*-coordinate increases to the right, and the *y*-coordinate increases downward. Note that the Java coordinate system differs from the conventional coordinate system, as shown in Figure 13.3.

The **Graphics** class—an abstract class—provides a device-independent graphics interface for displaying figures and images on the screen on different platforms. Whenever a component (e.g., a button, a label, or a panel) is displayed, the JVM automatically creates a **Graphics** object for the component on the native platform and passes this object to invoke the **paintComponent** method to display the drawings.

paintComponent

The signature of the **paintComponent** method is as follows:

```
protected void paintComponent(Graphics g)
```

This method, defined in the **JComponent** class, is invoked whenever a component is first displayed or redisplayed.

To draw on a component, you need to define a class that extends **JPanel** and overrides its **paintComponent** method to specify what to draw. Listing 13.1 gives an example that draws a line and a string on a panel, as shown in Figure 13.4.

java.awt.Graphics	
+setColor(color: Color): void	Sets a new color for subsequent drawings.
+setFont(font: Font): void	Sets a new font for subsequent drawings.
+drawString(s: String, x: int, y: int): void	Draws a string starting at point (x, y).
+drawLine(x1: int, y1: int, x2: int, y2: int): void	Draws a line from (x1, y1) to (x2, y2).
+drawRect(x: int, y: int, w: int, h: int): void	Draws a rectangle with specified upper-left corner point at (x,y) and width w and height h.
+fillRect(x: int, y: int, w: int, h: int): void	Draws a filled rectangle with specified upper-left corner point at (x, y) and width w and height h.
+drawRoundRect(x: int, y: int, w: int, h: int, aw: int, ah: int): void	Draws a round-cornered rectangle with specified arc width aw and arc height ah.
+fillRoundRect(x: int, y: int, w: int, h: int, aw: int, ah: int): void	Draws a filled round-cornered rectangle with specified arc width aw and arc height ah.
+draw3DRect(x: int, y: int, w: int, h: int, raised: boolean): void	Draws a 3-D rectangle raised above the surface or sunk into the surface.
+fill3DRect(x: int, y: int, w: int, h: int, raised: boolean): void	Draws a filled 3-D rectangle raised above the surface or sunk into the surface.
+drawOval(x: int, y: int, w: int, h: int): void	Draws an oval bounded by the rectangle specified by the parameters x, y, w, and h.
+fillOval(x: int, y: int, w: int, h: int): void	Draws a filled oval bounded by the rectangle specified by the parameters x, y, w, and h.
+drawArc(x: int, y: int, w: int, h: int, startAngle: int, arcAngle: int): void	Draws an arc conceived as part of an oval bounded by the rectangle specified by the parameters x, y, w, and h.
+fillArc(x: int, y: int, w: int, h: int, startAngle: int, arcAngle: int): void	Draws a filled arc conceived as part of an oval bounded by the rectangle specified by the parameters x, y, w, and h.
+drawPolygon(xPoints: int[], yPoints: int[], nPoints: int): void	Draws a closed polygon defined by arrays of x- and y-coordinates. Each pair of (x[i], y[i])-coordinates is a point.
+fillPolygon(xPoints: int[], yPoints: int[], nPoints: int): void	Draws a filled polygon defined by arrays of x- and y-coordinates. Each pair of (x[i], y[i])-coordinates is a point.
+drawPolygon(g: Polygon): void	Draws a closed polygon defined by a Polygon object.
+fillPolygon(g: Polygon): void	Draws a filled polygon defined by a Polygon object.
+drawPolyline(xPoints: int[], yPoints: int[], nPoints: int): void	Draws a polyline defined by arrays of x- and y-coordinates. Each pair of (x[i], y[i])-coordinates is a point.

FIGURE 13.2   The **Graphics** class contains the methods for drawing strings and shapes.

FIGURE 13.3   The Java coordinate system is measured in pixels, with (0, 0) at its upper-left corner.

LISTING 13.1 TestPaintComponent.java

```
1  import javax.swing.*;
2  import java.awt.Graphics;
3
```

create a panel

```
 4   public class TestPaintComponent extends JFrame {
 5     public TestPaintComponent() {
 6       add(new NewPanel());
 7     }
 8
 9     public static void main(String[] args) {
10       TestPaintComponent frame = new TestPaintComponent();
11       frame.setTitle("TestPaintComponent");
12       frame.setSize(200, 100);
13       frame.setLocationRelativeTo(null); // Center the frame
14       frame.setDefaultCloseOperation(JFrame.EXIT_ON_CLOSE);
15       frame.setVisible(true);
16     }
17   }
18
```

new panel class

override paintComponent
draw things in the superclass
draw line
draw string

```
19   class NewPanel extends JPanel {
20     @Override
21     protected void paintComponent(Graphics g) {
22       super.paintComponent(g);
23       g.drawLine(0, 0, 50, 50);
24       g.drawString("Banner", 0, 40);
25     }
26   }
```

FIGURE 13.4 A line and a string are drawn on a panel.

The **paintComponent** method is automatically invoked to paint graphics when the component is first displayed or whenever the component needs to be redisplayed. Invoking **super.paintComponent(g)** (line 22) invokes the **paintComponent** method defined in the superclass. This is necessary to ensure that the viewing area is cleared before a new drawing is displayed. Line 23 invokes the **drawLine** method to draw a line from (**0**, **0**) to (**50**, **50**). Line 24 invokes the **drawString** method to draw the string **Banner** at location (**0**, **40**).

All the drawing methods have parameters that specify the locations of the subjects to be drawn. In Java, all measurements are made in pixels.

The JVM invokes **paintComponent** to draw things on a component. The user should never invoke **paintComponent** directly. For this reason, the protected visibility is sufficient for **paintComponent**.

Panels are invisible and are used as small containers that group components to achieve a desired layout. Another important use of **JPanel** is for drawing. You can draw things on any Swing GUI component, but normally you should use a **JPanel** as a canvas upon which to draw things. What happens if you replace **JPanel** with **JLabel** in line 19 as follows?

```
class NewPanel extends JLabel {
```

extends JPanel?

The program will work, but it is not preferred, because **JLabel** is designed for creating a label, not for drawing. For consistency, this book will define a canvas class by subclassing **JPanel**.

Tip
Some textbooks define a canvas class by subclassing **JComponent**. The problem with
doing that is if you want to set a background in the canvas, you have to write the code
to paint the background color. A simple **setBackground(Color color)** method
will not set a background color in a **JComponent**.

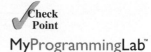
extends JComponent?

13.1 Suppose that you want to draw a new message below an existing message. Should the
x-coordinate, *y*-coordinate, or both increase or decrease?

13.2 How is a `Graphics` object created?

13.3 How is the `paintComponent` method invoked? How can a program invoke this
method?

13.4 Why is the `paintComponent` method `protected`? What happens if you change it
to `public` or `private` in a subclass? Why is `super.paintComponent(g)`
invoked in line 22 in Listing 13.1?

13.5 Can you draw things on any Swing GUI component? Why should you use a panel as
a canvas for drawings rather than a label or a button?

✓ **Check Point**

MyProgrammingLab™

13.3 Drawing Strings, Lines, Rectangles, and Ovals

You can draw strings, lines, rectangles, and ovals in a graphics context.

The **drawString(String s, int x, int y)** method draws a string starting at the point
(x, y), as shown in Figure 13.5a.

The **drawLine(int x1, int y1, int x2, int y2)** method draws a straight line
from point **(x1, y1)** to point **(x2, y2)**, as shown in Figure 13.5b.

🔑 **Key Point**

drawString

drawLine

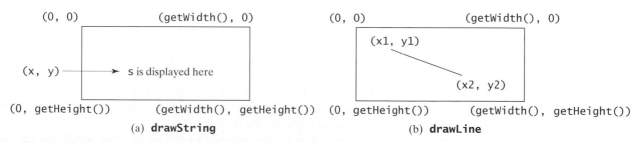

(a) **drawString** (b) **drawLine**

FIGURE 13.5 (a) The **drawString(s, x, y)** method draws a string starting at **(x, y)**. (b) The **drawLine(x1, y1,**
x2, y2) method draws a line between two specified points.

Java provides six methods for drawing the outline of rectangles or rectangles filled with
color. You can draw or fill plain rectangles, round-cornered rectangles, or three-dimensional
rectangles.

The **drawRect(int x, int y, int w, int h)** method draws a plain rectangle, and
the **fillRect(int x, int y, int w, int h)** method draws a filled rectangle. The
parameters **x** and **y** represent the upper-left corner of the rectangle, and **w** and **h** are its width
and height (see Figure 13.6).

The **drawRoundRect(int x, int y, int w, int h, int aw, int ah)** method
draws a round-cornered rectangle, and the **fillRoundRect(int x, int y, int w, int**
h, int aw, int ah) method draws a filled round-cornered rectangle. Parameters **x, y, w,**
and **h** are the same as in the **drawRect** method, parameter **aw** is the horizontal diameter of the
arcs at the corner, and **ah** is the vertical diameter of the arcs at the corner (see Figure 13.7a).

drawRect
fillRect

drawRoundRect
fillRoundRect

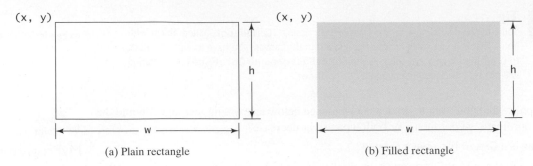

(a) Plain rectangle   (b) Filled rectangle

FIGURE 13.6 (a) The **drawRect(x, y, w, h)** method draws a rectangle. (b) The **fillRect(x, y, w, h)** method draws a filled rectangle.

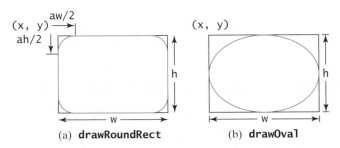

(a) **drawRoundRect**   (b) **drawOval**

FIGURE 13.7 (a) The **drawRoundRect(x, y, w, h, aw, ah)** method draws a round-cornered rectangle. (b) The **drawOval(x, y, w, h)** method draws an oval based on its bounding rectangle.

In other words, **aw** and **ah** are the width and the height of the oval that produces a quarter-circle at each corner.

draw3DRect
fill3DRect

The **draw3DRect(int x, int y, int w, int h, boolean raised)** method draws a 3-D rectangle and the **fill3DRect(int x, int y, int w, int h, boolean raised)** method draws a filled 3-D rectangle. The parameters **x, y, w,** and **h** are the same as in the **drawRect** method. The last parameter, a Boolean value, indicates whether the rectangle is raised above the surface or sunk into the surface.

drawOval
fillOval

Depending on whether you wish to draw an oval in outline or filled solid, you can use either the **drawOval(int x, int y, int w, int h)** method or the **fillOval(int x, int y, int w, int h)** method. An oval is drawn based on its bounding rectangle. Parameters **x** and **y** indicate the top-left corner of the bounding rectangle, and **w** and **h** indicate the width and height, respectively, of the bounding rectangle, as shown in Figure 13.7b.

Check
Point

MyProgrammingLab™

13.6 Describe the methods for drawing strings, lines, and the methods for drawing/filling rectangles, round-cornered rectangles, 3-D rectangles, and ovals.

13.7 Draw a thick line from (**10**, **10**) to (**70**, **30**). You can draw several lines next to each other to create the effect of one thick line.

13.8 Draw/fill a rectangle of width **100** and height **50** with the upper-left corner at (**10**, **10**).

13.9 Draw/fill a round-cornered rectangle with width **100**, height **200**, corner horizontal diameter **40**, and corner vertical diameter **20**.

13.10 Draw/fill a circle with radius **30**.

13.11 Draw/fill an oval with width **50** and height **100**.

13.4 Case Study: The **FigurePanel** Class

This case study develops the FigurePanel *class for displaying various figures.*

Key Point

This example develops a useful class for displaying various figures. The class enables the user to set the figure type and specify whether the figure is filled, and it displays the figure on a panel. The UML diagram for the class is shown in Figure 13.8. The panel can display lines, rectangles, round-cornered rectangles, and ovals. Which figure to display is decided by the type property. If the filled property is true, the rectangle, round-cornered rectangle, and oval are filled in the panel.

VideoNote

The FigurePanel class

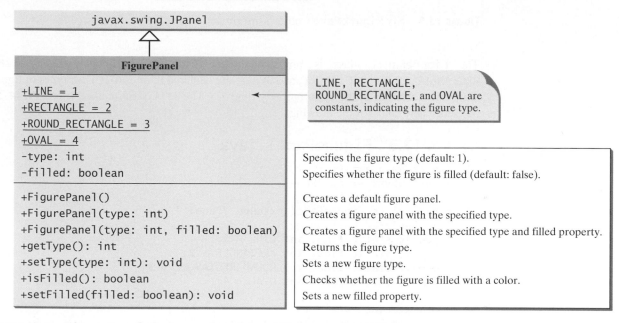

```
┌──────────────────────────────────┐
│        javax.swing.JPanel        │
└──────────────────────────────────┘
                 △
┌──────────────────────────────────┐
│           FigurePanel            │
├──────────────────────────────────┤
│ +LINE = 1                        │        LINE, RECTANGLE,
│ +RECTANGLE = 2                   │        ROUND_RECTANGLE, and OVAL are
│ +ROUND_RECTANGLE = 3             │        constants, indicating the figure type.
│ +OVAL = 4                        │
│ -type: int                       │        Specifies the figure type (default: 1).
│ -filled: boolean                 │        Specifies whether the figure is filled (default: false).
├──────────────────────────────────┤
│ +FigurePanel()                   │        Creates a default figure panel.
│ +FigurePanel(type: int)          │        Creates a figure panel with the specified type.
│ +FigurePanel(type: int, filled: boolean) │  Creates a figure panel with the specified type and filled property.
│ +getType(): int                  │        Returns the figure type.
│ +setType(type: int): void        │        Sets a new figure type.
│ +isFilled(): boolean             │        Checks whether the figure is filled with a color.
│ +setFilled(filled: boolean): void│        Sets a new filled property.
└──────────────────────────────────┘
```

FIGURE 13.8 FigurePanel displays various types of figures on the panel.

The UML diagram serves as the contract for the FigurePanel class. The user can use the class without knowing how the class is implemented. Let us begin by writing a program in Listing 13.2 that uses the class to display six figure panels, as shown in Figure 13.9.

LISTING 13.2 TestFigurePanel.java

```
1   import java.awt.*;
2   import javax.swing.*;
3
4   public class TestFigurePanel extends JFrame {
5     public TestFigurePanel() {
6       setLayout(new GridLayout(2, 3, 5, 5));
7       add(new FigurePanel(FigurePanel.LINE));                          create figures
8       add(new FigurePanel(FigurePanel.RECTANGLE));
9       add(new FigurePanel(FigurePanel.ROUND_RECTANGLE));
10      add(new FigurePanel(FigurePanel.OVAL));
11      add(new FigurePanel(FigurePanel.RECTANGLE, true));
12      add(new FigurePanel(FigurePanel.ROUND_RECTANGLE, true));
13    }
14
15    public static void main(String[] args) {
16      TestFigurePanel frame = new TestFigurePanel();
17      frame.setSize(400, 200);
18      frame.setTitle("TestFigurePanel");
```

```
19      frame.setLocationRelativeTo(null); // Center the frame
20      frame.setDefaultCloseOperation(JFrame.EXIT_ON_CLOSE);
21      frame.setVisible(true);
22    }
23  }
```

FIGURE 13.9 Six **FigurePanel** objects are created to display six figures.

The **FigurePanel** class is implemented in Listing 13.3. Four constants—**LINE**, **RECTANGLE**, **ROUND_RECTANGLE**, and **OVAL**—are declared in lines 6–9. Four types of figures are drawn according to the **type** property (line 37). The **setColor** method (lines 39, 44, 53, 62) sets a new color for the drawing.

LISTING 13.3 FigurePanel.java

```
1   import java.awt.*;
2   import javax.swing.JPanel;
3
4   public class FigurePanel extends JPanel {
5     // Declare constants
6     public static final int LINE = 1;
7     public static final int RECTANGLE = 2;
8     public static final int ROUND_RECTANGLE = 3;
9     public static final int OVAL = 4;
10
11    private int type = 1;
12    private boolean filled = false;
13
14    /** Construct a default FigurePanel */
15    public FigurePanel() {
16    }
17
18    /** Construct a FigurePanel with the specified type */
19    public FigurePanel(int type) {
20      this.type = type;
21    }
22
23    /** Construct a FigurePanel with the specified type and filled */
24    public FigurePanel(int type, boolean filled) {
25      this.type = type;
26      this.filled = filled;
27    }
28
29    @Override // Draw a figure on the panel
30    protected void paintComponent(Graphics g) {
31      super.paintComponent(g);
32
33      // Get the appropriate size for the figure
34      int width = getWidth();
35      int height = getHeight();
36
37      switch (type) {
38        case LINE: // Display two cross lines
```

constants

override
  paintComponent(g)

check type

```
39          g.setColor(Color.BLACK);
40          g.drawLine(10, 10, width - 10, height - 10);      draw lines
41          g.drawLine(width - 10, 10, 10, height - 10);
42          break;
43        case RECTANGLE: // Display a rectangle
44          g.setColor(Color.BLUE);
45          if (filled)
46            g.fillRect((int)(0.1 * width), (int)(0.1 * height),    fill a rectangle
47              (int)(0.8 * width), (int)(0.8 * height));
48          else
49            g.drawRect((int)(0.1 * width), (int)(0.1 * height),    draw a rectangle
50              (int)(0.8 * width), (int)(0.8 * height));
51          break;
52        case ROUND_RECTANGLE: // Display a round-cornered rectangle
53          g.setColor(Color.RED);
54          if (filled)
55            g.fillRoundRect((int)(0.1 * width), (int)(0.1 * height),   fill round-cornered rect
56              (int)(0.8 * width), (int)(0.8 * height), 20, 20);
57          else
58            g.drawRoundRect((int)(0.1 * width), (int)(0.1 * height),   draw round-cornered rect
59              (int)(0.8 * width), (int)(0.8 * height), 20, 20);
60          break;
61        case OVAL: // Display an oval
62          g.setColor(Color.BLACK);
63          if (filled)
64            g.fillOval((int)(0.1 * width), (int)(0.1 * height),    fill an oval
65              (int)(0.8 * width), (int)(0.8 * height));
66          else
67            g.drawOval((int)(0.1 * width), (int)(0.1 * height),    draw an oval
68              (int)(0.8 * width), (int)(0.8 * height));
69      }
70    }
71
72    /** Set a new figure type */
73    public void setType(int type) {
74      this.type = type;
75      repaint();                                               repaint panel
76    }
77
78    /** Return figure type */
79    public int getType() {
80      return type;
81    }
82
83    /** Set a new filled property */
84    public void setFilled(boolean filled) {
85      this.filled = filled;
86      repaint();                                               repaint panel
87    }
88
89    /** Check if the figure is filled */
90    public boolean isFilled() {
91      return filled;
92    }
93
94    @Override // Specify preferred size
95    public Dimension getPreferredSize() {                      override
96      return new Dimension(80, 80);                              getPreferredSize()
97    }
98  }
```

The **repaint** method (lines 75, 86) is defined in the **Component** class. Invoking **repaint** causes the **paintComponent** method to be called. The **repaint** method is invoked to refresh the viewing area. Typically, you call it if you have new things to display.

don't invoke
  paintComponent

Caution

The **paintComponent** method should never be invoked directly. It is invoked either by the JVM whenever the viewing area changes or by the **repaint** method. You should override the **paintComponent** method to tell the system how to paint the viewing area, but never override the **repaint** method.

request repaint using
  repaint()

Note

The **repaint** method lodges a request to update the viewing area and returns immediately. Its effect is asynchronous, meaning that it is up to the JVM to execute the **paintComponent** method on a separate thread.

The **getPreferredSize()** method (lines 95–97), defined in **Component**, is overridden in **FigurePanel** to specify the preferred size for the layout manager to consider when laying out a **FigurePanel** object. This property may or may not be considered by the layout manager, depending on its rules. For example, a component uses its preferred size in a container with a **FlowLayout** manager, but its preferred size is ignored if it is placed in a container with a **GridLayout** manager. It is a good practice to override **getPreferredSize()** in a subclass of **JPanel** to specify a preferred size, because the default width and height for a **JPanel** is **0**. You will see nothing if a **JPanel** component with a default **0** width and height is placed in a **FlowLayout** container.

why override
  getPreferredSize()?

 Check Point

MyProgrammingLab™

13.12 Why should you override the **preferredSize** method in a subclass of **JPanel**?

13.13 How do you **get** and **set** colors and fonts in a **Graphics** object?

13.5 Drawing Arcs

 Key Point

An arc is conceived as part of an oval bounded by a rectangle.

The methods to draw or fill an arc are as follows:

```
drawArc(int x, int y, int w, int h, int startAngle, int arcAngle)
fillArc(int x, int y, int w, int h, int startAngle, int arcAngle)
```

Parameters x, y, w, and h are the same as in the **drawOval** method; parameter **startAngle** is the starting angle; and **arcAngle** is the spanning angle (i.e., the angle covered by the arc). Angles are measured in degrees and follow the usual mathematical conventions (i.e., **0** degrees is in the easterly direction, and positive angles indicate counterclockwise rotation from the easterly direction); see Figure 13.10.

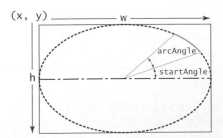

FIGURE 13.10 The **drawArc** method draws an arc based on an oval with specified angles.

Listing 13.4 is an example of how to draw arcs; the output is shown in Figure 13.11.

LISTING 13.4 DrawArcs.java

```
1   import javax.swing.JFrame;
2   import javax.swing.JPanel;
3   import java.awt.Graphics;
4
5   public class DrawArcs extends JFrame {
6     public DrawArcs() {
7       setTitle("DrawArcs");
8       add(new ArcsPanel());                              add a panel
9     }
10
11    /** Main method */
12    public static void main(String[] args) {
13      DrawArcs frame = new DrawArcs();
14      frame.setSize(250, 300);
15      frame.setLocationRelativeTo(null); // Center the frame
16      frame.setDefaultCloseOperation(JFrame.EXIT_ON_CLOSE);
17      frame.setVisible(true);
18    }
19  }
20
21  // The class for drawing arcs on a panel
22  class ArcsPanel extends JPanel {
23    @Override // Draw four blades of a fan
24    protected void paintComponent(Graphics g) {          override paintComponent
25      super.paintComponent(g);
26
27      int xCenter = getWidth() / 2;
28      int yCenter = getHeight() / 2;
29      int radius = (int)(Math.min(getWidth(), getHeight()) * 0.4);
30
31      int x = xCenter - radius;
32      int y = yCenter - radius;
33
34      g.fillArc(x, y, 2 * radius, 2 * radius, 0, 30);     30° arc from 0°
35      g.fillArc(x, y, 2 * radius, 2 * radius, 90, 30);    30° arc from 90°
36      g.fillArc(x, y, 2 * radius, 2 * radius, 180, 30);   30° arc from 180°
37      g.fillArc(x, y, 2 * radius, 2 * radius, 270, 30);   30° arc from 270°
38    }
39  }
```

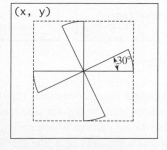

FIGURE 13.11 The program draws four filled arcs.

negative degrees

Angles may be negative. A negative starting angle sweeps clockwise from the easterly direction, as shown in Figure 13.12. A negative spanning angle sweeps clockwise from the starting angle. The following two statements draw the same arc:

```
g.fillArc(x, y, 2 * radius, 2 * radius, -30, -20);
g.fillArc(x, y, 2 * radius, 2 * radius, -50, 20);
```

The first statement uses negative starting angle **-30** and negative spanning angle **-20**, as shown in Figure 13.12a. The second statement uses negative starting angle **-50** and positive spanning angle **20**, as shown in Figure 13.12b.

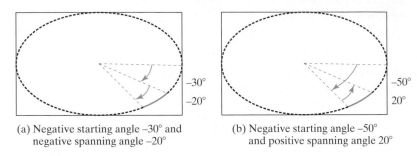

(a) Negative starting angle –30° and negative spanning angle –20°

(b) Negative starting angle –50° and positive spanning angle 20°

FIGURE 13.12 Angles may be negative.

13.14 Describe the methods for drawing/filling arcs.

13.15 Draw the upper half of a circle with radius **50**.

MyProgrammingLab™

13.16 Fill the lower half of a circle with radius **50** using the red color.

13.6 Drawing Polygons and Polylines

You can draw a polygon or a polyline that connects a set of points.

To draw a polygon, first create a **Polygon** object using the **Polygon** class, as shown in Figure 13.13.

java.awt.Polygon	
+xpoints: int[]	x-coordinates of all points in the polygon.
+ypoints: int[]	y-coordinates of all points in the polygon.
+npoints: int	The number of points in the polygon.
+Polygon()	Creates an empty polygon.
+Polygon(xpoints: int[], ypoints: int[], npoints: int)	Creates a polygon with the specified points.
+addPoint(x: int, y: int): void	Appends a point to the polygon.
+contains(x: int, y: int): boolean	Returns true if the specified point (x, y) is contained in the polygon.

FIGURE 13.13 The **Polygon** class models a polygon.

A polygon is a closed two-dimensional region. This region is bounded by an arbitrary number of line segments, each being one side (or edge) of the polygon. A polygon comprises a list of **(x, y)**-coordinate pairs in which each pair defines a vertex of the polygon, and two successive pairs are the endpoints of a line that is a side of the polygon. The first and final points are joined by a line segment that closes the polygon.

Here is an example of creating a polygon and adding points into it:

```
Polygon polygon = new Polygon();
polygon.addPoint(40, 20);
polygon.addPoint(70, 40);
polygon.addPoint(60, 80);
polygon.addPoint(45, 45);
polygon.addPoint(20, 60);
```

After these points are added, `xpoints` is {40, 70, 60, 45, 20}, `ypoints` is {20, 40, 80, 45, 60}, and `npoints` is 5. `xpoints`, `ypoints`, and `npoints` are public data fields in `Polygon`, which is a bad design. If the user changes a `Polygon`'s `npoints` data field without properly changing its `xpoints` and `ypoints` data fields, this will cause inconsistent data in the `Polygon` object.

To draw or fill a polygon, use one of the following methods in the `Graphics` class:

```
drawPolygon(Polygon polygon);
fillPolygon(Polygon polygon);

drawPolygon(int[] xpoints, int[] ypoints, int npoints);
fillPolygon(int[] xpoints, int[] ypoints, int npoints);
```

For example:

```
int x[] = {40, 70, 60, 45, 20};
int y[] = {20, 40, 80, 45, 60};
g.drawPolygon(x, y, x.length);
```

The drawing method opens the polygon by drawing lines between point (`x[i]`, `y[i]`) and point (`x[i+1]`, `y[i+1]`) for `i = 0, ... , x.length-1`; it closes the polygon by drawing a line between the first and last points (see Figure 13.14a).

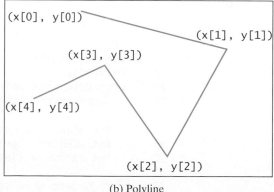

(a) Polygon   (b) Polyline

FIGURE 13.14 The `drawPolygon` method draws a polygon, and the `drawPolyLine` method draws a polyline.

To draw a polyline, use the `drawPolyline(int[] x, int[] y, int nPoints)` method, which draws a sequence of connected lines defined by arrays of *x*- and *y*-coordinates. For example, the following code draws the polyline like the one shown in Figure 13.14b.

```
int x[] = {40, 70, 60, 45, 20};
int y[] = {20, 40, 80, 45, 60};
g.drawPolyline(x, y, x.length);
```

Listing 13.5 is an example of how to draw a hexagon, with the output shown in Figure 13.15.

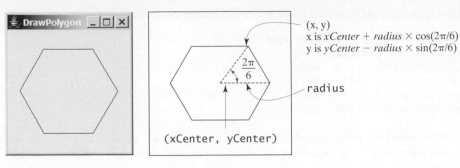

FIGURE 13.15 The program uses the **drawPolygon** method to draw a hexagon.

LISTING 13.5 DrawPolygon.java

```
 1  import javax.swing.JFrame;
 2  import javax.swing.JPanel;
 3  import java.awt.Graphics;
 4  import java.awt.Polygon;
 5
 6  public class DrawPolygon extends JFrame {
 7    public DrawPolygon() {
 8      setTitle("DrawPolygon");
 9      add(new PolygonsPanel());
10    }
11
12    /** Main method */
13    public static void main(String[] args) {
14      DrawPolygon frame = new DrawPolygon();
15      frame.setSize(200, 250);
16      frame.setLocationRelativeTo(null); // Center the frame
17      frame.setDefaultCloseOperation(JFrame.EXIT_ON_CLOSE);
18      frame.setVisible(true);
19    }
20  }
21
22  // Draw a polygon in the panel
23  class PolygonsPanel extends JPanel {
24    @Override
25    protected void paintComponent(Graphics g) {
26      super.paintComponent(g);
27
28      int xCenter = getWidth() / 2;
29      int yCenter = getHeight() / 2;
30      int radius = (int)(Math.min(getWidth(), getHeight()) * 0.4);
31
32      // Create a Polygon object
33      Polygon polygon = new Polygon();
34
35      // Add points to the polygon in this order
36      polygon.addPoint(xCenter + radius, yCenter);
37      polygon.addPoint((int)(xCenter + radius *
38        Math.cos(2 * Math.PI / 6)), (int)(yCenter - radius *
39        Math.sin(2 * Math.PI / 6)));
40      polygon.addPoint((int)(xCenter + radius *
41        Math.cos(2 * 2 * Math.PI / 6)), (int)(yCenter - radius *
42        Math.sin(2 * 2 * Math.PI / 6)));
43      polygon.addPoint((int)(xCenter + radius *
44        Math.cos(3 * 2 * Math.PI / 6)), (int)(yCenter - radius *
45        Math.sin(3 * 2 * Math.PI / 6)));
```

add a panel

paintComponent

add a point

```
46       polygon.addPoint(((int)(xCenter + radius *
47         Math.cos(4 * 2 * Math.PI / 6)), (int)(yCenter - radius *
48         Math.sin(4 * 2 * Math.PI / 6)));
49       polygon.addPoint(((int)(xCenter + radius *
50         Math.cos(5 * 2 * Math.PI / 6)), (int)(yCenter - radius *
51         Math.sin(5 * 2 * Math.PI / 6)));
52
53       // Draw the polygon
54       g.drawPolygon(polygon);
55   }
56 }
```
draw polygon

13.17 Draw a polygon connecting the following points: (20, 40), (30, 50), (40, 90), (90, 10), (10, 30).

Check Point

13.18 Create a `Polygon` object and add points (20, 40), (30, 50), (40, 90), (90, 10), (10, 30) in this order. Fill the polygon with the red color. Draw a polyline with a yellow color to connect all these points.

MyProgrammingLab™

13.7 Centering a String Using the **FontMetrics** Class

You can use the FontMetrics *class to measure the width and height of a string in the graphics context.*

Key Point

You can display a string at any location in a panel. Can you display it centered? Yes; to do so, you need to use the `FontMetrics` class to measure the exact width and height of the string for a particular font. `FontMetrics` can measure the following attributes for a given font (see Figure 13.16):

- **Leading,** pronounced *ledding*, is the amount of space between lines of text.

- **Ascent** is the distance from the baseline to the ascent line. The top of most characters in the font will be under the ascent line, but some may extend above the ascent line.

- **Descent** is the distance from the baseline to the descent line. The bottom of most descending characters (e.g., *j*, *y*, and *g*) in the font will be above the descent line, but some may extend below the descent line.

- **Height** is the sum of leading, ascent, and descent.

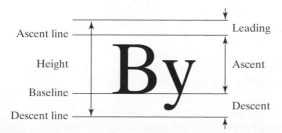

FIGURE 13.16 The `FontMetrics` class can be used to determine the font properties of characters for a given font.

`FontMetrics` is an abstract class. To get a `FontMetrics` object for a specific font, use the following **getFontMetrics** methods defined in the **Graphics** class:

- **public** FontMetrics getFontMetrics(Font font)

This method returns the font metrics of the specified font.

- **public** FontMetrics getFontMetrics()

This method returns the font metrics of the current font.
You can use the following instance methods in the **FontMetrics** class to obtain the attributes of a font and the width of a string when it is drawn using the font:

```
public int getAscent() // Return the ascent
public int getDescent() // Return the descent
public int getLeading() // Return the leading
public int getHeight() // Return the height
public int stringWidth(String str) // Return the width of the string
```

Listing 13.6 gives an example that displays a message in the center of the panel, as shown in Figure 13.17.

LISTING 13.6 TestCenterMessage.java

```
 1  import javax.swing.*;
 2  import java.awt.*;
 3
 4  public class TestCenterMessage extends JFrame {
 5    public TestCenterMessage() {
 6      CenterMessage messagePanel = new CenterMessage();
 7      add(messagePanel);
 8      messagePanel.setBackground(Color.WHITE);
 9      messagePanel.setFont(new Font("Californian FB", Font.BOLD, 30));
10    }
11
12    /** Main method */
13    public static void main(String[] args) {
14      TestCenterMessage frame = new TestCenterMessage();
15      frame.setSize(300, 150);
16      frame.setTitle("CenterMessage");
17      frame.setLocationRelativeTo(null); // Center the frame
18      frame.setDefaultCloseOperation(JFrame.EXIT_ON_CLOSE);
19      frame.setVisible(true);
20    }
21  }
22
23  class CenterMessage extends JPanel {
24    @Override /** Paint the message */
25    protected void paintComponent(Graphics g) {
26      super.paintComponent(g);
27
28      // Get font metrics for the current font
29      FontMetrics fm = g.getFontMetrics();
30
31      // Find the center location to display
32      int stringWidth = fm.stringWidth("Welcome to Java");
33      int stringAscent = fm.getAscent();
34
35      // Get the position of the leftmost character in the baseline
36      int xCoordinate = getWidth() / 2 - stringWidth / 2;
37      int yCoordinate = getHeight() / 2 + stringAscent / 2;
38
39      g.drawString("Welcome to Java", xCoordinate, yCoordinate);
40    }
41  }
```

create a message panel
add a message panel
set background
set font

override paintComponent

get FontMetrics

This is a MessagePanel object

(xCoordinate, yCoordinate)
xCoordinate = getWidth / 2 - stringWidth / 2;
yCoordinate = getHeight / 2 - stringAscent / 2;

FIGURE 13.17 The program uses the FontMetrics class to measure the string width and height and displays it at the center of the panel.

The methods getWidth() and getHeight() (lines 36–37) defined in the Component class return the component's width and height, respectively.

Since the message is centered, the first character of the string should be positioned at (xCoordinate, yCoordinate), as shown in Figure 13.17.

13.19 How do you find the leading, ascent, descent, and height of a font?

13.20 How do you find the exact length in pixels of a string in a Graphics object?

Check
Point

MyProgrammingLab™

13.8 Case Study: The **MessagePanel** Class

This case study develops a useful class that displays a message in a panel. The class enables the user to set the location of the message, center the message, and move the message a specified interval.

Key
Point

The contract of the MessagePanel class is shown in Figure 13.18.

Let us first write a test program in Listing 13.7 that uses the MessagePanel class to display four message panels, as shown in Figure 13.19.

VideoNote

The MessagePanel class

LISTING 13.7 TestMessagePanel.java

```
1  import java.awt.*;
2  import javax.swing.*;
3
4  public class TestMessagePanel extends JFrame {
5    public TestMessagePanel() {
6      MessagePanel messagePanel1 = new MessagePanel("Welcome to Java");      create message panel
7      MessagePanel messagePanel2 = new MessagePanel("Java is fun");
8      MessagePanel messagePanel3 = new MessagePanel("Java is cool");
9      MessagePanel messagePanel4 = new MessagePanel("I love Java");
10     messagePanel1.setFont(new Font("SansSerif", Font.ITALIC, 20));         set font
11     messagePanel2.setFont(new Font("Courier", Font.BOLD, 20));
12     messagePanel3.setFont(new Font("Times", Font.ITALIC, 20));
13     messagePanel4.setFont(new Font("Californian FB", Font.PLAIN, 20));
14     messagePanel1.setBackground(Color.RED);                                set background
15     messagePanel2.setBackground(Color.CYAN);
16     messagePanel3.setBackground(Color.GREEN);
17     messagePanel4.setBackground(Color.WHITE);
```

```
18        messagePanel1.setCentered(true);
19
20        setLayout(new GridLayout(2, 2));
21        add(messagePanel1);
22        add(messagePanel2);
23        add(messagePanel3);
24        add(messagePanel4);
25      }
26
27      public static void main(String[] args) {
28        TestMessagePanel frame = new TestMessagePanel();
29        frame.setSize(300, 200);
30        frame.setTitle("TestMessagePanel");
31        frame.setLocationRelativeTo(null); // Center the frame
32        frame.setDefaultCloseOperation(JFrame.EXIT_ON_CLOSE);
33        frame.setVisible(true);
34      }
35    }
```

add message panel

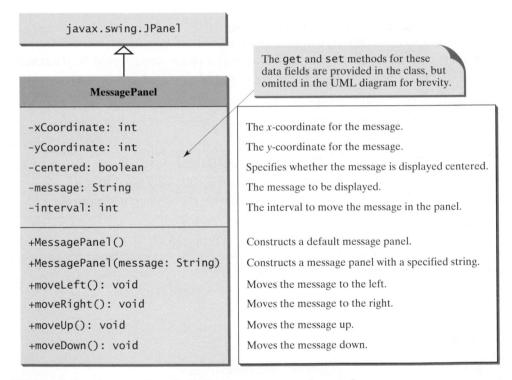

FIGURE 13.18 MessagePanel displays a message on the panel.

FIGURE 13.19 TestMessagePanel uses MessagePanel to display four message panels.

The rest of this section explains how to implement the MessagePanel class. Since you can use the class without knowing how it is implemented, you may skip the implementation if you wish.

skip implementation?

The **MessagePanel** class is implemented in Listing 13.8. The program seems long but is actually simple, because most of the methods are **get** and **set** methods, and each method is relatively short and easy to read.

LISTING 13.8 MessagePanel.java

```java
1  import java.awt.FontMetrics;
2  import java.awt.Dimension;
3  import java.awt.Graphics;
4  import javax.swing.JPanel;
5
6  public class MessagePanel extends JPanel {
7    /** The message to be displayed */
8    private String message = "Welcome to Java";
9
10   /** The x-coordinate where the message is displayed */
11   private int xCoordinate = 20;
12
13   /** The y-coordinate where the message is displayed */
14   private int yCoordinate = 20;
15
16   /** Indicate whether the message is displayed in the center */
17   private boolean centered;
18
19   /** The interval for moving the message horizontally
20    * and vertically */
21   private int interval = 10;
22
23   /** Construct with default properties */
24   public MessagePanel() {
25   }
26
27   /** Construct a message panel with a specified message */
28   public MessagePanel(String message) {
29     this.message = message;
30   }
31
32   /** Return message */
33   public String getMessage() {
34     return message;
35   }
36
37   /** Set a new message */
38   public void setMessage(String message) {
39     this.message = message;
40     repaint();                                                    repaint panel
41   }
42
43   /** Return xCoordinator */
44   public int getXCoordinate() {
45     return xCoordinate;
46   }
47
48   /** Set a new xCoordinator */
49   public void setXCoordinate(int x) {
50     this.xCoordinate = x;
51     repaint();                                                    repaint panel
52   }
53
54   /** Return yCoordinator */
```

```
55      public int getYCoordinate() {
56        return yCoordinate;
57      }
58
59      /** Set a new yCoordinator */
60      public void setYCoordinate(int y) {
61        this.yCoordinate = y;
62        repaint();
63      }
64
65      /** Return centered */
66      public boolean isCentered() {
67        return centered;
68      }
69
70      /** Set true or false to tell whether the message is centered */
71      public void setCentered(boolean centered) {
72        this.centered = centered;
73        repaint();
74      }
75
76      /** Return interval */
77      public int getInterval() {
78        return interval;
79      }
80
81      /** Set a new interval */
82      public void setInterval(int interval) {
83        this.interval = interval;
84        repaint();
85      }
86
87      @Override /** Paint the message */
88      protected void paintComponent(Graphics g) {
89        super.paintComponent(g);
90
91        if (centered) {
92          // Get font metrics for the current font
93          FontMetrics fm = g.getFontMetrics();
94
95          // Find the center location to display
96          int stringWidth = fm.stringWidth(message);
97          int stringAscent = fm.getAscent();
98          // Get the position of the leftmost character in the baseline
99          xCoordinate = getWidth() / 2 - stringWidth / 2;
100         yCoordinate = getHeight() / 2 + stringAscent / 2;
101       }
102
103       g.drawString(message, xCoordinate, yCoordinate);
104     }
105
106     /** Move the message left */
107     public void moveLeft() {
108       xCoordinate -= interval;
109       repaint();
110     }
111
112     /** Move the message right */
113     public void moveRight() {
114       xCoordinate += interval;
```

repaint panel (line 62)

repaint panel (line 73)

repaint panel (line 84)

override paintComponent (line 87)

check centered (line 91)

```
115        repaint();
116    }
117
118    /** Move the message up */
119    public void moveUp() {
120      yCoordinate -= interval;
121      repaint();
122    }
123
124    /** Move the message down */
125    public void moveDown() {
126      yCoordinate += interval;
127      repaint();
128    }
129
130    @Override /** Override get method for preferredSize */
131    public Dimension getPreferredSize() {
132      return new Dimension(200, 30);
133    }
134  }
```

override
getPreferredSize

The `paintComponent` method displays the message centered, if the **centered** property is **true** (line 91). **message** is initialized to **Welcome to Java** in line 8. If it were not initialized, a **NullPointerException** runtime error would occur when you created a **MessagePanel** using the no-arg constructor, because **message** would be **null** in line 103.

Caution

The **MessagePanel** class uses the properties **xCoordinate** and **yCoordinate** to specify the position of the message displayed on the panel. Do not use the property names **x** and **y**, because they are already defined in the **Component** class to return the position of the component in the parent's coordinate system using **getX()** and **getY()**.

Note

The **Component** class has the **setBackground**, **setForeground**, and **setFont** methods. These methods are for setting colors and fonts for the entire component. If you wanted to draw several messages in a panel with different colors and fonts, you would have to use the **setColor** and **setFont** methods in the **Graphics** class to set the color and font for the current drawing.

Note

A key feature of Java programming is the reuse of classes. Throughout this book, reusable classes are developed and later reused. **MessagePanel** is an example, as are **Loan** in Listing 10.2 and **FigurePanel** in Listing 13.3. **MessagePanel** can be reused whenever you need to display a message on a panel. To make your class reusable in a wide range of applications, you should provide a variety of ways to use it. **MessagePanel** provides many properties and methods that will be used in several examples in the book.

design classes for reuse

13.21 If **message** is not initialized in line 8 in Listing 13.8, MessagePanel.java, what will happen when you create a **MessagePanel** using its no-arg constructor?

13.22 The following program is supposed to display a message on a panel, but nothing is displayed. There are problems in lines 2 and 15. Correct them.

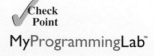

```
1   public class TestDrawMessage extends javax.swing.JFrame {
2     public void TestDrawMessage() {
3       add(new DrawMessage());
4     }
5
6     public static void main(String[] args) {
7       javax.swing.JFrame frame = new TestDrawMessage();
8       frame.setSize(100, 200);
9       frame.setVisible(true);
10    }
11  }
12
13  class DrawMessage extends javax.swing.JPanel {
14    @Override
15    protected void PaintComponent(java.awt.Graphics g) {
16      super.paintComponent(g);
17      g.drawString("Welcome to Java", 20, 20);
18    }
19  }
```

13.9 Case Study: The `StillClock` Class

VideoNote

The `StillClock` class

Key Point

This case study develops a class that displays a clock on a panel.

The contract of the `StillClock` class is shown in Figure 13.20.

FIGURE 13.20   `StillClock` displays an analog clock.

Let us first write a test program in Listing 13.9 that uses the `StillClock` class to display an analog clock and uses the `MessagePanel` class to display the hour, minute, and second in a panel, as shown in Figure 13.21a.

LISTING 13.9 DisplayClock.java

```
1   import java.awt.*;
2   import javax.swing.*;
3
4   public class DisplayClock extends JFrame {
```

```
5      public DisplayClock() {
6        // Create an analog clock for the current time
7        StillClock clock = new StillClock();
8
9        // Display hour, minute, and second in the message panel
10       MessagePanel messagePanel = new MessagePanel(clock.getHour() +
11         ":" + clock.getMinute() + ":" + clock.getSecond());
12       messagePanel.setCentered(true);
13       messagePanel.setForeground(Color.blue);
14       messagePanel.setFont(new Font("Courier", Font.BOLD, 16));
15
16       // Add the clock and message panel to the frame
17       add(clock);
18       add(messagePanel, BorderLayout.SOUTH);
19     }
20
21     public static void main(String[] args) {
22       DisplayClock frame = new DisplayClock();
23       frame.setTitle("DisplayClock");
24       frame.setSize(300, 350);
25       frame.setLocationRelativeTo(null); // Center the frame
26       frame.setDefaultCloseOperation(JFrame.EXIT_ON_CLOSE);
27       frame.setVisible(true);
28     }
29   }
```

create a clock

create a message panel

add a clock
add a message panel

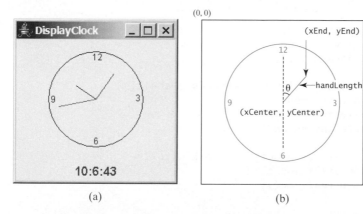

(a)   (b)

FIGURE 13.21   (a) The `DisplayClock` program displays a clock that shows the current time. (b) The endpoint of a clock hand can be determined, given the spanning angle, the hand length, and the center point.

The rest of this section explains how to implement the `StillClock` class. Since you can use the class without knowing how it is implemented, you may skip the implementation if you wish.

skip implementation?

To draw a clock, you need to draw a circle and three hands for the second, minute, and hour. To draw a hand, you need to specify the two ends of the line. As shown in Figure 13.21b, one end is the center of the clock at `(xCenter, yCenter)`; the other end, at `(xEnd, yEnd)`, is determined by the following formula:

implementation

```
xEnd = xCenter + handLength × sin(θ)
yEnd = yCenter - handLength × cos(θ)
```

Since there are 60 seconds in one minute, the angle for the second hand is

$$second \times (2\pi/60)$$

The position of the minute hand is determined by the minute and second. The exact minute value combined with seconds is `minute + second/60`. For example, if the time is 3 minutes and 30 seconds, the total minutes are 3.5. Since there are 60 minutes in one hour, the angle for the minute hand is

$$(minute + second/60) \times (2\pi/60)$$

Since one circle is divided into 12 hours, the angle for the hour hand is

$$(hour + minute/60 + second/(60 \times 60)) \times (2\pi/12)$$

For simplicity in computing the angles of the minute hand and hour hand, you can omit the seconds, because they are negligibly small. Therefore, the endpoints for the second hand, minute hand, and hour hand can be computed as:

```
xSecond = xCenter + secondHandLength × sin(second × (2π/60))
ySecond = yCenter - secondHandLength × cos(second × (2π/60))
xMinute = xCenter + minuteHandLength × sin(minute × (2π/60))
yMinute = yCenter - minuteHandLength × cos(minute × (2π/60))
xHour = xCenter + hourHandLength × sin((hour + minute/60) × (2π/12))
yHour = yCenter - hourHandLength × cos((hour + minute/60) × (2π/12))
```

The `StillClock` class is implemented in Listing 13.10.

LISTING 13.10 StillClock.java

```java
1   import java.awt.*;
2   import javax.swing.*;
3   import java.util.*;
4
5   public class StillClock extends JPanel {
6     private int hour;
7     private int minute;
8     private int second;
9
10    /** Construct a default clock with the current time*/
11    public StillClock() {
12      setCurrentTime();
13    }
14
15    /** Construct a clock with specified hour, minute, and second */
16    public StillClock(int hour, int minute, int second) {
17      this.hour = hour;
18      this.minute = minute;
19      this.second = second;
20    }
21
22    /** Return hour */
23    public int getHour() {
24      return hour;
25    }
26
27    /** Set a new hour */
28    public void setHour(int hour) {
29      this.hour = hour;
30      repaint();
31    }
32
33    /** Return minute */
```

repaint panel

```
34    public int getMinute() {
35      return minute;
36    }
37
38    /** Set a new minute */
39    public void setMinute(int minute) {
40      this.minute = minute;
41      repaint();                                              repaint panel
42    }
43
44    /** Return second */
45    public int getSecond() {
46      return second;
47    }
48
49    /** Set a new second */
50    public void setSecond(int second) {
51      this.second = second;
52      repaint();                                              repaint panel
53    }
54
55    @Override /** Draw the clock */
56    protected void paintComponent(Graphics g) {               override paintComponent
57      super.paintComponent(g);
58
59      // Initialize clock parameters
60      int clockRadius =
61        (int)(Math.min(getWidth(), getHeight()) * 0.8 * 0.5);
62      int xCenter = getWidth() / 2;
63      int yCenter = getHeight() / 2;
64
65      // Draw circle
66      g.setColor(Color.BLACK);
67      g.drawOval(xCenter - clockRadius, yCenter - clockRadius,
68        2 * clockRadius, 2 * clockRadius);
69      g.drawString("12", xCenter - 5, yCenter - clockRadius + 12);
70      g.drawString("9", xCenter - clockRadius + 3, yCenter + 5);
71      g.drawString("3", xCenter + clockRadius - 10, yCenter + 3);
72      g.drawString("6", xCenter - 3, yCenter + clockRadius - 3);
73
74      // Draw second hand
75      int sLength = (int)(clockRadius * 0.8);
76      int xSecond = (int)(xCenter + sLength *
77        Math.sin(second * (2 * Math.PI / 60)));
78      int ySecond = (int)(yCenter - sLength *
79        Math.cos(second * (2 * Math.PI / 60)));
80      g.setColor(Color.red);
81      g.drawLine(xCenter, yCenter, xSecond, ySecond);
82
83      // Draw minute hand
84      int mLength = (int)(clockRadius * 0.65);
85      int xMinute = (int)(xCenter + mLength *
86        Math.sin(minute * (2 * Math.PI / 60)));
87      int yMinute = (int)(yCenter - mLength *
88        Math.cos(minute * (2 * Math.PI / 60)));
89      g.setColor(Color.blue);
90      g.drawLine(xCenter, yCenter, xMinute, yMinute);
91
92      // Draw hour hand
93      int hLength = (int)(clockRadius * 0.5);
```

```
 94          int xHour = (int)(xCenter + hLength *
 95            Math.sin((hour % 12 + minute / 60.0) * (2 * Math.PI / 12)));
 96          int yHour = (int)(yCenter - hLength *
 97            Math.cos((hour % 12 + minute / 60.0) * (2 * Math.PI / 12)));
 98          g.setColor(Color.green);
 99          g.drawLine(xCenter, yCenter, xHour, yHour);
100        }
101
102        public void setCurrentTime() {
103          // Construct a calendar for the current date and time
```
get current time
```
104          Calendar calendar = new GregorianCalendar();
105
106          // Set current hour, minute, and second
107          this.hour = calendar.get(Calendar.HOUR_OF_DAY);
108          this.minute = calendar.get(Calendar.MINUTE);
109          this.second = calendar.get(Calendar.SECOND);
110        }
111
112        @Override
```
override
  getPreferredSize
```
113        public Dimension getPreferredSize() {
114          return new Dimension(200, 200);
115        }
116      }
```

The program enables the clock size to adjust as the frame resizes. Every time you resize the frame, the `paintComponent` method is automatically invoked to paint a new clock. The `paintComponent` method displays the clock in proportion to the panel width (`getWidth()`) and height (`getHeight()`) (lines 60–63 in `StillClock`).

13.10 Displaying Images

Key Point

You can draw images in a graphics context.

You learned how to create image icons and display them in labels and buttons in Section 12.10, Image Icons. For example, the following statements create an image icon and display it in a label:

```
ImageIcon imageIcon = new ImageIcon("image/us.gif");
JLabel jlblImage = new JLabel(imageIcon);
```

An image icon displays a fixed-size image. To display an image in a flexible size, you need to use the `java.awt.Image` class. An image can be created from an image icon using the `getImage()` method as follows:

```
Image image = imageIcon.getImage();
```

Using a label as an area for displaying images is simple and convenient, but you don't have much control over how the image is displayed. A more flexible way to display images is to use the `drawImage` method of the `Graphics` class on a panel. Four versions of the `drawImage` method are shown in Figure 13.22.

`ImageObserver` specifies a GUI component for receiving notifications of image information as the image is constructed. To draw images using the `drawImage` method in a Swing component, such as `JPanel`, override the `paintComponent` method to tell the component how to display the image in the panel.

Listing 13.11 gives the code that displays an image from **image/us.gif**. The file **image/us.gif** (line 20) is under the class directory. An `Image` object is obtained in line 21. The `drawImage` method displays the image to fill in the whole panel, as shown in Figure 13.23.

java.awt.Graphics	
+drawImage(image: Image, x: int, y: int, bgcolor: Color, observer: ImageObserver): void	Draws the image in a specified location. The image's top-left corner is at (x, y) in the graphics context's coordinate space. Transparent pixels in the image are drawn in the specified color bgcolor. The observer is the object on which the image is displayed. The image is cut off if it is larger than the area it is being drawn on.
+drawImage(image: Image, x: int, y: int, observer: ImageObserver): void	Same as the preceding method except that it does not specify a background color.
+drawImage(image: Image, x: int, y: int, width: int, height: int, observer: ImageObserver): void	Draws a scaled version of the image that can fill all of the available space in the specified rectangle.
+drawImage(image: Image, x: int, y: int, width: int, height: int, bgcolor: Color, observer: ImageObserver): void	Same as the preceding method except that it provides a solid background color behind the image being drawn.

FIGURE 13.22 You can apply the **drawImage** method on a **Graphics** object to display an image on a GUI component.

LISTING 13.11 DisplayImage.java

```java
1  import java.awt.*;
2  import javax.swing.*;
3
4  public class DisplayImage extends JFrame {
5    public DisplayImage() {
6      add(new ImagePanel());                              add panel
7    }
8
9    public static void main(String[] args) {
10     JFrame frame = new DisplayImage();
11     frame.setTitle("DisplayImage");
12     frame.setSize(300, 300);
13     frame.setLocationRelativeTo(null); // Center the frame
14     frame.setDefaultCloseOperation(JFrame.EXIT_ON_CLOSE);
15     frame.setVisible(true);
16   }
17 }
18
19 class ImagePanel extends JPanel {                        panel class
20   private ImageIcon imageIcon = new ImageIcon("image/us.gif");   create image icon
21   private Image image = imageIcon.getImage();            get image
22
23   @Override /** Draw image on the panel */
24   protected void paintComponent(Graphics g) {            override paintComponent
25     super.paintComponent(g);
26
27     if (image != null)
28       g.drawImage(image, 0, 0, getWidth(), getHeight(), this);   draw image
29   }
30 }
```

FIGURE 13.23 An image is displayed in a panel.

13.11 Case Study: The **ImageViewer** Class

Key
Point

*This case study develops the **ImageViewer** class for displaying an image in a panel.*

Displaying an image is a common task in Java programming. This case study develops a reusable component named **ImageViewer** that displays an image on a panel. The class contains the properties **image**, **stretched**, **xCoordinate**, and **yCoordinate**, with associated accessor and mutator methods, as shown in Figure 13.24.

FIGURE 13.24 The **ImageViewer** class displays an image on a panel.

stretchable image

You can use images in Swing components such as **JLabel** and **JButton**, but these images are not stretchable. The image in an **ImageViewer** can be stretched.

Let us write a test program in Listing 13.12 that displays six images using the **ImageViewer** class. Figure 13.25 shows a sample run of the program.

LISTING 13.12 SixFlags.java

create image

create image viewer

```
 1  import javax.swing.*;
 2  import java.awt.*;
 3
 4  public class SixFlags extends JFrame {
 5    public SixFlags() {
 6      Image image1 = new ImageIcon("image/us.gif").getImage();
 7      Image image2 = new ImageIcon("image/ca.gif").getImage();
 8      Image image3 = new ImageIcon("image/india.gif").getImage();
 9      Image image4 = new ImageIcon("image/uk.gif").getImage();
10      Image image5 = new ImageIcon("image/china.gif").getImage();
11      Image image6 = new ImageIcon("image/norway.gif").getImage();
12
13      setLayout(new GridLayout(2, 0, 5, 5));
14      add(new ImageViewer(image1));
15      add(new ImageViewer(image2));
16      add(new ImageViewer(image3));
17      add(new ImageViewer(image4));
18      add(new ImageViewer(image5));
19      add(new ImageViewer(image6));
20    }
21
22    public static void main(String[] args) {
23      SixFlags frame = new SixFlags();
24      frame.setTitle("SixFlags");
25      frame.setSize(400, 320);
26      frame.setLocationRelativeTo(null); // Center the frame
```

```
27        frame.setDefaultCloseOperation(JFrame.EXIT_ON_CLOSE);
28        frame.setVisible(true);
29      }
30    }
```

FIGURE 13.25   Six images are displayed in six **ImageViewer** components.

The **ImageViewer** class is implemented in Listing 13.13. (*Note: You may skip the imple-*   implementation
mentation.) The accessor and mutator methods for the properties **image**, **stretched**,   skip implementation?
xCoordinate, and **yCoordinate** are easy to implement. The **paintComponent** method
(lines 27–36) displays the image on the panel. Line 30 ensures that the image is not **null**
before displaying it. Line 31 checks whether the image is stretched or not.

LISTING 13.13 **ImageViewer.java**

```
1   import java.awt.*;
2   import javax.swing.*;
3
4   public class ImageViewer extends JPanel {
5     /** Hold value of property image */
6     private java.awt.Image image;                                   properties
7
8     /** Hold value of property stretched */
9     private boolean stretched = true;
10
11    /** Hold value of property xCoordinate */
12    private int xCoordinate;
13
14    /** Hold value of property yCoordinate */
15    private int yCoordinate;
16
17    /** Construct an empty image viewer */
18    public ImageViewer() {                                          constructor
19    }
20
21    /** Construct an image viewer for a specified Image object */
22    public ImageViewer(Image image) {                               constructor
23      this.image = image;
24    }
25
26    @Override
27    protected void paintComponent(Graphics g) {
28      super.paintComponent(g);
29
30      if (image != null)                                            image null?
31        if (isStretched())
32          g.drawImage(image, xCoordinate, yCoordinate,              stretched
33            getWidth(), getHeight(), this);
34        else
35          g.drawImage(image, xCoordinate, yCoordinate, this);       nonstretched
36    }
```

```
37
38    /** Return value of property image */
39    public java.awt.Image getImage() {
40      return image;
41    }
42
43    /** Set a new value for property image */
44    public void setImage(java.awt.Image image) {
45      this.image = image;
46      repaint();
47    }
48
49    /** Return value of property stretched */
50    public boolean isStretched() {
51      return stretched;
52    }
53
54    /** Set a new value for property stretched */
55    public void setStretched(boolean stretched) {
56      this.stretched = stretched;
57      repaint();
58    }
59
60    /** Return value of property xCoordinate */
61    public int getXCoordinate() {
62      return xCoordinate;
63    }
64
65    /** Set a new value for property xCoordinate */
66    public void setXCoordinate(int xCoordinate) {
67      this.xCoordinate = xCoordinate;
68      repaint();
69    }
70
71    /** Return value of property yCoordinate */
72    public int getYCoordinate() {
73      return yCoordinate;
74    }
75
76    /** Set a new value for property yCoordinate */
77    public void setYCoordinate(int yCoordinate) {
78      this.yCoordinate = yCoordinate;
79      repaint();
80    }
81  }
```

13.23 How do you create an `Image` object from the `ImageIcon` object?

13.24 How do you create an `ImageIcon` object from an `Image` object?

13.25 Describe the `drawImage` method in the `Graphics` class.

13.26 Explain the differences between displaying images in a `JLabel` and in a `JPanel`.

13.27 Which package contains `ImageIcon`, and which contains `Image`?

CHAPTER SUMMARY

I.   Each component has its own coordinate system with the origin (0, 0) at the upper-left corner of the window. In Java, the x-coordinate increases to the right, and the y-coordinate increases downward.

2. Whenever a component (e.g., a button, a label, or a panel) is displayed, the JVM automatically creates a `Graphics` object for the component on the native platform and passes this object to invoke the `paintComponent` method to display the drawings.

3. Normally you use `JPanel` as a canvas. To draw on a `JPanel`, you create a new class that extends `JPanel` and overrides the `paintComponent` method to tell the panel how to draw graphics.

4. Invoking `super.paintComponent(g)` is necessary to ensure that the viewing area is cleared before a new drawing is displayed. The user can request the component to be redisplayed by invoking the `repaint()` method defined in the `Component` class. Invoking `repaint()` causes `paintComponent` to be invoked by the JVM. The user should never invoke `paintComponent` directly. For this reason, the protected visibility is sufficient for `paintComponent`.

5. The `Component` class has the `setBackground`, `setForeground`, and `setFont` methods. These methods are used to set colors and fonts for the entire component. If you want to draw several messages in a panel with different colors and fonts, you have to use the `setColor` and `setFont` methods in the `Graphics` class to set the color and font for the current drawing.

6. `FontMetrics` can be used to compute the exact length and width of a string, which is helpful for measuring the size of a string in order to display it in the right position.

7. To display an image, first create an image icon. You can then use `ImageIcon`'s `getImage()` method to get an `Image` object for the image and draw the image using the `drawImage` method in the `java.awt.Graphics` class.

TEST QUESTIONS

Do the test questions for this chapter online at www.cs.armstrong.edu/liang/intro9e/test.html.

PROGRAMMING EXERCISES

MyProgrammingLab™

Sections 13.2–13.7

*13.1   (*Display a 3 × 3 grid*) Write a program that displays a 3 × 3 grid, as shown in Figure 13.26a. Use red color for vertical lines and blue for horizontals.

**13.2   (*Create a custom button class*) Develop a custom button class named `OvalButton` that extends `JButton` and displays the button text inside an oval. Figure 13.26b shows two buttons created using the `OvalButton` class.

*13.3   (*Display a checkerboard*) Programming Exercise 12.10 displays a checkerboard in which each white and black cell is a `JButton`. Rewrite a program that draws a checkerboard on a `JPanel` using the drawing methods in the `Graphics` class, as shown in Figure 13.26c. Use the `drawRect` method to draw each cell in the checkerboard.

*13.4   (*Display a multiplication table*) Write a program that displays a multiplication table in a panel using the drawing methods, as shown in Figure 13.27a.

(a) (b) (c)

FIGURE 13.26 (a) Exercise 13.1 displays a grid. (b) Exercise 13.2 displays two objects of `OvalButton`. (c) Exercise 13.3 displays a checkerboard.

**13.5 (*Display numbers in a triangular pattern*) Write a program that displays numbers in a triangular pattern, as shown in Figure 13.27b. The number of lines in the display changes to fit the window as the window resizes.

(a) (b)

FIGURE 13.27 (a) Exercise 13.4 displays a multiplication table. (b) Exercise 13.5 displays numbers in a triangle formation.

**13.6 (*Improve `FigurePanel`*) The `FigurePanel` class in Listing 13.3 can display lines, rectangles, round-cornered rectangles, and ovals. Add appropriate new code in the class to display arcs and polygons. Write a test program to display the shapes as shown in Figure 13.28a using the new `FigurePanel` class.

**13.7 (*Display a tic-tac-toe board*) Create a custom panel that displays X, O, or nothing. What to display is randomly decided whenever a panel is repainted. Use the `Math.random()` method to generate an integer 0, 1, or 2, which corresponds to displaying X, O, or nothing. Create a frame that contains nine custom panels, as shown in Figure 13.28b.

**13.8 (*Draw an octagon*) Write a program that draws an octagon, as shown in Figure 13.28c.

(a)   (b)   (c)

FIGURE 13.28 (a) Four panels of geometric figures are displayed in a frame of `GridLayout`. (b) `TicTacToe` cells randomly display X, O, or nothing. (c) Exercise 13.8 draws an octagon.

*13.9 (*Create four fans*) Write a program that places four fans in a frame of `GridLayout` with two rows and two columns, as shown in Figure 13.29a.

*13.10 (*Display a cylinder*) Write a program that draws a cylinder, as shown in Figure 13.29b.

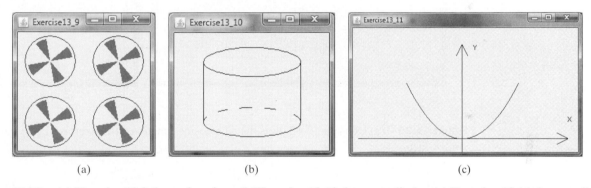

(a)   (b)   (c)

FIGURE 13.29 (a) Exercise 13.9 draws four fans. (b) Exercise 13.10 draws a cylinder. (c) Exercise 13.11 draws a diagram for function $f(x) = x^2$.

*13.11 (*Plot the square function*) Write a program that draws a diagram for the function
$f(x) = x^2$ (see Figure 13.29c).

Hint: Add points to a polygon **p** using the following loop:

```
double scaleFactor = 0.1;

for (int x = -100; x <= 100; x++) {
  p.addPoint(x + 200, 200 - (int)(scaleFactor * x * x));
}
```

Connect the points using `g.drawPolyline(p.xpoints,  p.ypoints, p.npoints)` for a `Graphics` object **g**. `p.xpoints` returns an array of x-coordinates, `p.ypoints` an array of y-coordinates, and `p.npoints` the number of points in `Polygon` object **p**.

**13.12 (*Plot the sine and cosine functions*) Write a program that plots the sine function in red and cosine in blue, as shown in Figure 13.30a.

VideoNote

Plot a function

Hint: The Unicode for π is `\u03c0`. To display −2π, use `g.drawString("-2\u03c0", x, y)`. For a trigonometric function like `sin(x)`, x is in radians. Use the following loop to add the points to a polygon **p**:

```
for (int x = -170; x <= 170; x++) {
  p.addPoint(x + 200,
    100 - (int)(50 * Math.sin((x / 100.0) * 2 * Math.PI)));
}
```

−2π is at (**100, 100**), the center of the axis is at (**200, 100**), and 2π is at (**300, 100**). Use the **drawPolyline** method in the **Graphics** class to connect the points.

**13.13 (*Paint a smiley face*) Write a program that paints a smiley face, as shown in Figure 13.30b.

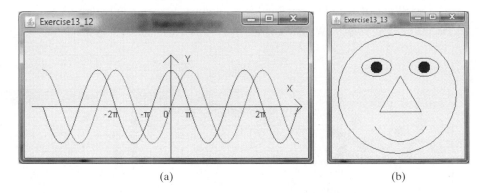

(a)   (b)

FIGURE 13.30 (a) Exercise 13.12 plots the sine/cosine functions. (b) Exercise 13.13 paints a smiley face.

13.14 (*Display a bar chart*) Write a program that uses a bar chart to display the percentages of the overall grade represented by projects, quizzes, midterm exams, and the final exam, as shown in Figure 13.1a. Suppose that projects take **20 percent and are displayed in red, quizzes take **10** percent and are displayed in blue, midterm exams take **30** percent and are displayed in green, and the final exam takes **40** percent and is displayed in orange.

13.15 (*Display a pie chart*) Write a program that uses a pie chart to display the percentages of the overall grade represented by projects, quizzes, midterm exams, and the final exam, as shown in Figure 13.31a. Suppose that projects take **20 percent and are displayed in red, quizzes take **10** percent and are displayed in blue, midterm exams take **30** percent and are displayed in green, and the final exam takes **40** percent and is displayed in orange.

13.16 (*Obtain font information*) Write a program that displays the message **Java is fun** in a panel. Set the panel's font to **TimesRoman**, **bold**, and **20** pixel. Display the font's leading, ascent, descent, height, and the string width as a tool tip text for the panel, as shown in Figure 13.31b.

13.17 (*Game: hangman*) Write a program that displays a drawing for the popular hangman game, as shown in Figure 13.31c.

VideoNote

Plot a bar chart

FIGURE 13.31 (a) Exercise 13.15 uses a pie chart to show the percentages of projects, quizzes, midterm exams, and final exam in the overall grade. (b) Exercise 13.16 displays font properties in a tool tip text. (c) Exercise 13.17 draws a sketch for the hangman game.

13.18 (*Use the StillClock class*) Write a program that displays two clocks. The hour, minute, and second values are **4**, **20**, **45** for the first clock and **22**, **46**, **15** for the second clock, as shown in Figure 13.32a.

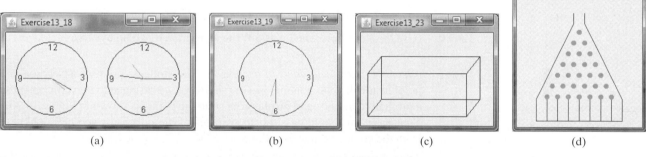

FIGURE 13.32 (a) Exercise 13.18 displays two clocks. (b) Exercise 13.19 displays a clock with random hour and minute values. (c) Exercise 13.23 displays a rectanguloid. (d) Exercise 13.24 simulates a bean machine.

*13.19 (*Random time*) Modify the **StillClock** class with three new Boolean properties—**hourHandVisible**, **minuteHandVisible**, and **secondHandVisible**—and their associated accessor and mutator methods. You can use the **set** methods to make a hand visible or invisible. Write a test program that displays only the hour and minute hands. The hour and minute values are randomly generated. The hour is between **0** and **11**, and the minute is either **0** or **30**, as shown in Figure 13.32b.

13.20 (*Draw a detailed clock*) Modify the **StillClock class in Section 13.9 to draw the clock with more details on the hours and minutes, as shown in Figure 13.1b.

13.21 (*Display a tic-tac-toe board with images*) Rewrite Programming Exercise 12.7 to display an image in a **JPanel instead of displaying an image icon in a **JLabel**.

*13.22 (*Display a STOP sign*) Write a program that displays a STOP sign, as shown in Figure 13.1c. The hexagon is in red and the sign is in white. (*Hint*: See Listing 13.5, DrawPolygon.java, and Listing 13.6, TestCenterMessage.java.)

13.23 (*Display a rectanguloid*) Write a program that displays a rectanguloid, as shown in Figure 13.32c. The cube should grow and shrink as the frame grows or shrinks.

**13.24 (*Game: bean machine*) Write a program that displays a bean machine introduced in Programming Exercise 6.21. The bean machine should be centered in a resizable panel, as shown in Figure 13.32d.

**13.25 (*Geometry: display an n-sided regular polygon*) Define a subclass of `JPanel`, named `RegularPolygonPanel`, to paint an *n*-sided regular polygon. The class contains a property named `numberOfSides`, which specifies the number of sides in the polygon. The polygon is centered in the panel. The size of the polygon is proportional to the size of the panel. Create a pentagon, hexagon, heptagon, octagon, nonagon, and decagon from `RegularPolygonPanel` and display them in a frame, as shown in Figure 13.33a.

(a)   (b)   (c)

FIGURE 13.33 (a) Exercise 13.25 displays several n-sided polygons. (b) Exercise 13.26 uses `MessagePanel` to display four strings. (c) The polygon and its strategic point are displayed.

Sections 13.8–13.11

13.26 (*Use the `MessagePanel` class*) Write a program that displays four messages, as shown in Figure 13.33b.

**13.27 (*Geometry: strategic point of a polygon*) The strategic point of a polygon is a point inside the polygon that has the shortest total distance to all vertices. Write a program that finds and displays the strategic point, as shown in Figure 13.33c. Your program should pass the coordinates of the polygon's vertices clockwise from the command line as follows:

```
java Exercise13_27 x1 y1 x2 y2 x3 y3 . . .
```

The program displays the polygon and its strategic point in the frame. (*Hint*: To find the strategic point, consider every pixel point inside the polygon to see if it is a strategic point. Use the `contains` method to check whether a point is inside the polygon.)

**13.28 (*Draw an arrow line*) Write a static method that draws an arrow line from a starting point to an ending point using the following method header:

```
public static void drawArrowLine(int x1, int y1,
  int x2, int y2, Graphics g)
```

Write a test program that randomly draws an arrow line, as shown in Figure 13.34a. Whenever you resize the frame, a new arrow line is drawn.

*13.29 (*Two circles and their distance*) Write a program that draws two filled circles with radius 15 pixels, centered at random locations, with a line connecting the two circles. The distance between the two centers is displayed on the line, as shown in Figure 13.34b-c. Whenever you resize the frame, the circles are redisplayed in new random locations.

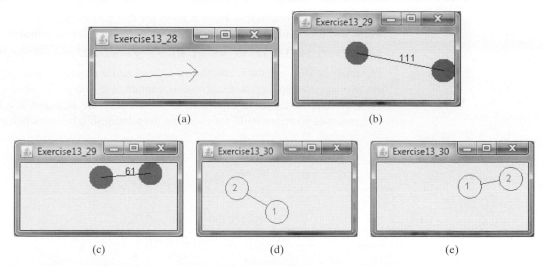

FIGURE 13.34 (a) The program displays an arrow line. (b-c) Exercise 13.29 connects the centers of two filled circles. (d-e) Exercise 13.30 connects two circles from their perimeter.

*13.30 (*Connect two circles*) Write a program that draws two filled circles with radius 15 pixels, centered at random locations, with a line connecting the two circles. The line should not cross inside the circles, as shown in Figure 13.34d-e. When you resize the frame, the circles are redisplayed in new random locations.

*13.31 (*Geometry: Inside a polygon?*) Write a program that passes the coordinates of five points from the command line as follows:

```
java Exercise13_31 x1 y1 x2 y2 x3 y3 x4 y4 x5 y5
```

The first four points form a polygon, and the program displays the polygon in a panel and a message in a label that indicates whether the fifth point is inside the polygon, as shown in Figure 13.35a.

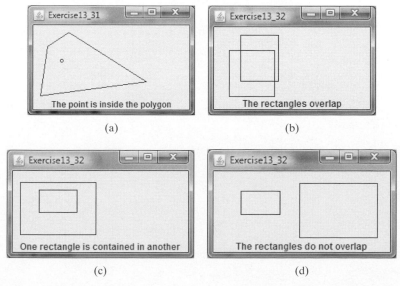

FIGURE 13.35 (a) The polygon and a point are displayed. (b-d) Two rectangles are displayed.

*13.32 (*Geometry: two rectangles*) Write a program that passes the center coordinates, width, and height of two rectangles from the command line as follows:

```
java Exercise13_32 x1 y1 w1 h1 x2 y2 w2 h2
```

The program displays the rectangles in a panel and a message indicating whether the two are overlapping, whether one is contained in the other, or whether they don't overlap, as shown in Figure 13.35b-d. Display the message in a label. See Programming Exercise 10.13 for checking the relationship between two rectangles.

EXCEPTION HANDLING AND TEXT I/O

Objectives

- To get an overview of exceptions and exception handling (§14.2).

- To explore the advantages of using exception handling (§14.2).

- To distinguish exception types: `Error` (fatal) vs. `Exception` (nonfatal) and checked vs. unchecked (§14.3).

- To declare exceptions in a method header (§14.4.1).

- To throw exceptions in a method (§14.4.2).

- To write a `try-catch` block to handle exceptions (§14.4.3).

- To explain how an exception is propagated (§14.4.3).

- To obtain information from an exception object (§14.4.4).

- To develop applications with exception handling (§14.4.5).

- To use the `finally` clause in a `try-catch` block (§14.5).

- To use exceptions only for unexpected errors (§14.6).

- To rethrow exceptions in a `catch` block (§14.7).

- To create chained exceptions (§14.8).

- To define custom exception classes (§14.9).

- To discover file/directory properties, to delete and rename files/directories, and to create directories using the `File` class (§14.10).

- To write data to a file using the `PrintWriter` class (§14.11.1).

- To read data from a file using the `Scanner` class (§14.11.2).

- To understand how data is read using a `Scanner` (§14.11.3).

- To develop a program that replaces text in a file (§14.11.4).

- To open files using a file dialog box (§14.12).

- To read data from the Web (§14.13).

14.1 Introduction

Exception handling enables a program to deal with exceptional situations and continue its normal execution.

Runtime errors occur while a program is running if the JVM detects an operation that is impossible to carry out. For example, if you access an array using an index that is out of bounds, you will get a runtime error with an `ArrayIndexOutOfBoundsException`. If you enter a `double` value when your program expects an integer, you will get a runtime error with an `InputMismatchException`.

exception

In Java, runtime errors are thrown as exceptions. An *exception* is an object that represents an error or a condition that prevents execution from proceeding normally. If the exception is not handled, the program will terminate abnormally. How can you handle the exception so that the program can continue to run or else terminate gracefully? This chapter introduces this subject and text input and output.

14.2 Exception-Handling Overview

Exceptions are thrown from a method. The caller of the method can catch and handle the exception.

VideoNote

Exception-handling advantages

To demonstrate exception handling, including how an exception object is created and thrown, let's begin with the example in Listing 14.1, which reads in two integers and displays their quotient.

LISTING 14.1 Quotient.java

```
1  import java.util.Scanner;
2
3  public class Quotient {
4    public static void main(String[] args) {
5      Scanner input = new Scanner(System.in);
6
7      // Prompt the user to enter two integers
8      System.out.print("Enter two integers: ");
9      int number1 = input.nextInt();
10     int number2 = input.nextInt();
11
12     System.out.println(number1 + " / " + number2 + " is " +
13       (number1 / number2));
14   }
15 }
```

reads two integers

integer division

```
Enter two integers: 5 2  ↵Enter
5 / 2 is 2
```

```
Enter two integers: 3 0  ↵Enter
Exception in thread "main" java.lang.ArithmeticException: / by zero
    at Quotient.main(Quotient.java:11)
```

If you entered **0** for the second number, a runtime error would occur, because you cannot divide an integer by **0**. (*Recall that a floating-point number divided by* **0** *does not raise an exception.*) A simple way to fix this error is to add an `if` statement to test the second number, as shown in Listing 14.2.

LISTING 14.2 QuotientWithIf.java

```java
 1  import java.util.Scanner;
 2
 3  public class QuotientWithIf {
 4    public static void main(String[] args) {
 5      Scanner input = new Scanner(System.in);
 6
 7      // Prompt the user to enter two integers
 8      System.out.print("Enter two integers: ");
 9      int number1 = input.nextInt();                          reads two integers
10      int number2 = input.nextInt();
11
12      if (number2 != 0)                                       test number2
13        System.out.println(number1 + " / " + number2
14          + " is " + (number1 / number2));
15      else
16        System.out.println("Divisor cannot be zero ");
17    }
18  }
```

```
Enter two integers: 5 0 ⏎Enter
Divisor cannot be zero
```

To demonstrate the concept of exception handling, we can rewrite Listing 14.2 to compute a quotient using a method, as shown in Listing 14.3.

LISTING 14.3 QuotientWithMethod.java

```java
 1  import java.util.Scanner;
 2
 3  public class QuotientWithMethod {
 4    public static int quotient(int number1, int number2) {   quotient method
 5      if (number2 == 0) {
 6        System.out.println("Divisor cannot be zero");
 7        System.exit(1);                                       terminate the program
 8      }
 9
10      return number1 / number2;
11    }
12
13    public static void main(String[] args) {
14      Scanner input = new Scanner(System.in);
15
16      // Prompt the user to enter two integers
17      System.out.print("Enter two integers: ");
18      int number1 = input.nextInt();                          reads two integers
19      int number2 = input.nextInt();
20
21      int result = quotient(number1, number2);                invoke method
22      System.out.println(number1 + " / " + number2 + " is "
23        + result);
24    }
25  }
```

```
Enter two integers: 5 3  ↵Enter
5 / 3 is 1
```

```
Enter two integers: 5 0  ↵Enter
Divisor cannot be zero
```

The method **quotient** (lines 4–11) returns the quotient of two integers. If **number2** is **0**, it cannot return a value, so the program is terminated in line 7. This is clearly a problem. You should not let the method terminate the program—the *caller* should decide whether to terminate the program.

How can a method notify its caller an exception has occurred? Java enables a method to throw an exception that can be caught and handled by the caller. Listing 14.3 can be rewritten, as shown in Listing 14.4.

LISTING 14.4 QuotientWithException.java

```
 1  import java.util.Scanner;
 2
 3  public class QuotientWithException {
 4    public static int quotient(int number1, int number2) {
 5      if (number2 == 0)
 6        throw new ArithmeticException("Divisor cannot be zero");
 7
 8      return number1 / number2;
 9    }
10
11    public static void main(String[] args) {
12      Scanner input = new Scanner(System.in);
13
14      // Prompt the user to enter two integers
15      System.out.print("Enter two integers: ");
16      int number1 = input.nextInt();
17      int number2 = input.nextInt();
18
19      try {
20        int result = quotient(number1, number2);
21        System.out.println(number1 + " / " + number2 + " is "
22          + result);
23      }
24      catch (ArithmeticException ex) {
25        System.out.println("Exception: an integer " +
26          "cannot be divided by zero ");
27      }
28
29      System.out.println("Execution continues ...");
30    }
31  }
```

quotient method

throw exception

reads two integers

try block
invoke method

If an Arithmetic Exception occurs

catch block

```
Enter two integers: 5 3  ↵Enter
5 / 3 is 1
Execution continues ...
```

```
Enter two integers: 5 0  ↵Enter
Exception: an integer cannot be divided by zero
Execution continues ...
```

If **number2** is **0**, the method throws an exception (line 6) by executing

> **throw new** ArithmeticException("Divisor cannot be zero");   throw statement

The value thrown, in this case **new ArithmeticException("Divisor cannot be zero")**,
is called an *exception*. The execution of a **throw** statement is called *throwing an exception*. The   exception
exception is an object created from an exception class. In this case, the exception class is   throwing exception
java.lang.ArithmeticException. The constructor **ArithmeticException(str)** is
invoked to construct an exception object, where **str** is a message that describes the exception.

When an exception is thrown, the normal execution flow is interrupted. As the name suggests, to "throw an exception" is to pass the exception from one place to another. The statement for invoking the method is contained in a **try** block and a **catch** block. The **try** block
(lines 19–23) contains the code that is executed in normal circumstances. The exception is
caught by the **catch** block. The code in the **catch** block is executed to *handle the exception*.   handle exception
Afterward, the statement (line 29) after the **catch** block is executed.

The **throw** statement is analogous to a method call, but instead of calling a method, it calls
a **catch** block. In this sense, a **catch** block is like a method definition with a parameter that
matches the type of the value being thrown. Unlike a method, however, after the **catch** block
is executed, the program control does not return to the **throw** statement; instead, it executes
the next statement after the **catch** block.

The identifier **ex** in the **catch**–block header

> **catch** (ArithmeticException ex)

acts very much like a parameter in a method. Thus, this parameter is referred to as a
catch–block parameter. The type (e.g., **ArithmeticException**) preceding **ex** specifies   catch–block parameter
what kind of exception the **catch** block can catch. Once the exception is caught, you can
access the thrown value from this parameter in the body of a **catch** block.

In summary, a template for a **try-throw-catch** block may look like this:

```
try {
  Code to run;
  A statement or a method that may throw an exception;
  More code to run;
}
catch (type ex) {
  Code to process the exception;
}
```

An exception may be thrown directly by using a **throw** statement in a **try** block, or by invoking a method that may throw an exception.

The main method invokes **quotient** (line 20). If the quotient method executes normally,
it returns a value to the caller. If the **quotient** method encounters an exception, it throws the
exception back to its caller. The caller's **catch** block handles the exception.

Now you can see the *advantage* of using exception handling: It enables a method to throw   advantage
an exception to its caller, enabling the caller to handle the exception. Without this capability,
the called method itself must handle the exception or terminate the program. Often the called
method does not know what to do in case of error. This is typically the case for the library
methods. The library method can detect the error, but only the caller knows what needs to be

done when an error occurs. The key benefit of exception handling is separating the detection of an error (done in a called method) from the handling of an error (done in the calling method).

Many library methods throw exceptions. Listing 14.5 gives an example that handles an **InputMismatchException** when reading an input.

LISTING 14.5 InputMismatchExceptionDemo.java

```
 1  import java.util.*;
 2
 3  public class InputMismatchExceptionDemo {
 4    public static void main(String[] args) {
 5      Scanner input = new Scanner(System.in);
 6      boolean continueInput = true;
 7
 8      do {
 9        try {
10          System.out.print("Enter an integer: ");
11          int number = input.nextInt();
12
13          // Display the result
14          System.out.println(
15            "The number entered is " + number);
16
17          continueInput = false;
18        }
19        catch (InputMismatchException ex) {
20          System.out.println("Try again. (" +
21            "Incorrect input: an integer is required)");
22          input.nextLine(); // Discard input
23        }
24      } while (continueInput);
25    }
26  }
```

create a Scanner

try block

If an InputMismatch Exception occurs

catch block

```
Enter an integer: 3.5  ⏎Enter
Try again. (Incorrect input: an integer is required)
Enter an integer: 4  ⏎Enter
The number entered is 4
```

When executing **input.nextInt()** (line 11), an **InputMismatchException** occurs if the input entered is not an integer. Suppose **3.5** is entered. An **InputMismatchException** occurs and the control is transferred to the **catch** block. The statements in the **catch** block are now executed. The statement **input.nextLine()** in line 22 discards the current input line so that the user can enter a new line of input. The variable **continueInput** controls the loop. Its initial value is **true** (line 6), and it is changed to **false** (line 17) when a valid input is received. Once a valid input is received, there is no need to continue the input.

 √Check Point

MyProgrammingLab

14.1 What is the advantage of using exception handling?

14.2 Which of the following statements will throw an exception?

```
System.out.println(1 / 0);
System.out.println(1.0 / 0);
```

14.3 Point out the problem in the following code. Does the code throw any exceptions?

```
long value = Long.MAX_VALUE + 1;
System.out.println(value);
```

14.4 What does the JVM do when an exception occurs? How do you catch an exception?

14.5 What is the printout of the following code?

```
public class Test {
  public static void main(String[] args) {
    try {
      int value = 30;
      if (value < 40)
        throw new Exception("value is too small");
    }
    catch (Exception ex) {
      System.out.println(ex.getMessage());
    }
    System.out.println("Continue after the catch block");
  }
}
```

What would be the printout if the line

```
int value = 30;
```

were changed to

```
int value = 50;
```

14.6 Show the output of the following code.

```
public class Test {
  public static void main(String[] args) {
    for (int i = 0; i < 2; i++) {
      System.out.print(i + " ");
      try {
        System.out.println(1 / 0);
      }
      catch (Exception ex) {
      }
    }
  }
}
```

(a)

```
public class Test {
  public static void main(String[] args) {
    try {
      for (int i = 0; i < 2; i++) {
        System.out.print(i + " ");
        System.out.println(1 / 0);
      }
    }
    catch (Exception ex) {
    }
  }
}
```

(b)

14.3 Exception Types

Exceptions are objects, and objects are defined using classes. The root class for exceptions is `java.lang.Throwable`.

Key Point

The preceding section used the classes **ArithmeticException** and **InputMismatch-Exception**. Are there any other types of exceptions you can use? Can you define your own exception classes? Yes. There are many predefined exception classes in the Java API. Figure 14.1 shows some of them, and in Section 14.9 you will learn how to define your own exception classes.

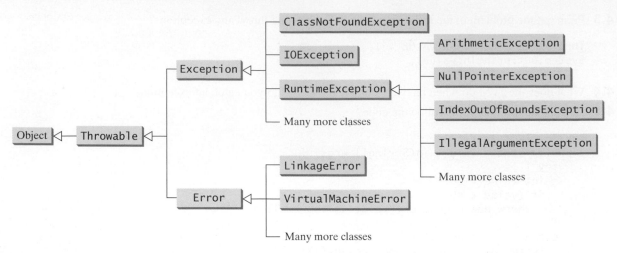

FIGURE 14.1 Exceptions thrown are instances of the classes shown in this diagram, or of subclasses of one of these classes.

Note

The class names **Error**, **Exception**, and **RuntimeException** are somewhat confusing. All three of these classes are exceptions, and all of the errors occur at runtime.

The **Throwable** class is the root of exception classes. All Java exception classes inherit directly or indirectly from **Throwable**. You can create your own exception classes by extending **Exception** or a subclass of **Exception**.

The exception classes can be classified into three major types: system errors, exceptions, and runtime exceptions.

system error

■ *System errors* are thrown by the JVM and are represented in the **Error** class. The **Error** class describes internal system errors, though such errors rarely occur. If one does, there is little you can do beyond notifying the user and trying to terminate the program gracefully. Examples of subclasses of **Error** are listed in Table 14.1.

TABLE 14.1 Examples of Subclasses of **Error**

Class	Reasons for Exception
LinkageError	A class has some dependency on another class, but the latter class has changed incompatibly after the compilation of the former class.
VirtualMachineError	The JVM is broken or has run out of the resources it needs in order to continue operating.

exception

■ *Exceptions* are represented in the **Exception** class, which describes errors caused by your program and by external circumstances. These errors can be caught and handled by your program. Examples of subclasses of **Exception** are listed in Table 14.2.

TABLE 14.2 Examples of Subclasses of **Exception**

Class	Reasons for Exception
ClassNotFoundException	Attempt to use a class that does not exist. This exception would occur, for example, if you tried to run a nonexistent class using the **java** command, or if your program were composed of, say, three class files, only two of which could be found.
IOException	Related to input/output operations, such as invalid input, reading past the end of a file, and opening a nonexistent file. Examples of subclasses of **IOException** are **InterruptedIOException**, **EOFException** (EOF is short for End of File), and **FileNotFoundException**.

■ *Runtime exceptions* are represented in the `RuntimeException` class, which describes programming errors, such as bad casting, accessing an out-of-bounds array, and numeric errors. Runtime exceptions are generally thrown by the JVM. Examples of subclasses are listed in Table 14.3.

runtime exception

TABLE 14.3   Examples of Subclasses of `RuntimeException`

Class	Reasons for Exception
`ArithmeticException`	Dividing an integer by zero. Note that floating-point arithmetic does not throw exceptions (see Appendix E, Special Floating-Point Values).
`NullPointerException`	Attempt to access an object through a `null` reference variable.
`IndexOutOfBoundsException`	Index to an array is out of range.
`IllegalArgumentException`	A method is passed an argument that is illegal or inappropriate.

`RuntimeException`, `Error`, and their subclasses are known as *unchecked exceptions*. All other exceptions are known as *checked exceptions*, meaning that the compiler forces the programmer to check and deal with them in a `try-catch` block or declare it in the method header. Declaring an exception in the method header will be covered in Section 14.4.

unchecked exception
checked exception

In most cases, unchecked exceptions reflect programming logic errors that are unrecoverable. For example, a `NullPointerException` is thrown if you access an object through a reference variable before an object is assigned to it; an `IndexOutOfBoundsException` is thrown if you access an element in an array outside the bounds of the array. These are logic errors that should be corrected in the program. Unchecked exceptions can occur anywhere in a program. To avoid cumbersome overuse of `try-catch` blocks, Java does not mandate that you write code to catch or declare unchecked exceptions.

✓ Check Point

14.7 Describe the Java `Throwable` class, its subclasses, and the types of exceptions.

14.8 What `RuntimeException` will the following programs throw, if any?

MyProgrammingLab™

```java
public class Test {
  public static void main(String[] args) {
    System.out.println(1 / 0);
  }
}
```
(a)

```java
public class Test {
  public static void main(String[] args) {
    int[] list = new int[5];
    System.out.println(list[5]);
  }
}
```
(b)

```java
public class Test {
  public static void main(String[] args) {
    String s = "abc";
    System.out.println(s.charAt(3));
  }
}
```
(c)

```java
public class Test {
  public static void main(String[] args) {
    Object o = new Object();
    String d = (String)o;
  }
}
```
(d)

```java
public class Test {
  public static void main(String[] args) {
    Object o = null;
    System.out.println(o.toString());
  }
}
```
(e)

```java
public class Test {
  public static void main(String[] args) {
    System.out.println(1.0 / 0);
  }
}
```
(f)

14.4 More on Exception Handling

Key Point

A handler for an exception is found by propagating the exception backward through a chain of method calls, starting from the current method.

The preceding sections gave you an overview of exception handling and introduced several predefined exception types. This section provides an in-depth discussion of exception handling.

Java's exception-handling model is based on three operations: *declaring an exception*, *throwing an exception*, and *catching an exception*, as shown in Figure 14.2.

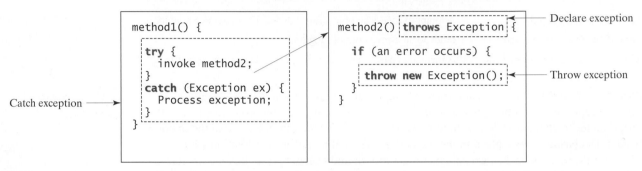

FIGURE 14.2 Exception handling in Java consists of declaring exceptions, throwing exceptions, and catching and processing exceptions.

14.4.1 Declaring Exceptions

declare exception

In Java, the statement currently being executed belongs to a method. The Java interpreter invokes the **main** method to start executing a program. Every method must state the types of checked exceptions it might throw. This is known as *declaring exceptions*. Because system errors and runtime errors can happen to any code, Java does not require that you declare **Error** and **RuntimeException** (unchecked exceptions) explicitly in the method. However, all other exceptions thrown by the method must be explicitly declared in the method header so that the caller of the method is informed of the exception.

To declare an exception in a method, use the **throws** keyword in the method header, as in this example:

```
public void myMethod() throws IOException
```

The **throws** keyword indicates that **myMethod** might throw an **IOException**. If the method might throw multiple exceptions, add a list of the exceptions, separated by commas, after **throws**:

```
public void myMethod()
  throws Exception1, Exception2, ..., ExceptionN
```

Note
If a method does not declare exceptions in the superclass, you cannot override it to declare exceptions in the subclass.

14.4.2 Throwing Exceptions

throw exception

A program that detects an error can create an instance of an appropriate exception type and throw it. This is known as *throwing an exception*. Here is an example: Suppose the program detects that an argument passed to the method violates the method contract (e.g., the argument must be nonnegative, but a negative argument is passed); the program can create an instance of `IllegalArgumentException` and throw it, as follows:

```
IllegalArgumentException ex =
    new IllegalArgumentException("Wrong Argument");
throw ex;
```

Or, if you prefer, you can use the following:

```
throw new IllegalArgumentException("Wrong Argument");
```

 Note

`IllegalArgumentException` is an exception class in the Java API. In general, each exception class in the Java API has at least two constructors: a no-arg constructor, and a constructor with a `String` argument that describes the exception. This argument is called the *exception message*, which can be obtained using `getMessage()`.

exception message

 Tip

The keyword to declare an exception is `throws`, and the keyword to throw an exception is `throw`.

throws vs. throw

14.4.3 Catching Exceptions

You now know how to declare an exception and how to throw an exception. When an exception is thrown, it can be caught and handled in a `try-catch` block, as follows:

catch exception

```
try {
    statements; // Statements that may throw exceptions
}
catch (Exception1 exVar1) {
    handler for exception1;
}
catch (Exception2 exVar2) {
    handler for exception2;
}
...
catch (ExceptionN exVar3) {
    handler for exceptionN;
}
```

If no exceptions arise during the execution of the `try` block, the `catch` blocks are skipped.

If one of the statements inside the `try` block throws an exception, Java skips the remaining statements in the `try` block and starts the process of finding the code to handle the exception. The code that handles the exception is called the *exception handler*; it is found by *propagating the exception* backward through a chain of method calls, starting from the current method. Each `catch` block is examined in turn, from first to last, to see whether the type of the exception object is an instance of the exception class in the `catch` block. If so, the exception object is assigned to the variable declared, and the code in the `catch` block is executed. If no handler is found, Java exits this method, passes the exception to the method that invoked the method, and continues the same process to find a handler. If no handler is found in the chain of methods being invoked, the program terminates and prints an error message on the console. The process of finding a handler is called *catching an exception*.

exception handler
exception propagation

Suppose the `main` method invokes `method1`, `method1` invokes `method2`, `method2` invokes `method3`, and `method3` throws an exception, as shown in Figure 14.3. Consider the following scenario:

- If the exception type is `Exception3`, it is caught by the `catch` block for handling exception `ex3` in `method2`. `statement5` is skipped, and `statement6` is executed.

- If the exception type is `Exception2`, `method2` is aborted, the control is returned to `method1`, and the exception is caught by the `catch` block for handling exception `ex2` in `method1`. `statement3` is skipped, and `statement4` is executed.

- If the exception type is `Exception1`, `method1` is aborted, the control is returned to the `main` method, and the exception is caught by the `catch` block for handling exception `ex1` in the `main` method. `statement1` is skipped, and `statement2` is executed.

- If the exception type is not caught in `method2`, `method1`, or `main`, the program terminates, and `statement1` and `statement2` are not executed.

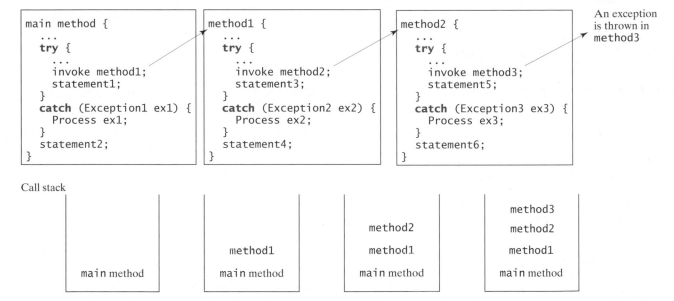

FIGURE 14.3 If an exception is not caught in the current method, it is passed to its caller. The process is repeated until the exception is caught or passed to the `main` method.

catch block

Note
Various exception classes can be derived from a common superclass. If a `catch` block catches exception objects of a superclass, it can catch all the exception objects of the subclasses of that superclass.

order of exception handlers

Note
The order in which exceptions are specified in `catch` blocks is important. A compile error will result if a catch block for a superclass type appears before a catch block for a subclass type. For example, the ordering in (a) on the next page is erroneous, because `RuntimeException` is a subclass of `Exception`. The correct ordering should be as shown in (b).

```
try {
  ...
}
catch (Exception ex) {
  ...
}
catch (RuntimeException ex) {
  ...
}
```
(a) Wrong order

```
try {
  ...
}
catch (RuntimeException ex) {
  ...
}
catch (Exception ex) {
  ...
}
```
(b) Correct order

 Note

catch or declare checked exceptions

Java forces you to deal with checked exceptions. If a method declares a checked exception (i.e., an exception other than **Error** or **RuntimeException**), you must invoke it in a **try-catch** block or declare to throw the exception in the calling method. For example, suppose that method **p1** invokes method **p2**, and **p2** may throw a checked exception (e.g., **IOException**); you have to write the code as shown in (a) or (b) below.

```
void p1() {
  try {
    p2();
  }
  catch (IOException ex) {
    ...
  }
}
```
(a) Catch exception

```
void p1() throws IOException {

  p2();

}
```
(b) Throw exception

 Note

JDK 7 multi-catch

You can use the new JDK 7 multi-catch feature to simplify coding for the exceptions with the same handling code. The syntax is:

```
catch (Exception1 | Exception2 | ... | Exceptionk ex) {
  // Code to handle exceptions
}
```

Each exception type is separated from the next with a vertical bar (|). If one of the exceptions is caught, the handling code is executed.

14.4.4 Getting Information from Exceptions

An exception object contains valuable information about the exception. You may use the following instance methods in the **java.lang.Throwable** class to get information regarding the exception, as shown in Figure 14.4. The **printStackTrace()** method prints stack trace

methods in Throwable

FIGURE 14.4 **Throwable** is the root class for all exception objects.

information on the console. The `getStackTrace()` method provides programmatic access to the stack trace information printed by `printStackTrace()`.

Listing 14.6 gives an example that uses the methods in `Throwable` to display exception information. Line 4 invokes the `sum` method to return the sum of all the elements in the array. There is an error in line 23 that causes the `ArrayIndexOutOfBoundsException`, a subclass of `IndexOutOfBoundsException`. This exception is caught in the `try-catch` block. Lines 7, 8, and 9 display the stack trace, exception message, and exception object and message using the `printStackTrace()`, `getMessage()`, and `toString()` methods, as shown in Figure 14.5. Line 12 brings stack trace elements into an array. Each element represents a method call. You can obtain the method (line 14), class name (line 15), and exception line number (line 16) for each element.

FIGURE 14.5 You can use the `printStackTrace()`, `getMessage()`, `toString()`, and `getStackTrace()` methods to obtain information from exception objects.

LISTING 14.6 TestException.java

```
1  public class TestException  {
2    public static void main(String[] args) {
3      try {
4        System.out.println(sum(new int[] {1, 2, 3, 4, 5}));
5      }
6      catch (Exception ex) {
7        ex.printStackTrace();
8        System.out.println("\n" + ex.getMessage());
9        System.out.println("\n" + ex.toString());
10
11       System.out.println("\nTrace Info Obtained from getStackTrace");
12       StackTraceElement[] traceElements = ex.getStackTrace();
13       for (int i = 0; i < traceElements.length; i++) {
14         System.out.print("method " + traceElements[i].getMethodName());
15         System.out.print("(" + traceElements[i].getClassName() + ":");
16         System.out.println(traceElements[i].getLineNumber() + ")");
17       }
18     }
19   }
20
21   private static int sum(int[] list) {
22     int result = 0;
23     for (int i = 0; i <= list.length; i++)
```

invoke sum

printStackTrace()
getMessage()
toString()

```
24        result += list[i];
25      return result;
26    }
27  }
```

14.4.5 Example: Declaring, Throwing, and Catching Exceptions

This example demonstrates declaring, throwing, and catching exceptions by modifying the setRadius method in the Circle class in Listing 8.9, CircleWithPrivateDataFields.java. The new setRadius method throws an exception if the radius is negative.

Listing 14.7 defines a new circle class named CircleWithException, which is the same as CircleWithPrivateDataFields except that the setRadius(double newRadius) method throws an IllegalArgumentException if the argument newRadius is negative.

LISTING 14.7   CircleWithException.java

```
1   public class CircleWithException {
2     /** The radius of the circle */
3     private double radius;
4
5     /** The number of the objects created */
6     private static int numberOfObjects = 0;
7
8     /** Construct a circle with radius 1 */
9     public CircleWithException() {
10      this(1.0);
11    }
12
13    /** Construct a circle with a specified radius */
14    public CircleWithException(double newRadius) {
15      setRadius(newRadius);
16      numberOfObjects++;
17    }
18
19    /** Return radius */
20    public double getRadius() {
21      return radius;
22    }
23
24    /** Set a new radius */
25    public void setRadius(double newRadius)
26      throws IllegalArgumentException {                           declare exception
27      if (newRadius >= 0)
28        radius = newRadius;
29      else
30        throw new IllegalArgumentException(                       throw exception
31          "Radius cannot be negative");
32    }
33
34    /** Return numberOfObjects */
35    public static int getNumberOfObjects() {
36      return numberOfObjects;
37    }
38
39    /** Return the area of this circle */
40    public double findArea() {
41      return radius * radius * 3.14159;
42    }
43  }
```

A test program that uses the new `Circle` class is given in Listing 14.8.

LISTING 14.8 `TestCircleWithException.java`

```
1  public class TestCircleWithException {
2    public static void main(String[] args) {
3      try {
4        CircleWithException c1 = new CircleWithException(5);
5        CircleWithException c2 = new CircleWithException(-5);
6        CircleWithException c3 = new CircleWithException(0);
7      }
8      catch (IllegalArgumentException ex) {
9        System.out.println(ex);
10     }
11
12     System.out.println("Number of objects created: " +
13       CircleWithException.getNumberOfObjects());
14   }
15 }
```

try

catch

```
java.lang.IllegalArgumentException: Radius cannot be negative
Number of objects created: 1
```

The original `Circle` class remains intact except that the class name is changed to `CircleWithException`, a new constructor `CircleWithException(newRadius)` is added, and the `setRadius` method now declares an exception and throws it if the radius is negative.

The `setRadius` method declares to throw `IllegalArgumentException` in the method header (lines 25–32 in CircleWithException.java). The `CircleWithException` class would still compile if the `throws IllegalArgumentException` clause were removed from the method declaration, since it is a subclass of `RuntimeException` and every method can throw `RuntimeException` (an unchecked exception) regardless of whether it is declared in the method header.

The test program creates three `CircleWithException` objects—`c1`, `c2`, and `c3`—to test how to handle exceptions. Invoking `new CircleWithException(-5)` (line 5 in Listing 14.8) causes the `setRadius` method to be invoked, which throws an `IllegalArgumentException`, because the radius is negative. In the `catch` block, the type of the object `ex` is `IllegalArgumentException`, which matches the exception object thrown by the `setRadius` method, so this exception is caught by the `catch` block.

The exception handler prints a short message, `ex.toString()` (line 9 in Listing 14.8), about the exception, using `System.out.println(ex)`.

Note that the execution continues in the event of the exception. If the handlers had not caught the exception, the program would have abruptly terminated.

The test program would still compile if the `try` statement were not used, because the method throws an instance of `IllegalArgumentException`, a subclass of `RuntimeException` (an unchecked exception). If a method throws an exception other than `RuntimeException` or `Error`, the method must be invoked within a `try-catch` block.

Check Point

MyProgrammingLab™

14.9 What is the purpose of declaring exceptions? How do you declare an exception, and where? Can you declare multiple exceptions in a method header?

14.10 What is a checked exception, and what is an unchecked exception?

14.11 How do you throw an exception? Can you throw multiple exceptions in one `throw` statement?

14.12 What is the keyword `throw` used for? What is the keyword `throws` used for?

14.13 Suppose that `statement2` causes an exception in the following `try-catch` block:

```
try {
  statement1;
  statement2;
  statement3;
}
catch (Exception1 ex1) {
}
catch (Exception2 ex2) {
}

statement4;
```

Answer the following questions:

■ Will `statement3` be executed?

■ If the exception is not caught, will `statement4` be executed?

■ If the exception is caught in the `catch` block, will `statement4` be executed?

14.14 What is displayed when the following program is run?

```
public class Test {
  public static void main(String[] args) {
    try {
      int[] list = new int[10];
      System.out.println("list[10] is " + list[10]);
    }
    catch (ArithmeticException ex) {
      System.out.println("ArithmeticException");
    }
    catch (RuntimeException ex) {
      System.out.println("RuntimeException");
    }
    catch (Exception ex) {
      System.out.println("Exception");
    }
  }
}
```

14.15 What is displayed when the following program is run?

```
public class Test {
  public static void main(String[] args) {
    try {
      method();
      System.out.println("After the method call");
    }
    catch (ArithmeticException ex) {
      System.out.println("ArithmeticException");
    }
    catch (RuntimeException ex) {
      System.out.println("RuntimeException");
    }
    catch (Exception e) {
      System.out.println("Exception");
    }
  }

  static void method() throws Exception {
```

```java
      System.out.println(1 / 0);
  }
}
```

14.16 What is displayed when the following program is run?

```java
public class Test {
  public static void main(String[] args) {
    try {
      method();
      System.out.println("After the method call");
    }
    catch (RuntimeException ex) {
      System.out.println("RuntimeException in main");
    }
    catch (Exception ex) {
      System.out.println("Exception in main");
    }
  }

  static void method() throws Exception {
    try {
      String s ="abc";
      System.out.println(s.charAt(3));
    }
    catch (RuntimeException ex) {
      System.out.println("RuntimeException in method()");
    }
    catch (Exception ex) {
      System.out.println("Exception in method()");
    }
  }
}
```

14.17 What does the method `getMessage()` do?

14.18 What does the method `printStackTrace` do?

14.19 Does the presence of a `try-catch` block impose overhead when no exception occurs?

14.20 Correct a compile error in the following code:

```java
public void m(int value) {
  if (value < 40)
    throw new Exception("value is too small");
}
```

14.5 The `finally` Clause

Key
Point

The `finally` clause is always executed regardless whether an exception occurred or not.

Occasionally, you may want some code to be executed regardless of whether an exception occurs or is caught. Java has a `finally` clause that can be used to accomplish this objective. The syntax for the `finally` clause might look like this:

```java
try {
  statements;
}
catch (TheException ex) {
  handling ex;
}
```

```
finally {
  finalStatements;
}
```

The code in the **finally** block is executed under all circumstances, regardless of whether an exception occurs in the **try** block or is caught. Consider three possible cases:

- If no exception arises in the **try** block, **finalStatements** is executed, and the next statement after the **try** statement is executed.

- If a statement causes an exception in the **try** block that is caught in a **catch** block, the rest of the statements in the **try** block are skipped, the **catch** block is executed, and the **finally** clause is executed. The next statement after the **try** statement is executed.

- If one of the statements causes an exception that is not caught in any **catch** block, the other statements in the **try** block are skipped, the **finally** clause is executed, and the exception is passed to the caller of this method.

The **finally** block executes even if there is a **return** statement prior to reaching the **finally** block.

Note

The **catch** block may be omitted when the **finally** clause is used.   omitting catch block

A common use of the **finally** clause is in I/O programming. To ensure that a file is closed under all circumstances, you may place a file closing statement in the **finally** block. Text I/O will be introduced later in this chapter.

14.21 Suppose that **statement2** causes an exception in the following statement:

```
try {
  statement1;
  statement2;
  statement3;
}
catch (Exception1 ex1) {
}
finally {
  statement4;
}
statement5;
```

Answer the following questions:

- If no exception occurs, will **statement4** be executed, and will **statement5** be executed?

- If the exception is of type **Exception1**, will **statement4** be executed, and will **statement5** be executed?

- If the exception is not of type **Exception1**, will **statement4** be executed, and will **statement5** be executed?

14.6 When to Use Exceptions

A method should throw an exception if the error needs to be handled by its caller.

The **try** block contains the code that is executed in normal circumstances. The **catch** block contains the code that is executed in exceptional circumstances. Exception handling separates error-handling code from normal programming tasks, thus making programs easier to read and to modify. Be aware, however, that exception handling usually requires more time and resources, because it requires instantiating a new exception object, rolling back the call stack, and propagating the exception through the chain of methods invoked to search for the handler.

An exception occurs in a method. If you want the exception to be processed by its caller, you should create an exception object and throw it. If you can handle the exception in the method where it occurs, there is no need to throw or use exceptions.

In general, common exceptions that may occur in multiple classes in a project are candidates for exception classes. Simple errors that may occur in individual methods are best handled without throwing exceptions. This can be done by using `if` statements to check for errors.

When should you use a `try-catch` block in the code? Use it when you have to deal with unexpected error conditions. Do not use a `try-catch` block to deal with simple, expected situations. For example, the following code

```java
try {
  System.out.println(refVar.toString());
}
catch (NullPointerException ex) {
  System.out.println("refVar is null");
}
```

is better replaced by

```java
if (refVar != null)
  System.out.println(refVar.toString());
else
  System.out.println("refVar is null");
```

Which situations are exceptional and which are expected is sometimes difficult to decide. The point is not to abuse exception handling as a way to deal with a simple logic test.

14.22 The following method checks whether a string is a numeric string:

```java
public static boolean isNumeric(String token) {
  try {
    Double.parseDouble(token);
    return true;
  }
  catch (java.lang.NumberFormatException ex) {
    return false;
  }
}
```

Is it correct? Rewrite it without using exceptions.

14.7 Rethrowing Exceptions

Java allows an exception handler to rethrow the exception if the handler cannot process the exception or simply wants to let its caller be notified of the exception.

The syntax for rethrowing an exception may look like this:

```java
try {
  statements;
}
catch (TheException ex) {
```

```
      perform operations before exits;
      throw ex;
  }
```

The statement `throw ex` rethrows the exception to the caller so that other handlers in the caller get a chance to process the exception `ex`.

14.23 Suppose that `statement2` causes an exception in the following statement:

```
try {
  statement1;
  statement2;
  statement3;
}
catch (Exception1 ex1) {
}
catch (Exception2 ex2) {
  throw ex2;
}
finally {
  statement4;
}
statement5;
```

Answer the following questions:

- If no exception occurs, will `statement4` be executed, and will `statement5` be executed?

- If the exception is of type `Exception1`, will `statement4` be executed, and will `statement5` be executed?

- If the exception is of type `Exception2`, will `statement4` be executed, and will `statement5` be executed?

- If the exception is not `Exception1` nor `Exception2`, will `statement4` be executed, and will `statement5` be executed?

14.8 Chained Exceptions

Throwing an exception along with another exception forms a chained exception.

In the preceding section, the `catch` block rethrows the original exception. Sometimes, you may need to throw a new exception (with additional information) along with the original exception. This is called *chained exceptions*. Listing 14.9 illustrates how to create and throw chained exceptions.

chained exception

LISTING 14.9 ChainedExceptionDemo.java

```
1  public class ChainedExceptionDemo {
2    public static void main(String[] args) {
3      try {
4        method1();
5      }
6      catch (Exception ex) {
7        ex.printStackTrace();
8      }
9    }
10
```

stack trace

```
11    public static void method1() throws Exception {
12      try {
13        method2();
14      }
15      catch (Exception ex) {
16        throw new Exception("New info from method1", ex);
17      }
18    }
19
20    public static void method2() throws Exception {
21      throw new Exception("New info from method2");
22    }
23  }
```

chained exception

throw exception

```
java.lang.Exception: New info from method1
  at ChainedExceptionDemo.method1(ChainedExceptionDemo.java:16)
  at ChainedExceptionDemo.main(ChainedExceptionDemo.java:4)
Caused by: java.lang.Exception: New info from method2
  at ChainedExceptionDemo.method2(ChainedExceptionDemo.java:21)
  at ChainedExceptionDemo.method1(ChainedExceptionDemo.java:13)
  ... 1 more
```

The **main** method invokes **method1** (line 4), **method1** invokes **method2** (line 13), and **method2** throws an exception (line 21). This exception is caught in the **catch** block in **method1** and is wrapped in a new exception in line 16. The new exception is thrown and caught in the catch block in the **main** method in line 6. The sample output shows the output from the **printStackTrace()** method in line 7. The new exception thrown from **method1** is displayed first, followed by the original exception thrown from **method2**.

14.9 Defining Custom Exception Classes

Key
Point

You can define a custom exception class by extending the java.lang.Exception *class.*

Java provides quite a few exception classes. Use them whenever possible instead of defining your own exception classes. However, if you run into a problem that cannot be adequately described by the predefined exception classes, you can create your own exception class, derived from **Exception** or from a subclass of **Exception**, such as **IOException**.

In Listing 14.7, CircleWithException.java, the **setRadius** method throws an exception if the radius is negative. Suppose you wish to pass the radius to the handler. In that case, you can define a custom exception class, as shown in Listing 14.10.

VideoNote

Create custom exception classes

LISTING 14.10 InvalidRadiusException.java

extends Exception

```
1  public class InvalidRadiusException extends Exception {
2    private double radius;
3
4    /** Construct an exception */
5    public InvalidRadiusException(double radius) {
6      super("Invalid radius " + radius);
7      this.radius = radius;
8    }
9
10   /** Return the radius */
11   public double getRadius() {
12     return radius;
13   }
14 }
```

This custom exception class extends **java.lang.Exception** (line 1). The **Exception** class extends **java.lang.Throwable**. All the methods (e.g., **getMessage()**, **toString()**, and **printStackTrace()**) in **Exception** are inherited from **Throwable**. The **Exception** class contains four constructors. Among them, the following two constructors are often used:

java.lang.Exception	
+Exception()	Constructs an exception with no message.
+Exception(message: String)	Constructs an exception with the specified message.

Line 6 invokes the superclass's constructor with a message. This message will be set in the exception object and can be obtained by invoking **getMessage()** on the object.

Tip
Most exception classes in the Java API contain two constructors: a no-arg constructor and a constructor with a message parameter.
To create an **InvalidRadiusException**, you have to pass a radius. Therefore, the **setRadius** method in Listing 14.7 can be modified as shown in Listing 14.11.

LISTING 14.11 TestCircleWithCustomException.java

```
1  public class TestCircleWithCustomException {
2    public static void main(String[] args) {
3      try {
4        new CircleWithCustomException(5);
5        new CircleWithCustomException(-5);
6        new CircleWithCustomException(0);
7      }
8      catch (InvalidRadiusException ex) {
9        System.out.println(ex);
10     }
11
12     System.out.println("Number of objects created: " +
13       CircleWithException.getNumberOfObjects());
14   }
15 }
16
17 class CircleWithCustomException {
18   /** The radius of the circle */
19   private double radius;
20
21   /** The number of objects created */
22   private static int numberOfObjects = 0;
23
24   /** Construct a circle with radius 1 */
25   public CircleWithCustomException() throws InvalidRadiusException {   declare exception
26     this(1.0);
27   }
28
29   /** Construct a circle with a specified radius */
30   public CircleWithCustomException(double newRadius)                   throw exception
31     throws InvalidRadiusException {
32     setRadius(newRadius);
33     numberOfObjects++;
34   }
35
36   /** Return radius */
```

```
37    public double getRadius() {
38      return radius;
39    }
40
41    /** Set a new radius */
42    public void setRadius(double newRadius)
43        throws InvalidRadiusException {
44      if (newRadius >= 0)
45        radius = newRadius;
46      else
47        throw new InvalidRadiusException(newRadius);
48    }
49
50    /** Return numberOfObjects */
51    public static int getNumberOfObjects() {
52      return numberOfObjects;
53    }
54
55    /** Return the area of this circle */
56    public double findArea() {
57      return radius * radius * 3.14159;
58    }
59  }
```

```
InvalidRadiusException: Invalid radius -5.0
Number of objects created: 0
```

The `setRadius` method in `CircleWithCustomException` throws an `InvalidRadius-Exception` when radius is negative (line 47). Since `InvalidRadiusException` is a checked exception, the `setRadius` method must declare it in the method header (line 42). Since the constructors for `CircleWithCustomException` invoke the `setRadius` method to a set a new radius and it may throw an `InvalidRadiusException`, the constructors are declared to throw `InvalidRadiusException` (lines 25, 31).

Invoking `new CircleWithCustomException(-5)` throws an `InvalidRadius-Exception`, which is caught by the handler. The handler displays the radius in the exception object `ex`.

checked custom exception

 Tip
Can you define a custom exception class by extending `RuntimeException`? Yes, but it is not a good way to go, because it makes your custom exception unchecked. It is better to make a custom exception checked, so that the compiler can force these exceptions to be caught in your program.

✓Check
Point
MyProgrammingLab™

14.24 How do you define a custom exception class?

14.25 Suppose the `setRadius` method throws the `InValidRadiusException` defined in Listing 14.10. What is displayed when the following program is run?

```
public class Test {
  public static void main(String[] args) {
    try {
      method();
      System.out.println("After the method call");
    }
    catch (RuntimeException ex) {
      System.out.println("RuntimeException in main");
```

```
      }
      catch (Exception ex) {
        System.out.println("Exception in main");
      }
    }

    static void method() throws Exception {
      try {
        Circle c1 = new Circle(1);
        c1.setRadius(-1);
        System.out.println(c1.getRadius());
      }
      catch (RuntimeException ex) {
        System.out.println("RuntimeException in method()");
      }
      catch (Exception ex) {
        System.out.println("Exception in method()");
        throw ex;
      }
    }
  }
```

14.10 The File Class

The File class contains the methods for obtaining the properties of a file/directory and for renaming and deleting a file/directory.

Key Point

Having learned exception handling, you are ready to step into file processing. Data stored in the program are temporary; they are lost when the program terminates. To permanently store the data created in a program, you need to save them in a file on a disk or other permanent storage device. The file can then be transported and read later by other programs. Since data are stored in files, this section introduces how to use the File class to obtain file/directory properties, to delete and rename files/directories, and to create directories. The next section introduces how to read/write data from/to text files.

why file?

Every file is placed in a directory in the file system. An *absolute file name* (or *full name*) contains a file name with its complete path and drive letter. For example, **c:\book\Welcome.java** is the absolute file name for the file **Welcome.java** on the Windows operating system. Here **c:\book** is referred to as the *directory path* for the file. Absolute file names are machine dependent. On the UNIX platform, the absolute file name may be **/home/liang/book/Welcome.java**, where **/home/liang/book** is the directory path for the file **Welcome.java**.

absolute file name

directory path

A *relative file name* is in relation to the current working directory. The complete directory path for a relative file name is omitted. For example, **Welcome.java** is a relative file name. If the current working directory is **c:\book**, the absolute file name would be **c:\book\Welcome.java**.

relative file name

The File class is intended to provide an abstraction that deals with most of the machine-dependent complexities of files and path names in a machine-independent fashion. The File class contains the methods for obtaining file and directory properties and for renaming and deleting files and directories, as shown in Figure 14.6. However, *the File class does not contain the methods for reading and writing file contents.*

The file name is a string. The File class is a wrapper class for the file name and its directory path. For example, `new File("c:\\book")` creates a File object for the directory **c:\book**, and `new File("c:\\book\\test.dat")` creates a File object for the file **c:\book\test.dat**, both on Windows. You can use the File class's `isDirectory()` method to check whether the object represents a directory, and the `isFile()` method to check whether the object represents a file.

java.io.File	
+File(pathname: String)	Creates a File object for the specified path name. The path name may be a directory or a file.
+File(parent: String, child: String)	Creates a File object for the child under the directory parent. The child may be a file name or a subdirectory.
+File(parent: File, child: String)	Creates a File object for the child under the directory parent. The parent is a File object. In the preceding constructor, the parent is a string.
+exists(): boolean	Returns true if the file or the directory represented by the File object exists.
+canRead(): boolean	Returns true if the file represented by the File object exists and can be read.
+canWrite(): boolean	Returns true if the file represented by the File object exists and can be written.
+isDirectory(): boolean	Returns true if the File object represents a directory.
+isFile(): boolean	Returns true if the File object represents a file.
+isAbsolute(): boolean	Returns true if the File object is created using an absolute path name.
+isHidden(): boolean	Returns true if the file represented in the File object is hidden. The exact definition of *hidden* is system-dependent. On Windows, you can mark a file hidden in the File Properties dialog box. On Unix systems, a file is hidden if its name begins with a period(.) character.
+getAbsolutePath(): String	Returns the complete absolute file or directory name represented by the File object.
+getCanonicalPath(): String	Returns the same as getAbsolutePath() except that it removes redundant names, such as "." and "..", from the path name, resolves symbolic links (on Unix), and converts drive letters to standard uppercase (on Windows).
+getName(): String	Returns the last name of the complete directory and file name represented by the File object. For example, new File("c:\\book\\test.dat").getName() returns test.dat.
+getPath(): String	Returns the complete directory and file name represented by the File object. For example, new File("c:\\book\\test.dat").getPath() returns c:\book\test.dat.
+getParent(): String	Returns the complete parent directory of the current directory or the file represented by the File object. For example, new File("c:\\book\\test.dat").getParent() returns c:\book.
+lastModified(): long	Returns the time that the file was last modified.
+length(): long	Returns the size of the file, or 0 if it does not exist or if it is a directory.
+listFile(): File[]	Returns the files under the directory for a directory File object.
+delete(): boolean	Deletes the file or directory represented by this File object. The method returns true if the deletion succeeds.
+renameTo(dest: File): boolean	Renames the file or directory represented by this File object to the specified name represented in dest. The method returns true if the operation succeeds.
+mkdir(): boolean	Creates a directory represented in this File object. Returns true if the the directory is created successfully.
+mkdirs(): boolean	Same as mkdir() except that it creates directory along with its parent directories if the parent directories do not exist.

FIGURE 14.6 The File class can be used to obtain file and directory properties, to delete and rename files and directories, and to create directories.

\ in file names

Caution
The directory separator for Windows is a backslash (\). The backslash is a special character in Java and should be written as \\ in a string literal (see Table 2.6).

Note
Constructing a File instance does not create a file on the machine. You can create a File instance for any file name regardless whether it exists or not. You can invoke the exists() method on a File instance to check whether the file exists.

relative file name

Java directory separator (/)

Do not use absolute file names in your program. If you use a file name such as c:\\book\\Welcome.java, it will work on Windows but not on other platforms. You should use a file name relative to the current directory. For example, you may create a File object using new File("Welcome.java") for the file **Welcome.java** in the current directory. You may create a File object using new File("image/us.gif") for the file **us.gif** under the **image** directory in the current directory. The forward slash (/) is the Java directory separator, which is the same as on UNIX. The statement new File("image/us.gif") works on Windows, UNIX, and any other platform.

Listing 14.12 demonstrates how to create a File object and use the methods in the File class to obtain its properties. The program creates a File object for the file **us.gif**. This file is stored under the **image** directory in the current directory.

LISTING 14.12 TestFileClass.java

```
1  public class TestFileClass {
2    public static void main(String[] args) {
3      java.io.File file = new java.io.File("image/us.gif");        create a File object
4      System.out.println("Does it exist? " + file.exists());        exists()
5      System.out.println("The file has " + file.length() + " bytes");  length()
6      System.out.println("Can it be read? " + file.canRead());       canRead()
7      System.out.println("Can it be written? " + file.canWrite());    canWrite()
8      System.out.println("Is it a directory? " + file.isDirectory()); isDirectory()
9      System.out.println("Is it a file? " + file.isFile());          isFile()
10     System.out.println("Is it absolute? " + file.isAbsolute());    isAbsolute()
11     System.out.println("Is it hidden? " + file.isHidden());        isHidden()
12     System.out.println("Absolute path is " +
13       file.getAbsolutePath());                                     getAbsolutePath()
14     System.out.println("Last modified on " +
15       new java.util.Date(file.lastModified()));                    lastModified()
16   }
17 }
```

The lastModified() method returns the date and time when the file was last modified, measured in milliseconds since the beginning of UNIX time (00:00:00 GMT, January 1, 1970). The Date class is used to display it in a readable format in lines 14–15.

Figure 14.7a shows a sample run of the program on Windows, and Figure 14.7b, a sample run on UNIX. As shown in the figures, the path-naming conventions on Windows are different from those on UNIX.

(a) On Windows

(b) On UNIX

FIGURE 14.7   The program creates a File object and displays file properties.

14.26 What is wrong about creating a File object using the following statement?

```
new File("c:\book\test.dat");
```

14.27 How do you check whether a file already exists? How do you delete a file? How do you rename a file? Can you find the file size (the number of bytes) using the File class? How do you create a directory?

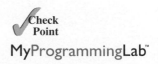

Check
Point

MyProgrammingLab™

14.28 Can you use the `File` class for I/O? Does creating a `File` object create a file on the disk?

14.11 File Input and Output

Use the Scanner class for reading text data from a file and the `PrintWriter` class for writing text data to a file.

VideoNote

Write and read data

A `File` object encapsulates the properties of a file or a path, but it does not contain the methods for creating a file or for writing/reading data to/from a file (referred to as data *input* and *output*, or *I/O* for short). In order to perform I/O, you need to create objects using appropriate Java I/O classes. The objects contain the methods for reading/writing data from/to a file. There are two types of files: text and binary. Text files are essentially strings on disk. This section introduces how to read/write strings and numeric values from/to a text file using the `Scanner` and `PrintWriter` classes. Binary files will be introduced in Chapter 19.

14.11.1 Writing Data Using `PrintWriter`

The `java.io.PrintWriter` class can be used to create a file and write data to a text file. First, you have to create a `PrintWriter` object for a text file as follows:

```
PrintWriter output = new PrintWriter(filename);
```

Then, you can invoke the `print`, `println`, and `printf` methods on the `PrintWriter` object to write data to a file. Figure 14.8 summarizes frequently used methods in `PrintWriter`.

java.io.PrintWriter	
+PrintWriter(file: File)	Creates a `PrintWriter` object for the specified file object.
+PrintWriter(filename: String)	Creates a `PrintWriter` object for the specified file-name string.
+print(s: String): void	Writes a string to the file.
+print(c: char): void	Writes a character to the file.
+print(cArray: char[]): void	Writes an array of characters to the file.
+print(i: int): void	Writes an `int` value to the file.
+print(l: long): void	Writes a `long` value to the file.
+print(f: float): void	Writes a `float` value to the file.
+print(d: double): void	Writes a `double` value to the file.
+print(b: boolean): void	Writes a `boolean` value to the file.
Also contains the overloaded `println` methods.	A `println` method acts like a `print` method; additionally, it prints a line separator. The line-separator string is defined by the system. It is \r\n on Windows and \n on Unix.
Also contains the overloaded `printf` methods.	The `printf` method was introduced in §3.16, "Formatting Console Output."

FIGURE 14.8 The `PrintWriter` class contains the methods for writing data to a text file.

Listing 14.13 gives an example that creates an instance of `PrintWriter` and writes two lines to the file **scores.txt**. Each line consists of a first name (a string), a middle-name initial (a character), a last name (a string), and a score (an integer).

LISTING 14.13 WriteData.java

throws an exception

create File object

file exist?

```
1 public class WriteData {
2   public static void main(String[] args) throws IoException {
3     java.io.File file = new java.io.File("scores.txt");
4     if (file.exists()) {
```

```
5         System.out.println("File already exists");
6         System.exit(1);
7       }
8
9       // Create a file                                                    create PrintWriter
10      java.io.PrintWriter output = new java.io.PrintWriter(file);
11
12      // Write formatted output to the file                               print data
13      output.print("John T Smith ");
14      output.println(90);
15      output.print("Eric K Jones ");          John T Smith 90  scores.txt
16      output.println(85);                     Eric K Jones 85
17
18      // Close the file                                                   close file
19      output.close();
20    }
21  }
```

Lines 4–7 check whether the file scores.txt exists. If so, exit the program (line 6).

Invoking the constructor of **PrintWriter** will create a new file if the file does not exist. If   create a file
the file already exists, the current content in the file will be discarded without verifying with
the user.

Invoking the constructor of **PrintWriter** may throw an I/O exception. Java forces you to   throws IOException
write the code to deal with this type of exception. For simplicity, we declare **throws**
IOException in the main method header (line 2).

You have used the **System.out.print**, **System.out.println**, and   print method
System.out.printf methods to write text to the console. **System.out** is a standard
Java object for the console. You can create **PrintWriter** objects for writing text to any file
using **print**, **println**, and **printf** (lines 13–16).

The **close()** method must be used to close the file. If this method is not invoked, the data   close file
may not be saved properly in the file.

14.11.2 Reading Data Using Scanner

The **java.util.Scanner** class was used to read strings and primitive values from the console in Section 2.3, Reading Input from the Console. A **Scanner** breaks its input into tokens
delimited by whitespace characters. To read from the keyboard, you create a **Scanner** for
System.in, as follows:

```
Scanner input = new Scanner(System.in);
```

To read from a file, create a **Scanner** for a file, as follows:

```
Scanner input = new Scanner(new File(filename));
```

Figure 14.9 summarizes frequently used methods in **Scanner**.

Listing 14.14 gives an example that creates an instance of **Scanner** and reads data from
the file **scores.txt**.

LISTING 14.14 ReadData.java

```
1  import java.util.Scanner;
2
3  public class ReadData {
4    public static void main(String[] args) throws Exception {
5      // Create a File instance
6      java.io.File file = new java.io.File("scores.txt");                  create a file
7
8      // Create a Scanner for the file
```

create a Scanner

```
 9    Scanner input = new Scanner(file);
10
11    // Read data from a file
12    while (input.hasNext()) {
13      String firstName = input.next();
14      String mi = input.next();
15      String lastName = input.next();
16      int score = input.nextInt();
17      System.out.println(
18        firstName + " " + mi + " " + lastName + " " + score);
19    }
20
21    // Close the file
22    input.close();
23  }
24 }
```

has next?
read items

scores.txt

John T Smith 90
Eric K Jones 85

close file

java.util.Scanner	
+Scanner(source: File)	Creates a Scanner that produces values scanned from the specified file.
+Scanner(source: String)	Creates a Scanner that produces values scanned from the specified string.
+close()	Closes this scanner.
+hasNext(): boolean	Returns true if this scanner has more data to be read.
+next(): String	Returns next token as a string from this scanner.
+nextLine(): String	Returns a line ending with the line separator from this scanner.
+nextByte(): byte	Returns next token as a byte from this scanner.
+nextShort(): short	Returns next token as a short from this scanner.
+nextInt(): int	Returns next token as an int from this scanner.
+nextLong(): long	Returns next token as a long from this scanner.
+nextFloat(): float	Returns next token as a float from this scanner.
+nextDouble(): double	Returns next token as a double from this scanner.
+useDelimiter(pattern: String): Scanner	Sets this scanner's delimiting pattern and returns this scanner.

FIGURE 14.9 The Scanner class contains the methods for scanning data.

Note that new Scanner(String) creates a Scanner for a given string. To create a Scanner to read data from a file, you have to use the java.io.File class to create an instance of the File using the constructor new File(filename) (line 6), and use new Scanner(File) to create a Scanner for the file (line 9).

File class

Invoking the constructor new Scanner(File) may throw an I/O exception, so the main method declares throws Exception in line 4.

throws Exception

Each iteration in the while loop reads the first name, middle initial, last name, and score from the text file (lines 12–19). The file is closed in line 22.

It is not necessary to close the input file (line 22), but it is a good practice to do so to release the resources occupied by the file.

close file

14.11.3 How Does Scanner Work?

The nextByte(), nextShort(), nextInt(), nextLong(), nextFloat(), nextDouble(), and next() methods are known as *token-reading methods*, because they read tokens separated by delimiters. By default, the delimiters are whitespace. You can use the useDelimiter(String regex) method to set a new pattern for delimiters.

token-reading method
change delimiter

How does an input method work? A token-reading method first skips any delimiters (white-space by default), then reads a token ending at a delimiter. The token is then automatically converted into a value of the **byte**, **short**, **int**, **long**, **float**, or **double** type for **nextByte()**, **nextShort()**, **nextInt()**, **nextLong()**, **nextFloat()**, and **nextDouble()**, respectively. For the **next()** method, no conversion is performed. If the token does not match the expected type, a runtime exception **java.util.InputMismatchException** will be thrown.

InputMismatchException

Both methods **next()** and **nextLine()** read a string. The **next()** method reads a string delimited by delimiters, and **nextLine()** reads a line ending with a line separator.

next() vs. nextLine()

Note
The line-separator string is defined by the system. It is \r\n on Windows and \n on UNIX. To get the line separator on a particular platform, use

line separator

```
String lineSeparator = System.getProperty("line.separator");
```

If you enter input from a keyboard, a line ends with the *Enter* key, which corresponds to the \n character.

The token-reading method does not read the delimiter after the token. If the **nextLine()** method is invoked after a token-reading method, this method reads characters that start from this delimiter and end with the line separator. The line separator is read, but it is not part of the string returned by **nextLine()**.

behavior of nextLine()

Suppose a text file named **test.txt** contains a line

input from file

```
34 567
```

After the following code is executed,

```
Scanner input = new Scanner(new File("test.txt"));
int intValue = input.nextInt();
String line = input.nextLine();
```

intValue contains **34** and **line** contains the characters **' '**, **5**, **6**, and **7**.

What happens if the input is *entered from the keyboard*? Suppose you enter **34**, press the *Enter* key, then enter **567** and press the *Enter* key for the following code:

input from keyboard

```
Scanner input = new Scanner(System.in);
int intValue = input.nextInt();
String line = input.nextLine();
```

You will get **34** in **intValue** and an empty string in **line**. Why? Here is the reason. The token-reading method **nextInt()** reads in **34** and stops at the delimiter, which in this case is a line separator (the *Enter* key). The **nextLine()** method ends after reading the line separator and returns the string read before the line separator. Since there are no characters before the line separator, **line** is empty.

You can read data from a file or from the keyboard using the **Scanner** class. You can also scan data from a string using the **Scanner** class. For example, the following code

scan a string

```
Scanner input = new Scanner("13 14");
int sum = input.nextInt() + input.nextInt();
System.out.println("Sum is " + sum);
```

displays

```
The sum is 27
```

14.11.4 Case Study: Replacing Text

Suppose you are to write a program named **ReplaceText** that replaces all occurrences of a string in a text file with a new string. The file name and strings are passed as command-line arguments as follows:

```
java ReplaceText sourceFile targetFile oldString newString
```

For example, invoking

```
java ReplaceText FormatString.java t.txt StringBuilder StringBuffer
```

replaces all the occurrences of **StringBuilder** by **StringBuffer** in the file **FormatString.java** and saves the new file in **t.txt**.

Listing 14.15 gives the program. The program checks the number of arguments passed to the **main** method (lines 7–11), checks whether the source and target files exist (lines 14–25), creates a **Scanner** for the source file (line 28), creates a **PrintWriter** for the target file, and repeatedly reads a line from the source file (line 32), replaces the text (line 33), and writes a new line to the target file (line 34). You must close the output file (line 38) to ensure that data are saved to the file properly.

LISTING 14.15 ReplaceText.java

```
 1  import java.io.*;
 2  import java.util.*;
 3
 4  public class ReplaceText {
 5    public static void main(String[] args) throws Exception {
 6      // Check command-line parameter usage
 7      if (args.length != 4) {
 8        System.out.println(
 9          "Usage: java ReplaceText sourceFile targetFile oldStr newStr");
10        System.exit(1);
11      }
12
13      // Check if source file exists
14      File sourceFile = new File(args[0]);
15      if (!sourceFile.exists()) {
16        System.out.println("Source file " + args[0] + " does not exist");
17        System.exit(2);
18      }
19
20      // Check if target file exists
21      File targetFile = new File(args[1]);
22      if (targetFile.exists()) {
23        System.out.println("Target file " + args[1] + " already exists");
24        System.exit(3);
25      }
26
27      // Create a Scanner for input and a PrintWriter for output
28      Scanner input = new Scanner(sourceFile);
29      PrintWriter output = new PrintWriter(targetFile);
30
31      while (input.hasNext()) {
32        String s1 = input.nextLine();
33        String s2 = s1.replaceAll(args[2], args[3]);
34        output.println(s2);
35      }
36
```

check command usage

source file exists?

target file exists?

create a Scanner
create a PrintWriter

has next?
read a line

```
37        input.close();                                                      close file
38        output.close();
39    }
40 }
```

In a normal situation, the program is terminated after a file is copied. The program is terminated abnormally if the command-line arguments are not used properly (lines 7–11), if the source file does not exist (lines 14–18), or if the target file already exists (lines 22–25). The exit status code 1, 2, and 3 are used to indicate these abnormal terminations (lines 10, 17, 24).

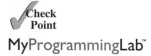

14.29 How do you create a `PrintWriter` to write data to a file? What is the reason to declare `throws Exception` in the main method in Listing 14.13, WriteData.java? What would happen if the `close()` method were not invoked in Listing 14.13?

14.30 Show the contents of the file **temp.txt** after the following program is executed.

```java
public class Test {
  public static void main(String[] args) throws Exception {
    java.io.PrintWriter output = new
      java.io.PrintWriter("temp.txt");
    output.printf("amount is %f %e\r\n", 32.32, 32.32);
    output.printf("amount is %5.4f %5.4e\r\n", 32.32, 32.32);
    output.printf("%6b\r\n", (1 > 2));
    output.printf("%6s\r\n", "Java");
    output.close();
  }
}
```

14.31 How do you create a `Scanner` to read data from a file? What is the reason to define `throws Exception` in the main method in Listing 14.14, ReadData.java? What would happen if the `close()` method were not invoked in Listing 14.14?

14.32 What will happen if you attempt to create a `Scanner` for a nonexistent file? What will happen if you attempt to create a `PrintWriter` for an existing file?

14.33 Is the line separator the same on all platforms? What is the line separator on Windows?

14.34 Suppose you enter `45 57.8 789`, then press the *Enter* key. Show the contents of the variables after the following code is executed.

```java
Scanner input = new Scanner(System.in);
int intValue = input.nextInt();
double doubleValue = input.nextDouble();
String line = input.nextLine();
```

14.35 Suppose you enter `45`, press the *Enter* key, `57.8`, press the *Enter* key, `789`, and press the *Enter* key. Show the contents of the variables after the following code is executed.

```java
Scanner input = new Scanner(System.in);
int intValue = input.nextInt();
double doubleValue = input.nextDouble();
String line = input.nextLine();
```

14.12 File Dialogs

JFileChooser is a GUI component for displaying a file dialog.

Java provides the `javax.swing.JFileChooser` class for displaying a file dialog, as shown in Figure 14.10. From this dialog box, the user can choose a file.

FIGURE 14.10 `JFileChooser` can be used to display a file dialog for opening a file.

Listing 14.16 gives a program that prompts the user to choose a file and displays its contents on the console.

LISTING 14.16 ReadFileUsingJFileChooser.java

```
1  import java.util.Scanner;
2  import javax.swing.JFileChooser;
3
4  public class ReadFileUsingJFileChooser {
5    public static void main(String[] args) throws Exception {
6      JFileChooser fileChooser = new JFileChooser();
7      if (fileChooser.showOpenDialog(null)
8          == JFileChooser.APPROVE_OPTION) {
9        // Get the selected file
10       java.io.File file = fileChooser.getSelectedFile();
11
12       // Create a Scanner for the file
13       Scanner input = new Scanner(file);
14
15       // Read text from the file
16       while (input.hasNext()) {
17         System.out.println(input.nextLine());
18       }
19
20       // Close the file
21       input.close();
22     }
23     else {
24       System.out.println("No file selected");
25     }
26   }
27 }
```

create a JFileChooser
display file chooser
check status

getSelectedFile

The program creates a `JFileChooser` in line 6. The **showOpenDialog(null)** method displays a dialog box, as shown in Figure 14.10. The method returns an **int** value, either **APPROVE_OPTION** or **CANCEL_OPTION**, which indicates whether the *Open* button or the *Cancel* button was clicked.

The **getSelectedFile()** method (line 10) returns the selected file from the file dialog box. Line 13 creates a scanner for the file. The program continuously reads the lines from the file and displays them to the console (lines 16–18).

showOpenDialog

APPROVE_OPTION

getSelectedFile

Check Point

MyProgrammingLab™

14.36 How do you create a File Open dialog box? What is returned from invoking **getSelectFile()** on a `JFileChooser` object?

14.13 Reading Data from the Web

Just like you can read data from a file on your computer, you can read data from a file on the Web.

In addition to reading data from a local file on a computer or file server, you can also access data from a file that is on the Web if you know the file's URL (Uniform Resource Locator—the unique address for a file on the Web). For example, www.google.com/index.html is the URL for the file **index.html** located on the Google Web server. When you enter the URL in a Web browser, the Web server sends the data to your browser, which renders the data graphically. Figure 14.11 illustrates how this process works.

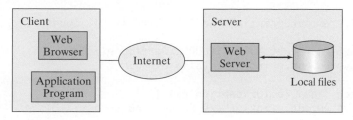

FIGURE 14.11 The client retrieves files from a Web server.

For an application program to read data from a URL, you first need to create a **URL** object using the **java.net.URL** class with this constructor:

public URL(String spec) **throws** MalformedURLException

For example, the following statement creates a URL object for http://www.google .com/index.html.

```
1  try {
2    URL url = new URL("http://www.google.com/index.html");
3  }
4  catch (MalformedURLException ex) {
5    ex.printStackTrace();
6  }
```

A `MalformedURLException` is thrown if the URL string has a syntax error. For example, the URL string "http:/www.google.com/index.html" would cause a `MalformedURLException` runtime error because two slashes (`//`) are required after the colon (`:`). Note that the `http://` prefix is required for the `URL` class to recognize a valid URL. It would be wrong if you replace line 2 with the following code:

URL url = **new** URL("www.google.com/index.html");

After a `URL` object is created, you can use the `openStream()` method defined in the `URL` class to open an input stream and use this stream to create a `Scanner` object as follows:

Scanner input = **new** Scanner(url.openStream());

Now you can read the data from the input stream just like from a local file. The example in Listing 14.17 prompts the user to enter a URL and displays the size of the file.

LISTING 14.17 ReadFileFromURL.java

```
1  import java.util.Scanner;
2
```

enter a URL

create a URL object

create a Scanner object
more to read?
read a line

MalformedURLException

IOException

```
3   public class ReadFileFromURL {
4     public static void main(String[] args) {
5       System.out.print("Enter a URL: ");
6       String URLString = new Scanner(System.in).next();
7
8       try {
9         java.net.URL url = new java.net.URL(URLString);
10        int count = 0;
11        Scanner input = new Scanner(url.openStream());
12        while (input.hasNext()) {
13          String line = input.nextLine();
14          count += line.length();
15        }
16
17        System.out.println("The file size is " + count + " bytes");
18      }
19      catch (java.net.MalformedURLException ex) {
20        System.out.println("Invalid URL");
21      }
22      catch (java.io.IOException ex) {
23        System.out.println("I/O Errors: no such file");
24      }
25    }
26  }
```

```
Enter a URL: http://cs.armstrong.edu/liang/data/Lincoln.txt  ↵Enter
The file size is 1469 bytes
```

```
Enter a URL: http://www.yahoo.com  ↵Enter
The file size is 190006 bytes
```

MalformedURLException

The program prompts the user to enter a URL string (line 6) and creates a URL object (line 9). The constructor will throw a `java.net.MalformedURLException` (line 19) if the URL isn't formed correctly.

The program creates a Scanner object from the input stream for the URL (line 11). If the URL is formed correctly but does not exist, an `IOException` will be thrown (line 22). For example, http://google.com/index1.html uses the appropriate form, but the URL itself does not exist. An `IOException` would be thrown if this URL was used for this program.

✓ Check
Point

MyProgrammingLab™

14.37 How do you create a Scanner object for reading text from a URL?

KEY TERMS

absolute file name   541
chained exception   537
checked exception   525
declare exception   526
directory path   541

exception   518
exception propagation   527
relative file name   541
throw exception   526
unchecked exception   525

CHAPTER SUMMARY

1. Exception handling enables a method to throw an exception to its caller.

2. A Java *exception* is an instance of a class derived from `java.lang.Throwable`. Java provides a number of predefined exception classes, such as `Error`, `Exception`, `RuntimeException`, `ClassNotFoundException`, `NullPointerException`, and `ArithmeticException`. You can also define your own exception class by extending `Exception`.

3. Exceptions occur during the execution of a method. `RuntimeException` and `Error` are *unchecked exceptions*; all other exceptions are *checked*.

4. When *declaring a method*, you have to declare a checked exception if the method might throw it, thus telling the compiler what can go wrong.

5. The keyword for declaring an exception is `throws`, and the keyword for throwing an exception is `throw`.

6. To invoke the method that declares checked exceptions, enclose it in a `try` statement. When an exception occurs during the execution of the method, the `catch` block catches and handles the exception.

7. If an exception is not caught in the current method, it is passed to its caller. The process is repeated until the exception is caught or passed to the `main` method.

8. Various exception classes can be derived from a common superclass. If a `catch` block catches the exception objects of a superclass, it can also catch all the exception objects of the subclasses of that superclass.

9. The order in which exceptions are specified in a `catch` block is important. A compile error will result if you specify an exception object of a class after an exception object of the superclass of that class.

10. When an exception occurs in a method, the method exits immediately if it does not catch the exception. If the method is required to perform some task before exiting, you can catch the exception in the method and then rethrow it to its caller.

11. The code in the `finally` block is executed under all circumstances, regardless of whether an exception occurs in the `try` block or whether an exception is caught if it occurs.

12. Exception handling separates error-handling code from normal programming tasks, thus making programs easier to read and to modify.

13. Exception handling should not be used to replace simple tests. You should perform simple test using `if` statements whenever possible, and reserve exception handling for dealing with situations that cannot be handled with `if` statements.

14. The `File` class is used to obtain file properties and manipulate files. It does not contain the methods for creating a file or for reading/writing data from/to a file.

15. You can use **Scanner** to read string and primitive data values from a text file and use **PrintWriter** to create a file and write data to a text file.

16. The **JFileChooser** class can be used to display file dialogs for choosing files.

17. You can read from a file on the Web using the **URL** class.

TEST QUESTIONS

Do the test questions for this chapter online at www.cs.armstrong.edu/liang/intro9e/test.html.

PROGRAMMING EXERCISES

Sections 14.2–14.9

*14.1   (*NumberFormatException*) Listing 9.5, Calculator.java, is a simple command-line calculator. Note that the program terminates if any operand is nonnumeric. Write a program with an exception handler that deals with nonnumeric operands; then write another program without using an exception handler to achieve the same objective. Your program should display a message that informs the user of the wrong operand type before exiting (see Figure 14.12).

FIGURE 14.12   The program performs arithmetic operations and detects input errors.

*14.2   (*InputMismatchException*) Write a program that prompts the user to read two integers and displays their sum. Your program should prompt the user to read the number again if the input is incorrect.

*14.3   (*ArrayIndexOutOfBoundsException*) Write a program that meets the following requirements:

   ■ Creates an array with **100** randomly chosen integers.
   ■ Prompts the user to enter the index of the array, then displays the corresponding element value. If the specified index is out of bounds, display the message **Out of Bounds**.

*14.4   (*IllegalArgumentException*) Modify the **Loan** class in Listing 10.2 to throw **IllegalArgumentException** if the loan amount, interest rate, or number of years is less than or equal to zero.

*14.5   (*IllegalTriangleException*) Programming Exercise 11.1 defined the **Triangle** class with three sides. In a triangle, the sum of any two sides is greater than the other side. The **Triangle** class must adhere to this rule. Create the **IllegalTriangleException** class, and modify the constructor of the

Triangle class to throw an IllegalTriangleException object if a triangle is created with sides that violate the rule, as follows:

```
/** Construct a triangle with the specified sides */
public Triangle(double side1, double side2, double side3)
  throws IllegalTriangleException {
  // Implement it
}
```

*14.6 (*NumberFormatException*) Listing 9.2 implements the hexToDecimal(String hexString) method, which converts a hex string into a decimal number. Implement the hexToDecimal method to throw a NumberFormatException if the string is not a hex string.

*14.7 (*NumberFormatException*) Programming Exercise 9.8 specifies the binaryToDecimal(String binaryString) method, which converts a binary string into a decimal number. Implement the binaryToDecimal method to throw a NumberFormatException if the string is not a binary string.

*14.8 (*HexFormatException*) Exercise 14.6 implements the hexToDecimal method to throw a NumberFormatException if the string is not a hex string. Define a custom exception called HexFormatException. Implement the hexToDecimal method to throw a HexFormatException if the string is not a hex string.

VideoNote

HexFormatException

*14.9 (*BinaryFormatException*) Exercise 14.7 implements the binaryToDecimal method to throw a BinaryFormatException if the string is not a binary string. Define a custom exception called BinaryFormatException. Implement the binaryToDecimal method to throw a BinaryFormatException if the string is not a binary string.

*14.10 (*OutOfMemoryError*) Write a program that causes the JVM to throw an OutOfMemoryError and catches and handles this error.

Sections 14.10–14.12

**14.11 (*Remove text*) Write a program that removes all the occurrences of a specified string from a text file. For example, invoking

```
java Exercise14_11 John filename
```

removes the string John from the specified file. Your program should get the arguments from the command line.

**14.12 (*Reformat Java source code*) Write a program that converts the Java source code from the next-line brace style to the end-of-line brace style. For example, the following Java source in (a) uses the next-line brace style. Your program converts it to the end-of-line brace style in (b).

```
public class Test
{
  public static void main(String[] args)
  {
    // Some statements
  }
}
```

```
public class Test {
  public static void main(String[] args) {
    // Some statements
  }
}
```

| (a) Next-line brace style | (b) End-of-line brace style |

Your program can be invoked from the command line with the Java source-code file as the argument. It converts the Java source code to a new format. For example, the following command converts the Java source-code file **Test.java** to the end-of-line brace style.

```
java Exercise14_12 Test.java
```

*14.13 (*Count characters, words, and lines in a file*) Write a program that will count the number of characters, words, and lines in a file. Words are separated by whitespace characters. The file name should be passed as a command-line argument, as shown in Figure 14.13.

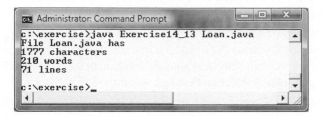

FIGURE 14.13 The program displays the number of characters, words, and lines in the given file.

*14.14 (*Process scores in a text file*) Suppose that a text file contains an unspecified number of scores separated by blanks. Write a program that prompts the user to enter the file, reads the scores from the file, and displays their total and average. Scores are separated by blanks.

*14.15 (*Write/read data*) Write a program to create a file named **Exercise14_15.txt** if it does not exist. Write **100** integers created randomly into the file using text I/O. Integers are separated by spaces in the file. Read the data back from the file and display the sorted data.

**14.16 (*Replace text*) Listing 14.15, ReplaceText.java, gives a program that replaces text in a source file and saves the change into a new file. Revise the program to save the change into the original file. For example, invoking

```
java Exercise14_16 file oldString newString
```

replaces `oldString` in the source file with `newString`.

***14.17 (*Game: hangman*) Rewrite Exercise 9.25. The program reads the words stored in a text file named **hangman.txt**. Words are delimited by spaces.

14.18 (*Add package statement*) Suppose you have Java source files under the directories **chapter1, **chapter2**, ..., **chapter34**. Write a program to insert the statement **package chapteri;** as the first line for each Java source file under the directory **chapteri**. Suppose **chapter1**, **chapter2**, ..., **chapter34** are under the root directory **srcRootDirectory**. The root directory and **chapteri** directory may contain other folders and files. Use the following command to run the program:

```
java Exercise14_18 srcRootDirectory
```

*14.19 (*Count words*) Write a program that counts the number of words in President Abraham Lincoln's Gettysburg address from http://cs.armstrong.edu/liang/data/Lincoln.txt.

^^14.20 (*Remove package statement*) Suppose you have Java source files under the directories `chapter1`, `chapter2`, ..., `chapter34`. Write a program to remove the statement `package chapteri;` in the first line for each Java source file under the directory `chapteri`. Suppose `chapter1`, `chapter2`, ..., `chapter34` are under the root directory `srcRootDirectory`. The root directory and `chapteri` directory may contain other folders and files. Use the following command to run the program:

```
java Exercise14_20 srcRootDirectory
```

**14.21 (*Display a graph*) A graph consists of vertices and edges that connect vertices. Write a program that reads a graph from a file and displays it on a panel. The first line in the file contains a number that indicates the number of vertices (`n`). The vertices are labeled as `0, 1, ..., n-1`. Each subsequent line, with the format `u x y v1 v2 ...`, describes that the vertex `u` is located at position (`x`, `y`) with edges (`u`, `v1`), (`u`, `v2`), and so on. Figure 14.14a gives an example of the file for a graph. Your program prompts the user to enter the name of the file, reads data from the file, and displays the graph on a panel, as shown in Figure 14.14b. Write another program that reads data from a Web URL such as http://cs.armstrong.edu/liang/data/graph.txt. This program should prompt the user to enter the URL for the file.

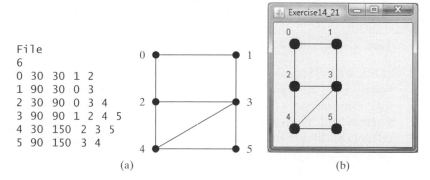

```
File
6
0  30   30  1 2
1  90   30  0 3
2  30   90  0 3 4
3  90   90  1 2 4 5
4  30  150  2 3 5
5  90  150  3 4
```
(a)   (b)

FIGURE 14.14 Exercise 14.21 reads the information about the graph and displays it visually.

**14.22 (*Replace text*) Revise Exercise 14.16 to replace a string in a file with a new string for all files in the specified directory using the command:

```
java Exercise14_22 dir oldString newString
```

**14.23 (*Process scores in a text file on the Web*) Suppose that the text file on the Web http://cs.armstrong.edu/liang/data/Scores.txt contains an unspecified number of scores. Write a program that reads the scores from the file and displays their total and average. Scores are separated by blanks.

*14.24 (*Create large dataset*) Create a data file with 1,000 lines. Each line in the file consists of a faculty member's first name, last name, rank, and salary. The faculty member's first name and last name for the *i*th line are FirstName*i* and LastName*i*. The rank is randomly generated as assistant, associate, and full. The salary is randomly generated as a number with two digits after the decimal point. The salary for an assistant professor should be in the range from 50,000 to

80,000, for associate professor from 60,000 to 110,000, and for full professor from 75,000 to 130,000. Save the file in **Salary.txt**. Here are some sample data:

FirstName1 LastName1 assistant 60055.95

FirstName2 LastName2 associate 81112.45

. . .

FirstName1000 LastName1000 full 92255.21

*14.25 (*Process large dataset*) A university posts its employees' salaries at http://cs.armstrong.edu/liang/data/Salary.txt. Each line in the file consists of a faculty member's first name, last name, rank, and salary (see Exercise 14.24). Write a program to display the total salary for assistant professors, associate professors, full professors, and all faculty, respectively, and display the average salary for assistant professors, associate professors, full professors, and all faculty, respectively.

**14.26 (*Create a directory*) Write a program that prompts the user to enter a directory name and creates a directory using the `File`'s `mkdirs` method. The program displays the message "Directory created successfully" if a directory is created or "Directory already exists" if the directory already exists.

14.27 (*Replace words*) Suppose you have a lot of files in a directory that contain words **Exercise*i*_*j*, where *i* and *j* are digits. Write a program that pads a 0 before *i* if *i* is a single digit and 0 before *j* if *j* is a single digit. For example, the word **Exercise2_1** in a file will be replaced by **Exercise02_01**. In Java, when you pass the symbol * from the command line, it refers to all files in the directory (see Supplement III.AC). Use the following command to run your program.

```
java Exercise14_27 *
```

14.28 (*Rename files*) Suppose you have a lot of files in a directory named **Exercise*i*_*j*, where *i* and *j* are digits. Write a program that pads a 0 before *i* if *i* is a single digit. For example, a file named **Exercise2_1** in a directory will be renamed to **Exercise02_1**. In Java, when you pass the symbol * from the command line, it refers to all files in the directory (see Supplement III.AC). Use the following command to run your program.

```
java Exercise14_28 *
```

14.29 (*Rename files*) Suppose you have a lot of files in a directory named **Exercise*i*_*j*, where *i* and *j* are digits. Write a program that pads a 0 before *j* if *j* is a single digit. For example, a file named **Exercise2_1** in a directory will be renamed to **Exercise2_01**. In Java, when you pass the symbol * from the command line, it refers to all files in the directory (see Supplement III.AC). Use the following command to run your program.

```
java Exercise14_29 *
```

ABSTRACT CLASSES AND INTERFACES

Objectives

- To design and use abstract classes (§15.2).

- To generalize numeric wrapper classes, `BigInteger`, and `BigDecimal` using the abstract `Number` class (§15.3).

- To process a calendar using the `Calendar` and `GregorianCalendar` classes (§15.4).

- To specify common behavior for objects using interfaces (§15.5).

- To define interfaces and define classes that implement interfaces (§15.5).

- To define a natural order using the `Comparable` interface (§15.6).

- To make objects cloneable using the `Cloneable` interface (§15.7).

- To explore the similarities and differences among concrete classes, abstract classes, and interfaces (§15.8).

- To design the `Rational` class for processing rational numbers (§15.9).

15.1 Introduction

Key Point

A superclass defines common behavior for related subclasses. An interface *can be used to define common behavior for classes (including unrelated classes).*

problem
interface

You have learned how to write simple programs to create and display GUI components. Can you write the code to respond to user actions, such as clicking a button to perform an action?

In order to write such code, you have to know about interfaces. An *interface* is for defining common behavior for classes (including unrelated classes). Before discussing interfaces, we introduce a closely related subject: abstract classes.

15.2 Abstract Classes

An abstract class cannot be used to create objects. An abstract class can contain abstract methods, which are implemented in concrete subclasses.

VideoNote

Abstract GeometricObject class

abstract class

In the inheritance hierarchy, classes become more specific and concrete *with each new subclass.* If you move from a subclass back up to a superclass, the classes become more general and less specific. Class design should ensure that a superclass contains common features of its subclasses. Sometimes a superclass is so abstract that it cannot have any specific instances. Such a class is referred to as an *abstract class.*

In Chapter 11, `GeometricObject` was defined as the superclass for `Circle` and `Rectangle`. `GeometricObject` models common features of geometric objects. Both `Circle` and `Rectangle` contain the `getArea()` and `getPerimeter()` methods for computing the area and perimeter of a circle and a rectangle. Since you can compute areas and perimeters for all geometric objects, it is better to define the `getArea()` and `getPerimeter()` methods in the `GeometricObject` class. However, these methods cannot be implemented in the `GeometricObject` class, because their implementation depends on the specific type of geometric object. Such methods are referred to as *abstract methods* and are denoted using the **abstract** modifier in the method header. After you define the methods in `GeometricObject`, it becomes an abstract class. Abstract classes are denoted using the **abstract** modifier in the class header. In UML graphic notation, the names of abstract classes and their abstract methods are italicized, as shown in Figure 15.1. Listing 15.1 gives the source code for the new `GeometricObject` class.

abstract method

abstract modifier

LISTING 15.1 GeometricObject.java

abstract class

```java
1  public abstract class GeometricObject {
2    private String color = "white";
3    private boolean filled;
4    private java.util.Date dateCreated;
5
6    /** Construct a default geometric object */
7    protected GeometricObject() {
8      dateCreated = new java.util.Date();
9    }
10
11   /** Construct a geometric object with color and filled value */
12   protected GeometricObject(String color, boolean filled) {
13     dateCreated = new java.util.Date();
14     this.color = color;
15     this.filled = filled;
16   }
17
18   /** Return color */
19   public String getColor() {
20     return color;
```

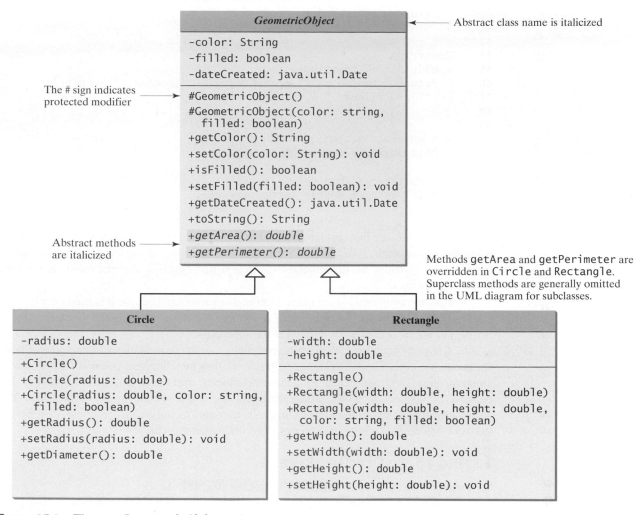

Abstract class name is italicized

The # sign indicates protected modifier

Abstract methods are italicized

Methods getArea and getPerimeter are overridden in Circle and Rectangle. Superclass methods are generally omitted in the UML diagram for subclasses.

FIGURE 15.1 The new GeometricObject class contains abstract methods.

```
21    }
22
23    /** Set a new color */
24    public void setColor(String color) {
25      this.color = color;
26    }
27
28    /** Return filled. Since filled is boolean,
29     *  the get method is named isFilled */
30    public boolean isFilled() {
31      return filled;
32    }
33
34    /** Set a new filled */
35    public void setFilled(boolean filled) {
36      this.filled = filled;
37    }
38
39    /** Get dateCreated */
40    public java.util.Date getDateCreated() {
```

```
41        return dateCreated;
42    }
43
44    @Override
45    public String toString() {
46        return "created on " + dateCreated + "\ncolor: " + color +
47            " and filled: " + filled;
48    }
49
```

abstract method
```
50    /** Abstract method getArea */
51    public abstract double getArea();
52
```

abstract method
```
53    /** Abstract method getPerimeter */
54    public abstract double getPerimeter();
55 }
```

Abstract classes are like regular classes, but you cannot create instances of abstract classes using the **new** operator. An abstract method is defined without implementation. Its implementation is provided by the subclasses. A class that contains abstract methods must be defined as abstract.

why protected constructor?

The constructor in the abstract class is defined as protected, because it is used only by subclasses. When you create an instance of a concrete subclass, its superclass's constructor is invoked to initialize data fields defined in the superclass.

The **GeometricObject** abstract class defines the common features (data and methods) for geometric objects and provides appropriate constructors. Because you don't know how to compute areas and perimeters of geometric objects, **getArea** and **getPerimeter** are defined as abstract methods. These methods are implemented in the subclasses. The implementation of **Circle** and **Rectangle** is the same as in Listings 15.2 and 15.3, except that they extend the **GeometricObject** class defined in this chapter.

implementing Circle
implementing Rectangle

LISTING 15.2 Circle.java

extends abstract
  GeometricObject
```
1  public class Circle extends GeometricObject {
2      // Same as lines 3-48 in Listing 11.2, so omitted
3  }
```

LISTING 15.3 Rectangle.java

extends abstract
  GeometricObject
```
1  public class Rectangle extends GeometricObject {
2      // Same as lines 3-51 in Listing 11.3, so omitted
3  }
```

15.2.1 Why Abstract Methods?

You may be wondering what advantage is gained by defining the methods **getArea** and **getPerimeter** as abstract in the **GeometricObject** class. The example in Listing 15.4 shows the benefits of defining them in the **GeometricObject** class. The program creates two geometric objects, a circle and a rectangle, invokes the **equalArea** method to check whether they have equal areas, and invokes the **displayGeometricObject** method to display them.

LISTING 15.4 TestGeometricObject.java

```
1  public class TestGeometricObject {
2      /** Main method */
3      public static void main(String[] args) {
4          // Create two geometric objects
```
create a circle
```
5          GeometricObject geoObject1 = new Circle(5);
```
create a rectangle
```
6          GeometricObject geoObject2 = new Rectangle(5, 3);
```

```
 7
 8      System.out.println("The two objects have the same area? " +
 9        equalArea(geoObject1, geoObject2));
10
11      // Display circle
12      displayGeometricObject(geoObject1);
13
14      // Display rectangle
15      displayGeometricObject(geoObject2);
16    }
17
18    /** A method for comparing the areas of two geometric objects */
19    public static boolean equalArea(GeometricObject object1,            equalArea
20        GeometricObject object2) {
21      return object1.getArea() == object2.getArea();
22    }
23
24    /** A method for displaying a geometric object */
25    public static void displayGeometricObject(GeometricObject object) {    displayGeometricObject
26      System.out.println();
27      System.out.println("The area is " + object.getArea());
28      System.out.println("The perimeter is " + object.getPerimeter());
29    }
30  }
```

```
The two objects have the same area? false

The area is 78.53981633974483
The perimeter is 31.41592653589793

The area is 15.0
The perimeter is 16.0
```

The methods **getArea()** and **getPerimeter()** defined in the **GeometricObject** class are overridden in the **Circle** class and the **Rectangle** class. The statements (lines 5–6)

```
GeometricObject geoObject1 = new Circle(5);
GeometricObject geoObject2 = new Rectangle(5, 3);
```

create a new circle and rectangle and assign them to the variables **geoObject1** and **geoObject2**. These two variables are of the **GeometricObject** type.

When invoking **equalArea(geoObject1, geoObject2)** (line 9), the **getArea()** method defined in the **Circle** class is used for **object1.getArea()**, since **geoObject1** is a circle, and the **getArea()** method defined in the **Rectangle** class is used for **object2.getArea()**, since **geoObject2** is a rectangle.

Similarly, when invoking **displayGeometricObject(geoObject1)** (line 12), the methods **getArea()** and **getPerimeter()** defined in the **Circle** class are used, and when invoking **displayGeometricObject(geoObject2)** (line 15), the methods **getArea** and **getPerimeter** defined in the **Rectangle** class are used. The JVM dynamically determines which of these methods to invoke at runtime, depending on the actual object that invokes the method.

Note that you could not define the **equalArea** method for comparing whether two geometric objects have the same area if the **getArea** method were not defined in **GeometricObject**. Now you have seen the benefits of defining the abstract methods in   why abstract methods?
GeometricObject.

15.2.2 Interesting Points about Abstract Classes

The following points about abstract classes are worth noting:

abstract method in abstract class

- An abstract method cannot be contained in a nonabstract class. If a subclass of an abstract superclass does not implement all the abstract methods, the subclass must be defined as abstract. In other words, in a nonabstract subclass extended from an abstract class, all the abstract methods must be implemented. Also note that abstract methods are nonstatic.

object cannot be created from abstract class

- An abstract class cannot be instantiated using the **new** operator, but you can still define its constructors, which are invoked in the constructors of its subclasses. For instance, the constructors of `GeometricObject` are invoked in the `Circle` class and the `Rectangle` class.

abstract class without abstract method

- A class that contains abstract methods must be abstract. However, it is possible to define an abstract class that doesn't contain any abstract methods. In this case, you cannot create instances of the class using the **new** operator. This class is used as a base class for defining subclasses.

superclass of abstract class may be concrete

- A subclass can be abstract even if its superclass is concrete. For example, the `Object` class is concrete, but its subclasses, such as `GeometricObject`, may be abstract.

concrete method overridden to be abstract

- A subclass can override a method from its superclass to define it as abstract. This is *very unusual*, but it is useful when the implementation of the method in the superclass becomes invalid in the subclass. In this case, the subclass must be defined as abstract.

abstract class as type

- You cannot create an instance from an abstract class using the **new** operator, but an abstract class can be used as a data type. Therefore, the following statement, which creates an array whose elements are of the `GeometricObject` type, is correct.

```
GeometricObject[] objects = new GeometricObject[10];
```

You can then create an instance of `GeometricObject` and assign its reference to the array like this:

```
objects[0] = new Circle();
```

15.1 Which of the following classes defines a legal abstract class?

```
class A {
  abstract void unfinished() {
  }
}
```
(a)

```
public class abstract A {
  abstract void unfinished();
}
```
(b)

```
class A {
  abstract void unfinished();
}
```
(c)

```
abstract class A {
  protected void unfinished();
}
```
(d)

```
abstract class A {
  abstract void unfinished();
}
```
(e)

```
abstract class A {
  abstract int unfinished();
}
```
(f)

15.2 The `getArea` and `getPerimeter` methods may be removed from the `GeometricObject` class. What are the benefits of defining `getArea` and `getPerimeter` as abstract methods in the `GeometricObject` class?

15.3 True or false?

    a. An abstract class can be used just like a nonabstract class except that you cannot use the `new` operator to create an instance from the abstract class.

    b. An abstract class can be extended.

    c. A subclass of a nonabstract superclass cannot be abstract.

    d. A subclass cannot override a concrete method in a superclass to define it as abstract.

    e. An abstract method must be nonstatic.

15.3 Case Study: the Abstract **Number** Class

Number is an abstract superclass for numeric wrapper classes, `BigInteger`, and `BigDecimal`.

Key Point

Section 10.12 introduced numeric wrapper classes and Section 10.14 introduced the `BigInteger` and `BigDecimal` classes. These classes have common methods `byteValue()`, `shortValue()`, `intValue()`, `longValue()`, `floatValue()`, and `doubleValue()` for returning a `byte`, `short`, `int`, `long`, `float`, and `double` value from an object of these classes. These common methods are actually defined in the `Number` class, which is a superclass for the numeric wrapper classes, `BigInteger`, and `BigDecimal`, as shown in Figure 15.2.

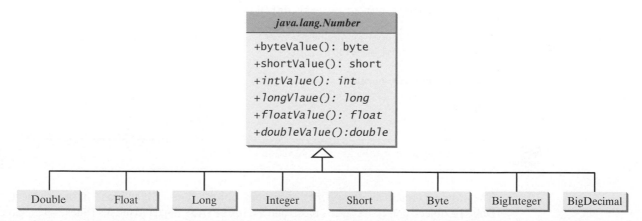

FIGURE 15.2 The `Number` class is an abstract superclass for `Double`, `Float`, `Long`, `Integer`, `Short`, `Byte`, `BigInteger` and `BigDecimal`.

Since the `intValue()`, `longValue()`, `floatValue()`, and `doubleValue()` methods cannot be implemented in the `Number` class, they are defined as abstract methods in the `Number` class. The `Number` class is therefore an abstract class. The `byteValue()` and `shortValue()` method are implemented from the `intValue()` method as follows:

```
public byte byteValue() {
  return (byte)intValue();
}
```

```
                    public short shortValue() {
                      return (short)intValue();
                    }
```

With **Number** defined as the superclass for the numeric classes, we can define methods to perform common operations for numbers. Listing 15.5 gives a program that finds the largest number in a list of **Number** objects.

LISTING 15.5 LargestNumbers.java

```
 1   import java.util.ArrayList;
 2   import java.math.*;
 3
 4   public class LargestNumbers {
 5     public static void main(String[] args) {
 6       ArrayList<Number> list = new ArrayList<Number>();
 7       list.add(45); // Add an integer
 8       list.add(3445.53); // Add a double
 9       // Add a BigInteger
10       list.add(new BigInteger("3432323234344343101"));
11       // Add a BigDecimal
12       list.add(new BigDecimal("2.0909090989091343433344343"));
13
14       System.out.println("The largest number is " +
15         getLargestNumber(list));
16     }
17
18     public static Number getLargestNumber(ArrayList<Number> list) {
19       if (list == null || list.size() == 0)
20         return null;
21
22       Number number = list.get(0);
23       for (int i = 1; i < list.size(); i++)
24         if (number.doubleValue() < list.get(i).doubleValue())
25           number = list.get(i);
26
27       return number;
28     }
29   }
```

create an array list
add number to list

invoke getLargestNumber

doubleValue

The largest number is 3432323234344343101

The program creates an **ArrayList** of **Number** objects (line 6). It adds an **Integer** object, a **Double** object, a **BigInteger** object, and a **BigDecimal** object to the list (lines 7–12). Note that **45** is automatically converted into an **Integer** object and added to the list in line 7 and that **3445.53** is automatically converted into a **Double** object and added to the list in line 8 using autoboxing.

Invoking the **getLargestNumber** method returns the largest number in the list (line 15). The **getLargestNumber** method returns **null** if the list is **null** or the list size is **0** (lines 19–20). To find the largest number in the list, the numbers are compared by invoking their **doubleValue()** method (line 24). The **doubleValue()** method is defined in the **Number** class and implemented in the concrete subclass of **Number**. If a number is an **Integer** object, the **Integer**'s **doubleValue()** is invoked. If a number is a **BigDecimal** object, the **BigDecimal**'s **doubleValue()** is invoked.

If the **doubleValue()** method is not defined in the **Number** class. You will not be able to find the largest number among different types of numbers using the **Number** class.

15.4 Why do the following two lines of code compile but cause a runtime error?

```
Number numberRef = new Integer(0);
Double doubleRef = (Double)numberRef;
```

15.5 Why do the following two lines of code compile but cause a runtime error?

```
Number[] numberArray = new Integer[2];
numberArray[0] = new Double(1.5);
```

15.6 Show the output of the following code.

```
public class Test {
  public static void main(String[] args) {
    Number x = 3;
    System.out.println(x.intValue());
    System.out.println(x.doubleValue());
  }
}
```

15.7 What is wrong in the following code? (Note that the **compareTo** method for the **Integer** and **Double** classes was introduced in Section 10.12.)

```
public class Test {
  public static void main(String[] args) {
    Number x = new Integer(3);
    System.out.println(x.intValue());
    System.out.println(x.compareTo(new Integer(4)));
  }
}
```

15.8 What is wrong in the following code?

```
public class Test {
  public static void main(String[] args) {
    Number x = new Integer(3);
    System.out.println(x.intValue());
    System.out.println((Integer)x.compareTo(new Integer(4)));
  }
}
```

15.4 Case Study: **Calendar** and **GregorianCalendar**

GregorianCalendar is a concrete subclass of the abstract class Calendar.

An instance of **java.util.Date** represents a specific instant in time with millisecond precision. **java.util.Calendar** is an abstract base class for extracting detailed calendar information, such as the year, month, date, hour, minute, and second. Subclasses of **Calendar** can implement specific calendar systems, such as the Gregorian calendar, the lunar calendar, and the Jewish calendar. Currently, **java.util.GregorianCalendar** for the Gregorian calendar is supported in Java, as shown in Figure 15.3. The **add** method is abstract in the **Calendar** class, because its implementation is dependent on a concrete calendar system.

You can use **new GregorianCalendar()** to construct a default **GregorianCalendar** with the current time and **new GregorianCalendar(year, month, date)** to construct a **GregorianCalendar** with the specified **year**, **month**, and **date**. The **month** parameter is **0** based—that is, **0** is for January.

VideoNote

Calendar and GregorianCalendar classes

abstract add method

constructing calendar

Key Point

java.util.Calendar	
#Calendar()	Constructs a default calendar.
+get(field: int): int	Returns the value of the given calendar field.
+set(field: int, value: int): void	Sets the given calendar to the specified value.
+set(year: int, month: int, dayOfMonth: int): void	Sets the calendar with the specified year, month, and date. The month parameter is 0-based; that is, 0 is for January.
+getActualMaximum(field: int): int	Returns the maximum value that the specified calendar field could have.
+add(field: int, amount: int): void	Adds or subtracts the specified amount of time to the given calendar field.
+getTime(): java.util.Date	Returns a Date object representing this calendar's time value (million second offset from the UNIX epoch).
+setTime(date: java.util.Date): void	Sets this calendar's time with the given Date object.

java.util.GregorianCalendar	
+GregorianCalendar()	Constructs a GregorianCalendar for the current time.
+GregorianCalendar(year: int, month: int, dayOfMonth: int)	Constructs a GregorianCalendar for the specified year, month, and date.
+GregorianCalendar(year: int, month: int, dayOfMonth: int, hour:int, minute: int, second: int)	Constructs a GregorianCalendar for the specified year, month, date, hour, minute, and second. The month parameter is 0-based, that is, 0 is for January.

FIGURE 15.3 The abstract Calendar class defines common features of various calendars.

get(field)

The **get(int field)** method defined in the **Calendar** class is useful for extracting the date and time information from a **Calendar** object. The fields are defined as constants, as shown in Table 15.1.

TABLE 15.1 Field Constants in the Calendar Class

Constant	Description
YEAR	The year of the calendar.
MONTH	The month of the calendar, with 0 for January.
DATE	The day of the calendar.
HOUR	The hour of the calendar (12-hour notation).
HOUR_OF_DAY	The hour of the calendar (24-hour notation).
MINUTE	The minute of the calendar.
SECOND	The second of the calendar.
DAY_OF_WEEK	The day number within the week, with 1 for Sunday.
DAY_OF_MONTH	Same as DATE.
DAY_OF_YEAR	The day number in the year, with 1 for the first day of the year.
WEEK_OF_MONTH	The week number within the month, with 1 for the first week.
WEEK_OF_YEAR	The week number within the year, with 1 for the first week.
AM_PM	Indicator for AM or PM (0 for AM and 1 for PM).

Listing 15.6 gives an example that displays the date and time information for the current time.

LISTING 15.6 TestCalendar.java

```
1  import java.util.*;
2
```

```
 3   public class TestCalendar {
 4     public static void main(String[] args) {
 5       // Construct a Gregorian calendar for the current date and time
 6       Calendar calendar = new GregorianCalendar();
 7       System.out.println("Current time is " + new Date());
 8       System.out.println("YEAR: " + calendar.get(Calendar.YEAR));
 9       System.out.println("MONTH: " + calendar.get(Calendar.MONTH));
10       System.out.println("DATE: " + calendar.get(Calendar.DATE));
11       System.out.println("HOUR: " + calendar.get(Calendar.HOUR));
12       System.out.println("HOUR_OF_DAY: " +
13         calendar.get(Calendar.HOUR_OF_DAY));
14       System.out.println("MINUTE: " + calendar.get(Calendar.MINUTE));
15       System.out.println("SECOND: " + calendar.get(Calendar.SECOND));
16       System.out.println("DAY_OF_WEEK: " +
17         calendar.get(Calendar.DAY_OF_WEEK));
18       System.out.println("DAY_OF_MONTH: " +
19         calendar.get(Calendar.DAY_OF_MONTH));
20       System.out.println("DAY_OF_YEAR: " +
21         calendar.get(Calendar.DAY_OF_YEAR));
22       System.out.println("WEEK_OF_MONTH: " +
23         calendar.get(Calendar.WEEK_OF_MONTH));
24       System.out.println("WEEK_OF_YEAR: " +
25         calendar.get(Calendar.WEEK_OF_YEAR));
26       System.out.println("AM_PM: " + calendar.get(Calendar.AM_PM));
27
28       // Construct a calendar for September 11, 2001
29       Calendar calendar1 = new GregorianCalendar(2001, 8, 11);
30       String[] dayNameOfWeek = {"Sunday", "Monday", "Tuesday", "Wednesday",
31         "Thursday", "Friday", "Saturday"};
32       System.out.println("September 11, 2001 is a " +
33         dayNameOfWeek[calendar1.get(Calendar.DAY_OF_WEEK) - 1]);
34     }
35   }
```

calendar for current time

extract fields in calendar

create a calendar

```
Current time is Sun Nov 27 17:48:15 EST 2011
YEAR: 2011
MONTH: 10
DATE: 27
HOUR: 5
HOUR_OF_DAY: 17
MINUTE: 48
SECOND: 15
DAY_OF_WEEK: 1
DAY_OF_MONTH: 27
DAY_OF_YEAR: 331
WEEK_OF_MONTH: 5
WEEK_OF_YEAR: 49
AM_PM: 1
September 11, 2001 is a Tuesday
```

The **set(int field, value)** method defined in the **Calendar** class can be used to set a field. For example, you can use **calendar.set(Calendar.DAY_OF_MONTH, 1)** to set the **calendar** to the first day of the month.

set(field, value)

The **add(field, value)** method adds the specified amount to a given field. For example, **add(Calendar.DAY_OF_MONTH, 5)** adds five days to the current time of the calendar. **add(Calendar.DAY_OF_MONTH, -5)** subtracts five days from the current time of the calendar.

add(field, amount)

getActualMaximum(field)

setTime(date)
getTime()

To obtain the number of days in a month, use **calendar** **.getActualMaximum(Calendar.DAY_OF_MONTH)**. For example, if the **calendar** were for March, this method would return **31**.

You can set a time represented in a **Date** object for the **calendar** by invoking **calendar.setTime(date)** and retrieve the time by invoking **calendar.getTime()**.

Check
Point

MyProgrammingLab

15.9 Can you create a **Calendar** object using the **Calendar** class?

15.10 Which method in the **Calendar** class is abstract?

15.11 How do you create a **Calendar** object for the current time?

15.12 For a **Calendar** object **c**, how do you get its year, month, date, hour, minute, and second?

15.5 Interfaces

Key
Point

VideoNote

The concept of interface

An interface is a class-like construct that contains only constants and abstract methods.

In many ways an interface is similar to an abstract class, but its intent is to specify common behavior for objects of related classes or unrelated classes. For example, using appropriate interfaces, you can specify that the objects are comparable, edible, and/or cloneable.

To distinguish an interface from a class, Java uses the following syntax to define an interface:

```
modifier interface InterfaceName {
  /** Constant declarations */
  /** Abstract method signatures */
}
```

Here is an example of an interface:

```
public interface Edible {
  /** Describe how to eat */
  public abstract String howToEat();
}
```

An interface is treated like a special class in Java. Each interface is compiled into a separate bytecode file, just like a regular class. You can use an interface more or less the same way you use an abstract class. For example, you can use an interface as a data type for a reference variable, as the result of casting, and so on. As with an abstract class, you cannot create an instance from an interface using the **new** operator.

You can use the **Edible** interface to specify whether an object is edible. This is accomplished by letting the class for the object implement this interface using the **implements** keyword. For example, the classes **Chicken** and **Fruit** in Listing 15.7 (lines 20, 39) implement the **Edible** interface. The relationship between the class and the interface is known as *interface inheritance*. Since interface inheritance and class inheritance are essentially the same, we will simply refer to both as *inheritance*.

interface inheritance

LISTING 15.7 TestEdible.java

```
1  public class TestEdible {
2    public static void main(String[] args) {
3      Object[] objects = {new Tiger(), new Chicken(), new Apple()};
4      for (int i = 0; i < objects.length; i++) {
5        if (objects[i] instanceof Edible)
6          System.out.println(((Edible)objects[i]).howToEat());
7
8        if (objects[i] instanceof Animal) {
9          System.out.println(((Animal)objects[i]).sound());
10       }
```

```
11        }
12      }
13    }
14
15    abstract class Animal {                                    Animal class
16      /** Return animal sound */
17      public abstract String sound();
18    }
19
20    class Chicken extends Animal implements Edible {           implements Edible
21      @Override
22      public String howToEat() {                               howToEat()
23        return "Chicken: Fry it";
24      }
25
26      @Override
27      public String sound() {
28        return "Chicken: cock-a-doodle-doo";
29      }
30    }
31
32    class Tiger extends Animal {                                Tiger class
33      @Override
34      public String sound() {
35        return "Tiger: RROOAARR";
36      }
37    }
38
39    abstract class Fruit implements Edible {                   implements Edible
40      // Data fields, constructors, and methods omitted here
41    }
42
43    class Apple extends Fruit {                                Apple class
44      @Override
45      public String howToEat() {
46        return "Apple: Make apple cider";
47      }
48    }
49
50    class Orange extends Fruit {                               Orange class
51      @Override
52      public String howToEat() {
53        return "Orange: Make orange juice";
54      }
55    }
```

```
Tiger: RROOAARR
Chicken: Fry it
Chicken: cock-a-doodle-doo
Apple: Make apple cider
```

This example uses several classes and interfaces. Their inheritance relationship is shown in Figure 15.4.

The `Animal` class defines the **sound** method (line 17). It is an abstract method and will be implemented by a concrete animal class.

The `Chicken` class implements `Edible` to specify that chickens are edible. When a class implements an interface, it implements all the methods defined in the interface with the exact

FIGURE 15.4 `Edible` is a supertype for `Chicken` and `Fruit`. `Animal` is a supertype for `Chicken` and `Tiger`. `Fruit` is a supertype for `Orange` and `Apple`.

signature and return type. The `Chicken` class implements the `howToEat` method (lines 22–24). `Chicken` also extends `Animal` to implement the `sound` method (lines 27–29).

The `Fruit` class implements `Edible`. Since it does not implement the `howToEat` method, `Fruit` must be denoted as **abstract** (line 39). The concrete subclasses of `Fruit` must implement the `howToEat` method. The `Apple` and `Orange` classes implement the `howToEat` method (lines 45, 52).

The `main` method creates an array with three objects for `Tiger`, `Chicken`, and `Apple` (line 3), and invokes the `howToEat` method if the element is edible (line 6) and the `sound` method if the element is an animal (line 9).

common behavior

In essence, the `Edible` interface defines common behavior for edible objects. All edible objects have the `howToEat` method.

Note

omitting modifiers

Since all data fields are *public static final* and all methods are *public abstract* in an interface, Java allows these modifiers to be omitted. Therefore the following interface definitions are equivalent:

```
public interface T {
    public static final int K = 1;

    public abstract void p();
}
```
Equivalent
```
public interface T {
    int K = 1;

    void p();
}
```

Tip

accessing constants

A constant defined in an interface can be accessed using the syntax `InterfaceName.CONSTANT_NAME` (e.g., `T.K`). It is a good practice to define common constants that are shared by many classes in an interface. For example, the constants `LEFT`, `CENTER`, `RIGHT`, `LEADING`, `TRAILING`, `TOP`, and `BOTTOM` used in `AbstractButton` are also used in many other Swing components. These constants are centrally defined in the `javax.swing.SwingConstants` interface. All Swing GUI components implement `SwingConstants`. You can reference the constants through `SwingConstants` or a GUI component. For example, `SwingConstants.CENTER` is the same as `JButton.CENTER`.

SwingConstants

15.13 Suppose `A` is an interface. Can you create an instance using `new A()`?

15.14 Suppose A is an interface. Can you declare a reference variable x with type A like this?

```
A x;
```

15.15 Which of the following is a correct interface?

```
interface A {
  void print() { };
}
```
(a)

```
abstract interface A extends I1, I2 {
  abstract void print() { };
}
```
(b)

```
abstract interface A {
  print();
}
```
(c)

```
interface A {
  void print();
}
```
(d)

15.16 Explain why `SwingConstants.LEFT`, `AbstractButton.LEFT`, `JButton.LEFT`, `JCheckBox.LEFT`, `JRadioButton.LEFT`, and `JLabel.LEFT` all have the same value.

15.6 The **Comparable** Interface

The `Comparable` *interface defines the* `compareTo` *method for comparing objects.*

Key Point

Suppose you want to design a generic method to find the larger of two objects of the same type, such as two students, two dates, two circles, two rectangles, or two squares. In order to accomplish this, the two objects must be comparable, so the common behavior for the objects must be comparable. Java provides the `Comparable` interface for this purpose. The interface is defined as follows:

```
// Interface for comparing objects, defined in java.lang
package java.lang;

public interface Comparable<E> {
  public int compareTo(E o);
}
```

`java.lang.Comparable`

The `compareTo` method determines the order of this object with the specified object `o` and returns a negative integer, zero, or a positive integer if this object is less than, equal to, or greater than `o`.

The `Comparable` interface is a generic interface. The generic type `E` is replaced by a concrete type when implementing this interface. Many classes in the Java library implement `Comparable` to define a natural order for objects. The classes `Byte`, `Short`, `Integer`, `Long`, `Float`, `Double`, `Character`, `BigInteger`, `BigDecimal`, `Calendar`, `String`, and `Date` all implement the `Comparable` interface. For example, the `Integer`, `BigInteger`, `String`, and `Date` classes are defined as follows in the Java API:

```
public class Integer extends Number
    implements Comparable<Integer> {
  // class body omitted

  @Override
  public int compareTo(Integer o) {
    // Implementation omitted
  }
}
```

```
public class BigInteger extends Number
    implements Comparable<BigInteger> {
  // class body omitted

  @Override
  public int compareTo(BigInteger o) {
    // Implementation omitted
  }
}
```

```
public class String extends Object
    implements Comparable<String> {
  // class body omitted

  @Override
  public int compareTo(String o) {
    // Implementation omitted
  }
}
```

```
public class Date extends Object
    implements Comparable<Date> {
  // class body omitted

  @Override
  public int compareTo(Date o) {
    // Implementation omitted
  }
}
```

Thus, numbers are comparable, strings are comparable, and so are dates. You can use the **compareTo** method to compare two numbers, two strings, and two dates. For example, the following code

```
1  System.out.println(new Integer(3).compareTo(new Integer(5)));
2  System.out.println("ABC".compareTo("ABE"));
3  java.util.Date date1 = new java.util.Date(2013, 1, 1);
4  java.util.Date date2 = new java.util.Date(2012, 1, 1);
5  System.out.println(date1.compareTo(date2));
```

displays

```
-1
-2
 1
```

Line 1 displays a negative value since **3** is less than **5**. Line 2 displays a negative value since **ABC** is less than **ABE**. Line 5 displays a positive value since **date1** is greater than **date2**.

Let **n** be an **Integer** object, **s** be a **String** object, and **d** be a **Date** object. All the following expressions are **true**.

```
n instanceof Integer
n instanceof Object
n instanceof Comparable
```

```
s instanceof String
s instanceof Object
s instanceof Comparable
```

```
d instanceof java.util.Date
d instanceof Object
d instanceof Comparable
```

Since all **Comparable** objects have the **compareTo** method, the **java.util.Arrays.sort(Object[])** method in the Java API uses the **compareTo** method to compare and sorts the objects in an array, provided that the objects are instances of the **Comparable** interface. Listing 15.8 gives an example of sorting an array of strings and an array of **BigInteger** objects.

LISTING 15.8 SortComparableObjects.java

```
1  import java.math.*;
2
3  public class SortComparableObjects {
4    public static void main(String[] args) {
5      String[] cities = {"Savannah", "Boston", "Atlanta", "Tampa"};
6      java.util.Arrays.sort(cities);
7      for (String city: cities)
8        System.out.print(city + " ");
9      System.out.println();
10
11     BigInteger[] hugeNumbers = {new BigInteger("2323231092923992"),
```

create an array
sort the array

create an array

```
12        new BigInteger("432232323239292"),
13        new BigInteger("54623239292")};
14     java.util.Arrays.sort(hugeNumbers);                          sort the array
15     for (BigInteger number: hugeNumbers)
16        System.out.print(number + " ");
17   }
18 }
```

```
Atlanta Boston Savannah Tampa
54623239292 432232323239292 2323231092923992
```

The program creates an array of strings (line 5) and invokes the **sort** method to sort the strings (line 6). The program creates an array of **BigInteger** objects (lines 11–13) and invokes the **sort** method to sort the **BigInteger** objects (line 14).

You cannot use the **sort** method to sort an array of **Rectangle** objects, because **Rectangle** does not implement **Comparable**. However, you can define a new rectangle class that implements **Comparable**. The instances of this new class are comparable. Let this new class be named **ComparableRectangle**, as shown in Listing 15.9.

LISTING 15.9 ComparableRectangle.java

```
1  public class ComparableRectangle extends Rectangle
2       implements Comparable<ComparableRectangle> {                implements Comparable
3     /** Construct a ComparableRectangle with specified properties */
4     public ComparableRectangle(double width, double height) {
5        super(width, height);
6     }
7
8     @Override // Implement the compareTo method defined in Comparable
9     public int compareTo(ComparableRectangle o) {                  implement compareTo
10       if (getArea() > o.getArea())
11          return 1;
12       else if (getArea() < o.getArea())
13          return -1;
14       else
15          return 0;
16    }
17
18    @Override // Implement the toString method in GeometricObject
19    public String toString() {                                     implement toString
20       return super.toString() + " Area: " + getArea();
21    }
22 }
```

ComparableRectangle extends **Rectangle** and implements **Comparable**, as shown in Figure 15.5. The keyword **implements** indicates that **ComparableRectangle** inherits all the constants from the **Comparable** interface and implements the methods in the interface. The **compareTo** method compares the areas of two rectangles. An instance of **ComparableRectangle** is also an instance of **Rectangle**, **GeometricObject**, **Object**, and **Comparable**.

You can now use the **sort** method to sort an array of **ComparableRectangle** objects, as in Listing 15.10.

Notation:
The interface name and the
method names are italicized.
The dashed lines and hollow
triangles are used to point to
the interface.

FIGURE 15.5 `ComparableRectangle` extends `Rectangle` and implements `Comparable`.

LISTING 15.10 SortRectangles.java

```
1  public class SortRectangles {
2    public static void main(String[] args) {
3      ComparableRectangle[] rectangles = {
4        new ComparableRectangle(3.4, 5.4),
5        new ComparableRectangle(13.24, 55.4),
6        new ComparableRectangle(7.4, 35.4),
7        new ComparableRectangle(1.4, 25.4)};
8      java.util.Arrays.sort(rectangles);
9      for (Rectangle rectangle: rectangles) {
10       System.out.print(rectangle + " ");
11       System.out.println();
12     }
13   }
14 }
```

create an array

sort the array

```
Width: 3.4 Height: 5.4 Area: 18.36
Width: 1.4 Height: 25.4 Area: 35.559999999999995
Width: 7.4 Height: 35.4 Area: 261.96
Width: 13.24 Height: 55.4 Area: 733.496
```

benefits of interface

An interface provides another form of generic programming. It would be difficult to use a generic `sort` method to sort the objects without using an interface in this example, because multiple inheritance would be necessary to inherit `Comparable` and another class, such as `Rectangle`, at the same time.

The `Object` class contains the `equals` method, which is intended for the subclasses of the `Object` class to override in order to compare whether the contents of the objects are the same. Suppose that the `Object` class contains the `compareTo` method, as defined in the `Comparable` interface; the `sort` method can be used to compare a list of *any* objects. Whether a `compareTo` method should be included in the `Object` class is debatable. Since the `compareTo` method is not defined in the `Object` class, the `Comparable` interface is defined in Java to enable objects to be compared if they are instances of the `Comparable` interface. It is strongly recommended (though not required) that `compareTo` should be consistent with `equals`. That is, for two objects `o1` and `o2`, `o1.compareTo(o2) == 0` if and only if `o1.equals(o2)` is `true`.

MyProgrammingLab

15.17 True or false? If a class implements `Comparable`, the object of the class can invoke the `compareTo` method.

15.18 Which of the following is the correct method header for the `compareTo` method in
the `String` class?

```
public int compareTo(String o)
public int compareTo(Object o)
```

15.19 Can the following code be compiled? Why?

```
Integer n1 = new Integer(3);
Object n2 = new Integer(4);
System.out.println(n1.compareTo(n2));
```

15.20 You can define the `compareTo` method in a class without implementing the
`Comparable` interface. What are the benefits of implementing the `Comparable`
interface?

15.21 True or false? If a class implements `Comparable`, the object of the class can invoke
the `compareTo` method.

15.7 The **Cloneable** Interface

The `Cloneable` *interface defines the* `compareTo` *method for comparing objects.*

 **Key
Point**

Often it is desirable to create a copy of an object. To do this, you need to use the `clone`
method and understand the `Cloneable` interface.

An interface contains constants and abstract methods, but the `Cloneable` interface is a
special case. The `Cloneable` interface in the `java.lang` package is defined as follows:

```
package java.lang;

public interface Cloneable {
}
```

java.lang.Cloneable

This interface is empty. An interface with an empty body is referred to as a *marker interface.*
A marker interface does not contain constants or methods. It is used to denote that a class possesses certain desirable properties. A class that implements the `Cloneable` interface is
marked cloneable, and its objects can be cloned using the `clone()` method defined in the
`Object` class.

marker interface

Many classes in the Java library (e.g., `Date`, `Calendar`, and `ArrayList`) implement
`Cloneable`. Thus, the instances of these classes can be cloned. For example, the following code

```
1  Calendar calendar = new GregorianCalendar(2013, 2, 1);
2  Calendar calendar1 = calendar;
3  Calendar calendar2 = (Calendar)calendar.clone();
4  System.out.println("calendar == calendar1 is " +
5    (calendar == calendar1));
6  System.out.println("calendar == calendar2 is " +
7    (calendar == calendar2));
8  System.out.println("calendar.equals(calendar2) is " +
9    calendar.equals(calendar2));
```

displays

```
calendar == calendar1 is true
calendar == calendar2 is false
calendar.equals(calendar2) is true
```

In the preceding code, line 2 copies the reference of `calendar` to `calendar1`, so `calendar`
and `calendar1` point to the same `Calendar` object. Line 3 creates a new object that is the

clone of **calendar** and assigns the new object's reference to **calendar2**. **calendar2** and **calendar** are different objects with the same contents.

The following code

```
1  ArrayList<Double> list1 = new ArrayList<Double>();
2  list1.add(1.5);
3  list1.add(2.5);
4  list1.add(3.5);
5  ArrayList<Double> list2 = (ArrayList<Double>)list1.clone();
6  ArrayList<Double> list3 = list1;
7  list2.add(4.5);
8  list3.remove(1.5);
9  System.out.println("list1 is " + list1);
10 System.out.println("list2 is " + list2);
11 System.out.println("list3 is " + list3);
```

displays

```
list1 is [2.5, 3.5]
list2 is [1.5, 2.5, 3.5, 4.5]
list3 is [2.5, 3.5]
```

In the preceding code, line 5 creates a new object that is the clone of **list1** and assigns the new object's reference to **list2**. **list2** and **list1** are different objects with the same contents. Line 6 copies the reference of **list1** to **list3**, so **list1** and **list3** point to the same **ArrayList** object. Line 7 adds **4.5** into **list2**. Line 8 removes **1.5** from **list3**. Since **list1** and **list3** point to the same **ArrayList**, line 9 and 11 display the same content.

clone arrays

You can clone an array using the **clone** method. For example, the following code

```
1  int[] list1 = {1, 2};
2  int[] list2 = list1.clone();
3  list1[0] = 7;
4  list2[1] = 8;
5  System.out.println("list1 is " + list1[0] + ", " + list1[1]);
6  System.out.println("list2 is " + list2[0] + ", " + list2[1]);
```

displays

```
list1 is 7, 2
list2 is 1, 8
```

how to implement Cloneable

To define a custom class that implements the **Cloneable** interface, the class must override the **clone()** method in the **Object** class. Listing 15.11 defines a class named **House** that implements **Cloneable** and **Comparable**.

LISTING 15.11   House.java

```
1  public class House implements Cloneable, Comparable<House> {
2    private int id;
3    private double area;
4    private java.util.Date whenBuilt;
5
6    public House(int id, double area) {
7      this.id = id;
8      this.area = area;
9      whenBuilt = new java.util.Date();
10   }
11
12   public int getId() {
```

```
13        return id;
14      }
15
16      public double getArea() {
17        return area;
18      }
19
20      public java.util.Date getWhenBuilt() {
21        return whenBuilt;
22      }
23
24      @Override /** Override the protected clone method defined in
25         the Object class, and strengthen its accessibility */
26      public Object clone() throws CloneNotSupportedException {
27        return super.clone();
28      }
29
30      @Override // Implement the compareTo method defined in Comparable
31      public int compareTo(House o) {
32        if (area > o.area)
33          return 1;
34        else if (area < o.area)
35          return -1;
36        else
37          return 0;
38      }
39   }
```

This exception is thrown if House does not implement Cloneable

The **House** class implements the **clone** method (lines 26–28) defined in the **Object** class. The header is:

protected native Object clone() **throws** CloneNotSupportedException;

The keyword **native** indicates that this method is not written in Java but is implemented in the JVM for the native platform. The keyword **protected** restricts the method to be accessed in the same package or in a subclass. For this reason, the **House** class must override the method and change the visibility modifier to **public** so that the method can be used in any package. Since the **clone** method implemented for the native platform in the **Object** class performs the task of cloning objects, the **clone** method in the **House** class simply invokes **super.clone()**. The **clone** method defined in the **Object** class may throw **CloneNotSupportedException**.

CloneNotSupportedException

The **House** class implements the **compareTo** method (lines 31–38) defined in the **Comparable** interface. The method compares the areas of two houses.

You can now create an object of the **House** class and create an identical copy from it, as follows:

```
House house1 = new House(1, 1750.50);
House house2 = (House)house1.clone();
```

house1 and **house2** are two different objects with identical contents. The **clone** method in the **Object** class copies each field from the original object to the target object. If the field is of a primitive type, its value is copied. For example, the value of **area** (**double** type) is copied from **house1** to **house2**. If the field is of an object, the reference of the field is copied. For example, the field **whenBuilt** is of the **Date** class, so its reference is copied into **house2**, as shown in Figure 15.6. Therefore, **house1.whenBuilt == house2.when-Built** is true, although **house1 == house2** is false. This is referred to as a *shallow copy* rather than a *deep copy*, meaning that if the field is of an object type, the object's reference is copied rather than its contents.

shallow copy
deep copy

FIGURE 15.6 The default `clone` method performs a shallow copy.

deep copy

To perform a deep copy for a **House** object, replace the **clone()** method in lines 26–27 with the following code:

```
public Object clone() throws CloneNotSupportedException {
    // Perform a shallow copy
    House houseClone = (House)super.clone();
    // Deep copy on whenBuilt
    houseClone.whenBuilt = (java.util.Date)(whenBuilt.clone());
    return houseClone;
}
```

or

```
public Object clone() {
    try {
        // Perform a shallow copy
        House houseClone = (House)super.clone();
        // Deep copy on whenBuilt
        houseClone.whenBuilt = (java.util.Date)(whenBuilt.clone());
        return houseClone;
    }
    catch (CloneNotSupportedException ex) {
        return null;
    }
}
```

Now if you clone a **House** object in the following code:

```
House house1 = new House(1, 1750.50);
House house2 = (House)house1.clone();
```

`house1.whenBuilt == house2.whenBuilt` will be **false**. **house1** and **house2** reference two different **Date** objects.

15.22 Can you invoke the **clone()** method to clone an object if the class for the object does not implement the **java.lang.Cloneable**? Does the **Date** class implement **Cloneable**?

15.23 What would happen if the **House** class (defined in Listing 15.9) did not override the **clone()** method or if **House** did not implement **java.lang.Cloneable**?

15.24 Show the printout of the following code:

```java
java.util.Date date = new java.util.Date();
java.util.Date date1 = date;
java.util.Date date2 = (java.util.Date)(date.clone());
System.out.println(date == date1);
System.out.println(date == date2);
System.out.println(date.equals(date2));
```

15.25 Show the printout of the following code:

```java
ArrayList<String> list = new ArrayList<String>();
list.add("New York");
ArrayList<String> list1 = list;
ArrayList<String> list2 = (ArrayList<String>)(list.clone());
list.add("Atlanta");
System.out.println(list == list1);
System.out.println(list == list2);
System.out.println("list is " + list);
System.out.println("list1 is " + list1);
System.out.println("list2.get(0) is " + list2.get(0));
System.out.println("list2.size() is " + list2.size());
```

15.26 What is wrong in the following code?

```java
public class Test {
  public static void main(String[] args) {
    GeometricObject x = new Circle(3);
    GeometricObject y = x.clone();
    System.out.println(x == y);
  }
}
```

15.8 Interfaces vs. Abstract Classes

A class can implement multiple interfaces, but it can only extend one superclass.

Key Point

An interface can be used more or less the same way as an abstract class, but defining an interface is different from defining an abstract class. Table 15.2 summarizes the differences.

TABLE 15.2 Interfaces vs. Abstract Classes

	Variables	Constructors	Methods
Abstract class	No restrictions.	Constructors are invoked by subclasses through constructor chaining. An abstract class cannot be instantiated using the new operator.	No restrictions.
Interface	All variables must be `public static final`.	No constructors. An interface cannot be instantiated using the new operator.	All methods must be public abstract instance methods

Java allows only *single inheritance* for class extension but allows *multiple extensions* for interfaces. For example,

single inheritance

multiple inheritance

```java
public class NewClass extends BaseClass
    implements Interface1, . . ., InterfaceN {
  . . .
}
```

subinterface

An interface can inherit other interfaces using the **extends** keyword. Such an interface is called a *subinterface*. For example, `NewInterface` in the following code is a subinterface of `Interface1, . . .`, and `InterfaceN`.

```
public interface NewInterface extends Interface1, . . . , InterfaceN {
    // constants and abstract methods
}
```

A class implementing `NewInterface` must implement the abstract methods defined in `NewInterface`, `Interface1, . . .`, and `InterfaceN`. An interface can extend other interfaces but not classes. A class can extend its superclass and implement multiple interfaces.

All classes share a single root, the `Object` class, but there is no single root for interfaces. Like a class, an interface also defines a type. A variable of an interface type can reference any instance of the class that implements the interface. If a class implements an interface, the interface is like a superclass for the class. You can use an interface as a data type and cast a variable of an interface type to its subclass, and vice versa. For example, suppose that `c` is an instance of `Class2` in Figure 15.7. `c` is also an instance of `Object`, `Class1`, `Interface1`, `Interface1_1`, `Interface1_2`, `Interface2_1`, and `Interface2_2`.

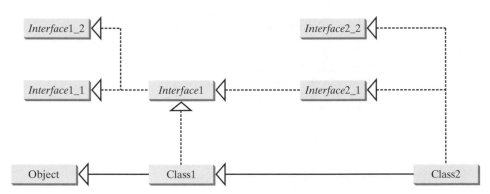

FIGURE 15.7 `Class1` implements `Interface1`; `Interface1` extends `Interface1_1` and `Interface1_2`. `Class2` extends `Class1` and implements `Interface2_1` and `Interface2_2`.

naming convention

Note
Class names are nouns. Interface names may be adjectives or nouns.

Design Guide
Abstract classes and interfaces can both be used to specify common behavior of objects. How do you decide whether to use an interface or a class? In general, a *strong is-a relationship* that clearly describes a parent-child relationship should be modeled using classes. For example, Gregorian calendar is a calendar, so the relationship between the class `java.util.GregorianCalendar` and `java.util.Calendar` is modeled

is-a relationship
is-kind-of relationship

using class inheritance. A *weak is-a relationship*, also known as an *is-kind-of relationship*, indicates that an object possesses a certain property. A weak is-a relationship can be modeled using interfaces. For example, all strings are comparable, so the `String` class implements the `Comparable` interface.

interface preferred

In general, interfaces are preferred over abstract classes because an interface can define a common supertype for unrelated classes. Interfaces are more flexible than classes. Consider the `Animal` class. Suppose the `howToEat` method is defined in the `Animal` class, as follows:

```
abstract class Animal {
  public abstract String howToEat();
}
```
Animal class

Two subclasses of `Animal` are defined as follows:

```
class Chicken extends Animal {
  @Override
  public String howToEat() {
    return "Fry it";
  }
}
```
Chicken class

```
class Duck extends Animal {
  @Override
  public String howToEat() {
    return "Roast it";
  }
}
```
Duck class

Given this inheritance hierarchy, polymorphism enables you to hold a reference to a `Chicken` object or a `Duck` object in a variable of type `Animal`, as in the following code:

```
public static void main(String[] args) {
  Animal animal = new Chicken();
  eat(animal);

  animal = new Duck();
  eat(animal);
}

public static void eat(Animal animal) {
  animal.howToEat();
}
```

The JVM dynamically decides which `howToEat` method to invoke based on the actual object that invokes the method.

You can define a subclass of `Animal`. However, there is a restriction: The subclass must be for another animal (e.g., `Turkey`).

Interfaces don't have this restriction. Interfaces give you more flexibility than classes, because you don't have to make everything fit into one type of class. You may define the `howToEat()` method in an interface and let it serve as a common supertype for other classes. For example,

```
public static void main(String[] args) {
  Edible stuff = new Chicken();
  eat(stuff);

  stuff = new Duck();
  eat(stuff);

  stuff = new Broccoli();
  eat(stuff);
}
```

```
                        public static void eat(Edible stuff) {
                          stuff.howToEat();
                        }

Edible interface        interface Edible {
                          public String howToEat();
                        }

Chicken class           class Chicken implements Edible {
                          @Override
                          public String howToEat() {
                            return "Fry it";
                          }
                        }

Duck class              class Duck implements Edible {
                          @Override
                          public String howToEat() {
                            return "Roast it";
                          }
                        }

Broccoli class          class Broccoli implements Edible {
                          @Override
                          public String howToEat() {
                            return "Stir-fry it";
                          }
                        }
```

To define a class that represents edible objects, simply let the class implement the `Edible` interface. The class is now a subtype of the `Edible` type, and any `Edible` object can be passed to invoke the `eat` method.

MyProgrammingLab™

15.27 Give an example to show why interfaces are preferred over abstract classes.

15.28 Define the terms abstract classes and interfaces. What are the similarities and differences between abstract classes and interfaces?

15.28 True or false?

 a. An interface is compiled into a separate bytecode file.

 b. An interface can have static methods.

 c. An interface can extend one or more interfaces.

 d. An interface can extend an abstract class.

 e. An abstract class can extend an interface.

15.9 Case Study: The `Rational` Class

This section shows how to design the `Rational` class for representing and processing rational numbers.

A rational number has a numerator and a denominator in the form `a/b`, where `a` is the numerator and `b` the denominator. For example, `1/3`, `3/4`, and `10/4` are rational numbers.

A rational number cannot have a denominator of `0`, but a numerator of `0` is fine. Every integer `i` is equivalent to a rational number `i/1`. Rational numbers are used in exact computations involving fractions—for example, `1/3 = 0.33333. . . .` This number cannot be precisely represented in floating-point format using either the data type **double** or **float**. To obtain the exact result, we must use rational numbers.

Java provides data types for integers and floating-point numbers, but not for rational numbers. This section shows how to design a class to represent rational numbers.

Since rational numbers share many common features with integers and floating-point numbers, and Number is the root class for numeric wrapper classes, it is appropriate to define Rational as a subclass of Number. Since rational numbers are comparable, the Rational class should also implement the Comparable interface. Figure 15.8 illustrates the Rational class and its relationship to the Number class and the Comparable interface.

Rational	
-numerator: long	The numerator of this rational number.
-denominator: long	The denominator of this rational number.
+Rational()	Creates a rational number with numerator 0 and denominator 1.
+Rational(numerator: long, denominator: long)	Creates a rational number with a specified numerator and denominator.
+getNumerator(): long	Returns the numerator of this rational number.
+getDenominator(): long	Returns the denominator of this rational number.
+add(secondRational: Rational): Rational	Returns the addition of this rational number with another.
+subtract(secondRational: Rational): Rational	Returns the subtraction of this rational number with another.
+multiply(secondRational: Rational): Rational	Returns the multiplication of this rational number with another.
+divide(secondRational: Rational): Rational	Returns the division of this rational number with another.
+toString(): String	Returns a string in the form "numerator/denominator." Returns the numerator if denominator is 1.
-gcd(n: long, d: long): long	Returns the greatest common divisor of n and d.

FIGURE 15.8 The properties, constructors, and methods of the Rational class are illustrated in UML.

A rational number consists of a numerator and a denominator. There are many equivalent rational numbers—for example, 1/3 = 2/6 = 3/9 = 4/12. The numerator and the denominator of 1/3 have no common divisor except 1, so 1/3 is said to be in *lowest terms*.

To reduce a rational number to its lowest terms, you need to find the greatest common divisor (GCD) of the absolute values of its numerator and denominator, then divide both the numerator and denominator by this value. You can use the method for computing the GCD of two integers n and d, as suggested in Listing 4.9, GreatestCommonDivisor.java. The numerator and denominator in a Rational object are reduced to their lowest terms.

As usual, let us first write a test program to create two Rational objects and test its methods. Listing 15.12 is a test program.

LISTING 15.12 TestRationalClass.java

```java
public class TestRationalClass {
  /** Main method */
  public static void main(String[] args) {
    // Create and initialize two rational numbers r1 and r2
```

create a Rational
create a Rational

add

```
5      Rational r1 = new Rational(4, 2);
6      Rational r2 = new Rational(2, 3);
7
8      // Display results
9      System.out.println(r1 + " + " + r2 + " = " + r1.add(r2));
10     System.out.println(r1 + " - " + r2 + " = " + r1.subtract(r2));
11     System.out.println(r1 + " * " + r2 + " = " + r1.multiply(r2));
12     System.out.println(r1 + " / " + r2 + " = " + r1.divide(r2));
13     System.out.println(r2 + " is " + r2.doubleValue());
14   }
15 }
```

```
2 + 2/3 = 8/3
2 - 2/3 = 4/3
2 * 2/3 = 4/3
2 / 2/3 = 3
2/3 is 0.6666666666666666
```

The `main` method creates two rational numbers, `r1` and `r2` (lines 5–6), and displays the results of `r1 + r2`, `r1 - r2`, `r1 x r2`, and `r1 / r2` (lines 9–12). To perform `r1 + r2`, invoke `r1.add(r2)` to return a new `Rational` object. Similarly, invoke `r1.subtract(r2)` for `r1 - r2`, `r1.multiply(r2)` for `r1 x r2`, and `r1.divide(r2)` for `r1 / r2`.

The `doubleValue()` method displays the double value of `r2` (line 13). The `double-Value()` method is defined in `java.lang.Number` and overridden in `Rational`.

Note that when a string is concatenated with an object using the plus sign (+), the object's string representation from the `toString()` method is used to concatenate with the string. So `r1 + " + " + r2 + " = " + r1.add(r2)` is equivalent to `r1.toString() + " + " + r2.toString() + " = " + r1.add(r2).toString()`.

The `Rational` class is implemented in Listing 15.13.

LISTING 15.13   Rational.java

```java
1  public class Rational extends Number implements Comparable<Rational> {
2    // Data fields for numerator and denominator
3    private long numerator = 0;
4    private long denominator = 1;
5
6    /** Construct a rational with default properties */
7    public Rational() {
8      this(0, 1);
9    }
10
11   /** Construct a rational with specified numerator and denominator */
12   public Rational(long numerator, long denominator) {
13     long gcd = gcd(numerator, denominator);
14     this.numerator = ((denominator > 0) ? 1 : -1) * numerator / gcd;
15     this.denominator = Math.abs(denominator) / gcd;
16   }
17
18   /** Find GCD of two numbers */
19   private static long gcd(long n, long d) {
20     long n1 = Math.abs(n);
21     long n2 = Math.abs(d);
22     int gcd = 1;
```

```
23
24        for (int k = 1; k <= n1 && k <= n2; k++) {
25          if (n1 % k == 0 && n2 % k == 0)
26            gcd = k;
27        }
28
29        return gcd;
30      }
31
32      /** Return numerator */
33      public long getNumerator() {
34        return numerator;
35      }
36
37      /** Return denominator */
38      public long getDenominator() {
39        return denominator;
40      }
41
42      /** Add a rational number to this rational */
43      public Rational add(Rational secondRational) {
44        long n = numerator * secondRational.getDenominator() +
45          denominator * secondRational.getNumerator();
46        long d = denominator * secondRational.getDenominator();
47        return new Rational(n, d);
48      }
49
50      /** Subtract a rational number from this rational */
51      public Rational subtract(Rational secondRational) {
52        long n = numerator * secondRational.getDenominator()
53          - denominator * secondRational.getNumerator();
54        long d = denominator * secondRational.getDenominator();
55        return new Rational(n, d);
56      }
57
58      /** Multiply a rational number by this rational */
59      public Rational multiply(Rational secondRational) {
60        long n = numerator * secondRational.getNumerator();
61        long d = denominator * secondRational.getDenominator();
62        return new Rational(n, d);
63      }
64
65      /** Divide a rational number by this rational */
66      public Rational divide(Rational secondRational) {
67        long n = numerator * secondRational.getDenominator();
68        long d = denominator * secondRational.numerator;
69        return new Rational(n, d);
70      }
71
72      @Override
73      public String toString() {
74        if (denominator == 1)
75          return numerator + "";
76        else
77          return numerator + "/" + denominator;
78      }
79
80      @Override // Override the equals method in the Object class
81      public boolean equals(Object other) {
82        if ((this.subtract((Rational)(other))).getNumerator() == 0)
```

$\frac{a}{b} + \frac{c}{d} = \frac{ad + bc}{bd}$

$\frac{a}{b} - \frac{c}{d} = \frac{ad - bc}{bd}$

$\frac{a}{b} \times \frac{c}{d} = \frac{ac}{bd}$

$\frac{a}{b} \div \frac{c}{d} = \frac{ad}{bc}$

```
83            return true;
84         else
85            return false;
86      }
87
88      @Override // Implement the abstract intValue method in Number
89      public int intValue() {
90         return (int)doubleValue();
91      }
92
93      @Override // Implement the abstract floatValue method in Number
94      public float floatValue() {
95         return (float)doubleValue();
96      }
97
98      @Override // Implement the doubleValue method in Number
99      public double doubleValue() {
100        return numerator * 1.0 / denominator;
101     }
102
103     @Override // Implement the abstract longValue method in Number
104     public long longValue() {
105        return (long)doubleValue();
106     }
107
108     @Override // Implement the compareTo method in Comparable
109     public int compareTo(Rational o) {
110        if (this.subtract(o).getNumerator() > 0)
111           return 1;
112        else if (this.subtract(o).getNumerator() < 0)
113           return -1;
114        else
115           return 0;
116     }
117  }
```

The rational number is encapsulated in a `Rational` object. Internally, a rational number is represented in its lowest terms (line 13), and the numerator determines its sign (line 14). The denominator is always positive (line 15).

The `gcd` method (lines 19–30 in the `Rational` class) is private; it is not intended for use by clients. The `gcd` method is only for internal use by the `Rational` class. The `gcd` method is also static, since it is not dependent on any particular `Rational` object.

The `abs(x)` method (lines 20–21 in the `Rational` class) is defined in the `Math` class and returns the absolute value of x.

Two `Rational` objects can interact with each other to perform add, subtract, multiply, and divide operations. These methods return a new `Rational` object (lines 43–70).

The methods `toString` and `equals` in the `Object` class are overridden in the `Rational` class (lines 72–86). The `toString()` method returns a string representation of a `Rational` object in the form **numerator/denominator**, or simply **numerator** if **denominator** is 1. The `equals(Object other)` method returns true if this rational number is equal to the other rational number.

The abstract methods `intValue`, `longValue`, `floatValue`, and `doubleValue` in the `Number` class are implemented in the `Rational` class (lines 88–106). These methods return the `int`, `long`, `float`, and `double` value for this rational number.

The `compareTo(Rational other)` method in the `Comparable` interface is implemented in the `Rational` class (lines 108–116) to compare this rational number to the other rational number.

Tip

The **get** methods for the properties **numerator** and **denominator** are provided in the **Rational** class, but the **set** methods are not provided, so, once a **Rational** object is created, its contents cannot be changed. The **Rational** class is immutable. The **String** class and the wrapper classes for primitive type values are also immutable.

immutable

Tip

The numerator and denominator are represented using two variables. It is possible to use an array of two integers to represent the numerator and denominator (see Programming Exercise 15.16). The signatures of the public methods in the **Rational** class are not changed, although the internal representation of a rational number is changed. This is a good example to illustrate the idea that the data fields of a class should be kept private so as to encapsulate the implementation of the class from the use of the class.

encapsulation

The **Rational** class has serious limitations and can easily overflow. For example, the following code will display an incorrect result, because the denominator is too large.

overflow

```java
public class Test {
  public static void main(String[] args) {
    Rational r1 = new Rational(1, 123456789);
    Rational r2 = new Rational(1, 123456789);
    Rational r3 = new Rational(1, 123456789);
    System.out.println("r1 * r2 * r3 is " +
      r1.multiply(r2.multiply(r3)));
  }
}
```

```
r1 * r2 * r3 is -1/2204193661661244627
```

To fix it, you can implement the **Rational** class using the **BigInteger** for numerator and denominator (see Programming Exercise 15.21).

15.30 Show the printout of the following code?

```java
Rational r1 = new Rational(-2, 6);
System.out.println(r1.getNumerator());
System.out.println(r1.getDenominator());
System.out.println(r1.intValue());
System.out.println(r1.doubleValue());
```

15.31 Why is the following code wrong?

```java
Rational r1 = new Rational(-2, 6);
Object r2 = new Rational(1, 45);
System.out.println(r2.compareTo(r1));
```

15.32 Why is the following code wrong?

```java
Object r1 = new Rational(-2, 6);
Rational r2 = new Rational(1, 45);
System.out.println(r2.compareTo(r1));
```

Check Point

MyProgrammingLab™

KEY TERMS

abstract class 560	marker interface 577
abstract method 560	shallow copy 579
deep copy 579	subinterface 582
interface 560	

CHAPTER SUMMARY

1. *Abstract classes* are like regular classes with data and methods, but you cannot create instances of abstract classes using the **new** operator.

2. An *abstract method* cannot be contained in a nonabstract class. If a subclass of an abstract superclass does not implement all the inherited abstract methods of the superclass, the subclass must be defined as abstract.

3. A class that contains abstract methods must be abstract. However, it is possible to define an abstract class that doesn't contain any abstract methods.

4. A subclass can be abstract even if its superclass is concrete.

5. An *interface* is a class-like construct that contains only constants and abstract methods. In many ways, an interface is similar to an abstract class, but an abstract class can contain constants and abstract methods as well as variables and concrete methods.

6. An interface is treated like a special class in Java. Each interface is compiled into a separate bytecode file, just like a regular class.

7. The `java.lang.Comparable` interface defines the `compareTo` method. Many classes in the Java library implement `Comparable`.

8. The `java.lang.Cloneable` interface is a *marker interface*. An object of the class that implements the `Cloneable` interface is cloneable.

9. A class can extend only one superclass but can implement one or more interfaces.

10. An interface can extend one or more interfaces.

TEST QUESTIONS

Do the test questions for this chapter online at www.cs.armstrong.edu/liang/intro9e/test.html.

MyProgrammingLab™

PROGRAMMING EXERCISES

Sections 15.2–15.3

**15.1 (*Plot functions using abstract methods*) Write an abstract class that draws the diagram for a function. The class is defined as follows:

```
public abstract class AbstractDrawFunction extends JPanel {
  /** Polygon to hold the points */
  private Polygon p = new Polygon();
```

```
  protected AbstractDrawFunction () {
    drawFunction();
  }

  /** Return the y-coordinate */
  abstract double f(double x);

  /** Obtain points for x-coordinates 100, 101, . . ., 300 */
  public void drawFunction() {
    for (int x = -100; x <= 100; x++) {
      p.addPoint(x + 200, 200 - (int)f(x));
    }
  }

  @Override /** Draw axes, labels, and connect points */
  protected void paintComponent(Graphics g) {
    // To be completed by you
  }
}
```

Test the class with the following functions:

a. $f(x) = x^2$;
b. $f(x) = \sin(x)$;
c. $f(x) = \cos(x)$;
d. $f(x) = \tan(x)$;
e. $f(x) = \cos(x) + 5\sin(x)$;
f. $f(x) = 5\cos(x) + \sin(x)$;
g. $f(x) = \log(x) + x^2$;

For each function, create a class that extends the **AbstractDrawFunction** class and implements the **f** method. Figure 15.9 displays the drawings for the first three functions.

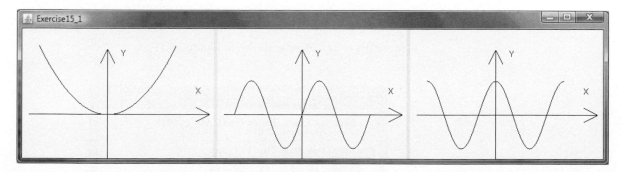

FIGURE 15.9   Exercise 15.1 draws the square, sine, and cosine functions.

15.2   (*Triangle class*) Design a new **Triangle class that extends the abstract **GeometricObject** class. Draw the UML diagram for the classes **Triangle** and **GeometricObject** and then implement the **Triangle** class. Write a test program that prompts the user to enter three sides of the triangle, a color, and a Boolean value to indicate whether the triangle is filled. The program should create a **Triangle** object with these sides and set the color and filled properties using the input. The program should display the area, perimeter, color, and true or false to indicate whether it is filled or not.

*15.3 (*Shuffle ArrayList*) Write the following method that shuffles an **ArrayList** of numbers:

```
public static void shuffle(ArrayList<Number> list)
```

*15.4 (*Sort ArrayList*) Write the following method that sorts an **ArrayList** of numbers.

```
public static void sort(ArrayList<Number> list)
```

15.5 (*Display a calendar*) Write a program that displays the calendar for the current month, as shown in Figure 15.10. Use labels, and set text on the labels to display the calendar. Use the **GregorianCalendar class to obtain the information for the month, year, first day of the month, and number of days in the month.

FIGURE 15.10 The program displays the calendar for the current month.

15.6 (*Display calendars*) Rewrite the **PrintCalendar class in Listing 5.12 to display a calendar for a specified month using the **Calendar** and **GregorianCalendar** classes. Your program receives the month and year from the command line. For example:

java Exercise15_06 1 2012

This displays the calendar shown in Figure 15.11.

FIGURE 15.11 The program displays a calendar for January 2012.

You also can run the program without the year. In this case, the year is the current year. If you run the program without specifying a month and a year, the month is the current month.

Sections 15.4–15.8

*15.7 (*Enable `GeometricObject` comparable*) Modify the `GeometricObject` class to implement the `Comparable` interface, and define a static `max` method in the `GeometricObject` class for finding the larger of two `GeometricObject` objects. Draw the UML diagram and implement the new `GeometricObject` class. Write a test program that uses the `max` method to find the larger of two circles and the larger of two rectangles.

*15.8 (*The `ComparableCircle` class*) Define a class named `ComparableCircle` that extends `Circle` and implements `Comparable`. Draw the UML diagram and implement the `compareTo` method to compare the circles on the basis of area. Write a test class to find the larger of two instances of `ComparableCircle` objects.

*15.9 (*The `Colorable` interface*) Design an interface named `Colorable` with a `void` method named `howToColor()`. Every class of a colorable object must implement the `Colorable` interface. Design a class named `Square` that extends `GeometricObject` and implements `Colorable`. Implement `howToColor` to display the message `Color all four sides`.

Draw a UML diagram that involves `Colorable`, `Square`, and `GeometricObject`. Write a test program that creates an array of five `GeometricObject`s. For each object in the array, invoke its `howToColor` method if it is colorable.

*15.10 (*Revise the `MyStack` class*) Rewrite the `MyStack` class in Listing 11.9 to perform a deep copy of the `list` field.

*15.11 (*Enable `Circle` comparable*) Rewrite the `Circle` class in Listing 15.2 to extend `GeometricObject` and implement the `Comparable` interface. Override the `equals` method in the `Object` class. Two `Circle` objects are equal if their radii are the same. Draw the UML diagram that involves `Circle`, `GeometricObject`, and `Comparable`.

*15.12 (*Enable `Rectangle` comparable*) Rewrite the `Rectangle` class in Listing 15.3 to extend `GeometricObject` and implement the `Comparable` interface. Override the `equals` method in the `Object` class. Two `Rectangle` objects are equal if their areas are the same. Draw the UML diagram that involves `Rectangle`, `GeometricObject`, and `Comparable`.

VideoNote

Redesign the `Rectangle` class

*15.13 (*The `Octagon` class*) Write a class named `Octagon` that extends `GeometricObject` and implements the `Comparable` and `Cloneable` interfaces. Assume that all eight sides of the octagon are of equal size. The area can be computed using the following formula:

$$area = (2 + 4/\sqrt{2}) * side * side$$

Draw the UML diagram that involves `Octagon`, `GeometricObject`, `Comparable`, and `Cloneable`. Write a test program that creates an `Octagon` object with side value `5` and displays its area and perimeter. Create a new object using the `clone` method and compare the two objects using the `compareTo` method.

*15.14 (*Sum the areas of geometric objects*) Write a method that sums the areas of all the geometric objects in an array. The method signature is:

public static double sumArea(GeometricObject[] a)

Write a test program that creates an array of four objects (two circles and two rectangles) and computes their total area using the `sumArea` method.

*15.15 (*Enable the Course class cloneable*) Rewrite the **Course** class in Listing 10.6 to add a **clone** method to perform a deep copy on the **students** field.

Section 15.9

*15.16 (*Demonstrate the benefits of encapsulation*) Rewrite the **Rational** class in Listing 15.13 using a new internal representation for the numerator and denominator. Create an array of two integers as follows:

```
private long[] r = new long[2];
```

Use **r[0]** to represent the numerator and **r[1]** to represent the denominator. The signatures of the methods in the **Rational** class are not changed, so a client application that uses the previous **Rational** class can continue to use this new **Rational** class without being recompiled.

*15.17 (*Use BigInteger for the Rational class*) Redesign and implement the **Rational** class in Listing 15.11 using **BigInteger** for the numerator and denominator.

*15.18 (*Create a rational-number calculator*) Write a program similar to Listing 9.5, Calculator.java. Instead of using integers, use rationals, as shown in Figure 15.12a. You will need to use the **split** method in the **String** class, introduced in Section 9.2.6, Converting, Replacing, and Splitting Strings, to retrieve the numerator string and denominator string, and convert strings into integers using the **Integer.parseInt** method.

(a)   (b)

FIGURE 15.12   (a) The program takes three arguments (operand1, operator, and operand2) from the command line and displays the expression and the result of the arithmetic operation. (b) A complex number can be interpreted as a point in a plane.

*15.19 (*Math: The Complex class*) A complex number is a number in the form $a + bi$, where a and b are real numbers and i is $\sqrt{-1}$. The numbers **a** and **b** are known as the real part and imaginary part of the complex number, respectively. You can perform addition, subtraction, multiplication, and division for complex numbers using the following formulas:

$$a + bi + c + di = (a + c) + (b + d)i$$

$$a + bi - (c + di) = (a - c) + (b - d)i$$

$$(a + bi)*(c + di) = (ac - bd) + (bc + ad)i$$

$$(a + bi)/(c + di) = (ac + bd)/(c^2 + d^2) + (bc - ad)i/(c^2 + d^2)$$

You can also obtain the absolute value for a complex number using the following formula:

$$|a + bi| = \sqrt{a^2 + b^2}$$

(A complex number can be interpreted as a point on a plane by identifying the (a,b) values as the coordinates of the point. The absolute value of the complex number corresponds to the distance of the point to the origin, as shown in Figure 15.12b.)

Design a class named **Complex** for representing complex numbers and the methods **add**, **subtract**, **multiply**, **divide**, and **abs** for performing complex-number operations, and override **toString** method for returning a string representation for a complex number. The **toString** method returns **(a + bi)** as a string. If **b** is **0**, it simply returns **a**.

Provide three constructors **Complex(a, b)**, **Complex(a)**, and **Complex()**. **Complex()** creates a **Complex** object for number **0** and **Complex(a)** creates a **Complex** object with **0** for **b**. Also provide the **getRealPart()** and **getImaginaryPart()** methods for returning the real and imaginary part of the complex number, respectively.

Write a test program that prompts the user to enter two complex numbers and displays the result of their addition, subtraction, multiplication, and division. Here is a sample run:

```
Enter the first complex number: 3.5 5.5  ↵Enter
Enter the second complex number: -3.5 1  ↵Enter
(3.5 + 5.5i) + (-3.5 + 1.0i) = 0.0 + 6.5i
(3.5 + 5.5i) - (-3.5 + 1.0i) = 7.0 + 4.5i
(3.5 + 5.5i) * (-3.5 + 1.0i) = -17.75 + -15.75i
(3.5 + 5.5i) / (-3.5 + 1.0i) = -0.5094 + -1.7i
|(3.5 + 5.5i)| = 6.519202405202649
```

**15.20 (*Mandelbrot fractal*) Mandelbrot fractal is a well-known image created from a Mandelbrot set (see Figure 15.13a). A Mandelbrot set is defined using the following iteration:

$$z_{n+1} = z_n^2 + c$$

c is a complex number and the starting point of iteration is $z_0 = 0$. For a given c, the iteration will produce a sequence of complex numbers: $\{z_0, z_1, \ldots, z_n, \ldots\}$. It can be shown that the sequence either tends to infinity or stays bounded, depending on the value of c. For example, if c is **0**, the sequence is $\{0, 0, \ldots\}$, which is bounded. If c is i, the sequence is $\{0, i, -1 + i, -i, -1 + i, i, \ldots\}$, which is bounded. If c is $1 + i$, the sequence is $\{0, 1 + i, 1 + 3i, \ldots\}$, which is unbounded. It is known that if the absolute value of a complex value z_i in the sequence is greater than 2, then the sequence is unbounded. The Mandelbrot set consists of the c value such that the sequence is bounded. For example, 0 and i are in the Mandelbrot set. A Mandelbrot image can be created using the following code:

```
1 class MandelbrotCanvas extends JPanel {
2    final static int COUNT_LIMIT = 60;
```

```
 3
 4    @Override /** Paint a Mandelbrot image */
 5    protected void paintComponent(Graphics g) {
 6      super.paintComponent(g);
 7
 8      for (double x = -2.0; x < 2.0; x += 0.01)
 9        for (double y = -2.0; y < 2.0; y += 0.01) {
10          int c = count(new Complex(x, y));
11          if (c == COUNT_LIMIT)
12            g.setColor(Color.BLACK); // c is in a Mandelbrot set
13          else
14            g.setColor(new Color(
15              c * 77 % 256, c * 58 % 256, c * 159 % 256));
16
17          g.drawRect((int)(x * 100) + 200, (int)(y * 100) + 200,
18            1, 1); // Fill a tiny rectangle with the specified color
19        }
20    }
21
22    /** Return the iteration count */
23    static int count(Complex c) {
24      Complex z = new Complex(0, 0); // z0
25
26      for (int i = 0; i < COUNT_LIMIT; i++) {
27        z = z.multiply(z).add(c); // Get z1, z2, . . .
28        if (z.abs() > 2) return i; // The sequence is unbounded
29      }
30
31      return COUNT_LIMIT; // Indicate a bounded sequence
32    }
33  }
```

The `count(Complex c)` method (lines 23–32) computes $z_1, z_2, \ldots, z_{60}$. If none of their absolute values exceeds **2**, we assume c is in the Mandelbrot set. Of course, there could always be an error, but **60 (COUNT_LIMIT)** iterations usually are enough. Once we find that the sequence is unbounded, the method returns the

(a)   (b)

FIGURE 15.13 A Mandelbrot image is shown in (a) and a Julia set image is shown in (b).

iteration count (line 28). The method returns `COUNT_LIMIT` if the sequence is bounded (line 31).

The loop in lines 8–9 examines each point (x, y) for $-2 < x < 2$ and $-2 < y < 2$ with interval 0.01 to see if its corresponding complex number $c = x + yi$ is in the Mandelbrot set (line 10). If so, paint the point black (line 12). If not, set a color that is dependent on its iteration count (line 15). Note that the point is painted in a square with width u and height 1. All the points are scaled and mapped to a grid of 400-by-400 pixels (lines 14–15). Note that the values $77, 58$, and 159 are set arbitrarily. You may set different numbers to get new colors.

Complete the program to draw a Mandelbrot image, as shown in Figure 15.13a.

**15.21 (*Julia set*) The preceding exercise describes Mandelbrot sets. The Mandelbrot set consists of the complex c value such that the sequence $z_{n+1} = z_n^2 + c$ is bounded with z_0 fixed and c varying. If we fix c and vary $z_0 (= x + yi)$, the point (x, y) is said to be in a Julia set for a fixed complex value c, if the function $z_{n+1} = z_n^2 + c$ stays bounded. Revise Exercise 15.20 to draw a Julia set as shown in Figure 15.13b. Note that you only need to revise the `count` method by using a fixed c value $(-0.3 + 0.6i)$.

15.22 (*Use the `Rational` class*) Write a program that computes the following summation series using the `Rational` class:

$$\frac{1}{2} + \frac{2}{3} + \frac{3}{4} + \ldots + \frac{98}{99} + \frac{99}{100}$$

You will discover that the output is incorrect because of integer overflow (too large). To fix this problem, see Programming Exercise 15.17.

EVENT-DRIVEN PROGRAMMING

Objectives

- To get a taste of event-driven programming (§16.1).

- To describe events, event sources, and event classes (§16.2).

- To define listener classes, register listener objects with the source object, and write the code to handle events (§16.3).

- To define listener classes using inner classes (§16.4).

- To define listener classes using anonymous inner classes (§16.5).

- To explore various coding styles for creating and registering listener classes (§16.6).

- To develop a GUI application for a loan calculator (§16.7).

- To write programs to deal with MouseEvents (§16.8).

- To simplify coding for listener classes using listener interface adapters (§16.9).

- To write programs to deal with KeyEvents (§16.10).

- To use the javax.swing.Timer class to control animations (§16.11).

16.1 Introduction

 Key Point

You can write code to process events such as a button click or a timer.

problem

Suppose you want to write a GUI program that lets the user enter a loan amount, annual interest rate, and number of years and click the *Compute Payment* button to obtain the monthly payment and total payment, as shown in Figure 16.1a. How do you accomplish the task? You have to use *event-driven programming* to write the code to respond to the button-clicking event.

| (a) | (b) | (c) | (d) |

FIGURE 16.1 (a) The program computes loan payments. (b)–(d) A flag is rising upward.

Suppose you want to write a program that animates a rising flag, as shown in Figure 16.1b–d. How do you accomplish the task? There are several ways to program this. An effective one is to use a timer in event-driven programming, which is the subject of this chapter.

problem

Before delving into event-driven programming, it is helpful to get a taste using a simple example. The example displays two buttons in a frame, as shown in Figure 16.2.

| (a) | (b) |

FIGURE 16.2 (a) The program displays two buttons. (b) A message is displayed in the console when a button is clicked.

To respond to a button click, you need to write the code to process the button-clicking action. The button is an *event source object*—where the action originates. You need to create an object capable of handling the action event on a button. This object is called an *event listener*, as shown in Figure 16.3.

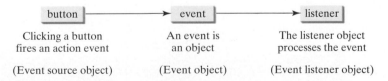

| button | event | listener |

| Clicking a button fires an action event | An event is an object | The listener object processes the event |
| (Event source object) | (Event object) | (Event listener object) |

FIGURE 16.3 A listener object processes the event fired from the source object.

Not all objects can be listeners for an action event. To be a listener of an action event, two requirements must be met:

`ActionListener` interface

1. The object must be an instance of the `ActionListener` interface. This interface defines the common behavior for all action listeners.

`addActionListener (listener)`

2. The `ActionListener` object `listener` must be registered with the event source object using the method `source.addActionListener(listener)`.

The `ActionListener` interface contains the `actionPerformed` method for processing the event. Your listener class must override this method to respond to the event. Listing 16.1 gives the code that processes the `ActionEvent` on the two buttons. When you click the *OK* button, the message "OK button clicked" is displayed. When you click the *Cancel* button, the message "Cancel button clicked" is displayed, as shown in Figure 16.2.

LISTING 16.1 HandleEvent.java

```
1  import javax.swing.*;
2  import java.awt.event.*;
3
4  public class HandleEvent extends JFrame {
5    public HandleEvent() {
6      // Create two buttons
7      JButton jbtOK = new JButton("OK");
8      JButton jbtCancel = new JButton("Cancel");
9
10     // Create a panel to hold buttons
11     JPanel panel = new JPanel();
12     panel.add(jbtOK);
13     panel.add(jbtCancel);
14
15     add(panel); // Add panel to the frame
16
17     // Register listeners
18     OKListenerClass listener1 = new OKListenerClass();        create listener
19     CancelListenerClass listener2 = new CancelListenerClass();
20     jbtOK.addActionListener(listener1);                       register listener
21     jbtCancel.addActionListener(listener2);
22   }
23
24   public static void main(String[] args) {
25     JFrame frame = new HandleEvent();
26     frame.setTitle("Handle Event");
27     frame.setSize(200, 150);
28     frame.setLocation(200, 100);
29     frame.setDefaultCloseOperation(JFrame.EXIT_ON_CLOSE);
30     frame.setVisible(true);
31   }
32 }
33
34 class OKListenerClass implements ActionListener {              listener class
35   @Override
36   public void actionPerformed(ActionEvent e) {                 process event
37     System.out.println("OK button clicked");
38   }
39 }
40
41 class CancelListenerClass implements ActionListener {          listener class
42   @Override
43   public void actionPerformed(ActionEvent e) {                 process event
44     System.out.println("Cancel button clicked");
45   }
46 }
```

Two listener classes are defined in lines 34–46. Each listener class implements `ActionListener` to process `ActionEvent`. The object `listener1` is an instance of `OKListenerClass` (line 18), which is registered with the button `jbtOK` (line 20). When the *OK* button is clicked, the `actionPerformed(ActionEvent)` method (line 36) in

`OKListenerClass` is invoked to process the event. The object `listener2` is an instance of `CancelListenerClass` (line 19), which is registered with the button `jbtCancel` in line 21. When the *Cancel* button is clicked, the `actionPerformed(ActionEvent)` method (line 43) in `CancelListenerClass` is invoked to process the event.

You now have seen a glimpse of event-driven programming in Java. You probably have many questions, such as why a listener class is defined to implement the `ActionListener`. The following sections will give you all the answers.

16.2 Events and Event Sources

Key Point

An event *is an object created from an event source. Firing an event* means to create an event and delegate the listener to handle the event.

event-driven programming
event

When you run a Java GUI program, the program interacts with the user, and the events drive its execution. This is called *event-driven programming*. An *event* can be defined as a signal to the program that something has happened. Events are triggered either by external user actions, such as mouse movements, button clicks, and keystrokes, or by internal program activities, such as a timer. The program can choose to respond to or ignore an event. The example in the preceding section gave you a taste of event-driven programming.

fire event

event source object

source object

The component that creates an event and fires it is called the *event source object*, or simply *source object* or *source component*. For example, a button is the source object for a button-clicking action event. An event is an instance of an event class. The root class of the event classes is `java.util.EventObject`. The hierarchical relationships of some event classes are shown in Figure 16.4.

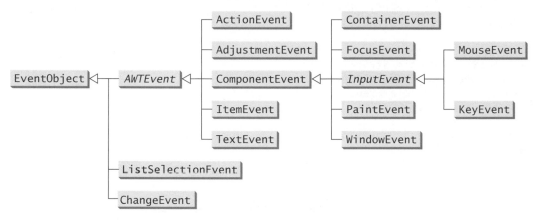

FIGURE 16.4 An event is an object of the `EventObject` class.

event object

getSource()

An *event object* contains whatever properties are pertinent to the event. You can identify the source object of an event using the `getSource()` instance method in the `EventObject` class. The subclasses of `EventObject` deal with specific types of events, such as action events, window events, component events, mouse events, and key events. The first three columns in Table 16.1 list some external user actions, source objects, and event types fired. For example, when clicking a button, the button creates and fires an `ActionEvent`, as indicated in the first line of this table. Here the button is an event source object and an `ActionEvent` is the event object fired by the source object, as shown in Figure 16.2.

Note
If a component can fire an event, any subclass of the component can fire the same type of event. For example, every GUI component can fire `MouseEvent` and `KeyEvent`, since `Component` is the superclass of all GUI components.

TABLE 16.1 User Action, Source Object, Event Type, Listener Interface, and Handler

User Action	Source Object	Event Type Fired	Listener Interface	Listener Interface Methods
Click a button	`JButton`	`ActionEvent`	`ActionListener`	`actionPerformed(ActionEvent e)`
Press Enter in a text field	`JTextField`	`ActionEvent`	`ActionListener`	`actionPerformed(ActionEvent e)`
Select a new item	`JComboBox`	`ActionEvent` `ItemEvent`	`ActionListener` `ItemListener`	`actionPerformed(ActionEvent e)` `itemStateChanged(ItemEvent e)`
Check or uncheck	`JRadioButton`	`ActionEvent` `ItemEvent`	`ActionListener` `ItemListener`	`actionPerformed(ActionEvent e)` `itemStateChanged(ItemEvent e)`
Check or uncheck	`JCheckBox`	`ActionEvent` `ItemEvent`	`ActionListener` `ItemListener`	`actionPerformed(ActionEvent e)` `itemStateChanged(ItemEvent e)`
Select a new item	`JComboBox`	`ActionEvent` `ItemEvent`	`ActionListener` `ItemListener`	`actionPerformed(ActionEvent e)` `itemStateChanged(ItemEvent e)`
Mouse pressed	`Component`	`MouseEvent`	`MouseListener`	`mousePressed(MouseEvent e)`
Mouse released				`mouseReleased(MouseEvent e)`
Mouse clicked				`mouseClicked(MouseEvent e)`
Mouse entered				`mouseEntered(MouseEvent e)`
Mouse exited				`mouseExited(MouseEvent e)`
Mouse moved			`MouseMotionListener`	`mouseMoved(MouseEvent e)`
Mouse dragged				`mouseDragged(MouseEvent e)`
Key pressed	`Component`	`KeyEvent`	`KeyListener`	`keyPressed(KeyEvent e)`
Key released				`keyReleased(KeyEvent e)`
Key typed				`keyTyped(KeyEvent e)`

Note

All the event classes in Figure 16.4 are included in the `java.awt.event` package except `ListSelectionEvent` and `ChangeEvent`, which are in the `javax.swing.event` package. AWT events were originally designed for AWT components, but many Swing components fire them.

16.1 What is an event source object? What is an event object? Describe the relationship between an event source object and an event object.

16.2 Can a button fire a `MouseEvent`? Can a button fire a `KeyEvent`? Can a button fire an `ActionEvent`?

16.3 Listeners, Registrations, and Handling Events

A listener is an object that must be registered with an event source object, and it must be an instance of an appropriate event-handling interface.

Key Point

Java uses a delegation-based model for event handling: a source object fires an event, and an object interested in the event handles it. The latter object is called an *event listener* or simply *listener*. For an object to be a listener for an event on a source object, two things are needed, as shown in Figure 16.5.

event delegation
event listener

1. *The listener object must be an instance of the corresponding event-listener interface* to ensure that the listener has the correct method for processing the event. Java provides a listener interface for every type of event. The listener interface is usually named *XListener* for *XEvent*, with the exception of `MouseMotionListener`. The last

event-listener interface

XListener/XEvent

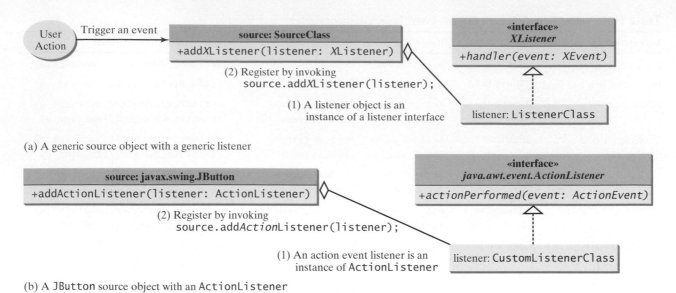

(a) A generic source object with a generic listener

(b) A JButton source object with an ActionListener

FIGURE 16.5 A listener must be an instance of a listener interface and must be registered with a source object.

event handler

three columns in Table 16.1 list event types, the corresponding listener interfaces, and the methods defined in the listener interfaces. The listener interface contains the method(s), known as the *event handler(s)*, for processing the event. For example, as shown in the first line of this table, the corresponding listener interface for **ActionEvent** is **ActionListener**; each listener for **ActionEvent** should implement the **ActionListener** interface; the **ActionListener** interface contains the handler **actionPerformed(ActionEvent)** for processing an **ActionEvent**.

register listener

2. *The listener object must be registered by the source object.* Registration methods depend on the event type. For **ActionEvent**, the method is **addActionListener**. In general, the method is named **add***X***Listener** for *X***Event**. A source object may fire several types of events, and for each event the source object maintains a list of registered listeners and notifies them by invoking the *handler* of the listener object to respond to the event, as shown in Figure 16.6. (Note that this figure shows the internal implementation of a source class. You don't have to know how a source class such as **JButton** is implemented in order to use it, but this knowledge will help you understand the Java event-driven programming framework.)

(a) Internal function of a generic source object   (b) Internal function of a JButton object

FIGURE 16.6 The source object notifies the listeners of the event by invoking the listener object's handler.

Let's revisit Listing 16.1, HandleEvent.java. Since a **JButton** object fires **ActionEvent**, a listener object for **ActionEvent** must be an instance of **ActionListener**, so the listener class implements **ActionListener** in line 34. The source object invokes **addActionListener(listener)** to register a listener, as follows:

```
JButton jbtOK = new JButton("OK"); // Line 7 in Listing 16.1
```
create source object

```
OKListenerClass listener1
    = new OKListenerClass(); // Line 18 in Listing 16.1
```
create listener object

```
jbtOK.addActionListener(listener1); // Line 20 in Listing 16.1
```
register listener

When you click the button, the **JButton** object fires an **ActionEvent** and passes it to invoke the listener's **actionPerformed** method to handle the event.

The event object contains information pertinent to the event, which can be obtained using the methods, as shown in Figure 16.7. For example, you can use **e.getSource()** to obtain the source object that fired the event. For an action event, you can use **e.getWhen()** to obtain the time when the event occurred.

FIGURE 16.7 You can obtain useful information from an event object.

We now write a program that uses two buttons to control the size of a circle, as shown in Figure 16.8.

FIGURE 16.8 The user clicks the *Enlarge* and *Shrink* buttons to enlarge and shrink the size of the circle.

We will develop this program incrementally. First we will write the program in Listing 16.2 that displays the user interface with a circle in the center (line 14) and two buttons on the bottom (line 15).

first version

LISTING 16.2 ControlCircleWithoutEventHandling.java

buttons

circle canvas

```
 1  import javax.swing.*;
 2  import java.awt.*;
 3
 4  public class ControlCircleWithoutEventHandling extends JFrame {
 5    private JButton jbtEnlarge = new JButton("Enlarge");
 6    private JButton jbtShrink = new JButton("Shrink");
 7    private CirclePanel canvas = new CirclePanel();
 8
 9    public ControlCircleWithoutEventHandling() {
10      JPanel panel = new JPanel(); // Use the panel to group buttons
11      panel.add(jbtEnlarge);
12      panel.add(jbtShrink);
13
14      this.add(canvas, BorderLayout.CENTER); // Add canvas to center
15      this.add(panel, BorderLayout.SOUTH); // Add buttons to the frame
16    }
17
18    /** Main method */
19    public static void main(String[] args) {
20      JFrame frame = new ControlCircleWithoutEventHandling();
21      frame.setTitle("ControlCircleWithoutEventHandling");
22      frame.setLocationRelativeTo(null); // Center the frame
23      frame.setDefaultCloseOperation(JFrame.EXIT_ON_CLOSE);
24      frame.setSize(200, 200);
25      frame.setVisible(true);
26    }
27  }
28
29  class CirclePanel extends JPanel {
30    private int radius = 5; // Default circle radius
31
32    @Override /** Repaint the circle */
33    protected void paintComponent(Graphics g) {
34      super.paintComponent(g);
35      g.drawOval(getWidth() / 2 - radius, getHeight() / 2 - radius,
36        2 * radius, 2 * radius);
37    }
38  }
```

CirclePanel class

paint the circle

How do you use the buttons to enlarge or shrink the circle? When the *Enlarge* button is clicked, you want the circle to be repainted with a larger radius. How can you accomplish this? You can expand the program in Listing 16.2 into Listing 16.3 with the following features:

second version

1. Define a listener class named `EnlargeListener` that implements `ActionListener` (lines 31–36).

2. Create a listener and register it with `jbtEnlarge` (line 18).

3. Add a method named `enlarge()` in `CirclePanel` to increase the radius, then repaint the panel (lines 42–45).

4. Implement the `actionPerformed` method in `EnlargeListener` to invoke `canvas.enlarge()` (line 34).

5. To make the reference variable `canvas` accessible from the `actionPerformed` method, define `EnlargeListener` as an inner class of the `ControlCircle` class (lines 31–36). (*Inner classes* are defined inside another class. We will introduce inner classes in the next section.)

inner class

6. To avoid compile errors, the `CirclePanel` class (lines 38–53) now is also defined as an inner class in `ControlCircle`, since another `CirclePanel` class is already defined in Listing 16.2.

LISTING 16.3 ControlCircle.java

VideoNote

Listener and its registration

```java
1   import javax.swing.*;
2   import java.awt.*;
3   import java.awt.event.*;
4
5   public class ControlCircle extends JFrame {
6     private JButton jbtEnlarge = new JButton("Enlarge");
7     private JButton jbtShrink = new JButton("Shrink");
8     private CirclePanel canvas = new CirclePanel();
9
10    public ControlCircle() {
11      JPanel panel = new JPanel(); // Use the panel to group buttons
12      panel.add(jbtEnlarge);
13      panel.add(jbtShrink);
14
15      this.add(canvas, BorderLayout.CENTER); // Add canvas to center
16      this.add(panel, BorderLayout.SOUTH); // Add buttons to the frame
17
18      jbtEnlarge.addActionListener(new EnlargeListener());
19    }
20
21    /** Main method */
22    public static void main(String[] args) {
23      JFrame frame = new ControlCircle();
24      frame.setTitle("ControlCircle");
25      frame.setLocationRelativeTo(null); // Center the frame
26      frame.setDefaultCloseOperation(JFrame.EXIT_ON_CLOSE);
27      frame.setSize(200, 200);
28      frame.setVisible(true);
29    }
30
31    class EnlargeListener implements ActionListener { // Inner class
32      @Override
33      public void actionPerformed(ActionEvent e) {
34        canvas.enlarge();
35      }
36    }
37
38    class CirclePanel extends JPanel { // Inner class
39      private int radius = 5; // Default circle radius
40
41      /** Enlarge the circle */
42      public void enlarge() {
43        radius++;
44        repaint();
45      }
46
47      @Override
48      protected void paintComponent(Graphics g) {
49        super.paintComponent(g);
50        g.drawOval(getWidth() / 2 - radius, getHeight() / 2 - radius,
51          2 * radius, 2 * radius);
52      }
53    }
54  }
```

create/register listener

listener class

CirclePanel class

enlarge method

the *Shrink* button

Similarly, you can add the code for the *Shrink* button to display a smaller circle when the *Shrink* button is clicked.

16.3 Why must a listener be an instance of an appropriate listener interface? Explain how to register a listener object and how to implement a listener interface.

16.4 Can a source have multiple listeners? Can a listener listen to multiple sources? Can a source be a listener for itself?

16.5 How do you implement a method defined in the listener interface? Do you need to implement all the methods defined in the listener interface?

16.6 What method do you use to get the timestamp for an action event?

16.4 Inner Classes

Key Point

An inner class, or nested class, is a class defined within the scope of another class. Inner classes are useful for defining listener classes.

We now introduce inner classes in this section and anonymous inner classes in the next section and use them to define listener classes. First let us see the code in Figure 16.9. The code in Figure 16.9a defines two separate classes, `Test` and `A`. The code in Figure 16.9b defines `A` as an inner class in `Test`.

```
public class Test {
    ...
}

public class A {
    ...
}
```
(a)

```
public class Test {
    ...

    // Inner class
    public class A {
        ...
    }
}
```
(b)

```
// OuterClass.java: inner class demo
public class OuterClass {
    private int data;

    /** A method in the outer class */
    public void m() {
        // Do something
    }

    // An inner class
    class InnerClass {
        /** A method in the inner class */
        public void mi() {
            // Directly reference data and method
            // defined in its outer class
            data++;
            m();
        }
    }
}
```
(c)

FIGURE 16.9 Inner classes combine dependent classes into the primary class.

The class `InnerClass` defined inside `OuterClass` in Figure 16.9c is another example of an inner class. An inner class may be used just like a regular class. Normally, you define a class as an inner class if it is used only by its outer class. An inner class has the following features:

■ An inner class is compiled into a class named `OuterClassName$InnerClassName.class`. For example, the inner class `A` in `Test` is compiled into `Test$A.class` in Figure 16.9b.

■ An inner class can reference the data and methods defined in the outer class in which it nests, so you need not pass the reference of an object of the outer class to the constructor of the inner class. For this reason, inner classes can make programs simple and concise.

For example, `canvas` is defined in `ControlCircle` in Listing 16.3 (line 8). It can be referenced in the inner class `EnlargeListener` in line 34.

■ An inner class can be defined with a visibility modifier subject to the same visibility rules applied to a member of the class.

■ An inner class can be defined as `static`. A `static` inner class can be accessed using the outer class name. A `static` inner class cannot access nonstatic members of the outer class.

■ Objects of an inner class are often created in the outer class. But you can also create an object of an inner class from another class. If the inner class is nonstatic, you must first create an instance of the outer class, then use the following syntax to create an object for the inner class:

```
OuterClass.InnerClass innerObject = outerObject.new InnerClass();
```

■ If the inner class is static, use the following syntax to create an object for it:

```
OuterClass.InnerClass innerObject = new OuterClass.InnerClass();
```

A simple use of inner classes is to combine dependent classes into a primary class. This reduces the number of source files. It also makes class files easy to organize, since they are all named with the primary class as the prefix. For example, rather than creating the two source files **Test.java** and **A.java** in Figure 16.9a, you can merge class A into class Test and create just one source file, **Test.java** in Figure 16.9b. The resulting class files are **Test.class** and **Test$A.class**.

Another practical use of inner classes is to avoid class-naming conflicts. Two versions of `CirclePanel` are defined in Listings 16.2 and 16.3. You can define them as inner classes to avoid a conflict.

A listener class is designed specifically to create a listener object for a GUI component (e.g., a button). The listener class will not be shared by other applications and therefore is appropriate to be defined inside the frame class as an inner class.

16.7 Can an inner class be used in a class other than the class in which it nests?

16.8 Can the modifiers `public`, `private`, and `static` be used for inner classes?

✓ **Check Point**

MyProgrammingLab™

16.5 Anonymous Class Listeners

An anonymous inner class *is an inner class without a name. It combines defining an inner class and creating an instance of the class into one step.*

🔑 **Key Point**

Inner-class listeners can be shortened using *anonymous inner classes*. The inner class in Listing 16.3 can be replaced by an anonymous inner class as shown below.

anonymous inner class

```
public ControlCircle() {
  // Omitted

  jbtEnlarge.addActionListener(
    new EnlargeListener());
}

class EnlargeListener
    implements ActionListener {
  @Override
  public void actionPerformed(ActionEvent e) {
    canvas.enlarge();
  }
}
```

(a) Inner class `EnlargeListener`

```
public ControlCircle() {
  // Omitted

  jbtEnlarge.addActionListener(
    new class EnlargeListener
        implements ActionListener() {
    @Override
    public void actionPerformed(ActionEvent e) {
      canvas.enlarge();
    }
  });
}
```

(b) Anonymous inner class

The syntax for an anonymous inner class is:

```
new SuperClassName/InterfaceName() {
  // Implement or override methods in superclass or interface

  // Other methods if necessary
}
```

Since an anonymous inner class is a special kind of inner class, it is treated like an inner class with the following features:

- An anonymous inner class must always extend a superclass or implement an interface, but it cannot have an explicit **extends** or **implements** clause.

- An anonymous inner class must implement all the abstract methods in the superclass or in the interface.

- An anonymous inner class always uses the no-arg constructor from its superclass to create an instance. If an anonymous inner class implements an interface, the constructor is **Object()**.

- An anonymous inner class is compiled into a class named **OuterClassName$***n***.class**. For example, if the outer class **Test** has two anonymous inner classes, they are compiled into **Test$1.class** and **Test$2.class**.

Listing 16.4 gives an example that handles the events from four buttons, as shown in Figure 16.10.

FIGURE 16.10 The program handles the events from four buttons.

VideoNote

Anonymous listener

LISTING 16.4 AnonymousListenerDemo.java

```
1  import javax.swing.*;
2  import java.awt.event.*;
3
4  public class AnonymousListenerDemo extends JFrame {
5    public AnonymousListenerDemo() {
6      // Create four buttons
7      JButton jbtNew = new JButton("New");
8      JButton jbtOpen = new JButton("Open");
9      JButton jbtSave = new JButton("Save");
10     JButton jbtPrint = new JButton("Print");
11
12     // Create a panel to hold buttons
13     JPanel panel = new JPanel();
14     panel.add(jbtNew);
15     panel.add(jbtOpen);
16     panel.add(jbtSave);
17     panel.add(jbtPrint);
18
19     add(panel);
```

```
20
21        // Create and register anonymous inner-class listener
22        jbtNew.addActionListener(new ActionListener() {          anonymous listener
23            @Override                                             handle event
24            public void actionPerformed(ActionEvent e) {
25                System.out.println("Process New");
26            }
27        }
28        );
29
30        jbtOpen.addActionListener(new ActionListener() {
31            @Override
32            public void actionPerformed(ActionEvent e) {
33                System.out.println("Process Open");
34            }
35        }
36        );
37
38        jbtSave.addActionListener(new ActionListener() {
39            @Override
40            public void actionPerformed(ActionEvent e) {
41                System.out.println("Process Save");
42            }
43        }
44        );
45
46        jbtPrint.addActionListener(new ActionListener() {
47            @Override
48            public void actionPerformed(ActionEvent e) {
49                System.out.println("Process Print");
50            }
51        }
52        );
53    }
54
55    /** Main method */
56    public static void main(String[] args) {
57        JFrame frame = new AnonymousListenerDemo();
58        frame.setTitle("AnonymousListenerDemo");
59        frame.setLocationRelativeTo(null); // Center the frame
60        frame.setDefaultCloseOperation(JFrame.EXIT_ON_CLOSE);
61        frame.pack();
62        frame.setVisible(true);
63    }
64 }
```

The program creates four listeners using anonymous inner classes (lines 22–52). Without using anonymous inner classes, you would have to create four separate classes. An anonymous listener works the same way as an inner class listener. The program is condensed using an anonymous inner class.

Anonymous inner classes are compiled into `OuterClassName$#.class`, where # starts at `1` and is incremented for each anonymous class the compiler encounters. In this example, the anonymous inner classes are compiled into `AnonymousListenerDemo$1.class`, `AnonymousListenerDemo$2.class`, `AnonymousListenerDemo$3.class`, and `AnonymousListenerDemo$4.class`.

Instead of using the `setSize` method to set the size for the frame, the program uses the `pack()` method (line 61), which automatically sizes the frame according to the size of the components placed in it.   pack()

16.9 If class **A** is an inner class in class **B**, what is the .class file for **A**? If class B contains two anonymous inner classes, what are the .class file names for these two classes?

MyProgrammingLab™ **16.10** What is wrong in the following code?

```java
import java.swing.*;
import java.awt.*;

public class Test extends JFrame {
  public Test() {
    JButton jbtOK = new JButton("OK");
    add(jbtOK);
  }

  private class Listener
      implements ActionListener {
    public void actionPerform
        (ActionEvent e) {
      System.out.println
        (jbtOK.getActionCommand());
    }
  }

  /** Main method omitted */
}
```

(a)

```java
import java.awt.event.*;
import javax.swing.*;

public class Test extends JFrame {
  public Test() {
    JButton jbtOK = new JButton("OK");
    add(jbtOK);
    jbtOK.addActionListener(
      new ActionListener() {
        public void actionPerformed
          (ActionEvent e) {
          System.out.println
            (jbtOK.getActionCommand());
        }
    } // Something missing here
  }

  /** Main method omitted */
}
```

(b)

16.11 What is the difference between the `setSize(width, height)` method and the `pack()` method in `JFrame`?

16.6 Alternative Ways of Defining Listener Classes

Using an inner class or an anonymous inner class is preferred for defining listener classes.

There are many other ways to define the listener classes. For example, you can rewrite Listing 16.4 by creating just one listener, register the listener with the buttons, and let the listener detect the event source—that is, which button fires the event—as shown in Listing 16.5.

LISTING 16.5 `DetectSourceDemo.java`

```java
1  import javax.swing.*;
2  import java.awt.event.*;
3
4  public class DetectSourceDemo extends JFrame {
5    // Create four buttons
6    private JButton jbtNew = new JButton("New");
7    private JButton jbtOpen = new JButton("Open");
8    private JButton jbtSave = new JButton("Save");
9    private JButton jbtPrint = new JButton("Print");
10
11   public DetectSourceDemo() {
12     // Create a panel to hold buttons
13     JPanel panel = new JPanel();
14     panel.add(jbtNew);
15     panel.add(jbtOpen);
16     panel.add(jbtSave);
17     panel.add(jbtPrint);
18
```

```
19      add(panel);
20
21      // Create a listener
22      ButtonListener listener = new ButtonListener();          create listener
23
24      // Register listener with buttons
25      jbtNew.addActionListener(listener);                      register listener
26      jbtOpen.addActionListener(listener);
27      jbtSave.addActionListener(listener);
28      jbtPrint.addActionListener(listener);
29    }
30
31    class ButtonListener implements ActionListener {          listener class
32      @Override
33      public void actionPerformed(ActionEvent e) {            handle event
34        if (e.getSource() == jbtNew)
35          System.out.println("Process New");
36        else if (e.getSource() == jbtOpen)
37          System.out.println("Process Open");
38        else if (e.getSource() == jbtSave)
39          System.out.println("Process Save");
40        else if (e.getSource() == jbtPrint)
41          System.out.println("Process Print");
42      }
43    }
44
45    /** Main method */
46    public static void main(String[] args) {
47      JFrame frame = new DetectSourceDemo();
48      frame.setTitle("DetectSourceDemo");
49      frame.setLocationRelativeTo(null); // Center the frame
50      frame.setDefaultCloseOperation(JFrame.EXIT_ON_CLOSE);
51      frame.pack();
52      frame.setVisible(true);
53    }
54  }
```

This program defines just one inner listener class (lines 31–43), creates a listener from the class (line 22), and registers it to four buttons (lines 25–28). When a button is clicked, the button fires an **ActionEvent** and invokes the listener's **actionPerformed** method. The **actionPerformed** method checks the source of the event using the **getSource()** method for the event (lines 34, 36, 38, 40) and determines which button fired the event.

Defining one listener class for handling a large number of events is efficient. In this case, you create just one listener object. Using anonymous inner classes, you would create four listener objects.

You could also rewrite Listing 16.4 by defining the custom frame class that implements **ActionListener**, as shown in Listing 16.6.

LISTING 16.6 FrameAsListenerDemo.java

```
1  import javax.swing.*;
2  import java.awt.event.*;
3
4  public class FrameAsListenerDemo extends JFrame
5      implements ActionListener {                             implement ActionListener
6    // Create four buttons
7    private JButton jbtNew = new JButton("New");
8    private JButton jbtOpen = new JButton("Open");
9    private JButton jbtSave = new JButton("Save");
```

```
10      private JButton jbtPrint = new JButton("Print");
11
12      public FrameAsListenerDemo() {
13        // Create a panel to hold buttons
14        JPanel panel = new JPanel();
15        panel.add(jbtNew);
16        panel.add(jbtOpen);
17        panel.add(jbtSave);
18        panel.add(jbtPrint);
19
20        add(panel);
21
22        // Register listener with buttons
23        jbtNew.addActionListener(this);
24        jbtOpen.addActionListener(this);
25        jbtSave.addActionListener(this);
26        jbtPrint.addActionListener(this);
27      }
28
29      @Override /** Implement actionPerformed */
30      public void actionPerformed(ActionEvent e) {
31        if (e.getSource() == jbtNew)
32          System.out.println("Process New");
33        else if (e.getSource() == jbtOpen)
34          System.out.println("Process Open");
35        else if (e.getSource() == jbtSave)
36          System.out.println("Process Save");
37        else if (e.getSource() == jbtPrint)
38          System.out.println("Process Print");
39      }
40
41      /** Main method */
42      public static void main(String[] args) {
43        JFrame frame = new FrameAsListenerDemo();
44        frame.setTitle("FrameAsListenerDemo");
45        frame.setLocationRelativeTo(null); // Center the frame
46        frame.setDefaultCloseOperation(JFrame.EXIT_ON_CLOSE);
47        frame.pack();
48        frame.setVisible(true);
49      }
50    }
```

register listeners *(margin note beside lines 23)*

handle event *(margin note beside line 30)*

The frame class extends **JFrame** and implements **ActionListener** (line 5), so the class is a listener class for action events. The listener is registered to four buttons (lines 23–26). When a button is clicked, the button fires an **ActionEvent** and invokes the listener's **actionPerformed** method. The **actionPerformed** method checks the source of the event using the **getSource()** method for the event (lines 31, 33, 35, 37) and determines which button fired the event.

This design is not desirable, however, because it puts too many responsibilities into one class. It is better to design a listener class that is solely responsible for handling events, which makes the code easy to read and easy to maintain.

Which way is preferred? *(margin note)*

You should define listener classes using either inner classes or anonymous inner classes—choose whichever produces shorter, clearer, and cleaner code. In general, use anonymous inner classes if the code in the listener is short and the listener is registered for one event source. Use inner classes if the code in the listener is long or the listener is registered for multiple event sources.

16.12 Why should you avoid defining the custom frame class that implements **ActionListener**?

MyProgrammingLab™ **16.13** What method do you use to get the source object from an event object **e**?

16.7 Case Study: Loan Calculator

This case study uses GUI components and events.

Key Point

Now we will write the program for the loan-calculator problem presented at the beginning of this chapter. Here are the major steps in the program:

1. Create the user interface, as shown in Figure 16.11.

   a. Create a panel of a `GridLayout` with 5 rows and 2 columns. Add labels and text fields to the panel. Set the title "Enter loan amount, interest rate, and years" for the panel.

   b. Create another panel with a `FlowLayout(FlowLayout.RIGHT)` and add a button to the panel.

   c. Add the first panel to the center of the frame and the second panel on the south side of the frame.

2. Process the event.

   Create and register the listener for processing the button-clicking action event. The handler obtains the user input on the loan amount, interest rate, and number of years, computes the monthly and total payments, and displays the values in the text fields.

JPanel of
GridLayout (5, 2)

JPanel of Flowlayout
right aligned

FIGURE 16.11 The program computes loan payments.

The complete program is given in Listing 16.7.

LISTING 16.7 LoanCalculator.java

```java
import java.awt.*;
import java.awt.event.*;
import javax.swing.*;
import javax.swing.border.TitledBorder;

public class LoanCalculator extends JFrame {
  // Create text fields for interest rate, years,
  // loan amount, monthly payment, and total payment
  private JTextField jtfAnnualInterestRate = new JTextField();      text fields
  private JTextField jtfNumberOfYears = new JTextField();
  private JTextField jtfLoanAmount = new JTextField();
  private JTextField jtfMonthlyPayment = new JTextField();
  private JTextField jtfTotalPayment = new JTextField();

  // Create a Compute Payment button
  private JButton jbtComputeLoan = new JButton("Compute Payment");   button
```

```
17
18   public LoanCalculator() {
19     // Panel p1 to hold labels and text fields
20     JPanel p1 = new JPanel(new GridLayout(5, 2));
21     p1.add(new JLabel("Annual Interest Rate"));
22     p1.add(jtfAnnualInterestRate);
23     p1.add(new JLabel("Number of Years"));
24     p1.add(jtfNumberOfYears);
25     p1.add(new JLabel("Loan Amount"));
26     p1.add(jtfLoanAmount);
27     p1.add(new JLabel("Monthly Payment"));
28     p1.add(jtfMonthlyPayment);
29     p1.add(new JLabel("Total Payment"));
30     p1.add(jtfTotalPayment);
31     p1.setBorder(new
32       TitledBorder("Enter loan amount, interest rate, and years"));
33
34     // Panel p2 to hold the button
35     JPanel p2 = new JPanel(new FlowLayout(FlowLayout.RIGHT));
36     p2.add(jbtComputeLoan);
37
38     // Add the panels to the frame
39     add(p1, BorderLayout.CENTER);
40     add(p2, BorderLayout.SOUTH);
41
42     // Register listener
43     jbtComputeLoan.addActionListener(new ButtonListener());
44   }
45
46   /** Handle the Compute Payment button */
47   private class ButtonListener implements ActionListener {
48     @Override
49     public void actionPerformed(ActionEvent e) {
50       // Get values from text fields
51       double interest =
52         Double.parseDouble(jtfAnnualInterestRate.getText());
53       int year = Integer.parseInt(jtfNumberOfYears.getText());
54       double loanAmount =
55         Double.parseDouble(jtfLoanAmount.getText());
56
57       // Create a loan object. Loan defined in Listing 10.2
58       Loan loan = new Loan(interest, year, loanAmount);
59
60       // Display monthly payment and total payment
61       jtfMonthlyPayment.setText(String.format("%.2f",
62         loan.getMonthlyPayment()));
63       jtfTotalPayment.setText(String.format("%.2f",
64         loan.getTotalPayment()));
65     }
66   }
67
68   public static void main(String[] args) {
69     LoanCalculator frame = new LoanCalculator();
70     frame.pack();
71     frame.setTitle("LoanCalculator");
72     frame.setLocationRelativeTo(null); // Center the frame
73     frame.setDefaultCloseOperation(JFrame.EXIT_ON_CLOSE);
74     frame.setVisible(true);
75   }
76 }
```

Margin notes:

create UI (line 20)

add to frame (line 35)

register listener (line 43)

get input (line 51)

create loan (line 58)

set result (line 61)

The user interface is created in the constructor (lines 18–44). The button is the source of the event. A listener is created and registered with the button (line 43).

The `ButtonListener` class (lines 47–66) implements the `actionPerformed` method. When the button is clicked, the `actionPerformed` method is invoked to get the interest rate (line 51), number of years (line 53), and loan amount (line 54). Invoking `jtfAnnualInterestRate.getText()` returns the string text in the `jtfAnnualInterestRate` text field. The `Loan` class is used for computing the loan payments. This class was introduced in Listing 10.2, Loan.java. Invoking `loan.getMonthlyPayment()` returns the monthly payment for the loan (line 62). The `String.format` method, introduced in Section 9.2.11, is used to format a number into a desirable format and returns it as a string (lines 61, 63). Invoking the `setText` method on a text field sets a string value in the text field (line 61).

16.8 Mouse Events

A mouse event is fired whenever a mouse button is pressed, released, or clicked, the mouse is moved, or the mouse is dragged onto a component.

Key Point

The `MouseEvent` object captures the event, such as the number of clicks associated with it, the location (the *x*- and *y*-coordinates) of the mouse, or which button was pressed, as shown in Figure 16.12.

java.awt.event.InputEvent	
+getWhen(): long	Returns the timestamp when this event occurred.
+isAltDown(): boolean	Returns true if the Alt key is pressed on this event.
+isControlDown(): boolean	Returns true if the Control key is pressed on this event.
+isMetaDown(): boolean	Returns true if the Meta mouse button is pressed on this event.
+isShiftDown(): boolean	Returns true if the Shift key is pressed on this event.

java.awt.event.MouseEvent	
+getButton(): int	Indicates which mouse button has been clicked.
+getClickCount(): int	Returns the number of mouse clicks associated with this event.
+getPoint(): java.awt.Point	Returns a Point object containing the *x*- and *y*-coordinates.
+getX(): int	Returns the *x*-coordinate of the mouse point.
+getY(): int	Returns the *y*-coordinate of the mouse point.

Figure 16.12 The `MouseEvent` class encapsulates information for mouse events.

Since the `MouseEvent` class inherits `InputEvent`, you can use the methods defined in the `InputEvent` class on a `MouseEvent` object. For example, the `isControlDown()` method detects whether the *CTRL* key was pressed when a `MouseEvent` is fired.

Three `int` constants—`BUTTON1`, `BUTTON2`, and `BUTTON3`—are defined in `MouseEvent` to indicate the left, middle, and right mouse buttons. You can use the `getButton()` method to detect which button is pressed. For example, `getButton() == MouseEvent.BUTTON3` indicates that the right button was pressed.

detect mouse buttons

The `java.awt.Point` class represents a point on a component. The class contains two public variables, `x` and `y`, for coordinates. To create a `Point`, use the following constructor:

Point class

```
Point(int x, int y)
```

This constructs a `Point` object with the specified *x*- and *y*-coordinates. Normally, the data fields in a class should be private, but this class has two public data fields.

Java provides two listener interfaces, `MouseListener` and `MouseMotionListener`, to handle mouse events, as shown in Figure 16.13. Implement the `MouseListener` interface to listen for such actions as pressing, releasing, entering, exiting, or clicking the mouse, and implement the `MouseMotionListener` interface to listen for such actions as dragging or moving the mouse.

«interface» *java.awt.event.MouseListener*	
+mousePressed(e: MouseEvent): void	Invoked after the mouse button has been pressed on the source component.
+mouseReleased(e: MouseEvent): void	Invoked after the mouse button has been released on the source component.
+mouseClicked(e: MouseEvent): void	Invoked after the mouse button has been clicked (pressed and released) on the source component.
+mouseEntered(e: MouseEvent): void	Invoked after the mouse enters the source component.
+mouseExited(e: MouseEvent): void	Invoked after the mouse exits the source component.

«interface» *java.awt.event.MouseMotionListener*	
+mouseDragged(e: MouseEvent): void	Invoked after a mouse button is moved with a button pressed.
+mouseMoved(e: MouseEvent): void	Invoked after a mouse button is moved without a button pressed.

FIGURE 16.13 The `MouseListener` interface handles mouse pressed, released, clicked, entered, and exited events. The `MouseMotionListener` interface handles mouse dragged and moved events.

To demonstrate using mouse events, we give an example that displays a message in a panel and enables the message to be moved using a mouse. The message moves as the mouse is dragged, and it is always displayed at the mouse point. Listing 16.8 gives the program. A sample run of the program is shown in Figure 16.14.

FIGURE 16.14 You can move the message by dragging the mouse.

VideoNote

Move message using the mouse

LISTING 16.8 MoveMessageDemo.java

```
1  import java.awt.*;
2  import java.awt.event.*;
3  import javax.swing.*;
4
5  public class MoveMessageDemo extends JFrame {
6    public MoveMessageDemo() {
```

```
7       // Create a MovableMessagePanel instance for moving a message
8       MovableMessagePanel p = new MovableMessagePanel          create a panel
9         ("Welcome to Java");
10
11      // Place the message panel in the frame
12      add(p);
13    }
14
15    /** Main method */
16    public static void main(String[] args) {
17      MoveMessageDemo frame = new MoveMessageDemo();
18      frame.setTitle("MoveMessageDemo");
19      frame.setSize(200, 100);
20      frame.setLocationRelativeTo(null); // Center the frame
21      frame.setDefaultCloseOperation(JFrame.EXIT_ON_CLOSE);
22      frame.setVisible(true);
23    }
24
25    // Inner class: MovableMessagePanel draws a message
26    static class MovableMessagePanel extends JPanel {          inner class
27      private String message = "Welcome to Java";
28      private int x = 20;
29      private int y = 20;
30
31      /** Construct a panel to draw string s */
32      public MovableMessagePanel(String s) {
33        message = s;                                           set a new message
34        addMouseMotionListener(new MouseMotionListener() {     anonymous listener
35          @Override /** Handle mouse-dragged event */
36          public void mouseDragged(MouseEvent e) {             override handler
37            // Get the new location and repaint the screen
38            x = e.getX();                                      new location
39            y = e.getY();
40            repaint();                                         repaint
41          }
42
43          @Override /** Handle mouse-moved event */
44          public void mouseMoved(MouseEvent e) {
45          }
46        });
47      }
48
49      @Override
50      protected void paintComponent(Graphics g) {              paint message
51        super.paintComponent(g);
52        g.drawString(message, x, y);
53      }
54    }
55  }
```

The `MovableMessagePanel` class extends `JPanel` to draw a message (line 26). Additionally, it handles redisplaying the message when the mouse is dragged. This class is defined as an inner class inside the main class because it is used only in this class. Furthermore, the inner class is defined as static because it does not reference any instance members of the main class.

The `MouseMotionListener` interface contains two handlers, `mouseMoved` and `mouseDragged`, for handling mouse-motion events. When you move the mouse with a button pressed, the `mouseDragged` method is invoked to repaint the viewing area and display the message at the mouse point. When you move the mouse without pressing a button, the **mouseMoved** method is invoked. Because the listener is interested only in the mouse-dragged event, the **mouseDragged** method is implemented (lines 36–41).

The **mouseDragged** method is invoked when you move the mouse with a button pressed. This method obtains the mouse location using the **getX** and **getY** methods (lines 38–39) in the **MouseEvent** class. This becomes the new location for the message. Invoking the **repaint()** method (line 40) causes **paintComponent** to be invoked (line 50), which displays the message in a new location.

MyProgrammingLab™

16.14 What method do you use to get the mouse-point position for a mouse event?

16.15 What is the listener interface for mouse pressed, released, clicked, entered, and exited? What is the listener interface for mouse moved and dragged?

16.9 Listener Interface Adapters

A listener interface adapter is a class that provides the default implementation for all the methods in the listener interface.

listener interface adapter

Because the methods in the **MouseMotionListener** interface are abstract, you must implement all of them even if your program does not care about some of the events. Java provides support classes, called *listener interface adapters*, that provide default implementations for all the methods in the listener interface. The default implementation is simply an empty body. Java provides listener interface adapters for every AWT listener interface with multiple handlers. A listener interface adapter is named *X*Adapter for *X*Listener. For example, **MouseMotionAdapter** is a listener interface adapter for **MouseMotionListener**. Table 16.2 lists some listener interface adapters used in this book.

TABLE 16.2 Listener Interface Adapters

Adapter	Interface
MouseAdapter	MouseListener
MouseMotionAdapter	MouseMotionListener
KeyAdapter	KeyListener
WindowAdapter	WindowListener

Using **MouseMotionAdapter**, the code in lines 34–46 in Listing 16.8 (shown in (a)) can be replaced by the following code, as shown in (b).

```
addMouseMotionListener(
    new MouseMotionListener() {
  @Override /** Handle mouse-dragged event */
  public void mouseDragged(MouseEvent e){
    x = e.getX();
    y = e.getY();
    repaint();
  }

  @Override /** Handle mouse-moved event */
  public void mouseMoved(MouseEvent e) {
  }
});
```

(a) Using a listener interface

```
addMouseMotionListener(
    new MouseMotionAdapter() {
  @Override /** Handle mouse-dragged event */
  public void mouseDragged(MouseEvent e){
    x = e.getX();
    y = e.getY();
    repaint();
  }
});
```

(b) Using a listener interface adapter

16.16 Why does the `ActionListener` interface have no listener interface adapter?

16.17 What is the advantage of using a listener interface adapter rather than a listener interface?

16.10 Key Events

A key event is fired whenever a key is pressed, released, or typed on a component.

Key events enable the use of the keys to control and perform actions or get input from the keyboard. The `KeyEvent` object describes the nature of the event (namely, that a key has been pressed, released, or typed) and the value of the key, as shown in Figure 16.15. Java provides the `KeyListener` interface to handle key events, as shown in Figure 16.16.

FIGURE 16.15 The `KeyEvent` class encapsulates information about key events.

FIGURE 16.16 The `KeyListener` interface handles key pressed, released, and typed events.

The `keyPressed` handler is invoked when a key is pressed, the `keyReleased` handler is invoked when a key is released, and the `keyTyped` handler is invoked when a Unicode character is entered. If a key does not have a Unicode (e.g., function keys, modifier keys, action keys, and control keys), the `keyTyped` handler will not be invoked.

Every key event has an associated key character or key code that is returned by the `getKeyChar()` or `getKeyCode()` method in `KeyEvent`. The key codes are constants defined in the `KeyEvent` class. Table 16.3 lists some constants. See the Java API for a complete list of the constants. For a key of the Unicode character, the key code is the same as the Unicode value. For the key-pressed and key-released events, `getKeyCode()` returns the value as defined in the table. For the key-typed event, `getKeyCode()` returns `VK_UNDEFINED` (0), and `getKeyChar()` returns the character entered.

The program in Listing 16.9 displays a user-input character. The user can move the character up, down, left, and right, using the arrow keys `VK_UP`, `VK_DOWN`, `VK_LEFT`, and `VK_RIGHT`. Figure 16.17 contains a sample run of the program.

TABLE 16.3 Key Constants

Constant	Description	Constant	Description
VK_HOME	The Home key	VK_SHIFT	The Shift key
VK_END	The End key	VK_BACK_SPACE	The Backspace key
VK_PGUP	The Page Up key	VK_CAPS_LOCK	The Caps Lock key
VK_PGDN	The Page Down key	VK_NUM_LOCK	The Num Lock key
VK_UP	The up-arrow key	VK_ENTER	The Enter key
VK_DOWN	The down-arrow key	VK_UNDEFINED	The **keyCode** unknown
VK_LEFT	The left-arrow key	VK_F1 to VK_F12	The function keys from F1 to F12
VK_RIGHT	The right-arrow key		
VK_ESCAPE	The Esc key	VK_0 to VK_9	The number keys from 0 to 9
VK_TAB	The Tab key	VK_A to VK_Z	The letter keys from A to Z
VK_CONTROL	The Control key		

FIGURE 16.17 The program responds to key events by displaying a character and moving it up, down, left, or right.

LISTING 16.9 KeyEventDemo.java

```
1   import java.awt.*;
2   import java.awt.event.*;
3   import javax.swing.*;
4
5   public class KeyEventDemo extends JFrame {
6     private KeyboardPanel keyboardPanel = new KeyboardPanel();
7
8     /** Initialize UI */
9     public KeyEventDemo() {
10      // Add the keyboard panel to accept and display user input
11      add(keyboardPanel);
12
13      // Set focus
14      keyboardPanel.setFocusable(true);
15    }
16
17    /** Main method */
18    public static void main(String[] args) {
19      KeyEventDemo frame = new KeyEventDemo();
20      frame.setTitle("KeyEventDemo");
21      frame.setSize(300, 300);
22      frame.setLocationRelativeTo(null); // Center the frame
23      frame.setDefaultCloseOperation(JFrame.EXIT_ON_CLOSE);
24      frame.setVisible(true);
25    }
26
27    // Inner class: KeyboardPanel for receiving key input
28    static class KeyboardPanel extends JPanel {
```

create a panel

focusable

inner class

```
29    private int x = 100;
30    private int y = 100;
31    private char keyChar = 'A'; // Default key
32
33    public KeyboardPanel() {
34      addKeyListener(new KeyAdapter() {          register listener
35        @Override
36        public void keyPressed(KeyEvent e) {      override handler
37          switch (e.getKeyCode()) {
38            case KeyEvent.VK_DOWN: y += 10; break;
39            case KeyEvent.VK_UP: y -= 10; break;
40            case KeyEvent.VK_LEFT: x -= 10; break;
41            case KeyEvent.VK_RIGHT: x += 10; break;
42            default: keyChar = e.getKeyChar();     get the key pressed
43          }
44
45          repaint();                              repaint
46        }
47      });
48    }
49
50    @Override /** Draw the character */
51    protected void paintComponent(Graphics g) {
52      super.paintComponent(g);
53
54      g.setFont(new Font("TimesRoman", Font.PLAIN, 24));
55      g.drawString(String.valueOf(keyChar), x, y);   redraw character
56    }
57  }
58 }
```

The KeyboardPanel class extends JPanel to display a character (line 28). This class is defined as an inner class inside the main class, because it is used only in this class. Furthermore, the inner class is defined as static, because it does not reference any instance members of the main class.

Because the program gets input from the keyboard, it listens for KeyEvent and extends KeyAdapter to handle key input (line 34).

When a key is pressed, the keyPressed handler is invoked. The program uses e.getKeyCode() to obtain the key code and e.getKeyChar() to get the character for the key. When a nonarrow key is pressed, the character is displayed (line 42). When an arrow key is pressed, the character moves in the direction indicated by the arrow key (lines 38–41).

Only a focused component can receive KeyEvent. To make a component focusable, set its focusable property to true (line 14).

focusable

Every time the component is repainted, a new font is created for the Graphics object in line 54. This is not efficient—it would be better to create the font once as a data field.

efficient?

We can now add more control for our ControlCircle example in Listing 16.3 to increase/decrease the circle radius by clicking the left/right mouse button or by pressing the UP and DOWN arrow keys. The new program is given in Listing 16.10.

LISTING 16.10 ControlCircleWithMouseAndKey.java

```
1  import javax.swing.*;
2  import java.awt.*;
3  import java.awt.event.*;
4
5  public class ControlCircleWithMouseAndKey extends JFrame {
6    private JButton jbtEnlarge = new JButton("Enlarge");
7    private JButton jbtShrink = new JButton("Shrink");
```

```
 8      private CirclePanel canvas = new CirclePanel();
 9
10    public ControlCircleWithMouseAndKey() {
11      JPanel panel = new JPanel(); // Use the panel to group buttons
12      panel.add(jbtEnlarge);
13      panel.add(jbtShrink);
14
15      this.add(canvas, BorderLayout.CENTER); // Add canvas to center
16      this.add(panel, BorderLayout.SOUTH); // Add buttons to the frame
17
18      jbtEnlarge.addActionListener(new ActionListener() {
19        @Override
20        public void actionPerformed(ActionEvent e) {
21          canvas.enlarge();
22          canvas.requestFocusInWindow();
23        }
24      });
25
26      jbtShrink.addActionListener(new ActionListener() {
27        @Override
28        public void actionPerformed(ActionEvent e) {
29          canvas.shrink();
30          canvas.requestFocusInWindow();
31        }
32      });
33
34      canvas.addMouseListener(new MouseAdapter() {
35        @Override
36        public void mouseClicked(MouseEvent e) {
37          if (e.getButton() == MouseEvent.BUTTON1)
38            canvas.enlarge();
39          else if (e.getButton() == MouseEvent.BUTTON3)
40            canvas.shrink();
41        }
42      });
43
44      canvas.setFocusable(true);
45      canvas.addKeyListener(new KeyAdapter() {
46        @Override
47        public void keyPressed(KeyEvent e) {
48          if (e.getKeyCode() == KeyEvent.VK_UP)
49            canvas.enlarge();
50          else if (e.getKeyCode() == KeyEvent.VK_DOWN)
51            canvas.shrink();
52        }
53      });
54    }
55
56    /** Main method */
57    public static void main(String[] args) {
58      JFrame frame = new ControlCircleWithMouseAndKey();
59      frame.setTitle("ControlCircle");
60      frame.setLocationRelativeTo(null); // Center the frame
61      frame.setDefaultCloseOperation(JFrame.EXIT_ON_CLOSE);
62      frame.setSize(200, 200);
63      frame.setVisible(true);
64    }
65
66    class CirclePanel extends JPanel { // Inner class
67      private int radius = 5; // Default circle radius
```

create/register listener

request focus

request focus

left button?

right button?

UP pressed?

DOWN pressed?

```
68
69       /** Enlarge the circle */
70       public void enlarge() {
71         radius++;
72         repaint();
73       }
74
75       /** Shrink the circle */
76       public void shrink() {
77         if (radius >= 1) radius--;
78         repaint();
79       }
80
81       @Override
82       protected void paintComponent(Graphics g) {
83         super.paintComponent(g);
84         g.drawOval(getWidth() / 2 - radius, getHeight() / 2 - radius,
85           2 * radius, 2 * radius);
86       }
87     }
88 }
```

A listener for **MouseEvent** is created to handle mouse-clicked events in lines 34–42. If the left mouse button is clicked, the circle is enlarged (lines 37–38); if the right mouse button is clicked, the circle is shrunk (lines 39–40).

    A listener for **KeyEvent** is created to handle key-pressed events in lines 45–53. If the UP arrow key is pressed, the circle is enlarged (lines 48–49); if the DOWN arrow key is pressed, the circle is shrunk (lines 50–51).

    Invoking **setFocusable** on **canvas** makes **canvas** focusable. However, once a button is clicked, the canvas is no longer focused. Invoking **canvas.requestFocusInWindow()** (lines 22, 30) resets the focus on **canvas** so that **canvas** can listen for key events.

MouseEvent

KeyEvent

setFocusable
requestFocusInWindow()

16.18 What method do you use to get the timestamp for an action event, a mouse event, or a key event?

16.19 What method do you use to get the key character for a key event?

16.20 How do you set focus on a component so it can listen for key events?

16.21 Does every key in the keyboard have a Unicode? Is a key code in the **KeyEvent** class equivalent to a Unicode?

16.22 Is the **keyPressed** handler invoked after a key is pressed? Is the **keyReleased** handler invoked after a key is released? Is the **keyTyped** handler invoked after *any* key is typed?

✓Check
Point

MyProgrammingLab™

16.11 Animation Using the **Timer** Class

*A **Timer** is a source object that fires **ActionEvent** at a fixed rate.*

Key
Point

Not all source objects are GUI components. The **javax.swing.Timer** class is a source component that fires an **ActionEvent** at a predefined rate. Figure 16.18 lists some of the methods in the class.

    A **Timer** object serves as the source of an **ActionEvent**. The listeners must be instances of **ActionListener** and registered with a **Timer** object. You create a **Timer** object using its sole constructor with a delay and a listener, where **delay** specifies the number of milliseconds between two action events. You can add additional listeners using the **addActionListener** method and adjust the **delay** using the **setDelay** method. To start the timer, invoke the **start()** method; to stop the timer, invoke the **stop()** method.

javax.swing.Timer	
+Timer(delay: int, listener: ActionListener)	Creates a Timer object with a specified delay in milliseconds and an ActionListener.
+addActionListener(listener: ActionListener): void	Adds an ActionListener to the timer.
+start(): void	Starts this timer.
+stop(): void	Stops this timer.
+setDelay(delay: int): void	Sets a new delay value for this timer.

FIGURE 16.18   A Timer object fires an ActionEvent at a fixed rate.

The Timer class can be used to control animations. Listing 16.11 gives a program that displays two messages in separate panels (see Figure 16.19). You can use the mouse button to control the animation speed for each message. The speed increases when the left mouse button is clicked and decreases when the right button is clicked.

FIGURE 16.19   Two messages move in the panels.

LISTING 16.11   AnimationDemo.java

```java
1   import java.awt.*;
2   import java.awt.event.*;
3   import javax.swing.*;
4
5   public class AnimationDemo extends JFrame {
6     public AnimationDemo() {
7       // Create two MovingMessagePanel for displaying two moving messages
8       this.setLayout(new GridLayout(2, 1));
9       add(new MovingMessagePanel("message 1 moving?"));
10      add(new MovingMessagePanel("message 2 moving?"));
11    }
12
13    /** Main method */
14    public static void main(String[] args) {
15      AnimationDemo frame = new AnimationDemo();
16      frame.setTitle("AnimationDemo");
17      frame.setLocationRelativeTo(null); // Center the frame
18      frame.setDefaultCloseOperation(JFrame.EXIT_ON_CLOSE);
19      frame.setSize(280, 100);
20      frame.setVisible(true);
21    }
22
23    // Inner class: Displaying a moving message
24    static class MovingMessagePanel extends JPanel {
25      private String message = "Welcome to Java";
26      private int xCoordinate = 0;
27      private int yCoordinate = 20;
28      private Timer timer = new Timer(1000, new TimerListener());
```

create message panel

create timer

```
29
30      public MovingMessagePanel(String message) {
31        this.message = message;
32
33        // Start timer for animation
34        timer.start();
35
36        // Control animation speed using mouse buttons
37        this.addMouseListener(new MouseAdapter() {
38          @Override
39          public void mouseClicked(MouseEvent e) {
40            int delay = timer.getDelay();
41            if (e.getButton() == MouseEvent.BUTTON1)
42              timer.setDelay(delay > 10 ? delay - 10 : 0);
43            else if (e.getButton() == MouseEvent.BUTTON3)
44              timer.setDelay(delay < 50000 ? delay + 10 : 50000);
45          }
46        });
47      }
48
49      @Override /** Paint the message */
50      protected void paintComponent(Graphics g) {
51        super.paintComponent(g);
52
53        if (xCoordinate > getWidth()) {
54          xCoordinate = -20;
55        }
56        xCoordinate += 5;
57        g.drawString(message, xCoordinate, yCoordinate);
58      }
59
60      class TimerListener implements ActionListener {
61        @Override
62        public void actionPerformed(ActionEvent e) {
63          repaint();
64        }
65      }
66    }
67  }
```

set message

start timer

mouse listener

reset *x*-coordinate

move message

listener class
event handler
repaint

Two instances of MovingMessagePanel are created to display two messages (lines 9–10). The MovingMessagePanel class extends JPanel to display a message (line 24). This class is defined as an inner class inside the main class, because it is used only in this class. Furthermore, the inner class is defined as static, because it does not reference any instance members of the main class.

An inner class listener is defined in line 60 to listen for ActionEvent from a timer. Line 28 creates a Timer for the listener, and the timer is started in line 34. The timer fires an ActionEvent every 1 second initially, and the listener responds in line 62 to repaint the panel. When a panel is painted, its *x*-coordinate is increased (line 56), so the message is displayed to the right. When the *x*-coordinate exceeds the bound of the panel, it is reset to -20 (line 54), so the message continues moving from left to right circularly.

A mouse listener is registered with the panel to listen for the mouse click event (lines 37–46). When the left mouse button is clicked, a new reduced delay time is set for the timer (lines 41–42). When the right mouse button is clicked, a new increased delay time is set for the timer (lines 43–44). The minimum delay time is 0 and the maximum can be Integer.MAX_VALUE, but it is set to 50000 in this program (line 44).

In Section 13.9, Case Study: The StillClock Class, you drew a StillClock to show the current time. The clock does not tick after it is displayed. What can you do to make the clock display a new current time every second? The key to making the clock tick is to repaint it every second with a new current time. You can use a timer to control the repainting of the clock with the code in Listing 16.12.

VideoNote

Animate a clock

create a clock

create a timer
start timer

listener class

implement handler

set new time
repaint

LISTING 16.12 ClockAnimation.java

```java
 1  import java.awt.event.*;
 2  import javax.swing.*;
 3
 4  public class ClockAnimation extends JFrame {
 5    private StillClock clock = new StillClock();
 6
 7    public ClockAnimation() {
 8      add(clock);
 9
10      // Create a timer with delay 1000 ms
11      Timer timer = new Timer(1000, new TimerListener());
12      timer.start();
13    }
14
15    private class TimerListener implements ActionListener {
16      @Override /** Handle the action event */
17      public void actionPerformed(ActionEvent e) {
18        // Set new time and repaint the clock to display current time
19        clock.setCurrentTime();
20        clock.repaint();
21      }
22    }
23
24    /** Main method */
25    public static void main(String[] args) {
26      JFrame frame = new ClockAnimation();
27      frame.setTitle("ClockAnimation");
28      frame.setSize(200, 200);
29      frame.setLocationRelativeTo(null); // Center the frame
30      frame.setDefaultCloseOperation(JFrame.EXIT_ON_CLOSE);
31      frame.setVisible(true);
32    }
33  }
```

The program displays a running clock, as shown in Figure 16.20. `ClockAnimation` creates a `StillClock` (line 5). Line 11 creates a `Timer` for a `ClockAnimation`. The timer is started in line 12. The timer fires an `ActionEvent` every second, and the listener responds to set a new time (line 19) and repaint the clock (line 20). The `setCurrentTime()` method defined in `StillClock` sets the current time in the clock.

FIGURE 16.20 A live clock is displayed in the panel.

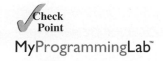

16.23 How do you create a timer? How do you start a timer? How do you stop a timer?

16.24 Does the `Timer` class have a no-arg constructor? Can you add multiple listeners to a timer?

KEY TERMS

anonymous inner class 609	event source object 602
event 602	event listener object 603
event-driven programming 602	inner class 606
event handler 604	listener interface adapter 620
event-listener interface 603	source object 602
event object 602	

CHAPTER SUMMARY

1. The root class of the event classes is `java.util.EventObject`. The subclasses of `EventObject` deal with special types of events, such as action events, window events, component events, mouse events, and key events. You can identify the source object of an event by using the `getSource()` instance method in the `EventObject` class. If a component can fire an event, any subclass of the component can fire the same type of event.

2. The listener object's class must implement the corresponding *event-listener interface*. Java provides a listener interface for every event class. The listener interface is usually named *X*`Listener` for *X*`Event`, with the exception of `MouseMotionListener`. For example, the corresponding listener interface for `ActionEvent` is `ActionListener`; each listener for `ActionEvent` should implement the `ActionListener` interface. The listener interface contains the method(s), known as the *handler(s)*, which process the events.

3. The listener object must be registered by the *source object*. Registration methods depend on the event type. For `ActionEvent`, the method is `addActionListener`. In general, the method is named `add`*X*`Listener` for *X*`Event`.

4. An *inner class*, or *nested class*, is defined within the scope of another class. An inner class can reference the data and methods defined in the outer class in which it nests, so you need not pass the reference of the outer class to the constructor of the inner class.

5. *Listener interface adapters* are support classes that provide default implementations for all the methods in the listener interface. Java provides listener interface adapters for every AWT listener interface with multiple handlers. A listener interface adapter is named *X*`Adapter` for *X*`Listener`.

6. A source object may fire several types of events. For each event, the source object maintains a list of registered listeners and notifies them by invoking the *handler* on the listener object to process the event.

7. A `MouseEvent` is fired whenever a mouse is pressed, released, clicked, entered, exited, moved, or dragged on a component. The mouse-event object captures the event, such as the number of clicks associated with it or the location (*x*- and *y*-coordinates) of the mouse point.

8. Java provides two listener interfaces, `MouseListener` and `MouseMotionListener`, to handle mouse events. Java implements the `MouseListener` interface to listen for such actions as mouse pressed, released, clicked, entered, or exited, and the `MouseMotionListener` interface to listen for such actions as mouse dragged or moved.

9. A `KeyEvent` is fired when a key is pressed, released, or typed. The key value and key character can be obtained from the key-event object.

10. A listener's `keyPressed` handler is invoked when a key is pressed, its `keyReleased` handler is invoked when a key is released, and its `keyTyped` handler is invoked when a Unicode character key is entered. If a key does not have a Unicode (e.g., function keys, modifier keys, action keys, and control keys), a listener's `keyTyped` handler will be not be invoked.

11. You can use the `Timer` class to control Java animations. A timer fires an `ActionEvent` at a fixed rate. The listener updates the painting to simulate an animation.

TEST QUESTIONS

Do the test questions for this chapter online at www.cs.armstrong.edu/liang/intro9e/test.html.

MyProgrammingLab™

PROGRAMMING EXERCISES

Sections 16.2–16.7

*16.1 (*Pick four cards*) Write a program that lets the user click the *Refresh* button to display four cards from a deck of 52 cards, as shown in Figure 16.21a. (*Hint*: See Listing 6.2 on how to draw four cards randomly.)

(a)

(b)

(c)

FIGURE 16.21   (a) Exercise 16.1 displays four cards randomly. (b) Exercise 16.3 uses the buttons to move the ball. (c) Exercise 16.4 performs addition, subtraction, multiplication, and division on double numbers.

16.2 (*Find which button has been clicked on the console*) Add the code to Programming Exercise 12.1 that will display a message on the console indicating which button has been clicked.

*16.3 (*Move the ball*) Write a program that moves the ball in a panel. You should define a panel class for displaying the ball and provide the methods for moving the ball left, right, up, and down, as shown in Figure 16.21b. Check the boundary to prevent the ball from moving out of sight completely.

*16.4 (*Create a simple calculator*) Write a program to perform addition, subtraction, multiplication, and division, as shown in Figure 16.21c.

*16.5 (*Create an investment-value calculator*) Write a program that calculates the future value of an investment at a given interest rate for a specified number of years. The formula for the calculation is:

```
futureValue = investmentAmount * (1 + monthlyInterestRate)^(years*12)
```

Use text fields for the investment amount, number of years, and annual interest rate. Display the future amount in a text field when the user clicks the *Calculate* button, as shown in Figure 16.22a.

(a)   (b)   (c)

FIGURE 16.22   (a) The user enters the investment amount, years, and interest rate to compute future value. (b) Exercise 16.8 displays the mouse position. (c) Exercise 16.9 uses the arrow keys to draw the lines.

Sections 16.8–16.9

**16.6 (*Alternate two messages*) Write a program to rotate with a mouse click the two messages `Java is fun` and `Java is powerful` displayed on a panel.

*16.7 (*Set background color using a mouse*) Write a program that displays the background color of a panel as black when the mouse button is pressed and as white when the mouse button is released.

*16.8 (*Display the mouse position*) Write two programs, such that one displays the mouse position when the mouse button is clicked (see Figure 16.22b) and the other displays the mouse position when the mouse button is pressed and ceases to display it when the mouse button is released.

Section 16.10

*16.9 (*Draw lines using the arrow keys*) Write a program that draws line segments using the arrow keys. The line starts from the center of the frame and draws toward east, north, west, or south when the right-arrow key, up-arrow key, left-arrow key, or down-arrow key is pressed, as shown in Figure 16.22c.

**16.10 (*Enter and display a string*) Write a program that receives a string from the keyboard and displays it on a panel. The *Enter* key signals the end of a string. Whenever a new string is entered, it is displayed on the panel.

*16.11 (*Display a character*) Write a program to get a character input from the keyboard and display the character where the mouse points.

Section 16.11

**16.12 (*Display a running fan*) Listing 13.4, DrawArcs.java, displays a motionless fan. Write a program that displays a running fan.

16.13 (*Slide show*) Twenty-five slides are stored as image files (slide0.jpg**, **slide1.jpg**, . . ., **slide24.jpg**) in the **image** directory downloadable along with the source code in the book. The size of each image is 800 × 600. Write a Java application that automatically displays the slides repeatedly. Each slide is shown for a second. The slides are displayed in order. When the last slide finishes, the first slide is redisplayed, and so on. (*Hint*: Place a label in the frame and set a slide as an image icon in the label.)

VideoNote

Animate a rising flag

**16.14 (*Raise flag*) Write a Java program that animates raising a flag, as shown in Figure 16.1. (See Section 13.10, Displaying Images, for how to display images.)

**16.15 (*Racing car*) Write a Java program that simulates car racing, as shown in Figure 16.23a. The car moves from left to right. When it hits the right end, it restarts from the left and continues the same process. You can use a timer to control animation. Redraw the car with a new base coordinates (x, y), as shown in Figure 16.23b. Also let the user pause/resume the animation with a button press/release and increase/decrease the car speed by pressing the UP and DOWN arrow keys.

(a) (b)

FIGURE 16.23 (a) Exercise 16.15 displays a moving car. (b) You can redraw a car with a new base point.

*16.16 (*Display a flashing label*) Write a program that displays a flashing label. (*Hint*: To make the label flash, you need to repaint the panel alternately with the label and without it (a blank screen) at a fixed rate. Use a **boolean** variable to control the alternation.)

*16.17 (*Control a moving label*) Modify Listing 16.11, AnimationDemo.java, to control a moving label using the mouse. The label freezes when the mouse is pressed, and moves again when the button is released.

Comprehensive

*16.18 (*Move a circle using keys*) Write a program that moves a circle up, down, left, or right using the arrow keys.

VideoNote

Check mouse point location

16.19 (*Geometry: inside a circle?*) Write a program that draws a fixed circle centered at (100**, **60**) with radius **50**. Whenever the mouse is moved, display a message indicating whether the mouse point is inside the circle at the mouse point or outside of it, as shown in Figure 16.24a.

(a) (b) (c)

FIGURE 16.24 Detect whether a point is inside a circle, a rectangle, or a polygon.

**16.20 (*Geometry: inside a rectangle?*) Write a program that draws a fixed rectangle centered at (100, 60) with width 100 and height 40. Whenever the mouse is moved, display a message indicating whether the mouse point is inside the rectangle at the mouse point or outside of it, as shown in Figure 16.24b. To detect whether a point is inside a rectangle, use the `MyRectangle2D` class defined in Programming Exercise 10.13.

**16.21 (*Geometry: inside a polygon?*) Write a program that draws a fixed polygon with points at (40, 20), (70, 40), (60, 80), (45, 45), and (20, 60). Whenever the mouse is moved, display a message indicating whether the mouse point is inside the polygon at the mouse point or outside of it, as shown in Figure 16.24c. To detect whether a point is inside a polygon, use the `contains` method defined in the `Polygon` class (see Figure 13.13).

***16.22 (*Game: bean-machine animation*) Write a program that animates the bean machine introduced in Programming Exercise 6.21. The animation terminates after ten balls are dropped, as shown in Figure 16.25.

FIGURE 16.25 The balls are dropped into the bean machine.

***16.23 (*Geometry: closest pair of points*) Write a program that lets the user click on the panel to dynamically create points. Initially, the panel is empty. When a panel has two or more points, highlight the pair of closest points. Whenever a new point is created, a new pair of closest points is highlighted. Display the points using small circles and highlight the points using filled circles, as shown in Figure 16.26a–c. (*Hint*: store the points in an `ArrayList`.)

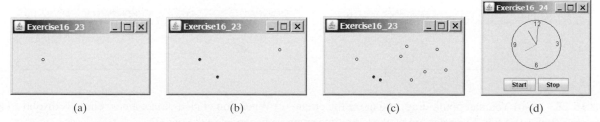

(a) (b) (c) (d)

FIGURE 16.26 Exercise 16.23 allows the user to create new points with a mouse click and highlights the pair of the closest points. Exercise 16.24 allows the user to start and stop a clock.

*16.24 (*Control a clock*) Modify Listing 16.12, ClockAnimation.java, to add the two methods `start()` and `stop()` to start and stop the clock. Write a program that lets the user control the clock with the *Start* and *Stop* buttons, as shown in Figure 16.26d.

***16.25 (*Game: hit balloons*) Write a program that displays a balloon in a random position in a panel (Figure 16.27a). Use the left- and right-arrow keys to point the gun left or right to aim at the balloon (Figure 16.27b). Press the up-arrow key to fire a small ball from the gun (Figure 16.27c–d). Once the ball hits the balloon, the debris is displayed (Figure 16.27e) and a new balloon is displayed in a random location (Figure 16.27f). If the ball misses the balloon, the ball disappears once it hits the boundary of the panel. You can then press the up-arrow key to fire another ball. Whenever you press the left- or the right-arrow key, the gun turns 5 degrees left or right. (Instructors may modify the game as follows: 1. Display the number of the balloons destroyed; 2. display a countdown timer (e.g., 60 seconds) and terminate the game once the time expires; and/or 3. allow the balloon to rise dynamically.)

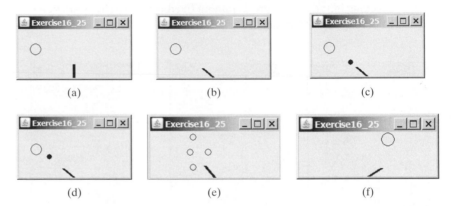

(a)   (b)   (c)

(d)   (e)   (f)

FIGURE 16.27 (a) A balloon is displayed in a random location. (b) Press the left-/right-arrow keys to aim at the balloon. (c) Press the up-arrow key to fire a ball. (d) The ball moves straight toward the balloon. (e) The ball hits the balloon. (f) A new balloon is displayed in a random position.

**16.26 (*Move a circle using mouse*) Write a program that displays a circle with radius 10 pixels. You can point the mouse inside the circle and drag (i.e., move with mouse pressed) the circle wherever the mouse goes, as shown in Figure 16.28a–b.

(a)   (b)   (c)   (d)

FIGURE 16.28 (a–b) You can point, drag, and move the circle. (c) When you click a circle, a new circle is displayed at a random location. (d) After 20 circles are clicked, the time spent is displayed in the panel.

***16.27 (*Game: eye-hand coordination*) Write a program that displays a circle of radius 10 pixels filled with a random color at a random location on a panel, as shown in Figure 16.28c. When you click the circle, it disappears and a new random-color circle is displayed at another random location. After twenty circles are clicked, display the time spent in the panel, as shown in Figure 16.28d.

***16.28   (*Simulation: self-avoiding random walk*) A self-avoiding walk in a lattice is a path from one point to another that does not visit the same point twice. Self-avoiding walks have applications in physics, chemistry, and mathematics. They can be used to model chain-like entities such as solvents and polymers. Write a program that displays a random path that starts from the center and ends at a point on the boundary, as shown in Figure 16.29a, or ends at a dead-end point (i.e., surrounded by four points that have already been visited), as shown in Figure 16.29b. Assume the size of the lattice is 16 by 16.

FIGURE 16.29   (a) A path ends at a boundary point. (b) A path ends at dead-end point. (c–d) Animation shows the progress of a path step by step.

***16.29   (*Animation: self-avoiding random walk*) Revise the preceding exercise to display the walk step by step in an animation, as shown in Figure 16.29c–d.

**16.30   (*Simulation: self-avoiding random walk*) Write a simulation program to show that the chance of getting dead-end paths increases as the grid size increases. Your program simulates lattices with size from 10 to 80. For each lattice size, simulate a self-avoiding random walk 10,000 times and display the probability of the dead-end paths, as shown in the following sample output:

```
For a lattice of size 10, the probability of dead-end paths is 10.6%
For a lattice of size 11, the probability of dead-end paths is 14.0%
. . .
For a lattice of size 80, the probability of dead-end paths is 99.5%
```

*16.31   (*Geometry: display an n-sided regular polygon*) Programming Exercise 13.25 created the `RegularPolygonPanel` for displaying an *n*-sided regular polygon. Write a program that displays a regular polygon and uses two buttons named *+1* and *−1* to increase or decrease the size of the polygon, as shown in Figure 16.30a–b. Also enable the user to increase or decrease the size by clicking the right or left mouse button and by pressing the UP and DOWN arrow keys.

**16.32   (*Geometry: add and remove points*) Write a program that lets the user click on a panel to dynamically create and remove points (see Figure 16.30c). When the user right-clicks the mouse, a point is created and displayed at the mouse point. The user can remove a point by pointing to it and left-clicking the mouse.

**16.33   (*Geometry: pendulum*) Write a program that animates a pendulum swinging, as shown in Figure 16.31. Press the UP arrow key to increase the speed and the DOWN key to decrease it. Press the *S* key to stop animation and the *R* key to resume it.

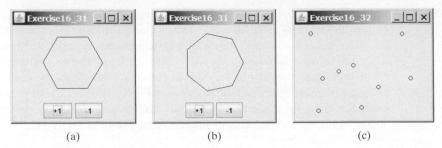

FIGURE 16.30   Clicking the $+1$ or -1 button increases or decreases the number of sides of a regular polygon in Exercise 16.31. Exercise 16.32 allows the user to create/remove points dynamically.

FIGURE 16.31   Exercise 16.33 animates a pendulum swinging.

**16.34   (*Game: hangman*) Write a program that animates a hangman game swinging, as shown in Figure 16.32. Press the UP arrow key to increase the speed and the DOWN arrow key to decrease it. Press the *S* key to stop animation and the *R* key to resume it.

FIGURE 16.32   The program animates a hangman game swinging.

***16.35   (*Animation: ball on curve*) Write a program that animates a ball moving along a sine curve, as shown in Figure 16.33. When the ball gets to the right border, it starts over from the left. Enable the user to resume/pause the animation with a click on the left/right mouse button.

*16.36   (*Flip coins*) Write a program that displays heads (**H**) or tails (**T**) for each of nine coins, as shown in Figure 16.34a–b. When a cell is clicked, the coin is flipped. A cell is a **JLabel**. Write a custom cell class that extends **JLabel**

Figure 16.33 The program animates a ball travelling along a sine curve.

(a) (b) (c) (d)

Figure 16.34 (a–b) Exercise 16.36 enables the user to click a cell to flip a coin. (c) The user can drag the circles. (d) Exercise 16.38 draws an arrow line randomly.

with the mouse listener for handling the clicks. When the program starts, all cells initially display **H**.

*16.37 (*Two movable vertices and their distances*) Write a program that displays two circles with radius **20** at location (**20, 20**) and (**120, 50**) with a line connecting the two circles, as shown in Figure 16.34c. The distance between the circles is displayed along the line. The user can drag a circle. When that happens, the circle and its line are moved and the distance between the circles is updated. Your program should not allow the circles to get too close. Keep them at least **70** pixels apart between the two circles' centers.

**16.38 (*Draw an arrow line*) Write a static method that draws an arrow line from a starting point to an ending point using the following method header:

```
public static void drawArrowLine(int x1, int y1,
   int x2, int y2, Graphics g)
```

Write a test program that randomly draws an arrow line when the *Draw a Random Arrow Line* button is clicked, as shown in Figure 16.34d.

16.39 (*Geometry: find the bounding rectangle*) Write a program that enables the user to add and remove points in a two-dimensional plane dynamically, as shown in Figure 16.35a–b. A minimum bounding rectangle is updated as the points are added and removed. Assume the radius of each point is **10 pixels.

*16.40 (*Display random 0 or 1*) Write a program that displays a 10-by-10 square matrix, as shown in Figure 16.35c. Each element in the matrix is 0 or 1, randomly generated with a click of the *Refresh* button. Display each number centered in a label.

FIGURE 16.35 (a–b) Exercise 16.39 enables the user to add/remove points dynamically and displays the bounding rectangle. (c) Exercise 16.40 displays 0s and 1s randomly with a click of the *Refresh* button.

GUI COMPONENTS

Objectives

- To create graphical user interfaces with various user-interface components (§§17.2–17.8).

- To create listeners for `JCheckBox`, `JRadioButton`, and `JTextField` (§17.2).

- To enter multiple-line texts using `JTextArea` (§17.3).

- To select a single item using `JComboBox` (§17.4).

- To select a single or multiple items using `JList` (§17.5).

- To select a range of values using `JScrollBar` (§17.6).

- To select a range of values using `JSlider` and explore differences between `JScrollBar` and `JSlider` (§17.7).

- To display multiple windows in an application (§17.8).

17.1 Introduction

Swing provides many GUI components for developing a comprehensive user interface.

Previous chapters briefly introduced `JButton`, `JCheckBox`, `JRadioButton`, `JLabel`, `JTextField`, and `JPasswordField`. This chapter introduces in detail how the events are processed for these components. We will also introduce `JTextArea`, `JComboBox`, `JList`, `JScrollBar`, and `JSlider`. More GUI components such as `JMenu`, `JToolBar`, `JTabbedPane`, `JSplitPane`, `JSpinner`, `JTree`, and `JTable` will be introduced in bonus Web Chapters 36–40.

17.2 Events for **JCheckBox**, **JRadioButton**, and **JTextField**

A GUI component may fire many types of events. `ActionEvent` *is commonly processed for* `JCheckBox`, `JRadioButton`, *and* `JTextField`, *and* `ItemEvent` *can be used for* `JCheckBox` *and* `JRadioButton`.

In the previous chapter, you learned how to handle an action event for `JButton`. This section introduces handling events for check boxes, radio buttons, and text fields.

When a `JCheckBox` or a `JRadioButton` is clicked (that is, checked or unchecked), it fires an `ItemEvent` and then an `ActionEvent`. When you press the *Enter* key on a `JTextField`, it fires an `ActionEvent`.

Listing 17.1 gives a program that demonstrates how to handle events from check boxes, radio buttons, and text fields. The program displays a label and allows the user to set the colors of the text in the label using radio buttons, set fonts using check boxes, and set new text entered from a text field, as shown in Figure 17.1.

FIGURE 17.1 The program demonstrates check boxes, radio buttons, and text fields.

LISTING 17.1 GUIEventDemo.java

```
1   import java.awt.*;
2   import java.awt.event.*;
3   import javax.swing.*;
4   import javax.swing.border.*;
5
6   public class GUIEventDemo extends JFrame {
7     private JLabel jlblMessage = new JLabel("Hello", JLabel.CENTER);
8
9     // Create check boxes to set the font for the message
10    private JCheckBox jchkBold = new JCheckBox("Bold");
11    private JCheckBox jchkItalic = new JCheckBox("Italic");
12
13    // Create three radio buttons to set message colors
14    private JRadioButton jrbRed = new JRadioButton("Red");
15    private JRadioButton jrbGreen = new JRadioButton("Green");
16    private JRadioButton jrbBlue = new JRadioButton("Blue");
17
18    // Create a text field for setting a new message
```

create label

create check boxes

create radio buttons

```
19    private JTextField jtfMessage = new JTextField(10);          create text field
20
21    public static void main(String[] args) {
22      GUIEventDemo frame = new GUIEventDemo();                    create frame
23      frame.pack();                                              pack frame
24      frame.setTitle("GUIEventDemo");
25      frame.setLocationRelativeTo(null); // Center the frame
26      frame.setDefaultCloseOperation(JFrame.EXIT_ON_CLOSE);
27      frame.setVisible(true);
28    }
29
30    public GUIEventDemo() {                                       create UI
31      jlblMessage.setBorder(new LineBorder(Color.BLACK, 2));
32      add(jlblMessage, BorderLayout.CENTER);                     place label
33
34      // Create a panel to hold check boxes
35      JPanel jpCheckBoxes = new JPanel();                        panel for check boxes
36      jpCheckBoxes.setLayout(new GridLayout(2, 1));
37      jpCheckBoxes.add(jchkBold);
38      jpCheckBoxes.add(jchkItalic);
39      add(jpCheckBoxes, BorderLayout.EAST);
40
41      // Create a panel to hold radio buttons
42      JPanel jpRadioButtons = new JPanel();                      panel for radio buttons
43      jpRadioButtons.setLayout(new GridLayout(3, 1));
44      jpRadioButtons.add(jrbRed);
45      jpRadioButtons.add(jrbGreen);
46      jpRadioButtons.add(jrbBlue);
47      add(jpRadioButtons, BorderLayout.WEST);
48
49      // Create a radio-button group to group three buttons
50      ButtonGroup group = new ButtonGroup();                     group buttons
51      group.add(jrbRed);
52      group.add(jrbGreen);
53      group.add(jrbBlue);
54
55      // Set initial message color to blue
56      jrbBlue.setSelected(true);
57      jlblMessage.setForeground(Color.blue);
58
59      // Create a panel to hold label and text field
60      JPanel jpTextField = new JPanel();                         panel for text field
61      jpTextField.setLayout(new BorderLayout(5, 0));
62      jpTextField.add(
63        new JLabel("Enter a new message"), BorderLayout.WEST);
64      jpTextField.add(jtfMessage, BorderLayout.CENTER);
65      jtfMessage.setHorizontalAlignment(JTextField.RIGHT);
66      add(jpTextField, BorderLayout.NORTH);
67
68      // Set mnemonic keys for check boxes and radio buttons
69      jchkBold.setMnemonic('B');                                 set mnemonics
70      jchkItalic.setMnemonic('I');
71      jrbRed.setMnemonic('E');
72      jrbGreen.setMnemonic('G');
73      jrbBlue.setMnemonic('U');
74
75      // Register listeners with check boxes
76      jchkBold.addActionListener(new ActionListener() {          register listener
77        @Override
78        public void actionPerformed(ActionEvent e) {
```

```
79            setNewFont();
80          }
81        });
82        jchkItalic.addActionListener(new ActionListener() {
83          @Override
84          public void actionPerformed(ActionEvent e) {
85            setNewFont();
86          }
87        });
88
89        // Register listeners for radio buttons
90        jrbRed.addActionListener(new ActionListener() {
91          @Override
92          public void actionPerformed(ActionEvent e) {
93            jlblMessage.setForeground(Color.red);
94          }
95        });
96        jrbGreen.addActionListener(new ActionListener() {
97          @Override
98          public void actionPerformed(ActionEvent e) {
99            jlblMessage.setForeground(Color.green);
100         }
101       });
102       jrbBlue.addActionListener(new ActionListener() {
103         @Override
104         public void actionPerformed(ActionEvent e) {
105           jlblMessage.setForeground(Color.blue);
106         }
107       });
108
109       // Register listener for text field
110       jtfMessage.addActionListener(new ActionListener() {
111         @Override
112         public void actionPerformed(ActionEvent e) {
113           jlblMessage.setText(jtfMessage.getText());
114           jtfMessage.requestFocusInWindow();
115         }
116       });
117     }
118
119     private void setNewFont() {
120       // Determine a font style
121       int fontStyle = Font.PLAIN;
122       fontStyle += (jchkBold.isSelected() ? Font.BOLD : Font.PLAIN);
123       fontStyle += (jchkItalic.isSelected() ? Font.ITALIC : Font.PLAIN);
124
125       // Set font for the message
126       Font font = jlblMessage.getFont();
127       jlblMessage.setFont(
128         new Font(font.getName(), fontStyle, font.getSize()));
129     }
130   }
```

register listener (line 82)

register listener (line 90)

register listener (line 96)

register listener (line 102)

register listener (line 110)

set a new font (line 127)

The program creates a label, check boxes, radio buttons, and a text field (lines 7–19). It places a label in the center of the frame (lines 31–32), check boxes in the east (lines 35–39), radio buttons in the west (lines 42–47), and a text field in the north (lines 60–66).

mnemonic keys

The program also sets mnemonics for check boxes and radio buttons (lines 69–73). You can use a mouse click or a shortcut key to select a check box or a radio button.

The program registers action listeners for check boxes, radio buttons, and the text field (lines 76–116).

register listeners

When a check box is checked or unchecked, the listener's **actionPerformed** method is invoked to process the event (lines 79, 85). The current font name and size used in **JLabel** are obtained from **jlblMessage.getFont()** using the **getName()** and **getSize()** methods (line 128). The font styles (**Font.BOLD** and **Font.ITALIC**) are specified in the check boxes. If no font style is selected, the default font style is **Font.PLAIN** (line 121). The font style is an integer 0 for **Font.PLAIN**, 1 for **Font.BOLD**, and 2 for **Font.ITALIC**. The font style can be combined by adding together the integers that represent the fonts (lines 122–123). For example, **Font.BOLD + Font.ITALIC** is 3, which represents a combined font of bold and italic.

check boxes

The **setFont** method (line 127) defined in the **Component** class is inherited in the **JLabel** class. This method automatically invokes the **repaint** method. Invoking **setFont** on **jlblMessage** automatically repaints **jlblMessage**.

A check box fires an **ItemEvent** and then an **ActionEvent** when it is clicked. You could process either the **ItemEvent** or the **ActionEvent** to redisplay the message. The program in this example processes the **ActionEvent**. If you want to process the **ItemEvent**, create a listener for **ItemEvent** and register it with a check box. The listener must implement the **itemStateChanged** handler to process an **ItemEvent**. For example, the following code registers an **ItemListener** with **jchkBold**:

```java
// To listen for ItemEvent
jchkBold.addItemListener(new ItemListener() {
  @Override /** Handle ItemEvent */
  public void itemStateChanged(ItemEvent e) {
    setNewFont();
  }
});
```

When a radio button is clicked, its action event listener sets the corresponding foreground color in **jlblMessage** (lines 93, 99, 105).

radio buttons

The program creates a **ButtonGroup** and puts three **JRadioButton** instances (**jrbRed**, **jrbGreen**, and **jrbBlue**) in the group (lines 50–53) so they can only be selected exclusively—the text will be either red *or* green *or* blue.

radio button group

A radio button fires an **ItemEvent** and then an **ActionEvent** when it is selected or deselected. You could process either the **ItemEvent** or the **ActionEvent** to choose a color. This program processes the **ActionEvent**. As an exercise, rewrite the code using the **ItemEvent**.

After you type a new message in the text field and press the *Enter* key, a new message is displayed. Pressing the *Enter* key on the text field triggers an action event. The listener sets a new message in **jlblMessage** (line 113).

ActionEvent for
   JTextField

The **requestFocusInWindow()** method (line 114) defined in the **Component** class requests the component to receive input focus. Thus, **jtfMessage.requestFocusInWindow()** requests the input focus on **jtfMessage**. You will see the cursor on **jtfMessage** after the **actionPerformed** method is invoked.

requestFocusInWindow()

The **pack()** method (line 23) automatically sizes the frame according to the size of the components placed in it.

pack()

17.1 Can a **JButton**, **JLabel**, **JCheckBox**, **JRadioButton**, and **JTextField** fire an **ActionEvent**?

17.2 Can a **JButton**, **JLabel**, **JCheckBox**, **JRadioButton**, and **JTextField** fire an **ItemEvent**?

17.3 What happens after invoking **jtfMessage.requestFocusInWindow()**?

✓Check
   Point

MyProgrammingLab™

17.3 Text Areas

Key
Point

A JTextArea enables the user to enter multiple lines of text.

If you want to let the user enter multiple lines of text, you may create several instances of JTextField. A better alternative is to use JTextArea, which enables the user to enter multiple lines of text. Figure 17.2 lists the constructors and methods in JTextArea.

FIGURE 17.2 JTextArea enables you to enter or display multiple lines of characters.

Like JTextField, JTextArea inherits JTextComponent, which contains the methods getText, setText, isEditable, and setEditable. You can specify whether a line is wrapped in the lineWrap property. If lineWrap is true, you can specify how line is wrapped in the wrapStyleWord property. If wrapStyleWord is true, line is wrapped on words. If it is false, line is wrapped on characters. The following example creates a text area with 5 rows and 20 columns, line-wrapped on words, red foreground color, and Courier font, bold, 20 pixels.

```
JTextArea jtaNote = new JTextArea("This is a text area", 5, 20);
jtaNote.setLineWrap(true);
jtaNote.setWrapStyleWord(true);
jtaNote.setForeground(Color.red);
jtaNote.setFont(new Font("Courier", Font.BOLD, 20));
```
wrap line
wrap word

JTextArea does not handle scrolling, but you can create a JScrollPane object to hold an instance of JTextArea and let JScrollPane handle scrolling for JTextArea, as follows:

```
// Create a scroll pane to hold text area
JScrollPane scrollPane = new JScrollPane(jtaNote);
add(scrollPane, BorderLayout.CENTER);
```

JScrollPane

 Tip
You can place any swing GUI component in a JScrollPane. JScrollPane provides vertical and horizontal scrolling automatically if the component is too large to fit in the viewing area.

Listing 17.3 gives a program that displays an image and a text in a label, and a text in a text area, as shown in Figure 17.3.

FIGURE 17.3 The program displays an image in a label, a title in a label, and text in the text area.

Here are the major steps in the program:

1. Define a class named `DescriptionPanel` that extends `JPanel`, as shown in Listing 17.2. This class contains a text area inside a scroll pane, and a label for displaying an image icon and a title. The class `DescriptionPanel` will be reused in later examples.

2. Define a class named `TextAreaDemo` that extends `JFrame`, as shown in Listing 17.3. Create an instance of `DescriptionPanel` and add it to the center of the frame. The relationship between `DescriptionPanel` and `TextAreaDemo` is shown in Figure 17.4.

FIGURE 17.4 `TextAreaDemo` uses `DescriptionPanel` to display an image, title, and text description of a national flag.

LISTING 17.2 DescriptionPanel.java

```
1  import javax.swing.*;
2  import java.awt.*;
3
4  public class DescriptionPanel extends JPanel {
5    /** Label for displaying an image icon and a title */
6    private JLabel jlblImageTitle = new JLabel();               label
7
8    /** Text area for displaying text */
9    private JTextArea jtaDescription = new JTextArea();         text area
10
11   public DescriptionPanel() {
12     // Center the icon and text and place the text under the icon
13     jlblImageTitle.setHorizontalAlignment(JLabel.CENTER);      label properties
14     jlblImageTitle.setHorizontalTextPosition(JLabel.CENTER);
15     jlblImageTitle.setVerticalTextPosition(JLabel.BOTTOM);
16
```

```
17      // Set the font in the label and the text field
18      jlblImageTitle.setFont(new Font("SansSerif", Font.BOLD, 16));
19      jtaDescription.setFont(new Font("Serif", Font.PLAIN, 14));
20
21      // Set lineWrap and wrapStyleWord true for the text area
22      jtaDescription.setLineWrap(true);
23      jtaDescription.setWrapStyleWord(true);
24      jtaDescription.setEditable(false);
25
26      // Create a scroll pane to hold the text area
27      JScrollPane scrollPane = new JScrollPane(jtaDescription);
28
29      // Set BorderLayout for the panel, add label and scroll pane
30      setLayout(new BorderLayout(5, 5));
31      add(scrollPane, BorderLayout.CENTER);
32      add(jlblImageTitle, BorderLayout.WEST);
33    }
34
35    /** Set the title */
36    public void setTitle(String title) {
37      jlblImageTitle.setText(title);
38    }
39
40    /** Set the image icon */
41    public void setImageIcon(ImageIcon icon) {
42      jlblImageTitle.setIcon(icon);
43    }
44
45    /** Set the text description */
46    public void setDescription(String text) {
47      jtaDescription.setText(text);
48    }
49 }
```

wrap line (22)
wrap word (23)
read only (24)
scroll pane (27)

The text area is inside a **JScrollPane** (line 27), which provides scrolling functions for the text area. Scroll bars automatically appear if there is more text than the physical size of the text area.

The **lineWrap** property is set to **true** (line 22) so that the line is automatically wrapped when the text cannot fit in one line. The **wrapStyleWord** property is set to **true** (line 23) so that the line is wrapped on words rather than characters. The text area is set as noneditable (line 24), so you cannot edit the description in the text area.

It is not necessary to create a separate class for **DescriptionPanel** in this example. However, this class was created for reuse in the next section, where you will use it to display a description panel for various images.

LISTING 17.3 TextAreaDemo.java

```
1  import java.awt.*;
2  import javax.swing.*;
3
4  public class TextAreaDemo extends JFrame {
5    // Declare and create a description panel
6    private DescriptionPanel descriptionPanel = new DescriptionPanel();
7
8    public static void main(String[] args) {
9      TextAreaDemo frame = new TextAreaDemo();
10     frame.pack();
11     frame.setLocationRelativeTo(null); // Center the frame
```

create descriptionPanel (6)
create frame (9)

```
12        frame.setDefaultCloseOperation(JFrame.EXIT_ON_CLOSE);
13        frame.setTitle("TextAreaDemo");
14        frame.setVisible(true);
15    }
16
17    public TextAreaDemo() {                                              create UI
18        // Set title, text, and image in the description panel
19        descriptionPanel.setTitle("Canada");
20        String description = "The Canadian national flag...";
21        descriptionPanel.setImageIcon(new ImageIcon("image/ca.gif"));
22        descriptionPanel.setDescription(description);
23
24        // Add the description panel to the frame
25        setLayout(new BorderLayout());
26        add(descriptionPanel, BorderLayout.CENTER);                      add descriptionPanel
27    }
28  }
```

The program in Listing 17.3 creates an instance of **DescriptionPanel** (line 6) and sets the title (line 19), image (line 21), and text in the description panel (line 22). **DescriptionPanel** is a subclass of **JPanel**. **DescriptionPanel** contains a label for displaying an image icon and a text title, and a text area for displaying a description of the image.

✓ **Check Point**

MyProgrammingLab™

17.4 How do you create a text area with **10** rows and **20** columns?

17.5 How do you insert or append three lines into the text area?

17.6 How do you create a scrollable text area?

17.7 What method do you use to get the text from a text area? How do you get the line count in the text area?

17.8 How do you specify a line wrap? How do you specify wrapping on characters? How do you specify wrapping on words?

17.4 Combo Boxes

A combo box, also known as a choice list *or* drop-down list, *contains a list of items from which the user can choose.*

🔑 **Key Point**

A combo box is useful for limiting a user's range of choices and avoids the cumbersome validation of data input. Figure 17.5 lists several frequently used constructors and methods in **JComboBox**.

The following statements create a combo box with four items, red foreground, white background, and the second item selected.

```
JComboBox jcb = new JComboBox(new Object[]
    {"Item 1", "Item 2", "Item3", "Item 4"});
jcb.setForeground(Color.red);
jcb.setBackground(Color.white);
jcb.setSelectedItem("Item 2");
```

JComboBox can fire **ItemEvent** and **ActionEvent** among many other events. Whenever an item is selected, an **ActionEvent** is fired. Whenever a new item is selected, **JComboBox** fires **ItemEvent** twice: once for deselecting the previously selected item, and the other for selecting the currently selected item. Note that no **ItemEvent** is fired if the current item is reselected. To respond to an **ItemEvent**, you need to implement the **itemStateChanged(ItemEvent e)** handler for processing a choice. To get data from a **JComboBox** menu, you can use **getSelectedItem()** to return the currently selected item, or the **e.getItem()** method to get the item from the **itemStateChanged(ItemEvent e)** handler.

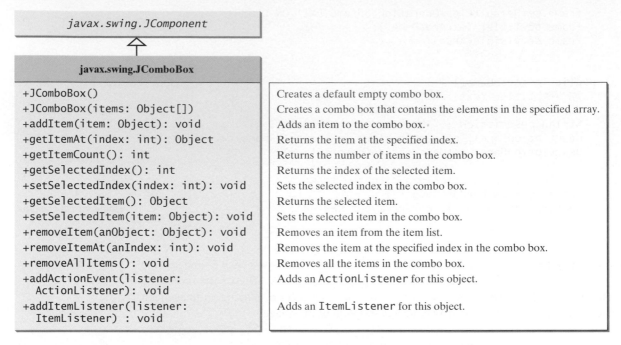

FIGURE 17.5 JComboBox enables you to select an item from a set of items.

Listing 17.4 gives a program that lets users view an image and a description of a country's flag by selecting the country from a combo box, as shown in Figure 17.6.

FIGURE 17.6 Information about a country, including an image and a description of its flag, is displayed when the country is selected in the combo box.

Here are the major steps in the program:

1. Create the user interface.
   Create a combo box with country names as its selection values. Create a DescriptionPanel object (the DescriptionPanel class was introduced in the preceding section). Place the combo box in the north of the frame and the description panel in the center of the frame.

2. Process the event.
   Create a listener to implement the itemStateChanged handler to set the flag title, image, and text in the description panel for the selected country name.

LISTING 17.4 ComboBoxDemo.java

```java
1   import java.awt.*;
2   import java.awt.event.*;
3   import javax.swing.*;
4
5   public class ComboBoxDemo extends JFrame {
6     // Create an array of Strings for flag titles
7     private String[] flagTitles = {"Canada", "China", "Denmark",           country
8       "France", "Germany", "India", "Norway", "United Kingdom",
9       "United States of America"};
10
11    // Declare an ImageIcon array for the national flags of 9 countries
12    private ImageIcon[] flagImage = {                                       image icon
13      new ImageIcon("image/ca.gif"),
14      new ImageIcon("image/china.gif"),
15      new ImageIcon("image/denmark.gif"),
16      new ImageIcon("image/fr.gif"),
17      new ImageIcon("image/germany.gif"),
18      new ImageIcon("image/india.gif"),
19      new ImageIcon("image/norway.gif"),
20      new ImageIcon("image/uk.gif"),
21      new ImageIcon("image/us.gif")
22    };
23
24    // Declare an array of strings for flag descriptions
25    private String[] flagDescription = new String[9];                       description
26
27    // Declare and create a description panel
28    private DescriptionPanel descriptionPanel = new DescriptionPanel();
29
30    // Create a combo box for selecting countries
31    private JComboBox jcbo = new JComboBox(flagTitles);                      combo box
32
33    public static void main(String[] args) {
34      ComboBoxDemo frame = new ComboBoxDemo();
35      frame.pack();
36      frame.setTitle("ComboBoxDemo");
37      frame.setLocationRelativeTo(null); // Center the frame
38      frame.setDefaultCloseOperation(JFrame.EXIT_ON_CLOSE);
39      frame.setVisible(true);
40    }
41
42    public ComboBoxDemo() {
43      // Set text description
44      flagDescription[0] = "The Canadian national flag...";
45      flagDescription[1] = "Description for China ... ";
46      flagDescription[2] = "Description for Denmark ... ";
47      flagDescription[3] = "Description for France ... ";
48      flagDescription[4] = "Description for Germany ... ";
49      flagDescription[5] = "Description for India ... ";
50      flagDescription[6] = "Description for Norway ... ";
51      flagDescription[7] = "Description for UK ... ";
52      flagDescription[8] = "Description for US ... ";
53
54      // Set the first country (Canada) for display
55      setDisplay(0);                                                        create UI
56
57      // Add combo box and description panel to the frame
58      add(jcbo, BorderLayout.NORTH);
```

```
59          add(descriptionPanel, BorderLayout.CENTER);
60
61          // Register listener
62          jcbo.addItemListener(new ItemListener() {
63            @Override /** Handle item selection */
64            public void itemStateChanged(ItemEvent e) {
65              setDisplay(jcbo.getSelectedIndex());
66            }
67          });
68        }
69
70        /** Set display information on the description panel */
71        public void setDisplay(int index) {
72          descriptionPanel.setTitle(flagTitles[index]);
73          descriptionPanel.setImageIcon(flagImage[index]);
74          descriptionPanel.setDescription(flagDescription[index]);
75        }
76      }
```

listener

The listener listens to **ItemEvent** from the combo box and implements **ItemListener** (lines 62–67). Instead of using **ItemEvent**, you could rewrite the program to use **ActionEvent** for handling combo-box item selection.

The program stores the flag information in three arrays: **flagTitles**, **flagImage**, and **flagDescription** (lines 7–25). The array **flagTitles** contains the names of nine countries, the array **flagImage** contains images of the nine countries' flags, and the array **flagDescription** contains descriptions of the flags.

The program creates an instance of **DescriptionPanel** (line 28), which was presented in Listing 17.2, DescriptionPanel.java. The program creates a combo box with initial values from **flagTitles** (line 31). When the user selects an item in the combo box, the **itemStateChanged** handler is executed. The handler finds the selected index and sets its corresponding flag title, flag image, and flag description on the panel.

MyProgrammingLab™

17.9 How do you create a combo box and add three items to it?

17.10 How do you retrieve an item from a combo box? How do you retrieve a selected item from a combo box?

17.11 How do you get the number of items in a combo box? How do you retrieve an item at a specified index in a combo box?

17.12 What events would a **JComboBox** fire upon selecting a new item?

17.5 Lists

A list is a component that basically performs the same function as a combo box, but it enables the user to choose a single value or multiple values.

The Swing **JList** is very versatile. Figure 17.7 lists several frequently used constructors and methods in **JList**.

selectionMode is one of the three values (**SINGLE_SELECTION**, **SINGLE_INTERVAL_SELECTION**, and **MULTIPLE_INTERVAL_SELECTION**) defined in **javax.swing.ListSelectionModel** that indicate whether a single item, single-interval item, or multiple-interval item can be selected. Single selection allows only one item to be selected. Single-interval selection allows multiple selections, but the selected items must be contiguous. Multiple-interval selection allows selections of multiple contiguous items without restrictions, as shown in Figure 17.8. The default value is **MULTIPLE_INTERVAL_SELECTION**.

FIGURE 17.7 JList enables you to select multiple items from a set of items.

(a) Single selection   (b) Single-interval selection   (c) Multiple-interval selection

FIGURE 17.8 JList has three selection modes: single selection, single-interval selection, and multiple-interval selection.

The following statements create a list with six items, **red** foreground, **white** background, **pink** selection foreground, **black** selection background, and visible row count **4**.

```
1  JList jlst = new JList(new String[]
2    {"Item 1", "Item 2", "Item 3", "Item 4", "Item 5", "Item 6"});
3  jlst.setForeground(Color.RED);
4  jlst.setBackground(Color.WHITE);
5  jlst.setSelectionForeground(Color.PINK);
6  jlst.setSelectionBackground(Color.BLACK);
7  jlst.setVisibleRowCount(4);
```

Lists do not scroll automatically. To make a list scrollable, create a scroll pane and add the list to it.

JList fires **javax.swing.event.ListSelectionEvent** to notify the listeners of the selections. The listener must implement the **valueChanged** handler in the **javax.swing.event.ListSelectionListener** interface to process the event.

Listing 17.5 gives a program that lets users select countries in a list and displays the flags of the selected countries in the labels. Figure 17.9 shows a sample run of the program.

JList inside a scroll pane

JPanel with GridLayout

An image is displayed on a Jlabel

FIGURE 17.9 When the countries in the list are selected, corresponding images of their flags are displayed in the labels.

Here are the major steps in the program:

1. Create the user interface.
   Create a list with nine country names as selection values, and place the list inside a scroll pane. Place the scroll pane in the west of the frame. Create nine labels to be used to display the countries' flag images. Place the labels in the panel, and place the panel in the center of the frame.

2. Process the event.
   Create a listener to implement the **valueChanged** method in the **ListSelectionListener** interface to set the selected countries' flag images in the labels.

LISTING 17.5 ListDemo.java

```
1  import java.awt.*;
2  import javax.swing.*;
3  import javax.swing.event.*;
4
5  public class ListDemo extends JFrame {
6    final int NUMBER_OF_FLAGS = 9;
7
8    // Declare an array of Strings for flag titles
9    private String[] flagTitles = {"Canada", "China", "Denmark",
10     "France", "Germany", "India", "Norway", "United Kingdom",
11     "United States of America"};
12
13   // The list for selecting countries
14   private JList jlst = new JList(flagTitles);
15
16   // Declare an ImageIcon array for the national flags of 9 countries
17   private ImageIcon[] imageIcons = {
18     new ImageIcon("image/ca.gif"),
19     new ImageIcon("image/china.gif"),
20     new ImageIcon("image/denmark.gif"),
21     new ImageIcon("image/fr.gif"),
22     new ImageIcon("image/germany.gif"),
23     new ImageIcon("image/india.gif"),
24     new ImageIcon("image/norway.gif"),
25     new ImageIcon("image/uk.gif"),
26     new ImageIcon("image/us.gif")
27   };
28
```

```
29      // Arrays of labels for displaying images
30      private JLabel[] jlblImageViewer = new JLabel[NUMBER_OF_FLAGS];
31
32      public static void main(String[] args) {                          create frame
33        ListDemo frame = new ListDemo();
34        frame.setSize(650, 500);
35        frame.setTitle("ListDemo");
36        frame.setLocationRelativeTo(null); // Center the frame
37        frame.setDefaultCloseOperation(JFrame.EXIT_ON_CLOSE);
38        frame.setVisible(true);
39      }
40
41      public ListDemo() {
42        // Create a panel to hold nine labels
43        JPanel p = new JPanel(new GridLayout(3, 3, 5, 5));             create UI
44
45        for (int i = 0; i < NUMBER_OF_FLAGS; i++) {
46          p.add(jlblImageViewer[i] = new JLabel());
47          jlblImageViewer[i].setHorizontalAlignment
48            (SwingConstants.CENTER);
49        }
50
51        // Add p and the list to the frame
52        add(p, BorderLayout.CENTER);
53        add(new JScrollPane(jlst), BorderLayout.WEST);
54
55        // Register listeners
56        jlst.addListSelectionListener(new ListSelectionListener() {
57          @Override /** Handle list selection */
58          public void valueChanged(ListSelectionEvent e) {             event handler
59            // Get selected indices
60            int[] indices = jlst.getSelectedIndices();
61
62            int i;
63            // Set icons in the labels
64            for (i = 0; i < indices.length; i++) {
65              jlblImageViewer[i].setIcon(imageIcons[indices[i]]);
66            }
67
68            // Remove icons from the rest of the labels
69            for (; i < NUMBER_OF_FLAGS; i++) {
70              jlblImageViewer[i].setIcon(null);
71            }
72          }
73        });
74      }
75    }
```

The anonymous inner-class listener listens to `ListSelectionEvent` for handling the selection of country names in the list (lines 56–73). `ListSelectionEvent` and `ListSelectionListener` are defined in the `javax.swing.event` package, so this package is imported into the program (line 3).

The program creates an array of nine labels for displaying flag images for nine countries. The program loads the images of the nine countries into an image array (lines 17–27) and creates a list of the nine countries in the same order as in the title array (lines 9–11). Thus, the index 0 of the image array corresponds to the first country in the list.

The list is placed in a scroll pane (line 53) so that it can be scrolled when the number of items in the list extends beyond the viewing area.

By default, the selection mode of the list is multiple-interval, which allows the user to select multiple items from different blocks in the list. When the user selects countries in the list, the `valueChanged` handler (lines 58–72) is executed, which gets the indices of the selected items and sets their corresponding image icons in the label to display the flags.

17.13 How do you create a list with an array of strings?

17.14 How do you set the visible row count in a list?

17.15 What selection modes are available for a list? How do you set a selection mode?

17.16 How do you set the foreground and background color of a list? How do you set the foreground and background color of the selected items?

17.6 Scroll Bars

Key Point

`JScrollBar` is a component that enables the user to select from a range of values.

Figure 17.10 shows a scroll bar. Normally, the user changes the value of the scroll bar by making a gesture with the mouse. For example, the user can drag the scroll bar's bubble up and down, or click in the scroll bar's unit-increment or block-increment areas. Keyboard gestures can also be mapped to the scroll bar. By convention, the *Page Up* and *Page Down* keys are equivalent to clicking in the scroll bar's block-increment and block-decrement areas.

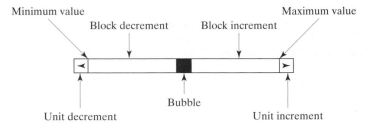

FIGURE 17.10 A scroll bar represents a range of values graphically.

Note

The width of the scroll bar's track corresponds to `maximum + visibleAmount`. When a scroll bar is set to its maximum value, the left side of the bubble is at `maximum`, and the right side is at `maximum + visibleAmount`.

`JScrollBar` has the following properties, as shown in Figure 17.11.

When the user changes the value of the scroll bar, the scroll bar fires an `AdjustmentEvent`. A listener class for this event must implement the `adjustmentValueChanged` handler in the `java.awt.event.AdjustmentListener` interface.

Listing 17.6 gives a program that uses horizontal and vertical scroll bars to control a message displayed on a panel. The horizontal scroll bar is used to move the message to the left and the right, and the vertical scroll bar to move it up and down. A sample run of the program is shown in Figure 17.12.

Here are the major steps in the program:

1. Create the user interface.
   Create a `MessagePanel` object and place it in the center of the frame. Create a vertical scroll bar and place it in the east of the frame. Create a horizontal scroll bar and place it in the south of the frame.

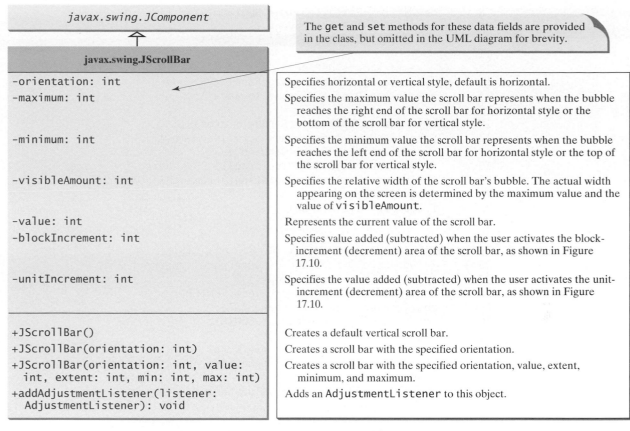

FIGURE 17.11 JScrollBar enables you to select from a range of values.

FIGURE 17.12 The scroll bars move the message on a panel horizontally and vertically.

2. Process the event.

Create listeners to implement the **adjustmentValueChanged** handler to move the message according to the bar movement in the scroll bars.

LISTING 17.6 ScrollBarDemo.java

```
1  import java.awt.*;
2  import java.awt.event.*;
3  import javax.swing.*;
4
5  public class ScrollBarDemo extends JFrame {
6    // Create horizontal and vertical scroll bars
7    private JScrollBar jscbHort =                              horizontal scroll bar
```

```
                          8        new JScrollBar(JScrollBar.HORIZONTAL);
vertical scroll bar       9      private JScrollBar jscbVert =
                         10        new JScrollBar(JScrollBar.VERTICAL);
                         11
                         12      // Create a MessagePanel
                         13      private MessagePanel messagePanel =
                         14        new MessagePanel("Welcome to Java");
                         15
                         16      public static void main(String[] args) {
create frame             17        ScrollBarDemo frame = new ScrollBarDemo();
                         18        frame.setTitle("ScrollBarDemo");
                         19        frame.setLocationRelativeTo(null); // Center the frame
                         20        frame.setDefaultCloseOperation(JFrame.EXIT_ON_CLOSE);
                         21        frame.pack();
                         22        frame.setVisible(true);
                         23      }
                         24
                         25      public ScrollBarDemo() {
                         26        // Add scroll bars and message panel to the frame
create UI                27        setLayout(new BorderLayout());
                         28        add(messagePanel, BorderLayout.CENTER);
add scroll bar           29        add(jscbVert, BorderLayout.EAST);
                         30        add(jscbHort, BorderLayout.SOUTH);
                         31
                         32        // Register listener for the scroll bars
adjustment listener      33        jscbHort.addAdjustmentListener(new AdjustmentListener() {
                         34          @Override
                         35          public void adjustmentValueChanged(AdjustmentEvent e) {
                         36            // getValue() and getMaximumValue() return int, but for better
                         37            // precision, use double
                         38            double value = jscbHort.getValue();
                         39            double maximumValue = jscbHort.getMaximum();
                         40            double newX = (value * messagePanel.getWidth() /
                         41              maximumValue);
                         42            messagePanel.setXCoordinate((int)newX);
                         43          }
                         44        });
adjustment listener      45        jscbVert.addAdjustmentListener(new AdjustmentListener() {
                         46          @Override
                         47          public void adjustmentValueChanged(AdjustmentEvent e) {
                         48            // getValue() and getMaximum() return int, but for better
                         49            // precision, use double
                         50            double value = jscbVert.getValue();
                         51            double maximumValue = jscbVert.getMaximum();
                         52            double newY = (value * messagePanel.getHeight() /
                         53              maximumValue);
                         54            messagePanel.setYCoordinate((int)newY);
                         55          }
                         56        });
                         57      }
                         58    }
```

The program creates two scroll bars (**jscbVert** and **jscbHort**) (lines 7–10) and an instance of **MessagePanel** (**messagePanel**) (lines 13–14). **messagePanel** is placed in the center of the frame (line 28); **jscbVert** and **jscbHort** are placed in the east and south sections of the frame (lines 29–30), respectively.

You can specify the orientation of the scroll bar in the constructor or use the **setOrientation** method. By default, the property value is **100** for **maximum**, **0** for **minimum**, **10** for **blockIncrement**, and **10** for **visibleAmount**.

When the user drags the bubble, or clicks the increment or decrement unit, the value of the scroll bar changes. An instance of **AdjustmentEvent** is fired and passed to the listener by invoking the **adjustmentValueChanged** handler. The listener for the vertical scroll bar moves the message up and down (lines 33–44), and the listener for the horizontal bar moves the message to the right and left (lines 45–56).

The maximum value of the vertical scroll bar corresponds to the height of the panel, and the maximum value of the horizontal scroll bar corresponds to the width of the panel. The ratio between the current and maximum values of the horizontal scroll bar is the same as the ratio between the x value and the width of the message panel. Similarly, the ratio between the current and maximum values of the vertical scroll bar is the same as the ratio between the y value and the height of the message panel. The *x*-coordinate and *y*-coordinate are set in response to the scroll bar adjustments (lines 39, 50).

17.17 How do you create a horizontal scroll bar? How do you create a vertical scroll bar?

17.18 What event can a scroll bar fire when the user changes the value on a scroll bar? What is the corresponding interface for the event? What is the handler defined in the interface?

17.19 How do you get the value from a scroll bar? How do you get the maximum value from a scroll bar?

17.7 Sliders

JSlider is similar to JScrollBar, but JSlider has more properties and can appear in many forms.

Figure 17.13 shows two sliders. **JSlider** lets the user graphically select a value by sliding a knob within a bounded interval. The slider can show both major tick marks and minor tick marks between them. The number of pixels between the tick marks is controlled by the **majorTickSpacing** and **minorTickSpacing** properties. Sliders can be displayed horizontally and/or vertically, with or without ticks, and with or without labels.

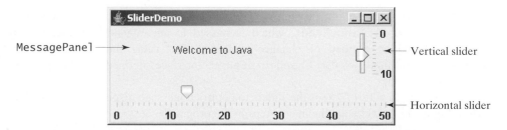

FIGURE 17.13 The sliders move the message on a panel horizontally and vertically.

The frequently used constructors and properties in **JSlider** are shown in Figure 17.14.

Note

The values of a vertical scroll bar increase from top to bottom, but the values of a vertical slider decrease from top to bottom by default.

Note

All the properties listed in Figure 17.14 have the associated **get** and **set** methods, but they are omitted for brevity. By convention, the **get** method for a Boolean property is named *is<PropertyName>()*. In the **JSlider** class, the **get** methods for

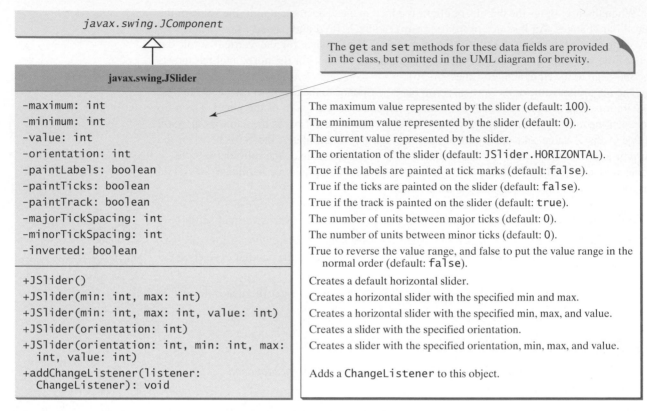

FIGURE 17.14 JSlider enables you to select from a range of values.

paintLabels, paintTicks, paintTrack, and inverted are getPaintLabels(), getPaintTicks(), getPaintTrack(), and getInverted(), which violate the naming convention.

When the user changes the value of the slider, the slider fires an instance of **javax.swing.event.ChangeEvent**, which is passed to any registered listeners. Any object that should be notified of changes to the slider's value must implement the **stateChanged** method in the **ChangeListener** interface defined in the package **javax.swing.event**.

The program in Listing 17.7 uses the sliders to control a message displayed on a panel, as shown in Figure 17.14. Here are the major steps in the program:

1. Create the user interface.
   Create a **MessagePanel** object and place it in the center of the frame. Create a vertical slider and place it in the east of the frame. Create a horizontal slider and place it in the south of the frame.

2. Process the event.
   Create listeners to implement the **stateChanged** handler in the **ChangeListener** interface to move the message according to the knot movement in the slider.

LISTING 17.7 SliderDemo.java

```
1  import java.awt.*;
2  import javax.swing.*;
3  import javax.swing.event.*;
```

```
4
5   public class SliderDemo extends JFrame {
6     // Create horizontal and vertical sliders
7     private JSlider jsldHort = new JSlider(JSlider.HORIZONTAL);        horizontal slider
8     private JSlider jsldVert = new JSlider(JSlider.VERTICAL);          vertical slider
9
10    // Create a MessagePanel
11    private MessagePanel messagePanel =
12      new MessagePanel("Welcome to Java");
13
14    public static void main(String[] args) {
15      SliderDemo frame = new SliderDemo();                            create frame
16      frame.setTitle("SliderDemo");
17      frame.setLocationRelativeTo(null); // Center the frame
18      frame.setDefaultCloseOperation(JFrame.EXIT_ON_CLOSE);
19      frame.pack();
20      frame.setVisible(true);
21    }
22
23    public SliderDemo() {                                             create UI
24      // Add sliders and message panel to the frame
25      setLayout(new BorderLayout(5, 5));
26      add(messagePanel, BorderLayout.CENTER);
27      add(jsldVert, BorderLayout.EAST);
28      add(jsldHort, BorderLayout.SOUTH);
29
30      // Set properties for sliders
31      jsldHort.setMaximum(50);                                        slider properties
32      jsldHort.setPaintLabels(true);
33      jsldHort.setPaintTicks(true);
34      jsldHort.setMajorTickSpacing(10);
35      jsldHort.setMinorTickSpacing(1);
36      jsldHort.setPaintTrack(false);
37      jsldVert.setInverted(true);
38      jsldVert.setMaximum(10);
39      jsldVert.setPaintLabels(true);
40      jsldVert.setPaintTicks(true);
41      jsldVert.setMajorTickSpacing(10);
42      jsldVert.setMinorTickSpacing(1);
43
44      // Register listener for the sliders
45      jsldHort.addChangeListener(new ChangeListener() {               listener
46        @Override /** Handle scroll-bar adjustment actions */
47        public void stateChanged(ChangeEvent e) {
48          // getValue() and getMaximumValue() return int, but for better
49          // precision, use double
50          double value = jsldHort.getValue();
51          double maximumValue = jsldHort.getMaximum();
52          double newX = (value * messagePanel.getWidth() /
53            maximumValue);
54          messagePanel.setXCoordinate((int)newX);
55        }
56      });
57      jsldVert.addChangeListener(new ChangeListener() {               listener
58        @Override /** Handle scroll-bar adjustment actions */
59        public void stateChanged(ChangeEvent e) {
60          // getValue() and getMaximum() return int, but for better
61          // precision, use double
62          double value = jsldVert.getValue();
63          double maximumValue = jsldVert.getMaximum();
```

```
64              double newY = (value * messagePanel.getHeight() /
65                maximumValue);
66              messagePanel.setYCoordinate((int)newY);
67            }
68        });
69      }
70    }
```

`JSlider` is similar to `JScrollBar` but has more features. As shown in this example, you can specify maximum, labels, major ticks, and minor ticks on a `JSlider` (lines 31–35). You can also choose to hide the track (line 36). Since the default values of a vertical slider decrease from top to bottom, the `setInverted` method reverses the order (line 37).

`JSlider` fires `ChangeEvent` when the slider is changed. The listener needs to implement the `stateChanged` handler in `ChangeListener` (lines 45–68). Note that `JScrollBar` fires `AdjustmentEvent` when the scroll bar is adjusted.

Check Point

MyProgrammingLab™

17.20 How do you create a horizontal slider? How do you create a vertical slider?

17.21 What event can a slider fire when the user changes the value on a slider? What is the corresponding interface for the event? What is the handler defined in the interface?

17.22 How do you get the value from a slider? How do you get the maximum value from a slider?

17.8 Creating Multiple Windows

Key Point

Multiple windows can be created in one program.

Occasionally, you may want to create multiple windows in an application so that the application can open a new window to perform a specified task. The new windows are called *subwindows*, and the main frame is called the *main window*.

Listing 17.8 gives a program that creates a main window with a text area in the scroll pane and a button named *Show Histogram*. When the user clicks the button, a new window appears that displays a histogram to show the occurrences of the letters in the text area. Figure 17.15 contains a sample run of the program.

Figure 17.15 The histogram is displayed in a separate frame.

Here are the major steps in the program:

1. Define a main class for the frame named `MultipleWindowsDemo` in Listing 17.8. Add a text area inside a scroll pane, and place the scroll pane in the center of the frame. Create a button *Show Histogram* and place it in the south of the frame.

2. Define a subclass of `JPanel` named `Histogram` in Listing 17.9. The class contains a data field named `count` of the `int[]` type, which counts the occurrences of 26 letters. The values in `count` are displayed in the histogram.

3. Implement the `actionPerformed` handler in `MultipleWindowsDemo`, as follows:

   a. Create an instance of `Histogram`. Count the letters in the text area and set the count in the `Histogram` object.

   b. Create a new frame and place the `Histogram` object in the center of frame. Display the frame.

LISTING 17.8 MultipleWindowsDemo.java

```java
 1  import java.awt.*;
 2  import java.awt.event.*;
 3  import javax.swing.*;
 4
 5  public class MultipleWindowsDemo extends JFrame {
 6    private JTextArea jta;
 7    private JButton jbtShowHistogram = new JButton("Show Histogram");
 8    private Histogram histogram = new Histogram();
 9
10    // Create a new frame to hold the histogram panel
11    private JFrame histogramFrame = new JFrame();                          create subframe
12
13    public MultipleWindowsDemo() {                                         create UI
14      // Store text area in a scroll pane
15      JScrollPane scrollPane = new JScrollPane(jta = new JTextArea());
16      scrollPane.setPreferredSize(new Dimension(300, 200));
17      jta.setWrapStyleWord(true);
18      jta.setLineWrap(true);
19
20      // Place scroll pane and button in the frame
21      add(scrollPane, BorderLayout.CENTER);
22      add(jbtShowHistogram, BorderLayout.SOUTH);
23
24      // Register listener
25      jbtShowHistogram.addActionListener(new ActionListener() {
26        @Override /** Handle the button action */
27        public void actionPerformed(ActionEvent e) {
28          // Count the letters in the text area
29          int[] count = countLetters();
30
31          // Set the letter count to histogram for display
32          histogram.showHistogram(count);
33
34          // Show the frame
35          histogramFrame.setVisible(true);                                 display subframe
36        }
37      });
38
39      // Add the histogram panel to the frame
40      histogramFrame.add(histogram);
41      histogramFrame.pack();
42      histogramFrame.setTitle("Histogram");
43    }
44
45    /** Count the letters in the text area */
46    private int[] countLetters() {
47      // Count for 26 letters
48      int[] count = new int[26];
49
50      // Get contents from the text area
```

```
51      String text = jta.getText();
52
53      // Count occurrences of each letter (case insensitive)
54      for (int i = 0; i < text.length(); i++) {
55        char character = text.charAt(i);
56
57        if (character >= 'A' && character <= 'Z') {
58          count[character - 'A']++;
59        }
60        else if (character >= 'a' && character <= 'z') {
61          count[character - 'a']++;
62        }
63      }
64
65      return count; // Return the count array
66    }
67
68    public static void main(String[] args) {
69      MultipleWindowsDemo frame = new MultipleWindowsDemo();
70      frame.setLocationRelativeTo(null); // Center the frame
71      frame.setDefaultCloseOperation(JFrame.EXIT_ON_CLOSE);
72      frame.setTitle("MultipleWindowsDemo");
73      frame.pack();
74      frame.setVisible(true);
75    }
76  }
```

create main frame

LISTING 17.9 Histogram.java

```
1  import javax.swing.*;
2  import java.awt.*;
3
4  public class Histogram extends JPanel {
5    // Count the occurrences of 26 letters
6    private int[] count;
7
8    /** Set the count and display histogram */
9    public void showHistogram(int[] count) {
10     this.count = count;
11     repaint();
12   }
13
14   @Override /** Paint the histogram */
15   protected void paintComponent(Graphics g) {
16     if (count == null) return; // No display if count is null
17
18     super.paintComponent(g);
19
20     // Find the panel size and bar width and interval dynamically
21     int width = getWidth();
22     int height = getHeight();
23     int interval = (width - 40) / count.length;
24     int individualWidth = (int)(((width - 40) / 24) * 0.60);
25
26     // Find the maximum count. The maximum count has the highest bar
27     int maxCount = 0;
28     for (int i = 0; i < count.length; i++) {
29       if (maxCount < count[i])
30         maxCount = count[i];
31     }
```

paint histogram

```
32
33     // x is the start position for the first bar in the histogram
34     int x = 30;
35
36     // Draw a horizontal base line
37     g.drawLine(10, height - 45, width - 10, height - 45);
38     for (int i = 0; i < count.length; i++) {
39       // Find the bar height
40       int barHeight =
41         (int)(((double)count[i] / (double)maxCount) * (height - 55));
42
43       // Display a bar (i.e., rectangle)
44       g.drawRect(x, height - 45 - barHeight, individualWidth,
45         barHeight);
46
47       // Display a letter under the base line
48       g.drawString((char)(65 + i) + "", x, height - 30);
49
50       // Move x for displaying the next character
51       x += interval;
52     }
53   }
54
55   @Override
56   public Dimension getPreferredSize() {                          preferredSize
57     return new Dimension(300, 300);
58   }
59 }
```

The program contains two classes: `MultipleWindowsDemo` and `Histogram`. Their relationship is shown in Figure 17.16.

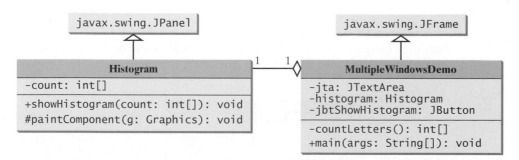

FIGURE 17.16 `MultipleWindowsDemo` uses `Histogram` to display a histogram of the occurrences of the letters in a text area in the frame.

`MultipleWindowsDemo` is a frame that holds a text area in a scroll pane and a button. `Histogram` is a subclass of `JPanel` that displays a histogram for the occurrences of letters in the text area.

In Listing 17.8, MultipleWindowsDemo.java, when the user clicks the *Show Histogram* button, the handler counts the occurrences of letters in the text area (line 29). Letters are counted regardless of their case. Nonletter characters are not counted. The count is stored in an `int` array of `26` elements (line 48). The first element in the array stores the count for the letter `a` or `A`, and the last element stores the count for the letter `z` or `Z` (lines 57–63). The `count` array is passed to the histogram for display (line 32).

The `MultipleWindowsDemo` class contains a `main` method. The `main` method creates an instance of `MultipleWindowsDemo` and displays the frame (lines 69–74). The

MultipleWindowsDemo class also contains an instance of JFrame, named histogramFrame (line 8), which holds an instance of Histogram. When the user clicks the *Show Histogram* button, histogramFrame is set as visible to display the histogram (line 35).

The height and width of the bars in the histogram are determined dynamically according to the window size of the histogram.

You cannot add an instance of JFrame to a container. For example, adding histogramFrame to the main frame would cause a runtime exception. However, you can create a frame instance and set it visible to launch a new window.

Check Point

MyProgrammingLab™

17.23 Explain how to create and show multiple windows in an application.

CHAPTER SUMMARY

1. You learned how to handle events for JCheckBox, JRadioButton, and JTextField.

2. You learned how to create graphical user interfaces using the Swing GUI components JTextArea, JComboBox, JList, JScrollBar, and JSlider. You also learned how to handle events on these components.

3. You learned how to launch multiple windows using JFrame.

TEST QUESTIONS

Do the test questions for this chapter online at www.cs.armstrong.edu/liang/intro9e/test.html.

MyProgrammingLab™

PROGRAMMING EXERCISES

Sections 17.2–17.5

*17.1 (*Use radio buttons*) Write a GUI program as shown in Figure 17.17. You can use buttons to move the message left and right and use the radio buttons to change the background color for the message displayed in the message panel.

FIGURE 17.17 The <= and => buttons move the message on the panel, and the radio buttons change the background color for the message.

*17.2 (*Select geometric figures*) Write a program that draws various figures, as shown in Figure 17.18. The user selects a figure from a radio button and uses a check box to specify whether it is filled. (*Hint*: Use the FigurePanel class introduced in Listing 13.3 to display a figure.)

**17.3 (*Traffic lights*) Write a program that simulates a traffic light. The program lets the user select one of three lights: red, yellow, or green. When a radio button is selected, the light is turned on, and only one light can be on at a time (see Figure 17.19). No light is on when the program starts.

FIGURE 17.18 The program displays lines, rectangles, and ovals when you select a shape type.

FIGURE 17.19 The radio buttons are grouped to let you select only one color in the group to control a traffic light.

Sections 17.6–17.8

**17.4 (*Text viewer*) Write a program that displays a text file in a text area, as shown in Figure 17.20a. The user enters a file name in a text field and clicks the *View* button; the file is then displayed in a text area.

(a) (b)

FIGURE 17.20 (a) The program displays the text from a file in a text area. (b) The program displays a histogram that shows the occurrences of each letter in the file.

17.5 (*Create a histogram* for *occurrences of letters*) The program in Listing 17.8, MultipleWindowsDemo.java, displays a histogram to show the occurrences of each letter in a text area. Reuse the **Histogram class created in Listing 17.9 to write a program that will display a histogram on a panel. The histogram should show the occurrences of each letter in a text file, as shown in Figure 17.20b. Assume that the letters are not case sensitive.

- Place the panel that will display the histogram in the center of the frame.
- Place a label and a text field in a panel, and put the panel in the south side of the frame. The text file will be entered from this text field.
- Pressing the *Enter* key on the text field causes the program to count the occurrences of each letter and display the count in a histogram.

*17.6 (*Create a miles/kilometers converter*) Write a program that converts miles and kilometers, as shown in Figure 17.21. If you enter a value in the Mile text field and press the *Enter* key, the corresponding kilometer measurement is displayed in the Kilometer text field. Likewise, if you enter a value in the Kilometer text field and press the *Enter* key, the corresponding miles is displayed in the Mile text field.

Panel with `GridLayout` for two labels

Panel with `BorderLayout`

Panel with `GridLayout` for two text fields

FIGURE 17.21 The program converts miles to kilometers, and vice versa.

*17.7 (*Set clock time*) Write a program that displays a clock and sets the time with the input from three text fields, as shown in Figure 17.22. Use the `StillClock` in Listing 13.10.

`StillClock`

Panel with `FlowLayout`

FIGURE 17.22 The program displays the time specified in the text fields.

**17.8 (*Select a font*) Write a program that can dynamically change the font of a message to be displayed on a panel. The message can be displayed in bold and italic at the same time, and/or it can be displayed in the center of the panel. You can select the font name or font size from combo boxes, as shown in Figure 17.23. The available font names can be obtained using `getAvailableFontFamilyNames()` in `GraphicsEnvironment` (see Section 12.8, The `Font` Class). The combo box for the font size is initialized with numbers from 1 to 100.

Panel with `BorderLayout`

Panel with `BorderLayout`

Panel with `BorderLayout`

FIGURE 17.23 You can dynamically set the font for the message.

**17.9 (*Demonstrate JLabel properties*) Write a program to let the user dynamically set the properties `horizontalAlignment`, `verticalAlignment`, `horizontalTextAlignment`, and `verticalTextAlignment`, as shown in Figure 17.24.

FIGURE 17.24 You can set the alignment and text-position properties of a label dynamically.

*17.10 (*Mandelbrot fractal*) Programming Exercise 15.20 displays Mandelbrot fractal. Note that the values `77`, `58`, and `159` in line 15 in the `MandelbrotCanvas` class in Programming Exercise 15.20 impact the color of the image. Revise the program to let the user enter these values from text fields dynamically, as shown in Figure 17.25a.

FIGURE 17.25 (a) The program enables the user to set the colors dynamically. (b) You can set a text field's properties for the horizontal alignment and column size dynamically.

*17.11 (*Demonstrate **JTextField** properties*) Write a program that sets the horizontal-alignment and column-size properties of a text field dynamically, as shown in Figure 17.25b.

*17.12 (*Demonstrate **JTextArea** properties*) Write a program that demonstrates the wrapping styles of the text area. The program uses a check box to indicate whether the text area is wrapped. If the text area is wrapped, you can specify whether it is wrapped by characters or by words, as shown in Figure 17.26.

FIGURE 17.26 You can set the options to wrap a text area dynamically by characters or by words.

*17.13 (*Compare loans with various interest rates*) Rewrite Programming Exercise 4.21 to create a user interface, as shown in Figure 17.27. Your program should let the user enter the loan amount and loan period in the number of years from a text field, and it should display the monthly and total payments for each interest rate starting from 5 percent to 8 percent, with increments of one-eighth, in a text area.

FIGURE 17.27 The program displays a table for monthly payments and total payments on a given loan based on various interest rates.

*17.14 (*Use **JComboBox** and **JList***) Write a program that demonstrates selecting items in a list. The program uses a combo box to specify a selection mode, as shown in Figure 17.28. When you select items, they are displayed in a label below the list.

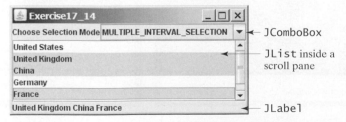

FIGURE 17.28 You can choose single selection, single-interval selection, or multiple-interval selection in a list.

Sections 17.6–17.8

**17.15 (*Use JScrollBar*) Write a program that uses scroll bars to select the foreground color for a label, as shown in Figure 17.29. Three horizontal scroll bars
are used for selecting the color's red, green, and blue components. Use a title
border on the panel that holds the scroll bars.

Panel with
GridLayout
for three labels

Panel with BorderLayout

Panel with GridLayout
for three scroll bars

FIGURE 17.29 The foreground color changes in the label as you adjust the scroll bars.

**17.16 (*Use JSlider*) Revise the preceding exercise using sliders.

***17.17 (*Display a calendar*) Write a program that displays the calendar for the current
month. You can use the *Prior* and *Next* buttons to show the calendar of the previous or next month. Display the dates in the current month in black and display the dates in the previous month and next month in gray, as shown in
Figure 17.30.

Exercise17_17						
			November 2012			
Sunday	Monday	Tuesday	Wednesday	Thursday	Friday	Saturday
28	29	30	31	1	2	3
4	5	6	7	8	9	10
11	12	13	14	15	16	17
18	19	20	21	22	23	24
25	26	27	28	29	30	

Prior   Next

JLabel

JPanel with
GridLayout

Each cell is
a JLabel

FIGURE 17.30 The program displays the calendar for the current month.

*17.18 (*Revise Listing 17.8, MultipleWindowsDemo.java*) Instead of displaying the
occurrences of the letters using the **Histogram** component in Listing 17.8,
use a bar chart, so that the display is as shown in Figure 17.31.

FIGURE 17.31 The number of occurrences of each letter is displayed in a bar chart.

17.19 (*Display country flag and flag description*) Listing 17.4, ComboBoxDemo.java, gives a program that lets users view a country's flag image and description by selecting the country from a combo box. The description is a string coded in the program. Rewrite the program to read the text description from a file. Suppose that the descriptions are stored in the files **description0.txt, . . ., and **description8.txt** under the **text** directory for the nine countries Canada, China, Denmark, France, Germany, India, Norway, the United Kingdom, and the United States, in this order.

17.20 (*Slide show*) Programming Exercise 16.13 developed a slide show using images. Rewrite that program to develop a slide show using text files. Suppose ten text files named **slide0.txt, **slide1.txt**, . . ., and **slide9.txt** are stored in the **text** directory. Each slide displays the text from one file. Each slide is shown for one second, and the slides are displayed in order. When the last slide finishes, the first slide is redisplayed, and so on. Use a text area to display the slide.

**17.21 (*Retrieve files from Web*) Write a Java program that retrieves a file from a Web server, as shown in Figure 17.32. The user interface includes a text field in which to enter the URL of the file name, a text area in which to show the file, and a button that can be used to submit an action. A label is added at the bottom of the applet to indicate the status, such as *File loaded successfully* or *Network connection problem*.

FIGURE 17.32 The program displays the contents of a specified file on the Internet.

APPLETS AND MULTIMEDIA

Objectives

- To convert GUI applications into applets (§18.2).

- To embed applets in Web pages (§18.3).

- To run applets from Web browsers and from the **appletviewer** command (§§18.3.1–18.3.2).

- To understand the applet security sandbox model (§18.4).

- To write a Java program that can run both as an application and as an applet (§18.5).

- To override the applet life-cycle methods `init`, `start`, `stop`, and `destroy` (§18.6).

- To pass string values to applets from HTML (§18.7).

- To develop an animation for a bouncing ball (§18.8).

- To develop an applet for the tic-tac-toe game (§18.9).

- To locate resources (images and audio) using the `URL` class (§18.10).

- To play audio in any Java program (§18.11).

18.1 Introduction

Key Point

Java applets are Java programs running from a Web browser.

When browsing the Web, often the graphical user interface and animation you see have been developed using Java. The Java programs that run from a Web browser are called *Java applets*. How do you write Java applets with graphics, images, and audio? This chapter will show you how.

18.2 Developing Applets

Key Point

Java applets are instances of the `Applet` *class.* `JApplet` *is a subclass of* `Applet`, *and it is suitable for developing applets using Swing components.*

VideoNote

First applet

So far, you have used and written Java applications. Everything you have learned about writing applications, however, applies also to writing applets. Applications and applets share many common programming features, although they differ slightly in some aspects. For example, every application must have a `main` method, which is invoked by the Java interpreter. Java applets, on the other hand, do not need a `main` method. They run in the Web browser environment. Because applets are embedded in a Web page, Java provides special features that enable applets to run from a Web browser.

The `Applet` class provides the essential framework that enables applets to be run from a Web browser. While every Java application has a `main` method that is executed when the application starts, applets, because they don't have a `main` method, depend on the browser to run them. Every applet is an instance of `java.applet.Applet`. The `Applet` class is an AWT class and is not designed to work with Swing components. To use Swing components in Java applets, you need to define a Java applet that extends `javax.swing.JApplet`, which is a subclass of `java.applet.Applet`.

Every Java GUI program you have developed can be converted into an applet by replacing `JFrame` with `JApplet` and deleting the `main` method. Figure 18.1a shows a Java GUI application program, which can be converted into a Java applet as shown in Figure 18.1b.

```
import javax.swing.*;

public class DisplayLabel extends JFrame {
  public DisplayLabel() {
    add(new JLabel("Great!", JLabel.CENTER));
  }

  public static void main(String[] args) {
    JFrame frame = new DisplayLabel();
    frame.setTitle("DisplayLabel");
    frame.setSize(200, 100);
    frame.setLocationRelativeTo(null);
    frame.setDefaultCloseOperation(
      JFrame.EXIT_ON_CLOSE);
    frame.setVisible(true);
  }
}
```

(a) GUI application

```
import javax.swing.*;
                                   JApplet
public class DisplayLabel extends JFrame {
  public DisplayLabel() {
    add(new JLabel("Great!", JLabel.CENTER));
  }

  public static void main(String[] args) {
    JFrame frame = new DisplayLabel();
    frame.setTitle("DisplayLabel");
    frame.setSize(200, 100);
    frame.setLocationRelativeTo(null);
    frame.setDefaultCloseOperation(
      JFrame.EXIT_ON_CLOSE);
    frame.setVisible(true);
  }
}
```

(b) Applet

FIGURE 18.1 You can convert a GUI application into an applet.

Listing 18.1 gives the complete code for the applet.

LISTING 18.1 `DisplayLabel.java`

```
1  import javax.swing.*;
2
3  public class DisplayLabel extends JApplet {
```

extend JApplet

```
4    public DisplayLabel() {
5      add(new JLabel("Great!", JLabel.CENTER));
6    }
7  }
```

Like `JFrame`, `JApplet` is a container that can contain other GUI components (see the GUI class diagrams in Figure 12.1). The default layout manager for `JApplet` is `BorderLayout`. So, the label is placed in the center of the applet (line 5).

18.1 Is every applet an instance of `java.applet.Applet`?

18.2 Is `javax.swing.JApplet` a subclass of `java.applet.Applet`?

Check Point

MyProgrammingLab™

18.3 The HTML File and the `<applet>` Tag

To run an applet, you need to create an HTML file with an `<applet>` tag for embedding the applet.

Key Point

HTML is a markup language that presents static documents on the Web. It uses *tags* to instruct the Web browser how to render a Web page and contains a tag called `<applet>` that incorporates applets into a Web page.

HTML

The HTML file in Listing 18.2 embeds the applet **DisplayLabel.class**.

LISTING 18.2 DisplayLabel.html

```html
<html>
  <head>
    <title>Java Applet Demo</title>
  </head>
  <body>
    <applet
      code = "DisplayLabel.class"
      width = 250
      height = 50>
    </applet>
  </body>
</html>
```

applet class

An HTML *tag* is an instruction to the Web browser. The browser interprets the tag and decides how to display or otherwise treat the subsequent contents of the HTML document. Tags are enclosed inside brackets (< >). The first word in a tag, called the *tag name*, describes tag functions. A tag can have additional attributes, sometimes with values after an equals sign, which further define the tag's action. For example, in the preceding HTML file, `<applet>` is the tag name, and `code`, `width`, and `height` are attributes. The `width` and `height` attributes specify the rectangular viewing area of the applet.

tag

`<applet>` tag

Most tags have a *start tag* and a corresponding *end tag*. The tag has a specific effect on the region between the start tag and the end tag. For example, `<applet...>...</applet>` tells the browser to display an applet. An end tag is always the start tag's name preceded by a slash.

An HTML document begins with the `<html>` tag, which declares that the document is written in HTML. Each document has two parts, a *head* and a *body*, defined by `<head>` and `<body>` tags, respectively. The head part contains the document title, including the `<title>` tag and other information the browser can use when rendering the document, and the body part holds the actual contents of the document. The header is optional. For more information, refer to Supplement V.A, HTML and XHTML Tutorial.

The complete syntax of the `<applet>` tag is as follows:

```
<applet
  [codebase = applet_url]
```

```
        code = classfilename.class
        width = applet_viewing_width_in_pixels
        height = applet_viewing_height_in_pixels
        [archive = archivefile]
        [vspace = vertical_margin]
        [hspace = horizontal_margin]
        [align = applet_alignment]
        [alt = alternative_text]
    >
```

<param> tag

```
    <param name = param_name1 value = param_value1>
    <param name = param_name2 value = param_value2>
    ...
    <param name = param_namei value = param_valuei>
    </applet>
```

The `code`, `width`, and `height` attributes are required; all the others are optional. The `<param>` tag will be introduced in Section 18.7, Passing Strings to Applets. The other attributes are explained below.

codebase attribute

- `codebase` specifies the base from which your classes are loaded. If this attribute is not used, the Web browser loads the applet from the directory in which the HTML page is located. If your applet is located in a different directory from the HTML page, you must specify the `applet_url` for the browser to load the applet. This attribute enables you to load the class from anywhere on the Internet. The classes used by the applet are dynamically loaded when needed.

archive attribute

- `archive` instructs the browser to load an archive file that contains all the class files needed to run the applet. Archiving allows the Web browser to load all the classes from a single compressed file at one time, thus reducing loading time and improving performance. To create archives, see Supplement III.Q, Packaging and Deploying Java Projects.

- `vspace` and `hspace` specify the size, in pixels, of the blank margin to pad around the applet vertically and horizontally.

- `align` specifies how the applet will be aligned in the browser. One of nine values is used: `left`, `right`, `top`, `texttop`, `middle`, `absmiddle`, `baseline`, `bottom`, or `absbottom`.

- `alt` specifies the text to be displayed in case the browser cannot run Java.

18.3.1 Viewing Applets from a Web Browser

To display an applet from a Web browser, open the applet's HTML file (e.g., **DisplayLabel.html**). Its output is shown in Figure 18.2a.

To make your applet accessible on the Web, you need to store the **DisplayLabel.class** and **DisplayLabel.html** files on a Web server, as shown in Figure 18.3. You can view the applet

(a)

(b)

FIGURE 18.2 The DisplayLabel program is loaded from a local host in (a) and from a Web server in (b).

FIGURE 18.3 A Web browser requests an HTML file from a Web server.

from an appropriate URL. For example, I have uploaded these two files on Web server www.cs.armstrong.edu/. As shown in Figure 18.2b, you can access the applet from www.cs.armstrong.edu/liang/intro9e/book/DisplayLabel.html.

18.3.2 Viewing Applets Using the Applet Viewer Utility

You can test the applet using the applet viewer utility, which can be launched from the DOS prompt using the **appletviewer** command, as shown in Figure 18.4a. Its output is shown in Figure 18.4b.

appletviewer

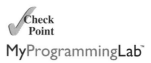

(a)   (b)

FIGURE 18.4 The **appletviewer** command runs a Java applet in the applet viewer utility.

The applet viewer functions as a browser. It is convenient for testing applets during development without launching a Web browser.

18.3 Describe the `<applet>` HTML tag. How do you embed an applet in a web page?

18.4 How do you test an applet using the **appletviewer** command?

✓Check Point

MyProgrammingLab™

18.4 Applet Security Restrictions

Applet security restrictions ensure that safety is maintained when running applets.

Key Point

Java uses the so-called "sandbox security model" for executing applets to prevent destructive programs from damaging the system on which the browser is running. Applets are not allowed to use resources outside the "sandbox." Specifically, the sandbox restricts the following activities:

- Applets are not allowed to read from, or write to, the file system of the computer. Otherwise, they could damage the files and spread viruses.

- Applets are not allowed to run programs on the browser's computer. Otherwise, they might call destructive local programs and damage the local system on the user's computer.

- Applets are not allowed to establish connections between the user's computer and any other computer, except for the server where the applets are stored. This restriction prevents the applet from connecting the user's computer to another computer without the user's knowledge.

signed applet

> **Note**
> You can create *signed applets* to circumvent the security restrictions. See Supplement
> III.S, Signed Applets, for detailed instructions on how to create signed applets.

18.5 List some security restrictions on applets.

MyProgrammingLab™

VideoNote

Run applets standalone

18.5 Enabling Applets to Run as Applications

You can add a main method in the applet to enable the applet to run as a standalone application.

Despite some differences, the `JFrame` class and the `JApplet` class have a lot in common. Since they both are subclasses of the `Container` class, all their user-interface components, layout managers, and event-handling features are the same. Applications, however, are invoked from the static `main` method by the Java interpreter, and applets are run by the Web browser. The Web browser creates an instance of the applet using the applet's no-arg constructor and controls and executes the applet.

In general, an applet can be converted into an application without loss of functionality. An application can be converted into an applet as long as it does not violate the security restrictions imposed on applets. You can implement a `main` method in an applet to enable the applet to run as an application. This feature has both theoretical and practical implications. Theoretically, it blurs the difference between applets and applications: You can write a class that is both an applet and an application. From the standpoint of practicality, it is convenient to be able to run a program both ways.

How do you write such programs? Suppose you have an applet named `MyApplet`. To enable it to run as an application, you only need to add a `main` method in the applet, as follows:

```
public static void main(String[] args) {
    // Create a frame
    JFrame frame = new JFrame("Applet is in the frame");

    // Create an instance of the applet
    MyApplet applet = new MyApplet();

    // Add the applet to the frame
    frame.add(applet, BorderLayout.CENTER);

    // Display the frame
    frame.setSize(300, 300);
    frame.setLocationRelativeTo(null); // Center the frame
    frame.setDefaultCloseOperation(JFrame.EXIT_ON_CLOSE);
    frame.setVisible(true);
}
```

create frame

create applet

add applet

show frame

run standalone

You can revise the `DisplayLabel` class in Listing 18.1 to enable it to run as a standalone application (often abbreviated as "run standalone") by adding a `main` method, as shown in Listing 18.3.

LISTING 18.3 New DisplayLabel.java with a main Method

```
1  import javax.swing.*;
2
3  public class DisplayLabel extends JApplet {
4    public DisplayLabel() {
5      add(new JLabel("Great!", JLabel.CENTER));
6    }
7
```

```
 8    public static void main(String[] args) {
 9       // Create a frame
10       JFrame frame = new JFrame("Applet is in the frame");
11
12       // Create an instance of the applet
13       DisplayLabel applet = new DisplayLabel();
14
15       // Add the applet to the frame
16       frame.add(applet);
17
18       // Display the frame
19       frame.setSize(300, 100);
20       frame.setLocationRelativeTo(null); // Center the frame
21       frame.setDefaultCloseOperation(JFrame.EXIT_ON_CLOSE);
22       frame.setVisible(true);
23    }
24 }
```

new main method

When the applet is run from a Web browser, the browser creates an instance of the applet and displays it. When the applet is run standalone, the main method is invoked to create a frame (line 10) to hold the applet. The applet is created (line 13) and added to the frame (line 16). The frame is displayed in line 22.

Note that you can add an applet to a container, but not a frame to a container. A frame is a top-level container that cannot be embedded in another container.

18.6 How do you add components to a `JApplet`? What is the default layout manager of `JApplet`?

18.7 Can you place a frame in an applet?

18.8 Can you place an applet in a frame?

18.9 What are the differences between applications and applets? How do you run an application, and how do you run an applet? Is the compilation process different for applications and applets?

MyProgrammingLab™

18.6 Applet Life-Cycle Methods

The Web browser controls and executes applets using the applet life-cycle methods.

Applets are actually run from the *applet container*, which is a plug-in of a Web browser. A plug-in is a software component that can be added into a larger software to provide additional functions. The `Applet` class contains the `init()`, `start()`, `stop()`, and `destroy()` methods, known as the *life-cycle methods*. These methods are called by the applet container to control the execution of an applet. They are implemented with an empty body in the `Applet` class, so they do nothing by default. You may override them in a subclass of `Applet` to perform desired operations. Figure 18.5 shows how the applet container calls these methods.

applet container

FIGURE 18.5 The applet container uses the `init`, `start`, `stop`, and `destroy` methods to control the applet.

18.6.1 The `init` Method

init()

The `init` method is invoked after the applet is created. If a subclass of **Applet** has an initialization to perform, it should override this method. The functions usually implemented in this method include getting string parameter values from the `<applet>` tag in the HTML page.

18.6.2 The `start` Method

start()

The `start` method is invoked after the `init` method. It is also called when the user returns to the Web page containing the applet after surfing other pages.

A subclass of **Applet** overrides this method if it has any operation that needs to be performed whenever the Web page containing the applet is visited. An applet with animation, for example, might start the timer to resume animation.

18.6.3 The `stop` Method

stop()

The `stop` method is the opposite of the `start` method. The `start` method is called when the user moves back to the page that contains the applet. The `stop` method is invoked when the user leaves the page.

A subclass of **Applet** overrides this method if it has any operation to be performed each time the Web page containing the applet is no longer visible. An applet with animation, for example, might stop the timer to pause animation.

18.6.4 The `destroy` Method

destroy()

The `destroy` method is invoked when the browser exits normally to inform the applet that it is no longer needed and should release any resources it has allocated. The `stop` method is always called before the `destroy` method.

A subclass of **Applet** overrides this method if it has any operation to be performed before it is destroyed. Usually, you won't need to override this method unless you want to release specific resources that the applet created.

18.10 Describe the `init()`, `start()`, `stop()`, and `destroy()` methods in the **Applet** class.

MyProgrammingLab™

18.11 Why does the applet in (a) below display nothing? Why does the applet in (b) have a runtime `NullPointerException` on the highlighted line?

```
import javax.swing.*;

public class WelcomeApplet extends JApplet {
  public void WelcomeApplet() {
    JLabel jlblMessage =
      new JLabel("It is Java");
  }
}
```
(a)

```
import javax.swing.*;

public class WelcomeApplet extends JApplet {
  private JLabel jlblMessage;

  public WelcomeApplet() {
    JLabel jlblMessage =
      new JLabel("It is Java");
  }

  @Override
  public void init() {
    add(jlblMessage);
  }
}
```
(b)

18.7 Passing Strings to Applets

You can pass string parameters from an HTML file to an applet.

In Section 9.7, Command-Line Arguments, you learned how to pass strings to Java applications from a command line. Strings are passed to the `main` method as an array of strings. When the application starts, the `main` method can use these strings. There is no `main` method in an applet, however, and applets are not run from the command line by the Java interpreter.

How, then, can applets accept arguments? In this section, you will learn how to pass strings to Java applets. To be passed to an applet, a parameter must be defined in the HTML file and must be read by the applet when it is initialized. Parameters are defined using the `<param>` tag. The `<param>` tag must be embedded in the `<applet>` tag. Its syntax is:

```
<param name = parametername value = stringvalue />
```

The `<param>` tag defines a parameter and its corresponding string value.

 Note

No comma separates the parameter name from the parameter value in the HTML code. The HTML parameter names are not case sensitive.

Suppose you want to write an applet to display a message. The message is passed as a parameter. In addition, you want the message to be displayed at a specific location with *x*-coordinate and *y*-coordinate, which are passed as two parameters. The parameters and their values are listed in Table 18.1.

TABLE 18.1   Parameter Names and Values for the `DisplayMessage` Applet

Parameter Name	*Parameter Value*
MESSAGE	"Welcome to Java"
X	20
Y	30

The HTML source file is given in Listing 18.4.

LISTING 18.4 DisplayMessage.html

```
<html>
  <head>
    <title>Passing Strings to Java Applets</title>
  </head>
  <body>
    <p>This applet gets a message from the HTML
      page and displays it.</p>
    <applet
      code = "DisplayMessage.class"
      width = 200
      height = 50
      alt = "You must have a Java-enabled browser to view the applet"
    >
      <param name = MESSAGE value = "Welcome to Java" />
      <param name = X value = 20 />
```

```
        <param name = Y value = 30 />
      </applet>
    </body>
  </html>
```

To read the parameter from the applet, use the following method defined in the **Applet** class:

```
public String getParameter(String parametername);
```

This returns the value of the specified parameter.

The applet is given in Listing 18.5. A sample run of the applet is shown in Figure 18.6.

LISTING 18.5 DisplayMessage.java

getParameter

add to applet

```
 1  import javax.swing.*;
 2
 3  public class DisplayMessage extends JApplet {
 4    @Override /** Initialize the applet */
 5    public void init() {
 6      // Get parameter values from the HTML file
 7      String message = getParameter("MESSAGE");
 8      int x = Integer.parseInt(getParameter("X"));
 9      int y = Integer.parseInt(getParameter("Y"));
10
11      // Create a message panel
12      MessagePanel messagePanel = new MessagePanel(message);
13      messagePanel.setXCoordinate(x);
14      messagePanel.setYCoordinate(y);
15
16      // Add the message panel to the applet
17      add(messagePanel);
18    }
19  }
```

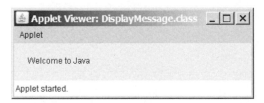

FIGURE 18.6 The applet displays the message `Welcome to Java` passed from the HTML page.

The program gets the parameter values from the HTML file in the `init` method. The values are strings obtained using the `getParameter` method (lines 7–9). Because `x` and `y` are `int`s, the program uses `Integer.parseInt(string)` to parse a digital string into an `int` value.

If you change *Welcome to Java* in the HTML file to *Welcome to HTML*, and reload the HTML file in the Web browser, you should see *Welcome to HTML* displayed. Similarly, the `x` and `y` values can be changed to display the message in a desired location.

Caution

The **Applet**'s `getParameter` method can be invoked only after an instance of the applet is created. Therefore, this method cannot be invoked in the constructor of the applet class. You should invoke it from the `init` method.

You can add a main method to enable this applet to run as a standalone application. The applet takes the parameters from the HTML file when it runs as an applet and takes the parameters from the command line when it runs standalone. The program, as shown in Listing 18.6, is identical to `DisplayMessage` except for the addition of a new **main** method and of a variable named `isStandalone` to indicate whether it is running as an applet or as an application.

LISTING 18.6 `DisplayMessageApp.java`

```java
1  import javax.swing.*;
2  import java.awt.Font;
3  import java.awt.BorderLayout;
4
5  public class DisplayMessageApp extends JApplet {
6    private String message = "A default message"; // Message to display
7    private int x = 20; // Default x-coordinate
8    private int y = 20; // Default y-coordinate
9
10   /** Determine whether it is an application */
11   private boolean isStandalone = false;                              isStandalone
12
13   @Override /** Initialize the applet */
14   public void init() {
15     if (!isStandalone) {
16       // Get parameter values from the HTML file
17       message = getParameter("MESSAGE");                            applet params
18       x = Integer.parseInt(getParameter("X"));
19       y = Integer.parseInt(getParameter("Y"));
20     }
21
22     // Create a message panel
23     MessagePanel messagePanel = new MessagePanel(message);
24     messagePanel.setFont(new Font("SansSerif", Font.BOLD, 20));
25     messagePanel.setXCoordinate(x);
26     messagePanel.setYCoordinate(y);
27
28     // Add the message panel to the applet
29     add(messagePanel);
30   }
31
32   /** Main method to display a message
33      @param args[0] x-coordinate
34      @param args[1] y-coordinate
35      @param args[2] message
36   */
37   public static void main(String[] args) {
38     // Create a frame
39     JFrame frame = new JFrame("DisplayMessageApp");
40
41     // Create an instance of the applet
42     DisplayMessageApp applet = new DisplayMessageApp();
43
44     // It runs as an application
45     applet.isStandalone = true;                                     standalone
46
47     // Get parameters from the command line
48     applet.getCommandLineParameters(args);                          command params
49
50     // Add the applet instance to the frame
51     frame.add(applet, BorderLayout.CENTER);
```

```
52
53       // Invoke applet's init method
54       applet.init();
55       applet.start();
56
57       // Display the frame
58       frame.setSize(300, 300);
59       frame.setLocationRelativeTo(null); // Center the frame
60       frame.setDefaultCloseOperation(JFrame.EXIT_ON_CLOSE);
61       frame.setVisible(true);
62     }
63
64     /** Get command-line parameters */
65     private void getCommandLineParameters(String[] args) {
66       // Check usage and get x, y and message
67       if (args.length != 3) {
68         System.out.println(
69           "Usage: java DisplayMessageApp x y message");
70         System.exit(1);
71       }
72       else {
73         x = Integer.parseInt(args[0]);
74         y = Integer.parseInt(args[1]);
75         message = args[2];
76       }
77     }
78   }
```

When you run the program as an applet, the **main** method is ignored. When you run it as an application, the **main** method is invoked. Sample runs of the program as an application and as an applet are shown in Figure 18.7.

(a)   (b)

FIGURE 18.7   The DisplayMessageApp class can run as an applet in (a) and as an application in (b).

The **main** method creates a **JFrame** object **frame** and creates a **JApplet** object **applet**, then places the applet **applet** into the frame **frame** and invokes its **init** method. The application runs just like an applet.

The **main** method sets **isStandalone** as **true** (line 45) so that it does not attempt to retrieve HTML parameters when the **init** method is invoked.

The **setVisible(true)** method (line 61) is invoked *after* the components are added to the applet, and the applet is added to the frame to ensure that the components will be visible. Otherwise, the components are not shown when the frame starts.

Important Pedagogical Note

omitting main method

From now on, all the GUI examples will be created as applets with a **main** method. Thus, you will be able to run the program either as an applet or as an application. For brevity, the **main** method is not listed in the text.

✓ Check Point

MyProgrammingLab™

18.12   How do you pass parameters to an applet?

18.13   Where is the **getParameter** method defined?

18.14 What is wrong if the `DisplayMessage` applet is revised as follows?

```java
public class DisplayMessage extends JApplet {
  /** Initialize the applet */
  public DisplayMessage() {
    // Get parameter values from the HTML file
    String message = getParameter("MESSAGE");
    int x =
      Integer.parseInt(getParameter("X"));
    int y =
      Integer.parseInt(getParameter("Y"));

    // Create a message panel
    MessagePanel messagePanel =
      new MessagePanel(message);
    messagePanel.setXCoordinate(x);
    messagePanel.setYCoordinate(y);

    // Add the message panel to the applet
    add(messagePanel);
  }
}
```

(a) Revision 1

```java
public class DisplayMessage extends JApplet {
  private String message;
  private int x;
  private int y;

  @Override /** Initialize the applet */
  public void init() {
    // Get parameter values from the HTML file
    message = getParameter("MESSAGE");
    x = Integer.parseInt(getParameter("X"));
    y = Integer.parseInt(getParameter("Y"));
  }

  public DisplayMessage() {
    // Create a message panel
    MessagePanel messagePanel =
      new MessagePanel(message);
    messagePanel.setXCoordinate(x);
    messagePanel.setYCoordinate(y);

    // Add the message panel to the applet
    add(messagePanel);
  }
}
```

(b) Revision 2

18.8 Case Study: Bouncing Ball

This section presents an applet that displays a ball bouncing in a panel.

Key Point

The applet uses two buttons to suspend and resume the bouncing movement, and uses a scroll bar to control the bouncing speed, as shown in Figure 18.8.

FIGURE 18.8 The ball's movement is controlled by the *Suspend* and *Resume* buttons and the scroll bar.

Here are the major steps to write this program:

1. Define a subclass of **JPanel** named **Ball** to display a ball bouncing, as shown in Listing 18.7.

2. Define a subclass of **JPanel** named **BallControl** to set the ball speed with a scroll bar, and two control buttons *Suspend* and *Resume*, as shown in Listing 18.8.

3. Define an applet named **BounceBallApp** to contain an instance of **BallControl** and enable the applet to run as a standalone application, as shown in Listing 18.9.

The relationship among these classes is shown in Figure 18.9.

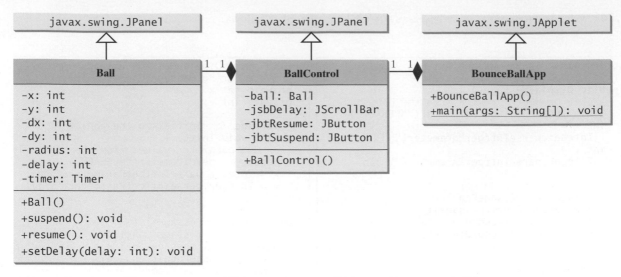

FIGURE 18.9 BounceBallApp contains BallControl, and BallControl contains Ball.

LISTING 18.7 Ball.java

```
1   import javax.swing.Timer;
2   import java.awt.*;
3   import javax.swing.*;
4   import java.awt.event.*;
5
6   public class Ball extends JPanel {
7     private int delay = 10;
8
9     // Create a timer with the specified delay in milliseconds
10    private Timer timer = new Timer(delay, new TimerListener());
11
12    private int x = 0; private int y = 0; // Current ball position
13    private int radius = 5; // Ball radius
14    private int dx = 2; // Increment on ball's x-coordinate
15    private int dy = 2; // Increment on ball's y-coordinate
16
17    public Ball() {
18      timer.start();
19    }
20
21    private class TimerListener implements ActionListener {
22      @Override /** Handle the action event */
23      public void actionPerformed(ActionEvent e) {
24        repaint();
25      }
26    }
27
28    @Override
29    protected void paintComponent(Graphics g) {
30      super.paintComponent(g);
31
32      g.setColor(Color.red);
33
34      // Check boundaries
35      if (x < 0 || x > getWidth())
36        dx *= -1;
```

Margin notes:

timer delay — line 7
create timer — line 10
start timer — line 18
timer listener — line 21
repaint ball — line 24
paint ball — line 29

```
37      if (y < 0 || y > getHeight())
38        dy *= -1;
39
40      // Adjust ball position
41      x += dx;
42      y += dy;
43      g.fillOval(x - radius, y - radius, radius * 2, radius * 2);
44    }
45
46    public void suspend() {
47      timer.stop(); // Suspend timer
48    }
49
50    public void resume() {
51      timer.start(); // Resume timer
52    }
53
54    public void setDelay(int delay) {
55      this.delay = delay;
56      timer.setDelay(delay);
57    }
58  }
```

The use of `Timer` to control animation was introduced in Section 16.11, Animation Using the `Timer` Class. `Ball` extends `JPanel` to display a moving ball. The timer listener implements `ActionListener` to listen for `ActionEvent` (line 21). Line 10 creates a `Timer` for a `Ball`. The timer is started in line 18 when a `Ball` is constructed. The timer fires an `ActionEvent` at a fixed rate. The listener responds in line 24 to repaint the ball to animate ball movement. The center of the ball is at (x, y), which changes to $(x + dx, y + dy)$ on the next display (lines 41–42). When the ball is out of the horizontal boundary, the sign of `dx` is changed (from positive to negative, or vice versa) (lines 35–36). This causes the ball to change its horizontal movement direction. When the ball is out of the vertical boundary, the sign of `dy` is changed (from positive to negative, or vice versa) (lines 37–38). This causes the ball to change its vertical movement direction. The `suspend` and `resume` methods (lines 46–52) can be used to stop and start the timer. The `setDelay(int)` method (lines 54–57) sets a new delay.

LISTING 18.8 BallControl.java

```
1  import javax.swing.*;
2  import java.awt.event.*;
3  import java.awt.*;
4
5  public class BallControl extends JPanel {
6    private Ball ball = new Ball();
7    private JButton jbtSuspend = new JButton("Suspend");           button
8    private JButton jbtResume = new JButton("Resume");
9    private JScrollBar jsbDelay = new JScrollBar();                scroll bar
10
11   public BallControl() {                                         create UI
12     // Group buttons in a panel
13     JPanel panel = new JPanel();
14     panel.add(jbtSuspend);
15     panel.add(jbtResume);
16
17     // Add ball and buttons to the panel
18     ball.setBorder(new javax.swing.border.LineBorder(Color.red));
19     jsbDelay.setOrientation(JScrollBar.HORIZONTAL);
20     ball.setDelay(jsbDelay.getMaximum());
21     setLayout(new BorderLayout());
```

```
22        add(jsbDelay, BorderLayout.NORTH);
23        add(ball, BorderLayout.CENTER);
24        add(panel, BorderLayout.SOUTH);
25
26        // Register listeners
27        jbtSuspend.addActionListener(new ActionListener() {
28          @Override
29          public void actionPerformed(ActionEvent e) {
30            ball.suspend();
31          }
32        });
33        jbtResume.addActionListener(new ActionListener() {
34          @Override
35          public void actionPerformed(ActionEvent e) {
36            ball.resume();
37          }
38        });
39        jsbDelay.addAdjustmentListener(new AdjustmentListener() {
40          @Override
41          public void adjustmentValueChanged(AdjustmentEvent e) {
42            ball.setDelay(jsbDelay.getMaximum() - e.getValue());
43          }
44        });
45      }
46    }
```

register listener

suspend

register listener

resume

register listener

new delay

The `BallControl` class extends `JPanel` to display the ball with a scroll bar and two control buttons. When the *Suspend* button is clicked, the ball's `suspend()` method is invoked to suspend the ball's movement (line 30). When the *Resume* button is clicked, the ball's `resume()` method is invoked to resume the ball's movement (line 36). The bouncing speed can be changed using the scroll bar.

LISTING 18.9 `BounceBallApp.java`

```
1  import java.awt.*;
2  import javax.swing.*;
3
4  public class BounceBallApp extends JApplet {
5    public BounceBallApp() {
6      add(new BallControl());
7    }
8  }
```

add BallControl

main method omitted

The `BounceBallApp` class simply places an instance of `BallControl` in the applet. The `main` method is provided in the applet (not displayed in the listing for brevity) so that you can also run it standalone.

Check
Point

MyProgrammingLab™

18.15 How does the program make the ball moving?

18.16 How does the code in Listing 18.7 Ball.java change the direction of the ball movement?

18.17 What does the program do when the *Suspend* button is clicked? What does the program do when the *Resume* button is clicked?

18.9 Case Study: Developing a Tic-Tac-Toe Game

Key
Point

This section develops an applet for playing tic-tac-toe.

VideoNote

TicTacToe

From the many examples in this and earlier chapters you have learned about objects, classes, arrays, class inheritance, GUI, event-driven programming, and applets. Now it is time to put what you have learned to work in developing comprehensive projects. In this section, we will develop a Java applet with which to play the popular game of tic-tac-toe.

Two players take turns marking an available cell in a 3 × 3 grid with their respective tokens (either X or O). When one player has placed three tokens in a horizontal, vertical, or diagonal row on the grid, the game is over and that player has won. A draw (no winner) occurs when all the cells on the grid have been filled with tokens and neither player has achieved a win. Figure 18.10 shows the representative sample runs of the example.

(a) The X player won the game   (b) Draw—no winners   (c) The O player won the game

FIGURE 18.10 Two players play a tic-tac-toe game.

All the examples you have seen so far show simple behaviors that are easy to model with classes. The behavior of the tic-tac-toe game is somewhat more complex. To create classes that model the behavior, you need to study and understand the game.

Assume that all the cells are initially empty, and that the first player takes the X token and the second player the O token. To mark a cell, the player points the mouse to the cell and clicks it. If the cell is empty, the token (X or O) is displayed. If the cell is already filled, the player's action is ignored.

From the preceding description, it is obvious that a cell is a GUI object that handles the mouse-click event and displays tokens. Such an object could be either a button or a panel. Drawing on panels is more flexible than drawing on buttons, because on a panel the token (X or O) can be drawn in any size, but on a button it can be displayed only as a text label. Therefore, a panel should be used to model a cell. How do you know the state of the cell (empty, X, or O)? You use a property named **token** of the **char** type in the **Cell** class. The **Cell** class is responsible for drawing the token when an empty cell is clicked, so you need to write the code for listening to the **MouseEvent** and for painting the shapes for tokens X and O. The **Cell** class can be defined as shown in Figure 18.11.

FIGURE 18.11 The **Cell** class paints the token in a cell.

The tic-tac-toe board consists of nine cells, created using `new Cell[3][3]`. To determine which player's turn it is, you can introduce a variable named `whoseTurn` of the `char` type. `whoseTurn` is initially `'X'`, then changes to `'O'`, and subsequently changes between `'X'` and `'O'` whenever a new cell is occupied. When the game is over, set `whoseTurn` to `' '`.

How do you know whether the game is over, whether there is a winner, and who the winner, if any, is? You can define a method named `isWon(char token)` to check whether a specified token has won and a method named `isFull()` to check whether all the cells are occupied.

Clearly, two classes emerge from the foregoing analysis. One is the `Cell` class, which handles operations for a single cell; the other is the `TicTacToe` class, which plays the whole game and deals with all the cells. The relationship between these two classes is shown in Figure 18.12.

FIGURE 18.12 The `TicTacToe` class contains nine cells.

Since the `Cell` class is only to support the `TicTacToe` class, it can be defined as an inner class in `TicTacToe`. The complete program is given in Listing 18.10.

LISTING 18.10 TicTacToe.java

```
1  import java.awt.*;
2  import java.awt.event.*;
3  import javax.swing.*;
4  import javax.swing.border.LineBorder;
5
6  public class TicTacToe extends JApplet {
7    // Indicate which player has a turn; initially it is the X player
8    private char whoseTurn = 'X';
9
10   // Create and initialize cells
11   private Cell[][] cells =  new Cell[3][3];
12
13   // Create and initialize a status label
14   private JLabel jlblStatus = new JLabel("X's turn to play");
15
16   /** Initialize UI */
17   public TicTacToe() {
18     // Panel p to hold cells
```

main class TicTacToe

```
19        JPanel p = new JPanel(new GridLayout(3, 3, 0, 0));
20        for (int i = 0; i < 3; i++)
21          for (int j = 0; j < 3; j++)
22            p.add(cells[i][j] = new Cell());
23
24        // Set line borders on the cells' panel and the status label
25        p.setBorder(new LineBorder(Color.red, 1));
26        jlblStatus.setBorder(new LineBorder(Color.yellow, 1));
27
28        // Place the panel and the label for the applet
29        add(p, BorderLayout.CENTER);
30        add(jlblStatus, BorderLayout.SOUTH);
31      }
32
33      /** Determine whether the cells are all occupied */
34      public boolean isFull() {                               check isFull
35        for (int i = 0; i < 3; i++)
36          for (int j = 0; j < 3; j++)
37            if (cells[i][j].getToken() == ' ')
38              return false;
39
40        return true;
41      }
42
43      /** Determine whether the player with the specified token wins */
44      public boolean isWon(char token) {
45        for (int i = 0; i < 3; i++)                           check rows
46          if ((cells[i][0].getToken() == token)
47              && (cells[i][1].getToken() == token)
48              && (cells[i][2].getToken() == token)) {
49            return true;
50          }
51
52        for (int j = 0; j < 3; j++)                           check columns
53          if ((cells[0][j].getToken() ==  token)
54              && (cells[1][j].getToken() == token)
55              && (cells[2][j].getToken() == token)) {
56            return true;
57          }
58
59        if ((cells[0][0].getToken() == token)                 check major diagonal
60            && (cells[1][1].getToken() == token)
61            && (cells[2][2].getToken() == token)) {
62          return true;
63        }
64
65        if ((cells[0][2].getToken() == token)                 check subdiagonal
66            && (cells[1][1].getToken() == token)
67            && (cells[2][0].getToken() == token)) {
68          return true;
69        }
70
71        return false;
72      }
73
74      // An inner class for a cell
75      public class Cell extends JPanel {                      inner class Cell
76        // Token used for this cell
77        private char token = ' ';
78
```

register listener

paint cell

listener class

main method omitted

```
 79      public Cell() {
 80        setBorder(new LineBorder(Color.black, 1)); // Set cell's border
 81        addMouseListener(new MyMouseListener());  // Register listener
 82      }
 83
 84      /** Return token */
 85      public char getToken() {
 86        return token;
 87      }
 88
 89      /** Set a new token */
 90      public void setToken(char c) {
 91        token = c;
 92        repaint();
 93      }
 94
 95      @Override /** Paint the cell */
 96      protected void paintComponent(Graphics g) {
 97        super.paintComponent(g);
 98
 99        if (token == 'X') {
100          g.drawLine(10, 10, getWidth() - 10, getHeight() - 10);
101          g.drawLine(getWidth() - 10, 10, 10, getHeight() - 10);
102        }
103        else if (token == 'O') {
104          g.drawOval(10, 10, getWidth() - 20, getHeight() - 20);
105        }
106      }
107
108      private class MyMouseListener extends MouseAdapter {
109        @Override /** Handle mouse click on a cell */
110        public void mouseClicked(MouseEvent e) {
111          // If cell is empty and game is not over
112          if (token == ' ' && whoseTurn != ' ') {
113            setToken(whoseTurn); // Set token in the cell
114
115            // Check game status
116            if (isWon(whoseTurn)) {
117              jlblStatus.setText(whoseTurn + " won! The game is over");
118              whoseTurn = ' '; // Game is over
119            }
120            else if (isFull()) {
121              jlblStatus.setText("Draw! The game is over");
122              whoseTurn = ' '; // Game is over
123            }
124            else {
125              // Change the turn
126              whoseTurn = (whoseTurn == 'X') ? 'O' : 'X';
127              // Display whose turn
128              jlblStatus.setText(whoseTurn + "'s turn");
129            }
130          }
131        }
132      }
133    }
134  }
```

The TicTacToe class initializes the user interface with nine cells placed in a panel of GridLayout (lines 19–22). A label named jlblStatus is used to show the status of the game (line 14). The variable whoseTurn (line 8) is used to track the next type of token to be placed in a cell. The methods `isFull` (lines 34–41) and `isWon` (lines 44–72) are for checking the status of the game.

Since `Cell` is an inner class in `TicTacToe`, the variable (`whoseTurn`) and methods (`isFull` and `isWon`) defined in `TicTacToe` can be referenced from the `Cell` class. The inner class makes programs simple and concise. If `Cell` were not defined as an inner class of `TicTacToe`, you would have to pass an object of `TicTacToe` to `Cell` in order for the variables and methods in `TicTacToe` to be used in `Cell`. You will rewrite the program without using an inner class in Programming Exercise 18.6.

The listener for `MouseEvent` is registered for the cell (line 81). If an empty cell is clicked and the game is not over, a token is set in the cell (line 113). If the game is over, `whoseTurn` is set to `' '` (lines 118, 122). Otherwise, `whoseTurn` is alternated to a new turn (line 126).

 Tip
Use an incremental approach in developing and testing a Java project of this kind. For example, this program can be divided into five steps:

incremental development and testing

1. Lay out the user interface and display a fixed token X on a cell.
2. Enable the cell to display a fixed token X upon a mouse click.
3. Coordinate between the two players so as to display tokens X and O alternately.
4. Check whether a player wins, or whether all the cells are occupied without a winner.
5. Implement displaying a message on the label upon each move by a player.

18.18 When the game starts, what value is in `whoseTurn`? When the game is over, what value is in `whoseTurn`?

18.19 What happens when the user clicks on an empty cell if the game is not over? What happens when the user clicks on an empty cell if the game is over?

18.20 How does the program check whether a player wins? How does the program check whether all cells are filled?

18.21 Delete `super.paintComponent(g)` on line 97 in TicTacToe.java in Listing 18.10 and run the program to see what happens.

✓ **Check Point**

MyProgrammingLab™

18.10 Locating Resources Using the **URL** Class

You can use the URL class to load a resource file for an applet, as long as the resource file is located in the applet's class directory.

🔑 **Key Point**

You have used the `ImageIcon` class to create an icon from an image file and used the `setIcon` method or the constructor to place the icon in a GUI component, such as a button or a label. For example, the following statements create an `ImageIcon` and set it on a `JLabel` object `jlbl`:

```
ImageIcon imageIcon = new ImageIcon("c:\\book\\image\\us.gif");
jlbl.setIcon(imageIcon);
```

This approach presents a problem. The file location is fixed, because it uses the absolute file path on the Windows platform. As a result, the program cannot run on other platforms and cannot run as an applet. Assume that **image/us.gif** is under the class directory. You can circumvent this problem by using a relative path as follows:

```
ImageIcon imageIcon = new ImageIcon("image/us.gif");
```

This works fine with Java applications on all platforms but not with Java applets, because applets cannot load local files. To enable it to work with both applications and applets, you need to locate the file's *URL* (Uniform Resource Locator).

why URL class?

The `java.net.URL` class was used to locate a text file on the Internet in Section 14.13. It can also be used to locate image files and audio files on the Internet. In general, a `URL` object is a pointer to a "resource" on a local machine or a remote host. A resource can be a file or a directory.

The `URL` class can be used to locate a resource file from a class in a way that is independent of the file's location, as long as the resource file is located in the class directory. Recall that the class directory is where the class is stored. To obtain the `URL` object for a file from a class, use the following statement in the applet or application:

```
Class metaObject = this.getClass();
URL url = metaObject.getResource(resourceFilename);
```

meta object

The `getClass()` method returns an instance of the `java.lang.Class` class for the current class. This instance is automatically created by the JVM for every class loaded into the memory. This instance, also known as a *meta object*, contains the information about the class file such as class name, constructors, and methods. You can obtain a `URL` object for a file in the class path by invoking the `getResource(filename)` method on the meta object. For example, if the class file is in **c:\book**, the following statements obtain a `URL` object for **c:\book\image\us.gif**.

```
Class metaObject = this.getClass();
URL url = metaObject.getResource("image/us.gif");
```

You can now create an `ImageIcon` using

```
ImageIcon imageIcon = new ImageIcon(url);
```

Listing 18.11 gives the code that displays an image from **image/us.gif** in the class directory. The file **image/us.gif** is under the class directory, and its `URL` object is obtained using the `getResource` method (line 5). A label with an image icon is created in line 6. The image icon is obtained from the `URL` object.

LISTING 18.11 DisplayImageWithURL.java

```
1  import javax.swing.*;
2
3  public class DisplayImageWithURL extends JApplet {
```

```
4      public DisplayImageWithURL() {
5        java.net.URL url = this.getClass().getResource("image/us.gif");
6        add(new JLabel(new ImageIcon(url)));
7      }
8    }
```

get image URL
create a label

main method omitted

If you replace the code in lines 5–6 with the following code,

```
add(new JLabel(new ImageIcon("image/us.gif")));
```

you can still run the program as a standalone application, but not as an applet from a browser, as shown in Figure 18.13.

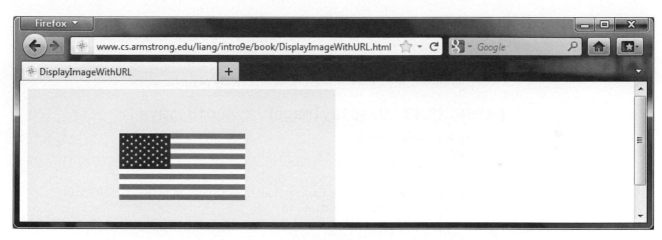

FIGURE 18.13   The applet loads an image from an image file located in the same directory as the applet.

18.22   How do you create a URL object for the file **image/us.gif** in the class directory?

18.23   How do you create an ImageIcon from the file **image/us.gif** in the class directory?

18.11 Playing Audio in Any Java Program

The Applet class contains the methods for obtaining an AudioClip object for an audio file. The AudioClip object contains the methods for playing audio files.

There are several formats for audio files. Java programs can play audio files in the WAV, AIFF, MIDI, AU, and RMF formats.

To play an audio file in Java (application or applet), first create an *audio clip object* for the file. The audio clip is created once and can be played repeatedly without reloading the file. To create an audio clip, use the static method newAudioClip() in the **java.applet.Applet** class:

```
AudioClip audioClip = Applet.newAudioClip(url);
```

Audio originally could be played only from Java applets. For this reason, the AudioClip interface is in the **java.applet** package. Since JDK 1.2, audio can be played in any Java program.

The following statements, for example, create an AudioClip for the **beep.au** audio file in the class directory:

```
Class metaObject = this.getClass();
URL url = metaObject.getResource("beep.au");
AudioClip audioClip = Applet.newAudioClip(url);
```

To manipulate a sound for an audio clip, use the `play()`, `loop()`, and `stop()` methods in `java.applet.AudioClip`, as shown in Figure 18.14.

«interface» *java.applet.AudioClip*	
+*play()*	Starts playing this audio clip. Each time this method is called, the clip is restarted from the beginning.
+*loop()*	Plays the clip repeatedly.
+*stop()*	Stops playing the clip.

FIGURE 18.14   The `AudioClip` interface provides the methods for playing sound.

Listing 18.12 gives the code that displays the Danish flag and plays the Danish national anthem repeatedly. The image file **image/denmark.gif** and audio file **audio/denmark.mid** are stored under the class directory. Line 12 obtains the `URL` object for the audio file, line 13 creates an audio clip for the file, and line 14 repeatedly plays the audio.

LISTING 18.12   `DisplayImagePlayAudio.java`

```
1   import javax.swing.*;
2   import java.net.URL;
3   import java.applet.*;
4
5   public class DisplayImagePlayAudio extends JApplet {
6     private AudioClip audioClip;
7
8     public DisplayImagePlayAudio() {
9       URL urlForImage = getClass().getResource("image/denmark.gif");
10      add(new JLabel(new ImageIcon(urlForImage)));
11
12      URL urlForAudio = getClass().getResource("audio/denmark.mid");
13      audioClip = Applet.newAudioClip(urlForAudio);
14      audioClip.loop();
15    }
16
17    @Override
18    public void start() {
19      if (audioClip != null) audioClip.loop();
20    }
21
22    @Override
23    public void stop() {
24      if (audioClip != null) audioClip.stop();
25    }
26  }
```

get image URL (line 9)
create a label (line 10)

get audio URL (line 12)
create an audio clip (line 13)
play audio repeatedly (line 14)

start audio (lines 18–20)

stop audio (lines 23–25)
main method omitted (line 26)

The `stop` method (lines 23–25) stops the audio when the applet is not displayed, and the `start` method (lines 18–20) restarts the audio when the applet is redisplayed. Try to run this applet without the `stop` and `start` methods from a browser and observe the effect.

Run this program as a standalone application from the main method and from a Web browser to test it. Recall that, for brevity, the `main` method in all applets is not printed in the text.

✓Check Point

18.24   What types of audio files are used in Java?

18.25   How do you create an audio clip from the file **anthem/us.mid** in the class directory?

MyProgrammingLab™

18.26   How do you play, repeatedly play, and stop an audio clip?

18.12 Case Study: National Flags and Anthems

This case study presents an applet that displays a nation's flag and plays its anthem.

Key Point

The images in the applet are for seven national flags, named **flag0.gif**, **flag1.gif**, . . ., **flag6.gif** for Denmark, Germany, China, India, Norway, the U.K., and the U.S. They are stored under the **image** directory in the class path. The audio consists of national anthems for these seven nations, named **anthem0.mid**, **anthem1.mid**, . . ., and **anthem6.mid**. They are stored under the **audio** directory in the class path.

The program enables the user to select a nation from a combo box and then displays its flag and plays its anthem. The user can suspend the audio by clicking the *Suspend* button and resume it by clicking the *Resume* button, as shown in Figure 18.15.

FIGURE 18.15 The applet displays a sequence of images and plays audio.

The program is given in Listing 18.13.

LISTING 18.13 FlagAnthem.java

```java
1   import java.awt.*;
2   import java.awt.event.*;
3   import javax.swing.*;
4   import java.applet.*;
5
6   public class FlagAnthem extends JApplet {
7     private final static int NUMBER_OF_NATIONS = 7;
8     private int current = 0;
9     private ImageIcon[] icons = new ImageIcon[NUMBER_OF_NATIONS];
10    private AudioClip[] audioClips = new AudioClip[NUMBER_OF_NATIONS];
11    private AudioClip currentAudioClip;
12
13    private JLabel jlblImageLabel = new JLabel();
14    private JButton jbtResume = new JButton("Resume");
15    private JButton jbtSuspend = new JButton("Suspend");
16    private JComboBox jcboNations = new JComboBox(new Object[]
17      {"Denmark", "Germany", "China", "India", "Norway", "UK", "US"});
18
19    public FlagAnthem() {
20      // Load image icons and audio clips
21      for (int i = 0; i < NUMBER_OF_NATIONS; i++) {
22        icons[i] = new ImageIcon(getClass().getResource(
23          "image/flag" + i + ".gif"));
24        audioClips[i] = Applet.newAudioClip(
25          getClass().getResource("audio/anthem" + i + ".mid"));
26      }
27
28      JPanel panel = new JPanel();
```

VideoNote

Audio and image

image icons
audio clips
current audio clip

GUI components

create icons

create audio clips

create UI

```
29        panel.add(jbtResume);
30        panel.add(jbtSuspend);
31        panel.add(new JLabel("Select"));
32        panel.add(jcboNations);
33        add(jlblImageLabel, BorderLayout.CENTER);
34        add(panel, BorderLayout.SOUTH);
35
36        jbtResume.addActionListener(new ActionListener() {
37          @Override
38          public void actionPerformed(ActionEvent e) {
39            start();
40          }
41        });
42        jbtSuspend.addActionListener(new ActionListener() {
43          @Override
44          public void actionPerformed(ActionEvent e) {
45            stop();
46          }
47        });
48        jcboNations.addActionListener(new ActionListener() {
49          @Override
50          public void actionPerformed(ActionEvent e) {
51            stop();
52            current = jcboNations.getSelectedIndex();
53            presentNation(current);
54          }
55        });
56
57        jlblImageLabel.setIcon(icons[0]);
58        jlblImageLabel.setHorizontalAlignment(JLabel.CENTER);
59        currentAudioClip = audioClips[0];
60        currentAudioClip.play();
61      }
62
63      private void presentNation(int index) {
64        jlblImageLabel.setIcon(icons[index]);
65        jcboNations.setSelectedIndex(index);
66        currentAudioClip = audioClips[index];
67        currentAudioClip.play();
68      }
69
70      @Override
71      public void start() {
72        currentAudioClip.play();
73      }
74
75      @Override
76      public void stop() {
77        currentAudioClip.stop();
78      }
79    }
```

Margin notes (left column):
- register listener (line 36)
- start audio (line 39)
- register listener (line 42)
- stop audio (line 45)
- register listener (line 48)
- select a nation (line 52)
- present a nation (line 53)
- play a clip (line 72)
- stop audio clip (line 77)
- main method omitted (line 79)

A label is created in line 13 to display a flag image. An array of flag images for seven nations is created in lines 22–23. An array of audio clips is created in lines 24–25. The image files and audio files are stored in the same directory as the applet class file so these files can be located using the **getResource** method.

The combo box for country names is created in lines 16–17. When a new country name in the combo box is selected, the current presentation is stopped and a new selected nation is presented (lines 51–53).

The `presentNation(index)` method (lines 63–68) presents a nation with the specified index. It sets a new image in the label (line 64), synchronizes with the combo box by setting the selected index (line 65), and plays the new audio (line 67).

The applet's `start` and `stop` methods are overridden to resume and suspend the audio (lines 70–78).

18.27 Which code sets the initial image icon? Which code plays the initial audio clip?

18.28 What does the program do when the *Suspend* button is clicked? What does the program do when the *Resume* button is clicked?

KEY TERMS

applet 673	HTML 673
applet container 677	signed applet 676
archive 674	tag 673

CHAPTER SUMMARY

1. `JApplet` is a subclass of `Applet`. It is used for developing Java applets with Swing components.

2. The applet class file must be specified, using the `<applet>` *tag* in an *HTML file* to tell the Web browser where to find the applet. The applet can accept string parameters from HTML using the `<param>` tag.

3. The *applet container* controls and executes applets through the `init`, `start`, `stop`, and `destroy` methods in the `Applet` class.

4. When an applet is loaded, the applet container creates an instance of it by invoking its no-arg constructor. The `init` method is invoked after the applet is created. The `start` method is invoked after the `init` method. It is also called whenever the applet becomes active again after the page containing the applet is revisited. The `stop` method is invoked when the applet becomes inactive.

5. The `destroy` method is invoked when the browser exits normally to inform the applet that it is no longer needed and should release any resources it has allocated. The `stop` method is always called before the `destroy` method.

6. Applications and applets are very similar. An applet can easily be converted into an application, and vice versa. Moreover, an applet can be written with a `main` method to run standalone.

7. You can pass arguments to an applet using the `param` attribute in the applet's tag in HTML. To retrieve the value of the parameter, invoke the `getParameter(paramName)` method.

8. The `Applet`'s `getParameter` method can be invoked only after an instance of the applet is created. Therefore, this method cannot be invoked in the constructor of the applet class. You should invoke this method from the `init` method.

9. You learned how to incorporate images and audio in Java applications and applets. To load audio and images for Java applications and applets, you have to create a `URL` object for the audio and image file. The resource files must be stored in the class directory.

10. To play an audio, create an audio clip from the **URL** object for the audio source. You can use the **AudioClip**'s **play()** method to play it once, the **loop()** method to play it repeatedly, and the **stop()** method to stop it.

TEST QUESTIONS

Do the test questions for this chapter online at www.cs.armstrong.edu/liang/intro9e/test.html.

MyProgrammingLab™

PROGRAMMING EXERCISES

Pedagogical Note

For every applet in the exercise, add a main method to enable it to run as a stand-alone application.

Sections 18.2–18.6

18.1 (*Loan calculator*) Revise Listing 16.7, LoanCalculator.java, to be an applet for computing loan payment.

18.2 (*Convert applications to applets*) Rewrite **ClockAnimation** in Listing 16.12 as an applet and enable it to run standalone.

*18.3 (*Guess capitals and states*) Revise Programming Exercise 9.17 to write an applet that repeatedly prompts the user to enter a capital for a state or vice versa, as shown in Figure 18.16a. Upon clicking the *Answer* button, the program gets the user input from the text field, reports whether the answer is correct in a message dialog box (Figure 18.16b–c), shows the correct count and total count, and then displays the next question. The user can specify whether to let the program generate a question randomly or sequentially, and whether to generate questions for a capital or a state.

(a) (b) (c)

FIGURE 18.16 The applet tests the user knowledge on states and capitals.

*18.4 (*Pass strings to applets*) Rewrite Listing 18.5, DisplayMessage.java, to display a message with a standard color, font, and size. The **message**, **x**, **y**, **color**, **fontname**, and **fontsize** are parameters in the **<applet>** tag, as shown below:

```
<applet
  code = "Exercise18_04.class"
  width = 200
  height = 50
  alt = "You must have a Java-enabled browser to view the applet"
>
  <param name = MESSAGE value = "Welcome to Java" />
  <param name = X value = 40 />
  <param name = Y value = 50 />
  <param name = COLOR value = "red" />
```

```
        <param name = FONTNAME value = "Monospaced" />
        <param name = FONTSIZE value = 20 />
    </applet>
```

**18.5 (*Game: a clock learning tool*) Develop a clock applet to show a first-grade student how to read a clock. Modify Programming Exercise 13.19 to display a detailed clock with an hour hand and a minute hand in an applet, as shown in Figure 18.17a. The hour and minute values are randomly generated. The hour is between 0 and 11, and the minute is 0, 15, 30, or 45. Upon a mouse click, a new random time is displayed on the clock.

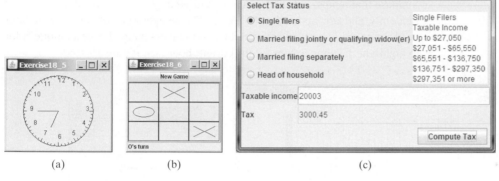

(a)	(b)	(c)

FIGURE 18.17 (a) Upon a mouse click on the clock, the clock time is randomly displayed. (b) Clicking the *New Game* button starts a new game. (c) The tax calculator computes the tax for the specified taxable income and tax status.

**18.6 (*Game: tic-tac-toe*) Rewrite the program in Listing 18.10 TicTacToe.java with the following modifications:

- Define `Cell` as a separate class rather than an inner class.
- Add a button named *New Game*, as shown in Figure 18.17b. Clicking the *New Game* button starts a new game.

**18.7 (*Financial application: tax calculator*) Create an applet to compute tax, as shown in Figure 18.17c. The applet lets the user select the tax status and enter the taxable income to compute the tax based on the 2001 federal tax rates, as shown in Programming Exercise 10.8.

***18.8 (*Create a calculator*) Use various panels of `FlowLayout`, `GridLayout`, and `BorderLayout` to lay out the following calculator and to implement addition (+), subtraction (-), division (/), square root (`sqrt`), and modulus (%) functions (see Figure 18.18a).

(a)	(b)

FIGURE 18.18 (a) Exercise 18.8 is a Java implementation of a popular calculator. (b) Exercise 18.9 converts between decimal, hex, and binary numbers.

*18.9 (*Convert numbers*) Write an applet that converts between decimal, hex, and binary numbers, as shown in Figure 18.18b. When you enter a decimal value in the decimal-value text field and press the *Enter* key, its corresponding hex and binary numbers are displayed in the other two text fields. Likewise, you can enter values in the other fields and convert them accordingly.

**18.10 (*Repaint a partial area*) When you repaint the entire viewing area of a panel, sometimes only a tiny portion of the viewing area is changed. You can improve the performance by repainting only the affected area, but do not invoke `super.paintComponent(g)` when repainting the panel, because this will cause the entire viewing area to be cleared. Use this approach to write an applet to display the temperatures of each hour during the last 24 hours in a histogram. Suppose that temperatures between 50 and 90 degrees Fahrenheit are obtained randomly and are updated every hour. The temperature of the current hour needs to be redisplayed, while the others remain unchanged. Use a unique color to highlight the temperature for the current hour (see Figure 18.19a).

(a)   (b)

FIGURE 18.19 (a) The histogram displays the average temperature of every hour in the last 24 hours. (b) The program simulates a running fan.

18.11 (*Simulation: a running fan*) Write a Java applet that simulates a running fan, as shown in Figure 18.19b. The buttons *Start*, *Stop*, and *Reverse* control the fan. The scrollbar controls the fan's speed. Create a class named **Fan, a subclass of **JPanel**, to display the fan. This class also contains the methods to suspend and resume the fan, set its speed, and reverse its direction. Create a class named **FanControl** that contains a fan, and three buttons and a scroll bar to control the fan. Create a Java applet that contains an instance of **FanControl**.

**18.12 (*Control a group of fans*) Write a Java applet that displays three fans in a group, with control buttons to start and stop all of them, as shown in Figure 18.20.

FIGURE 18.20 The program runs and controls a group of fans.

***18.13 (*Create an elevator simulator*) Write an applet that simulates an elevator going up and down (see Figure 18.21). The buttons on the left indicate the floor where the passenger is now located. The passenger must click a button on the left to request that the elevator come to his or her floor. On entering the elevator, the passenger clicks a button on the right to request that it go to the specified floor.

FIGURE 18.21 The program simulates elevator operations.

VideoNote

Control a group of clocks

*18.14 (*Control a group of clocks*) Write a Java applet that displays three clocks in a group, with control buttons to start and stop all of them, as shown in Figure 18.22.

(clocks figure — Exercise18_14)

FIGURE 18.22 Three clocks run independently with individual control and group control.

Sections 18.10–18.12

*18.15 (*Enlarge and shrink an image*) Write an applet that will display a sequence of images from a single image file in different sizes. Initially, the viewing area for this image has a width of 300 and a height of 300. Your program should continuously shrink the viewing area by 1 in width and 1 in height until it reaches a width of 50 and a height of 50. At that point, the viewing area should continuously enlarge by 1 in width and 1 in height until it reaches a width of 300 and a height of 300. The viewing area should shrink and enlarge (alternately) to create animation for the single image.

***18.16 (*Simulate a stock ticker*) Write a Java applet that displays a stock-index ticker (see Figure 18.23). The stock-index information is passed from the `<param>` tag in the HTML file. Each index has four parameters: Index Name (e.g., S&P

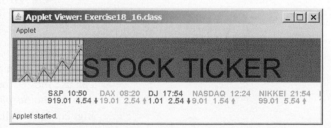

FIGURE 18.23 The program displays a stock-index ticker.

500), Current Time (e.g., 15:54), the index from the previous day (e.g., 919.01), and Change (e.g., 4.54). Use at least five indexes, such as Dow Jones, S&P 500, NASDAQ, NIKKEI, and Gold & Silver Index. Display positive changes in green and negative changes in red. The indexes move from right to left in the applet's viewing area. The applet freezes the ticker when the mouse button is pressed; it moves again when the mouse button is released.

**18.17 (*Racing cars*) Write an applet that simulates four cars racing, as shown in Figure 18.24a. You can set the speed for each car, with maximum 100.

             (a)   (b)

FIGURE 18.24 (a) You can set the speed for each car. (b) This applet shows each country's flag, name, and description, one after another, and reads the description that is currently shown.

18.18 (*Show national flags*) Write an applet that introduces national flags, one after the other, by presenting each one's photo, name, and description (see Figure 18.24b) along with audio that reads the description. Suppose your applet displays the flags of eight countries. Assume that the photo image files, named **flag0.gif, **flag1.gif**, and so on, up to **flag7.gif**, are stored in a subdirectory named **image** in the applet's directory. The length of each audio is less than 10 seconds. Assume that the name and description of each country's flag are passed from the HTML using the parameters **name0**, **name1**, . . . , **name7**, and **description0**, **description1**, . . . , and **description7**. Pass the number of countries as an HTML parameter using **numberOfCountries**. Here is an example:

```
<param name = "numberOfCountries" value = 8>
<param name = "name0" value = "Canada">
<param name = "description0" value = "The Canadian ... ">
```

 Hint
Use the **DescriptionPanel** class to display the image, name, and the text. The **DescriptionPanel** class was introduced in Listing 17.2.

***18.19 (*Bouncing balls*) The example in Section 18.8 simulates a bouncing ball. Extend the example to allow multiple balls, as shown in Figure 18.25a. You can use the +*1* or −*1* button to increase or decrease the number of the balls, and use the *Suspend* and *Resume* buttons to freeze the balls or resume bouncing. For each ball, assign a random color.

FIGURE 18.25 (a) The applet allows you to add or remove bouncing balls. (b) Click *Play* to play an audio clip once, click *Loop* to play an audio repeatedly, and click *Stop* to terminate playing.

*18.20 (*Play, loop, and stop a sound clip*) Write an applet that meets the following requirements:

■ Get an audio file from the class directory.
■ Place three buttons labeled *Play*, *Loop*, and *Stop*, as shown in Figure 18.25b.
■ If you click the *Play* button, the audio file is played once. If you click the *Loop* button, the audio file keeps playing repeatedly. If you click the *Stop* button, the playing stops.
■ The applet can run as an application.

**18.21 (*Create an alarm clock*) Write an applet that will display a digital clock with a large display panel that shows the hour, minute, and second. This clock should allow the user to set an alarm. Figure 18.26a shows an example of such a clock. To turn on the alarm, check the *Alarm* check box. To specify the alarm time, click the *Set alarm* button to display a new frame, as shown in Figure 18.26b. You can set the alarm time in the frame.

FIGURE 18.26 The program displays the current hour, minute, and second and enables you to set an alarm.

**18.22 (*Create an image animator with audio*) Create animation using the applet shown in Figure 18.27 to meet the following requirements:

■ Allow the user to specify the animation speed in a text field.
■ Get the number of frames and the image's file-name prefix from the user. For example, if the user enters **n** for the number of frames and **L** for the image prefix, then the files are **L1**, **L2**, and so on, to **L**n. Assume that the images are stored in the **image** directory, a subdirectory of the applet's directory.
■ Allow the user to specify an audio file name. The audio file is stored in the same directory as the applet. The sound is played while the animation runs.

FIGURE 18.27 This applet lets the user select image files, an audio file, and the animation speed.

**18.23 (*Simulation: raise flag and play anthem*) Create an applet that displays a flag rising up, as shown in Figure 16.1b–d. As the national flag rises, play the national anthem. (You may use a flag image and anthem audio file from Listing 18.13.)

Comprehensive

***18.24 (*Game: bean-machine animation*) Write an applet that enhances the bean machine animation in Programming Exercise 16.22. The applet lets you set the number of slots, as shown in Figure 18.28. Click *Start* to start or restart the animation and click *Stop* to stop.

(a)   (b)   (c)

FIGURE 18.28 The applet controls a bean-machine animation.

**18.25 (*Game: guess birthdays*) Listing 3.3, GuessBirthday.java, gives a program for guessing a birthday. Create an applet for guessing birthdays as shown in Figure 18.29. The applet prompts the user to check whether the date is in any of the five sets. The date is displayed in the text field upon clicking the *Guess Birthday* button.

***18.26 (*Game: math quiz*) Listing 3.1, AdditionQuiz.java, and Listing 3.4, SubtractionQuiz.java, generate and grade math quizzes. Write an applet that allows

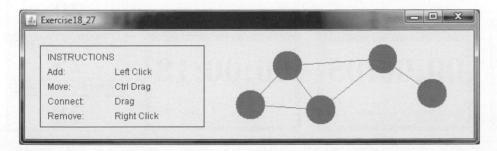

FIGURE 18.29 This applet guesses the birthday.

the user to select a question type and difficulty level, as shown in Figure 18.30a. When the user clicks the *Start* button, the program begins to generate a question. After the user enters an answer with the *Enter* key, a new question is displayed. When the user clicks the *Start* button, the elapsed time is displayed. The time is updated every second until the *Stop* button is clicked. The correct count is updated whenever a correct answer is made.

(a) Before a session starts   (b) After a session is started

FIGURE 18.30 The applet tests math skills.

***18.27 (*Graphs*) A graph consists of vertices and edges that connect vertices. Write a program that enables the user to draw vertices and edges dynamically, as shown in Figure 18.31. The radius of each vertex is **20** pixels. Implement the following functions: (1) The user clicks the left-mouse button to place a vertex centered at the mouse point, provided that the mouse point is not inside or too

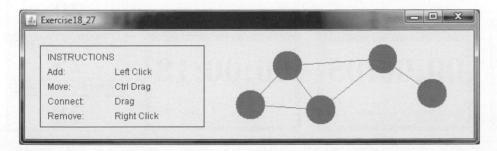

FIGURE 18.31 The applet enables users to draw a graph dynamically.

close to an existing vertex. (2) The user clicks the right-mouse button inside an existing vertex to remove the vertex. (3) The user presses a mouse button inside a vertex and drags to another vertex and then releases the button to create an edge. (4) The user drags a vertex while pressing the *CTRL* key to move a vertex.

**18.28 (*Geometry: two circles intersect?*) The `Circle2D` class was defined in Programming Exercise 10.11. Write an applet that enables the user to specify the location and size of the circles and displays whether the two circles intersect, as shown in Figure 18.32a. Enable the user to point the mouse inside a circle and drag it. As the circle is being dragged, the circle's center coordinates in the text fields are updated.

(a)   (b)   (c)

FIGURE 18.32 Check whether two circles, two rectangles, and two triangles are overlapping.

**18.29 (*Geometry: two rectangles intersect?*) The `MyRectangle2D` class was defined in Programming Exercise 10.13. Write an applet that enables the user to specify the location and size of the rectangles and displays whether the two rectangles intersect, as shown in Figure 18.32b. Enable the user to point the mouse inside a rectangle and drag it. As the rectangle is being dragged, the rectangle's center coordinates in the text fields are updated.

**18.30 (*Geometry: two triangles intersect?*) The `Triangle2D` class was defined in Programming Exercise 10.12. Write an applet that enables the user to specify the location of the two triangles and displays whether the two triangles intersect, as shown in Figure 18.32c.

*18.31 (*Count-up stopwatch*) Write an applet that simulates a stopwatch, as shown in Figure 18.33a. When the user clicks the *Start* button, the button's label

(a)   (b)   (c)   (d)

FIGURE 18.33 (a)–(c) The applet counts up the time. (d) The applet counts down the time.

is changed to *Pause*, as shown in Figure 18.33b. When the user clicks the *Pause* button, the button's label is changed to *Resume*, as shown in Figure 18.33c. The *Clear* button resets the count to 0 and resets the button's label to *Start*.

*18.32 (*Count-down stopwatch*) Write an applet that allows the user to enter time in seconds in the text field and press the *Enter* key to count down the minutes, as shown in Figure 18.33(d). The remaining seconds are redisplayed every one second. When the minutes are expired, the program starts to play music continuously.

**18.33 (*Pattern recognition: consecutive four equal numbers*) Write an applet for Programming Exercise 7.19, as shown in Figure 18.34a–b. Let the user enter the numbers in the text fields in a grid of 6 rows and 7 columns. The user can click the *Solve* button to highlight a sequence of four equal numbers, if it exists.

| (a) | (b) | (c) |

FIGURE 18.34 (a)–(b) Clicking the *Solve* button to highlight the four consecutive numbers in a row, a column, or a diagonal. (c) The applet enables two players to play the connect-four game.

***18.34 (*Game: connect four*) Programming Exercise 7.20 enables two players to play the connect-four game on the console. Rewrite the program using an applet, as shown in Figure 18.34c. The applet enables two players to place red and yellow discs in turn. To place a disk, the player needs to click on an available cell. An *available cell* is unoccupied and its downward neighbor is occupied. The applet flashes the four winning cells if a player wins and reports no winners if all cells are occupied with no winners.

***18.35 (*Game: play connect four with computer*) Revise Exercise 18.34 to play the game with the computer. The program lets the user make a move first, followed by a move by the computer. The minimum requirement is for the computer to make a legal move. You are encouraged to design good strategies for the computer to make intelligent moves.

**18.36 (*Geometry: display angles*) Write a program that enables the user to drag the vertices of a triangle and displays the angles dynamically as the triangle shape changes, as shown in Figure 18.35a. Change the mouse cursor to the cross-hair shape when the mouse is moved close to a vertex. The formula to compute angles A, B, and C are as follows (see Figure 18.35b):

```
A = Math.acos((a * a - b * b - c * c) / (-2 * b * c))
B = Math.acos((b * b - a * a - c * c) / (-2 * a * c))
C = Math.acos((c * c - b * b - a * a) / (-2 * a * b))
```

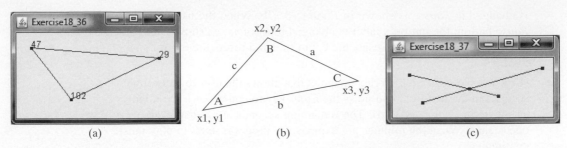

Figure 18.35 (a–b) Exercise18.36 enables the user to drag vertices and display the angles dynamically. (c) Exercise18.37 enables the user to drag vertices and display the lines and their intersecting point dynamically.

**18.37 (*Geometry: intersecting point*) Write a program that displays two line segments with their end points, and their intersecting point. Initially, the end points are at (20, 20) and (56, 130) for line 1 and at (100, 20) and (16, 130) for line 2. The user can use the mouse to drag a point and dynamically display the intersecting point, as shown in Figure 18.35c. *Hint*: See Programming Exercise 3.25 for finding the intersecting point of two unbounded lines.

BINARY I/O

Objectives

- To discover how I/O is processed in Java (§19.2).

- To distinguish between text I/O and binary I/O (§19.3).

- To read and write bytes using `FileInputStream` and `FileOutputStream` (§19.4.1).

- To filter data using the base classes `FilterInputStream` and `FilterOutputStream` (§19.4.2).

- To read and write primitive values and strings using `DataInputStream` and `DataOutputStream` (§19.4.3).

- To improve I/O performance by using `BufferedInputStream` and `BufferedOutputStream` (§19.4.4).

- To write a program that copies a file (§19.5).

- To store and restore objects using `ObjectOutputStream` and `ObjectInputStream` (§19.6).

- To implement the `Serializable` interface to make objects serializable (§19.6.1).

- To serialize arrays (§19.6.2).

- To read and write files using the `RandomAccessFile` class (§19.7).

19.1 Introduction

**Key
Point**

Java provides many classes for performing text I/O and binary I/O.

text file

binary file

Files can be classified as either text or binary. A file that can be processed (read, created, or modified) using a text editor such as Notepad on Windows or vi on UNIX is called a *text file*. All the other files are called *binary files*. You cannot read binary files using a text editor—they are designed to be read by programs. For example, Java source programs are stored in text files and can be read by a text editor, but Java class files are stored in binary files and are read by the JVM.

Although it is not technically precise and correct, you can envision a text file as consisting of a sequence of characters and a binary file as consisting of a sequence of bits. Characters in a text file are encoded using a character encoding scheme such as ASCII or Unicode. For example, the decimal integer **199** is stored as the sequence of the three characters **1**, **9**, **9** in a text file, and the same integer is stored as a byte-type value **C7** in a binary file, because decimal **199** equals hex **C7** ($199 = 12 \times 16^1 + 7$). The advantage of binary files is that they are more efficient to process than text files.

why binary I/O?

text I/O

binary I/O

Java offers many classes for performing file input and output. These can be categorized as *text I/O classes* and *binary I/O classes*. In Section 14.11, File Input and Output, you learned how to read and write strings and numeric values from/to a text file using **Scanner** and **PrintWriter**. This chapter introduces the classes for performing binary I/O.

19.2 How Is Text I/O Handled in Java?

**Key
Point**

*Text data is read using the **Scanner** class and written using the **PrintWriter** class.*

Recall that a **File** object encapsulates the properties of a file or a path but does not contain the methods for reading/writing data from/to a file. In order to perform I/O, you need to create objects using appropriate Java I/O classes. The objects contain the methods for reading/writing data from/to a file. For example, to write text to a file named **temp.txt**, you can create an object using the **PrintWriter** class as follows:

```
PrintWriter output = new PrintWriter("temp.txt");
```

You can now invoke the **print** method on the object to write a string to the file. For example, the following statement writes **Java 101** to the file.

```
output.print("Java 101");
```

The next statement closes the file.

```
output.close();
```

There are many I/O classes for various purposes. In general, these can be classified as input classes and output classes. An *input class* contains the methods to read data, and an *output class* contains the methods to write data. **PrintWriter** is an example of an output class, and **Scanner** is an example of an input class. The following code creates an input object for the file **temp.txt** and reads data from the file.

```
Scanner input = new Scanner(new File("temp.txt"));
System.out.println(input.nextLine());
```

If **temp.txt** contains the text **Java 101**, **input.nextLine()** returns the string **"Java 101"**.

stream

input stream

output stream

Figure 19.1 illustrates Java I/O programming. An input object reads a *stream* of data from a file, and an output object writes a stream of data to a file. An input object is also called an *input stream* and an output object an *output stream*.

Program

Input object
created from an
input class

Input stream

01011...1001

File

Output object
created from an
output class

11001...1011

File

Output stream

FIGURE 19.1 The program receives data through an input object and sends data through an output object.

19.1 What is a text file, and what is a binary file? Can you view a text file or a binary file using a text editor?

19.2 How do you read or write text data in Java? What is a stream?

19.3 Text I/O vs. Binary I/O

Binary I/O does not involve encoding or decoding and thus is more efficient than text I/O.

Computers do not differentiate between binary files and text files. All files are stored in binary format, and thus all files are essentially binary files. Text I/O is built upon binary I/O to provide a level of abstraction for character encoding and decoding, as shown in Figure 19.2a. Encoding and decoding are automatically performed for text I/O. The JVM converts Unicode to a file-specific encoding when writing a character, and it converts a file-specific encoding to Unicode when reading a character. For example, suppose you write the string **"199"** using text I/O to a file. Each character is written to the file. Since the Unicode for character **1** is **0x0031**, the Unicode **0x0031** is converted to a code that depends on the encoding scheme for the file. (Note that the prefix **0x** denotes a hex number.) In the United States, the default encoding for text files on Windows is ASCII. The ASCII code for character **1** is **49** (**0x31** in

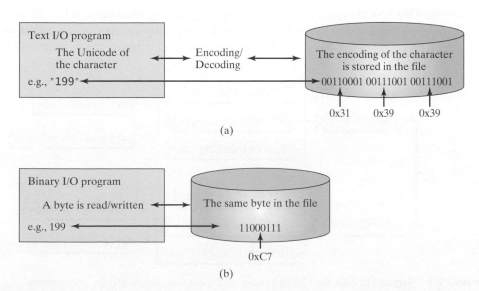

Text I/O program
The Unicode of
the character

Encoding/
Decoding

The encoding of the character
is stored in the file

e.g., "199"

00110001 00111001 00111001

0x31   0x39   0x39

(a)

Binary I/O program

A byte is read/written

The same byte in the file

e.g., 199

11000111

0xC7

(b)

FIGURE 19.2 Text I/O requires encoding and decoding, whereas binary I/O does not.

hex) and for character **9** is **57** (**0x39** in hex). Thus, to write the characters **199**, three bytes—**0x31**, **0x39**, and **0x39**—are sent to the output, as shown in Figure 19.2a.

Binary I/O does not require conversions. If you write a numeric value to a file using binary I/O, the exact value in the memory is copied into the file. For example, a byte-type value **199** is represented as **0xC7** ($199 = 12 \times 16^1 + 7$) in the memory and appears exactly as **0xC7** in the file, as shown in Figure 19.2b. When you read a byte using binary I/O, one byte value is read from the input.

In general, you should use text input to read a file created by a text editor or a text output program, and use binary input to read a file created by a Java binary output program.

Binary I/O is more efficient than text I/O, because binary I/O does not require encoding and decoding. Binary files are independent of the encoding scheme on the host machine and thus are portable. Java programs on any machine can read a binary file created by a Java program. This is why Java class files are binary files. Java class files can run on a JVM on any machine.

.txt and .dat

Note
For consistency, this book uses the extension **.txt** to name text files and **.dat** to name binary files.

Check Point

MyProgrammingLab™

19.3 What are the differences between text I/O and binary I/O?

19.4 How is a Java character represented in the memory, and how is a character represented in a text file?

19.5 If you write the string **"ABC"** to an ASCII text file, what values are stored in the file?

19.6 If you write the string **"100"** to an ASCII text file, what values are stored in the file? If you write a numeric byte-type value **100** using binary I/O, what values are stored in the file?

19.7 What is the encoding scheme for representing a character in a Java program? By default, what is the encoding scheme for a text file on Windows?

19.4 Binary I/O Classes

Key Point

*The abstract **InputStream** is the root class for reading binary data and the abstract **OutputStream** is the root class for writing binary data.*

The design of the Java I/O classes is a good example of applying inheritance, where common operations are generalized in superclasses, and subclasses provide specialized operations. Figure 19.3 lists some of the classes for performing binary I/O. **InputStream** is the root for

FIGURE 19.3 **InputStream**, **OutputStream**, and their subclasses are for performing binary I/O.

java.io.InputStream	
+read(): int	Reads the next byte of data from the input stream. The value byte is returned as an int value in the range 0 to 255. If no byte is available because the end of the stream has been reached, the value –1 is returned.
+read(b: byte[]): int	Reads up to b.length bytes into array b from the input stream and returns the actual number of bytes read. Returns –1 at the end of the stream.
+read(b: byte[], off: int, len: int): int	Reads bytes from the input stream and stores them in b[off], b[off+1], . . ., b[off+len-1]. The actual number of bytes read is returned. Returns –1 at the end of the stream.
+available(): int	Returns an estimate of the number of bytes that can be read from the input stream.
+close(): void	Closes this input stream and releases any system resources occupied by it.
+skip(n: long): long	Skips over and discards n bytes of data from this input stream. The actual number of bytes skipped is returned.
+markSupported(): boolean	Tests whether this input stream supports the mark and reset methods.
+mark(readlimit: int): void	Marks the current position in this input stream.
+reset(): void	Repositions this stream to the position at the time the mark method was last called on this input stream.

FIGURE 19.4   The abstract `InputStream` class defines the methods for the input stream of bytes.

binary input classes, and `OutputStream` is the root for binary output classes. Figures 19.4 and 19.5 list all the methods in the classes `InputStream` and `OutputStream`.

> **Note**
> All the methods in the binary I/O classes are declared to throw `java.io.IOException` or a subclass of `java.io.IOException`.

`throws IOException`

java.io.OutputStream	
+write(int b): void	Writes the specified byte to this output stream. The parameter b is an int value. (byte)b is written to the output stream.
+write(b: byte[]): void	Writes all the bytes in array b to the output stream.
+write(b: byte[], off: int, len: int): void	Writes b[off], b[off+1],. . ., b[off+len-1] into the output stream.
+close(): void	Closes this output stream and releases any system resources occupied by it.
+flush(): void	Flushes this output stream and forces any buffered output bytes to be written out.

FIGURE 19.5   The abstract `OutputStream` class defines the methods for the output stream of bytes.

19.4.1 `FileInputStream`/`FileOutputStream`

`FileInputStream`/`FileOutputStream` is for reading/writing bytes from/to files. All the methods in these classes are inherited from `InputStream` and `OutputStream`. `FileInputStream`/`FileOutputStream` does not introduce new methods. To construct a `FileInputStream`, use the constructors shown in Figure 19.6.

A `java.io.FileNotFoundException` will occur if you attempt to create a `FileInputStream` with a nonexistent file.

`FileNotFoundException`

To construct a `FileOutputStream`, use the constructors shown in Figure 19.7.

If the file does not exist, a new file will be created. If the file already exists, the first two constructors will delete the current content of the file. To retain the current content and append new data into the file, use the last two constructors and pass **true** to the **append** parameter.

FIGURE 19.6 `FileInputStream` inputs a stream of bytes from a file.

FIGURE 19.7 `FileOutputStream` outputs a stream of bytes to a file.

IOException

Almost all the methods in the I/O classes throw `java.io.IOException`. Therefore, you have to declare `java.io.IOException` to throw in the method or place the code in a try-catch block, as shown below:

Declaring exception in the method

```java
public static void main(String[] args)
    throws IOException {
  // Perform I/O operations
}
```

Using try-catch block

```java
public static void main(String[] args) {
  try {
    // Perform I/O operations
  }
  catch (IOException ex) {
    ex.printStackTrace();
  }
}
```

Listing 19.1 uses binary I/O to write ten byte values from **1** to **10** to a file named **temp.dat** and reads them back from the file.

LISTING 19.1 TestFileStream.java

import

output stream

output

```java
 1  import java.io.*;
 2
 3  public class TestFileStream {
 4    public static void main(String[] args) throws IOException {
 5      // Create an output stream to the file
 6      FileOutputStream output = new FileOutputStream("temp.dat");
 7
 8      // Output values to the file
 9      for (int i = 1; i <= 10; i++)
10        output.write(i);
11
12      // Close the output stream
13      output.close();
14
```

```
15      // Create an input stream for the file
16      FileInputStream input = new FileInputStream("temp.dat");         input stream
17
18      // Read values from the file
19      int value;
20      while ((value = input.read()) != -1)                             input
21        System.out.print(value + " ");
22
23      // Close the output stream
24      input.close();                                                   
25    }
26  }
```

```
1 2 3 4 5 6 7 8 9 10
```

A `FileOutputStream` is created for the file **temp.dat** in line 6. The `for` loop writes ten byte values into the file (lines 9–10). Invoking `write(i)` is the same as invoking `write((byte)i)`. Line 13 closes the output stream. Line 16 creates a `FileInputStream` for the file **temp.dat**. Values are read from the file and displayed on the console in lines 19–21. The expression `((value = input.read()) != -1)` (line 20) reads a byte from `input.read()`, assigns it to `value`, and checks whether it is −1. The input value of −1 signifies the end of a file.

end of a file

The file **temp.dat** created in this example is a binary file. It can be read from a Java program but not from a text editor, as shown in Figure 19.8.

Binary data ⟶

FIGURE 19.8   A binary file cannot be displayed in text mode.

Tip

When a stream is no longer needed, always close it using the `close()` method. Not closing streams may cause data corruption in the output file, or other programming errors.

close stream

Note

The root directory for the file is the classpath directory. For the example in this book, the root directory is **c:\book**, so the file **temp.dat** is located at **c:\book**. If you wish to place **temp.dat** in a specific directory, replace line 6 with

where is the file?

```
FileOutputStream output =
  new FileOutputStream ("directory/temp.dat");
```

Note

An instance of `FileInputStream` can be used as an argument to construct a `Scanner`, and an instance of `FileOutputStream` can be used as an argument to construct a `PrintWriter`. You can create a `PrintWriter` to append text into a file using

appending to text file

```
new PrintWriter(new FileOutputStream("temp.txt", true));
```

If **temp.txt** does not exist, it is created. If **temp.txt** already exists, new data are appended to the file.

19.4.2 `FilterInputStream`/`FilterOutputStream`

Filter streams are streams that filter bytes for some purpose. The basic byte input stream provides a `read` method that can be used only for reading bytes. If you want to read integers, doubles, or strings, you need a filter class to wrap the byte input stream. Using a filter class enables you to read integers, doubles, and strings instead of bytes and characters. `FilterInputStream` and `FilterOutputStream` are the base classes for filtering data. When you need to process primitive numeric types, use `DataInputStream` and `DataOutputStream` to filter bytes.

19.4.3 `DataInputStream`/`DataOutputStream`

`DataInputStream` reads bytes from the stream and converts them into appropriate primitive type values or strings. `DataOutputStream` converts primitive type values or strings into bytes and outputs the bytes to the stream.

`DataInputStream` extends `FilterInputStream` and implements the `DataInput` interface, as shown in Figure 19.9. `DataOutputStream` extends `FilterOutputStream` and implements the `DataOutput` interface, as shown in Figure 19.10.

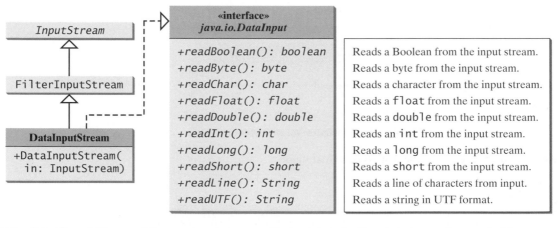

FIGURE 19.9 `DataInputStream` filters an input stream of bytes into primitive data type values and strings.

`DataInputStream` implements the methods defined in the `DataInput` interface to read primitive data type values and strings. `DataOutputStream` implements the methods defined in the `DataOutput` interface to write primitive data type values and strings. Primitive values are copied from memory to the output without any conversions. Characters in a string may be written in several ways, as discussed in the next section.

Characters and Strings in Binary I/O

A Unicode character consists of two bytes. The `writeChar(char c)` method writes the Unicode of character `c` to the output. The `writeChars(String s)` method writes the Unicode for each character in the string `s` to the output. The `writeBytes(String s)` method writes the lower byte of the Unicode for each character in the string `s` to the output. The high byte of the Unicode is discarded. The `writeBytes` method is suitable for strings that consist

FIGURE 19.10 `DataOutputStream` enables you to write primitive data type values and strings into an output stream.

of ASCII characters, since an ASCII code is stored only in the lower byte of a Unicode. If a string consists of non-ASCII characters, you have to use the `writeChars` method to write the string.

The `writeUTF(String s)` method writes two bytes of length information to the output stream, followed by the modified UTF-8 representation of every character in the string `s`. UTF-8 is a coding scheme that allows systems to operate with both ASCII and Unicode. Most operating systems use ASCII. Java uses Unicode. The ASCII character set is a subset of the Unicode character set. Since most applications need only the ASCII character set, it is a waste to represent an 8-bit ASCII character as a 16-bit Unicode character. The modified UTF-8 scheme stores a character using one, two, or three bytes. Characters are coded in one byte if their code is less than or equal to `0x7F`, in two bytes if their code is greater than `0x7F` and less than or equal to `0x7FF`, or in three bytes if their code is greater than `0x7FF`.

The initial bits of a UTF-8 character indicate whether a character is stored in one byte, two bytes, or three bytes. If the first bit is `0`, it is a one-byte character. If the first bits are `110`, it is the first byte of a two-byte sequence. If the first bits are `1110`, it is the first byte of a three-byte sequence. The information that indicates the number of characters in a string is stored in the first two bytes preceding the UTF-8 characters. For example, `writeUTF("ABCDEF")` actually writes eight bytes (i.e., `00 06 41 42 43 44 45 46`) to the file, because the first two bytes store the number of characters in the string.

UTF-8 scheme

The `writeUTF(String s)` method converts a string into a series of bytes in the UTF-8 format and writes them into an output stream. The `readUTF()` method reads a string that has been written using the `writeUTF` method.

The UTF-8 format has the advantage of saving a byte for each ASCII character, because a Unicode character takes up two bytes and an ASCII character in UTF-8 only one byte. If most of the characters in a long string are regular ASCII characters, using UTF-8 is more efficient.

Creating `DataInputStream`/`DataOutputStream`

`DataInputStream`/`DataOutputStream` are created using the following constructors (see Figures 19.9 and 19.10):

```
public DataInputStream(InputStream instream)
public DataOutputStream(OutputStream outstream)
```

The following statements create data streams. The first statement creates an input stream for the file **in.dat**; the second statement creates an output stream for the file **out.dat**.

```
DataInputStream input =
  new DataInputStream(new FileInputStream("in.dat"));
DataOutputStream output =
  new DataOutputStream(new FileOutputStream("out.dat"));
```

Listing 19.2 writes student names and scores to a file named **temp.dat** and reads the data back from the file.

LISTING 19.2 TestDataStream.java

```
 1  import java.io.*;
 2
 3  public class TestDataStream {
 4    public static void main(String[] args) throws IOException {
 5      // Create an output stream for file temp.dat
 6      DataOutputStream output =
 7        new DataOutputStream(new FileOutputStream("temp.dat"));
 8
 9      // Write student test scores to the file
10      output.writeUTF("John");
11      output.writeDouble(85.5);
12      output.writeUTF("Susan");
13      output.writeDouble(185.5);
14      output.writeUTF("Kim");
15      output.writeDouble(105.25);
16
17      // Close output stream
18      output.close();
19
20      // Create an input stream for file temp.dat
21      DataInputStream input =
22        new DataInputStream(new FileInputStream("temp.dat"));
23
24      // Read student test scores from the file
25      System.out.println(input.readUTF() + " " + input.readDouble());
26      System.out.println(input.readUTF() + " " + input.readDouble());
27      System.out.println(input.readUTF() + " " + input.readDouble());
28    }
29  }
```

Margin notes: output stream (line 6), output (line 10), close stream (line 18), input stream (line 21), input (line 25)

```
John 85.5
Susan 185.5
Kim 105.25
```

A **DataOutputStream** is created for file **temp.dat** in lines 6–7. Student names and scores are written to the file in lines 10–15. Line 18 closes the output stream. A **DataInputStream** is created for the same file in lines 21–22. Student names and scores are read back from the file and displayed on the console in lines 25–27.

DataInputStream and **DataOutputStream** read and write Java primitive type values and strings in a machine-independent fashion, thereby enabling you to write a data file on one machine and read it on another machine that has a different operating system or file structure. An application uses a data output stream to write data that can later be read by a program using a data input stream.

Caution
You have to read data in the same order and format in which they are stored. For example, since names are written in UTF-8 using `writeUTF`, you must read names using `readUTF`.

Detecting the End of a File

If you keep reading data at the end of an `InputStream`, an `EOFException` will occur. This exception can be used to detect the end of a file, as shown in Listing 19.3. EOFException

LISTING 19.3 DetectEndOfFile.java

```java
1   import java.io.*;
2
3   public class DetectEndOfFile {
4     public static void main(String[] args) {
5       try {
6         DataOutputStream output =
7           new DataOutputStream(new FileOutputStream("test.dat"));
8         output.writeDouble(4.5);
9         output.writeDouble(43.25);
10        output.writeDouble(3.2);
11        output.close();
12
13        DataInputStream input =
14          new DataInputStream(new FileInputStream("test.dat"));
15        while (true) {
16          System.out.println(input.readDouble());
17        }
18      }
19      catch (EOFException ex) {
20        System.out.println("All data were read");
21      }
22      catch (IOException ex) {
23        ex.printStackTrace();
24      }
25    }
26  }
```

output stream

output

close stream

input stream

input

EOFException

```
4.5
43.25
3.2
All data were read
```

The program writes three double values to the file using `DataOutputStream` (lines 6–10), and reads the data using `DataInputStream` (lines 13–14). When reading past the end of the file, an `EOFException` is thrown. The exception is caught in line 19.

19.4.4 BufferedInputStream/BufferedOutputStream

`BufferedInputStream`/`BufferedOutputStream` can be used to speed up input and output by reducing the number of disk reads and writes. Using `BufferedInputStream`, the whole block of data on the disk is read into the buffer in the memory once. The individual data are then delivered to your program from the buffer, as shown in Figure 19.11a. Using `BufferedOutputStream`, the individual data are first written to the buffer in the memory. When the buffer is full, all data in the buffer is written to the disk once, as shown in Figure 19.11b.

FIGURE 19.11 Buffer I/O places data in a buffer for fast processing.

BufferedInputStream/BufferedOutputStream does not contain new methods. All the methods in BufferedInputStream/BufferedOutputStream are inherited from the InputStream/OutputStream classes. BufferedInputStream/BufferedOutputStream manages a buffer behind the scene and automatically reads/writes data from/to disk on demand.

You can wrap a BufferedInputStream/BufferedOutputStream on any InputStream/OutputStream using the constructors shown in Figures 19.12 and 19.13.

FIGURE 19.12 BufferedInputStream buffers an input stream.

FIGURE 19.13 BufferedOutputStream buffers an output stream.

If no buffer size is specified, the default size is `512` bytes. You can improve the performance of the `TestDataStream` program in Listing 19.2 by adding buffers in the stream in lines 6–7 and 21–22, as follows:

```
DataOutputStream output = new DataOutputStream(
  new BufferedOutputStream(new FileOutputStream("temp.dat")));

DataInputStream input = new DataInputStream(
  new BufferedInputStream(new FileInputStream("temp.dat")));
```

> **Tip**
> You should always use buffered I/O to speed up input and output. For small files, you may not notice performance improvements. However, for large files—over 100 MB—you will see substantial improvements using buffered I/O.

19.8 Why do you have to declare to throw `IOException` in the method or use a try-catch block to handle `IOException` for Java I/O programs?

19.9 Why should you always close streams?

19.10 The `read()` method in `InputStream` reads a byte. Why does it return an `int` instead of a `byte`? Find the abstract methods in `InputStream` and `OutputStream`.

19.11 Does `FileInputStream`/`FileOutputStream` introduce any new methods beyond the methods inherited from `InputStream`/`OutputStream`? How do you create a `FileInputStream`/`FileOutputStream`?

19.12 What will happen if you attempt to create an input stream on a nonexistent file? What will happen if you attempt to create an output stream on an existing file? Can you append data to an existing file?

19.13 How do you append data to an existing text file using `java.io.PrintWriter`?

19.14 Suppose a file contains an unspecified number of `double` values. Theses values were written to the file using the `writeDouble` method using a `DataOutputStream`. How do you write a program to read all these values? How do you detect the end of a file?

19.15 What is written to a file using `writeByte(91)` on a `FileOutputStream`?

19.16 How do you check the end of a file in an input stream (`FileInputStream`, `DataInputStream`)?

19.17 What is wrong in the following code?

```java
import java.io.*;

public class Test {
  public static void main(String[] args) {
    try {
      FileInputStream fis = new FileInputStream("test.dat");
    }
    catch (IOException ex) {
      ex.printStackTrace();
    }
    catch (FileNotFoundException ex) {
      ex.printStackTrace();
    }
  }
}
```

19.18 Suppose you run the program on Windows using the default ASCII encoding. After the program is finished, how many bytes are in the file **t.txt**? Show the contents of each byte.

```java
public class Test {
  public static void main(String[] args)
      throws java.io.IOException {
    java.io.PrintWriter output =
      new java.io.PrintWriter("t.txt");
    output.printf("%s", "1234");
    output.printf("%s", "5678");
    output.close();
  }
}
```

19.19 After the program is finished, how many bytes are in the file **t.dat**? Show the contents of each byte.

```java
import java.io.*;

public class Test {
  public static void main(String[] args) throws IOException {
    DataOutputStream output = new DataOutputStream(
      new FileOutputStream("t.dat"));
    output.writeInt(1234);
    output.writeInt(5678);
    output.close();
  }
}
```

19.20 For each of the following statements on a `DataOutputStream output`, how many bytes are sent to the output?

```java
output.writeChar('A');
output.writeChars("BC");
output.writeUTF("DEF");
```

19.21 What are the advantages of using buffered streams? Are the following statements correct?

```java
BufferedInputStream input1 =
  new BufferedInputStream(new FileInputStream("t.dat"));

DataInputStream input2 = new DataInputStream(
  new BufferedInputStream(new FileInputStream("t.dat")));

ObjectInputStream input3 = new ObjectInputStream(
  new BufferedInputStream(new FileInputStream("t.dat")));
```

19.5 Case Study: Copying Files

This section develops a useful utility for copying files.

In this section, you will learn how to write a program that lets users copy files. The user needs to provide a source file and a target file as command-line arguments using the command:

VideoNote

Copy file

```
java Copy source target
```

The program copies the source file to the target file and displays the number of bytes in the file. The program should alert the user if the source file does not exist or if the target file already exists. A sample run of the program is shown in Figure 19.14.

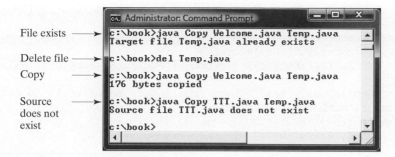

File exists

Delete file

Copy

Source
does not
exist

FIGURE 19.14 The program copies a file.

To copy the contents from a source file to a target file, it is appropriate to use an input stream to read bytes from the source file and an output stream to send bytes to the target file, regardless of the file's contents. The source file and the target file are specified from the command line. Create an `InputFileStream` for the source file and an `OutputFileStream` for the target file. Use the `read()` method to read a byte from the input stream, and then use the `write(b)` method to write the byte to the output stream. Use `BufferedInputStream` and `BufferedOutputStream` to improve the performance. Listing 19.4 gives the solution to the problem.

LISTING 19.4 Copy.java

```java
import java.io.*;

public class Copy {
  /** Main method
     @param args[0] for source file
     @param args[1] for target file
  */
  public static void main(String[] args) throws IOException {
    // Check command-line parameter usage
    if (args.length != 2) {                                          // check usage
      System.out.println(
        "Usage: java Copy sourceFile targetFile");
      System.exit(1);
    }

    // Check whether source file exists
    File sourceFile = new File(args[0]);                             // source file
    if (!sourceFile.exists()) {
      System.out.println("Source file " + args[0]
        + " does not exist");
      System.exit(2);
    }

    // Check whether target file exists
    File targetFile = new File(args[1]);                            // target file
    if (targetFile.exists()) {
      System.out.println("Target file " + args[1]
        + " already exists");
      System.exit(3);
    }

    // Create an input stream
    BufferedInputStream input =                                     // input stream
```

output stream

read
write

close stream

```
34        new BufferedInputStream(new FileInputStream(sourceFile));
35
36      // Create an output stream
37      BufferedOutputStream output =
38        new BufferedOutputStream(new FileOutputStream(targetFile));
39
40      // Continuously read a byte from input and write it to output
41      int r, numberOfBytesCopied = 0;
42      while ((r = input.read()) != -1) {
43        output.write((byte)r);
44        numberOfBytesCopied++;
45      }
46
47      // Close streams
48      input.close();
49      output.close();
50
51      // Display the file size
52      System.out.println(numberOfBytesCopied + " bytes copied");
53    }
54  }
```

The program first checks whether the user has passed the two required arguments from the command line in lines 10–14.

The program uses the `File` class to check whether the source file and target file exist. If the source file does not exist (lines 18–22) or if the target file already exists (lines 25–30), the program ends.

An input stream is created using `BufferedInputStream` wrapped on `FileInputStream` in lines 33–34, and an output stream is created using `BufferedOutputStream` wrapped on `FileOutputStream` in lines 37–38.

The expression `((r = input.read()) != -1)` (line 42) reads a byte from `input.read()`, assigns it to `r`, and checks whether it is `-1`. The input value of `-1` signifies the end of a file. The program continuously reads bytes from the input stream and sends them to the output stream until all of the bytes have been read.

MyProgrammingLab™

19.22 How does the program check if a file already exists?

19.23 How does the program detect the end of the file while reading data?

19.24 How does the program count the number of bytes read from the file?

19.6 Object I/O

`ObjectInputStream`/`ObjectOutputStream` classes can be used to read/write serializable objects.

VideoNote

Object I/O

`DataInputStream`/`DataOutputStream` enables you to perform I/O for primitive type values and strings. `ObjectInputStream`/`ObjectOutputStream` enables you to perform I/O for objects in addition to primitive type values and strings. Since `ObjectInputStream`/`ObjectOutputStream` contains all the functions of `DataInputStream`/`DataOutputStream`, you can replace `DataInputStream`/`DataOutputStream` completely with `ObjectInputStream`/`ObjectOutputStream`.

`ObjectInputStream` extends `InputStream` and implements `ObjectInput` and `ObjectStreamConstants`, as shown in Figure 19.15. `ObjectInput` is a subinterface of `DataInput` (`DataInput` is shown in Figure 19.9). `ObjectStreamConstants` contains the constants to support `ObjectInputStream`/`ObjectOutputStream`.

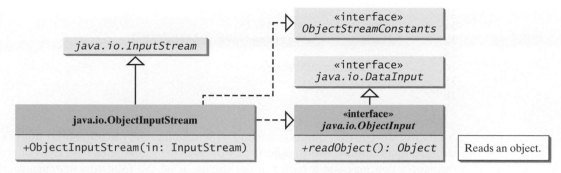

FIGURE 19.15 `ObjectInputStream` can read objects, primitive type values, and strings.

`ObjectOutputStream` extends `OutputStream` and implements `ObjectOutput` and `ObjectStreamConstants`, as shown in Figure 19.16. `ObjectOutput` is a subinterface of `DataOutput` (`DataOutput` is shown in Figure 19.10).

FIGURE 19.16 `ObjectOutputStream` can write objects, primitive type values, and strings.

You can wrap an `ObjectInputStream`/`ObjectOutputStream` on any `InputStream`/`OutputStream` using the following constructors:

```
// Create an ObjectInputStream
public ObjectInputStream(InputStream in)

// Create an ObjectOutputStream
public ObjectOutputStream(OutputStream out)
```

Listing 19.5 writes student names, scores, and the current date to a file named **object.dat**.

LISTING 19.5 TestObjectOutputStream.java

```
1  import java.io.*;
2
3  public class TestObjectOutputStream {
4    public static void main(String[] args) throws IOException {
5      // Create an output stream for file object.dat
6      ObjectOutputStream output =
7        new ObjectOutputStream(new FileOutputStream("object.dat"));
8
9      // Write a string, double value, and object to the file
```

output stream

```
10        output.writeUTF("John");
11        output.writeDouble(85.5);
12        output.writeObject(new java.util.Date());
13
14        // Close output stream
15        output.close();
16    }
17  }
```

An `ObjectOutputStream` is created to write data into the file **object.dat** in lines 6–7. A string, a double value, and an object are written to the file in lines 10–12. To improve performance, you may add a buffer in the stream using the following statement to replace lines 6–7:

```
ObjectOutputStream output = new ObjectOutputStream(
    new BufferedOutputStream(new FileOutputStream("object.dat")));
```

Multiple objects or primitives can be written to the stream. The objects must be read back from the corresponding `ObjectInputStream` with the same types and in the same order as they were written. Java's safe casting should be used to get the desired type. Listing 19.6 reads data from **object.dat**.

LISTING 19.6 `TestObjectInputStream.java`

```
1   import java.io.*;
2
3   public class TestObjectInputStream {
4     public static void main(String[] args)
5       throws ClassNotFoundException, IOException {
6       // Create an input stream for file object.dat
```
input stream
```
7       ObjectInputStream input =
8         new ObjectInputStream(new FileInputStream("object.dat"));
9
10      // Write a string, double value, and object to the file
```
input
```
11      String name = input.readUTF();
12      double score = input.readDouble();
13      java.util.Date date = (java.util.Date)(input.readObject());
14      System.out.println(name + " " + score + " " + date);
15
16      // Close input stream
17      input.close();
18    }
19  }
```

```
John 85.5 Sun Dec 04 10:35:31 EST 2011
```

ClassNotFoundException

The `readObject()` method may throw `java.lang.ClassNotFoundException`, because when the JVM restores an object, it first loads the class for the object if the class has not been loaded. Since `ClassNotFoundException` is a checked exception, the `main` method declares to throw it in line 5. An `ObjectInputStream` is created to read input from **object.dat** in lines 7–8. You have to read the data from the file in the same order and format as they were written to the file. A string, a double value, and an object are read in lines 11–13. Since `readObject()` returns an `Object`, it is cast into `Date` and assigned to a `Date` variable in line 13.

19.6.1 The `Serializable` Interface

Not every object can be written to an output stream. Objects that can be so written are said to be *serializable*. A serializable object is an instance of the `java.io.Serializable` interface, so the object's class must implement `Serializable`.

serializable

The `Serializable` interface is a marker interface. Since it has no methods, you don't need to add additional code in your class that implements `Serializable`. Implementing this interface enables the Java serialization mechanism to automate the process of storing objects and arrays.

To appreciate this automation feature, consider what you otherwise need to do in order to store an object. Suppose you want to store a `JButton` object. To do this you need to store all the current values of the properties (e.g., color, font, text, alignment) in the object. Since `JButton` is a subclass of `AbstractButton`, the property values of `AbstractButton` have to be stored as well as the properties of all the superclasses of `AbstractButton`. If a property is of an object type (e.g., `background` of the `Color` type), storing it requires storing all the property values inside this object. As you can see, this would be a very tedious process. Fortunately, you don't have to go through it manually. Java provides a built-in mechanism to automate the process of writing objects. This process is referred to as *object serialization*, which is implemented in `ObjectOutputStream`. In contrast, the process of reading objects is referred to as *object deserialization*, which is implemented in `ObjectInputStream`.

serialization

deserialization

Many classes in the Java API implement `Serializable`. The utility classes, such as `java.util.Date`, and all the Swing GUI component classes implement `Serializable`. Attempting to store an object that does not support the `Serializable` interface would cause a `NotSerializableException`.

NotSerializableException

When a serializable object is stored, the class of the object is encoded; this includes the class name and the signature of the class, the values of the object's instance variables, and the closure of any other objects referenced by the object. The values of the object's static variables are not stored.

Note
nonserializable fields

If an object is an instance of `Serializable` but contains nonserializable instance data fields, can it be serialized? The answer is no. To enable the object to be serialized, mark these data fields with the **transient** keyword to tell the JVM to ignore them when writing the object to an object stream. Consider the following class:

transient

```
public class C implements java.io.Serializable {
  private int v1;
  private static double v2;
  private transient A v3 = new A();
}

class A { } // A is not serializable
```

When an object of the `C` class is serialized, only variable `v1` is serialized. Variable `v2` is not serialized because it is a static variable, and variable `v3` is not serialized because it is marked **transient**. If `v3` were not marked **transient**, a `java.io.NotSerializableException` would occur.

Note
duplicate objects

If an object is written to an object stream more than once, will it be stored in multiple copies? No, it will not. When an object is written for the first time, a serial number is created for it. The JVM writes the complete contents of the object along with the serial number into the object stream. After the first time, only the serial number is stored if the same object is written again. When the objects are read back, their references are the same, since only one object is actually created in the memory.

19.6.2 Serializing Arrays

An array is serializable if all its elements are serializable. An entire array can be saved into a file using **writeObject** and later can be restored using **readObject**. Listing 19.7 stores an array of five **int** values and an array of three strings and reads them back to display on the console.

LISTING 19.7 TestObjectStreamForArray.java

```
1  import java.io.*;
2
3  public class TestObjectStreamForArray {
4    public static void main(String[] args)
5        throws ClassNotFoundException, IOException {
6      int[] numbers = {1, 2, 3, 4, 5};
7      String[] strings = {"John", "Susan", "Kim"};
8
9      // Create an output stream for file array.dat
10     ObjectOutputStream output = new ObjectOutputStream(new
11       FileOutputStream("array.dat", true));
12
13     // Write arrays to the object output stream
14     output.writeObject(numbers);
15     output.writeObject(strings);
16
17     // Close the stream
18     output.close();
19
20     // Create an input stream for file array.dat
21     ObjectInputStream input =
22       new ObjectInputStream(new FileInputStream("array.dat"));
23
24     int[] newNumbers = (int[])(input.readObject());
25     String[] newStrings = (String[])(input.readObject());
26
27     // Display arrays
28     for (int i = 0; i < newNumbers.length; i++)
29       System.out.print(newNumbers[i] + " ");
30     System.out.println();
31
32     for (int i = 0; i < newStrings.length; i++)
33       System.out.print(newStrings[i] + " ");
34
35     // Close the stream
36     input.close();
37   }
38 }
```

output stream (lines 10–11)
store array (lines 14–15)
input stream (lines 21–22)
restore array (lines 24–25)

```
1 2 3 4 5
John Susan Kim
```

Lines 14–15 write two arrays into file **array.dat**. Lines 24–25 read two arrays back in the same order they were written. Since **readObject()** returns **Object**, casting is used to cast the objects into **int[]** and **String[]**.

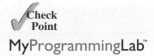

19.25 What types of objects can be stored using the `ObjectOutputStream`? What is the method for writing an object? What is the method for reading an object? What is the return type of the method that reads an object from `ObjectInputStream`?

19.26 If you serialize two objects of the same type, will they take the same amount of space? If not, give an example.

19.27 Is it true that any instance of `java.io.Serializable` can be successfully serialized? Are the static variables in an object serialized? How do you mark an instance variable not to be serialized?

19.28 Can you write an array to an `ObjectOutputStream`?

19.29 Is it true that `DataInputStream`/`DataOutputStream` can always be replaced by `ObjectInputStream`/`ObjectOutputStream`?

19.30 What will happen when you attempt to run the following code?

```
import java.io.*;

public class Test {
  public static void main(String[] args) throws IOException {
    ObjectOutputStream output =
      new ObjectOutputStream(new FileOutputStream("object.dat"));

    output.writeObject(new A());
  }
}

class A implements Serializable {
  B b = new B();
}

class B {
}
```

19.7 Random-Access Files

Java provides the `RandomAccessFile` class to allow a file to be read from and written to at random locations.

All of the streams you have used so far are known as *read-only* or *write-only* streams. The external files of these streams are *sequential* files that cannot be updated without creating a new file. However, it is often necessary to modify files. Java provides the `RandomAccessFile` class to allow a file to be read from and written to at *random* locations.

read-only
write-only
sequential
random-access file

The `RandomAccessFile` class implements the `DataInput` and `DataOutput` interfaces, as shown in Figure 19.17. The `DataInput` interface (see Figure 19.9) defines the methods for reading primitive type values and strings (e.g., `readInt`, `readDouble`, `readChar`, `readBoolean`, `readUTF`), and the `DataOutput` interface (see Figure 19.10) defines the methods for writing primitive type values and strings (e.g., `writeInt`, `writeDouble`, `writeChar`, `writeBoolean`, `writeUTF`).

When creating a `RandomAccessFile`, you can specify one of two modes: `r` or `rw`. Mode `r` means that the stream is read-only, and mode `rw` indicates that the stream allows both read and write. For example, the following statement creates a new stream, `raf`, that allows the program to read from and write to the file **test.dat**:

```
RandomAccessFile raf = new RandomAccessFile("test.dat", "rw");
```

If **test.dat** already exists, `raf` is created to access it; if **test.dat** does not exist, a new file named **test.dat** is created, and `raf` is created to access the new file. The method `raf.length()` returns the number of bytes in **test.dat** at any given time. If you append new data into the file, `raf.length()` increases.

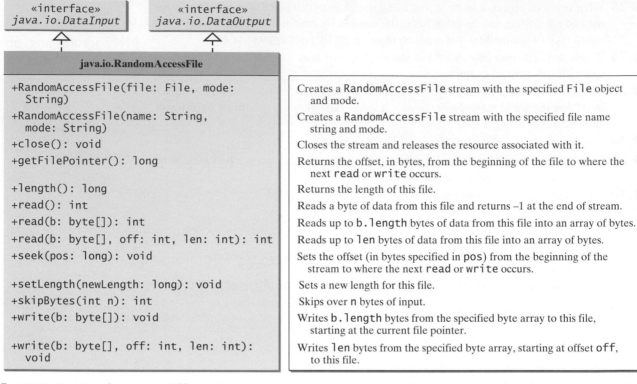

FIGURE 19.17 RandomAccessFile implements the **DataInput** and **DataOutput** interfaces with additional methods to support random access.

Tip

If the file is not intended to be modified, open it with the r mode. This prevents unintentional modification of the file.

file pointer

A random-access file consists of a sequence of bytes. A special marker called a *file pointer* is positioned at one of these bytes. A read or write operation takes place at the location of the file pointer. When a file is opened, the file pointer is set at the beginning of the file. When you read or write data to the file, the file pointer moves forward to the next data item. For example, if you read an **int** value using **readInt()**, the JVM reads 4 bytes from the file pointer, and now the file pointer is 4 bytes ahead of the previous location, as shown in Figure 19.18.

For a **RandomAccessFile raf**, you can use the **raf.seek(position)** method to move the file pointer to a specified position. **raf.seek(0)** moves it to the beginning of the file, and **raf.seek(raf.length())** moves it to the end of the file. Listing 19.8 demonstrates

FIGURE 19.18 After an **int** value is read, the file pointer is moved 4 bytes ahead.

RandomAccessFile. A large case study of using RandomAccessFile to organize an address book is given in Supplement VI.B.

LISTING 19.8 TestRandomAccessFile.java

```java
 1  import java.io.*;
 2
 3  public class TestRandomAccessFile {
 4    public static void main(String[] args) throws IOException {
 5      // Create a random-access file
 6      RandomAccessFile inout = new RandomAccessFile("inout.dat", "rw");
 7
 8      // Clear the file to destroy the old contents, if any
 9      inout.setLength(0);
10
11      // Write new integers to the file
12      for (int i = 0; i < 200; i++)
13        inout.writeInt(i);
14
15      // Display the current length of the file
16      System.out.println("Current file length is " + inout.length());
17
18      // Retrieve the first number
19      inout.seek(0); // Move the file pointer to the beginning
20      System.out.println("The first number is " + inout.readInt());
21
22      // Retrieve the second number
23      inout.seek(1 * 4); // Move the file pointer to the second number
24      System.out.println("The second number is " + inout.readInt());
25
26      // Retrieve the tenth number
27      inout.seek(9 * 4); // Move the file pointer to the tenth number
28      System.out.println("The tenth number is " + inout.readInt());
29
30      // Modify the eleventh number
31      inout.writeInt(555);
32
33      // Append a new number
34      inout.seek(inout.length()); // Move the file pointer to the end
35      inout.writeInt(999);
36
37      // Display the new length
38      System.out.println("The new length is " + inout.length());
39
40      // Retrieve the new eleventh number
41      inout.seek(10 * 4); // Move the file pointer to the next number
42      System.out.println("The eleventh number is " + inout.readInt());
43
44      inout.close();
45    }
46  }
```

RandomAccessFile

empty file

write

move pointer
read

close file

```
Current file length is 800
The first number is 0
The second number is 1
The tenth number is 9
The new length is 804
The eleventh number is 555
```

A `RandomAccessFile` is created for the file named **inout.dat** with mode **rw** to allow both read and write operations in line 6.

`inout.setLength(0)` sets the length to 0 in line 9. This, in effect, destroys the old contents of the file.

The `for` loop writes 200 `int` values from 0 to 199 into the file in lines 12–13. Since each `int` value takes 4 bytes, the total length of the file returned from `inout.length()` is now 800 (line 16), as shown in the sample output.

Invoking `inout.seek(0)` in line 19 sets the file pointer to the beginning of the file. `inout.readInt()` reads the first value in line 20 and moves the file pointer to the next number. The second number is read in line 24.

`inout.seek(9 * 4)` (line 27) moves the file pointer to the tenth number. `inout.readInt()` reads the tenth number and moves the file pointer to the eleventh number in line 28. `inout.write(555)` writes a new eleventh number at the current position (line 31). The previous eleventh number is destroyed.

`inout.seek(inout.length())` moves the file pointer to the end of the file (line 34). `inout.writeInt(999)` writes a 999 to the file. Now the length of the file is increased by 4, so `inout.length()` returns 804 (line 38).

`inout.seek(10 * 4)` moves the file pointer to the eleventh number in line 41. The new eleventh number, 555, is displayed in line 42.

19.31 Can `RandomAccessFile` streams read and write a data file created by `DataOutputStream`? Can `RandomAccessFile` streams read and write objects?

19.32 Create a `RandomAccessFile` stream for the file **address.dat** to allow the updating of student information in the file. Create a `DataOutputStream` for the file **address.dat**. Explain the differences between these two statements.

19.33 What happens if the file **test.dat** does not exist when you attempt to compile and run the following code?

```java
import java.io.*;

public class Test {
  public static void main(String[] args) {
    try {
      RandomAccessFile raf =
        new RandomAccessFile("test.dat", "r");
      int i = raf.readInt();
    }
    catch (IOException ex) {
      System.out.println("IO exception");
    }
  }
}
```

KEY TERMS

binary I/O   710
deserialization   727
file pointer   730
random-access file   729

sequential-access file   729
serialization   727
stream   710
text I/O   710

Chapter Summary

1. I/O can be classified into *text I/O* and *binary I/O*. Text I/O interprets data in sequences of characters. Binary I/O interprets data as raw binary values. How text is stored in a file depends on the encoding scheme for the file. Java automatically performs encoding and decoding for text I/O.

2. The `InputStream` and `OutputStream` classes are the roots of all binary I/O classes. `FileInputStream`/`FileOutputStream` associates a file for input/output. `BufferedInputStream`/`BufferedOutputStream` can be used to wrap any binary I/O stream to improve performance. `DataInputStream`/`DataOutputStream` can be used to read/write primitive values and strings.

3. `ObjectInputStream`/`ObjectOutputStream` can be used to read/write objects in addition to primitive values and strings. To enable object *serialization*, the object's defining class must implement the `java.io.Serializable` marker interface.

4. The `RandomAccessFile` class enables you to read and write data to a file. You can open a file with the `r` mode to indicate that it is read-only, or with the `rw` mode to indicate that it is updateable. Since the `RandomAccessFile` class implements `DataInput` and `DataOutput` interfaces, many methods in `RandomAccessFile` are the same as those in `DataInputStream` and `DataOutputStream`.

Test Questions

Do the test questions for this chapter online at www.cs.armstrong.edu/liang/intro9e/test.html.

Programming Exercises

MyProgrammingLab™

Section 19.3

*19.1 (*Create a text file*) Write a program to create a file named **Exercise19_01.txt** if it does not exist. Append new data to it if it already exists. Write 100 integers created randomly into the file using text I/O. Integers are separated by a space.

Section 19.4

*19.2 (*Create a binary data file*) Write a program to create a file named **Exercise19_02.dat** if it does not exist. Append new data to it if it already exists. Write 100 integers created randomly into the file using binary I/O.

*19.3 (*Sum all the integers in a binary data file*) Suppose a binary data file named **Exercise19_03.dat** has been created and its data are created using `writeInt(int)` in `DataOutputStream`. The file contains an unspecified number of integers. Write a program to find the sum of the integers.

*19.4 (*Convert a text file into UTF*) Write a program that reads lines of characters from a text file and writes each line as a UTF-8 string into a binary file. Display the sizes of the text file and the binary file. Use the following command to run the program:

```
java Exercise19_04 Welcome.java Welcome.utf
```

Section 19.6

*19.5 (*Store objects and arrays in a file*) Write a program that stores an array of the five `int` values 1, 2, 3, 4 and 5, a `Date` object for the current time, and the `double` value 5.5 into the file named **Exercise19_05.dat**.

*19.6 (*Store Loan objects*) The `Loan` class in Listing 10.2 does not implement `Serializable`. Rewrite the `Loan` class to implement `Serializable`. Write a program that creates five `Loan` objects and stores them in a file named **Exercise19_06.dat**.

*19.7 (*Restore objects from a file*) Suppose a file named **Exercise19_07.dat** has been created using the `ObjectOutputStream`. The file contains `Loan` objects. The `Loan` class in Listing 10.2 does not implement `Serializable`. Rewrite the `Loan` class to implement `Serializable`. Write a program that reads the `Loan` objects from the file and computes the total loan amount. Suppose you don't know how many `Loan` objects are in the file. Use `EOFException` to end the loop.

Section 19.7

*19.8 (*Update count*) Suppose you want to track how many times a program has been executed. You can store an `int` to count the file. Increase the count by 1 each time this program is executed. Let the program be **Exercise19_08** and store the count in **Exercise19_08.dat**.

***19.9 (*Address book*) Supplement VI.B has a case study of using random-access files for creating and manipulating an address book. Modify the case study by adding an *Update* button, as shown in Figure 19.19, to enable the user to modify the address that is being displayed.

FIGURE 19.19 The application can store, retrieve, and update addresses from a file.

Comprehensive

VideoNote

Split a large file

*19.10 (*Split files*) Suppose you want to back up a huge file (e.g., a 10-GB AVI file) to a CD-R. You can achieve it by splitting the file into smaller pieces and backing up these pieces separately. Write a utility program that splits a large file into smaller ones using the following command:

```
java Exercise19_10 SourceFile numberOfPieces
```

The command creates the files **SourceFile.1**, **SourceFile.2**, ..., **SourceFile.n**, where **n** is `numberOfPieces` and the output files are about the same size.

**19.11 (*Split files GUI*) Rewrite Exercise 19.10 with a GUI, as shown in Figure 19.20a.

*19.12 (*Combine files*) Write a utility program that combines the files together into a new file using the following command:

```
java Exercise19_12 SourceFile1 . . . SourceFilen TargetFile
```

The command combines SourceFile1, ..., and SourceFilen into TargetFile.

(a)   (b)

FIGURE 19.20   (a) The program splits a file. (b) The program combines files into a new file.

*19.13   (*Combine files GUI*) Rewrite Exercise 19.12 with a GUI, as shown in Figure 19.20b.

19.14   (*Encrypt files*) Encode the file by adding 5 to every byte in the file. Write a program that prompts the user to enter an input file name and an output file name and saves the encrypted version of the input file to the output file.

19.15   (*Decrypt files*) Suppose a file is encrypted using the scheme in Programming Exercise 19.14. Write a program to decode an encrypted file. Your program should prompt the user to enter an input file name for the encrypted file and an output file name for the unencrypted version of the input file.

19.16   (*Frequency of characters*) Write a program that prompts the user to enter the name of an ASCII text file and displays the frequency of the characters in the file.

19.17   (*BitOutputStream*) Implement a class named `BitOutputStream`, as shown in Figure 19.21, for writing bits to an output stream. The `writeBit(char bit)` method stores the bit in a byte variable. When you create a `BitOutputStream`, the byte is empty. After invoking `writeBit('1')`, the byte becomes `00000001`. After invoking `writeBit("0101")`, the byte becomes `00010101`. The first three bits are not filled yet. When a byte is full, it is sent to the output stream. Now the byte is reset to empty. You must close the stream by invoking the `close()` method. If the byte is neither empty nor full, the `close()` method first fills the zeros to make a full 8 bits in the byte, and then outputs the byte and closes the stream. For a hint, see Programming Exercise 4.46. Write a test program that sends the bits `010000100100001001101` to the file named **Exercise19_17.dat.

FIGURE 19.21   `BitOutputStream` outputs a stream of bits to a file.

*19.18   (*View bits*) Write the following method that displays the bit representation for the last byte in an integer:

```
public static String getBits(int value)
```

For a hint, see Programming Exercise 4.46. Write a program that prompts the user to enter a file name, reads bytes from the file, and displays each byte's binary representation.

*19.19 (*View hex*) Write a program that prompts the user to enter a file name, reads bytes from the file, and displays each byte's hex representation. (*Hint*: You can first convert the byte value into an 8-bit string, then convert the bit string into a two-digit hex string.)

**19.20 (*Binary editor*) Write a GUI application that lets the user enter a file name in the text field and press the *Enter* key to display its binary representation in a text area. The user can also modify the binary code and save it back to the file, as shown in Figure 19.22a.

(a)   (b)

FIGURE 19.22 The programs enable the user to manipulate the contents of the file in (a) binary and (b) hex.

**19.21 (*Hex editor*) Write a GUI application that lets the user enter a file name in the text field and press the *Enter* key to display its hex representation in a text area. The user can also modify the hex code and save it back to the file, as shown in Figure 19.22b.

RECURSION

Objectives

- To describe what a recursive method is and the benefits of using recursion (§20.1).

- To develop recursive methods for recursive mathematical functions (§§20.2–20.3).

- To explain how recursive method calls are handled in a call stack (§§20.2–20.3).

- To solve problems using recursion (§20.4).

- To use an overloaded helper method to design a recursive method (§20.5).

- To implement a selection sort using recursion (§20.5.1).

- To implement a binary search using recursion (§20.5.2).

- To get the directory size using recursion (§20.6).

- To solve the Towers of Hanoi problem using recursion (§20.7).

- To draw fractals using recursion (§20.8).

- To discover the relationship and difference between recursion and iteration (§20.9).

- To know tail-recursive methods and why they are desirable (§20.10).

20.1 Introduction

Key Point

Recursion is a technique that leads to elegant solutions to problems that are difficult to program using simple loops.

search word problem

Suppose you want to find all the files under a directory that contain a particular word. How do you solve this problem? There are several ways to do so. An intuitive and effective solution is to use recursion by searching the files in the subdirectories recursively.

H-tree problem

H-trees, depicted in Figure 20.1, are used in a very large-scale integration (VLSI) design as a clock distribution network for routing timing signals to all parts of a chip with equal propagation delays. How do you write a program to display H-trees? A good approach is to use recursion.

(a)   (b)   (c)   (d)

FIGURE 20.1 An H-tree can be displayed using recursion.

recursive method

To use recursion is to program using *recursive methods*—that is, to use methods that invoke themselves. Recursion is a useful programming technique. In some cases, it enables you to develop a natural, straightforward, simple solution to an otherwise difficult problem. This chapter introduces the concepts and techniques of recursive programming and illustrates with examples of how to "think recursively."

20.2 Case Study: Computing Factorials

Key Point

A recursive method is one that invokes itself.

Many mathematical functions are defined using recursion. Let's begin with a simple example. The factorial of a number n can be recursively defined as follows:

```
0! = 1;
n! = n × (n - 1)!; n > 0
```

How do you find $n!$ for a given n? To find $1!$ is easy, because you know that $0!$ is 1, and $1!$ is $1 \times 0!$. Assuming that you know $(n - 1)!$, you can obtain $n!$ immediately by using $n \times (n - 1)!$. Thus, the problem of computing $n!$ is reduced to computing $(n - 1)!$. When computing $(n - 1)!$, you can apply the same idea recursively until n is reduced to 0.

Let `factorial(n)` be the method for computing $n!$. If you call the method with $n = 0$, it immediately returns the result. The method knows how to solve the simplest case, which is

base case or stopping condition

referred to as the *base case* or the *stopping condition*. If you call the method with $n > 0$, it reduces the problem into a subproblem for computing the factorial of $n - 1$. The *subproblem* is essentially the same as the original problem, but it is simpler or smaller. Because the sub-problem has the same property as the original problem, you can call the method with a differ-

recursive call

ent argument, which is referred to as a *recursive call*.

The recursive algorithm for computing `factorial(n)` can be simply described as follows:

```
if (n == 0)
    return 1;
```

```
    else
      return n * factorial(n - 1);
```

A recursive call can result in many more recursive calls, because the method keeps on dividing a subproblem into new subproblems. For a recursive method to terminate, the problem must eventually be reduced to a stopping case, at which point the method returns a result to its caller. The caller then performs a computation and returns the result to its own caller. This process continues until the result is passed back to the original caller. The original problem can now be solved by multiplying **n** by the result of **factorial(n - 1)**.

Listing 20.1 gives a complete program that prompts the user to enter a nonnegative integer and displays the factorial for the number.

LISTING 20.1 ComputeFactorial.java

```java
1  import java.util.Scanner;
2
3  public class ComputeFactorial {
4    /** Main method */
5    public static void main(String[] args) {
6      // Create a Scanner
7      Scanner input = new Scanner(System.in);
8      System.out.print("Enter a nonnegative integer: ");
9      int n = input.nextInt();
10
11     // Display factorial
12     System.out.println("Factorial of " + n + " is " + factorial(n));
13   }
14
15   /** Return the factorial for the specified number */
16   public static long factorial(int n) {
17     if (n == 0) // Base case                                    base case
18       return 1;
19     else
20       return n * factorial(n - 1); // Recursive call            recursion
21   }
22 }
```

```
Enter a nonnegative integer: 4 ↵Enter
Factorial of 4 is 24
```

```
Enter a nonnegative integer: 10 ↵Enter
Factorial of 10 is 3628800
```

The **factorial** method (lines 16–21) is essentially a direct translation of the recursive mathematical definition for the factorial into Java code. The call to **factorial** is recursive because it calls itself. The parameter passed to **factorial** is decremented until it reaches the base case of **0**.

You see how to write a recursive method. How does recursion work? Figure 20.2 illustrates the execution of the recursive calls, starting with **n = 4**. The use of stack space for recursive calls is shown in Figure 20.3.

how does it work?

740 Chapter 20   Recursion

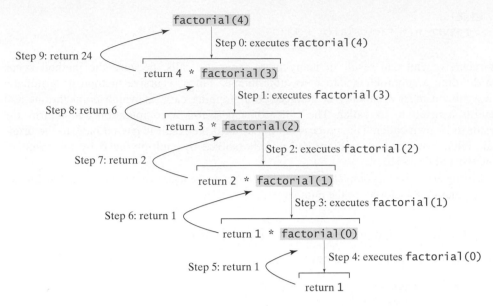

FIGURE 20.2 Invoking `factorial(4)` spawns recursive calls to `factorial`.

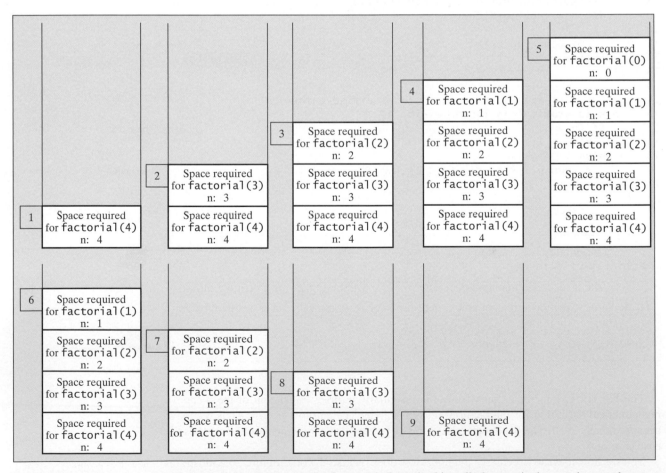

FIGURE 20.3 When `factorial(4)` is being executed, the `factorial` method is called recursively, causing stack space to dynamically change.

Pedagogical Note

It is simpler and more efficient to implement the `factorial` method using a loop. However, we use the recursive `factorial` method here to demonstrate the concept of recursion. Later in this chapter, we will present some problems that are inherently recursive and are difficult to solve without using recursion.

If recursion does not reduce the problem in a manner that allows it to eventually converge into the base case, *infinite recursion* can occur. For example, suppose you mistakenly write the `factorial` method as follows:

infinite recursion

```java
public static long factorial(int n) {
  return n * factorial(n - 1);
}
```

The method runs infinitely and causes a `StackOverflowError`.

The example discussed in this section shows a recursive method that invokes itself. This is known as *direct recursion*. It is also possible to create *indirect recursion*. This occurs when method A invokes method B, which in turn invokes method A. There can even be several more methods involved in the recursion. For example, method A invokes method B, which invokes method C, which invokes method A.

direct recursion
indirect recursion

20.1 What is a recursive method? What is an infinite recursion?

20.2 How many times is the `factorial` method in Listing 20.1 invoked for `factorial(6)`?

20.3 Show the output of the following programs and identify base cases and recursive calls.

Check Point

MyProgrammingLab™

```java
public class Test {
  public static void main(String[] args) {
    System.out.println(
      "Sum is " + xMethod(5));
  }

  public static int xMethod(int n) {
    if (n == 1)
      return 1;
    else
      return n + xMethod(n - 1);
  }
}
```

```java
public class Test {
  public static void main(String[] args) {
    xMethod(1234567);
  }

  public static void xMethod(int n) {
    if (n > 0) {
      System.out.print(n % 10);
      xMethod(n / 10);
    }
  }
}
```

20.4 Write a recursive mathematical definition for computing 2^n for a positive integer n.

20.5 Write a recursive mathematical definition for computing x^n for a positive integer n and a real number x.

20.6 Write a recursive mathematical definition for computing $1 + 2 + 3 + \ldots + n$ for a positive integer.

20.3 Case Study: Computing Fibonacci Numbers

In some cases, recursion enables you to create an intuitive, straightforward, simple solution to a problem.

Key Point

The `factorial` method in the preceding section could easily be rewritten without using recursion. In this section, we show an example for creating an intuitive solution to a problem using recursion. Consider the well-known Fibonacci-series problem:

The series: 0 1 1 2 3 5 8 13 21 34 55 89 ...
indices: 0 1 2 3 4 5 6 7 8 9 10 11

The Fibonacci series begins with 0 and 1, and each subsequent number is the sum of the preceding two. The series can be recursively defined as:

```
fib(0) = 0;
fib(1) = 1;
fib(index) = fib(index - 2) + fib(index - 1); index >= 2
```

The Fibonacci series was named for Leonardo Fibonacci, a medieval mathematician, who originated it to model the growth of the rabbit population. It can be applied in numeric optimization and in various other areas.

How do you find `fib(index)` for a given `index`? It is easy to find `fib(2)`, because you know `fib(0)` and `fib(1)`. Assuming that you know `fib(index - 2)` and `fib(index - 1)`, you can obtain `fib(index)` immediately. Thus, the problem of computing `fib(index)` is reduced to computing `fib(index - 2)` and `fib(index - 1)`. When doing so, you apply the idea recursively until `index` is reduced to 0 or 1.

The base case is `index = 0` or `index = 1`. If you call the method with `index = 0` or `index = 1`, it immediately returns the result. If you call the method with `index >= 2`, it divides the problem into two subproblems for computing `fib(index - 1)` and `fib(index - 2)` using recursive calls. The recursive algorithm for computing `fib(index)` can be simply described as follows:

```
if (index == 0)
  return 0;
else if (index == 1)
  return 1;
else
  return fib(index - 1) + fib(index - 2);
```

Listing 20.2 gives a complete program that prompts the user to enter an index and computes the Fibonacci number for that index.

LISTING 20.2 ComputeFibonacci.java

```java
 1  import java.util.Scanner;
 2
 3  public class ComputeFibonacci {
 4    /** Main method */
 5    public static void main(String[] args) {
 6      // Create a Scanner
 7      Scanner input = new Scanner(System.in);
 8      System.out.print("Enter an index for a Fibonacci number: ");
 9      int index = input.nextInt();
10
11      // Find and display the Fibonacci number
12      System.out.println("The Fibonacci number at index "
13        + index + " is " + fib(index));
14    }
15
16    /** The method for finding the Fibonacci number */
17    public static long fib(long index) {
18      if (index == 0) // Base case
19        return 0;
```

base case

```
20        else if (index == 1) // Base case
21           return 1;
22        else  // Reduction and recursive calls
23           return fib(index - 1) + fib(index - 2);
24      }
25   }
```

base case

recursion

```
Enter an index for a Fibonacci number: 1  ↵Enter
The Fibonacci number at index 1 is 1
```

```
Enter an index for a Fibonacci number: 6  ↵Enter
The Fibonacci number at index 6 is 8
```

```
Enter an index for a Fibonacci number: 7  ↵Enter
The Fibonacci number at index 7 is 13
```

The program does not show the considerable amount of work done behind the scenes by the computer. Figure 20.4, however, shows the successive recursive calls for evaluating `fib(4)`. The original method, `fib(4)`, makes two recursive calls, `fib(3)` and `fib(2)`, and then returns `fib(3) + fib(2)`. But in what order are these methods called? In Java, operands are evaluated from left to right, so `fib(2)` is called after `fib(3)` is completely evaluated. The labels in Figure 20.4 show the order in which the methods are called.

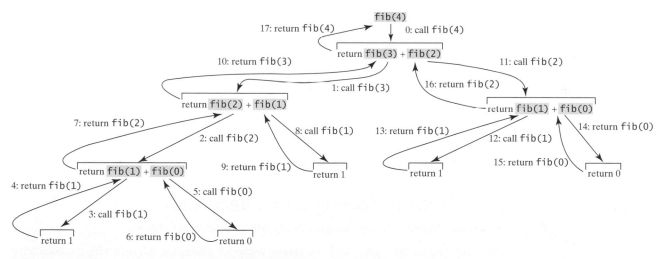

FIGURE 20.4   Invoking `fib(4)` spawns recursive calls to `fib`.

As shown in Figure 20.4, there are many duplicated recursive calls. For instance, `fib(2)` is called twice, `fib(1)` three times, and `fib(0)` twice. In general, computing `fib(index)` requires roughly twice as many recursive calls as does computing `fib(index - 1)`. As you try larger index values, the number of calls substantially increases, as shown in Table 20.1.

TABLE 20.1   Number of Recursive Calls in `fib(index)`

index	2	3	4	10	20	30	40	50
# of calls	3	5	9	177	21891	2,692,537	331,160,281	2,075,316,483

Pedagogical Note

The recursive implementation of the `fib` method is very simple and straightforward, but it isn't efficient, since it requires more time and memory to run recursive methods. See Programming Exercise 20.2 for an efficient solution using loops. Though it is not practical, the recursive `fib` method is a good example of how to write recursive methods.

20.7 Show the output of the following two programs:

```java
public class Test {
  public static void main(String[] args) {
    xMethod(5);
  }

  public static void xMethod(int n) {
    if (n > 0) {
      System.out.print(n + " ");
      xMethod(n - 1);
    }
  }
}
```

```java
public class Test {
  public static void main(String[] args) {
    xMethod(5);
  }

  public static void xMethod(int n) {
    if (n > 0) {
      xMethod(n - 1);
      System.out.print(n + " ");
    }
  }
}
```

20.8 What is wrong in the following method?

```java
public class Test {
  public static void main(String[] args) {
    xMethod(1234567);
  }

  public static void xMethod(double n) {
    if (n != 0) {
      System.out.print(n);
      xMethod(n / 10);
    }
  }
}
```

```java
public class Test {
  public static void main(String[] args) {
    Test test = new Test();
    System.out.println(test.toString());
  }

  public Test() {
    Test test = new Test();
  }
}
```

20.9 How many times is the `fib` method in Listing 20.2 invoked for `fib(6)`?

20.4 Problem Solving Using Recursion

If you think recursively, you can solve many problems using recursion.

The preceding sections presented two classic recursion examples. All recursive methods have the following characteristics:

recursion characteristics

if-else
- The method is implemented using an `if-else` or a `switch` statement that leads to different cases.

base cases
- One or more base cases (the simplest case) are used to stop recursion.

reduction
- Every recursive call reduces the original problem, bringing it increasingly closer to a base case until it becomes that case.

In general, to solve a problem using recursion, you break it into subproblems. Each subproblem is the same as the original problem but smaller in size. You can apply the same approach to each subproblem to solve it recursively.

Recursion is everywhere. It is fun to *think recursively*. Consider drinking coffee. You may describe the procedure recursively as follows:

think recursively

```java
public static void drinkCoffee(Cup cup) {
  if (!cup.isEmpty()) {
    cup.takeOneSip(); // Take one sip
    drinkCoffee(cup);
  }
}
```

Assume **cup** is an object for a cup of coffee with the instance methods **isEmpty()** and **takeOneSip()**. You can break the problem into two subproblems: one is to drink one sip of coffee and the other is to drink the rest of the coffee in the cup. The second problem is the same as the original problem but smaller in size. The base case for the problem is when the cup is empty.

Consider the problem of printing a message **n** times. You can break the problem into two subproblems: one is to print the message one time and the other is to print it **n - 1** times. The second problem is the same as the original problem but it is smaller in size. The base case for the problem is **n == 0**. You can solve this problem using recursion as follows:

```java
public static void nPrintln(String message, int times) {
  if (times >= 1) {
    System.out.println(message);
    nPrintln(message, times - 1);
  } // The base case is times == 0
}
```

recursive call

Note that the **fib** method in the preceding section returns a value to its caller, but the **drinkCoffee** and **nPrintln** methods are **void** and they do not return a value.

If you *think recursively*, you can use recursion to solve many of the problems presented in earlier chapters of this book. Consider the palindrome problem in Listing 9.1. Recall that a string is a palindrome if it reads the same from the left and from the right. For example, "mom" and "dad" are palindromes, but "uncle" and "aunt" are not. The problem of checking whether a string is a palindrome can be divided into two subproblems:

think recursively

- Check whether the first character and the last character of the string are equal.

- Ignore the two end characters and check whether the rest of the substring is a palindrome.

The second subproblem is the same as the original problem but smaller in size. There are two base cases: (1) the two end characters are not the same, and (2) the string size is **0** or **1**. In case 1, the string is not a palindrome; in case 2, the string is a palindrome. The recursive method for this problem can be implemented as shown in Listing 20.3.

LISTING 20.3   RecursivePalindromeUsingSubstring.java

```java
 1  public class RecursivePalindromeUsingSubstring {
 2    public static boolean isPalindrome(String s) {
 3      if (s.length() <= 1) // Base case
 4        return true;
 5      else if (s.charAt(0) != s.charAt(s.length() - 1)) // Base case
 6        return false;
 7      else
 8        return isPalindrome(s.substring(1, s.length() - 1)) ;
 9    }
10
11    public static void main(String[] args) {
```

method header
base case

base case

recursive call

```
12          System.out.println("Is moon a palindrome? "
13            + isPalindrome("moon"));
14          System.out.println("Is noon a palindrome? "
15            + isPalindrome("noon"));
16          System.out.println("Is a a palindrome? " + isPalindrome("a"));
17          System.out.println("Is aba a palindrome? " +
18            isPalindrome("aba"));
19          System.out.println("Is ab a palindrome? " + isPalindrome("ab"));
20      }
21  }
```

```
Is moon a palindrome? false
Is noon a palindrome? true
Is a a palindrome? true
Is aba a palindrome? true
Is ab a palindrome? false
```

The `substring` method in line 8 creates a new string that is the same as the original string except without the first and last characters. Checking whether a string is a palindrome is equivalent to checking whether the substring is a palindrome if the two end characters in the original string are the same.

Check Point
MyProgrammingLab

20.10 Describe the characteristics of recursive methods.

20.11 For the `isPalindrome` method in Listing 20.3, what are the base cases? How many times is this method called when invoking `isPalindrome("abdxcxdba")`?

20.12 Show the call stack for `isPalindrome("abcba")` using the method defined in Listing 20.3.

20.5 Recursive Helper Methods

Sometimes you can find a recursive solution by slightly changing the original problem. This new method is called a recursive helper method.

The recursive `isPalindrome` method in Listing 20.3 is not efficient, because it creates a new string for every recursive call. To avoid creating new strings, you can use the low and high indices to indicate the range of the substring. These two indices must be passed to the recursive method. Since the original method is `isPalindrome(String s)`, you have to create the new method `isPalindrome(String s, int low, int high)` to accept additional information on the string, as shown in Listing 20.4.

LISTING 20.4 `RecursivePalindrome.java`

```
1  public class RecursivePalindrome {
2    public static boolean isPalindrome(String s) {
3      return isPalindrome(s, 0, s.length() - 1);
4    }
5
6    private static boolean isPalindrome(String s, int low, int high) {
7      if (high <= low) // Base case
8        return true;
9      else if (s.charAt(low) != s.charAt(high)) // Base case
10       return false;
11     else
12       return isPalindrome(s, low + 1, high - 1);
13   }
14
```

helper method
base case

base case

```
15    public static void main(String[] args) {
16      System.out.println("Is moon a palindrome? "
17        + isPalindrome("moon"));
18      System.out.println("Is noon a palindrome? "
19        + isPalindrome("noon"));
20      System.out.println("Is a a palindrome? " + isPalindrome("a"));
21      System.out.println("Is aba a palindrome? " + isPalindrome("aba"));
22      System.out.println("Is ab a palindrome? " + isPalindrome("ab"));
23    }
24  }
```

Two overloaded `isPalindrome` methods are defined. The first, `isPalindrome(String s)`, checks whether a string is a palindrome, and the second, `isPalindrome(String s, int low, int high)`, checks whether a substring `s(low..high)` is a palindrome. The first method passes the string `s` with `low = 0` and `high = s.length() - 1` to the second method. The second method can be invoked recursively to check a palindrome in an ever-shrinking substring. It is a common design technique in recursive programming to define a second method that receives additional parameters. Such a method is known as a *recursive helper method*.

recursive helper method

Helper methods are very useful in designing recursive solutions for problems involving strings and arrays. The sections that follow give two more examples.

20.5.1 Recursive Selection Sort

Selection sort was introduced in Section 6.11.1. Recall that it finds the smallest element in the list and swaps it with the first element. It then finds the smallest element remaining and swaps it with the first element in the remaining list, and so on until the remaining list contains only a single element. The problem can be divided into two subproblems:

■ Find the smallest element in the list and swap it with the first element.

■ Ignore the first element and sort the remaining smaller list recursively.

The base case is that the list contains only one element. Listing 20.5 gives the recursive sort method.

LISTING 20.5 RecursiveSelectionSort.java

```
1  public class RecursiveSelectionSort {
2    public static void sort(double[] list) {
3      sort(list, 0, list.length - 1); // Sort the entire list
4    }
5
6    private static void sort(double[] list, int low, int high) {
7      if (low < high) {
8        // Find the smallest number and its index in list[low .. high]
9        int indexOfMin = low;
10       double min = list[low];
11       for (int i = low + 1; i <= high; i++) {
12         if (list[i] < min) {
13           min = list[i];
14           indexOfMin = i;
15         }
16       }
17
18       // Swap the smallest in list[low .. high] with list[low]
19       list[indexOfMin] = list[low];
20       list[low] = min;
21
```

helper method
base case

```
22          // Sort the remaining list[low+1 .. high]
23          sort(list, low + 1, high);
24       }
25    }
26 }
```

Two overloaded **sort** methods are defined. The first method, **sort(double[] list)**, sorts an array in **list[0..list.length - 1]** and the second method, **sort(double[] list, int low, int high)**, sorts an array in **list[low..high]**. The second method can be invoked recursively to sort an ever-shrinking subarray.

20.5.2 Recursive Binary Search

Binary search was introduced in Section 6.10.2. For binary search to work, the elements in the array must be in an increasing order. The binary search first compares the key with the element in the middle of the array. Consider the following three cases:

- Case 1: If the key is less than the middle element, recursively search for the key in the first half of the array.

- Case 2: If the key is equal to the middle element, the search ends with a match.

- Case 3: If the key is greater than the middle element, recursively search for the key in the second half of the array.

Case 1 and Case 3 reduce the search to a smaller list. Case 2 is a base case when there is a match. Another base case is that the search is exhausted without a match. Listing 20.6 gives a clear, simple solution for the binary search problem using recursion.

LISTING 20.6 Recursive Binary Search Method

```
1  public class RecursiveBinarySearch {
2     public static int recursiveBinarySearch(int[] list, int key) {
3        int low = 0;
4        int high = list.length - 1;
5        return recursiveBinarySearch(list, key, low, high);
6     }
7
8     private static int recursiveBinarySearch(int[] list, int key,
9           int low, int high) {
10       if (low > high)  // The list has been exhausted without a match
11          return -low - 1;
12
13       int mid = (low + high) / 2;
14       if (key < list[mid])
15          return recursiveBinarySearch(list, key, low, mid - 1);
16       else if (key == list[mid])
17          return mid;
18       else
19          return recursiveBinarySearch(list, key, mid + 1, high);
20    }
21 }
```

The first method finds a key in the whole list. The second method finds a key in the list with index from **low** to **high**.

The first **binarySearch** method passes the initial array with **low = 0** and **high = list.length - 1** to the second **binarySearch** method. The second method is invoked recursively to find the key in an ever-shrinking subarray.

20.13 Show the call stack for `isPalindrome("abcba")` using the method defined in Listing 20.4.

**Check
Point**

20.14 Show the call stack for `selectionSort(new double[]{2, 3, 5, 1})` using the method defined in Listing 20.5.

MyProgrammingLab™

20.15 What is a recursive helper method?

20.6 Case Study: Finding the Directory Size

Recursive methods are efficient for solving problems with recursive structures.

**Key
Point**

The preceding examples can easily be solved without using recursion. This section presents a problem that is difficult to solve without using recursion. The problem is to find the size of a directory. The size of a directory is the sum of the sizes of all files in the directory. A directory d may contain subdirectories. Suppose a directory contains files $f_1, f_2, \ldots, f_m$ and subdirectories $d_1, d_2, \ldots, d_n$, as shown in Figure 20.5.

VideoNote

Directory size

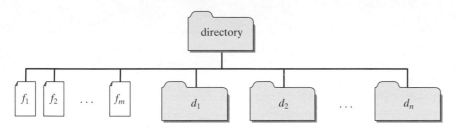

FIGURE 20.5 A directory contains files and subdirectories.

The size of the directory can be defined recursively as follows:

$$size(d) = size(f_1) + size(f_2) + \ldots + size(f_m) + size(d_1) + size(d_2) + \ldots + size(d_n)$$

The `File` class, introduced in Section 14.10, can be used to represent a file or a directory and obtain the properties for files and directories. Two methods in the `File` class are useful for this problem:

- The `length()` method returns the size of a file.

- The `listFiles()` method returns an array of `File` objects under a directory.

Listing 20.7 gives a program that prompts the user to enter a directory or a file and displays its size.

LISTING 20.7 DirectorySize.java

```
1  import java.io.File;
2  import java.util.Scanner;
3
4  public class DirectorySize {
5    public static void main(String[] args) {
6      // Prompt the user to enter a directory or a file
7      System.out.print("Enter a directory or a file: ");
8      Scanner input = new Scanner(System.in);
9      String directory = input.nextLine();
10
11     // Display the size
12     System.out.println(getSize(new File(directory)) + " bytes");
13   }
14
```

invoke method

getSize method

```
15  public static long getSize(File file) {
16    long size = 0; // Store the total size of all files
17
18    if (file.isDirectory()) {
```
is directory?
all subitems
```
19      File[] files = file.listFiles(); // All files and subdirectories
20      for (int i = 0; files != null && i < files.length; i++) {
```
recursive call
```
21        size += getSize(files[i]); // Recursive call
22      }
23    }
```
base case
```
24    else { // Base case
25      size += file.length();
26    }
27
28    return size;
29  }
30 }
```

```
Enter a directory or a file: c:\book  ↵ Enter
48619631 bytes
```

```
Enter a directory or a file: c:\book\Welcome.java  ↵ Enter
172 bytes
```

```
Enter a directory or a file: c:\book\NonExistentFile  ↵ Enter
0 bytes
```

If the `file` object represents a directory (line 18), each subitem (file or subdirectory) in the directory is recursively invoked to obtain its size (line 21). If the `file` object represents a file (line 24), the file size is obtained (line 25).

What happens if an incorrect or a nonexistent directory is entered? The program will detect that it is not a directory and invoke `file.length()` (line 25), which returns **0**. Thus, in this case, the `getSize` method will return **0**.

testing all cases

Tip
To avoid mistakes, it is a good practice to test all cases. For example, you should test the program for an input of file, an empty directory, a nonexistent directory, and a nonexistent file.

Check Point

MyProgrammingLab™

20.16 What is the base case for the `getSize` method?

20.17 How does the program get all files and directories under a given directory?

20.18 How many times will the `getSize` method be invoked for a directory if the directory has three subdirectories and each subdirectory has four files?

20.7 Case Study: Towers of Hanoi

Key Point

The Towers of Hanoi problem is a classic problem that can be solved easily using recursion, but it is difficult to solve otherwise.

The problem involves moving a specified number of disks of distinct sizes from one tower to another while observing the following rules:

- There are *n* disks labeled 1, 2, 3, . . . , *n* and three towers labeled A, B, and C.
- No disk can be on top of a smaller disk at any time.

■ All the disks are initially placed on tower A.

■ Only one disk can be moved at a time, and it must be the smallest disk on a tower.

The objective of the problem is to move all the disks from A to B with the assistance of C. For example, if you have three disks, the steps to move all of the disks from A to B are shown in Figure 20.6.

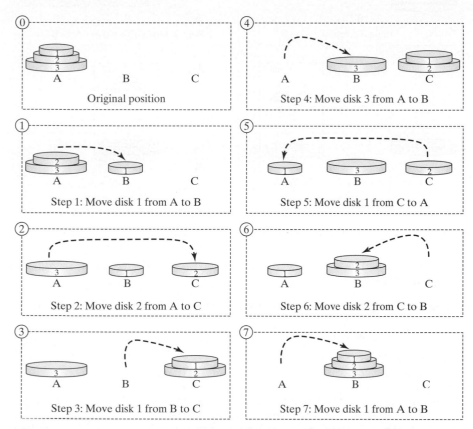

FIGURE 20.6 The goal of the Towers of Hanoi problem is to move disks from tower A to tower B without breaking the rules.

Note

The Towers of Hanoi is a classic computer-science problem, to which many websites are devoted. One of them worth looking at is www.cut-the-knot.com/recurrence/hanoi.html.

In the case of three disks, you can find the solution manually. For a larger number of disks, however—even for four—the problem is quite complex. Fortunately, the problem has an inherently recursive nature, which leads to a straightforward recursive solution.

The base case for the problem is n = 1. If n == 1, you could simply move the disk from A to B. When n > 1, you could split the original problem into the following three subproblems and solve them sequentially.

1. Move the first n - 1 disks from A to C with the assistance of tower B, as shown in Step 1 in Figure 20.7.

2. Move disk n from A to B, as shown in Step 2 in Figure 20.7.

3. Move n - 1 disks from C to B with the assistance of tower A, as shown in Step 3 in Figure 20.7.

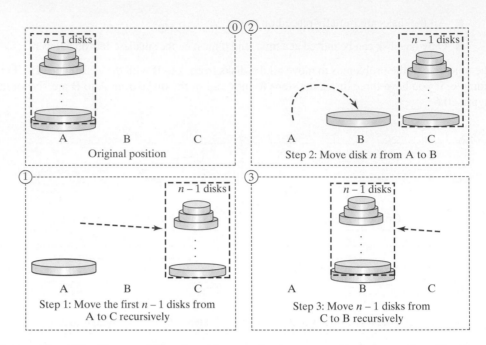

FIGURE 20.7 The Towers of Hanoi problem can be decomposed into three subproblems.

The following method moves n disks from the **fromTower** to the **toTower** with the assistance of the **auxTower**:

```
void moveDisks(int n, char fromTower, char toTower, char auxTower)
```

The algorithm for the method can be described as:

```
if (n == 1) // Stopping condition
  Move disk 1 from the fromTower to the toTower;
else {
  moveDisks(n - 1, fromTower, auxTower, toTower);
  Move disk n from the fromTower to the toTower;
  moveDisks(n - 1, auxTower, toTower, fromTower);
}
```

Listing 20.8 gives a program that prompts the user to enter the number of disks and invokes the recursive method **moveDisks** to display the solution for moving the disks.

LISTING 20.8 TowersOfHanoi.java

```java
1  import java.util.Scanner;
2
3  public class TowersOfHanoi {
4    /** Main method */
5    public static void main(String[] args) {
6      // Create a Scanner
7      Scanner input = new Scanner(System.in);
8      System.out.print("Enter number of disks: ");
9      int n = input.nextInt();
10
11     // Find the solution recursively
12     System.out.println("The moves are:");
13     moveDisks(n, 'A', 'B', 'C');
14   }
15
```

```
16    /** The method for finding the solution to move n disks
17       from fromTower to toTower with auxTower */
18    public static void moveDisks(int n, char fromTower,
19       char toTower, char auxTower) {
20      if (n == 1) // Stopping condition                          base case
21        System.out.println("Move disk " + n + " from " +
22          fromTower + " to " + toTower);
23      else {
24        moveDisks(n - 1, fromTower, auxTower, toTower);          recursion
25        System.out.println("Move disk " + n + " from " +
26          fromTower + " to " + toTower);
27        moveDisks(n - 1, auxTower, toTower, fromTower);          recursion
28      }
29    }
30  }
```

```
Enter number of disks: 4 ↵Enter
The moves are:
Move disk 1 from A to C
Move disk 2 from A to B
Move disk 1 from C to B
Move disk 3 from A to C
Move disk 1 from B to A
Move disk 2 from B to C
Move disk 1 from A to C
Move disk 4 from A to B
Move disk 1 from C to B
Move disk 2 from C to A
Move disk 1 from B to A
Move disk 3 from C to B
Move disk 1 from A to C
Move disk 2 from A to B
Move disk 1 from C to B
```

This problem is inherently recursive. Using recursion makes it possible to find a natural, simple solution. It would be difficult to solve the problem without using recursion.

Consider tracing the program for n = 3. The successive recursive calls are shown in Figure 20.8. As you can see, writing the program is easier than tracing the recursive calls. The

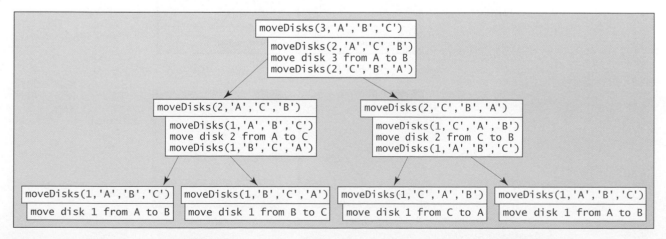

FIGURE 20.8 Invoking moveDisks(3, 'A', 'B', 'C') spawns calls to moveDisks recursively.

system uses stacks to manage the calls behind the scenes. To some extent, recursion provides a level of abstraction that hides iterations and other details from the user.

Check Point

20.19 How many times is the `moveDisks` method in Listing 20.8 invoked for `moveDisks(5, 'A', 'B', 'C')`?

MyProgrammingLab™

20.8 Case Study: Fractals

Key Point

Using recursion is ideal for displaying fractals, because fractals are inherently recursive.

VideoNote

Fractal (Sierpinski triangle)

A *fractal* is a geometrical figure, but unlike triangles, circles, and rectangles, fractals can be divided into parts, each of which is a reduced-size copy of the whole. There are many interesting examples of fractals. This section introduces a simple fractal, the *Sierpinski triangle*, named after a famous Polish mathematician.

A Sierpinski triangle is created as follows:

1. Begin with an equilateral triangle, which is considered to be a Sierpinski fractal of order (or level) **0**, as shown in Figure 20.9a.

2. Connect the midpoints of the sides of the triangle of order **0** to create a Sierpinski triangle of order **1** (Figure 20.9b).

3. Leave the center triangle intact. Connect the midpoints of the sides of the three other triangles to create a Sierpinski triangle of order **2** (Figure 20.9c).

4. You can repeat the same process recursively to create a Sierpinski triangle of order **3**, **4**, . . . , and so on (Figure 20.9d).

The problem is inherently recursive. How do you develop a recursive solution for it? Consider the base case when the order is **0**. It is easy to draw a Sierpinski triangle of order **0**.

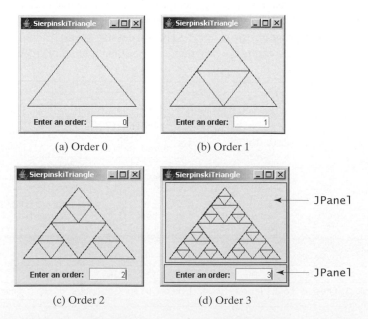

(a) Order 0   (b) Order 1

(c) Order 2   (d) Order 3

FIGURE 20.9 A Sierpinski triangle is a pattern of recursive triangles.

How do you draw a Sierpinski triangle of order 1? The problem can be reduced to drawing three Sierpinski triangles of order 0. How do you draw a Sierpinski triangle of order 2? The problem can be reduced to drawing three Sierpinski triangles of order 1, so the problem of drawing a Sierpinski triangle of order n can be reduced to drawing three Sierpinski triangles of order $n - 1$.

Listing 20.9 gives a Java applet that displays a Sierpinski triangle of any order, as shown in Figure 20.9. You can enter an order in a text field to display a Sierpinski triangle of the specified order.

LISTING 20.9 SierpinskiTriangle.java

```java
 1  import javax.swing.*;
 2  import java.awt.*;
 3  import java.awt.event.*;
 4
 5  public class SierpinskiTriangle extends JApplet {
 6    private JTextField jtfOrder = new JTextField("0", 5); // Order
 7    private SierpinskiTrianglePanel trianglePanel =
 8      new SierpinskiTrianglePanel(); // To display the pattern
 9
10    public SierpinskiTriangle() {
11      // Panel to hold label, text field, and a button
12      JPanel panel = new JPanel();
13      panel.add(new JLabel("Enter an order: "));
14      panel.add(jtfOrder);
15      jtfOrder.setHorizontalAlignment(SwingConstants.RIGHT);
16
17      // Add a Sierpinski triangle panel to the applet
18      add(trianglePanel);
19      add(panel, BorderLayout.SOUTH);
20
21      // Register a listener
22      jtfOrder.addActionListener(new ActionListener() {                    listener
23        @Override
24        public void actionPerformed(ActionEvent e) {
25          trianglePanel.setOrder(Integer.parseInt(jtfOrder.getText()));    set a new order
26        }
27      });
28    }
29
30    static class SierpinskiTrianglePanel extends JPanel {
31      private int order = 0;
32
33      /** Set a new order */
34      public void setOrder(int order) {
35        this.order = order;
36        repaint();
37      }
38
39      @Override
40      protected void paintComponent(Graphics g) {
41        super.paintComponent(g);
42
43        // Select three points in proportion to the panel size
44        Point p1 = new Point(getWidth() / 2, 10);                          three initial points
45        Point p2 = new Point(10, getHeight() - 10);
46        Point p3 = new Point(getWidth() - 10, getHeight() - 10);
47
```

```
48              displayTriangles(g, order, p1, p2, p3);
49          }
50
51          private static void displayTriangles(Graphics g, int order,
52              Point p1, Point p2, Point p3) {
53              if (order == 0) {
54                  // Draw a triangle to connect three points
55                  g.drawLine(p1.x, p1.y, p2.x, p2.y);
56                  g.drawLine(p1.x, p1.y, p3.x, p3.y);
57                  g.drawLine(p2.x, p2.y, p3.x, p3.y);
58              }
59              else {
60                  // Get the midpoint on each edge of the triangle
61                  Point p12 = midpoint(p1, p2);
62                  Point p23 = midpoint(p2, p3);
63                  Point p31 = midpoint(p3, p1);
64
65                  // Recursively display three triangles
66                  displayTriangles(g, order - 1, p1, p12, p31);
67                  displayTriangles(g, order - 1, p12, p2, p23);
68                  displayTriangles(g, order - 1, p31, p23, p3);
69              }
70          }
71
72          private static Point midpoint(Point p1, Point p2) {
73              return new Point((p1.x + p2.x) / 2, (p1.y + p2.y) / 2);
74          }
75      }
76  }
```

draw a triangle (line 55)

top subtriangle (line 66)
left subtriangle (line 67)
right subtriangle (line 68)

main method omitted (line 76)

displayTriangle method

The initial triangle has three points set in proportion to the panel size (lines 44–46). If `order == 0`, the `displayTriangles(g, order, p1, p2, p3)` method displays a triangle that connects the three points `p1`, `p2`, and `p3` in lines 55–57, as shown in Figure 20.10a. Otherwise, it performs the following tasks:

1. Obtain the midpoint between `p1` and `p2` (line 61), the midpoint between `p2` and `p3` (line 62), and the midpoint between `p3` and `p1` (line 63), as shown in Figure 20.10b.

2. Recursively invoke `displayTriangles` with a reduced order to display three smaller Sierpinski triangles (lines 66–68). Note that each small Sierpinski triangle is structurally identical to the original big Sierpinski triangle except that the order of a small triangle is one less, as shown in Figure 20.10b.

A Sierpinski triangle is displayed in a `SierpinskiTrianglePanel`. The `order` property in the inner class `SierpinskiTrianglePanel` specifies the order for the Sierpinski triangle. The `Point` class, introduced in Section 16.8, Mouse Events, represents a point on a component. The `midpoint(Point p1, Point p2)` method returns the midpoint between `p1` and `p2` (lines 72–74).

20.20 How do you obtain the midpoint between two points?

20.21 What is the base case for the `displayTriangles` method?

20.22 How many times is the `displayTriangles` method invoked for a Sierpinski triangle of order 0, order 1, order 2, and order n?

MyProgrammingLab™

FIGURE 20.10 Drawing a Sierpinski triangle spawns calls to draw three small Sierpinski triangles recursively.

20.9 Recursion vs. Iteration

Recursion is an alternative form of program control. It is essentially repetition without a loop.

 Key Point

When you use loops, you specify a loop body. The repetition of the loop body is controlled by the loop control structure. In recursion, the method itself is called repeatedly. A selection statement must be used to control whether to call the method recursively or not.

Recursion bears substantial overhead. Each time the program calls a method, the system must allocate memory for all of the method's local variables and parameters. This can consume considerable memory and requires extra time to manage the memory.

Any problem that can be solved recursively can be solved nonrecursively with iterations. Recursion has some negative aspects: it uses up too much time and too much memory. Why, then, should you use it? In some cases, using recursion enables you to specify a clear, simple solution for an inherently recursive problem that would otherwise be difficult to obtain. Examples are the directory-size problem, the Towers of Hanoi problem, and the fractal problem, which are rather difficult to solve without using recursion.

The decision whether to use recursion or iteration should be based on the nature of, and your understanding of, the problem you are trying to solve. The rule of thumb is to use whichever approach can best develop an intuitive solution that naturally mirrors the problem. If an iterative solution is obvious, use it. It will generally be more efficient than the recursive option.

recursion overhead

recursion advantages

recursion or iteration?

 Note
Recursive programs can run out of memory, causing a `StackOverflowError`.

`StackOverflowError`

performance concern

Tip
If you are concerned about your program's performance, avoid using recursion, because it takes more time and consumes more memory than iteration. In general, recursion can be used to solve the inherent recursive problems such as Towers of Hanoi, recursive directories, and Sierpinski triangles.

20.23 Which of the following statements are true?

   a. Any recursive method can be converted into a nonrecursive method.

   b. Recursive methods take more time and memory to execute than nonrecursive methods.

   c. Recursive methods are *always* simpler than nonrecursive methods.

   d. There is always a selection statement in a recursive method to check whether a base case is reached.

20.24 What is a cause for a stack-overflow exception?

20.10 Tail Recursion

A tail recursive method is efficient for reducing stack size.

tail recursion

A recursive method is said to be *tail recursive* if there are no pending operations to be performed on return from a recursive call, as illustrated in Figure 20.11a. However, method **B** in Figure 20.11b is not tail recursive because there are pending operations after a method call is returned.

Recursive method A	Recursive method B
. . .	. . .
. . .	. . .
	Invoke method B recursively
. . .	. . .
Invoke method A recursively	. . .
(a) Tail recursion	(b) Nontail recursion

FIGURE 20.11 A tail-recursive method has no pending operations after a recursive call.

For example, the recursive `isPalindrome` method (lines 6–13) in Listing 20.4 is tail recursive because there are no pending operations after recursively invoking `isPalindrome` in line 12. However, the recursive `factorial` method (lines 16–21) in Listing 20.1 is not tail recursive, because there is a pending operation, namely multiplication, to be performed on return from each recursive call.

Tail recursion may be desirable: because the method ends when the last recursive call ends, there is no need to store the intermediate calls in the stack. Some compilers can optimize tail recursion to reduce stack size.

A nontail-recursive method can often be converted to a tail-recursive method by using auxiliary parameters. These parameters are used to contain the result. The idea is to incorporate the pending operations into the auxiliary parameters in such a way that the recursive call no longer has a pending operation. You can define a new auxiliary recursive method with the auxiliary parameters. This method may overload the original method with the same name but a different signature. For example, the `factorial` method in Listing 20.1 is written in a tail-recursive way in Listing 20.10.

LISTING 20.10 ComputeFactorialTailRecursion.java

```
 1  public class ComputeFactorialTailRecursion {
 2    /** Return the factorial for a specified number */
 3    public static long factorial(int n) {                          original method
 4      return factorial(n, 1); // Call auxiliary method             invoke auxiliary method
 5    }
 6
 7    /** Auxiliary tail-recursive method for factorial */
 8    private static long factorial(int n, int result) {             auxiliary method
 9      if (n == 0)
10        return result;
11      else
12        return factorial(n - 1, n * result); // Recursive call     recursive call
13    }
14  }
```

The first **factorial** method (line 3) simply invokes the second auxiliary method (line 4). The second method contains an auxiliary parameter **result** that stores the result for the factorial of **n**. This method is invoked recursively in line 12. There is no pending operation after a call is returned. The final result is returned in line 10, which is also the return value from invoking **factorial(n, 1)** in line 4.

20.25 Identify tail-recursive methods in this chapter.

20.26 Rewrite the **fib** method in Listing 20.2 using tail recursion.

✓ **Check Point**

MyProgrammingLab™

KEY TERMS

base case 738	recursive helper method 747
direct recursion 741	recursive method 738
indirect recursion 741	stopping condition 738
infinite recursion 741	tail recursion 758

CHAPTER SUMMARY

1. A *recursive method* is one that directly or indirectly invokes itself. For a recursive method to terminate, there must be one or more *base cases*.

2. *Recursion* is an alternative form of program control. It is essentially repetition without a loop control. It can be used to specify simple, clear solutions for inherently recursive problems that would otherwise be difficult to solve.

3. Sometimes the original method needs to be modified to receive additional parameters in order to be invoked recursively. A *recursive helper method* can be defined for this purpose.

4. Recursion bears substantial overhead. Each time the program calls a method, the system must allocate memory for all of the method's local variables and parameters. This can consume considerable memory and requires extra time to manage the memory.

5. A recursive method is said to be *tail recursive* if there are no pending operations to be performed on return from a recursive call. Some compilers can optimize tail recursion to reduce stack size.

TEST QUESTIONS

Do the test questions for this chapter online at www.cs.armstrong.edu/liang/intro9e/test.html.

PROGRAMMING EXERCISES

Sections 20.2–20.3

*20.1   (*Factorial*) Using the `BigInteger` class introduced in Section 10.14, you can find the factorial for a large number (e.g., `100!`). Implement the `factorial` method using recursion. Write a program that prompts the user to enter an integer and displays its factorial.

*20.2   (*Fibonacci numbers*) Rewrite the `fib` method in Listing 20.2 using iterations.

Hint: To compute `fib(n)` without recursion, you need to obtain `fib(n - 2)` and `fib(n - 1)` first. Let `f0` and `f1` denote the two previous Fibonacci numbers. The current Fibonacci number would then be `f0 + f1`. The algorithm can be described as follows:

```
f0 = 0; // For fib(0)
f1 = 1; // For fib(1)

for (int i = 1; i <= n; i++) {
  currentFib = f0 + f1;
  f0 = f1;
  f1 = currentFib;
}
// After the loop, currentFib is fib(n)
```

Write a test program that prompts the user to enter an index and displays its Fibonacci number.

*20.3   (*Compute greatest common divisor using recursion*) The `gcd(m, n)` can also be defined recursively as follows:

- If `m % n` is `0`, `gcd(m, n)` is `n`.
- Otherwise, `gcd(m, n)` is `gcd(n, m % n)`.

Write a recursive method to find the GCD. Write a test program that prompts the user to enter two integers and displays their GCD.

20.4   (*Sum series*) Write a recursive method to compute the following series:

$$m(i) = 1 + \frac{1}{2} + \frac{1}{3} + \ldots + \frac{1}{i}$$

Write a test program that displays `m(i)` for $i = 1, 2, \ldots, 10$.

20.5   (*Sum series*) Write a recursive method to compute the following series:

$$m(i) = \frac{1}{3} + \frac{2}{5} + \frac{3}{7} + \frac{4}{9} + \frac{5}{11} + \frac{6}{13} + \ldots + \frac{i}{2i + 1}$$

Write a test program that displays `m(i)` for $i = 1, 2, \ldots, 10$.

*20.6   (*Sum series*) Write a recursive method to compute the following series:

$$m(i) = \frac{1}{2} + \frac{2}{3} + \ldots + \frac{i}{i + 1}$$

Write a test program that displays `m(i)` for $i = 1, 2, \ldots, 10$.

*20.7 (*Fibonacci series*) Modify Listing 20.2, ComputeFibonacci.java, so that the program finds the number of times the `fib` method is called. (*Hint*: Use a static variable and increment it every time the method is called.)

Section 20.4

*20.8 (*Print the digits in an integer reversely*) Write a recursive method that displays an `int` value reversely on the console using the following header:

```
public static void reverseDisplay(int value)
```

For example, `reverseDisplay(12345)` displays `54321`. Write a test program that prompts the user to enter an integer and displays its reversal.

*20.9 (*Print the characters in a string reversely*) Write a recursive method that displays a string reversely on the console using the following header:

```
public static void reverseDisplay(String value)
```

For example, `reverseDisplay("abcd")` displays `dcba`. Write a test program that prompts the user to enter a string and displays its reversal.

*20.10 (*Occurrences of a specified character in a string*) Write a recursive method that finds the number of occurrences of a specified letter in a string using the following method header:

```
public static int count(String str, char a)
```

For example, `count("Welcome", 'e')` returns 2. Write a test program that prompts the user to enter a string and a character, and displays the number of occurrences for the character in the string.

*20.11 (*Sum the digits in an integer using recursion*) Write a recursive method that computes the sum of the digits in an integer. Use the following method header:

```
public static int sumDigits(long n)
```

For example, `sumDigits(234)` returns $2 + 3 + 4 = 9$. Write a test program that prompts the user to enter an integer and displays its sum.

Section 20.5

**20.12 (*Print the characters in a string reversely*) Rewrite Exercise 20.9 using a helper method to pass the substring `high` index to the method. The helper method header is:

```
public static void reverseDisplay(String value, int high)
```

*20.13 (*Find the largest number in an array*) Write a recursive method that returns the largest integer in an array. Write a test program that prompts the user to enter a list of eight integers and displays the largest element.

*20.14 (*Find the number of uppercase letters in a string*) Write a recursive method to return the number of uppercase letters in a string. Write a test program that prompts the user to enter a string and displays the number of uppercase letters in the string.

*20.15 (*Occurrences of a specified character in a string*) Rewrite Exercise 20.10 using a helper method to pass the substring `high` index to the method. The helper method header is:

```
public static int count(String str, char a, int high)
```

*20.16   (*Find the number of uppercase letters in an array*) Write a recursive method to return the number of uppercase letters in an array of characters. You need to define the following two methods. The second one is a recursive helper method.

```
public static int count(char[] chars)
public static int count(char[] chars, int high)
```

Write a test program that prompts the user to enter a list of characters in one line and displays the number of uppercase letters in the list.

*20.17   (*Occurrences of a specified character in an array*) Write a recursive method that finds the number of occurrences of a specified character in an array. You need to define the following two methods. The second one is a recursive helper method.

```
public static int count(char[] chars, char ch)
public static int count(char[] chars, char ch, int high)
```

Write a test program that prompts the user to enter a list of characters in one line, and a character, and displays the number of occurrences of the character in the list.

Sections 20.6–20.10

*20.18   (*Towers of Hanoi*) Modify Listing 20.8, TowersOfHanoi.java, so that the program finds the number of moves needed to move *n* disks from tower A to tower B. (*Hint*: Use a static variable and increment it every time the method is called.)

*20.19   (*Sierpinski triangle*) Revise Listing 20.9 to develop an applet that lets the user use the + and − buttons to increase or decrease the current order by 1, as shown in Figure 20.12a. The initial order is 0. If the current order is 0, the *Decrease* button is ignored.

(a)   (b)

FIGURE 20.12   (a) Exercise 20.19 uses the + and − buttons to increase or decrease the current order by 1. (b) Exercise 20.20 draws ovals using a recursive method.

*20.20   (*Display circles*) Write a Java applet that displays ovals, as shown in Figure 20.12b. The ovals are centered in the panel. The gap between two adjacent ovals is 10 pixels, and the gap between the border of the panel and the largest oval is also 10.

*20.21   (*Decimal to binary*) Write a recursive method that converts a decimal number into a binary number as a string. The method header is:

```
public static String decimalToBinary(int value)
```

Write a test program that prompts the user to enter a decimal number and displays its binary equivalent.

*20.22 (*Decimal to hex*) Write a recursive method that converts a decimal number into a hex number as a string. The method header is:

```
public static String decimalToHex(int value)
```

Write a test program that prompts the user to enter a decimal number and displays its hex equivalent.

*20.23 (*Binary to decimal*) Write a recursive method that parses a binary number as a string into a decimal integer. The method header is:

```
public static int binaryToDecimal(String binaryString)
```

Write a test program that prompts the user to enter a binary string and displays its decimal equivalent.

*20.24 (*Hex to decimal*) Write a recursive method that parses a hex number as a string into a decimal integer. The method header is:

```
public static int hexToDecimal(String hexString)
```

Write a test program that prompts the user to enter a hex string and displays its decimal equivalent.

**20.25 (*String permutation*) Write a recursive method to print all the permutations of a string. For example, for the string abc, the printout is

```
abc
acb
bac
bca
cab
cba
```

(*Hint*: Define the following two methods. The second is a helper method.)

```
public static void displayPermutation(String s)
public static void displayPermutation(String s1, String s2)
```

The first method simply invokes `displayPermutation(" ", s)`. The second method uses a loop to move a character from `s2` to `s1` and recursively invokes it with a new `s1` and `s2`. The base case is that `s2` is empty and prints `s1` to the console.

Write a test program that prompts the user to enter a string and displays all its permutations.

**20.26 (*Create a maze*) Write an applet that will find a path in a maze, as shown in Figure 20.13a. The maze is represented by an 8 × 8 board. The path must meet the following conditions:

■ The path is between the upper-left corner cell and the lower-right corner cell in the maze.
■ The applet enables the user to place or remove a mark on a cell. A path consists of adjacent unmarked cells. Two cells are said to be adjacent if they are horizontal or vertical neighbors, but not if they are diagonal neighbors.
■ The path does not contain cells that form a square. The path in Figure 20.13b, for example, does not meet this condition. (The condition makes a path easy to identify on the board.)

(a) Correct path   (b) Illegal path

FIGURE 20.13 The program finds a path from the upper-left corner to the bottom-right corner.

**20.27 (*Koch snowflake fractal*) The text presented the Sierpinski triangle fractal. In this exercise, you will write an applet to display another fractal, called the *Koch snowflake*, named after a famous Swedish mathematician. A Koch snowflake is created as follows:

1. Begin with an equilateral triangle, which is considered to be the Koch fractal of order (or level) **0**, as shown in Figure 20.14a.
2. Divide each line in the shape into three equal line segments and draw an outward equilateral triangle with the middle line segment as the base to create a Koch fractal of order **1**, as shown in Figure 20.14b.
3. Repeat Step 2 to create a Koch fractal of order **2**, **3**, . . . , and so on, as shown in Figure 20.14c–d.

(a)   (b)   (c)   (d)

FIGURE 20.14 A Koch snowflake is a fractal starting with a triangle.

**20.28 (*Nonrecursive directory size*) Rewrite Listing 20.7, DirectorySize.java, without using recursion.

*20.29 (*Number of files in a directory*) Write a program that prompts the user to enter a directory and displays the number of the files in the directory.

VideoNote

Search a string in a directory

**20.30 (*Find words*) Write a program that finds all occurrences of a word in all the files under a directory, recursively. Pass the parameters from the command line as follows:

```
java Exercise20_30 dirName word
```

**20.31 (*Replace words*) Write a program that replaces all occurrences of a word with a new word in all the files under a directory, recursively. Pass the parameters from the command line as follows:

```
java Exercise20_31 dirName oldWord newWord
```

***20.32   (*Game: Knight's Tour*) The Knight's Tour is an ancient puzzle. The objective is to move a knight, starting from any square on a chessboard, to every other square once, as shown in Figure 20.15a. Note that the knight makes only L-shaped moves (two spaces in one direction and one space in a perpendicular direction). As shown in Figure 20.15b, the knight can move to eight squares. Write a program that displays the moves for the knight in an applet, as shown in Figure 20.15c.

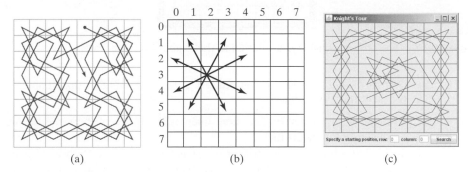

(a)   (b)   (c)

FIGURE 20.15   (a) A knight traverses all squares once. (b) A knight makes an L-shaped move. (c) An applet displays a Knight's Tour path.

(*Hint*: A brute-force approach for this problem is to move the knight from one square to another available square arbitrarily. Using such an approach, your program will take a long time to finish. A better approach is to employ some heuristics. A knight has two, three, four, six, or eight possible moves, depending on its location. Intuitively, you should attempt to move the knight to the least accessible squares first and leave those more accessible squares open, so there will be a better chance of success at the end of the search.)

***20.33   (*Game: Knight's Tour animation*) Write an applet for the Knight's Tour problem. Your applet should let the user move a knight to any starting square and click the *Solve* button to animate a knight moving along the path, as shown in Figure 20.16.

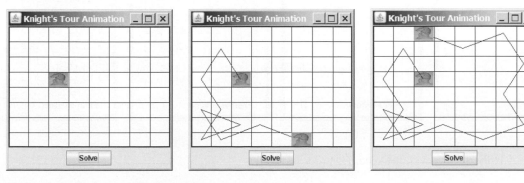

FIGURE 20.16   A knight traverses along the path.

**20.34   (*Game: Eight Queens*) The Eight Queens problem is to find a solution to place a queen in each row on a chessboard such that no two queens can attack each other. Write a program to solve the Eight Queens problem using recursion and display the result as shown in Figure 20.17.

FIGURE 20.17   The program displays a solution to the Eight Queens problem.

**20.35   (*H-tree fractal*) An H-tree (introduced at the beginning of this chapter) is a fractal defined as follows:

1. Begin with a letter H. The three lines of the H are of the same length, as shown in Figure 20.1a.
2. The letter H (in its sans-serif form, H) has four endpoints. Draw an H centered at each of the four endpoints to an H-tree of order **1**, as shown in Figure 20.1b. These Hs are half the size of the H that contains the four endpoints.
3. Repeat Step 2 to create an H-tree of order **2**, **3**, . . . , and so on, as shown in Figure 20.1c–d.

Write an applet that draws an H-tree, as shown in Figure 20.1.

**20.36   (*Hilbert curve*) The Hilbert curve, first described by German mathematician David Hilbert in 1891, is a space-filling curve that visits every point in a square grid with a size of 2×2, 4×4, 8×8, 16×16, or any other power of 2. Write a Java applet that displays a Hilbert curve for the specified order, as shown in Figure 20.18.

(a)   (b)   (c)   (d)

FIGURE 20.18   A Hilbert curve with the specified order is drawn.

20.37   (*Sierpinski triangle*) Write a program that prompts the user to enter the order and display the filled Sierpinski triangles as shown in Figure 20.19.

**20.38   (*Recursive tree*) Write an applet to display a recursive tree as shown in Figure 20.20.

FIGURE 20.19 A filled Sierpinski triangle is displayed.

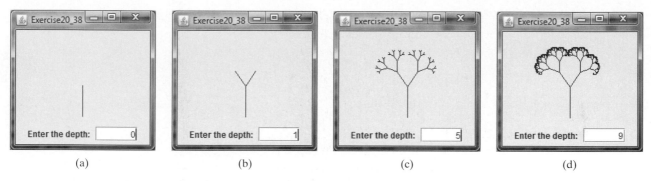

FIGURE 20.20 A recursive tree with the specified depth is drawn.

**20.39 (*Dragging the tree*) Revise Exercise 20.38 to move the tree to where the mouse is dragged.

APPENDIXES

Appendix A
Java Keywords

Appendix B
The ASCII Character Set

Appendix C
Operator Precedence Chart

Appendix D
Java Modifiers

Appendix E
Special Floating-Point Values

Appendix F
Number Systems

Appendix G
Bitwise Operations

Java Keywords

The following fifty keywords are reserved for use by the Java language:

abstract	double	int	super
assert	else	interface	switch
boolean	enum	long	synchronized
break	extends	native	this
byte	final	new	throw
case	finally	package	throws
catch	float	private	transient
char	for	protected	try
class	goto	public	void
const	if	return	volatile
continue	implements	short	while
default	import	static	
do	instanceof	strictfp*	

The keywords **goto** and **const** are C++ keywords reserved, but not currently used, in Java. This enables Java compilers to identify them and to produce better error messages if they appear in Java programs.

The literal values **true**, **false**, and **null** are not keywords, just like literal value 100. However, you cannot use them as identifiers, just as you cannot use 100 as an identifier. In the code listing, we use the keyword color for **true**, **false**, and **null** to be consistent with their coloring in Java IDEs.

assert is a keyword added in JDK 1.4 and **enum** is a keyword added in JDK 1.5.

---

*The **strictfp** keyword is a modifier for a method or class that enables it to use strict floating-point calculations. Floating-point arithmetic can be executed in one of two modes: *strict* or *nonstrict*. The strict mode guarantees that the evaluation result is the same on all Java Virtual Machine implementations. The nonstrict mode allows intermediate results from calculations to be stored in an extended format different from the standard IEEE floating-point number format. The extended format is machine-dependent and enables code to be executed faster. However, when you execute the code using the nonstrict mode on different JVMs, you may not always get precisely the same results. By default, the nonstrict mode is used for floating-point calculations. To use the strict mode in a method or a class, add the **strictfp** keyword in the method or the class declaration. Strict floating-point may give you slightly better precision than nonstrict floating-point, but the distinction will only affect some applications. Strictness is not inherited; that is, the presence of **strictfp** on a class or interface declaration does not cause extended classes or interfaces to be strict.

APPENDIX B

The ASCII Character Set

Tables B.1 and B.2 show ASCII characters and their respective decimal and hexadecimal codes. The decimal or hexadecimal code of a character is a combination of its row index and column index. For example, in Table B.1, the letter **A** is at row 6 and column 5, so its decimal equivalent is 65; in Table B.2, letter **A** is at row 4 and column 1, so its hexadecimal equivalent is 41.

TABLE B.1 ASCII Character Set in the Decimal Index

	0	1	2	3	4	5	6	7	8	9
0	nul	soh	stx	etx	eot	enq	ack	bel	bs	ht
1	nl	vt	ff	cr	so	si	dle	dc1	dc2	dc3
2	dc4	nak	syn	etb	can	em	sub	esc	fs	gs
3	rs	us	sp	!	"	#	$	%	&	'
4	(	)	*	+	,	-	.	/	0	1
5	2	3	4	5	6	7	8	9	:	;
6	<	=	>	?	@	A	B	C	D	E
7	F	G	H	I	J	K	L	M	N	O
8	P	Q	R	S	T	U	V	W	X	Y
9	Z	[	\	]	^	_	`	a	b	c
10	d	e	f	g	h	i	j	k	l	m
11	n	o	p	q	r	s	t	u	v	w
12	x	y	z	{	|	}	~	del		

TABLE B.2 ASCII Character Set in the Hexadecimal Index

	0	1	2	3	4	5	6	7	8	9	A	B	C	D	E	F
0	nul	soh	stx	etx	eot	enq	ack	bel	bs	ht	nl	vt	ff	cr	so	si
1	dle	dc1	dc2	dc3	dc4	nak	syn	etb	can	em	sub	esc	fs	gs	rs	us
2	sp	!	"	#	$	%	&	'	(	)	*	+	,	-	.	/
3	0	1	2	3	4	5	6	7	8	9	:	;	<	=	>	?
4	@	A	B	C	D	E	F	G	H	I	J	K	L	M	N	O
5	P	Q	R	S	T	U	V	W	X	Y	Z	[	\	]	^	_
6	`	a	b	c	d	e	f	g	h	i	j	k	l	m	n	o
7	p	q	r	s	t	u	v	w	x	y	z	{	|	}	~	del

APPENDIX C

Operator Precedence Chart

The operators are shown in decreasing order of precedence from top to bottom. Operators in the same group have the same precedence, and their associativity is shown in the table.

Operator	Name	Associativity
()	Parentheses	Left to right
()	Function call	Left to right
[]	Array subscript	Left to right
.	Object member access	Left to right
++	Postincrement	Right to left
--	Postdecrement	Right to left
++	Preincrement	Right to left
--	Predecrement	Right to left
+	Unary plus	Right to left
-	Unary minus	Right to left
!	Unary logical negation	Right to left
(type)	Unary casting	Right to left
new	Creating object	Right to left
*	Multiplication	Left to right
/	Division	Left to right
%	Remainder	Left to right
+	Addition	Left to right
-	Subtraction	Left to right
<<	Left shift	Left to right
>>	Right shift with sign extension	Left to right
>>>	Right shift with zero extension	Left to right
<	Less than	Left to right
<=	Less than or equal to	Left to right
>	Greater than	Left to right
>=	Greater than or equal to	Left to right
instanceof	Checking object type	Left to right

Operator	Name	Associativity
==	Equal comparison	Left to right
!=	Not equal	Left to right
&	(Unconditional AND)	Left to right
^	(Exclusive OR)	Left to right
|	(Unconditional OR)	Left to right
&&	Conditional AND	Left to right
||	Conditional OR	Left to right
?:	Ternary condition	Right to left
=	Assignment	Right to left
+=	Addition assignment	Right to left
-=	Subtraction assignment	Right to left
*=	Multiplication assignment	Right to left
/=	Division assignment	Right to left
%=	Remainder assignment	Right to left

APPENDIX D

Java Modifiers

Modifiers are used on classes and class members (constructors, methods, data, and class-level blocks), but the `final` modifier can also be used on local variables in a method. A modifier that can be applied to a class is called a *class modifier*. A modifier that can be applied to a method is called a *method modifier*. A modifier that can be applied to a data field is called a *data modifier*. A modifier that can be applied to a class-level block is called a *block modifier*. The following table gives a summary of the Java modifiers.

Modifier	*Class*	*Constructor*	*Method*	*Data*	*Block*	*Explanation*
(default)*	√	√	√	√	√	A class, constructor, method, or data field is visible in this package.
public	√	√	√	√		A class, constructor, method, or data field is visible to all the programs in any package.
private		√	√	√		A constructor, method, or data field is only visible in this class.
protected		√	√	√		A constructor, method, or data field is visible in this package and in subclasses of this class in any package.
static			√	√	√	Define a class method, a class data field, or a static initialization block.
final	√		√	√		A final class cannot be extended. A final method cannot be modified in a subclass. A final data field is a constant.
abstract	√		√			An abstract class must be extended. An abstract method must be implemented in a concrete subclass.
native			√			A native method indicates that the method is implemented using a language other than Java.

*Default access doesn't have a modifier associated with it. For example: `class Test {}`

Modifier	Class	Constructor	Method	Data	Block	Explanation
`synchronized`			√		√	Only one thread at a time can execute this method.
`strictfp`	√		√			Use strict floating-point calculations to guarantee that the evaluation result is the same on all JVMs.
`transient`				√		Mark a nonserializable instance data field.

The modifiers default (no modifier), `public`, `private`, and `protected` are known as *visibility* or *accessibility modifiers* because they specify how classes and class members are accessed.

The modifiers `public`, `private`, `protected`, `static`, `final`, and `abstract` can also be applied to inner classes.

Appendix E

Special Floating-Point Values

Dividing an integer by zero is invalid and throws `ArithmeticException`, but dividing a floating-point value by zero does not cause an exception. Floating-point arithmetic can overflow to infinity if the result of the operation is too large for a `double` or a `float`, or underflow to zero if the result is too small for a `double` or a `float`. Java provides the special floating-point values `POSITIVE_INFINITY`, `NEGATIVE_INFINITY`, and `NaN` (Not a Number) to denote these results. These values are defined as special constants in the `Float` class and the `Double` class.

If a positive floating-point number is divided by zero, the result is `POSITIVE_INFINITY`. If a negative floating-point number is divided by zero, the result is `NEGATIVE_INFINITY`. If a floating-point zero is divided by zero, the result is `NaN`, which means that the result is undefined mathematically. The string representations of these three values are `Infinity`, `-Infinity`, and `NaN`. For example,

```
System.out.print(1.0 / 0);  // Print Infinity
System.out.print(-1.0 / 0); // Print -Infinity
System.out.print(0.0 / 0);  // Print NaN
```

These special values can also be used as operands in computations. For example, a number divided by `POSITIVE_INFINITY` yields a positive zero. Table E.1 summarizes various combinations of the /, *, %, +, and - operators.

TABLE E.1 Special Floating-Point Values

x	y	x/y	x*y	x%y	x + y	x − y
Finite	± 0.0	± infinity	± 0.0	NaN	Finite	Finite
Finite	± infinity	± 0.0	± 0.0	x	± infinity	infinity
± 0.0	± 0.0	NaN	± 0.0	NaN	± 0.0	± 0.0
± infinity	Finite	± infinity	± 0.0	NaN	± infinity	± infinity
± infinity	± infinity	NaN	± 0.0	NaN	± infinity	infinity
± 0.0	± infinity	± 0.0	NaN	± 0.0	± infinity	± 0.0
NaN	Any	NaN	NaN	NaN	NaN	NaN
Any	NaN	NaN	NaN	NaN	NaN	NaN

Note
If one of the operands is NaN, the result is NaN.

Number Systems

F.I Introduction

Computers use binary numbers internally, because computers are made naturally to store and process 0s and 1s. The binary number system has two digits, 0 and 1. A number or character is stored as a sequence of 0s and 1s. Each 0 or 1 is called a *bit* (binary digit).

binary numbers

In our daily life we use decimal numbers. When we write a number such as 20 in a program, it is assumed to be a decimal number. Internally, computer software is used to convert decimal numbers into binary numbers, and vice versa.

decimal numbers

We write computer programs using decimal numbers. However, to deal with an operating system, we need to reach down to the "machine level" by using binary numbers. Binary numbers tend to be very long and cumbersome. Often hexadecimal numbers are used to abbreviate them, with each hexadecimal digit representing four binary digits. The hexadecimal number system has 16 digits: 0–9 and A–F. The letters A, B, C, D, E, and F correspond to the decimal numbers 10, 11, 12, 13, 14, and 15.

hexadecimal number

The digits in the decimal number system are 0, 1, 2, 3, 4, 5, 6, 7, 8, and 9. A decimal number is represented by a sequence of one or more of these digits. The value that each digit represents depends on its position, which denotes an integral power of 10. For example, the digits 7, 4, 2, and 3 in decimal number 7423 represent 7000, 400, 20, and 3, respectively, as shown below:

$$\boxed{7 \mid 4 \mid 2 \mid 3} = 7 \times 10^3 + 4 \times 10^2 + 2 \times 10^1 + 3 \times 10^0$$

$$10^3 \; 10^2 \; 10^1 \; 10^0 = 7000 + 400 + 20 + 3 = 7423$$

The decimal number system has ten digits, and the position values are integral powers of 10. We say that 10 is the *base* or *radix* of the decimal number system. Similarly, since the binary number system has two digits, its base is 2, and since the hex number system has 16 digits, its base is 16.

base
radix

If 1101 is a binary number, the digits 1, 1, 0, and 1 represent 1×2^3, 1×2^2, 0×2^1, and 1×2^0, respectively:

$$\boxed{1 \mid 1 \mid 0 \mid 1} = 1 \times 2^3 + 1 \times 2^2 + 0 \times 2^1 + 1 \times 2^0$$

$$2^3 \; 2^2 \; 2^1 \; 2^0 \quad = 8 + 4 + 0 + 1 = 13$$

If 7423 is a hex number, the digits 7, 4, 2, and 3 represent 7×16^3, 4×16^2, 2×16^1, and 3×16^0, respectively:

$$\boxed{7 \mid 4 \mid 2 \mid 3} = 7 \times 16^3 + 4 \times 16^2 + 2 \times 16^1 + 3 \times 16^0$$

$$16^3 \; 16^2 \; 16^1 \; 16^0 = 28672 + 1024 + 32 + 3 = 29731$$

binary to decimal

F.2 Conversions Between Binary and Decimal Numbers

Given a binary number $b_n b_{n-1} b_{n-2} \ldots b_2 b_1 b_0$, the equivalent decimal value is

$$b_n \times 2^n + b_{n-1} \times 2^{n-1} + b_{n-2} \times 2^{n-2} + \ldots + b_2 \times 2^2 + b_1 \times 2^1 + b_0 \times 2^0$$

Here are some examples of converting binary numbers to decimals:

Binary	Conversion Formula	Decimal
10	$1 \times 2^1 + 0 \times 2^0$	2
1000	$1 \times 2^3 + 0 \times 2^2 + 0 \times 2^1 + 0 \times 2^0$	8
10101011	$1 \times 2^7 + 0 \times 2^6 + 1 \times 2^5 + 0 \times 2^4 + 1 \times 2^3 + 0 \times 2^2 + 1 \times 2^1 + 1 \times 2^0$	171

decimal to binary

To convert a decimal number d to a binary number is to find the bits $b_n, b_{n-1}, b_{n-2}, \ldots, b_2, b_1$, and b_0 such that

$$d = b_n \times 2^n + b_{n-1} \times 2^{n-1} + b_{n-2} \times 2^{n-2} + \ldots + b_2 \times 2^2 + b_1 \times 2^1 + b_0 \times 2^0$$

These bits can be found by successively dividing d by 2 until the quotient is 0. The remainders are $b_0, b_1, b_2, \ldots, b_{n-2}, b_{n-1}$, and b_n.

For example, the decimal number 123 is 1111011 in binary. The conversion is done as follows:

Tip
The Windows Calculator, as shown in Figure F.1, is a useful tool for performing number conversions. To run it, search for *Calculator* from the *Start* button and launch Calculator, then under *View* select *Scientific*.

FIGURE F.1 You can perform number conversions using the Windows Calculator.

F.3 Conversions Between Hexadecimal and Decimal Numbers

Given a hexadecimal number $h_n h_{n-1} h_{n-2} \ldots h_2 h_1 h_0$, the equivalent decimal value is

hex to decimal

$$h_n \times 16^n + h_{n-1} \times 16^{n-1} + h_{n-2} \times 16^{n-2} + \ldots + h_2 \times 16^2 + h_1 \times 16^1 + h_0 \times 16^0$$

Here are some examples of converting hexadecimal numbers to decimals:

Hexadecimal	Conversion Formula	Decimal
7F	$7 \times 16^1 + 15 \times 16^0$	127
FFFF	$15 \times 16^3 + 15 \times 16^2 + 15 \times 16^1 + 15 \times 16^0$	65535
431	$4 \times 16^2 + 3 \times 16^1 + 1 \times 16^0$	1073

To convert a decimal number d to a hexadecimal number is to find the hexadecimal digits $h_n, h_{n-1}, h_{n-2}, \ldots, h_2, h_1$, and h_0 such that

decimal to hex

$$d = h_n \times 16^n + h_{n-1} \times 16^{n-1} + h_{n-2} \times 16^{n-2} + \ldots + h_2 \times 16^2$$
$$+ h_1 \times 16^1 + h_0 \times 16^0$$

These numbers can be found by successively dividing d by 16 until the quotient is 0. The remainders are $h_0, h_1, h_2, \ldots, h_{n-2}, h_{n-1}$, and h_n.

For example, the decimal number 123 is 7B in hexadecimal. The conversion is done as follows:

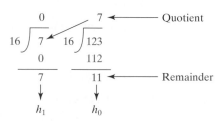

F.4 Conversions Between Binary and Hexadecimal Numbers

To convert a hexadecimal to a binary number, simply convert each digit in the hexadecimal number into a four-digit binary number, using Table F.1.

hex to binary

For example, the hexadecimal number 7B is 1111011, where 7 is 111 in binary, and B is 1011 in binary.

To convert a binary number to a hexadecimal, convert every four binary digits from right to left in the binary number into a hexadecimal number.

binary to hex

For example, the binary number 1110001101 is 38D, since 1101 is D, 1000 is 8, and 11 is 3, as shown below.

TABLE F.I Converting Hexadecimal to Binary

Hexadecimal	Binary	Decimal
0	0000	0
1	0001	1
2	0010	2
3	0011	3
4	0100	4
5	0101	5
6	0110	6
7	0111	7
8	1000	8
9	1001	9
A	1010	10
B	1011	11
C	1100	12
D	1101	13
E	1110	14
F	1111	15

Note

Octal numbers are also useful. The octal number system has eight digits, 0 to 7. A decimal number 8 is represented in the octal system as 10.

Here are some good online resources for practicing number conversions:

- http://forums.cisco.com/CertCom/game/binary_game_page.htm
- http://people.sinclair.edu/nickreeder/Flash/binDec.htm
- http://people.sinclair.edu/nickreeder/Flash/binHex.htm

F.1 Convert the following decimal numbers into hexadecimal and binary numbers:

100; 4340; 2000

F.2 Convert the following binary numbers into hexadecimal and decimal numbers:

1000011001; 100000000; 100111

F.3 Convert the following hexadecimal numbers into binary and decimal numbers:

FEFA9; 93; 2000

APPENDIX G

Bitwise Operations

To write programs at the machine-level, often you need to deal with binary numbers directly and perform operations at the bit-level. Java provides the bitwise operators and shift operators defined in Table G.1.

The bit operators apply only to integer types (`byte`, `short`, `int`, and `long`). A character involved in a bit operation is converted to an integer. All bitwise operators can form bitwise assignment operators, such as =, |=, <<=, >>=, and >>>=.

TABLE G.1

Operator	Name	Example (using bytes in the example)	Description
&	Bitwise AND	10101110 & 10010010 yields 10000010	The AND of two corresponding bits yields a 1 if both bits are 1.
|	Bitwise inclusive OR	10101110 | 10010010 yields 10111110	The OR of two corresponding bits yields a 1 if either bit is 1.
^	Bitwise exclusive OR	10101110 ^ 10010010 yields 00111100	The XOR of two corresponding bits yields a 1 only if two bits are different.
~	One's complement	~10101110 yields 01010001	The operator toggles each bit from 0 to 1 and from 1 to 0.
<<	Left shift	10101110 << 2 yields 10111000	The operator shifts bits in the first operand left by the number of bits specified in the second operand, filling with 0s on the right.
>>	Right shift with sign extension	10101110 >> 2 yields 11101011 00101110 >> 2 yields 00001011	The operator shifts bit in the first operand right by the number of bits specified in the second operand, filling with the highest (sign) bit on the left.
>>>	Unsigned right shift with zero extension	10101110 >>> 2 yields 00101011 00101110 >>> 2 yields 00001011	The operator shifts bit in the first operand right by the number of bits specified in the second operand, filling with 0s on the left.

INDEX

Symbols

-- (decrement operator), 54–56

- (subtraction operator), 46, 50

. (dot operator), 23, 304

. (object member access operator), 304, 427

/ (division operator), 46, 50

//, in line comment syntax, 25

/*, in block comment syntax, 25

/**.*/ (Javadoc comment syntax), 25

/= (division assignment operator), 53–54

; (semicolons), common errors, 93

\ (backslash character), as directory separator, 542

\ (escape characters), 63–64

|| (or logical operator), 102–105

+ (addition operator), 46, 50

+ (string concatenation operator), 38, 340

++ (increment operator), 54–56

+= (addition assignment operator), augmented, 53–54

= (assignment operator), 42–43, 53–54

= (equals operator), 82

-= (subtraction assignment operator), 53–54

== (comparison operator), 82, 430

== (equal to operator), 82

! (not logical operator), 102–105

!= (not equal to comparison operator), 82

$ (dollar sign character), use in source code, 40

% (remainder or modulo operator), 46, 50

%= (remainder assignment operator), 53–54

&& (and logical operator), 102–105

( ) (parentheses), 18, 203

* (multiplication operator), 19, 46, 50

*= (multiplication assignment operator), 53–54

^ (exclusive or logical operator), 102–105

{} (curly braces), 17–18, 85, 93

< (less than comparison operator), 82

<= (less than or equal to comparison operator), 82

> (greater than comparison operator), 82

>= (greater than or equal to comparison operator), 82

A

abs method, Math class, 199–200, 588

Absolute file name, 541

Abstract classes

    case study: abstract number class, 565–567

    case study: Calendar and GregorianCalendar
        classes, 567–568

    characteristics of, 564–565

    Circle.java and Rectangle.java examples, 562

    compared with interfaces, 581–584

    Component and JComponent as, 447

    FontMetrics as, 493

    GeometricObject.java example, 560–562

    InputStream and OutputStream classes, 712–713

    interfaces compared to, 570

    key terms, 590

    overview of, 559–560

    questions and exercises, 590–598

    Rational.java example, 586–589

    reasons for using abstract methods, 562

    summary, 590

    TestCalendar.java example, 568–570

    TestGeometricObject.java example, 562–563

    TestRationalClass.java example, 585–586

Abstract data type (ADT), 375

Abstract methods

    characteristics of, 564

    GeometricObject class, 561–562

    implementing in subclasses, 560

    in interfaces, 570

    in Number class, 588

    reasons for using, 562–563

abstract modifier, for denoting abstract methods, 560

Abstract number class

    LargestNumbers.java, 566–567

    overview of, 565–567

Abstract Windows Toolkit. see AWT (Abstract Windows Toolkit)

AbstractButton class

    alignment, 470

    overview of, 468–469

Abstraction

    classes, 375–376

    methods, 203–204

Accessor methods. see Getter (accessor) methods

acos method, trigonometry, 197–198

ActionEvents

    GUI components firing, 640

    JComboBox class, 647, 650

    processing with event handlers, 604–605

    Timer class firing, 625–626

ActionListener interface

    animation using Timer class, 625

    ControlCircle.java, 607–608

    DetectSourceDemo.java, 613–614

    event handlers and register listeners and, 604–605

    overview of, 600–602

Actions (behaviors), object, 296

Activation records, invoking methods and, 182

Actual parameters, defining methods and, 179

Ada, high-level languages, 11

add method, for adding components to frames, 450–451
addActionListener method, 600
Addition (+) operator, 46, 50
Addition (+=) assignment operator, augmented assignment
 operators, 53–54
Adjustment listeners, 656
ADT (abstract data type), 375
Aggregating classes, 382
Aggregating objects, 382
Aggregation relationships, objects, 382–383
AIFF audio files, 693
Algorithms, 34
Alignment, **JButton** class and, 470
Ambiguous invocation, of methods, 195
American Standard Code for Information Interchange (ASCII).
 see ASCII (American Standard Code for Information
 Interchange)
Anagrams, 364
And (&&) logical operator, 102–105
Android phones, use of Java on, 15
Animation
 AnimationDemo.java, 626–628
 ClockAnimation.java, 628–629
 using **Timer** class for, 625–626
Anonymous arrays, 238
Anonymous class listeners
 AnonymousListenerDemo.java, 610–612
 ListDemo.java, 653
 MoveMessageDemo.java, 619
 overview of, 609–610
Anonymous objects, 305
APIs (Application Program Interfaces), 16
Applet class
 developing applets, 672
 as top-level container, 447
Applet Viewer utility, 675
<applet> tag, HTML, 673
Applets
 case study: bouncing ball, 683–686
 case study: national flags and anthems, 695–697
 case study: tic-tac-toe game, 686–688
 containers, 447, 677
 developing, 672
 DisplayImagePlayAudio.java, 694
 DisplayImageWithURL.java, 692–693
 DisplayLabel.html, 673–674
 DisplayLabel.java, 672–673, 676–677
 DisplayMessageApp.java, 681–683
 DisplayMessage.html, 679–680
 DisplayMessage.java, 680–681
 enabling to run as application, 676–677
 HTML **<applet>** tag, 673
 Java, 14
 key terms, 697
 life-cycle methods, 677–678
 locating resources using **URL** class, 691–692

overview of, 671–672
 passing strings to, 679
 playing audio files, 693–694
 questions and exercises, 698–708
 security restrictions, 675–676
 summary, 697–698
 TicTacToe.java, 688–691
 viewing from Web browser, 674–675
 viewing with Applet Viewer utility, 675
appletviewer command, 675
Application, enabling applets to run as, 676–677
Application Program Interfaces (APIs), 16
Apps, developing on Web servers, 14
Archive attribute, applets, 674
Arcs, drawing, 488–490
Arguments
 defining methods and, 179
 passing by values, 186–189
 receiving string arguments from command line, 358–359
 variable-length argument lists, 244–245
ArithmeticException class, 521
Arithmetic/logic units, CPU components, 3
Array initializers, 227
Array variables, 226
arraycopy method, **System** class, 236
ArrayIndexOutOfBoundsException, 230
ArrayList class
 case study: custom stack class, 436–437
 cloning arrays, 578
 creating and adding numbers to array lists, 566–567
 DistinctNumbers.java example, 434–436
 storing list of objects in, 430–431
 TestArrayList.java example, 431–434
Arrays, multi-dimensional
 case study: daily temperature and humidity, 278–279
 case study: guessing birthdays, 279
 overview of, 277–278
 questions and exercises, 281–294
 summary, 281
Arrays, single-dimensional
 ArrayList class, 433–434
 Arrays class, 252–253
 case study: counting occurrences of letters, 241–244
 case study: deck of cards, 234–236
 case study: lotto numbers, 231–234
 constructing strings from, 336
 converting strings to/from, 343–344
 copying, 236–237
 creating, 225–226, 574–576
 declaring, 225
 for-each loops, 229–231
 indexed variables, 226–227
 initializers, 227
 key terms, 253
 of objects, 326–328
 overview of, 223–225

passing to methods, 237–240
processing, 227–229
questions and exercises, 255–262
returning from methods, 240–241
searching, 245–248
serializing, 728–729
size and default values, 226
sorting, 248–252, 574–576
summary, 253–254
treating as objects in Java, 304
variable-length argument lists, 244–245
Arrays, two-dimensional
  case study: finding closest pair of points, 272–273
  case study: grading multiple-choice test, 270–272
  case study: Sudoku, 274–277
  declaring variables and creating two-dimensional arrays, 264–265
  obtaining length of two-dimensional arrays, 265–266
  overview of, 263–264
  passing to methods to two-dimensional arrays, 269–270
  processing two-dimensional arrays, 267–269
  questions and exercises, 281–294
  ragged arrays, 266–267
  summary, 281
`Arrays` class, 252–253
Arrows keys, on keyboards, 8
Ascent, in text fonts, 493
ASCII (American Standard Code for Information Interchange)
  character data type (`char`) and, 63
  data input and output streams, 717
  encoding scheme, 4
  text encoding, 710
  text I/O vs. binary I/O, 711
`asin` method, trigonometry, 197–198
Assemblers, 10
Assembly language, 10
Assignment operator (=)
  augmented, 53–54
  overview of, 42–43
Assignment statements (assignment expressions)
  assigning value to variables, 36
  overview of, 42–43
Associativity, of operators, 116
`atan` method, trigonometry, 197–198
Attributes, object, 296
AU files, audio formats, 693
Audio files
  applets for playing, 693–694
  case study: national flags and anthems, 695–697
  `DisplayImagePlayAudio.java`, 694
`AudioClip` objects, 693–694
Autoboxing/Autounboxing, 396–397
AWT (Abstract Windows Toolkit)
  `Applet` class, 447, 672
  `Color` class, 460–462
  `Component` class. *see* `Component` class

`Container` class. *see* Containers/ `Container` class
`Date` class, 308–309, 567–568
`Dialog` class, 447
`Dimension` class, 448
`Error` class, 524, 526
event classes in, 603
`EventObject` class, 602–603, 605
exceptions. *see* `Exception` class
`FigurePanel` class, 485–488
`File` class, 541–543, 710
`FlowLayout` class. *see* FlowLayout class
`Font` class, 461–462
`Frame` class, 447
`GeometricObject` class, 560–563
`Graphics` class. *see* `Graphics` class
`GregorianCalendar` class in. *see* `GregorianCalendar` class
`GridLayout` class. *see* `GridLayout` class
`GuessDate` class, 388–391
`IllegalArgumentException` class, 527
`Image` class, 504
`ImageViewer` class, 506–508
`InputMismatchException` class, 522–523, 547
`KeyEvent` class, 621
`LayoutManager` class, 448
`MalformedURLException` class, 551
`MessagePanel` class, 495–497
`MouseEvent` class, 617–619
`Point` class, 617–618
`Polygon` class, 490
`Scanner` class. *see* `Scanner` class
`String` class, 336
Swing vs., 446

B

Babylonian method, 217
Background color, setting, 463
Backslash character (\), as directory separator, 542
Base cases, in recursion, 744
BASIC, high-level languages, 11
Bean machine game, 258–259, 514, 633
`beginIndex` method, for obtaining substrings from strings, 341
Behaviors (actions), object, 296
Behind the scene evaluation, expressions, 116
`BigDecimal` class, 397–398, 565
Binary
  files, 710
  machine language as binary code, 9–10
  operators, 47
  searches, 246–248, 748–749
binary digits (Bits), 4
Binary I/O
  `BufferedInputStream` and `BufferedOutputStream` classes, 719–722
  characters and strings in, 716

Binary I/O (*continued*)
   classes, 712–713
     `DataInputStream` and `DataOutputStream` classes, 716–718
     `DetectEndOfFile.java`, 719
     `FileInputStream` and `FileOutputStream` classes, 713–714
     `FilterInputStream` and `FilterOutputStream` classes, 716
     overview of, 710
     `TestDataStream.java`, 718–719
     `TestFileStream.java`, 714–716
     vs. text I/O, 711–712
Binary numbers
   converting to decimal, 763
   converting to/from, 364
`binarySearch` method, Arrays class, 252–253
Bits (binary digits), 4
Block comments, in `Welcome.java`, 17
Block style, programming style, 25–26
Blocks, in `Welcome.java`, 17
BMI (Body Mass Index), 97–99, 379–382
Boolean accessor method, 320
`boolean` data type
   `java.util.Random`, 309–310
   overview of, 82–84
Boolean expressions
   case study: determining leap year, 105–106
   conditional expressions, 111–112
   defined, 82
   `if` statements and, 84–85
   `if-else` statements, 89–91
   writing, 95
Boolean literals, 83
Boolean values
   defined, 82
   as format specifier, 113
   inability to cast, 104
   logical operators and, 101–102
   redundancy in testing, 94
Boolean variables
   assigning, 95
   overview of, 83
   redundancy in testing, 94
`BorderLayout` class
   overview of, 456
   properties of, 457
   `ShowBorderLayout.java` example, 456–457
Borders
   `JComponent` class, 463
   setting, 463–464
   sharing, 466
Bottom-up implementation, 205–207
Boxing, converting wrapper object to primitive value, 396
Braces. *see* Curly braces (`{}`)
`break` statements
   controlling loops, 159–162
   using with `switch` statements, 109

Breakpoints, setting for debugging, 120
Bubble sorts, 258
`BufferedInputStream` and `BufferedOutputStream` classes, 719–722
Bugs (logic errors), 27–28, 119–120
Bus, function of, 2–3
`ButtonListener` class, 617
Buttons
   adding to `BorderLayout`, 457
   creating, 311, 451
   grouping, 641
   icons used with, 469
   image icons displayed as, 466
   `JButton` class. *see* `JButton` class
   `JRadioButton` class. *see* `JRadioButton` class
   text positions, 470–471
   types of, 468
`byte` type, numeric types, 45
Bytecode
   translating Java source file into, 20–21
   verifier, 22
Bytes
   defined, 4
   measuring storage capacity in, 5

C

C, high-level languages, 11
C++, high-level languages, 11
Cable modems, 8
`Calendar` class, 567–568
Call stacks
   displaying in debugging, 120
   invoking methods and, 182
Calling
   methods, 180–182
   objects, 305
`canRead` method, `File` class, 542–543
`canWrite` method, `File` class, 542–543
`capacity` method, `StringBuilder` class, 355–356
Case sensitivity
   identifiers and, 40
   in `Welcome.java`, 18
Casting. *see* Type casting
Casting objects
   `CastingDemo.java` example, 426–429
   overview of, 425–426
Catching exceptions
   `catch` block omitted when `finally` clause is used, 535
   `CircleWithException.java` example, 532
   `InputMismatchExceptionDemo.java` example, 522
   `QuotientWithException.java` example, 520–521
   `try-catch` blocks, 527–529
CDs (compact discs), as storage device, 6
Cells
   in Sudoku grid, 274
   in tic-tac-toe case study, 687–691

Celsius, converting to/from Fahrenheit, 50–51, 213
Chained exceptions, 537–538
Character class, 350–351
Characters/ character data type (char)
    applying numeric operators to, 201–202
    in binary I/O, 716–717
    case study: counting monetary units, 65–68
    case study: ignoring nonalphanumeric characters when
        checking palindromes, 356–358
    casting to/from numeric types, 63–65
    Character class, 350–351
    comparing, 82
    constructing strings from arrays of, 336
    converting to strings, 344
    CountEachLetter.java example, 351–353
    escape characters, 63–64
    finding, 342–343
    overview of, 62
    RandomCharacter.java, 202
    retrieving in strings, 339–340
    TestRandomCharacter.java, 202–203
    Unicode and ASCII and, 62–63
charAt (index) method
    retrieving characters in strings, 339–340
    StringBuilder class, 355–356
charValue method, Character class, 350
Check boxes
    creating, 311
    events, 640–643
    JCheckBox class, 471–472
    types of buttons, 468
Checked exceptions, 525
Choice lists. *see* Combo boxes
Circle class, 296–297
Clarity, class design guidelines, 392
Class abstraction, 375
Class diagrams, UML, 297
Class encapsulation, 375–376
Class loaders, 22
Class variables, 312
ClassCastException, 426
Classes
    abstract. *see* Abstract classes
    abstraction and encapsulation in, 375–376
    case study: designing class for stacks, 386–388
    case study: designing Course class, 384–386
    in CircleWithPrivateDataFields.java example,
        320–321
    in CircleWithStaticMembers.java example, 313–314
    clients of, 299
    commenting, 25
    in ComputeExpression.java, 19
    data field encapsulation for maintaining, 319–320
    defining custom exception classes, 538–541
    defining for objects, 296–298
    design guidelines, 391–393
    designing for reuse, 499

    for displaying GUI components, 310–312
    event classes, 603
    event listeners. *see* Listener classes
    identifiers, 40
    inner (nested) classes. *see* Inner (nested) classes
    from Java Library, 308
    names/naming conventions, 17, 44
    preventing extension of, 439–440
    for primitive data types, 350
    static variables, constants, and methods, 312–313
    in TestCircleWithPrivateDataFields.java example,
        321–322
    in TestCircleWithStaticMembers.java example,
        314–317
    in UML diagram, 298
    variable scope and, 371–372
    visibility modifiers, 317–319
    in Welcome.java, 17
    in WelcomeWithThreeMessages.java, 18
Classes, binary I/O
    BufferedInputStream and BufferedOutputStream
        classes, 719–722
    DataInputStream and DataOutputStream classes,
        716–718
    DetectEndOfFile.java, 719
    FileInputStream and FileOutputStream classes,
        713–714
    FilterInputStream and FilterOutputStream classes,
        716
    overview of, 712–713
    TestDataStream.java, 718–719
    TestFileStream.java, 714–716
Class's contract, 375
Clock speed, CPUs, 3
clone method, shallow and deep copies, 579–580
Cloneable interface
    House.java example, 578–581
    overview, 577–578
Closest pair problem, two-dimensional array applied to, 272–273
COBOL, high-level languages, 11
Code
    arrays for simplifying, 229
    comments and, 109
    programming. *see* Programs/programming
    reuse. *see* Reusable code
    sharing. *see* Sharing code
Codebase attribute, applets, 674
Coding (Implementation)
    incremental development, 137
    in software development process, 60–61
Coherent purpose, class design guidelines, 391
Color
    Component class and, 499
    setting background and foreground color, 463
Color class
    helper classes, 446, 448
    in Java GUI API, 460–462

Combo boxes
  `ComboBoxDemo.java`, 648–649
  creating, 310–312
  overview of, 647–648
Command-line arguments, 358–361
Comments
  code maintainability and, 109
  programming style and, 25
  in `Welcome.java`, 17
Common denominator, finding greatest common denominator.
    see Gcd (greatest common denominator)
Communication devices, computers and, 8–9
Compact discs (CDs), as storage device, 6
`Comparable` interface
  `ComparableRectangle.java` example, 575–576
  overview of, 573–574
  `Rational` class implementing, 585
  `SortComparableObjects.java` example, 574–575
  `SortRectangles.java` example, 576–577
`compareTo` method
  `Character` class, 350–351
  `Cloneable` interface and, 577
  `Comparable` interface defining, 573–574
  `ComparableRectangle.java` example, 575–576
  comparing strings, 338
  implementing in `Rational` class, 588
  wrapper classes and, 394
`compareToIgnoreCase` method, strings, 338–339
Comparing strings, 337–339
Comparison operator (==), 82, 430
Compile errors (Syntax errors)
  common errors, 18
  debugging, 119–120
  programming errors, 26–27
Compilers
  ambiguous invocation and, 195
  reporting syntax errors, 26
  translating Java source file into bytecode file, 20–21
  translating source program into machine code, 10–11
Completeness, class design guidelines, 392
Complex numbers, `Math` class, 594
`Component` class
  as abstract class, 447
  color and font methods, 499
  common features of `Component`, `Container`,
    and `JComponent`, 462
  subclasses of, 446, 451
Components
  adding to `BorderLayout` to, 456
  adding to frames, 450–451
  combo boxes, 647–648
  `ComboBoxDemo.java`, 648–649
  common features of, 462
  comparing Swing and AWT components, 446
  component classes, 446–447
  `DescriptionPanel.java`, 645–646
  events, 640

  `GUIEventDemo.java`, 640–643
  `Histogram.java`, 662–664
  `JComponent` class. *see* `JComponent` class
  `JFrame` displaying, 449
  `JTextComponent` class, 474–475
  `ListDemo.java`, 652–654
  lists, 649–652
  multiple windows, 660–661
  `MultipleWindowsDemo.java`, 661–662
  naming conventions, 468
  overview of, 639–640
  questions and exercises, 664–670
  scroll bars, 654–655
  `ScrollBarDemo.java`, 655–657
  `SliderDemo.java`, 658–660
  sliders, 657–658
  summary, 664
  text areas, 644–645
  `TextAreaDemo.java`, 646–647
Composition relationships
  between `ArrayList` and `MyStack`, 436–437
  objects and, 382–383
Compute expression, 19
Computers
  communication devices, 8–9
  CPUs, 3–4
  input/output devices, 7–8
  memory, 4–5
  OSs (operating systems), 12–13
  overview of, 2–3
  programming languages, 9–12
  storage devices, 5–7
`concat method`, 340
Concatenate strings, 36, 68, 340
Conditional AND operator, 104
Conditional expressions, 111–112
Confirmation dialogs
  controlling loops, 164–165
  making selections, 117–119
Connect four game, 288
Consistency, class design guidelines, 391
Consoles
  defined, 16
  formatting output, 112–115
  input, 16
  output, 16
  reading input, 37–40
Constants
  accessing in interfaces, 572
  class, 312–313
  declaring, 313
  in `FigurePanel.java`, 486
  identifiers, 40
  key constants, 622
  named constants, 43
  naming conventions, 44
  wrapper classes and, 394

Constructor chaining, 415–417
Constructors
    in abstract classes, 562
    for `BMI` class, 381
    calling subclass constructors, 414–415
    for `Character` class, 350
    creating objects with, 303
    creating `Random` objects, 310
    for `DataInputStream` and `DataOutputStream` classes, 717
    for `Date` class, 309
    for `GuessDate` class, 390–391
    in `ImageViewer.java` example, 507
    interfaces vs. abstract classes, 581
    invoking with `this` reference, 374–375
    for `Loan` class, 377–379
    object methods and, 296–297
    `private`, 319
    in `SimpleCircle` example, 299–300
    for `String` class, 336
    for `StringBuilder` class, 353
    in `TV.java` example, 300
    UML diagram of, 298
    wrapper classes and, 393
Containers/ `Container` class
    common features in `Component`, `Container`,
        and `JComponent` classes, 462
    `JPanel` as subclass of, 459–460
    overview of, 446, 447–448
Content pane, in `JFrame` class, 450–451
Content-pane delegation, 451
`continue` statements, for controlling loops, 159–162
Contract, object class as, 296
Control units, CPUs, 3
Control variables, in `for` loops, 147–148
Conversion methods, for wrapper classes, 394
Converting strings
    to/from arrays, 343–344
    to/from numeric values, 344
    overview of, 341
Coordinates
    drawing polygons, 490–491
    Java coordinate system, 481
    in `MessagePanel` class, 499
Copying
    arrays, 236–237
    files, 722–723
Core, of CPU, 4
cos method, trigonometry, 197–198
Cosine function, 511
Counter-controlled loops, 135
Coupon collector's problem, 260
`Course` class, 384–386
CPUs (central processing units), 3–4
Curly braces ({})
    in block syntax, 17–18
    dangers of omitting, 85
    forgetting to use, 93

`currentTimeMillis` method, 51–52
Cursor, mouse, 8
`Cursor` class, 463

D

.dat files (binary), 712
Data, arrays for referencing, 224
Data fields
    accessing object data, 304–305
    encapsulating, 319–320, 391–392
    in interfaces, 572
    object state represented by, 296–297
    referencing, 305, 373–374
    in `SimpleCircle` example, 299–300
    in `TV.java` example, 301
    UML diagram of, 298
Data streams. *see* `DataInputStream`/`DataOutputStream` classes
Data types
    ADT (abstract data type), 375
    `boolean`, 82–84, 309–310
    characters. *see* Characters/ character data type (`char`)
    `double`. *see* `double` (double precision) data type
    `float`. *see* Floating-point numbers/float data type
    fundamental. *see* Primitive types
    integers. *see* Integers (`int` data type)
    `long` data type. *see* `long` data type
    numeric, 44–46, 56–58
    reference types. *see* Reference types
    specifying, 35
    strings, 68–69
    types of, 41
    using abstract class as, 564
`DataInputStream`/`DataOutputStream` classes
    `DetectEndOfFile.java`, 719
    overview of, 716–718
    `TestDataStream.java`, 718–719
`Date` class
    case study: `Calendar` and `GregorianCalendar` classes,
        567–568
    `java.util`, 308–309
De Morgan's law, 104
Debugging
    benefits of stepwise refinement, 210
    code modularization and, 189
    selections, 119–120
Decimal numbers
    `BigDecimal` class, 397–398
    converting to hexadecimals, 191–193, 348–350, 763
    converting to/from binary, 364, 763
    division of, 51
Declaring constants, 43, 313
Declaring exceptions
    `CircleWithException.java` example, 531
    `ReadData.java` example, 546
    `TestCircleWithCustomException.java` example, 539
    `throws` keyword for, 526

Declaring static methods, 313
Declaring variables
  array variables, 225
  overview of, 41
  specifying data types and, 35–36
  two-dimensional array variables, 264–265
Decrement (−−) operator, 54–56
Deep copies, 579–580
Default field values, for data fields, 305–306
Delete key, on keyboards, 8
Delimiters, token reading methods and, 546–547
Denominator. *see* Gcd (greatest common denominator)
Denominators, in rational numbers, 584
Deployment, in software development process, 59
Descent, in text fonts, 493
`DescriptionPanel` class, 645–647
Descriptive names
  benefits of, 40
  for variables, 35
Deserialization, of objects, 727
Design guidelines, classes, 391–393
`destroy` method, applet life-cycle, 677–678
Dialog boxes
  confirmation dialogs, 117–119, 164–165
  `Dialog` class, 447
  displaying file dialogs, 549–550
  input dialogs, 70, 72
  `JDialog` class, 447–448
  message dialogs, 22–23
`Dialog` class, 447
Dial-up modems, 8
Digital subscriber lines (DSLs), 8
Digital versatile disc (DVDs), 6
Digits, matching, 107
`Dimension` class, 448
Direct recursion, 741
Directories
  case study: determining directory size, 749
  `DirectorySize.java`, 749–750
  `File` class and, 542
  file paths, 541
Disks, as storage device, 6
Display message
  in dialog box, 22–24
  in `Welcome.java`, 17
  in `WelcomeWithThreeMessages.java`, 18
Divide-and-conquer strategy. *see* Stepwise refinement
Division (/=) assignment operator, 53–54
Division operator (/), 46, 50
Documentation, programming and, 24
Dot operator (.), 23, 304
Dot pitch, measuring sharpness of displays, 8
`double` (double precision) data type
  converting characters and numeric values to strings, 344
  converting strings to numbers, 70
  declaring variables and, 41
  `java.util.Random`, 309–310

overview of numeric types, 45
precision of, 154–155
`do-while` loops
  deciding when to use, 150–151
  overview of, 144–146
Downcasting objects, 425
`drawArc` method, 488–490
`drawImage` method, 504–505
`drawLine` method, 483
`drawOval` method, 484, 488
`drawPolygon` method, 491
`drawPolyline` method, 491
`drawRect` method, 483–484
`drawString` method, 483
Drives, 6
Drop-down lists. *see* Combo boxes
DSLs (digital subscriber lines), 8
DVDs (Digital versatile disc), 6
Dynamic binding, inheritance and, 422–425

E

Eclipse
  built in debugging, 119
  creating/editing Java source code, 19
  stopping programs with Terminate button, 450
Eight Queens puzzle, 259, 262, 765–766
Element type, specifying for arrays, 225
Emirp, 218
Encapsulation
  in `CircleWithPrivateDataFields.java` example, 320–321
  class design guidelines, 391
  of classes, 375–376
  of data fields, 319–320
  in `GuessDate` class, 391
  information hiding with, 203
  of `Rational` class, 589
  strings and, 339
Encoding schemes
  defined, 4
  mapping characters to binary equivalents, 61
End of file exception (`EOFException`), 719
`endIndex` method, for obtaining substrings from strings, 341
End-of-line style, block styles, 25–26
Equal (=) operator, for assignment, 82
Equal to (==) operator, for comparison, 82
`equalArea` method, for comparing areas of geometric objects, 563
`equals` method
  `Arrays` class, 253
  `Character` class, 350–351
  comparing strings, 337
  `Object` class, 429–430
`equalsIgnoreCase` method, comparing strings, 338–339
`Error` class, 524, 526
Errors, programming. *see* Programming errors
Escape characters (\), 63–64

Event delegation, 603
Event handlers/event handling, 601–602
    anonymous class listeners, 611
    `DetectSourceDemo.java`, 613–614
    `ListDemo.java`, 653
    overview of, 604
Event listener object, 603
Event listeners, 603–604. *see also* Listener classes
Event source object, 602–603
Event-driven programming
    alternatives for defining listener classes, 612
    animation using `Timer` class, 625–626
    `AnimationDemo.java`, 626–628
    anonymous class listeners, 609–610
    `AnonymousListenerDemo.java`, 610–612
    case study: loan calculator, 615
    `ClockAnimation.java`, 628–629
    `ControlCircle.java`, 607–608
    `ControlCircleWithMouseAndKey.java`, 623–625
    `ControlCircleWithoutEventHandling.java`, 606–607
    defined, 602
    `DetectSourceDemo.java`, 612–613
    event handlers, 604
    event listeners, 603–604
    events and event sources, 602–603
    `FrameAsListenerDemo.java`, 613–614
    `HandleEvent.java`, 601–602
    inner classes, 608–609
    key events, 621–622
    key terms, 629
    `KeyEventDemo.java`, 622–623
    listener interface adapters, 620–621
    `LoanCalculator.java`, 615–617
    mouse events, 617–618
    `MoveMessageDemo.java`, 618–620
    overview of, 600–601
    questions and exercises, 630–638
    register listeners, 604–605
    summary, 629–630
Event-listener interface, 603
`EventObject` class, `java.util`, 602–603, 605
Events
    `ControlCircleWithMouseAndKey.java`, 623–625
    event sources and, 602–603
    GUI component, 640
    `GUIEventDemo.java`, 640–643
    `JList` class, 651
    key events, 621–622
    `KeyEventDemo.java`, 622–623
    mouse events, 617–618
    `MoveMessageDemo.java`, 618–620
    `Timer` class firing `ActionEvents`, 625–626
`Exception` class
    exceptions in, 524
    extending, 538
    in `java.lang`, 539
    subclasses of, 524–525

Exception handling. *see also* Programming errors
    catching exceptions, 527–529, 531
    chained exceptions, 537–538
    `CircleWithException.java` example, 531–532
    declaring exceptions (`throws`), 526, 531
    defining custom exception classes, 538–541
    `finally` clause in, 534–535
    getting information about exceptions, 529–530
    `InputMismatchExceptionDemo.java` example, 522–523
    key terms, 552
    overview of, 39, 517–518
    questions and exercises, 554–558
    `Quotient.java` example, 518
    `QuotientWithException.java` example, 520–522
    `QuotientWithIf.java` example, 519
    `QuotientWithMethod.java` example, 519–520
    rethrowing exceptions, 536–537
    summary, 553–554
    `TestCircleWithException.java` example, 532–534
    `TestException.java` example, 530
    throwing exceptions, 526–527, 531
    types of exceptions, 523–525
    when to use exceptions, 535–536
Exception propagation, 527
Exceptions. *see also* Programming errors
    catching (`try-catch`), 527–529
    checked and unchecked, 525
    `ClassCastException`, 426
    declaring, 526
    defined, 518
    `EOFException`, 719
    in `Exception` class, 524
    `FileNotFoundException`, 713
    handling. *see* Exception handling
    in `House.java` example, 579
    `IOException`, 713–714
    `NotSerializableException`, 727
    throwing, 526–527
Exclusive or (∧) logical operator, 102–105
Execution stacks. *see* Call stacks
`exists` method, for checking file instances, 542–543
Explicit casting, 56–57, 425
Exponent method, `Math` class, 198–199
Exponent operations, 48
Expressions
    assignment statements and, 42
    behind the scene evaluation, 116
    Boolean. *see* Boolean expressions
    evaluating, 50–51
`extends` keyword, interface inheritance and, 582

F

Factorials
    case study: computing factorials, 738–739
    `ComputeFactorial.java`, 739–741
    `ComputeFactorialTailRecusion.java`, 759
    tail recursion and, 758–759

Fahrenheit, converting Celsius to/from, 50–51, 213
Fall-through behavior, `switch` statements, 109
Feet, converting to/from meters, 213–214
`fib` method, 742–744
Fibonacci, Leonardo, 742
Fibonacci numbers
    case study: computing, 741–742
    `ComputeFibonacci.java`, 742–744
    computing recursively, 761
`FigurePanel` class
    `FigurePanel.java`, 486–488
    overview of, 485
    `TestFigurePanel.java`, 485–486
`File` class, 541–543, 710
File I/O. *see* I/O (input/output)
File pointers, random-access files and, 730
`FileInputStream`/`FileOutputStream` classes
    overview of, 713–714
    `TestFileStream.java`, 714–716
Files
    case study: copying files, 722–723
    case study: replacing text in, 548–549
    displaying file dialogs, 549–550
    `File` class, 541–543, 710
    input/output, 544
    `JFileChooser`class, 550
    key terms, 552
    questions and exercises, 554–558
    reading data from, 545–547
    reading data from Web, 551–552
    summary, 553–554
    `TestFileClass.java`, 543–544
    writing data to, 544–545
`FilterInputStream`/`FilterOutputStream` classes, 716
`final` keyword, for declaring constants, 43
`final` modifier, for preventing classes from being extended, 439–440
`finally` clause, in exception handling, 534–535
Floating-point literals, 49
Floating-point numbers/`float` data type
    approximation of, 47
    converting characters and numeric values to strings, 344
    converting to integers, 56
    `java.util.Random`, 309–310
    minimizing numeric errors related to loops, 154–155
    numeric types for, 45
    overview of numeric types, 45
    specifying data types, 35
    specifying precision, 114
Flowcharts
    `do-while` loops, 145
    `if` statements, 84–85
    `if-else` statements, 90
    `for` loops, 147
    `switch` statements, 108
    `while` loops, 135
`FlowLayout` class
    overview of, 452

    properties of, 457
    `ShowFlowLayout.java` example, 452–454
`Font` class
    helper classes, 446, 448
    in Java GUI API, 461–462
`FontMetrics` class
    centering a string using, 493–494
    helper classes, 446, 448
    `TestCenterMessage.java` example, 494–495
Fonts
    `Component` class, 499
    creating, 463
    `GUIEventDemo.java`, 642
    setting for message panel, 495
`for` loops
    deciding when to use, 151
    nesting, 152, 267
    overview of, 146–149
    processing arrays with, 227
    variable scope and, 196
`for-each` (enhanced) loops, 229–231
Foreground color, 463–464
Formal parameters. *see* Parameters
`format` method, strings, 344–347
Format specifiers, 113–115
FORTRAN, high-level languages, 11
Fractals
    case study, 754–755
    H-tree fractals, 766
    Koch snowflake fractal, 764
    `SierpinskiTriangle.java`, 755–757
Frames (windows)
    adding components to, 450–451
    creating, 310–312, 449, 457, 641, 676
    `DisplayLabel.java`, 677
    `Frame` class, 447
    `JFrame` class. *see* `JFrame` class
    `ListDemo.java`, 653
    `MultipleWindowsDemo.java`, 661–662
    `MyFrame.java` example, 449–450
    `ScrollBarDemo.java`, 656
    `SliderDemo.java`, 659
Free cells, in Sudoku grid, 274
Function keys, on keyboards, 7
Functions, 179. *see also* Methods
Fundamental types (Primitive types). *see* Primitive types

G

Galton box, 258–259
Garbage collection, JVM and, 236
GBs (gigabytes), of storage, 5
Gcd (greatest common denominator)
    case study: finding greatest common denominator, 155–157
    computing recursively, 760
    `gcd method`, 189–190
    `gcd` method, 588
    `Rational` class and, 585

Gene sequences, 367
Genome, 367
`GeometricObject` class
  `Circle.java` and `Rectangle.java`, 562
  overview of, 560
  `TestGeometricObject.java`, 562–563
`getAbsolutePath` method, `File` class, 542–543
`getArea` method, `SimpleCircle` example, 299
`getArray` method, 269–270
`getBMI` method, `BMI` class, 381
`getChars` method, converting strings into arrays, 343
`getDateCreated` method, `Date` class, 370
`getFontMetrics` method, `Graphics` class, 493–494
`getHeight` method, `FontMetrics` class, 495
`getIndex` method, `ArrayList` class, 433
`getPerimeter` method, `SimpleCircle` example, 299
`getRadius` method, `CircleWithPrivateDataFields.java`
  example, 321
`getRandomLowerCaseLetter` method, 241, 243
`getSize` method, finding directory size, 750
`getSource` method, events, 602
`getStackTrace` method, for getting information about
  exceptions, 529
`getStatus` method, `BMI` class, 381
Getter (accessor) methods
  `ArrayList` class and, 434
  encapsulation of data fields and, 320–322
`getTime` method, `Date` class, 309
`getWidth` method, `FontMetrics` class, 495
GIF (Graphics Interchange Format), 465
Gigabytes (GBs), of storage, 5
Gigahertz (GHz), clock speed, 4
GMT (Greenwich Mean Time), 51
Gosling, James, 13
Graphics
  case study: `FigurePanel` class, 485–488
  case study: `ImageViewer` class, 506–507
  case study: `MessagePanel` class, 495–497
  case study: `StillClock` class, 500
  centering a string using `FontMetrics` class, 493–495
  `DisplayClock.java` example, 500–502
  `DisplayImage.java` example, 505
  displaying images, 504–505
  drawing arcs, 488–490
  drawing polygons and polylines, 490–493
  drawing strings, lines, rectangles, and ovals, 483–484
  `ImageViewer.java` example, 507–508
  `Message.Panel.java` example, 497–500
  overview of, 479–480
  questions and exercises, 509–516
  `SixFlags.java` example, 506–507
  `StillClock.java` example, 502–504
  summary, 508–509
  `TestPaintComponent.java` example, 481–483
Graphics class
  `GetFontMetrics` method, 493
  helper classes, 446, 448
  overview of, 480–481

Graphics Interchange Format (GIF), 465
Greater than (>) comparison operator, 82
Greater than or equal to (>=) comparison operator, 82
Greatest common denominator. *see* Gcd (greatest common
  denominator)
Greenwich Mean Time (GMT), 51
`GregorianCalendar` class
  `Cloneable` interface and, 577–578
  in `java.util` package, 331
  overview of, 567–568
  `TestCalendar.java`, 568–569
`GridLayout` class
  overview of, 454–455
  properties of, 457
  `ShowGridLayout.java` example, 455–456
Grids
  `GridLayout` manager, 454–456
  representing using two-dimensional array, 274
`GuessDate` class, 388–391
GUI (graphical user interface)
  alignment, 470
  `BorderLayout` class, 456–457
  classes for GUI components, 310–312
  `Color` class, 460–462
  common features of Swing GUI components, 462–465
  `Component` class, 447
  components. *see* Components
  `Container` class, 447–448
  converting GUI applications into applets, 672
  `FlowLayout` class, 452–454
  `Font` class, 461–462
  frames, 449–451
  `GridLayout` class, 454–456
  GUI objects created from classes, 296
  helper classes, 448
  icons, pressed icons, and rollover icons, 469
  image icons, 465–467
  Java GUI API, 446–447
  `JButton` class, 467–469
  `JCheckBox` class, 471–472
  `JLabel` class, 473–474
  `JRadioButton` class, 472–473
  `JTextField` class, 474–475
  key terms, 475
  layout managers, 451
  overview of, 445–446
  panels used as subcontainers, 458–460
  properties of layout managers, 457–458
  questions and exercises, 476–478
  summary, 475–476
  Swing vs. AWT, 446
  text positions, 470–471

H

Hand-traces, for debugging, 119–120
Hangman game, 367, 512, 556, 636
Hard disks, as storage device, 6

Hardware, 2
Has-a relationships
    in aggregation models, 382–383
    composition and, 437
Heap, dynamic memory allocation and, 239
Height, in text fonts, 493
Helper classes, 448
Helper methods, recursive
    overview of, 746
    `RecursivePalindrome.java`, 746–747
Hertz (Hz), clock speed in, 3
Hex integer literals, 49
Hexadecimal numbers
    converting to/from binary, 364, 763
    converting to/from decimals, 191–193, 348–350, 763
Hexagons, drawing, 491–492
Hidden data fields, referencing, 373–374
High-level languages, 10–12
Hilbert curve, 766
Horizontal scroll bars, 655
Horizontal sliders, 657, 659
Horizontal text positioning, 470
HTML (Hypertext Markup Language)
    `<applet>` tag, 673
    defining applet parameters, 679
    `DisplayLabel.html`, 673–674
    `DisplayMessage.html`, 679–680
    scripting language for document layout, 14
    viewing applets from Web browser, 674
H-trees
    fractals, 766
    recursive approach to, 738
Hz (Hertz), clock speed in, 3

I

Icons. *see* Image icons
Identifiers, 40
IDEs (integrated development environments)
    for creating/editing Java source code, 19–20
    overview of, 16
IEEE (Institute of Electrical and Electronics Engineers), floating
        point standard (IEEE 754), 45
`if` statements
    common errors, 93–95
    in computing body mass index, 97–99
    in computing taxes, 99–101
    conditional operator used with, 112
    nesting, 91
    overview of, 84–85
    `SimpleIfDemo.java` example, 85–86
`if-else` statements
    conditional expressions and, 112
    dangling else ambiguity, 94–95
    multi-way, 91–93
    overview of, 89–91
    recursion and, 744

`IllegalArgumentException` class, 527
`Image` class, 504
Image icons
    `ComboBoxDemo.java`, 649
    creating and placing, 691–692
    default icons, pressed icons, and rollover icons, 469
    displaying images, 504
    overview of `ImageIcon` class, 465–466
    `TestImageIcon.java` example, 466–467
Images
    case study: `ImageViewer` class, 506–507
    `DisplayImage.java` example, 505
    displaying, 504–505
    `ImageViewer.java` example, 507–508
    `SixFlags.java` example, 506–507
`ImageViewer` class
    `ImageViewer.java` example, 507–508
    overview of, 506–507
Immutable
    `BigInteger` and `BigDecimal` classes, 397–398
    class, 370
    objects, 370–371
    `Rational` class, 589
    `String` object, 336–337
    wrapper classes, 394
Implementation (coding), in software development process,
        59–61
Implementation methods, 207–210
Implicit casting, 64, 425
Importing
    importing package into program, 23–24
    `JFrame` package, 449
    types of `import` statements, 24
Increment (++) operator, 54–56
`increment` method, in `Increment.java` example, 186–187
Incremental development
    benefits of stepwise refinement, 210
    coding incrementally, 137
    testing and, 61
Indentation, programming style, 25
Indexed variables, 226–227
Indexes
    accessing elements in arrays, 224, 226
    finding characters/substrings in a string, 342–343
    string index range, 340
`indexOf` method, 342–343
Indirect recursion, 741
Infinite loops, 136
Infinite recursion, 741
Information
    getting information about exceptions, 529–530
    hiding (encapsulation), 203
Inheritance
    `ArrayList` object, 430–431
    calling subclass constructors, 414–415
    calling superclass methods, 417
    case study: custom stack class, 436–437

casting objects and, 425–426
CastingDemo.java example, 426–429
CircleFromGeometricObject.java example, 410–412
constructor chaining and, 415–417
DistinctNumbers.java example, 434–436
dynamic binding and, 422–425
equals method of Object class, 429–430
interface inheritance, 570–571, 582
is-a relationships and, 437
key terms, 440
Object class and, 420–421
overriding methods and, 418–420
overview of, 407–408
preventing classes from being extended or overridden, 439–440
protected data and methods, 437–440
questions and exercises, 442–444
RectangleFromGeometricObject.java example, 412–413
SimpleGeometricObject.java example, 409–410
summary, 440–441
superclasses and subclasses and, 408–409
TestArrayList.java example, 431–434
TestCircleRectangle.java example, 413–414
using super keyword, 414
init method, applet life-cycle methods, 677–678
Initializing variables
arrays, 227–228
declaring variables and, 41
LottoNumbers.java, 232
multidimensional arrays, 265
two-dimensional arrays, 267
Inner (nested) classes
AnimationDemo.java, 627
anonymous, 609–610
AnonymousListenerDemo.java, 610–612
for defining listener classes, 608–609
KeyEventDemo.java, 622
MoveMessageDemo.java, 619
TicTacToe.java, 689
Input. see also I/O (input/output)
reading from console, 37–40
redirecting using while loops, 143–144
runtime errors, 27
streams. see InputStream classes
Input, process, output (IPO), 39–40
Input dialog boxes
getting input via, 70–72
ShowInputDialog method, 70, 72
InputMismatchException class, 522–523, 547
Input/output devices, computers and, 7–8
InputStream classes
BufferedInputStream, 719–722
case study: copying files, 723–724
DataInputStream, 716–718
deserialization and, 727
DetectEndOfFile.java, 719

FileInputStream, 713–714
FilterInputStream, 716
ObjectInputStream class, 724–725
overview of, 712–713
TestDataStream.java, 718–719
TestFileStream.java, 714–716
TestObjectInputStream.java, 726
Insert key, on keyboards, 8
Insertion sorts, arrays, 250–252
Instance methods
accessing object data and methods, 305
in CircleWithStaticMembers.java, 314
class design guidelines, 392–393
invoking, 377, 380
when to use instance methods vs. static, 313–314
Instance variables
accessing object data and methods, 305
class design guidelines, 392–393
static variables compared with, 312–313
in TestCircleWithStaticMembers.java, 314
when to use instance variables vs. static, 316
Instances. see also Objects
checking file instantiation, 542
checking object instantiation, 296, 426
Institute of Electrical and Electronics Engineers (IEEE), floating point standard (IEEE 754), 45
Integer literals, 48–49
Integers (int data type)
ArrayList for, 435
BigInteger class, 397–398
casting to/from char types, 63
converting characters and numeric values to strings, 344
converting strings to numbers, 70
declaring variables and, 41
division of, 46, 51, 518–522
finding larger between two, 179
floating-point numbers converted to, 56
java.util.Random, 309–310
numeric types for, 44–45
specifying data types, 35
Integrated development environments (IDEs)
for creating/editing Java source code, 19–20
overview of, 16
Intelligent guesses, 137
Interface adapters, listener classes, 620–621
Interfaces
abstract classes compared with, 581–584
benefits of, 576
case study: Rational class, 584–585
Cloneable interface, 577–578
Comparable interface, 573–574
ComparableRectangle.java example, 575–576
for defining common class behaviors, 560
House.java example, 578–581
key terms, 590
overview of, 570
questions and exercises, 590–598

Interfaces (*continued*)
SortComparableObjects.java example, 574–575
SortRectangles.java example, 576–577
summary, 590
TestEdible.java example, 570–573
Interned strings, 336–337
Interpreters, translating source program into machine code, 10–11
Invoking methods, 180–182, 305
I/O (input/output)
binary I/O classes, 712–713
BufferedInputStream and BufferedOutputStream classes, 719–722
case study: copying files, 722–723
case study: replacing text, 548–549
Copy.java, 723–724
DataInputStream and DataOutputStream classes, 716–718
DetectEndOfFile.java, 719
displaying file dialogs, 549–550
FileInputStream and FileOutputStream classes, 713–714
FilterInputStream and FilterOutputStream classes, 716
handling text I/O in Java, 710–711
key terms, 732
object I/O, 724–725
overview of, 544, 709–710
questions and exercises, 733–736
random-access files, 729–731
reading data from file using Scanner class, 545–547
reading data from Web, 551–552
serializable interface, 727–728
serializing arrays, 728–729
summary, 733
TestDataStream.java, 718–719
TestFileStream.java, 714–716
TestObjectInputStream.java, 726
TestObjectOutputStream.java, 725–726
TestRandomAccessFile.java, 731–732
text I/O vs. binary I/O, 711–712
types of I/O devices, 7–8
writing data to file using PrintWriter class, 544–545
IOException, 713–714
IPO (input, process, output), 39–40
Is-a relationships
design guide for when to use interfaces vs. classes, 582
inheritance and, 437
isAbsolute method, File class, 542–543
isDigit method, Character class, 351, 356–357
isDirectory method, File class, 542–543
isFile method, File class, 542–543
isHidden method, File class, 542–543
Is-kind-of relationships, 582
isLetter method, Character class, 351, 356–357
isLowerCase method, Character class, 351
isPalindrome method
RecursivePalindrome.java, 746–747
as tail-recursive method, 758
isPrime method, prime numbers, 191
isUpperCase method, Character class, 351

isValid method, applying to grid, 276
ItemEvents
GUI components firing, 640
JComboBox class, 647, 650
Iterations
loops and, 134
recursion compared with, 757–758

J

JApplet class
container classes, 446, 448
developing applets, 672
JFrame class compared with, 676–677
top-level containers, 447
java command, for executing Java program, 21
Java Development Toolkit (JDK)
jdb debugger in, 119
overview of, 16
Java EE (Java Enterprise Edition), 16
Java GUI API, 446–447
Java language specification, 16
Java Library, 308
Java ME (Java Micro Edition), 16
Java programming
creating, compiling, and executing programs, 19–22
displaying text in message dialog box, 22–24
high-level languages, 11
introduction to, 13–15
simple examples, 16–19
Java SE (Java Standard Edition), 16
Java Virtual Machine. *see* JVM (Java Virtual Machine)
java.awt classes. *see* AWT (Abstract Windows Toolkit)
javac command, for compiling Java program, 21
Javadoc comments (/**.*/), 25
java.io
File class, 541–543
PrintWriter class, 544–545
RandomAccessFile class, 730
java.lang
Class class, 692
Comparable interface, 573
Exception class, 539
Number class, 565
packages, 61
Throwable class, 523–525, 529–530
java.net
MalformedURLException class, 551
URL class, 551, 691–692
java.util
Arrays class, 252–253
Calandar class, 567–568
Date class, 308–309, 567
EventObject class, 602–603, 605
GregorianCalendar class, 331, 567–568
Random class, 309–310
Scanner class, 38, 545–547

`javax.swing`. *see* Swing
`JButton` class
    alignment, 470
    creating buttons, 310–312, 451
    creating push button, 467–469
    default icons, pressed icons, and rollover icons, 469
    image icons displayed as buttons, 466
    inheriting from `Container` class, 460
    text positions, 470–471
`JCheckBox` class
    creating check boxes, 311
    events, 640–643
    overview of, 471–472
    types of buttons, 468
`JComboBox` class
    `ComboBoxDemo.java`, 648–649
    creating combo boxes, 310–312
    GUI components, 647–648
`JComponent` class
    as abstract class, 447
    common features in `Component`, `Container`, and `JComponent` classes, 462–463
    overview of, 446–447
    `paintComponent` method, 480
    subclassing, 483
jdb debugger, 119
`JDialog` class, 447, 448
JDK (Java Development Toolkit)
    jdb debugger in, 119
    overview of, 16
`JFileChooser`class, 550
`JFrame` class
    adding components to frames, 450–451
    as container class, 446, 447–448
    creating frames, 310–312, 449, 641, 676
    `JApplet` class compared with, 676
    `ShowFlowLayout` class extending, 452–454
`JLabel` class
    adding labels to frames, 452
    adding labels to grids, 455
    creating and placing image icons on, 691
    creating labels, 311
    image icons displayed as labels, 466
    overview of, 473–474
`JList` class
    creating lists, 310–312
    `ListDemo.java`, 652–654
    overview of lists, 650–652
Joint Photographic Experts Group (JPEG), 465
`JOptionPane` class
    as predefined Java class, 22
    `showConfirmDialog` method, 117–119
    `showInputDialog` method, 70, 72
`JPanel` class
    `Ball` subclass, 683–684
    `Cell` subclass, 687–688
    as container class, 446, 448

`DescriptionPanel` extending, 645–646
    `FigurePanel` class, 485
    `ImageViewer` class, 506–507
    `paintComponent` method, 480
    panels used as subcontainers, 458–459
    `StillClock` class, 500
    subclassing, 482
    `TestPanels.java` example, 459–460
JPEG (Joint Photographic Experts Group), 465
`JRadioButton` class
    creating radio buttons, 310–312
    events, 640
    overview of, 472–473
    types of buttons, 468
`JScrollBar` class
    `BallControl.java`, 685
    controlling bouncing speed in bouncing ball case study, 683
    overview of, 654–655
    `ScrollBarDemo.java`, 655–657
`JScrollPane` class
    `DescriptionPanel.java`, 646
    overview of, 644
    scrolling lists, 644
`JSlider` class
    overview of, 657–658
    `SliderDemo.java`, 658–660
`JTextArea` class
    overview of, 644–645
    `TextAreaDemo.java`, 646–647
`JTextComponent` class, 474–475
`JTextField` class
    adding text fields to frames, 452
    adding text fields to grids, 455
    creating text fields, 311
    events, 640
    overview of, 474–475
JVM (Java Virtual Machine)
    defined, 21
    detecting runtime errors, 518
    garbage collection, 236
    heap as storage area in, 239
    interned string and, 337

K

KBs (kilobytes), 5
Key constants, 622
Keyboards, 7
`KeyEvents`
    `ControlCircleWithMouseAndKey.java`, 625
    `KeyEventDemo.java`, 622–623
    overview of, 621–622
`KeyListener` interface, 621
Keywords (reserved words)
    syntax of, 426
    in `Welcome.java`, 17

Kilobytes (KBs), 5
Knight's Tour, 765
Koch snowflake fractal, 764

L

Labels
    adding to frames, 452
    adding to grids, 455
    creating, 311
    `DescriptionPanel.java`, 645–646
    image icons displayed as, 466
    `JLabel` class. *see* `JLabel` class
    placing, 641
LANs (local area networks), 8–9, 645–646
`lastIndexOf` method, strings, 342–343
`lastModified` method, `File` class, 542–543
Latin square, 293–294
Layout managers
    `BorderLayout`, 456–457
    `FlowLayout`, 452–454
    `GridLayout`, 454–456
    `LayoutManager` class, 448
    overview of, 451
    properties of, 457–458
Leading, in text fonts, 493
Length, strings, 339–340, 355–356
`length` method, `File` class, 542–543
Less than (<) comparison operator, 82
Less than or equal to (<=) comparison operator, 82
Letters, counting, 352–353
Libraries, APIs as, 16
Life-cycle methods, applets, 677–678
Line comments, in `Welcome.java`, 17
Line numbers, in `Welcome.java`, 17
Linear searches, arrays, 245–246
Lines, drawing, 483–484, 487
Linux OS, 12
Listener classes
    `ActionListener` interface, 600–602
    adjustment listeners, 656
    alternatives for defining, 612
    `AnimationDemo.java`, 627
    anonymous listeners for defining, 609–610
    `AnonymousListenerDemo.java`, 610–612
    `BallControl.java`, 686
    `ButtonListener` class, 617
    case study: national flags and anthems, 696
    `ClockAnimation.java`, 628
    `ComboBoxDemo.java`, 650
    `ControlCircle.java`, 607–608
    `ControlCircleWithoutEventHandling.java`, 606–607
    `DetectSourceDemo.java`, 612–613
    event listeners, 603–604
    `FrameAsListenerDemo.java`, 613–614
    `HandleEvent.java`, 601–602
    inner classes for defining, 608–609

    interface adapters, 620–621, 651–652
    register listeners, 604–605
    `SliderDemo.java`, 659
    `TicTacToe.java`, 690
Listener interface adapters
    `KeyEvents`, 621
    `ListSelectionListener` interface, 651–652
    `MouseEvents`, 620–621
Lists
    creating, 310–312
    `ListDemo.java`, 652–654
    overview of `JList` class, 650–652
`ListSelectionListener` interface, 651–652
Literals
    Boolean literals, 83
    character literals, 61
    constructing strings from string literal, 336
    defined, 48
    floating-point literals, 49
    integer literals, 48–49
LiveLab grading system, 15
Loans
    interest rates in loan computation example, 71–72
    Loan calculator case study, in event-driven programming, 615–617
    `Loan.java` object, 377–379
Local area networks (LANs), 8–9, 645–646
Local variables, 196
Locker puzzle, 260
Logic errors (bugs), 27–28, 119–120
Logical operators (Boolean operators)
    overview of, 101–102
    `TestBooleanOperators.java` example, 103–105
    truth tables, 102–103
`long` data type
    converting characters and numeric values to strings, 344
    integer literals and, 49
    `java.util.Random`, 309–310
    overview of numeric types, 45
Loop body, 134
Loop-continuation-condition
    `do-while` loop, 144–145
    loop design and, 139
    in multiple subtraction quiz, 140
    overview of, 134–135
Loops
    `break` and `continue` keywords as controls in, 159–162
    case study: displaying prime numbers, 162–164
    case study: finding greatest common denominator, 155–157
    case study: guessing numbers, 137–139
    case study: Monte Carlo simulation, 158–159
    case study: multiple subtraction quiz, 139–141
    case study: predicting future tuition, 157
    controlling with confirmation dialog, 164–165
    creating arrays, 237
    deciding which to use, 150–151
    design strategies, 139

`do-while` loop, 144–146
  input and output redirections, 143–144
  iteration compared with recursion, 757–758
  key terms, 165
  `for` loop, 146–149
  minimizing numeric errors related to, 154–155
  nesting, 152–153
  overview of, 133–134
  questions and exercises, 166–175
  sentinel-controlled, 141–143
  summary, 166
  `while` loop, 133–137
Low-level languages, 10

M

Mac OS, 12
Machine language
  bytecode compared with, 21
  overview of, 9–10
  translating source program into, 10–11
Machine stacks. *see* Call stacks
Main class
  defined, 297
  in `TestSimpleCircle.java` example, 298
`main` method
  in `ComputeExpression.java`, 19
  invoking, 181
  main class vs., 297
  receiving string arguments from command line, 358–359
  in `SimpleCircle.java` example, 300–301
  in `TestSimpleCircle.java` example, 298
  in `TestTV.java` example, 300–301
  in `Welcome.java`, 17
  in `WelcomeWithThreeMessages.java`, 18
Main windows, 660
Maintenance, in software development process, 59
`MalformedURLException` class, 552
Mandelbrot fractal, 595–597
Marker interfaces, 577
Markov matrix, 290
Match braces, in `Welcome.java`, 17
`matches` method, strings, 342
`Math` class
  `BigInteger` and `BigDecimal` classes, 397–398
  complex numbers, 594–595
  exponent methods, 198–199
  invoking object methods, 305
  methods generally, 197
  `pow(a, b)` method, 48
  `random` method, 96–97, 106–108, 200–203
  rounding methods, 199
  service methods, 199–200
  trigonometric methods, 197–198
Matrices
  `GridLayout` manager for, 454
  two-dimensional arrays for storing, 264–265

`max` method, `Math` class
  defining and invoking, 180–182
  overloading, 194–195
  overview of, 199–200
`maxRow` variable, for finding largest sum, 268
Mbps (million bits per second), 8
MBs (megabytes), of storage, 5
Megabytes (MBs), of storage, 5
Megahertz (MHz), clock speed, 3
Memory, computers, 4–5
Mersenne prime, 218
Message dialog boxes, 22–23
`MessagePanel` class
  `DisplayClock.java`, 500–502
  `MessagePanel.java`, 497–500
  overview of, 495
  `StillClock.java`, 502–503
  `TestMessagePanel.java`, 495–496
Meta objects, 692
Meters, converting to/from feet, 213–214
Method header, 179
Method signature, 179
Methods
  abstraction, 203–204
  accessing object methods, 304–305
  calling, 180–182
  case study: converting decimals to hexadecimals, 191–193
  case study: generating random numbers, 201–203
  class, 312–313
  commenting, 25
  defining, 178–180
  identifiers, 40
  implementation details, 207–210
  invoking object methods, 305
  key terms, 210
  `Math` class, 197, 199–201
  modularizing code, 189–191
  naming conventions, 44
  object actions defined by, 296–297
  overloading, 193–196
  overview of, 177–178
  passing arrays to, 237–240
  passing objects to, 322–326
  passing parameters by values, 186–189
  passing to two-dimensional arrays, 269–270
  questions and exercises, 211–222
  recursive methods, 738
  returning arrays from, 240–241
  rounding, 199
  in `SimpleCircle.java` example, 300–301
  static, 313
  stepwise refinement, 203–204, 210
  summary, 211
  top-down and/or bottom-up implementation, 205–207
  top-down design, 204–205
  tracing or stepping over as debugging technique, 119
  trigonometric, 197–198

Methods (*continued*)
    variable scope and, 196–197
    `void` method example, 183–185
MHz (Megahertz), clock speed, 3
Microsoft Windows, 12
MIDI files, 693
Million bits per second (Mbps), 8
`min` method, `Math` class, 199–200
Mnemonics
    in assembly language, 10
    for check boxes and radio buttons, 641–643
Modems (modulator/demodulator), 8
Modifier keys, on keyboards, 8
Modifiers, method, 179
Modularizing code
    `GreatestCommonDivisorMethod.java`, 189–190
    overview of, 189
    `PrimeNumberMethod.java`, 190–191
Monitors, 8
Monte Carlo simulation, 158–159
Motherboard, 3
Mouse
    `Cursor` class, 463
    as I/O device, 8
`MouseEvents`
    `ControlCircleWithMouseAndKey.java`, 625
    event-driven programming, 617–618
    listener interface adapters, 620–621
    `MoveMessageDemo.java`, 618–620
`MouseListener` interface, 618, 627
`MouseMotionListener` interface, 619–620
Multi-dimensional arrays. *see* Arrays, multi-dimensional
Multimedia. *see* Applets
Multiple choice test, 270–272
Multiplication (`*=`) assignment operator, 53–54
Multiplication operator (`*`), 19, 46, 50
Multiplication table, 152
Multiplicities, in object composition, 382
Multiprocessing, 13
Multiprogramming, 13
Multithreading, 13
Multi-way `if-else` statements
    in computing taxes, 99–101
    overview of, 91–93
Mutator methods. *see* Setter (mutator) methods

N

Named constants. *see* Constants
Naming conventions
    class design guidelines, 391
    components, 468
    interfaces, 582
    programming and, 44
    wrapper classes, 393
Naming rules, identifiers, 40
N-by-*n* matrix, 215

Negative angles, drawing arcs, 490
Nested `if` statements
    in computing body mass index, 97–99
    in computing taxes, 99–101
    overview of, 91
Nested loop, 152–153, 267
NetBeans
    built in debugging, 119
    for creating/editing Java source code, 19
    stopping programs with Terminate button, 450
Network interface cards (NICs), 8
`new` operator
    creating arrays, 225
    creating objects, 303
`next` method, whitespace characters and, 69
`nextLine` method, whitespace characters and, 69
Next-line style, block styles, 25
NICs (network interface cards), 8
No-arg constructors
    class design guidelines, 391
    `Loan` class, 377
    wrapper classes not having, 394
Not (`!`) logical operator, 102–105
Not equal to (`!=`) comparison operator, 82
`NotSerializableException`, 727
`null` values, objects, 305–306
`NullPointerException`, as runtime error, 306
`Number` class
    case study: abstract number class, 564
    as root class for numeric wrapper classes, 585
Numbers/numeric types
    abstract number class, 565–567
    binary. *see* Binary numbers
    case study: converting hexadecimals to decimals, 348–350
    case study: displaying prime numbers, 162–164
    case study: generating random numbers, 201–203
    case study: guessing numbers, 137–139
    casting to/from `char` types, 63
    conversion between numeric types, 56–58, 364
    converting to/from strings, 70, 344
    decimal. *see* Decimal numbers
    double. *see* `double`
    floating-point. *see* Floating-point numbers/`float` data type
    generating random numbers, 96–97
    `GreatestCommonDivisorMethod.java`, 189–190
    hexadecimal. *see* Hexadecimal numbers
    integers. *see* Integers (`int` data type)
    `LargestNumbers.java`, 566–567
    overview of, 44–46
    `PrimeNumberMethod.java`, 190–191
    processing large numbers, 397–398
Numerators, in rational numbers, 584
Numeric keypads, on keyboards, 8
Numeric literals, 48–49
Numeric operators
    applied to characters, 64
    overview of, 46–47

O

`Object` class, 420–421, 429–430
`Object I/O.` *see*
    `ObjectInputStream/ObjectOutputStream` classes
Object member access operator (`.`), 304, 427
Object reference variables, 304
`ObjectInputStream/ObjectOutputStream` classes
  overview of, 724–725
  `serializable` interface, 727–728
  Serializing arrays, 728–729
  `TestObjectInputStream.java`, 726
  `TestObjectOutputStream.java`, 725–726
Object-oriented programming (OOP), 296, 304, 379–382
Objects
  accessing data and methods of, 304–305
  accessing via reference variables, 304
  array of, 326–327
  `ArrayList` class, 430–431
  arrays as, 239
  `AudioClip` class, 693–694
  automatic conversion between primitive types and wrapper
    class types, 396–397
  `BigInteger` and `BigDecimal` classes, 397–398
  cannot be created from abstract classes, 564
  case study: designing class for stacks, 386–388
  case study: designing `Course` class, 384–386
  case study: designing `GuessDate` class, 388–391
  casting, 425–426
  `CircleWithPrivateDataFields.java` example, 320–321
  `CircleWithStaticMembers.java` example, 313–314
  class abstraction and encapsulation, 375–376
  class design guidelines, 391–393
  classes for displaying GUI components, 310–312
  classes from Java Library, 308
  comparing primitive variables with reference variables,
    306–308
  composing, 382–383
  constructors, 303
  creating, 298–299
  data field encapsulation for maintaining classes, 319–320
  `Date` class, 308–309
  defining classes for, 296–298
  `equals` method of `Object` class, 429–430
  event listener object, 603
  event objects, 602
  immutable, 370–371
  inheritance. *see* inheritance
  key terms, 328–329, 399
  `Loan.java`, 377–379
  meta objects, 692
  `null` values, 305–306
  `Object` class, 420–421
  object-oriented thinking, 379–382
  overview of, 295–296, 369–370
  passing to methods, 322–326
  polymorphism, 421–422
  processing primitive data type values as, 393–396
  questions and exercises, 330–334, 399–406
  `Random` class, 309–310
  reference data fields and, 305
  `SimpleCircle.java` example, 300–301
  static variables, constants, and methods and, 312–313
  summary, 329, 399
  `TestCircleWithPrivateDataFields.java` example, 321–322
  `TestCircleWithStaticMembers.java` example, 314–317
  `TestLoanClass.java`, 376–377
  `TestSimpleCircle.java` example, 298–300
  `TestTV.java` example, 302–303
  `this` reference and, 373–375
  `TotalArea.java` example, 327–328
  `TV.java` example, 301–302
  variable scope and, 371–372
  visibility modifiers, 317–319
Octal integer literals, 49
Off-by-one errors
  arrays and, 230
  in loops, 136
OOP (object-oriented programming), 296, 304, 379–382
Operands
  defined, 46
  incompatible, 104
Operators
  assignment operator (=), 42–43
  augmented assignment operators, 53–54
  comparison operators, 82
  increment and decrement operators, 54–56
  numeric operators, 46–47
  precedence and associativity, 115–117
  precedence rules, 50–51
  unary and binary, 47
Option panes
  predefined Java classes, 22
  `showConfirmDialog` method, 117–119
  `showInputDialog` method, 70, 72
Or (`||`) logical operator, 102–105
OSs (operating systems)
  overview of, 12
  tasks of, 12–13
Output redirection, 143–144
Output streams, 710–711. *see also* I/O (input/output)
`OutputStream` classes
  `BufferedOutputStream` classes, 719–722
  case study: copying files, 723–724
  `DataOutputStream` classes, 716–718
  `DetectEndOfFile.java`, 719
  `FileOutputStream` classes, 713–714
  `FilterOutputStream` classes, 716
  `ObjectOutputStream` class, 724–725
  overview of, 712–713
  serialization and, 727
  `TestDataStream.java`, 718–719
  `TestFileStream.java`, 715–716
  `TestObjectOutputStream.java`, 725–726

Ovals, drawing, 483–484, 487
Overflows
   `Rational` class, 589
   variables, 45
Overloading methods, 193–196
Overriding methods, 418–420

P

π (pi), estimating, 158–159, 215
Package-private (package-access) visibility modifiers, 317
Packages
   importing, 23–24
   importing `JFrame` package, 449
   organizing classes in, 318
   organizing programs in, 22
   predefined classes grouped into, 23
Page Down key, on keyboards, 8
Page Up key, on keyboards, 8
`paintComponent` method
   `DisplayImage.java` example, 505
   drawing arcs and, 488–489
   `DrawPolygon.java` example, 492–493
   `JComponent` class, 480, 482
   `MessagePanel.java`, 494
   `StillClock.java`, 503
   `TestCenterMessage.java` example, 494
Palindromes
   case study: checking if string is a palindrome, 347–348
   case study: ignoring nonalphanumeric characters when checking palindromes, 356–358
   palindrome integers, 212
   palindromic primes, 218
   `RecursivePalindrome.java`, 746–747
   `RecursivePalindromeUsingSubstring.java`, 745–746
Panels
   adding, 489
   adding for `DisplayImage.java` example, 505
   check boxes and radio buttons for, 641
   creating, 311–312, 482
   `DescriptionPanel` class, 645–647
   `FigurePanel` class. *see* `FigurePanel` class
   `JPanel` class. *see* `JPanel` class
   `MessagePanel` class. *see* `MessagePanel` class
   as subcontainers, 458–460
`<param>` tag, applets, 679
Parameters
   actual parameters, 179
   defining methods and, 178–179
   as local variable, 196
   order association, 186
   passing by values, 186–189
   variable-length argument lists, 244–245
Parentheses (`( )`)
   defining and invoking methods and, 203
   in `Welcome.java`, 18
Parsing methods, 395
Pascal, high-level languages, 11

Pass-by-sharing
   arrays to methods, 238
   objects to methods, 323–324
Pass-by-value
   arrays to methods, 238
   `Increment.java` example, 186–187
   objects to methods, 322–323
   overview of, 186
   `TestPassByValue.java` example, 187–189
Passwords, checking if string is valid password, 362
Pentagonal numbers, 212
Pixels (picture elements)
   coordinates measure in, 481
   defined, 450
   measuring resolution in, 8
PNG (Portable Network Graphics), 465
`Point` class, 617–618
Polygons
   drawing, 490–492
   `DrawPolygon.java`, 492–493
Polylines, drawing, 491
Polymorphism
   `CastingDemo.java` example, 426–429
   overview of, 421
   `PolymorphismDemo.java` example, 421–422
Portable Network Graphics (PNG), 465
Postfix decrement operator, 54–55
Postfix increment operator, 54–55
`pow method`, `Math` class, 48
Precedence, operator, 115–117
Prefix decrement operator, 54–55
Prefix increment operator, 54–55
Pressed icons, 469
Prime numbers
   case study: displaying prime numbers, 162–164
   `PrimeNumberMethod.java`, 190–191
   types of, 218
Primitive types (fundamental types)
   automatic conversion between primitive types and wrapper class types, 396–397
   casting, 427
   classes for, 350
   comparing parameters of primitive type with parameters of reference types, 324
   comparing primitive variables with reference variables, 306–308
   converting wrapper object to/from (boxing/unboxing), 396
   creating arrays of, 326
   processing primitive data type values as objects, 393–396
   specifying data types, 35
`print` method, `PrintWriter` class, 38, 544–545
`printf` method, `PrintWriter` class, 544
Printing arrays, 267
`println` method, `PrintWriter` class, 38, 544
`printStackTrace` method, 529
`PrintWriter` class
   case study: replacing text, 548–549

writing data to file using, 544–545
for writing text data, 710
`private`
  encapsulation of data fields and, 319–320
  visibility modifier, 318–319, 437–440
Problems
  breaking into subproblems, 164
  creating programs to address, 34
  solving with recursion, 744–745
Procedural paradigm, compared with object-oriented paradigm, 381–382
Procedures, 179. *see also* Methods
Processing arrays, 227–229
Programming errors. *see also* Exceptions
  `ClassCastException`, 426
  common class design errors, 393
  debugging, 119–120
  logic errors, 27–28
  minimizing numeric errors related to loops, 154–155
  runtime errors, 27
  selections, 93–95
  syntax errors, 18, 26–27
Programming languages
  assembly language, 10
  high-level languages, 10–12
  Java. *see* Java programming
  machine language, 9–10
  overview of, 2
Programming style
  block styles, 25–26
  comments and, 25
  indentation and spacing, 25
  overview of, 24–25
Programs/programming
  assignment statements and expressions, 42–43
  augmented assignment operators, 53–54
  case study: counting monetary units, 65–68
  case study: displaying current time, 51–53
  character data type, 62–65
  coding incrementally, 137
  evaluating expressions and operator precedence rules, 50–51
  exponent operations, 48
  identifiers, 40
  increment and decrement operators, 54–56
  input dialogs, 70–72
  introduction to, 34
  key terms, 72–73
  modularizing code, 189–191
  named constants, 43
  naming conventions, 44
  numeric literals, 48–49
  numeric operators, 46–47
  numeric type conversions, 56–58
  numeric types, 44–46
  overview of, 2
  questions and exercises, 74–80
  reading input from console, 37–40
  recursive methods in, 738
  software development process, 58–62
  `string` data type, 68–69
  summary, 73–74
  variables, 40–42
  writing a simple program, 34–37
Properties
  layout manager, 457–458
  object, 296
`Protected` data and methods, inheritance and, 437–440
`protected` visibility modifier, 318, 437–440
Pseudocode, 34
Public classes, 299
`public` method, 321
`public` visibility modifier, 317–319, 437–440
Python, high-level languages, 11

Q
Quincunx, 258–259
Quotients
  `Quotient.java` example, 518
  `QuotientWithException.java` example, 520–522
  `QuotientWithIf.java` example, 519
  `QuotientWithMethod.java` example, 519–520

R
Radio buttons
  creating, 310–312
  events, 640
  `GUIEventDemo.java`, 640–643
  `JRadioButton` class. *see* `JRadioButton` class
  overview of, 472–473
  for panels, 641
  types of buttons, 468
Ragged arrays, 266–267
RAM (random-access memory), 5–6
`Random` class, `java.util`, 309–310
`random` method
  case study: generating random numbers, 201–203
  case study: lottery, 106–108
  `Math` class, 96–97, 200–201
Random numbers
  case study: generating random numbers, 201–203
  case study: lottery, 106–108
  case study: Monte Carlo simulation, 158–159
  generating, 96–97
Random-access files
  overview of, 729–731
  `TestRandomAccessFile.java`, 731–732
Random-access memory (RAM), 5–6
`Rational` class
  overview of, 584–585
  `Rational.java` example, 586–589
  `TestRationalClass.java` example, 585–586
Rational numbers, representing and processing, 584–586
`readASolution` method, applying to Sudoku grid, 276

Read-only streams, 729. *see also* `InputStream` class
Rectangles, drawing, 483–484, 487
Recursion
   binary searches, 748–749
   case study: computing factorials, 738–739
   case study: computing Fibonacci numbers, 741–742
   case study: determining directory size, 749
   case study: fractals, 754–755
   case study: Towers of Hanoi, 750–752
   `ComputeFactorial.java`, 739–741
   `ComputeFactorialTailRecursion.java`, 759
   `ComputeFibonacci.java`, 742–744
   `DirectorySize.java`, 749–750
   helper methods, 746
   iteration compared with, 757–758
   key terms, 759
   overview of, 737–738
   problem solving by thinking recursively, 744–745
   questions and exercises, 760–767
   `RecursivePalindrome.java`, 746–747
   `RecursivePalindromeUsingSubstring.java`, 745–746
   `RecursiveSelectionSort.java`, 747–748
   selection sorts, 747
   `SierpinskiTriangle.java`, 755–757
   summary, 759
   tail recursion, 758
   `TowersOfHanoi.java`, 752–754
Recursive methods, 738
Reduction, characteristics of recursion, 744
Reference types
   classes as, 304
   comparing parameters of primitive type with parameters of
     reference types, 324
   comparing primitive variables with, 306–308
   reference data fields, 305
   `string` data type as, 68
Reference variables
   accessing objects with, 304
   array of objects as array of, 326
   comparing primitive variables with, 306–308
`regionMatches` method, strings, 338–339
Register listeners
   `ControlCircle.java`, 607–608
   `ControlCircleWithMouseAndKey.java`, 624
   `DetectSourceDemo.java`, 613–614
   `GUIEventDemo.java`, 641–643
   `KeyEventDemo.java`, 623
   `LoanCalculator.java`, 616
   overview of, 604–605
Regular expressions, matching strings with, 342
Relative file names, 541–542
Remainder (%) or modulo operator, 46, 50
Remainder (%=) assignment operator, 53–54
`repaint` method
   applying to message panel, 497–498
   `StillClock.java`, 502–503
Repetition. *see* Loops

`replace` method, strings, 341
`replaceAll` method, strings, 342
`replaceFirst` method, strings, 341
Requirements specification, in software development process,
   58–59
Reserved words (keywords)
   syntax of, 426
   in `Welcome.java`, 17
Resolution, pixels and, 450
Resource files, locating for applets using `URL` class, 691–692
Resources, role of OSs in allocating, 12
Responsibilities, separation as class design principle, 391
`return` statements, 181
Return value type
   constructors not having, 303
   in defining methods, 179
Reusable code
   benefits of stepwise refinement, 210
   code modularization and, 189
   designing classes for, 499
   method enabling, 182
   methods for, 178
reverse method, returning arrays from methods,
   240–241
RGB color model, 460
RMF files, 693
Rollover icons, 469
Rounding methods, `Math` class, 199
Runtime errors
   debugging, 119–120
   declaring, 525–526
   exception handling and, 39, 518
   `NullPointerException` as, 306
   programming errors, 27
Runtime stacks. *see* Call stacks

S

Sandbox security model, 675
`Scanner` class
   obtaining input with, 72
   for reading console input, 37–39
   reading data from file using, 545–547
   for reading text data, 710
Scanners
   case study: replacing text, 548–549
   creating, 522
Scheduling operations, 13
Scientific notation, of integer literals, 49
Scope, of variables, 42, 196–197
Screen resolution, 8
Scroll bars
   `BallControl.java`, 685
   controlling bouncing speed in bouncing ball case
     study, 683
   overview of, 654–655
   `ScrollBarDemo.java`, 655–657

Scroll panes
   `DescriptionPanel.java`, 646
   overview of, 644
   scrolling lists, 651
Searches
   arrays, 245
   binary searches, 246–248, 748–749
   linear searches, 245–246
   recursive approach to searching for words, 738
Security restrictions, applets, 675–676
Selection sorts
   arrays, 245, 249–250
   `RecursiveSelectionSort.java`, 747–748
   using recursion, 747
Selection statements, 82, 84
Selections
   `Addition.Quiz.java` example, 83–84
   `boolean` data type, 82–84
   case study: computing Body Mass Index, 97–99
   case study: computing taxes, 99–101
   case study: determining leap year, 105–106
   case study: guessing birthdays, 86–89
   case study: lottery, 106–108
   common errors, 93–95
   conditional expressions, 111–112
   confirmation dialogs, 117–119
   debugging, 119–120
   formatting console output, 112–115
   generating random numbers, 96–97
   `if` statements, 84–86
   `if-else` statements, 89–91
   key terms, 120
   logical operators, 101–105
   nested `if` statements and multi-way `if-else` statements, 91–93
   operator precedence and associativity, 115–117
   overview of, 81–82
   questions and exercises, 121–131
   summary and exercises, 120–121
   `switch` statements, 108–111
Semicolons (;), common errors, 93
Sentinel-controlled loops, 141–143, 164–165
Sequential files, input/output streams, 729
Serialization
   of arrays, 728–729
   of objects, 727
`setBackground` method, `Component` class, 499
`setFont` method, `Component` class, 499
`setForeground` method, `Component` class, 499
`setLayout` method, `Component` class, 451
`setLength` method, `StringBuilder` class, 355–356
`setRadius` method
   `CircleWithPrivateDataFields.java` example, 321
   `SimpleCircle` example, 299
Setter (mutator) methods
   `ArrayList` class and, 434
   encapsulation of data fields and, 320–322

Shallow copies, `clone` method and, 579–580
Sharing code, 182
`short` numeric type, 45
Short-circuited OR operator, 104
`showConfirmDialog` method, `JOptionPane` class, 117–119
`showInputDialog` method, `JOptionPane` class, 70, 72
`showMessageDialog method`, 22–23
Shuffling arrays, 228–229, 268
Sierpinski triangle
   case study, 754–755
   computing recursively, 762, 766–767
   `SierpinskiTriangle.java`, 755–757
Signed applets, 676
`sin` method, trigonometry, 197–198
Sine function, 511
Single precision numbers. *see* Floating-point numbers/`float` data type
Single-dimensional arrays. *see* Arrays, single-dimensional
Sinking sorts, 258
Sliders
   overview of, 657–658
   `SliderDemo.java`, 658–660
Software
   development process, 58–62
   programs as, 2
`sort` method
   `Arrays` class, 252
   `ComparableRectangle.java` example, 575–576
   `SortRectangles.java` example, 576–577
   using recursion, 747–748
Sorting arrays
   bubble sorts, 258
   insertion sorts, 250–252
   overview of, 248
   selection sorts, 245, 249–250
Source objects, event sources and, 602–603
Source program or source code, 10, 40
Spacing, programming style and, 25
Special characters, 18
Specific import, 24
Splash screens, 467
`split` method, strings, 341, 342
`StackOfIntegers` class, 386–387
`StackOverflowError`, recursion causing, 757
Stacks
   case study: custom stack class, 436–437
   case study: designing class for stacks, 386–388
`start` method, applet life-cycle methods, 677–678
State, of objects, 296
Statements
   executing one at a time, 119
   executing repeatedly (loops), 134
   in high-level languages, 10
   terminators, 17
Static data, in `GuessDate` class, 388, 390

Static methods
  in `CircleWithStaticMembers.java`, 313–314
  class design guidelines, 392–393
  declaring, 313
  defined, 312
  in `GuessDate` class, 388–391
  invoking, 23
  when to use instance methods vs. static, 313–314
  wrapper classes and, 395
Static variables
  in `CircleWithStaticMembers.java`, 313–314
  class, 312–313
  class design guidelines, 392–393
  declaring, 313
  instance variables compared with, 312
  in `TestCircleWithStaticMembers.java`, 314
  when to use instance variables vs. static, 316
Stepwise refinement
  benefits of, 210
  implementation details, 207–210
  method abstraction, 203–204
  top-down and/or bottom-up implementation, 205–207
  top-down design, 204–205
`stop` method, applet life-cycle methods, 677–678
Storage devices
  CDs and DVDs, 6
  disks, 6
  overview of, 5
  USB flash drives, 7
Storage units, for measuring memory, 4–5
`String` class, 336
String concatenation operator (+), 36, 340
String literals, 336
String variables, 336
`StringBuffer` class, 336, 353, 357
`StringBuilder` class
  case study: ignoring nonalphanumeric characters when checking palindromes, 356–358
  modifying strings in, 353–355
  overview of, 336, 353
  `toString`, `capacity`, `length`, `setLength`, and `charAt` methods, 355–356
Strings
  in binary I/O, 716–717
  case study: checking if string is a palindrome, 347–348
  case study: converting hexadecimals to decimals, 348–350
  case study: ignoring nonalphanumeric characters when checking palindromes, 356–358
  `Character` class, 350–351
  command-line arguments, 358–361
  comparing, 337–339
  concatenating, 36, 68
  constructing, 336
  converting, replacing, and splitting, 341
  converting to `double`, 71–72
  converting to/from arrays, 343–344
  converting to/from numbers, 70, 344

`CountEachLetter.java` example, 351–353
  finding characters or substrings in, 342–343
  formatting, 344–347
  immutable and interned, 336–337
  key terms, 361
  matching, replacing, and splitting by patterns, 342
  obtaining length, getting individual characters, and combining, 339–340
  overview of, 335–336
  passing to applets, 679
  questions and exercises, 362–368
  `string` data type, 68–69
  `StringBuilder` and `StringBuffer` classes, 353–356
  substrings, 37, 340–341
  summary, 361–362
  in `Welcome.java`, 17
Strings (graphics)
  centering using `FontMetrics` class, 493–495
  drawing, 483–484
Subclasses
  abstract methods and, 560
  abstracting, 564
  constructors, 414–415
  creating graphics canvas, 482–483
  of Exception class, 524–525
  inheritance and, 408–409
  of `RuntimeException` class, 525
Subcontainers, panels as, 458–460
Subdirectories, 749
Subinterfaces, 582
`substring` method, 340, 746
Substrings, 340–343
Subtraction (−) operator, 46, 50
Subtraction (−=) assignment operator, 53–54
Subwindows, 660
Sudoku puzzle, 274–277
`sum` method, 269–270
`super` keyword, 414
Superclass methods, 417
Superclasses
  of abstract class can be concrete, 564
  classes extending, 581
  common features in `Component`, `Container`, and `JComponent` classes, 462
  `Container` class as, 460
  inheritance and, 408–409
  subclasses related to, 560
Supplementary characters, Unicode, 62
`swap` method
  swapping elements in an array, 239–240
  in `TestPassByValue.java` example, 187–189
Swing
  `AbstractButton` class, 468–469
  applets. *see* `JApplet` class
  AWT vs., 446
  buttons. *see* `JButton` class
  check boxes. *see* `JCheckBox` class

combo boxes. *see* `JComboBox` class

common features of Swing GUI components, 462–465

components. *see* `JComponent` class

constants, 572–573

creating user interfaces with, 468

dialogs. *see* `JDialog` class

event classes in, 603

file choosers (`JFileChooser` class), 550, 551–552

frames. *see* `JFrame` class

labels. *see* `JLabel` class

lists. *see* `JList` class

option panes (`JOptionPane` class), 72

panels. *see* `JPanel` class

radio buttons. *see* `JRadioButton` class

scroll bars. *see* `JScrollBar class`

scroll panes, 644, 646

sliders (`JSlider` class), 657–660

text areas. *see* `JTextArea` class

text classes, 644

text components (`JTextComponent` class), 474–475

text fields. *see* `JTextField` class

`switch` statements

    `ChineseZodiac.java` example, 110–111

    overview of, 108–110

Syntax errors (compile errors)

    common errors, 18

    debugging, 119–120

    programming errors, 26–27

Syntax rules, in `Welcome.java`, 18

System activities, role of OSs, 12

System analysis, in software development process, 58–59

System design, in software development process, 58, 60

System errors, 524

System resources, allocating, 12

`System.in`, 37

`System.out`, 37, 112–115

T

Tables, storing, 264

Tags, HTML, 673–674

Tail recursion

    `ComputeFactorialTailRecusion.java`, 759

    overview of, 758

tan `method`, trigonometry, 197–198

TBs (terabytes), of storage, 5

Teamwork, facilitated by stepwise refinement, 210

Terabytes (TBs), of storage, 5

Testing

    benefits of stepwise refinement, 210

    in software development process, 59, 61–62

Text

    case study: replacing text, 548–549

    displaying in message dialog box, 22–24

    files, 710

    font attributes, 493

    positioning with `JButton` class, 470–471

    `.txt` files (text), 712

Text areas

    `DescriptionPanel.java`, 645–646

    overview of, 644–645

    `TextAreaDemo.java`, 646–647

Text fields

    adding to frames, 452

    adding to grid, 455

    creating, 311

    events, 640

    `JTextField` class, 474–475

    panel for, 641

Text I/O

    vs. binary I/O, 711–712

    handling in Java, 710–711

    overview of, 710

TextPad, for creating/editing Java source code, 19

`this` reference

    invoking constructors with, 374–375

    overview of, 373–375

    referencing hidden data fields with, 373–374

Three-dimensional arrays. *see* Arrays, multi-dimensional

`throw` keyword

    chained exceptions, 538

    `throw ex` for rethrowing exceptions, 537

    for throwing exceptions, 527

`Throwable` class

    getting information about exceptions, 529–530

    `java.lang`, 523–525

Throwing exceptions

    `CircleWithException.java` example, 531

    `QuotientWithException.java` example, 521

    rethrowing, 536–537

    `TestCircleWithCustomException.java` example, 539

    `throw` keyword for, 526–527

`throws` keyword

    for declaring exceptions, 527

    `IOException`, 712–713

Tic-tac-toe game, 283

`Timer` class

    animation using, 625–626

    `AnimationDemo.java`, 626–628

    `Ball.java`, 684–685

    `ClockAnimation.java`, 628–629

`toCharArray` method, converting strings into arrays, 343

Toggle buttons, 468

Token reading methods, `Scanner` class, 546–547

`toLowerCase` method, `Character` class, 341

`toLowerCase` method, `Character` class, 351

Tool tips, for components, 462

Top-down design, 204–205

Top-down implementation, 205–207

Top-level containers, 447–448

`toString` method

    `ArrayList` class, 433

    `Arrays` class, 253

`toString` method (*continued*)
   `Date` class, 309
   `Object` class, 429
   `StringBuilder` class, 355–356
`total` variable, for storing sums, 268
`toUpperCase` method, `Character` class, 341, 351
Towers of Hanoi problem
   case study, 750–752
   computing recursively, 762
   `TowersOfHanoi.java`, 752–754
Tracing a program, 36
`transient` keyword, serialization and, 727
Transistors, CPUs, 3
Trigonometric methods, `Math` class, 197–198
`trim` method, strings, 341
True/false (Boolean) values, 82
Truth tables, 102–103
`try` block
   `InputMismatchExceptionDemo.java` example, 522
   `QuotientWithException.java` example, 520
   when to use exceptions, 535–536
`try-catch` blocks
   catching exceptions, 525, 527–529
   chained exceptions, 537–538
   `CircleWithException.java` example, 532–533
   rethrowing exceptions, 536–537
   when to use exceptions, 535–536
Twin primes, 218
Two-dimensional arrays. *see* Arrays, two-dimensional
`.txt` files (text), 712
Type casting
   between `char` and numeric types, 63
   loss of precision, 67
   for numeric type conversion, 56–57

U

UI (user interface)
   `BallControl.java`, 685
   `ComboBoxDemo.java`, 649
   creating, 641
   `ListDemo.java`, 653
   `MultipleWindowsDemo.java`, 661
   `ScrollBarDemo.java`, 656
   `SliderDemo.java`, 659
   `TextAreaDemo.java`, 647
UML (Unified Modeling Language)
   aggregation shown in, 382
   class diagrams with, 297
   diagram for `Loan` class, 376
   diagram of `StackOfIntegers`, 386
   diagram of static variables and methods, 312–313
Unary operators, 47
Unboxing, 396
Unchecked exceptions, 525
Underflow, floating point numbers, 45

Unicode
   character data type (`char`) and, 62–65
   comparing characters, 82
   data input and output streams, 717
   generating random numbers and, 201
   text encoding, 710
   text I/O vs. binary I/O, 711
Unified Modeling Language. *see* UML (Unified Modeling Language)
Uniform Resource Locators. *see* URLs (Uniform Resource Locators)
Unique addresses, for each byte of memory, 5
Universal serial bus (USB) flash drives, 7
UNIX epoch, 51
Upcasting objects, 425
`URL` class
   `DisplayImagePlayAudio.java`, 694
   `DisplayImageWithURL.java`, 692–693
   `java.net`, 551
   locating resources using, 691–692
URLs (Uniform Resource Locators)
   `ReadFileFromURL.java` example, 551–552
   reading data from Web, 551
USB (universal serial bus) flash drives, 7
User interface. *see* UI (user interface)
UTF-8, 717. *see also* Unicode

V

`valueOf` methods
   converting strings into arrays, 344
   wrapper classes and, 395
Value-returning methods
   `return` statements required by, 181
   `TestReturnGradeMethod.java`, 183–185
   `void` method and, 179
Variable-length argument lists, 244–245
Variables
   Boolean variables. *see* Boolean variables
   comparing primitive variables with reference variables, 306–308
   control variables in `for` loops, 147–148
   declaring, 35–36, 41
   declaring array variables, 225
   declaring for two-dimensional arrays, 264–265
   displaying/modifying, 120
   hidden, 372
   identifiers, 40
   indexed array variables, 226–227
   naming conventions, 44
   overflow, 45
   overview of, 40–41
   reference variables, 304
   scope of, 42, 196–197, 371–372
   static variables, 312–313
Vertical alignment, `AbstractButton` class, 470

Vertical scroll bars, 656
Vertical sliders, 657, 659
Vertical text position, 470–471
Virtual machines (VMs), 21. *see also* JVM (Java Virtual Machine)
Visibility (accessibility) modifiers
    classes and, 317–319
    `protected`, `public`, and `private`, 437–440
Visual Basic, high-level languages, 11
VLSI (very large-scale integration), 738
VMs (virtual machines), 21. *see also* JVM (Java Virtual Machine)
`void` method
    defined, 179
    defining and invoking, 183
    `TestVoidMethod.java`, 183

W

WAV file, 693
Web, reading file data from, 551–552
Web browsers
    controlling applet execution and life-cycle, 677
    viewing applets, 674–675
Web servers, developing apps on, 628
`while` loops
    case study: guessing numbers, 137–139
    case study: multiple subtraction quiz, 139–141
    case study: predicting future tuition, 157
    deciding when to use, 150–151
    design strategies, 139

`do-while` loop. *see* `do-while` loop
    input and output redirections, 143–144
    overview of, 134–136
    RepeatAdditionQuiz.java example, 136–137
    sentinel-controlled, 141–143
    syntax of, 134
Whitespace
    characters, 69
    as delimiter in token reading methods, 546–547
Wildcard import, 24
Windows. *see* Frames (windows)
Windows, multiple
    `Histogram.java`, 662–664
    `MultipleWindowsDemo.java`, 661–662
    overview of, 660–661
`Windows` class, 447
Windows OSs, 12
Wireless networking, 8
Wrapper classes
    automatic conversion between primitive types and wrapper class types, 396–397
    `File` class as, 541
    numeric, 585
    primitive types and, 350, 393–396
Wrapping lines of text or words, 644, 646
Write-only streams, 729. *see also* `OutputStream` class

X

`XListener/XEvent` listener interface, 603–604

Java Quick Reference

Console Input

```
Scanner input = new Scanner(System.in);
int intValue = input.nextInt();
long longValue = input.nextLong();
double doubleValue = input.nextDouble();
float floatValue = input.nextFloat();
String string = input.next();
```

Console Output

```
System.out.println(anyValue);
```

GUI Input Dialog

```
String string = JOptionPane.showInputDialog(
    "Enter input");
int intValue = Integer.parseInt(string);
double doubleValue =
    Double.parseDouble(string);
```

Message Dialog

```
JOptionPane.showMessageDialog(null,
    "Enter input");
```

Primitive Data Types

byte	8 bits
short	16 bits
int	32 bits
long	64 bits
float	32 bits
double	64 bits
char	16 bits
boolean	true/false

Arithmetic Operators

+	addition
–	subtraction
*	multiplication
/	division
%	remainder
++var	preincrement
--var	predecrement
var++	postincrement
var--	postdecrement

Assignment Operators

=	assignment
+=	addition assignment
-=	subtraction assignment
*=	multiplication assignment
/=	division assignment
%=	remainder assignment

Relational Operators

<	less than
<=	less than or equal to
>	greater than
>=	greater than or equal to
==	equal to
!=	not equal

Logical Operators

&&	short circuit AND
||	short circuit OR
!	NOT
^	exclusive OR

if Statements

```
if (condition) {
  statements;
}

if (condition) {
  statements;
}
else {
  statements;
}

if (condition1) {
  statements;
}
else if (condition2) {
  statements;
}
else {
  statements;
}
```

switch Statements

```
switch (intExpression) {
  case value1:
    statements;
    break;
  ...
  case valuen:
    statements;
    break;
  default:
    statements;
}
```

loop Statements

```
while (condition) {
  statements;
}

do {
  statements;
} while (condition);

for (init; condition;
  adjustment) {
  statements;
}
```

Companion Web site: www.pearsonhighered.com/liang